MANAGEMENT: A PRACTICAL INTRODUCTION, 2024 RELEASE

Published by McGraw Hill LLC, 1325 Avenue of the Americas, New York, NY 10019. Copyright © 2024 by McGraw Hill LLC. All rights reserved. Printed in the United States of America. Previous editions ©2022, 2020, and 2018. No part of this publication may be reproduced or distributed in any form or by any means, or stored in a database or retrieval system, without the prior written consent of McGraw Hill LLC, including, but not limited to, in any network or other electronic storage or transmission, or broadcast for distance learning.

Some ancillaries, including electronic and print components, may not be available to customers outside the United States.

This book is printed on acid-free paper.

1 2 3 4 5 6 7 8 9 LWI 29 28 27 26 25 24

ISBN 978-1-265-79537-5 (bound edition)
MHID 1-265-79537-1 (bound edition)
ISBN 978-1-265-06099-2 (loose-leaf edition)
MHID 1-265-06099-1 (loose-leaf edition)

Portfolio Director: *Michael Ablassmeir*
Product Developer: *Anne Ehrenworth*
Executive Marketing Manager: *Debbie Clare*
Content Project Managers: *Harvey Yep (Core)/Emily Windelborn (Assessment)*
Manufacturing Project Manager: *Nancy Flaggman*
Content Licensing Specialists: *Brianna Kirschbaum*
Cover Image: *Kapook2981/iStock/Getty Images*
Compositor: *Aptara®, Inc*

All credits appearing on page or at the end of the book are considered to be an extension of the copyright page.

Library of Congress Cataloging-in-Publication Data

Names: Kinicki, Angelo, author. | Soignet, Denise Breaux, author. | Hartnell, Chad, author.
Title: Management : a practical introduction / Angelo Kinicki, Arizona State University, Kent State University, Denise Breaux Soignet, University of Arkansas, Chad Hartnell, Georgia State University.
Description: 2024 Release. | Dubuque, IA : McGraw Hill LLC, [2024] | Revised edition of Management, [2020]
Identifiers: LCCN 2023035215 (print) | LCCN 2023035216 (ebook) | ISBN 9781265795375 (hardcover) | ISBN 9781265060992 (spiral bound) | ISBN 9781265801069 (ebook) | ISBN 9781265079031 (ebook other)
Subjects: LCSH: Management.
Classification: LCC HD31 .K474 2024 (print) | LCC HD31 (ebook) | DDC 658–dc23/eng/20230807
LC record available at https://lccn.loc.gov/2023035215
LC ebook record available at https://lccn.loc.gov/2023035216

The Internet addresses listed in the text were accurate at the time of publication. The inclusion of a website does not indicate an endorsement by the authors or McGraw Hill Education, and McGraw Hill Education does not guarantee the accuracy of the information presented at these sites.

mheducation.com/highered

brief contents

Walkthrough Preface xix

DEI Diversity, Equity, and Inclusion (DE&I) DEI-1

PART 1
Introduction
1. The Exceptional Manager: What You Do, How You Do It 2
2. Management Theory: Essential Background for the Successful Manager 38

PART 2
The Environment of Management
3. The Manager's Changing Work Environment and Ethical Responsibilities: Doing the Right Thing 60

Learning Module 1: Shared Value and Sustainable Development: A New Way to Think about Leading and Managing 88

4. Global Management: Managing across Borders 108

PART 3
Planning
5. Planning: The Foundation of Successful Management 142
6. Strategic Management: How Exceptional Managers Realize a Grand Design 168

Learning Module 2: Entrepreneurship 198

7. Individual and Group Decision Making: How Managers Make Things Happen 218

PART 4
Organizing
8. Organizational Culture and Structure: Drivers of Strategic Implementation 262
9. Human Resource Management: Getting the Right People for Managerial Success 302
10. Organizational Change and Innovation: Lifelong Challenges for the Exceptional Manager 348

PART 5
Leading
11. Managing Individual Differences and Behavior: Supervising People as People 386
12. Motivating Employees: Achieving Superior Performance in the Workplace 420
13. Groups and Teams: Increasing Cooperation, Reducing Conflict 466
14. Power, Influence, and Leadership: From Becoming a Manager to Becoming a Leader 500
15. Interpersonal and Organizational Communication: Mastering the Exchange of Information 538

PART 6
Controlling
16. Control Systems and Quality Management: Techniques for Enhancing Organizational Effectiveness 578

Appendix 622
Chapter Notes CN-1

Name Index IND1
Organization Index IND4

Glossary/Subject Index IND8

about the authors

Angelo Kinicki

Angelo Kinicki is an emeritus professor of management and held the Weatherup/Overby Chair in Leadership from 2005 to 2015 at the W. P. Carey School of Business at Arizona State University. He joined the faculty in 1982, the year he received his doctorate in business administration from Kent State University. He was inducted into the W. P. Carey Faculty Hall of Fame in 2016. Angelo currently is the Dean's Scholar in Residence at Kent State University. He is conducting seminars on the implementation of active learning in the classroom and publishing scholarly research. He also serves on the Dean's National Advisory Board.

Angelo is the recipient of six teaching awards from Arizona State University, where he taught in its nationally ranked undergraduate, MBA, and PhD programs. He also received several research awards and was selected to serve on the editorial review boards for four scholarly journals. His current research interests focus on the dynamic relationships among leadership, organizational culture, organizational change, and individual, group, and organizational performance. Angelo has published over 95 articles in a variety of academic journals and proceedings and is co-author of eight textbooks (37 including revisions) that are used by hundreds of universities around the world. Several of his books have been translated into multiple languages, and two of his books were awarded revisions of the year by McGraw Hill. Out of 15,317 scientists in the field of Social Sciences and Humanities, Angelo was ranked as the 984th (top 6%) best scientist in the United States by Research.com in 2023. He also was identified as being among the top 100 most influential (top 0.6%) Organizational Behavioral authors in 2018 out of a total of 16,289 academics.

Angelo is a busy international consultant and co-founder of Kinicki and Associates, Inc., a management consulting firm that works with top management teams to create organizational change aimed at increasing organizational effectiveness and profitability. He has worked with many Fortune 500 firms as well as numerous entrepreneurial organizations in diverse industries. His expertise includes facilitating strategic/operational planning sessions, diagnosing the causes of organizational and work-unit problems, conducting organizational culture interventions, implementing performance management systems, designing and implementing performance appraisal systems, developing and administering surveys to assess employee attitudes, and leading management/executive education programs. He developed a 360-degree leadership feedback instrument called the Performance Management Leadership Survey (PMLS) that is used by companies throughout the world.

Angelo and his wife of 42 years, Joyce, have enjoyed living in the beautiful Arizona desert for 41 years. They are both natives of Cleveland, Ohio. They enjoy traveling, hiking, watching movies, and walking Gracie, their adorable golden retriever. Angelo also has a passion for golfing.

Denise Breaux Soignet is an associate teaching professor of management and director of the Tyson Center for Faith-Friendly Workplaces at the Sam M. Walton College of Business at the University of Arkansas. She joined the University of Arkansas faculty in 2010 after receiving her PhD in business administration from Florida State University. Denise has received awards both for her teaching and her work to promote inclusion and diversity within the university and professional communities. She has taught courses in the Walton College's nationally ranked undergraduate and MBA programs, has developed multiple online undergraduate courses, and sees active learning as a key component of all of her courses, both face-to-face and online. Denise's research interests include dysfunctional workplace behavior, inclusion and diversity, leadership, social influence, and job stress, and her work has been published in multiple premier management journals.

Denise is a Certified Professional for the Society for Human Resource Management, and she consults with public- and private-sector organizations. Her expertise includes diagnosing the causes of interpersonal problems in the workplace, implementing management solutions that enhance the quality of supervisor–subordinate relationships, assessing workplace religious inclusion and tolerance, and designing and delivering organizational learning and development programs. She also has specialized expertise in resolving the unique interpersonal challenges that arise in poultry production and has years of experience working with managers and technicians at some of the industry's largest firms.

Denise lives in Northwest Arkansas with her husband, Joe, and their two children. She is also the lucky stepmom of two bonus adult children. Denise and her family are natives of South Louisiana and Cajuns at heart. They enjoy watching their two favorite football teams—the New Orleans Saints (WHO DAT!) and the Nicholls State University Colonels—and can often be found making food and cocktails for friends, gardening, listening to jazz, and traveling.

Cydney A Soignet

Chad Hartnell is an Associate Professor of Management in the J. Mack Robinson College of Business at Georgia State University (GSU). He joined the GSU faculty in 2012 after receiving his PhD in Business Administration from Arizona State University. Chad has received 16 Certificates of Recognition for Outstanding Teaching Performance at GSU and consistently earns among the highest teaching ratings in the business school. He has taught courses at the undergraduate and doctoral levels in topics such as organizational behavior, leadership, and teams. He is passionate about developing strong relationships with his students, challenging them to grow their critical thinking and problem-solving skills, and equipping them to learn, improve, and ultimately succeed at a high academic level.

Chad currently serves on the editorial review board for *Personnel Psychology*. His current research interests focus on leadership, organizational culture, and team dynamics. Chad has published over 15 peer-reviewed articles in premier management journals. His work has been cited over 6,000 times according to Google Scholar. His work has gained attention in popular press outlets like *Harvard Business Review, Talent Quarterly, Wall Street Journal, Forbes, Financial Times,* and *Atlanta Business Chronicle*.

Chad lives in Atlanta, Georgia, with his wife, Sandy, his four children, and his playful golden retriever, Tucker. He cherishes his role as a husband and father. He enjoys making memories with his family at professional soccer matches (Atlanta United) and baseball games (Atlanta Braves). He also loves to play tennis, hike, and tell dad jokes.

Chad Hartnell

dedication

To Joyce Kinicki, the love of my life, best friend, and the wind beneath my wings.

—**Angelo**

To Joe, my snug harbor.

—**Denise**

To Sandy Hartnell, the one who adds beauty to life and rhythm to my step. You are my heart's beat, my encourager, and my best friend.

—**Chad**

new to the 2024 release

It Begins with a New Member of the Author Team

Denise and I are very excited to introduce our new co-author, Dr. Chad Hartnell. I recommended Chad as a new co-author because of what I learned about him from our long-standing relationship that began as his advisor in the doctoral program at Arizona State University. Through many years of working together on research projects, I learned that Chad, like Denise, possesses all the skills and traits I desire in a co-author. His content knowledge is vast, and his work ethic and values are similar to mine. Chad is an outstanding teacher and cares deeply about developing students and assisting them in achieving well-being and success. Most importantly, Chad is a friend and he and Denise are well suited for each other. They like each other, love their families, believe in integrity and doing things for the greater good, and are equally committed to maintaining the long-standing tradition of excellence within our product. In conclusion, Denise and Chad are my "dream team" and I look forward to working with them for years to come.

We are Pleased to Share these Exciting New Additions and Updates!

All of our changes were based on the goal of providing the most up-to-date theory, research, and practical examples.

The 2024 Release incorporated five major changes. The first involved writing a new chapter on diversity, equity, and inclusion (DE&I). The second concentrated on updating and expanding our strategic theme of career readiness. The third entailed a concerted effort to discuss leading edge hot topics such as hybrid work schedules and artificial intelligence (AI). Fourth, we enhanced our Teaching Resource Manual 2.0 (TRM) to facilitate ease of use and added guidance for using Application-Based Activities (ABAs) and Manager's Hot Seat videos to foster higher-levels of learning. Finally, we reduced the length of the product while still covering the fundamentals and the most recent theory and concepts.

Diversity, Equity, and Inclusion

The first change you'll notice in the 2024 Release is a new chapter on diversity, equity, and inclusion right up front. As you can imagine, adding a chapter to an already packed textbook is not a light decision. We believed that a full chapter on DE&I was incredibly important, and we are grateful for the reviewers and users who pushed us to add this chapter over the years. Our chapter begins with a discussion of the true meaning behind the term *DE&I*—we explore each component in depth and introduce the term *DE&I management* to ground the research, theory, examples, and advice we provide throughout the chapter. We challenge readers to think beyond single identifiers of diversity and instead consider the intersection of various diverse identities. In the second section of the chapter, we describe how DE&I management has evolved over time and explore emerging concepts that modern organizations are currently grappling with. The third section of the chapter presents research, theory, and examples to help readers understand why many organizations have such a difficult time getting DE&I right. We next describe what it takes for DE&I management practices to be successful at the managerial and organizational levels. We conclude with a Career Corner that provides practical advice to help readers build several important career readiness competencies related to DE&I management.

Updated and Expanded Coverage of Career Readiness

Our ninth edition was the first textbook to introduce a strategic theme on career readiness, with the goal of helping students develop their career readiness competencies so that they would be more employable upon graduation. This was an important theme because research shows that employers believe college graduates are not career ready. We have expanded this theme in the 2024 Release.

Our first change involved refining our model of career readiness in Chapter 1 based on recent research findings. The new model starts with eight core competencies—a set of competencies that are vital across jobs, occupations, and industries. We then categorize 19 additional career readiness competencies into four categories: knowledge, soft skills, attitudes, and other characteristics (KSAOs, see Figure 1.4). McGraw Hill also conducted a series of executive interviews from global managers across a variety of industries asking them to comment on the importance of developing various career readiness competencies. Our second change involved integrating these video interviews within the developmental guidance provided in the Career Corner for every chapter.

> ❝ [This] book is widely adopted, strongly supported, . . . and comprehensive. [The] integrated career readiness component to the materials bolsters what already is a strong product. ❞
>
> —Michael Shane Spiller,
> Western Kentucky University

Integrated Coverage of Hybrid Work Schedules and Artificial Intelligence

The additive effects of the Great Resignation, quiet quitting, and the pandemic have created the need to consider how management theories apply to today's workers. For example, the associated labor shortages and preferences for hybrid work schedules have spawned a new psychological contract between employers and employees. Consider that employers are having to offer higher pay, better working conditions, and improved benefits to attract and retain employees. Today's work environment has fundamentally changed, and we desired to reflect these changes in our product. In recognition, we integrated the discussion of a new psychological contract and hybrid work schedules within 10 chapters.

Moreover, the management functions of plan, organize, lead, and control are being impacted by the growth of AI applications. Some believe that AI will usher in a completely new way of working. Although the impacts of AI are being realized on a real-time basis, we decided to integrate a discussion of AI's managerial implications and applications across 10 chapters.

> ❝ (Management) provides insights on a wide range of micro and macro management topics with an emphasis on practical application to students' lives and careers. ❞
>
> —Zahir Latheef,
> University of Houston—Downtown

Enhanced Teaching Resource Manual 2.0 (TRM)

This is the third edition in which we focused on improving our Teaching Resource Manual (TRM). Our goal continues to be one of providing instructors with a turnkey solution for implementing active learning with their students. Feedback on the TRM has been extremely positive, but a few changes were suggested. The first was to provide some type of onboarding for how best to use our vast repertoire of teaching resources. We responded by creating a new chapter entitled the "TRM Orientation Guide." It is structured around a five-step class planning process model that guides the process of creating an overall chapter-level lesson plan. It also provides instructions for using ABAs and Hot Seat Videos to foster higher levels of learning, thereby developing students' career readiness competencies.

The second suggestion pertained to ease of navigation within the many chapter-level resources we provide. We thus developed a navigation process built on hot links across various sections of teaching resources within a chapter. The Orientation Guide explains and demonstrates how to use this navigation system.

The third request was for more resources that foster higher levels of learning that develop students' core career readiness competencies. We met this request in two ways. First, we selected our favorite ABA and Manager's Hot Seat Video for every chapter and then created teaching guides for using these Connect assets with techniques associated with active learning. Our approach is based upon engaging students in critical thinking and problem solving by having them apply the four steps within a generalized rational decision-making model: define the problem, determine the causes, develop alternative solutions, and decide on a solution. Second, we created an AI group exercise for each chapter that provides ideas and instructions to help students interface with and think critically about AI-based applications like ChatGPT.

> *I have found that this TRM is the very, very best of all (Instructor's Manuals) provided across publishers and management courses. Well done. Even (without) Connect, we would choose this textbook based on the strength of the TRM. This course often has adjuncts and new faculty teaching it, so th(e) TRM is a real value-added aspect to this textbook.*
>
> —Gerald Schoenfeld,
> Florida Gulf Coast University

> *I manage 16–18 sections of Principles of Management taught by adjuncts, lecturers, etc. The TRM is an invaluable resource that provides me with a detailed guide and vault of activities other instructors can benefit from. Without the TRM, I would be spending countless hours creating one so this has saved me a lot of time! It is one of the primary reasons for using Kinicki.*
>
> —Zahir I. Latheef,
> University of Houston—Downtown

> *(The) TRM is an excellent tool to plan and implement active learning in my management classes; it . . . increase(s) student engagement in the classroom learning environment.*
>
> —Jessie Lee Bellflowers,
> Fayetteville Technical Community College

Reduced the Length of the Product

We received feedback that the product was too long and that all topics could not be covered. We heard you! We made a concerted effort to reduce the length of each chapter by about five pages. This was accomplished by covering the fundamental principles of management as well as the most recent theory and concepts.

Completely Revamped, Revised, and Updated Chapters

In each chapter, we refreshed examples (we replaced or updated 281 of them to illustrate the principles of management), research (approximately 50% of our citations are from 2022 and 2023), figures, tables, statistics, and photos, as well as modified the design to accommodate new changes to the 2024 Release. We also have largely replaced topics in such popular features as Example boxes and Practical Action boxes. To make the most of certain cornerstone features—the Management in Action cases and Legal/Ethical Challenge cases—we have fully updated or created them anew and moved them into Connect, making them fully assignable for students. We linked these two cases by focusing them on the same company or issue. This enables instructors to link ethical considerations within the broader context of a Management in Action Case.

> *You are the leader in the field for the Principles of Management course by a far margin. Your work in soliciting feedback help[s] to ensure that you retain your advantage. Angelo and now with Denise, along with everyone at McGraw Hill, are to be commended for all of their efforts to continually enrich this textbook. A true example of continuous improvement.*
>
> —Gerald Schoenfeld,
> Florida Gulf Coast University

While the following list does not encompass all the updates and revisions, it does highlight some of the more notable changes.

CHAPTER DEI

This material is new to the 2024 Release:

- Fourteen new timely examples woven throughout the chapter to illustrate various concepts in DE&I management.
- Manage U: Using Inclusive Language.
- Section DEI.1—Introduces the concepts of DE&I. Defines diversity, equity, and inclusion, and describes how these interrelated parts form the whole of a concept called DE&I management. Introduces a figure of the diversity wheel and discusses the idea of intersectionality as it relates to the multiple dimensions of diversity contained in the wheel. Presents a new table of the qualities of fair and unbiased HR procedures. Describes the hallmarks of inclusion and presents the concept of inclusion climate.
- Section DEI.2—Summarizes how DE&I in organizations has evolved over many years. Presents a table with a timeline of key legislation related to protected class status in modern organizations. Describes the emerging concepts of neurodiversity and gender identity in DE&I. Discusses the ever-present tensions related to the evolution of DE&I in organizations.
- Section DEI.3—Describes key challenges of effective DE&I management in organizations. Categorizes challenges as either person factors or environmental factors. Discusses person factors including fear, misperceptions (including stereotypes), and expectations and attributions. Discusses environmental factors including leadership, HR practices, and organizational culture.
- Section DEI.4—Describes effective DE&I management practices at the managerial and organizational levels. Managerial practices discussed include those that facilitate belongingness and value employees' uniqueness. Organizational practices discussed include making DE&I a part of business strategy, encouraging meaningful conversations, and effectively tracking and using data.
- Section DEI.5—Illustrates how the career readiness competencies discussed in the section connect with the chapter's Executive Interview Series video. Introduces the concept of perspective taking and provides practical advice for seeing things from others' perspectives. Introduces the concept of an ally and provides practical advice for being a better ally in the workplace. Introduces the concept of being a "good-ish" person and provides practical tips for engaging in these behaviors.

CHAPTER 1

- Seven new or updated examples and/or boxes.
- Updated Manage U: Using Management Skills for College Success
- Section 1.1—Updated Example box on effectiveness vs. efficiency in the lab-grown meat industry. Updated statistics on managers' salaries and formal mentoring programs.
- Section 1.3—Revised discussion of the importance of middle managers. New examples of nonprofit general managers. Updated discussion of nonprofit organizations.
- Section 1.4—Reconfigured discussion of how managers spend their time to enhance readability and focus on connections between Mintzberg's classic work and the modern work of Porter and Nohria. New example of how CEO Sundar Pichai plays an informational role at Google.
- Section 1.5—Updated the running example on Mary Barra.
- Section 1.6—Updated management challenge #1, Managing for Competitive Advantage—Staying Ahead of Rivals, with the addition of being responsive to employees in light of the new psychological contract that has emerged in the employment relationship. Introduced *psychological contract* as a new key term. Updated the Example box on direct-to-consumer genetics testing. New example of the Russia–Ukraine war to illustrate management challenge #4, Managing for Globalization. Updated discussion of managing for globalization. Updated example of the Houston Astros ethical scandal. Updated the Practical Action box on doing the right thing when you're tempted to cheat. New example of the Salesforce Citizen Philanthropy program to illustrate managing for happiness and meaningfulness.
- Section 1.7—Updated Figure 1.3 on the gap between employers' and new college graduates' perceptions of new college graduates' career readiness. Updated Figure 1.4 (Model of career readiness) to better align with the most recent NACE research and the career readiness competencies desired by today's employers. Added "diversity, equity, and inclusion" as a core career readiness competency. Updated Practical Action box on developing your soft skills (formerly located in Section 1.5).

CHAPTER 2

- Twelve new or updated examples and/or boxes.
- New Manage U: Using Theory as Your Guide to Solve Problems.
- Section 2.1—Revised Figure 2.1 "Progression of management perspectives" to include focal outcome (people/processes) for each management perspective.
- Section 2.2—Streamlined coverage of the classical viewpoint of management. New example to illustrate how scientific management principles are being used in today's businesses.
- Section 2.3—New examples to illustrate Theory X and Theory Y.
- Section 2.4—New examples of the Houston Astros, General Motors, and Novartis to illustrate the concept of quantitative management.
- Section 2.5—Consolidated discussion of the systems viewpoint. New example of Peloton to describe a closed system view of management.
- Section 2.6—Updated Example box on the contingency viewpoint and the creative steps manufacturers are taking to recruit future talent.
- Section 2.7—Updated Example box on examples of high-performance work practices.
- Section 2.8—Illustrated how the career readiness competencies discussed in the section connect with the chapter's Executive Interview Series video.

CHAPTER 3

- Nine new or updated examples and/or boxes.
- Updated Manage U: Being Courageous at Work.
- Section 3.1—Revised introduction to enhance the focus and readability of the chapter by presenting the dilemma businesses face when considering what it means to do the "right" thing. Revised discussion of the triple bottom line. Updated section on younger workers' search for meaning with recent data on Gen Z workers.
- Section 3.2—Updated introduction to focus readers on how the organization's environment relates to the central dilemma posed in Section 3.1 (i.e., what does it mean for businesses to do the "right" thing?). Updated statistics on Hilton hotels.
- Section 3.3—New example of the grocery delivery wars between Amazon, Walmart, and Target to illustrate competitors in an organization's environment. New example of the auto industry's current semiconductor chip shortage to illustrate suppliers. New example of Warner Music and Rothco to illustrate the concept of strategic allies. Updated statistics regarding unions, unemployment, and interest rates. Updated example of governmental regulation of drones. New example of changing work arrangements to illustrate technological forces. Updated figure showing states where marijuana is legal. New example of TikTok bans to illustrate international forces.
- Section 3.4—Various updates to streamline content and better connect discussion with broader chapter content. Updated discussion of MIT donations in introduction to better align with the central dilemma posed in Section 3.1. Revised definition of ethical dilemma. New example of the Walt Disney Company to illustrate organizational values. New statistics on white collar crime. New example of pandemic relief fraud to illustrate white-collar crime. New example of ExxonMobil to illustrate SarbOx. Updated example of and statistics on workplace cheating.
- Section 3.5—Revised introduction to align with the central dilemma posed in Section 3.1. Updated statistics on CSR.

New to the 2024 release

- Updated statistics on philanthropy and the Giving Pledge. Updated research in Table 3.2 on how being ethical and socially responsible pays off.
- Section 3.6—Revised introduction and streamlined text in entire section for enhanced readability and connection to chapter content.
- Section 3.7—Illustrated how the career readiness competencies discussed in the section connect with the chapter's Executive Interview Series video. Updated discussion of fostering positive emotions in yourself and others.

LEARNING MODULE 1: SHARED VALUE AND SUSTAINABLE DEVELOPMENT

- Seven new or updated examples and/or boxes.
- Section LM 1.1—Updated statistics on CSR initiatives. Revised discussion of traditional CSR to connect with the central dilemma (what does it mean for businesses to do the "right" thing?) posed in Chapter 3. Updated example of how Reliance Jio creates shared value. Updated example of Novartis Pharmaceuticals used to illustrate discovery of new products, markets, and opportunities. New example of Flex Ltd. used to illustrate transformation of the value chain. Updated Example box on CSV at Campbell Soup.
- Section LM 1.2—Updated statistics on poverty, access to safe drinking water, and air pollution in the introduction. New example of the UN COP Meetings to illustrate the SDGs as an opportunity for CSV. Updated example of Merck to illustrate how big businesses are engaging in CSV. New example of Zipline to illustrate small businesses engaging in CSV. Updated section on the approaches business schools are taking to teach the concept of shared value. Updated statistics on job searchers' interest in organizations' commitment to sustainability.
- Section LM 1.3—Revised introduction for enhanced readability and connection to chapter content. Updated statistics on corporate engagement with the SDGs throughout section. Updated statistics on progress toward SDG #5 (Gender Equality) to be more inclusive. Updated statistics on progress toward SDG #15 (Life on Land). New statistics on progress toward SDG #17 (Partnerships for the Goals). Revised discussion of areas of concern regarding the SDGs to account for the deleterious impacts of the COVID-19 pandemic on progress toward the goals.

CHAPTER 4

- Nine new or updated examples and/or boxes.
- Section 4.1—Updated statistics on U.S. imports. Redesigned section on competition and globalization with a discussion of the four facets of competitiveness in global business. Updated statistics on the world's most competitive countries. Updated statistics on Internet use, social media use, and U.S. e-commerce sales. New Example box on globalization and supply chain vulnerabilities that discusses the vulnerability of supply chains in the context of international events.
- Section 4.2—Revised introduction to enhance connection between career readiness competencies and international management. Updated list of the 10 largest American multinational corporations. Revised discussion of ethnocentric managers to include new example of the 2022 Clean Vehicle Credit. Updated discussion of polycentric managers to include advantages and disadvantages.
- Section 4.3—Revised the iPhone example in the introduction to better illustrate international business. Updated discussion of new markets as a reason for international expansion. Updated statistics on the China Investment Corporation, reshoring, and overseas franchises. Updated table on the world's leading export countries. New examples of joint ventures and wholly owned subsidiaries.
- Section 4.4—Updated table on the top U.S. trading partners in goods. Revised discussion of the U.S.–China trade war to illustrate the concept of tariffs. Revised discussion of sanctions and embargoes including updated and new examples. Updated the current events in table on organizations promoting international trade. Updated discussion of trade across North America, including the USMCA. Revised section on the European Union to include a discussion of the significance of BREXIT and the EU's dependence on Russia. Updated Example box on dealing with currency. Revised discussion of the BRICS countries, including new statistics on the economies of India, China, and Brazil.
- Section 4.5—Revised introduction to enhance connection between career readiness competencies and the value of understanding cultural differences. Revised discussion of cultural dimensions including a new example of video games to illustrate high context cultures. Reconfigured discussion of Hofstede's model of four cultural dimensions for enhanced readability. Updated statistics on the world's most spoken languages. Revised section on cultural differences in religion to enhance connection between religious culture and global business. New figure illustrating the world's major religions by geographic area. New example of French labor protests to illustrate political instability. Updated statistics on global corruption. Completely revamped section on U.S. managers on foreign assignments to include issues related to expatriate selection, ongoing adjustment, and repatriation.
- Section 4.6—Illustrated how the career readiness competencies discussed in the section connect with the chapter's Executive Interview Series video. Revised section to align with the core career readiness competency of diversity, equity, and inclusion.

CHAPTER 5

- Nine new or updated examples and/or boxes.
- Updated Manage U: Start Your Career Off Right by Planning.

- Section 5.1—Revised figure on planning and strategic management. The figure is now the same as Figure 6.2. This change shows the similar processes involved with planning and strategic management. It creates more continuity between Chapter 5 and Chapter 6 and reinforces student learning by using the same figure in Chapter 6.
- Section 5.2—Revised figure about making plans to vertically depict three levels of management. Updated Example box on the mission, vision, and values of Coca Cola. Updated Example box on Coca-Cola's strategies.
- Section 5.3—New example of Walker & Dunlop to illustrate long-term and short-term goals. New example of Air France/KLM to describe an organization's contingency plans.
- Section 5.4—Updated Practical Action box on how small businesses can set goals.
- Section 5.5—Revised figure on the planning/control cycle to be the same as Figure 6.8. This change creates more continuity between Chapter 5 and Chapter 6 in the discussion of maintaining strategic control. It also reinforces student learning by using the same figure in Chapter 6.
- Section 5.6—Expanded set of career readiness competencies that are used in planning. Illustrated how the career readiness competencies discussed in the section connect with the chapter's Executive Interview Series video.

CHAPTER 6

- Fifteen new or updated examples and/or boxes.
- Updated Manage U: Your Personal Brand Requires a Strategy.
- Section 6.1—Updated Neutrogena example to illustrate trade-offs associated with a strategy. Updated Dunkin' example to illustrate the concept of functional-level strategies.
- Section 6.2—Updated Microsoft running example. Revised figure on the strategic management process to be the same as Figure 5.1. This change shows the similar processes involved with planning and strategic management. It creates more continuity between Chapter 5 and Chapter 6 and reinforces student learning by using a familiar figure to describe the strategic management process.
- Section 6.3—Revised figure on the SWOT analysis to expand the discussion of opportunities and threats to include the external general environment. Revised table on SWOT characteristics applicable to a college to include the external general environment. Introduced new content using PESTEL to analyze macro opportunities and threats from six societal forces. Revised end of section content to focus on scenario analysis rather than contingency planning, a topic discussed in Section 5.3. Updated statistics in figure on airline benchmarks.
- Section 6.4—Revised figure on the BCG matrix to streamline the content and enhance applicability.
- Section 6.5—Updated examples from Warby Parker to illustrate the differentiation strategy and Viking Cruises as an application of the focused-differentiation strategy.
- Section 6.6—Revised figure on strategic implementation at Kroger. Updated Kroger running example. New figure on the planning/control cycle. It is the same as Figure 5.5 introduced in Section 5.5. This change creates more continuity between Chapter 5 and Chapter 6 in the discussion of maintaining strategic control. It also reinforces student learning by using a familiar figure to describe the planning/control process.
- Section 6.7—Expanded set of career readiness competencies that are used in strategic decision making. Illustrated how the career readiness competencies discussed in the section connect with the chapter's Executive Interview Series video.

LEARNING MODULE 2: ENTREPRENEURSHIP

- Eleven new or updated examples and/or boxes.
- Updated Manage U: So You Want to Start a Business?
- Section LM 2.1—New section introduction using *Shark Tank* to create an example students can role play and relate to throughout the LM. New table on the difference between being self-employed and being an entrepreneur. Introduced new definition and description of social entrepreneurship. New table on the five types of social entrepreneurship organizations. Introduced new figure outlining research-based characteristics of entrepreneurs. Organized seven entrepreneur characteristics within three categories: entrepreneurial mindset, entrepreneurial orientation, and entrepreneurial confidence. Updated table listing valuable facts about small businesses.
- Section LM 2.2—New section introduction with a *Shark Tank* pitch competition scenario. Introduced new content using the Business Model Canvas template to communicate nine building blocks of writing a business plan with associated questions.

CHAPTER 7

- Twenty-four new or updated examples and/or boxes.
- Updated Manage U: How to Make Good Decisions.
- Section 7.1—Updated Example box on getting the most from intuition.
- Section 7.2—Updated research on ethical lapses in organizations and how companies are responding to them.
- Section 7.3—Expanded linkage to career readiness competencies in section opening. Introduced new figure integrating evidence-based decision making, big data, artificial intelligence, and analytics. Introduced new definitions for descriptive analytics, machine learning, and predictive analytics. New figure on the 5 V's of big data. New content on big data's core characteristics.
- Section 7.4—New figure on the four functions of artificial intelligence. New content on four types of AI: automate,

New to the 2024 release xiii

analyze, advise, and anticipate. New Example box on how ChatGPT is ushering in a new era. Updated figure on the benefits of AI. Updated Practical Action box on how career readiness competencies can enhance collaboration with robots.

- Section 7.5—Introduced new running example of decision-making styles using HR professionals handling sexual harassment claims in their companies.
- Section 7.6—Updated examples and research on decision-making biases.
- Section 7.7—New table on the symptoms and attitudes associated with groupthink and the preventative measures to avoid it. Changed project post-mortems to the more contemporary concept of after action reviews, and updated research on the topic.
- Section 7.8—Expanded set of career readiness competencies that are used in decision making. Illustrated how the career readiness competencies discussed in the section connect with the chapter's Executive Interview Series video.

CHAPTER 8

- Twenty-nine new or updated examples and/or boxes.
- Updated the Manage U to situate recommendations within the context of modern work arrangements.
- Section 8.1—Updated Southwest example illustrating how culture can support strategy. Updated P&G example illustrating how structure can support strategy. Updated In-N-Out Burger example of how HR practices can support strategy. Updated UPS example illustrating how leadership can align culture, structure, and HR practices.
- Section 8.2—Revised introduction for enhanced readability, relevance, and connection to the modern work environment. New example of Gitlab to illustrate observable artifacts. New example of Cadence to illustrate espoused values. New Red Robin example to illustrate enacted values. New restaurant industry example to illustrate basic assumptions. New example of Nelly Cheboi to illustrate heroes. New example of McKinsey & Company to illustrate rites and rituals. Re-formatted content on the three phases of organizational socialization for enhanced readability. Updated example of NYU to illustrate socialization. Updated example of Wegmans to illustrate clan culture. Updated example of Baxter International to illustrate adhocracy culture. Updated example of Tyson Foods to illustrate market culture. Updated example of McDonald's to illustrate hierarchy culture. Reconfigured section on P–O fit by breaking content into two smaller sections—the first focusing on how organizations use interviews to assess candidates' levels of P–O fit (and recommendations for doing so correctly), and the second focusing on helping students understand how to assess their own fit with potential employers.
- Section 8.3—Updated example of HubSpot illustrating formal statements. New example of companies that have changed their slogans. Updated example of Pinterest illustrating rites and rituals. New example of the UNHCR to illustrate stories, legends, and myths. New example of Adidas to illustrate leader reactions to crises. Updated example of companies that use reverse role modeling. New example of companies using the physical design of neighborhoods in the new world of hybrid work. New example of Ford to illustrate organizational goals and performance criteria. Updated example of employee monitoring to illustrate measurable and controllable activities. Updated example of Zappos to illustrate organizational structure. Updated example of Google to illustrate organizational systems and procedures. Revamped section on P-O fit to account for two important issues: (1) what happens when poor P–O fit causes dysfunctional turnover and the implications for culture change, and (2) what happens when high P–O fit hinders DE&I efforts, leads to homogeneity, and engenders a resistance to organizational change.
- Section 8.4—Updated Practical Action box on how to delegate effectively.
- Section 8.5—Streamlined introduction for enhanced readability and connection with chapter content. Revised discussion of ExxonMobil's organizational structure. Updated example of Boeing to illustrate modular structure. New example of Zapier to illustrate virtual structure.
- Section 8.6—Illustrated how the career readiness competencies discussed in the section connect with the chapter's Executive Interview Series video. New example of taking ownership and accepting responsibility to illustrate how readers can become more adaptable.

CHAPTER 9

- Twenty-four new or updated examples and/or boxes.
- Updated Manage U: How to Prepare for a Job Interview.
- Section 9.1—Streamlined introduction for enhanced readability and clarity. Revised figure on human resource practices to better reflect how HR practices fit together to form an effective HRM strategy. New examples of organizations leading the way with the HR practices. Revised discussion of internal and external HR fit for enhanced clarity and connection to the overall goals of the chapter. New example of IBM to illustrate internal HR fit. Updated example of Airbnb to illustrate external HR fit. New example of Rocket Companies to illustrate how companies generate competitive advantage through their HR practices. New example of the U.S. Marine Corps to illustrate talent management. New example of P&G to illustrate high performance work systems.
- Section 9.2—Revised introduction for increased clarity and readability. New statistics on skills gaps in today's workplace. Introduced the concept of talent marketplaces as part of internal recruiting. New example of Schneider Electric to

illustrate talent marketplaces. New example of the U.S. Air Force to illustrate external recruiting. Updated example of UKG (formerly Kronos) to illustrate boomerangs. New example of George Santos to illustrate dishonesty on resumes. New example of Accenture to illustrate skills-based hiring. Streamlined section on employment tests for enhanced readability.

- Section 9.3—Streamlined introduction for enhanced readability and connection with modern compensation and benefits issues. New example of Goldman Sachs to illustrate compensation packages. Revised incentives section to focus on the new world of hybrid work. New data on the pros and cons of hybrid work arrangements. Updated discussion of the benefits preferred by Gen Z workers.

- Section 9.4—Streamlined discussion of the outcomes of onboarding. Updated content on practices for onboarding. New example of Carrefour to illustrate L&D. Streamlined discussion of L&D for enhanced readability.

- Section 9.5—Updated data on performance feedback in the introduction. Updated example of Adobe illustrating frequent feedback. New example of Synchrony to illustrate future-oriented feedback. Updated example of patient experience surveys illustrating performance information. Revised discussion of 360-degree performance assessments including risks when used incorrectly and likelihood of use. New example of Cox Communications to illustrate 360-degree assessments. Streamlined discussion of forced ranking and updated example of GE.

- Section 9.6—Streamlined introduction for enhanced readability and connection to chapter content. Revised discussion of the importance of fairness in promotions. New example of how various companies use transfers. Introduced the concept of a performance improvement plan (PIP) as part of disciplining and demotion. New example of the technology sector to illustrate layoffs. Revised discussion on firings. Enhanced content on exit interviews, including when they are likely to be used.

- Section 9.7—Updated statistics on minimum wage and workplace discrimination. Introduced discussion of new laws banning workplaces from inquiring about applicants' prior salaries. New example of AI-based selection tools to illustrate workplace discrimination. Updated Harvard example illustrating affirmative action. Streamlined content on workplace bullying and updated statistics.

- Section 9.8—Updated statistics in table on today's U.S. labor union movement. Updated statistics on right-to-work laws. Revised discussion of two-tier wage contracts and included a new example using multiple companies. New example of the Ending Forced Arbitration of Sexual Assault and Sexual Harassment act to illustrate arbitration.

- Section 9.9—Illustrated how the career readiness competencies discussed in the section connect with the chapter's Executive Interview Series video. Streamlined introduction. Revised content on learning how to listen.

CHAPTER 10

- Thirty-one new or updated examples and/or boxes.
- Updated Manage U: How Can I Be More Creative at Work?
- Section 10.1—Revised introduction to enhance understanding of chapter content. Added a sixth supertrend shaping the future of business to account for today's shifting employment landscape. Updated discussion of today's increasingly segmented marketplace, including new data on consumer expectations and a new example of custom clothing. Updated discussion of speed-to-market, including new data on firm performance and a new example of lithium-ion batteries. Updated Example box on radical change in the movie industry. Revised discussion of how offshore suppliers are changing the way we work. Updated statistics on knowledge work. New example of robotic surgery to illustrate how AI can assist knowledge workers. New discussion of the shifting employment landscape, including the implication of the new psychological contract between employers and employees and an illustrative example using Dropbox. New example of solar power to illustrate reactive change. New example of Microsoft to illustrate proactive change. Multiple new and revised examples illustrating the various forces for change originating inside and outside the organization.

- Section 10.2—Updated examples of adaptive and innovative change. New example of radically innovative change using the shift to remote work during the COVID-19 pandemic. New example of Diligent Robotics woven throughout the discussion of the three stages in Lewin's model of change.

- Section 10.3—Revised introduction to enhance readability and understanding of organizational development. New example of USC to illustrate how OD can be used to improve individual, team, and organizational performance. New example of Aramis Group to illustrate how OD can be used to transform organizations. Updated statistics on mergers. Revised and updated discussion on recommendations for using OD successfully.

- Section 10.4—Revised introduction and updated statistics on American spending patterns. Updated example of food delivery to illustrate process innovation. New examples to illustrate product, improvement, and new-direction innovation. New example of ChatGPT to illustrate the risks of innovation going too far. Clarified innovation as the product of all the elements in an innovation system working together. New example of Ambow Education to illustrate commitment from senior leaders. Updated data in table on the most innovative companies. Updated Practical Action box (formerly an Example box) on IDEO's approach to innovation to provide practical advice for readers wishing to improve their ability to generate creative and innovative ideas. Updated example of innovation competitions to illustrate crowdsourcing. Revised discussion on developing the necessary human capital, including content from recent global surveys indicating the most important competencies that organizations seek in prospective

New to the 2024 release xv

employees. New example of Nestlé USA to illustrate developing the necessary human capital. Updated CarMax example illustrating HR policies, practices, and procedures. New statistics on upskilling and new example of Guild to illustrate how organizations develop the appropriate resources.

- Section 10.5—Revised content on the reasons employees resist change, including a new table developed for enhanced readability and understanding.
- Section 10.6—Illustrated how the career readiness competencies discussed in the section connect with the chapter's Executive Interview Series video. Revised introduction to enhance connection to openness to change. Revised discussion of self-affirmation theory.

CHAPTER 11

- Six new or updated examples and/or boxes.
- Updated Manage U: Making Positive First Impressions.
- Section 11.1—Updated statistics on the use of personality tests in Fortune 500 companies. Enhanced connection of content with career readiness competencies. New example of how personality testing can aid team-building efforts. Updated discussion of emotional intelligence. Updated Practical Action box on using technology to develop emotional intelligence.
- Section 11.2—Revised introduction to enhance connection to and understanding of how values, attitudes, and behavior relate to managing individual differences. Revised discussion of values. Updated example of generational differences to illustrate attitudes. New example of cognitive dissonance.
- Section 11.3—Revised entire discussion of distortions in perception for brevity and enhanced readability. New statistics on workplace stereotypes and implicit bias. Revised discussion of the recency effect for enhanced clarity. Revised discussion of the fundamental attribution bias and the self-serving bias. Revised discussion of the Pygmalion effect.
- Section 11.4—Updated table with recent statistics on global employee engagement. New example of Nordstrom to illustrate employee engagement. Updated statistics on how managers can increase employee engagement. New statistics on job satisfaction. Updated Example box on rudeness in the workplace. Revised material on absenteeism and turnover, including a new discussion of the difference between functional and dysfunctional turnover.
- Section 11.5—Completely new, with a revised introduction to clarify the importance of learning about workplace stress. New statistics on stress in the workplace. Enhanced discussion of burnout as a result of too much work stress. Introduced new model and discussion of the stress process. Updated content on the sources of job-related stress, including revised discussions of stress arising from work roles and group demands, and a new section discussing the demands created by remote and hybrid work schedules.

- Section 11.6—Completely new, illustrating how the career readiness competencies discussed in the section connect with the chapter's Executive Interview Series video. Enhanced discussion of "good attitude" behaviors with new material on gratitude.

CHAPTER 12

- Twenty-nine new or updated examples and/or boxes.
- Updated Manage U: Managing for Motivation: Building Your Own Motivation.
- Section 12.1—Added relational job characteristics to the discussion of job design theories.
- Section 12.2—Revised figure on Maslow's hierarchy of needs. The updated figure and subsequent discussion organizes Maslow's five needs into three buckets: basic, psychological, and self-fulfillment needs. Expanded discussion of need for managers to be attentive to employees' different and changing needs. Updated discussion of employee benefits programs as they relate to two-factor theory.
- Section 12.3—Consolidated discussion of cognitive dissonance. Revised figure on equity theory to clarify equity as a ratio of outcomes to inputs. Updated Example box on Dr. Anne-Marie Imafidon.
- Section 12.4—New opening statistics related to engagement and quiet quitting. New discussion of relational job design that covers prosocial motivation, research explaining its benefits, and ways to increase it. New figure on prosocial motivation and how it impacts employee outcomes.
- Section 12.5—Streamlined introduction. Added example of ghosting to the discussion of extinction.
- Section 12.6—Updated research-based conclusions about money and motivation. Added new example on healthcare providers to illustrate the concept of gainsharing. Changed the term *flex-time* to *flexible work arrangements*. Updated Practical Action box on how managers can encourage gratitude. Added new research linking flourishing to quiet quitting.
- Section 12.7—Expanded set of career readiness competencies that are used in motivation. Illustrated how the career readiness competencies discussed in the section connect with the chapter's Executive Interview Series video.

CHAPTER 13

- Twelve new or updated examples and/or boxes.
- Updated Manage U: Managing Team Conflict Like a Pro.
- Section 13.1—Streamlined introduction to focus on outlining the learning objectives for the section. Expanded discussion of the benefits of and challenges associated with virtual work. Introduced a new section with a new figure that presents an organizing framework for understanding team

functioning. The figure outlines the content in the remainder of the chapter and provides a framework to define several key terms.

- Section 13.2—Revised figure on the five stages of group and team development to enhance readability and recall. Illustrated punctuated equilibrium using AI's impact on business.
- Section 13.3—Reduced eight team effectiveness competencies to seven: moved content under "Effective Team Processes" to new section (Section 13.6) called "Managing Team Dysfunction."
- Section 13.4—New examples using MetroHealth and Pixar to illustrate dysfunctional and functional conflict, respectively. New examples using the former and current Disney CEO to illustrate personality conflict, Manny Machado to illustrate envy-based conflict, and Meta to illustrate cross-cultural conflict. Focused discussion on how to stimulate constructive conflict with programmed conflict. Revised figure on the five common styles for handing conflict to enhance its descriptiveness and usability.
- Section 13.5—Expanded set of career readiness competencies that are used in teams. Illustrated how the career readiness competencies discussed in the section connect with the chapter's Executive Interview Series video.
- Section 13.6—Introduced a new a-head called "Managing Team Dysfunction." Introduced new figure on five team dysfunctions that lists the major team dysfunctions, how to recognize them, and how to manage them. This section features a practical running example about a typical student team to illustrate each dysfunction.

CHAPTER 14

- Twenty-five new or updated examples and/or boxes.
- Updated Manage U: Improving Your Leadership Skills.
- Section 14.1—Included new and updated examples in the table on nine common influence tactics. New discussion of the outcomes of influence tactics that focuses on three common outcomes of influence attempts: commitment, compliance, and resistance.
- Section 14.2 – Updated table on key task-oriented traits and interpersonal attributes by adding proactive personality to positive task-oriented traits, and adding collectivism, trait empathy, and moral identity to positive interpersonal traits. Updated research on gender differences in leadership. Introduced a new discussion of changing gender stereotypes and more equitable HR practices that support equitable access to leadership development.
- Section 14.3—New examples to illustrate task-oriented and relationship-oriented leadership using CEOs from Adidas and TIAA, respectively.
- Section 14.4—Revised figure on the general representation of House's revised path-goal theory by organizing eight leader behaviors into two categories: task-oriented and relationship-oriented. Introduced new example of path-goal leadership. Updated Practical Action box on the application of situational leadership theories.
- Section 14.5—Updated Example box on leaders who are both transactional and transformational. Introduced a new running example of Coach Pat Summitt to illustrate four key behaviors of transformational leaders.
- Section 14.6—Updated example of FEED to illustrate leading for autonomy. Added new discussion on the effects of empowering leadership on employees and key research on empowering leadership's effectiveness. Introduced new material on research related to the effectiveness of ethical leadership. Updated Practical Action box on how to be a good leader by being a good follower.
- Section 14.7—Expanded set of career readiness competencies that are used in leadership. Illustrated how the career readiness competencies discussed in the section connect with the chapter's Executive Interview Series video.

CHAPTER 15

- Eleven new or updated examples and/or boxes.
- Updated Manage U: Improving Your Use of Empathy
- Section 15.1—Streamlined section on the definition of communication, including new data on the importance of the career readiness competency of communication. New example of multilingual signage to illustrate eliminating semantic noise. New example of your authoring team to illustrate selecting the right medium. Enhanced discussion of media richness.
- Section 15.2—Enhanced discussions of downward and upward communication, including new examples. Revised material on horizontal communication, including new Example box on internal communication in the modern work environment. New example of Wendy's illustrating external communication. Updated statistics on the grapevine as a communication system. Updated discussion of basic principles for making the most of face-to-face communication at work. Updated Practical Action box on improving meetings.
- Section 15.3—Enhanced discussion of variations in the way we process and interpret information. New statistics on generational differences in communication. Updated example of Dutch communication to illustrate style differences. Updated Example box on improving your cross-cultural communication fluency. Streamlined content on gender differences to increase inclusion.
- Section 15.4—Updated statistics on the use of social media. New example of National Geographic to illustrate an organization embracing social media. Updated figure on age distribution across social networks. Streamlined discussion of social media and managerial and organizational effectiveness. Revised discussion of social media in

employment recruiting. New example of Burger King UK to illustrate corporate reputation and social media. New example on microaggressions in social media. Updated statistics on privacy. Revised discussion of false information, including new example of searching for statistics and new recommendations for defending against being fooled by false information. Updated table on effective social media policy.

- Section 15.5—Updated table on the antecedents of defensive and nondefensive communication. Updated example of Danish schools illustrating empathy.

- Section 15.6—Illustrated how the career readiness competencies discussed in the section connect with the chapter's Executive Interview Series video. Updated statistics on networking. Revised discussion of building personal connections.

CHAPTER 16

- Twenty new or updated examples and/or boxes.
- New Manage U: Managing Your Personal and Professional Satisfaction.
- Section 16.1—This section begins with an overview of a new three-part series of Practical Action boxes that helps students apply what they learned in the section to their own goals. The three-part series helps students to (1) set long-term career goals, (2) develop short-term SMART goals needed to accomplish the long-term career goals, and (3) define behaviors to measure progress toward the SMART goals and make adjustments as needed to ensure they achieve their goals. Revised figure on controlling for effective performance to illustrate the connection between controlling and planning. New Practical Action box on determining your overall career objective.
- Section 16.2—New table summarizing the different performance standards among nonprofit, for-profit, and service organizations. Reframed three types of controls around their time-related focus: future, present, and past.

- Section 16.3—Revised table on popular financial ratios. Expanded discussion of differences between benchmarking and best practices. New Practical Action box on developing your career management competency. Updated strategy map for Keurig Dr Pepper.

- Section 16.4—New Practical Action box on using the PDCA model to control your career management action plan. New table that presents an action plan to help readers measure progress toward goals. Created new example on Hyundai Genesis to illustrate the concept of people orientation. Revised and updated Example box on Trader Joe's service excellence. New discussion of Lean Six Sigma 4.0. Moved content from "Reducing Errors and Defects" in Section 16.5 to Lean Six Sigma 4.0. Updated the number of ISO 9000 standards from eight to seven.

- Section 16.5—Moved "Reducing Errors and Defects" discussion to Section 16.4 under Lean Six Sigma 4.0. Updated content on how AI can improve productivity. Updated discussion of employee tracking and monitoring to focus on flexible work arrangements and added state of the science research conclusions about its effectiveness. New table on the top non-work activities that hybrid and remote workers reported engaging in during work hours. Summarized text discussion of pros/cons of employee tracking in new table on the advantages and disadvantages of employee tracking and monitoring. New research-based recommendations to effectively deploy employee tracking and monitoring.

- Section 16.6—Expanded set of career readiness competencies that are used in the control process. Illustrated how the career readiness competencies discussed in the section connect with the chapter's Executive Interview Series video. Updated section that explains how to apply the control process to career management. New figure presenting a model of continuous self-improvement that describes the connection between the control process and the process of continuous self-improvement. The section concludes with recommendations for students' career management formerly found in the epilogue.

Walkthrough Preface

Kinicki, Breaux Soignet, and Hartnell's *Management: A Practical Introduction 2024 Release* **empowers** students to develop the management career skills necessary in everyday life through the practical and relevant application of theory. Developed to help students learn management with a purpose, Kinicki, Breaux Soignet, and Hartnell's 2024 Release takes a student-centered approach. **The revision includes a new chapter on DE&I, expanded coverage of its strategic career readiness theme, and new coverage of practical, leading edge hot topics.** The hallmark strengths that have made it the market best-seller have been maintained and include:

- A student-centered approach to learning.
- Imaginative writing for readability and reinforcement.
- Emphasis on practicality.
- Resources that work.

Our product covers the principles that most management instructors have come to expect in an introductory text—planning, organizing, leading, and controlling—plus current issues that students need to be to be aware of to succeed: career readiness, DE&I, hybrid work schedules, customer focus, globalism, ethics, sustainability, social media, entrepreneurship, teams, innovation, artificial intelligence, big data, and person–organization fit.

> " *This book and its ancillary materials (are) vastly superior to any other management textbook on the market. The text coverage and rich examples, colorful pages, and visuals enhance its readability and engagement for students.* "
>
> **—Gerald Schoenfeld,**
> *Florida Gulf Coast University*

> " *Management is an excellent textbook. It is easy to read, interesting, and relevant.* "
>
> **—Maureen Sutton,**
> *County College of Morris*

> " *(Management) is easy to read and follow; there is no escape from learning if a student is truly motivated to learn! Examples and illustrations are excellent and aid in learning. SmartBook questions are of superb quality and help students to learn in the most effective way. This is one of the very few textbooks in the market that is a joy to read! Connect homework package is excellent and included self-assessments, mini-simulations, and Hot Seats. Based on student feedback, students truly enjoy doing their homework.* "
>
> **—Elina Ibrayeva,**
> *University of Nebraska—Lincoln*

Based on a wealth of instructor feedback and blending Angelo's scholarship, teaching, publishing, and management-consulting with Denise's and Chad's academic backgrounds and writing ability, we have worked tirelessly to create a research-based yet highly readable, practical, and motivational product for the introductory principles of management course. Our goal is to make a difference in your life and the lives of your students.

Focus on Career Readiness

Global research shows that employers struggle to find college graduates who possess the skills needed to be successful. These employers want colleges and universities to do a better job making students career ready. Our goal in the 2024 Release is to contribute to solving this problem in two ways. First, we refined our model of career readiness (first presented in Chapter 1) to better align with the latest research. Second, we incorporated a new series of executive interviews conducted with global managers across a variety of industries into each chapter's Career Corner. As always, we provide activities for both online and face-to-face teaching that professors can use to develop students' career readiness competencies in our novel Teaching Resources Manual (TRM).

Building Your Career Readiness

Chapter 1 contains a section devoted to explaining the need, value, and process for becoming career ready. It includes a model of career readiness along with a table of competencies desired by employers.

> **SELF-ASSESSMENT 1.2   CAREER READINESS**
>
> **To What Extent Do You Accept Responsibility for Your Actions?**
> This survey is designed to assess the extent to which you accept responsibility for your actions. Please complete Self-Assessment 1.2 if your instructor has assigned it in Connect.

Self-Assessments

Of the 65 Self-Assessments in this text, over 35 of them allow students to assess the extent to which they possess aspects of the career readiness competencies desired by employers.

Career Corner

Each chapter concludes with a section entitled "Career Corner: Managing Your Career Readiness." The material provides students with practical tips for developing targeted career readiness competencies and links with the advice of modern global executives and managers. It also explains the linkage between the content covered in the chapter and the career readiness competencies desired by employers.

> ### 1.8 Career Corner: Managing Your Career Readiness
>
> The goal of this section is to help you apply what you learn to building your career readiness. Let's begin with three keys to success:
>
> 1. It's your responsibility to manage your career. Don't count on others.
> 2. Personal reflection, motivation, commitment, and experimentation are essential.
> 3. Success is achieved by following a process. A **process** is defined as a series of actions or steps followed to bring about a desired result.
>
> **LO 1-8**
> Describe the process for managing your career readiness.
>
> #### A Process for Developing Career Readiness
>
> Figure 1.5 illustrates a process to guide the pursuit of managing your career readiness. We recommend the following four steps:
>
> **Step 1** The first step entails examining the list of career readiness competencies in Table 1.3 and picking a few that impact your current performance at school, work, or other activities. Then, assess your skill level for these competencies. This product contains 64 self-assessments you can take for this purpose. The first two were presented earlier in this chapter.

> 66 *The examples and cases are relevant and engaging. I especially like the self-assessments and the career readiness focus. I think anytime students use experiential learning is time well spent, and can be eye opening for all.* 99
>
> —**Sandra Ryan,**
> *Texas Tech University*

Concept Mastery

New exercises in Connect allow students to demonstrate lower levels of learning regarding career readiness. The TRM provides opportunities for higher levels of learning for career readiness competencies.

xxi

Student-Centered Approach to Learning

Our writing style and product design is based on neuroscience research showing that greater learning occurs when information is "chunked" to keep students' attention. We break down topics into easily digestible portions with purposeful pedagogy to make theories and concepts easier to learn and apply. We are intentional in our use of color, images, bulleted lists, and headings to appeal to the visual sensibilities, time constraints, and diverse learning styles of today's students.

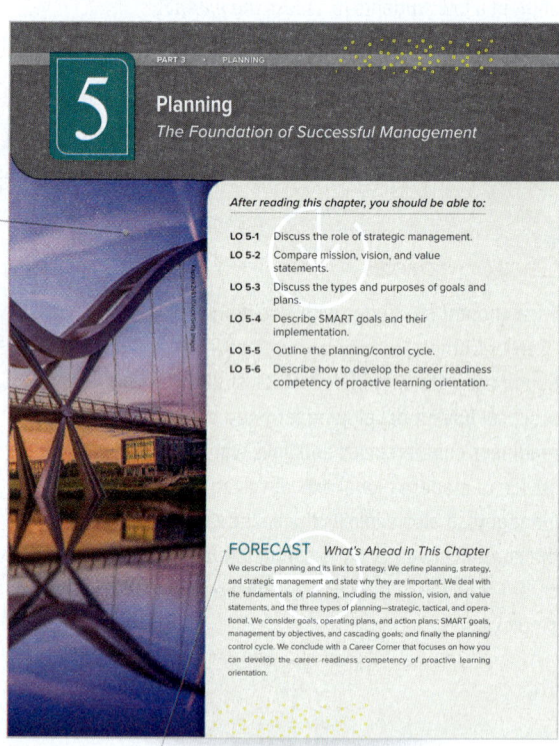

Chapter Openers

Each chapter begins with a list of key learning objectives to answer students' question of "what's in it for me?" and to help them read with purpose.

Chapter Sections

Within each chapter, sections are organized according to the major learning objectives. Generous use of headings and bulleted lists provide students with bite-sized chunks of information to facilitate retention. Each section begins with a recap of the **Learning Objective** and includes **The Big Picture**, which presents an overview of how the section addresses the stated objective.

Forecast

Following the learning objectives, the forecast provides a high-level summary of what is covered in the chapter.

> *Out of all the management textbooks on today's market, the textbook is the very best package to support active student learning in today's classroom learning environment. The textbook clearly supports the student-learning approach to learning and [I] strongly recommend any instructor to use the book in both face-to-face and online management classes.*
>
> —Jessie Lee Bellflowers,
> *Fayetteville Technical Community College*

xxii

Imaginative Writing for Readability and Reinforcement

Research shows that products written in an imaginative, story-telling style significantly improve students' ability to retain information. We employ numerous journalistic devices to make the material engaging and relevant to students' lives.

Example boxes

Our Example boxes emphasize the practical applications of business. These mini cases use snapshots of real-world companies to explain the concepts in the text. "Your Call" questions stimulate class discussions and help students develop their critical thinking skills.

EXAMPLE: Coca-Cola's Mission, Vision, and Values

The Coca-Cola Company is one of the world's largest beverage companies. It has more than 500 brands and nearly one out of four dollars spent on nonalcoholic drinks worldwide are spent on a Coca-Cola brand. Headquartered in Atlanta, the company is more than 135 years old. It employs about 700,000 people worldwide and had more than $42.3 billion in revenues in 2022. Some of its best-known brands include Coke, Coke Zero, Sprite, Dr Pepper, Fanta, Schweppes, Minute Maid, Powerade, Dasani, Honest Tea, and Smart Water. Many of its beverages are available in low-calorie or no-calorie versions.[26]

The company's chair and CEO, James Quincey, describes Coca-Cola's mission, vision, and values as follows.

Our Mission[27]
Our purpose: *"Refresh the world. Make a difference."*

Our Vision
Our vision for our next stage of growth has three connected pillars:[28]

- **Loved Brands.** "We craft meaningful brands and a choice of drinks that people love, enjoy, and that refresh them in body and spirit."
- **Done Sustainably.** "We grow our business in ways that achieve positive change in the world and build a more sustainable future for our planet."
- **For a Better Shared Future.** "We invest to improve people's lives, from our employees, to all those who touch our business system, to our investors, to the communities we call home."

Core Values
Our values represent our compass and the conscience we follow:[29]

- **Courage and a Growth Mindset:** Learn continuously and adopt a broader perspective of what's possible.
- **Curiosity:** Explore, imagine, and wonder how our products, service, or our impact on the world could be better or different.
- **Empowerment:** Be accountable. Be proactive.
- **Inclusion:** Draw on the diversity of talent and experiences to generate better ideas and make better decisions.
- **Agility:** Learn quickly and continuously improve.
- **Honesty:** If we make mistakes, we own them and act quickly to correct them.
- **Integrity:** Do the right thing. Always.

YOUR CALL
What do you think of Coca-Cola's mission, vision, and values? Are they explicit enough to guide employee behavior and company actions? Why or why not? Could any of them apply equally well to other businesses? Why or why not?

Heavy consumption. Coca-Cola has hundreds of brands, including Coca-Cola Classic, Sprite, and Fanta. Alignment among its mission, vision, and values isn't just important for employees, it's also important for the brand as the company has millions of customers around the world. Did you know that over 1.9 billion servings of Coca-Cola beverages are consumed in more than 200 countries every day? Chones/Shutterstock

> ❝ Very practical (and) easy to follow.... A good foundation for later management courses. The examples are relevant and enjoyable. ❞
>
> —**Kelli Crickey,**
> *University of North Georgia*

> ❝ Very practical, well-suited for undergraduates at the introductory level, suitable for various levels of academic preparedness and ability. Highly structured in a way that rewards the student for study effort and helps the student make efficient use of their study time. Avoids an overly academic and abstract approach. ❞
>
> —**Edward B. Hubbard,**
> *Rutgers Business School*

> ❝ Excellent, easy to read textbook with great company examples. ❞
>
> —**Elena Ibrayeva,**
> *University of Nebraska—Lincoln*

Extended Emphasis on Practicality

Students are more engaged and motivated when they connect with the material being taught. This means that the examples and illustrations we use must be relevant to our readers. The 2024 Release includes more than 280 new or updated practical examples of management concepts. Of these, more than 30 related to the management opportunities and challenges presented by the seismic shift to hybrid and remote work, and more than 40 related to how businesses and managers are adjusting to modern applications of artificial intelligence.

We want this 2024 Release to be a cherished resource that students keep as they move into future courses and their future careers. We give students a great deal of practical advice in addition to covering the fundamental concepts of management.

Practical Action Boxes Practical Action boxes offer students practical and interesting advice on issues they will face in the workplace.

PRACTICAL ACTION — Setting Goals for a Small Business

Goal setting can seem like an intimidating process, but it's both a necessary and a helpful one for the millions of small businesses (defined as having 500 or fewer employees) in the United States. In fact, a research study of 231 small businesses found that goal setting had a positive impact on the firm's performance.[53] These findings are important, particularly because small businesses account for 44% of U.S. economic activity and 62% of the nation's new jobs.[54]

The Great Lakes Brewing Company, Ohio's first craft brewery, is a good example of goal setting in small businesses.[55]

1. **Break large goals down into smaller ones:** Growth is a key indicator in the craft brewing industry. Great Lakes faced declining beer production for seven years from its peak in 2014. The company's CEO, Mark King, identified innovation as the strategic key to the company's turnaround. He focused on three smaller goals to achieve his strategic objective: rebranding the core brands, new products, and a new canning line. We'll focus on rebranding the core brands, which the brewery breaks down into areas such as redesigned labels, marketing via new platforms, and leveraging key partners—like the Cleveland Guardians—to build brand recognition and strengthen brand reputation. Rebranding the core brands is then broken down into a more specific measurable goal, which is sales growth at grocery stores, a critical distribution channel during the pandemic, at or above the industry average for any given year.

2. **Track progress toward goals:** The company monitors its sales growth/decline from its core brands at grocery stores annually. It then compares the sales figures to the industry average to determine if it is meeting its goal.

3. **Keep the goal in sight:** The brewery's management knows it must take action to ensure its sales goals are met. For example, Great Lakes redesigned the labels for its core brands using bright, colorful imagery with designs inspired by significant events in the company's and its founding city's (Cleveland, Ohio) history. In addition to redesigning the packaging to attract consumers' attention in a grocery store, the brewer created point of sale display pieces to entice new customers to try their product.

4. **Celebrate success:** Great Lakes stopped its decline and celebrated achieving 18% sales growth in grocery stores in 2021 compared to 2020. Regarding the company's turnaround performance, King commented, "We're the best-performing top-25 craft brewery in the U.S. And we are only one of two that is in positive numbers. That's really exciting."

YOUR CALL

What major goal of your own have you broken into smaller parts? If you have never done this, for what future goal do you think it would be an effective strategy for you?

SELF-ASSESSMENT 5.2

What Is the Quality of Goal Setting within a Current or Past Employer?

This survey is designed to assess the quality of goal setting in a company. Please complete Self-Assessment 5.2 if your instructor has assigned it in Connect.

Self-Assessments Self-Assessment evaluations help students relate what they are learning to their own experiences and promote self-reflection, engagement, and development of their career readiness. Of the more than 65 total Self-Assessments included, over 35 of them pertain to a career readiness competency. For each of these, students are asked to consider how they might display the competency in an employment interview.

xxiv

Management in Action Cases (Available in Connect) Rather than using stories about companies, the new Management in Action cases now focus on higher levels of learning by asking students to solve real organizational problems using relevant management concepts. These cases develop students' core career readiness competencies of critical thinking and problem solving.

Legal/Ethical Challenge Cases (Available in Connect) Legal/Ethical Challenge cases ask students to resolve real ethical challenges faced by managers and organizations. They help develop students' critical thinking and problem-solving skills around ethical issues. The Management in Action and Legal/Ethical Challenge cases are linked. This enables instructors to integrate ethical issues within the broader context of the Management in Action case.

Boeing Continuing Case (Available in Connect) The updated continuing case asks students to synthesize and apply what they've learned across the course to recent events occurring at Boeing. Based on reviewer feedback, we present the continuing case at the part level within Connect.

> *Provides students a well-written text with comprehensive topic coverage, includes real-world examples, is geared toward helping students understand the connection between coursework and career. It provides many applicable exercises (Manage U, Management in Action, Legal/Ethical Challenges, Practical Action, Self-Assessments and Application-Based Activities, and group exercises for each section of the chapter). As the title states, it takes a very practical approach to the course material.*
>
> **—Suzanne Clinton,**
> University of Central Oklahoma

> *Management covers the basic concepts required for a Principles of Management course in an engaging way for students that allows them to not only learn theory but also how to apply it in their lives now and as their careers progress.*
>
> **—Kirk Silvernail,**
> University of Nevada—Las Vegas

xxv

Resources That Work

No matter how you teach your course—face-to-face, hybrid, or online—you're in the driver's seat. We offer the most robust set of resources to enhance your Principles of Management course. In addition to our unique Teaching Resource Manual 2.0 (TRM), packed with additional activities and supplemental teaching tools, PowerPoint presentations, and Test Bank questions, we have a wealth of assignable resources available in Connect®.

Connect®

The 2024 Release continues to build on the power of Connect and furthers our quest to help students move from comprehension to application. McGraw Hill Connect® is a personalized teaching and learning tool powered by adaptive technologies so your students learn more efficiently, retain more, and achieve better outcomes. We used this platform to create exercises that are auto-graded in order to assist students in developing their career readiness. Here you will find a wide variety of learning resources that develop students' higher-order thinking skills, including:

- **SmartBook®** An adaptive learning and reading tool, SmartBook prompts students with questions based on the material they are studying. By assessing individual answers, SmartBook learns what each student knows and identifies which topics they need to practice. This technology gives each student a personalized learning experience and path to success. SmartBook provides students with a seamless combination of practice, assessment, and remediation.

- **Matching and Multiple Choice** These activities help make the connection between theory and application through matching, ranking, or grouping. Every Career Corner has an exercise to help you assess students' understanding about how to improve targeted career readiness competencies.

- **iSeeIt Animated Videos** These brief, contemporary videos offer dynamic student-centered introductions, illustrations, and animations to guide students through challenging concepts. Ideal for before class as an introduction, during class to launch or clarify a topic, or after class for formative assessment.

- **Self-Assessments** Designed to promote student self-awareness and self-reflection, these research-based activities also provide personal and professional development. For this edition, five new assessments were created to measure different career readiness competencies. In addition, new structured feedback explains how students should interpret their scores.

- **Case Analyses and Video Cases** Our assortment of written and video cases challenge students to analyze concepts as they manifest in scenarios related to a real-life product or company, fostering students' ability to think critically in lecture and beyond. Thought-provoking questions check the students' application of the course material and develop their workplace readiness skills.

- **Manager's Hot Seat videos** These actor-portrayed videos depict real-life situations where a manager is faced with a dilemma that needs to be analyzed based on management concepts. These videos enable students to see how managers in realistic situations deal with employees and complex issues. Students use their critical thinking skills to apply, analyze, and evaluate these managerial challenges while learning from the manager's mistakes. Each Hot Seat includes follow-up multiple-choice questions that are assignable and auto-gradable.

- **Boeing Continuing Case** Students understand the application of and relationship between different concepts by applying them to the same company throughout the semester. Instructors can use the continuing case on Boeing as a summary case for each part. Each part-ending case includes multiple-choice questions that are assignable and auto-gradable, as well as essay-based questions.

- **Application-Based Activities** McGraw Hill's Application-Based Activities are highly interactive, automatically graded online exercises that provide students with a safe space to practice using problem-solving skills to apply their knowledge to realistic scenarios. Each scenario addresses key concepts and skills that students must use to work through and solve course-specific problems, resulting in improved critical thinking and relevant workplace skills. Students progress from understanding basic concepts to using their knowledge to analyze complex scenarios and solve real-life problems. Along the way, students see the implications of their decisions and are provided with feedback on how management theory should be informing their actions. They also receive detailed feedback at the conclusion of the activity.

- **Writing Assignments** Available within McGraw Hill Connect,® the Writing Assignment tool delivers a learning experience to help students improve their written communication skills and conceptual understanding. As an instructor you can assign, monitor, grade, and provide feedback on writing more efficiently and effectively.

> " When I first started teaching this course, the size and scope of the TRM seemed daunting. I was also concerned about the recommended timing for each chapter's sections, as it seemed to require much more time than I had available. I finally settled on using the TRM's recommended lesson plan for each chapter as a starting point which I then modified to fit the particular constraints of my course. I've also found it to be a useful tool for developing a different approach in the classroom when I perceive that the level of student engagement has been less than desired. "
>
> —**Christopher Mann,**
> *Clemson University*

> " Management and its associated Connect materials have everything your management students need to develop a sound foundation. We all know that management is a learned skill. This text and Connect duo will give them all they need to step into the rigors of management. I'd say, these students will have an advantage that others could only wish to have. "
>
> —**Ed Drozda,**
> *Bryant University*

xxvii

A complete course platform

Connect enables you to build deeper connections with your students through cohesive digital content and tools, creating engaging learning experiences. We are committed to providing you with the right resources and tools to support all your students along their personal learning journeys.

65%
Less Time Grading

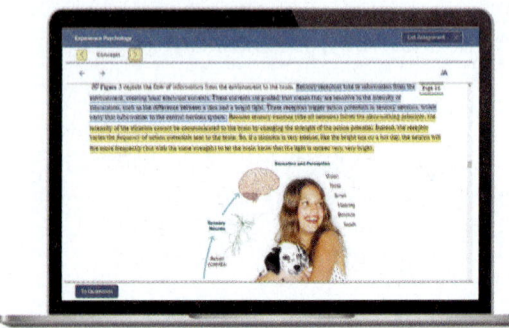

Laptop: Getty Images; Woman/dog: George Doyle/Getty Images

Every learner is unique

In Connect, instructors can assign an adaptive reading experience with SmartBook® 2.0. Rooted in advanced learning science principles, SmartBook 2.0 delivers each student a personalized experience, focusing students on their learning gaps, ensuring that the time they spend studying is time well spent.
mheducation.com/highered/connect/smartbook

Study anytime, anywhere

Encourage your students to download the free ReadAnywhere® app so they can access their online eBook, SmartBook® 2.0, or Adaptive Learning Assignments when it's convenient, even when they're offline. And since the app automatically syncs with their Connect account, all of their work is available every time they open it. Find out more at **mheducation.com/readanywhere**

> *"I really liked this app— it made it easy to study when you don't have your textbook in front of you."*
>
> Jordan Cunningham, a student at *Eastern Washington University*

Effective tools for efficient studying

Connect is designed to help students be more productive with simple, flexible, intuitive tools that maximize study time and meet students' individual learning needs. Get learning that works for everyone with Connect.

Education for all

McGraw Hill works directly with Accessibility Services departments and faculty to meet the learning needs of all students. Please contact your Accessibility Services Office, and ask them to email **accessibility@mheducation.com**, or visit **mheducation.com/about/accessibility** for more information.

Affordable solutions, added value

Make technology work for you with LMS integration for single sign-on access, mobile access to the digital textbook, and reports to quickly show you how each of your students is doing. And with our Inclusive Access program, you can provide all these tools at the lowest available market price to your students. Ask your McGraw Hill representative for more information.

Solutions for your challenges

A product isn't a solution. Real solutions are affordable, reliable, and come with training and ongoing support when you need it and how you want it. Visit **supportateverystep.com** for videos and resources both you and your students can use throughout the term.

Updated and relevant content

Our new Evergreen delivery model provides the most current and relevant content for your course, hassle-free. Content, tools, and technology updates are delivered directly to your existing McGraw Hill Connect® course. Engage students and freshen up assignments with up-to-date coverage of select topics and assessments, all without having to switch editions or build a new course.

acknowledgments

We have the pleasure of working with one of the best teams in the business. Their dedication and effort significantly contributed to the quality of this revision. It all begins with the captain of the team, Michael Ablassmeir. As our editorial director, he provides the internal support to launch and manage the revision process. He also spends much time traveling in support of our products. Thanks for your continuing support over the last 14 years! To Anne Ehrenworth, senior product developer, thank you for paying attention to the details, keeping us all focused on the schedule, coordinating all the moving pieces, and your timely responses to all our questions. You are a joy to work with!

To Debbie Clare, executive marketing manager, you are the energizer bunny who works tirelessly in support of this product. Your creativity, passion, and effort make you the absolute best at your job, and you push us more than anyone to raise our "marketing" game. Thank you! To Harvey Yep, your knowledge and experience with the production process keep us on schedule and responsive to all the change requests. We also appreciate your flexibility and creativity when solving production-related issues. And finally, to Emily Windelborn, assessment content project manager, we appreciate all you do in support of our product in Connect.

To Jennifer Coonce and Doreen MacAulay, your collaboration on the Teaching Resource Manual has been invaluable. Thank you for your commitment to our product. We would also like to thank Jennifer Sexton for her assistance in creating some of the Management in Action and Legal/Ethical Challenge cases; Jack Kirn for his work on the PowerPoint slides, Laci Lyons for her work on the Test Bank and Quizzes; and Kawanna Strong for her work on the Connect exercises. We are also indebted to Patrick Soleymani for all of the Application-Based Activities he has created, as well as all of the incredible Manager's Hot Seat videos that he has spearheaded for our product.

To the McGraw Hill company, a world-class publisher, we are grateful to be members of the family.

Warmest thanks and appreciation go to the individuals who provided valuable input during the developmental stages of this edition, as follows:

Laura L. Alderson,
University of Memphis

Jessie Bellflowers,
Fayetteville Technical Community College

Brenda Brown,
Lansing Community College

Suzanne Clinton,
University of Central Oklahoma

Anastasia Cortes,
Virginia Tech

Kelli Crickey,
University of North Georgia

Justin L. Davis,
University of West Florida

Jamie Nelson Derrick,
Stephen F. Austin State University

Ed Drozda,
Bryant University

Trudy Dunson,
Gwinnett Technical College

Candace Esken,
Bradley University

Tracy Ethridge,
Tri-County Technical College

Edward B. Hubbard,
Rutgers Business School

Elina Ibrayeva,
University of Nebraska–Lincoln

James Latham,
Northern Arizona University

Zahir Latheef,
University of Houston–Downtown

K. Doreen MacAulay,
University of South Florida

Cheryl Macon,
Butler County Community College

Christopher Mann,
Clemson University

Vivianne Moore,
Davenport University

John Olotewo,
Essex County College

William Paczkowski,
Florida Atlantic University

Ken Ross,
University of Kansas

Sandra Ryan,
Texas Tech University–Rawls College of Business

Gerald Schoenfeld,
Florida Gulf Coast University

Kirk Silvernail,
University of Nevada–Las Vegas

Shane Spiller,
Western Kentucky University

Samuel Stapleton,
Morehead State University

Maureen Sutton,
County College of Morris

Debbie Vance,
Tri-County Technical College

We would also like to thank the following colleagues who served as manuscript reviewers during the development of previous editions:

Steven Abram, Kirkwood Community College

G. Stoney Alder, University of Nevada–Las Vegas

Phyllis C. Alderdice, Jefferson Community and Technical College

M. Ruhul Amin, Bloomsburg University of Pennsylvania

Danielle Beu Ammeter, University of Mississippi

William Scott Anchors, University of Maine at Orono

Jeffrey L. Anderson, Ohio University

Darlene Andert, Florida Gulf Coast University

Joel Andexler, Cuyahoga Community College

John Anstey, University of Nebraska at Omaha

Joseph Aranyosi, University of Phoenix

Lindy Archambeau, Warrington College of Business, University of Florida

Maria Aria, Camden County College

Mihran Aroian, University of Texas at Austin

Shelly Arneson, Colorado State University

Lisa Augustyniak, Lake Michigan College

Mona Bahl, Illinois State University

Tanya Balcom, Macomb Community College

Pamela Ball, Clark State Community College

Amy S. Banta, Ohio University

Valerie Barnett, Kansas State University

Lynn Becker, University of Central Florida

William Belcher, Troy University

James D. Bell, Texas State University–San Marcos

Michael Bento, Owens Community College

Victor Berardi, Kent State University

George Bernard, Seminole State College of Florida

Patricia Bernson, County College of Morris

David Bess, University of Hawaii

Stephen Betts, William Paterson University

Jim Bishop, New Mexico State University

Randy Blass, Florida State University

Audrey Blume, Wilmington University

Larry Bohleber, University of Southern Indiana

Alison Bolton, Solano Community College

Melanie Bookout, Greenville Technical College

Robert S. Boothe, University of Southern Mississippi

Susan M. Bosco, Roger Williams University

Scott Boyar, University of Alabama–Birmingham

Anne Brantley, Central Piedmont Community College

David Allen Brown, Ferris State University

Roger Brown, Northwestern Oklahoma State University

Reginald Bruce, University of Louisville

Marit Brunsell, Madison Area Technical College

Jon Bryan, Bridgewater State University

Becky Bryant, Texas Woman's University

Paul Buffa, Jefferson College, Missouri Baptist University

Mark David Burdsall, University of Pittsburgh

Neil Burton, Clemson University

Regina Cannon, Tarrant County College

Barbara A. Carlin, University of Houston

Shari Carpenter, Eastern Oregon University

Tara Carr, University of Wisconsin–Green Bay

Pamela Carstens, Coe College

Julie J. Carwile, John Tyler Community College

Daniel A. Cernas Ortiz, University of North Texas

Glen Chapuis, St. Charles Community College

Rod Christian, Mesa Community College

Mike Cicero, Highline College

Jack Cichy, Davenport University

Anthony Cioffi, Lorain County Community College

Deborah Clark, Santa Fe Community College

J. Dana Clark, Appalachian State University

Dean Cleavenger, University of Central Florida

Sharon Clinebell, University of Northern Colorado

Loretta Fergus Cochran, Arkansas Tech University

Glenda Coleman, South University

Ron Cooley, South Suburban College

Melissa M. Cooper, School of Management, Texas Woman's University

Acknowledgments xxxi

Gary Corona, Florida State College

Susie Cox, University of Louisiana–Monroe

Keith Credo, University of Louisiana–Lafayette

Derek E. Crews, Texas Woman's University

Daniel J. Curtin, Lakeland Community College

Ajay Das, Baruch College

Tom Deckelman, Owens Community College

Linda I. DeLong, University of La Verne

Margaret Deck, Virginia Tech

Kate Demarest, University of Baltimore

E. Gordon DeMeritt, Shepherd University

Kathleen DeNisco, Erie Community College

Anant R. Deshpande, SUNY Empire State College

John DeSpagna, Nassau Community College

Carrie L. Devone, Mott Community College

Pamela A. Dobies, University of Missouri–Kansas City

David Dore, Pima Community College

Lon Doty, San Jose State University

Ron Dougherty, Ivy Tech Community College/Columbus Campus

Scott Droege, Western Kentucky University

Ken Dunegan, Cleveland State University

Steven Dunphy, Indiana University Northwest

Linda Durkin, Delaware County Community College

Subhash Durlabhji, Northwestern State University of Louisiana

Jack Dustman, Northern Arizona University

Jennifer Egrie, Keiser University

Ray Eldridge, Lipscomb University

Bob Eliason, James Madison University

Valerie Evans, Kansas State University

W. Randy Evans, University of Tennessee at Chattanooga

Paul A. Fadil, University of North Florida

Crystal Saric Fashant, Metropolitan State University

Jud Faurer, Metropolitan State University of Denver

Bennie Felts, North Carolina Wesleyan College

Judy Fitch, Augusta State University

Carla Flores, Ball State University

Christopher Flynn, University of North Florida

David Foote, Middle Tennessee State University

Lucy R. Ford, Saint Joseph's University

Charla Fraley, Columbus State Community College

Gail E. Fraser, Kean University

Dana Frederick, Missouri State University

Tony Frontera, Binghamton University

Dane Galden, Columbus State Community College

Patricia Galitz, Southeast Community College

Michael Garcia, Liberty University

Barbara Garrell, Delaware County Community College

Evgeniy Gentchev, Northwood University

Lydia Gilmore, Columbus State Community College

Terry Girdon, Pennsylvania College of Technology

James Glasgow, Villanova University

Ronnie Godshalk, Penn State University

Connie Golden, Lakeland Community College

Lacey Gonzalez-Horan, Lehigh Carbon Community College

Deborah Cain Good, University of Pittsburgh

Kathleen Gosser, University of Louisville

Kris Gossett, Mercyhurst University

Marie Gould, Horizons University

Tita Gray, Maryland University of Integrative Health

Ryan Greenbaum, Oklahoma State University–Stillwater

Jan Grimes, Georgia Southern University

Kevin S. Groves, Pepperdine University

Joyce Guillory, Austin Community College

William Habacivch, Central Penn College

Gordon Haley, Palm Beach State College

Reggie Hall, Tarleton State University

Stephen F. Hallam, University of Akron

Marie D.K. Halvorsen-Ganepola, University of Notre Dame

Charles T. Harrington, Pasadena City College

Lisa M. Harris, Southeast Community College

Joanne Hartsell, East Carolina University

Santhi Harvey, Central State University

Ahmad Hassan, Morehead State University

Karen H. Hawkins, Miami Dade College, Kendall Campus

Samuel Hazen, Tarleton State University

Jack Heinsius, Modesto Junior College

Duane Helleloid, University of North Dakota

Jacob Heller, Tarleton State University

Cathy Henderson, Stephen F. Austin State University

Evelyn Hendrix, Lindenwood University

Nhung Hendy, Towson University

Kim Hester, Arkansas State University

Mark Hiatt, Kennesaw State University

Lara Hobson, Western Michigan University

Anne Hoel, University of Wisconsin–Stout

Gregory A. Hoffeditz, Southern Illinois University–Carbondale

Mary Hogue, Kent State University

David Hollomon, Victor Valley College

James Hopkins, University of Georgia

Tammy Hunt, University of North Carolina–Wilmington

Perwaiz Ismaili, Metropolitan State University

Aviad Israeli, Kent State University

Jacquelyn Jacobs, University of Tennessee

Edward Johnson, University of North Florida

Nancy M. Johnson, Madison Area Technical College

Paul D. Johnson, University of Mississippi

Sue Joiner, Tarleton State University

Kathleen Jones, University of North Dakota

Rusty Juban, Southeastern Louisiana University

Dmitriy Kalyagin, Chabot College

Heesam Kang, Trident University International

Marvin Karlins, University of South Florida

Marcella Kelly, Santa Monica College

Richard Kimbrough, University of Nebraska–Lincoln

Renee N. King, Eastern Illinois University

John Kirn, University of Kentucky

Shaun C. Knight, Penn State University

Bobbie Knoblauch, Wichita State University

Todd Korol, Monroe Community College

Leo C. Kotrodimos, NC Wesleyan College

Sal Kukalis, California State University–Long Beach

Chalmer E. Labig Jr., Oklahoma State University

Wendy Lam, Hawaii Pacific University

Patricia Lanier, University of Louisiana at Lafayette

Dave Lanzilla, College of Central Florida

Barbara Larson, Northeastern University

Robert L. Laud, William Paterson University

Blaine Lawlor, University of West Florida

Rebecca Legleiter, Tulsa Community College

David Leonard, Chabot College

Chris Levan, University of Tennessee–Chattanooga

David Levy, United States Air Force Academy

Chi Lo Lim, Northwest Missouri State University

Natasha Lindsey, University of North Alabama

Benjamin Lipschutz, Central Penn College

Beverly Little, Western Carolina University

Guy Lochiatto, MassBay Community College

Mary Lou Lockerby, College of DuPage

Michael Dane Loflin, York Technical College

Jessica Lofton, University of Mount Olive

Paul Londrigan, Charles Stewart Mott Community College

Tom Loughman, Columbus State University

Ivan Lowe, York Technical College

Gregory Luce, Bucks County Community College

Margaret Lucero, Texas A&M–Corpus Christi

Charles Lyons, University of Georgia

Zengie Mangaliso, University of Massachusetts–Amherst

James Manicki, Northwestern College

Christine Marchese, Nassau Community College

Christine I. Mark, University of Southern Mississippi

Marcia A. Marriott, Monroe Community College

Dr. David Matthews, SUNY Adirondack

Brenda McAleer, University of Maine at Augusta

Daniel W. McAllister, University of Nevada–Las Vegas

David McArthur, Utah Valley University

Tom McFarland, Mount San Antonio College

Joe McKenna, Howard Community College

David Kim McKinnon, Arizona State University

Benjamin David McLarty, Mississippi State University

Erin McLaughlin, University of Alabama–Huntsville

Acknowledgments

Zack McNeil, Metropolitan Community College

Jeanne McNett, Assumption College

Spencer Mehl, Coastal Carolina Community College

Mary Meredith, University of Louisiana

Lori Merlak, Kirkwood Community College

Douglas Micklich, Illinois State University

Christine Miller, Tennessee Tech University

Val Miskin, Washington State University

Lorianne Mitchell, East Tennessee State University

Kelly Mollica, University of Memphis

Debra L. Moody, Virginia Commonwealth University

Gregory Moore, Middle Tennessee State University

Rob Moorman, Elon University

Byron Morgan, Texas State University

Jaideep Motwani, Grand Valley State University

Troy Mumford, Colorado State University

Jennifer Muryn, Robert Morris University

Robert Myers, University of Louisville

Christopher P. Neck, Arizona State University

Patrick J. Nedry, Monroe County Community College

Francine Newth, Providence College

Margie Nicholson, Columbia College, Chicago

Troy Nielson, Brigham Young University

Thomas J. Norman, California State University–Dominguez Hills

Paul O'Brien, Keiser University

Nathan Oliver, University of Alabama at Birmingham

Joanne Orabone, Community College of Rhode Island

John Orife, Indiana University of Pennsylvania

Eren Ozgen, Florida State University–Panama City

Rhonda Palladi, Georgia State University

Fernando Pargas, James Madison University

Jack Partlow, Northern Virginia Community College

Don A. Paxton, Pasadena City College

John Paxton, Wayne State College

John Pepper, University of Kansas

Clifford R. Perry, Florida International University

Sheila Petcavage, Cuyahoga Community College–Western Campus

Barbara Petzall, Maryville University

Thomas Philippe, St. Petersburg College

Shaun Pichler, Mihaylo College of Business, California State University–Fullerton

Michael Pirson, Fordham University

Anthony Plunkett, Harrison College

Beth Polin, Eastern Kentucky University

Tracy H. Porter, Cleveland State University

Paula Potter, Western Kentucky University

Elizabeth Prejean, Northwestern State University

Cynthia Preston, University of Northwestern Ohio

Ronald E. Purser, San Francisco State University

Gregory R. Quinet, Kennesaw State University

Kenneth Rasheed, Chattahoochee Technical College

George Redmond, Franklin University

Deborah Reed, Benedictine College

Chelsea Hood Reese, Southeast Community College

Rosemarie Reynolds, Embry Riddle Aeronautical University

Tammy Rich, Pennsylvania College of Technology

H. Lynn Richards, Johnson County Community College

Leah Ritchie, Salem State College

Gary B. Roberts, Kennesaw State University

Martha Robinson, University of Memphis

Sean E. Rogers, University of Rhode Island

Katherine Rosenbusch, George Mason University

Barbara Rosenthal, Miami Dade Community College–Wolfson Campus

Gary Ross, Cardinal Stritch University

David Ruderman, University of Colorado–Denver

Catherine Ruggieri, St. John's University–Staten Island

Storm Russo, Valencia Community College

Cindy Ruszkowski, Illinois State University

William Salyer, Illinois State University

Diane R. Scott, Wichita State University

Alex J. Scrimpshire, Xavier University

Marina Sebastijanovic, University of Houston

Marianne Sebok, College of Southern Nevada

Thomas J. Shaughnessy, Illinois Central College

Joanna Shaw, Tarleton State University

Sarah Shike,
Western Illinois University

Randi Sims,
Nova Southeastern University

Raj K. Singh,
University of California–Riverside

Frederick J. Slack,
Indiana University of Pennsylvania

Erika E. Small,
Coastal Carolina University

Jim Smas,
Kent State University

Dustin Smith,
Webster University

Gerald F. Smith,
University of Northern Iowa

Joy Turnheim Smith,
Elizabeth City State University

Mark Smith,
University of Southwest Louisiana

Paula Kirch Smith,
Cincinnati State

Jeff Stauffer,
Ventura College

George E. Stevens,
Kent State University

Jerry Stevens,
Texas Tech University

Martin St. John,
Westmoreland County Community College

Raymond Stoudt,
DeSales University

Barb Stuart,
Daniels College of Business

Robert Scott Taylor,
Moberly Area Community College

Ronda Taylor,
Ivy Tech Community College

Virginia Anne Taylor,
William Patterson University

Wynn Teasley,
University of West Florida

Marguerite Teubner,
Nassau Community College

Jerry Thomas,
Arapahoe Community College

C. Justice Tillman,
Baruch College–City University of New York

Jody Tolan,
University of Southern California, Marshall School of Business

Joseph Tomkiewicz,
East Carolina University

Jennifer Trout,
Rasmussen College

Robert Trumble,
Virginia Commonwealth University

Jim Turner,
Davenport University

Isaiah Ugboro,
North Carolina Agricultural & Technical State University

Brandi Ulrich,
Anne Arundel Community College

Anthony Uremovic,
Joliet Junior College

George Valcho,
Bossier Parish Community College

Barry Van Hook,
Arizona State University

Scot W. Vaver,
University of Wisconsin–Stout

Susan Verhulst,
Grand View University

Annie Viets,
Prince Mohammad Bin Fahd University

Tom Voigt Jr.,
Judson University

Tim Waid,
University of Missouri

Carolyn Waits,
Cincinnati State

Bruce C. Walker,
University of Louisiana at Monroe

Kevin Walker,
Eastern Oregon University

Wendy Walker,
University of North Georgia

Charlene Walters,
Strayer University

Ray D. Walters,
Fayetteville Technical Community College

Tekle O. Wanorie,
Northwest Missouri State University

Charles Warren,
Salem State College

Kerry Webb,
Texas Woman's University

Rick Webb,
Johnson County Community College

Brian D. Webster,
Ball State University

Velvet Weems-Landingham,
Kent State University–Geauga

Allen Weimer,
University of Tampa

Anthony Weinberg,
Daymar College

David A. Wernick,
Florida International University

James Whelan,
Manhattan College

John Whitelock,
Community College of Baltimore/Catonsville Campus

Eric S. Williams,
University of Alabama–Tuscaloosa

Wallace Alexander Williams Jr.,
Texas A&M University–Commerce

Joette Wisnieski,
Indiana University of Pennsylvania

Dr. Linsey Willis,
Florida Atlantic University

Colette Wolfson,
Ivy Tech Community College

Tiffany Woodward,
East Carolina University

M. Susan Wurtz,
University of Northern Iowa

Wendy V. Wysocki,
Monroe County Community College

Carol Bormann Young,
Metropolitan State University

Ned D. Young,
Sinclair Community College

Jan T. Zantinga,
University of Georgia

Mark Zarycki,
Hillsborough Community College (Brandon)

Mary E. Zellmer-Bruhn,
University of Minnesota

Mark Zorn,
Butler County Community College

From Angelo –
I would like to thank my wife, Joyce, for being understanding, patient, and encouraging throughout the process of writing this edition. We have been at this for many years, and I could not do what I do without you. Your continued love and support helped me endure the trials of completing this revision. I also want to thank Denise and Chad. I am proud to be your co-author and friend.

From Denise –
I would like to thank the mentors who have been part of building the foundation for the work I am so fortunate to do with this product. They include my late mother (librarian, English teacher, and avid writer/editor), Andrea Hymel and Ron Harrist (two extraordinary teachers I will never forget), many professors at my beloved Nicholls State University (especially Dr. Sonya Premeaux and Dr. John Lajaunie), Dr. Pam Perrewé (the GOAT), and last but certainly not least, Angelo. May all the students who read this product be fortunate enough to learn from the wisdom of people such as these, and may you someday become mentors to others.

From Chad –
I would like to thank my parents, brother, and two sisters who shaped my character, sharpened the questions I ask, and supported me through the highest and lowest seasons in life. To my wife, Sandy—you continually amaze, inspire, and captivate me with your unconditional love, patience, wisdom, and support. This revision was possible because of your sacrifices and encouragement. To my four children: Emily, Richard, Marie, and Clark—you bring joy to my life and inspiration to my writing. The future is exceedingly bright because of the gifts that are blossoming within you. I'm proud to be your Dad.

    We hope you enjoy reading and applying the product. Best wishes for success in your career.

Angelo Kinicki

Denise Breaux Soignet

Chad Hartnell

contents

Walkthrough Preface xix

CHAPTER DEI
Diversity, Equity, and Inclusion (DEI) DEI-1

DEI.1 Managing DE&I: The What, How, and Why DEI-3
- Diversity (The What) DEI-3
- Equity (The How) DEI-5
- Inclusion (The Why) DEI-6

DEI.2 The Evolution of DE&I in Organizations DEI-9
- A History of Protections DEI-9
- A History of Changes DEI-10
- A History of Tensions DEI-11

DEI.3 Challenges of Effective DE&I Management DEI-12
- Person Factors DEI-13
- Environmental Factors DEI-15

DEI.4 Effective DE&I Management Practices DEI-20
- Managerial Practices DEI-21
- Organizational Practices DEI-22

DEI.5 Career Corner DEI-25
- Practice Seeing Things from Others' Perspectives DEI-25
- Work on Being an Ally DEI-26
- Accept That You Won't Be Perfect (Be a Good-ish Person) DEI-27

Key Terms Used in This Chapter DEI-29

PART 1
Introduction

CHAPTER ONE
The Exceptional Manager: What You Do, How You Do It 2

1.1 Management: What It Is, What Its Benefits Are 4
- The Rise of a Leader 4
- Key to Career Growth: "Doing Things I've Never Done Before" 4
- The Art of Management Defined 5
- Why Organizations Value Managers: The Multiplier Effect 6
- What Are the Rewards of Studying and Practicing Management? 7

1.2 What Managers Do: The Four Principal Functions 8
- Planning: Discussed in Part 3 of This Book 9
- Organizing: Discussed in Part 4 of This Book 9
- Leading: Discussed in Part 5 of This Book 9
- Controlling: Discussed in Part 6 of This Book 9

1.3 Pyramid Power: Levels and Areas of Management 9
- The Traditional Management Pyramid: Levels and Areas 10
- Four Levels of Management 10
- Areas of Management: Functional Managers versus General Managers 11
- Managers for Three Types of Organizations: For-Profit, Nonprofit, Mutual-Benefit 12
- Different Organizations, Different Management? 13

1.4 Roles Managers Must Play Successfully 13
- The Manager's Roles: How Do Managers Spend Their Time? 13
- Three Types of Managerial Roles: Interpersonal, Informational, and Decisional 14

1.5 The Skills Exceptional Managers Need 16
1. Technical Skills—The Ability to Perform a Specific Job 16
2. Conceptual Skills—The Ability to Think Analytically 16
3. Human Skills—"Soft Skills," the Ability to Interact Well with People 17
- The Most Valued Traits in Managers 18

1.6 Seven Challenges to Being an Exceptional Manager 18
- Challenge #1: Managing for Competitive Advantage—Staying Ahead of Rivals 18
- Challenge #2: Managing for Technological Advances—Dealing with the "New Normal" 20
- Challenge #3: Managing for Inclusion and Diversity—The Future Won't Resemble the Past 22
- Challenge #4: Managing for Globalization—The Expanding Management Universe 22
- Challenge #5: Managing for Ethical Standards 23
- Challenge #6: Managing for Sustainable Development—The Business of Green 24
- Challenge #7: Managing for Happiness and Meaningfulness 25
- How Strong Is Your Motivation to Be a Manager? The First Self-Assessment 26

1.7 Building Your Career Readiness 27
- A Model of Career Readiness 28
- Developing Career Readiness 32
- Let Us Help 33

xxxvii

1.8 Career Corner: Managing Your Career Readiness 33

  A Process for Developing Career Readiness 33
  Make It a Habit 34

  Key Terms Used in This Chapter 36
  Key Points 36

CHAPTER TWO
Management Theory: Essential Background for the Successful Manager 38

2.1 Evolving Viewpoints: How We Got to Today's Management Outlook 40

  Creating Modern Management: The Handbook of Peter Drucker 40
  Six Practical Reasons for Studying This Chapter 41
  The Progression of Management Viewpoints 41

2.2 Classical Viewpoint: Scientific and Administrative Management 42

  Scientific Management: Pioneered by Taylor and the Gilbreths 43
  Administrative Management: Pioneered by Spaulding, Fayol, and Weber 44
  The Problem with the Classical Viewpoint: Too Mechanistic 45

2.3 Behavioral Viewpoint: Behaviorism, Human Relations, and Behavioral Science 45

  Early Behaviorism: Pioneered by Follett and Mayo 45
  The Human Relations Movement: Pioneered by Maslow and McGregor 46
  The Behavioral Science Approach 47

2.4 Quantitative Viewpoints: Operations Management and Evidence-Based Management 48

  Operations Management: Being More Effective 48
  Evidence-Based Management: Facing Hard Facts, Rejecting Nonsense 49

2.5 Systems Viewpoint 49

  The Systems Viewpoint 50

2.6 Contingency Viewpoint 51

2.7 Contemporary Approaches: The Learning Organization, High-Performance Work Practices, and Shared Value and Sustainable Development 52

  The Learning Organization: Sharing Knowledge and Modifying Behavior 52
  High-Performance Work Practices 54
  Shared Value and Sustainable Development: Going beyond Profits 55

2.8 Career Corner: Managing Your Career Readiness 55

  Key Terms Used in This Chapter 58
  Key Points 58

PART 2
The Environment of Management

CHAPTER THREE
The Manager's Changing Work Environment and Ethical Responsibilities: Doing the Right Thing 60

3.1 The Goals of Business: More Than Making Money 62

  The Triple Bottom Line: People, Planet, and Profit 62
  Younger Workers' Search for Meaning 63

3.2 The Community of Stakeholders Inside the Organization 63

  Internal and External Stakeholders 63
  Internal Stakeholders 63

3.3 The Community of Stakeholders Outside the Organization 65

  The Task Environment 66
  The General Environment 68

3.4 The Ethical Responsibilities Required of You as a Manager 71

  Defining Ethics and Values 71
  Four Approaches to Resolving Ethical Dilemmas 72
  White-Collar Crime, SarbOx, and Ethical Training 75
  How Organizations Can Promote Ethics 77

3.5 The Social Responsibilities Required of You as a Manager 78

  Corporate Social Responsibility: The Top of the Pyramid 79
  Is Social Responsibility Worthwhile? Opposing and Supporting Viewpoints 80
  One Type of Social Responsibility: Climate Change, Sustainable Development, and Natural Capital 80
  Another Type of Social Responsibility: Undertaking Philanthropy, "Not Dying Rich" 81
  Does Being Good Pay Off? 81

3.6 Corporate Governance 82

  Corporate Governance and Ethics 82
  Corporate Governance and Social Responsibility 82

3.7 Career Corner: Managing Your Career Readiness 83

  Focus on the Greater Good and on Being More Ethical 84
  Become an Ethical Consumer 84

  Key Terms Used in This Chapter 86
  Key Points 86

LEARNING MODULE 1: Shared Value and Sustainable Development: A New Way to Think about Leading and Managing 88

1.1 From Corporate Social Responsibility to Creating Shared Value 89
Traditional CSR 90
Creating Shared Value 90
A Model of Shared Value Creation 91
How CSR and CSV Are Fundamentally Different 95

1.2 The Roles of Various Stakeholders in CSV 96
Global Collaboration: The Role of the United Nations 96
The Role of Businesses, Big and Small 98
The Role of Entrepreneurs 99
The Role of Business Schools 100

1.3 Progress, Challenges, and Recommendations for CSV 102
Current Progress and Challenges in Shared Value and Sustainable Development 102
Recommendations for Transitioning to a Shared-Value Mindset 104

Key Terms Used in This Learning Module 106
Key Points 106

CHAPTER FOUR
Global Management: Managing across Borders 108

4.1 Globalization: The Collapse of Time and Distance 110
Competition and Globalization: Who Will Be No. 1 Tomorrow? 110
The Rise of the "Global Village" and Electronic Commerce 111
One Big World Market: The Global Economy 111

4.2 You and International Management 113
Why Learn about International Management? 114
The Successful International Manager: Geocentric, Not Ethnocentric or Polycentric 115

4.3 Why and How Companies Expand Internationally 116
Why Companies Expand Internationally 116
How Companies Expand Internationally 117

4.4 The World of Free Trade: Regional Economic Cooperation and Competition 120
Barriers to International Trade 120
Organizations Promoting International Trade 121
Major Trading Blocs 122
Most Favored Nation Trading Status 124
Exchange Rates 124
The BRICS Countries: Important International Competitors 125

4.5 The Value of Understanding Cultural Differences 126
The Importance of National Culture 127
Cultural Dimensions: The Hofstede and GLOBE Project Models 127
Other Cultural Variations: Language, Interpersonal Space, Communication, Time Orientation, Religion, and Law and Political Stability 131
U.S. Managers on Foreign Assignments: Why Do They Fail? 135

4.6 Career Corner: Managing Your Career Readiness 136
1. Listen and Observe 137
2. Become Aware of the Context 137
3. Choose Something Basic 138

Key Terms Used in This Chapter 139
Key Points 139

PART 3
Planning

CHAPTER FIVE
Planning: The Foundation of Successful Management 142

5.1 Planning and Strategy 144
Planning, Strategy, and Strategic Management 144
Why Planning and Strategic Management Are Important 146

5.2 Fundamentals of Planning 148
Mission, Vision, and Values Statements 149
Three Types of Planning for Three Levels of Management: Strategic, Tactical, and Operational 152

5.3 Goals and Plans 154
Long-Term and Short-Term Goals 154
The Operating Plan and Action Plan 154
Plans Are Great, But . . . 154

5.4 Promoting Consistencies in Goals: SMART Goals, Management by Objectives, and Goal Cascading 155
SMART Goals 155
Management by Objectives: The Four-Step Process for Motivating Employees 156
Cascading Goals: Making Lower-Level Goals Align with Top Goals 158

5.5 The Planning/Control Cycle 160

5.6 Career Corner: Managing Your Career Readiness 162
Becoming More Proactive 163
Keeping an Open Mind and Suspending Judgment 163

Key Terms Used in This Chapter 165
Key Points 165

Contents   xxxix

CHAPTER SIX
Strategic Management: How Exceptional Managers Realize a Grand Design 168

6.1 Strategic Positioning and Levels of Strategy 170
Strategic Positioning and Its Principles 170
Levels of Strategy 171
Does Strategic Management Work for Small as Well as Large Firms? 172

6.2 The Strategic-Management Process 172
The Five Steps of the Strategic-Management Process 173

6.3 Assessing the Current Reality 175
SWOT Analysis 175
Using VRIO to Assess Competitive Potential: Value, Rarity, Imitability, and Organization 177
Forecasting: Predicting the Future 179
Benchmarking: Comparing with the Best 180

6.4 Establishing Corporate-Level Strategy 181
Three Overall Types of Corporate Strategy 181
The BCG Matrix 182
Diversification Strategy 184

6.5 Establishing Business-Level Strategy 185
Porter's Five Competitive Forces 185
Porter's Four Competitive Strategies 186
An Executive's Approach toward Strategy Development 188

6.6 Strategic Implementation: Creating, Executing, and Controlling Functional-Level Strategies 189
Strategic Implementation: Creating, Executing, and Controlling Functional-Level Strategies 189
Execution: Getting Things Done 190
The Three Core Processes of Business: People, Strategy, and Operations 191
Execution Roadblocks 192
Maintaining Strategic Control 192

6.7 Career Corner: Managing Your Career Readiness 193
Why Is Strategic Thinking Important to New Graduates? 194
Developing Strategic Thinking 194

Key Terms Used in This Chapter 196
Key Points 196

LEARNING MODULE 2: Entrepreneurship 198

2.1 Entrepreneurship: Its Foundations and Importance 200
Entrepreneurship: It's Not the Same as Self-Employment 200
Social Entrepreneurship 201
Characteristics of Entrepreneurs 203
Entrepreneurship Matters across the Globe 205

2.2 Starting a Business 207
Businesses Start with an Idea 208
Franchising: Building on Someone Else's Idea 209
Writing the Business Plan 210
Choosing a Legal Structure 212
Obtaining Financing 213
Creating the "Right" Organizational Culture and Design 215
Why Entrepreneurial Ventures Fail 216

Key Terms Used in This Learning Module 217
Key Points 217

CHAPTER SEVEN
Individual and Group Decision Making: How Managers Make Things Happen 218

7.1 Two Kinds of Decision Making: Rational and Nonrational 220
Rational Decision Making: Managers Should Make Logical and Optimal Decisions 220
Stage 1: Identify the Problem or Opportunity—Determining the Actual versus the Desirable 221
Stage 2: Think Up Alternative Solutions—Both the Obvious and the Creative 221
Stage 3: Evaluate Alternatives and Select a Solution—Ethics, Feasibility, and Effectiveness 221
Stage 4: Implement and Evaluate the Solution Chosen 221
What's Wrong with the Rational Model? 222
Nonrational Decision Making: Managers Find It Difficult to Make Optimal Decisions 223

7.2 Making Ethical Decisions 225
The Dismal Record of Business Ethics 226
Road Map to Ethical Decision Making: A Decision Tree 227

7.3 Evidence-Based Decision Making and Data Analytics 229
Evidence-Based Decision Making 229
In Praise of Data Analytics 232
Big Data: What It Is, How It's Used 232

7.4 Artificial Intelligence Is a Powerful Decision-Making Resource 236
Types of AI 236
AI's Benefits 240
AI's Drawbacks 241

7.5 Four General Decision-Making Styles 243
Value Orientation and Tolerance for Ambiguity 244
1. The Directive Style: Action-Oriented Decision Makers Who Focus on Facts 244
2. The Analytical Style: Careful Decision Makers Who Like Lots of Information and Alternative Choices 245
3. The Conceptual Style: Decision Makers Who Rely on Intuition and Have a Long-Term Perspective 245

4. The Behavioral Style: The Most People-Oriented Decision Makers 246

Which Style Do You Have? 246

7.6 Decision-Making Biases 247

Ten Common Decision-Making Biases: Rules of Thumb, or "Heuristics" 247

7.7 Group Decision Making: How to Work with Others 250

Advantages and Disadvantages of Group Decision Making 251

Groupthink 252

Characteristics of Group Decision Making 253

Group Problem-Solving Techniques: Reaching for Consensus 254

More Group Problem-Solving Techniques 254

7.8 Career Corner: Managing Your Career Readiness 257

Improving Your Critical Thinking and Problem-Solving Skills 258

Reflect on Past Decisions 258

Establish a Decision Methodology 259

Demonstrating These Competencies during a Job Interview 259

Key Terms Used in This Chapter 260
Key Points 260

PART 4
Organizing

CHAPTER EIGHT
Organizational Culture and Structure: Drivers of Strategic Implementation 262

8.1 Aligning Culture, Structure, and Human Resource (HR) Practices to Support Strategy 264

How an Organization's Culture, Structure, and HR Practices Support Strategic Implementation 264

8.2 What Kind of Organizational Culture Will You Be Operating In? 267

The Three Levels of Organizational Culture 268

How Employees Learn Culture: Symbols, Stories, Heroes, Rites and Rituals, and Organizational Socialization 270

Four Types of Organizational Culture: Clan, Adhocracy, Market, and Hierarchy 272

The Importance of Culture 274

Preparing to Assess Person–Organization Fit before a Job Interview 276

8.3 The Process of Culture Change 278

1. Formal Statements 278
2. Slogans and Sayings 279
3. Rites and Rituals 279
4. Stories, Legends, and Myths 279
5. Leader Reactions to Crises 280
6. Role Modeling, Training, and Coaching 280
7. Physical Design 280
8. Rewards, Titles, Promotions, and Bonuses 281
9. Organizational Goals and Performance Criteria 281
10. Measurable and Controllable Activities 282
11. Organizational Structure 282
12. Organizational Systems and Procedures 283

Using Multiple Mechanisms to Drive Culture Change 283

Don't Forget about Person–Organization Fit 284

8.4 The Major Features of an Organization 285

Major Features of Organizations: Four Proposed by Edgar Schein 286

Major Features of Organizations: Three More That Most Authorities Agree On 287

The Organization Chart 289

8.5 Eight Types of Organizational Structure 290

1. Traditional Designs: Simple, Functional, Divisional, and Matrix Structures 291
2. The Horizontal Design: Eliminating Functional Barriers to Solve Problems 294
3. Designs That Open Boundaries between Organizations: Hollow, Modular, and Virtual Structures 294

8.6 Career Corner: Managing Your Career Readiness 296

Understanding the Business and Where You "Fit" In 297

Becoming More Adaptable 297

Key Terms Used in This Chapter 299
Key Points 299

CHAPTER NINE
Human Resource Management: Getting the Right People for Managerial Success 302

9.1 Strategic Human Resource Management 304

Human Resource Management: Managing an Organization's Most Important Resource 304

Internal and External HR Fit Promote Strategic HR Management 305

The Role of Human and Social Capital 307

What Is the Best Approach to Strategic Human Resource Management? 307

9.2 Recruitment and Selection: Putting the Right People into the Right Jobs 309

Recruitment: How to Attract Qualified Applicants 310

Selection: How to Choose the Best Person for the Job 312

9.3 Managing an Effective Workforce: Compensation and Benefits 317
- Wages or Salaries 318
- Incentives 319
- Benefits 319

9.4 Onboarding and Learning and Development 320
- Onboarding: Helping Newcomers Learn the Ropes 320
- Learning and Development: Helping People Perform Better 321

9.5 Performance Management 323
- Performance Management in Human Resources 323
- Performance Appraisals: Are They Worthwhile? 324
- Two Kinds of Performance Appraisal: Objective and Subjective 325
- Who Should Make Performance Appraisals? 326
- Effective Performance Feedback 328

9.6 Managing Promotions, Transfers, Disciplining, and Dismissals 329
- Promotion: Moving Upward 329
- Transfer: Moving Sideways 330
- Disciplining and Demotion: The Threat of Moving Downward 330
- Dismissal: Moving Out of the Organization 331

9.7 The Legal Requirements of Human Resource Management 332
- 1. Labor Relations 334
- 2. Compensation and Benefits 334
- 3. Health and Safety 335
- 4. Equal Employment Opportunity 335
- Workplace Discrimination, Affirmative Action, Sexual Harassment, and Bullying 335

9.8 Labor–Management Issues 339
- How Workers Organize 340
- How Unions and Management Negotiate a Contract 340
- The Issues Unions and Management Negotiate About 340
- Settling Labor–Management Disputes 342

9.9 Career Corner: Managing Your Career Readiness 343
- Becoming a Better Receiver 344

Key Terms Used in This Chapter 346
Key Points 346

CHAPTER TEN
Organizational Change and Innovation: Lifelong Challenges for the Exceptional Manager 348

10.1 The Nature of Change in Organizations 350
- Fundamental Change: What Will You Be Called On to Deal With? 350
- Two Types of Change: Reactive and Proactive 355
- The Forces for Change Outside and Inside the Organization 356

10.2 Forms and Models of Change 359
- Three Forms of Change: From Least Threatening to Most Threatening 359
- Lewin's Change Model: Unfreezing, Changing, and Refreezing 361
- A Systems Approach to Change 362

10.3 Organizational Development: What It Is, What It Can Do 366
- What Can OD Be Used For? 366
- How OD Works 367
- The Effectiveness of OD 368

10.4 Organizational Innovation 369
- Approaches to Innovation 369
- An Innovation System: The Supporting Forces for Innovation 371

10.5 The Threat of Change: Managing Employee Fear and Resistance 376
- The Causes of Resistance to Change 377
- Ten Reasons Employees Resist Change 378

10.6 Career Corner: Managing Your Career Readiness 379
- Applying Self-Affirmation Theory 379
- Practicing Self-Compassion 381

Key Terms Used in This Chapter 383
Key Points 383

PART 5
Leading

CHAPTER ELEVEN
Managing Individual Differences and Behavior: Supervising People as People 386

11.1 Personality and Individual Behavior 388
- The Big Five Personality Dimensions 388
- Core Self-Evaluations 389
- Emotional Intelligence: Understanding Your Emotions and the Emotions of Others 392

11.2 Values, Attitudes, and Behavior 394
- Organizational Behavior: Trying to Explain and Predict Workplace Behavior 394
- Values: What Are Your Consistent Beliefs and Feelings about All Things? 395
- Attitudes: What Are Your Consistent Beliefs and Feelings about Specific Things? 395
- Behavior: How Values and Attitudes Affect People's Actions and Judgments 397

11.3 Perception and Individual Behavior 397
- The Four Steps in the Perceptual Process 398

Five Distortions in Perception 398
The Self-Fulfilling Prophecy, or Pygmalion Effect 401

11.4 Work-Related Attitudes and Behaviors Managers Need to Deal With 402
1. Employee Engagement: How Connected Are You to Your Work? 403
2. Job Satisfaction: How Much Do You Like or Dislike Your Job? 405
3. Organizational Commitment: How Much Do You Identify with Your Organization? 405
Important Workplace Behaviors 405

11.5 Understanding Stress and Individual Behavior 408
The Toll of Workplace Stress 408
How Does Stress Work? 409
The Sources of Job-Related Stress 410
Reducing Stressors in the Organization 413

11.6 Career Corner: Managing Your Career Readiness 414
Fostering a Positive Approach 414
Self-Managing Your Emotions 416

Key Terms Used in This Chapter 418
Key Points 418

CHAPTER TWELVE
Motivating Employees: Achieving Superior Performance in the Workplace 420

12.1 Motivating for Performance 422
Motivation: What It Is, Why It's Important 422
The Four Major Perspectives on Motivation: An Overview 425

12.2 Content Perspectives on Employee Motivation 426
Maslow's Hierarchy of Needs Theory: Five Levels 426
McClelland's Acquired Needs Theory: Achievement, Affiliation, and Power 428
Deci and Ryan's Self-Determination Theory: Competence, Autonomy, and Relatedness 429
Herzberg's Two-Factor Theory: From Dissatisfying Factors to Satisfying Factors 431

12.3 Process Perspectives on Employee Motivation 434
Equity/Justice Theory: How Fairly Do You Think You're Being Treated in Relation to Others? 434
Expectancy Theory: How Much Do You Want and How Likely Are You to Get It? 439
Goal-Setting Theory: Objectives Should Be Specific and Challenging but Achievable 441

12.4 Job Design Perspectives on Motivation 443
Fitting People to Jobs 444
Fitting Jobs to People 444
The Job Characteristics Model: Five Job Attributes for Better Work Outcomes 445
Relational Job Design 447

12.5 Reinforcement Perspectives on Motivation 448
The Four Types of Behavior Modification: Positive Reinforcement, Negative Reinforcement, Extinction, and Punishment 449
Using Behavior Modification to Motivate Employees 450

12.6 Using Compensation, Nonmonetary Incentives, and Other Rewards to Motivate: In Search of the Positive Work Environment 451
Is Money the Best Motivator? 452
Motivation and Compensation 452
Nonmonetary Ways of Motivating Employees 454

12.7 Career Corner: Managing Your Career Readiness 459
The Self-Management Process 460
Recharging 461

Key Terms Used in This Chapter 463
Key Points 463

CHAPTER THIRTEEN
Groups and Teams: Increasing Cooperation, Reducing Conflict 466

13.1 Groups versus Teams 468
Groups and Teams: How Do They Differ? 468
Formal versus Informal Groups 469
Types of Teams 469
An Organizing Framework 473

13.2 Stages of Group and Team Development 474
Tuckman's Five-Stage Model 474
Punctuated Equilibrium 477

13.3 Building Effective Teams 478
1. Collaboration—the Foundation of Teamwork 478
2. Trust: "We Need to Have Reciprocal Faith in Each Other" 479
3. Performance Goals and Feedback 479
4. Motivation through Mutual Accountability and Interdependence 479
5. Team Composition 480
6. Roles: How Team Members Are Expected to Behave 480
7. Norms: Unwritten Rules for Team Members 482
Putting It All Together 482

13.4 Managing Conflict 483
The Nature of Conflict: Disagreement Is Normal 483
Can Too Little or Too Much Conflict Affect Performance? 484
Four Kinds of Conflict: Personality, Envy, Intergroup, and Cross-Cultural 485

How to Stimulate Constructive Conflict 487
Career Readiness Competencies to Help You to Better Handle Conflict 487
Dealing with Disagreements: Five Conflict-Handling Styles 488

13.5 Career Corner: Managing Your Career Readiness 490
Become a More Effective Team Member 490
Become a More Effective Collaborator 491

13.6 Managing Team Dysfunction 492
The 5 Dysfunctions of a Team 493
Recommendations to Solve the 5 Team Dysfunctions 496

Key Terms Used in This Chapter 498
Key Points 498

CHAPTER FOURTEEN
Power, Influence, and Leadership: From Becoming a Manager to Becoming a Leader 500

14.1 The Nature of Leadership: The Role of Power and Influence 502
What Is the Difference between Leading and Managing? 502
Managerial Leadership: Can You Be *Both* a Manager and a Leader? 503
Six Sources of Power 504
Common Influence Tactics 506
Outcomes of Influence Tactics 508

14.2 Trait Approaches: Do Leaders Have Distinctive Traits and Personal Characteristics? 508
Positive Task-Oriented Traits and Positive/Negative Interpersonal Attributes 509
What Do We Know about Gender and Leadership? 510
Are Knowledge and Skills Important? 512
So What Do We Know about Leadership Traits? 512

14.3 Behavioral Approaches: Do Leaders Show Distinctive Patterns of Behavior? 513
Task-Oriented Leader Behaviors 514
The Focus of Task-Oriented Leadership: "Here's What We Do to Get the Job Done" 514
Relationship-Oriented Leader Behavior 514
The Focus of Relationship-Oriented Leadership: "The Concerns and Needs of My Employees Are Highly Important" 514
So What Do We Know about the Behavioral Approaches? 515

14.4 Situational Approaches: Does Leadership Vary with the Situation? 515
1. The Contingency Leadership Model: Fiedler's Approach 515
2. The Path–Goal Leadership Model: House's Approach 517

So What Do We Know about the Situational Approaches? 519

14.5 The Full-Range Model: Using Transactional and Transformational Leadership 520
Transactional and Transformational Leadership 521
The Best Leaders Are Both Transactional and Transformational 522
Four Key Behaviors of Transformational Leaders 522
So What Do We Know about Transformational Leadership? 524

14.6 Contemporary Perspectives and Concepts 525
Leader–Member Exchange Leadership: Having Different Relationships with Different Subordinates 525
Servant Leadership 527
The Power of Humility 527
Empowering Leadership 529
Ethical Leadership 530
Followers: What Do They Want, How Can They Help? 531
Abusive Supervision 532

14.7 Career Corner: Managing Your Career Readiness 533
Becoming More Self-Aware 534

Key Terms Used in This Chapter 536
Key Points 536

CHAPTER FIFTEEN
Interpersonal and Organizational Communication: Mastering the Exchange of Information 538

15.1 The Communication Process: What It Is, How It Works 540
Communication Defined: The Transfer of Information and Understanding 540
How the Communication Process Works 540
Selecting the Right Medium for Effective Communication 543

15.2 How Managers Fit into the Communication Process 545
Formal Communication Channels: Up, Down, Sideways, and Outward 545
Informal Communication Channels 547

15.3 Barriers to Communication 550
1. Physical Barriers: Sound, Time, Space 551
2. Personal Barriers: Individual Attributes That Hinder Communication 551
3. Cross-Cultural Barriers 553
4. Nonverbal Communication: How Unwritten and Unspoken Messages May Mislead 555
5. Gender Differences 556

15.4 Social Media and Management 556
- The Use of Social Media Has Changed the Fabric of Our Lives 556
- Social Media and Managerial and Organizational Effectiveness 558
- Downsides of Social Media 560
- Managerial Considerations in Creating Social Media Policies 564

15.5 Improving Communication Effectiveness 565
- Nondefensive Communication 566
- Using Empathy 567
- Being an Effective Listener 567
- Being an Effective Writer 570
- Being an Effective Speaker 570

15.6 Career Corner: Managing Your Career Readiness 572
- Improve Your Face-to-Face Networking Skills 572

Key Terms Used in This Chapter 575
Key Points 575

PART 6
Controlling

CHAPTER SIXTEEN

Control Systems and Quality Management: Techniques for Enhancing Organizational Effectiveness 578

16.1 Control: When Managers Monitor Performance 580

16.2 The Control Process and Types of Control 582
- Steps in the Control Process 582
- Types of Controls 586

16.3 What Should Managers Control? 587
- The Balanced Scorecard: A Comprehensive Approach to Managerial Control 588
- Financial Perspective: "What Does Success Look Like to Our Shareholders?" 588
- Customer Perspective: "How Do We Appear to Our Customers?" 592
- Internal Business Perspective: "What Must We Do Extremely Well?" 594
- Innovation and Learning Perspective: "Are We Equipped for Continued Value and Improvement?" 596
- Strategy Mapping: Visual Representation of the Path to Organizational Effectiveness 599

16.4 Total Quality Management 601
- Quality Control and Quality Assurance 601
- Deming Management: The Contributions of W. Edwards Deming to Improved Quality 601
- Core TQM Principles: Deliver Customer Value and Strive for Continuous Improvement 604
- Applying TQM to Services 605
- Some TQM Tools, Techniques, and Standards 607
- Takeaways from TQM Research 609

16.5 Contemporary Control Issues 610
- Using Artificial Intelligence to Control 610
- Employee Tracking and Monitoring 612

16.6 Career Corner: Managing Your Career Readiness 614
- The Control Process and Career Management 614
- Continuous Self-Improvement 616
- Life Lessons for Your Career Management 618

Key Terms Used in This Chapter 620
Key Points 620

APPENDIX: THE PROJECT PLANNER'S TOOLKIT 622

CHAPTER NOTES CN-1
NAME INDEX IND1
ORGANIZATION INDEX IND4
GLOSSARY/SUBJECT INDEX IND8

Chapter
Diversity, Equity, and Inclusion (DE&I)

After reading this chapter, you should be able to:

LO DEI-1 Describe the concepts of diversity, equity, and inclusion in organizations.

LO DEI-2 Summarize the evolution of DE&I management in organizations.

LO DEI-3 Explain the person and environmental factors that can undermine effective DE&I management.

LO DEI-4 Describe effective DE&I management practices.

LO DEI-5 Discuss how to develop career readiness competencies related to DE&I management.

FORECAST *What's Ahead in This Chapter*

In this chapter we explore diversity, equity, and inclusion (DE&I) in organizations. First, we discuss the meaning of the terms *diversity, equity,* and *inclusion* and introduce the idea of DE&I management. Next, we describe the evolution of DE&I management in organizations. Then, we explore person and environmental factors that can make DE&I management challenging. We next introduce practices that managers and organizations can use to improve their DE&I management efforts. Finally, we conclude with a Career Corner that provides advice for you to develop several career readiness competencies related to DE&I management.

Using Inclusive Language

Research suggests workers and teams perform better when there are strong norms for respecting others and calling out exclusive language.[1] As a manager, you can build a more inclusive and respectful work environment by avoiding harmful language, intentionally using inclusive terms, and helping your team members do the same.

Inclusive language is a key communication skill that can enhance your career readiness and help others feel like they belong. It's easy to make mistakes, as many common words and phrases have underlying meanings we may not realize are problematic. The goal of this feature is to help you recognize exclusive language and give you tools to practice being more inclusive in the future.

Step 1: Be Intentional with Your Words

Avoid common exclusive or harmful terms. You can select an inclusive term so that your meaning is more accurate and your words are more respectful. See Table DEI.1 for examples of exclusive and inclusive language.

TABLE DEI.1 Examples of Exclusive and Inclusive Language

	INSTEAD OF...	SAY THIS:	WHY? TO BE INCLUSIVE OF
Referring to people	husband or wife	spouse	LGBTQ+
	epileptic	has epilepsy	neurodivergent
	ladies and gentlemen	friends, folks	LGBTQ+
	illegal aliens	immigrants	everyone, regardless of country of birth
	confined to a wheelchair	person who uses a wheelchair	all abilities
Phrases and sayings	fell on deaf ears	ignored the issue	all abilities
	master copy	primary copy	descendants of enslaved people
	manpower	workers	all genders
	blacklist	blocklist	descendants of enslaved people
	Christmas break	winter break	all faith traditions
	peanut gallery	audience, crowd	everyone, regardless of socioeconomic background
	long time no see	great to see you again	those for whom English is an additional language

Step 2: Make Inclusive Language a Priority

Below are four ways you can prioritize using more inclusive language beginning today.

1. Try using the names, pronouns, and terms others use to self-identify. Doing this demonstrates respect and celebrates differences.
2. Select descriptive words that are relevant to the situation. For example, only mention someone's sexual orientation or physical disability if it's necessary to make your meaning clear.
3. Avoid exclusive terms whenever possible so that you do not promote unconscious bias. For example, instead of chairman or stewardess, try inclusive terms like chairperson or flight attendant.
4. Keep your language current. *Mentally retarded* was once the medically acceptable term to describe people with intellectual functioning limitations.[2] The term's connotation shifted negatively, so the medical community established *intellectual development disorders* as the appropriate term in official documents.[3] Great communicators adapt their language to keep up with changes over time.

Step 3: Practice Makes Perfect

Using inclusive language is a skill, and all skills can be learned with practice. Remember to aim for progress, not perfection. Over time, you will build your skill and confidence in selecting inclusive terms. Language changes over time, so you, as a lifelong learner, must learn and embrace inclusive language each and every day.

DEI.1 Managing DE&I: The What, How, and Why

THE BIG PICTURE
Diversity, equity, and inclusion are three separate but interrelated terms that form the acronym DE&I. The concept of DE&I is more than the sum of its parts. Effective DE&I management begins with understanding how diversity, equity, and inclusion relate to one another.

LO DEI-1
Describe the concepts of diversity, equity, and inclusion in organizations.

Hundreds of studies demonstrate the value that a diverse workforce brings in terms of company growth, financial performance, innovation, customer satisfaction, and employee engagement, well-being, and job performance.[4] Propy CEO Natalia Karayaneva considers diversity "essential in business today as a healthy variety of people from different backgrounds and cultures provides us with the balance of voices and diversity of thought that we need."[5] Other organizational leaders agree, with 95% of the 200 CEOs surveyed in a recent study saying that their companies would be focusing on DE&I in the coming years.[6] Diversity is important to job seekers and employees, too. Consider that over 75% of respondents to a recent survey of 2,745 U.S. adults named company diversity as a key factor they use to evaluate the attractiveness of job offers.[7] The lesson is clear—organizations need diversity to thrive in today's marketplace.

Corporate efforts related to diversity typically fall under the umbrella term **DE&I**, an acronym that stands for diversity, equity, and inclusion. A critical characteristic of corporate DE&I programs is that they acknowledge the mere existence of diversity isn't enough. Organizations and their leaders also need the knowledge and tools to manage diverse perspectives properly. In this chapter we focus on **DE&I management**—the process of identifying, acquiring, developing, deploying, and integrating diverse perspectives throughout an organization. As a manager, one of your jobs will be to engage with the DE&I management process. In this section, we walk you through the three interrelated components of DE&I—the "what" (diversity), "how" (equity), and "why" (inclusion).

Lightspring/Shutterstock

Diversity (The What)

Diversity refers to the presence of differences among a group of people. Diversity represents the *what* in DE&I management because it describes what organizations look like, both literally and figuratively, in terms of their workforces. We often describe organizations with little diversity as *homogenous,* and organizations with considerable diversity as *heterogeneous.* Homogenous organizations are made of up employees who are highly similar in terms of characteristics such as race, gender, age, political ideology, and educational background. Heterogenous organizations are made up of highly dissimilar employees, with great variance across these and many other dimensions of human diversity. Organizations with high levels of diversity are heterogenous because they have

FIGURE DEI.1

The diversity wheel

Sources: Figure adapted from: B.W. Hawkins, M. Morris, T. Nguyen, J. Siegel, and E. Vardell, "Advancing the Conversation: Next Steps for Lesbian, Gay, Bisexual, Trans, and Queer (LGBTQ) Health Sciences Librarianship," Journal of the Medical Library Association, Vol. 105, No. 4 (2017), p. 316; Rasmussen University. Diversity, Equity, and Inclusion: Diversity. https://guides.rasmussen.edu/DEI/Diversity.

employees that represent a multitude of identities, experiences, and perspectives. Understanding the facets of human diversity is essential for effective DE&I management.

The Diversity Wheel   Researchers have created various models over the years to depict the ways human beings identify themselves and others.[8] Your **identity represents your own description of who you are** and is based on your alignment with and membership in various groups.[9] Figure DEI.1 presents these dimensions of diversity as a wheel with two primary layers—an inner circle and an outer circle. You can describe your identity using the various dimensions in the wheel.

The inner circle of the diversity wheel represents diversity dimensions that are generally stable and less likely to vary greatly. Your age, for example, is what it is, and only changes each year on your birthday. Some dimensions in the inner circle, such as gender identity, are more fluid. In general, though, the diversity dimensions in the inner circle are less likely to change than those in the outer circle. The diversity dimensions in the outer circle represent characteristics that are more malleable and are likely to vary throughout your life. For example, your education levels are changing as you progress through your college degree program, and your organizational role will change each time you get a new job, receive a promotion, or take on extra responsibilities at work.

SELF-ASSESSMENT DEI.1

Assessing Your Attitudes Toward Diversity

This survey is designed to assess how you feel about diversity in organizations. Please complete Self-Assessment DEI.1 if your instructor has assigned it in Connect.

Intersectionality Try describing yourself according to Figure DEI.1. How does your description sound? It's likely you refer to more than one category when describing yourself. This is because identities are made up of more than one dimension, and who you are is a function of the interplay of all your various identity categories. The way multiple dimensions of our identities work together to influence our experiences, opportunities, and outcomes is called **intersectionality**, defined as the way various dimensions of individual identity overlap to create unique experiences not attributable to individual dimensions.[10]

You may think that the women in this photo have highly similar experiences. But this assumption ignores how the constellation of categories with which one identifies can impact their outcomes in life. Intersectionality reminds us to consider the multiple identity groups that these women belong to, including their various abilities, educational experiences, religions, ethnic backgrounds, and family status. Djomas/Shutterstock

Intersectionality research studies the experiences of individuals who belong to two or more marginalized identity groups. The term *marginalize* originated with the common writing practice of placing less important information in the margins of a page instead of including it in the central text.[11] Marginalization has since come to refer to a phenomenon whereby societies have historically relegated members of various demographic groups to positions that hold little influence, prestige, or power.[12] Intersectionality researchers argue that the current methods and frameworks we use in studying diversity at work are not adequate to address the experiences of individuals who belong to two or more marginalized identity groups.[13] As we work to understand the challenges in managing DE&I and the ways we can do better, we must understand not only the experiences of individuals who belong to a single marginalized group, but also the experiences of those with various intersecting marginalized identities.[14]

Research Example—Intersectionality: Gender and race are two identity dimensions that intersect to influence workplace outcomes. As one example, studies suggest that women in the United States earn 86% of what men earn for doing comparable work.[15] Further, data show that Black employees earn 80% of what white employees earn for doing comparable work.[16] But when we look at the intersection of gender and race, we learn that Black women earn just 63% of what white men earn for doing comparable work.[17]

The previous example shows we can't fully understand others' perspectives unless we understand how the intersection of their various identity dimensions impacts their outcomes.[18] Said Serena Fong, vice president for strategic engagement at Catalyst, "If you're talking about how women as a group face the glass ceiling, what we've always heard is women of color face a concrete one. ... And that is due to the systemic barriers that exist in terms of talent management and advancement."[19]

Equity (The How)

Organizations need to know how to manage diversity properly, and this is where equity comes into the equation. **Equity** exists when employees perceive that they receive fair and unbiased treatment with respect to their opportunities, resources, and outcomes in organizations.[20] Equity is the *how* in DE&I management because it refers to the rules,

TABLE DEI.2 Qualities of Fair and Unbiased HR Procedures

PROCEDURAL RULE	EXPLANATION
Consistency	Is applied consistently across employees and situations.
Bias suppression	Is not subject to the influence of decision makers' personal interests.
Accuracy	Is based on accurate and complete information.
Correctability	Contains avenues for unfair decisions to be revisited and corrected.
Representativeness	Represents the perspectives and needs of all parties impacted by decisions.
Ethicality	Aligns with prevailing ethical and moral standards.

Information in Table 3.3 based on: Leventhal, G. S., J. Karuza, and W. R. Fry. "Beyond Fair Theory of Allocation Preferences." In Justice and Interactions, *edited by G. Mikulka, 167–218. New York: Springer, 1980.*

methods, and tools organizations use to manage diverse groups of employees effectively and fairly. In other words, if you want to know how to manage diversity well, you should look to the principles of equity. In equitable organizations, employees believe that their outcomes reflect the relative value they bring to the workplace. Here we highlight two key points about equity.

Employees Assess Equity through Social Comparisons Our workplace equity perceptions reflect the extent to which we believe what we're getting out of our jobs (our outcomes such as pay, status, benefits, respect, and access to resources) is fair relative to what we're putting into our jobs (our inputs such as knowledge, skill, ability, experience, and effort). We assess this fairness by comparing ourselves to others in the organization who we view as similar in terms of inputs.[21] For example, if you and I do the same job in the same company and have the same objective inputs (e.g., education, job experience, tenure, performance history), but your salary is half the size of mine, you're going to view that as unfair. This is because our outcome/input ratios are very different. This example represents the type of social comparison employees use to determine whether they're being treated fairly. You'll study equity in depth in Chapter 12.

HR Practices Drive Equity Perceptions Equity exists when employees perceive that their organizations make fair and unbiased decisions about the opportunities, resources, and outcomes they receive. Any decisions that affect employees' careers (e.g., hiring, promotion, salary, benefits) should be based on objective, performance-relevant criteria, rather than on non-job-related employee characteristics. Organizations use various HR practices to encourage objectivity and remove biases in decision making. These practices are thoroughly discussed in Chapter 10.

HR practices include the various activities associated with recruiting, hiring, appraising, compensating, promoting, and developing employees. Organizations should design their HR practices to be free from bias and should provide training for managers on how to implement the practices properly.[22] Research on organizational justice (which you'll learn about in Chapter 12) provides a set of rules to follow when designing and deploying employment decision-making practices and procedures.[23] Specifically, fair procedures have the following qualities summarized in Table DEI.2.

The use of HR practices that align with the rules in Table DEI.2 demonstrates to employees that the organization values fairness and makes decisions based on objective, job-relevant criteria. This drives employees' perceptions of equity.

Inclusion (The Why)

Inclusion represents the extent to which employees feel heard, valued, involved, and respected. Inclusion is the *why* in DE&I because it is the ultimate goal of DE&I

management. When employees are included, they have fair access to opportunities and resources, are appropriately sought out and involved in critical workplace conversations, and feel commensurate influence over organizational decision making.[24] Research suggests that feeling included enhances many desirable outcomes, including employee well-being as well as both individual and team performance.[25] Here are two important points about inclusion:

1. **Equity is necessary, but not sufficient, for inclusion.** Equitable HR practices might get you a chair at the table where you deserve to sit, but they won't ensure you'll be treated as though you belong there.[26] If you've ever been part of a group (e.g., family, friendship, work, school), then you know there's a difference between (1) being a physical member of the group and (2) feeling like a valued member of the group. We feel included when we're invited to contribute to the group's key outcomes and when other group members treat us as though our presence is important.

2. **Inclusion isn't a free-for-all.** It can be easy to oversimplify the notion of inclusion and assume we're suggesting the only way to be inclusive is to allow everyone in the organization to be equally involved in every decision at all times. But this isn't a formula for inclusion—it's a recipe for disaster. Organizations are social systems, and social systems require authority, decision hierarchies, and complementary roles to make progress toward achieving goals. Inclusive organizations don't assume that every employee gets an equal say in every conversation. Rather, inclusive organizations evaluate employees based on their objective value, place employees in roles and positions commensurate with their job-relevant knowledge, skills, and abilities, and treat employees as though they belong in the roles they occupy.

Hallmarks of Inclusion

According to a perspective in psychology called *optimal distinctiveness theory*, we all have two important needs related to inclusion in social groups: (1) belongingness and (2) uniqueness.[27] These needs capture our desire to be accepted in social groups while maintaining what makes us who we are while participating in those groups.

1. **Belongingness.** Our sense of belongingness is increased when we build strong and lasting relationships with other group members. We wish to feel that we are a true part of the group.

2. **Uniqueness.** Our sense of uniqueness is increased when others fully accept and respect what makes us different. We wish to feel that we can be ourselves and will not have to hide important aspects of our identities to be accepted by the group.

Optimal distinctiveness, then, is the state of having the perfect balance of both belongingness and uniqueness. Diverse employees achieve an optimal level of distinctiveness in organizational groups when they are accepted as part of the group and integrated into the decision-making process in a way that capitalizes on the unique value they add. According to Dorae CEO Aba Schubert, "The more differences of perspective and experience we can gather around us, the more we can know ... having a diverse team means we 'connect the dots' in new ways, because we can borrow novel perspectives from each other and build on an experience set that spans the world and generations."[28] Dorae is an example of an organization where employees are encouraged to be part of the group by placing their uniqueness front and center.

Research suggests optimal distinctiveness is important for realizing the potential performance advantages of

Have you ever been part of a group and felt a sense of both belonging and uniqueness? What was the experience like?
Rawpixel.com/Shutterstock

diversity. For example, a recent study of women entering top management teams (TMTs) found that organizations are more likely to reap the full benefit of a female perspective when newly appointed women are well-integrated into the TMT. When women are added to upper echelons merely as tokens of diversity, organizations do not see the same level of benefit.[29] In terms of DE&I, managers must remember that a critical part of inclusion is recognizing, honoring, and equally valuing the unique perspectives and talents that diverse employees bring to the table.[30]

Inclusion Climate   One way that organizations gauge the success of DE&I management efforts is by measuring something called the inclusion climate. **Inclusion climate represents employees' shared beliefs about the degree to which they feel valued, welcomed, accepted, and important in the organization.**[31] Inclusion climates should be stronger when HR practices are equitable and when employees feel a balanced sense of belongingness and uniqueness.

Let's talk a bit more about what the word climate means and how it's different from an organization's culture. An organization's culture (defined and discussed in Section DEI.4 and covered at length in Chapter 8) is its identity—*culture* describes an organization in the same way that the diversity wheel describes an individual. When employees speak about culture, they describe who the organization is and what it values. An organization's *climate,* on the other hand, refers to employees' shared sense of what it feels like to work in that organization (much like the weather climate in your current location describes what it feels like to live there). Specifically, an organization's **climate is defined as the set of perceptions that employees share, based on their interrelated experiences, regarding the organization's procedures and policies.** Employees' beliefs about their organizations' climates stem, in part, from organizational culture. A highly inclusive climate is characterized by employees who feel welcomed, valued, and respected, no matter who they are.[32] Organizations build strong inclusion climates by focusing on three key things:[33]

1. **Equitable employment decision-making practices.** Employees want to know that the organizational decisions that affect them are made according to just process (refer to Table DEI.2). In other words, they want to know that procedures in the organization are fair and unbiased. The use of unbiased procedures sends a signal to employees that the organization values fairness.
2. **Integration of differences.** Employees want to be invited and accepted into their work groups and organizations just as they are. In inclusive organizations, employees are not expected to be like everyone else. Rather, their differences are embraced and honored. In other words, employees can maintain uniqueness.
3. **Inclusion in decision making.** In inclusive climates, managers actively seek out diverse employee perspectives and value those perspectives just as much as more conventional perspectives. In other words, all employees have a strong sense of belongingness.

SELF-ASSESSMENT DEI.2   INCLUSION CLIMATE

Try taking Self-Assessment DEI.2 in Connect, if your instructor has assigned it, to consider the extent to which a current or previous employer had an inclusive climate.

Our emphasis in this chapter is on the importance of using effective DE&I management to integrate and capitalize on diverse perspectives in organizations. Some researchers call this the *value-in-diversity hypothesis,* which suggests that categorical dissimilarity (i.e., having lots of variation across and among the different dimensions of diversity) is beneficial because it increases the variety of knowledge, skills, abilities, and experiences in a group, which should therefore lead to a wider range of perspectives and ideas.[34] An abundance of research supports the assertion that heterogeneous groups show problem-solving and performance advantages over homogenous groups.[35] But we can't realize these advantages unless all of the members of heterogeneous groups feel comfortable sharing their perspectives and believe that the team will respect and value their unique contributions. This is where equity and inclusion play a role in DE&I management, and it's the reason that all three elements—the what, how, and why—are equally important.

DEI.2 The Evolution of DE&I in Organizations

THE BIG PICTURE
Understanding the history of DE&I management helps managers to realize its importance and anticipate its challenges.

LO DEI-2

Summarize the evolution of DE&I management in organizations.

One hundred percent of Fortune 100 companies have DE&I management programs in place, and data suggest that over 80% of all U.S. employers use DE&I initiatives.[36] But diversity hasn't always received this level of attention in the corporate world. The federal government only began mandating broad workplace protections for various groups about 60 years ago. This early legislation (and related legislation around the world) paved the way for modern corporate DE&I management efforts. Here we briefly explore this legal history, as well as the accompanying history of social tensions.

A History of Protections

One of the most important outcomes of early employment legislation was the introduction of protections for workers that ensured they could not be discriminated against in the workplace due to non-work-related personal characteristics. The term **protected class** refers to a group of people protected from employment discrimination based on a specific characteristic or identity they share. Table DEI.3 presents a timeline of key legislation,

TABLE DEI.3 The Evolution of Protected Class Status in Modern Organizations

TIME FRAME	1960s	1970s	1990s	2000–2019	Present
Key legislation, rulings, and milestones	Civil Rights Act of 1964/ Title VII Creation of EEOC Age Discrimination in Employment Act of 1967	Pregnancy Discrimination Act of 1978	Americans with Disabilities Act of 1990	Uniformed Services Employment and Reemployment Rights Act of 2013 Genetic Information Nondiscrimination Act of 2008	*Bostock v. Clayton County*, U.S. Supreme Court Case (2020)
Employers may not discriminate on the basis of	Race Sex Color Religion National origin Age	Pregnancy (as part of sex)	Disability status	Veteran status Genetic information Family medical history	Sexual orientation (as part of sex) Gender identity (as part of sex)

Table developed using information from: https://www.dol.gov/agencies/vets/programs/userra/USERRA-Pocket-Guide#:~:text=USERRA%20applies%20to%20 virtually%20all,State%20and%20Local%20Government%20employers; https://www.eeoc.gov/youth/timeline-important-eeoc-events; https://www.eeoc.gov/laws/guidance/protections-against-employment-discrimination-based-sexual-orientation-or-gender
Source: www.dol.gov.

court rulings, and employment law milestones that provided federal protections for employees and established various protected classes through the years.

All employees are protected by this legislation by virtue of their membership in various groups. For example, it is illegal for employers to base employment decisions on factors like employees' skin color, national origin, or religious beliefs (including atheism/agnosticism). One of your authors remembers her mother explaining that, as a schoolteacher in the 1960s, she could only keep her job until her pregnancies were physically visible. It may be difficult to imagine today, but before the Pregnancy Discrimination Act of 1978, an organization could have legally fired or refused to hire her mother simply because she was pregnant. After 1978, organizations had to comply with federal legislation protecting pregnant workers' rights. Early DE&I management programs focused more on ensuring this type of compliance than on building inclusive climates. We discuss compliance with EEOC legislation in detail in Chapter 10.

A History of Changes

A quick glance at Table DEI.3 shows that our beliefs about which aspects of employee identity should be legally protected in the workplace evolve over time. The law is reactive in nature, and we see new legislation emerge when certain aspects of diversity become more widely understood.

An increased understanding of and ability to empathize with diverse employees helps organizations to better support workers' needs and build feelings of inclusion. This requires managers to operate outside of their comfort zones and be willing to adapt to workers' needs in novel ways. This can feel daunting, and research suggests the fear of making mistakes is a primary factor that keeps managers from fully engaging with DE&I.[37] Managers should be prepared to be proactive learners (a key career readiness competency) when it comes to supporting their employees. Mistakes are normal and even necessary. Here we discuss two emerging concepts related to employee diversity.

Emerging Concepts in Diversity Much of our existing knowledge on diversity in organizations revolves around dimensions like race, disability, and religion because researchers have focused the most attention on these categories. However, in recent years, we've seen increasing interest in better understanding other dimensions of diversity, including neurodiversity and gender identity.

1. **Neurodiversity.** **Neurodiversity** is the idea that there are differences in the way people learn, think, and interact.[38] Scientists have studied neurodiversity for decades, so the concept itself is not new. What is emergent is our understanding of neurodiversity. Outdated approaches viewed neurological conditions like autism, ADHD, and dyslexia as pathologies that limited individuals and needed to be minimized or fixed. Fortunately, we now realize these natural variations should not only be accommodated but also represent unique abilities and perspectives.[39] Consider the following example:

    Neurodiversity Example—Ultranauts: At Ultranauts, a quality engineering firm, more than 75% of the employees are neurodivergent. According to co-founder Rajesh Anandan, "We started our company with the intention that neurodiversity, including autism, could be a competitive advantage for business." Anandan's previous experience working with people with autism revealed that neurodiverse individuals often find that the workplace is simply not designed for their needs. He and co-founder Art Schectman intentionally focused their recruiting efforts to identify individuals with autism who possessed the **KSAs (essential knowledge, skills, and abilities)** needed for quality engineering work. These strengths include logical reasoning, pattern recognition, and systems thinking. According to the two co-founders, after one year, their new hires on the autism spectrum were outperforming seasoned quality engineers who were considered neurotypical. Said Anandan in a recent interview, "We fundamentally believe if we're able to bring together different brain types, different thinking styles, different processing models onto the same team and focused on the same work, we can do better, we can solve more complex problems."[40]

2. **Gender identity.** "Gender identity refers to a person's internal sense of being male, female, a combination of both, or neither."[41] While a person's sex is determined by anatomy and biology, gender relates to social expectations for how a person's sex (their "femaleness" or "maleness") is expressed. Gender identity, therefore, pertains to how individuals feel about and express this aspect of the self. A person may have female (male) anatomy but identify and express themselves in ways that society would expect from a male (female). A person who identifies as gender nonbinary may see themselves in more neutral terms.

   Gender Identity Example—Dell: Two former Dell systems engineers recently shared their experiences with exclusion in an interview with NPR. Helen Harris is gender nonconforming (meaning that she does not conform to conventional expectations for how a woman should behave, dress, etc.) and identifies as a woman but chooses to dress in men's clothing. Cecilia Gilbert is a transgender woman.[42] Both individuals say they experienced pervasive and systemic bias at Dell based on their gender identities. Harris described being repeatedly heckled by co-workers and pressured to dress more in line with social expectations for women. She also felt the company intentionally and repeatedly prevented her from interacting with customers due to her appearance. Gilbert recalls the day a transgender co-worker told her that if she came out as transgender at work, her career would be over. Both of these individuals felt excluded, devalued, and unappreciated in their jobs at Dell.

A History of Tensions

It may be very difficult for you to imagine yourself refusing to send a pregnant worker out on a sales call for a politically conservative customer. But what if instead of being pregnant, the worker was transgender? Are you less clear on how you'd react when you consider the latter scenario? Remember that the law can change overnight, but viewpoints and habits do not, and since the dawn of equal employment opportunity, employers and managers have had to wrestle with the tensions between what the law said they *had* to do and what they believed they *should* do. We call this out for two reasons:

1. **All of us will experience these tensions.** Feelings of discomfort related to DE&I management are normal, and all of us—no matter who we are—will experience these tensions at some point in our professional lives. You will encounter problems that feel extremely challenging to solve, and at times you will find yourself wondering if it's possible to know what the "right" decision is. Consider the following example:

   DE&I Management Tensions Example—Transgender Athletes: In March 2022, Lia Thomas became the first transgender woman to win a Division I National Collegiate Athletic Association (NCAA) swimming competition.[43] Thomas, a student at the University of Pennsylvania, was born a biological male and began the process of transitioning genders in 2019. A media frenzy erupted in the weeks prior to the event as people spoke out about the NCAA's decision to allow Thomas to race in the women's competition. Parents of some of Thomas' competitors argued that allowing her to compete was an injustice to their daughters.[44] Women's athletic advocacy groups requested that the NCAA adopt fairer, evidence-based transgender guidelines for eligibility.[45] Hundreds of current and former competitive swimmers petitioned the NCAA to include Thomas in the women's event.[46] The common thread on all sides of the issue was the argument for fairness. Some felt that it wasn't fair to include a swimmer born a biological male in a competition against biological females, and others felt it was an injustice to exclude Thomas from the women's event. Some proposed the NCAA create a third, "open" category for transgender athletes to occupy in future competitions.

2. **Inclusion requires that we confront these tensions.** Federal law will guide you on how to do the bare minimum to protect your organization from legal action, but it won't help you to make everyone who has a legal right to be in your organization feel like they are truly welcomed and respected there. Working through these tensions to build a sense of inclusion is hard work, and we believe it's a worthwhile cause. Remember that effective DE&I management does not require you to be comfortable with or even personally accepting of everything; rather, it asks you to work toward equity and inclusion in your organization in spite of any personal discomfort you may experience. Displaying this type of personal adaptability in the face of changing norms is a key career readiness competency.

> **Research Example:** Consider that meta-analytic data suggests members of marginalized groups experience decreased well-being when they believe their position or status in the organization is due namely to their protected class status (e.g., being hired through an affirmative action program).[47] On the flip side, research suggests that workers who belong to marginalized identity groups experience enhanced well-being and performance when they believe their competence, rather than their protected class membership, is the reason they hold a seat at the table.[48]

Managers must regularly wrestle with complex issues that don't have simple answers and that are often uncomfortable. Organizations are struggling with these issues, and so will you. In your own career you can expect to grapple with questions such as: (1) what does equity really mean in various situations (spoiler alert: it's complicated); (2) is there a such thing as being too inclusive (e.g., to the point that inclusion disrupts decision making or consensus building); and (3) how can a manager build an inclusive culture and climate while also maintaining their own personal beliefs and sense of identity? Managing for inclusion requires knowledge, openness, practice, patience, lots of errors, and above all, career readiness skills such as critical thinking and problem solving, because the decisions that inclusion requires are tough ones.[49]

DEI.3 Challenges of Effective DE&I Management

THE BIG PICTURE
Multiple person and environmental factors underlie common DE&I management challenges.

Eighty percent of the HR leaders who responded to a recent survey felt their organizations were simply "going through the motions" with regard to DE&I.[50] This highlights the reality that having a DE&I program and effectively managing DE&I are two different things. Consider what a recent survey of 804 HR professionals representing a variety of industries found:[51]

1. Over 75% of companies have no formal DE&I goals and do not include DE&I in leadership or employee learning and development.
2. Approximately 40% of employees believe that their organizations' diversity efforts are merely in place to prevent or respond to legal and ethical problems.

Research overwhelmingly shows corporate boards and executive leadership in U.S. organizations continue to lack diversity, and employees that belong to marginalized

LO DEI-3

Explain the person and environmental factors that can undermine effective DE&I management.

groups experience mistreatment in the workplace and struggle to build the social networks that are critical for career advancement.[52]

In this section, we discuss person and environmental factors that make DE&I management challenging. This distinction is common in management science and is based on psychologist Kurt Lewin's enduring theory that important outcomes in organizations are a function of these two sets of factors:[53]

1. **Person factors** are the various individual differences that make individuals the unique people they are. They include personality, values, attitudes, emotions, and various other aspects of identity.
2. **Environmental factors** are external forces and elements that contribute to people's outcomes. They include the organization's culture, structure, leadership, human resource policies, and the way jobs are designed.

Lewin's work tells us if we want to understand the root causes of our outcomes, we must understand both the individual and situational variables that are jointly influencing those outcomes. Here we use these two sets of factors to better understand the causes of common DE&I management challenges.

Person Factors

Organizations must understand the person, or individual, factors that get in the way of their DE&I management efforts. Three categories of person factors that explain struggles with DE&I management are: (1) fear, (2) misperceptions, and (3) expectations and attributions.

Have you ever avoided a conversation with someone different from you out of fear that you would offend them? This fear is quite common, and it is one of the person factors that inhibits DE&I work in organizations. Imagehit Limited Exclusive Contributor/123RF

1. Fear Fear is the first category of person factors that make effective DE&I management challenging. Fear represents our basic human tendency to avoid things that we are unsure of. Specifically, when we believe that someone is different from us on various dimensions of diversity, we naturally fear interacting with them. Researchers call this phenomenon **intercultural communication apprehension**, and it represents the anxiety, stress, and general avoidance we experience when we are confronted with the possibility of spending time with someone we perceive as different. As you might imagine, anxiety, stress, and avoidance are the opposite of well-being. We don't enjoy these feelings, and as a result, we seek to avoid them by avoiding anything that might cause them.

Research suggests that spending time talking, communicating, and building relationships with those from backgrounds different than our own improves our levels of tolerance, builds better communities, and reduces the incidence of dysfunctional conflict.[54] These interactions also increase our well-being and help us build the valuable social networks that are essential for career progression and performance.[55] Unfortunately, our fear of the unknown often prevents us from taking the first step toward engaging with diverse others.

2. Misperceptions Misperceptions are the second category of person factors that make effective DE&I management challenging. As you'll learn in Chapter 12, perceptions are important inputs into decision making, but our perceptions of others are often inaccurate. When we misperceive someone, we make an incorrect judgment about *who they are,* and this can adversely affect our interactions with them.

Various stereotypes and biases (discussed in Chapter 12) can lead to misperceptions that cloud our ability to perceive the people and things around us accurately. Specifically, **stereotypes** are generalizations that we make about groups of people. When we stereotype someone, we make an assumption about who they are simply because they belong to a certain identity group. Applying negative stereotypes can impact our DE&I efforts because doing so may prevent us from seeing the value that others bring to organizational decisions. Instead, we see what our stereotypes tell us to see, and we risk judging people's intentions and abilities incorrectly. We all carry perceptual biases. You can increase your career readiness competency of self-awareness if you work to identify these biases in yourself. This also will help to minimize the negative effects of biases.

3. Expectations and Attributions Expectations and attributions are the third category of person factors that make effective DE&I management challenging. Expectations relate to how we think someone should behave, and attributions are the explanations we make for others' behaviors and outcomes.

- *Expectations* relate to the subconscious social expectations we hold for members of various identity groups. We expect that people belonging to certain groups will (1) behave in certain ways and (2) hold certain types of job roles. A simple yet effective self-test is to imagine a doctor and a nurse. If you are like many people raised in U.S. society, the first images that popped into your mind were likely of a male doctor and a female nurse. These are examples of social expectations related to the people we see as fit for different types of job roles. These expectations impede DE&I efforts in a couple of ways. First, we are less likely to value someone's opinions or see them as a viable candidate for certain positions if our social expectations tell us they are not likely to have a valuable perspective or to be competent to fill the position. Second, we are more likely to judge someone's performance in their existing job role as unacceptable if our subconscious social expectations tell us that the person should not occupy that role.[56] In other words, inaccurate expectations prevent marginalized group members from both obtaining and succeeding in important jobs.

    Expectations Example—NFL Coaches and Owners: Almost 70% of NFL football players are Black, but 27 of the league's 32 head coaches, and all but 2 of its team owners, are white.[57] The lack of racial diversity in its upper echelon is not a new problem for the NFL, but the issue recently came to the forefront when former Miami Dolphins head coach Brian Flores sued the league for using discriminatory hiring practices. According to federal court filings, Flores received a text from Bill Belichick—his former boss and the head coach of the New England Patriots—congratulating him for winning the New York Giants head coaching job. The problem was, Flores' interview with the Giants wasn't scheduled to happen for three more days. Further texts between the two, according to the lawsuit, revealed that Belichick intended to send the message to Brian Daboll, another contender for (and ultimate winner of) the position. Flores believes the NFL scheduled his interview in order to comply with its own "Rooney Rule," which requires that at least one person of color is interviewed for every head coaching position.[58] He described the process as a "sham" intended to create the impression that the league was seriously considering a Black candidate for the head coaching job.

- *Attributions* relate to our subconscious need to explain why things happen, both to ourselves and others. We make attributions about the causes of our and others' behavior. One attributional issue that hinders effective DE&I management is the **fundamental attribution error**, defined as the tendency to assume that others' negative outcomes are attributable to their person factors rather than to factors in their environment. The fundamental attribution error prevents us from asking questions and digging deeper when we witness discrimination against members of marginalized groups. Instead, we assume that their outcomes were their own fault, and we fail to consider external influences such as unfair HR practices or biased decision making on the part of leadership.[59]

Fears, misperceptions, and expectations and attributions are person factors that hinder effective DE&I management. These factors prevent us from developing deep relationships and cloud our ability to evaluate others accurately. The result is that individuals who belong to marginalized identity groups feel excluded, devalued, and ignored.

Environmental Factors

Managers need to understand the various environmental factors that obstruct DE&I efforts. Three environmental factors that can cause difficulties with DE&I management are: (1) leadership, (2) HR practices, and (3) organizational culture.

Leadership Employees look to leadership to get a sense of what kind of organization they are working for. Leaders' actions are often highly visible, and thus employees view their decisions as representative of the organization's values and priorities. Employees form perceptions of an organization's commitment to DE&I by seeking information about two things:

1. **Alignment.** One way that employees use leadership to gauge whether their organization is truly committed to DE&I is by assessing whether organizational leaders' public statements regarding DE&I align with the organization's actions and decisions that affect DE&I outcomes.[60] Research suggests that employees become cynical, develop negative attitudes, and are more likely to leave the company when they believe leaders are merely "talking the talk" but not "walking the walk" in DE&I.[61] Further, both current and prospective employees see an organization as lacking in integrity and less attractive when its actions and words regarding DE&I are misaligned.

2. **Representation.** A second way employees use leadership to gauge whether their organization is truly committed to DE&I is by assessing whether there is diverse representation in the upper echelon. Recent data from a Gartner survey of 3,500 workers across 20+ industries indicate that women account for less than 30% of executive positions but comprise over 50% of the front-line workforce. These data also show that although BIPOC (Black, Indigenous, and other people of color) workers account for over 30% of front-line workers, they occupy only 17% of executive positions.[62] Senior leadership teams are highly visible to both organizational insiders and outsiders, and homogenous leadership teams signal that the organization does not truly value diverse perspectives.[63]

   Alignment and Representation Example—Fortune 500 Leadership Teams: A recent article questioned the alignment between the words and actions of multiple Fortune 500 companies.[64] Specifically, the author presented photos of firms' social media posts regarding the Black Lives Matter movement alongside photos of the firms' executive leadership teams. The piece made a powerful statement about both the lack of alignment between corporate words and deeds, as well as the lack of representation of Black executives on senior leadership teams.

Does a statement such as this one indicate that an organization truly values DE&I? james anderson/Alamy Stock Photo

HR Practices HR practices are another environmental factor rife with potential to harm DE&I efforts. As you learned in Section DEI.1, HR practices include the various policies, procedures, and tools organizations use to recruit, hire, appraise, compensate, promote, and develop employees. Firms that succeed at DE&I management are strategic about implementing HR practices that drive diversity, equity, and inclusion. For example, Salesforce committed to increasing the U.S. representation of both senior leaders and employees from Black, Indigenous, Latinx, and multiracial communities by 50% by the end of 2023. Firms winning at DE&I management also design and implement HR practices that are not only fair but that actively encourage decision makers to reject their own biases and seek out diverse perspectives. A recent article in the *Harvard Business Review* highlights the problems common in various HR practices.[65] These issues are found in HR practices such as:

1. **Recruiting.** Recruiting practices determine which applicants the organization considers when hiring for various positions. There are several ways that faulty recruiting practices harm DE&I efforts.

    - **Biased job postings.** Job postings can deter or even eliminate older applicants when they imply or state that the organization is looking for "digital natives," "recent graduates," or "candidates with 1–5 years of experience."[66]

    - **Narrow recruiting efforts.** Recruiting efforts can rule out members of various identity groups if recruiters fail to cast a wide net when they seek out applicants. It can be easy and more efficient for recruiters to return to their tried-and-true sources, such as one or two universities in the area. However, this practice fails to consider recruiting sources that are likely to contain highly qualified candidates that belong to diverse identity groups.

        Narrow Recruiting Example—WayUp: The WayUp job site focuses on connecting diverse college students and recent college graduates with hiring organizations. Nia Lewis partnered with WayUp when she took on the role of global talent acquisition senior specialist at Colgate-Palmolive. Lewis' goal was to increase the diversity of her organization's talent, and she realized quickly that the company was primarily recruiting from only a few schools close to their headquarters. The partnership with WayUp provided Colgate-Palmolive with access to a database of more than 5 million diverse students and recent grads hailing from more than 7,000 institutions.[67]

    - **Overreliance on referrals.** Referrals are highly popular tools for recruiting new job applicants. When a current, high-performing employee provides a referral, the recruiter spends less time sourcing applicants and has more confidence that the candidate will be successful in the role.[68] Unfortunately, referrals often serve to increase homogeneity in organizations. This is because current employees are likely to refer candidates who are similar to them in terms of identity.[69]

2. **Selection.** Selection practices determine which candidate the organization ultimately hires for a job position. The goal of a selection system is to accurately select the candidate who is most likely to perform the job well. In other words, selection is about predicting future performance. Selection devices need to be free from bias and should capture only that information which is directly related to performance in a specific job. Unfortunately, many organizations operate with deficient or even discriminatory selection practices. Here are some of the ways faulty selection practices harm DE&I efforts:

One way that organizations can improve the accuracy of interviews and rule out potential bias is by using panels of interviewers rather than a single interviewer. fizkes/123RF

- **Overreliance on interviews.** Interviews remain one of the most popular techniques for differentiating among job applicants.[70] They also remain one of the most inaccurate techniques, largely because they tend to be poorly designed, poorly implemented, or both. Interviews should be structured, questions should be scientifically designed to capture relevant aspects of job performance, and interviewers should be properly trained to deliver them.[71] Instead, interviews tend to consist of informal conversations, and interviewers tend to select candidates based more on subconscious judgments of personal liking and similarity than objective job qualifications.[72] Interviews can be useful selection tools, but even when they are designed and implemented well, interviews should be only one part of a broader set of selection devices.

- **Discriminatory selection tools.** As you'll learn in Chapter 10, firms can be held liable for discrimination in employment decisions even when they do not realize the selection devices they're using are biased. Sadly, it's not uncommon for selection devices to inadvertently discriminate against various identity groups in ways that are difficult to detect on the surface. Organizations are responsible for ensuring that the selection devices they use are non-discriminatory. Consider this example of documented bias in AI-based selection tools:

    Discriminatory Selection Tools Example—Bias in AI: More and more firms are relying on artificial intelligence (AI) in employment decisions.[73] One way technology companies market these programs is as a tool for increasing efficiency in the hiring process; algorithms purport to analyze candidates' video interviews and screen out those deemed a poor fit for certain jobs based on their facial expressions, movements, and other characteristics that the programs supposedly identify. But numerous experts warn that the science behind this technology is far too new to be either valid or accurate.[74] Further, studies reveal that algorithms designed to recognize facial expressions, mood, character traits, and body movements are rife with both race and gender bias.[75] For example, researchers at Stanford and MIT found that a prominent U.S. tech firm used a data set that was 83% white and 77% male to train its facial recognition algorithm.[76] The warning is clear—AI can be just as biased as the humans who develop its underlying algorithms, and companies who consider implementing these tools should proceed with extreme caution.

3. **Training.** Data suggest nearly all Fortune 500 companies conduct some type of diversity training.[77] However, according to a recent review of the organizational diversity literature, numerous issues persist in this type of training.[78] Let's discuss three of these issues:

    - **Messaging invokes fear.** One reason diversity training fails to improve DE&I management is that organizational leaders inadvertently (or deliberately) convey the message that if employees mess up in terms of diversity, something bad will happen. In other words, employees often view diversity training as fear-based, and fear hinders our ability to open our minds and learn.

    - **Training is mandatory.** Another reason diversity training fails to produce desired DE&I outcomes is that companies often make training—and the specific content it contains—mandatory. Employees tend to feel angry and/or defensive when they think they're being forced to learn something, particularly when the subject matter relates to their own shortcomings.[79]

    - **Training is reactionary.** A final reason that diversity training often misses the mark with DE&I is that organizations tend to implement it in response to specific and public incidents involving discrimination. Employees want

Equal access to resources is important. How would you feel if your team was given access to the weight room on the right, but your competition was given access to the weight room on the left? (left) fotoandy/Shutterstock; (right) PhotoSunnyDays/Shutterstock

to know that their organizations truly value diversity. When training only happens because someone messed up, employees get the message that DE&I is not a priority for the organization.

Reactionary DE&I Efforts Example—NCAA Women's Basketball Tournament: The NCAA came under fire in 2021 after Sedona Prince—a forward on the University of Oregon's basketball team—called the organization out for clear and alarming disparities in the weightlifting equipment it provided for the women's versus men's basketball players at its annual March Madness tournament. Soon after the discovery, other female athletes began sharing numerous additional ways that they felt devalued and underappreciated, including receiving less-accurate COVID-19 tests than male athletes.[80] This incident was not the first time that the public has questioned the NCAA's commitment to women's athletics. However, in reaction, the organization upgraded the women's weightlifting facilities overnight, and NCAA President Mark Emmert made a public apology and statement explaining that the incident should not have happened and would not happen in the future.

4. **Performance evaluations.** Most mid-size and large firms rely on performance appraisal ratings as a primary input into decisions regarding employee pay and promotion. But, as with other practices, performance evaluations can hinder DE&I management if managers don't conduct them properly. The main problem with performance evaluations as they relate to DE&I is that the numerical ratings these evaluations produce come from managers' assessments of employee performance. As you'll learn in Chapter 12, people—including managers—are notoriously inaccurate and biased in their perceptions. Successful DE&I requires objective and unbiased ratings of employee performance, and this is often difficult to achieve. Consider the following example:

Gender Bias in Performance Evaluations—Research Example: Kieran Snyder, linguist and CEO/co-founder of Textio, conducted a study to better understand the types of performance feedback that managers give to male and female employees.[81] Snyder's data set included 248 performance reviews given by 180 different male and female managers across 28 companies. Her findings revealed that 76% of female employees received negative performance feedback related to their personalities, while only 2% of male employees received such criticism. The issue here is not that female employees received personality-based feedback, but rather that managers in the study—both male and female—didn't deem it necessary to give this type of feedback to male employees. Further, the words that managers used to describe aspects of female employees' personalities contrasted starkly with those used to describe male employees. For example, female and male employees were labeled as abrasive and assertive, respectively, for exhibiting similar workplace behaviors.

5. **Grievance procedures.** Grievance procedures are intended to allow employees a safe avenue for reporting problems in the organization related to DE&I. As you learned in Section DEI.1, fair procedures need mechanisms for correctability—if a procedure isn't fair, there must be a way for managers to find out and make corrections to it. In theory, grievance procedures provide this element of correctability, but in reality, employees are often afraid to use them. Even when organizations promise anonymity, workers fear that managers will retaliate against them for speaking up about mistreatment, unfairness, and other problems related to DE&I.[82] This leads to a second problem: When employees don't speak up about problems, leaders assume that there are no problems, and thus the organization makes no effort to course correct.

A recent article in the *Harvard Business Review* suggests that organizations thoroughly investigate their HR practices related to talent management to identify which practices are limiting opportunities for workers who identify with marginalized groups. Organizations should then devise specific measures to correct the problems.[83]

EXAMPLE — HR Practices: Class-Action Lawsuit Prompts Riot Games to Improve HR Practices

Video game developer Riot Games paid a hefty price for ignoring DE&I in its HR practices. The company recently settled a class-action lawsuit filed on behalf of more than 2,000 current and former female employees and contract workers. The lawsuit accused Riot of gender discrimination in its HR practices, among other things, and the company eventually agreed to pay $100 million in damages and legal fees.

What Went Wrong?
Many females who worked for Riot believed they were repeatedly passed over for jobs, promotions, and pay raises simply due to their gender.[84] Some female employees recalled having to prove that they played video games as part of their interviews.[85] The original complaint filed in Los Angeles in 2018 cited the company's "bro culture" and alleged multiple examples of male employees and executives harassing, objectifying, and belittling female employees.[86] At the time, Riot had no females on its executive leadership team, no executive position or team devoted to DE&I, and no HR practices aimed at achieving gender pay equity.[87]

What's Changed?
Riot has pledged to do better since the lawsuit. The company now has a dedicated DE&I team and chief diversity officer, and around 20% of its leadership team is female. Further, Riot agreed to make changes to limit "subjectivity and implicit bias in hiring and selection processes."[88] The company now requires that women and members of ethnic minority groups be part of all candidate lists given to hiring managers, and all selection panels must include a woman or member of an underrepresented identity group.

Riot has made specific changes to some of its hiring practices. For example, prior to the lawsuit, hiring managers would often directly ask female candidates if they were actual "gamers" or would simply assume they didn't possess the skills and knowledge that gaming requires. The company now uses rubrics written around the KSAs necessary for specific positions.[89] Riot has also begun conducting annual analyses of its pay data to look for, and correct, issues with pay equity. As part of the settlement, Riot agreed to allow a third party to monitor its HR practices for a three-year period.

Organizational Culture Organizational culture is a third environmental factor that can inhibit well-intentioned DE&I management efforts. **Organizational culture** is the set of shared, taken-for-granted, implicit assumptions that a group holds and that determines how it perceives, thinks about, and reacts to its various environments.[90] You can glean information about an organization's culture by paying attention to visible factors such as its mission statement, dress code, and décor. Culture also is evident in an organization's statement of its values.

As we mentioned in Section DEI.1, you can think of an organization's culture as its identity. This metaphor is useful because identity serves as a tool to help us make sense out of others' decisions. For example, if your pal is late to a movie, you may tell yourself it's because they're outgoing and friendly and tend to get caught up visiting with everyone around them instead of watching the clock. If your bestie won't go skydiving with you, perhaps you'll understand it's because they're not a risk taker and prefer to play it safe. Knowledge of identity helps us to understand why others do what they do, and organizational culture helps us understand why organizations do what they do. Culture, as you'll read more about in Chapter 8, is evident in various aspects of organizational life, including:

1. **Slogans and sayings.** Companies often express who they are through various slogans, sayings, and catchy acronyms. This language provides insight into the things the organization cares most about. For example, Hilton Brands' core values are Hospitality, Integrity, Leadership, Teamwork, Ownership, Now.[91] Each letter in the acronym tells you something about what Hilton Brands values as an organization.

2. **Rites and rituals.** Many firms engage in regular activities designed to celebrate, commemorate, or call attention to issues that matter to them. For example, Cisco held weekly employee check-in meetings throughout the duration of their COVID-19-driven work-from-home order. Employees in attendance heard from various medical experts and had the chance to discuss both physical and mental health issues.[92] Cisco's devotion of organizational time and resources to this initiative signaled that they valued their employees' mental and physical health.

3. **Rewards.** Employees pay close attention to the kinds of behaviors their organizations reward. As you'll discover in Chapter 12, we are more likely to engage in behaviors that are incentivized. E.ON, a German utility company, encourages employees at all levels to write thank-you notes to each other to recognize outstanding behaviors at work.[93] The organization likely uses this practice to encourage certain behaviors by directly thanking employees for engaging in them. Employees discern which behaviors their organization values by paying attention to which behaviors generate thank-you notes.

4. **Organizational goals.** Goals motivate us to achieve the things that matter most to us. We can get a sense of what a company values by looking at its goals. For example, Bloomberg recently set a goal to reach net-zero carbon emissions by the year 2025.[94] This decision indicates that the company cares about its impact on the natural environment.

All the these aspects of culture provide a window into an organization's values. Employees learn what's most important in their workplaces through these and other expressions of culture, and they use this information to make sense out of organizational decisions. Organizational culture also impacts important outcomes such as employee well-being and performance, according to recent research. Specifically, meta-analytic studies support a significant relationship between organizational culture and positive job attitudes and behaviors.[95]

DEI.4 Effective DE&I Management Practices

THE BIG PICTURE
Implementing the right practices at the managerial and organizational levels can improve DE&I management outcomes.

Organizations are catching on to the importance of creating and supporting diverse workforces. The number of new chief diversity officer (CDO) positions created by S&P 500 companies has almost tripled in recent years.[96] But some evidence suggests that many companies are struggling to achieve meaningful progress with their DE&I management

LO DEI-4
Describe effective DE&I management practices.

efforts. For example, a recent multi-industry survey of 1,000 managers and employees found that although over 90% of respondents identified DE&I as a high priority, only about one-third saw it as a strength in their organizations.[97] In another study, only 9% of 367 HR professionals surveyed characterized the DE&I management programs in their companies as highly effective.[98]

According to Sonja Gittens Ottley—Asana's head of diversity, inclusion, and belonging—DE&I management can only be successful when organizations and managers are equipped with the right tools to effectively execute initiatives.[99] Even the most well-intentioned companies will encounter roadblocks such as those we presented in Section DEI.3 if they don't know the best ways to manage DE&I. Organizations and their leaders need to approach DE&I management with the necessary knowledge, resources, and training. In this section we highlight managerial and organizational practices that foster effective DE&I management.

Banana Oil/Shutterstock

Managerial Practices

Managers are instrumental in driving successful DE&I efforts. Specifically, those in supervisory and leadership roles are visible and powerful members of the organization, and to followers, their actions represent the organization's true values and priorities. In other words, we look to our superiors to learn what's important in our workplaces. It's not possible to achieve strong inclusion climates unless leaders know how to facilitate inclusion and provide employees with the supports they need to be successful.[100] Recall that optimal distinctiveness theory proposes that all of us want to achieve belongingness in our groups while maintaining uniqueness in our identities.[101] Management experts suggest that leaders should engage in two different sets of behaviors: those that drive belongingness and those that show that the organization values uniqueness.

Facilitate Belongingness A recent multinational study of approximately 4,900 employees who'd recently quit their jobs found that a lack of belonging was a major driver of turnover for over 50% of respondents. The study also showed that employees from underrepresented identity groups were more likely to feel this way than employees who belonged to majority identity groups.[102] Research suggests that leaders should repeatedly and intentionally engage in behaviors that facilitate a sense of belongingness for their team members.[103] Here are three behaviors leaders can implement to foster belongingness:

1. **Support team members as part of the group.** Leaders should be genuinely interested in the needs of different team members. As a manager, take the time to develop relationships with subordinates, learn about their experiences, and demonstrate in your actions that your team members' needs are an important consideration in decisions. The work experience can be significantly more difficult for members of marginalized groups when leaders fail to foster a sense of belongingness. Consider a recent study that found members of marginalized groups are less likely to ask for deadline extensions at work than members of majority groups because they fear being a burden to others or being judged as incompetent.[104] This amounts to members of marginalized groups being mentally taxed and overwhelmed, which harms both their personal well-being and their job performance. Inclusive leaders make it clear to employees if and when certain deadlines are flexible and show group members that missed deadlines often indicate the desire to do a better job as opposed to a lack of competence or hard work.

2. **Promote equity and fairness.** In equitable environments, all employees have fair access to resources, opportunities, and information. As a manager you should proactively consider how any decision you make might disproportionately

benefit or harm certain groups of employees. For example, it may sound like fun to invite the team to strategize over cocktails on the weekend. An inclusive leader would think about the fact that caregivers, members of certain faith groups, or individuals who don't drink alcohol for a variety of reasons may be uncomfortable with and/or unable to participate in this gathering and would thus miss out on the opportunity to strategize and drive team decisions.

3. **Share decision-making authority.** A third way managers can facilitate a sense of belongingness is by intentionally sharing decision power with team members. Specifically, inclusive leaders consult with diverse members of the group, ask those with different experiences to provide input on work methods and group decisions, and create a culture where authority is shared and not concentrated at the top or with a few majority group members.

Value Uniqueness In addition to creating feelings of belongingness, managers who wish to improve DE&I management must behave in ways that assure group members that their uniqueness is something the organization values.[105] Here are two practices managers can implement to accomplish this goal:

1. **Encourage a variety of perspectives.** Inclusive managers are proactive about seeking out multiple viewpoints before making decisions. As a manager, you should make it clear that providing a unique perspective on an issue is something that is both valued and rewarded on your team. One way to encourage this is to simply state something like "ok, that's one idea on the board. Now let's try to come up with three wildly different ways of solving this problem." Team members are more likely to contribute something that might be unpopular or atypical if they know their leader has specifically asked for this type of contribution.

2. **Ensure diverse group members can contribute.** Inclusive leaders are mindful of the fact that different people do things in different ways. Leaders need to be sure that all group members can contribute to discussions and decision making. This involves providing accessible options that account for the various ways that communication may happen differently for different employees, including neurodiverse team members and those with disabilities.[106]

> **Diverse Contributions Example—Author Example:** Your authoring team has adopted decision-making rules based on ensuring all members can contribute in the way that suits them. For example, Angelo Kinicki is a quick decision maker; he often prefers to discuss issues in the moment, reach an immediate resolution with the team, and move on. Denise Breaux Soignet prefers to take time to process information and think through larger decisions before forming an opinion about the best solution. Angelo and Denise often joke about this disparity, but after years of working together, they have made a conscious choice to allow time and space for processing whenever big decisions related to this product are on the table. This has proven worthwhile to the team on many occasions, and our relationships are stronger because we have a team culture of respecting each other's needs.

Managers can encourage successful DE&I efforts by ensuring all employees are starting from the same line in terms of their access to resources, opportunities, and information. Image Source/Getty Images

Organizational Practices

Successful DE&I management requires that organizations take a long-term, company-wide approach and commit to providing the necessary time, money, and resources.[107] According to a recent study, organizations that do the work to create and sustain strong DE&I programs are better at adapting to changing market needs and are more likely to exceed their financial goals, retain happy customers, and generate employee engagement than organizations without strong DE&I programs.[108] Here are three broad organizational practices for succeeding with DE&I management.

Make It Part of Business Strategy
Nearly 90% of the 113 HR leaders surveyed in a recent Gartner study believed their organizations had failed to make meaningful strides toward increasing representation of diverse identities in the workplace despite efforts to improve DE&I.[109] This is not surprising, given that data suggest more than 70% of attempted organizational changes ultimately flop.[110] An important reason organizations often fail to make significant progress is that change efforts are not successfully integrated into the core business strategy. Instead, programs amount to a hodgepodge of isolated initiatives with no common thread and no link to measurable short-term and long-term company goals. Successfully building diverse, equitable, inclusive organizations requires that DE&I be infused into the business strategy in the same vein as goals related to revenue generation, shareholder wealth, and so on.[111]

You'll learn about setting strategy in depth in Chapter 6, but broadly speaking, strategic DE&I management begins with analyzing your organization's weaknesses and then setting and monitoring specific, measurable goals for improvement. This amounts to asking "where are we now? what's not working? where do we want to be in what amount of time? how do we plan to get there? and how will we measure our progress?"

Pay gaps are one example of a DE&I-related issue that requires strategic focus.[112] This is due in part to the complexities involved with identifying the reasons for, and remedying, these gaps. Data suggest that disparities in pay related to factors such as race, gender, and disability status are prevalent in organizations all over the world.[113] But a recent survey of 374 HR professionals found that only about one-third of companies included dedicated funding for closing diversity-related pay gaps in their firms' budgets.[114] Another DE&I-related issue that should be addressed at the strategic level is increasing the representation of diverse talent in applicant pools. Consider that over 70% of respondents to a recent multinational survey of 4,500 senior executives, HR professionals, and DE&I specialists said that recruiting members of underrepresented groups was their single biggest challenge.[115]

The authors of a recent *Harvard Business Review* article suggested that organizations assign measurable goals for managers and leaders as part of strategic DE&I efforts.[116] These goals, according to the authors, should focus on two distinct categories of results: (1) representation results (e.g., metrics that assess career mobility, hiring, promotion, etc. for diverse employee groups) and (2) inclusion results (e.g., equity perceptions and measures of employee engagement from diverse employee groups). At the British Broadcasting Corporation (BBC), leaders are evaluated in part based on equity goals related to various employee identity categories. At Target, corporate assigns managers specific targets related to diversity and includes outcomes in the calculation of performance evaluation scores.[117]

Encourage Meaningful Conversations
Strong relationships with others from a variety of identity categories can help individuals to grow and can facilitate the creation of inclusive organizational climates. The trust built over time in close relationships leads to conversations that provide deeper insight into and respect for the value of others' perspectives and ideas.[118] This argument is based on a long-standing psychological theory called the *contact hypothesis,* which suggests we can reduce prejudice and build inclusion by encouraging and nurturing contact among diverse identity groups.[119] Consider this example:

> **Meaningful Conversations Example—The Coffee Project:** Your author Denise Breaux Soignet spends most of her work hours advocating for organizations to be more faith-friendly. Faith-friendly organizations are inclusive of all employees, regardless of religious background (including atheism and agnosticism). Faith-friendly organizations don't encourage employees to have religion; rather, they allow employees to bring their whole selves to work and provide the accommodations and supports that honor this important part of workers' identities. Denise's favorite activity is something called

The Coffee Project, where her students each receive $20 and the e-mail address/phone number of another student on campus who (1) they have never met, and (2) observes a faith tradition very different from their own. The only requirement is that the students get together, that they spend the money on food and drink (coffee, water, tea, bagels ... whatever they'd each like), and that they talk to each other. The results of this simple project are astounding, and multiple new friendships blossom every semester because two people who would likely never have spoken realize how much they have in common, and how much they stand to learn from one another. This photo was taken at the very first coffee project in Denise's religious inclusion course.

Two students from different religious backgrounds get to know each other over coffee as part of an ongoing project at the Tyson Center for Faith-Friendly Workplaces at the University of Arkansas.
Sam M. Walton College of Business, University of Arkansas

Organizational scholars Jane Dutton and Emily Heaphy believe that high-quality connections built on a foundation of repeated, positive interactions build inclusion and transform the way employees experience their work environments.[120] This is because when employees engage with dissimilar others on multiple occasions, they learn more about their own identities, understand others' perspectives better, and build confidence in their ability to communicate across differences. Mistakes are a normal part of the learning and growth that stem from these conversations, and we've provided some best practices to help build your self-efficacy around having respectful conversations in the Manage U at the beginning of this chapter. Over time, relationships built between diverse teammates foster enhanced psychological safety, functional disagreement, creative problem solving, and work group performance. Organizations can encourage meaningful conversations among employees by building in habitual and prominent opportunities for diverse teammates to have high-quality interactions in various settings and for a multitude of positive purposes.[121]

Track the Data (and Use It) Data are hard to ignore. Making behavioral changes is easier when we can see reality in front of us in an objective, easy-to-interpret format.[122] Technological advances have made it possible for organizations—even small ones—to easily collect data on a multitude of important employee-related variables. Organizations can use the data they collect to identify DE&I issues, create goals, and track progress over time. Consider the following example:

> **Accountability for Results—Colgate-Palmolive Example:** Consumer products company Colgate-Palmolive uses a dashboard to track data related to diverse representation in roles across the organization. Specifically, the company monitors the career progression of employees according to various identity categories to learn whether some groups are not advancing in the organization as quickly as other groups. The company also strives to meet specific diversity targets for candidate pools for each open position.[123]

According to the Society for Human Resource Management (SHRM), less than 20% of S&P 500 companies say they tie senior management pay to diversity-related data.[124] This is discouraging considering that setting targets and tracking progress through data is an important way that organizations demonstrate commitment to DE&I. Research suggests that organizations use data to evaluate and incentivize leaders for their work toward meeting DE&I objectives. In a recent *Harvard Business Review* article, experts Siri Chilazi and Iris Bohnet stated that organizations should approach DE&I management "in exactly the same rigorous and data-driven way you manage the rest of your business. Achieving DEI objectives requires no more and no less than the use of the same planning, feedback, and accountability processes that are deployed to reach targets in sales, product development, and budgeting. Data drives targeted action and creates accountability in these domains, and so it should in DEI as well."[125]

DEI.5 Career Corner

LO DEI-5
Discuss how to develop career readiness competencies related to DE&I management.

Figure DEI.2 shows the model of career readiness that we introduce in Chapter 1. Multiple links exist between DE&I management and the competencies in Figure DEI.2. Specifically, managing DE&I requires the career readiness competencies of oral/written communication; professionalism/work ethic; diversity, equity, and inclusion; social intelligence; networking; showing commitment; proactive learning orientation; positive approach; personal adaptability; self-awareness; a service/others orientation; and openness to change.

This career corner focuses on a subset of the competencies involved in DE&I management. Read on to discover ways to improve your competencies of service/others orientation; diversity, equity, and inclusion; social intelligence; professionalism/work ethic; proactive learning orientation; and positive approach.

Practice Seeing Things from Others' Perspectives

Our worldviews, attitudes, behaviors, and decisions all stem from the unique perspectives we hold. These perspectives develop due to the experiences we have throughout our lives. No two people hold identical perspectives, and the more categorical dissimilarity two people have, the more variance we're likely to find between their

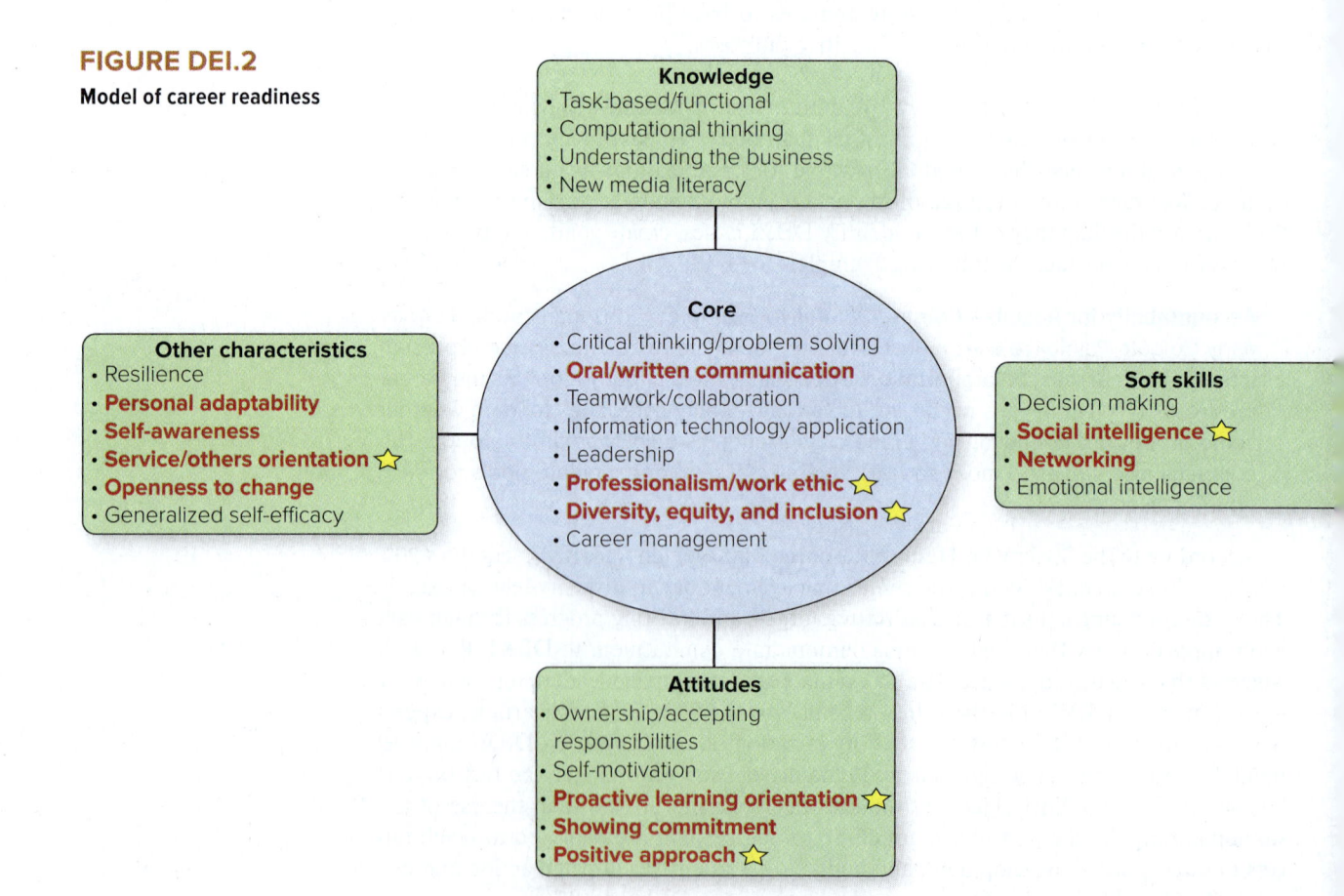

FIGURE DEI.2
Model of career readiness

Knowledge
- Task-based/functional
- Computational thinking
- Understanding the business
- New media literacy

Core
- Critical thinking/problem solving
- Oral/written communication
- Teamwork/collaboration
- Information technology application
- Leadership
- Professionalism/work ethic ⭐
- Diversity, equity, and inclusion ⭐
- Career management

Other characteristics
- Resilience
- Personal adaptability
- Self-awareness
- Service/others orientation ⭐
- Openness to change
- Generalized self-efficacy

Soft skills
- Decision making
- Social intelligence ⭐
- Networking
- Emotional intelligence

Attitudes
- Ownership/accepting responsibilities
- Self-motivation
- Proactive learning orientation ⭐
- Showing commitment
- Positive approach ⭐

perspectives. To increase your career readiness related to DE&I management, try practicing something called perspective taking, defined as viewing the world from another person's perspective.[126] The leaders in this chapter's Executive Interview Series video suggest that you do everything you can to see the world from others' perspectives. Seeing things from a different point of view allows you to put others' needs over your own (service/others orientation), builds your awareness of what makes others unique (diversity, equity, and inclusion), and provides the opportunity for you to generate meaningful connections and build strong relationships (social intelligence).

We suggest two different ways for you to practice perspective taking:

1. **Make an effort.** It's not easy to understand others and how the world appears to them. We often think we know another's perspective because we know a few facts about them. In reality, how someone views the world is complex and difficult to grasp. First-hand accounts are a good way to build a better understanding of diverse perspectives, and we encourage you to read books, listen to podcasts, and pay attention for opportunities to hear another person's story. You'll never be able to live another person's life, but you can listen to their experiences and honor how those experiences have shaped their realities.

2. **Appreciate and nurture diverse relationships.** It's easier to understand someone when you have put the time and energy into investing in a relationship with them.[127] This is evident if you compare the relationships you have with your closest friends to those with your most casual acquaintances. It's likely that you understand close friends' perspectives far more than those of causal pals. In close friendships, we learn bits and pieces over time that contribute to a more complete picture of who someone is and how they view the world. Nurturing diverse relationships also helps to bring members of underrepresented groups into corporate social networks.

   Nurturing Diverse Relationships Example—Thesis: Thesis CEO Ryan Buchanan immediately noticed something unsettling when he walked into a social event for business executives in Portland, OR a few years ago. Nearly all the attendees were white males. Said Buchanan, "I was part of the problem because I hadn't been intentional about building relationships with entrepreneurs of color."[128] He further noted that his own company had "not been intentional about racial diversity and [gender] equity." Buchanan credits this moment with changing the trajectory of DE&I at his company and is now proud to report that of his 250+ employees, 42% are people of color and 61% identify as women. "We changed our hiring practices. It was like that pebble in the lake that helped us start creating relationships with folks who don't look like us," said Buchanan.

Executive Interview Series: Diversity, Equity, and Inclusion

Work on Being an Ally

An ally is a member of a majority group who champions DE&I by publicly and proactively calling attention to DE&I issues and working to drive improvements to an organization's systems.[129] Allies can be formidable forces for change because of the social power inherent in their membership in dominant social groups. In other words, people tend to listen when a member of the in-group talks. Using your social position to ensure others receive what they deserve demonstrates integrity and a concern for the greater good. Practicing the following three tips inspired by a recent *Harvard Business Review* article will help you to improve your career readiness competency of professionalism/work ethic:

1. **Bring diversity to the table.** Members of marginalized groups often experience the discomfort of being the only person in the room with characteristics that are different from majority members. An organization that truly values diverse perspectives is proactive about building groups that represent diverse experiences. Allies can help by ensuring that members of a variety of identity groups

Being an ally means using your own social capital to ensure that members of marginalized groups have a seat at the decision-making table.
Arthimedes/Shutterstock

are represented and valued in decision-making groups. Consider the following example of this powerful type of advocacy:

> **Advocating for Members of Marginalized Groups—Bill Campbell Example:** YouTube CEO Susan Wojcicki shared in a *Vanity Fair* article how the late Bill Campbell—football coach turned Silicon Valley legend—acted as a powerful ally for members of marginalized groups.[130] Wojcicki recalled learning she had not been invited to a highly important, invite-only industry conference just after she became YouTube's CEO. She knew some of tech's most important deals happened at these events and she reached out to Campbell for help with the situation. "This makes me so angry" he said, adding "of course you should be there!"[131] "He immediately recognized I had a rightful place at the event and within a day he worked his magic and I received my invitation," said Wojcicki.

2. **Accept feedback.** The best allies want to know their own biases and grow in their commitment to DE&I. This requires a willingness to accept feedback from others. If someone calls out your behavior as problematic, try taking a step back, saying "I hear you," and then asking, "how can I make this right?" When you work at improving your ability to accept DE&I-related feedback, you improve your career readiness competency of a positive approach and demonstrate the competency of proactive learning orientation.

3. **Call out unacceptable behavior.** People mess up, all the time. When other employees engage in behavior that is discriminatory or excluding, say something. Here's why this is so important. Members of marginalized groups often hold back when they witness or experience exclusionary or discriminatory behaviors because calling these things out publicly often means others will accuse them of "being too sensitive" or "playing the (insert identity category) card." Members of marginalized groups also experience frequent gaslighting (e.g., "calm down, it was just a joke" or "that's not what happened"). Allies have unique privilege in that their words are often more likely to be taken seriously or believed because they belong to dominant identity groups.

Accept That You Won't Be Perfect (Be a Good-ish Person)

Research by award-winning social psychologist Dolly Chugh and her colleagues encourages all of us to realize that we don't have to be perfect in our efforts to improve DE&I in our organizations.[132] Sadly, the assumption that advocacy is an all-or-nothing affair is often the reason many of us fail to do anything at all—it's too daunting and we give up. It's important to remind yourself that the desire to get better at something difficult demonstrates that you have a proactive learning orientation. Chugh suggests we remember that much of the social change throughout history has happened incrementally because of the small, combined efforts of many people over long periods of time. She calls this approach being a "good-ish" person. Here are two tips for being a good-ish person:

1. **Accept that you're going to make mistakes.** Any amount of learning and growth will require you to make mistakes. We'll say it again—you are going to mess up—and this is awesome. Mistakes equal growth. What matters is that you try and that you then use your failings to try something else. When others know that you are committed to improving DE&I, and when you are willing to

publicly and humbly learn from mistakes, you're making progress toward building more inclusive environments.

2. **Recognize and use your "ordinary privilege."** Chugh encourages us to label all the different dimensions of our identity and then consider which dimensions we rarely even have to think about. For example, someone who has perfect vision probably spends very little time thinking about the fact that they can see and rarely has to explain their good vision to others. Their vision is simply part of their identity, and the fact that it's good serves as what Chugh calls a "tailwind" for them. Any aspect of your identity that you don't have to think about, defend, or talk about represents a source of ordinary privilege, and thus a tailwind that propels you forward. The good news is you can use ordinary privilege to encourage more positive attitudes toward DE&I in your organization.

Key Terms Used in This Chapter

ally DEI-26
climate DEI-8
DE&I DEI-3
DE&I management DEI-3
diversity DEI-3
environmental factors DEI-13
equity DEI-5
fundamental attribution error DEI-14

gender identity DEI-11
identity DEI-4
inclusion DEI-6
inclusion climate DEI-8
intercultural communication apprehension DEI-13
intersectionality DEI-5

KSAs DEI-10
neurodiversity DEI-10
organizational culture DEI-19
person factors DEI-13
perspective taking DEI-26
protected class DEI-9
stereotypes DEI-13

PART 1 • INTRODUCTION

1 The Exceptional Manager
What You Do, How You Do It

After reading this chapter, you should be able to:

LO 1-1 Identify the rewards of being an exceptional manager.

LO 1-2 List the four principal functions of a manager.

LO 1-3 Describe the levels and areas of management.

LO 1-4 Identify the roles an effective manager must play.

LO 1-5 Discuss the skills of an outstanding manager.

LO 1-6 Identify the seven challenges faced by most managers.

LO 1-7 Define the core competencies, knowledge, soft skills, attitudes, and other characteristics needed for career readiness and discuss how they can be developed.

LO 1-8 Describe the process for managing your career readiness.

FORECAST   What's Ahead in This Chapter

We describe the rewards, benefits, and privileges managers might expect. We also describe the four principal functions of management—planning, organizing, leading, and controlling. We consider levels and areas of management and describe the three roles managers must play. We describe the three skills required of a manager and discuss seven challenges managers face in today's world. Next we focus on a model of career readiness and offer tips for building your career readiness. The chapter concludes with a Career Corner that presents a process that can be used to develop your career readiness.

Using Management Skills for College Success

Our goal is *to make this book as practical as possible for you*. One place we do this is in the "Manage U" features, like this one, that appear at the beginning of every chapter and offer practical advice for applying the topic of the chapter to your personal life and career. Here, for instance, we show you how the four functions of management—planning, organizing, leading, and controlling—relate to your teamwork skills. Recruiters are looking for teamwork skills when hiring college graduates.[1]

Applying the Functions of Management to School Projects

Consider the students in a Princeton University summer business program. Working in teams, they had 10 weeks to prepare a pitch for a start-up idea and ask for funding. One of the teams ran a four-week pilot after-school program for five Trenton, NJ, girls and asked for $324,000 to scale the program up to include 40 girls on a year-round basis. Their pitch was that the program would help more young women graduate from high school and have a positive effect on the entire community. The students planned their pilot program, its budget, and its schedule and curriculum; they organized the four weeks of activities for the girls they recruited; they led the girls through each day's events; and they used before and after surveys to control (that is, measure) the effects of their efforts. In other words, they relied on the four functions of management to ensure that they worked together to achieve their goals.[2]

Think about how you might make better use of planning and controlling in a team assignment for a course. You might draw up a detailed schedule of tasks and assign them to team members (planning), and then identify checkpoint dates on which you measure progress toward your deadline (controlling). You could set up a way to best use the resources at your disposal, such as time, library materials, personal expertise, and outside experts (organizing), and then use the progress checkpoints to motivate your fellow team members to continue putting forth their best effort (leading). The experience you can gain by using these essential management skills now will serve you well in your studies and throughout your career.

Applying the Functions of Management in Your Personal Life

Consider how you might use the functions of management to run your first 10K race. Your plan would include dates and times to exercise on your Google or Outlook calendar along with distances and ideas for how you will fuel your body on longer runs. You then would make sure you have the resources (time, clothing, support network, nutrition plan) to assist you along your journey (organizing). You also may find it valuable to have a running buddy during some of your workouts (leading). Alternatively, some people may find it motivational to have an accountability partner to review their time and distance totals each week (controlling).

1.1 Management: What It Is, What Its Benefits Are

THE BIG PICTURE

Management is defined as the efficient and effective pursuit of organizational goals. Organizations, or people who work together to achieve a specific purpose, value managers because of the multiplier effect: Good managers have an influence on the organization far beyond the results that can be achieved by one person acting alone. Managers are well paid, with the chief executive officers (CEOs) and presidents of even small and midsize businesses earning good salaries and many benefits.

LO 1-1

Identify the rewards of being an exceptional manager.

When Chief Executive Officer Mary Barra took the reins of Detroit-based General Motors (GM) in January 2014, she became the first female CEO of a global automaker in the world. She also became only the 22nd woman at the helm of a Fortune 500 company, one of the 500 U.S. companies that appear on the prestigious annual list compiled by *Fortune* magazine. (Other female CEOs of major companies include Thasunda Brown Duckett of TIAA, Michele Buck of Hershey, and Safra Catz of Oracle.)

What kind of a person is Barra, a 40+ year GM veteran? She has been called "nearly impossible to dislike" and is credited with bringing a much-needed "calm stability" to GM. Among her many people skills is the ability to engage and motivate others, including top executives who may have vied for her job but were persuaded to stay and work with her.[3] Are these qualities enough to propel someone to the top of a great organization?

The Rise of a Leader

Barra grew up in suburban Detroit, joined GM at age 18 as an intern on the factory floor, graduated from General Motors Institute (now Kettering University) with a degree in electrical engineering, and then became a plant engineer in GM's Pontiac Division. Spotting her talent, GM gave her a scholarship to Stanford University, where she earned a graduate degree in business. She then began moving up the GM ladder, first as the executive assistant to the CEO and then as the company's head of human resources—formerly often as high as female executives ever got in the auto industry and many others. In 2011, Barra's big break came when she was promoted to lead GM's $15 billion vehicle-development operations, a high-profile role that became the stepping-stone to the CEO spot. In 2016, she was also made chair of the board.[4]

Key to Career Growth: "Doing Things I've Never Done Before"

The driving force. One quality that stands out about General Motors CEO Mary Barra is her obvious enthusiasm for cars. She is said to be given to talking excitedly about whatever car she is currently driving and what it demonstrates about GM's product line. Do you think passion about one's work is a necessary quality for managerial success?
Mark Lennihan/AP Photo

Did it help that Barra has such deep experience in the auto industry and at GM in particular? No doubt it did. But there is another key to career growth—the ability to take risks. Jeff Bezos, the founder of Amazon.com, was holding down a lucrative job as a Wall Street hedge fund manager in the 1990s when he read that the Internet had recently grown 2,300% in a single year. Even though it meant leaving a stable job with a big bonus on the way, Bezos made the risky leap to the start-up he called Amazon, working out of a garage. "I knew that I might sincerely regret not having participated in this thing called the Internet that I thought was going to be a revolutionizing event," he says. "When I thought about it that way . . . it was incredibly easy to make the decision."[5] In addition to building Amazon into the largest e-commerce hub in the world, Bezos founded Blue Origin Aerospace company in 2000 and began launching human spaceflights in 2021. He is one of the richest people in the world.[6]

The Art of Management Defined

Is being an exceptional manager a gift, like a musician having perfect pitch? Not exactly. But a good part of it may be an art.[7] Fortunately, it is one that is teachable.

Management, said one pioneer of management ideas, is "the art of getting things done through people."[8]

Getting things done. Through people. Thus, managers are task oriented, achievement oriented, and people oriented. And they operate within an **organization**—a group of people who work together to achieve some specific purpose.

More formally, **management** is defined as (1) the pursuit of organizational goals efficiently and effectively by (2) integrating the work of people through (3) planning, organizing, leading, and controlling the organization's resources.

Note the words *efficiently* and *effectively,* which basically mean "doing things right."

- **Efficiency—the means.** Efficiency is the means of attaining the organization's goals. To be **efficient** means to use resources—people, money, raw materials, and the like—wisely and cost-effectively.

- **Effectiveness—the ends.** Effectiveness regards the organization's ends, the goals. To be **effective** means to achieve results, to make the right decisions, and to successfully carry them out so that they achieve the organization's goals.

Good managers focus on achieving both efficiency and effectiveness. Often, however, organizations erroneously strive for efficiency without being effective. Retired U.S. Army general Stanley McChrystal, former commander of all U.S. and coalition forces in Afghanistan, suggests that effectiveness is a more important outcome in today's organizations.[9]

EXAMPLE | **Effectiveness versus Efficiency: Have Scientists Found a Viable Solution to Address Rising Demands for Meat?**

Data suggest approximately 70% of Earth's land suitable for agriculture is used for livestock farming. If this sounds high, consider that experts predict a 70% increase in the demand for meat products by 2050 as Earth's population reaches 9 to 10 billion.[10] With younger generations of consumers showing a preference for healthier nutrition and more sustainable alternatives to traditional food production, how should the food industry evolve?

At least 30 start-ups across the globe think they have the answer. Scientists at companies like Mosa Meat, Finless Foods, Upside Foods, SuperMeat, and Future Meat Technologies are "growing" meat in laboratories using stem-cell samples taken from live animals—no slaughter required.[11] The resulting product is referred to interchangeably as "cultured meat," "clean meat," and "lab-grown meat," and it could potentially provide a healthier, less expensive, and more sustainable food source. Venture capitalists and industry giants have invested billions into lab-grown meat companies, and some analysts predict a nearly $500 million market for these products by 2030.[12]

Let's look at this issue from both an effectiveness and efficiency perspective.

Effectiveness. One problem cultured meat producers face is consumer sentiment because the idea of lab-grown meet feels unnatural and repulsive to many. If cultured meat producers wish to be successful, then they will need to supply food that consumers are willing to purchase and eat.

For those not completely turned off by the idea of a steak grown from stem cells, there are other concerns. For example, consumers are skeptical that cultured meats will taste the same as the farmed meats they are accustomed to eating. Taste tests have yielded positive results.[13] Still, many worry that laboratories won't be able to replicate the taste and texture of traditional animal meat.[14]

There are also widespread fears of unforeseen negative health consequences. According to researchers at Maastricht University in the Netherlands, growing meat in laboratories eliminates the need for antibiotics and gives scientists control over things like cholesterol and fat levels. But a substantial portion of consumers aren't ready to take the risk.[15]

Efficiency. Lab-grown meat start-ups claim to offer a more environmentally friendly solution to increasing meat demands. For example, some research suggests it may be possible to produce as many as 175 million quarter-pound hamburgers with the stem cells from only one cow. (It currently takes about 440,000 cows to produce the same amount of meat.)[16] Additional data suggests cultured meat production uses approximately 96% less land and water than livestock production.[17]

But some experts believe that growing meat in labs could foster climate change. "Lab meat doesn't solve anything from an environmental perspective, since the energy emissions are so high," said Marco Springmann, senior environmental researcher at the University of Oxford. Indeed, some research suggests the potential for high levels of carbon dioxide pollution. This would question the environmental benefit of lab-grown meat, given that CO_2 stays in the atmosphere for several hundred years, while the methane produced in cattle farming dissipates after about 12 years.[18]

There is also the issue of affordability. In 2013 a pound of lab-grown hamburger meat cost an astonishing $1.2 million, but process and technology improvements continue to drive these costs down. By 2021, the price to produce cultivated meat was around $50 per pound, and Future Meat announced it could produce a pound of cultivated chicken for $1.70.[19]

Lab-grown meat. Have scientists found a way to address rising food demands by growing meat in laboratories? Would you be willing to try a burger made from a cow's stem cells? nevodka/Shutterstock

Preliminary data surrounding all of these issues—from social acceptability to environmental impacts to costs—are mixed.[20] It will be difficult to answer any of these questions with precision until cultured meats are available to the mass market and more data are available.

YOUR CALL

Do you think that lab-grown meat companies will be effective in reaching their goals? Do you believe their processes will prove to be more or less efficient than traditional livestock production?

Why Organizations Value Managers: The Multiplier Effect

Some great achievements of history, such as scientific discoveries or works of art, were accomplished by individuals working quietly by themselves. But so much more has been achieved by people who were able to leverage their talents and abilities by being managers. For instance, of the top 10 great architectural wonders of the world named by the American Institute of Architects, none was built by just one person. All were triumphs of management, although some reflected the vision of an individual. (The wonders are the Great Wall of China, the Great Pyramid, Machu Picchu, the Acropolis, the Coliseum, the Taj Mahal, the Eiffel Tower, the Brooklyn Bridge, the Empire State Building, and Frank Lloyd Wright's Fallingwater house in Pennsylvania.)

Good managers create value. The reason is that in being a manager you have a *multiplier effect:* Your influence on the organization is multiplied far beyond the results that can be achieved by just one person acting alone. Thus, while a solo operator such as a salesperson might accomplish many things and incidentally make a very good living, their boss could accomplish a great deal more—and could well earn two to seven times the income. And the manager will undoubtedly have a lot more influence.

What Are the Rewards of Studying and Practicing Management?

Are you studying management with no plans to be a manager? Or are you learning techniques and concepts that will help you be an exceptional management practitioner? Either way, you will use what you learn. Managerial competencies including time management, people skills, mastery of interpersonal and electronic communication, and the capacity to organize and plan are essential in both managerial and nonmanagerial careers.

The Rewards of Studying Management Students sign up for an introductory management course for all kinds of reasons. Many, of course, are planning business careers, but others are taking it to fulfill a requirement or an elective. Regardless of the reason, studying management will benefit you in your life.

Here are just a few of the payoffs of studying management as a discipline:

- **You will have an insider's understanding of how to deal with organizations from the outside.** Since we all are in constant interaction with all kinds of organizations, it helps to understand how they work and how the people in them make decisions. Such knowledge may give you skills you can use in dealing with organizations from the outside, as a customer or investor, for example.

- **You will know from experience how to relate to your supervisors.** Since most of us work in organizations and most of us have bosses, studying management will enable you to understand the pressures managers deal with and how they will best respond to you.

- **You will better interact with co-workers.** The kinds of management policies in place can affect how your co-workers behave. Studying management can give you the understanding of teams and teamwork, cultural differences, conflict and stress, and negotiation and communication skills that will help you get along with fellow employees.

- **You will be able to manage yourself and your career.** Management courses in general, and this book in particular, give you the opportunity to realize insights about yourself—your personality, emotions, values, perceptions, needs, and goals. We help you build your skills in areas such as self-management, listening, handling change, managing stress, avoiding groupthink, and coping with organizational politics.

- **You might make more money during your career.** Managers are well compensated in comparison to other workers. Entry-level managers earn an average of $50,000 a year; mid-level manager salaries average over $80,000 annually, and that's before the various fringe benefits and status rewards that go with being a manager, ranging from health insurance to stock options to bonuses. And the higher you ascend in the management hierarchy, the more privileges may come your way.[21] (For examples of managerial salaries, go to www.bls.gov/ooh/management/home.html.)

The Rewards of Practicing Management Many young people want not only to make money but also to make a difference. As Swarthmore psychology professor Barry Schwartz, author of *Why We Work,* suggests, "We want work that is challenging and engaging, that enables us to exercise some discretion and control over what we do, and that provides us with opportunities to learn and grow."[22] Becoming a management practitioner offers many rewards apart from money and status. Practicing management will allow you to:

- **Experience a sense of accomplishment.** Every successful goal accomplished provides you not only with personal satisfaction but also with the satisfaction of all those employees you directed who helped you accomplish it.

- **Stretch your abilities and magnify your range.** Every promotion up the hierarchy of an organization stretches your abilities, challenges your talents and skills, and magnifies the range of your accomplishments.

- **Build a catalog of successful products or services.** Every product or service you provide—the personal Eiffel Tower or Empire State Building you build, as it were—becomes a monument to your accomplishments. Indeed, studying management may well help you in running your own business.
- **Become a mentor and help others.** Having a **mentor**—an experienced person who provides guidance to someone new to the work world—can be crucial to advancing your career.[23] The most successful U.S. companies clearly agree, with 100% of Fortune 100 companies and 84% of Fortune 500 companies relying on formal mentoring programs.[24] •

1.2 What Managers Do: The Four Principal Functions

THE BIG PICTURE
Management has four functions: *planning, organizing, leading,* and *controlling.*

LO 1-2

List the four principal functions of a manager.

What do you as a manager do to get things done—that is, to achieve the stated goals of the organization you work for? You perform what is known as the management process, also called the **four management functions**: planning, organizing, leading, and controlling. (The abbreviation POLC may help you to remember them.) As Figure 1.1 illustrates, all these functions affect one another, are ongoing, and are performed simultaneously.

Although the process of management can be quite varied, these four functions represent its essential principles. Indeed, as a glance at our text's table of contents shows, they form four of the part divisions of the book. Let's consider what the four functions are, using the management (or "administration," as it is called in nonprofit organizations) of your college to illustrate them.

FIGURE 1.1

The management process
What you as a manager do to get things done—to achieve the stated goals of your organization.

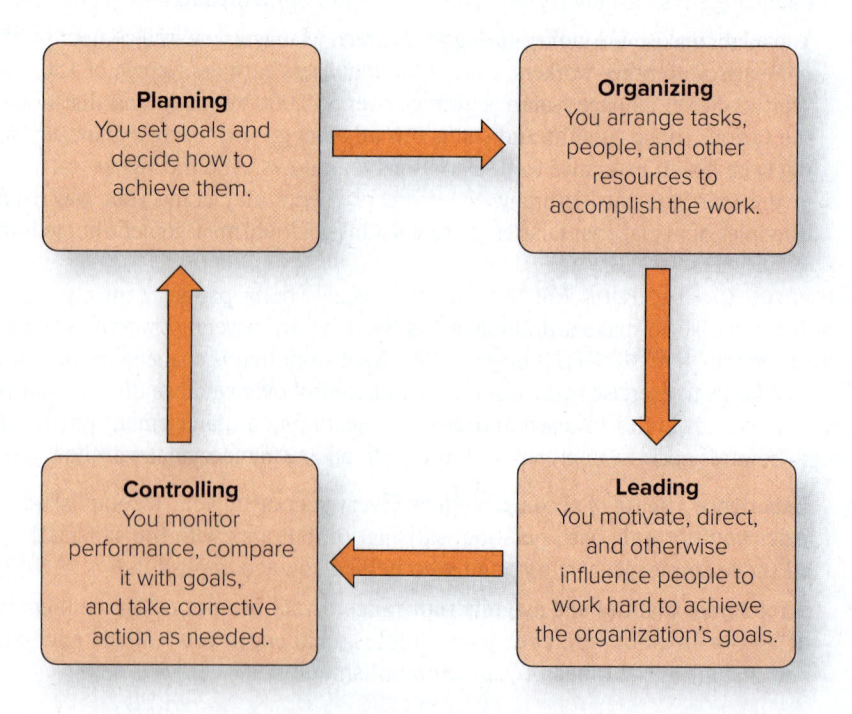

Planning — You set goals and decide how to achieve them.

Organizing — You arrange tasks, people, and other resources to accomplish the work.

Leading — You motivate, direct, and otherwise influence people to work hard to achieve the organization's goals.

Controlling — You monitor performance, compare it with goals, and take corrective action as needed.

Planning: Discussed in Part 3 of This Book

Planning is defined as setting goals and deciding how to achieve them. Your college was established for the purpose of educating students, and its present managers, or administrators, now must decide the best way to accomplish this. Which of several possible degree programs should be offered? Should the college be a residential or a commuter campus? What sort of students should be recruited and admitted? What kind of faculty should be hired? What kind of buildings and equipment are needed?

Organizing: Discussed in Part 4 of This Book

Organizing is defined as arranging tasks, people, and other resources to accomplish the work. College administrators must determine the tasks to be done, by whom, and what the reporting hierarchy is to be. Should the institution be organized into schools with departments, with department chairpersons reporting to deans who in return report to vice presidents? Should the college hire more full-time instructors than part-time instructors? Should English professors teach just English literature or also composition, developmental English, and "first-year experience" courses?

Leading: Discussed in Part 5 of This Book

Leading is defined as motivating, directing, and otherwise influencing people to work hard to achieve the organization's goals. At your college, leadership begins, of course, with the president (who would be the CEO in a for-profit organization). The president must inspire faculty, staff, students, alumni, wealthy donors, and residents of the surrounding community to help realize the college's goals. As you might imagine, these groups often have different needs and wants, so an essential part of leadership is resolving conflicts.

Controlling: Discussed in Part 6 of This Book

Controlling is defined as monitoring performance, comparing it with goals, and taking corrective action as needed. Is the college discovering that fewer students are majoring in nursing than they did five years ago? Is the fault with a change in the job market? With the quality of instruction? With the kinds of courses offered? Are the nursing department's student recruitment efforts not going well? Should the department's budget be reduced? Under the management function of controlling, college administrators must deal with these kinds of issues. •

1.3 Pyramid Power: Levels and Areas of Management

THE BIG PICTURE

Within an organization, there are four levels of managers: *top, middle,* and *first-line managers* as well as *team leaders*. Managers may also be *general managers,* or they may be *functional managers,* responsible for just one organizational activity, such as research and development (R&D), marketing, finance, production, or human resources. Managers may work for for-profit, nonprofit, or mutual-benefit organizations.

The workplace of the future may resemble a symphony orchestra, famed management theorist Peter Drucker said.[25] Employees, especially so-called knowledge workers—those who have a great deal of technical skills—can be compared to concert musicians. Their managers can be seen as conductors.

LO 1-3

Describe the levels and areas of management.

FIGURE 1.2

The levels and areas of management

Top managers make long-term decisions, middle managers implement those decisions, first-line managers make short-term decisions, and team leaders facilitate team activities toward achieving a goal.

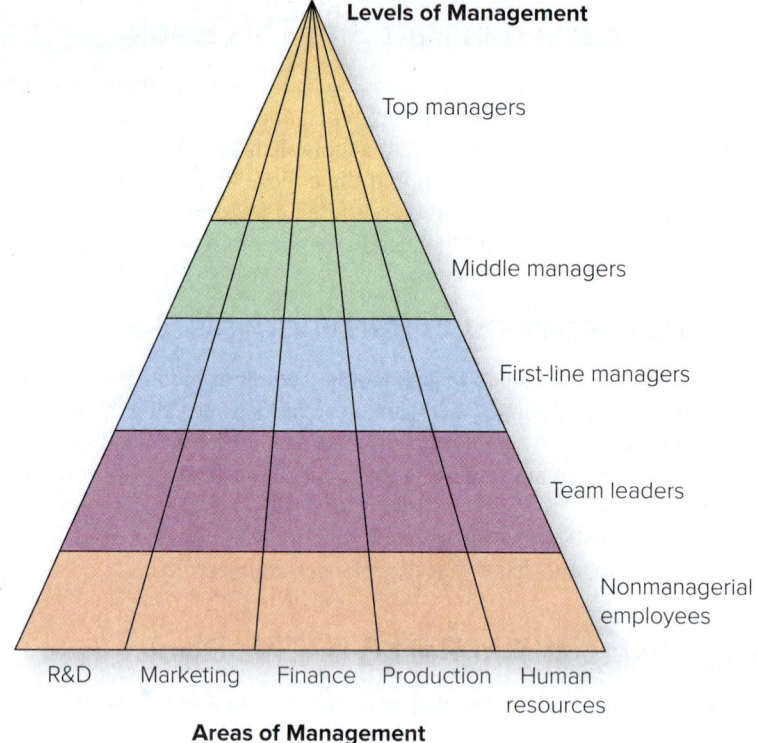

Levels of Management (from top to bottom of pyramid): Top managers, Middle managers, First-line managers, Team leaders, Nonmanagerial employees

Areas of Management: R&D, Marketing, Finance, Production, Human resources

Successful top manager. India-born Satya Nadella, who joined Microsoft in 1992, became CEO of the technology company in early 2014 and has helped transition it to cloud computing. Do you see yourself joining a company and staying with it for life, as Nadella has (after an earlier job at Sun Microsystems), or is that even possible anymore?
Justin Sullivan/Getty Images

In Drucker's analogy, musicians are used for some pieces of music—that is, work projects—and not others, and they are divided into different sections (teams) based on their instruments. The conductor's role is not to play each instrument better than the musicians but to lead them all through the most effective performance of a particular work.

This model differs from the traditional pyramid-like organizational model, where one leader sits at the top, with layers of managers beneath, each of whom must report to and justify their work to the manager above (what's called *accountability,* as we discuss in Chapter 8). Let's first look at the traditional arrangement.

The Traditional Management Pyramid: Levels and Areas

A new start-up staffed by a small group of young entrepreneurs who work from their home offices may be so small and so loosely organized that only one or two members may be said to be a manager. General Motors or the U.S. Army, in contrast, have thousands of managers doing thousands of different things. Is there a picture we can draw that applies to all the different kinds of organizations and describes them in ways that make sense? Yes: by levels and by areas, as the pyramid shows (see Figure 1.2).

Four Levels of Management

Not everyone who works in an organization is a manager, but those who are may be classified into four levels—top, middle, and first-line managers, and team leaders. Nonmanagerial employees represent the foundation of an organizational pyramid.

Top Managers: Determining Overall Direction   An organization's top managers tend to have titles such as chief executive officer (CEO), chief operating officer (COO), president, and senior vice president.

Some may be the stars in their fields, the people whose pictures appear on the covers of business magazines, people such as Lucasfilm president Kathleen Kennedy or Apple CEO Tim Cook, both of whom have been profiled in *Fortune*.

Top managers make long-term decisions about the overall direction of the organization and establish the objectives, policies, and strategies for it. They need to pay a lot of attention to the environment outside the organization, being alert for long-run opportunities and problems and devising strategies for dealing with them. Thus, executives at this level must be future oriented, strategic, and able to deal with uncertain, highly competitive conditions.

Middle Managers: Implementing Policies and Plans **Middle managers** implement the policies and plans of the top managers above them and supervise and coordinate the activities of the first-line managers below them. This definition illustrates the critical mediating role that middle managers play between the upper and lower levels of an organization.[26] Middle managers must act as followers to top management and leaders to lower-level managers and employees. They must possess the interpersonal skills needed to build relationships with people in various positions in the hierarchy, and they must somehow merge the interests of those they report to and those who report to them. Titles might include plant manager, district manager, and regional manager, among others. In the nonprofit world, middle managers may have titles such as clinic director, dean of student services, and the like.

Middle managers are critical for organizational success because they implement the strategic plans created by CEOs and top managers. (Strategic planning is discussed in Chapter 6.) In other words, these managers have the type of "high-touch" jobs—dealing with people rather than computer screens or voice-response systems—that can directly affect employees, customers, and suppliers.

First-Line Managers: Directing Daily Tasks The job titles at this level of the managerial pyramid tend to include department head, foreperson, or supervisor.

Following the plans of middle and top managers, **first-line managers** make short-term operating decisions, directing the daily tasks of nonmanagerial personnel, who work directly at their jobs but don't oversee the work of others.

Team Leaders Organizations use teams for tasks that can't be accomplished by one person alone because they require a variety of perspectives, knowledge, and skills. **Team leaders** facilitate team members' activities to help teams achieve their goals. In other words, team leaders see to it that their team members have everything they need to be successful.

Research published in *Harvard Business Review* suggests the most successful teams possess four key elements—compelling direction, strong structure, a supportive context, and a shared mindset—and that team leaders are uniquely positioned to positively impact these elements.[27] We discuss building effective teams in Chapter 13.

Nonmanagerial Employees **Nonmanagerial employees** either work alone on tasks or with others on a variety of teams. They do not formally supervise or manage other people, and they are the bulk of a company's workforce.

Areas of Management: Functional Managers versus General Managers

We can represent the levels of management by slicing the organizational pyramid horizontally. We can also slice the pyramid vertically to represent the organization's departments or functional areas, as we did in Figure 1.2.

In a for-profit technology company, these functional areas might include research and development, marketing, finance, production, and human resources. In a nonprofit college, these might be faculty, student support staff, finance, maintenance, and administration. Whatever the names of the departments, the organization is run by two types of managers—functional and general.

Functional Managers: Responsible for One Activity
If your title is vice president of production, director of finance, or administrator for human resources, you are a functional manager. A **functional manager** is responsible for just one organizational activity. Google is particularly noteworthy for its unusual functional management job titles, such as engineering, wearables, and experience design lead, and vice president of hardware.

General Managers: Responsible for Several Activities
If you are working in a small organization of 100 people and your title is executive vice president, you are probably a general manager over several departments, such as production, finance, and human resources. A **general manager** is responsible for several organizational activities, and they typically supervise other managers.

At the top of the pyramid, general managers are those who seem to be the subject of news stories in outlets such as *Bloomberg Businessweek, Fortune, Forbes,* and *Inc.* Examples are big-company CEOs Mark Clouse of Campbell Soup and Nicke Widyawati of Pertamina, as well as small-company CEOs such as Emily Weiss, who founded Glossier, an online beauty-product retailer. Examples of nonprofit general managers include Save the Children U.S. CEO Janti Soeripto and American Civil Liberties Union (ACLU) CEO Anthony Romero.

Managers for Three Types of Organizations: For-Profit, Nonprofit, Mutual-Benefit

There are three types of organizations classified according to the three purposes for which they are formed—*for-profit, nonprofit,* and *mutual-benefit.*

1. **For-profit organizations: For making money.** For-profit, or business, organizations are formed to make money, or profits, by offering products or services. When most people think of "management," they think of business organizations, ranging from Allstate to Zillow, from Adobe to Zoom. There are about 5,300 public companies in the United States today.[28] This is a sharp increase from the 4,100 listed in 2020.

2. **Nonprofit organizations: For offering services.** Managers in nonprofit organizations are often known as administrators. Nonprofit organizations may be either in the public sector, such as the University of California, or in the private sector, such as Stanford University. Either way, their purpose is to offer services. Although called nonprofits, these organizations can and often do operate in a surplus. The difference between nonprofit and for-profit organizations is that nonprofits put excess revenues back into their organizations rather than distribute them to shareholders. Examples of nonprofits are hospitals, colleges, and social-welfare agencies (the Salvation Army and the Red Cross). According to the National Center for Charitable Statistics (NCCS), more than 1.8 million nonprofit organizations are registered in the United States. This includes public charities, private foundations, and other types of nonprofits, including chambers of commerce, fraternal organizations, and civic leagues.[29]

   One particular type of nonprofit organization is called the *commonweal organization* (not to be confused with *commonwealth* organization). Unlike nonprofit service organizations, which offer services to *some* clients, commonweal organizations offer services to *all* clients within their jurisdictions. Examples are the military services, the U.S. Postal Service, and your local fire and police departments.

3. **Mutual-benefit organizations: For aiding members.** Mutual-benefit organizations are voluntary collections of members—political parties, farm cooperatives, labor unions, trade associations, and clubs—whose purpose is to advance members' interests. There are over 9,500 such organizations.[30]

Different Organizations, Different Management?

If you became a manager, would you be doing the same types of things regardless of the type of organization? Generally you would be; that is, you would be performing the four management functions—planning, organizing, leading, and controlling—that we described in Section 1.2.

The biggest difference, however, is that for-profit organizations measure success according to profits (or losses) generated. In the other two types of organizations, although income and expenditures are very important concerns, success is usually measured by the effectiveness of the services delivered—how many students were graduated, if you're a college administrator, or how many crimes were prevented or solved, if you're a police chief. •

1.4 Roles Managers Must Play Successfully

THE BIG PICTURE

Managers tend to work long hours, and their time is always in demand; their work is characterized by near constant communication with others; and their jobs require impeccable time-management skills. According to management scholar Henry Mintzberg, managers play three roles—*interpersonal, informational,* and *decisional.* Interpersonal roles include figurehead, leader, and liaison activities. Informational roles are monitor, disseminator, and spokesperson. Decisional roles are entrepreneur, disturbance handler, resource allocator, and negotiator.

Clearly, being a successful manager requires playing several different roles. We discuss these managerial roles in this section.

LO 1-4
Identify the roles an effective manager must play.

The Manager's Roles: How Do Managers Spend Their Time?

Maybe, you think, it might be interesting to follow some managers around to see what it is they actually do. That's exactly what management scholar Henry Mintzberg did when, in the late 1960s, he shadowed five chief executives for a week and recorded their working lives.[31] The portrait looked like this:

- "There was no break in the pace of activity during office hours."
- "The mail (average of 36 pieces per day), telephone calls (average of five per day), and meetings (average of eight) accounted for almost every minute from the moment these executives entered their offices in the morning until they departed in the evening."[32]

Although these findings have historical value, times have changed, and they may not reflect today's reality. Two management scholars—Michael Porter and Nitin Nohria—updated this research by examining how 27 CEOs of multi-billion-dollar companies spent their time on a daily basis over three months.[33]

See Table 1.1 for a summary of some of Porter and Nohria's key findings, important for any prospective manager. We follow with a discussion of how these findings compare with Mintzberg's earlier work:

TABLE 1.1 Key Findings from an Updated Study of How Managers Spend their Time

ACCORDING TO THE STUDY, MANAGERS...		
WERE ALWAYS WORKING AND WERE IN CONSTANT DEMAND	**SPENT VIRTUALLY ALL THEIR WORK TIME COMMUNICATING WITH OTHERS**	**HAD TO BE PURPOSEFUL AND PROACTIVE ABOUT TIME MANAGEMENT**
• Worked over 9 hours per day on average • Took few true breaks and were likely to work on most weekend and vacation days • Typically had 60+ hour workweeks • Spent most of their hours satisfying others' demands, including internal and external constituencies	• Spent 100% of their time communicating with others in some format • Attended an average of 37 meetings per week	• Operated from clear, meticulous agendas • Depended heavily upon direct reports (senior leadership teams) to accomplish many of the tasks on their plates • Relied on "broad integrating mechanisms" (e.g., strategy, relationships, employee development) to enable other organizational actors to make good decisions in their absence

What's Changed? What's changed in the time between these two studies? Not much, it turns out.

Long hours at work were and are still standard, and managers of both yesteryear and today rarely experienced "a true break" from dealing with constituencies.[34] Managers continue to be constant communicators, albeit through increasingly advanced communication methods that add complexity to an already demanding gig. Indeed, says Ed Reilly, who heads the American Management Association, all the e-mail, text messaging, and so on can lead people to end up "concentrating on the urgent rather than the important."[35] The ability to communicate effectively and to manage your communication demands is one of the most important career readiness competencies you can develop—it is essential not only for managers but in every single job. We'll explore this and other important career readiness competencies in Section 1.7.

Finally, Mintzberg saw workdays characterized by much of the same fragmentation, brevity, and variety we see today. A 9-minute task here, a 6-minute call there, followed by a 10-minute informal meeting and a 15-minute desk-work session. Only about one-tenth of the managerial activities observed by Mintzberg took more than an hour. "When free time appeared," wrote Mintzberg, "ever-present subordinates quickly usurped it."[36]

No wonder the executive's work time has been characterized as "the interrupt-driven day" and that many managers—such as GM's Mary Barra—are often in their offices by 6 a.m. to take advantage of a brief, quiet period in which to work undisturbed. No wonder that finding balance between work and family lives—work-life balance, as we consider in Chapter 13—is an ongoing concern. The division between work and nonwork hours is becoming increasingly blurred as people use technology 24/7 to stay linked to their jobs and an increasing number of workers—including managers—are doing their jobs from home.[37]

Three Types of Managerial Roles: Interpersonal, Informational, and Decisional

From his observations and other research, Mintzberg concluded that managers play three broad types of roles, or organized sets of behavior: *interpersonal, informational,* and *decisional.* (Porter and Nohria's discussion of the dimensions of the modern CEO role is consistent with the behaviors Mintzberg described).

1. Interpersonal Roles—Figurehead, Leader, and Liaison In their **interpersonal roles**, managers interact with people inside and outside their work units. The three interpersonal roles include *figurehead, leader,* and *liaison activities.*

2. Informational Roles—Monitor, Disseminator, and Spokesperson The most important part of a manager's job, Mintzberg believed, is information handling because accurate information is vital for making intelligent decisions. In their three **informational roles**—as monitor, disseminator, and spokesperson—managers receive and communicate information with other people inside and outside the organization.

Informational Roles Example—Sundar Pichai: At Google, CEO Sundar Pichai holds monthly companywide "all-hands" meetings to answer employees' questions about issues of concern. In the fall of 2022, Pichai used one such meeting to discuss companywide budget cuts. At the time, many employees felt perplexed that Google was "nickel-and-diming" them on travel and entertainment expenses even though the company was enjoying "record profits and huge cash reserves." Pichai urged employees to consider the company's external environment (which you'll read more about in Chapters 3 and 6) including an impending recession and skyrocketing inflation and interest rates. Pichai also provided detailed responses to employee questions about his goal to increase productivity by 20% and the company's return-to-office plans.[38]

3. Decisional Roles—Entrepreneur, Disturbance Handler, Resource Allocator, and Negotiator In their **decisional roles**, managers use information to make decisions to solve problems or take advantage of opportunities. The four decision-making roles are entrepreneur, disturbance handler, resource allocator, and negotiator. All of the roles are summarized in Table 1.2.

TABLE 1.2 Three Types of Managerial Roles: Interpersonal, Informational, and Decisional

BROAD MANAGERIAL ROLES	TYPES OF ROLES	DESCRIPTION
Interpersonal	Figurehead role	In your *figurehead* role, you show visitors around your company, attend employee birthday parties, and present ethical guidelines to your subordinates. In other words, you perform symbolic tasks that represent your organization.
	Leadership role	In your role of *leader,* you are responsible for the actions of your subordinates, as their successes and failures reflect on you. Your leadership is expressed in your decisions about training, motivating, and disciplining people.
	Liaison role	In your *liaison* role, you must act like a politician, working with other people outside your work unit and organization to develop alliances that will help you achieve your organization's goals.
Informational	Monitor role	As a *monitor,* you should be constantly alert for useful information, whether gathered from newspaper stories about the competition or from snippets of conversation with subordinates you meet in the hallway.
	Disseminator role	Are workers complaining they never know what's going on? That probably means their supervisor failed in the role of *disseminator.* Managers need to constantly disseminate important information to employees, via e-mail and meetings.
	Spokesperson role	You are expected, of course, to be a diplomat, to put the best face on the activities of your work unit or organization to people outside it. This is the informational role of *spokesperson.*
Decisional	Entrepreneur role	A good manager is expected to be an *entrepreneur,* to initiate and encourage change and innovation.
	Disturbance handler role	Unforeseen problems—from product defects to international currency crises—require you to be a *disturbance handler,* fixing problems.
	Resource allocator role	Because you'll never have enough time, money, and so on, you'll need to be a resource *allocator,* setting priorities about use of resources.
	Negotiator role	To be a manager is to be a continual *negotiator,* working with others inside and outside the organization to accomplish your goals.

Did anyone say a manager's job is easy? Certainly it's not for people who want to sit on the sidelines of life. Above all else, managers are *doers.* ●

1.5 The Skills Exceptional Managers Need

THE BIG PICTURE
Good managers need to work on developing three principal skills. The first is *technical*, the ability to perform a specific job. The second is *conceptual*, the ability to think analytically. The third is *human*, the ability to interact well with people.

LO 1-5

Discuss the skills of an outstanding manager.

Aspiring managers need to have the "right stuff" for succeeding in managerial roles. In the mid-1970s, researcher Robert Katz found that through education and experience managers acquire three principal skills—*technical, conceptual,* and *human*.[39]

1. Technical Skills—The Ability to Perform a Specific Job

Technical skills consist of the job-specific knowledge needed to perform well in a specialized field. Having the requisite technical skills seems to be most important at the lower levels of management—that is, among employees in their first professional job and first-line managers.

Mary Barra has a bachelor's degree in electrical engineering and a master's in business administration. She also has a well-rounded resume that includes important experience such as executive assistant to the CEO, being head of midsize car engineering, managing GM's Detroit-Hamtramck plant, and leading the company's human resources division. She also spent time as head of GM's huge worldwide product development. Barra said in a recent interview, "(I try) to make sure I understand key parts of the business, and having worked in an assembly plant, having been a plant manager, having been responsible for product development, having understood HR, all of those things really round out to give me a lot of the skills that I need ... as CEO."[40]

Said by her predecessor to be "one of the most gifted executives" he had met in his career, she displays an engineer's enthusiasm for cars, a quality not found among other car-company CEOs promoted from finance operations.[41] Indeed, says one account, "Ms. Barra can often be found on the company's test track putting vehicles through their paces at high speeds."[42]

Triple threat. Mary Barra announces that GM will invest $300 million in electric and self-driving vehicles at its Orion Assembly Plant. Barra seems to have the three skills—technical, conceptual, and human—necessary to be a terrific manager in the complex organization that is General Motors. Which skill do you think you need to work on the most?
Rebecca Cook/Newscom

2. Conceptual Skills—The Ability to Think Analytically

Conceptual skills consist of the ability to think analytically, to visualize an organization as a whole and understand how the parts work together. Conceptual skills are more important as you move up the management ladder, particularly for top managers, who must deal with problems that are ambiguous but could have far-reaching consequences. Today a top car executive must deal with radical trends including autonomous (self-driving) cars and a strong push for more electric-powered vehicles.

Said a GM executive about Barra, "When you put her in a position that's completely new to her, she does an amazing job of getting grounded, understanding what's important and what's not, and executing very well."[43] Or, as Barra said about her management approach, "Problems don't go away when you ignore them—they get bigger. In my experience, it is much better to get the right people together, to make a plan, and to address every challenge head on."[44]

At every stop along the way in rising through GM, Barra analyzed the situation and simplified things. For example, in her product-development job, she streamlined designs by using the same parts in many different models. She also assigned engineers to work in car dealerships to learn more about what customers want in their vehicles.[45] When promoted to CEO, she stepped into the middle of a safety crisis in which GM had to admit to misleading regulators and consumers about a defective ignition switch, and GM agreed to pay a $900 million penalty.[46]

Now she is dealing with bigger issues and trying to make GM a more nimble and forward-thinking company. The century-old company is leading the industry in connected-car technology and new electric and hybrid vehicles. Barra believes "we can either sit around and be disrupted or we can lead this transformation."[47]

3. Human Skills—"Soft Skills," the Ability to Interact Well with People

This may well be the most difficult set of skills to master. **Human skills** consist of the ability to work well in cooperation with other people to get things done—especially with people in teams, an important part of today's organizations. Groups and teams are thoroughly discussed in Chapter 13.

Often these are thought of as "soft skills." **Soft skills** are interpersonal "people" skills needed for success at all levels. As discussed in Section 1.7, developing your soft skills is an ongoing, lifelong effort (see the Practical Action box).

During her more than four decades at GM, Barra has demonstrated exceptionally strong soft skills. She has "an ability with people," says her previous boss, that is critical to GM's team-first approach.[48] "She is known inside GM as a consensus builder who calls her staff together on a moment's notice to brainstorm on pressing issues," says another report.[49] "She's fiercely intelligent yet humble and approachable," says a third account. "She's collaborative but is often the person who takes charge. And she's not afraid to make changes."[50]

Among her most significant changes: hiring people with "diverse views, diverse backgrounds, diverse experiences," she says, to try to reshape the company's notoriously insular corporate culture and to bring GM into the age of Apple and Google. "At the end of the day," says Barra, "the success of every company is about its people."[51]

PRACTICAL ACTION | Developing Your Soft Skills

Are you persistent, creative, curious? How do you deal with frustration or anxiety? Do you see yourself as part of a larger whole that gives your work purpose? How do you perceive problems—as temporary and solvable, or as a personal burden you are doomed to bear? Are you a good listener? Your answers will give you an idea about how well developed some of your soft skills are.

More than 90% of respondents to a recent Job Market Outlook survey by ZipRecruiter identified soft skills as a critical priority.[52] Many employers say these skills are hard to find in college graduates, who often value hard skills more highly.[53] The good news is that soft skills can be taught, and you can be proactive about developing your soft skills. Here are two ideas to get you started:

Get to know yourself. Employees often overestimate their levels of various career readiness competencies, including their soft skills. You can begin your journey to improving your soft skills by assessing your current levels of these skills. Use self-assessments, such as those we include for you in this product, to increase your awareness of your own soft skills. Then, you'll know which skills to target for improvement.

Take advantage of opportunities for development. A study conducted by Harvard University, Boston University, and the University of Michigan shows that training employees in soft skills doesn't just marginally improve individual performance and employee retention; it actually betters these metrics enough to provide a 256% return on the financial investment a company makes in training programs.[54] If your school or company offers opportunities for soft skills development, take advantage!

For those who want to learn online and at their own pace, many inexpensive online classes are available.[55] These short interactive programs are geared for everyone from CEOs to entry-level employees. They cover everything from self-confidence to emotional intelligence, coaching teams, building healthy work relationships, handling business etiquette, resolving conflicts, decision making, reading body language, negotiating, dealing with angry customers, and becoming a successful leader.

YOUR CALL

Look back at the first paragraph in this Practical Action box. Which of the soft skills listed there would you like to improve by the time you graduate, in order to make yourself a more attractive candidate to prospective employers?

The Most Valued Traits in Managers

Clearly, GM's Barra embodies the qualities sought in exceptional managers, especially top managers. "The style for running a company is different from what it used to be," says a top executive recruiter of CEOs. "Companies don't want dictators, kings, or emperors."[56] Instead of someone who gives orders, they want executives who ask probing questions and invite people to participate in decision making and power sharing.

Among the chief skills companies seek in top managers are the following:

- The ability to motivate and engage others.
- The ability to communicate.
- Work experience outside the United States.
- High energy levels to meet the demands of global travel and a 24/7 world.[57]

1.6 Seven Challenges to Being an Exceptional Manager

THE BIG PICTURE

Seven challenges face any manager: You need to manage for competitive advantage—to stay ahead of rivals. You need to manage for technological advances—to deal with the "new normal." You need to manage for inclusion and diversity because the future won't resemble the past. You need to manage for globalization and the expanding management universe. You also must maintain ethical standards, and you need to manage for sustainable development—to practice sound environmental policies. Finally, you need to manage for the achievement of your own happiness and life goals.

LO 1-6

Identify the seven challenges faced by most managers.

Would you agree that the ideal state many people seek is an emotional zone somewhere between boredom and anxiety? That's the view of psychologist Mihaly Csikszentmihalyi (pronounced Me-*high* Chick-sent-me-*high*-ee), founder of the Quality of Life Research Center at Claremont Graduate University.[58]

Boredom, he says, may arise because skills and challenges are mismatched: You are exercising your high level of skill in a job with a low level of challenge, such as licking envelopes. Anxiety arises when someone has low levels of skill but a high level of challenge, such as (for many people) suddenly being called upon to give a rousing speech to strangers.

As a manager, could you achieve a balance between these two states—between boredom and anxiety, or between action and serenity? Certainly, managers have enough challenges to keep their lives more than mildly interesting. Let's see what they are.

Challenge #1: Managing for Competitive Advantage—Staying Ahead of Rivals

Competitive advantage is the ability of an organization to produce goods or services more effectively than competitors do, thereby outperforming them. This means an organization must stay ahead in five areas: (1) being responsive to employees, (2) being responsive to customers, (3) innovation, (4) quality, and (5) efficiency.

1. Being Responsive to Employees Employers and employees develop a set of unspoken expectations regarding what each party owes to the other in the employment relationship. This is known as a **psychological contract**, which represents your perception of the terms that govern your exchange relationship with another party.[59] This contract looks dramatically different for many workers post-pandemic. Here are a few ways the psychological contract has shifted in recent years:

- **More employees expect the option to work remotely.** The pandemic offered millions of workers the chance to experience what it felt like to work from home, and many wish to continue to do their jobs remotely.[60] Employers seem to be taking notice, with one-third of the companies that participated in a recent survey allowing workers to choose whether they want to work in the office or remotely, and about one-fourth of companies requiring employees to be in the office fewer than five days per week. According to Gartner research and consulting firm, organizations risk losing almost 40% of their workers if they force a full return to the office.[61]

- **More employees demand increased work-life balance.** In a recent survey of more than 4,600 workers, 68% of respondents said they would consider changing their careers in order to achieve better work-life balance, even if staying in their current career meant higher pay.[62] Research suggests organizations see less turnover, higher employee productivity, and better employee physical and mental health outcomes when they invest in programs to promote work-life balance for employees. Post-pandemic, more workers expect to be able to achieve this type of balance. One important way organizations can promote work-life balance is through scheduling policies. Specifically, workers who are most at-risk for work-life balance issues (i.e., people of color and women) benefit greatly from having both choice regarding when to complete work and predictability in work schedules.[63] We discuss work-life balance in Chapter 12.

- **More employees want their organizations to show empathy and concern for their health.** The pandemic forced many employees to face complex emotional and personal needs that could not be separated from work. Of the corporations surveyed in a recent study conducted by Arizona State University, the World Economic Forum, and the Rockefeller Foundation, 58% reported an increased use of their companies' available mental health resources since the pandemic began.[64] Employees are now paying more attention to their own needs and are demanding more compassion, kindness, and concern for these needs from their organizations. Gartner suggests that workers want leaders who are willing to accept them for who they are, adapt to their unique needs, and show genuine concern for their situations.[65]

Clearly, workers have a new set of expectations about what they should receive from their employers. Managers will need to understand how to manage their employees in this new landscape and in light of this new psychological contract. New psychological contracts require organizations and their managers to be innovative and flexible in terms of human resource practices. Without this understanding, organizations risk losing employees to competitors.

2. Being Responsive to Customers The first law of business is *Take care of the customer*. Without customers—buyers, clients, consumers, shoppers, users, patrons, guests, investors, or whatever they're called—sooner or later there will be no organization. Nonprofit organizations are well advised to be responsive to their "customers," too, whether they're called citizens, members, or something else, because they are the justification for the organizations' existence.

3. Innovation Finding ways to deliver new or better goods or services is called *innovation*. No organization can allow itself to become complacent. We discuss innovation in Chapter 10.

4. Quality If your organization is the only one of its kind, customers may put up with less-than-stellar products or services (as they have with some airlines that have a near monopoly on flights out of certain cities), but only because they have no choice. If another organization comes along with a better-quality product or experience, you may find your company falling behind. Making improvements in quality has become an important management idea in recent times, as we shall discuss in Chapter 16.

5. Efficiency Today's organizations emphasize efficiency. Although many value employee loyalty, companies often simultaneously must strive to produce goods or services quickly using fewer employees and raw materials. A strategy that downgrades the value of employees might ultimately backfire—resulting in the loss of essential experience and skills and even customers—but an overstaffed organization may not be able to compete with leaner rivals.

Challenge #2: Managing for Technological Advances— Dealing with the "New Normal"

The challenge of managing for technological advances will require your unflagging attention. Some observers believe we are in the midst of a Fourth Industrial Revolution given the unprecedented speed, scope, and impact of technological breakthroughs in every industry, including artificial intelligence (AI), robotics, self-driving cars, 3D printers, the Internet of Things, and many more innovations.[66]

Some of the implications of technological advances that we will discuss throughout the product are as follows:

- **E-commerce**, or electronic commerce—the buying and selling of goods or services over computer networks—has reshaped entire industries and revamped the very notion of what a company is. U.S. consumers spent $870 billion online in 2021, over 13% of overall retail spending.[67] In addition, technological advances have led to the growth of **e-business**, using the Internet to facilitate every aspect of running a business. Because the Internet so dramatically lowers the cost of communication, it can radically alter any activity that depends heavily on the flow of information. The result is that disruption has become the "new normal," according to Forrester Research.[68]

- **Far-ranging electronic management: E-communication all the time.** Today's managers will be masters of e-communication, using mobile devices to create powerful messages to motivate and lead teams of specialists all over the world. The next section notes employers are looking to hire college graduates with information technology application skills. **Information technology application skills** reflect the extent to which you can effectively use information technology and learn new applications on an ongoing basis. You will want to excel at e-communication.

- **Data, data, and more data: A challenge to decision making.** The digital universe is growing at an incomprehensible speed, one that—according to web-hosting service 100Tb—contains an amount of data so vast it is "impossible for the human mind to quantify."[69] The Internet can assemble astonishing amounts of information and make them available to us instantaneously. This is possible through **cloud computing**—the storing of software and data on gigantic collections of computers located away from a company's principal site ("in the cloud")—and huge, interconnected **databases**—computerized collections of interrelated files. This has led to the phenomenon known as **big data**, stores of data so vast that conventional database management systems cannot handle them, so very sophisticated analysis software and supercomputers are required. The challenge: How do we deal with this massive amount of data to make useful decisions without violating people's right to privacy? We discuss big data in Chapter 7. (Check out the following Example Box on the use of big data in the healthcare industry.)

EXAMPLE: How Direct-to-Consumer Genetics Testing Companies Are Using Big Data to Disrupt the Healthcare Industry

Direct-to-consumer genetics testing companies use sophisticated data analytics and genotyping to home in on rich genealogical data and unearth users' ethnicities, family lineage, potential relatives, regions of origin, and fun facts like inherited traits and preferences.[70]

Advances in analytics along with a dramatic decrease in the cost of genetic sequencing have opened the door for consumers to be able to access this information quickly and affordably—all it takes is a few weeks, a small sample of saliva, and less than $200.[71]

Disruption through Data Analytics. DNA has tremendous potential. For example, scientists have uncovered thousands of links between genetic variants and diseases, meaning that your DNA has the potential to tell you whether you're likely to develop serious medical conditions or to respond to specific treatments.[72]

Could genetic testing be the missing link in disrupting the healthcare industry and shifting more knowledge and power into consumers' hands? Home genetic testing companies certainly think so and are working to tap into this potential in their massive data sets (more than 30 million people across the globe have shared their genetic data with these types of companies).[73] Let's look at two ways these companies are disrupting the healthcare paradigm.

First, home genetic testing companies are disrupting health care by sharing knowledge directly with consumers. Users can learn whether they carry genetic mutations or have propensities for various conditions.

Second, home genetic testing companies are disrupting the healthcare paradigm through medical research. Their data sets are helping medical scientists and pharmaceutical giants as they attempt to discover new links between genetics and disease.[74]

Ethical Concerns. Recent data breaches make clear that databases are susceptible to either malicious or accidental leaks no matter how well protected. Users sign waivers and consent forms and have some control over how their data are used and stored, but the fact remains that each user's genetic information is vulnerable.[75]

Further, genetic information stored with home genetic testing companies may be subpoenaed by law enforcement agencies in criminal investigations. Even without a subpoena, it is possible for forensic experts to identify perpetrators without the perpetrators' DNA; all that is needed may be the DNA samples of enough of the suspect's close family members, as was the case in the identification and arrest of Golden State Killer Joseph DeAngelo in 2018.[76]

The Future of DNA Testing. Proponents of direct-to-consumer genetics testing companies praise their efforts toward the "democratization of health care" and believe privacy concerns are outweighed by the benefits these services provide.[77] Consumers seem confident these companies will play a critical role in transforming the healthcare industry and consumers' access to health care.[78]

YOUR CALL

Do you think direct-to-consumer genetics testing companies will gain and sustain significant competitive advantages over existing healthcare options? If so, how? If not, why? What role will data analytics play in the future of consumer genetics testing?

- **The rise of artificial intelligence: More automation in the workforce.** Artificial intelligence (AI) is the discipline concerned with creating computer systems that simulate human reasoning and sensation, as represented by robots, natural language processing, pattern recognition, and similar technologies. Some people fear that increasingly sophisticated programs will eventually take over even those jobs previously considered too complex for automation, replacing surgeons, writers, lawyers, and airline pilots with AI technology. But others are more optimistic and argue for focusing on what technology has created rather than on what might be lost. Work will be transformed, these observers say, rather than eliminated, and the change will be slow enough for employers, and employees, to adapt.[79] What will be the implications of these events for you as a manager for staffing and training employees and for your own professional development?

- **Organizational changes: Shifts in structure, jobs, goals, and management.** Organizations and their employees are no longer as bound by time zones and locations. The "virtual" organization presents a variety of options for how work gets done, including the ability to:
    1. Telecommute or work from home or remote locations using a variety of information technologies.

2. **Videoconference** by using video and audio links along with computers to conduct meetings and allow people in different locations see, hear, and talk with one another.
3. Deliver and track a variety of functions digitally with programs such as eWorkbench that enable managers to create and track employee goals and deliver feedback.
4. Manage projects using **project management software** programs for planning and scheduling the people, costs, and resources to complete a project on time.

- **Knowledge management and collaborative computing.** The forms of interaction just described will require managers and employees to be more flexible, and there will be an increased emphasis on **knowledge management**—the implementing of systems and practices to increase the sharing of knowledge and information throughout an organization. In addition, **collaborative computing** will help people work better together through state-of-the-art computer software and hardware. Many hospitals, for example, now knit various functions together—patient histories, doctors' orders, lab results, prescription information, billing—in a single information system, parts of which patients can access themselves to schedule appointments, question doctors, and request prescription refills.

Challenge #3: Managing for Inclusion and Diversity—The Future Won't Resemble the Past

Diversity in organizations represents the extent to which employees are different from one another in terms of various characteristics. Equity relates to employees' perceptions that they are treated in a fair and unbiased manner at work. Inclusion represents the extent to which employees feel heard, valued, involved, and respected in the workplace. Organizations are increasing in diversity in a variety of ways. Consider two examples:

- In 2021, more than 46 million people in the United States were born in another country, representing 14.2% of the total population.[80] That number will exceed 50 million (14.6% of the population) by 2025, and by 2060, over 17% of the U.S. population will be made up of people born outside of the United States.[81]
- The coming years also will bring challenges related to age diversity in the general population, as well as in the workforce. For instance, the national median age has increased by 3.4 years since 2020, and by 2030, approximately 10% of the civilian labor force will be over 65.[82]

Some scholars think that diversity and variety in staffing produce organizational strength, as we will discuss in Chapter 11. A diverse organization holds the benefits of a variety of knowledge, skills, and experiences that can translate into increased innovation. Further, diverse organizations are well positioned to compete in an increasingly global economy. Clearly, the challenge for modern managers is to realize the value of a diverse group of employees while ensuring that everyone feels included.

Challenge #4: Managing for Globalization—The Expanding Management Universe

Business around the world is becoming increasingly interconnected, a phenomenon called globalization. Some critics push back against the idea that globalization is always a good idea, citing the risks inherent in relying too heavily on international economies. Consider the following example:

Challenges of Managing for Globalization—Russia–Ukraine War Example: Russia's invasion of Ukraine in 2022 led to a host of supply chain issues across the globe. For

Cross-border burger business. The manager of this Johnny Rockets hamburger store, which opened in Lagos, Nigeria, in 2012, found that to achieve an authentic, U.S.-style taste he needed to fly in the toppings—onions, mushrooms, and iceberg lettuce—which meant that he had to start prices at $14 for a single-patty burger.
Sunday Alamba/AP Images

example, Ukraine typically exports large amounts of grains as well as fertilizer for crops, and global food prices increased in part due to this supply being cut off. A related issue occurred with semiconductor chips, as half of the neon gas (a raw material necessary for chip production) in the world comes from Ukraine. Auto manufacturers felt the impacts of the war as well. BMW and Volkswagen had to shut down some of their assembly lines when Ukrainian-based wiring harness manufacturer Leoni was unable to continue fulfilling orders.[83]

Despite challenges, the fact is that we are living in, and reaping the many benefits of, a global economy. Globalization brings greater efficiencies, increased access to goods and services, and the potential for widespread innovation, among other things. The challenge for managers is understanding and navigating the complexities that accompany globalization. For example, business etiquette, social customs, and communication norms vary greatly around the world. Failure to understand these nuances can hinder an organization's ability to succeed in a global environment. Managing for globalization will be a complex, ongoing challenge, as we discuss at length in Chapter 4.

Challenge #5: Managing for Ethical Standards

Managers face a variety of ethical dilemmas, including pressure to meet sales, production, and other targets, and the temptation to falsify data.

How far would you go to satisfy demanding customers in a highly competitive international market? In an era of climate change, with increasingly severe storms and rising sea levels, what is your responsibility to "act green"—to avoid company policies that are damaging to the environment?

Ethical behavior is not just a nicety; it is an essential principle to follow in every industry, and one that is even more compelling when you are in a position of power. We hold leaders and managers accountable for unethical behaviors in their organizations even if they are not directly involved. This was evident in the case of the Houston Astros baseball organization.

Managing for Ethical Standards—Houston Astros Example: In early 2020, the Houston Astros fired general manager Jeff Luhnow and manager A.J. Hinch after an investigation revealed that Astros players and personnel had colluded to steal opposing teams' signs using camera footage during the 2017 and 2018 baseball seasons. Commissioner Robert Manfred acknowledged that Luhnow and Hinch were not directly involved with the scheme, but Manfred stressed that high-ranking officials were responsible for creating cultures where these types of behaviors are not able to take root. Major league baseball levied a $5 million dollar fine—the highest allowed—on the Astros organization. Years later, the team still deals with reputation damage from the scandal.[84]

Recent incidents point to serious repercussions when people fail to realize that thical standards must be followed in every area of life. Clearly ethical lapses have the potential to do great harm, and not only financial harm. How would you behave if you were in a position of power? We consider ethics in Chapter 3 and throughout the book and provide some advice to jumpstart your thinking in the Practical Action Box.

Challenge #6: Managing for Sustainable Development —The Business of Green

Our economic system has brought prosperity for many generations, but in doing so has often assumed an unlimited supply of natural resources. We now believe some of our economic actions and decisions have caused irreversible environmental damage, resulting in problems including deforestation, water shortages, and soil pollution.

The United Nations (UN) addressed these issues head-on in 2015 when all 193 members adopted a set of 17 Sustainable Development Goals (SDGs) meant to serve as a

PRACTICAL ACTION | Doing the Right Thing When You're Tempted to Cheat

Results from various survey studies estimate that between 60% and 90% of college students cheat.[85] Further, rates of cheating in college settings skyrocketed during the pandemic when most instruction moved online.[86] Cheating to get ahead in school or in your job is not only unethical, it can also ruin your future. Cheating in your professional life can be grounds for firing (in the case of lying on your resume or breaking company ethical policy) or forcible removal from professional organizations and certifying bodies.

The temptation to cheat is real for many of us, even if we understand the consequences. Here are two suggestions to help you resist this temptation.

Ask Yourself Why You're Tempted to Cheat. Some of the reasons we might decide to cheat include time pressure, performance anxiety, stress, peer pressure, or even a misunderstanding of policy. The next time you feel the urge to skirt academic dishonesty policies, ask yourself why you feel the need to break these rules. Then, consider whether your professional reputation is worth the risk of engaging in the dishonest behavior.[87] Talk to someone if you are experiencing an abundance of stress, pressure to cheat, or fear of failing.

Be Prepared. We may behave unethically simply because we don't have the experience, knowledge, or practice necessary to know how to behave in the "right" way in a situation. A great way to avoid this problem is to practice working through ethical dilemmas before they show up in your life. Medical professionals, for example, can find lists of common ethical dilemmas along with helpful guides for working through these tricky situations.[88] We have two suggestions for how you can better prepare yourself for facing the temptation to behave unethically. First, familiarize yourself with the academic dishonesty policies of your university, college, and/or classroom. If you aren't sure if something is considered cheating, ask your professor for guidance. Second, take advantage of opportunities presented to you in this product. Specifically, work through the "Legal/Ethical Challenge" cases that we include in Connect with every chapter. These will assist you in developing a more ethical orientation and will give you the practice you need to be able to make ethical decisions when faced with temptation.

YOUR CALL

What will you tell yourself the next time you're tempted to cheat or see someone cheating? What behaviors are you willing to commit to in order to avoid giving in to the temptation to cheat?

Working to meet the SDGs. A group of professors, ambassadors, and participants at a seminar addressing Taiwan's progress toward meeting the SDGs.
SOPA Images Limited/Alamy Stock Photo

blueprint for future economic planning.[89] **Sustainable development** focuses on meeting present needs while simultaneously ensuring that future generations will be able to meet their needs.[90] The UN SDGs include zero hunger and affordable and clean energy, among others.

A unique aspect of the UN's approach to sustainable development is that it encourages businesses to pursue strategies that are mutually beneficial to both society and the organizations' bottom lines.[91] The corporate world took notice of this quickly, and by 2022, over 60% of Fortune 500 companies were engaging with the SDGs and discussing their commitment to sustainable development on their websites.[92]

Recently, the CEOs of some of the most admired and profitable companies in the world (including Accenture, Apple, IBM, FedEx, Coca-Cola, and Amazon) came together collectively to address sustainable development. These CEOs are members of The Business Roundtable—a public policy advocacy group comprised of CEOs from about 200 leading U.S. companies. The group's 2019 statement on the purpose of a corporation was the first since 1997 that did not place shareholders above all other priorities. Instead, it stressed the value of environmental health and widespread economic opportunity, and it expressed that these leaders and their organizations would commit to, among other things, "protect the environment by embracing sustainable practices across our businesses."[93] Mary Barra led the Roundtable as chair from January 2022–January 2024.

Clearly, sustainable development is a critical issue facing businesses today. We will discuss these issues in depth in Learning Module 1.

Challenge #7: Managing for Happiness and Meaningfulness

Which would you rather have, a happy life or a meaningful life? We recommend both!

One study found that "Happiness was linked to being a taker rather than a giver, whereas meaningfulness went with being a giver rather than a taker," as a study author put it.[94] Happiness is getting what you want, having your desires fulfilled. **Meaningfulness** is the sense of "belonging to and serving something that you believe is bigger than the self."[95] Your authors derive meaning from writing this product because we believe it can enrich your life and help you manage others more effectively. Research clearly shows that a sense of meaningfulness in your life is associated with better health, work and life satisfaction, and performance.[96]

Finding meaning at work. Some organizations give their employees paid time off for volunteer work. Would you find it meaningful to put food and drinks into paper bags for charity?
LightField Studios/Shutterstock

We have three suggestions for building meaning into your life.

1. **Identify activities you love doing.** Try to do more of these activities or find ways to build them into your work role. Employees at St. Jude Children's Research Hospital embody this suggestion. They truly enjoy participating in the St. Jude Marathon weekend because it raises money for the children being treated at the hospital. One employee, a cancer survivor, commented, "Each year it provides me with another opportunity to give back so that we can help countless other children have anniversaries of their own."[97]

2. **Find a way to build your natural strengths into your personal and work life.** Doing this requires that you assess yourself along a host of competencies desired by employers. The next section identifies these competencies and discusses how you might evaluate your strengths and development opportunities.

3. **Go out and help someone.** Research shows that people derive a sense of meaningfulness from helping others.[98] Salesforce, ranked as the fourth best place to work by *Fortune* in 2022, follows this suggestion.[99]

Deriving Meaningfulness from Helping Others—Salesforce Example: Salesforce employees participate in a Citizen Philanthropy program. Each year, the company matches employee charitable donations up to $5,000 and provides employees with seven paid days off for volunteering.[100] Employees find volunteer opportunities that match with both their personal values and their unique skills. The logic is that this type of alignment will generate the most impactful outcomes for employees' communities and for the world.

How Strong Is Your Motivation to Be a Manager? The First Self-Assessment

As we stated at the beginning of this chapter, we desire to make this product *as practical as possible* for you. As an important means of advancing this goal, we developed 64 **self-assessments**—two to four per chapter—that allow you to gauge how you feel about the material you are reading and how you can make use of it.

Go to *connect.mheducation.com*, complete the self-assessment, then answer the self-assessment questions. (Note: These self-assessments are available only if your instructor uses *Connect* and assigns them to you). Taking the self-assessments is a valuable way to develop your self-awareness and career readiness, which is discussed in the next section. The first one assesses your motivation to lead. Do you desire to hold leadership positions? Find out by taking the self-assessment. ●

SELF-ASSESSMENT 1.1   CAREER READINESS

How Strong Is My Motivation to Lead?

This survey is designed to assess your motivation to lead. Please complete Self-Assessment 1.1 if your instructor has assigned it in Connect.

The Exceptional Manager | CHAPTER 1 | 27

1.7 Building Your Career Readiness

THE BIG PICTURE
Companies want to hire *career ready* college graduates. In this section we describe a model of career readiness and offer tips for building your readiness.

About 49,000 undergraduate students from 317 universities across the United States rated 2022's most attractive employers. The top 10 were (1) Google, (2) Apple, (3) JPMorgan Chase, (4) The Walt Disney Company, (5) Goldman Sachs, (6) Netflix, (7), Tesla, (8) Nike, (9) Spotify, and (10) Amazon.[101] Would you like to work at these companies or others like them? If so, you need to be career ready.

Career readiness represents the extent to which you possess the knowledge, skills, and attributes desired by employers. How ready do you believe you are? Recent surveys of college students and employers reveal a big gap in the degree of readiness each group perceives in students. Figure 1.3 shows some key results of a study of 157 employers and 2,140 graduating seniors. The majority of students rated themselves as career ready on all eight skills, whereas the majority of employers perceived students to be well prepared on only four of the skills. The three largest gaps were in leadership, professionalism, and communication, skills that are very important to employers.[102] Other studies have similarly demonstrated that employers see a major gap in college students' career readiness skills.[103]

LO 1-7
Define the core competencies, knowledge, soft skills, attitudes, and other characteristics needed for career readiness and discuss how they can be developed.

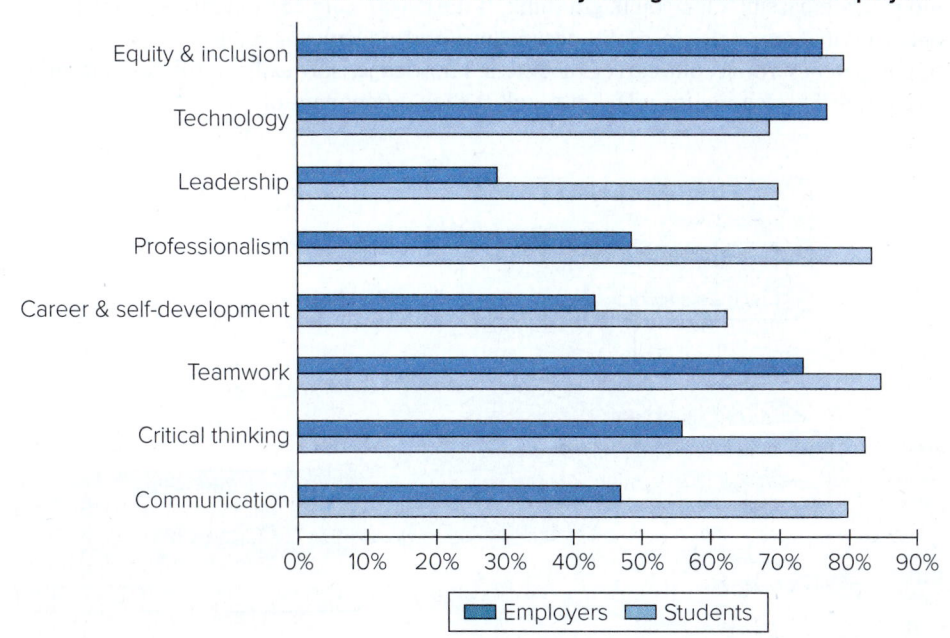

FIGURE 1.3
Employers and college grads disagree about levels of career readiness

Career Readiness Proficiency Ratings: Students vs. Employers

The good news is that merely acknowledging the existence of these gaps will impress potential employers because companies prefer to hire people with realistic self-perceptions. This underscores the need to obtain information about your strengths and weaknesses throughout your career.

More importantly, we think your awareness that employers expect more from you in these areas will be valuable for at least two reasons:

1. **You will be motivated to learn.** Studies of human behavior reveal that people won't spend time on personal development unless they feel the need. Overinflated perceptions of career readiness will not motivate you to develop the

attributes that enhance that readiness. Having a realistic picture will increase your motivation to learn and develop. It will also allow you to practice learning, which is something you will need to do throughout your career. You may be surprised to learn that the knowledge you gain from your college degree may be obsolete in as little as five years.[104] This is due to the rapidly changing nature of jobs, and it means that you should approach career readiness as a lifelong process rather than a one-time event that stops after graduation. A recent article in the *Harvard Business Review* suggested that hiring lifelong learners was an "economic imperative" and that organizations of the future will achieve sustainable competitive advantage through employees who consistently improve upon and build skills.[105]

2. **You will know where to focus your energy.** As you will learn in the upcoming section, the list of career readiness competencies is quite long, and some of the competencies will be more relevant to your personal career path than others. This can be daunting when you are trying to improve your career readiness—where should you begin? We're here to help. In comparing the results from multiple career readiness studies (including the NACE data presented in Figure 1.3), we noticed there were several competencies that employers consistently rated as essential.[106] We call these *core competencies*. Organizations across the board are on the prowl for employees who possess these basic competencies, many of which are reflected in the "gaps" you just learned about.

Let's consider a model of career readiness and how you can apply it in your life.

Visit your instructor's Connect course and access your eBook to view this video.

Executive Interview Series:
Cultural Awareness and Social Intelligence

A Model of Career Readiness

As you will see in this chapter's Executive Interview Series video, being career ready is more encompassing than you might think. It starts with **core competencies**—a set of competencies that are vital across jobs, occupations, and industries. Four additional categories of competency round out career readiness: knowledge, soft skills, attitudes, and other characteristics (see Figure 1.4). Let's look at each component of the model in detail.

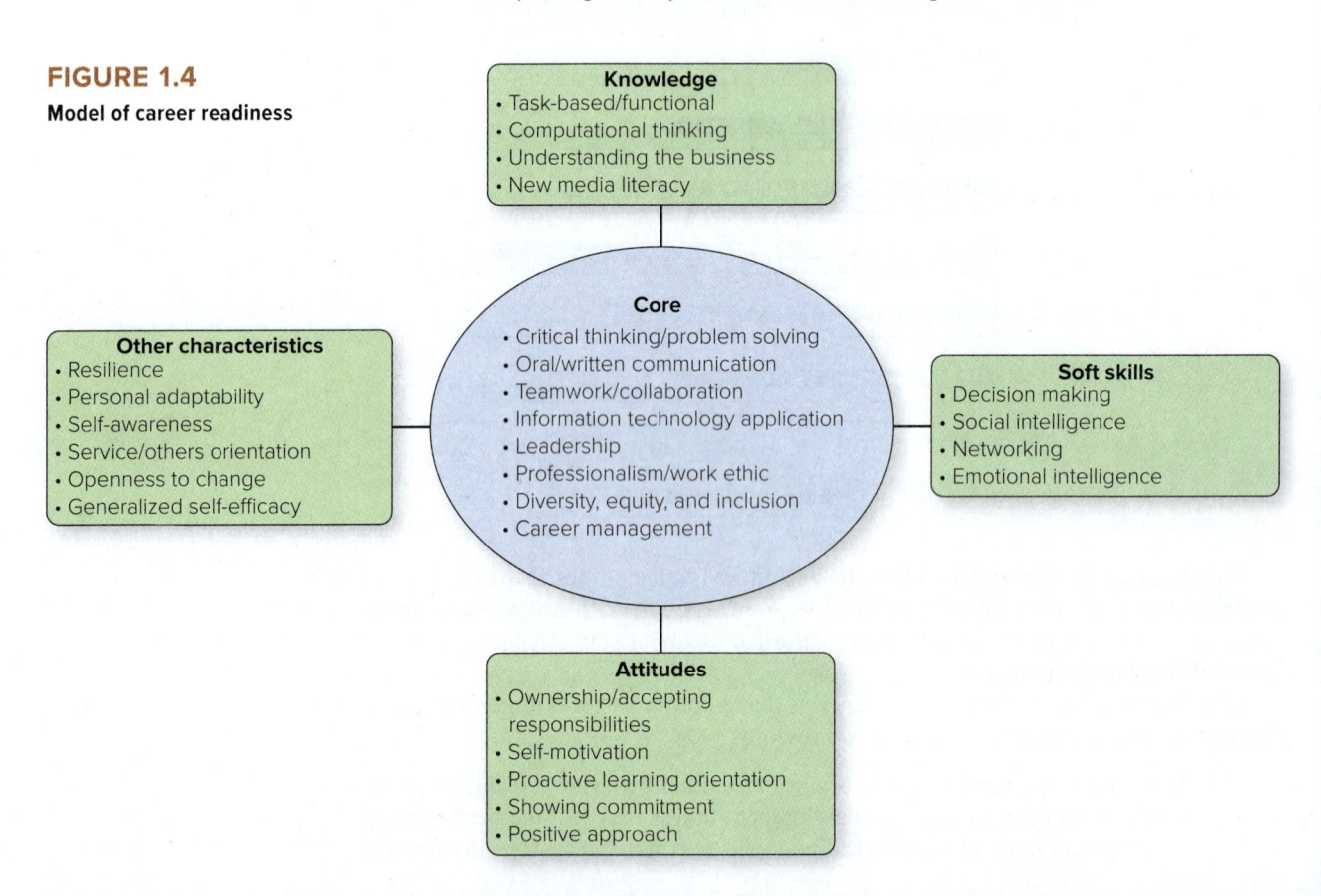

FIGURE 1.4
Model of career readiness

Knowledge
- Task-based/functional
- Computational thinking
- Understanding the business
- New media literacy

Core
- Critical thinking/problem solving
- Oral/written communication
- Teamwork/collaboration
- Information technology application
- Leadership
- Professionalism/work ethic
- Diversity, equity, and inclusion
- Career management

Other characteristics
- Resilience
- Personal adaptability
- Self-awareness
- Service/others orientation
- Openness to change
- Generalized self-efficacy

Soft skills
- Decision making
- Social intelligence
- Networking
- Emotional intelligence

Attitudes
- Ownership/accepting responsibilities
- Self-motivation
- Proactive learning orientation
- Showing commitment
- Positive approach

Core Competencies The eight competencies in the center of the model are necessary for success no matter what career path you pursue. The demand for things like communication and leadership ability, interpersonal skills, and information technology skills is predicted to grow substantially across all industries in the United States and Europe by the year 2030.[107] Still, employers consider many of these competencies to be rare in today's labor market. Kate Davidson, a reporter for *The Wall Street Journal,* concluded that "it is becoming increasingly difficult to find applicants who can communicate clearly, take initiative, problem-solve and get along with co-workers."[108] We think this provides excellent incentive for you to work on increasing your level of these competencies. Your efforts may translate to big advantages on the job market.

Knowledge Skills in the knowledge category, generally referred to as "hard skills," encompass the basic knowledge employers expect you to possess. They develop from your ability to apply academic and practical knowledge while performing the job. Your grade point average is one way to assess your current level of this type of knowledge.[109] Other types of knowledge desired by employers include computational thinking, understanding the business, and new media literacy (see Table 1.3).

TABLE 1.3 Description of the Competencies Needed for Career Readiness

CATEGORY	COMPETENCY	DESCRIPTION
Core	Critical Thinking/Problem Solving	Sound reasoning to analyze situations, make decisions, and solve problems. Ability to obtain, interpret, and analyze both qualitative and quantitative information while creatively solving problems.
	Oral/Written Communication	Ability to effectively express your thoughts, ideas, and messages to diverse people in oral and written form. Public speaking skills and ability to write/edit e-mails, letters, and technical reports.
	Teamwork/Collaboration	Ability to work effectively with and build collaborative relationships with diverse people, work within a team structure, and manage interpersonal conflict.
	Information Technology Application	Effective use of IT and learning new applications as needed.
	Leadership	Skill at influencing a group of people to achieve common goals. Ability to motivate, coach, and develop others.
	Professionalism/Work Ethic	Accountability and positive work habits such as punctuality, time management, appropriate dress and appearance, and willingness to go beyond a job description or ask for help when needed. Demonstrated integrity, ethical behavior, and concern for the greater good.
	Diversity, Equity, and Inclusion	Awareness of workers' differences; respect for diverse cultures, races, ethnicities, abilities, ages, genders, and religions; and demonstrated openness, inclusiveness, and ability to interact with diverse people.
	Career Management	Ability to proactively manage your career and identify opportunities for professional development.
Knowledge	Task-Based/Functional	Demonstrated ability to apply academic and practical knowledge in pursuit of organizational and individual goals/assignments.
	Computational Thinking	Ability to use numbers to distill abstract concepts and conduct data-based reasoning. Ability to work with and interpret big data.
	Understanding the Business	Understanding of the company's business and strategies and the needs of stakeholders, and ability to see how your work fits into the larger organizational puzzle.

(Continued)

TABLE 1.3 Description of the Competencies Needed for Career Readiness (*Continued*)

CATEGORY	COMPETENCY	DESCRIPTION
	New Media Literacy	Ability to develop, evaluate, and use new media forms, and to apply these media for persuasive communication. Ability to stay up-to-date with the latest media trends and to leverage them in the interest of the organization.
Soft Skills	Decision Making	Ability to collect, process, and analyze information in order to identify and choose from alternative solutions that lead to optimal outcomes.
	Social Intelligence	Ability to connect with others in a meaningful way, to recognize and understand another person's feelings and thoughts, and to use this information to stimulate positive relationships and beneficial interactions.
	Networking	Ability to build and maintain a strong, broad professional network of relationships.
	Emotional Intelligence	Ability to monitor your emotions and those of others, to discriminate among them, and to use this information to guide your thinking and behavior.
Attitudes	Ownership/Accepting Responsibility	Willingness to accept responsibility for your actions.
	Self-Motivation	Ability to work productively without constant direction, instruction, and praise. Ability to establish and maintain good work habits and consistent focus on organizational goals and personal development.
	Proactive Learning Orientation	Desire to learn and improve your knowledge, soft skills, and other characteristics in pursuit of personal development.
	Showing Commitment	Willingness to support others and positively work toward achieving individual and company goals.
	Positive Approach	Willingness to accept developmental feedback, to try and suggest new ideas, and to maintain a positive attitude at work.
Other Characteristics	Resilience	Ability to bounce back from adversity and to remain motivated when confronted with challenges.
	Personal Adaptability	Ability and willingness to adapt to changing situations.
	Self-Awareness	A realistic view of your strengths and weaknesses relative to a specific job and context, and the ability to create and implement a personal development plan.
	Service/Others Orientation	Willingness to put the needs of others over self-interests.
	Openness to Change	Flexibility when confronted with change, ability to see change as a challenge, and willingness to apply new ideas, processes, or directives.
	Generalized Self-Efficacy	Confidence in your ability to perform across a variety of situations.

Sources: Based on material in NACE Staff, "Career Readiness Defined," 2019, https://www.naceweb.org/career-readiness/competencies/career-readiness-defined; Alison Doyle, "Hard Skills vs. Soft Skill: What's the Difference? The Balance Careers, February 4, 2019, https://www.thebalancecareers.com/hard-skills-vs-soft-skills-2063780; Ashita Bhagra and Dinesh Kumar Sharma, "Changing Paradigm of Employability Skills in the Global Business World: A Review," IUP Journal of Soft Skills, 2018, pp. 7–24; and Fatima Suleman, "The Employability Skills of Higher Education Graduates: Insights into Conceptual Frameworks and Methodological Options," Higher Education, 2018, pp. 263–278.

Soft Skills We defined *soft skills* as the interpersonal "people" skills needed for success at all levels. These are not knowledge or technical skills. Soft skills are becoming increasingly important as companies outsource and automate routine tasks. For example, a *LinkedIn* survey of global talent trends reported that 92% of talent professionals believed soft skills were as important or more important than hard skills when making hiring decisions. Further, 89% said that identifying someone as a "bad hire" typically came down to a lack of soft skills.[110] Check out the Practical Action Box "Developing Your Soft Skills" in Section 1.5 for tips on how to develop your soft skills.

You can increase your career readiness by focusing on the four soft skills described in Table 1.3. You will learn more about each one as we progress through this product.

Attitudes Attitudes are beliefs and feelings directed toward *specific* objects, people, or events. More formally, an **attitude** is defined as a learned predisposition toward a given object. Attitudes are thoroughly discussed in Chapter 11.

Table 1.3 indicates that recruiters seek five attitudes in college graduates they hire. All have a positive and proactive focus. People perceive our attitudes by observing what we do and say. For example, taking ownership or responsibility is a key attitude recruiters prefer. It reflects the extent to which a person accepts responsibility for their actions. We suspect recruiters desire this attitude because it is positively associated with employees' commitment, job satisfaction, and engagement. Feelings of ownership also reduce employees' desire to quit.[111] All told, you can create more favorable impressions during interviews if you demonstrate this attitude. Find out where you stand on this attitude by taking Self-Assessment 1.2. It was designed to enhance your self-awareness about the extent to which you accept responsibility for your actions.

SELF-ASSESSMENT 1.2   CAREER READINESS

To What Extent Do You Accept Responsibility for Your Actions?

This survey is designed to assess the extent to which you accept responsibility for your actions. Please complete Self-Assessment 1.2 if your instructor has assigned it in Connect.

Other Characteristics This category contains a host of personal characteristics that help you to succeed and to effectively adapt to personal and work-related changes. Consider professionalism/work ethic and resilience. Aaron Michel, co-founder and CEO at PathSource, a career navigation and education software company, believes professionalism/work ethic "cannot be overvalued in the job market." He concluded that "just being on time and behaving responsibly can leave a strong impression."[112] Consider the competency of resilience.

Resilience is the ability to bounce back from adversity and to sustain yourself when faced with a challenge. Research shows that it is a key trait of successful people.[113] Consider the following example:

Bouncing back from adversity. Joe Burrow showed tremendous resilience during his college football career, culminating in a 2020 National Championship for the LSU Tigers.
Ken Murray/Icon Sportswire/Getty Images

Resilience Example—Joe Burrow: Heisman Trophy winner Joe Burrow displayed resilience in his college football career. After being rejected by his dream school Nebraska and then sitting on the bench at Ohio State for two seasons, Burrow broke his thumb and lost his chance to start in the 2018 season.[114] Instead of giving up on his dream, he transferred to LSU, where his persistence and dedication led the LSU Tigers to a 2020 National Championship. In describing his path to success, Burrow said, "Adversity is a key component in building the kind of players to succeed at the next level. I'm forever grateful I went through that adversity."[115] This type of cognitive reframing is key to becoming resilient.[116] Can you see why employers want to hire people who are professional and resilient?

Developing Career Readiness

We classify the many ways to develop career readiness into six categories: (1) *build self-awareness,* (2) *learn from educational activities,* (3) *model others possessing the desired competencies,* (4) *learn from on-the-job-activities,* (5) *seek experience from student groups and organizations,* and (6) *experiment.*

1. Build Self-Awareness   There are two ways to gather the data or information you need to make an accurate evaluation of your strengths and developmental opportunities:

- Ask for honest, targeted feedback from trusted students, co-workers, managers, teachers, and family.
- Take validated self-assessment surveys. This product provides 64 self-assessments for this purpose. Each includes developmental feedback, enabling you to devise a path toward improvement of a particular skill.

2. Learn from Educational Activities   To continue the lifelong process of learning, you need a proactive learning orientation. As defined in Table 1.3, a **proactive learning orientation** is the desire to learn and improve your knowledge, soft skills, and other characteristics in pursuit of personal development. To be more proactive in finding learning opportunities, you can:

- Take courses at your university or attend training seminars that focus on the competencies you need, such as time management or communication.
- Watch training videos and documentaries.
- Read books, magazines, and research in pursuit of developmental ideas.[117] This product is a good source. You can also consult the references we cite to find more detailed information about a variety of topics.
- Search the Internet for reputable content related to what you'd like to learn.

3. Model Others Possessing the Targeted Competencies   To learn from others around you, you can:

- Identify role models or mentors who possess the skills or traits you need and then interview them. Try to learn how they execute their competencies.
- Observe people who possess the targeted competency and learn from their behavior.
- Try out new behaviors and then discuss your results with a mentor, coach, or colleague.

4. Learn from On-the-Job Activities   To learn from on-the-job activities you can:

- Seek new assignments that require you to use one of your targeted competencies.
- Represent a member of management at a meeting or business function.
- Serve as a coach to another employee.
- Ask to serve as a team leader or project manager.
- Make presentations and facilitate meetings.
- Volunteer for special projects or committees.
- Transfer to another job to obtain new skills and experience.

5. Seek Experience from Student Groups and Organizations The following activities are useful:

- Join student groups and seek leadership positions.
- Join and network at student organizations such as Toastmasters.
- Volunteer at organizations where you can practice your developing skills.
- Enroll in internships, research projects, or service learning opportunities.
- Make presentations to professional or civic organizations.
- Volunteer in religious, civic, or community organizations.

6. Experiment Developing soft skills requires you to put new knowledge or information to use. Try these ideas:

- Identify new behaviors you want to master, then practice them. For example, if you want to build your leadership skills, volunteer to facilitate your next team meeting at school or work. Chapter 14
- Keep a journal. Record the details of your developmental efforts and learn from both successes and missteps. Collect stories about your strengths and the progress you've made, and use them during job interviews.

Let Us Help

Our two overriding goals for this product are to (1) assist you in leading a happy and meaningful life and (2) help you become career ready by learning about the principles of management. We thus created a feature for each chapter titled "Career Corner: Managing Your Career Readiness." Its purpose is to help you integrate what you learn in a chapter into the process of building your career readiness. The next section is our first installment. •

1.8 Career Corner: Managing Your Career Readiness

The goal of this section is to help you apply what you learn to building your career readiness. Let's begin with three keys to success:

1. It's your responsibility to manage your career. Don't count on others.
2. Personal reflection, motivation, commitment, and experimentation are essential.
3. Success is achieved by following a process. A **process** is defined as a series of actions or steps followed to bring about a desired result.

LO 1-8

Describe the process for managing your career readiness.

A Process for Developing Career Readiness

Figure 1.5 illustrates a process to guide the pursuit of managing your career readiness. We recommend the following four steps:

Step 1 The first step entails examining the list of career readiness competencies in Table 1.3 and picking a few that impact your current performance at school, work, or other activities. Then, assess your skill level for these competencies. This product contains 64 self-assessments you can take for this purpose. The first two were presented earlier in this chapter.

FIGURE 1.5

Process for managing career readiness

Kinicki and Associates, Inc. 2022.

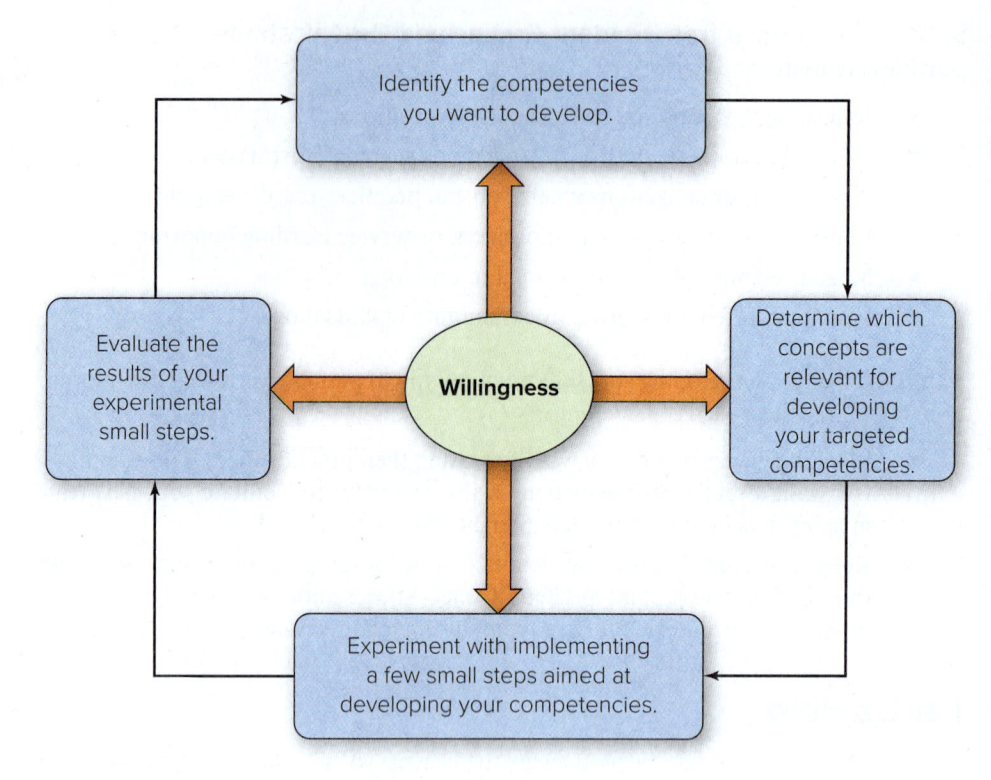

[Diagram: A circular process with "Willingness" at the center, connected by orange arrows to four boxes: "Identify the competencies you want to develop." (top), "Determine which concepts are relevant for developing your targeted competencies." (right), "Experiment with implementing a few small steps aimed at developing your competencies." (bottom), "Evaluate the results of your experimental small steps." (left). Black arrows connect the boxes in a clockwise cycle.]

Step 2 The second step requires you to consider how you can use the material covered in a chapter to develop your targeted career readiness competencies. For example, do your targeted competencies at this point relate to any of the challenges to being an exceptional manager? If yes, reflect on what you learned while reading that section of the chapter and consider how you can apply ideas, concepts, or suggestions you learned.

Step 3 The third step involves experimenting with small steps aimed at developing your targeted career readiness competencies.

Step 4 The final step is to evaluate what happened during your small-step experiments. This entails reflecting on what went right and wrong. Remember, you can learn as much from failure as success.

Figure 1.5 shows that *willingness* is at the center of developing your career readiness. This reinforces the point that it's up to you to shape and direct your future. We are confident that you can develop your career readiness by following this process and using the guidance provided at the end of every chapter.

Make It a Habit

We know from experience that self-improvement can be a difficult and often disappointing process. If you've ever tried to change something about yourself, you know it too. We want to set you up for success right from the start by offering a simple way to approach the task of managing your career readiness: Make it a habit.

Stanford University behavior scientist Dr. B.J. Fogg says the secret to successfully changing behavior lies in creating habits. You can use Dr. Fogg's three-step process to turn managing your career readiness into a habit.[118]

1. **Identify something specific you want to accomplish.** Choose something that excites you, because if the goal is one you truly want to accomplish, then motivation will come naturally. Suppose you want to improve the career readiness competency of networking. Perhaps you are energized imagining what it would feel like to have a

large network of professional contacts at your disposal. (Tickets to that sold-out concert? You'd know just whom to call. An interview with that exciting company? You'd be a mere text away.) An example of a specific outcome related to networking is to "add three new professionals to my contacts list over the next year."

2. **Identify a simple, tiny change you can implement.** Fogg says you should plan to make incremental progress toward your goal through a series of tiny, simple changes. Tiny changes are easy, which means you are more likely to stick with them. Take our previous example. If you want to get better at networking and your ultimate goal is to add three professional contacts to your list, start by identifying all of the little steps that would eventually get you to this goal. Your first tiny change might be as simple as peeking at your local young professionals Instagram every day. Once you've established this as a habit, your next tiny change might be to bookmark any post on that account that advertises an upcoming networking event. Again, do this until it becomes habitual. Next you might commit to adding each new bookmarked event to your personal calendar. Before you know it, you'll be attending networking events, meeting new people, and upsizing that professional contacts list.

3. **Attach the tiny change to an existing habit.** Fogg's method relies on the fact that we are already engaging in a slew of habits as part of our daily routines. Try to identify some of your existing habits. Maybe you head straight for the bathroom sink to brush your teeth when you wake up in the morning. Or perhaps you are useless until you get a cup of coffee. It's likely you can identify a long list of existing habits; choose one of them to prompt your new, tiny change. In the case of our networking example, if you are a daily coffee drinker, you might start by looking at your local young professionals Instagram each morning as you sip your latté. Over time, each successive tiny change should move you closer to your ultimate networking goal.

One final note—celebrate each time you engage in one of these tiny behaviors. It can be as simple as saying "nice job!" to yourself in your head. Fogg says that over time, these moments of positive reinforcement will go a long way toward making your new behaviors automatic, and therefore, toward helping you reach your goals. •

Key Terms Used in This Chapter

artificial intelligence (AI) 21
attitude 31
big data 20
career readiness 27
cloud computing 20
collaborative computing 22
competitive advantage 18
conceptual skills 16
controlling 9
core competencies 28
databases 20
decisional roles 15
e-business 20
e-commerce 20
effective 5
efficient 5
first-line managers 11
four management functions 8
functional manager 12
general manager 12
information technology application skills 20
informational roles 15
innovation 19
interpersonal roles 14
knowledge management 22
leading 9
management 5
meaningfulness 25
mentor 8
middle managers 11
nonmanagerial employees 11
organization 5
organizing 9
planning 9
proactive learning orientation 32
process 33
project management software 22
psychological contract 18
resilience 31
soft skills 17
sustainable development 25
team leaders 11
telecommute 21
top managers 11
videoconference 22

Key Points

1.1 Management: What It Is, What Its Benefits Are

- Management is defined as the pursuit of organizational goals efficiently through wise and cost-effective use of resources, and effectively through planning, organizing, leading, and controlling the organization's resources.

1.2 What Managers Do: The Four Principal Functions

- The management process consists of four functions: planning, organizing, leading, and controlling.

1.3 Pyramid Power: Levels and Areas of Management

- Within an organization, there are managers at four levels: top managers, middle managers, first-line managers, and team leaders.
- There are three types of organizations—for-profit, nonprofit, and mutual benefit. Each has a different purpose.

1.4 Roles Managers Must Play Successfully

- Porter and Nohria found that managers (1) are always working and in constant demand, (2) spend virtually all of their time at work communicating with others, and (3) have to be purposeful and proactive about managing their time.
- Mintzberg concluded that managers play three broad roles: (1) interpersonal—figurehead, leader, and liaison; (2) informational—monitor, disseminator, and spokesperson; and (3) decisional—entrepreneur, disturbance handler, resource allocator, and negotiator.

1.5 The Skills Exceptional Managers Need

- The three skills that exceptional managers cultivate are technical, conceptual, and human. Each uses different abilities.

1.6 Seven Challenges to Being an Exceptional Manager

- Managers face seven key challenges. These include managing for (1) competitive advantage, (2) technological advances, (3) inclusion and diversity, (4) globalization, (5) ethical standards, (6) sustainable development, and (7) happiness and meaningfulness.

1.7 Building Your Career Readiness

- Career readiness reflects the extent to which you possess the competencies desired by employers.
- Research uncovered 27 career readiness competencies preferred by employers (see Table 1.3).
- Six actions develop career readiness: (1) Build self-awareness, (2) learn from educational activities, (3) model others possessing the targeted competencies, (4) learn from on-the-job activities, (5) seek experience from student groups and organizations, and (6) experiment.

1.8 Career Corner: Managing Your Career Readiness

- A four-step process is recommended for managing your career readiness: (1) Identify the career readiness competencies you want to develop, (2) determine which concepts are relevant for developing your targeted career readiness competencies, (3) experiment with implementing a few small steps aimed at developing your career readiness competencies, and (4) evaluate the results of your experimental small steps.
- It takes willingness on your part to manage career readiness.
- You can turn developing career readiness into a habit by following three simple steps: (1) identify something specific you want to accomplish; (2) identify a simple, tiny change you can implement; and (3) attach the tiny change to an existing habit.

2

Management Theory
Essential Background for the Successful Manager

After reading this chapter, you should be able to:

LO 2-1 Describe the development of current viewpoints on management.

LO 2-2 Discuss the insights of the classical view of management.

LO 2-3 Describe the principles of the behavioral view of management.

LO 2-4 Discuss the two quantitative approaches to solving problems.

LO 2-5 Identify takeaways from the systems view of management.

LO 2-6 Explain why there is no one best way to manage in all situations.

LO 2-7 Define how managers foster a learning organization, high-performance work practices, and shared value and sustainable development.

LO 2-8 Describe how to develop the career readiness competency of understanding the business.

FORECAST   What's Ahead in This Chapter

This chapter gives you a short overview of the three principal viewpoints on management—classical, behavioral, and quantitative. It then describes three more recent viewpoints—systems, contingency, and contemporary. Contemporary approaches include the concepts of learning organizations, high-performance work practices, and shared value and sustainable development. We conclude with a Career Corner that focuses on how you can demonstrate the career readiness competency of understanding the business.

Using Theory as Your Guide to Solve Problems

We regularly tell our students that nothing is as practical as a good theory. The economic theory of supply and demand is an example. It proposes that prices go up when demand exceeds supply, thereby producing inflation. Simple, elegant, and practical. The same can be said about the management theories you will read about in this chapter.

Applying Management Theories

You apply theories when making decisions and solving problems. So let's begin by defining what we mean by a problem. Problems represent gaps between what you want and what you actually receive in a specific situation. Problems were quite simple as a toddler (share your toys) and an elementary schooler (be a good friend). They quickly become bigger and more complex as we age. Theories help you solve problems because they help you identify the causes of a problem and determine the best solutions. A good strategy to manage increasingly complicated problems, according to business professors Clayton Christensen and Michael Raynor, is to use the right theory at the right time.[1]

The goal of this chapter is to provide you a historical foundation of the many contemporary management theories you will learn throughout the text. The key to making the most of this information is to understand the basics of each theory so that you can apply the "best" one at the appropriate time (see Figure 2.1 for a summary). Below is a three-step process you can use when applying theory to solve problems.

1. What is the problem?

Defining a problem first is critically important so you have a clear sense of what you're aiming to resolve. Ask yourself, "what undesirable behaviors or outcomes are occurring?" Consider the following problems: Your best people are quitting; your employees are unproductive; your business is not profitable; your company is losing market share. Decades of management theory (summarized in Figure 2.1) suggests that business problems boil down to people, processes, or a combination of people and processes.

2. Why is the problem occurring?

A good theory is *useful*. It organizes evidence into clear and credible explanations for why business problems occur. In other words, theory offers insight into different factors that cause problems. For instance, your best employees may be quitting because their individual needs aren't being met, their direct managers are not supportive, or the organization doesn't provide enough opportunities for training and professional development. Theory is useful because it surfaces more potential causes than what your individual experience or intuition alone might lead you to consider. Figure 2.1 identifies multiple theories that explain why people- and process-related problems arise.

3. What actions can I take to solve the problem?

Theories are *usable* because they help identify root causes that can be overcome to eliminate problems. Researchers Herman Aguinis and Matt Cronin suggest theories are critical for managers because they offer a framework "to identify actions that effectively influence (i.e., improve) a situation and produce a desired outcome."[2]

Putting Theories into Practice

Once you have identified a problem and understand its causes, you are ready to use the underlying logic of a theory to solve the problem. Let's take the case of those employees from Starbucks who want to create a union.[3] To date, employees from over 300 stores in three dozen states have begun the process of forming a union. Why might this be happening and what can management do?

Figure 2.1 tells us that we clearly have a people problem and that behavioral theories might provide a solution. Equity theory, which you will learn about in Chapter 12, is one such theory. It is based on the logic that people seek unions when they feel unfairly treated. Management might want to investigate employees' feelings of inequity and try to overcome them based on the application of this theory. You can ponder the details once you learn more about equity theory. For now, we want you to consider the underlying premises of a host of management theories and then try to use our three-step process when solving problems.

For Discussion How can knowledge of management theories give you a broader understanding of organizational problems? How can management theories help you gain others' buy-in to your decisions?

2.1 Evolving Viewpoints: How We Got to Today's Management Outlook

THE BIG PICTURE

This section provides an overview of management history, starting with an overview of Peter Drucker's four fundamental principles of management. We also review six reasons for studying management theory.

LO 2-1

Describe the development of current viewpoints on management.

"The best way to predict the future is to create it," says Peter Drucker. Understanding management history can assist you in determining the type of management style you prefer in others and the type you want to adopt for yourself in the future. A good grasp of management history also enables you to utilize a host of different managerial viewpoints and techniques, thereby improving your ability to manage others.

Creating Modern Management: The Handbook of Peter Drucker

Who is Peter Drucker? "He was the creator and inventor of modern management," says management guru Tom Peters (author of *In Search of Excellence*).[4] *Business.com* suggests that Drucker's management theories "form the bedrock on which corporate America was built."[5]

An Austrian trained in economics and international law, Drucker came to the United States in 1937, where he worked as a correspondent for British newspapers and later became a college professor. In 1954, he published his famous text *The Practice of Management*, in which he proposed the important idea that *management was one of the major social innovations of the 20th century and should be treated as a profession*, like medicine or law.

In this and other books, he introduced several ideas that now underlie the organization and practice of management:

- Workers should be treated as assets.
- The corporation could be considered a human community.
- There is "no business without a customer."
- Institutionalized management practices are preferable to charismatic cult leaders.

True learner. Peter Drucker authored more than 35 books and numerous other publications, received the U.S. Presidential Medal of Freedom, and achieved near rock-star status for his innovative management ideas during his 70-year career.
Jonathan Alcorn/ZUMAPRESS/Newscom

Wegmans Food Markets Example: Wegmans supermarket chain, listed as one of *Fortune*'s "Best Companies to Work For" for 25 consecutive years, puts Drucker's principles in action by treating its workforce as assets. Colleen Wegman, president and CEO of Wegmans, says, "Our philosophy has always been to take care of our people, so they can take care of our customers."[6] Wegmans invests more than $50 million annually in employee scholarships, cooking technique certifications, and management trainee and leadership development programs.[7] Employees can also take online training seminars and workshops from the convenience of their homes. The company has seen its investment in its employees provide substantial returns in the form of customer satisfaction. Wegmans' customers love them so much that the company ranks #2 for providing the best customer service for a supermarket, according to *Newsweek*'s 2023 America's Best Customer Service ratings.[8]

Many ideas you will encounter in this book—decentralization, management by objectives, knowledge workers—are directly traceable to Drucker's pen. In our time, Drucker's rational approach has culminated in *evidence-based management,* as we describe in Section 2.4 in this chapter. Evidence-based management is grounded in good theory.

Six Practical Reasons for Studying This Chapter

"Theory," say business scholars Herman Aguinis and Matthew Cronin, "is essentially just a fancy word for 'Do we understand what's going on?'"[9] Managers rely on theories to understand and address organizational problems as well as improve organizational functioning.

No one approach to management is suited for all situations, so what could be more practical than studying different approaches to see which work best?

Indeed, there are six good reasons for studying theoretical viewpoints. Sound theories offer:

1. **Insight into past and present circumstances.** "Sound theories help us interpret the present, to understand what is happening and why," say business professors Clayton Christensen and Michael Raynor.[10] Or as scholars Scott Montgomery and Daniel Chirot argue, ideas "do not merely matter, they matter immensely, as they have been the source for decisions and actions that have structured the modern world."[11] Understanding history will help you understand why some practices are still favored, whether for right or wrong reasons.

2. **A guide to action.** Good theories help you make predictions and enable you to develop a set of principles that will guide your actions. For example, the theory of supply and demand tells us that prices go up when demand is high and supply is low. This is the situation with respect to the cost of labor in 2022 after the COVID-19 pandemic and during the Great Resignation. Firms had to pay more for workers due to the shortage of qualified employees looking for work.

3. **Sources of new ideas.** It can also provide new ideas that may be useful to you when you come up against new situations. For example, theories of employee engagement, which are discussed in Chapter 11, offer managers new ideas for how to best engage their workers. Contrary to the notion that compensation drives employee performance, these theories reveal that employees become engaged when an organization has the kind of culture that promotes employee development, recognition, and trust between management and employees.

4. **Clues to the meaning of your managers' decisions.** It can help you understand your firm's focus, where the top managers are "coming from."

5. **Clues to the meaning of outside events.** It may allow you to understand events outside the organization that could affect it or you.

6. **A path to achieve positive results.** It can help you understand why certain management practices—such as setting goals that stretch you to the limit (stretch goals), basing compensation and promotion on performance, and monitoring results—have been so successful for many firms.

The Progression of Management Viewpoints

In this chapter, we describe the complementary progression of management theories starting from the earliest to the most recent (see Figure 2.1). Notice how each theoretical viewpoint focuses on explaining different focal outcomes. Each of the following sections in this chapter is devoted to exploring these theoretical viewpoints and how they inform our current view of management.

FIGURE 2.1
Progression of management viewpoints

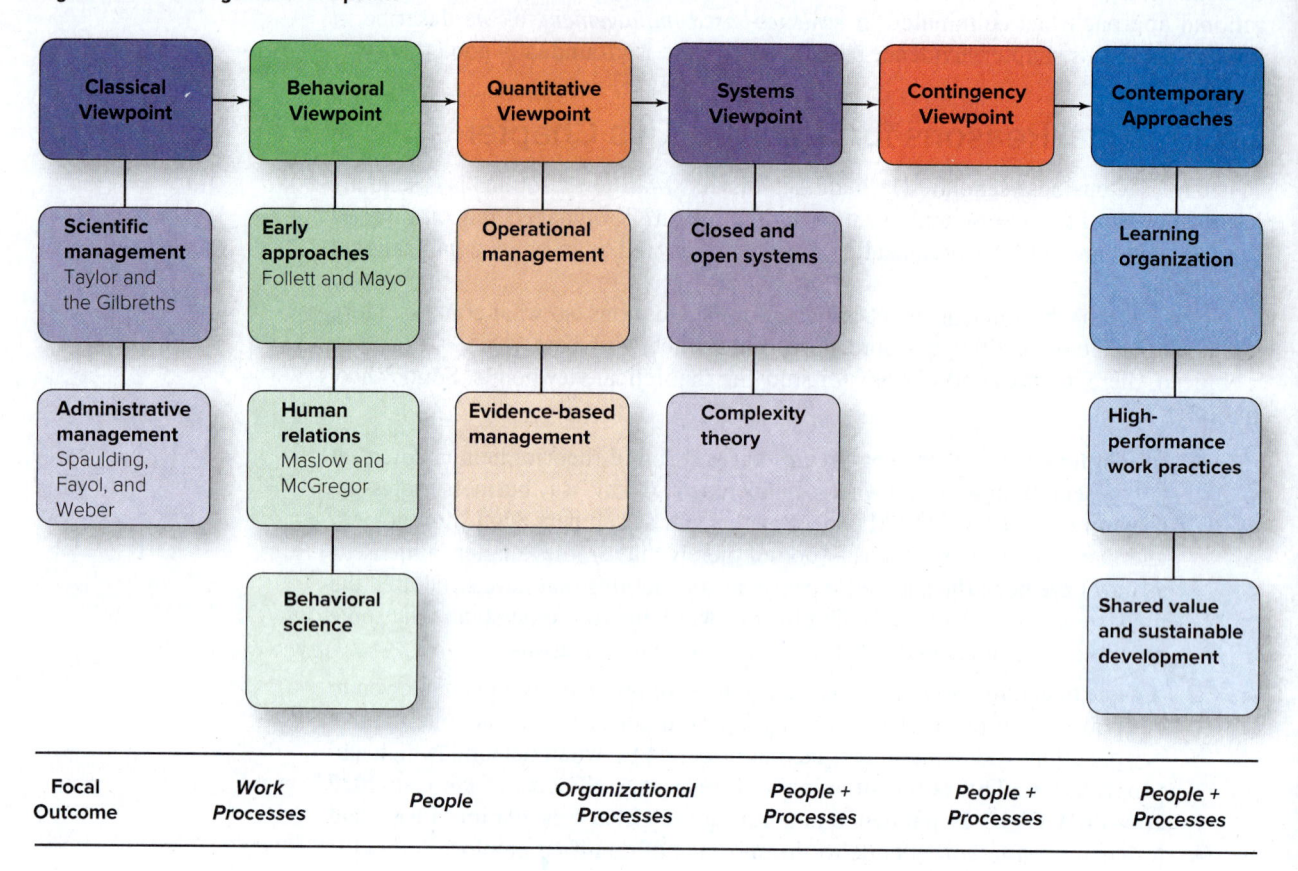

Classical Viewpoint	Behavioral Viewpoint	Quantitative Viewpoint	Systems Viewpoint	Contingency Viewpoint	Contemporary Approaches
Scientific management — Taylor and the Gilbreths	Early approaches — Follett and Mayo	Operational management	Closed and open systems		Learning organization
Administrative management — Spaulding, Fayol, and Weber	Human relations — Maslow and McGregor	Evidence-based management	Complexity theory		High-performance work practices
	Behavioral science				Shared value and sustainable development

Focal Outcome	Work Processes	People	Organizational Processes	People + Processes	People + Processes	People + Processes

2.2 Classical Viewpoint: Scientific and Administrative Management

THE BIG PICTURE

Here we'll discuss the classical viewpoint, which emphasized ways to manage work more efficiently. *Scientific management* emphasized the scientific study of work methods to improve the productivity of individual workers. *Administrative management* was concerned with managing the total organization.

LO 2-2

Discuss the insights of the classical view of management.

In this section, we describe the classical view of management, which originated during the early 1900s. The ==classical viewpoint==, which emphasized finding ways to manage work more efficiently, assumed that people are rational. It had two branches—scientific and administrative—each of which is identified with particular pioneering theorists. As shown in Figure 2.1, the classical view of management focused on improving work processes by increasing productivity and efficiency. Let's compare the two fundamental approaches.

Scientific Management: Pioneered by Taylor and the Gilbreths

The problem for which scientific management emerged as a solution was this: In the expansive economy of the early 20th century, labor was in such short supply that managers looked for ways to raise workers' productivity. **Scientific management applied the scientific study of work methods to improving the productivity of individual workers.** Two of its chief proponents were Frederick W. Taylor and the team of Frank and Lillian Gilbreth.

Frederick Taylor and the Four Principles of Scientific Management Considered to be the founder of scientific management, Taylor was an engineer from Philadelphia who believed managers could improve workers' productivity by applying four scientific principles:[12]

1. Evaluate a task by scientifically studying each part of it (not by using old imprecise methods). This approach leads to the establishment of realistic performance goals for a job.
2. Carefully select workers with the right abilities for the task.
3. Give workers the training and incentives to do the task with the proper work methods.
4. Use scientific principles to plan the work methods and ease the way for workers to do their jobs.

Taylor based his system on *motion studies,* in which he broke down each worker's job—for example, moving pig iron at a steel company—into basic physical motions and then trained workers to use the methods of their best-performing co-workers. He suggested employers institute a *differential rate system,* in which more efficient workers earned higher rates of pay. He also was a proponent of setting performance goals for employees.

Why Taylor Is Important: "Taylorism" met considerable resistance from workers, who feared it would lead to lost jobs except for the highly productive few. In fact, Taylor believed that increasing production would benefit both labor and management by increasing profits to the point where they no longer had to quarrel over them. If used correctly, the principles of scientific management can enhance productivity, and innovations like motion studies and differential pay are still used today.

Amazon Example: Amazon relies on Taylor's scientific management principles to maximize productivity and efficiency at its warehouses. Amazon's flagship fulfillment center, located in Kent, WA, ships more than 1 million items a day, more than tripling its capability from 10 years ago. Amazon uses technology to drive its efficiency. Software algorithms send product orders to warehouses based on their capacity and the product's final destination. Employees load and unload robots that race through the fulfillment center at high speeds transporting products to a network of conveyors leading to delivery trucks waiting to transport them to their destination.[13]

Frederick W. Taylor. Called the founder of scientific management, Taylor published *The Principles of Management* in 1911.
Bettmann/Getty Images

Amazon's distribution centers utilize cutting edge technology to improve their efficiency from product order to final delivery.
SWNS/Alamy Stock Photo

Frank and Lillian Gilbreth and Industrial Engineering Frank and Lillian Gilbreth took Taylor's ideas one step further by using movie cameras to film workers in order to isolate specific parts of a job. They identified 17 basic motions workers can perform. By identifying these basic motions, the Gilbreths helped workers eliminate unnecessary motions and reduce their fatigue, thereby increasing productivity.

Lillian Gilbreth was a pioneer in her own right. She was the first woman to receive a PhD in industrial psychology and the first to become a member of the Society of Industrial Engineers.[14] She also was a major contributor to management science. She found ways to improve workplace communication, nonfinancial incentive programs, and management training.[15]

Why the Gilbreth's Are Important: The Gilbreths reinforced the link between studying the physical movements in a job and workers' efficiency.[16] Today, companies such as Tesla and GM use the Gilbreths' management principles to automate physical production processes and increase efficiencies.

Administrative Management: Pioneered by Spaulding, Fayol, and Weber

Scientific management is concerned with improving individuals' productivity and efficiency. **Administrative management** is concerned with managing the total organization's productivity and efficiency. Among the pioneering theorists were Charles Clinton Spaulding, Henri Fayol, and Max Weber.

Charles Clinton Spaulding and the "Fundamental Necessities" of Management
Spaulding was the son of a farmer and had 13 siblings. He proposed eight "necessities" of management based on his experiences working in his father's fields as a boy and later leading the North Carolina Mutual Life Insurance Company. He is recognized as the founder of African American management and published his classic article in the *Pittsburgh Courier* in 1927.[17]

Why Spaulding Is Important: Spaulding's "necessities" went beyond the task orientation of scientific management, thereby broadening the view of what it takes to effectively manage people and organizations. He suggested that considerations such as the need for authority, division of labor, adequate capital, proper budgeting, and cooperation and teamwork were essential for smooth organizational operations. He also was one of the first management practitioners to highlight the need to enrich "the lives of his organizational and community family" while focusing on making a profit.[18]

Henri Fayol and the Functions of Management
Fayol was not the first to investigate management behavior, but he was the first to systematize it. A French engineer and industrialist, he became known to American business when his most important work, *General and Industrial Management,* was translated into English in 1930.

Why Fayol Is Important: Fayol was the first to identify the major functions of management—planning, organizing, leading, and controlling, as well as coordinating—the first four of which you'll recognize as the functions providing the framework for this and most other management books.[19]

Max Weber and the Rationality of Bureaucracy
In our time, the word *bureaucracy* has come to have negative associations: impersonality, inflexibility, red tape, a molasses-like response to problems. But to German sociologist Max Weber, a *bureaucracy* was a rational, efficient, ideal organization based on principles of logic. According to Weber, bureaucratic organizations improve organizational productivity and efficiency by reducing ambiguity in three ways: (1) defining a hierarchy of authority (who reports

Management Theory | CHAPTER 2

to whom?), (2) detailing a clear division of labor (who does what?), and (3) documenting formal rules and procedures (how should I do my work?).

Why Weber Is Important: Weber's work came to have an important influence on the structure of large corporations, such as the Coca-Cola Company, by identifying organizing principles that improve organizational consistency and efficiency.

The Problem with the Classical Viewpoint: Too Mechanistic

A flaw in the classical viewpoint is that it is mechanistic: It tends to view humans as cogs within a machine, not taking into account the importance of human needs. The behavioral viewpoint addressed this problem by swinging the pendulum from a focus on processes to a focus on people (shown in Figure 2.1), as we explain next.

McDonald's uses scientific management principles to improve employees' efficiency by organizing their work into specific tasks. What are the benefits and drawbacks to this management approach for employees?
Alex Segre/Alamy Stock Photo

Why the Classical Viewpoint Is Important: The essence of the classical viewpoint was that work activity was amenable to a rational approach, that productivity can be improved through applying scientific methods, time and motion studies, and job specialization. Indeed, these concepts are still in use today as scientific management principles are at the center of industries like quick-serve restaurants and manufacturing. The results are visible every time you visit a McDonald's, as shown in the accompanying photo, or see images of an auto manufacturing plant. The classical viewpoint also led to such innovations as management by objectives and goal setting. •

2.3 Behavioral Viewpoint: Behaviorism, Human Relations, and Behavioral Science

THE BIG PICTURE
The behavioral viewpoint emphasized the importance of understanding human behavior and of motivating employees toward achievement. The behavioral viewpoint developed over three phases: (1) *Early behaviorism,* (2) the *human relations movement,* and (3) *behavioral science.*

The **behavioral viewpoint** emphasized the importance of understanding human behavior and of motivating employees toward achievement. The behavioral viewpoint developed over three phases: (1) early behaviorism, (2) the human relations movement, and (3) behavioral science.

LO 2-3

Describe the principles of the behavioral view of management.

Early Behaviorism: Pioneered by Follett and Mayo

The two people who pioneered behavioral theory were Mary Parker Follett and Elton Mayo.

Mary Parker Follett and Power Sharing among Employees and Managers A Massachusetts social worker and social philosopher, Mary Parker Follett was lauded on her death in 1933 as a female pioneer in the fields of civics and sociology. Instead of following the usual hierarchical arrangement of managers as order givers and employees as order takers, Follett thought organizations should become more democratic, with managers and employees working cooperatively.

The following ideas were among her most important:

1. Organizations should be operated as "communities," with managers and subordinates working together in harmony.
2. Conflicts should be resolved by having managers and workers talk over differences and find solutions that would satisfy both parties—a process Follett called *integration*.
3. The work process should be under the control of workers with the relevant knowledge, rather than of managers who instead should act as facilitators.

Why Follett Is Important: With these and other ideas, Follett anticipated some of today's concepts of "self-managed teams," "worker empowerment," and "interdepartmental teams"—that is, members of different departments working together on joint projects.

Elton Mayo and the Supposed "Hawthorne Effect" Elton Mayo and his associates at Western Electric's Hawthorne plant near Chicago conducted an investigation into whether workplace lighting level affected worker productivity. Worker performance varied but tended to increase over time, leading Mayo and his colleagues to hypothesize what came to be known as the **Hawthorne effect**—namely, that employees worked harder when they received added attention, if they thought that managers cared about their welfare, and that supervisors paid special attention to them. However, later investigations disputed Mayo's conclusions. Critics point to factors other than receiving more attention that likely improved workers' productivity such as use of a particular instructional method or social innovation.[20]

Why the Hawthorne Studies Are Important: Although the Hawthorne studies were criticized, they succeeded in drawing attention to the importance of "social man" (social beings) and how managers using good human relations could improve worker productivity. This in turn led to the so-called human relations movement in the 1950s and 1960s.

The Human Relations Movement: Pioneered by Maslow and McGregor

The two theorists who contributed most to the **human relations movement**—which proposed that better human relations could increase worker productivity—were Abraham Maslow and Douglas McGregor.

Abraham Maslow and the Hierarchy of Needs Abraham Maslow, an academic and practicing psychologist, observed that his patients had certain basic innate needs that had to be satisfied before they could reach their fullest potential. Based on these observations, he proposed his famous *hierarchy of human needs* (physiological, safety, love, esteem, and self-actualization) in 1943.[21] As a humanist, Maslow advocated that employees have an innate desire to be self-actualized, which means to fully develop their abilities and fulfill their potential.[22]

We discuss Maslow's hierarchy in detail in Chapter 12, where we further explain why he is important and how his work has impacted motivation theory.

Douglas McGregor and Theory X versus Theory Y Having been a college president for a time (at Antioch College in Ohio), Douglas McGregor came to realize that it was not enough for managers to try to be liked (or be aware of employees' attitudes toward them); they also needed to be aware of their own attitudes toward employees.[23] McGregor suggested managers hold two fundamental assumptions about employees: Theory "X" or Theory "Y."

Theory X represents a pessimistic, negative view of workers. In this view, workers are considered to be irresponsible, to be resistant to change, to lack ambition, to hate work, and to want to be led rather than to lead.

Theory Y represents a human relations outlook—an optimistic, positive view of workers as capable of accepting responsibility, having self-direction and self-control, and being imaginative and creative.

Consider the contrast in the following managerial behaviors:

Theory X Example: Companies like Amazon, Kroger, UPS, UnitedHealth Group, and hospitals use desktop monitoring software and digital surveillance to track, record, and rank employees' productivity. Research indicates constant monitoring can cause employees to take less personal responsibility for their behavior and be more likely to engage in unethical behavior at work.[24]

Theory Y Example: U.S. retailer, Target, ranked number 1 on *People*'s "100 Companies that Care 2022" because of how the company takes care of its employees. One employee commented, "Target appreciates diversity and sees the skills I have to offer. They treat me the way I want to be treated. There's no other company with as much to offer. I'm home."[25]

Why Theory X/Theory Y Is Important: The principal contribution offered by the Theory X/Theory Y perspective is that it helps managers understand how their beliefs about employees affect their behavior toward them. Are your beliefs about others more consistent with Theory X or Theory Y? If you're not sure about which belief you align with, try the following two steps. First, ask those in your sphere of influence to describe how you behave toward them. Your beliefs about and attitudes toward others influence your interactions with them. Second, try the following self-assessment in Connect if your instructor has assigned it to you to identify your beliefs about others.

SELF-ASSESSMENT 2.1

What Is Your Orientation: Toward Theory X/Theory Y?

This self-assessment is designed to reveal your orientation as a manager—whether it tends toward Theory X or Theory Y. Please complete Self-Assessment 2.1 if your instructor has assigned it in Connect.

The Behavioral Science Approach

The human relations movement was a necessary correction to the sterile approach used within scientific management, but its optimism came to be considered too simplistic for practical use. More recently, the human relations view has been superseded by the behavioral science approach to management. **Behavioral science approach** relies on scientific research for developing theories about human behavior that can be used to provide practical tools for managers. This approach is the foundation for the study of organizational behavior (OB); all three of your authors specialized in OB during graduate school. Behavioral science draws from the following disciplines: psychology, sociology, anthropology, and economics. ●

2.4 Quantitative Viewpoints: Operations Management and Evidence-Based Management

THE BIG PICTURE

Quantitative viewpoints emphasize the application of quantitative techniques, such as statistics and computer simulations, to the practice of management. Two approaches to quantitative management are *operations management* and *evidence-based management*.

LO 2-4

Discuss the two quantitative approaches to solving problems.

Quantitative management is the application of quantitative techniques, such as statistics and computer simulations, to management. Whereas the classical viewpoint focused on work processes and behavioral viewpoints focused on people's motivation and attitudes, the quantitative viewpoint shifted management's focus to organizational processes (see Figure 2.1). Two branches of quantitative management are operations management and evidence-based management. Militaries, businesses, and sports franchises use these techniques to improve their decision making. For example, Major League Baseball teams use quantitative management to develop in-game strategies and to determine a player's financial value to the team.[26]

Houston Astros Example: The Houston Astros, the 2022 World Series champions, used data analytics to determine when to pull starting pitchers from the game, a strategy aimed to manage a pitcher's fatigue and maximize their pitching effectiveness. The Astros used three pitchers to produce a no-hitter in Game 4, a feat achieved for only the second time in the World Series' storied 115+ year history.[27]

The National Basketball Association (NBA) also uses quantitative management when scheduling games, developing a playoff structure, and setting draft lotteries. Evan Wasch, senior vice president of basketball strategy and analytics for the NBA, says that evidence-based management can prompt small changes that make a big difference.[28]

Operations Management: Being More Effective

Operations management focuses on managing the production and delivery of an organization's products or services more effectively. In the day-to-day running of the company, operations management consists of all the job functions and activities in which managers schedule and delegate work and job training, plan production to meet customer needs, design services customers want and how to deliver them, locate and design company facilities, and choose optimal levels of product inventory to keep costs down and reduce backorders. It governs managers' decisions about how to increase productivity and efficiency, as well as how to achieve the highest possible quality of both goods and services. Another major function of operations management is managing the **supply chain**, which is the process of creating the product, starting with designing and obtaining raw materials for physical goods or technology for services and going all the way through delivery to customers' hands, and sometimes even beyond to responsible disposal or recycling.

COVID-19 lockdowns created a significant disruption in the global supply chain because it left ports, which are responsible for inspecting and unloading container ships like the one in this picture, understaffed.
Fancy Collection/SuperStock

General Motors Example: Supply chains are only as strong as their weakest link, and multiple weak links appeared at the same time affecting General Motors' automobile manufacturing. Lingering COVID-19 lockdowns coupled with the Russia–Ukraine geopolitical conflict constrained exports and created kinks in the global supply chain. These weak links contributed to oil and semiconductor chip shortages, materials critical to manufacturing automobiles. Experts link supply chain disruptions to significantly higher manufacturing costs and record high automobile prices as consumer demand for vehicles far outpaces supply.[29]

Why Operations Management Is Important: Through the rational management of resources and distribution of goods and services, operations management helps ensure that business operations are efficient and effective.

Evidence-Based Management: Facing Hard Facts, Rejecting Nonsense

Evidence-based management entails translating principles based on best evidence into organizational practice, bringing rationality to the decision-making process.

As its two principal proponents, Stanford business scholars Jeffrey Pfeffer and Robert Sutton, put it, evidence-based management is based on the belief that "facing the hard facts about what works and what doesn't, understanding the dangerous half-truths that constitute so much conventional wisdom about management, and rejecting the total nonsense that too often passes for sound advice will help organizations perform better."[30]

Novartis Example: Swiss pharmaceutical company, Novartis, uses evidence-based management to drive innovation. It has invested substantially to integrate large amounts of data, derive insights from it, and share the insights across departments. The company's objective is to use big data, or sets of data so vast and complex that new methods have been developed to analyze them, and analytics to make the company more agile. Their specific goal is to accelerate the time from developing a new drug to bringing it to market from 12 years to 9 years.[31]

Learning to make managerial decisions based on evidence rather than intuition or anecdotes is the approach we hope you will learn to take after studying many other viewpoints we cover in this chapter. We will consider evidence-based management further, along with analytics and big data, in Chapter 7. •

2.5 Systems Viewpoint

THE BIG PICTURE

The *systems viewpoint* sees organizations as either a closed or open system. The systems viewpoint has led to the development of complexity theory, the study of how order and pattern arise from very complicated, apparently chaotic systems.

Could you run a present-day organization or a department according to the managerial theories you've just learned? Probably not. The reason: People are complicated and organizations are more complex than ever before. As shown in Figure 2.1, the earliest management perspectives focused either on processes *or* people. New management theories were needed to account for both processes *and* people to explain the

LO 2-5

Identify takeaways from the systems view of management.

complex challenges organizations face. The systems viewpoint explains the complexity surrounding today's businesses by breaking down organizations into separate but interrelated parts.

The Systems Viewpoint

The 27 bones in the hand. The monarchy of Great Britain. A weather storm front. Each of these is a system. A **system** is a set of interrelated parts that operate together to achieve a common purpose. Even though a system may not work very well—as in the inefficient way the Italian government collects taxes, for example—it is nevertheless still a system. Furthermore, if managers do not understand how the different parts of an organization come together to achieve its goals, they will not be able to diagnose problems and develop effective solutions.

The **systems viewpoint** regards the organization as a system of interrelated parts. By adopting this point of view, you can look at your organization both as (1) a collection of **subsystems**—parts making up the whole system like gears in a clock—and (2) a part of the larger environment. A university, for example, is made up of a collection of academic departments, support staffs, students, and the like. But it also exists as a system within the environment of education, having to be responsive to parents, alumni, legislators, nearby townspeople, and so on.

According to the systems viewpoint, an organization is like a set of interconnected gears. Effective managers understand how changing one gear will affect the others.
Natali _ Mis/Shutterstock

Closed and Open Systems
A **closed system** has little interaction with its environment; that is, it focuses exclusively on the organization's inner workings. The classical management viewpoint often considered an organization a closed system. So does the quantitative viewpoint, which simplifies organizations for purposes of analysis. However, any organization that ignores information from the environment opens itself up to possibly spectacular failures. Peloton is an example of the potentially devastating consequences associated with a closed system view of management.

Peloton Example: Interactive fitness equipment provider, Peloton, grew exponentially during the COVID-19 pandemic (valued at $52 billion in early 2021) as consumers clamored for equipment to work out from home, but it struggled to keep up with consumer demand. Peloton co-founder and CEO, John Foley, led the organization to acquire several companies in 2021 to ramp up its production capacity and capabilities. The CEO failed, however, to anticipate consumer demand for Peloton's products plunging once businesses reopened post-pandemic. Foley stepped down from his executive role at the company in 2022 amidst investor pressure as the company's market value shrunk to $2.85 billion.[32]

An **open system** continually interacts with its environment. Today nearly all organizations are, at least to some degree, open systems rather than closed. Open systems have the potential of producing synergy. **Synergy** (pronounced "sin-ur-jee") is the idea that two or more forces combined create an effect that is greater than the sum of their individual effects, as when a guitarist, drummer, and bassist combine to play a better version of a song than any of them would playing alone. Or a copywriter, art director, and photographer combine to create a magazine ad, each representing various influences from the environment.

Complexity Theory: The Ultimate Open System The systems viewpoint has led to the development of **complexity theory**, the study of how order and pattern arise from very complicated, apparently chaotic systems. Complexity theory recognizes that all complex systems are networks of many interdependent parts that interact with each other according to certain simple rules. Used in strategic management and organizational studies, the discipline seeks to understand how organizations, considered as relatively simple and partly connected structures, adapt to their environments.

Why the Systems Viewpoint—Particularly the Concept of Open Systems—Is Important: History is full of accounts of products that failed (such as Google Glass, Google's attempt in 2012 to combine eyeglasses and smartphone capabilities) because they were developed in closed systems and didn't have sufficient feedback. Open systems stress gathering and analyzing multiple waves of information from both inside and outside the organization, resulting in a continuous learning process to try to correct old mistakes and avoid new ones. ●

2.6 Contingency Viewpoint

THE BIG PICTURE
The *contingency viewpoint* emphasizes that a manager's approach should vary according to the individual and environmental situation.

The classical viewpoints advanced by Taylor, Spaulding, and Fayol assumed that their approaches had universal applications—that they were "the one best way" to manage organizations. The contingency viewpoint began to develop when managers discovered that under some circumstances better results could be achieved by breaking the one-best-way rule. The **contingency viewpoint** emphasizes that a manager's approach should vary according to—that is, be contingent on—the individual and the environmental situation. The contingency viewpoint thus takes both people and processes into account to determine the best managerial approach (see Figure 2.1).

Consider how you approach your studies. Do you study the same way for every course you take in college? Probably not. Let's say you are taking both anatomy and finance classes this semester. The anatomy course may require you to memorize the different parts of the body and their functions to pass the exam. In contrast, the technique of memorizing may not be as effective in your finance class. Finance requires you to perform calculations so you can master concepts such as the time value of money. In this case, however, you are more likely to obtain a better grade by doing sample problems. The point is that you are more likely to get higher grades in different classes by using methods of study that match the content being taught.

Why the Contingency Viewpoint Is Important: The contingency viewpoint would seem to be the most practical of the viewpoints discussed so far because it addresses problems on a case-by-case basis and provides solutions specific to a certain situation or dilemma. The career readiness competency of critical thinking/problem solving is essential when applying the contingency viewpoint.

LO 2-6

Explain why there is no one best way to manage in all situations.

> **EXAMPLE**
>
> **The Contingency Viewpoint: Manufacturers Get Creative to Pitch Jobs to the Next Generation**
>
> Parents around the country are increasingly worried about paying for their children to attend college, and college graduates are worried about getting that first real job that pays well, offers flexibility, and affords them lucrative opportunities for advancement. U.S. manufacturers are worried about how they're going to fill approximately 846,000 open positions in a very competitive labor market, nearly double the amount of job openings in the manufacturing sector from 2019.[33] These vacant jobs are increasingly problematic, according to a 2022 Deloitte survey, because 45% of surveyed manufacturing executives turned down business opportunities due to not having enough employees.[34]
>
> Historically, manufacturing jobs were attractive, stable positions. Manufacturing companies presented opportunities for young talent to progress from factory-line positions to top management. This is not the case anymore, possibly because manufacturing jobs do not seem to possess the "cool factor" touted by technology giants Amazon, Google, or Facebook in their job openings and benefits packages. In fact, a study found that 36% of younger workers expressed little or no interest in a manufacturing career.[35] Faced with this situation, manufacturing firms are having to take a contingency approach toward recruiting.
>
> Some U.S. manufacturers are taking several creative steps to recruit workers for critical and well-paid jobs. They are:[36]
>
> 1. Using social media platforms (such as Instagram, TikTok, and Twitter) and digital job boards (like LinkedIn) to reach younger generations.
> 2. Changing the industry's image. A common misconception among the Millennial and Gen Z workforce about modern manufacturing is that manufacturing work is equated with boring and strenuous manual labor. Organizations are highlighting how many manufacturing roles involve specialized training and interaction with cutting-edge technologies, an image that is much more attractive to digital natives.
> 3. Engaging with high schools and colleges. A manufacturer in Pennsylvania is raising high schoolers' and collegiate students' awareness about modern manufacturing through school visits and sponsoring robotics competitions.
>
> **YOUR CALL**
>
> What other contingency approaches can you suggest to help solve manufacturers' recruiting problem?

2.7 Contemporary Approaches: The Learning Organization, High-Performance Work Practices, and Shared Value and Sustainable Development

THE BIG PICTURE

Three contemporary approaches include learning organizations, high-performance work practices, and shared value and sustainable development. Learning organizations actively create, acquire, and transfer knowledge within themselves and are able to modify their behavior to reflect new knowledge. High-performance work practices require investment in and effective implementation of human resource systems. Shared value and sustainable development look beyond short-term profits and focus on the environmental and social costs of doing business.

LO 2-7

Define how managers foster a learning organization, high-performance work practices, and shared value and sustainable development.

Management theory continues to evolve to tackle the challenges facing companies today. Three contemporary approaches to management include *learning organizations, high-performance work practices,* and *shared value and sustainable development.* Figure 2.1 shows all three approaches consider the organization's impact on people and processes.

The Learning Organization: Sharing Knowledge and Modifying Behavior

Ultimately, the lesson we need to take from the historical management viewpoints we have described is this: Keep on learning. A key challenge for managers is to establish a culture of shared knowledge and values that will enhance their employees' ability to learn—to build so-called learning organizations. An additional advantage for tomorrow's managers is that Millennials and Gen Z actively *expect* to have learning opportunities at work.[37]

Learning organizations, says Massachusetts Institute of Technology professor Peter Senge, who coined the term, are places "where people continually expand their capacity to create the results they truly desire, where new and expansive patterns of thinking are nurtured, where collective aspiration is set free, and where people are continually learning how to learn together."[38]

More formally, a **learning organization** is an organization that actively creates, acquires, and transfers knowledge within itself and is able to modify its behavior to reflect new knowledge. Managers build learning organizations by empowering teams to make decisions and learn from their experiences and structuring teams to communicate and collaborate frequently with peers and customers.[39] Another helpful strategy for managers to build a learning organization is to develop a learning culture within the organization that encourages people to ask questions without negative consequences (such as being made to feel ignorant), consider how different perspectives can lead to new and better ideas, and engage in spirited discovery by experimenting with new ideas and trying new approaches.[40] Microsoft is a good illustration.

Microsoft Example: Microsoft is an exemplar of a learning organization as recognized by its #8 spot on *Fast Company*'s "2022 World's Most Innovative Companies." The company analyzed data from Microsoft 365, LinkedIn, brain research from the company's Human Factors Lab, and survey data from 30,000 people across 31 countries to bring the human element into work productivity, especially for hybrid and virtual work. For example, Microsoft developed a calendar tool that encourages breaks between meetings, a "together mode" on Microsoft teams that joins participants' videos in a virtual conference room, and a "virtual commute" option to help workers be more intentional about creating a buffer between work and home and mentally prepare for or decompress from the work day.[41]

A learning organization is like a lightbulb. It must be turned on before it creates value. How do you think organizations promote the value of continuous learning?
Photodisc/Getty Images

Microsoft is continuously learning to build a better virtual experience for workers like the "Together Mode" feature in Microsoft Teams, an attempt to make virtual meetings feel like everyone is in the same room.
Microsoft Corporation

Learning organizations are agile. They quickly adapt to market changes and emerging opportunities. Agile outcomes include innovation, faster decision making, operational efficiency, and customer satisfaction.[42] We'll examine organizational change and innovation in Chapter 10.

Have you ever worked for a learning organization? Try the following self-assessment in Connect, if your instructor has assigned it to you, to evaluate whether an organization you now work for or formerly worked for could be considered a serious learning organization. The survey items provide a good indication of what it takes to become a learning organization.

SELF-ASSESSMENT 2.2

Are You Working for a Learning Organization?

This self-assessment provides a measure of the extent to which an organization of your choice is a learning organization. Please complete Self-Assessment 2.2 if your instructor has assigned it in Connect.

High-Performance Work Practices

High-performance work practices are an extension of the behavioral and systems viewpoints. It grew from research by Jeff Pfeffer, a professor at Stanford, and Jim Collins, a former Stanford professor who became a consultant. Pfeffer and Collins suggested employees are an organization's most important asset, and management should focus on attracting, developing, and motivating the best talent.[43] Management's central job, according to this viewpoint, is to create human resource (HR) practices that foster employee development and overall well-being.[44] **High-performance work practices (HPWPs)** build employees' knowledge, skills, and abilities (KSAs), improve their motivation, and afford them opportunities to make important work-related decisions and take responsibility for work outcomes. These work practices are called "high performance" because they improve an organization's performance by reducing turnover and absenteeism and increasing employee satisfaction, commitment, and extra-role behavior.[45]

There is one conclusion about this contemporary viewpoint that is important to remember. It's not enough to have one type of HPWP. The best outcomes are obtained when managers integrate bundles of work practices into one overall organizational HR system. We will discuss high-performance work systems in depth in Chapter 9.

Let's consider how three organizations have incorporated high-performance work practices into their HR systems.

EXAMPLE — Three Examples of High-Performance Work Practices

High-performance work practices are utilized across many different industries. Here are three examples:[46]

Enterprise Rent-A-Car
As the largest car rental company in the United States, Enterprise understands the importance of recruiting top talent. The company has successfully used selective hiring to recruit "people people," whom they categorize as those with excellent interpersonal skills. Specifically, Enterprise targets college students who are more prone to understanding the importance of working as a team. The company was awarded "2022 Top Entry-Level Employer" by CollegeGrad.com.

Whole Foods
The Amazon-owned supermarket chain known for its high-quality products also provides high-quality rewards for its employees. The company rewards employees with bonuses based on performance, including coming in under budget on labor costs. Whole Foods keeps its Team Members motivated by offering programs that promote and maintain their physical, mental, and financial well-being such as total health immersion getaways, in-person counseling sessions, and competitive compensation.

Ritz-Carlton Hotels
The luxury hotel chain, with 97 hotels in 30 countries, is known for the high quality of its customer service. Management's approach to customer service includes providing employees with autonomy in decision making. For example, Ritz-Carlton lists gold standards on its website, which include employees being empowered to "create unique, memorable and personal experiences for our guests."[47] How empowered are Ritz employees? They have discretion to spend up to $2,000 if they believe it would benefit the customer and uphold the hotel's mission.

Shared Value and Sustainable Development: Going beyond Profits

Fashion Week 2022 in New York City wasn't just about glitz and glamour. Iconic brands, such as Dior, Louis Vuitton, and Burberry, were focusing on sustainability campaigns. Whether creating new clothes from old fabric or implementing responsible land management for the production of cotton, wool, and hemp, there is a growing consensus in the fashion industry that doing right by the planet makes good business sense.[48] And this industry isn't alone.

Shared value and sustainable development look beyond short-term profits and focus on the environmental and social costs of doing business. The term *sustainable*, according to scientists Dennis and Donella Meadows, describes a "state of global equilibrium" in which the world would not have a sudden and uncontrolled collapse and would be able to satisfy the basic requirements of its people.[49] As we discussed in Chapter 1, sustainable development focuses on meeting the needs of the present without compromising the ability of future generations to meet their own needs.[50]

Green innovations. Some managers believe sustainable practices can be costly when in fact they can make companies more competitive. Can you think of some sustainable practices that can be profitable for both organizations and the Earth?
AnjuChoudhary/Shutterstock

Harvard Professor Michael Porter argued in 1995 that sustainability "can trigger innovations that lower the total cost of a product or improve its value . . . making companies more competitive, not less."[51] Thus, shared value and sustainable development is where business and sustainability intersect. Organizations that focus on creating value not only for their shareholders but also for a broader set of stakeholders position themselves and future members of society to reap rewards. In the decades that followed Porter's statement, more and more organizations viewed sustainability as a source of competitive advantage. A global survey of 3,000 CEOs encompassing 40 countries and 28 industries revealed 51% listed sustainability as the top business challenge in 2022 and 80% expected corporate sustainability investments to bolster business results in the next five years.[52]

Companies have now developed management positions such as chief sustainability officer, VP of corporate responsibility, and environmental program manager to be accountable for their company's sustainability strategy, policies, and initiatives. Shared value and sustainable development is prevalent in a range of industries, as evidenced by companies who have hired or promoted staff to support their sustainability goals. These include Disney, Mastercard, Zendesk, and Kroger.[53]

We'll discuss shared value and sustainable development in depth in Learning Module 1.

2.8 Career Corner: Managing Your Career Readiness

Figure 2.2 shows the model of career readiness we discussed in Chapter 1. What does a chapter on management history have to do with your career readiness? How about its application to the Knowledge competency of *understanding the business?* This competency was defined in Table 1.3 as the extent to which you understand a company's business and strategies and the needs of its stakeholders. It comes into play whenever you interview for a job. Listen to what the executives in this chapter's Executive Interview Series video say about why demonstrating knowledge about your prospective employer's business will set you apart from 90% of the other applicants.

LO 2-8

Describe how to develop the career readiness competency of understanding the business.

FIGURE 2.2

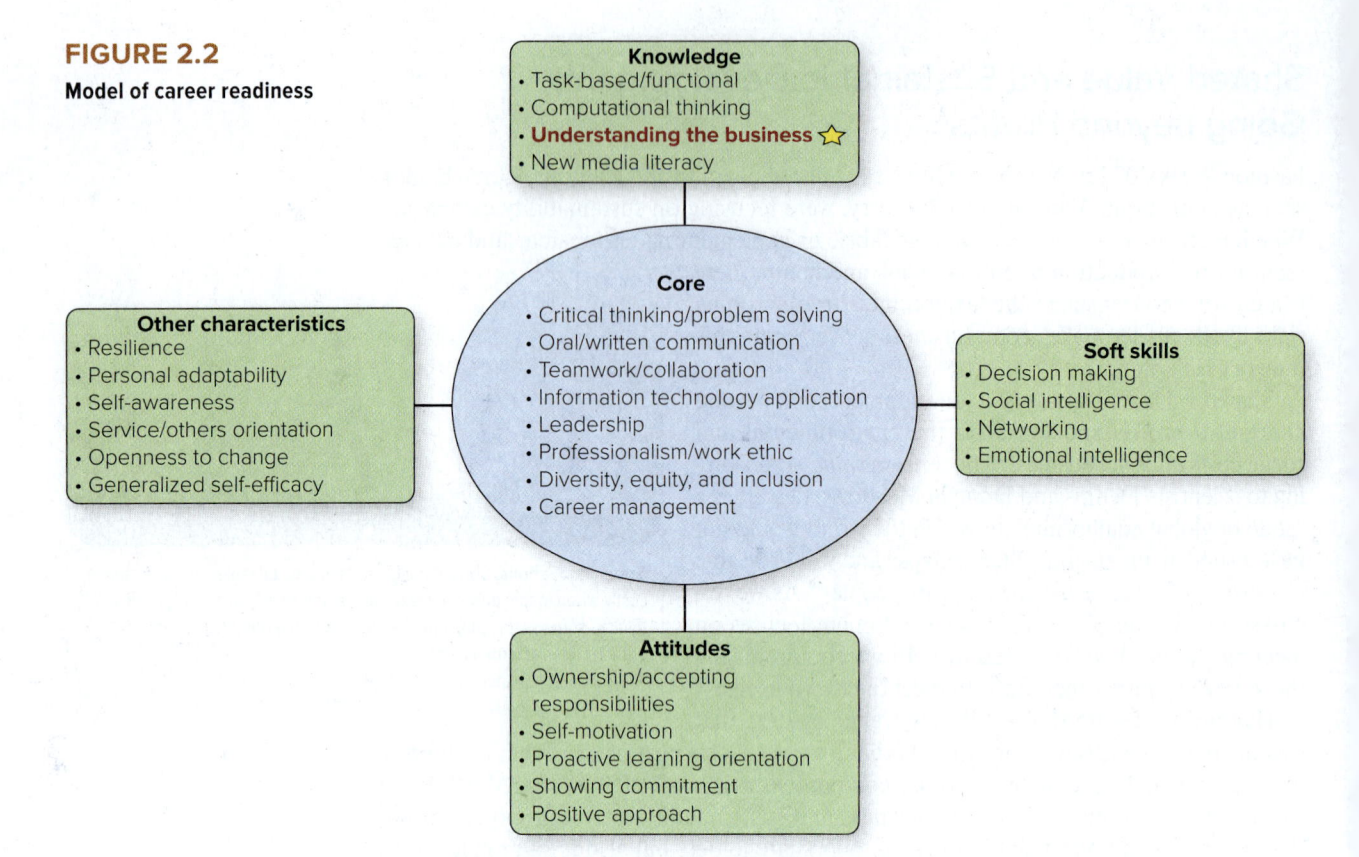

Model of career readiness

Knowledge
- Task-based/functional
- Computational thinking
- **Understanding the business** ⭐
- New media literacy

Core
- Critical thinking/problem solving
- Oral/written communication
- Teamwork/collaboration
- Information technology application
- Leadership
- Professionalism/work ethic
- Diversity, equity, and inclusion
- Career management

Other characteristics
- Resilience
- Personal adaptability
- Self-awareness
- Service/others orientation
- Openness to change
- Generalized self-efficacy

Soft skills
- Decision making
- Social intelligence
- Networking
- Emotional intelligence

Attitudes
- Ownership/accepting responsibilities
- Self-motivation
- Proactive learning orientation
- Showing commitment
- Positive approach

McGraw Hill Connect

Visit your instructor's Connect course and access your eBook to view this video.

Kristine Remedios
Global Head of Inclusion, Diversity, and Equity, KPMG

Executive Interview Series:
Understanding the Business

Recruiters expect you to do some research, just as you would for a class assignment. They want you to act like Sherlock Holmes and do some snooping. That's good for both you and a potential employer because it helps identify the likely level of fit between the two of you. Good fit, in turn, is associated with more positive work attitudes and task performance, lower intentions to quit, and less job-related stress.[54] Moreover, doing your homework on a company makes you a more attractive job candidate. It shows interest on your part, and recruiters are impressed by the fact that you took the time to learn about the business.[55] It also prepares you to ask smart questions, a behavior recruiters want to see. Remember, sometimes it's the small things like this that help land a job.

So, what does it take to demonstrate that you understand a business? We recommend that you learn the following eight things about a company before showing up at a job interview:[56]

1. **The company's mission and vision statements.** These statements tell you why the company exists and what it wants to become or achieve over time. The question to answer is whether you support these pursuits and would like to be part of the journey. If you do, you will be a better fit for the company. This is important because employees are more likely to be productive and stay at a company when they fit in. For example, if you like outdoor activities, you will most likely be a better fit at Recreational Equipment, Inc. (REI), which sells sporting goods, camping gear, and outdoor clothing, than at Whole Foods. You can find this information on the company's website.

2. **The company's core values and culture.** The values an organization endorses represent the foundation of its culture. You can find clues about this by studying a company's website. Try to find a list of company values. What do these values tell you about the company? Next, look for statements that inform you about how the company treats its employees. For example, does

the company support empowerment and employee development? Look at any photos posted online and consider what they tell you. If you see pictures only of products and not of people, for instance, it suggests the company really cares about products. What type of goals is the company pursuing? Does the company care about the environment, quality, or customers' opinions?

3. **The history of the company.** When was the company founded? What were the values and background of the founder(s)? Try to find out how the company evolved, grew, or changed over the years.

4. **Key organizational players.** It's important to demonstrate this knowledge during a job interview. Who holds important positions in the company? What are their backgrounds? You can find this out by reading the employer's "About" page and top employees' bios. You might check them out on LinkedIn or read what they say on Twitter.

5. **Who are you interviewing with?** Aside from key organizational players, you should also find out the names and titles of the people you're likely to interview with, particularly those higher up the chain of command. Knowing the interviewers' titles and responsibilities will help you better answer their questions in a way that shows your appreciation for their roles.

6. **The company's products, services, and clients.** What are people saying about the company's products and services? You can explore this by locating reviews or comments about the company's products and services. It would also be useful to try the company's products and services. This would enable you to speak directly from experience. You should also let the interviewer know that you've done your research by sharing three concrete ideas about how you can help the company with its products and services.

7. **Current events and accomplishments.** Look for current news stories about the company and examine its website for a list of accomplishments. Note what this information reveals about the company and decide whether it matches what you learned about the company's mission, vision, stated values, and organizational culture. Inconsistencies are a red flag.

8. **Comments from current or previous employees.** Talk to anyone you know at the company. Ask their opinion about working there and how they feel about management and corporate policies. Search websites like Glassdoor to find inside information such as salary ranges and company reviews.

These activities will increase your career readiness and chances of getting a desired job. They also demonstrate that you care about or even have passion about working at the company. This will distinguish you from others who did not do their research. Remember, it is important to stand out from other applicants when looking for a job. More important, understanding the business will help you determine if you are a good fit for an employer. Go get 'em! •

You must do research to understand a business. This takes time and attention. At what point in the interview process should you investigate a potential employer?
Kraska/Shutterstock

Key Terms Used in This Chapter

administrative management 44
behavioral science approach 47
behavioral viewpoint 45
classical viewpoint 42
closed system 50
complexity theory 51
contingency viewpoint 51
evidence-based management 49
Hawthorne effect 46
high-performance work practices (HPWPs) 54
human relations movement 46
learning organization 53
open system 50
operations management 48
quantitative management 48
scientific management 43
subsystems 50
supply chain 48
synergy 50
system 50
systems viewpoint 50

Key Points

2.1 Evolving Viewpoints: How We Got to Today's Management Outlook

- Principal management viewpoints include classical, behavioral, and quantitative. More recent viewpoints include systems, contingency, and contemporary.
- Six practical reasons for studying theoretical perspectives are that they provide (1) insight into past and present circumstances, (2) a guide to action, (3) sources of new ideas, (4) clues to the meaning of your managers' decisions, (5) clues to the meaning of outside events, and (6) a path to achieve positive results.

2.2 Classical Viewpoint: Scientific and Administrative Management

- The first viewpoint is the classical viewpoint, which emphasized finding ways to manage work more efficiently. It had two branches, scientific management and administrative management.
- Scientific management emphasized the scientific study of work methods to improve productivity by individual workers. It was pioneered by Frederick W. Taylor, who offered four principles of science that could be applied to management, and by Frank and Lillian Gilbreth, who refined motion studies that broke down job tasks into physical motions.
- Administrative management was concerned with managing the total organization. Among its pioneers were Charles Clinton Spaulding, the founder of African American management; Henri Fayol, who identified the major functions of management (planning, organizing, leading, controlling); and Max Weber, who identified positive bureaucratic features in a well-performing organization.

2.3 Behavioral Viewpoint: Behaviorism, Human Relations, and Behavioral Science

- The second viewpoint is the behavioral viewpoint, which emphasized the importance of understanding human behavior and of motivating employees toward achievement. It developed over three phases: (1) early behaviorism, (2) the human relations movement, and (3) the behavioral science approach.
- Early behaviorism had two pioneers: (1) Mary Parker Follett thought organizations should be democratic, with employees and managers working together; (2) Elton Mayo hypothesized a so-called Hawthorne effect, suggesting that employees worked harder if they received added attention from managers.
- The human relations movement suggested that better relationships between managers and employees could increase worker productivity. Among its pioneers were Abraham Maslow, who proposed a hierarchy of human needs, and Douglas McGregor, who proposed Theory X (managers have pessimistic views of workers) and Theory Y (managers have positive views of workers).
- The behavioral science approach relies on scientific research for developing theories about human behavior that can be used to provide practical tools for managers.

2.4 Quantitative Viewpoints: Operations Management and Evidence-Based Management

- The third viewpoint is the quantitative viewpoint, which emphasized the application of quantitative techniques to management.
- Two approaches are (1) operations management, which focuses on managing the production and delivery of an organization's products or services more effectively, and (2) evidence-based management, which means translating principles based on best evidence into organizational practice, bringing rationality to the decision-making process.

2.5 Systems Viewpoint

- The systems viewpoint regards the organization as a system of interrelated parts or collection of subsystems that operate together to achieve a common purpose.

- A system can be closed, having little interaction with the environment, or open, continually interacting with it.

2.6 Contingency Viewpoint

- The contingency viewpoint emphasizes that a manager's approach should vary according to the individual and the environmental situation.

2.7 Contemporary Approaches: The Learning Organization, High-Performance Work Practices, and Shared Value and Sustainable Development

- A learning organization is one that actively creates, acquires, and transfers knowledge within itself and is able to modify its behavior to reflect new knowledge.
- High-performance work practices improve an organization's ability to effectively attract, select, hire, develop, and retain high-performing personnel.
- Shared value and sustainable development looks beyond short-term profits and focuses on the environmental and social costs of doing business.

2.8 Career Corner: Managing Your Career Readiness

- You can increase the competency of understanding the business by engaging in eight activities: (1) learn the company's mission and vision; (2) identify the company's core values and culture; (3) learn the history of the company; (4) identify the key organizational players; (5) know whom you are talking to; (6) learn about the company's products, services, and clients; (7) study current events and accomplishments about the company; and (8) talk to current or former employees.

Boeing Continuing Case

Learn more about Boeing's history and management perspectives, starting from the beginning to the company's current challenges in developing the Boeing 737 MAX.

Assess your ability to apply concepts discussed in Chapters 1 and 2 to the case by going to Connect.

PART 2 • THE ENVIRONMENT OF MANAGEMENT

3. The Manager's Changing Work Environment and Ethical Responsibilities

Doing the Right Thing

After reading this chapter, you should be able to:

LO 3-1 Describe the triple bottom line of people, planet, and profit and its importance to younger workers.

LO 3-2 Identify important stakeholders inside the organization.

LO 3-3 Identify important stakeholders outside the organization.

LO 3-4 Explain the importance of ethics and values in effective management.

LO 3-5 Describe the concept of social responsibility and its role in today's organizations.

LO 3-6 Discuss the role of corporate governance in building ethical and socially responsible organizations.

LO 3-7 Describe how to develop the career readiness competency of professionalism/work ethic.

FORECAST   What's Ahead in This Chapter

The triple bottom line of people, planet, and profit represents a new standard of success for businesses. This helps define the new world in which managers must operate and their responsibilities, including the community of stakeholders, both internal and external, to which they are accountable. The chapter also considers a manager's ethical and social responsibilities, as well as the importance of corporate governance. We conclude with a Career Corner that focuses on how you can develop the career readiness competency of professionalism/work ethic.

Being Courageous at Work

More than 50% of employees report witnessing unethical behavior at their jobs.[1] This means that workplace ethics violations are common, and it's likely you will find yourself in an unethical work environment at some point. Sadly, although most employees intend to report ethics violations, only about 40% of workers who witness unethical workplace behavior actually find the courage to do so.[2]

Behaving with courage means taking intentional and deliberate action in the name of a worthy cause and enduring in this act despite the risk of serious personal consequences such as retaliation, disapproval, or rejection.[3] Here's how you can develop your capacity to behave courageously at work.

1. Practice in a Low-Risk Setting

Executive coach Peter Bregman says the best way to get better at something scary is to practice it in a low-risk environment. Want to be a better negotiator? Try negotiating with your roommate the next time you both want to pick the music station. Interested in being more assertive when a co-worker repeatedly interrupts you during meetings? Think about how you'd want to respond, then engage a close friend in a debate over something mundane such as which Starbucks drink is best. Chances are your friend will interrupt you at some point, giving you the opportunity to practice your skill.

2. Plan for an Endurance Event

Imagine that you are about to head out into the snow on a freezing day. You'll likely dress in multiple layers of warm clothing to shield your body from the cold, right? Researchers Debra Comer and Leslie Sekerka suggest that you prepare yourself to behave courageously much like you prepare yourself for a day in the snow.

Part of being courageous is the willingness to *endure* hardship.[4] Courage requires a series of actions, and you should be prepared for a lengthy and uncomfortable journey that may not go completely your way. You should also plan to face resistance from others. Anticipating a challenging process will "insulate" you from difficulties that may otherwise cause you to abandon your decision to behave courageously, just like your thermal shirt, down jacket, and warm gloves help you stay out in the snow for a longer period of time.[5]

3. Rely on Self-Regulation after the Act of Courage

If anticipating a difficult journey works like a set of warm and cozy winter layers, then practicing self-regulation *after* a courageous act is akin to a steamy mug of hot cocoa that warms you from the inside out and gives you the strength to go back out in the snow after a rest. In other words, self-regulation techniques fortify you each time you grow weary, reinforcing your energy to sustain your convictions in the face of resistance. Comer and Sekerka recommend three self-regulation practices:

- *Self-Affirmation*—One way to keep going when others are unsupportive is to think about past accomplishments. Maybe you finally got through your backlog of class readings or assignments. Or perhaps you ranked first in a competition earlier in life such as a spelling bee, swim meet, or debate. Remembering successes generates positive emotions that help you to continue behaving courageously.
- *Self-Compassion*—Another way to fortify yourself is to focus on what you can learn from the experience rather than on the resistance. Avoid the temptation to abandon your mission. Instead, be kind to yourself the way you would be to a close friend going through the same thing. Remind yourself that you did the "right" thing and that you will adjust to any setbacks and forge ahead on a courageous path.
- *Social Support*—Share your experience with people who support you when you find it difficult to sustain your campaign. Their willingness to listen and provide advice and encouragement will validate your belief that you are doing the right thing and supply you with the sustenance you need to stay strong.

For Discussion Have you ever wanted to behave courageously but decided to stay silent? What do you think prevented you from acting with courage? What are one or two ways that you can practice courage in a low-risk environment? What can you do to ensure that you will both insulate and fortify yourself when you are confronted with a situation that requires you to behave with courage?

3.1 The Goals of Business: More Than Making Money

THE BIG PICTURE

Many businesses, small and large, are beginning to subscribe to a new standard of success—the triple bottom line, representing people, planet, and profit. This outlook has found favor with many younger workers who are more concerned with finding meaning than material success.

LO 3-1

Describe the triple bottom line of people, planet, and profit and its importance to younger workers.

This chapter focuses on what it means to do the "right" thing as a manager and as an organization. You'll learn that doing the right thing involves considering all the stakeholders that are impacted by an organization's actions. You'll also learn about the ethical and social responsibilities that govern many managerial decisions. As you read, remember that doing what's right isn't always easy, and many of the decisions you make as a manager will be more challenging than you anticipate. In fact, there won't be an obvious "right" answer to a great deal of the problems you're asked to resolve. How, then, will you know what it means to do the right thing in your role as a manager?

Milton Friedman, one of the most influential economists of the 20th century, believed businesses existed to make profits for shareholders. In his view, doing the right thing as a manager meant taking the course of action that maximized shareholder wealth and complied with the law. But views about what constitutes the right thing for organizations are changing, as you'll discover in this section and in the remainder of the chapter.

The Triple Bottom Line: People, Planet, and Profit

"If you're a company that isn't creating value for society, why do you exist?" asked former Siemens USA CEO Barbara Humpton on a *Washington Post Live* podcast.[6] In Humpton's view, making money should be only one goal of business, and the right decisions should account for more than just profit. Humpton, and many other influential leaders like her, believe organizations and managers have broad responsibilities beyond their fiscal duties to shareholders. This sentiment reflects the reality that organizations do not exist in a vacuum. Rather, businesses operate within a broad environment that they affect and that also affects them, and gauging performance requires considering your impacts on various elements of this environment.

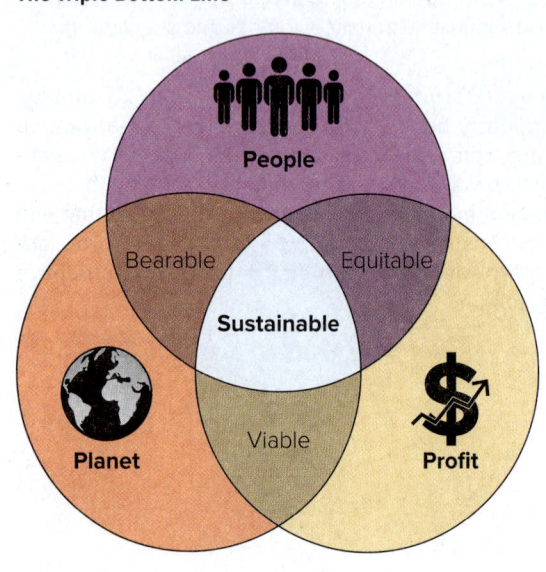

The **triple bottom line (TBL)**—representing people, planet, and profit (the 3 Ps)—measures an organization's social, environmental, and financial performance. In this view of corporate performance, an organization is accountable to its employees and to the wider community (people); is committed to sustainable development (planet); and includes the costs of pollution, worker displacement, and other factors in its financial calculations (profit).[7]

Proponents of the TBL argue that organizations can only achieve sustainable development (defined in Chapter 1 as meeting present needs while ensuring that future generations will be able to meet their needs) if they define success according to all three of these elements.

FIGURE 3.1
The Triple Bottom Line

Younger Workers' Search for Meaning

Gen Zers (people born after 1997)[8] make up more than 25% of the U.S. workforce.[9] Recent data suggests these younger workers expect their organizations to do the right thing and to consider the TBL when measuring corporate performance. In a recent survey, over 75% of Gen Z respondents indicated that they need alignment between their employers' values and their own, and many are not interested in jobs with companies that don't care about sustainable development and ethics.[10] Gen Z workers are strongly driven by a desire for purpose, fulfillment, and meaning in their jobs. A study of 18- to 25-year-old workers across six different countries revealed that almost 90% of respondents ranked having a positive impact on the environment and society near the top of their priority lists.[11]

3.2 The Community of Stakeholders Inside the Organization

THE BIG PICTURE

Managers operate in two organizational environments—internal and external—both made up of stakeholders, the people whose interests are affected by the organization. The first, or internal, environment consists of employees, owners, and the board of directors.

Doing the right thing requires managers to consider all the parties that affect—and may be affected by—the organization's actions. These parties are known as **stakeholders**—the people whose interests are affected by an organization's activities. The stakeholders inside and outside the organization make up the organization's environment.

LO 3-2
Identify important stakeholders inside the organization.

Internal and External Stakeholders

Figure 3.2 illustrates that managers operate in two organizational environments, both made up of various stakeholders. We separate these stakeholders into two buckets that represent the organization's internal and external environments. Let's consider each.

Internal Environment. In the internal environment are the stakeholders involved with the organization's internal activities on a regular basis. These **internal stakeholders** consist of employees, owners, and the board of directors, if any.

External Environment. An organization's **external stakeholders** consist of all the parties outside the organization that have a stake in its decisions. The external environment comprises two sub-environments:

1. The **task environment** consists of 10 groups that interact with the organization on a regular basis.
2. The **general environment**, or **macroenvironment**, is the set of broad, uncontrollable forces in the external environment that impact the organization.

This section focuses on internal stakeholders, and we discuss external stakeholders in Section 3.3.

Internal Stakeholders

Managers need to know what matters to their organizations' internal stakeholders. These parties—the employees, owners, and board of directors—have both an important

FIGURE 3.2

The organization's environment
The two main groups are internal and external stakeholders.

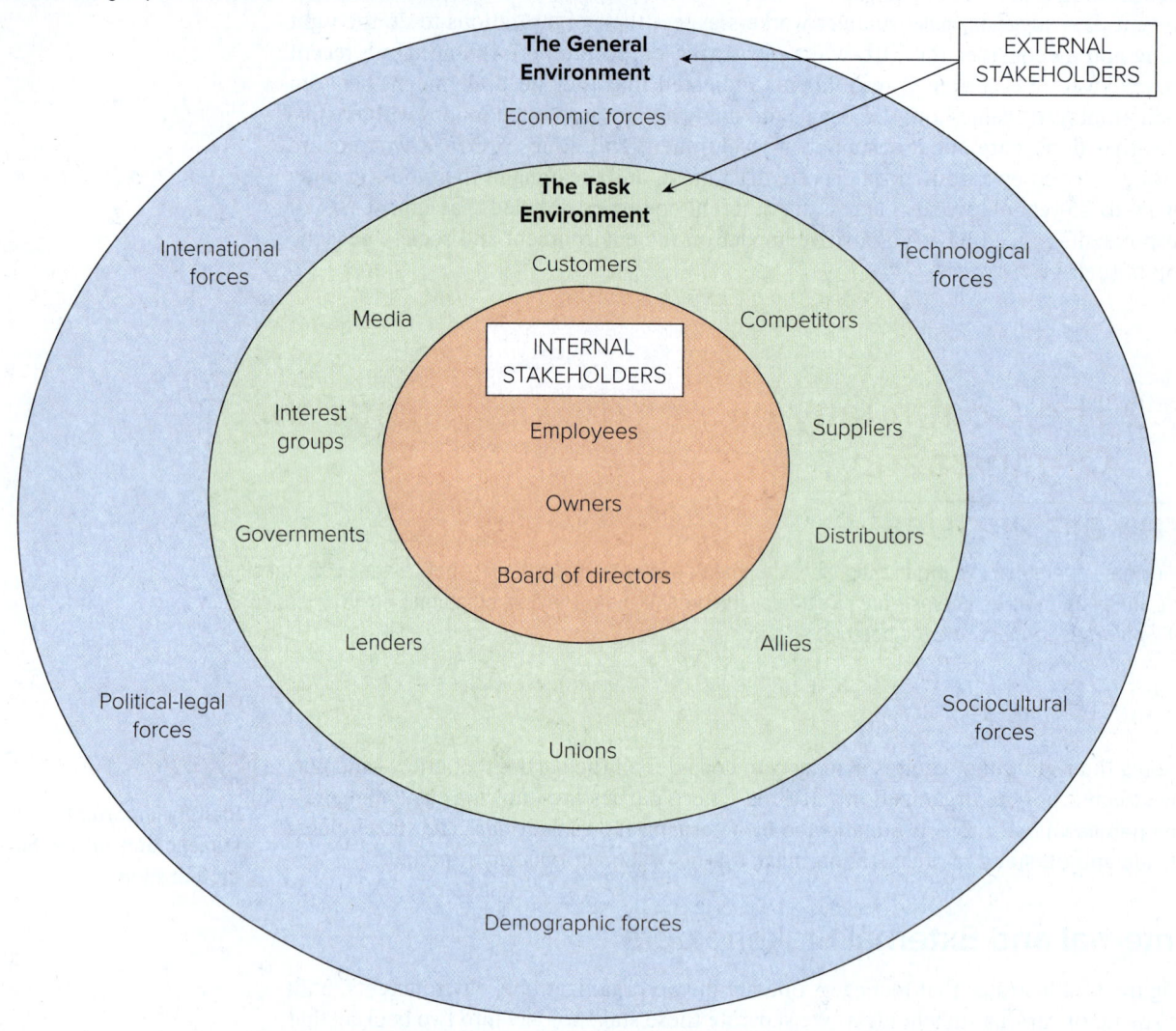

The General Environment ← EXTERNAL STAKEHOLDERS
- Economic forces
- International forces
- Technological forces
- Political-legal forces
- Sociocultural forces
- Demographic forces

The Task Environment
- Customers
- Media
- Competitors
- Interest groups
- Suppliers
- Governments
- Distributors
- Lenders
- Allies
- Unions

INTERNAL STAKEHOLDERS
- Employees
- Owners
- Board of directors

Source: Adapted from Diverse Teams at Work by Lee Gardenswartz. Published by the Society for Human Resource Management.

stake in how the organization performs and the power to shape its future.[12] Let's consider each category of internal stakeholders in turn.

Employees As a manager, could you do your job well if you were constantly in conflict with your employees? Labor history, of course, is full of accounts of just this. But such conflict may lower the company's performance, thereby hurting everyone's stake. In many modern organizations, employees—a.k.a. "the talent"—are seen as the most important resource.

"We are in a people business—a business that relies upon the talent and passion of our team to deliver incredible experiences to our guests," said Hilton president and CEO Christopher Nassetta. "We do this through our relentless focus on creating an exceptional workplace culture for all."[13] Hilton was ranked #2 on *Fortune*'s 2023 list of "100 Best Companies to Work For."[14] The hotel chain treats its employees exceptionally well, as evidenced by a recent survey that found that 86% of Hilton's employees considered it a "great place to work." Further, 87% of Hilton employees indicated that their jobs have "special meaning," and 82% believed that managers involved employees in decisions that would affect them.[15]

Owners The **owners** of an organization consist of all those who can claim it as their legal property, such as Walmart's stockholders. There are five principal types of owners.

- **Sole proprietors:** In the for-profit world, if you're running a one-person graphic design firm, the owner is just you—you're what is known as a sole proprietorship. There are currently more than 17 million sole proprietorships in the United States.[16]
- **Partners:** If you're in an Internet start-up with your sister-in-law and you're both owners—you're a partnership, and the two of you are considered partners.
- **Private investors:** If you're a member of a family running a car dealership and you're all owners—you're investors in a privately owned company.
- **Employee owners:** If you work for a company that is more than half owned by its employees (such as Tucson-based Barrio Brewing Company, producer of 15,000 barrels of craft beer per year), you're part of an employee stock ownership plan (ESOP).[17]
- **Stockholders:** If you've purchased stock in a company whose shares are listed for sale on the New York Stock Exchange, such as General Motors, you're one of thousands of owners—you're a stockholder.

In all these examples, of course, the stated goal of the owners is to make a profit.

Board of Directors Who hires the chief executive of a for-profit or nonprofit organization? The answer is the **board of directors**—the group of people elected to oversee the firm's activities and ensure that management acts in shareholders' best interests. In nonprofit organizations, such as universities or hospitals, the board may be called the *board of trustees* or *board of regents*. Board members are important in setting the organization's overall strategic goals and approving major decisions and top management salaries.

Some of the directors in a large corporation (inside directors) may be top executives of the firm. The rest (outside directors) are elected from outside. The board of directors at Meta (formerly Facebook), for instance, includes not only insiders CEO Mark Zuckerberg and former Chief Operating Officer (COO) Sheryl Sandberg, but also executives from outside firms including PayPal, Dropbox, and DoorDash.[18]

We consider directors further in Section 3.6, "Corporate Governance." •

3.3 The Community of Stakeholders Outside the Organization

THE BIG PICTURE
The external environment of stakeholders consists of the task environment and the general environment. The task environment consists of customers, competitors, suppliers, distributors, strategic allies, employee associations, local communities, financial institutions, government regulators, and special-interest groups. The general environment consists of economic, technological, sociocultural, demographic, political–legal, and international forces.

In Section 3.2 we described the environment inside the organization. Here let's consider the people or groups in the organization's external environment that impact and are impacted by its decisions. Recall that external stakeholders reside in one of two sub-environments:

- The task environment.
- The general environment.

LO 3-3

Identify important stakeholders outside the organization.

The Task Environment

The first sub-environment in an organization's external environment is the task environment, defined in Section 3.2 as consisting of 10 groups that interact with the organization on a regular basis. The task environment is made up of customers, competitors, suppliers, distributors, strategic allies, employee organizations, local communities, financial institutions, government regulators, and special-interest groups.

1. Customers The first law of business (even for nonprofits), as we've said, is *take care of the customer.* Customers are those who pay to use an organization's goods or services. Many customers are generally frustrated by poor customer relations at airlines, banks, and cable providers, in part because many of these companies have few competitors and thus don't have to worry about making decisions in line with their customers' needs, values, or expectations.

2. Competitors Competitors are the people or organizations that compete for customers or resources, such as talented employees or raw materials. Some of the most hated companies in America have little competition—but every organization has to be on the lookout for *possible* competitors, even if not yet in sight.

Competitors Example—Grocery Delivery: Rapid digital disruption and an increased demand for grocery delivery has stimulated intense competition between companies like Amazon, Walmart, and Target in recent years. AmazonFresh boasts a two-hour delivery window for all orders, but the company recently upset customers when it began charging delivery fees for all orders under $150.[19] Walmart is building more fulfillment centers throughout the country and using drones for delivery in at least seven states.[20] In early 2023, Target announced it was investing $100 million into efforts to better compete with Amazon and Walmart in the delivery space.[21]

3. Suppliers A supplier, or vendor, is a person or an organization that provides supplies—that is, raw materials, services, equipment, labor, or energy—to other organizations. Suppliers in turn have their own suppliers. Firms may turn to their suppliers for help with product improvements and innovations.[22] Consider how suppliers—an important stakeholder in an organization's external environment—can impact a firm's decisions and outcomes:

Suppliers Example—Auto Industry: Modern vehicles use semiconductor chips in a variety of functions, including emergency brakes, airbag deployment mechanisms, vehicle touchscreens, and backup cameras. In 2022, the world experienced a global shortage of semiconductors that sent big shockwaves through the auto manufacturing industry.[23] The shortage stemmed from the Russia–Ukraine war and the fact that Ukraine and Russia have historically supplied the world with around 70% of the neon and 40% of the palladium used in semiconductor chip manufacturing, respectively.[24] Auto manufacturers responded in various ways. Ford, for example, focused on putting its limited supply of available chips into its most profitable vehicles, including the F-150 Lightning fully electric pickup truck.[25] Audi, BMW, and Kia all announced that some features would not be available on certain vehicle models until further notice.

4. Distributors A distributor, sometimes called a middleperson, is a person or an organization that helps another organization sell its goods and services to customers. Magazine publishers, for instance, don't sell directly to newsstands; rather, they go through a distributor, or wholesaler. A venue may sell tickets for a concert directly, but distributors such as Ticketmaster, LiveNation, and StubHub also handle these transactions. Distributors can be quite important because in some industries (such as movie theaters and magazines), there is not a lot of competition, and the distributor has a lot of power over the ultimate price of the product. Millions of fans learned this the hard way when they tried to purchase tickets for Taylor Swift's Eras tour through Ticketmaster in 2022. Consider the following example of the complex interplay between companies and stakeholders in their external environments, including distributors:

> **Distributors Example—Is Direct-to-Consumer Losing Steam?:** The advent of e-commerce meant that many companies—including popular brands like Allbirds and Warby Parker—were able to remove distributors entirely and sell directly to consumers. However, forces in these companies' external environments have made their direct-to-consumer strategies more difficult. These include sharply increasing costs to advertise on social media and ship goods. For example, by some estimates, the cost to reach customers through Facebook advertisements has nearly tripled in recent years.[26]

5. Strategic Allies Companies frequently link up with other organizations (even competing ones) in order to realize strategic advantages.[27] The term **strategic allies describes the relationship between two organizations who join forces to achieve advantages neither can perform as well alone.** Strategic alliances allow firms to access new technologies, knowledge, capital, and markets, while sharing the costs and risks.[28]

> **Strategic Allies Example—Warner Music and Rothco:** A strategic alliance between Warner Music and Rothco means children in speech therapy now have access to specially curated playlists to make speech practice more engaging. The song lists, called "Saylists," provide the opportunity for repetition of sounds that are often difficult for children with speech challenges, including "s," "ch," and "k." Songs included in the Saylists include Ed Sheeran's "I Don't Care" and Dua Lipa's "Don't Start Now."[29]

6. Employee Organizations: Unions and Associations As a rule of thumb, labor unions (such as the United Auto Workers or the Teamsters Union) tend to represent hourly workers; professional associations (such as the National Education Association or The Newspaper Guild) tend to represent salaried workers. Nevertheless, during a labor dispute, salary-earning teachers in the American Federation of Teachers might well act in sympathy with the wage-earning custodians in the Service Employees International Union. In recent years, the percentage of the U.S. labor force represented by unions has steadily declined (from 35% in the 1950s to 10.1% in 2022).[30] In contrast, a much larger percentage of the workforce in the European Union is unionized, with a range of 60+% in Finland to a low of around 8% in Hungary and Lithuania.[31] We discuss labor unions in detail in Chapter 9.

7. Local Communities The role of local communities as stakeholders becomes evident not only when a big organization arrives in town, but also when it leaves, sending local government officials scrambling to find new industry to replace it. Schools and municipal governments rely on the organization for their tax base. Families and merchants may depend on its employee payroll for their livelihoods. In addition, everyone from the United Way to the Little League may rely on it for some financial support. Organizations realize significant benefits when they invest time and resources into understanding and meeting the needs of the local communities surrounding their various locations.[32]

If a community gives a company tax breaks in return for the promise of new jobs and the company fails to deliver, does the community have the right to institute **clawbacks—rescinding the tax breaks when firms don't deliver promised jobs?** Further, should companies be getting these tax breaks to begin with? These questions represent ethical dilemmas involving companies and their external stakeholders.

8. Financial Institutions Want to launch a small company? Banks, savings and loans, and credit unions may loan you the money to do so if you have a good credit history or can secure the loan with property such as a house. You might also receive help from venture capitalists. **Venture capital** is money provided by investors to start-up firms and small businesses with high risk but perceived long-term growth potential, in return for an ownership stake. Established companies also often need loans to tide them over when revenues are down or to finance expansion, but they rely on lenders such as commercial banks, investment banks, and insurance companies for assistance.

During the Great Recession, when even good customers found loans hard to get, a new kind of financing emerged called **crowdfunding**, raising money for a project or venture by obtaining many small amounts of money from many people ("the crowd"), using websites such as Kickstarter. We discuss crowdfunding further in Chapter 15.

9. Government Regulators

The preceding groups are external stakeholders in your organization because they clearly affect and are affected by its activities. But why would **government regulators**—regulatory agencies that establish ground rules under which organizations may operate—be considered stakeholders?

We are talking here about an alphabet soup of agencies, boards, and commissions that have the legal authority to prescribe or proscribe the conditions under which you may conduct business. To these may be added local and state regulators on the one hand and foreign governments and international agencies (such as the World Trade Organization, which oversees international trade and standardization efforts) on the other. The Federal Aviation Agency (FAA), for example, specifies how far planes must stay apart to prevent midair collisions. When airlines want to add more flights on certain routes, the FAA may have to add more flight controllers and radar equipment because those are the agency's responsibility.

Government Regulators Example—FAA: The FAA regulates the use of drones in the United States, where there are now around 800,000 commercial and 1.5 million recreational drones in operation.[33] New regulations will implement more sophisticated identification and tracking systems, place tighter restrictions on where drones can be flown, and require that all drone users pass an aeronautical knowledge and safety exam.[34] The FAA now requires Remote ID capability for most drones that operate in U.S. airspace. Remote ID equips the drone to broadcast data regarding its location, altitude, and identity to necessary agencies.

10. Special-Interest Groups

Special-interest groups are groups whose members try to influence specific issues, some of which may affect your organization. Examples are People for the Ethical Treatment of Animals, Mothers Against Drunk Driving, the National Organization for Women, and the National Rifle Association.

Special-interest groups may try to exert political influence over an organization's activities by contributing funds to lawmakers' election campaigns, launching letter-writing efforts to officials, or organizing marches. This was the case in 2023 when 20-year-old Greta Thunberg led thousands of people in a protest against expanding a coal mine in Lützerath, Germany.[35]

Protestors often go to great lengths to demonstrate their commitment to causes. Would you be willing to be arrested in order to influence an organization's decisions? Roberto Pfeil/dpa/Alamy Stock Photo

The General Environment

The second sub-environment in an organization's external environment is the general environment, or macroenvironment—defined in Section 3.2 as the set of broad, uncontrollable forces in the external environment that impact the organization. The general environment includes six forces: economic, technological, sociocultural, demographic, political–legal, and international.

1. **Economic Forces** **Economic forces** consist of the general economic conditions and trends—such as unemployment, interest rates, and trade balance—that may affect an organization's decisions. These are forces in your world, region, and nation, over which you and your organization probably have no control, such as the events during and after the Great Recession and the COVID-19 pandemic.

- **Unemployment.** Is the unemployment rate rising? Then maybe you'll have more job applicants to hire from, yet fewer customers with money to spend. Conversely, declining unemployment will mean you'll have to vie for top talent (often by offering more competitive wages and benefits), but you may enjoy increased consumer spending. The national unemployment rate rose to its highest level since the Great Depression during the COVID-19 pandemic, and by 2023 it had fallen to 3.4%–the lowest in over 50 years.[36]

- **Interest rates.** The Federal Reserve began raising interest rates in 2021/2022 to reduce inflation, and by 2023 interest rates hit a 15-year high. This stifled growth in the economy because it cost more to borrow money to open new stores or build new plants. When the Federal Reserve lowers interest rates, small businesses may be in a better position to expand.[37]

- **Trade balance.** The **trade balance**, or balance of trade, is the difference between the monetary value of a country's imports and exports.[38] When the United States imports more than it exports it is said to have a *trade deficit*. If exports exceed imports, there is a *trade surplus*. Although the word surplus sounds positive and the word deficit sounds negative, economists generally do not view a trade surplus as inherently good, nor do they view a trade deficit as inherently bad.[39]

These and other economic forces greatly impact organizations, and it is important that managers consider them in concert with one another rather than as isolated indices.[40]

2. **Technological Forces** **Technological forces** are new developments in methods for transforming resources into goods or services. The way we manufacture goods and provide services has changed dramatically in recent years and will continue to evolve as technologies improve. Technological forces such as artificial intelligence, which we discuss in Chapter 7, have overhauled not only how humans interact with the workplace but also the amount and type of human interaction that is necessary.[41]

Technological Forces Example—Changing Work Arrangements: Proponents of remote and hybrid work believe that productivity and innovation don't always require face-to-face interaction. But flexible working arrangements are only as good as the technology that supports them. A recent Qualtrics study found that workers were over 200% more engaged and over 80% more likely to remain in their jobs for 3+ years if they had the right technology and tech support in place. Unfortunately, many organizations have struggled to implement the technology necessary to sustain these arrangements. An Adobe study of 1,400 managers and workers found that hybrid workers spent at least five hours each week troubleshooting technology, and 70% of respondents said that tech issues were one of the biggest challenges of remote and hybrid work.[42] Flexible working arrangements are especially important to younger generations of workers, and technological advances have greatly increased firms' capacity to offer remote and hybrid work options.[43] The key is for organizations to take advantage of the appropriate technology that makes these arrangements successful.[44]

3. **Sociocultural Forces** **Sociocultural forces** are influences and trends originating in a country's, a society's, or a culture's human relationships and values that may affect an organization or industry. Attitudes about marijuana represent an important sociocultural force. Medical marijuana is now legal in 37 states, and for recreational use in 21 states and the District of Columbia (see Figure 3.3), reflecting the fact that about two-thirds of

FIGURE 3.3

States where marijuana is legal

Sources: I. Pereira, "Recreational Marijuana Legalized in 2 States, Rejected in 3 in 2022 Election Referendums," ABC News, November 9, 2022, https://abcnews.go.com/Politics/recreational-marijuana-legalized-states-rejected/story?id=92683852; Will Yakowicz, "Where Is Cannabis Legal: A Guide to All 50 States," Forbes, May 30, 2023, https://www.forbes.com/sites/willyakowicz/2023/01/06/where-is-cannabis-legal-a-guide-to-all-50-states/?sh=643bf1831619.

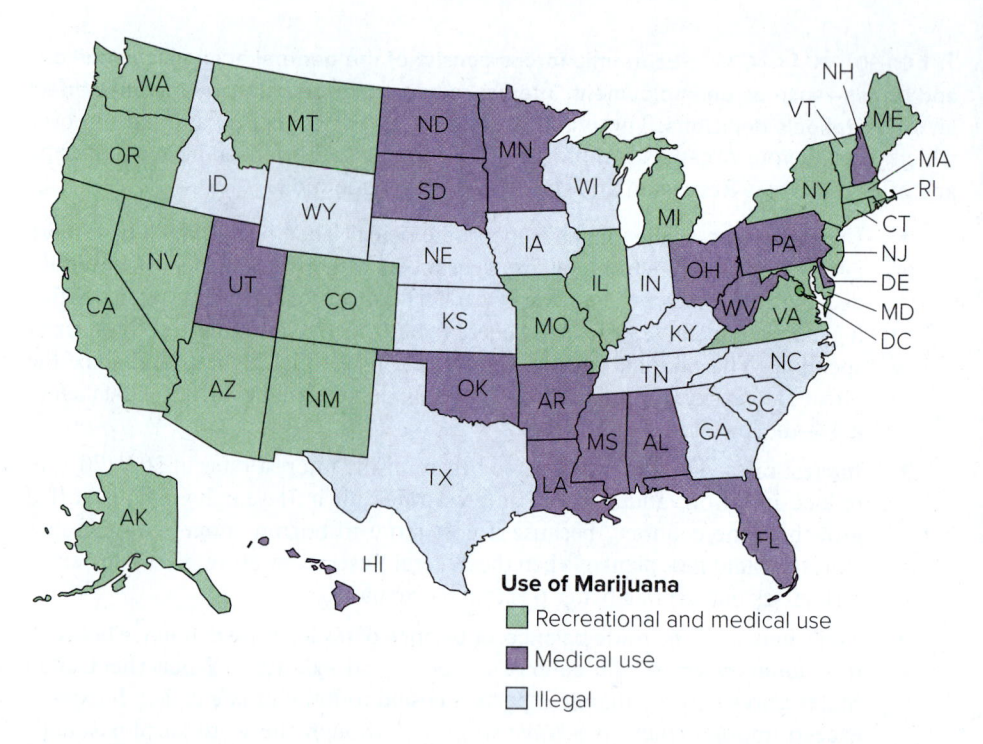

Use of Marijuana
- Recreational and medical use
- Medical use
- Illegal

U.S. adults now support legalization.[45] It's safe to assume that decision makers at well-known pharmacy and grocery chains are already working through the ethical dilemma of whether they should sell marijuana in their stores, given that the substance was viewed negatively for so long and is now gaining widespread acceptance. Circle K recently formed a partnership with Green Thumb Industries to begin selling marijuana in some of its gas stations.[46] Federal marijuana legislation is in flux at the time of this writing.

4. Demographic Forces

Demographic forces are influences on an organization arising from changes in the characteristics of a population, such as age, gender, or ethnic origin. *Demographics* derives from the ancient Greek word for "people"—*demos*—and deals with statistics relating to human populations. Age, gender, race, sexual orientation, occupation, income, and family size are examples of demographic characteristics when they are used to express measurements of certain groups.

In Chapter 1 we mentioned several instances of major impending shifts related to workforce and national demographics. The job for managers is to adapt their decisions to these evolving demographics in the workforce and broader environment. Important evolving demographic forces include decreasing birth rates, increasing secularism, and more widespread acceptance of same-sex marriage.[47] Many firms now have chief diversity officers to support increasing workforce diversity.[48] We consider demographic and diversity matters in detail in Chapter DEI.

5. Political–Legal Forces

Political–legal forces are changes in the way politics shape laws and laws shape the opportunities for and threats to an organization. In the United States, the currently dominant political view may be reflected in the way the government addresses environmental and sustainable development issues, such as those we described in Chapter 1 and in the upcoming Learning Module 1. For instance, should coal mining be allowed on public lands?[49] How should public money be spent on climate change and ocean warming?[50]

As for legal forces, some countries have more fully developed legal systems than others. And some countries have more lawyers per capita. (The United States reportedly has approximately one lawyer for every 250 people versus one for every 1,200 people in France.)[51] U.S. companies may be more willing to use the legal system to advance their interests, as in suing competitors to gain competitive advantage. But they must also watch that others don't do the same to them.

6. International Forces **International forces** are changes in the economic, political, legal, and technological global system that may affect organizations. This category represents a huge variety of influences. TikTok bans are a notable recent example of international forces impacting business:

> **International Forces Example—TikTok Bans:** More than 1 billion people around the world had a TikTok account by early 2023, and major companies like Microsoft, Starbucks, Google, and McDonald's were capitalizing on the platform to build and maintain customer bases.[52] Around the same time, global concerns about the security of TikTok users' data came to a head. At least 27 U.S. states banned TikTok on government devices[53], as did countries including Taiwan, India, Canada, Denmark, New Zealand, and France. The U.S. government issued an ultimatum to the social media platform's owners to either sell their share of the company or risk a nationwide ban.[54] The possibility of a TikTok ban was especially troublesome for small businesses that relied on the platform to build brand awareness.[55]

3.4 The Ethical Responsibilities Required of You as a Manager

THE BIG PICTURE
Managers need to be aware of what constitutes ethics, values, the four approaches to ethical dilemmas, and how organizations can promote ethics.

LO 3-4
Explain the importance of ethics and values in effective management.

MIT received $800,000 in donations from billionaire Jeffrey Epstein over the course of 20 years. When Epstein was indicted for sex trafficking in 2019, MIT president L. Rafael Reif announced that the university would not keep the money and would instead donate $800,000 to a charity to benefit sexual abuse victims.[56] Do you think this took courage? We do. This decision removed financial resources from MIT's short-term financial bottom line, but it also considered the longer-term implications of the decision on the university and on many additional stakeholders. Rescinding close to a million dollars in donations couldn't have been an easy decision for those who also had to consider the impact on stakeholders such as students who would have benefited greatly from a donation of this size.

It would not have been illegal for MIT to keep the $800,000 that Epstein gave to them. Strictly speaking, retaining the donation would have satisfied the conditions set forth in Friedman's perspective—the institution would have increased its wealth in a way that complied with the law. But MIT's decision makers believed retaining the money would be unethical and was therefore not the right thing to do. Further, they chose to use the money to increase the welfare of stakeholders in their environment that had been victimized by Epstein and others like him.

Making this kind of decision requires that managers understand (1) what's most important to them and to the organizations they represent. It also requires (2) the ability to think critically about ethical dilemmas and (3) a high level of moral development. In this section, we consider each of these requirements of managing for ethical standards.

Defining Ethics and Values

A report from the Ethics & Compliance Initiative (ECI) revealed that 49% of U.S. workers surveyed had witnessed ethical misconduct at work.[57] Further, the report revealed that managers experienced more pressure to compromise ethical standards at work than nonmanagers. It's likely you will experience this type of pressure in your role as a manager, and you need to know how determine right from wrong in these situations. Here we explore ethics and values as they relate to important managerial decisions.

Ethics Ethics are the standards of right and wrong that influence behavior. These standards may vary among countries and among cultures. Ethical behavior is behavior that is accepted as "right" as opposed to "wrong" according to prevailing standards. Managing for ethical standards is a considerable challenge because these standards are relative, and managers often must balance conflicting sets of ethical standards when considering the needs of multiple stakeholders in a decision.

Research suggests that one of the most common sources of ethical conflict for managers is the choice between *economic performance* and *social performance*.[58] This is an example of an ethical dilemma, a situation in which you have to decide whether to pursue a course of action that may benefit you or your organization but that may harm one or more stakeholders in your environment. Ethical dilemmas often arise because of a conflict between the different values held by two or more parties.

Values Values are the relatively permanent and deeply held underlying beliefs and attitudes that help determine a person's behavior, such as the belief that "fairness means hiring according to ability, not family background." Our values indicate what is most important to us, and just as managers have their own personal values, so do organizations.[59] Organizations' value systems represent the pattern of values within an organization. One way that organizations express their value systems is by taking a stance on broader issues. Consider these examples:

> **Organizational Value Systems Example—Taking a Stance:** Should corporations take a stance on social and/or political issues? According to recent Gallup data, nearly 60% of adults aged 18 to 29 say yes.[60] The Walt Disney Company appeared to take a stance against legislation that prevented the discussion of sexual orientation and gender identity in Florida schools when it signed on to host the Out and Equal Workplace Summit in 2023 and 2024. Walgreens seemed to express a stance on medical termination of pregnancy when it announced it would not distribute mifepristone in states where the legislature was against it, even if the distribution was within state law.[61] Taking a social or political stance carries both benefits and risks for an organization. For example, consider that recent survey data suggests nearly two-thirds of consumers globally say they will actively boycott or buy from a company due to its stance on social and/or political issues.[62]

Companies are bound to make some stakeholders happy while alienating others when making decisions based on a set of deeply held values. As a manager, you will have to think through decisions that present conflicts between your organization's values and those of various stakeholder groups. You also will encounter decisions that pit your own personal values against those of your organization. Table 3.1 presents some common ethical dilemmas that managers face.

Four Approaches to Resolving Ethical Dilemmas

A second factor that influences your ability to determine the right thing to do as a manager is your ability to think critically about ethical dilemmas (this type of thinking also represents a core career readiness competency). Remember that ethical dilemmas are called dilemmas because they are difficult to resolve, and there's a big difference between wanting to do the right thing and having the knowledge and skills to determine what the best resolution is.

TABLE 3.1   **Common Managerial Ethical Dilemmas**

DILEMMA	EXPLANATION	EXAMPLE
Should I hire my buddies and/or family members?	Managers may be tempted to make decisions that favor one employee or party over another. Nepotism—showing preference for your friends and/or family members in hiring decisions—is an example of this. As a manager, you may have to decide whether hiring someone you know is the right decision for your stakeholders.	Sam Bankman-Fried (SBF) founded the cryptocurrency companies FTX and Alameda Research. Federal authorities arrested SBF in 2022, charging him with two counts of wire fraud and conspiracy.[i] Sources close to the company and its employees claim that the small group running the company were all close friends and, in many instances, current or former romantic partners.[ii]
Can something really hurt stakeholders if they don't know about it?	Managers lie when they intentionally misrepresent the truth to various organizational stakeholders. You may encounter the dilemma of whether to withhold information from one set of stakeholders in order to satisfy the demands of another set of stakeholders.	Volkswagen avoided making legally required updates to their automobiles and instead deliberately installed cheating software in more than 500,000 diesel passenger cars sold in the United States plus 10 million other cars sold around the world to get around emissions requirements. The scandal resulted in billions of dollars in fines and penalties and multiple prison sentences.[iii]
Is this a conflict of interest?	Conflicts of interest occur when the potential for personal benefit—or benefit to family or friends—makes it difficult for a manager to make the right decision for their organization. Conflicts of interest often involve the issue of whether an employee of one organization can accept gifts from another organization.	It's illegal for pharmaceutical firms to pay physicians to prescribe specific drugs. But doctors can legally accept payments for consulting and speaking jobs. Data suggest that the pharmaceutical industry spends billions annually on these types of payments.[iv] Many believe these behaviors represent unethical attempts to influence drug sales. Others see it as a legitimate business relationship.
Is it ever ok to mistreat subordinates?	Managers are under tremendous pressure to get things done and to do things right. They often are tempted to take out their frustration on employees. This can manifest as **abusive supervision, which occurs when managers repeatedly display verbal and nonverbal hostility toward their subordinates.**[v] Abusive supervision does not include physical contact. Rather, it focuses on behaviors such as public humiliation, insults, shouting, name-calling, gossiping, and ignoring subordinates.[vi]	In early 2023, René Redzepi announced he would be closing his three-Michelin-starred restaurant, Noma, which had garnered international fame as the world's best restaurant. Redzepi has admitted to yelling at, pushing, and bullying his kitchen staff throughout his years in the culinary business in past interviews.[vii] In his announcement, Redzepi called for broad changes to the dysfunctional culture that permeates professional kitchens.[viii]
Do health and safety regulations really matter?	Different jobs come with different sets of rules about what constitutes safe and healthy behavior. In a hospital setting, for example, employees must wash their hands frequently and thoroughly; at a construction site, hard hats, goggles, and steel-toed boots are necessary protections. Experts agree that a major contributing factor to accidents and injuries across the board is the overconfidence that can accompany violations of health and safety regulations over time. It's easy for managers to become complacent and wonder if certain regulations really matter.	OSHA recently fined Ohio-based tile manufacturer NOX US LLC over $1 million for its failure to resolve hazardous workplace conditions. At least 20 employees reportedly suffered severe injuries between 2017 and 2022 as a result of health and safety violations committed by the company. Said Todd Jensen, an OSHA area director involved with the case, "NOX US LLC continues to put profit before safety, and the company's efforts when it comes to worker safety are unacceptable."[ix]

Source: Table based in part on Ethics & Compliance Initiative. *2021 Global Business Ethics Survey Report.* 2021. https://www.ethics.org/just-released-2021-global-business-ethics-survey-report/.

i R. Goswami and M. Sigalos, "Sam Bankman-Fried Pleads Not Guilty to Federal Fraud Charges in New York," CNBC, January 3, 2023, https://www.cnbc.com/2023/01/03/sam-bankman-fried-pleads-not-guilty-to-fraud-charges-in-new-york.html#:~:text=Former%20FTX%20CEO%20Sam%20Bankman,wire%20fraud%20and%20securities%20fraud.

ii T. Wong and CoinDesk, "Sam Bankman-Fried's Crypto Empire 'Was Run by a Gang of Kids in the Bahamas' Who All Dated Each Other," Fortune, November 11, 2022, https://fortune.com/2022/11/11/sam-bankman-fried-crypto-empire-ftx-alameda-run-gang-kids-bahamas-who-all-dated-each-other/

iii G. Kell, "From Emissions Cheater to Climate Leader: VW's Journey from Dieselgate to Embracing e-Mobility," Forbes, December 5, 2022, https://www.forbes.com/sites/georgkell/2022/12/05/from-emissions-cheater-to-climate-leader-vws-journey-from-dieselgate-to-embracing-e-mobility/?sh=f8b66ff68a55.

iv M. Totty, "Research Brief: Public Disclosure of Drug Company Gifts: High-Prescribing Physicians Unaffected," UCLA Anderson Review, August 31, 2022, https://anderson-review.ucla.edu/public-disclosure-of-drug-company-gifts-high-prescribing-physicians-unaffected/

v B.J. Tepper, "Consequences of Abusive Supervision," Academy of Management Journal, Vol. 43, No. 2 (April 2000), p. 178.

vi Z. Lyubykh, J. Bozeman, M.S. Hershcovis, N. Turner, and J.V. Shan, "Employee Performance and Abusive Supervision: The Role of Supervisor Over-Attributions," Journal of Organizational Behavior, Vol. 43, No. 1 (2022), pp.125–145.

vii L. Ochoa, "Does Rene Redzepi Closing Noma Really Mean the End of Fine Dining?" Los Angeles Times, January 14, 2023, https://www.latimes.com/food/newsletter/2023-01-14/rene-redzepi-closing-noma-help-fix-restaurant-inequities-tasting-notes.

viii "'This Is Too Hard. We Have to Work a Different Way': Noma and the Future of Fine Dining," The Irish Times, January 9, 2023, https://www.irishtimes.com/food/restaurants/2023/01/09/we-have-to-completely-rethink-the-industry-noma-and-the-future-of-fine-dining/

ix News Release, "Ohio Manufacturer Faces $1.2 M in Penalties after 7th Worker in 5 Years Suffers Severe Injuries When Caught in Machine Employer Failed to Lock Out," U.S. Department of Labor, October 27, 2022, https://www.dol.gov/newsroom/releases/osha/osha20221027.

CVS made waves when it announced it would no longer carry tobacco products in its stores. Do you think all of the company's stakeholders were happy with the decision? CVS likely gained and lost business when it took this stance. Matti/Alamy Stock Photo

The work of philosophers and ethics scholars provides us with a set of approaches to use when attempting to resolve ethical dilemmas. Each approach views a dilemma from a different angle, and there is no one "best" approach guaranteed to produce a superior decision. Rather, managers should use a variety of approaches to achieve a holistic understanding of a dilemma and to make what they feel is the best decision.

1. The Utilitarian Approach: For the Greatest Good Ethical behavior in the **utilitarian approach** is guided by what will result in the greatest good for the greatest number of people. Managers often use the utilitarian approach, using financial performance—such as efficiency and profit—to guide their decisions.[63] Under this approach, a utilitarian "cost–benefit" analysis might show firing thousands of employees may improve a company's bottom line and provide immediate benefits for shareholders in the short term. The drawback of this approach, however, is that it may result in decisions that damage workforce morale and strip the organization of employees with valuable experience and skills—actions not so readily measurable in dollars.

2. The Individual Approach: For Your Greatest Self-Interest Long Term, which Will Help Others Ethical behavior in the **individual approach** is guided by what will result in the individual's best long-term interests, which ultimately are in everyone's self-interest. The assumption here is that you will act ethically in the short run to avoid others harming you in the long run. The flaw here, however, is that one person's short-term self-gain may *not*, in fact, be good for everyone in the long term. After all, placing a series of eight dams around the Columbia and Snake rivers helped mitigate the effects of water shortages, improved the wheat export process, and bolstered access to food sources, but the fishing industries downstream have ultimately suffered as the increased water temperatures and blocked migration routes drastically reduced the number of fish. Indeed, this is one reason why Puget Sound Chinook, or king salmon, has been threatened with extinction in the Pacific Northwest.[64]

3. The Moral-Rights Approach: Respecting Fundamental Rights Shared by Everyone Ethical behavior in the **moral-rights approach** is guided by respect for the fundamental rights of human beings, such as those expressed in the U.S. Constitution's Bill of Rights. For example, most of us tend to agree that denying people the right to life, liberty, privacy, health and safety, and due process is unethical. This is why you likely feel some level of moral outrage when you hear about a child dying from a curable condition simply because their parents didn't have any money and the hospital turned them away. The difficulty with this approach occurs when rights are in conflict, such as employer and employee rights. For example, consider the case of an employee who knowingly enters the workplace while suffering from a highly contagious disease. Does that employees' right to keep their medical information private supersede their co-workers' right to work in a healthy and safe workplace?

4. The Justice Approach: Respecting Impartial Standards of Fairness Ethical behavior in the **justice approach** is guided by respect for impartial standards of fairness and equity. One consideration here is whether an organization's policies—such as those governing promotions or sexual harassment cases—are administered impartially and fairly regardless of employees' membership in protected classes. Fairness matters to employees, as you learned in Chapter DEI when you read about the importance of equity in DE&I management. For instance, many employees are loudly resentful when a CEO's pay is hundreds of times higher than that of their employees—and when CEOs that are fired for performance problems or ethical violations still receive a "golden parachute," or extravagant package of separation pay and benefits.

What are your views on ethics? If your instructor has assigned it, complete Self-Assessment 3.1 in Connect to assess your perspective on ethics.

SELF-ASSESSMENT 3.1   CAREER READINESS

Assessing My Perspective on Ethics

This survey is designed to assess your views about ethics. Please complete Self-Assessment 3.1 if your instructor has assigned it in Connect.

White-Collar Crime, SarbOx, and Ethical Training

In this section we discuss important factors relating to ethical decision making in organizations. We begin with a look at white-collar crime and legislation that aims to prevent it. We then explore a psychological theory of how managers learn ethics and which criteria they use to determine right from wrong.

White-Collar Crime   At the beginning of the 21st century, U.S. business erupted in an array of scandals represented in such names as Enron, WorldCom, Tyco, and Adelphia, and their chief executives went to prison on various fraud convictions. Executives' deceits generated a great deal of public outrage, and as a result Congress passed the Sarbanes–Oxley Act, as we'll describe. Did that stop the raft of business scandals? Not quite.

Next to hit the headlines were cases of **insider trading**, **the illegal trading of a company's stock by people using confidential company information.** The federal government launched a six-year crackdown on insider trading on Wall Street that resulted in 87 convictions (14 of which were dismissed or lost on appeal; one ended in acquittal).[65]

In 2022 the U.S. Department of Justice named Associate Deputy Attorney General Kevin Chambers as the Director for COVID-19 Fraud Enforcement. The position oversees legal action related to the misuse of over $6 billion in federal pandemic relief funding. Consider the following example:

White-Collar Crime Example—Pandemic Relief: A federal judge sentenced Patrick Parker Walsh to over five years in federal prison for stealing nearly $8 million in pandemic relief funds.[66] Throughout the pandemic, Walsh submitted multiple fraudulent applications for both Paycheck Protection Program (PPP) loans and Economic Injury Disaster Loans (EIDLs). Prosecutors said Walsh funneled millions of dollars in federal relief funding into luxury real estate, including a private island and a ski lodge, rather than using the money for its intended business purposes.[67]

The Sarbanes–Oxley Reform Act   The **Sarbanes–Oxley Act of 2002**, often shortened to SarbOx, or SOX, established requirements for proper financial record keeping for public companies and penalties of as much as 25 years in prison for noncompliance.[68] Administered by the Securities and Exchange Commission (SEC), SarbOx requires a company's chief executive officer (CEO) and chief financial officer (CFO) to personally certify the organization's financial reports, prohibits them from taking personal loans or lines of credit, and makes them reimburse the organization for bonuses and stock options when required by restatement of corporate profits. It also requires the company to have established procedures and guidelines for audit committees and provides whistleblower protection for employees who report SarbOx violations.[69]

SarbOx Example—ExxonMobil: The U.S. Department of Labor (DOL) ordered ExxonMobil to reinstate the employment status of two fired employees and pay them more than $800,000 in compensatory damages, back pay, and interest.[70] An investigation showed that ExxonMobil wrongfully terminated the employees when it learned they had leaked information to the *Wall Street Journal*. The employees (both computational scientists) believed the company had overstated future production estimates and property valuations in its SEC filings. The DOL determined that the employees acted within their whistleblower rights under SarbOx when they communicated their concerns with the media outlet.

Managers at ExxonMobil, like those in numerous other instances of ethical and legal misconduct, made decisions that violated standards of "right" behavior. Up next we explore Kohlberg's theory on the reasoning we use to justify moral decisions.

How Do People Learn Ethics? Kohlberg's Theories

A third factor that influences your ability to determine the right thing to do as a manager is your level of moral development. Psychologist Laurence Kohlberg proposed that human beings develop the capacity for moral reasoning in a series of sequential stages.[71] These stages comprise three levels of personal moral development—preconventional, conventional, and postconventional. Your level of personal moral development is one of the factors that influences your ability to determine the right thing to do as a manager.

Levels of Moral Development: Kohlberg's theory suggests that we all begin life at the first (lowest) level of moral development and improve our moral reasoning as we experience life, grow in maturity, and face increasingly complex moral dilemmas.

- Level 1, preconventional—follows rules. People at the preconventional level of moral development tend to follow rules and obey authority because doing so allows them to avoid unpleasant consequences. Managers at Level 1 tend to be autocratic or coercive, expecting employees to be obedient for obedience's sake.

- Level 2, conventional—follows expectations of others. People at the conventional level of moral development are conformist but not submissive. Rather than simply seeking to avoid unpleasant consequences, they consider society's expectations when determining right and wrong. Level 2 managers lead by encouragement and cooperation and are more group and team oriented. Most managers are at this level.

- Level 3, postconventional—guided by internal values. People at the highest level of moral development—postconventional—are independent thinkers guided by their own values and standards. Level 3 managers focus on the needs of their employees and try to lead by empowering those working for them. Only about one-fifth of American managers are said to reach this level.

Evidence suggests that many managers display lower levels of moral development. Consider the scandals that pepper U.S. business history, from railroad tycoons trying to corner the gold market (the 1872 Crédit Mobilier scandal) to bank customer service representatives swindling older customers out of their finances. These examples depict decision makers motivated by self-interest rather than the greater good.

Have you ever lied, scammed, or deceived someone to advance your own interests? **Workplace cheating** consists of unethical behaviors that result in employees receiving benefits or advantages to which they are otherwise not entitled.[72] Workplace cheating is common. As one example, Ernst & Young was recently ordered to pay a $100 million fine to the SEC after it was discovered that the company's auditors had cheated on the CPA exam's ethics section as well as in continuing education courses.[73]

Cheating among college students is also common, and its proliferation suggests business schools are ushering managers with questionable moral reasoning abilities into the workforce. A poll of 30,000 students revealed that about 61% admitted to cheating, and 16.5% didn't regret it.[74] These behaviors may persist because professors don't want to deal with the hassle of reporting cheating, fear legal trouble, or believe they have no control over the problem.[75] They also occur in response to performance pressures to deliver results or face negative consequences.[76] It is no wonder that now many colleges and universities require formal ethics education.

Linking Moral Development with Ethical Action: University of Virginia Darden School of Business Professor Mary Gentile developed an ethics curriculum for business schools called *Giving Voice to Values* (GVV). The GVV program is built on the assumption that the problem in organizations is not necessarily a lack of values, but rather a lack of training in how to voice and act on our existing values successfully. The program centers on giving people the opportunity to practice voicing their values so that they are better prepared to do so when ethical dilemmas arise in the workplace. GVV has been implemented in more than 1,000 business schools and organizations to date.[77] The good news is that more graduate business schools are changing their curriculums to teach ethics, although there is still much progress to be made to ensure the effectiveness of ethics education.[78]

How Organizations Can Promote Ethics

Ethics needs to be an everyday affair, not a one-time thing. This is why many large U.S. companies now have a *chief ethics officer*, whose job is to make ethical conduct a priority issue.

There are several ways an organization may promote high ethical standards on the job, as follows.[79]

1. Creating a Strong Ethical Climate The first step is to foster an ethical climate. An ethical climate represents employees' perceptions about the extent to which work environments support ethical behavior. This climate manifests in employees' shared sense of "how things are done around here." It is important for managers to foster ethical climates because they significantly affect the frequency of ethical behavior, which in turn impacts employee performance and firm profitability.[80] Managers can promote ethical climates through the policies, procedures, and practices that are used on a daily basis.[81]

2. Screening Prospective Employees Companies try to screen out dishonest, irresponsible employees by checking applicants' resumes and references. Some also use personality and integrity testing to identify potentially dishonest people. As we will discuss in detail in Chapter 7 and Chapter 9, AI technology is being harnessed to streamline employee screening. For example, bots can quickly analyze candidates' social media accounts, and algorithms can scan interview videos for content, emotional cues, tone of voice, and information about temperament. Experts caution that many AI screening tools need further refinement to address serious validity, privacy, and equal employment opportunity concerns.[82]

3. Instituting Ethics Codes and Training Programs A code of ethics consists of a formal written set of ethical standards guiding an organization's actions. Most codes offer guidance on how to treat customers, suppliers, competitors, and other stakeholders. Their purpose is to clearly state top management's expectations for all employees.[83] As you might expect, most codes prohibit bribes, kickbacks, misappropriation of corporate assets, conflicts of interest, and "cooking the books"—falsifying accounting statements and other records. Other areas frequently covered in ethics codes are political contributions, workforce diversity, and confidentiality of corporate information.

4. Rewarding Ethical Behavior: Protecting Whistleblowers It's not enough to simply punish bad behavior; managers must also reward ethical behavior, as in encouraging (or at least not discouraging) whistleblowers.[84]

A **whistleblower is an employee, or even an outside consultant, who reports organizational misconduct such as health and safety violations, waste, corruption, or overcharging of customers, to the public.**[85] For instance, the law that created the Occupational Safety and Health Administration (OSHA) gives employees and their representatives the right to file a complaint and request an OSHA inspection of their workplace if they "believe there is a serious hazard" or their employer is "not following OSHA standards."[86] In some cases, whistleblowers may receive a reward; the Internal Revenue Service (IRS), for instance, is authorized to pay tipsters rewards as high as 30% in cases involving large amounts of money.[87]

The number of whistleblower tips received by the Securities and Exchange Commission (SEC), for example, is now over 12,000 a year.[88] Whistleblowers sometimes risk their jobs by coming forward and thus deserve protection. Federal law prohibits organizations from retaliating against whistleblowers, and the SEC has the authority to impose severe penalties on companies that violate these protections (as you previously saw in the SarbOx example on ExxonMobil).[89] Still, retaliation against whistleblowers is not uncommon and includes social rejection, verbal abuse, demotion, and firing.[90]

5. Using a Multi-Faceted Approach The four suggestions offered above highlight the need for organizations to promote ethical behaviors by addressing both individual factors such as personality, and organizational factors such as training, reward systems, and climate. Indeed, there is abundant evidence to suggest that unethical behaviors stem both from workers' personalities and their work environments.[91] In short, it is not enough to screen out the bad apples—we also must repair the bad barrels and prevent the good barrels from rotting.

All told, it is important for you to learn more about your ethical tendencies. This will help you to behave in ways that are consistent with your values and beliefs, even when your environment isn't ideal. •

3.5 The Social Responsibilities Required of You as a Manager

THE BIG PICTURE
Managers need to be aware of the viewpoints supporting and opposing social responsibility and whether being and doing good pays off financially for the organization.

LO 3-5

Describe the concept of social responsibility and its role in today's organizations.

If ethical responsibility is about being a good individual citizen, social responsibility is about being a good *organizational citizen*. More and more companies now believe that being socially responsible—attending to the triple bottom line of people, planet, and profit—is simply the "right thing" for firms to do.[92] **Corporate social responsibility (CSR) is the notion that corporations are expected to go above and beyond following the law and making a profit.** Areas of CSR include the environment, philanthropy, and ethical labor practices.[93]

Recent estimates say that Fortune 500 companies funnel an estimated $20 billion into CSR initiatives each year.[94]

Corporate Social Responsibility: The Top of the Pyramid

According to University of Georgia business scholar Archie B. Carroll, CSR rests at the top of a pyramid of a corporation's obligations, right up there with economic, legal, and ethical obligations. Some people might hold that a company's first and only duty is to make a profit. However, Carroll suggests the responsibilities of an organization in the global economy should take the following priorities, with profit being the most fundamental (at the base of the pyramid) and corporate citizenship at the top:[95]

- *Be a good global corporate citizen,* as defined by your stakeholder's expectations.
- *Be ethical in its practices,* taking stakeholders' standards into consideration.
- *Obey the law* of host countries as well as international law.
- *Make a profit* consistent with expectations for international business.

These priorities are illustrated in the pyramid in Figure 3.4.

As shown in Figure 3.4, Carroll's CSR pyramid includes, as its foundation, Friedman's view of what it means for a business to do the right thing. Specifically, economic responsibility (profits) forms the base of the pyramid, while legal compliance makes up the next layer.

Carroll goes further by suggesting that the right decisions for an organization also must account for ethical responsibilities that go beyond legal compliance. One of a manager's major challenges, as we stated in Chapter 1, is managing for ethical standards. **Ethics**, as you learned in Section 3.4, are the standards of right and wrong that influence behavior, and ethical behavior is that which is accepted as "right" as opposed

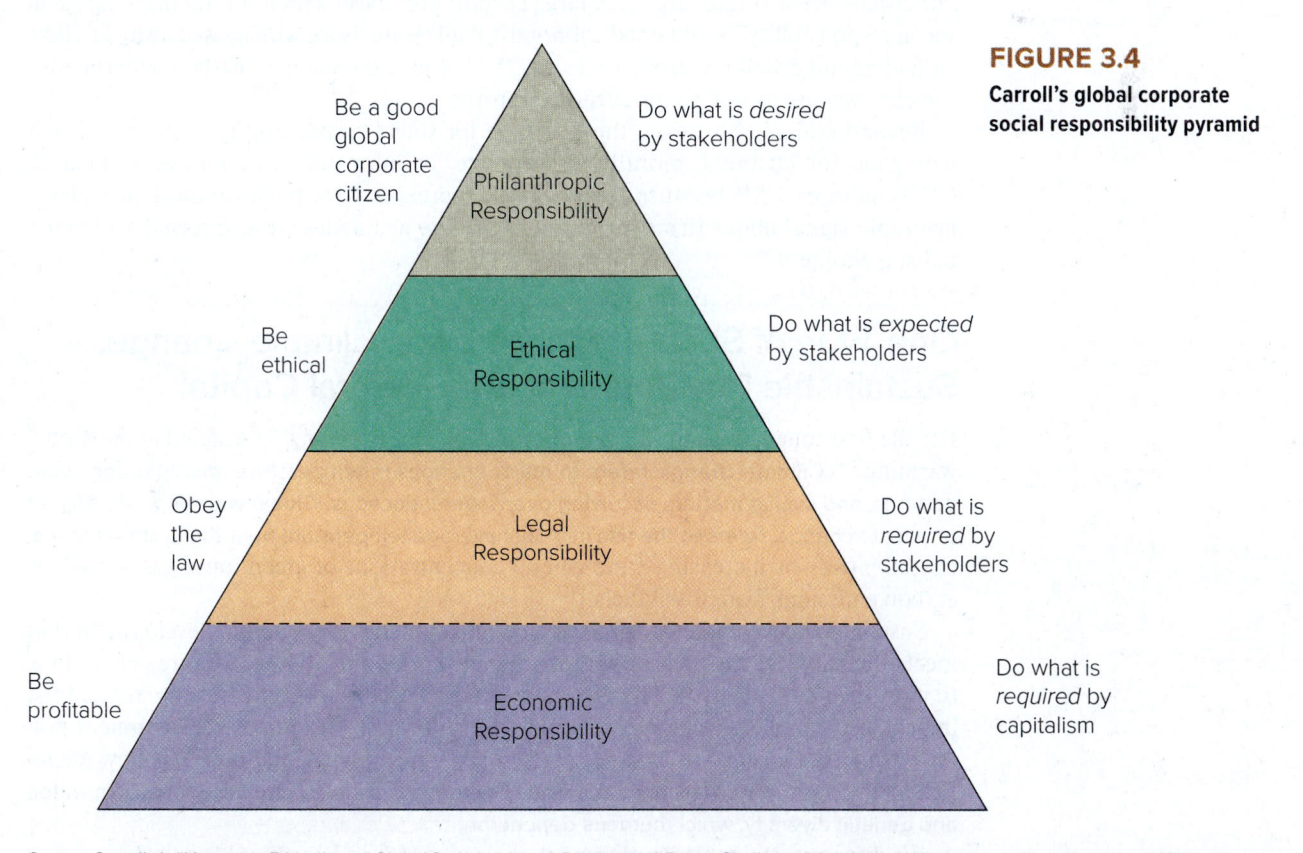

FIGURE 3.4

Carroll's global corporate social responsibility pyramid

Pyramid (bottom to top):
- Economic Responsibility — Be profitable — Do what is *required* by capitalism
- Legal Responsibility — Obey the law — Do what is *required* by stakeholders
- Ethical Responsibility — Be ethical — Do what is *expected* by stakeholders
- Philanthropic Responsibility — Be a good global corporate citizen — Do what is *desired* by stakeholders

Source: Carroll, A. "Managing Ethically and Global Stakeholders: A Present and Future Challenge." *Academy of Management Executive (May 2004):* 116.

to "wrong" according to prevailing standards. Managing for ethical standards is a considerable challenge because these standards are relative, and managers often must balance conflicting sets of ethical standards when considering the needs of multiple stakeholders in a decision.

Is Social Responsibility Worthwhile? Opposing and Supporting Viewpoints

In the old days of cutthroat capitalism, social responsibility was hardly a thought. A company's most important goal was to make money pretty much any way it could—consequences be damned. Today, for-profit enterprises in the United States and Europe—along with an increasing number of multinational firms from developing nations—generally make a point of "putting something back" into society in conjunction with taking something out.[96]

Not everyone, however, agrees with these priorities. Let's consider the two viewpoints.

Against Social Responsibility "Few trends could so thoroughly undermine the very foundations of our free society," argued the late free-market economist Milton Friedman, "as the acceptance by corporate officials of social responsibility other than to make as much money for their stockholders as possible."[97]

Friedman represents the view that, as he said, "The social responsibility of business is to make profits." That is, unless a company focuses on maximizing profits, it will become distracted and fail to provide goods and services, benefit the stockholders, create jobs, and expand economic growth—the real social justification for the firm's existence.

This view would presumably support the efforts of companies to set up headquarters in name only in offshore tax havens (while keeping their actual headquarters in the United States) in order to minimize their tax burden.

For Social Responsibility "A large corporation these days not only may engage in social responsibility," said famed economist Paul Samuelson, who passed away in 2009, "it had damned well better try to do so."[98] That is, a company must be concerned for society's welfare as well as for corporate profits.

Beyond ethical obligation, the rationale for social responsibility is the belief that it is good for business, morally appropriate, or important to employees. That is, CEOs support CSR because they think it increases firm performance, provides a favorable signal about firms, or garners positive accolades from internal and external stakeholders.[99]

One Type of Social Responsibility: Climate Change, Sustainable Development, and Natural Capital

For the first time in history, the majority of U.S. adults are highly worried about global warming.[100] **Climate change** refers to major changes in temperature, precipitation, wind patterns, and similar matters occurring over several decades. **Global warming**, one aspect of climate change, refers to the rise in global average temperature near the Earth's surface, caused mostly by increasing atmospheric concentrations of greenhouse gases, such as carbon emissions from fossil fuels.[101]

Sustainable development, as introduced in Chapter 1, is economic development that meets the needs of the present without compromising the ability of future generations to meet their own needs.[102] The UN, in the company of many scholars, has stressed the importance of natural capital accounting for informing sustainable development policy.[103] Indeed, planet (of the triple bottom line people, planet, and profit) is now identified by the name **natural capital**, the value of natural resources, such as topsoil, air, water, and genetic diversity, which humans depend on.

We discuss sustainable development goals at length in Learning Module 1.

Another Type of Social Responsibility: Undertaking Philanthropy, "Not Dying Rich"

"He who dies rich dies thus disgraced," 19th-century steel magnate Andrew Carnegie is supposed to have said, after he turned his interests from making money to **philanthropy**, making charitable donations to benefit humankind. Carnegie became well known as a supporter of free libraries.

Warren Buffett, one of the richest people in the world, has pledged to donate 99% of his $94 billion dollar fortune before he dies.[104] Buffet has been joined by 200+ other billionaires from 22 countries—including fashion designer Diane von Fürstenberg, philanthropist MacKenzie Scott, and others—in taking the Giving Pledge, a commitment to dedicate a majority of their wealth to philanthropy.[105]

Does Being Good Pay Off?

We answered this question by reviewing relevant research. Our conclusion is that indeed it pays to be ethical and socially responsible. Supportive findings are shown in Table 3.2.

Have you ever considered the degree of importance you place on ethics and social responsibility? An organization's commitment to CSR may be an important factor for you to consider during job searches. Take a few minutes to complete Self-Assessment 3.2, if your instructor has assigned it, to get a better idea of your attitude toward corporate responsibility. •

TABLE 3.2 Being Ethical and Socially Responsible Pays Off

	RESEARCH FINDINGS
Employees	• Younger generations of workers are more likely to join and stay with a company when management is committed to helping society. • Employees are more likely to do the right thing when faced with an ethical dilemma when the organization has a strong ethical climate.
Customers	• Customers believe it's important to purchase from socially responsible companies. • Customers make purchases and plan to spend more with socially responsible companies in the future.
Revenue	• Investing in responsible companies is predicted to top $30 trillion by 2026. • A focus on social responsibility is essential for long-term revenue growth.
Profits	• Companies that earn B Corp status (a designation related to high ethical standards, accountability, and social responsibility) are more profitable than companies without this status. • America's Most Just Companies earn a 4.5% higher profit margin and a 2.3% higher return-on-equity than competition.

Sources: Research findings compiled from McKinsey & Company. "Consumers Care about Sustainability—and Back it Up With their Wallets." February 6, 2023. https://www.mckinsey.com/industries/consumer-packaged-goods/our-insights/consumers-care-about-sustainability-and-back-it-up-with-their-wallets; PWC. ESG-Focused Institutional Investment Seen Soaring 84% to US$33.9 Trillion in 2026, Making up 21.5% of Assets Under Management: PWC Report. October 10, 2022. https://www.pwc.com/gx/en/news-room/press-releases/2022/awm-revolution-2022-report.html; Malik, Z. "$4 Trillion Increase in Revenue for Businesses Placing Greater Importance on ESG." International Accounting Bulletin. September 16, 2022. https://www.internationalaccountingbulletin.com/analysis/4-trillion-increase-in-revenue-for-businesses-placing-greater-importance-on-esg/; Al-Shammari, M. A., S. N. Banerjee, and A. A. Rasheed. "Corporate Social Responsibility and Firm Performance: A Theory of Dual Responsibility." Management Decision 60, no. 6 (2022): 1513–1540; Stevens, L. "Ethics in Business: Why Ethical Businesses are More Profitable." HCM Sales, Marketing & Alliance Excellence 21, no. 7 (2022): 25–27; "JUST Capital and CNBC Release Annual 'JUST 100,' the Only Comprehensive Ranking of How Corporations Perform on the American People's Priorities." CNBC. January 10, 2023. https://www.cnbc.com/2023/01/10/just-capital-and-cnbc-release-annual-just-100-the-only-comprehensive-ranking-of-how-corporations-perform-on-the-american-peoples-priorities.html; Al Halbusi, H., T. L. P. Tang, K. A. Williams, and T. Ramayah. "Do Ethical Leaders Enhance Employee Ethical Behaviors? Organizational Justice And Ethical Climate as Dual Mediators and Leader Moral Attentiveness as a Moderator—Evidence From Iraq's Emerging Market." Asian Journal of Business Ethics 11, no. 1 (2022):105–135.

SELF-ASSESSMENT 3.2 CAREER READINESS

Assessing Your Attitudes toward Corporate Responsibility

This self-assessment assesses your attitudes toward corporate responsibility. Please complete Self-Assessment 3.2 if your instructor has assigned it in Connect.

3.6 Corporate Governance

THE BIG PICTURE
Good corporate governance can contribute to more ethical and socially responsible organizations. CEO accountability, board composition, and CSR contracting are important governance factors for organizations and their boards to consider.

LO 3-6

Discuss the role of corporate governance in building ethical and socially responsible organizations.

Corporate governance is the system of governing a company so that the interests of corporate owners and other stakeholders are protected. Shareholders should elect directors who they believe will run the company according to the interests of the organization's stakeholders, but this doesn't always turn out to be the case. Poor corporate governance was apparent in the infamous cases involving fraud allegations, bankruptcy filings, and prison terms at companies like Enron, WorldCom, and Tyco. Good corporate governance, on the other hand, can contribute to more ethical and socially responsible organizations.

Corporate Governance and Ethics

Is there any connection between corporate governance and ethics? Certainly, says scholar Henrik Syse. Corporate governance is about such matters as long-term strategies, sustainable finances, accurate reporting, and positive work environments. All are tied to ethics because they are concerned with how a firm relates to and impacts its internal and external stakeholders.[106]

How organizations approach ethics will vary according to the unique compositions of their boards. Companies should actively seek to build boards with characteristics that are likely to encourage the organization to be more ethical. One study in the *Journal of Business Ethics* analyzed 43 publicly traded companies from 13 different countries and found that the presence of board characteristics that reflect stronger oversight and monitoring are positively related to financial firms' ethical reputations.[107] Specifically, companies with boards that are larger, more gender-diverse, and whose members serve—on average—on fewer than three other boards, have better ethical reputations. The authors theorize that these characteristics signal that a board will be more sensitive to and able to focus on ethical issues.

Corporate Governance and Social Responsibility

Boards of directors are tasked with designing compensation packages for CEOs and upper-level managers, and modern executive compensation is increasingly likely to be linked to additional metrics beyond traditional performance indicators.[108] In particular, more firms are integrating social responsibility into executive compensation.[109] This practice is often referred to as **CSR contracting**—the linking of executive compensation to CSR criteria such as environmental and social performance.[110]

Firms see increases in value, long-term orientation, and engagement in CSR initiatives when boards include CSR criteria in executive compensation. Further, CSR contracting leads to reduced carbon emissions and a stronger pursuit of "green" innovations. Importantly, CSR contracting is more effective when a substantial portion of executive compensation is tied to CSR criteria.[111]

Would you agree that factors such as board composition and the inclusion of CSR in executive compensation are important drivers of ethical and socially responsible organizations?

3.7 Career Corner: Managing Your Career Readiness

Figure 3.5 shows the model of career readiness we discussed in Chapter 1. We see one clear link between the content of this chapter and this model. It's the career readiness competency of *professionalism/work ethic*. The relevant aspect of this competency for this chapter is "demonstrated integrity, ethical behavior, and concern for the greater good" (look back at Figure 1.4).

The leaders in this chapter's executive interview series video discuss integrity and work ethic as some of the most important factors for advancing in your career. These executives highlight the importance of doing what's right (even when no one is looking), following through on your commitments, and working hard for the greater good of everyone around you. You can develop your professionalism/work ethic competency by engaging in activities that facilitate a habit of showing integrity, ethicality, and concern for the greater good. Doing so will give you behavioral examples of your *professionalism/work ethic* to discuss during job interviews.

LO 3-7

Describe how to develop the career readiness competency of professionalism/work ethic.

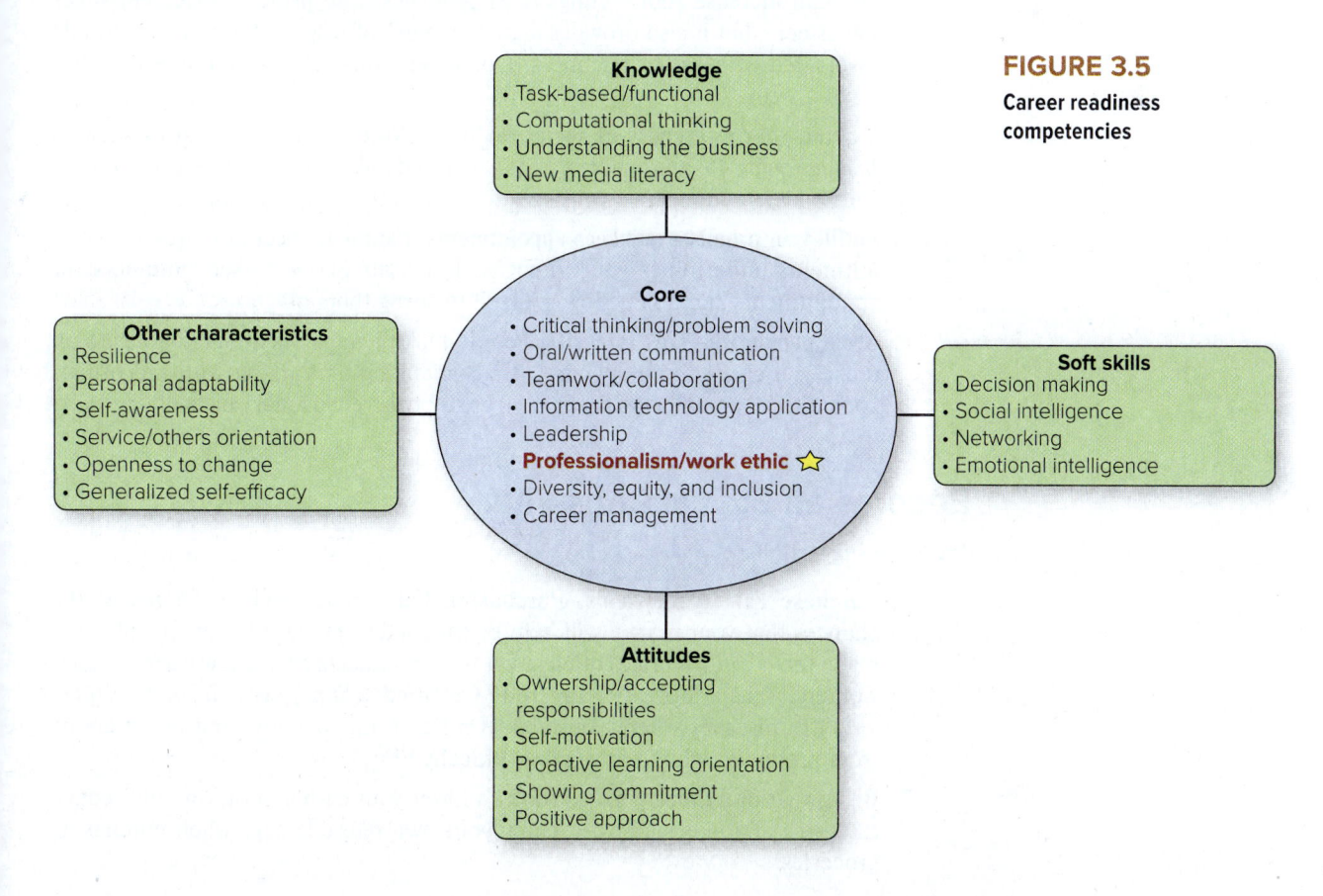

FIGURE 3.5

Career readiness competencies

Knowledge
- Task-based/functional
- Computational thinking
- Understanding the business
- New media literacy

Core
- Critical thinking/problem solving
- Oral/written communication
- Teamwork/collaboration
- Information technology application
- Leadership
- **Professionalism/work ethic** ⭐
- Diversity, equity, and inclusion
- Career management

Other characteristics
- Resilience
- Personal adaptability
- Self-awareness
- Service/others orientation
- Openness to change
- Generalized self-efficacy

Soft skills
- Decision making
- Social intelligence
- Networking
- Emotional intelligence

Attitudes
- Ownership/accepting responsibilities
- Self-motivation
- Proactive learning orientation
- Showing commitment
- Positive approach

Visit your instructor's Connect course and access your eBook to view this video.

Executive Interview Series: Professionalism and Work Ethic

Focus on the Greater Good and on Being More Ethical

Experiment with implementing some of the following:

1. **Reduce your carbon footprint.** Activities include ride-sharing, walking, or using public transportation more frequently; turning off lights when you leave a room; unplugging devices that are not in use; using whatever water bottles, jars, and totes you own until they fall apart; eating more plants and less meat; avoiding fast fashion; reducing your use of air conditioning; and annually servicing your home's air-conditioning/heating units.[112]

2. **Foster positive emotions in yourself and others.** Research suggests workers who make an effort to express genuinely positive feelings toward their co-workers experience better work relationships than workers who simply "fake it" in order to get through the day.[113] Positivity and helping others can also beget positivity and helping behavior, thereby enhancing the greater good. In fact, research suggests the benefits of positive emotions are more intense and longer lasting when the experience is shared by two or more people.[114] Focus on displaying the positive emotions of joy, gratitude, hope, pride, inspiration, and love. Start by thinking every day of one thing you are thankful for. You can also practice thinking of the qualities you genuinely admire in your co-workers when you are together.

3. **Spend time in nature.** Research shows that people are more helpful, trusting, and generous when they have recently experienced natural beauty. This occurs because positive emotions are associated with time spent in nature.[115]

4. **Get the proper amount of sleep.** Research shows that people are more likely to succumb to temptation to engage in deviant and unethical work behaviors when they are sleep-deprived.[116] For better sleep, try going to bed at the same time each night and avoiding screens for at least an hour before bedtime.

5. **Increase your level of exercise.** Besides providing obvious health benefits, exercise can increase your feelings of virtuousness and pride.[117] Pride enhances self-esteem, but it also provides a greater sense of responsibility, a key attitude associated with career readiness. Don't like gyms? Go for a long walk a few times a week.

6. **Expand your awareness of social realities.** Watching documentaries such as *Inequality for All*, and reading books by reputable commentators can increase your understanding of social issues that affect the greater good.[118]

7. **Fulfill your promises and keep appointments.** Failing to meet promises and commitments undermines your integrity. Use your phone to set reminders for appointments and don't allow yourself to shrug them off.

8. **Avoid people who lack integrity.** People make judgments about you based on those you choose to associate with. Socializing or working with individuals known to be unethical will detract from a positive personal image.[119]

Become an Ethical Consumer

Try these suggestions:

1. **Purchase Fair Trade items.** Purchasing Fair Trade products increases the chances that your money will help provide a decent wage for the people who made them.[120] Low prices often result from producers paying low wages to their workers. Take a look at "Fair Trade Certified" (*https://www.fairtradecertified.org/*) to discover where you might find clothing, alcohol, and home goods from producers who treat workers ethically.[121]

2. **Bring your own grocery bags.** You can lower your carbon footprint and reduce the price of goods sold by bringing your own reusable bags when purchasing groceries.

3. **Don't purchase items that aren't ethically made or sourced.** Research where and how a company makes its products. You may pay more for your purchases, but passing on low prices to support more ethical companies supports the greater good.[122]
4. **Don't buy knockoffs.** Cheap counterfeit and illegal merchandise are often made in sweatshop conditions. Although forgoing the low prices on such items may hurt your pocketbook, it's another way you can help the greater good. •

Key Terms Used in This Chapter

abusive supervision 73
board of directors 65
clawbacks 67
climate change 80
code of ethics 77
competitors 66
corporate governance 82
corporate social responsibility (CSR) 78
courage 61
crowdfunding 68
CSR contracting 82
customers 66
demographic forces 70
distributor 66
economic forces 69
ethical behavior 72
ethical climate 77
ethical dilemma 72
ethics 72
external stakeholders 63
general environment 63
global warming 80
government regulators 68
individual approach 74
insider trading 75
internal stakeholders 63
international forces 71
justice approach 74
macroenvironment 63
moral-rights approach 74
natural capital 80
owners 65
philanthropy 81
political–legal forces 70
Sarbanes–Oxley Act of 2002 75
sociocultural forces 69
special-interest groups 68
stakeholders 63
strategic allies 67
supplier 66
task environment 63
technological forces 69
trade balance 69
triple bottom line (TBL) 62
utilitarian approach 74
value system 72
values 72
venture capital 68
whistleblower 78
workplace cheating 76

Key Points

3.1 The Goals of Business: More Than Making Money

- Many businesses subscribe to a new standard of success—the triple bottom line, representing people, planet, and profit.
- The triple bottom line has particular appeal to younger workers who are less concerned with financial success and material goods than with meaningful work and sustainable development.

3.2 The Community of Stakeholders inside the Organization

- Managers operate in two organizational environments—internal and external—both made up of stakeholders.
- The internal environment includes employees, owners, and the board of directors.
- The external environment of stakeholders consists of the task environment and the general environment.

3.3 The Community of Stakeholders outside the Organization

- The task environment consists of 10 groups that present the manager with daily tasks to deal with: (1) customers, (2) competitors, (3) suppliers, (4) distributors, (5) strategic allies, (6) employee organizations, (7) local communities, (8) financial institutions, (9) government regulators, and (10) special-interest groups.

- The general environment consists of six forces: (1) economic, (2) technological, (3) sociocultural, (4) demographic, (5) political-legal, and (6) international.

3.4 The Ethical Responsibilities Required of You as a Manager

- Ethics are the standards of right and wrong that influence behavior. Ethical behavior is behavior that is accepted as "right" as opposed to "wrong" according to those standards.
- Ethical dilemmas often occur due to conflicts between value systems.
- The four approaches to resolving ethical dilemmas are: (1) utilitarian, (2) individual, (3) moral-rights, and (4) justice.
- Public outrage over white-collar crime (Enron, Tyco) led to the creation of the Sarbanes–Oxley Act of 2002 (SarbOx).
- Laurence Kohlberg proposed three levels of personal moral development: (1) preconventional, (2) conventional, and (3) postconventional.
- The five ways an organization can promote high ethical standards are: (1) creating a strong ethical climate, (2) screening prospective employees, (3) instituting ethics codes and training programs, (4) rewarding ethical behavior, and (5) using a multi-faceted approach.

3.5 The Social Responsibilities Required of You as a Manager

- Archie Carroll suggests organizations in the global economy should have the following priorities: (1) be a good global corporate citizen, (2) be ethical in its practices, (3) obey the law, and (4) make a profit.
- The idea of social responsibility has opposing and supporting viewpoints.
- One type of social responsibility focuses on climate change, sustainable development, and natural capital.
- Another type of social responsibility is undertaking philanthropy.
- Positive ethical behavior and social responsibility can pay off in the form of customer satisfaction, employee and customer loyalty, revenue growth, and enhanced long-term profits.

3.6 Corporate Governance

- Corporate governance is the system of governing a company so that the interests of corporate owners and other stakeholders are protected.
- Ways to use corporate governance to build more ethical and socially responsible organizations include holding CEOs accountable for ethical (mis)behaviors, ensuring that boards are composed of the right mix of people, and integrating social responsibility into executive compensation.

3.7 Career Corner: Managing Your Career Readiness

- You can develop the competency of professionalism/work ethic by engaging in activities that facilitate a habit of showing integrity, ethicality, and concern for the greater good.

LEARNING MODULE 1

Shared Value and Sustainable Development:

A New Way to Think about Leading and Managing

After reading this learning module, you should be able to:

LM 1-1   Describe how the concept of creating shared value improves upon the traditional approach to corporate social responsibility.

LM 1-2   Discuss the roles various stakeholders play in creating shared value.

LM 1-3   Explain recommendations for creating shared value in light of current progress and challenges.

MANAGE U

How Can You Contribute to a More Sustainable Future?

It's easy to think that sustainable development is a problem for big businesses and governments to solve, but we all can contribute. The United Nations' "Lazy Person's Guide to Saving the World" suggests activities at four levels, ranging from things you can accomplish during a Netflix binge to things you can try at your job.[1] Here are some of their ideas:

1. **Level 1: Things You Can Do from Your Couch**

   - **Like and Share.** If you see an interesting social media post about an issue related to one or more of the SDGs, share it so folks in your network see it too. Use the hashtag #globalgoals to share with the UN and give others ideas for contributing. These efforts can have a big ripple effect.
   - **Report online bullies.** If you notice harassment online, flag it. Calling out the behavior prevents others from being harmed and gives you practice at speaking up when it's important.
   - **Stay informed.** Follow local and national news outlets on social media. Doing so means you'll automatically learn about anything noteworthy when it comes across your feed.

2. **Level 2: Things You Can Do at Home**

   - **Air dry your clothes.** You'll use less energy and preserve your clothes for longer. This translates into less carbon and less consumption, with the bonus of saving money.
   - **Reconsider the preheat.** Think about whether you really need to preheat your oven. If you're just reheating a plate of leftovers, skip this step and instead stick your plate in as soon as you turn on the oven. This will drastically reduce the amount of energy your oven uses.

3. **Level 3: Things You Can Do Outside Your House**

   - **Purchase ugly foods.** Misfits Market purchases ugly produce (the stuff grocers won't put on their shelves because it doesn't adhere to size, shape, or other appearance standards) from local, organic farmers and bundles it in food subscription boxes that it ships

right to your door.[2] This strategy cuts down on food waste and gives farmers a chance to earn something on crops that would otherwise go into the garbage.
- **Shop smart**. Plan your meals so that you don't buy more than you need. The eMeals app takes it a step further by generating a shopping list based on the meals you choose.

4. **Level 4: Things You Can Do at Work**
- **Share**. If you don't want your apple or snack, don't toss it—send an e-mail on the listserv or offer it to a colleague—people love free stuff—especially food.
- **Speak up**. Raise your voice against discrimination in your office. If you're feeling unsure about how to do this the right way, flip back to the Chapter 3 ManageU feature for advice.
- **Engage locally.** Always be thinking about ways your company may be able to help the local community achieve its goals. Focus on your firm's core business activities for ideas on how your company can create the most impact.

FORECAST — *What's Ahead in This Learning Module*

This learning module discusses shared value and sustainable development as a new approach to leading and managing, which replaces more traditional forms of corporate social responsibility (CSR). We briefly review CSR and its shortcomings before introducing the concept and model of creating shared value. Next, we explore the roles that various stakeholders play in the creation of shared value, including the United Nations and its set of 17 sustainable development goals. We then examine progress that has been made toward creating shared value and managing for sustainable development and the challenges that have arisen in this process. We conclude with recommendations for managing for shared value and sustainable development.

1.1 From Corporate Social Responsibility to Creating Shared Value

THE BIG PICTURE
Traditional CSR programs are one way organizations have attempted to contribute to society. Creating shared value is a new approach that incorporates capitalism to improve upon the limitations of CSR.

By now you have completed your work on Chapter 2 and hopefully remember a few facts about management history. Do you recall the contemporary perspective on management that says firms should look beyond making short-term profits for shareholders and also consider the environmental and social costs of doing business? Chapter 3 revealed that corporate social responsibility (CSR) captures the idea that organizations have obligations to a much broader group of stakeholders than just the people who own shares of the company's stock.

In this section we take a look at traditional CSR and some of the criticisms of this approach in practice. We then turn our discussion to the concept of shared value.

LM 1-1

Describe how the concept of creating shared value improves upon the traditional approach to corporate social responsibility.

Traditional CSR

As you learned in Chapter 3, an increasing number of companies see engaging in social responsibility as the "right thing" to do.[3] In fact, recent estimates show that Fortune 500 companies funnel an estimated $20 billion into CSR initiatives each year.[4]

Does Traditional CSR Run Counter to Shareholders' Interests? What do you think Milton Friedman, one of the most influential economists of the 20th century, would say about the popularity of CSR? Recall from Chapter 3 that Friedman believed the only social responsibility a business should worry about was making profits for shareholders.

It's clear that doing the right thing in today's global environment requires managers to consider the impacts of their decisions on a host of stakeholders in addition to their shareholders. Still, many firms remain hesitant to move beyond making minimally acceptable investments in social initiatives. This is because the prevailing wisdom—heavily influenced by Friedman's paradigm—depicts CSR as a "necessary expense" which can quickly turn into an irresponsible way to spend shareholders' dollars.[5] In this view, there is a "fixed pie" of value available in the marketplace, and by spending money in one area (social responsibility) a company reduces the money available for another area (shareholders). This viewpoint characterizes social responsibility as a zero-sum game.

Moving beyond the "Fixed Pie" Perspective Do you think organizations are doomed if they "give up" a portion of shareholders' profits and redistribute them as charity in order to be socially responsible? A quick review of Table 3.1 in Chapter 3 will remind you of evidence that suggests some organizations are actually better off financially after engaging in CSR. Perhaps maximizing shareholder wealth and creating social benefit aren't necessarily mutually exclusive propositions. In fact, some organizations are using CSR strategically as a way to solve social problems while growing their organizations. This perspective is known as creating shared value (CSV).

Creating Shared Value

According to Harvard Business School professors Michael Porter and Mark Kramer, organizations often miss out on how best to impact society through CSR because they fail to align CSR initiatives with their core business strategies. This failure, they say, stems from a limited view of capitalism's potential to create value, which in turn generates extensive corporate philanthropy, but few meaningful solutions for long-term societal improvement.[6] Porter and Kramer conclude that, "Businesses acting as businesses, not as charitable donors, are the most powerful force for addressing the pressing issues we face."[7]

Does this mean firms should abandon CSR all together and return to a purely profit-driven mindset? Not exactly. Porter and Kramer propose that organizations focus instead on **creating shared value (CSV)—implementing policies and operating practices that enhance the competitiveness of a company while simultaneously advancing the economic and social conditions in the communities in which it operates.** CSV accounts for people and planet in addition to profit, and rather than representing a fixed pie of value, it advocates that organizations can make the entire pie bigger by doing the right thing and working toward the benefit of their stakeholders. Consider the following example of a company engaging in CSV:

> **Creating Shared Value Example—Reliance Jio:** This wireless carrier invested billions of dollars to create a modern 4G network in India in 2016. Prior to this, only about 150 million people in India (out of more than 1 billion) had access to a mobile network, and existing cellular service was unreliable and expensive. By 2022, Reliance Jio had over 421 million subscribers on its network and had attracted huge investments, including $5.7 billion from Facebook in exchange for a 9.9% stake in the company.[8] The company offers low-cost data and also sells inexpensive smartphones. The

existence of a reliable mobile network provides a plethora of opportunities for economic growth in developing regions because businesses have more access to customers, real-time information, and mobile financial services. Reliance Jio's network benefits a huge number of people in India, and the company has experienced unprecedented growth and soaring profits.[9]

The firm mentioned in this example leveraged the power of capitalism to generate financial wealth while simultaneously solving large-scale social problems. The opportunities created by their initiatives will drive continued economic growth in these once underserved regions. In this example, the "fixed pie" perspective is replaced by one that allows for the whole pie to grow. The CSV approach requires a major shift in the way we think about capitalism and CSR. Let's consider two important points.

Affordable and reliable 4G. A Reliance Jio employee demonstrates the JioTV app that provides live-streaming TV content to its almost 400 million subscribers. The 4G access Reliance Jio provides has transformed India's digital economy. soumen82hazra/Shutterstock

CSV Generates Sustainable Competitive Advantages The beauty of CSV is that it shifts the concept of CSR from *a way to use profits* toward *a way to make profits*.[10] Successful CSV is strategic—it stems from opportunities that are closely aligned with a firm's specific business. Firms seeking CSV should evaluate opportunities for social benefit in the same way they evaluate firm-level strategic decisions. This means the right decisions for an organization are those that allow it to thrive, grow, and create long-term value for shareholders while also generating broader value for society.

CSV Is Gaining Traction The private sector has grown increasingly supportive of the idea that firms are uniquely positioned to enact solutions to some of the world's most pressing problems—issues like poverty, poor education, and inequality—while maximizing shareholder value.[11] You can find evidence of this in the *Fortune* annual Change the World List, which recognizes firms that are using their core business models to tackle major societal issues. Editors at *Fortune* say these companies "understand that doing good for society and the planet can help them bring in more revenue, which can help them do more good, in a self-reinforcing loop."[12]

Let's consider how organizations can work toward successful CSV.

A Model of Shared Value Creation

Figure LM 1.1 shows a model of CSV based on Porter and Kramer's work. The figure is structured around the classic Input-Process-Output (IPO) management perspective that shows how key processes transform inputs into outputs. The idea is that managers create desired outputs by fostering a specific set of inputs and processes. As business students and professors, we know that the overarching goal of firms is to provide economic value for shareholders in the form of increased profits. Figure LM 1.1 shows how CSV contributes to this goal.

The model shows that the amount of economic value a firm ultimately produces for shareholders is most directly affected by the extent to which it is able to create shared value. CSV occurs when the firm generates meaningful, lasting benefits for its myriad internal and external stakeholders in addition to maximizing shareholders' profits. Let's consider the processes and inputs that drive shared value.

Key Processes for Creating Shared Value Managers need to understand the processes that enable CSV to approach business decisions from this perspective. Figure LM 1.1 highlights three key processes at play:

1. ***Discovery of new products, markets, and opportunities.*** One key process for CSV is the discovery of potential new products and/or services that the firm can offer, new markets the firm can enter, and new opportunities for the firm to reposition or differentiate itself in its current landscape. The following example illustrates this key process:

FIGURE LM 1.1

A model of creating shared value

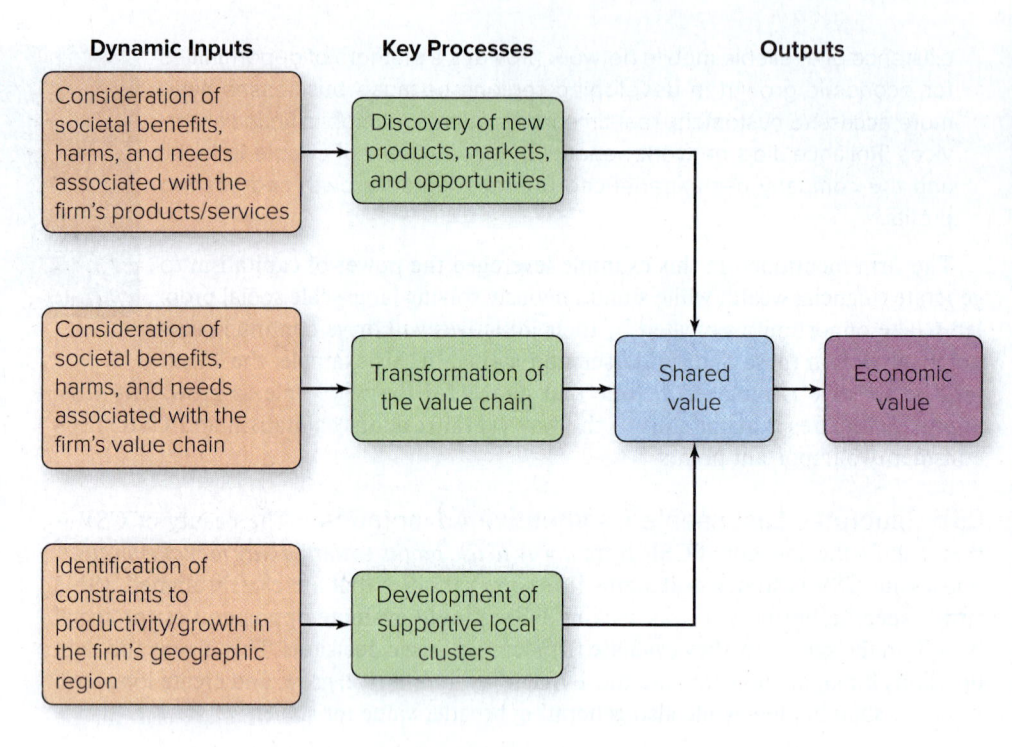

Dynamic Inputs	Key Processes	Outputs
Consideration of societal benefits, harms, and needs associated with the firm's products/services	Discovery of new products, markets, and opportunities	
Consideration of societal benefits, harms, and needs associated with the firm's value chain	Transformation of the value chain	Shared value → Economic value
Identification of constraints to productivity/growth in the firm's geographic region	Development of supportive local clusters	

Discovery of New Products, Markets, and Opportunities Example—Novartis Pharmaceuticals: A shared-value approach led Novartis pharmaceuticals to discover a lucrative new market that now spans 22,000 rural villages in India. The company launched a program called Arogya Parivar (Hindi for "healthy family") with the goal of increasing access to doctors and medications and improving health literacy for the millions of residents of these villages.[13] The program enlists health educators familiar with local customs to travel from village to village offering free health camps. The residents, most of whom earn the equivalent of less than $5 a day, gain access to information about things like disease prevention, hygiene, and nutrition. Local doctors often volunteer to join the educators, seeing patients at no cost but gaining potential future patients in the process. The program's corporate wing sells inexpensive medications for conditions that are common in the villages. The increased demand for these medications allowed the program to turn a profit for Novartis after only three years. Villagers' doctor visits tripled in this time, meaning that millions of people—many of whom had never seen a doctor—had increased access to important medical care. Novartis has expanded the initiative to Kenya, Vietnam, and Uganda.[14]

Without a shared-value perspective, it is highly unlikely that Novartis would have seen the potential to market its products to millions of people in rural India who had little money for medicine and almost no access to doctors.

2. *Transformation of the value chain.* A second key process for CSV is transformation of the firm's value chain. A **value chain** consists of all of the processes a company uses to add value to its products or services. The value chain includes activities involved in production, marketing, and ongoing customer support. Value chains are important because they represent the primary means through which firms derive sustainable competitive advantages. For

example, a firm that develops innovative technology for assembling and packaging its products can benefit from substantially lower costs in these areas relative to competitors. If competitors can't figure out how to mimic the technology, the innovation translates into longer-term advantages for the firm. As another example, firms derive advantages through the relationships they develop with suppliers. A company is more likely to reap benefits such as special pricing and fast shipping if it has consistently made prompt payments or invested in improving the supplier's operations.[15] CSV requires firms to consider improvements and enhancements across their value chains. Consider the following example:

> **Transformation of the Value Chain Example—Flex Ltd.:** Flex Ltd. (Flex) is a multinational manufacturing company with more than 100 facilities in 30 countries. Flex manufactures for a variety industries including healthcare, automotive, and communications, and the company has 170,000 employees and 16,000 suppliers.[16] Flex facilities around the world use advanced technologies to "deliver better business outcomes for our customers" and to "advance sustainable manufacturing and production throughout various manufacturing processes."[17] The company's 2030 goals include helping its suppliers to reduce greenhouse gas emissions and reducing the amount of water used in its manufacturing facilities located in water scarce areas.[18] According to the company's website, "Building on 20 years of sustainability investment, our disciplined practices stand strong to help address broader environmental and social challenges, cultivate a workplace that empowers every team member to thrive, lead with integrity, and accelerate a more sustainable value chain."[19]

3. ***Development of supportive local clusters.*** The third and final key process that enables CSV is the development of supportive **clusters**—geographic concentrations of interrelated entities such as competitors, suppliers, universities, and other organizations that result in benefits for the firm in the local operating environment.

Employees in the various firms comprising a cluster are likely to engage in face-to-face interactions because they are near to one another and face similar operational challenges arising from the local operating environment. Over time, these close interactions create trust, and this forms the basis for the open and transparent sharing of ideas, knowledge, and resources that characterizes supportive clusters. Innovation results from working through problems with employees from competing and supporting firms, universities, governments, and trade associations.[20] Cluster-related activities improve the broader local environment in the form of, for example, job creation and larger skilled labor pools.[21] Deficiencies in local clusters represent constraints to firm productivity and profitability. Cisco learned this first-hand and used a shared-value perspective to address cluster weaknesses.

> **Development of Supportive Local Clusters Example—Cisco:** A lack of qualified candidates in the local labor pool represented a critical constraint for Cisco's operations in Brazil, South Africa, and other markets. The company addressed this weakness by establishing its Networking Academy—a collaboration with nonprofits, government bodies, schools, and other entities through which Cisco leverages its cloud technology expertise to deliver IT training and education and foster career readiness for students and veterans that may not otherwise have the opportunity to enhance their education or career prospects.[22]

An example of a value chain. All of the activities involved in getting food on the table—from sowing seeds through cooking a meal—are part of the food value chain. One of the ways firms create shared value is by transforming their value chain activities. elenabs/iStock/Getty Images

FOOD VALUE CHAIN

PRODUCTION — CULTIVATION — HARVESTING
PROCESSING/PACKAGING
DISTRIBUTION — RETAIL — HOME PREPARATION — RESTAURANT — RESTAURANT PREPARATION — CONSUMER

Dynamic Inputs Figure LM 1.1 shows that each key process is affected by a unique dynamic input. We call these dynamic because organizations' rapidly changing environments create constant opportunities for reassessment and adjustment. Let's consider the dynamic inputs managers can use to promote the processes that create shared value.

1. *Consideration of societal benefits, harms, and needs associated with the firm's products/services.* The first set of dynamic inputs requires that firms continually envision all of the ways their products and services might be used to address current and potential societal needs. This set of dynamic inputs also asks companies to get real about the ways their business might be harming or benefiting society. Figure LM 1.1 shows that this set of inputs drives the key process of discovery of new products, markets, and opportunities.

2. *Consideration of societal benefits, harms, and needs associated with the firm's value chain.* The second set of dynamic inputs requires that firms continually consider all of the current and potential ways their value chain activities meet societal needs and/or and create societal benefit or harm. Figure LM 1.1 shows that this set of inputs drives the key process of transformation of the value chain. Experts emphasize the need for firms to be brutally honest with themselves when considering the societal impacts of their value chains. It is highly likely that managers will discover value chain activities that are counterproductive to the goals of CSV. What is important is to acknowledge the existence of these issues and then make a detailed plan for improvement.[23]

3. *Identification of constraints to productivity/growth in the firm's geographic region.* The third set of dynamic inputs requires that firms continually monitor their cluster for things that might restrain firm productivity and growth.

Figure LM 1.1 shows that this set of inputs drives the key process of development of supportive local clusters.

How CSR and CSV Are Fundamentally Different

Historically speaking, CSR approaches have been largely ineffective at addressing large-scale societal problems. This is because CSR initiatives tend to be narrow in scope and misaligned with firms' core businesses. Campbell Soup presents a great example of the difference between a failed CSR effort and a vibrant CSV strategy (see the Example box).

EXAMPLE: A Shift in Perspective at the Campbell Soup Company

CSR at Campbell Soup

In 2010 the Campbell Soup Company announced that it was doing its part to combat heart disease by reducing the sodium content in its soups by up to 45%. It didn't go over well—customers revolted against the loss of flavor and by mid-2011, the company had added most of the sodium back.[24] Campbell Soup made a noble attempt to do the socially responsible thing, but the project only addressed one specific concern and was not implemented as a strategic initiative.

CSV at Campbell Soup

Fast-forward to present day and you'll find Campbell Soup engaged in a full-blown campaign to improve the agricultural supply chain of tomatoes. The company educates its farmers on environmental impact and efficient resource utilization. It encourages and supports the installation of drip irrigation, a strategy that helped the company reduce the amount of water required to produce a pound of tomatoes by 15%. The company is now working toward a 20% reduction in its overall water usage by 2025, and it continues to educate farmers on soil nutrient preservation and optimal fertilizer use. These initiatives benefit local watersheds and increase the long-term viability of soil for crop production.[25]

According to the Campbell Soup website, the company is "Focusing on combating climate change, promoting sustainable water supplies, working to eliminate waste, and improving circularity in packaging. We're committed to building a more resilient, sustainable food system that improves the planet we share. We believe in food from farms that nurture the land, made and packaged in ways that conserve natural resources, to create a sustainable future for generations to come."[26]

Moving from CSR to CSV. For Campbell Soup, the decision to remove salt was socially responsible but not strategically valuable. By focusing instead on the environmental impact of its agricultural supply chains, the company has begun to create shared value.
(left): FoodCollection; *(right):* David R. Frazier Photolibrary, Inc./Alamy Stock Photo

YOUR CALL

What are the key differences between the two initiatives at Campbell Soup? What additional opportunities might the company have to create shared value through its core business activities?

The contrasting examples within Campbell Soup illustrate the importance that a shift in managers' perspectives can have on a company's ability to create shared value. While CSR focuses on isolated issues or on minimizing or making up for firms' collateral damage to society, CSV places profit maximization at the center of solutions to complex, wide-ranging global challenges.[27]

1.2 The Roles of Various Stakeholders in CSV

THE BIG PICTURE

CSV involves multiple stakeholders. The United Nations introduced the Sustainable Development Goals to help stakeholders across the globe understand how to work together to solve global crises. The stakeholders most relevant to leading and managing for CSV include big and small businesses, entrepreneurs, and business schools.

LM 1-2

Discuss the roles various stakeholders play in creating shared value.

The world is facing serious problems, and many of them are getting bigger. For example:

- More than 650 million people in the world live in extreme poverty, and the percentage of people who live with hunger is growing.
- More than 10% of the world's population has no access to safe drinking water.
- 99% of people living in urban areas are breathing polluted air, and 25% of urban residents live in slum-like conditions. Rapidly increasing urbanization is adding to these problems.[28]

Do you think businesses and managers can make a difference in these and other global issues? Solving problems of this scale represents a remarkable challenge, and research suggests that societal change efforts can only be successful when a wide range of stakeholders get involved.[29] In this section, we discuss several stakeholder groups that must work together to solve global challenges through the creation of shared value.

Global Collaboration: The Role of the United Nations

The United Nations (UN) took an aggressive stance on global issues in 2016 when all 193 member countries agreed to adopt a set of 17 Sustainable Development Goals (SDGs). These goals, introduced in Chapter 1, represent a roadmap for economic planning and development that allows the current population to meet its needs without compromising the ability of future generations to do the same.[30] The SDGs address serious, persistent, global issues such as threats to human and animal life, destruction of the natural environment, and unequal access to basic necessities. We summarize the 17 SDGs in *Figure LM 1.2*.

The SDGs Are an Opportunity for CSV
The SDGs emphasize the need for key stakeholders to join forces in creating mutually beneficial solutions to global problems. In other words, the SDGs are a veritable menu of opportunities for organizations to join with governments and communities to create shared value.[31] Dr. Mark Kramer explained the connection between the SDGs and CSV as "a new revenue model for business," adding, "You can actually quantify the market potential of for-profit business to meet the needs of the SDGs."[32] Here is one example:

Creating Shared Value through the SDGs Example—UN COP Meetings:
Each year, the UN brings together businesses, government officials, and entrepreneurs from all over the world for its Conference of the Parties (COP) meeting. The meeting focuses specifically on achieving SDG #13—Climate Action. The COP27 meeting, held in Sharm el-Sheikh, Egypt in November of 2022, centered on ensuring that countries had the resources, knowledge, and tools to enable follow-through on climate-related goals they'd previously set.[33] The key outcome of COP27 was the establishment of a fund to aid countries that have been especially vulnerable to and affected by climate change. The fund reached over $200 million in pledges by the end of 2022.[34]

FIGURE LM 1.2

Summary of the 17 UN Sustainable Development Goals

#	Goal	Description
1	NO POVERTY	10% of the world's population lives in extreme poverty. Economic growth must be inclusive to reduce poverty and provide sustainable jobs.
2	ZERO HUNGER	Investments in agriculture and sustainable food production systems are needed to help alleviate hunger.
3	GOOD HEALTH AND WELL-BEING	Good health for all ages is imperative for sustainable development. Improved sanitation and hygiene as well as access to doctors can save millions.
4	QUALITY EDUCATION	A quality education is the foundation for sustainable development. Education equips people with the tools needed to help solve the world's problems.
5	GENDER EQUALITY	Women and girls must be provided with access to equal education, health care and work to create sustainable economies, benefit societies, and humanity at large.
6	CLEAN WATER AND SANITATION	40% of the world's population struggles with water scarcity. Investment in freshwater ecosystems and sanitation facilities is needed to create fresh water for all.
7	AFFORDABLE AND CLEAN ENERGY	Energy is vital to every challenge and opportunity in the world. Access to clean fuel, technology, and renewable energy is essential for sustainability.
8	DECENT WORK AND ECONOMIC GROWTH	Conditions where people have quality jobs that stimulate the economy but don't harm the environment are needed for sustainable economic growth.
9	INDUSTRY, INNOVATION AND INFRASTRUCTURE	Transportation, irrigation, energy and information, and communication technology are vital infrastructure needs for sustainable development.
10	REDUCED INEQUALITIES	Policies that are universal and include the needs of the disadvantaged and marginalized populations need to be created in order to reduce inequality.
11	SUSTAINABLE CITIES AND COMMUNITIES	Sustainable development requires cities to provide opportunities for all, including clean air, access to basic services, energy, housing, transportation, and more.
12	RESPONSIBLE CONSUMPTION AND PRODUCTION	Sustainable consumption and production—"doing more and better with less"—reduces resource use, degradation, and pollution while increasing quality of life.
13	CLIMATE ACTION	Climate change is affecting every country, disrupting economies and affecting lives. Renewable energy and emissions reduction are needed to create a low carbon world.
14	LIFE BELOW WATER	The world's oceans make the earth habitable for humankind. Careful management including control of overfishing, pollution, and ocean acidification is needed.
15	LIFE ON LAND	Forests cover 30.7% of the earth and they are key to combating climate change, protecting biodiversity, and combating desertification.
16	PEACE, JUSTICE AND STRONG INSTITUTIONS	Sustainable development includes justice for all and effective, accountable institutions. Efficient and transparent regulations are vital.
17	PARTNERSHIPS FOR THE GOALS	Sustainable development requires partnerships—along with shared goals and visions—between governments, the private sector, and civil society.

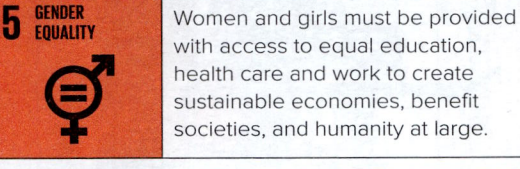

Source: Used with permission of the United Nations, www.un.org/sustainabledevelopment/. The content of this publication has not been approved by the United Nations and does not reflect the views of the United Nations or its officials or Members States.

Private-Sector Involvement Is Critical for Achieving the SDGs Did you know that the SDGs were designed specifically to enlist businesses and managers in solving global problems through the creation of shared value?[35] The private sector's participation is essential because it carries unparalleled financial resources and capabilities. According to UN Secretary-General António Guterres, investment from the private sector is "critical" for achieving the SDGs.[36]

The Role of Businesses, Big and Small

According to the UN, global CSV initiatives represent a $12 trillion opportunity and carry the potential to create 380 million new jobs across the globe by 2030.[37] Businesses both large and small can make an impact.

Big Businesses What do GM, Walmart, IBM, and Apple have in common? For starters, and as you've probably already guessed, these are some of the largest and most recognizable companies in the world. But you may be surprised to learn that these firms also share a commitment to shared value creation. They belong to a growing body of industry titans pledging to embrace sustainable business practices by working to benefit *all* of their stakeholders rather than just their shareholders.[38]

This is good news for advocates of shared value and the SDGs for at least two reasons:

1. *Big businesses are influencers*—These firms have the reputations, reach, and social media presence to shine a spotlight on societal issues.[39] Their actions inspire others to follow suit.
2. *Big businesses can mobilize big solutions*—Companies with extensive resources can deliver sizable impact.[40] And collaborations across big businesses have the potential to—quite literally—change the world.

Here's one example of recent strides big businesses have made in creating shared value:

Big Businesses Creating Shared Value Example—Merck: Kenneth Frazier, former CEO of Merck, once said that, "While a fundamental responsibility of business leaders is to create value for shareholders, I think businesses also exist to deliver value to society."[41] The pharmaceutical company is currently using its core business strategy and strengths to increase global access to Human Papillomavirus (HPV) vaccines.[42] Merck has committed more than 91 million doses of the HPV vaccine for countries in dire need of increased access to vaccines.[43] According to CEO Robert Davis, "Our commitment and efforts in this space reflect Merck's distinguished legacy of operating responsibly and creating value for society."[44]

Joerg Boethling/Alamy Stock Photo

Small Businesses It may be difficult to believe that small businesses can have an impact on global issues after reading examples of large companies improving *billions* of lives with their CSV initiatives. But did you know that 90% of businesses in the world are small businesses?[45] These companies are responsible for almost 70% of the world's jobs and GDP, and they occupy the front lines for eradicating poverty, boosting income generation, and creating jobs. Small businesses are an essential player in shared value creation and sustainable development.[46]

Need more proof that small firms can make big strides? Consider *Fortune*'s 2022 Change the World List—it featured 18 companies with annual revenues of less than $1 billion.[47] Here is one example of a small business creating shared value:

Small Businesses Creating Shared Value Example—Zipline: Zipline is a delivery and logistics company that specializes in drone delivery. According to the company's website, Zipline is "on a mission to create the first logistics system that serves all humans equally."[48] Zipline is using its capabilities to make progress toward SDG#3—Good Health and Well-Being. Specifically, the company uses its drones to deliver life-saving medical supplies, vaccines, and many other necessary medical items from its bases to its targeted zones in rapid time. Zipline has delivered more than 1 million doses of the COVID-19 vaccine to medical facilities in Ghaha, and during the pandemic, Zipline's drones transported more than 5 million critical routine vaccine doses to the area at a time when lockdowns made it nearly impossible for healthcare facilities to access them otherwise.[49] The company has also made more than 60,000 deliveries of emergency medical supplies to areas in Rwanda that are otherwise difficult to access.

The Role of Entrepreneurs

Do you dream of starting your own business? Then we have good news for you as it pertains to your ability to make decisions that create shared value. According to two experts, "Lasting societal change is catalyzed by starting enterprises." This statement highlights the critical role entrepreneurship plays in creating shared value.[50] In fact, experts believe entrepreneurs are one of the groups that has driven the most progress toward the SDGs to date.[51]

Here are two reasons entrepreneurs are well-positioned to create shared value:

- **Entrepreneurs' environments are less constrained.** Big businesses may have the advantage of deep pockets, but there's one thing they don't have—agility. Recall from Figure LM 1.1 that societal needs are dynamic. This means organizations must monitor their environments regularly and be poised to respond to new or changing opportunities for CSV as they arise. Unfortunately, large and established companies often suffer from inertia—the tendency for firms to resist change in favor of their current modes of operation—and this is where entrepreneurs have a unique advantage. Unlike large organizations, entrepreneurial ventures are not locked in by pre-existing policies, routines, or expectations, and this enables them to be nimble and responsive to changing needs.[52]

- **Entrepreneurs possess important traits.** CSV is uncharted territory for many firms and doing something completely new is both difficult and scary. Entrepreneurs have two traits that are advantageous in this situation: creativity and risk propensity. (We discuss entrepreneurs' traits in detail in Learning Module 2.)

    1. *Creativity.* Entrepreneurs are more likely to be innovative, which is beneficial when devising solutions to highly complex societal problems for which there is no precedent. Entrepreneurs have a gift for seeing *possibilities* when others see lost causes.
    2. *Risk propensity.* Entrepreneurs are willing to take risks. This means they are more comfortable trying something even though it may not be successful. Their bold moves, in turn, often clear the way for industrywide changes later on.[53]

Consider the following example of how entrepreneurship is creating shared value for famers.

Entrepreneurship Example—Ricult: The rise in global access to smartphones is a ripe opportunity for entrepreneurs to create shared value.[54] MIT-based start-up Ricult uses smartphone technology to empower rural farmers in developing countries to break free from systemic factors that previously held them in poverty. "Farmers are at the bottom of the pyramid in developing countries, so if you want to drive these countries forward and reduce inequality, you have to transform the agricultural sector," said co-founder Aukrit Unahalekhaka. Along with Usman Javaid, Jonathan Stoller, and Gabriel Torres, Unahalekhaka created the service to give farmers direct access to credit, a digital marketplace for farm supplies, and buyers. The farmers also receive personalized advice for their operations based on their unique weather and soil conditions. So far, farmers using Ricult have seen their yields increase by an average of 50%, and their profits have gone up by 30–40%. This kind of growth is life-changing for the rural farmers the company serves. Unahalekhaka said, "Before the farmer had to decide, 'Should I send my kid to school or should I save that money to pay for food or health care?' All of those things are necessary for a quality life. With more money, they don't have to make those tough choices anymore."[55]

The Role of Business Schools

Younger generations of workers expect organizations to create shared value. In one recent survey, nearly two-thirds of Gen Zers said they aren't interested in applying for jobs at companies that negatively impact the environment.[56] Further, Gen Zers' values and rising earnings potential are driving financial advising firms to incorporate more socially responsible investments in their portfolios.[57] Let's take a look at what we can learn from the business schools leading the charge in shared value and sustainable development education for these younger generations of future managers.

Business Schools Take Varied Approaches to Teaching Shared Value

The Association to Advance Collegiate Schools of Business (AACSB) reports that more and more colleges and universities are contributing to advancing the SDGs with innovative and meaningful approaches.[58] Evidence suggests institutes of higher education incorporate these ideas at four levels:

1. **Coursework.** We found various examples of courses dedicated to the study of shared value, sustainable development, and related concepts. For example, Columbia College at New York's Columbia University offers courses such as *Challenges of Sustainable Development* and *Economic & Financial Methods for Sustainable Development*.[59] At the University of Michigan, the Marsal Family School of Education offers a course called *Introduction to Environmental Education for Sustainable Development*.[60] There are many more examples of business school coursework focused on these ideas.

2. **Experiential learning.** Another approach for teaching the principles of shared value and sustainable development is to provide students with opportunities for hands-on experience. An example is the Keough School Integration Lab at the University of Notre Dame. Students in the Master of Global Affairs program participate in a 3-semester *Global Partner Experience,* during which they work with high-impact organizations to address global challenges.[61]

3. **Certificate and degree programs.** The University of Iowa offers a Master of Science in Sustainable Development.[62] Courses include *The UN Sustainable Development Goals: A Blueprint for a Sustainable Future* and *Skills for Future Leaders in Sustainable Development.* Says Professor Lucie Laurian, "The ideal student for the program is one who has a sense of where they're going, but don't know how

to get there. They know sustainability, climate, or justice is something they care about. They're planning on being in the world and doing something that matters."[63]

4. **Cultural infusion.** Some business school leaders embed shared value at a deep, cultural level. For example, Dr. Cathy DuBois leads the Responsible Leadership Initiative at the Kent State University College of Business. The initiative advocates for business as a force for good and weaves the SDGs into research, teaching, and practice activities throughout the college. Through this program, Kent State business students are immersed in principles of shared value. The college integrates the SDGs and related concepts into nearly 60 courses and offers multiple study abroad programs built around sustainable development and social responsibility. Faculty members participate in workshops and resource groups, and between 2013 and 2018, 36% of faculty research publications related to at least one of the SDGs.

The Association to Advance Collegiate Schools of Business (AACSB)—the world's most recognized accrediting body for business schools—ensures colleges of business prepare students to respond to relevant and dynamic global needs. The AACSB recently added *Engagement and Societal Impact* as one of the standards schools must meet in order to achieve and retain accreditation.[64]

Engaging the next generation of leadership in CSV and sustainable development. In 2022, the Gordon S. Lang School of Business and Economics at Canada's University of Guelph ranked # 5 on the Corporate Knights Better World MBA list. The School houses 4 unique centers and institutes that focus on sustainability and the SDGs.
Courtesy of John F. Wood Centre for Business and Student Enterprise at the Lang School of Business and Economics

Your Knowledge of CSV and the SDGs Enhances Your Career Readiness

You can use the knowledge you gain from this learning module to gain an advantage on the job market, even if your university doesn't incorporate shared value and/or sustainable development into its programs just yet. Recent survey data suggests at least 70% of U.S. workers would consider a firm's commitment to sustainability when determining whether to accept a job with the company.[65] We suggest taking time to research an organization's history with shared value and sustainable development before your interview. This will increase your career readiness competency of *understanding the business*, and you'll demonstrate to the company that you have a *proactive learning orientation*.

1.3 Progress, Challenges, and Recommendations for CSV

THE BIG PICTURE

In this section we discuss progress to date on shared value and sustainable development, examine the challenges firms face as they work toward shared value creation, and provide recommendations for addressing these challenges and moving forward.

LM 1-3

Explain recommendations for creating shared value in light of current progress and challenges.

It is clear that the private sector is adopting the view that profitable businesses and social change go hand-in-hand. For example, a recent study from the Global Reporting Initiative found that over 80% of companies surveyed include a specific commitment to advancing the SDGs in their corporate sustainability reports.[66] However, many companies still have difficulty turning commitment into measurable action. This was evidenced by a recent qualitative study of more than 1,300 corporate sustainability reports that found "a superficial engagement with the SDGs for the vast majority of organizations."[67] In this section we explore progress that has been made toward the SDGs as well as with challenges that those pursuing these goals must overcome.

Current Progress and Challenges in Shared Value and Sustainable Development

Much progress in fostering shared value and sustainable development has occurred in recent years. Organizations, for example, are becoming increasingly comfortable with the notion of CSV and have started to implement shared value in strategic decisions.

Areas of Progress Corporate engagement with shared value and sustainable development is relatively new, but already we see improvements in two broad areas:

1. *Awareness of and engagement with CSV and the SDGs.* A growing number of organizations are updating their existing, outdated CSR programs with the language of shared value and sustainable development.[68] There also is increasing awareness and understanding of shared value and sustainable development in the corporate community, and more CEOs are engaging their organizations with the SDGs at a strategic level.[69] According to a recent PWC study, 41% of companies surveyed plan to embed the SDGs into their strategic frameworks over the next 5 years.[70]

2. *Progress toward specific goals.* Societies have made significant strides toward achieving some of the SDGs. For example:
    - SDG #5: Gender Equality[71]
        - The number of transgender elected officials in the United States rose by almost 10% between 2021 and 2022.
        - A record number of women—150 total—served in the 118th U.S. Congress beginning in 2023.
    - SDG #15: Life on Land[72]
        - Almost 50% of areas identified as key biodiversity areas (including freshwater, terrestrial, and mountain) are now protected.
        - An increasing number of countries include biodiversity and ecosystem metrics in their national reporting and accounting systems.

Progress toward equality for women. The 118th Congress was the most diverse in history in terms of gender, race, and ethnicity. Anna Moneymaker/Getty Images

- SDG #17: Partnerships for the Goals[73]
  - Foreign Direct Investments (FDI)—a critical driver of a nation's prosperity and sustainable economic growth—reached over $1.5 trillion by 2022.
  - In developing countries, international investments in sectors related to the SDGs increased 70% between 2021 and 2022.

Areas of Concern The UN's most recent progress report revealed alarmingly negative impacts of the COVID-19 pandemic on progress toward the SDGs. In addition, the private sector has continued to struggle with advancing solutions for important global issues. At this rate, it is unlikely the world will meet the UN's original objective to accomplish the SDGs by 2030.[74] Here are some areas of concern:

1. *More of the same.* One reason we don't see more progress toward CSV in the private sector is that firms are doing the same things they did before. Traditional philanthropy and CSR have been dressed up in fancy new titles. There is an abundance of enthusiasm for adopting a new mindset, but many firms still lack the necessary tools for funneling that energy into a complex plan for creating shared value.[75]

2. *Lack of commitment at the top.* Another roadblock is a lack of CEO engagement with shared value. A recent report on the state of the SDGs suggests the implementation of these goals still ranks fairly low on CEO agendas.[76] Managers also struggle to suppress the impulse to prioritize decisions that maximize short-term profits. Infusing an organization with a shared-value outlook requires a dramatic shift in perspective along with strong commitment, participation, and continual support from the top down.

3. *Misalignment with strategy.* A final concern is that firms are struggling to incorporate shared-value principles with core business strategies. CSV isn't possible

without a nuanced understanding of how core capabilities and strategic objectives align with specific opportunities for addressing societal issues.[77] Outdated organizational policies and procedures that support CSR instead of CSV can further complicate the process.[78]

Recommendations for Transitioning to a Shared-Value Mindset

In this section we offer three recommendations for transitioning to a shared-value mindset and overcoming the challenges discussed in the last section. Managers can use the practical advice and examples we share to help manage with a new CSV lens.

Set Priorities to Overcome Problems with Strategic Alignment
As a manager you will need to prioritize opportunities for shared value creation. Look for opportunities to maximize impact, and don't pursue goals that aren't a good fit for your unique business. Recall from the model of CSV in Figure LM 1.1 that the best opportunities for shared value aren't always immediately obvious. Keep this in mind as you evaluate your firm's potential to make progress on one of the SDGs.

Encourage a Long-Term Mindset to Gain Support across the Organization
Creating shared value requires that companies adopt a longer-term perspective on earnings than they have in the past. Unfortunately, the importance of short-term rewards is deeply embedded in executive compensation systems, and managers face intense pressure to prioritize short-term earnings over other goals.[79] Some experts believe this obsession with the short-term is the reason more firms in the private sector have yet to engage with the SDGs.

Boards of directors and CEOs are encouraged to take a long-term perspective that focuses on multiple stakeholders. This shift in perspective is essential for CSV because projects aimed at achieving the SDGs often won't produce quick returns.[80] Here are two recommendations for building a long-term mindset in your organization:

- *Designate special-purpose funds.* In some firms, investors contribute to separate funds that are earmarked for longer-term opportunities. This provides the chance for investors to adjust to a long-term perspective in a relatively risk-free environment. Over time, investors may become more amenable to additional long-term projects that focus on creating shared value.[81]
- *Reconfigure executive compensation.* Executive pay often revolves around short-term results like stock performance, and this leads managers to prioritize decisions that prop up short-term stock price over decisions that may grow the business.[82] Executives are more likely to adopt a long-term focus if they are rewarded for long-term performance rather than short-term earnings.

Break Out of Old Routines by Thinking Bigger
It can be difficult to switch from a traditional CSR business model to a shared-value perspective.[83] In fact, studies suggest that many business have made only weak progress toward achieving these goals.[84]

As a manager, adopting a shared value and sustainable development approach means that you can no longer view your organization in isolation from its larger environment. Instead, you must consider yourself in conjunction with the larger ecosystem that includes your community, local cluster participants, value chain, and other stakeholders. Creating shared value is virtually impossible without collaboration across the ecosystem.[85]

Consider the case of Revolution Foods in the following Example box.

EXAMPLE: Revolution Foods Navigates Its Ecosystem to Create Shared Value

Kristin Richmond and Kirsten Tobey became friends in 2006 in an MBA class at UC Berkeley. The former educators shared a vision of getting nutritious, appetizing, affordable meals into school cafeterias, and Revolution Foods was born. The owners quickly realized they were operating within a complex web of federal government–mandated lunch prices, existing food-service companies, and schools that seemed closed off to changes in their existing routines.[86]

In response, Richmond and Tobey developed a keen understanding of their ecosystem and devised strategies for innovation that relied on collaboration with key stakeholders. For example, Richmond and Tobey figured out that suppliers were willing to offer big discounts on pricey and nutritious food items because demand from school lunch providers is high and consistent. This discount allowed them to keep their meal prices at or below the federal maximum, a necessity if they wanted to sell their meals in the public school system.

When they finally got the chance to serve their lunches at a few schools, they experienced immediate pushback from students and administrators because their meals contained whole grains and vegetables instead of chips and sodas. Once again, Richmond and Tobey took the opportunity to collaborate with their stakeholders. They visited the schools and educated lunchroom staff and administrators about nutrition and its impacts on children's behavior and health outcomes. They won their case, and Revolution Foods now provides nutritious meals for thousands of schools across the country.[87]

Revolution Foods' success—which can be measured by its progress toward SDG #3 (good health and well-being) and its healthy revenue stream—is the result of strategic collaboration with stakeholders and a nuanced understanding of how Revolution Foods fits into its unique ecosystem. Experts believe that efforts to create shared value and deliver on the SDGs will be most successful if firms collaborate with stakeholders in this fashion.[88]

A school lunch revolution at Revolution Foods. Revolution Foods provides nutritious, colorful, innovative meals and wants to change the conversation about school lunch. Did your school lunches look anything like this? ikvyatkovskaya/123RF

YOUR CALL
Why do you think it is so important for companies to understand and collaborate with their ecosystems in order to create shared value?

Conclusion A shared value and sustainable development approach means that shareholder returns and societal benefit are no longer in competition. A CSV approach gives managers more clarity about what it means to do the right thing along with a systematic way for evaluating decisions and opportunities.

Key Terms Used in This Learning Module

clusters 93
creating shared value (CSV) 90
inertia 99
value chain 92

Key Points

LM 1.1 From Corporate Social Responsibility to Creating Shared Value

- Organizations have traditionally used CSR programs to contribute to societal welfare.
- Creating shared value (CSV) is a new way to think about an organization's role in tackling societal issues.
- CSV is defined as implementing policies and operating practices that enhance the competitiveness of a company while simultaneously advancing the economic and social conditions in the communities in which it operates.

LM 1.2 The Roles of Various Stakeholders in CSV

- Multiple stakeholders are involved in creating shared value.
- The United Nations' 17 Sustainable Development Goals (SDGs) represent the efforts of the multinational organization's 193 member countries to tackle global issues.
- The private sector, entrepreneurs, and business schools are important stakeholders in the process of creating shared value.

LM 1.3 Progress, Challenges, and Recommendations for CSV

- There is more awareness of and engagement with CSV and the SDGs, and there has been progress made toward meeting specific goals.
- Three important areas of concern in CSV are (1) more of the same—organizations not doing enough to change existing CSR programs, (2) lack of commitment at the top, and (3) misalignment with organizational strategies.
- Three recommendations for CSV are (1) set priorities to overcome problems with strategic alignment; (2) encourage a long-term mindset to gain support across the organization, and (3) break out of old routines by thinking bigger.

4 Global Management
Managing across Borders

After reading this chapter, you should be able to:

LO 4-1 Identify three influential effects of globalization.

LO 4-2 Describe the characteristics of a successful international manager.

LO 4-3 Outline the ways in which companies can expand internationally.

LO 4-4 Discuss barriers to free trade and ways companies try to overcome them.

LO 4-5 Explain the value to managers of understanding cultural differences.

LO 4-6 Describe how to develop your diversity, equity, and inclusion competency.

FORECAST   What's Ahead in This Chapter

This chapter covers the impact of globalization—the rise of the global village, of one big market, of both worldwide megafirms and minifirms. We also describe the characteristics of the successful international manager and why and how companies expand internationally. We describe the barriers to free trade, the major organizations promoting trade, and the major competitors. We discuss some of the cultural differences you may encounter if you become an international manager, and we conclude with a Career Corner that focuses on how you can develop the career readiness competency of diversity, equity, and inclusion.

Working Successfully Abroad: Developing Cultural Awareness

Whether you travel abroad on your own or on a work assignment for your company, there are many ways to develop cultural awareness to help ensure your international experience enhances your career success.[1] The general idea is to be global in your focus but think in terms of your local environment.

Do Your Research

Don't wait until you arrive to start the process of familiarizing yourself with the culture of your new environment. Start reading books and articles and watching videos well in advance. Study the geography and the transportation systems ahead of time. Talk to people who have been there, and before you leave, begin seeking out and contacting people from the local area who can help you now or in the future. A few general rules always apply when you are the outsider: Learn by listening more than you speak; follow the example of others; and be moderate, open-minded, and humble.

Check Your Attitude

In a recent interview with *Business Insider*, Karoli Hindriks, CEO of Jobbatical, the international tech marketplace, offered some good advice about leaving biased attitudes at home.[2] "Don't move abroad if you're looking to find things to be exactly like they were back home," she says. "Only when you open your mind to the experience and grasp all the quirks that your new home has in store for you, will the journey boost your creativity and become positive." Be ready to embrace the opportunity, and don't let minor problems or the novelty of your experience throw you. Maintain a positive, can-do attitude and overcome the small stuff.

Learn the Appropriate Behavior

Before you go, spend some time learning about patterns of interpersonal communication and interaction. A quick online search can clue you in about expectations in the particular country or areas where you'll be living or working. Pay attention to social customs about such everyday behaviors as making introductions, being introduced, order of speaking in a meeting or group, use and nonuse of humor, dining etiquette, and the norms for personal space, which can be very different from what you're used to.

Global events. A trio of business people chat during an international conference. How would you start a conversation with someone from another country if you were attending such a conference?
Rawpixel.com/Shutterstock

Become at Least Minimally Skilled in the Language

Whatever foreign country you're in, learn a few key phrases—such as "hello," "please," and "thank you"—in your host country's language. The effort you make to do this will go a long way to enhancing your relationships with others, even if your grammar and accent aren't perfect.

Pack Wisely

Packing wisely means more than just bringing the right clothes for the climate, although you should do that, too. But also inform yourself about the attire that's appropriate for the places you'll visit and the events you'll attend. More conservative clothing is often the norm abroad, and you'll want to be sensitive to your cultural surroundings. Consider, too, that living spaces are often smaller in other countries. Pack light, bring outfits that are versatile and easy to care for, and don't anticipate a walk-in closet.

Finally, Be Prepared

Get a head start on making sure all your paperwork is in order—a valid passport (with an expiration date at least six months in the future), a visa and work permit if needed, debit and credit cards that are accepted in your host country, and health insurance that covers you outside the United States. Know your rights, too; working abroad is not the same as being a tourist. Be prepared for emergencies, such as running out of cash unexpectedly (though you should always have some in reserve), and have a plan that will help you stay calm and focused while you resolve the issue.

For Discussion You've just accepted an internship at a telecommunications company in Seoul, South Korea. Before leaving for Korea, how would you plan on developing your cross-cultural awareness to ensure success?

4.1 Globalization: The Collapse of Time and Distance

THE BIG PICTURE

Globalization, the trend of the world economy toward becoming a more interdependent system, is reflected in three developments: the rise of the "global village" and e-commerce, the trend of the world becoming one big market, and the rise of both megafirms and Internet-enabled minifirms worldwide.

LO 4-1

Identify three influential effects of globalization.

Is everything sold in the United States now made abroad? What does that mean for U.S. consumers and the economy? Although it is one of the largest exporters in the world, the United States imports more than it exports. In 2022, the nation imported over $3 trillion in goods and $600 billion in services. Consumer goods account for almost $654 billion of U.S. imports, consisting mostly of cell phones, TVs, and pharmaceuticals.[3]

Competition and Globalization: Who Will Be No. 1 Tomorrow?

It goes without saying that the world is a competitive place. What exactly does it mean for a country to be competitive in a global business environment?

The International Institute for Management Development (IMD) defines competitiveness as how well countries "manage their competencies to achieve long-term value creation."[4] The IMD ranks countries each year based on the following four facets of competitiveness in the global business environment:

1. **Economic performance.** Indicators of a country's economic performance include international trade markers such as export data, various employment statistics including employment growth and unemployment rates, and price indices including the cost-of-living index and food and gasoline prices.

2. **Government efficiency.** Indicator's of a country's government efficiency include corporate and personal tax policies, societal data such as income distribution and gender (in)equality, and business legislation including immigration policies and tariffs.

3. **Business efficiency.** Indicators of a country's business efficiency include labor market measures such as growth and availability of skills, management practices including corporate governance and social responsibility, and attitudes and values such as workforce adaptability and attitudes toward globalization.

4. **Infrastructure.** Indicators of a country's infrastructure include basic factors like density of railroads and roadways, technological factors such as telecom investments and availability of broadband networks, and education factors including public expenditures per student and the number of women with college degrees.

According to IMD's report, the top 10 most competitive countries in 2022 were (in order beginning with #1) Denmark; Switzerland; Singapore; Sweden; Hong Kong SAR; Netherlands; Taiwan, China; Finland; Norway; and the United States. These types of lists provide an informative snapshot of global business conditions at a moment in time, but we think it's important that managers view these data with caution. Specifically, a country's competitiveness can fluctuate for a number of reasons. Executives indicated that some of the most pressing current trends impacting global business and countries' competitiveness included inflation, geopolitical conflicts, supply chain issues, and remote/hybrid work arrangements.

There are many reasons the highest-scoring countries on this list achieved their status, but one thing is clear: They didn't do it all by themselves; other countries were involved. Our world is changing rapidly due to **globalization**—**the trend of the world economy toward becoming a more interdependent system.** Time and distance have now virtually collapsed, as reflected in three important developments we shall discuss:[5]

1. The rise of the "global village" and electronic commerce.
2. The world becoming one market instead of many national ones.
3. The rise of both megafirms and Internet-enabled minifirms worldwide.

The Rise of the "Global Village" and Electronic Commerce

The hallmark of great civilizations has been their systems of communication. In the beginning, communication was based on transportation: The Roman Empire had its network of roads, as did other ancient civilizations such as the Incas. Later, the great European powers had their far-flung navies. In the 19th century, the United States and Canada unified North America by building transcontinental railroads. Later the airplane reduced travel time between continents.

From Transportation to Communication Transportation began to yield to the electronic exchange of information. Beginning in 1844, the telegraph ended the short existence of the Pony Express and, beginning in 1876, found itself in competition with the telephone. The amplifying vacuum tube, invented in 1906, led to commercial radio. Television came into being in England in 1925. During the 1950s and 1960s, as television exploded throughout the world, communications philosopher Marshall McLuhan posed the notion of a "global village," where we all share our hopes, dreams, and fears in a "worldpool" of information. The **global village** refers to the "shrinking" of time and space as air travel and the electronic media have made it easier for the people around the globe to communicate with one another.

Then the world became even faster and smaller. When AT&T launched the first cellular communications system in 1983, it predicted there would be fewer than a million users by 2000. By 2027, there will be over 7 billion smartphone subscriptions worldwide.[6]

The Net, the Web, and the World Then came the Internet, the worldwide computer-linked "network of networks." Today, of the 8 billion people in the world, around 63% are Internet users and around 59% use social media.[7] The arrival of the web quickly led to the introduction of e-commerce, or electronic commerce, defined in Chapter 1 as the buying and selling of products and services through computer networks. U.S. e-commerce sales surpassed $900 billion in 2022 and are projected to reach $1.7 trillion by 2027.[8]

One Big World Market: The Global Economy

"We are seeing the results of things started in 1988 and 1989," said Rosabeth Moss Kantor of the Harvard Business School, referring to three historic global changes.[9] The first was in the late 1980s when the Berlin Wall came down, signaling the beginning of the end of communism in Eastern Europe. The second was when Asian countries began to open their economies to foreign investors. The third was the worldwide trend of governments deregulating their economies. These three events set up conditions by which goods, people, and money could move more freely throughout the world—a global economy. The **global economy** refers to the increasing tendency of the economies of the world to interact with one another as one market instead of many national markets.

It's no secret the economies of the world are increasingly tied together, connected by information arriving instantaneously through currency traders' screens, CNN news reports, social media networks, text messages, and other technology. Money, represented by digital blips, changes hands globally in a matter of keystrokes. Let's consider the positive and negative effects of globalization.

Positive Effects   A global economy has a number of benefits. In the past, people on different continents could not interact without difficulty. The Internet, high-speed travel, and other innovations have lessened the "friction of distance," shrinking the world and eliminating borders.[10]

Spreading soda. A Coca-Cola employee unloads a truck in Phuket, Thailand. The company sells its products in over 200 countries and territories.
Lou Linwei/Alamy Stock Photo

Rapid technological improvements can result from increased communication and information sharing, and as we've seen, many products and services can be produced more cheaply due to innovation and economies of scale.[11] People and information aren't the only two things moving quickly across the globe; money is as well. Electronic transfers and the ability to invest in developing countries has increased access to capital, allowing for greater market growth across different global economies.[12]

In addition, in some industries foreign firms are building plants in the United States, revitalizing some industrial areas. For example, recent changes to government policy along with hefty federal funding have boosted semiconductor manufacturing in the United States. Taiwan Semiconductor Manufacturing Company recently pledged more than $12 billion for a manufacturing facility in Arizona.[13]

Negative Effects   The large-scale effects of the rise of global economy have included much-publicized job losses across the United States. Despite an apparent rise in protectionist sentiment in some of the world's largest economies, some of those jobs will not return. Other negative effects of globalization are more closely tied to individual managers' day-to-day challenges. These include potential threats to information security because data must be shared, possible loss of control over quality and standards because products or components are made hundreds or thousands of miles away, and the risk of hidden or unanticipated costs, especially transportation costs, that can offset some of the savings expected from moving manufacturing to countries with lower labor costs.[14] An interconnected world also has other risks. For example, if a nation is heavily depended on by others, and its economy falters, there can be instant regional or global instability.[15] Consider the impacts of global economic factors on supply chains by reading the Example Box. •

EXAMPLE | Globalization and Supply Chain Vulnerabilities

Companies all over the world have taken steps to decrease their reliance on global supply chains in recent years.[16] One major reason for this trend is the stark realization that supply chains are exceedingly vulnerable to international events. Consider how the following events have impacted the world's supply chains in recent years.

China's Zero-COVID policy
In recent years, China has accounted for anywhere from 20% to 30% of the world's manufacturing output.[17] This is due to factors such as availability of raw materials and low costs of labor and production. This global dependence became increasingly salient throughout the pandemic and the years that followed, when China's governmental policies aimed to keep COVID-19 numbers as close to zero as possible. Rolling lockdowns impacted the exportation of numerous goods. For example, homebuilders reported significant shortages in key materials such as roofing, framing lumber, and wallboard.[18] Medical supplies also were heavily impacted. From raw materials used in prescription drugs to acetaminophen and ibuprofen tablets, the effects of lockdowns at Chinese manufacturing and production facilities found consumers around the world scrambling to find items such as pain medicines and antibiotics.[19] Supplies of critical chemicals such as those used in X-rays also were stunted.

Egypt's Suez Canal Blockage
In March 2021, one of the world's largest container ships—The Ever Given—became wedged in a diagonal across Egypt's Suez Canal. Over 10% of the world's trade is shipped through the Suez Canal, and the resulting six-day blockage held up approximately $60 billion in cargo (being carried by more than 350 shipping vessels).[20] Analysts estimated that the blockage, which lasted less than a week, disrupted global supply chains for months.[21]

The Russia–Ukraine War
The Russian invasion of Ukraine on February 24, 2022 had tremendous impacts on the global availability of numerous important materials. For example, Ukraine and Russia produce around one-third of the wheat, one-fourth of the barley, and three-fourths of the sunflower oil in the world.[22] These commodities are critical food sources for many countries. Fifteen percent of the world's nickel, a key commodity necessary for lithium-ion battery production, also comes from Russia.[23] Russian sanctions and port blockages cut off the supply of these and other exports, including 25% of the world's nitrogen fertilizer.[24] One painful impact was a sharp increase in global commodity and food prices. Between February and June of 2022, global prices of wheat, gas, and corn increased approximately 60%, 54%, and 24%, respectively.[25]

YOUR CALL
Do you think that companies should work to decrease their reliance on global supply chains? Are there risks of making supply chains too concentrated?

4.2 You and International Management

THE BIG PICTURE
Studying international management prepares you to work with foreign customers or suppliers, for a foreign firm in the United States, or for a U.S. firm overseas. Successful international managers aren't ethnocentric or polycentric but geocentric.

LO 4-2
Describe the characteristics of a successful international manager.

Can you see yourself working overseas? Recruiters believe international experience can be a big professional advantage because it builds career readiness competencies like resilience, critical thinking/problem solving, and adaptability.[26] But how does this content help you if you don't plan to work overseas? The answer is simple. In today's global economy, it's more than likely that you'll engage with international colleagues, suppliers, customers, customer service representatives, vendors, or collaborators. This chapter can enhance your ability to work with people from other countries.

Why Learn about International Management?

International management is management that oversees the conduct of operations in or with organizations in foreign countries, whether it's through a multinational corporation or a multinational organization.

Multinational Corporations A **multinational corporation**, or multinational enterprise, is a business with operations in several countries. For example, McDonald's is a well-known multinational corporation with more than 38,000 restaurants in more than 100 countries.[27] In terms of sales revenue, the 10 largest American multinational corporations in 2022 were Wal-Mart, Amazon, Apple, CVS Health, UnitedHealth Group, Exxon Mobil, Berkshire Hathaway, Alphabet, McKesson, and AmerisourceBergen.[28] The 10 largest foreign firms were State Grid (Chinese utility), China National Petroleum, Sinopec Group (Chinese oil company), Saudi Aramco (Saudi Arabian oil company), Volkswagen, China State Construction Engineering, Toyota Motor, Shell, Samsung Electronics, and Trifigura Group (Singaporean commodity trading company).[29]

Multinational Organizations A **multinational organization** is a nonprofit organization with operations in several countries. Multinational organizations operate independently of any government and are sometimes called non-governmental organizations (NGOs). Examples are the World Health Organization, the International Red Cross, and the Church of Jesus Christ of Latter-day Saints.

Even if you never travel beyond North America (an unlikely proposition, we think), the world will surely come to you. That, in a nutshell, is why you need to learn about international management.

More specifically, consider yourself in the following situations:

You May Deal with Foreign Customers or Partners While working for a U.S. company, you may engage with foreign customers or work with a foreign company in some sort of joint venture. The people you're working with may be outside the United States or visitors to the country. Either way you would hate to blow a deal—and maybe all future deals—because you were ignorant of one or more cultural aspects you could easily have learned about.

You May Deal with Foreign Employees or Suppliers You may have to purchase important components, raw materials, or services for your U.S. employer from a foreign supplier. And you never know where foreign practices may diverge from what you're accustomed to. Many software developer jobs, for instance, have moved outside the United States to places such as India, New Zealand, and Eastern Europe.

You May Work for a Foreign Firm in the United States You may take a job with a foreign firm doing business in the United States, such as Unilever, Anheuser-Busch, or Toyota. In this instance, you'll work with managers above and below you whose outlook may be different from yours. If you work for the German supermarket company Aldi, for example, you may find its slim approach to staffing and its policies regarding store operating hours a bit unusual. This is because many of Aldi's policies reflect cultural aspects of its German ownership rather than its U.S. locations.[30]

You May Work for a U.S. Firm outside the United States—or for a Foreign One You might easily find yourself working abroad in the foreign operation of a U.S. company. Most big U.S. corporations—including Microsoft, Johnson & Johnson, and Marriott International—have overseas subsidiaries or divisions. On the other hand, you might also work for a foreign firm in a foreign country, such as Infosys in Bangalore, India or Nestlé in Vevey, Switzerland.

The Successful International Manager: Geocentric, Not Ethnocentric or Polycentric

Maybe you don't really care that you don't have much understanding of the foreign culture you're dealing with. "What's the point?" you may think. "The main thing is to get the job done." Managers with this perspective have what are called *ethnocentric* attitudes, one of three primary attitudes among international managers. International managers can also have *polycentric* and *geocentric* attitudes.[31]

Ethnocentric Managers—"We Know Best" What do foreign executives fluent in English think when they hear Americans using an endless array of baseball, basketball, and American football phrases (such as "touch base," "out of left field," or "Hail Mary pass")? **Ethnocentric managers** believe that their native country, culture, language, and behavior are superior to all others. The ethnocentric viewpoint is often more attributable to ignorance than to conscious prejudice, and studies suggest building cross-cultural awareness makes us less likely to hold ethnocentric viewpoints.[32] Ethnocentrism might also be called **parochialism**—that is, a narrow view in which people see things solely through their own perspective.

Ethnocentric views also affect our purchasing decisions. For example, some people have a strong preference for purchasing products made in their home country.[33] President Biden's 2022 Clean Vehicle Credit instituted a federal tax credit of up to $7,500 for certain types of new electric vehicles (EVs) purchased beginning in 2023. The EVs must be used primarily in the United States and must undergo final assembly in North America.[34] What are your views about being an ethnocentric consumer? If your instructor has assigned it, try taking Self-Assessment 4.1 in Connect.

SELF-ASSESSMENT 4.1

Assessing Your Consumer Ethnocentrism

This survey is designed to assess your consumer ethnocentrism. Please complete Self-Assessment 4.1 if your instructor has assigned it in Connect.

Polycentric Managers—"They Know Best"
Polycentric managers take the view that native managers best understand personnel and practices in their home countries, and so the home office should defer to them. Thus, the attitude of polycentric managers is nearly the opposite of that of ethnocentric managers. The potential advantages of polycentric management over ethnocentric management include fewer relocation costs, more established local social networks, and higher team morale. Potential disadvantages of polycentric management include the home office having less control over and connection with subsidiaries.[35]

Geocentric Managers—"What's Best Is What's Effective, Regardless of Origin"
Geocentric managers accept that there are differences and similarities between home and foreign personnel and practices and that they should use whichever techniques are most effective. Clearly, being an ethno- or polycentric manager takes less work. But the payoff for being a geocentric manager can be far greater. ●

4.3 Why and How Companies Expand Internationally

THE BIG PICTURE
Multinationals expand to take advantage of availability of supplies, new markets, lower labor costs, access to finance capital, or avoidance of tariffs and import quotas. Five ways they do so are by global outsourcing; importing, exporting, and countertrading; licensing and franchising; joint ventures; and wholly owned subsidiaries.

LO 4-3

Outline the ways in which companies can expand internationally.

Operating internationally may be the most efficient and effective way for a particular business to offer its products or services. Consider the following example:

The Benefits of Doing Business Internationally—iPhone Example: Who makes Apple's iPhone? That's actually difficult to answer. This is because Apple and its iPhone are a good example of a complex supply chain. The accelerometer may come from Germany; the battery is likely manufactured in China; an Australian company may make the camera and LCD screen; the gyroscope probably comes from the UAE or South Africa; and the Wi-Fi chip could be made in the United States.[36]

There are many reasons U.S. companies are going global. Let us consider why and how they are expanding beyond U.S. borders.

Why Companies Expand Internationally

Why do companies make the decision to expand their businesses internationally? There are at least five reasons, all of which relate to making or saving money.

1. Availability of Supplies Mining companies, banana growers, sellers of hard woods—all have to go where their basic supplies or raw materials are located. Oil companies, for example, have for years expanded their activities outside the United States to seek cheaper or more plentiful sources of oil.

2. New Markets Sometimes a company will find that demand for their product (cigarettes, for example) has declined domestically but not necessarily overseas. Or sometimes a company will launch a concerted effort to expand into foreign markets, as Coca-Cola did under the leadership of CEO Roberto Goizueta. Costco is another U.S. company that has been successful internationally. Taking advantage of a growing middle class in China, the warehouse giant opened its first store in Shanghai in August 2019 to crowds so large it was forced to suspend business due to safety concerns. Amazon expanded to Australia in 2017 and opened its first Australian robotics fulfillment center in 2022.[37]

A Middle Eastern Gem. The gross domestic product of Dubai has grown from $82 billion in U.S. dollars in 2008 to over $600 billion in 2022. This tremendous economic growth has resulted in the development of the beautiful skyscrapers at the Dubai Marina in the United Arab Emirates. Boule/Shutterstock

3. Lower Labor Costs The decline in manufacturing jobs in the United States is partly attributable to the fact that U.S. companies have found it cheaper to manufacture internationally. For example, the rationale for using maquiladoras—foreign-owned manufacturing plants allowed to operate in Mexico with special privileges in return for employing Mexican citizens—is that they provide less expensive labor for assembling everything from appliances to cars. Sometimes companies even move operations from one foreign country to another in order to reduce labor costs. For example, Apple moved a significant portion of iPhone production from China to India, where production costs are nearly 60% less than in China.[38] Even professional and service jobs, such as computer programming, often are shipped overseas.

4. Access to Finance Capital The prospects of capital investments from foreign companies or subsidies from foreign governments may entice companies into going abroad. A sovereign wealth fund is a government-owned investment fund that often invests in foreign assets. China's sovereign wealth fund, China Investment Corporation (CIC), started in a joint venture with Goldman Sachs called the China-U.S. Industrial Cooperation Fund. The joint venture raised $2.5 billion for investments in U.S. industrial firms.[39]

5. Avoidance of Tariffs and Import Quotas Countries place tariffs (fees) on imported goods or impose import quotas—limitations on the numbers of products allowed in—for the purpose of protecting their own domestic industries. For example, Japan imposes tariffs on agricultural products—such as meat, tea, and produce—imported from the United States. To avoid these penalties, a company might create a subsidiary to produce the product in the foreign country.

How Companies Expand Internationally

Most companies don't start out as multinational operations. Companies generally edge their way into international business, beginning with minimal investments and minimal risks (see Figure 4.1).

Let's consider the five ways of expanding internationally shown in Figure 4.1.

1. Global Outsourcing Outsourcing—using suppliers outside the company to provide goods and services—is a common practice of many companies. For example, airlines outsource much of their aircraft maintenance to other companies. Management

FIGURE 4.1

Five ways of expanding internationally

These range from lowest risk and investment (*left*) to highest risk and investment (*right*).

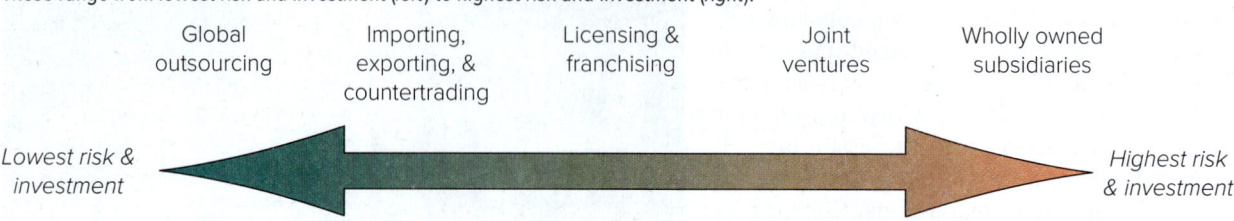

| Global outsourcing | Importing, exporting, & countertrading | Licensing & franchising | Joint ventures | Wholly owned subsidiaries |

Lowest risk & investment ←——————————————→ Highest risk & investment

philosopher Peter Drucker believed that in the near future organizations might be outsourcing all work that consists of "support services"—such as information systems—because they don't generate revenue for the company.

Global outsourcing extends this technique outside the United States. **Global outsourcing**, or **offshoring**, is defined as using suppliers outside the United States to provide labor, goods, or services. One reason for global outsourcing is access to suppliers with resources not available in the United States, such as Italian marble. Another reason is access to special expertise, such as weavers in Pakistan. Another, and quite common, reason for global outsourcing is access to labor that is more affordable than domestic labor. As a manager, your first business trip outside the United States might be to inspect the production lines of one of your outsourced suppliers.

Interestingly, in a countertrend called "reshoring," some companies are moving production back home in order to respond to consumer trends with greater speed and flexibility. A recent Deloitte study of 305 transport and manufacturing firm executives found that over 60% of companies surveyed had begun reshoring some of their production operations. The report estimated that U.S. firms reshored nearly 350,000 jobs in 2022 alone. Reasons for this trend include pandemic-induced supply chain nightmares, restrictions on exports, and financial incentives outlined in the Inflation Reduction Act of 2022 and other federal legislation aimed at returning manufacturing jobs to North America.[40]

2. Importing, Exporting, and Countertrading

When **importing**, a company buys goods outside the country and resells them domestically. Nothing might seem to be more American than Caterpillar tractors, but they are made not only in the United States but also in Mexico, from which they are imported and made available for sale in the United States.[41] Many of the products used in the United States are imported, ranging from LG televisions (South Korea) to Chevron gasoline (Saudi Arabia).

When **exporting**, a company produces goods domestically and sells them outside the country. China was the world's top export country in 2021, and the United States was second (see Table 4.1). The top U.S. exports include medicines and medical devices, computer chips, mineral fuels, and passenger vehicles.[42]

Sometimes other countries may wish to import U.S. goods but lack the currency to pay for them. In that case, the exporting U.S. company may resort to **countertrading**—that is, bartering goods for goods. Countertrading can be beneficial in situations where goods are a better medium of exchange than currency.

3. Licensing and Franchising

Licensing and franchising are two aspects of the same thing, although licensing is used by manufacturing companies and franchising is used more frequently by service companies.

In **licensing**, a company allows a foreign company to pay it a fee to make or distribute the first company's product or service. For example, DuPont might license a company in Brazil to make Teflon, the nonstick substance found on some frying pans. Thus, DuPont, the licensor, can make money without having to invest large sums to conduct

TABLE 4.1 Top 10 Exporting Countries, 2021

| 1. China |
| 2. United States |
| 3. Germany |
| 4. Netherlands |
| 5. Japan |
| 6. Hong Kong |
| 7. South Korea |
| 8. Italy |
| 9. France |
| 10. Belgium |

Source: "Leading export countries worldwide in 2021." Statista. Aug 5, 2022. https://www.statista.com/statistics/264623/leading-export-countries-worldwide/.

At McDonald's franchises in India, menu items are customized to fit with local dietary customs and preferences. Homeland photos/Alamy Stock Photo

business directly in a foreign company. Moreover, the Brazilian firm, the licensee, knows the local market better than DuPont probably would.

Franchising is a form of licensing in which a company allows a foreign company to pay it a fee and a share of its profit in return for using the first company's brand name and a package of materials and services. For example, Burger King, Hertz, and Hilton Hotels, all well-known brands, might provide the use of their names plus their operating knowledge (facility design, equipment, recipes, management systems) to companies in the Philippines in return for an up-front fee plus a percentage of profits.

Today, so-called U.S. stores are opening everywhere, and many franchise chains are experiencing the bulk of their growth overseas. Kentucky Fried Chicken dominates the Franchise Direct 2022 report, followed by 7-Eleven, McDonald's, Marriott International, and Burger King.[43] We'll discuss franchising further when we cover entrepreneurship in Learning Module 2.

4. Joint Ventures *Strategic allies* (described in Chapter 3) are two organizations that have joined forces to realize strategic advantages that neither would have if operating alone. A U.S. firm may form a joint venture, also known as a strategic alliance, with a foreign company to share the risks and rewards of starting a new enterprise together in a foreign country. For instance, in 2022 Chevron and Baseload Capital (headquartered in Stockholm, Sweden) announced a joint venture to create geothermal project opportunities in the United States.[44] LG Energy Solution and Honda Motor Company formed a joint venture in 2023 to manufacture lithium-ion batteries in the United States for Honda and Acura EVs manufactured for North America.[45]

5. Wholly Owned Subsidiaries A **wholly owned subsidiary** is a foreign subsidiary that is totally owned and controlled by another organization. The foreign subsidiary may be an existing company that is purchased outright. For example, the Walt Disney Company—which does not have sole ownership of many of its foreign theme parks—purchased 100% of Disneyland Paris. A **greenfield venture** is a foreign subsidiary that the owning organization has built from scratch. •

4.4 The World of Free Trade: Regional Economic Cooperation and Competition

THE BIG PICTURE

Barriers to free trade include tariffs, import quotas, and embargoes. Organizations promoting international trade are the World Trade Organization, the World Bank, and the International Monetary Fund. We discuss two major trading blocs, NAFTA (now USMCA) and the EU. Major competitors with the United States are the "BRICS" countries—Brazil, Russia, India, China, and South Africa.

LO 4-4

Discuss barriers to free trade and ways companies try to overcome them.

If you live in the United States, you see foreign products on a daily basis—cars, appliances, clothes, foods, beers, wines, and so on. Based on what you see every day, which countries would you think are our most important trading partners? China? Japan? Germany? United Kingdom? South Korea?

These five countries do indeed appear among the top leading U.S. trading partners. Interestingly, however, some of our foremost trading partners are our immediate neighbors—Canada and Mexico—whose products may not be quite so visible (see Table 4.2).

Let's begin to consider **free trade**, the movement of goods and services among nations without political or economic obstruction.

Barriers to International Trade

Countries often use **trade protectionism**—the use of government regulations to limit the import of goods and services—to protect their domestic industries against foreign competition. The justification they often use is that this saves jobs. Actually, protectionism is not considered beneficial, mainly because of what it does to the overall trading atmosphere.

The devices by which countries try to exert protectionism consist of *tariffs, import quotas,* and *trade sanctions* and *embargoes.*

1. Tariffs A **tariff** is a trade barrier in the form of a customs duty, or tax, levied mainly on imports. At one time, for instance, to protect the American shoe industry, the United States imposed a tariff on Italian shoes. Tariffs come in one of two forms: A *revenue tariff* is designed simply to raise money for the government, such as a tax on all oil imported into the United States. A *protective tariff* is intended to raise the price of imported goods to make the prices of domestic products more competitive. Consider how tariffs affect the economic relationship between two countries by reading the following example:

Tariffs Example—The U.S.–China Trade War: Between 2018 and 2019, the Trump administration imposed over $350 billion worth of tariffs on Chinese goods, sparking what experts have called the "U.S.–China Trade War." These goods ranged from footwear to diapers to flat-screen televisions. In response, China retaliated with $185 billion worth of tariffs on American goods.[46] The Biden administration kept these policies in place, and the United States saw Chinese imports as a percentage of its total imports decrease from 22% to 18% between 2018 and late 2022.[47] Imports on products subject to these tariffs—including furniture, smartwatches, routers, and data servers—decreased substantially as a percentage of total U.S. imports between 2017 and 2022. Imports on products not subject to these tariffs—including video game consoles, toys, and computer monitors—increased during the same time period.

2. Import Quotas An *import quota* is a trade barrier in the form of a limit on the quantity of a product that can be imported. Like a tariff, its intent is to protect domestic industry by restricting the availability of foreign products. Consumers in countries using tariffs and import quotas are likely to find price increases due to the reduction of imported products. This was the case in Israel post-pandemic as consumers and suppliers struggled with sharp rises in living costs. In February 2022, Israel's government relaxed its import quotas to allow 10 times more honey and 2 times more fresh eggs to be imported, respectively, in order to help lower prices for these goods.[48]

3. Sanctions and Embargoes A *sanction* is the trade prohibition on certain types of products, services, or technology to another country for specific reasons, including nuclear nonproliferation, terrorism, and humanitarian concerns. The key words here are *certain types of products*. For example, following the 2022 invasion of Ukraine, the federal government-imposed sanctions on Russia to prevent the country from accessing technology that could be used to produce weapons.[49] The sanctions did not target medical and agricultural trade due to the extent to which this could impact global prices and supplies.[50]

An *embargo* is a complete ban or prohibition of trade of one country with another so that no goods or services can be imported or exported from or to the embargoed nation. The key word here is *complete*, as in "complete ban." President John F. Kennedy imposed a trade embargo on Cuba in 1962, and as of this writing, it remains in place as the longest-standing trade embargo in the history of U.S. foreign policy.[51] The UN has pressured the United States to lift this embargo for more than 30 years.

A sanction is different from an embargo. Sanctions may be considered "partial embargoes," since they restrict trade in certain areas.[52] For instance, since 2005 the United States has placed various sanctions on Iranian individuals, companies, and sectors to prohibit the growth of its nuclear program, but food and medicine are generally exempt from sanctions.[53]

TABLE 4.2 Top U.S. Trading Partners in Goods, November 2022

TOP 10 NATIONS THE UNITED STATES EXPORTS TO	TOP 10 NATIONS THE UNITED STATES IMPORTS FROM
1. Canada	1. China
2. Mexico	2. Mexico
3. China	3. Canada
4. United Kingdom	4. Germany
5. Japan	5. Japan
6. Germany	6. South Korea
7. Netherlands	7. Vietnam
8. South Korea	8. Taiwan
9. India	9. Ireland
10. France	10. India

Source: U.S. Census Bureau. "Top Trading Partners—November 2022." https://www.census.gov/foreign-trade/statistics/highlights/topcm.html (accessed January 28, 2023).

Organizations Promoting International Trade

The institution of tariff barriers in the 1920s and early 1930s was intended to protect jobs, but instead it depressed the demand for goods and services, thereby worsening job loss and partially fueling the massive unemployment seen during the Great Depression.[54] Post–World War II, the world's advanced nations began to realize that if all countries could freely exchange what each could produce most efficiently, prices would decrease all around. Thus began the removal of barriers to free trade.

The three principal organizations designed to facilitate international trade are the *World Trade Organization,* the *World Bank,* and the *International Monetary Fund.* Table 4.3 summarizes the background of each organization.

TABLE 4.3 Organizations Promoting International Trade

ORGANIZATIONS PROMOTING INTERNATIONAL TRADE					
PRINCIPAL ORGANIZATIONS	**PURPOSE**	**ESTABLISHED**	**MEMBER COUNTRIES**	**IN THE NEWS**
World Trade Organization (WTO)	To monitor and enforce trade agreements	1995 in Geneva to replace the General Agreement on Tariffs and Trade	164	The 12th Ministerial Conference (MC12) of the WTO in 2022 secured the "Geneva package" as a response to current challenges including those involving global fish populations, vaccine production, e-commerce, and global food insecurity.*
World Bank	To provide low-interest loans to developing nations for improving transportation, education, health, and telecommunications	After WWII to help European countries rebuild	189	In January 2023, the World Bank announced a new Country Partnership Framework (CPF) to help the Lao People's Democratic Republic with sustainable development, economic growth, and the stabilization of its economy.**
International Monetary Fund (IMF)	Designed to assist in smoothing the flow of money between nations	1945	189	In 2022 the IMF established the Resilience and Sustainability Trust (RST). The RST aims to ensure member countries can sustain growth and achieve economic stability in the face of external shocks such as geopolitical events and global pandemics.***

Sources: * "MC12 'Geneva package' - In Brief." World Trade Organization. (accessed January 30, 2023). https://www.wto.org/english/thewto_e/minist_e/mc12_e/geneva_package_e.htm.
** "World Bank Group Adopts New Country Partnership Framework for the Lao PDR." The World Bank. January 26, 2023. https://www.worldbank.org/en/news/press-release/2023/01/24/world-bank-group-adopts-new-country-partnership-framework-for-the-lao-pdr.
*** "IMF Executive Board Approves Establishment of the Resilience and Sustainability Trust." International Monetary Fund. April 18, 2022. https://www.imf.org/en/News/Articles/2022/04/18/pr22119-imf-executive-board-approves-establishment-of-the-rst.

Major Trading Blocs

A **trading bloc**, also known as an economic community, is a group of nations within a geographical region that have agreed to remove trade barriers with one another. The first trading blocs we'll consider are *NAFTA/USMCA* and the *European Union*. We'll then turn our focus to others.

Trade across North America Formed in 1994, the **North American Free Trade Agreement (NAFTA)** was a trading bloc consisting of the United States, Canada, and Mexico, encompassing 444 million people. The agreement was intended to eliminate 99% of the tariffs and quotas between these countries, allowing for freer flow of goods, services, and capital. It is difficult to isolate all the real effects of the trade agreement, given the many other factors in each country's economy, but overall, the United States appears to have lost low-skilled manufacturing jobs and gained employment in autos and aerospace, according to the Economic Policy Institute.[55] According to former U.S. Trade Representative Carla Hills, the NAFTA created one of the "most vibrant" supply chains in world trade, and its positive impacts on things like prices, economic growth, and foreign direct investment were considerable.[56]

Still, the NAFTA was not without its problems, and the three countries renegotiated the agreement in 2018. The new policy, known as the **United States–Mexico–Canada**

Agreement (USMCA), includes new chapters covering digital trade, anti-corruption, and regulatory practices. Congress approved the USMCA in January 2020, and it took effect later that year.[57] Some refer to the USMCA as "NAFTA 2.0" due to its attempt to modernize and improve upon the progress that the NAFTA enabled.

The EU—The 27 Countries of the European Union

Formed in 1957, the **European Union (EU)** consists of 27 trading partners in Europe, covering nearly 500 million consumers.[58]

Nearly all internal trade barriers were eliminated (including movement of labor between countries), making the EU a union of borderless neighbors and one of the world's largest free markets. The EU had a gross domestic product of approximately $16 trillion in 2022.[59]

One of the most significant events impacting the EU in the past decade was the United Kingdom's exit from the trade block, an event known as BREXIT (a combination of Britain and exit). Reasons for BREXIT were varied and complex, but some of the most prominent disagreements centered on how the EU had addressed economic challenges after the Great Recession as well as the ability of member nations to enact their own immigration policies.[60] It will take many years to determine the impacts of

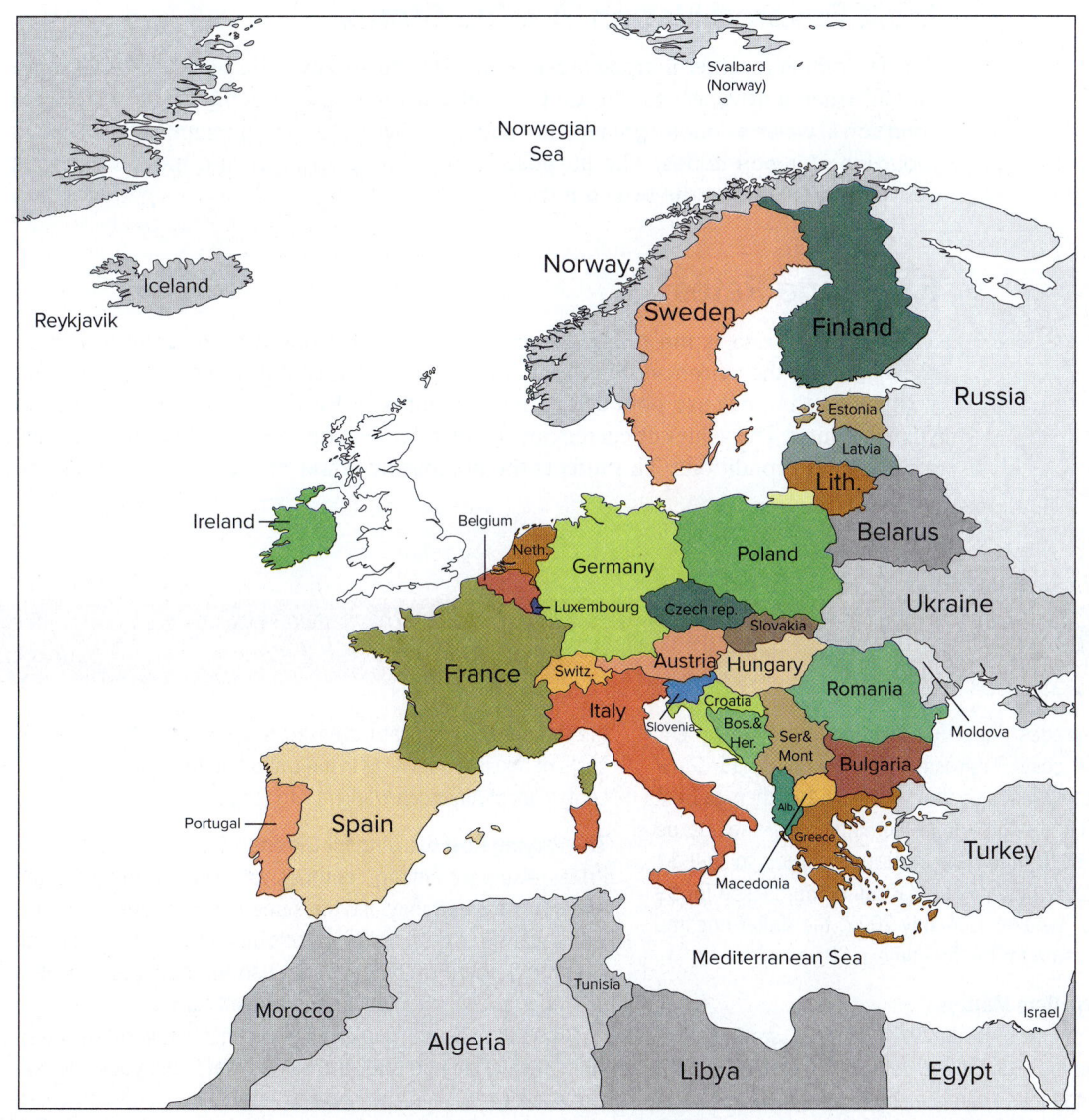

Martm/123RF

Show me the money! The United Nations recognizes 180 currencies that are used in 195 countries across the world. Maria Toutoudaki/Photodisc/Getty Images

BREXIT, but initial indicators suggest that the United Kingdom has suffered since the separation. For example, between June 2016 (the time of the United Kingdom's initial vote to leave the EU) and December 2022, the British pound lost almost 20% of its value.[61] In late 2022, the Organization for Economic Co-operation and Development (OECD) forecast that the United Kingdom would experience the second-largest economic contraction of all the G20 economies in 2023, with only Russia predicted to experience a worse decline.[62]

In recent years, the EU struggled to come to an agreement on how it would collectively decrease its energy dependence on Russia amid the Russia–Ukraine war. Some countries in the trading bloc were more confident than others about their ability to weather a complete ban on Russian oil, given that such a decision could substantially increase oil prices in EU member countries. In December 2022, the EU countries agreed to a $60 per barrel price cap on Russian crude oil, with a plan to revisit and adjust every two months along with market shifts.[63]

Most Favored Nation Trading Status

Besides joining together in trade blocs, countries will also extend special, "most favored nation" trading privileges to one another. **Most favored nation** trading status describes a condition in which a country grants other countries favorable trading treatment such as the reduction of import duties. The purpose is to promote stronger and more stable ties between companies in the two countries.

Exchange Rates

The **exchange rate** is the rate at which the currency of one area or country can be exchanged for the currency of another. Americans in the United States deal in dollars with each other, but use pounds in England, euros in Europe, pesos in Mexico, and yuan in China. The values of currencies fluctuate in relation to each other due to changing economic conditions. This affects the purchasing power of a U.S. dollar at a given time.

EXAMPLE — Dealing with Currency—How Much Do Those Jeans *Really* Cost?

Assume that $1 trades equal to 1 euro, symbolized by €1. Thus, an item that costs 3 euros (€3) can be bought for $3. If the exchange rate changes so that $1 buys €1.5, then an item that costs €3 can be bought for $2 (i.e., the dollar is said to be "stronger" against the euro). If the rate changes so that $1 buys only €0.5, an item that costs €6 can be purchased for $9 (i.e., the dollar is "weaker"). In July 2022, the dollar became stronger than the euro for the first time in 20 years.[64]

How the Exchange Rate Matters
At the time of this writing, $1 buys €0.92. Thus, staying in EU countries has become less expensive for U.S. travelers. And for expatriates working for U.S. companies and being paid in dollars, the standard of living has increased. Some suggest the increased costs of housing and living in the United States have fueled a recent influx of American workers into European countries.[65]

The Varying Cost of Living for Different Cities
Prices also vary among countries and cities throughout the world, even when they use the same currency. Table 4.4 provides a sense of what a U.S. visitor's purchasing power is worth in two different EU countries that use the euro (estimated in U.S. dollars, computed on www.expatistan.com):

With this example, you can see why it's important to understand how exchange rates work and what value your U.S. dollars actually have in different countries.

TABLE 4.4 Comparison of Prices in Zürich and Lisbon

AVERAGE COSTS FOR:	ZÜRICH	LISBON
2-liter Coke	$3.18	$2.50
Combo meal (Big Mac or similar)	$16.28	$7.60
Monthly rent, furnished studio (expensive area)	$3,977.71	$1,629.71
Monthly rent, furnished studio (average area)	$2,823.24	$1,129.51
Pair of Levi's	$134.54	$92.23
Nike or similar sports shoes	$119.35	$87.89
Monthly public transportation pass	$97.65	$40.15
Two movie tickets	$42.32	$16.28

Source: www.expatistan.com.

YOUR CALL

Planning to visit any EU countries (e.g., Germany, France) that use the euro? Go online to www.x-rates.com and figure out the exchange rate of the U.S. dollar and that country's currency. Then go to www.expatistan.com and figure out what things cost in that country's principal city versus a U.S. city near you. Could you afford to go?

The BRICS Countries: Important International Competitors

Coined by a financial analyst who saw the countries as promising markets for finance capital in the 21st century, the term *BRICS* stands for the five major emerging economies of Brazil, Russia, India, China, and South Africa.[66]

Though not a trading bloc as such, the BRICS are important because they hold over 40% of the world's population. By comparison, the United States has just about 4.3% of the world's population.[67] Let's consider the largest of these countries in the order of their population size: India, China, and Brazil.

India Analysts estimated that India's population grew to surpass China's in early 2023. India's advantages have been its large English-speaking population, its technological and scientific expertise, and its reputation in services, such as "back office" accounting systems and software engineering. Services, and especially IT, make up almost half of India's GDP.[68] The OECD predicted that India would have the second-fastest growing economy of all the G20 economies in fiscal year 2022–2023.[69]

China China's economy is currently the second largest in the world after that of the United States, and analysts predict that both China and India may surpass the United States by 2075.[70] China's middle class has expanded significantly, with somewhere between 30% to 50% of its population now considered middle class, compared to around 3% in 2000.[71]

Brazil As one of the top 10 largest economies in the world, Brazil benefits from agriculture, mining, manufacturing, and services. Brazil experienced a decade of economic and social progress from 2003 to 2014, lifting 29 million people out of poverty.[72] The country suffered economically in recent years due to COVID-19 and gained infamy as one of the pandemic's worst affected countries in the world.[73] After struggling for several years with inflation and unemployment, Brazil's economy seems to be making a slow comeback, with economic growth of about 2.7% in 2022.[74]

4.5 The Value of Understanding Cultural Differences

THE BIG PICTURE

Managers trying to understand other cultures need to understand the importance of national culture and cultural dimensions and basic cultural perceptions embodied in language, interpersonal space, communication, time orientation, religion, and law and political stability.

LO 4-5

Explain the value to managers of understanding cultural differences.

Whether you are abroad or at home, you are likely to find yourself working with people whose cultural norms and traditions are very different from your own. This is why it is especially important that you develop **cross-cultural awareness**, defined as the ability to operate in different cultural settings. Cross-cultural awareness is a key component of the career readiness competency of diversity, equity, and inclusion.

What time you arrive for a business meeting, where you sit in the room, how you introduce yourself or introduce people to each other, whether you tip in a restaurant and how much, and even what you eat and whether you share it with others at the table are just a few behaviors influenced by culture.

How Culture Influences Business—Author Example: One of your authors, Angelo Kinicki, encountered several of these scenarios during recent business trips to the United Arab Emirates. He was surprised to see men, who were very familiar with each other, touch noses when saying hello. He also realized that Emiratis have a much more fluid and flexible orientation toward time than people in the United States. Angelo also had to adjust his style of introducing himself to women: no shaking hands unless a woman offered her hand. The start of business meetings is quite different than in the United States. Emiratis like to spend more time engaging in pleasantries before getting down to business.

Another outcome heavily influenced by culture is a company's ability to market and sell certain products and services. As one example, Western manufacturers of personal care products have faced an uphill battle to introduce deodorant products in China and other Asian countries, in part because people there do not perceive sweating as embarrassing. "The traditional thinking [in China] is that sweating is good because it helps people detox," said Unilever's assistant manager for skin care. "There is a marketing barrier that is really hard to overcome." Unilever's cowboy- and boxer-themed ads also missed the mark for cultural reasons. "The series of advertisements we designed relied on the Western sense of humor," said the company's creative director. "Not many Chinese would understand this."[75]

Understanding cultural differences is an essential component of your success as a global manager. rawpixel/123RF

The Importance of National Culture

A nation's culture is the shared set of beliefs, values, knowledge, and patterns of behavior common to a group of people. We begin learning our culture starting at an early age through everyday interaction with people around us. This is why, from the outside looking in, a nation's culture can seem so intangible and perplexing. As cultural anthropologist Edward T. Hall puts it, "Since much of culture operates outside our awareness, frequently we don't even know what we know. . . . We unconsciously learn what to notice and what not to notice, how to divide time and space, how to walk and talk and use our bodies, how to behave as men or women, how to relate to other people, how to handle responsibility. . . ."[76] Indeed, says Hall, what we think of as "mind" is really internalized culture.

Because a culture is made up of so many nuances, visitors to a different and unfamiliar culture may experience feelings of discomfort and disorientation. These feelings are generally associated with "not understanding the verbal and nonverbal communication of the host culture" and the need for adaptability to accommodate "differences in lifestyles, living conditions and business practices in another cultural setting."[77]

Cultural Dimensions: The Hofstede and GLOBE Project Models

Misunderstandings and miscommunications often arise in international business relationships because people don't properly interpret messages coming from other side. Hall suggested that in order to communicate effectively in international business, we must understand the extent to which context impacts the meaning of the words people say. A person from North America, Great Britain, Scandinavia, Germany, or Switzerland, for example, comes from a low-context culture, in which shared meanings are primarily derived from written and spoken words. In a low-context culture, what a person says is the same thing as what they mean, more or less. Someone from China, Korea, Japan, Vietnam, Mexico, or many Arab countries, on the other hand, comes from a high-context culture, in which people rely heavily on situational and nonverbal cues for meaning when communicating with others. In a high-context culture, the meaning of what a person says doesn't come from the words they speak, but, rather, from the context surrounding the words. In high-context cultures, your job as the recipient of a communication is to figure out the true message underlying the words being spoken.

Understanding High-Context Culture—Video Game Example: A Japanese video game called *KUUKIYOMI: Consider It* (available in the United States on Nintendo Switch) requires players to "read the air" in order to perform well. Players' scores depend on how well they interpret contextual cues in more than 100 situations. Rochelle Kopp, founder of Illinois-based cross-cultural training company Japan Intercultural Consulting, believes it is essential for international managers to work on developing their ability to interpret messages correctly in high-context communication. And while a video game won't educate you on the historical and cultural nuances that underlie communication in a particular culture, it allows you to practice paying attention to context when determining how to behave in a particular situation and what to glean from a communication.[78]

An important way to avoid cultural collisions is to have an understanding of various cultural dimensions, as expressed in the Hofstede model and the GLOBE project.[79]

Hofstede's Model of Four Cultural Dimensions

Thirty years ago, Dutch researcher and IBM psychologist Geert Hofstede collected data from 116,000 IBM employees in 53 countries and proposed the **Hofstede model of four cultural dimensions**, which identified four dimensions along which national cultures can be described:[80]

- *Individualism/collectivism* indicates how much people prefer a loosely knit social framework in which people are expected to take care of themselves (as in the United States and Canada) or a tightly knit social framework in which people and organizations are expected to look after each other (as in Mexico and China).

- *Power distance* refers to the degree to which people accept inequality in social situations (high in Mexico and India, low in Sweden and Australia).

- *Uncertainty avoidance* expresses people's intolerance for uncertainty and risk (high in Japan, low in the United States).

- *Masculinity/femininity* expresses how much people value performance-oriented traits (masculinity: high in Mexico) or how much they embrace relationship-oriented traits (femininity: high in Norway).

In general, the United States ranked very high on individualism, relatively low on power distance, low on uncertainty avoidance, and moderately high on masculinity. Hofstede's work has attracted critics despite its groundbreaking contribution to understanding cultural differences. One criticism is that it views a country's population as a homogenous whole. However, most nations, such as the United States, France, and Germany, are groups of ethnic units not necessarily bound by borders. Another criticism is that Hofstede based this work solely on IBM employees, a group that may not be representative of an entire country's culture.[81]

The GLOBE Project's Nine Cultural Dimensions

Started in 1993 by University of Pennsylvania professor Robert J. House, the **GLOBE project** is a massive and ongoing cross-cultural investigation of nine cultural dimensions involved in leadership and organizational processes.[82] (GLOBE stands for Global Leadership and Organizational Behavior Effectiveness.) GLOBE extends Hofstede's theory and results and has evolved into an ongoing research network of more than 200 scholars from 62 societies. Most of these researchers are native to the particular cultures being studied. The nine cultural dimensions are as follows:

- **Power distance—how much unequal distribution of power should there be in organizations and society?** *Power distance* expresses the degree to which a society's members expect power to be unequally shared.

- **Uncertainty avoidance—how much should people rely on social norms and rules to avoid uncertainty?** *Uncertainty avoidance* expresses the extent to which a society relies on social norms and procedures to alleviate the unpredictability of future events.
- **Institutional collectivism—how much should leaders encourage and reward loyalty to the social unit?** *Institutional collectivism* expresses the extent to which individuals are encouraged and rewarded for loyalty to the group as opposed to pursuing individual goals.
- **In-group collectivism—how much pride and loyalty should people have for their family or organization?** In contrast to individualism, *in-group collectivism* expresses the extent to which people should take pride in being members of their family, circle of close friends, and their work organization.[83]
- **Gender egalitarianism—how much should society maximize gender role differences?** *Gender egalitarianism* expresses the extent to which a society should minimize gender discrimination and role inequalities.
- **Assertiveness—how confrontational and dominant should individuals be in social relationships?** *Assertiveness* represents the extent to which a society expects people to be confrontational and competitive as opposed to tender and modest.
- **Future orientation—how much should people delay gratification by planning and saving for the future?** *Future orientation* expresses the extent to which a society encourages investment in the future, as by planning and saving.
- **Performance orientation—how much should individuals be rewarded for improvement and excellence?** *Performance orientation* expresses the extent to which society encourages and rewards its members for performance improvement and excellence.
- **Humane orientation—how much should society encourage and reward people for being kind, fair, friendly, and generous?** *Humane orientation* represents the degree to which individuals are encouraged to be altruistic, caring, kind, generous, and fair.

Data from 18,000 managers yielded the GLOBE country profiles shown in Table 4.5.

TABLE 4.5 Countries Ranking Highest and Lowest on the GLOBE Cultural Dimensions

DIMENSION	DESCRIPTION	HIGHEST	LOWEST
Power distance	Society's members expect power to be unequally shared.	Morocco, Argentina, Thailand, Spain, Russia	Denmark, Netherlands, South Africa (Black sample), Israel, Costa Rica
Uncertainty avoidance	A society relies on social norms and procedures to alleviate the unpredictability of future events.	Switzerland, Sweden, Germany (former West), Denmark, Austria	Russia, Hungary, Bolivia, Greece, Venezuela
Institutional collectivism	Individuals are encouraged and rewarded for loyalty to the group as opposed to pursuing individual goals.	Sweden, South Korea, Japan, Singapore, Denmark	Greece, Hungary, Germany (former East), Argentina, Italy

(Continued)

TABLE 4.5 Countries Ranking Highest and Lowest on the GLOBE Cultural Dimensions (*Continued*)

DIMENSION	DESCRIPTION	HIGHEST	LOWEST
In-group collectivism	People should take pride in being members of their family, circle of close friends, and their work organization.	Iran, India, Morocco, China, Egypt	Denmark, Sweden, New Zealand, Netherlands, Finland
Gender egalitarianism	A society should minimize gender discrimination and role inequalities.	Hungary, Poland, Slovenia, Denmark, Sweden	South Korea, Egypt, Morocco, India, China
Assertiveness	A society expects people to be confrontational and competitive as opposed to tender and modest.	Germany (former East), Austria, Greece, United States, Spain	Sweden, New Zealand, Switzerland, Japan, Kuwait
Future orientation	A society encourages investment in the future, as by planning and saving.	Singapore, Switzerland, Netherlands, Canada (English speaking), Denmark	Russia, Argentina, Poland, Italy, Kuwait
Performance orientation	Society encourages and rewards its members for performance improvement and excellence.	Singapore, Hong Kong, New Zealand, Taiwan, United States	Russia, Argentina, Greece, Venezuela, Italy
Humane orientation	Individuals are encouraged to be altruistic, caring, kind, generous, and fair.	Philippines, Ireland, Malaysia, Egypt, Indonesia	Germany (former West), Spain, France, Singapore, Brazil

Source: "How Cultures Collide." *Psychology Today*, July 1976, p. 69.

The GLOBE study is now in its third wave of data collection, demonstrating the continued importance of understanding cultural dimensions in global business.[84] Have you thought about how you stand in relation to various norms—in both your society and others? Would your views affect your success in taking an international job? If your instructor has assigned it, try taking Self-Assessment 4.2 in Connect.

SELF-ASSESSMENT 4.2 CAREER READINESS

Assessing Your Standing on the GLOBE Dimensions

This survey is designed to assess your values in terms of the GLOBE dimensions. Please complete Self-Assessment 4.2 if your instructor has assigned it in Connect.

Recognizing Cultural Tendencies to Gain Competitive Advantage The GLOBE dimensions illuminate the interesting variety of cultural patterns around the world. For example, the U.S. managerial sample scored high on assertiveness and performance orientation—which is why Americans are widely perceived as being pushy and hardworking. Switzerland's high scores on uncertainty avoidance and future orientation help explain its centuries of political neutrality and world-renowned banking industry. Singapore is known as a great place to do business because it is clean and safe and its people are well educated and hardworking—no surprise, considering the country's high scores on social collectivism, future orientation, and performance orientation.

Understanding these dimensions is important for managers, especially those who are working overseas. For example, research suggests that the way employees react to performance feedback and goal-setting is impacted by where they stand on the dimensions of collectivism and uncertainty avoidance.[85] Research also has shown that employee career proactivity varies based on where that person stands on the GLOBE's cultural dimensions.[86] The practical lesson to draw from all this: *Knowing the cultural tendencies of foreign business partners and competitors increases your career readiness and can give you a strategic competitive advantage.*[87]

Other Cultural Variations: Language, Interpersonal Space, Communication, Time Orientation, Religion, and Law and Political Stability

How do you go about bridging cross-cultural gaps? It begins with understanding. Let's consider variations in six basic culture areas: (1) *language,* (2) *interpersonal space,* (3) *communication,* (4) *time orientation,* (5) *religion,* and (6) *law and political stability.*

Note, however, that such cultural differences are to be viewed as *tendencies* rather than absolutes. We all need to be aware that *individuals* may be exceptions to cultural rules. After all, there *are* talkative and aggressive individuals in Japan, just as there are quiet and deferential people in the United States, stereotypes notwithstanding.

1. Language More than 7,100 different languages are spoken throughout the world, and it's indeed true that global business speaks English, although Mandarin Chinese, Hindi, and Spanish consistently top lists of the world's most spoken languages.[88]

In communicating across cultures you have four options: (a) You can speak your own language. (b) You can use a translator. (c) You can use a translation app, such as Google Translate, which turns a smartphone into an interpreter. (d) You can learn the local language—by far the best option.

It's possible to gain some language proficiency online. Several free apps, like Duolingo and Memrise, can provide instruction and practice in many widely spoken languages, including Spanish, Chinese, Russian, French, Italian, Arabic, German, and more. Most of these apps are easy to use and customizable; you can choose the level at which you want to begin (so you can brush up on the language you studied in high school, for instance, or start a brand new one), and you can test yourself with quizzes, flashcards, memory games, and more.[89]

2. Interpersonal Space It is common for men to hold hands in friendship in the Middle East with no underlying sexual connotation. This is not necessarily the case in the United States, where such a display might indicate a romantic relationship.

People from different cultures have different ideas about what constitutes acceptable interpersonal space—that is, how close or far away one should be when communicating with another person. A global study of almost 9,000 people from 42 countries revealed some interesting patterns (see Figure 4.2). For instance, the people of North America and northern Europe tend to conduct business conversations at a range of 3.1 to 3.4 feet. For people in Asia, the range is about 3.6 to 4.2 feet. The average interpersonal space

FIGURE 4.2
Comfortable Interpersonal Space for Different Countries

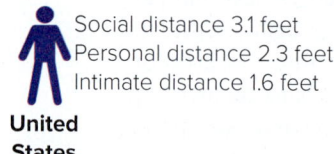

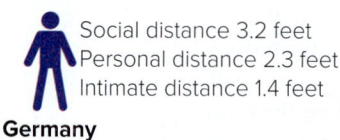

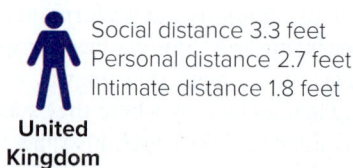

United States
Social distance 3.1 feet
Personal distance 2.3 feet
Intimate distance 1.6 feet

Canada
Social distance 3.4 feet
Personal distance 2.8 feet
Intimate distance 2.5 feet

Mexico
Social distance 3.3 feet
Personal distance 2.7 feet
Intimate distance 2.2 feet

Germany
Social distance 3.2 feet
Personal distance 2.3 feet
Intimate distance 1.4 feet

United Kingdom
Social distance 3.3 feet
Personal distance 2.7 feet
Intimate distance 1.8 feet

Russia
Social distance 3.4 feet
Personal distance 2.4 feet
Intimate distance 1.5 feet

Saudi Arabia
Social distance 4.2 feet
Personal distance 3.5 feet
Intimate distance 3.2 feet

India
Social distance 3.6 feet
Personal distance 2.9 feet
Intimate distance 1.9 feet

China
Social distance 3.8 feet
Personal distance 2.8 feet
Intimate distance 1.9 feet

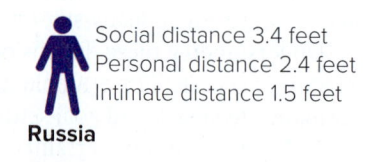

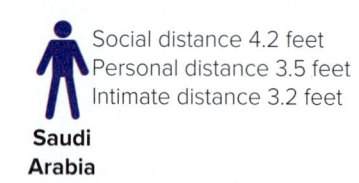

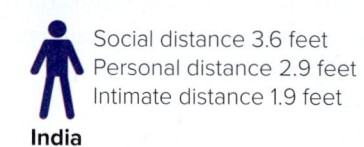

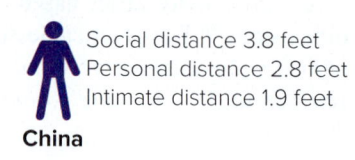

Source: Data taken from Sorokowska A., P. Sorokowski, P. Hilpert, K. Cantarero, T. Frackowiak, K. Ahmadi, et al. "Preferred Interpersonal Distances: A Global Comparison." Journal of Cross-Cultural Psychology (March 2017): 577–592.

for social distance, personal distance, and intimate distance across the 42 countries was 4.43 feet, 3 feet, and 1 foot, respectively.[90]

Interestingly, there are times when the world develops a standard for interpersonal space. For example, during the COVID-19 pandemic many countries adopted a 6-foot social distancing standard to keep people from spreading the virus to each other.

3. Communication Research has found that cross-cultural communication competence plays a critical role for expatriates to communicate effectively.[91] Angelo has tried to deal with this issue by reading books targeted for specific countries. For example, he read *Doing Business in the Middle East*[92] to prepare him for a consulting project in the United Arab Emirates (UAE). While he learned much from the book, a big takeaway was not to take everything at face value. For instance, it was suggested that females would not actively participate in classroom discussions and presenters should not try to encourage group discussion by randomly calling on people. He found that both of these recommendations did not fit for his managerial audience in Abu Dhabi. We consider communication matters in more detail in Chapter 15.

4. Time Orientation Time orientation is different across cultures. For example, people in the United States move at a different pace of business than people in China. In the United States, "time is money" and people are expected to be at meetings on time and meet deadlines. The Chinese, on the other hand, can be slower decision makers, preferring to build consensus and foster relationships before committing. During negotiations, people from the United States may find different attitudes toward time frustrating, especially if they don't understand the underlying reason.[93]

Anthropologist Hall made a useful distinction between *monochronic* time and *polychronic* time:

- **Monochronic time.** This kind of time is standard in U.S. business practice—at least until recently. That is, **monochronic time** is a preference for doing one thing at a time. In this perception, time is viewed as being limited, precisely segmented, and schedule driven. This perception of time prevails, for example, when you schedule a meeting with someone and then give the visitor your undivided attention during the allotted time.[94] Indeed, you probably practice monochronic time when you're in a job interview. You work hard at listening to what the interviewer says and even take careful notes. You don't answer your cell phone or gaze repeatedly out the window.

- **Polychronic time.** This outlook on time prevails in Mediterranean, Latin American, and especially Middle Eastern cultures. **Polychronic time is a preference for doing more than one thing at a time. Here time is viewed as being flexible and multidimensional.** This orientation can lead to work stress as people try to accomplish multiple things at once.[95] This perception of time prevails when you visit a Latin American client, find yourself sitting in the waiting room for 45 minutes, and then learn in the meeting that the client is dealing with three other people at the same time.

Research suggests that the distinction between monochronic and polychronic time is an important one, especially when it comes to work tasks. For example, when work tasks assume a polychronic view, but the workforce is monochronic, there will be conflict between the organization and the person. The end result is a stressful work environment.[96]

5. Religion If you grew up in the United States or another predominantly Christian country, then you may never have considered the profound influence religion has on work-related customs, practices, and values. The very ethos of American business is built upon values that underlie the Protestant work ethic, including individuality, the central importance of hard work, and a distaste for activities perceived as inefficient uses of time, money, and energy. The generally accepted American business calendar is also built around Protestant and Roman Catholic Christian calendars.

Working internationally requires you to understand and adapt to others' business cultures. It can be helpful for managers to grasp the religious traditions that inform various cultures around the world (see Figure 4.3).

Research suggests that a country's or region's predominant religious traditions influence a host of business-related factors. These include corporate accounting practices, risk-taking behaviors, and advertising decisions. Religion also informs organizational approaches to social responsibility and employee performance management.[97]

6. Law and Political Stability Doing business abroad means engaging with other countries' laws and business practices. This frequently involves calculations about political risk that might impact a company's assets or impair its foreign operations. Among the risks an organization might experience abroad are *instability, expropriation, corruption,* and *labor abuses.*

- **Instability.** Even in a developed country a company may encounter political instability, such as riots or civil disorders. This happened in 2023 when the French government proposed increasing the country's legal retirement age from 62 to 64 by 2030. The proposal was geared toward addressing impending deficits in the pension system, and French workers quickly responded. Thousands went on strike to protest the proposal, and more than one million marched in the streets against the announcement.[98] To increase pressure on the government, energy workers belonging to one of France's largest labor unions—the Confédération générale du travail (CGT)—began cutting power to President Macron's supporters and lowering energy rates for laborers.[99]

Many Muslims strive to pray five times a day, prostrating themselves on a prayer mat that faces the holy city of Mecca, located in Saudi Arabia. Many organizations provide a prayer space for employees as a way of promoting a culture of inclusion. Purestock/Getty Images

FIGURE 4.3

Major Religions by Geographic Area
All population counts are estimated.

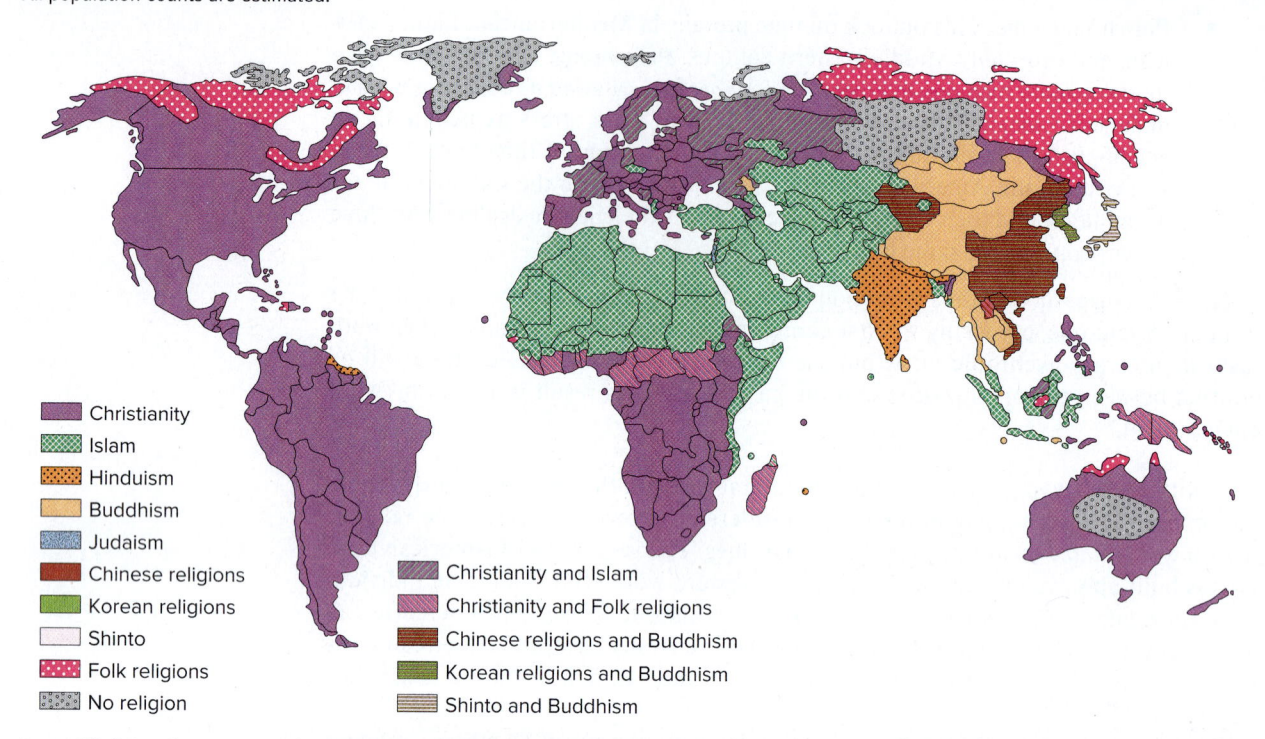

- Christianity
- Islam
- Hinduism
- Buddhism
- Judaism
- Chinese religions
- Korean religions
- Shinto
- Folk religions
- No religion
- Christianity and Islam
- Christianity and Folk religions
- Chinese religions and Buddhism
- Korean religions and Buddhism
- Shinto and Buddhism

Source: "Religious Composition by Country, 2010–2050," Pew Research Center, December 21, 2022, https://www.pewresearch.org/religion/interactives/religious-composition-by-country-2010-2050/.

- **Expropriation.** Expropriation is defined as a government's seizure of a domestic or foreign company's assets. Political instability in a foreign country can increase this type of risk for U.S. multinationals. In 2022, Exxon Mobil attempted to sell its 30% stake in the Sakhalin-1 oil venture in Russia. A spokesperson for Exxon said the Russian government transferred ownership of the project to a government company and gave Exxon one month to reapply for ownership under new terms. Exxon did not agree to the terms and instead exited Russia, incurring heavy losses.[100] Examples such as this call into question the processes that different countries may use for seizing a company's assets, which should be an important consideration for managers.

- **Corruption.** Bribery is considered an acceptable business practice in some countries. Among the countries where this type of corruption is seen as most common are Venezuela, Afghanistan, South Sudan, North Korea, Yemen, and Somalia.[101] U.S. businesspeople are prevented from participating in overseas bribes under the 1978 Foreign Corrupt Practices Act, which makes it illegal for employees of U.S. companies to make "questionable" or "dubious" contributions to political decision makers in foreign nations. While this creates a competitive disadvantage for those working in foreign countries in which government bribery may be the only way to obtain business, the United Nations Global Compact is attempting to level the playing field by promoting anti-corruption standards for business.

- **Labor abuses.** Overseas suppliers may offer low prices, but working conditions can be harsh, as has been the case for garment makers in Cambodia, Bangladesh, India, Myanmar, and Pakistan. Workers in Bangladesh interviewed for a recent research study reported physical abuse, salary deductions for drinking water or taking bathroom breaks, and 14-hour days with no rest or meal breaks.[102] Even worse, around 27 million people across the world are said to be forced to work with no pay.[103]

U.S. Managers on Foreign Assignments: Why Do They Fail?

The U.S. State Department estimates that about 9 million U.S. citizens live abroad.[104] These individuals are called **expatriates**—people living or working in a foreign country. It can be very costly to support expatriates and their families. For example, a family living in cities such as Geneva, Brussels, Dubai, or Hong Kong can cost a business between $5,000 and $6,500 a month.[105] Are employers who are subsidizing these costs getting their money's worth? Not always. Expatriate managers often have trouble adjusting to their host country's cultures, and this can lead to poor performance, decreased well-being, and higher turnover rates.[106] Researchers attempting to better understand issues expatriate managers experience have studied factors related to expatriate selection, ongoing adjustment, and return to the home country (i.e., repatriation).

Expatriate Selection Expatriates often leave their foreign assignments early due to the challenges of adjusting to everyday life in a different culture. Some research suggests that organizations should consider specific factors that may indicate readiness for expatriate roles. These include career readiness competencies such as self-motivation; diversity, equity, and inclusion; and resilience, emotional intelligence, social intelligence, and personal adaptability.[107] Factors such as family support and the ability to speak the host country's language also play an important role.[108]

Ongoing Expatriate Adjustment In addition to selecting managers who are more likely to succeed in expatriate roles, experts believe organizations must create working environments that help expats continually adjust throughout their foreign assignments.[109] This begins with providing adequate training on cross-cultural differences and facilitating the establishment of social contacts prior to and in the early stages of assignments.[110] Further, facilitating expatriate managers' adjustment requires ongoing support beyond these initial activities. This is because successful expatriate adjustment is a dynamic process that requires managers to continuously learn, reflect, and adapt.[111] Research suggests expatriate managers have better outcomes when they perceive strong ongoing support from their organizations.[112]

Repatriation Unfortunately, problems may continue when expatriates return home. For example, studies suggest that expatriates experience increased psychological distress due to the challenges of re-adapting to their home culture. Expatriates also report a sense of career disruption and a lack of integration with co-workers in their home office locations.[113] Research estimates that at least 25% of expatriates leave their organizations within two years of returning home, often due to the issues mentioned.[114] These studies underscore the importance of managing the repatriation process. The Society for Human Resource Management (SHRM) recommends organizations take the following steps to ensure successful repatriation of expatriate managers:[115]

- **Maintain communication and connection with the home office.** Expatriate managers often experience a lack of connection with home office employees upon returning home. Organizations can encourage ongoing connections in a variety of ways, including periodically flying expatriate managers in for important face-to-face meetings and including stories of expatriate experiences and successes in company newsletters and conversations.
- **Set clear expectations about career planning.** Expatriates may feel as though their international experiences don't count toward career progression and are instead seen as isolated assignments unrelated to their upward trajectories within their home organizations. Companies should include expatriate assignments as part of long-term career planning. This begins with expectations and plans set prior to the international assignment.

- **Ensure re-assignment reflects international experience.** Organizations should strongly consider expatriates' international experiences and resulting gained KSAOs when re-assigning these employees to home office roles. One suggestion is to fly expatriate managers to the home office for face-to-face interviews that allow them to discuss the nuances of what they have gained from international assignments. Another suggestion is to ask repatriates for updated resumes and KSAO lists, and to use this information to match them with the best-fitting available roles.

Do you think you have what it takes to be an effective global manager? Try taking Self-Assessment 4.3 in Connect, if your instructor has assigned it.

SELF-ASSESSMENT 4.3   CAREER READINESS

Assessing Your Global Manager Potential

This survey is designed to assess how well suited you are to becoming a global manager. Please complete Self-Assessment 4.3 if your instructor has assigned it in Connect.

4.6 Career Corner: Managing Your Career Readiness

LO 4-6

Describe how to develop your diversity, equity, and inclusion competency.

Executive Interview Series: Cross-Cultural Awareness and Self-Awareness

You may think this chapter won't build your career readiness if you have no plans to work overseas. Don't make this assumption! In our 24/7 globally connected world, cultural and national borders have all but disappeared. If your instructor has assigned it, you should check out what the executives in this chapter's Executive Interview Series video have to say about the importance of career readiness skills related to global management. Namely, whether you work in the United States or abroad, you need to understand, embrace, and use cultural awareness to enhance your personal and professional relationships.

Figure 4.4 shows the model of career readiness we discussed in Chapter 1. This chapter links with three of the competencies contained in this model. The most important one is the core competency of *diversity, equity, and inclusion*. This important career readiness competency includes respect for and openness to diverse cultures and identities. The remaining two are the characteristics of *personal adaptability* and *self-awareness*. Personal adaptability is important because it helps when interacting with diverse people and when living or working in another country. Self-awareness is essential for becoming more culturally aware.

It takes effort to improve these three competencies because they are firmly rooted in our personal experiences and belief systems. Said the author of a recent article on the influence of culture, "As long as one remains within one's own cultural boundaries, the ways of thinking, living, and behaving peculiar to that culture are transparent or invisible."[116] This means that how we see ourselves, how we view and treat others who differ from us, and our willingness to change our ways of thinking, perceiving, and behaving are all deeply influenced by our cultures. It's difficult for us to imagine reality outside of that cultural lens.

FIGURE 4.4
Career readiness competencies

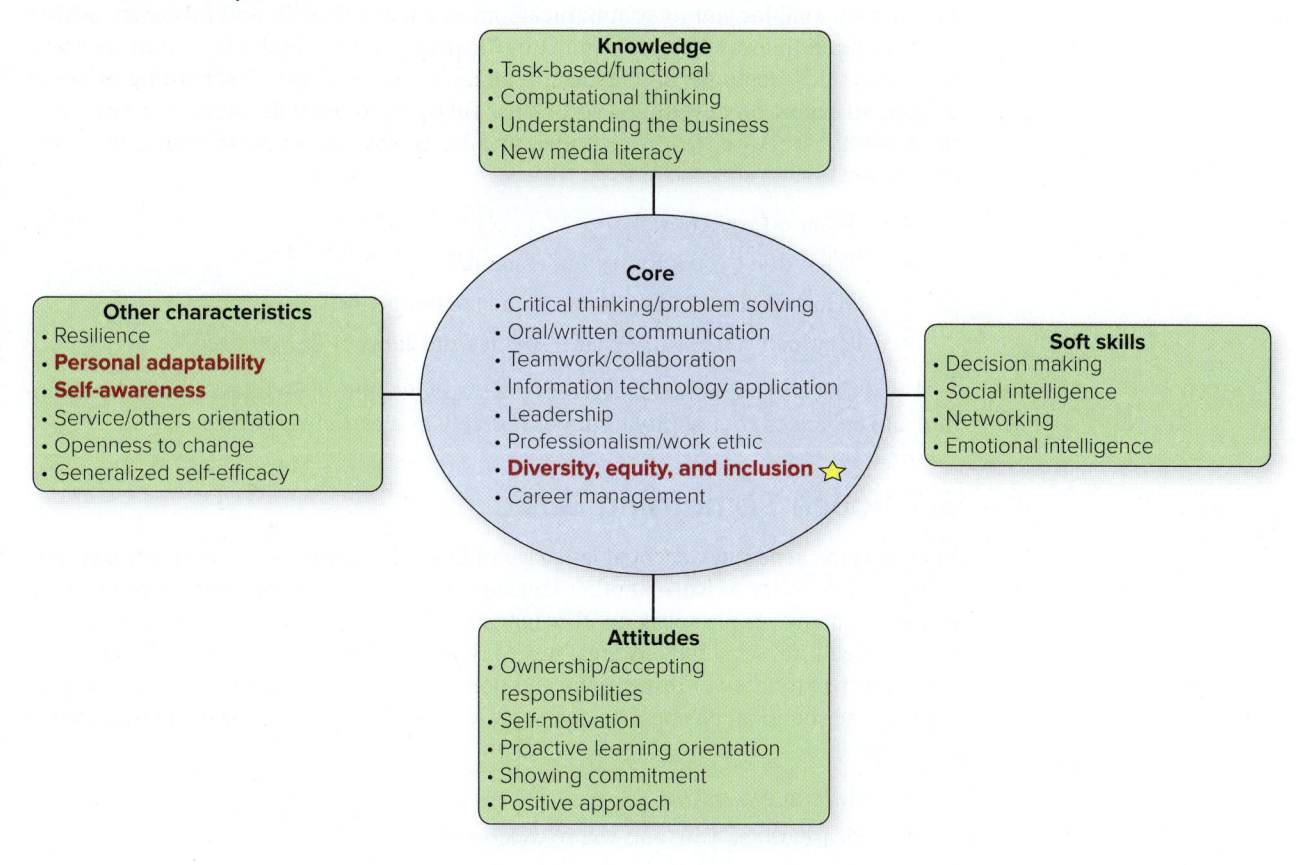

Knowledge
- Task-based/functional
- Computational thinking
- Understanding the business
- New media literacy

Other characteristics
- Resilience
- **Personal adaptability**
- **Self-awareness**
- Service/others orientation
- Openness to change
- Generalized self-efficacy

Core
- Critical thinking/problem solving
- Oral/written communication
- Teamwork/collaboration
- Information technology application
- Leadership
- Professionalism/work ethic
- **Diversity, equity, and inclusion** ⭐
- Career management

Soft skills
- Decision making
- Social intelligence
- Networking
- Emotional intelligence

Attitudes
- Ownership/accepting responsibilities
- Self-motivation
- Proactive learning orientation
- Showing commitment
- Positive approach

We recommend the following activities to help you see the world through a broader cultural lens and enhance the core career readiness competency of diversity, equity, and inclusion.

1. Listen and Observe

Try to take the perspective of a native when interacting with others in a new cultural context. Listening and observing are the foundations of this kind of perspective taking. If a behavior or statement seems odd or confusing to you, look for the cultural logic or set of values that may explain it. For example, Angelo's international students rarely challenged him in the classroom. He felt they were not adequately contributing to classroom discussion due to a lack of confidence or inability to speak English. This assumption was wrong! Their behavior was caused by cultural values that grant tremendous respect and esteem to the role of professor. By understanding this cross-cultural perspective, Angelo was able to encourage his international students to take a more critical and participative perspective during classroom activities. Remember, it is generally good practice to avoid making assumptions and instead check your understanding by asking questions of someone familiar with the context at hand.

2. Become Aware of the Context

Context refers to the situational or environmental characteristics that influence our behavior.[117] Recall what you learned from our discussion of high- and low-context cultures in Section 4.5. Specifically, in high-context cultures, it is nearly impossible to decipher the meaning of a spoken or written message without also understanding the context in which the message was delivered. Understanding context gives you insights that let you correctly interpret the "what" and "why" of someone's behavior. This in turn enables you to communicate more effectively with and influence others. You can develop awareness of context by "learning to read and adapt to the existing structure, rules, customs, and leaders in an unfamiliar situation," according to Bruce Tulgan, an expert on developing soft skills. Tulgan recommends answering four questions about structure, rules, customs, and leadership to increase your contextual awareness:

- "What do you know?"
- "What don't you know or understand?"
- "What do you need to know or understand better?"
- "How can you learn? What resources and support do you need?"[118]

Answering these questions increases your insights into the contextual effects of culture and enhances your ability to fit comfortably in a particular context.

3. Choose Something Basic

English is the generally accepted language of business. If you are a native speaker, it is still advisable to try to learn another language if you plan to work overseas or in a context where many people speak another language. Even a small effort shows respect and promotes cultural sensitivity. A great way to start is by learning basic words and phrases that allow you to interact respectfully and politely in another language.[119] Before engaging with international business partners, try learning to say the following in their native language:

- Hello and goodbye
- Please, thank you, and you're welcome
- Yes and no
- I'm sorry and excuse me
- My name is/what is your name?

A host of other activities can enhance your diversity, equity, and inclusion competency. The executives in this chapter's Executive Interview Series video encourage you to create opportunities to learn and diversify your experience, and we agree with them. Make it a goal to select several of them from the following list:[120]

- Study the principles or values of another religion, or visit a place of worship different from what you are accustomed to in your own faith background.
- Observe people and interact with people from other cultures.
- Participate in a sporting event related to a different culture (cricket, karate, rugby, bocce, pétanque).
- Learn about traditions and celebratory days from other countries.
- Watch international films.
- Try the cuisine of other countries.
- Attend seminars or speeches by culturally diverse speakers.
- Follow world news on a regular basis.
- Take courses in Black history, women's studies, Asian American studies, Chicano studies, and Native American studies.
- Take an anthropology class.

Key Terms Used in This Chapter

context 137
countertrading 118
cross-cultural awareness 126
culture 127
embargo 121
ethnocentric managers 115
European Union (EU) 123
exchange rate 124
expatriates 135
exporting 118
expropriation 134
Foreign Corrupt Practices Act 134
franchising 119
free trade 120
geocentric managers 116
global economy 111

globalization 111
global outsourcing 118
global village 111
GLOBE project 128
greenfield venture 119
high-context culture 127
Hofstede model of four cultural dimensions 128
import quota 121
importing 118
licensing 118
low-context culture 127
maquiladoras 117
monochronic time 132
most favored nation 124
multinational corporation 114

multinational organization 114
North American Free Trade Agreement (NAFTA) 122
offshoring 118
outsourcing 117
parochialism 115
polycentric managers 116
polychronic time 133
sanction 121
tariff 120
trade protectionism 120
trading bloc 122
United States–Mexico–Canada Agreement (USMCA) 122
wholly owned subsidiary 119

Key Points

4.1 Globalization: The Collapse of Time and Distance

- Globalization is the trend of the world economy toward becoming more interdependent.
- The rise of the "global village" refers to the "shrinking" of time and space as communications have become easier.
- The global economy is the increasing tendency of nations to interact with one another as one market.

4.2 You and International Management

- International management oversees operations in or with organizations in foreign countries.
- The successful international manager is not ethnocentric or polycentric but geocentric.

4.3 Why and How Companies Expand Internationally

- Companies expand internationally because they seek (1) supplies, (2) new markets, (3) lower labor costs, (4) access to finance capital, and (5) avoidance of tariffs or import quotas.
- Companies expand internationally through: (1) global outsourcing; (2) importing, exporting, and countertrading; (3) licensing and franchising; (4) joint ventures; or (5) wholly owned subsidiaries.

4.4 The World of Free Trade: Regional Economic Cooperation and Competition

- Free trade is international movement of goods and services without political or economic obstructions.
- Three barriers to free trade are tariffs, import quotas, and sanctions and embargoes.
- Three principal organizations exist to facilitate international trade: (1) the World Trade Organization, (2) the World Bank, and (3) the International Monetary Fund.
- A trading bloc is a group of nations within a geographical region that have agreed to remove trade barriers. Examples include (1) the United States–Mexico–Canada Agreement (USMCA) and (2) the European Union (EU).
- Managers must consider exchange rates, the rate at which the currency of one area or country can be exchanged for the currency of another, such as American dollars in relation to Mexican pesos or European euros.
- The term BRICS stands for the five major emerging economies of Brazil, Russia, India, China, and South Africa.

4.5 The Value of Understanding Cultural Differences

- In low-context cultures, shared meanings derive from written and spoken words. In high-context cultures, meanings derive more from situational cues.
- The Hofstede model identified four dimensions along which national cultures can be placed: (1) individualism/collectivism, (2) power distance, (3) uncertainty avoidance, and (4) masculinity/femininity.

- The GLOBE (Global Leadership and Organizational Behavior Effectiveness) Project is an ongoing cross-cultural investigation of nine cultural dimensions involved in business: (1) power distance, (2) uncertainty avoidance, (3) institutional collectivism, (4) in-group collectivism, (5) gender egalitarianism, (6) assertiveness, (7) future orientation, (8) performance orientation, and (9) humane orientation.
- A nation's culture is the shared set of beliefs, values, knowledge, and patterns of behavior common to a group of people. Managers trying to understand other cultures need to understand six basic cultural perceptions embodied in (1) language, (2) interpersonal space, (3) communication, (4) time orientation, (5) religion, and (6) law and political stability.

4.6 Career Corner: Managing Your Career Readiness

- You can develop your diversity, equity, and inclusion competency by remembering to: (1) listen and observe, (2) become aware of the context, and (3) choose something basic.

Boeing Continuing Case

Learn more about Boeing's ethical responsibilities in a globalized world, and the impact its decisions had on various stakeholders, including those outside the United States.

Assess your ability to apply concepts discussed in Chapters 3 and 4 to the case by going to Connect.

PART 3 • PLANNING

5

Planning
The Foundation of Successful Management

After reading this chapter, you should be able to:

LO 5-1 Discuss the role of strategic management.

LO 5-2 Compare mission, vision, and value statements.

LO 5-3 Discuss the types and purposes of goals and plans.

LO 5-4 Describe SMART goals and their implementation.

LO 5-5 Outline the planning/control cycle.

LO 5-6 Describe how to develop the career readiness competency of proactive learning orientation.

FORECAST   What's Ahead in This Chapter

We describe planning and its link to strategy. We define planning, strategy, and strategic management and state why they are important. We deal with the fundamentals of planning, including the mission, vision, and value statements, and the three types of planning—strategic, tactical, and operational. We consider goals, operating plans, and action plans; SMART goals, management by objectives, and cascading goals; and finally the planning/control cycle. We conclude with a Career Corner that focuses on how you can develop the career readiness competency of proactive learning orientation.

Start Your Career Off Right by Planning

The thought of starting a career (or switching to a new one) can be either intimidating or exciting. What's the difference? Having goals and a plan.

Setting Goals and Making a Plan

Here are some steps in the career-management process for you to consider as you start to build your career.[1]

1. Match your skills and aspirations to job opportunities.

Make two lists. In the first list, use the career readiness skill of self-awareness to write down your individual strengths, lifestyle preferences, passions, and work style. This should include an assessment of the career readiness competencies shown in Table 1.3. In the second list, identify the opportunities available to you through your networking, earlier work and volunteer experience, and other resources (don't forget the alumni and placement offices at your school). Now compare the two lists to discover where you should focus your career-building efforts.

2. Evaluate market conditions in your target field.

The career readiness skill of understanding the business will guide you to identify important labor market conditions like the demand for new hires in your chosen field or fields, the competencies expected of incoming employees, the likely salary range and opportunities for advancement, and the projected growth rate in the industry. Resources such as the Occupational Outlook Handbook (https://www.bls.gov/ooh/) are a great place to gather information about industry trends and strengthen your career readiness skill of understanding the business.

3. Create your action plan.

Using what you learned from steps 1 and 2, consider the following two questions: (1) What jobs match your strengths and career aspirations? (2) What skills and abilities do you need to develop? Write a list of actions you can take to achieve your goal of breaking into a new career. You are more likely to achieve your goals if they are "SMART"—specific, measurable against clear criteria to show progress, attainable with a 50% or greater chance of success, relevant to you, and time-bound with target dates for completion. We discuss the process of writing SMART goals in Section 5.4. Try to keep your steps or goals to a manageable number; somewhere between three and five is recommended. Prioritize and schedule them to create your plan.

4. Track your progress.

You'll see as you study this chapter that evaluating progress toward goals and making adjustments are an inherent part of the planning process. Plans aren't perfect. Unforeseen obstacles arise and unprecedented events occur. Consequently, you need to adapt or modify your plan along the way. Schedule periodic check-ups to evaluate your progress. What's going well? What's not? If steps in your plan don't work out as you had hoped, don't give up. Rely on the career readiness skills of a positive approach and personal adaptability to change your approach. Recalibrate your plan by capitalizing on what's effective and modifying what's ineffective. Then, implement your revised plan and continue making adjustments until you achieve your goal.

5. Stay resilient.

Draw on the career readiness competency of resilience to keep your hope alive during the twists and turns in the career-building process. It takes time to find a job, especially one that's a good fit for both you and the company that hires you. College graduates spend three to six months, on average, landing their first job after graduation. If you are already working, even part-time, stay in the job while you pursue a new one. It's always easier to find a job if you have one. If you are not working, consider accepting an internship that might open the door to key networking opportunities, or taking a short-term position, such as a part-time or seasonal job, to generate income while you continue to pursue your long-term career goals.[2]

For Discussion What fields or industries are interesting or appealing to you as places to work? What news and information about these areas can you start tracking now, and how will you do that? What skills and abilities do you need to develop to become an ideal candidate? Is there anyone in your network who can help increase your exposure to your ideal jobs? If not, how could you find someone?

5.1 Planning and Strategy

THE BIG PICTURE
The first of four functions in the management process is planning, which involves setting goals and deciding how to achieve them and which is linked to strategy. We define planning, strategy, and strategic management. We then describe three reasons strategic management and strategic planning are important.

LO 5-1

Discuss the role of strategic management.

The *management process,* as you'll recall (from Chapter 1), involves the four management functions of *planning, organizing, leading,* and *controlling,* which form four of the part divisions of this book. This chapter begins our exploration into the planning function by discussing the link between planning and strategy, the basics of planning, and the issues associated with creating goals and action plans. The next two chapters expand this coverage by focusing on strategic management and decision making.

Planning, Strategy, and Strategic Management

How important is planning for organizational success? The failure rate for new businesses is 50% within the first 5 years and 66% within 10 years, according to the U.S. Bureau of Labor Statistics.[3] Poor planning is one of the top reasons small businesses fail.[4] *Planning,* which we discuss in this chapter, is a broad umbrella term used in conjunction with *strategy* and *strategic management,* concepts we describe in detail in Chapter 6. Let's consider some definitions.

Navigating through uncertainty. Managing is like driving during a thunderstorm. Drivers must deal with the uncertainties of the storm (poor visibility, slick roads, etc.), while managers navigate their way through the uncertainty and ambiguity of market conditions, competitor actions, and supplier demands. ND700/Shutterstock

Planning: Coping with Uncertainty   As noted in Chapter 1, **planning** is defined as setting goals and deciding how to achieve them. Like a captain at the helm of a ship skillfully navigating through stormy seas, entrepreneurs and executives alike lead their companies through an uncertain business environment by carefully formulating courses of action to achieve specific results.[5] Planning aids managers in thinking through how they are going to position their company to survive, grow, and thrive into the future and thus avoid joining the two out of three business that fail within 10 years.

A **plan** is a document that outlines how goals are going to be met. It is a product of the planning process and represents a roadmap for future action.

One important type of plan is a **business plan**, a document that outlines a firm's goals, the strategy for achieving them, and the standards for measuring success.

Business Plan Example—Disney: Disney sought to accelerate the company's revenue and profitability by creating Disney+, a video streaming service, in November 2019. The company's goal is for Disney+ to become profitable by 2024. Their strategy to achieve profitability is strong subscriber growth and increased subscription revenues. By 2022, Disney+ reported nearly 164 million subscribers around the world (compared to Netflix's 223 million subscribers), and the company has instituted price increases in its streaming platform. It is on its way to achieving a profitable streaming business as an engine for the company's future growth.[6]

Strategy: Setting Long-Term Direction   A **strategy** sets the long-term goals and direction for an organization. It represents an "educated guess" about what long-term goals or direction to pursue for the survival or prosperity of the organization.

Strategy Example—Levi Strauss & Co.:   When you think of Levi Strauss & Co., do you think denim jeans? Levi Strauss, the global market share leader in men's jeans, is adopting a strategy to expand beyond denim jeans to global apparel and accessories (a market 16 times the size of the global jeans market). The company's strategy includes expanding its product portfolio to appeal to diverse lifestyles and produce offerings in women's apparel, men's and women's tops, and activewear and athleisure.[7]

Strategy is not something that can be decided on just once. It generally is reconsidered annually because of ever-changing business conditions.

Strategic Management: Involving All Managers in Strategy   In the late 1940s, most large U.S. companies were organized around a single idea or product line. By the 1970s, Fortune 500 companies were operating in more than one industry and had expanded overseas. It became apparent that to stay focused and efficient, companies had to begin taking a strategic-management approach. Today, companies are using strategic management to scale or focus their operations.

Strategic management is a process that involves managers from all parts of the organization in the formulation and the implementation of strategies and strategic goals. This definition doesn't mean that managers at the top dictate ideas to be followed by people lower in the organization. Indeed, precisely because middle managers in particular are the ones who will be asked to understand and implement the strategies, they should also help to formulate them.

As we will see, strategic management is a process that involves managers from all parts of the organization—top managers, middle managers, first-line managers, and team leaders—in the formulation, implementation, and execution of strategies and strategic goals to advance the purposes of the organization. Thus, planning covers not only

FIGURE 5.1

Planning and strategic management

The details of planning and strategic management are explained in Chapters 5 and 6.

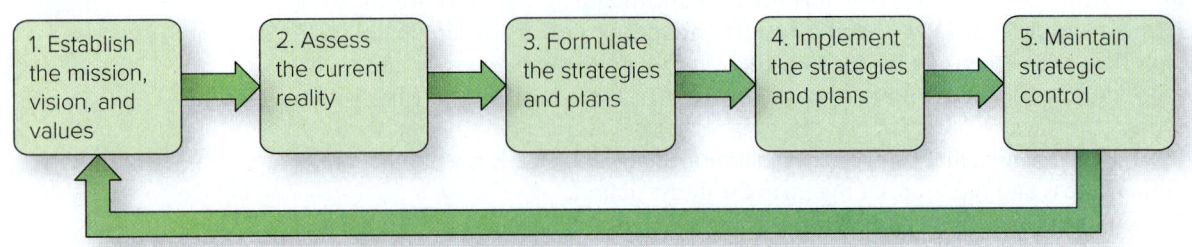

1. Establish the mission, vision, and values → 2. Assess the current reality → 3. Formulate the strategies and plans → 4. Implement the strategies and plans → 5. Maintain strategic control

Feedback: Revise actions, if necessary, based on feedback

strategic planning (done by top managers) but also tactical planning (done by middle managers) and operational planning (done by first-line managers and team leaders).

Planning and strategic management flow from an organization's mission and vision, as we describe in the next section (see Figure 5.1).

Why Planning and Strategic Management Are Important

An organization should adopt planning and strategic management for three reasons: They can (1) *provide direction and momentum,* (2) *encourage new ideas,* and above all (3) *develop a sustainable competitive advantage.*[8] Let's consider these three benefits in more detail.

1. Provide Direction and Momentum Planning and strategic management help people focus on the most critical short-term and long-term problems, choices, and opportunities. Without a plan, managers may well focus on whatever is in front of them, putting out fires until they get an unpleasant jolt when a competitor moves out in front because it has been able to take a long-range view of things and respond more quickly to changes in market dynamics or customer preferences. Consider the challenges facing Twitter.

> **Planning and Strategic Management Example—X, formerly known as Twitter:** Elon Musk purchased Twitter in October 2022 in the midst of a dramatic shift in the social media landscape. Social media is increasingly attracting government scrutiny while advertisers significantly reduce spending on social media platforms and users change how they interact with social media. Within one month, Musk fired nearly half of the company's staff and 50 of Twitter's top 100 advertisers stopped advertising on the platform (advertising accounted for 90% of Twitter's revenue in 2021). A strategic plan is needed to provide stability and a clear roadmap for how the company plans to increase its revenue and profitability over the long term.[9]

Research shows that established companies are more successful when they formulate a business plan, and founders benefit most from business planning 6 to 12 months after launching the business.[10] Of course, a poor plan can send an organization in the *wrong* direction. Bad planning usually results from not understanding the problem, poor assessment of an organization's capabilities, ineffective group dynamics, faulty assumptions about the future, and failure to use management control as a feedback mechanism.[11] And it needs to be said that while a detailed plan may be comforting, it's not necessarily a strategy.[12] Meta is a good example.

Planning and Strategic Management Example—Meta: Meta (formerly Facebook) CEO, Mark Zuckerberg, changed the name of his company and made a multibillion dollar strategic bet on shifting the company's focus from a traditional social media platform to a networked platform of immersive three-dimensional virtual worlds. Meta lost $20 billion on its investments developing the metaverse in 2021–2022 yet is accelerating its spending. At the same time, Meta faces stiff competition for market share in the social media arena from competitors like TikTok. Influential investors are beginning to wonder if the company is pursuing the wrong strategy or is straying too far from its core business.[13]

2. Encourage New Ideas Some people claim that planning can foster rigidity, that it reduces creative thinking and adaptability. "Setting oneself on a predetermined course in unknown waters," says one critic, "is the perfect way to sail straight into an iceberg."[14]

Far from being an innovative straitjacket, strategic planning encourages new ideas by stressing the importance of innovation in achieving long-range success.[15] A research study of 227 technology-related businesses, for example, found that firms that supported and rewarded risk taking in their strategic planning achieved both high returns and a high level of innovative activity.[16] Along these lines, management scholar Gary Hamel says that companies such as Apple have been successful because they have been able to unleash the spirit of "strategy innovation." Strategy innovation, he says, is the ability to reinvent the basis of competition within existing industries—"bold new business models that put incumbents on the defensive."[17]

Some successful innovators are companies moving into new lines of business to fuel customer engagement.

Innovative Ideas Example—Mattel: Mattel, maker of Barbie, Hot Wheels, and Uno saw a steady decline in sales, from $6.6 billion in 2013 to $4.3 billion in 2020.[18] The company is recovering lost revenue by adding avenues through which customers can engage with and experience its brands. In additional to digital gaming, Mattel is developing animated and live-action films based on its beloved brands and has more than a dozen film projects in the works with A-listers like Tom Hanks, Vin Diesel, and Margot Robbie.[19]

Innovative Ideas Example—Red Bull: Red Bull is another well-known brand strategically innovating by expanding to the sports and entertainment industries. The popular energy drink maker owns five soccer teams, a Formula One racing team, and now has a media arm, Red Bull Media House, which produces digital, TV, film, print, and music content.[20]

3. Develop a Sustainable Competitive Advantage Strategic management can provide a sustainable *competitive advantage,* which, you'll recall (from Chapter 1), is the ability of an organization to produce goods or services more effectively than its competitors do, thereby outperforming them. We discuss the manner in which companies create competitive advantage more thoroughly in Chapter 6. You will learn that companies must have products or services that are valuable, rare, and difficult to imitate, and an organization poised to exploit its strengths. Apple, Amazon, and Starbucks have all built a sustainable competitive advantage in their respective industries: Apple's products are built on its proprietary software, Amazon's distribution system enables the company to deliver a massive selection of products quickly to customers, and Starbuck's integrated supply chain gives it cost control over its ingredients and provides customers a farm-to-store experience.[21] •

5.2 Fundamentals of Planning

THE BIG PICTURE
Planning consists of translating an organization's mission and vision into objectives. The organization's purpose is expressed as a mission statement, and what it becomes is expressed as a vision statement; both should represent the organization's values, expressed in a values statement. From these are derived strategic planning, then tactical planning, then operational planning.

LO 5-2

Compare mission, vision, and value statements.

Are you hopeful? That's a good thing. Students who have more hope reportedly have higher grades and are more apt to finish college.

"Hope is the belief that the future will be better than the present," says columnist Elizabeth Bernstein, "and that you have some power to make it so." People who are hopeful "don't just have a goal or a wish, they have a strategy to achieve it and the motivation to implement their plan."[22]

First, however, you must determine your "goal or wish"—that is, your purpose. An organization must determine its purpose, too—what's known as its *mission*. And managers must have an idea of where they want the organization to go—the *vision*. Both mission and vision should express what's most important to the organization—its *values*. The approach to planning can be summarized in the following diagram, which shows how an organization's mission becomes translated into action plans (see Figure 5.2).

FIGURE 5.2

Making plans

An organization's reason for being is expressed in a *mission statement*. What the organization wishes to become is expressed in a *vision statement*. The values the organization wishes to emphasize are expressed in a *values statement*. From these are derived *strategic planning*, then *tactical planning*, and finally *operational planning*. The purpose of each kind of planning is to specify *goals* and *action plans* that ultimately pave the way toward achieving an organization's vision.

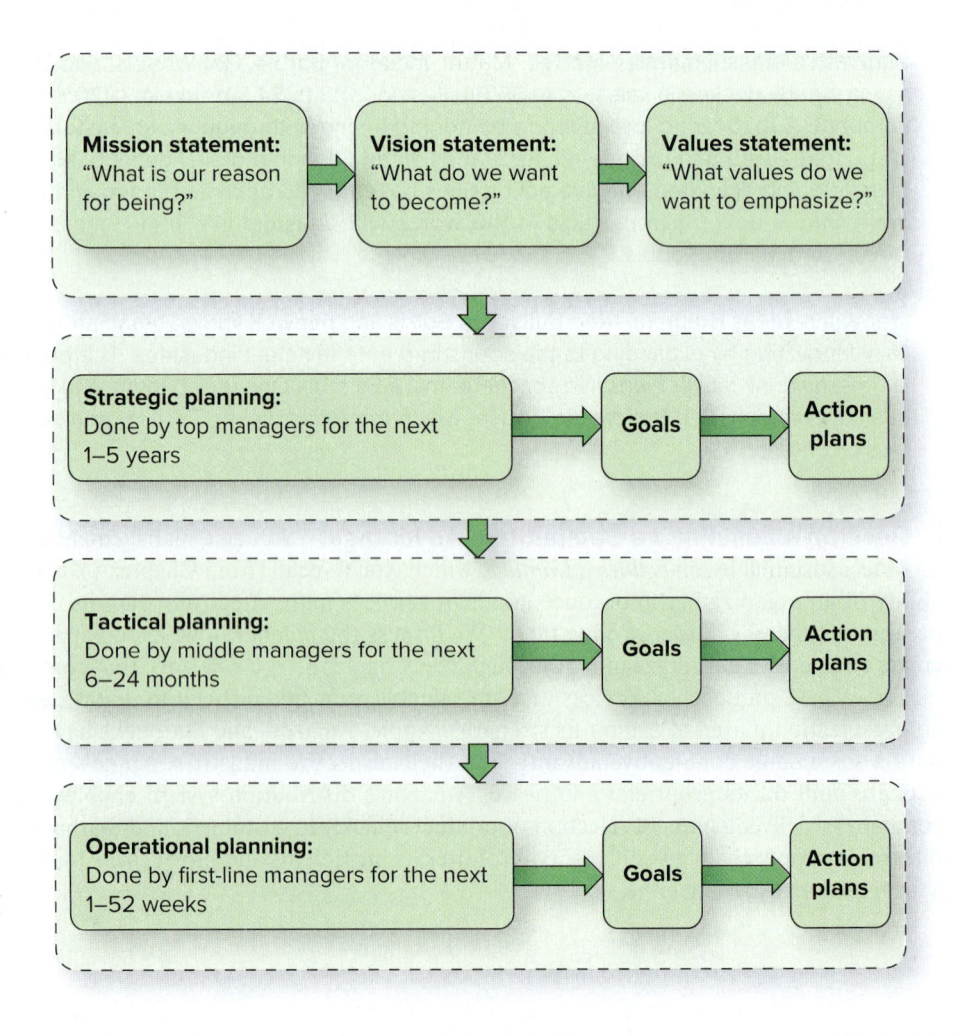

- **Mission statement:** "What is our reason for being?" → **Vision statement:** "What do we want to become?" → **Values statement:** "What values do we want to emphasize?"

- **Strategic planning:** Done by top managers for the next 1–5 years → Goals → Action plans

- **Tactical planning:** Done by middle managers for the next 6–24 months → Goals → Action plans

- **Operational planning:** Done by first-line managers for the next 1–52 weeks → Goals → Action plans

Mission, Vision, and Values Statements

The planning process begins with three attributes: a mission statement (which answers the question "What is our reason for being?"), a vision statement (which answers the question "What do we want to become?"), and a values statement (which answers the question "What values do we want to emphasize?") (See Table 5.1).

TABLE 5.1 Mission, Vision, and Values Statements

MISSION STATEMENTS: DOES YOUR COMPANY'S MISSION STATEMENT ANSWER THESE QUESTIONS?

1. Who are our customers?
2. What are our major products or services?
3. In what geographical areas do we compete?
4. What is our basic technology?
5. What is our commitment to economic objectives?
6. What are our basic beliefs, values, aspirations, and philosophical priorities?
7. What are our major strengths and competitive advantages?
8. What are our public responsibilities, and what image do we wish to project?
9. What is our attitude toward our employees?

VISION STATEMENTS: DOES YOUR COMPANY'S VISION STATEMENT ANSWER "YES" TO THESE QUESTIONS?

1. Is it appropriate for the organization and for the times?
2. Does it set standards of excellence and reflect high ideals?
3. Does it clarify purpose and direction?
4. Does it inspire enthusiasm and encourage commitment?
5. Is it well articulated and easily understood?
6. Does it reflect the uniqueness of the organization, its distinctive competence, what it stands for, what it's able to achieve?
7. Is it ambitious?

VALUES STATEMENTS: DOES YOUR COMPANY'S VALUES STATEMENT ANSWER "YES" TO THESE QUESTIONS?

1. Does it express the company's distinctiveness, its view of the world?
2. Is it intended to guide all the organization's actions, including how you treat employees, customers, and so on?
3. Is it tough, serving as the foundation on which difficult company decisions can be made?
4. Will it be unchanging, as valid 100 years from now as it is today?
5. Does it reflect the core beliefs the organization wants to guide all employee behavior?
6. Are the values expressed in the statement limited (five or so) and easy to remember, so that employees will have them top-of-mind when making decisions?
7. Would you want the organization to continue to hold these values, even if at some point they become a competitive disadvantage?

Sources: B. Nanus, Visionary Leadership: Creating a Compelling Sense of Direction for Your Organization (San Francisco: Jossey-Bass, 1992), pp. 28–29; S. Quain, "9 Characteristics of an Effective Mission Statement," Chron.com, March 9, 2019, https://smallbusiness.chron.com/9-characteristics-effective-mission-statement-18142.html; S. Blount and P. Leinwand, "Why Are We Here?" Harvard Business Review, November–December 2019. https://hbr.org/2019/11/why-are-we-here; S. Peek, "What Is a Vision Statement?" Business News Daily, November 22, 2022. https://www.businessnewsdaily.com/3882-vision-statement.html; P. Ingram and Y. Choi, "What Does Your Company Really Stand For?" Harvard Business Review, November–December 2022. https://hbr.org/2022/11/what-does-your-company-really-stand-for.

The Mission Statement—"What Is Our Reason for Being?"

An organization's **mission** is its purpose or reason for being. The questions in Table 5.1 reveal that a mission is present-focused and defines "who we are and what we do." Determining the mission is the responsibility of top management and the board of directors. It is up to them to formulate a **mission statement**, which expresses the purpose of the organization.

"Only a clear definition of the mission and purpose of the organization makes possible clear and realistic . . . objectives," said Peter Drucker.[23] Whether the organization is for-profit or nonprofit, the mission statement identifies the goods or services the organization provides and will provide. Sometimes it also gives the reasons for providing them (to make a profit or to achieve humanitarian goals, for example).

The Vision Statement—"What Do We Want to Become?"

A **vision** is a long-term goal describing "what" an organization wants to become. It casts a clear and motivational picture of the ultimate goal the organization wants to pursue. A vision is aspirational and inspirational. "The vision should motivate the team to make a difference and be part of something bigger than themselves," says Paige Arnof-Fenn, founder and CEO of Mavens & Moguls, a strategic marketing consulting firm.[24]

Research has found that vision statements exhibiting the following characteristics are most effective:[25]

- **Clarity:** Employees understand the vision statement.
- **Future focus:** The vision statement describes the future, not the current state.
- **Abstractness and challenge:** The future is described as hypothetical and difficult, but achievable.
- **Idealism:** The future is portrayed as being highly desirable.

After formulating a mission statement, top managers need to develop a **vision statement**, which expresses what the organization should become, where it wants to go strategically.

EXAMPLE: Coca-Cola's Mission, Vision, and Values

The Coca-Cola Company is one of the world's largest beverage companies. It has more than 500 brands and nearly one out of four dollars spent on nonalcoholic drinks worldwide are spent on a Coca-Cola brand. Headquartered in Atlanta, the company is more than 135 years old. It employs about 700,000 people worldwide and had more than $42.3 billion in revenues in 2022. Some of its best-known brands include Coke, Coke Zero, Sprite, Dr Pepper, Fanta, Schweppes, Minute Maid, Powerade, Dasani, Honest Tea, and Smart Water. Many of its beverages are available in low-calorie or no-calorie versions.[26]

The company's chair and CEO, James Quincey, describes Coca-Cola's mission, vision, and values as follows.

Our Mission[27]
Our purpose: *"Refresh the world. Make a difference."*

Our Vision
Our vision for our next stage of growth has three connected pillars:[28]

- **Loved Brands.** "We craft meaningful brands and a choice of drinks that people love, enjoy, and that refresh them in body and spirit."
- **Done Sustainably.** "We grow our business in ways that achieve positive change in the world and build a more sustainable future for our planet."
- **For a Better Shared Future.** "We invest to improve people's lives, from our employees, to all those who touch our business system, to our investors, to the communities we call home."

Core Values

Our values represent our compass and the conscience we follow:[29]

- **Courage and a Growth Mindset:** Learn continuously and adopt a broader perspective of what's possible.
- **Curiosity:** Explore, imagine, and wonder how our products, service, or our impact on the world could be better or different.
- **Empowerment:** Be accountable. Be proactive.
- **Inclusion:** Draw on the diversity of talent and experiences to generate better ideas and make better decisions.
- **Agility:** Learn quickly and continuously improve.
- **Honesty:** If we make mistakes, we own them and act quickly to correct them.
- **Integrity:** Do the right thing. Always.

YOUR CALL

What do you think of Coca-Cola's mission, vision, and values? Are they explicit enough to guide employee behavior and company actions? Why or why not? Could any of them apply equally well to other businesses? Why or why not?

Heavy consumption. Coca-Cola has hundreds of brands, including Coca-Cola Classic, Sprite, and Fanta. Alignment among its mission, vision, and values isn't just important for employees, it's also important for the brand as the company has millions of customers around the world. Did you know that over 1.9 billion servings of Coca-Cola beverages are consumed in more than 200 countries every day? Chones/Shutterstock

The concept of a vision statement also is important for individuals. Harvard professor Clayton Christensen believed that creating a personal life vision statement is akin to developing a strategy for your life. He found that people are happier and lead more meaningful lives when they are directed by personal vision statements.[30] For example, Angelo Kinicki, one of your authors, has a vision statement that says "to lead a life that influences the lives of others." This vision drives his motivation to write textbooks. Do you have a vision for your future career? Is it vague or specific? The following self-assessment was created to help you evaluate the quality of your career vision and plan. If your instructor has assigned the self-assessment, think back to the Manage U at the beginning of the chapter as you complete the self-assessment and make modifications to your career plan as needed.

SELF-ASSESSMENT 5.1   CAREER READINESS

Assessing Career Behaviors and Future Career Identity

This survey is designed to help you reflect on the vision of your career identity. Please complete Self-Assessment 5.1 if your instructor has assigned it in Connect.

The Values Statement—"What Values Do We Want to Emphasize?" *Values,* we said in Chapter 3, are the relatively permanent and deeply held underlying beliefs and attitudes that help determine a person's behavior: integrity, dedication, teamwork, excellence, compassion, or whatever. Values reflect the qualities that represent an organization's deeply held beliefs, highest priorities, and core guiding principles. Shared values are the glue that keep employees working together to achieve a common goal.

A compass is a great metaphor for values. A compass is a reliable source of direction when you feel lost or confused in your environment. Corporate values are a compass for the entire organization. They provide enduring guiding principles that instruct employees what to prioritize and how to behave, even in pressure packed moments. Mattjeacock/iStock/Getty Images

After formulating a vision statement, top managers are encouraged to develop a **values statement**, also called a *core values statement*, which expresses what the company stands for, its core priorities, the values its employees embody, and what its products contribute to the world.[31] Values statements "become the deeply ingrained principle and fabric that guide employee behavior and company decisions and actions—the behaviors the company and employees expect of themselves," says former executive Eric Jacobsen. "Without a statement, the company will lack soul."[32]

Values Statement Example—Lululemon: Lululemon, an athletic apparel company, created a values statement that is the foundation of its company culture and represents what employees stand for as a team. Its values include:

- Personal Responsibility
- Entrepreneurship
- Honesty
- Courage
- Connection
- Fun
- Inclusion

Values are so essential to the culture at Lululemon that Julie Averill, Lululemon's chief technology officer, looks to recruit top talent who embrace the company's values. She noted, "Top talent to us includes experience/expertise and values alignment. I don't want to hire someone who has an incredible pedigree but will not share knowledge and want to be part of a team."[33]

Three Types of Planning for Three Levels of Management: Strategic, Tactical, and Operational

Inspiring, clearly stated mission statements and vision statements provide the focal point of the entire planning process. Then three things happen:

- **Strategic planning by top management. Strategic planning** is a process that determines what the organization's long-term goals should be for the next one to five years with the resources they expect to have available. It begins once the mission and vision are established. A summary of 31 research studies concludes strategic planning has a significant positive impact on organizational performance.[34] A well-crafted strategic plan is integral to an organization's success because "[a] bad strategy will fail no matter how good your information is," says Microsoft cofounder Bill Gates.[35] Strategic plans communicate not only general goals about growth and profits but also ways to achieve them. Today, because of the frequency with which global competition and information technology alter marketplace conditions, a company's strategic planning should be reviewed every year.

- **Tactical planning by middle management.** The strategic priorities and policies are then passed down to middle managers, who must do **tactical planning**—that is, they determine what contributions their departments or similar work units can make with their given resources during the next 6–24 months.

- **Operational planning by first-line management and team leaders.** Middle managers then pass these plans along to first-line managers and team leaders to do **operational planning**—that is, they determine how to accomplish specific tasks with available resources within the next 1–52 weeks.

The three kinds of managers and their role in the planning process are illustrated in Figure 5.3. •

EXAMPLE: Coca-Cola's Strategies

Coca-Cola recently announced several business and sustainability-related actions as part of its overall growth strategy. Six of them include:[36]

1. **Optimize the brand portfolio.** The company is developing a balanced portfolio of global, regional, and local brands that appeal to a broader base of consumers and "address all drinking moments."
2. **Build great brands.** Coca-Cola is partnering with marketing agencies to expand avenues through which it interacts with consumers outside of traditional media outlets. This effort will result in more personalized consumer relationships, a broader consumer base, and more relatable brand messaging.
3. **Reduce sugar content.** The beverage company reformulated more than 1,000 beverages to remove more than 900,000 tons of added sugar. It is also introducing a greater variety of low- and no-sugar drinks to its beverage portfolio.
4. **Innovate.** The company is engaging in "intelligent innovation" by experimenting with new products and packaging in local markets and making rapid adjustments based on market feedback before scaling and distributing the initiatives geographically.
5. **Recycle and reuse.** Coca-Cola launched its World Without Waste initiative, which is focused on collecting and recycling a bottle or can for each one they sell by 2030. They collected or refilled an equivalent of 61% of the bottles and cans they introduced into the market in 2021. Refillable glass bottles are driving revenue growth in multiple geographic locations.
6. **Replenish the water supply.** The beverage company replenished the environment with more water than it used for beverages and production by reducing water usage and partnering with the World Wildlife Fund to restore wetlands, rivers, and floodplains in critical areas.

YOUR CALL
Coca-Cola combines its business and sustainability reports into one strategic document. What message is it sending to stakeholders by doing this?

FIGURE 5.3

Three levels of management, three types of planning

Each type of planning has different time horizons, although the times overlap because the plans are somewhat elastic.

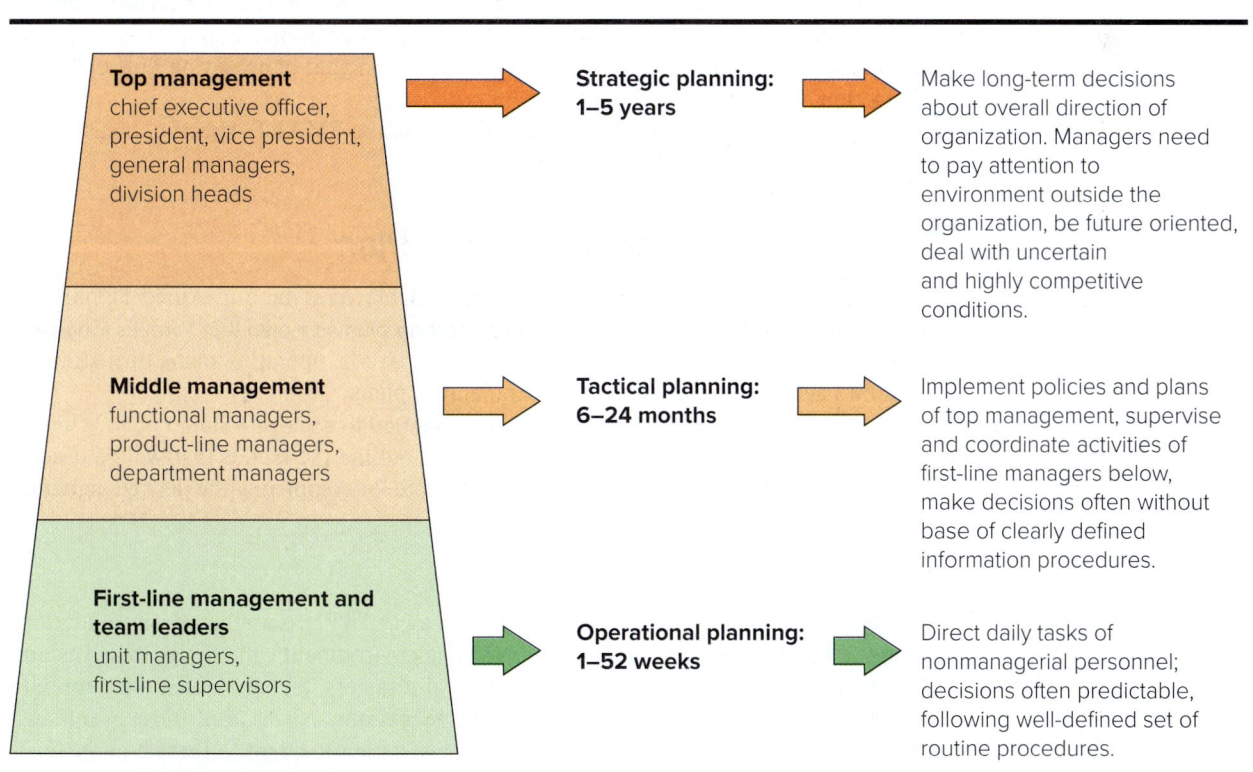

Top management: chief executive officer, president, vice president, general managers, division heads	**Strategic planning:** 1–5 years	Make long-term decisions about overall direction of organization. Managers need to pay attention to environment outside the organization, be future oriented, deal with uncertain and highly competitive conditions.
Middle management: functional managers, product-line managers, department managers	**Tactical planning:** 6–24 months	Implement policies and plans of top management, supervise and coordinate activities of first-line managers below, make decisions often without base of clearly defined information procedures.
First-line management and team leaders: unit managers, first-line supervisors	**Operational planning:** 1–52 weeks	Direct daily tasks of nonmanagerial personnel; decisions often predictable, following well-defined set of routine procedures.

5.3 Goals and Plans

THE BIG PICTURE
The purpose of planning is to set a goal and then an action plan. There are two types of goals, short term and long term, and they are connected by a means-end chain. Finally, it's important to understand that the proper execution of a plan is just as important as properly developing it.

LO 5-3

Discuss the types and purposes of goals and plans.

Long-Term and Short-Term Goals

A **goal**, also known as an **objective**, is a specific commitment to achieve a measurable result within a stated period of time. Goals may be long term or short term.

Long-term goals are generally referred to as **strategic goals**. They tend to span one to five years and focus on achieving the strategies identified in a company's strategic plan.

Long-term Goals Example—Walker & Dunlop: Walker & Dunlop, a commercial real estate finance company, developed a strategic plan entitled "Drive to '25" with a goal to increase annual revenues to $2 billion by 2025.[37]

Short-term goals are sometimes referred to as **tactical** or **operational goals**, or just plain goals. They generally span 12 months and are connected to strategic goals in a hierarchy known as a means-end chain.

Short-term Goals Example—Walker & Dunlop: Walker & Dunlop's short-term revenue goal is to increase revenue from $1.3 billion in 2022 to $1.4 billion in 2023 by building its brand reputation to expand business with existing customers and using technology to identify and attract new customers.[38]

A **means-end chain** shows how goals are connected or linked across an organization. For example, a low-level goal such as responding to customer inquiries in less than 24 hours is the means to accomplishing a higher-level goal of achieving 90% customer satisfaction.

As we will see later in Section 5.4, goals should be SMART—specific, measurable, attainable, results-oriented, and with target dates.

The Operating Plan and Action Plan

Larry Bossidy, former CEO of both Honeywell International and Allied Signal, and global consultant Ram Charan define an **operating plan** as a plan that "breaks long-term output into short-term targets" or goals.[39] In other words, operating plans turn strategic plans into actionable short-term goals and action plans.

An **action plan** defines the course of action needed to achieve a stated goal. Whether the goal is long term or short term, action plans outline the tactics that will be used to achieve a goal. Each tactic contains a projected date for completing the desired activities.

Plans Are Great, But . . .

"The best laid plans of mice and men often go awry."[40] Plans are based on predictions about the future that may not come to pass. The environment can change in an instant. Unforeseen circumstances arise such as natural disasters, global pandemics, geopolitical disputes, runaway inflation, or economic recessions. Any one of these events can threaten a company's survival if it doesn't have a plan to adapt to these emergencies. **Contingency plans** are responses to possible future events that could threaten a company's operations. For example, the COVID-19 pandemic disrupted the container-ship industry, and the Russian war in Ukraine disrupted the global supply of oil and natural gas, both of which led to inflation. These events highlight the need for companies to build a more resilient and flexible supply chain in which companies contract with multiple suppliers from multiple geographic locations and are able to move their goods via multiple modes of transportation.[41]

Contingency Plans Example—Air France-KLM: Fuel is a significant cost to airlines (an estimated 20% to 40% of an an airline's total expenses). Air France-KLM and other airlines practice fuel hedging as a contingency plan to reduce the volatility associated with fuel prices. The company saved $1 billion in 2022 due to their hedging policy because of higher fuel prices attributable to the Russian war in Ukraine.[42] •

The Russian war in Ukraine drastically impacted the global supply of oil and natural gas, leading to a significant spike in oil prices and leaving countries and organizations without contingency plans to scramble to find other sources to meet their energy needs. (left) Tunasalmon/Shutterstock; (right) Comstock Images/Getty Images

5.4 Promoting Consistencies in Goals: SMART Goals, Management by Objectives, and Goal Cascading

THE BIG PICTURE
This section discusses SMART goals—goals that are specific, measurable, attainable, results-oriented, and have target dates. It also briefly discusses a technique for setting goals, management by objectives (MBO), a four-step process for motivating employees. Finally, it introduces the concept of goal cascading, which attempts to ensure that higher-level goals are communicated and aligned with the goals at lower levels of the organizational hierarchy.

Anyone can define goals. But as we mentioned earlier, the five characteristics of a good goal are represented by the acronym SMART.

LO 5-4
Describe SMART goals and their implementation.

SMART Goals

A **SMART goal** is one that is specific, measurable, attainable, results-oriented, and has target dates.

FIGURE 5.4
Relationship between goal difficulty and performance

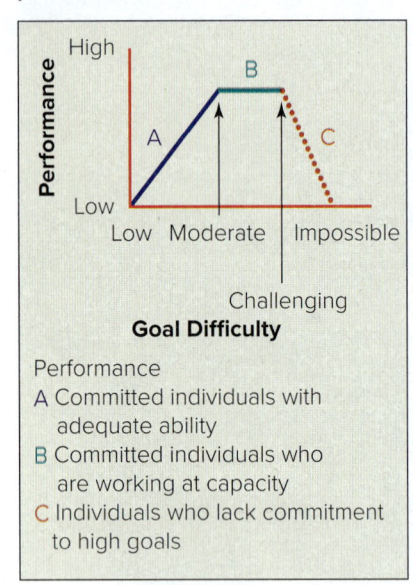

Performance
A Committed individuals with adequate ability
B Committed individuals who are working at capacity
C Individuals who lack commitment to high goals

Source: Adapted from Locke, A. E. and G. P. Latham. A Theory of Goal Setting and Task Performance (Englewood Cliffs, NJ: Prentice Hall, 1990).

Specific Goals should be stated in *specific* rather than vague terms. The goal "As many planes as possible should arrive on time" is too general. The goal that "Ninety percent of planes should arrive within 15 minutes of the scheduled arrival time" is specific.

Measurable Whenever possible, goals should be *measurable*, or quantifiable (as in "90% of planes should arrive within 15 minutes"). That is, there should be some way to measure the degree to which a goal has been reached.

Of course, some goals—such as those concerned with improving quality—are not precisely quantifiable. In that case, something on the order of "Improve the quality of customer relations by instituting 10 follow-up telephone calls every week" will do. You can certainly quantify how many follow-up phone calls were made.

Attainable Goals should be challenging, of course, but above all, they should be realistic and *attainable*. It may be best to set goals that are quite ambitious so as to challenge people to meet high standards. Always, however, the goals should be achievable within the scope of the time, equipment, and financial support available (see Figure 5.4).

If they are too easy (as in "half the flights should arrive on time"), goals won't compel people to put forth much effort. If goals are impossible ("all flights must arrive on time, regardless of weather"), employees won't even bother trying. Or they will try and continually fail, which will end up hurting morale. Finally, if goals are too difficult, employees may resort to cheating. Research indicates employees under high performance pressure cut corners and rationalize unethical behavior in an attempt to achieve unrealistic goals.[43]

Results-Oriented Only a few goals should be chosen—say, five for any work unit. And they should be *results-oriented*—they should support the organization's vision.

In writing out the goals, start with the word "To" and follow it with action-oriented verbs—"complete," "acquire," "increase" ("to decrease the time to get passengers settled in their seats before departure by 10%").

Some verbs should not be used in your goal statement because they imply activities rather than outcomes (such as having baggage handlers waiting). For example, you should not use "to develop," "to conduct," "to implement."

Target Dates Goals should specify the *target dates* or deadline dates when they are to be attained. For example, it's unrealistic to expect an airline to improve its on-time arrivals by 10% in a short period of time. However, you could set a target date—three to six months away, say—by which this goal is to be achieved. That allows enough time for lower-level managers and employees to revamp their systems and work habits and gives them a clear time frame in which they know what they are expected to do.

Management by Objectives: The Four-Step Process for Motivating Employees

First suggested by Peter Drucker in 1954, *management by objectives* has spread largely because of the appeal of its emphasis on converting general objectives into specific ones for all members of an organization.[44]

Management by objectives (MBO) is a four-step process:

1. Managers and employees jointly set objectives for the employee.
2. Managers develop action plans.

3. Managers and employees periodically review the employee's performance.
4. Managers make a performance appraisal and rewards the employee according to results.

The purpose of MBO is to *motivate* rather than to control subordinates by clearly defining goals, illustrating what success looks like, and rewarding for performance.

Before we discuss MBO's four steps, you may want to consider the quality of the goal-setting process in a current or former employer. Management by objectives will not work without an effective goal-setting process. Try the following self-assessment if your instructor has assigned it to you to gain insight into the quality of goal setting within an organization.

SELF-ASSESSMENT 5.2

What Is the Quality of Goal Setting within a Current or Past Employer?

This survey is designed to assess the quality of goal setting in a company. Please complete Self-Assessment 5.2 if your instructor has assigned it in Connect.

1. Jointly Set Objectives We recommend that managers jointly set objectives with their employees. Managers tend to set three types of objectives, shown in the following table (see Table 5.2). Remember what we learned about SMART goals. Managers garner greater acceptance to goal setting when employees believe the goal is attainable and they possess the skills and resources to achieve it.[45] One way to achieve buy-in is to involve employees in setting goals. Research shows employees set more difficult goals and are more committed to goals when they participate in goal setting rather than being assigned a goal.[46]

We want to briefly focus on the career readiness competency of *proactive learning orientation* because it fuels the achievement of learning objectives. Proactive learning orientation represents a desire to learn and improve one's knowledge, soft skills, and

TABLE 5.2 Three Types of Objectives Used in MBO: Performance, Behavioral, and Learning

PERFORMANCE OBJECTIVES
Express the objective as an outcome or end result. Examples: "Increase small appliance sales by 10%." "Reduce turnover by 15%."
BEHAVIORAL OBJECTIVES
Express the objective as the behaviors needed to achieve an outcome. Examples: "Greet all potential automobile customers with a smile and offer to assist." "Ensure food is stored in seal-proof containers." "Attend five days of leadership training." "Learn basics of Microsoft Office software by June 1."
LEARNING OBJECTIVES
Express the objective in terms of acquiring knowledge or competencies. Examples: "Attend diversity training class." "Learn how the features in our sports utility vehicles compare to competitors."

Source: These descriptions were based on G. Latham, G. Seijts, and J. Slocum, "The Goal Setting and Goal Orientation Labyrinth: Effective Ways for Increasing Employee Performance," Organizational Dynamics, October–December 2016, pp. 271–277.

other characteristics in pursuit of personal development. Employers value this attitude because it drives the creativity and innovation needed in today's global economy. Satya Nadella, CEO of Microsoft, remarked, "The learn-it-all will always do better than the know-it-all."[47] So where do you stand on this competency? Find out by taking the proactive learning orientation self-assessment if your instructor has assigned it to you.

SELF-ASSESSMENT 5.3   CAREER READINESS

Do I Have a Proactive Learning Orientation?

This survey is designed to assess the extent to which you possess a proactive learning orientation. Please complete Self-Assessment 5.3 if your instructor has assigned it in Connect.

2. Develop an Action Plan   Once objectives are set, employees are encouraged to prepare an action plan for attaining them. Action plans may be prepared for both individuals and work units, such as departments. Goals and plans that lack resources are likely to fail. Consequently, it is important for management to provide resources to support action plans. For example, the U.S. Department of Health and Human Services awarded $1.5 billion in 2022 to support states' efforts to combat the opioid crisis and support individuals in drug recovery programs.[48]

3. Periodically Review Performance   Employees and managers should meet reasonably often—either informally as needed or formally every three months—to review progress. During each meeting, managers should give employees feedback, and objectives should be updated or revised as necessary to reflect new realities. Feedback is essential for improving performance.[49]

4. Give Performance Appraisal and Rewards, if Any   Because the purpose of MBO is to *motivate* employees, performance that meets the objectives should be rewarded—with compliments, raises, bonuses, promotions, or other suitable benefits. Failure can be addressed by redefining the objectives for the next 6- or 12-month period, or even by taking stronger measures, such as demotion. Basically, however, MBO is viewed as being a learning process. After step 4, the MBO cycle begins anew.

Cascading Goals: Making Lower-Level Goals Align with Top Goals

For goal setting to be successful, the following three things have to happen.

1. Top Management and Middle Management Must Be Committed   According to research, "When top management commitment [to MBO] was high, the average gain in productivity was 56%. When commitment was low, the average gain in productivity was only 6%."[50]

Streaming goals. Onondaga Falls, at Ricketts Glen State Park, Pennsylvania. The downward flow of strategic goals to lower level ones resembles this type of cascading waterfall. Jon Bilous/Shutterstock

2. It Is Best to Cascade Goals The cascading process is most effective when goals are cascaded across the entire organization. According to a team of researchers, this broad-based approach is more likely to encourage collaboration and alignment across departments.[51]

3. Goals Must "Cascade"—Be Linked Consistently Down through the Organization Cascading goals is the process of ensuring that the strategic goals set at the top level align, or "cascade," downward with more specific short-term goals at lower levels within an organization, including employees' objectives and activities. Top managers set *strategic goals*, which are translated into *divisional goals*, which are translated into *departmental goals*, which are translated into *individual goals*. The cascading process ends when all individuals have a set of goals that support the company's overall strategic goals. This process helps employees understand how their work contributes to overall corporate success.

Cascading Goals Example—Dr. K: Dr. K worked with a Vice President of the Claims Division of an automobile insurance company. The company, which pays off requests (or claims) by customers seeking insurance payments to repair damage to their cars, established the SMART goal "to increase customer satisfaction in the Claims Division by 10% over last year." In the cascading goals process, the same goal was embraced by the Assistant Vice President of Claims and the Recovery Director below the VP in the organizational hierarchy. Further down the hierarchy, the Recovery Unit Manager reworded the goal to be more specific to their department: "To decrease the number of customer complaints about claims by 10% over last year's average." For the individual Recovery Analyst at the lowest level, the goal became: "To return all customer phone calls about claims within 24 hours."[52] You can see that the goals became more specific as they cascaded downward. The cascading process ensures that employees' goals are aligned with the major goal established by top management. ●

PRACTICAL ACTION: Setting Goals for a Small Business

Goal setting can seem like an intimidating process, but it's both a necessary and a helpful one for the millions of small businesses (defined as having 500 or fewer employees) in the United States. In fact, a research study of 231 small businesses found that goal setting had a positive impact on the firm's performance.[53] These findings are important, particularly because small businesses account for 44% of U.S. economic activity and 62% of the nation's new jobs.[54]

The Great Lakes Brewing Company, Ohio's first craft brewery, is a good example of goal setting in small businesses.[55]

1. **Break large goals down into smaller ones:** Growth is a key indicator in the craft brewing industry. Great Lakes faced declining beer production for seven years from its peak in 2014. The company's CEO, Mark King, identified innovation as the strategic key to the company's turnaround. He focused on three smaller goals to achieve his strategic objective: rebranding the core brands, new products, and a new canning line. We'll focus on rebranding the core brands, which the brewery breaks down into areas such as redesigned labels, marketing via new platforms, and leveraging key partners—like the Cleveland Guardians—to build brand recognition and strengthen brand reputation. Rebranding the core brands is then broken down into a more specific measurable goal, which is sales growth at grocery stores, a critical distribution channel during the pandemic, at or above the industry average for any given year.

2. **Track progress toward goals:** The company monitors its sales growth/decline from its core brands at grocery stores annually. It then compares the sales figures to the industry average to determine if it is meeting its goal.

3. **Keep the goal in sight:** The brewery's management knows it must take action to ensure its sales goals are met. For example, Great Lakes redesigned the labels for its core brands using bright, colorful imagery with designs inspired by significant events in the company's and its founding city's (Cleveland, Ohio) history. In addition to redesigning the packaging to attract consumers' attention in a grocery store, the brewer created point of sale display pieces to entice new customers to try their product.

4. **Celebrate success:** Great Lakes stopped its decline and celebrated achieving 18% sales growth in grocery stores in 2021 compared to 2020. Regarding the company's turnaround performance, King commented, "We're the best-performing top-25 craft brewery in the U.S. And we are only one of two that is in positive numbers. That's really exciting."

YOUR CALL

What major goal of your own have you broken into smaller parts? If you have never done this, for what future goal do you think it would be an effective strategy for you?

5.5 The Planning/Control Cycle

THE BIG PICTURE
The four-step planning/control cycle makes sure plans stay headed in the right direction.

LO 5-5

Outline the planning/control cycle.

Maintaining strategic control is the final step of the strategic management process. It is executed by using a four-step planning/control cycle (see Figure 5.5). The **planning/control cycle** is a continuous process managers use to evaluate the progress in achieving strategic goals and to make modifications as needed.

As shown in Figure 5.5, the planning/control process has two planning steps (1 and 2) and two control steps (3 and 4). Let's bring this process to life by considering a personal goal to lose five pounds; this is analogous to creating a strategic goal in Step 1. As part of Step 1, you also develop a plan to lose weight by changing your diet (e.g., eat three meals a day, reduce amount of carbohydrates eaten, and don't eat after 8 P.M.) and increasing your cardio exercise to 300 minutes per week. Step 2 simply amounts to

FIGURE 5.5

The planning/control cycle

This model describes a continuous feedback loop designed to ensure plans stay headed in the right direction.

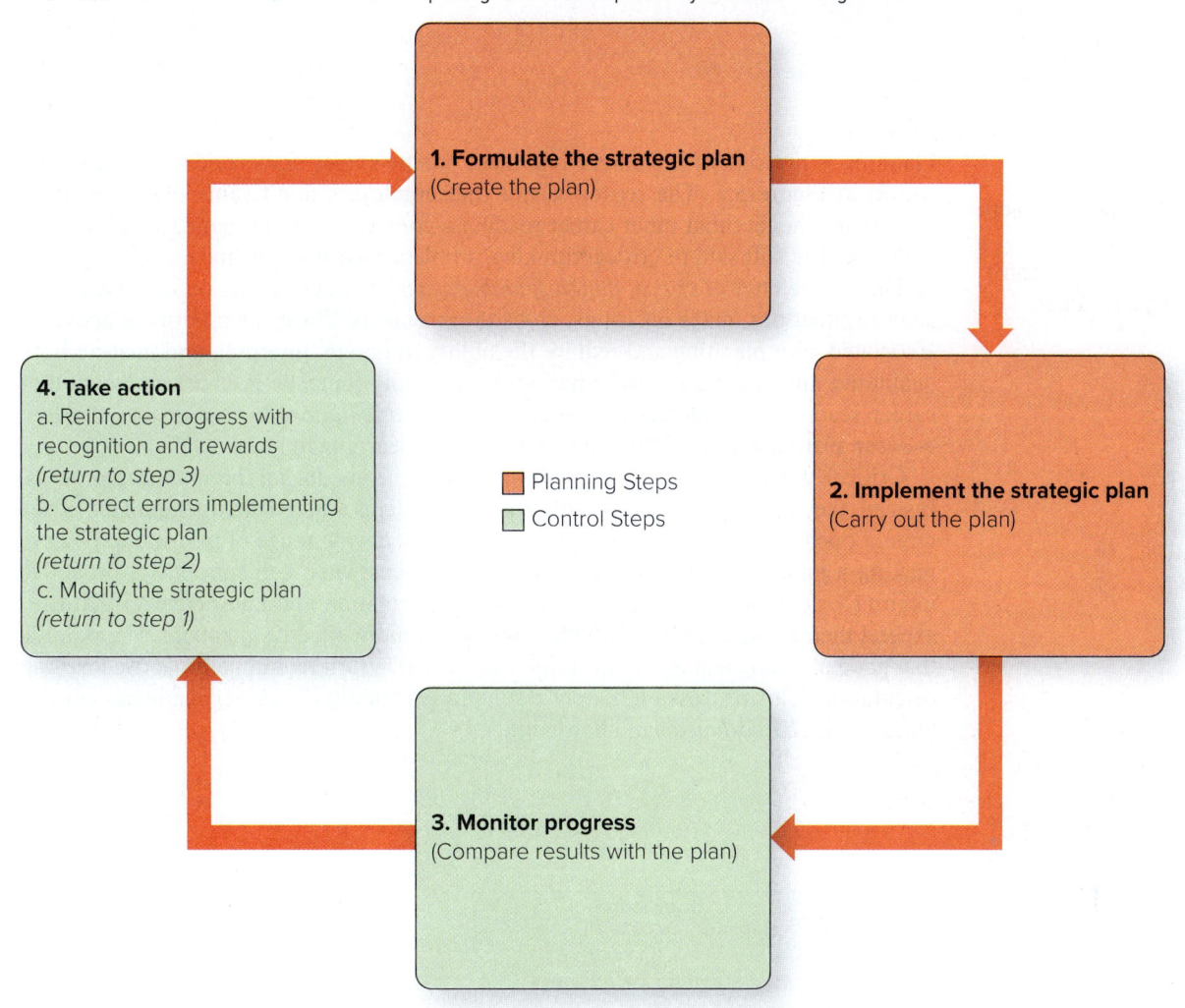

1. Formulate the strategic plan
(Create the plan)

2. Implement the strategic plan
(Carry out the plan)

3. Monitor progress
(Compare results with the plan)

4. Take action
a. Reinforce progress with recognition and rewards *(return to step 3)*
b. Correct errors implementing the strategic plan *(return to step 2)*
c. Modify the strategic plan *(return to step 1)*

■ Planning Steps
□ Control Steps

Source: Robert Kreitner, Management, *8th edition.*

implementing your plan and ensuring you have the needed resources to achieve the strategic goal. These two steps complete the planning component of the planning/control process.

In Step 3, you take the time to monitor your progress on both a macro (how much do I weigh) and micro (what is my daily intake of carbs and time spent exercising) level. This data is then used as input for Step 4—Take Action. It is important to note that taking action contains three options: (1) reinforce progress with recognition and rewards—purchase an album from iTunes, (2) correct errors implementing the plan—buy new running shoes or join a gym, or (3) modify the plan—increase cardio to 350 minutes a week.

As you might imagine, this process is much more complicated when dealing with actual strategic goals and action plans. That said, the four-step process remains the same. You can apply the planning/control cycle to manage each level of planning—strategic, tactical, and operational. At any level, the cycle results in a process of continuous improvement. We will see this model again in Chapter 6 regarding strategic implementation and echoed later in Chapter 16. ●

5.6 Career Corner: Managing Your Career Readiness

LO 5-6

Describe how to develop the career readiness competency of *proactive learning orientation*.

Planning is not one of the career readiness competencies associated with the model shown in Figure 5.6. The reason is not that employers don't value planning skills. Rather, it's the fact that other career readiness competencies are foundational to good planning. The soft skill of critical thinking/problem solving is a prime example.

The competency of *critical thinking/problem solving* is defined as sound reasoning to analyze situations, make decisions, and solve problems. These are all critical activities associated with planning and require the ability to obtain, interpret, and analyze both qualitative and quantitative information. In turn, this competency is driven by another career readiness competency: *proactive learning orientation*. Let's consider the link between planning, critical thinking, and proactive learning in more detail.

Critical thinkers don't make quick or rash decisions during the planning process. Instead, they consider alternative solutions to problems and remain open-minded. They remain open-minded by obtaining and considering a wide range of information before making a judgment. This is precisely what happens when someone has a proactive learning orientation. Proactive learners seek information and knowledge so that they expand their knowledge base, which makes them more effective planners. The point is that good planning requires critical thinking, which in turn requires a proactive learning orientation. This process ultimately results in expanding the career readiness competency of *task-based/functional* knowledge.

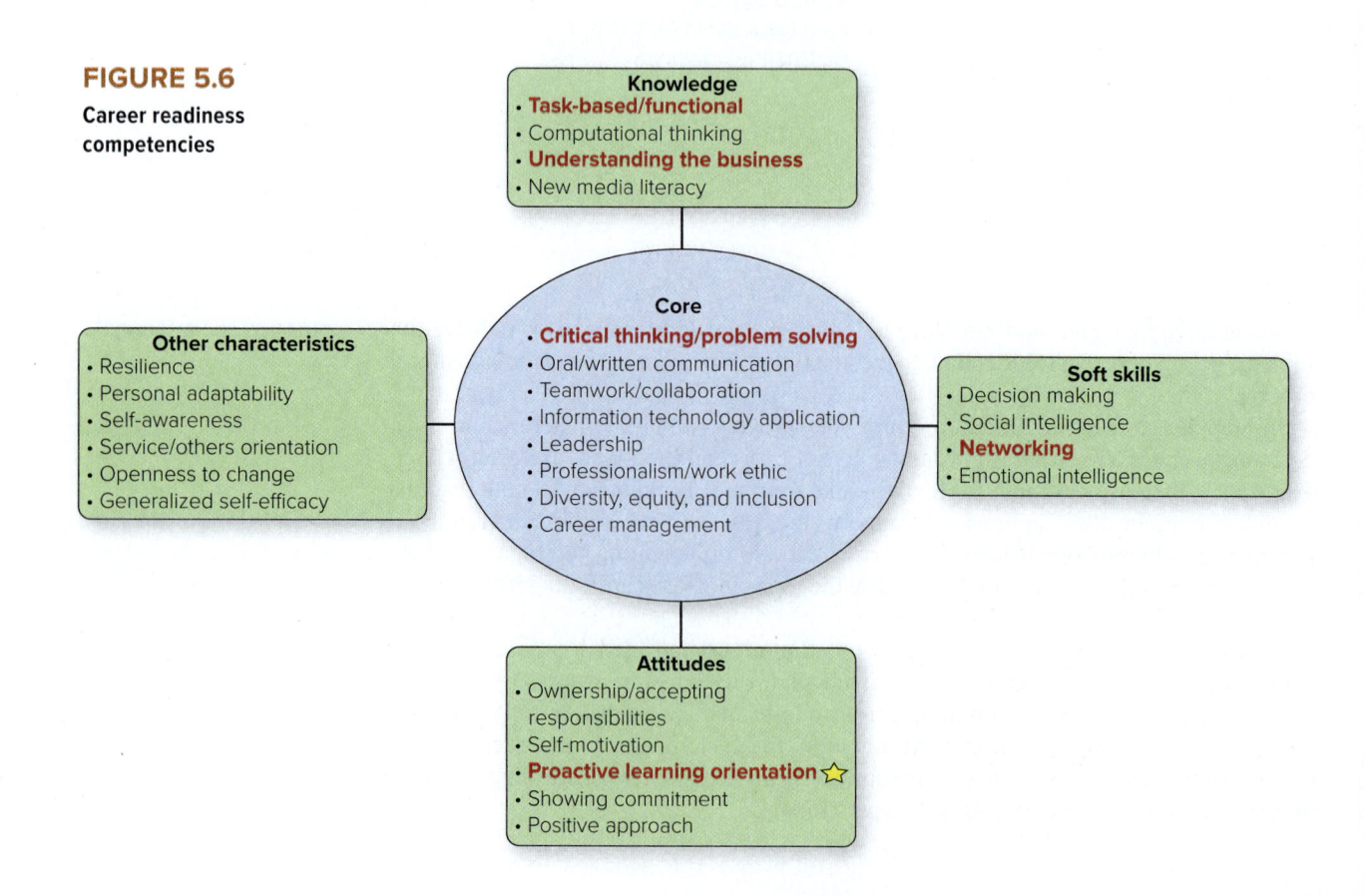

FIGURE 5.6

Career readiness competencies

Knowledge
- **Task-based/functional**
- Computational thinking
- **Understanding the business**
- New media literacy

Core
- **Critical thinking/problem solving**
- Oral/written communication
- Teamwork/collaboration
- Information technology application
- Leadership
- Professionalism/work ethic
- Diversity, equity, and inclusion
- Career management

Other characteristics
- Resilience
- Personal adaptability
- Self-awareness
- Service/others orientation
- Openness to change
- Generalized self-efficacy

Soft skills
- Decision making
- Social intelligence
- **Networking**
- Emotional intelligence

Attitudes
- Ownership/accepting responsibilities
- Self-motivation
- **Proactive learning orientation** ⭐
- Showing commitment
- Positive approach

Effective planning requires you to be a proactive learner in areas beyond the technicalities of your profession. It also applies to two additional career readiness competencies: *understanding the business* and *networking*. Organizations want all of us to stay abreast of what is happening in the industries and markets in which we work. Doing so enables us to consider a wider bandwidth of information when planning. For example, staying current about trends in higher education enables us as authors to do a better job in planning the revisions of this product. We also find that many people fail to keep their social and professional networks up to date over time. This is a mistake! Failing to proactively maintain such networks means that we are losing contacts and valuable information that can aid the planning process and our career progression. As authors, for instance, we rely on our social networks to get feedback about what students and educational institutions are looking for in a textbook. As you can see, effective planning is grounded in information that comes from staying current about events within the industry in which we work and with people in our social networks.

The five competencies that we've introduced are highlighted in Figure 5.6. For the purposes of this section, we will focus more closely on the proactive learning orientation competency of career readiness. But first check out what the executives in this chapter's Executive Interview Series say about how you can leverage a proactive learning orientation to set yourself apart as a job applicant or accelerate your career development with your current employer.

Visit your instructor's Connect course and access your eBook to view this video.

Executive Interview Series: Proactive Learning Orientation

Becoming More Proactive

Being "intentionally proactive" is the first step to becoming a proactive learner. "Being proactive means relying on your own choices instead of luck and circumstances. It's about controlling the situation rather than simply waiting for the outcomes," said one business writer.[56] Your proactivity may also lead others to be more proactive. To this point, self-made billionaire and Virgin Group founder, Sir Richard Branson says, "Simply put: positive, proactive behaviour spurs positive, proactive behaviour."[57] You can be more proactive by following four key recommendations:[58]

1. Focus on solutions rather than problems.
2. Take initiative and rely on yourself.
3. Set realistic goals and don't overpromise.
4. Participate and contribute to personal and professional conversations.

Keeping an Open Mind and Suspending Judgment

Keeping an open mind and suspending judgment are essential for developing a proactive learning orientation. This exercise was designed to assist you in this pursuit. Focus on your school work or a current job to practice the technique. You can repeat this process in the future whenever you desire to be open-minded.[59]

Step 1 Make a list of your current tasks, projects, or commitments at school or work.

Step 2 For each task listed in step one, identify the key moments it would be important to be open-minded and suspend judgment.

Step 3 For each of these moments, think of how you might apply the four key skills of being open-minded:[60]

1. Question your beliefs. Many of us make decisions based on false beliefs and assumptions. You can check yourself by asking: What specific evidence supports my view? Is my knowledge based on facts or my experience? Why am I arguing with others who have more experience and knowledge? Am I offering an opinion or being opinionated? Based on answers to these questions, you

can either proceed in the discussion or take a step back and allow your mind to take in new information.

2. Pause and seek feedback. Sometimes being open minded requires talking through a situation with someone else. Observe how others respond to your opinions and recommendations. Don't be married to a perspective, and admit it if you are wrong. If the goal of a discussion is to conduct better planning and make better decisions, then it does not matter whether people agree or disagree with your views. Your goal is to arrive at better decisions and help people to grow.

3. Watch for communication blocks. Be aware of words, concepts, or communication styles that elicit emotional responses from you and others. Train your brain to reframe negative thoughts and not jump to negative conclusions. Emotionality leads to defensiveness and is a barrier to listening.

4. Check the accuracy of your past judgments and predictions. If your judgments and predictions have been wrong, consider the reasons and adjust in the future. ●

Key Terms Used in This Chapter

action plan 154
business plan 145
cascading goals 159
contingency plans 154
goal 154
long-term goals 154
management by objectives (MBO) 156
means-end chain 154
mission 150

mission statement 150
objective 154
operating plan 154
operational goals 154
operational planning 152
plan 145
planning 145
planning/control cycle 160
short-term goals 154

SMART goal 155
strategic goals 154
strategic management 145
strategic planning 152
strategy 145
tactical goals 154
tactical planning 152
values statement 152
vision 150
vision statement 150

Key Points

5.1 Planning and Strategy

- Planning is defined as setting goals and deciding how to achieve them. It is also defined as coping with uncertainty by formulating future courses of action to achieve specified results.
- A plan is a document that outlines how goals are going to be met.
- A strategy, or strategic plan, sets the long-term goals and direction for an organization.
- Strategic management is a process that involves managers from all parts of the organization in the formulation and implementation of strategies and strategic goals.

5.2 Fundamentals of Planning

- An organization's reason for being is expressed in a mission statement.
- A vision is a long-term goal describing "what" an organization wants to become.
- Both mission and vision should express the organization's values. A values statement, or core values statement, expresses what the company stands for, its core priorities, the values its employees embody, and what its products contribute to the world.
- In strategic planning, managers determine what the organization's long-term goals should be for the next one to five years with the resources they expect to have available. In tactical planning, managers determine what contributions their work units can make with their given resources during the next 6–24 months. In operational planning, they determine how to accomplish specific tasks with available resources within the next 1–52 weeks.

5.3 Goals and Plans

- Long-term goals are generally referred to as strategic goals. They tend to span one to five years and focus on achieving the strategies identified in a company's strategic plan.
- Short-term goals are sometimes referred to as tactical goals, operational goals, or just plain goals. They generally span 12 months and are connected to strategic goals in a hierarchy known as a means-end chain.
- A means-end chain shows how goals are connected or linked across an organization. The accomplishment of low-level goals is the means leading to the accomplishment of high-level goals or ends.
- Strategic goals are set by and for top management and focus on objectives for the organization as a whole. Tactical goals are set by and for middle managers and focus on the actions needed to achieve strategic goals. Operational goals are set by first-line managers and team leaders and are concerned with short-term matters associated with realizing tactical goals.
- An operating plan is a plan that breaks long-term output into short-term targets or goals. Operational plans turn strategic plans into actionable short-term goals and action plans.
- An action plan defines the course of action needed to achieve the stated goal. Whether the goal is long term or short term, action plans outline the tactics that will be used to achieve the goal. Each tactic also contains a projected date for completing the desired activities.

5.4 Promoting Consistencies in Goals: SMART Goals, Management by Objectives, and Goal Cascading

- The five characteristics of a good goal are represented by the acronym SMART. A SMART goal is one that is specific, measurable, attainable, results-oriented, and has target dates.

- Management by objectives (MBO) is a four-step process in which (1) managers and employees jointly set objectives for the employee, (2) managers develop action plans, (3) managers and employees periodically review the employee's performance, and (4) managers make a performance appraisal and reward the employee according to results.
- The purpose of MBO is to motivate rather than to control subordinates.
- For goal setting to be successful, (1) top management and middle management must be committed, (2) it is best to cascade goals, and (3) goals must aligned consistently through the organization.

5.5 The Planning/Control Cycle

- Once plans are made, managers must maintain strategic control using the planning/control cycle, which has two planning steps (1 and 2) and two control steps (3 and 4), as follows: (1) Formulate the strategic plan; (2) Implement the strategic plan; (3) Monitor progress; (4) Take action—namely, by (a) reinforcing progress with recognition and rewards, (b) correcting errors implementing the strategic plan, or (c) modifying the strategic plan.

5.6 Career Corner: Managing Your Career Readiness

- Planning requires the use of multiple career readiness competencies, including critical thinking/problem solving, proactive learning orientation, task-based/functional knowledge, understanding the business, and networking.
- You can increase the competency of proactive learning orientation by becoming more intentionally proactive and keeping an open mind and suspending judgment.

6

Strategic Management
How Exceptional Managers Realize a Grand Design

After reading this chapter, you should be able to:

LO 6-1 Identify the three principles underlying strategic positioning.

LO 6-2 Outline the five steps in the strategic-management process.

LO 6-3 Explain how an organization assesses the competitive landscape.

LO 6-4 Explain the three methods of corporate-level strategy.

LO 6-5 Discuss Porter's and Welch's techniques for formulating a business-level strategy.

LO 6-6 Describe how to create, execute, and control a functional-level strategy.

LO 6-7 Describe how to enhance your strategic thinking.

FORECAST *What's Ahead in This Chapter*

We describe strategic positioning and three levels of strategy, and then consider the five steps in the strategic-management process. In assessing current reality, we describe the tools of SWOT analysis, VRIO, forecasting, and benchmarking. When discussing corporate-level strategy, we review three types of overall strategies, the BCG matrix, and diversification. In describing business-level strategy, we discuss Porter's five competitive forces and his four competitive strategies, as well as Welch's strategy formulation questions. When describing functional-level strategy, we discuss the importance of strategic implementation and control. We conclude with a Career Corner that focuses on how to develop your strategic thinking.

Your Personal Brand Requires a Strategy

As part of their overall competitive strategy, organizations create and build memorable brands for their products and services. Among the world's most valuable brands are Apple, Google, Microsoft, Coca-Cola, and Amazon, but brands don't have to be global to have value. For her blog about getting kids to eat vegetables, London mom Mandy Mazliah created a brand name, Sneaky Veg, and asked an artist to design a logo and distinctive graphics to help her creation stand out from the crowd.[1]

The term *branding* used to only be for businesses, but not anymore. Technological advancements, such as the advent of social media, mean individuals are in the public eye. In fact, 67% of employers use social media to screen candidates during the hiring process.[2] You'll need to build your own personal brand if you are looking to gain employment upon graduation.

Why You Need a Personal Brand

Ceejay Dawkins, a tax manager at Deloitte, advises the following to new college graduates:

> Build your brand. Whether it's being the first person at work in the morning or being the person that always asks intelligent questions—be known for something. Building that brand, building that solid reputation, will follow you through your career. People will notice that and will want you on their assignments.[3]

Quite simply, branding sells. Personal branding goes beyond having a resume or a Twitter, LinkedIn, or Instagram profile. It's presenting a carefully crafted image of how you want others to see you.[4] A strong personal brand lets potential employers learn about who you are, your passions, your areas of expertise, your relevant experience, and your aspirations. That's why it's a good idea for you to take control of the message you want to send employers about your career readiness and the information you want them to see on social media.[5]

How to Create Your Brand

Your personal brand should have two components. The first reflects your unique identity and strengths (this is part of a SWOT analysis, which we will discuss in Section 6.3). The second conveys the fact that you are career ready. Developing this type of brand increases your chances of obtaining a desired job and a rewarding career.

Create and promote your personal brand with these steps:

1. Identify Your Personal Brand's Core Message

Think about what motivates you and what you want to achieve. Write down any special training received, education, talents, skills, family background, and special challenges overcome. Where do you see yourself in five years? Ten?

2. Write a Personal Branding Statement

Your personal branding statement draws on your career readiness skill of self-awareness. It is a short paragraph describing who you are, what you stand for, and what you like to do. It emphasizes your unique knowledge and expertise as well as your personal principles and identity.[6]

3. Develop a Social Media Strategy[7]

Choose the most appropriate platform for your message (Twitter, YouTube, and LinkedIn have very different audiences and purposes); polish your oral/written communication career readiness skill; and make sure everything you share, whether in posts, comments, or a blog, is a good and truthful representation of your brand. Remember, everything an employer sees or reads about you tells a story about your brand. Ensure that your language and imagery are consistent across social media platforms so others can find you easily and have a clear sense of who you are.

4. Start networking

Don't wait until graduation to network; start now! Join groups and attend meetings for people in your field of interest. Meeting others in your industry, whether online or in person, can lead to great opportunities that will hone your teamwork/collaboration career readiness skill.

For Discussion Do you have a personal brand? How would you change your social media presence to make it more appealing to potential employers?

6.1 Strategic Positioning and Levels of Strategy

THE BIG PICTURE

Strategic positioning attempts to achieve sustainable competitive advantage by preserving what is distinctive about a company. It is based on the principles that strategy is the creation of a unique and valuable position, requires trade-offs in competing, and involves creating a "fit" among activities. There are three levels of strategy: corporate, business level, and functional.

LO 6-1
Identify the three principles underlying strategic positioning.

In this section, we describe the fundamentals of strategy by discussing strategic positioning and levels of strategy.

Strategic Positioning and Its Principles

According to Porter, **strategic positioning** attempts to achieve sustainable competitive advantage by preserving what is distinctive about a company. "It means," he says, "performing *different* activities from rivals, or performing *similar* activities in different ways."[8]

Strategic positioning is based on three key principles.[9]

1. Strategy Is the Creation of a Unique and Valuable Position   Strategic position emerges from three sources:[10]

- **Few needs, many customers.** Strategic position can be derived from serving the few needs of many customers. Example: Crocs sells only clogs and sandals, but it provides an array of personalized options that appeal to both younger and older generations.
- **Broad needs, few customers.** A strategic position may be based on serving the broad needs of a few customers. Example: buybuy Baby is the one stop shop that specializes in baby gear including clothing, strollers, cribs, and other accessories.
- **Broad needs, many customers.** Strategy may be oriented toward serving the broad needs of many customers. Example: PepsiCo is a food and beverage company that offers a portfolio of 21 brands offering soft drinks, snacks, and breakfast foods. PepsiCo's products are consumed an estimated 1 billion times each day by customers in more than 200 countries around the world.

2. Strategy Requires Trade-Offs in Competing   As a glance of the preceding choices shows, some strategies are incompatible. Thus, a company has to choose not only what strategy to follow but what strategy *not* to follow. Example: Neutrogena soap originally positioned itself more as a medicinal skin care product than as a generic cleansing agent. In achieving this narrower positioning, the company gave up sales in the broader deodorant and skin softener markets and gave up manufacturing efficiencies to preserve its soap's quality. Neutrogena has since built upon its "science-backed skin care" reputation to expand its product offerings beyond soap to cleansers, creams, sunscreen, and serums that address a broader array of skin care needs.[11]

3. Strategy Involves Creating a "Fit" among Activities   "Fit" has to do with the ways a company's activities interact and reinforce one another. Example: A mutual fund company such as Vanguard Group follows a low-cost strategy and aligns all its activities accordingly, selling funds directly to consumers and minimizing portfolio turnover.

Levels of Strategy

Strategic management takes places at three levels, each supporting the other (see Figure 6.1). Though each level is distinct, there needs to be alignment across them. For instance, one study showed that organizations are more competitive and agile when their corporate- and business-level strategies are aligned.[12]

FIGURE 6.1
Three levels of strategy

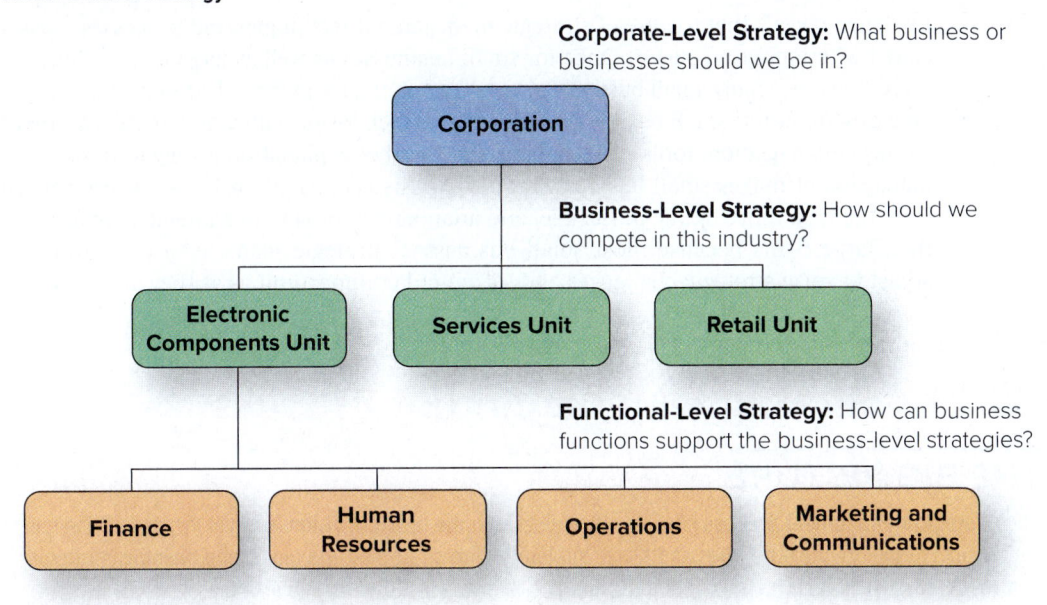

Corporate-Level Strategy: What business or businesses should we be in?

Corporation

Business-Level Strategy: How should we compete in this industry?

Electronic Components Unit — Services Unit — Retail Unit

Functional-Level Strategy: How can business functions support the business-level strategies?

Finance — Human Resources — Operations — Marketing and Communications

Level 1: Corporate-Level Strategy Corporate-level strategy focuses on the organization as a whole. Executives at the most senior levels, generally referred to as the "C-Suite," typically conduct this type of strategic planning. This analysis answers questions such as "what business are we in?" and "what products and services shall we offer?" Strategic decisions at this level can involve acquisitions, such as Amazon's acquisition of Whole Foods. Joint ventures also are considered corporate-level strategies. For example, Honda and Sony are setting up a joint venture to introduce a new electric car brand, Afeela, that focuses on a driver's feeling, or sensory experiences.[13]

Level 2: Business-Level Strategy Business-level strategy focuses on individual business units or product/service lines. Senior-level managers below the C-Suite typically are responsible for this level of strategy. Issues under consideration flow from decisions made at the corporate level and involve considerations such as how much to spend on marketing, new-product development, product expansion or contraction, facilities expansion or reduction, equipment, pricing, and employee development. For example, Dunkin' created Team Dunkin' to sponsor student athletes from universities across the country and leverage their partnerships to appeal to a younger generation of customers.[14]

Level 3: Functional-Level Strategy Functional-level strategy is a plan of action by each functional area of the organization to support higher level strategies. Functional managers lead planning discussions at this level, and the focus is on more tactical issues that support the execution of business-level strategies.

Functional-Level Strategy Example—Dunkin': Dunkin's decision to sponsor student athletes would require three related functional strategies. Marketing managers would first need to decide through which channels to market their partnership with student athletes to current and prospective customers. Store managers would then need to determine how best to use a student athlete's name, image, and likeness (NIL) in the store to influence customers' purchasing decisions. Finally, finance managers would need to determine how much to compensate each student athlete based on their sphere of influence.

Does Strategic Management Work for Small as Well as Large Firms?

Evidence reveals that the use of strategic management techniques and processes is associated with increased performance for small businesses as well as large firms.[15] Surprisingly, however, many small business owners do not engage in formal strategic planning.[16] One explanation is small business managers who lack formal education are less aware of strategic-management tools and techniques.[17] Another explanation is long-term strategic management makes small businesses too rigid. Instead, small business owners benefit from taking a more frequent, flexible, and adaptable approach to strategic management than large firms because most small businesses' strategic plans need to continually adjust to solve strategic challenges and seize market opportunities as they arise.[18]

6.2 The Strategic-Management Process

THE BIG PICTURE

The strategic-management process has five steps: Establish the mission, vision, and values; assess the current reality; formulate the strategies and plans; implement the strategies and plans; and maintain strategic control. All steps may be affected by feedback that enables taking constructive action.

LO 6-2

Outline the five steps in the strategic-management process.

When is a good time to begin the strategic-management process? There is not one correct answer. For instance, many large organizations review their strategy every three to five years. Organizations in fast-changing markets, such as technology and tourism, reevaluate their strategy every one or two years. Small businesses review and revise their strategies more often as they search for traction in the market.[19] Regardless of size or industry, market disruptions are often a catalyst for all organizations to revisit their strategic plans. A good example is artificial intelligence (AI) disrupting Google's market-leading Internet search engine.

Artificial intelligence (AI) is changing the way we search for information. Microsoft is working to incorporate AI to unseat Google's dominance in the Internet search engine market. Edward George/Alamy Stock Photo

Strategic Management Example—Google: Google's Internet search engine enjoyed a commanding 92.6% share of the market followed by Microsoft Bing with a 3.04% market share in 2023. Microsoft presented a significant challenge to Google's market dominance by investing $10 billion in AI tool ChatGPT and using the tool to power its search engine. AI is changing the rules of the game in Internet search by providing more direct answers and more concise results to users' questions. This AI-driven summary offers a more efficient search process than supplying a large collection of links for users to sift through. Google is developing its own AI chatbot (Bard) to counter Microsoft's innovative developments, but experts wonder if Google will cede market share and along with it billions of advertising revenue to its chief technology rival.[20]

The Five Steps of the Strategic-Management Process

The strategic-management process has five steps, plus a feedback loop, as shown in Figure 6.2. This figure was introduced in Chapter 5 (Figure 5.1) and focused on the planning process. Here, we apply the model to the strategic-management process. Let's consider these five steps and bring them to life by examining how Microsoft is using them to revamp its corporate strategy.

FIGURE 6.2

The strategic management process

The process has five steps.

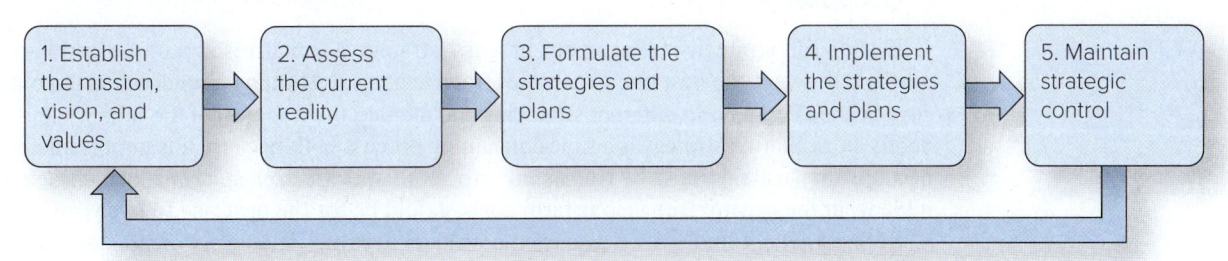

1. Establish the mission, vision, and values → 2. Assess the current reality → 3. Formulate the strategies and plans → 4. Implement the strategies and plans → 5. Maintain strategic control

Feedback: Revise actions, if necessary, based on feedback

Step 1: Establish the Mission, Vision, and Values We discussed mission, vision, and values statements in Chapter 5. The *mission statement,* you'll recall, expresses the organization's purpose or reason for being. The *vision statement* states what the organization wants to become, where it wants to go strategically. The *values statement* describes what the organization stands for, its core priorities, the values its employees embody, and what its products contribute to the world. Research has found that organizations that clearly articulate their values in their mission statement perform better.[21]

Mission and Values Statement Example—Microsoft: Microsoft identified a number of core values that support its mission "to empower every person and every organization on the planet to achieve more."[22] They include respect for colleagues', customers', and partners' points of view, integrity (being honest, ethical, and trustworthy), and accountability.[23]

Step 2: Assess the Current Reality The second step is to do a **current reality assessment**, or *organizational assessment,* to look at where the organization stands and see what is working and what could be done differently so as to maximize efficiency and effectiveness in achieving the organization's mission. Among the tools for assessing the current reality are SWOT analysis, VRIO analysis, forecasting, and benchmarking, all of which we discuss in Section 6.3.

The cloud, or remote access to on-demand computer system resources, is instrumental to fulfilling Microsoft's mission to empower individuals and organizations to store, access, and analyze more information than ever before. Nopparat Khokthong/Shutterstock

Current Reality Assessment Example—Microsoft: Microsoft is a good example of a firm whose current reality has radically changed. In 2008, competitors such as Amazon introduced cloud-based software, or software stored and accessed remotely using the Internet. Cloud innovation left Microsoft scrambling to pivot from desktop software to the cloud as customers were looking for new ways to keep their software current without manually installing updates on each physical device.[24] The competitive environment shifted again in 2022 as Google began talks to invest $200 million in an artificial intelligence (AI) startup. Microsoft needed to keep pace with these market changes or risk being left behind.

Step 3: Formulate the Strategies and Plans   The next step is to translate the broad mission and vision statements into a corporate strategy, which, after the assessment of the current reality, explains how the organization's mission is to be accomplished. Three common grand strategies are growth, stability, and defensive, as we'll describe.

Corporate Strategy Example—Microsoft: Microsoft knew it had to evolve if it wanted to grow and remain a market leader. The company quickly leveraged its resources and offered a solution for cloud computing when, in 2010, CEO Steve Ballmer formally introduced a mobile-first and cloud-first strategy utilizing Azure, the company's cloud-based platform. In 2022, Microsoft kicked off a multi-year collaboration with NVIDIA to build one of the world's most powerful AI supercomputers based on its Azure platform to provide a new suite of solutions that improves customers' productivity.[25]

During the strategic-management process, strategy alternatives should be evaluated properly to select the best one to achieve strategic goals.[26] **Strategy formulation** is the process of choosing among different strategies and altering them to best fit the organization's needs. Formulating strategy is a time-consuming process both because it is important and because the strategy must be translated into more specific *strategic plans,* which determine what the organization's long-term goals should be for the next one to five years.

In Sections 6.4 and 6.5 we discuss the process by which managers create corporate- and business-level strategy, respectively.

Step 4: Implement the Strategies and Plans   Putting strategic plans into effect is **strategy implementation**. Strategic planning isn't effective, of course, unless it can be translated into lower-level plans within the organization. This means that top managers need to check on possible roadblocks within the organization's structure and culture and see if the right people and control systems are available to execute the plans.[27] Strategic implementation, a concept we discuss in Section 6.6, is essential for success. It requires significant involvement by leadership and is considered to be one of the greatest challenges for managers.[28] Strategic dashboards are among the tools leaders use to implement strategy.

Strategy Implementation Example—Microsoft: Microsoft utilized its Azure platform as a foundation to execute new offerings, including software, gaming, and personal computing products. The company reorganized its structure and acquired dozens of cloud start-ups since 2013 (almost double that of Amazon) in order to gain market share in the fast-moving cloud market. In 2023, Microsoft placed a significant strategic bet on AI by investing approximately $10 billion in start-up research laboratory, OpenAI. CEO Satya Nadella believes this investment will allow it to lead the market by launching a new generation of AI-powered products and services.[29]

Step 5: Maintain Strategic Control: The Feedback Loop   **Strategic control** consists of monitoring the execution of strategy and making adjustments, if necessary. To keep strategic plans on track, managers need control systems to monitor progress and take corrective action—early and rapidly—when things start to go awry. Corrective action constitutes a feedback loop, as shown in Figure 6.2, in which a problem requires that managers return to an earlier step to rethink policies, redo budgets, or revise personnel arrangements. Monitoring strategy implementation and taking corrective action, the last two elements of the planning/control cycle introduced in Figure 5.5, are discussed further in Section 6.6.

Strategic Control Example—Microsoft: Microsoft Azure has an error reporting system which is designed to provide the company with real-time feedback when customers face issues with its software. The system allows the company to quickly become aware of errors and push out solutions to users. Microsoft uses its powerful computing capability to train AI models such that they develop more interpretable, accurate, and creative solutions. Azure's error reporting system and AI services both rely on feedback, or additional information, to continuously improve.[30]

All told, Microsoft's strategies are working. The company's revenue increased 11% between 2021 and 2022. The boost came from its cloud division, which saw a revenue increase of 24%, or $25.7 billion in year-over-year revenues.[31] Microsoft's cloud services have the second highest market share in the rapidly growing cloud infrastructure service market (second only to Amazon Web Services) with 21% in a market worth $217 billion.[32] AI breakthroughs are expected to drive Microsoft's revenue into the future. CEO Nadella remarked about the company's strategy, "In a world facing increasing headwinds, digital technology is the ultimate tailwind."[33]

The rest of this chapter reveals the details of the steps in the strategic-management process. Before you proceed, connect what you've learned to your own experience. Picture an organization that you worked for, currently work for, or would like to work for. Assess the organization's level of strategic thinking by taking the following self-assessment in Connect if your instructor has assigned it to you.

SELF-ASSESSMENT 6.1

Assessing Strategic Thinking

This survey is designed to assess an organization's level of strategic thinking. Please complete Self-Assessment 6.1 if your instructor has assigned it in Connect.

6.3 Assessing the Current Reality

THE BIG PICTURE

To develop a grand strategy, you need to gather data and make projections using tools such as SWOT analysis, VRIO analysis, forecasting, and benchmarking.

Figure 6.2 (and Chapter 5) demonstrate that the first step in the strategic-management process is to establish the organization's mission, vision, and values. The second step, *assess the current reality,* looks at where the organization stands internally and externally—to determine what's working and what's not, to see what can be changed to create sustainable competitive advantage. **Sustainable competitive advantage** exists when other companies cannot duplicate the value delivered to customers. An assessment develops an objective view of everything the organization does: its sources of revenue or funding, its work-flow processes, its organizational structure, client satisfaction, employee turnover, and other matters.

Among the tools for assessing the current reality are *SWOT analysis, VRIO analysis, forecasting,* and *benchmarking.*

LO 6-3
Explain how an organization assesses the competitive landscape.

SWOT Analysis

SWOT analysis is a good first step at gaining insight into whether or not a company has competitive advantage. **SWOT analysis** is a situational analysis in which a company assesses its strengths, weaknesses, opportunities, and threats. In Chapter 3 we introduced you to an organization's internal and external environment (see Figure 3.1). Recall that the external environment consists of the *task environment*—external groups an organization interacts with on a routine basis—and the *general environment*—macro

FIGURE 6.3

SWOT analysis

SWOT stands for strengths, weaknesses, opportunities, and threats.

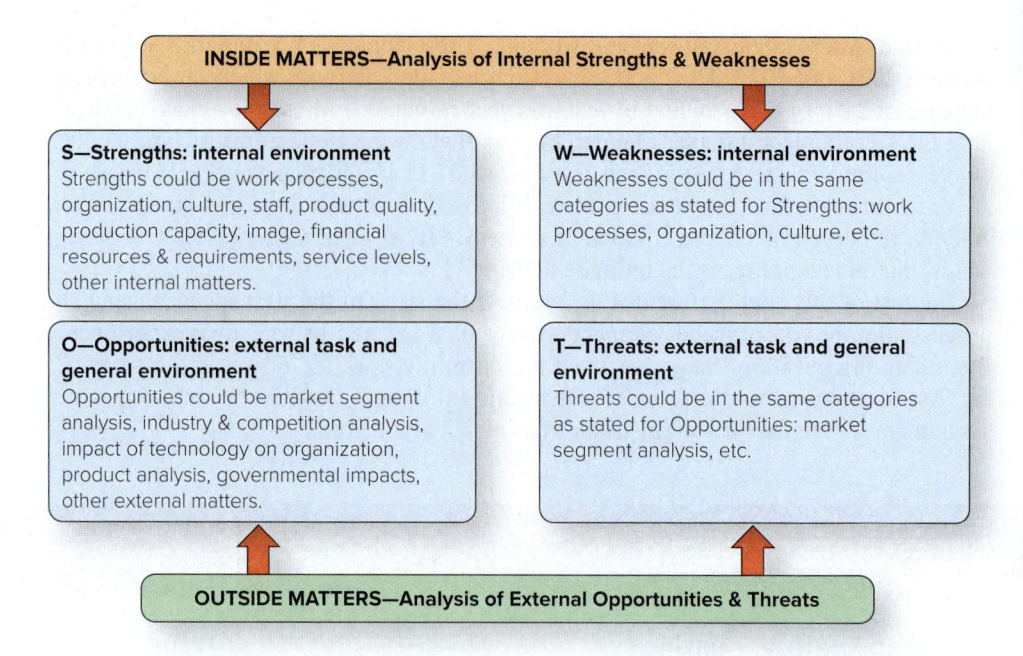

INSIDE MATTERS—Analysis of Internal Strengths & Weaknesses

S—Strengths: internal environment
Strengths could be work processes, organization, culture, staff, product quality, production capacity, image, financial resources & requirements, service levels, other internal matters.

W—Weaknesses: internal environment
Weaknesses could be in the same categories as stated for Strengths: work processes, organization, culture, etc.

O—Opportunities: external task and general environment
Opportunities could be market segment analysis, industry & competition analysis, impact of technology on organization, product analysis, governmental impacts, other external matters.

T—Threats: external task and general environment
Threats could be in the same categories as stated for Opportunities: market segment analysis, etc.

OUTSIDE MATTERS—Analysis of External Opportunities & Threats

external forces that influence an organization and are outside its control. A SWOT analysis provides you with a realistic understanding of your organization in relation to its internal and external environments so you can better formulate strategy in pursuit of its mission.[34] (See Figure 6.3.)

The SWOT analysis is divided into two parts: internal environment and external environment—that is, an analysis of *internal strengths and weaknesses* (internal environment) and an analysis of *external opportunities and threats* (external environment). The following table gives examples of SWOT characteristics that might apply to a college (see Table 6.1).

TABLE 6.1 SWOT Characteristics That Might Apply to a College

S—STRENGTHS (INTERNAL STRENGTHS)	W—WEAKNESSES (INTERNAL WEAKNESSES)
• Faculty teaching and research abilities • High-ability students • Loyal alumni • Strong interdisciplinary programs	• Limited programs in business • High teaching loads • Insufficient racial diversity • Lack of high-technology infrastructure
O—OPPORTUNITIES (EXTERNAL TASK ENVIRONMENT OPPORTUNITIES)	**T—THREATS (EXTERNAL TASK ENVIRONMENT THREATS)**
• Local college shuts down • Growth in many local skilled jobs • High schools partner with colleges to offer dual enrollment • Companies support employees' continuing college education	• Increased competition from other colleges • Students hesitant to acquire loans to pay for education • Parents question the affordability of a college education • Companies offer employees in-house training and development
O—OPPORTUNITIES (EXTERNAL GENERAL ENVIRONMENT OPPORTUNITIES)	**T—THREATS (EXTERNAL GENERAL ENVIRONMENT THREATS)**
• Local minority population increasing • College savings plans incentive parents to save for college • Technology reduces geographic barriers to college courses	• Depressed state and national economy • Fewer visas granted for international students • State governments reduce university funding

Internal Environment: Analysis of Internal Strengths and Weaknesses Does your organization have a skilled workforce? a superior reputation? a unique product? These are examples of **organizational strengths**—the skills and capabilities that give the organization special competencies and competitive advantages in executing strategies in pursuit of its vision.

Or does your organization have obsolete technology? outdated facilities? a shaky marketing operation? These are examples of **organizational weaknesses**—the drawbacks that hinder an organization in executing strategies in pursuit of its vision.

External Task Environment: Analysis of External Opportunities and Threats Consider your organization's task environment, or external forces that affect your company's day-to-day operations. Is your organization fortunate to have weak competitors? a strong relationship with suppliers and distributors? favorable financing terms with lenders? These are instances of **organizational opportunities**—environmental factors that the organization may exploit for competitive advantage.

Alternatively, is your organization having to deal with new governmental regulations? a shortage of resources? substitute products? These are some possible **organizational threats**—environmental factors that hinder an organization's achieving a competitive advantage.

External General Environment: Analysis of External Opportunities and Threats Whereas organizations have some control over opportunities and threats in their external task environment, they have little influence over opportunities and threats that emerge from broader societal forces. PESTEL is a strategic planning tool to analyze macro opportunities and threats stemming from six societal forces:

- **Political**—Tax policies, government incentives, corruption, trade tariffs.
- **Economic**—Inflation, exchange rates, interest rates, unemployment.
- **Social**—Population demographics, cultural norms, career attitudes, lifestyle.
- **Technological**—Research and development, automation, Internet infrastructure.
- **Environmental**—Climate, geographic resources, environmental policies.
- **Legal**—Employment laws, antitrust laws, intellectual property laws.

Managers use PESTEL for two applications: (1) to assess the risk associated with entering new markets or starting a new venture and (2) to analyze the macro external general environment.[35]

PESTEL Example—McDonald's: Fast-food restaurant, McDonald's, made the strategic decision to sell its business in Russia after operating there for 32 years citing social and political forces such as the humanitarian crisis caused by the country's conflict with Ukraine and the "unpredictable operating environment" in the country. Exiting the country cost McDonald's approximately $1.2 billion.[36]

Using VRIO to Assess Competitive Potential: Value, Rarity, Imitability, and Organization

How do managers determine if a company or its products possess a competitive advantage in the marketplace? Conduct a VRIO analysis to assess the company's resources and capabilities.[37]

VRIO (pronounced by its letters, "V-R-I-O") is a framework for analyzing a resource or capability to determine its competitive strategic potential by answering four questions about its value, rarity, imitability, and organization.[38] The questions are shown in Figure 6.4.

VRIO is a way to analyze a firm's competitive potential by asking four questions about value, rarity, imitability, and organization. A yes answer to each question means

FIGURE 6.4

Is the resource or capability . . .

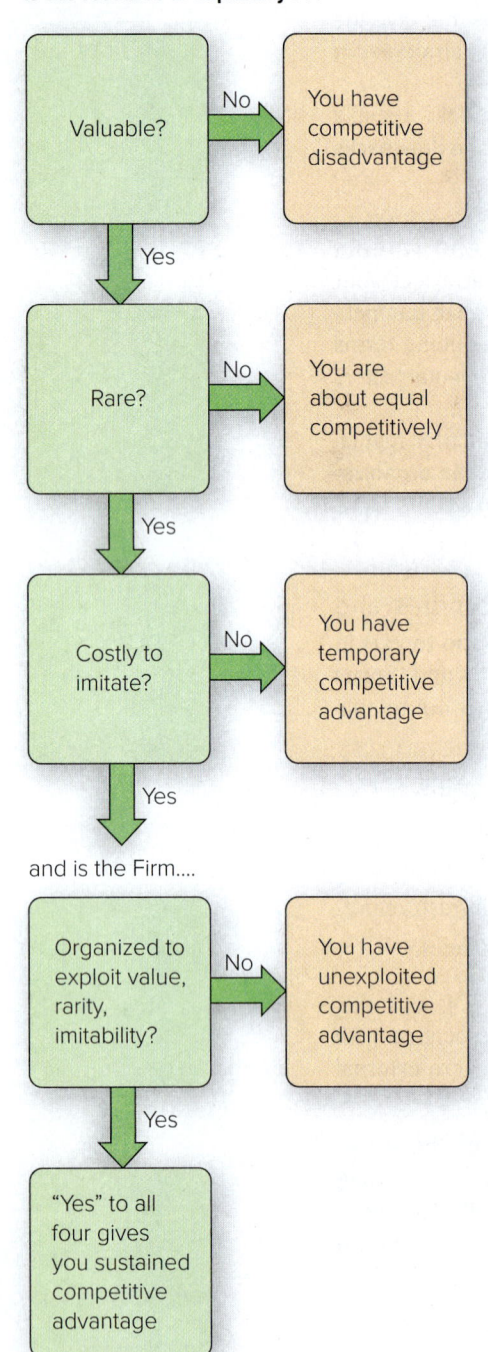

- Valuable? — No → You have competitive disadvantage
- Yes ↓
- Rare? — No → You are about equal competitively
- Yes ↓
- Costly to imitate? — No → You have temporary competitive advantage
- Yes ↓

and is the Firm....

- Organized to exploit value, rarity, imitability? — No → You have unexploited competitive advantage
- Yes ↓
- "Yes" to all four gives you sustained competitive advantage

Source: Adapted from Rothaermel, F. T. Strategic Management: Concepts and Cases. New York: McGraw Hill, 2012, 91.

---

the resource or capability—that is, the business idea—has a competitive advantage (see Figure 6.4). Let's better understand each part of the VRIO framework by applying it to assess how one of Toyota's capabilities—mass vehicle production—could impact its ability to rapidly gain market share in the electric vehicle market segment.

Value: Is the Resource or Capability Valuable?
Valuable means "Does the resource or capability allow your firm to exploit an opportunity or neutralize a threat?" If the answer is yes, the resource puts you in a competitive position. If no, then you're at a competitive disadvantage.

> **Value Example—Toyota:** Value is derived from Toyota's mass vehicle production capabilities. Toyota was the world's top-selling automaker in 2022 for the third consecutive year. It sold 10.5 million vehicles globally, 2.2 million more vehicles than the automobile industry's runner-up, Volkswagen. Toyota currently produces 2.7 million electrified (mostly hybrid) vehicles. The company's existing mass production capabilities enables it to produce vehicles cheaper than its competitors and positions it to manufacture and deliver electric vehicles at scale faster than its competitors.[39]

Rarity: Is the Resource or Capability Currently Controlled by Only a Few Firms or No Other Firms?
If the answer is yes, that status gives your firm at least some temporary competitive advantage. If the answer is no (because several competing firms exist), you're at least at equal competitive advantage because you're no worse than the competition.

> **Rarity Example—Toyota:** Toyota's automobile production capability is unrivaled in the industry. It controls 10.5% of the global automotive market share and more than doubles the market share controlled by any other automobile manufacturer except Volkswagen (6.4% market share). Such a strong hold on the global automobile market creates significant barriers for competitors to expand their production capabilities worldwide.[40]

Imitability: Is the Resource or Capability Costly for Other Firms to Imitate?
If the answer is yes, that gives you a definite competitive advantage. If no—because other firms can get into the market without much expense—that gives you only a temporary competitive advantage.

> **Imitability Example—Toyota:** Expanding production capability in the automobile industry is exceedingly difficult because it is resource intensive and involves a complex supply chain to source parts and distribute vehicles to a network of dealers. Tesla doubled its production capacity to 2 million cars a year in 2022 but estimates suggest they would need to spend $400 billion to build new vehicle assembly and battery plants to meet their 2030 goal of producing an ambitious 20 million vehicles per year. Other electric vehicle (EV) start-ups such as Rivian, Lucid Motors, Xiaopeng Motors, and Nio face a steeper uphill battle to quickly build production capacity in a market where traditional auto manufacturers are saturating the market with new EV models.[41] Toyota's existing production capability and supply chain provide it with a significant competitive advantage in the EV market.

Organization: Is the Firm Organized to Exploit the Resource or Capability? Research has found that organizational structure helps companies leverage their existing resources and capabilities.[42] If the firm has the necessary structure, culture, leadership, control systems, employee policies, and particularly financing—then, assuming yes answers on value, rarity, and imitability, it would seem the firm has the ability to exploit its resources and capabilities to achieve a competitive advantage. If no, it may only have a temporary competitive advantage.

Organization Example—Toyota: In 2022, Toyota announced it will invest $5.6 billion to expand its battery plants in the United States and Japan to achieve its goal to expand its EV offerings and sell 3.5 million EVs annually by 2030.[43] The company is leveraging its vast financial resources, technical expertise, and supply chain relationships to quickly develop a dedicated EV platform. According to Toyota's Chair, Akio Toyoda, "It takes a lot of money to design this architecture, but once it's ready, large volumes and multiple models can be built off similar blueprints, saving costs over the long term."[44] Toyota repositioned its leadership as well to support the exploitation of its capabilities. In 2023, long-time CEO and President Akio Toyoda appointed his successor, Koji Sato, to lead the company into the digitalization, electrification, and connectivity era. Taken together, Toyota is organizing its financial, operations, and leadership infrastructure to exploit its production capability and achieve a competitive advantage in the EV market.[45]

Toyota is building on its hybrid technology to make a strong push into the electric vehicle market segment. Sergiy Palamarchuk/Alamy Stock Photo

Forecasting: Predicting the Future

Once planners analyze their organization's strengths, weaknesses, opportunities, and threats, they need to forecast to develop a long-term strategy. A **forecast** is a vision or projection of the future. Accurate forecasting enables managers to acquire, use, expend, and reallocate organizational resources efficiently and effectively. But, according to baseball-playing philosopher Yogi Berra, "It's tough to make predictions, especially about the future."[46]

Lots of people make predictions; they are often wrong.[47] Cryptocurrency was predicted to become the single global currency by 2028. Bitcoin, the most popular cryptocurrency, soared to its all-time high $68,789 in November 2021. Governmental regulations, rising interest rates, and the arrest of Sam Bankman-Fried—the CEO of a leading cryptocurrency exchange—for fraud caused confidence in cryptocurrency to plummet. Only time will tell if cryptocurrency can fulfill its once-lofty expectations.[48]

Of course, the farther into the future one makes a prediction, the more difficult it is to be accurate, especially in matters of technology. Yet forecasting is a necessary part of planning, and research shows that managers who consider multiple points of view make better predictions than those who bet on one perspective.[49]

Cryptocurrencies such as Bitcoin, Ethereum, and Litecoin were predicted to make traditional currencies extinct. Those predictions have not materialized... yet. What role do you think cryptocurrency will play in the financial markets? Marc Bruxelle/Shutterstock

Trend Analysis A **trend analysis** is a hypothetical extension of a past series of events into the future. The basic assumption is that the picture of the present can be projected into the future. This is not a bad assumption if you have enough historical data, but it is always subject to surprises.[50] If your data are unreliable, they will produce erroneous trend projections.

An example of trend analysis is a time-series forecast, which predicts future data based on patterns of historical data. Time-series forecasts are used to predict long-term trends, cyclic patterns (as in the up-and-down nature of the business cycle), and seasonal variations (as in holiday sales versus summer sales).

Trend Analysis Example—Stamford Health: Stamford Health analyzed historical data concerning patients' length of hospital stays, conditions, the timing of medications, and patient outcomes. The time-series forecasts identified better times to give patients medication and reduced the average length of their hospital stay.[51]

Scenario Analysis: Predicting Alternative Futures Companies are vulnerable to changes in their environment, like the COVID-19 pandemic, that may unexpectedly render their business strategy ineffective.[52] **Scenario analysis is the creation of alternative hypothetical but equally likely future conditions.** Managers apply the technique by making alternative plans for different scenarios and then using the one that best fits the situation at hand.

Scenario Analysis Example—Shell: Shell Energy has relied on scenario planning for 50 years to envision future possibilities and understand uncertainties associated with global energy demands and their environmental impacts. The company describes how the world is changing and develops scenarios about the future to stretch its strategic thinking. For instance, imagine how society's energy demands would differ 10 years from now if it prioritized one of the three following outcomes: wealth, security, and health.[53]

Today's business environment is rapidly changing, and more organizations are using scenario planning to manage environmental uncertainty.[54] A 2021 McKinsey survey indicated 90% of CFOs in their sample reported using at least three scenarios to support their planning and 70% plan to hold back cash to navigate a potential crisis as a result of their scenario analysis.[55]

Benchmarking: Comparing with the Best

Benchmarking is a process by which a company compares its performance with that of high-performing organizations.[56] Consulting firm Bain & Company notes that "the objective of benchmarking is to find examples of superior performance and understand the processes and practices driving that performance. Companies then improve their performance by tailoring and incorporating these best practices into their own operations—not by imitating, but by innovating."[57] Quick-service restaurant chains such as Chick-fil-A, McDonald's, and Taco Bell, constantly benchmark against each other's drive-thru service to shorten wait times, take accurate orders, and deliver quality food. This benchmark is critical to these restaurants because 75% of their sales come from their drive-thru.[58] Benchmarking has led to innovations in drive-thru configurations such as changing the number of windows, the menu, speaker boards, and ordering approaches, all in the spirit of outperforming competitors.[59]

Aside from restaurants, research has found that benchmarking is a valuable tool to improve goal performance in a variety of industrial sectors.[60] These include investment firms, local governments, and airlines. For example, Charles Schwab may compare its rate of return on a certain stock portfolio against competitors. Cities similarly benchmark quality of life measures against other cities in the region, country, or world.

The airline industry regularly uses benchmarks to measure success. Figure 6.5 provides a 2022 comparison of nine U.S. airlines across benchmarks such as on-time arrivals, canceled flights, consumer complaints, and an overall ranking. Which airline do you think ranked the highest based on your own experience or what you may have heard from family and friends?

Delta Airlines is ranked #1 overall in the United States for the second consecutive year and five of the past six years. They had the best on-time arrival and fewest canceled flights of any carrier in 2022. Budget airline JetBlue came in last overall in the 2022 airline rankings because it had the highest rate of extreme delays of any airline. JetBlue's president blames its poor performance on 75% of its flights operating out of New York

FIGURE 6.5

Airline benchmarks, 2022

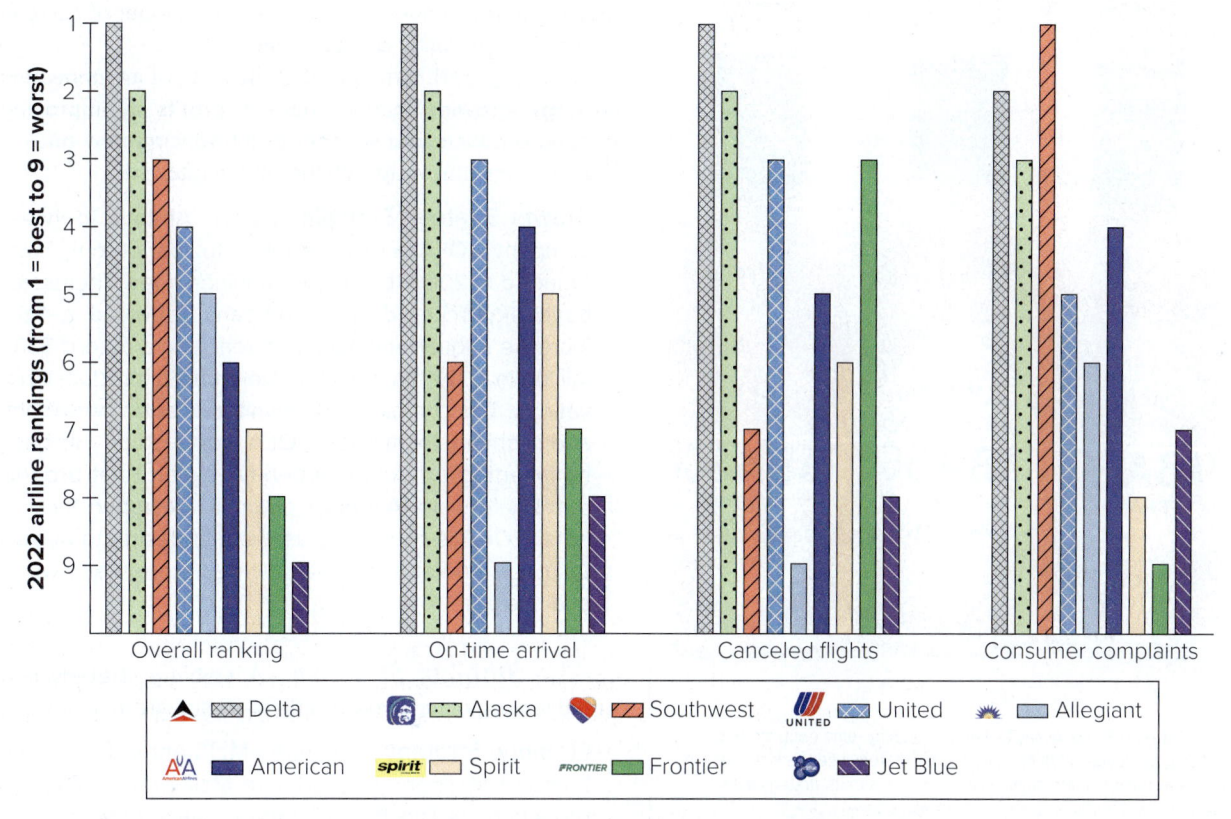

[Bar chart showing 2022 airline rankings (from 1 = best to 9 = worst) across four categories: Overall ranking, On-time arrival, Canceled flights, and Consumer complaints. Airlines shown: Delta, Alaska, Southwest, United, Allegiant, American, Spirit, Frontier, Jet Blue.]

Source: Based on D. Gilbertson, and A. Pohle, "The Best and Worst Airlines of 2022," *Wall Street Journal*, January 18, 2023, https://www.wsj.com/articles/best-worst-us-airlines-flights-cancellations-delays-baggage-11673982171?mod=Searchresults_pos5&page=1.

and surrounding cities in the Northeast, a region plagued by congested air traffic.[61] Southwest ranked #1 in fewest consumer complaints, but its operational meltdown during Christmas was not accounted for in the 2022 rankings. Southwest's outdated scheduling system contributed to the airline canceling over 16,000 flights because it could not handle the volume of rescheduling issues caused by adverse weather across the United States at the busiest travel time of the year, during the Christmas holiday. ●

6.4 Establishing Corporate-Level Strategy

THE BIG PICTURE

Common corporate-level grand strategies are growth, stability, or defensive strategies. The Boston Consulting Group (BCG) matrix and diversification considerations are used to formulate corporate strategy.

After assessing the current reality (Step 2 in the strategic-management process), it's time to formulate corporate-level strategies. Three methods to understand corporate-level strategies are common grand strategies, the Boston Consulting Group (BCG) matrix, and diversification.

LO 6-4

Explain the three methods of corporate-level strategy.

Three Overall Types of Corporate Strategy

The three common corporate-level grand strategies are *growth, stability,* and *defensive*.

Hot strategy? Tabasco may be keen on adding some excitement to entrées, but it doesn't think its corporate strategy needs a kick. Does a company need to make significant adjustments to its strategy if it's currently working? Prachaya Roekdeethaweesab/Shutterstock

1. The Growth Strategy A **growth strategy** is a grand strategy that involves expansion—as in sales revenues, market share, number of employees, or number of customers or (for nonprofits) clients served.

Often a growth strategy takes the form of an **innovation strategy**, growing market share or profits by improving existing products and services or introducing new ones.[62] We consider innovation further in Chapter 10.

Growth Strategy Example—HOKA: Athletic footwear company HOKA, a verb meaning "to soar or to fly," was founded in 2009 to improve running shoes. Their sales have skyrocketed. The company reported a 58% increase in quarterly net sales, reaching a record $333 million in 2022. Its growth is fueled by its product innovations. The company is known for its soft, lightweight, and cushiony foam base. HOKA improved on this base by inserting a flexible carbon-fiber plate that propels runners forward. Although originally designed for runners, HOKA is expanding its product design to appeal to other market segments such as streetwear, work, and leisure.[63]

2. The Stability Strategy A **stability strategy** is a grand strategy that involves little or no significant change.

Stability Strategy Example—McIlhenny Company: Edmund McIlhenny, founder of McIlhenny Company, produced the first Tabasco pepper sauce bottle in 1868 to give southern food "some flavor and excitement." Today, Tabasco sauce is labeled in 25 languages and dialects and sold in more than 180 countries. The company has added seven additional flavors to its offerings through the decades, but there hasn't been a significant change to the company's strategy.[64]

3. The Defensive Strategy A **defensive strategy**, or a *retrenchment strategy,* is a grand strategy that involves reduction in the organization's efforts.

Defensive Strategy Example—Bombardier: Canadian plane and train manufacturer Bombardier adopted a defensive strategy by selling its commercial aerospace and rail transportation divisions. The company used the proceeds to pay down debt and consolidate its business on "designing, building, and servicing the world's best business jets," says Bombardier's President and CEO Éric Martel.[65]

Table 6.2 shows different actions organizations take to implement each grand strategy.

The BCG Matrix

Developed by the Boston Consulting Group, the **BCG matrix** is a management strategy companies use to evaluate their portfolio of strategic business units on the basis of (1) their market growth rates and (2) their market share. Market growth rate describes how quickly the entire industry is growing. Market share is the business unit's share of the market in relation to competitors. The purpose of evaluating each business unit is to recalibrate the company's portfolio, or identify which business units to invest in and which ones to divest from. In general, the BCG matrix suggests that organizations allocate more resources to businesses in fast-growing markets than businesses in slow-growing markets. These concepts are illustrated in Figure 6.6.[66]

TABLE 6.2 How Companies Can Implement Each Corporate-Level Grand Strategy

GROWTH STRATEGY

- It can improve an existing product or service to attract more buyers.
- It can increase its promotion and marketing efforts to expand its market share.
- It can expand its operations by taking over distribution or manufacturing previously handled by someone else.
- It can expand into new products or services.
- It can acquire similar or complementary businesses.
- It can merge with another company to form a larger company.

STABILITY STRATEGY

- It can adopt a no-change strategy (if, for example, the company is effectively serving the needs of a niche market with no competitors threatening its market share).
- It can adopt a little-change strategy (if, for example, the company has been growing at a breakneck speed and feels it needs a period of consolidation).

DEFENSIVE STRATEGY

- It can reduce costs by freezing hiring or tightening expenses.
- It can sell off (liquidate) assets—land, buildings, inventories, and the like.
- It can gradually phase out product lines or services.
- It can divest part of its business by selling off entire divisions or subsidiaries.
- It can declare bankruptcy.
- It can attempt a turnaround—do some retrenching, with a view toward restoring profitability.

FIGURE 6.6

The BCG matrix

Market growth and market share are divided into two categories: low and high. In this matrix, *dogs* are undesirable business units, *question marks* are promising but unproven business units, *stars* are highly desirable business units, and *cash cows* are profitable but mature business units.

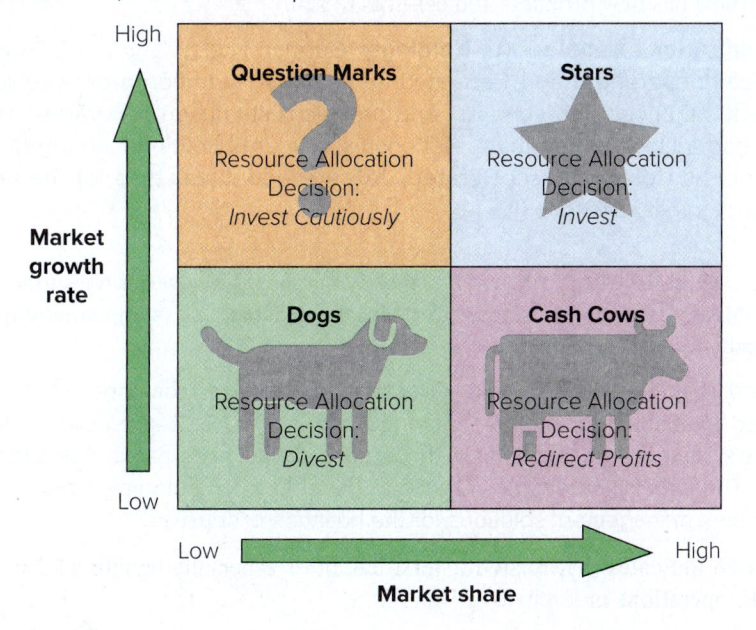

	Market share: Low	Market share: High
Market growth rate: High	**Question Marks** — Resource Allocation Decision: *Invest Cautiously*	**Stars** — Resource Allocation Decision: *Invest*
Market growth rate: Low	**Dogs** — Resource Allocation Decision: *Divest*	**Cash Cows** — Resource Allocation Decision: *Redirect Profits*

A company should usually operate by investing (or "milking") profits from one or more successful but slow-growing units, called *cash cows,* into new products or services called *stars* that have demonstrated success in growing markets. Investing in stars tends to support growth and generate more positive cash flows to fund further growth. A company should take a more cautious approach toward funding question marks, or business units with low market share in fast-growing markets. These business units typically churn through large amounts of cash in an attempt to gain market share. Question marks should be monitored closely because they can either become stars or dogs. *Dogs* consist of business units that are no longer succeeding relative to their competitors. They should be shut down or sold.

Let's apply the BCG matrix by analyzing Google.

BCG Matrix Example—Google: Search ads are a cash cow for the technology company bringing in $149 billion in revenue in 2021, or 36% of its total revenue.[67] Google has substantial market share here, which means it is still earning significant profits from its search ads which it can invest in its other products, particularly stars. Google's mobile video platform, YouTube, is a star with strong growth and high market share in a market that is still growing. It competes with content providers such as Amazon, Netflix, Disney, and traditional media companies. It also competes with music subscription businesses like Spotify and Apple Music. Google's entry into cloud computing is seen as a question mark because it accounts for only 11% of the market share, well behind market leaders Amazon Web Services and Microsoft Azure.[68] The cloud is a rapidly growing market, but Google's ability to grow its market share in a crowded market remains to be seen. Google Glass, a product developed to compete in the niche consumer smart glasses market, failed to gain traction among consumers. Google discontinued the product four years after it was first developed. High investment combined with low return made this Google product a dog.[69]

One drawback of the BCG matrix is that in practice it is fairly easy for managers to mischaracterize their business units, thereby erroneously drawing investment away from cash cows that still need it or writing off units or product lines as dogs when they still have the potential to flourish.

Diversification Strategy

The strategy of moving into new lines of business is called **diversification**. Companies generally diversify to either grow revenue or reduce risk. They grow revenue because the company now has new products and services to sell.

Diversification Example—JAB Holdings: German investment firm, JAB Holdings acquired beverage brand Core Hydration. Core Hydration produces premium, nutrient-enhanced bottled water and organic fruit-infused beverages. The company had a close distribution relationship with JAB Holdings' Keurig Dr Pepper division. As Core sales accelerated, JAB decided it was time for the beverage maker to join its portfolio.[70]

Related Diversification
When a company purchases a new business that is related to the company's existing business portfolio, the organization is implementing **related diversification**.

Related Diversification Example—Oracle: Cloud services company Oracle acquired Cerner, a health information technologies provider, in 2022 as an avenue to merge Oracle's computing capabilities with Cerner's clinical expertise and healthcare systems. The acquisition enables Oracle to develop more automated and integrated healthcare management solutions for the healthcare industry.[71]

Research indicates that related diversification is especially beneficial for organizations with operations in foreign markets.[72]

Unrelated Diversification   Companies sometimes attempt to reduce risk by using an unrelated diversification strategy. **Unrelated diversification** occurs when a company acquires another company in a completely unrelated business. This strategy reduces risk because losses in one business or industry can be offset by profits from other companies in the corporate portfolio.

Unrelated Diversification Example—Amazon: E-commerce company Amazon purchased Whole Foods, a high-end, specialty grocery chain in 2017. The deal provided Amazon with access to hundreds of physical stores and provided an entry point into the grocery market. Since the acquisition, Amazon incorporated operational and technological changes to increase Whole Foods' efficiency. As the COVID-19 pandemic faded and consumers' habits shifted from shopping online to in-person, Whole Foods offered Amazon an important source of revenue growth.[73]

Vertical Integration   Organizations also can pursue a diversification strategy through vertical integration. In **vertical integration,** a firm expands into businesses that provide the supplies it needs to make its products or that distribute and sell its products. For many years, Hollywood movie studios followed this model, not only producing movies but also distributing them and even owning their own theaters.[74] Today, Apple follows the same path by producing and distributing its own entertainment programming on Apple TV+. Starbucks has long followed a plan of vertical integration by buying and roasting all of its own coffee and then selling it directly to consumers through Starbucks stores.[75]

Research indicates vertical integration is desirable because it increases financial performance by increasing quality and lowering costs. It also reduces supply chain disruptions because organizations are less dependent on external suppliers to source resources or distribute products to end users.[76]

6.5 Establishing Business-Level Strategy

THE BIG PICTURE
Business-level strategy begins with an assessment of Porter's five competitive forces. Companies then are advised to select from one of four competitive strategies. We contrast this academic approach with a practical one proposed by Jack Welch, former CEO of General Electric. He recommended that leaders create business-level strategies by answering five key questions.

Business-level strategies flow from the details contained in corporate strategies. The objective of formulating a business-level strategy is to answer the question of how the company wants to compete in industries in which the business units operate. Harvard professor Michael Porter is credited with devising the models and processes for establishing business-level strategies. We start by focusing on his analysis of his five competitive forces and then delve into a discussion of his four key competitive strategies. We end this section with a practical approach proposed by Jack Welch.

LO 6-5

Discuss Porter's and Welch's techniques for formulating a business-level strategy.

Porter's Five Competitive Forces

What are the forces that influence the intensity of competition within a particular industry? After studying several kinds of businesses, strategic-management expert Michael Porter suggested, in his **Porter's model for industry analysis,** that business-level strategies originate by evaluating five competitive forces in the firm's environment: (1) threats of new entrants, (2) bargaining power of suppliers, (3) bargaining power of buyers, (4) threats of substitute products or services, and (5) rivalry among competitors.[77] Let's consider how Porter's model applies to video streaming services.

1. Threats of New Entrants New competitors can affect an industry almost overnight, taking away customers from existing organizations. For example, since Netflix found success by shifting its focus from in-store and mail-order DVD rentals to online streaming, legacy media networks such as HBO, NBC, CBS, and Discovery have started streaming services of their own. In addition, Amazon, Apple, and Disney have thrown their hats into the streaming market, creating what many have called the "streaming wars."[78]

2. Bargaining Power of Suppliers Some companies are readily able to switch suppliers in order to get components or services, but others are not. Streaming services like Netflix, Amazon, and Apple need to procure new movies and TV shows to keep their content offerings diverse and fresh. A reliance on licensing content provides suppliers, like film studios, with higher power to increase licensing fees because only a limited number of studios produce entertainment content. As a result, streaming services have turned to creating their own original content. This programming strategy is becoming the norm in the industry with Netflix Originals now making up 50% of all content on the streaming platform.[79]

3. Bargaining Power of Buyers Informed customers become better negotiators. For example, use of the Internet enabled one of your authors to get a higher trade-in on his current vehicle and a lower sales price on a new car. Netflix faces an uphill battle when it comes to customer switching costs. Subscribers don't have to worry about termination fees if they cancel their Netflix service, and acquiring competitors' services is as easy as downloading an app. Netflix is steadily losing market share to its competitors.[80]

4. Threats of Substitute Products or Services Like all programming providers, Netflix must ensure that customers continue to prefer its offerings to the many other options available. This includes alternatives like traditional cable providers (e.g., Xfinity, Spectrum, and Cox), discount Internet television services (e.g., DirecTV, Hulu, fuboTV, and YouTube TV), or even your local library.[81]

5. Rivalry among Competitors The preceding four forces influence the fifth force, rivalry among competitors. Think of the growing competition among online streaming networks engaged in the "streaming wars" and the number of services you can now utilize to watch your favorite shows. Once again, the Internet has intensified rivalries among all kinds of organizations.

Porter recommends that organizations conduct a SWOT analysis that examines these five competitive forces. He believes that this analysis enables companies to formulate effective strategy, using what he identified as four competitive strategies, as we discuss in the next section.

Streaming wars. Companies such as Netflix, Amazon, HBO, Hulu, and Disney are competing for your viewership. How do you feel about having so many options? Can too many be a bad thing? Ivan Marc/Shutterstock

Porter's Four Competitive Strategies

Porter's four competitive strategies (also called four generic strategies) are (1) cost-leadership, (2) differentiation, (3) cost-focus, and (4) focused-differentiation. The first two strategies focus on *wide* markets, the last two on *narrow* markets. WarnerMedia, one of the largest media and entertainment companies in the world, serves wide markets around the globe. Your neighborhood video store (if one still exists) serves a narrow market of local customers.

Let's look at these four strategies.

1. Cost-Leadership Strategy: Keeping Costs and Prices Low for a Wide Market
The **cost-leadership strategy** is to keep the costs, and hence prices, of a product or service below those of competitors and to target a wide market.

This puts the pressure on R&D managers to develop products or services that can be created cheaply, production managers to reduce production costs, and marketing managers to reach a wide variety of customers as inexpensively as possible.

Firms implementing the cost-leadership strategy include Timex, IKEA, computer maker Acer, retailers Walmart and Home Depot, and pen maker Bic.

2. Differentiation Strategy: Offering Unique and Superior Value for a Wide Market
The **differentiation strategy** is to offer products or services that are of unique and superior value compared with those of competitors and to target a wide market.

Because products are expensive, managers may have to spend more on R&D, marketing, and customer service. This is the strategy followed by Ritz-Carlton hotels and Lexus automobiles. Research indicates differentiation can lead to product innovation, higher customer satisfaction, and competitive advantage.[82]

The differentiation strategy also is pursued by companies trying to create *brands* to differentiate themselves from competitors.

> **Differentiation Strategy Example—Warby Parker:** Eyewear retailer Warby Parker invests in differentiation strategies for its glasses and contact lenses by making them fashionable. It also features world-class customer service in its stores and through social media. The company responds to every customer's tweets. They even create a short video to answer more complicated questions and then send customers a link to watch the video on YouTube. Warby Parker's product and service differentiation has fueled its growth in the eyeglass industry.[83]

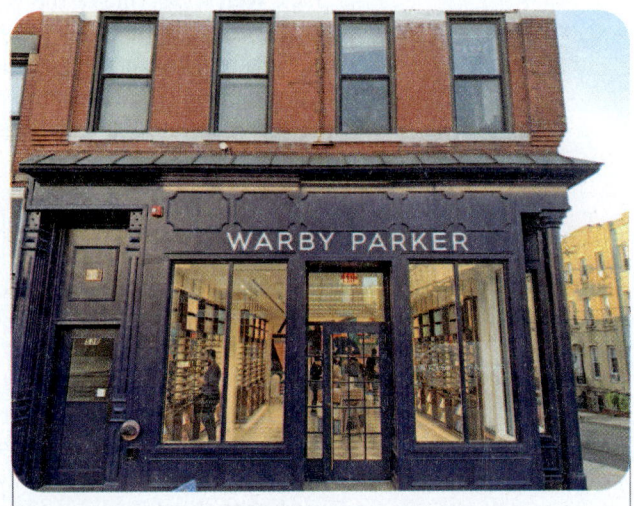

Warby Parker differentiates itself from the competition by offering fashionable eyeglasses at an affordable price. They are also well-known for their outstanding customer service. Dev Chatterjee/Shutterstock

3. Cost-Focus Strategy: Keeping Costs and Prices Low for a Narrow Market
The **cost-focus strategy** is to keep the costs, and hence prices, of a product or service below those of competitors and to target a narrow market.

This is a strategy often executed with low-end products sold in discount stores, such as Aldi, Dollar Tree, and Harbor Freight. Red Box, originally a kiosk-based video rental company, added a low-cost on-demand streaming service. This strategy is keeping the company afloat in the streaming era by offering its cost-conscious customers a more convenient avenue to watch movies.[84]

Needless to say, the pressure on managers to keep costs down in cost-focused companies is even more intense than it is in cost-leadership companies.

4. Focused-Differentiation Strategy: Offering Unique and Superior Value for a Narrow Market
The **focused-differentiation strategy** is to offer products or services that are of unique and superior value compared to those of competitors and to target a narrow market. Viking Cruises represents a good application of this strategy.

> **Focused-Differentiation Strategy Example—Viking:** Viking, founded in 1997, is a river, ocean, and expedition cruise provider based in Basel, Switzerland. Its founder and chair, Torstein Hagen, caters to wealthy, well-educated individuals who are over 55. "I do my market research in the mirror every morning," the 80-year-old jokes. Named both the #1 River Line and #1 Ocean Line by *Travel + Leisure,* Viking's cruises often sell out a year in advance.[85]

Formal strategic planning is essential to evaluate business-level strategies and select the best one for your organization. Research shows that business-level strategies improve firm performance and help organizations achieve sustainability goals.[86] Take Self-Assessment 6.2 in Connect to assess your own strategic planning skills if your instructor has assigned it to you.

SELF-ASSESSMENT 6.2   CAREER READINESS

Core Skills Required for Strategic Planning

This survey is designed to assess the skills needed in strategic planning. Please complete Self-Assessment 6.2 if your instructor has assigned it in Connect.

An Executive's Approach toward Strategy Development

Jack Welch was one of the world's most respected CEOs in the 20th century. During his 21 year tenure as CEO of General Electric (GE), Welch transformed it into the world's most admired and successful company with his innovative approach toward management. The company's revenue grew from $25 billion to $130 billion, and GE's market capitalization increased 30-fold to more than $400 billion under Welch's leadership.[87]

Welch's approach to strategy development was somewhat simplistic but obviously effective. He believed that business strategy should come from identifying a big strategic opportunity, or a clever, achievable, and timely way to gain sustainable competitive advantage. The former CEO created the company's business-level strategies by asking senior executives in GE's 10+ lines of business to answer the following five questions.[88]

What Does the Playing Field Look Like Now?   Managers need to understand who their competitors are, large and small. This includes veterans in the industry and potential new players. Each competitor's strengths and weaknesses should be analyzed (consider using a SWOT analysis, as we discussed in Section 6.3). Customers and buying habits should also be reviewed.

What Has the Competition Been Up To?   Strong competitors are always active. Managers need to understand what each competitor has done in the past year to change the playing field. Are there new products, technologies, or distribution channels that will change the market?

What Have You Been Up To?   In addition to an external analysis, managers also need to analyze what the company has done to change the competitive playing field. Has there been an acquisition, new product, or new technology that can be leveraged? Any lost competitive advantages, such as the departure of a key employee or proprietary technology, should be noted as well.

What's around the Corner?   Managers need to identify what they fear the most in the year ahead. For example, what are some moves a competitor can make that can hurt the company? It's also important to keep an eye out for potential competitors merging or acquiring one another. From an internal perspective, managers need to ensure that top talent is being cared for with competitive pay and perks, as well as an inspiring organizational culture.

What's Your Winning Move?   The final question is based on what the manager wants to do going forward. This includes possible acquisitions, the launch of a new product, securing better talent, or taking advantage of globalization. In the end, managers need to ensure that customers stick with the company more than ever before and more than any other competitor. •

6.6 Strategic Implementation: Creating, Executing, and Controlling Functional-Level Strategies

THE BIG PICTURE
Strategic implementation involves executing and controlling functional-level strategies. A company's overall ability to deliver results is a function of effectively executing according to three processes: people, strategy, and operations. In order for execution to be successful, managers must overcome common roadblocks. Finally, strategic control is necessary to monitor results and make corrections, if necessary.

Step 1 of the strategic-management process establishes an organization's mission, vision, and values. Step 2 assesses the organization's current reality. In step 3 of the process, the organization formulates its corporate, business, and functional strategies and plans. Now we come to the last two steps—step 4, implement the strategies and plans and step 5, maintain strategic control.

We earlier defined strategic implementation as the process of putting strategic plans into effect. Functional-level strategies are the key to successful implementation. We explain the strategic implementation process by first describing functional strategies. Next, we focus on how managers execute strategy through the three core internal processes and then review obstacles to execution. We end by discussing the role of strategic control.

LO 6-6

Describe how to create, execute, and control a functional-level strategy.

Strategic Implementation: Creating, Executing, and Controlling Functional-Level Strategies

A *functional strategy* is a plan of action by each functional area of the organization to support higher-level strategies. In other words, higher-level corporate- and business-level strategies flow down to the functional strategy. This is similar to goal cascading, which ensures that higher-level goals are communicated and aligned with the goals at the next levels down in the organizational hierarchy. (We discussed goal cascading in Chapter 5.) Typical functional areas include marketing, finance, human resources, operations, information technology, and supply chain. Let's look at how supermarket giant Kroger might create functional strategies to support the business-level and corporate-level strategies.

Strategic Implementation Example—Kroger: Kroger's corporate strategy is to invest in technology and innovation to deliver an 8% to 11% return on shareholders' investment.[89] The company targeted its technology/innovation investment in developing AI-powered self-checkouts. Kroger adopted Everseen's Visual Artificial Intelligence (AI) platform to grow sales and reduce loss at the self-checkout. Visual AI analyzes high-resolution video from checkout kiosks in real-time to notify customers when an item failed to scan. The system proceeds to alert a store associate for assistance if the customer is unable to resolve the problem. Kroger deployed AI-powered self-checkouts into more than 1,700 stores as a solution to achieve its in-store division business strategy: to reduce costs and improve customers' experiences. Self-checkouts were quick and convenient, but they caused (1) frustration for customers when barcodes didn't scan correctly and (2) inventory loss when customers failed to scan an item. Functional strategies to support the higher-level strategies might include training supermarket employees on this new system (human resource function),

FIGURE 6.7

An example of strategic implementation at Kroger

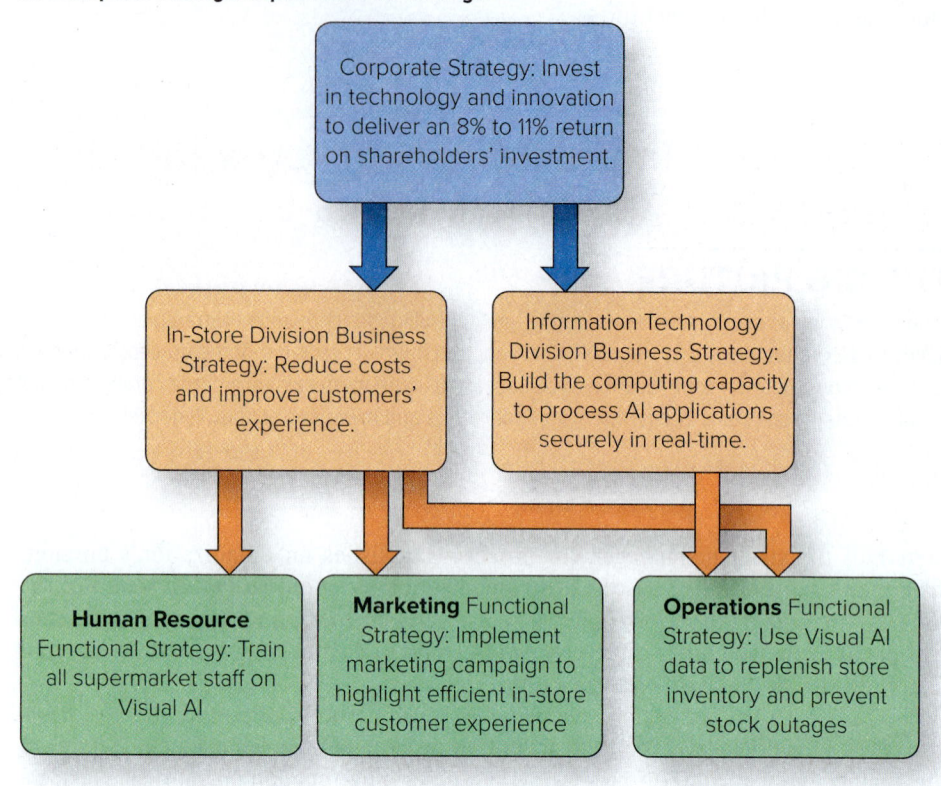

- **Corporate Strategy:** Invest in technology and innovation to deliver an 8% to 11% return on shareholders' investment.
  - **In-Store Division Business Strategy:** Reduce costs and improve customers' experience.
  - **Information Technology Division Business Strategy:** Build the computing capacity to process AI applications securely in real-time.
    - **Human Resource** Functional Strategy: Train all supermarket staff on Visual AI
    - **Marketing** Functional Strategy: Implement marketing campaign to highlight efficient in-store customer experience
    - **Operations** Functional Strategy: Use Visual AI data to replenish store inventory and prevent stock outages

ensuring word gets out about its efficient in-store customer experience (marketing function), and using Visual AI data to replenish store inventory and prevent stock outages (operations function). The new technology is already paying dividends for the company says Chris McCarrick, senior manager of asset protection solutions and technology at Kroger, who noted fewer errors at checkout "gives us a much more accurate view of what stock is going out of the store. This allows us to stay on top of replenishing inventory, which boosts on-shelf availability for customers and ultimately increases our sales."[90]

Figure 6.7 portrays what Kroger's Visual AI strategy may look like across all three strategic levels.

Execution: Getting Things Done

Once management has formulated functional-level strategies, it's time to move forward and get things done. Larry Bossidy, former CEO of AlliedSignal (later Honeywell), and Ram Charan, a business adviser to senior executives, are authors of *Execution: The Discipline of Getting Things Done.*[91] **Execution**, they say, is not simply tactics; it is a central part of any company's strategy. It consists of using questioning, analysis, and follow-through to mesh strategy with reality, align people with goals, and achieve results promised.

How important is execution to organizational success in today's global economy? A survey of more than 400 global CEOs found that their number one challenge was executional excellence. Another study of 8,000 managers, in over 250 companies, found that respondents were three times as likely to miss performance commitments due to insufficient support from colleagues.[92]

The Three Core Processes of Business: People, Strategy, and Operations

A company's overall ability to execute is a function of effectively managing three processes: *people, strategy,* and *operations*.[93] Because all work ultimately entails some human interaction, effort, or involvement, Bossidy and Charan believe that the *people* process is the most important. We'll illustrate each of these three processes by circling back to Kroger's plan for AI-powered self-checkouts.

The First Core Process—People: "You Need to Consider Who Will Benefit You in the Future"
"If you don't get the people process right," say Bossidy and Charan, "you will never fulfill the potential of your business." But today, most organizations focus on evaluating the jobs people are doing at present rather than considering which individuals can handle the jobs of the future. An effective leader tries to evaluate talent by linking people to particular strategic milestones, developing future leaders, dealing with nonperformers, and transforming the mission and operations of the human resource department.

> **People Example—Kroger:** Kroger needs the right people in the right positions if it wants to successfully launch AI-powered self-checkouts. For its human resource functional strategy, this means training existing clerks on the new technology so they trust its capabilities, respond quickly to its notifications, and allocate more time to keeping store shelves fully stocked.

The Second Core Process—Strategy: "You Need to Consider How Success Will Be Accomplished"
In most organizations, the strategies developed fail to consider the "how" of execution. In considering how the organization can execute the strategy, a leader must take a realistic and critical view of its capabilities and competencies. If it does not have the resources financially, technologically, and operationally to accomplish the vision, chances of success are drastically reduced.

> **Strategy Example—Kroger:** Kroger's AI-powered self-checkouts are being deployed at more grocery stores to reduce inventory loss and improve customers' in-store experience. With the technological capabilities in place, the company needs to entice customers to shop in store and experience the benefits of the innovative new process. For its marketing functional strategy, this includes advertising stocked shelves along with a quicker, more seamless self-checkout experience.

The Third Core Process—Operations: "You Need to Consider What Path Will Be Followed"
The strategy process defines where an organization wants to go, and the people process defines who's going to get it done. The third core process, operations, or the operating plan, provides the path for people to follow. The operating plan, described in Chapter 5, should address all the major activities in which the company will engage—marketing, production, sales, revenue, and so on—and then define short-term objectives for these activities to provide targets for people to aim for. We also discuss operations management in Chapter 16.

> **Operations Example—Kroger:** Kroger needs to leverage Visual AI data to improve its inventory management. For its operations functional strategy, this includes integrating the new technology with each store's inventory management system to ensure adequate product is delivered from Kroger's distribution centers to keep their shelves fully stocked.

By linking people, strategy, and operating plans, execution allows executives to direct and control the three core processes that will advance their strategic vision.

Execution Roadblocks

Execution doesn't always go smoothly. Managers may face obstacles to strategic implementation for many different reasons. Consider the following four roadblocks:

1. **Misaligned organizational culture.** Organizational culture is a system of shared values and beliefs within an organization that guides the behavior of its members. Effective execution is hampered when an organization's culture is misaligned with its strategies.[94] Renowned management expert Peter Drucker coined a slogan to reflect the importance of this alignment. He said, "culture eats strategy for breakfast." (Chapter 8 presents 12 ways managers can attempt to create an execution-oriented culture).[95]

2. **Poor performance management leadership.** Performance management is a set of activities designed to assess and improve employee performance as a means to improve organizational performance.[96] It includes a range of activities such as goal setting, providing feedback, coaching, communicating, and rewarding performance. Unfortunately, ineffective performance management behaviors are all too common. According to data from Gallup's international database containing more than 60 million employee responses, only 14% of employees believed that their company's performance management process inspired them to improve.[97] This sobering statistic suggests that organizations might consider leadership training to improve strategic implementation.

3. **Conflicting functional objectives.** Marketing's objective to appeal to customers by designing the most interesting and attractive product packaging may be at odds with manufacturing's goal to reduce materials costs and increase production-related efficiencies. Conflicting functional objectives cause departments to work against each other rather than toward a common goal. Effective execution occurs when departments' goals are aligned through the process of goal cascading.

4. **Employees' resistance to change.** Employees resist executing strategic plans when they feel the plans threaten their influence or livelihood. Signs of employee resistance to change include emotions like fear and anxiety or behaviors like disengagement and procrastination. Thus, top managers can't just announce strategic plans; they have to actively sell them to middle and supervisory managers. Winning employees' buy-in is the key to them accepting and participating in change efforts.[98]

Regardless of where the roadblock appears, research shows that initial obstacles can snowball and create bigger challenges that are even more difficult to overcome if they are not dealt with at the outset.[99] Self-Assessment 6.3 assesses five common obstacles to strategic execution. If your instructor has assigned it to you, take the assessment in Connect to evaluate your employer's proficiency at strategic execution.

SELF-ASSESSMENT 6.3

Assessing the Obstacles to Strategic Execution

This survey is designed to assess the obstacles to strategic execution that may be impacting an organization's ability to execute. Please complete Self-Assessment 6.3 if your instructor has assigned it in Connect.

Maintaining Strategic Control

The final step in the strategic-management process is maintaining strategic control. *Strategic control* consists of monitoring strategic implementation and taking appropriate action based on results. The planning/control cycle introduced in Chapter 5 (see Figure 6.8) is used for this purpose. Strategies are formulated and implemented in the planning

FIGURE 6.8
The planning/control cycle

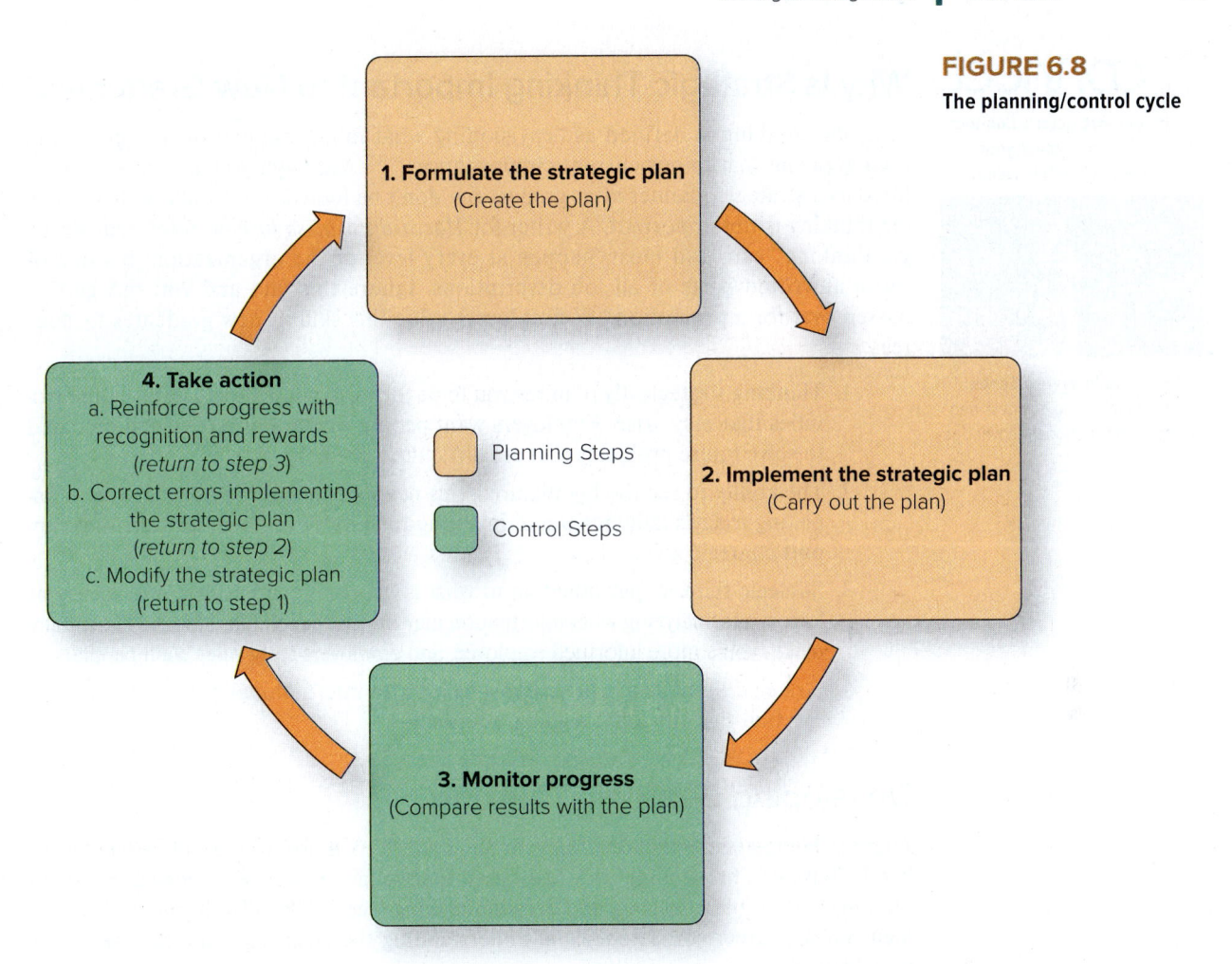

1. **Formulate the strategic plan** (Create the plan)

2. **Implement the strategic plan** (Carry out the plan)

3. **Monitor progress** (Compare results with the plan)

4. **Take action**
   a. Reinforce progress with recognition and rewards (*return to step 3*)
   b. Correct errors implementing the strategic plan (*return to step 2*)
   c. Modify the strategic plan (*return to step 1*)

Planning Steps
Control Steps

phase and progress is monitored and evaluated in the control phase. Bossidy and Charan recommend that managers meet on a regular basis to review the status of actual performance to desired goals. Dr. K follows this advice with his clients by encouraging them to meet on a monthly basis to discuss which goals are being met, exceeded, or underachieved. These meetings should be interactive, collaborative, and future focused.

Many practical tools exist to evaluate activities related to strategic implementation. Strategic control may take many forms, including strategic dashboards, budgets to monitor and control financial expenditures, and total quality management. We discuss these and other control mechanisms in Chapter 16. •

6.7 Career Corner: Managing Your Career Readiness

Strategic thinking is not one of the competencies in the career readiness model shown in Figure 6.9. The reason is because other, more specific, competencies drive your ability to think strategically. Four career readiness competencies drive your ability to think strategically (see Figure 6.9): understanding the business, task-based functional knowledge, critical thinking/problem solving, and decision making. Don't take our word for it. Listen to what the executives in this chapter's Executive Interview Series video say about how gaining knowledge about your job and the organization as a whole improve your strategic thinking and increase the value you add to your current or prospective employer.

LO 6-7
Describe how to enhance your strategic thinking.

Visit your instructor's Connect course and access your eBook to view this video.

Executive Interview Series:
Understanding the Business and Task-Based Functional Knowledge

Why Is Strategic Thinking Important to New Graduates?

Strategic thinking is defined as "envisioning what might happen in the future and then applying that to our current circumstances."[100] Although you are unlikely to be hired as a strategic planner after graduation, don't be fooled into thinking that strategic thinking is not important. A writer for *Harvard Business Review* noted that strategic thinking "can, and must, happen at every level of the organization; it's one of those unwritten parts of all job descriptions. Ignore this fact and you risk getting passed over for a promotion."[101] Employers value this skill in new graduates for four reasons.[102]

1. Thinking strategically requires you to be forward-looking and alert for opportunities that may arise. Employers want people who are proactive and prepared to solve future problems that are difficult to predict.

2. The ability to see the big picture helps people connect the dots between completing today's daily tasks and investing time in longer-term projects that support strategic goals.

3. Strategic thinkers pay attention to what is happening in business and society at large while analyzing what information may or not be credible. This skill essentially makes you a more informed employee, and employers truly value such people.

4. Strategic thinkers are more likely to have an international perspective, an orientation that fits today's global economy.

Developing Strategic Thinking

Four key competencies will develop your ability to think more strategically: understanding the business, broadening your task-based functional knowledge, engaging in critical thinking and problem solving, and decision making (see Figure 6.9). In this section, we focus on the career competencies of understanding the business and task-based functional knowledge.

Understand the Business This career readiness competency reflects the extent to which you understand a potential or current employer's business and strategies. This can be learned by studying a company's web page and annual report. You can look for any published SWOT analyses on a company or conduct one on your own.[103]

Once you are hired, you can extend your knowledge by networking with current employees, proactively seeking mentoring from experienced employees, participating in a job rotation program, and attending as many cross-functional or business meetings as possible.[104] The more you understand the business, the more you'll be able to align what you are doing internally to changes in the external environment. In fact, research confirms that organizations employing continuous alignment can enjoy up to 15% annual growth, compared to competitors.[105] You also might consider joining industry groups or other professional associations affiliated with the type of work you are doing.[106]

Broaden Your Task-Based Functional Knowledge Strategic thinking requires making connections between concepts, ideas, people, and events. The more ideas and experiences you have, the greater the ability to make connections. For example, international travel has enhanced our understanding about the nuances of cross-cultural behavior, which in turn has helped in writing about cross-cultural management. Make it a goal to try new things, visit new places, meet new people, and read about new topics. All of these activities will stimulate your mind and expand your base of knowledge.

FIGURE 6.9
Career readiness competencies

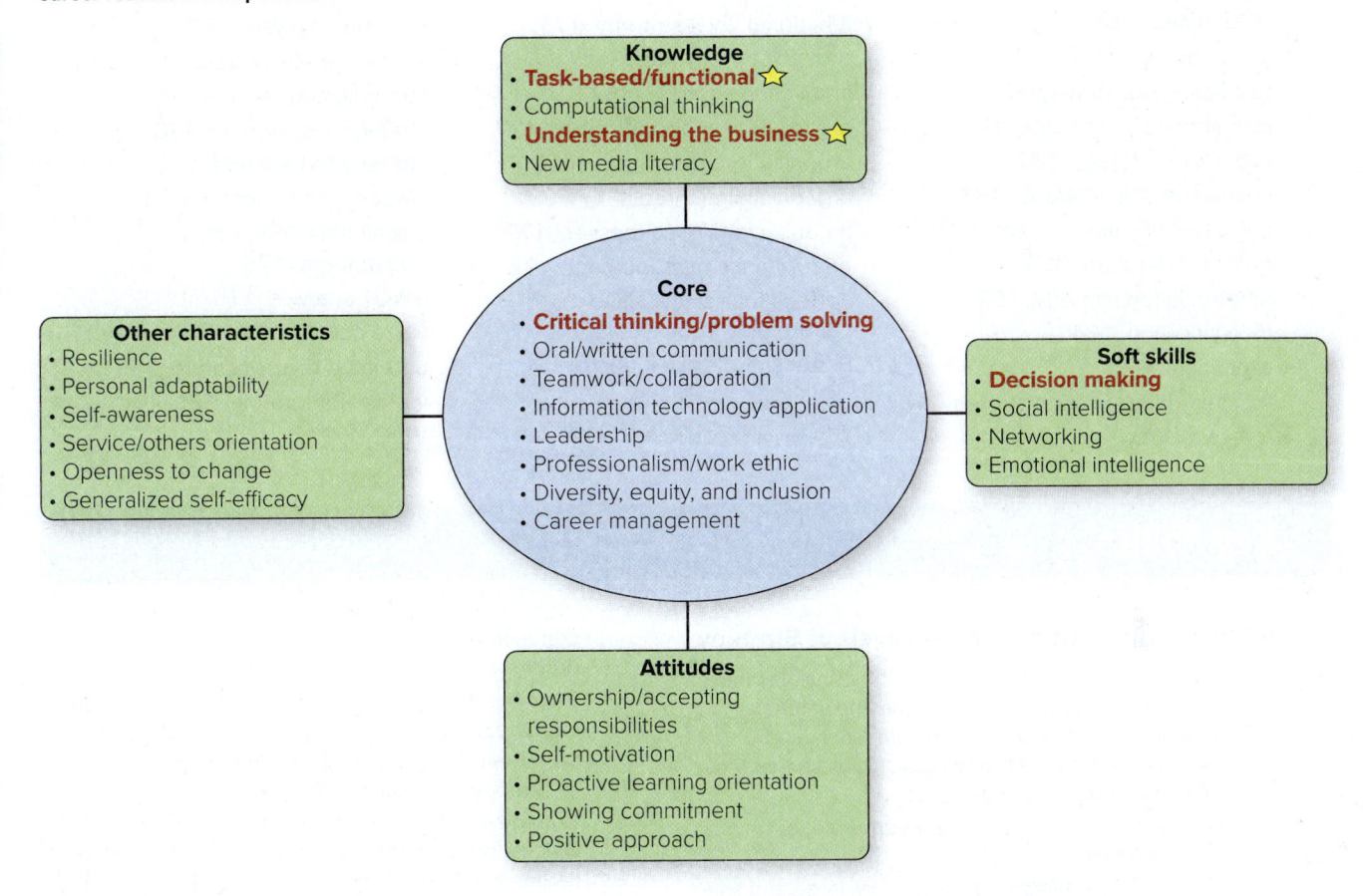

Knowledge
- **Task-based/functional** ⭐
- Computational thinking
- **Understanding the business** ⭐
- New media literacy

Other characteristics
- Resilience
- Personal adaptability
- Self-awareness
- Service/others orientation
- Openness to change
- Generalized self-efficacy

Core
- **Critical thinking/problem solving**
- Oral/written communication
- Teamwork/collaboration
- Information technology application
- Leadership
- Professionalism/work ethic
- Diversity, equity, and inclusion
- Career management

Soft skills
- **Decision making**
- Social intelligence
- Networking
- Emotional intelligence

Attitudes
- Ownership/accepting responsibilities
- Self-motivation
- Proactive learning orientation
- Showing commitment
- Positive approach

Some experts suggest that strategic thinkers have a knowledge base that represents a "T." The top of the "T" reflects your breadth of knowledge and the stem reflects the depth of understanding about your primary area of expertise.[107] So in addition to broadening your knowledge and experiences, dive deeper by learning about the finer aspects of your employer's industry. Here again, it would be useful to attend industry or functional conferences. The goal of doing this is twofold: learn about the industry and network. •

Key Terms Used in This Chapter

BCG matrix 182
benchmarking 180
business-level strategy 171
corporate-level strategy 171
cost-focus strategy 187
cost-leadership strategy 187
current reality assessment 173
defensive strategy 182
differentiation strategy 187
diversification 184
execution 190
focused-differentiation strategy 187
forecast 179
functional-level strategy 171
growth strategy 182
innovation strategy 182
organizational opportunities 177
organizational strengths 177
organizational threats 177
organizational weaknesses 177
performance management 192
Porter's four competitive strategies 186
Porter's model for industry analysis 185
related diversification 184
scenario analysis 180
stability strategy 182
strategic control 174
strategic positioning 170
strategy formulation 174
strategy implementation 174
sustainable competitive advantage 175
SWOT analysis 175
trend analysis 179
unrelated diversification 185
vertical integration 185
VRIO 177

Key Points

6.1 Strategic Positioning and Levels of Strategy

- Strategic positioning is based on the principles that strategy is the creation of a unique and valuable position, requires trade-offs in competing, and involves creating a "fit" among activities so that they interact and reinforce each other.
- The three levels of strategy are corporate, business, and functional.
- Strategic management works for both large and small firms.

6.2 The Strategic-Management Process

- The strategic-management process has five steps plus a feedback loop.
- Step 1 is to establish the mission, vision, and values statements. The mission statement expresses the organization's purpose or reason for being. The vision statement states what the organization wants to become and where it wants to go strategically. The values statement describes what the organization stands for, its core priorities, the values its employees embody, and what its products contribute to the world.
- Step 2 is to do a current reality assessment, to look at where the organization stands and see what is working and what could be different so as to maximize efficiency and effectiveness in achieving the organization's mission. Among the tools for assessing the current reality are SWOT analysis, VRIO analysis, forecasting, and benchmarking.
- Step 3 is to formulate corporate, business, and functional strategies. This means translating the company's broad mission and vision statements into a corporate strategy, which, after the assessment of the current reality, explains how the organization's mission is to be accomplished. Three common grand strategies are growth, stability, and defensive.
- Step 4 is strategy execution—putting strategic plans into effect.
- Step 5 is strategic control, monitoring the execution of strategy and making adjustments.
- Corrective action constitutes a feedback loop in which a problem requires that managers return to an earlier step to rethink policies, budgets, or personnel arrangements.

6.3 Assessing the Current Reality

- Step 2 in the strategic-management process, assess the current reality, looks at where the organization stands internally and externally—to determine what's working and what's not, to see what can be changed so as to increase efficiency and effectiveness in achieving the organization's vision.
- Among the tools for assessing the current reality are SWOT analysis, VRIO analysis, forecasting, and benchmarking.
- In SWOT, organizational strengths are the skills and capabilities that give the organization special competencies and competitive advantages. Organizational weaknesses are the drawbacks that hinder an organization in executing strategies. Organizational opportunities are environmental factors that the organization may exploit for competitive advantage. Organizational threats are environmental factors that hinder an organization's achieving a competitive advantage.
- VRIO is a framework for analyzing a resource or capability to determine its competitive strategic potential by answering four questions about its value, rarity, imitability, and organization.
- Forecasting is another tool for assessing current reality. Two types of forecasting are (1) trend analysis,

a hypothetical extension of a past series of events into the future, and (2) scenario analysis, the creation of alternative hypothetical but equally likely future conditions.
- Benchmarking is a process by which a company compares its performance with that of high-performing organizations.

6.4 Establishing Corporate-Level Strategy

- Three common corporate-level strategies are (1) a growth strategy involving expansion—as in sales revenues or market share—and one form of growth strategy is an innovation strategy, growing market share or profits by innovating improvements in products or services; (2) a stability strategy, which involves little or no significant change; and (3) a defensive strategy, which involves reduction in the organization's efforts.
- The BCG matrix is a means of evaluating strategic business units on the basis of (1) their business growth rates and (2) their share of the market. In general, organizations do better in fast-growing markets in which they have a high market share rather than slow-growing markets in which they have low market shares.
- A diversification strategy pertains to deciding whether to expand or grow into other businesses. There are two types of diversification strategies: related and unrelated diversification.

6.5 Establishing Business-Level Strategy

- Formulating the business-level strategy makes use of Porter's five competitive forces and his four competitive strategies.
- Porter's model for industry analysis suggests that business-level strategies originate in five primary competitive forces in the firm's environment: (1) threats of new entrants, (2) bargaining power of suppliers, (3) bargaining power of buyers, (4) threats of substitute products or services, and (5) rivalry among competitors.
- Porter's four competitive strategies are as follows: (1) The cost-leadership strategy is to keep the costs, and hence the prices, of a product or service below those of competitors and to target a wide market.

(2) The differentiation strategy is to offer products or services that are of unique and superior value compared with those of competitors and to target a wide market. (3) The cost-focus strategy is to keep the costs and hence prices of a product or service below those of competitors and to target a narrow market. (4) The focused-differentiation strategy is to offer products or services that are of unique and superior value compared with those of competitors and to target a narrow market.
- Jack Welch's questions for developing business-level strategy include: (1) What does the playing field look like now? (2) What has the competition been up to? (3) What have you been up to? (4) What's around the corner? (5) What's your winning move?

6.6 Strategic Implementation: Creating, Executing, and Controlling Functional-Level Strategies

- Strategic implementation is the process of putting strategic plans into effect.
- A functional strategy is a plan of action by each functional area of the organization to support higher-level strategies.
- Execution is not simply tactics; it is a central part of any company's strategy. Execution consists of using questioning, analysis, and follow-through to mesh strategy with reality, align people with goals, and achieve results promised.
- Three core processes of execution are people, strategy, and operations.
- Execution roadblocks can occur for four reasons: (1) misaligned organizational culture, (2) poor performance management leadership, (3) conflicting functional objectives, and (4) employees' resistance to change.
- Strategic control consists of monitoring the execution of strategy and taking corrective action, if necessary.

6.7 Career Corner: Managing Your Career Readiness

- Four career readiness competencies—understanding the business, task-based functional knowledge, critical thinking/problem solving, and decision making—drive your ability to think strategically.

LEARNING MODULE 2

Entrepreneurship

After reading this learning module, you should be able to:

LM 2-1   Define entrepreneurship and discuss its importance across the world.

LM 2-2   Identify how entrepreneurs get started.

MANAGE U

So You Want to Start a Business?

We would not be surprised if you answered yes, given the data shown in Figure LM 2.1. You can see that the number of start-ups has been growing since 2012, particularly in the last few years. Nearly 1.4 million businesses were established in the United States in 2021, up approximately 61% from 2011.[1] Businesses have also been exiting, which occurs when an establishment goes from having one employee to having none, and the business remains closed for one year. While the number of exits jumped during the peak of COVID-19 in 2020, small business start-ups have significantly outpaced exits in 2021 according to the Small Business Association's 2022 *Small Business Report*.[2]

Speaking from experience, we can tell you that owning your own business can be highly rewarding, but it's no picnic and requires perseverance and lots of hard work. As Biz Stone, co-founder of Twitter noted, "Timing, perseverance, and ten years of trying will eventually make you look like an overnight success."[3] Still interested in starting your own business?

FIGURE LM 2.1
Business start-ups and exits in the United States

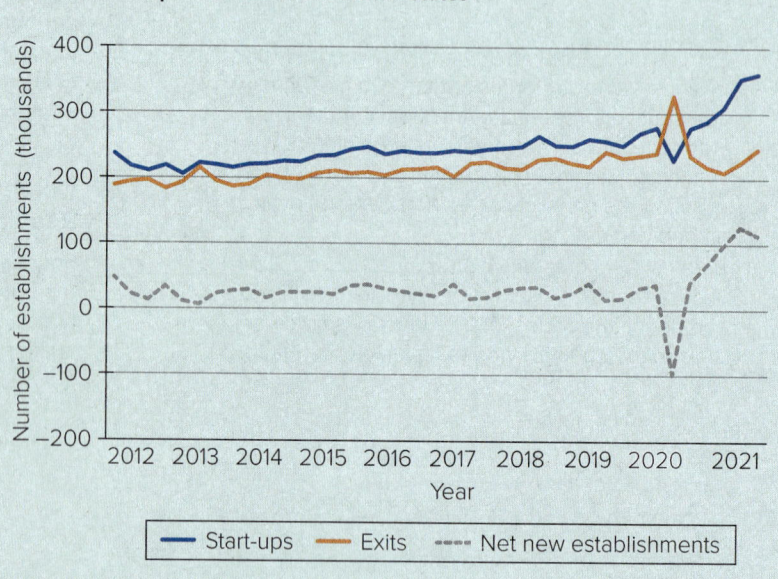

Source: "Economic News Release: Private Sector Establishment Births and Deaths, Seasonally Adjusted," U.S. Bureau of Labor Statistics, https://www.bls.gov/news.release/cewbd.t08.htm (accessed February 8, 2023).

Below are four issues to consider before your launch your business:[4]

1. Identify Your Motives
What do you hope to accomplish by starting a business? Be specific about what you want and stay open to change. For example, when one of your authors, Dr. K, began his consulting activities, he started with the goal of running a sole proprietorship while keeping his job at the university. This goal changed, as did the business decisions, when he and his wife, Joyce, decided to convert their business to a corporation. Joyce quit her job and served as president, running the company. Dr. K took a leave of absence from his university job. They grew the business to about nine employees and traveled around the world, but they realized they were unhappy and needed a change. After parting with all but one employee, Angelo went back to the university and Joyce continued to run the business. The business continued to operate through today, and everybody is happy.

2. Test Your Ideas
Successful founders intricately understand the needs and desires of their prospective customers.[5] If you are currently working and have a business idea, test it with potential clients before quitting your job. After all, your business idea won't work if you can't find people who want your product or service. Consider providing your product or service for free until you fine tune your product/service and build up market interest. A friend of Dr. K's is doing this as she attempts to market a new app. Her plan is to give it away, create demand, and then charge a nominal amount.

3. Surround Yourself with the Right People
Consider what Steve Jobs, co-founder of Apple, had to say about hiring the right people. "When you're in a start-up, the first ten people will determine whether the company succeeds or not. Each is ten percent of the company. So why wouldn't you take as much time as necessary to find all A-players?" We couldn't agree more. Hire people who complement your skills and abilities. Don't make the mistake of hiring only friends and family. Though these individuals may share your vision or agree to work for lower salaries, you need to have people on the team with the appropriate skill set, work ethic, and experience to make the venture a success.

4. Learn the Basics of Accounting
All owners need to understand financial statements. These tools are discussed in Chapter 16. For now, recognize the need to understand how to create and adhere to a budget and how to read a balance sheet and income statement. We also encourage you to hire a good accountant. And yes, those Introduction to Accounting courses are important!

For Discussion What excites you about the opportunity of starting a business, and what fears get in the way of your doing so? Explain.

FORECAST   *What's Ahead in This Learning Module*

This learning module discusses what entrepreneurship is, its role in the economy, and how entrepreneurs start new businesses. We begin by defining entrepreneurship and social entrepreneurship, with an emphasis on describing entrepreneurial orientation and entrepreneurs' impact around the world. We then explore the process of starting a new business or franchise. We review the basics of writing a business plan, choosing an appropriate legal structure, obtaining financing, and creating the "right" type of organizational culture and design. We conclude by discussing some of the reasons businesses fail.

2.1 Entrepreneurship: Its Foundations and Importance

THE BIG PICTURE

This section discusses entrepreneurship's foundations and its importance for society. Entrepreneurship means taking risks to create a new enterprise. Social entrepreneurship is a specific form of entrepreneurship that identifies, develops, funds, and pursues solutions to social issues. Entrepreneurs share common characteristics and have an important role in society.

LM 2-1

Define *entrepreneurship* and discuss its importance across the world.

Innovative. Trend-setting. Forward-thinking. Entrepreneurs are the movers and shakers in business around the world. They are individuals who start with an idea. Whether big or small, entrepreneurs develop their ideas and turn them into impactful products or services via hard work and entrepreneurial thinking.

Shark Tank is a popular reality show in which aspiring entrepreneurs pitch their products or services to five sharks—wealthy and successful entrepreneurs—to earn funding and additional resources to grow their business. Imagine you are in the hallway waiting for the closed double doors to open when you will have your long-awaited opportunity to pitch your product/service idea to the sharks. What questions should you anticipate from the sharks? How should you respond? This chapter will provide a basic framework for you to put your best foot forward and make the most of your moment in the Shark Tank.

This section lays the foundation for entrepreneurship by defining entrepreneurship and explaining how it is different from self-employment. We then discuss social entrepreneurship. Finally, we examine research on entrepreneurial characteristics and conclude by exploring why entrepreneurship is important around the world.

Shark Tank is a reality show for aspiring entrepreneurs to pitch their ideas and earn funding from five sharks. The five sharks pictured here (from left to right) are Robert Herjavec, Barbara Corcoran, Mark Cuban, Lori Greiner, and Kevin O'Leary.
Shutterstock/Kathy Hutchins

Entrepreneurship: It's Not the Same as Self-Employment

The number of small businesses in the United States totaled 32.5 million in 2022. Even more staggering, 99.9% of all U.S. businesses are small businesses.[6] Most small businesses originate with entrepreneurs, the people with the idea, the risk takers. The most successful entrepreneurs become wealthy and make the covers of business magazines: Oprah Winfrey (Harpo Productions); Jack Dorsey (Twitter); Larry Page and Sergey Brin (Google). Failed entrepreneurs may benefit from the experience to return and fight another day—as did J.K. Rowling, author of the Harry Potter series. Rowling's first Harry Potter book was rejected from twelve publishing houses before she found one who agreed to publish it.[7]

What Is Entrepreneurship? Although many definitions have been proposed, Harvard Business School simply defines **entrepreneurship** as "the pursuit of opportunity beyond resources controlled."[8] In other words, entrepreneurship involves risks to pursue novel business opportunities. Entrepreneurship can take place while leading a company or as an employee of a company.

- An **entrepreneur** is someone who identifies a business opportunity and takes the risk of creating or running an independent business to exploit the business opportunity.[9] Entrepreneurs start new businesses or lead an existing one because they perceive an opportunity to introduce, change, or transform a product or service to meet an unmet marketplace need. Steve Jobs, for example, saw an opportunity to meet a consumer need when his company invented the iPod and iPhone, innovations that merged technology, design, and convenience with commonly used products like portable music players and cellular phones.

- An **intrapreneur** is an employee working inside an existing organization who identifies a business opportunity and mobilizes the organization's resources to exploit the idea for their company.[10] This person might be a researcher or a scientist but could also be a manager who sees an opportunity to create a new product, process, service, or venture that might be profitable for their company. Research shows that intrapreneurship pays dividends through increasing a firm's business growth, innovation, performance, and value creation.[11]

How Is Entrepreneurship Different from Self-Employment? Entrepreneurs and self-employed individuals share the commonality of running a business, but they execute this role in very different ways. Let's explore these similarities and differences, starting with a definition of self-employment.

Self-employment is a way of working for yourself "as a freelancer or the owner of a business rather than for an employer."[12] As textbook writers, we are self-employed. We work for ourselves and hire contractors to help get things done. The same is true for many doctors, lawyers, accountants, insurance agents, electricians, and general contractors. Self-employed people are frequently experts in their fields and recognized members of their communities. They rely on their individual reputation and abilities to sustain their business. In contrast, entrepreneurs take financial risks to pursue innovation and business growth. As a result, entrepreneurs are much more likely to look to the sharks in the Shark Tank for financial resources to grow their business than are self-employed people. Table LM 2.1 summarizes the differences between self-employed people and entrepreneurs according to five categories: employees, risk, mindset, legal structure, and market scope.

TABLE LM 2.1 What's the Difference Between Being Self-Employed and Being An Entrepreneur?

	SELF-EMPLOYED PEOPLE...	**ENTREPRENEURS...**
EMPLOYEES	primarily rely on their own expertise but hire contractors as needed to get things done.	build a business by hiring employees and working with them to achieve the vision.
RISK	are generally risk-averse. They generally stay within their resource constraints.	take risks and seek external financing to grow the business.
MINDSET	focus on the short term and save costs to maximize profits.	focus on the long term and aren't afraid to invest significant sums of money to develop products and services.
LEGAL STRUCTURE	usually set up their business as a sole proprietorship.	usually have loftier aspirations for their business and set it up as a corporation.
MARKET SCOPE	target a specific geographic market.	target a national or international market to increase their business' revenue, profit, and market share.

Social Entrepreneurship

Social entrepreneurship combines entrepreneurship with a social mission. It identifies and pursues business opportunities to benefit society.[13] Social entrepreneurship can take shape in multiple ways. Table LM 2.2 summarizes five types of organizations that span the domain of social entrepreneurship. As shown in the table, social entrepreneurship differs based on the centrality of social goals and the purpose of profits to an organization. At the extremes, nonprofits exist exclusively to "do good" by providing a social service without regard to profit. For-profit businesses, in contrast, exist primarily to grow the business or maximize profit but engage with social causes as a means to fulfill their social responsibility or to further increase revenue by improving the company's reputation and employees' commitment to the organization. As a result, these businesses "do well financially by doing good."

Today, more than 50% of new and established entrepreneurs report considering social and environmental implications when making business decisions, according to the Global Entrepreneurship Monitor.[14] Why is social entrepreneurship becoming so popular? The answer may be related to corporate social responsibility (discussed in Chapter 3) and Porter's notion of *shared value* (discussed in Learning Module 1). As you may recall,

TABLE LM 2.2 Five Types of Social Entrepreneurship Organizations

TYPE OF ORGANIZATION	CENTRALITY OF SOCIAL GOALS	PURPOSE OF PROFITS	EXAMPLE
Nonprofits or non-governmental organizations (NGOs)	Organization's goals are exclusively social.	Organization does not make a profit because it doesn't sell its goods or services. "Do good."	Lighthouse Family Retreat is a faith-based nonprofit that offers all-expenses paid weeklong retreats to families with a child diagnosed with and receiving treatment for cancer. The organization relies on financial donations and volunteers to deliver its services to families in need.
Co-operatives	Organization's goals are exclusively social.	Organization directs profits to social benefit or reinvests them in the organization. "Do good."	Oneota Community Food Cooperative exists to buy organic products at lower prices or increase the range of organic product offerings for its members. The Co-op either reinvests profits to expand its services to its members or distributes profits back to its members through a dividend.
Social purpose business	Organization's goals are primarily, but not exclusively, social.	Organization directs profits to social benefit, reinvest in the organization, and then, as necessary, distribute to financial stakeholders. "Do more good by doing well."	Outdoor adventure outfitter, Cotopaxi, sells durable, ethically sourced, and sustainably produced gear with the purpose of fighting poverty and inequality especially in Latin American communities. In 2021, founder and CEO, Davis Smith, sought private equity investment from Bain Capital Double Impact to accelerate his efforts to build a billion-dollar business so Cotopaxi can have a bigger humanitarian impact.
Socially responsible business; B Corporation; public-benefit corporation	Organization's goals include social goals that are as important as other goals.	Organization directs profits to both social benefit and financial stakeholders. "Do good and do well."	Insurance provider, Lemonade, was founded to "make insurance a social good." The company is structured to benefit employees and create a positive social and environmental impact. Lemonade's Giveback program donates up to 40% of policyholders' premiums to a charity of their choice when they don't make a claim.
For-profit business	Organization's goals include social goals but they are less important than other goals.	Organization primarily directs profits to financial stakeholders and donates a portion of profit to social benefit. "Do well financially by doing good."	Bank of America matches up to $5,000 per year of an employee's donation to a charitable organization. It also funds nonprofits serving low-income communities through its charitable foundation. These social goals improve the company's reputation and employee satisfaction but are not central to the publicly owned company's core priorities.

Source: Based on A.M. Peredo and M. McLean, "Social Entrepreneurship: A Critical Review of the Concept," *Journal of World Business*, Vol. 41 (2006), pp. 56–65. Also see "ABOUT US," Lighthouse, https://www.lighthousefamilyretreat.org/about (accessed February 10, 2023); B. Pardee, "A Profitable Cooperative?" Oneota Cooperative, https://oneotacoop.com/scoop/a-profitable-cooperative/#:~:text=That%20is%2C%20when%20the%20Co (accessed February 10, 2023); "About Us," Cotopaxi, https://www.cotopaxi.com/pages/about-us?utm_source=google&utm_medium=cpc&utm_campaign=15137072837&utm_creative=642064760616&utm_placement=&utm_adposition=&utm_keyword=cotopaxi&gclid=CjwKCAiA0JKfBhBlEiwAPhZXDxVno1apA1Bdif96jAFoGqKfrrKkXGliuM7KEKGxO91WfY62Yb7mPxoCCPwQAvD_BwE (accessed February 10, 2023); E. Smith, "Cotopaxi CEO Outlines Goal to Become Billion-Dollar Brand," *Outside Online*, September 24, 2021, https://www.outsideonline.com/business-journal/brands/cotopaxi-ceo-outlines-goal-to-become-billion-dollar-brand/; "The B Corporation, Explained," Lemonade Blog, https://www.lemonade.com/blog/the-b-corporation-explained/ (accessed February 10, 2023); "Matching Gift Program & Employee Giving from Bank of America," Bank of America, https://about.bankofamerica.com/en/making-an-impact/matching-gifts-features-and-eligibility (accessed February 10, 2023).

shared value focuses on identifying and expanding the connections between societal and economic progress.[15] To Porter, the concept of shared value presents an opportunity for businesses to meet customers' social needs while generating revenue. Businesses that don't fulfill these needs risk being left behind.[16] In support, a survey of 8,000 consumers in eight global markets revealed 70% of Gen Z and Millennials believed a company's brand should have a purpose they personally believe in. But be careful. Taking a social stand can be a double-edged sword. 92% of Gen Zers and 90% of Millennials reported they would act in support of a purposeful brand they agreed with. On the flip side, 88% and 85% of Gen Zers and Millennials, respectively, would switch to a competitor, stop buying, or discourage others from buying a brand that supported a purpose they disagreed with.[17]

Though social entrepreneurs typically make a profit, they measure success by another metric—the positive impact they make in the community in the long run.[18] A recent study confirms that social entrepreneurship plays an especially important role in making today's world more equitable and sustainable.[19]

A nonprofit food pantry is an example of one type of a social entrepreneurship organization that directly benefits society by distributing food to those in need. SteveDebenport/E+/Getty Images

Characteristics of Entrepreneurs

What's the difference between an entrepreneur and a manager? An entrepreneur is driven to *start* a business; a manager is motivated to *grow or maintain* a business. Do you think being an entrepreneur and being a manager require different skills? Researchers address this question by comparing managers' and entrepreneurs' personal characteristics. Their answer is yes, the jobs require different traits, skills, and abilities. If you watch a couple episodes of *Shark Tank,* you'll quickly see that the sharks are looking for individuals who exhibit entrepreneurial characteristics. Although the list of entrepreneurial characteristics is extensive, we've reduced them to seven characteristics believed to be the most important. We organize them into three categories: entrepreneurial mindset, entrepreneurial orientation, and entrepreneurial confidence (see Figure LM 2.2).[20]

FIGURE LM 2.2
Research-based characteristics of entrepreneurs

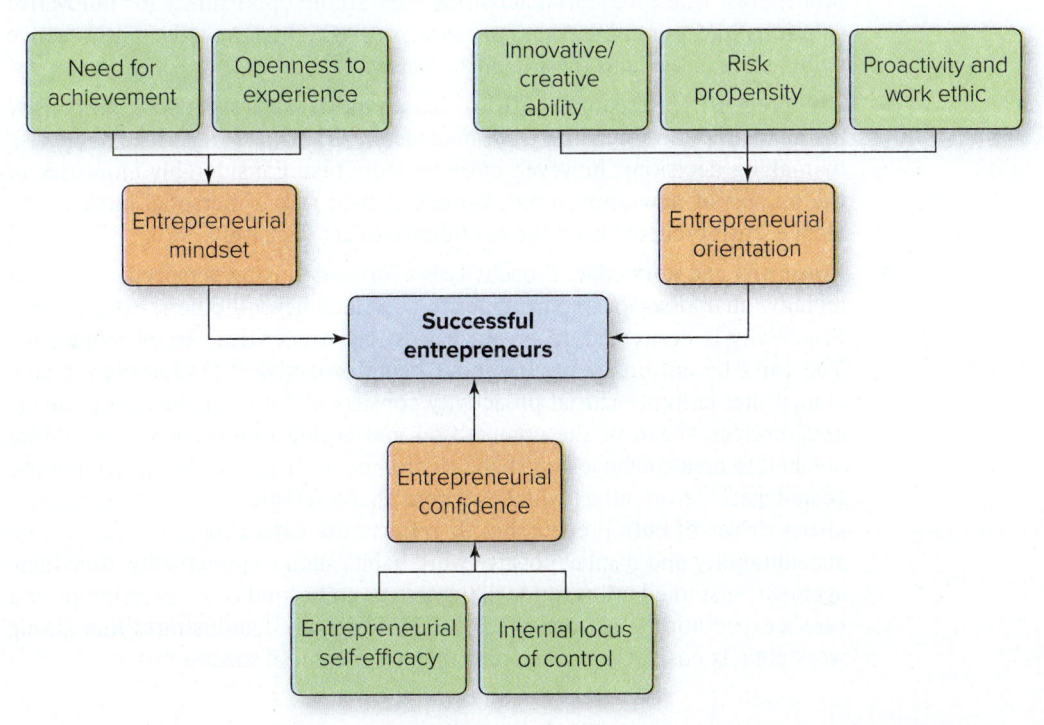

Entrepreneurial Mindset

Entrepreneurial mindset reflects an individual's adaptive ability to continuously gather information and make decisions in a complex, uncertain, and dynamic environment.[21] It describes how entrepreneurs think. An entrepreneurial mindset is fueled by two attributes: need for achievement and openness to experience.

- **Need for achievement.** Entrepreneurs are driven to attain excellence. This internal drive motivates them to take risks, accomplish goals, and devise better solutions to problems.[22] High need for achievement individuals are drawn to environments in which success is more likely to be a result of their own efforts than an employer's resources or constraints. As a result, entrepreneurs have a higher need for achievement than managers.[23] A meta-analysis of 41 studies concluded individuals who pursue entrepreneurial careers have a significantly higher need for achievement than those who chose other types of careers.[24]

- **Openness to experience.** Openness to experience describes individuals who are imaginative, curious, and broad-minded. It is one of the the Big Five characteristics that psychologists have concluded define the core of our personality. (The Big Five are discussed in detail in Chapter 11.) Research suggests that openness to experience is the biggest differentiator between entrepreneurs and managers.[25] Entrepreneurs' openness to experience increases their attraction to rapidly changing environments and new challenges. Entrepreneurs' tolerance for ambiguity—that is, comfort with unclear or incomplete information—leads them to generate imaginative and innovative solutions to ill-defined problems.[26]

Entrepreneurial Orientation

Entrepreneurial orientation describes an individual's tendency to engage in innovative, risk-taking, and proactive behaviors. We focus here on how innovative/creative ability, risk propensity, and proactivity and work ethic drive individuals to engage in entrepreneurial behavior and develop entrepreneurial organizations.

- **Innovative/creative ability.** *Innovation* leads to the creation of something new and useful that makes money. *Creativity* creates the building blocks for innovation by introducing new ideas about products, services, processes, and procedures. Entrepreneurial activities offer ample opportunity for innovative solutions and creative expression. Not surprisingly, innovative and creative ability steer individuals toward entrepreneurial behaviors.[27]

- **Risk propensity.** Research confirms that an individual's risk-taking propensity distinguishes entrepreneurs from managers.[28] Managers must take some risk by making decisions; however, entrepreneurs take considerably more risk in the pursuit of new opportunities—indeed, even risk of personal bankruptcy. Hence, entrepreneurs need the confidence to act decisively.

- **Proactivity and work ethic.** Proactivity is a forward-looking perspective in which an individual looks for opportunities to add value beyond others' expectations. Proactivity is desired by all organizations, but it is critical for entrepreneurs. You can't be entrepreneurial without being proactive.[29] One academic concluded that entrepreneurial proactivity consists of "introducing new products and services ahead of the competition and acting in anticipation of future demand to create change and shape environment, thereby creating a first move advantage."[30] Work ethic, which is a core characteristic of career readiness, is also a driver of entrepreneurship. It reflects the extent to which you accept accountability and display positive work habits such as punctuality, time management, sustained effort, and willingness to go beyond a job description or a boss's expectations (see again Table 1.3). Research demonstrates that strong work ethic is positively associated with entrepreneurial success.[31]

Entrepreneurial Confidence **Entrepreneurial confidence** describes an individual's generalized sense of self-assurance and control over outcomes.[32] Entrepreneurial confidence makes individuals feel more comfortable making tough decisions and taking decisive action—critical competencies for successful entrepreneurs. Indeed, research affirms that entrepreneurs tend to be more self-confident than non-entrepreneurs.[33] Two factors influence entrepreneurial confidence: entrepreneurial self-efficacy and internal locus of control.

- **Entrepreneurial self-efficacy.** Entrepreneurial self-efficacy is a person's confidence in their capability to succeed in entrepreneurial activities. Meta-analytic research shows that this characteristic is a stronger predictor of entrepreneurial success than generalized self-efficacy, or a general confidence about succeeding in different situations.[34] Research show that females became more confident in their entrepreneurial ability after training. Specifically, women had lower levels of entrepreneurial self-efficacy before training than men but had an equivalent level of entrepreneurial self-efficacy after training.[35]
- **Internal locus of control.** If you believe "I am the captain of my fate, the master of my soul," you have what is known as an *internal locus of control*, the belief that you control your own destiny and that external forces will have little influence. (*External locus of control* means the opposite—you don't believe you control your destiny but that external forces do.) Entrepreneurs were found to have higher levels of internal locus of control than managers.[36] A recent German study of 45 ultra-high net-worth individuals confirmed this finding, with 95% of participants describing themselves as someone who prefers to forge their own path.[37]

So where do you stand? How many entrepreneurial characteristics come naturally to you? The following self-assessment was created to provide you with feedback about your entrepreneurial spirit. Take the assessment in Connect if your instructor has assigned it to you.

SELF-ASSESSMENT LM 2.1   CAREER READINESS

To What Extent Do You Possess an Entrepreneurial Spirit?

This survey is designed to help you reflect on your entrepreneurial spirit. Please complete Self-Assessment LM 2.1 if your instructor has assigned it in Connect.

Entrepreneurship Matters across the Globe

Entrepreneurship continues to be an economic generator across industries and countries around the world. In this section, we discuss the importance of entrepreneurship from the perspective of startups, innovation, job creation, and global experience.

Start-ups Generate Wealth and Economic Development A **start-up** is a newly created company designed to grow fast.[38] All kinds of new endeavors are constantly being launched. Some of the recent start-up success stories include Instacart, Grammarly, SpaceX, and ByteDance (the developer behind TikTok).[39] Whether start-ups are small or large, all new start-ups share a common element: They are driven by an individual or group that relies on entrepreneurial thinking. Consider the following examples from Step, a small start-up, and Stripe, a large start-up.

Small Start-Up Example—Step: Founded in 2018, Step is one of *Fast Company*'s 2022 most innovative companies with fewer than 100 employees. It is a 28-employee financial platform that offers teenagers a free bank account, debit card, and peer-to-peer payment platform, like Venmo. Founders CJ MacDonald and Alexey Kalinichenko were motivated to afford teens an opportunity to learn budgeting and cash management while also building a credit history at an earlier age than the typical 18-year-old requirement for cash management accounts.[40]

Large Start-Up Example—Stripe: Founded in 2010 by brothers Patrick and John Collison, Stripe offers software for companies to accept payments and manage their businesses online. The company processed more than $640 billion in online payments in 2021 and is currently valued at $63 billion. The Collison brothers' skilled entrepreneurship is driving the growth and continued success of the firm.[41]

Entrepreneurship Drives Innovation Innovation is the fuel for economic development. It represents the foundation for entrepreneurial activities. Entrepreneurs and entrepreneurial firms propose and create new products and services sold around the world. **Patents**, licenses with which the government authorizes a person or company to exclude others from making, using, or selling an invention for a time, protect innovations. Patents protect a company's intellectual property from being stolen. Small businesses, usually defined as firms with fewer than 500 employees,[42] are an important source of patent creation in the United States. They recently generated about 18% of all U.S. patent applications according to the U.S. Small Business Administration.[43] Research indicates patents are important for firm survival. New firms with patents are less likely to go bankrupt and more likely to merge with existing companies than new firms without patents.[44] Table LM 2.3 reveals some interesting facts about small businesses in the United States.

TABLE LM 2.3 Valuable Facts about Small Businesses

• 99.9% of all firms in the United States are small businesses.
• 81% of small businesses don't have any employees.
• 46.4% of all U.S. employees are employed by small businesses.
• 66.6% of new jobs added to the economy since 1995 came from small businesses.
• 43% of small businesses are female-owned.
• 19% of small businesses are owned by members of a minority ethnic group.
• 68% of firms survive 2 years; 49% survive 5 years; 34% survive 10 years.

Sources: Data taken from K. Main, and C. Bottorff, "Small Business Statistics of 2023," Forbes, December 7, 2022, https://www.forbes.com/advisor/business/small-business-statistics/. Also see "Small Business Finance FAQ," U.S. Small Business Administration Office of Advocacy, February 2022, https://cdn.advocacy.sba.gov/wp-content/uploads/2022/02/15122206/FinanceFAQ-Final-Feb2022.pdf; "Frequently Asked Questions," U.S. Small Business Administration Office of Advocacy, December 2021, https://cdn.advocacy.sba.gov/wp-content/uploads/2021/12/06095731/Small-Business-FAQ-Revised-December-2021.pdf.

Entrepreneurship Drives Job Creation How often do we hear politicians run on a platform promising job creation? It's standard these days because job creation is good for citizens, communities, states, and countries. Historical figures show that small businesses employ over 46% of all private-sector employees. Moreover, from 1995 to 2020, small businesses created 12.7 million net new jobs while large businesses, or organizations with more than 500 employees, created 7.9 million.[45] This data confirms the importance of entrepreneurial firms.

Entrepreneurship Improves the World's Standard of Living The standard of living is the level of "necessaries, comforts and luxuries which a person is accustomed to enjoy."[46] Clearly, entrepreneurial job creation improves standards of living around the world by transferring profits from the business to employees (in the form of pay) and thus to communities as employees are better able to make purchases that maintain or improve their material life. So what is the status of entrepreneurial activity around the globe? The annual Global Entrepreneurship Monitor (GEM) has been studying global entrepreneurship for 23 consecutive years. Its 2022 report is a summary of more than 150,000 interviews with people from 50 countries. The good news is that entrepreneurial activity is generally positively perceived and actively pursued around the world. For example, in most countries in Europe and North America, two-thirds to three-fourths of people believe successful entrepreneurs have high status. In addition, most people see new business opportunities as a result of the COVID-19 pandemic. These two statistics suggest that people worldwide are interested in starting a business, but the report also reveals that fear of failure is holding them back from taking steps to start a business.[47] If you are fearful about starting your own business as well, the next section will demystify the process of starting a business and equip you with tools and techniques to launch a business successfully.

Patents, like copyrights and trademarks, protect a company's intellectual property from competitors and gives it time to develop and bring its ideas to market. ibreakstock/Shutterstock

2.2 Starting a Business

THE BIG PICTURE
Businesses start with an idea for a new product or service, or by licensing someone else's idea. Entrepreneurs then undertake a series of activities to build the foundation for getting the business off the ground. These activities include writing a business plan, choosing the company's legal structure, and arranging for financing. Once this foundation has been built, the job of building an organizational culture and design further helps the business take off. Finally, there are some common themes surrounding businesses that ultimately fail.

The doors to the *Shark Tank* just opened. You nervously walk into the room as the five sharks await your product demonstration. You illustrate how your product works and then inform the sharks how much money you are seeking to further develop your business. The sharks follow up with a series of questions. Their questions press you about your business idea, business plan, and financing. Entrepreneurs who leave *Shark Tank* empty handed usually fail because one of the three elements is poorly developed. The following sections will prepare you to earn the sharks' confidence and win an investment proposal.

LM 2-2

Identify how entrepreneurs get started.

The five sharks in the *Shark Tank* await the next entrepreneur to present their pitch. They will be listening closely for the entrepreneur's business plan.
(left): Adam Vilimek/Shutterstock; (right): ssi77/Shutterstock

Businesses Start with an Idea

Everyone has the potential to come up with a viable business idea. The following actions can assist any aspiring entrepreneur to uncover a business idea.

1. **Identify your passions, skills, and talents.** Your past experience and in-depth knowledge about an industry are great sources of new business ideas.

    Passion, Skills, and Talents Example—Dr. K: Dr. K and his wife Joyce started a consulting business that built on their passions, skills, and experience. The idea was conceived from their love of teaching and helping others to learn and develop. Joyce had extensive experience and skills in human resource management, and Angelo was a proven academic who could easily explain complicated concepts to managers. They put their skills together to offer services targeted at assisting companies in developing and achieving strategic plans. They also engaged in leadership development programs for aspiring managers. The company has operated for more than 30 years.

2. **Identify a problem or frustration.** Fresh, locally grown organic food using sustainable agricultural methods is hard to come by. Chris Tidmarsh started Green Bridge Growers with his mother Jan Pilarski to solve this problem in his hometown.

    Problem Identification Example—Green Bridge Growers: Green Bridge Growers is a commercial greenhouse that provides greens to local restaurants and flowers to florists. Tidmarsh has three college degrees: chemistry, environmental studies, and French. He was diagnosed with autism during preschool and struggled to find an employer and work role that benefited from his background and interpersonal style. To make the new venture work, Tidmarsh's mom performs the administrative activities like accounting, marketing, and sales. Chris "perfects the spacing between rows of kale and spinach and keeps close tabs on water chemistry and soil acidity. He spends hours researching natural and effective pesticides to deal with aphids. The solution: 4,500 ladybugs."[48] Green Bridge Growers actively blogs about its agricultural methods and the ways it is helping the planet.[49]

3. **Identify an opportunity or need.** You can find opportunities by considering markets that are not being served. Pay attention to current events and societal trends, then strike first so you can capitalize on the first-mover advantage.[50] For instance, the development of mobile devices triggered an opportunity for Uber's founders Garret Camp and Travis Kalanick. While searching for a cab in Paris, they discovered the need to create an app that would hail a vehicle. The rest is history. Finding opportunities and unmet market needs takes time, focus, and motivation. You have to be looking for them.

   Opportunity Identification Example—Amazon: Jeff Bezos, who was a stock market researcher and hedge fund manager, followed Internet usage as part of his job. He decided to start Amazon when he realized that the surge in Internet usage provided an opportunity for online retailing. He went on to build the largest online retailer in the world.

4. **Study customer complaints.** Customer complaints are a warning sign that something is wrong with a product or service. They represent an opportunity to improve the offering. Consider Apple's response to the way iPhone batteries degraded as the product aged.

   Customer Complaints Example—Apple: Apple secretly used software controls to slow iPhones down to prolong their lives. Users were furious! In response, the company decided to replace batteries in older phones for a reduced price and to provide more information about battery life within iOS.[51] Apple also was forced to pay up to $500 million in 2020 to settle a class action lawsuit stemming from its decision to slow down the devices.[52] Perhaps this customer backlash will lead to a breakthrough idea for phone batteries.

Are you a glass half full or half empty kind of person?
Entrepreneurs see opportunities when others see setbacks.
Elenathewise/iStock/Getty Images

Franchising: Building on Someone Else's Idea

Most entrepreneurs create their own business ideas, but some leverage the proven ideas of others. Franchising, which we discussed in Chapter 4, is when a company (typically called the franchisor) allows another entity (typically called the franchisee) to pay it a fee and a share of the profits in return for using the company's brand name and a package of materials and services. In 2022, there were an estimated 792,000 franchised businesses in the United States, producing over $827 billion and employing more than 8.5 million people.[53] McDonald's is the largest franchise with more than 38,000 restaurants in over 100 countries.[54] Other franchises include 7-Eleven, The UPS Store, and Planet Fitness. Franchises have certain advantages and disadvantages, as well as special considerations for starting:

- **Advantages of franchising.** Opening a franchise instead of going it alone has its benefits. Franchise owners can take advantage of a proven brand instead of opening an unknown entity. There are volume discounts for ordering supplies from the franchise company's designated supplier, access to employee training and development, and many franchise companies will offer loans to cover start-up costs.[55] Marketing and technology support is another advantage of owning a franchise. Take, for example, Chick-fil-A, ranked #1 in *Franchise Direct*'s top 2023 franchises. The company spent $156 million on nationwide advertising and promotions on behalf of its franchisees in 2021. The company also manages a food-ordering and rewards app so customers can order ahead of time and accrue points with each purchase to earn free food.[56]

- **Disadvantages of franchising.** Opening a franchise also has its downsides. Just as the franchise company provides support and guidelines on how to operate its locations, there also are restrictions on what a franchisee can and cannot do, taking away entrepreneurial autonomy. This may include restrictions on modifying menu items or prices, changing suppliers, and even the way you

Chick-fil-A tops the list of top franchises in 2023. Rob Wilson/Shutterstock

decorate a location.[57] Another disadvantage is the extra fees, known as royalties, you need to pay the franchise company for using its brand and services. Chick-fil-A franchise owners currently pay the company 15% royalty and 50% of all profits (because the franchise covers all of the capital, real estate, and equipment expenses). To get started, franchise owners undergo a highly selective interview process and pay a $10,000 one-time franchise fee for opening a new Chick-fil-A.[58]

- **Starting a franchise.** With these pros and cons of franchise ownership in mind, you should be aware of some important considerations prior to starting one. First, you'll need to budget extra money for the one-time franchise fee, which can be substantial for some franchises (e.g., McDonald's charges $45,000). You'll also need to do your research on the franchise you are interested in. What's the history of the franchise company and who is in charge? What does its finances look like? This research also should include a better understanding of the support the franchise company provides each location and the restrictions it has on franchise owner decision making. Finally, you should complete your due diligence by speaking to current or former franchise owners to understand their experience with the franchise company. Is there anything they wish they knew prior to starting their franchise?[59]

Writing the Business Plan

A business plan is much more than a funding plan. It answers critical questions such as, "What business are we in?" "What is our vision and where are we going?" and "What will we do to achieve our goals?" *Harvard Business Review* noted that "A plan helps detail how the opportunity is to be seized, what success looks like, and what resources are required, and it can be key to the investment decisions of angel investors, banks, and venture capitalists."[60] Most of the questions the sharks in *Shark Tank* are likely to ask you are related to your business plan.

A business plan is like a map that will help your startup navigate obstacles and get to its intended destination (a successful enterprise). SydaProductions/Shutterstock

The components of a business plan vary, and people disagree about the level of detail to be included. Some suggest a one-page plan,[61] while others recommend a longer plan (15 to 25 pages).[62] Alexander Osterwalder simplified the business plan by developing the Business Model Canvas (BMC), a one-page template that summarizes how a business intends to create, deliver, and capture value.[63] It is a useful way for entrepreneurs to clarify their thinking about and succinctly communicate to others how their organization plans to make money.

The BMC outlines nine sequential building blocks to build a business plan. Each building block answers a specific question. As you prepare your presentation for the sharks, make sure you have clear answers to each of the nine questions associated with their respective building blocks.[64]

1. Customer Segments   The first building block, customer segments, identifies your customers. It organizes multiple customers into groups based on common preferences, distribution channels needed to reach them, and types of relationships needed to serve them.

Question #1: Who are your core customers?

2. Value Proposition Value proposition, the second building block, describes how an organization's products and services solve a customer's problem or meets a customer's need. Entrepreneurs define this building block when they study the market, pay attention to customer complaints, and identify a problem, opportunity, or unmet need—all actions to develop a viable business idea described earlier. They then develop their products and services to address specific customer segments' needs.

Question #2: What problem does your product/service uniquely solve?

3. Channels The channels through which a company delivers its value proposition to customer segments is the third building block. Channels include communication, distribution, and sales. These channels provide information about how a company's products and services are promoted, sold, delivered, and supported.

Entrepreneurs can expand their reach to customers by selling their products through partner channels such as Walmart or Amazon. Alternatively, entrepreneurs can elect to make higher profit margins by reaching consumers directly through developing their own communication, distribution, and sales channels via developing their own website and marketing directly to customers.

Channels Example—Scrub Daddy Inc.: Scrub Daddy, a unique scrubbing sponge to clean dishes, is one of the best-selling products that appeared on *Shank Tank*. In addition to selling sponges and other products through major retailers like Walmart, Home Depot, Kroger, Target, and Meijer, founder Aaron Krause markets and sells directly to customers via Scrub Daddy's website.[65]

Question #3: How will you deliver your product/service to your customers?

4. Customer Relationships The fourth building block, customer relationships, is the heart of the business model. It describes the type of relationship an organization wants to establish with its customers. Customer relationships consider how you will acquire and retain customers as well as expand the customer relationship over time. Different customer relationship strategies are needed if an organization is focused primarily on customer acquisition, customer retention, or customer upselling.

Question #4: How will you acquire new customers, keep them, and derive more value from the customer relationship?

5. Revenue Streams Revenue streams is the fifth building block. It describes how you plan to generate revenue from your customer relationships. Organizations can generate revenue through one-time transactions such as selling a product, or through recurring revenues such as providing a service, customer support, or a license to use the product.

Question #5: How will you monetize customer relationships?

6. Key Resources Key resources, the sixth building block, describes the assets or infrastructure you need to create, deliver, and generate revenue from your value proposition.

Question #6: What assets and capabilities does your company need to develop produce your product/service?

7. Key Activities The seventh building block, key activities, describes the knowledge, skills, and abilities an organization needs to maintain to deliver its value proposition. For example, the Honest company is a product-based company that produces baby, beauty, and skincare products. This company's key activities include designing better products, understanding how customers use their existing products, and managing supply chain relationships to ensure product quality and availability for customers.

Question #7: Who are the key people in your company with the knowledge, skills, and abilities to develop and produce your product/service?

8. Key Partners Key partners are the eighth building block. They describe other firms that help an organization deliver its value proposition. Key partners for the Honest company include suppliers, manufacturers, distributors, and retail stores.

Question #8: Who are the suppliers, manufacturers, and distributors for your product/service?

9. Cost Structure The ninth building block is cost structure. How do your key resources, activities, and partners influence the cost associated with delivering your value proposition? What percentage of your costs are fixed or variable? Entrepreneurs develop sales projections and conduct a cash flow analysis during this step of the plan. Sales projections are based on other information contained in the plan such as market trends, sales strategies, and human resource needs.

Question #9: How costly are your operations and what is your break-even point?

Now that you've built your business plan, it's time to ask the sharks for the money you need to get the business running or to expand. Be realistic when you outline your funding requirements and set a range if you are unsure about exact future costs. Provide a timeline that links funding to expansion activities. You want to provide the sharks with realistic expectations about their return on investment.

Research affirms the value of developing a business plan. A six-year study of 1,000 would-be U.S. entrepreneurs compared planning practices and firm performance across one group that wrote formal plans and a second group that did not. The groups were balanced so that they were "statistical twins." Findings showed that entrepreneurs who planned were 16% more likely to survive than their identical nonplanning cohorts. Entrepreneurs tended to plan when the company was a high-growth–oriented start-up and when they were seeking funding.[66] If you want to succeed in the *Shark Tank,* it pays to plan.

Choosing a Legal Structure

Your choice of a legal structure is one of the most important decisions you will make as an entrepreneur. The reason is that this decision affects everything from the taxes you'll pay to your legal liability and control over the company. As we review the options, keep in mind that your choice depends on your personal and financial goals. Let's consider the four basic business entities: sole proprietorship, partnership, corporation, and limited liability (LLC).[67]

Choosing a legal structure is an important decision that affects an entrepreneur's taxes, legal liability, and control over the company.
MMG1/AlamyStock Photo

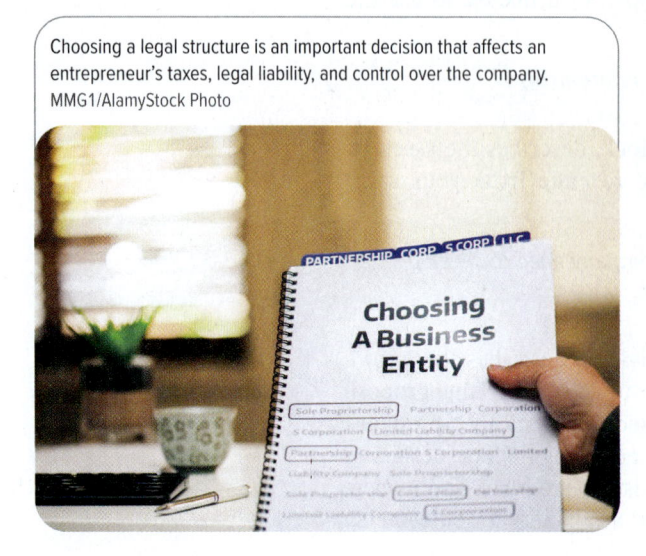

Sole Proprietorship The Internal Revenue Service (IRS) defines a sole proprietor as "someone who [completely] owns an unincorporated business."[68] It's the simplest form of business structure. The sole proprietor makes all the decisions and has total control over the business. The key drawback, however, is that the owner has unlimited liability. If someone sues, the owner's personal and business assets are put at risk. Dr. K discovered it was hard to get financial backing for his consulting business when it operated as a sole proprietorship because banks did not like the liability risk. As a result, they would not lend him money to grow the business.

Partnership The IRS defines a partnership as a relationship "between two or more persons who join to carry on a trade or business. Each person contributes money, labor or skill, and expects to share in the profits and losses of the business."[69] Partnerships generally begin with a common interest or experience. François Pelen is a good example. He left his position as a VP at Pfizer to start Groupe Point Vision with Patrice Pouts and Raphael Schnitzer, two fellow MBA students at HEC Paris. Groupe Point Vision now has 53 centers and has seen over 1.2 million patients.[70]

A partnership is an unincorporated business and there are two types: general and limited. In a *general partnership*, the partners equally share all profits and losses. In *limited partnerships*, "only one partner has control of its operation, while the other person or persons simply contribute to and receive only part of the profit."[71] This structure works well when you want to start a business with a family member or a friend. The drawbacks are the unlimited liability of the partners in general partnerships, and the risk of disagreements between them. Income and losses are "passed through" to the partners' individual taxable incomes.

Corporation A **corporation** is an entity that is separate from its owners, meaning "it has its own legal rights, independent of its owners—it can sue, be sued, own and sell property, and sell the rights of ownership in the form of stocks."[72] There are two key types of corporations: C corporations and S corporations.

- *C corporations* are owned by shareholders and are taxed as separate entities. The IRS states that this type of corporation "realizes net income or loss, pays taxes and distributes profits to shareholders. The profit of a corporation is taxed to the corporation when earned, and is taxed to the shareholders when distributed as dividends. This creates a double tax."[73] The benefit to the entrepreneur is that the legal entity and thus any liability exist separately from any individual owner of the business.

- *S corporations* "are corporations that elect to pass corporate income, losses, deductions, and credits through to their shareholders for federal tax purposes. Shareholders of S corporations report the flow-through of income and losses on their personal tax returns and are assessed at their individual income tax rates. This allows S corporations to avoid double taxation on the corporate income."[74] The benefit of an S corporation is that owners have limited liability and don't incur corporate tax.

Limited Liability Company (LLC) A **limited liability company (LLC)** is a hybrid structure that combines elements of sole proprietorship, partnership, and corporation. Each state may have different regulations regarding an LLC. "Limited liability means that its owners, also called members, are usually not personally responsible for the LLC's debts and lawsuits. . . . In the eyes of the IRS, LLC taxes usually resemble a sole proprietorship or partnership. The LLC does not pay income taxes itself: instead, the owners list business profits and losses on their personal tax returns."[75] Benefits of LLCs include fewer recordkeeping and reporting requirements than for corporations.

Conclusions You should not make a decision about the legal structure of a new business by yourself. The preceding information does not provide enough details for you to decide on your own. You want to obtain professional advice. The Kinickis, for instance, relied on the combined advice of their accountant and their attorney when deciding to transition their consulting company from a sole proprietorship to an S corporation. Our discussion here is not intended to provide all the information you need to start a business. We want to provide enough detail to enable you to ask good questions should you consider pursuing entrepreneurship.

Obtaining Financing

Whether they need equipment to start a small landscape business or a large investment to drive growth for a financial software firm like the Collison brothers' Stripe Inc., all entrepreneurs must eventually obtain financing. The amount depends on the nature of the business. Shopify's survey of 150 entrepreneurs and 300 small business owners in

How much money do you think it takes to start a business? Small Business Administration data show that 50% of new businesses were started with less than $25,000.[81] Palto/Shutterstock

the United States revealed start-up and first-year costs averaged $40,000. Product costs consumed 31.6% of the first-year budget.[76]

The availability of financing to start or grow a business can make the difference between pursuing an entrepreneurial dream and giving up. More than 33% of small businesses fail because they aren't able to receive adequate financing to continue operating.[77]

Below is a summary of financing options for start-ups:[78]

- **Personal funding.** A large percentage of entrepreneurs use their own savings or credit cards to initially fund a business. Banks like to see entrepreneurs invest in their own firms before they ask for a loan.

- **Family and friends (aka "love money").** Friends, parents, and other relatives are another common source of funding. You should expect to repay these loans as the business grows. Be careful when borrowing from or going into business with family and friends because people often have a hard time separating personal and business relationships.

- **Bank loans.** Bank loans are a more costly source of financing than the previous two options. Banks generally want to see a good business plan and personal guarantees before they will lend. Entrepreneurs frequently use their homes as collateral for bank loans. The Small Business Administration is another good source of loan financing. The SBA provides loans, "loan guarantees, contracts, counseling sessions and other forms of assistance to small businesses." It provides "an array of financing from the smallest needs in microlending—to substantial debt and equity investment capital."[79]

- **Venture capital. Venture capitalists (VCs)** exchange funds for an ownership share in the company. They generally look for high-growth potential in industries like information technology, biotechnology, and communication and desire a high return on their investment. VCs essentially invest money for a share in controlling the company. This can include "the right to supervise the company's management practices" and "often involves a seat on the board of directors and an assurance of transparency."[80]

Making a pitch to VCs, like the sharks in *Shark Tank,* is critical for entrepreneurs needing a larger investment to build their business. The process begins with a business plan and a formal presentation. Lakshmi Balachandra worked at two VC firms and observed a number of these entrepreneurial presentations. She wondered why some proposals looked so good on paper and then turned into nonstarters based on presentations. She spent 10 years studying these dynamics.

Dr. Balachandra is now a professor at Babson College and is publishing insights from her research. They include the following:

1. Entrepreneurs are more successful getting financing when they laugh during pitches.
2. Entrepreneurs are more likely to get financing when they have friends or acquaintances in common with the VCs.
3. Judges prefer a calmer demeanor than over-the-top passion and excitement. People apparently equate calmness with effective leadership.
4. Interest in a start-up was due more to the entrepreneur's character and trustworthiness than to perceptions of competence.
5. Gender stereotypes play a role in investment decisions. People displaying stereotypically female behaviors such as warmth, sensitivity, and expressiveness were less likely than others to get funded.[82]

Let's focus a bit more on this last insight as research on gender bias during VC pitches has uncovered some problematic patterns. Multiple studies have shown that there is a strong gender bias against females in the pitch process. In one study, researchers concluded that "Investors prefer pitches presented by male entrepreneurs compared with pitches made by female entrepreneurs, even when the content of the pitch is the same."[83] Research also uncovered that the most deserving women entrepreneurs ironically faced the most resistance from venture capitalists.[84] A third study suggests that venture capitalists should stop this practice and embrace stereotypically female behavior as these traits can be advantageous. Researchers believe this would increase female entry into entrepreneurship and foster a more diverse and robust economy.[85]

- Angels. Angel investors are wealthy individuals or retired executives who invest in small firms. "They are often leaders in their own field who not only contribute their experience and network of contacts but also their technical and/or management knowledge. Angels usually finance the early stages of the business with investments ranging from $25,000 to $100,000."[86] They like to mentor would-be entrepreneurs and thus prefer those who are responsive to feedback.[87] Finally, Angels tend to finance companies in the software, mass market consumer goods, and equipment industries.[88]

- Crowd investing. Crowd investing allows a group of people—the crowd—to invest in an entrepreneur or business online. The investors can take either an equity position in which they exchange money for stock or ownership in the company, or they can engage in debt investing by making a loan to the business.[89] GoFundMe, launched in 2010, is the world's largest, free social fundraising platform. The company has raised over $25 billion from over 200 million individual donations for personal, business, and charitable causes.[90]

Creating the "Right" Organizational Culture and Design

At this stage in starting a business, the entrepreneur has a viable idea for a new or improved product and service, an established legal structure, a physical location in which to operate, and some level of financing. It's now time to decide on the type of organizational culture and design to adopt. These are important decisions because they affect employee behavior and performance across the individual, group, and organizational levels.

Entrepreneurs learn that they can't complete all tasks alone. They need people. At the early stages of a business, entrepreneurs tend to hire people they trust or who have values similar to their own. This group frequently includes family, friends, or experts in the industry. People generally get along and the excitement and interest in the new business drives motivation and performance. As the business grows, however, the founder or founders need to hire people with different skills who may bring with them values and beliefs a little different from those of the current workforce. This is where organizational culture and design start to exert their influence on the business' success.

Organizational culture, discussed in detail in Chapter 8, helps the business articulate its own values and beliefs, which generally flow from the founder's. There are different types of organizational culture, and research confirms that entrepreneurs need to identify the type that best fits the organization's vision and strategies, and their leadership style.[91] The business's evolving culture matters because it will influence employees' work attitudes and performance outcomes such as level of customer satisfaction, market share, operational efficiency, product/service quality, innovation, and financial performance.[92]

Organizational design, discussed in Chapter 8, is the process of designing the optimal structure of accountability and responsibility an organization will use to execute its strategies. In many small firms, the structure tends to form haphazardly and is rather simple. People pick up tasks as needed and there are no clear reporting relationships. This is feasible at first, but it quickly becomes dysfunctional as the business grows.

Growth brings the need for better organization and decision making. Like its culture, an organization's structure needs to fit the vision and strategies the business is pursuing. Chapter 8 discusses eight different organizational designs entrepreneurs might choose to organize the business. In the end, this decision can be difficult for entrepreneurs because they now must contend with sharing power, control, and decision making.

Being an entrepreneur can be stressful. Knowledge about why new ventures fail can help you avoid common pitfalls and devise a more deliberate plan to guide your startup to success.
JOKE_PHATRAPONG/Shutterstock

Why Entrepreneurial Ventures Fail

Earlier you learned that many new businesses fail. According to the Small Business Association, 68% of businesses survive their first 2 years, but that number falls to around 34% by year 10.[93] This means that the vast majority of new businesses will not live to see their 10th anniversary. Although there are many reasons why businesses fail, four common themes exist.[94]

- **Lack of effective planning.** Many businesses fail because they had an ineffective business plan, deviated from an effective one, or didn't even plan in the first place. As we noted earlier, businesses that effectively plan have a higher likelihood of success. Plans should be realistic and based on accurate, current information.

- **Insufficient capital.** A common mistake for new business owners is not understanding the need for sufficient capital for day-to-day operations. This can lead to the business closing before it has had a fair chance to succeed. In fact, cash-flow issues are the cause of 82% of small business closures. When determining how much money is required for your business, don't just think about start-up costs. Successful new businesses plan for the costs of staying in business, especially when they know they may not make a profit for a year or two.

- **Poor management.** As we noted in Section LM 2.1, not all entrepreneurs are effective managers. New business owners frequently lack relevant management expertise in areas such as finance, purchasing, hiring, and communications. Successful business owners educate themselves on the skills they lack, hire those with the required skills, or outsource work to competent professionals.

- **Lack of customer interest.** A new product or service needs to solve a problem or fulfill an existing need. Excellent management skills and access to plenty of capital won't make up for the fact that nobody wants what you are offering. In actuality, 42% of small businesses fail due to lack of customer interest. A good way to avoid this problem is to conduct effective market research as part of your business planning.

Key Terms Used in This Learning Module

angel investor 215
corporation 213
crowd investing 215
entrepreneur 200
entrepreneurial confidence 205
entrepreneurial mindset 204
entrepreneurial orientation 204
entrepreneurship 200
intrapreneur 200
limited liability company (LLC) 213
partnership 212
patents 206
self-employment 201
social entrepreneurship 201
sole proprietor 212
standard of living 207
start-up 205
venture capitalists (VCs) 214

Key Points

LM 2.1 Entrepreneurship: Its Foundations and Importance

- Entrepreneurship is the pursuit of opportunity beyond the resources under one's control.
- Two types of entrepreneurship are entrepreneurs and intrapreneurs.
- Entrepreneurship is different from self-employment.
- Social entrepreneurship identifies and pursues business opportunities to benefit society.
- Entrepreneurs have an entrepreneurial mindset, entrepreneurial orientation, and have entrepreneurial confidence.
- Entrepreneurship matters around the globe because it (1) generates wealth and economic development, (2) drives innovation, (3) drives job creation, and (4) improves the world's standard of living.

LM 2.2 Starting a Business

- All businesses start with an idea. Ideas come from four sources: (1) the entrepreneur's passions, skills, and talents; (2) a problem or frustration; (3) an opportunity or need; and (4) customer complaints.
- Franchising occurs when a company allows another entity (the franchisee) to pay it a fee and a share of the profits in return for using the company's brand name and a package of materials and services.
- Business plans help set the direction of a new business. They answer questions such as "What business are we in?" "What is our vision and where are we going?" and "What will we do to achieve our goals?"
- The Business Model Canvas outlines nine sequential building blocks to build a business plan: (1) customer segments, (2) value proposition, (3) channels, (4) customer relationships, (5) revenue streams, (6) key resources, (7) key activities, (8) key partners, and (9) cost structure.
- There are four fundamental legal structures entrepreneurs can use when starting a business: sole proprietorship, partnership, corporation, and limited liability company (LLC).
- There are a variety of funding sources entrepreneurs use to start and grow their new business. They include personal funding, loans from family and friends, bank loans, venture capital, angel investors, and crowd investing.
- Entrepreneurs need to establish an organizational culture and design that fit the vision and strategies being pursued by the new business.
- Common reasons why new businesses fail are lack of effective planning, insufficient capital, poor management, and lack of customer interest.

7.1 Two Kinds of Decision Making: Rational and Nonrational

THE BIG PICTURE

Decision making, the process of identifying and choosing alternative courses of action, may sound rational, but it is often nonrational. Four steps in making a rational decision are (1) identify the problem or opportunity, (2) think up alternative solutions, (3) evaluate alternatives and select a solution, and (4) implement and evaluate the solution chosen. Two examples of nonrational models of decision making are (1) satisficing and (2) intuition.

LO 7-1

Compare rational and nonrational decision making.

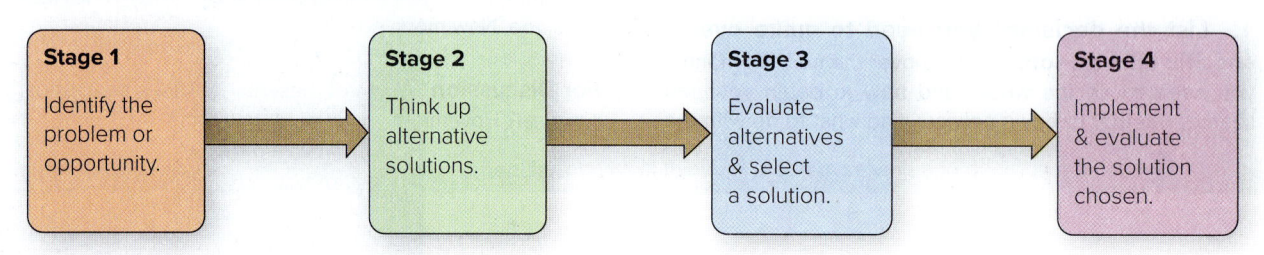

Leaders are under increasing pressure to make fast, high-quality decisions. But fast decisions don't always work out. For example, McKinsey reported only 20% of 1,228 executives surveyed believed their company made fast, high-quality decisions that improved firm performance. In contrast, a majority of respondents suggested most of the time spent making decisions in their company was used ineffectively. One key to success for "winners" is delegating decisions to employees at lower levels of the organization who are on the front lines.[8] These results suggest your decisions in your current or future job will be instrumental to your organization's success.

This section helps develop your critical thinking/problem solving and decision making career readiness competencies. We'll first introduce the steps to making a rational decision. The focus then turns to nonrational decision making, which includes satisficing and intuition. Finally, we'll provide tips for improving your intuition.

Rational Decision Making: Managers Should Make Logical and Optimal Decisions

A **decision** is a choice made from available alternatives. **Decision making** is the process of identifying and choosing among alternative courses of action. The **rational model of decision making**, also called the classical model, explains how managers should make decisions. The rational model emerged from ideas published in Scottish economist Adam Smith's 1759 book titled *The Theory of Moral Sentiments*. Smith, the architect of modern economics, introduced a theory of human decision making that assumes people make rational decisions based on an analysis of all potential outcomes.[9] It predicts managers will make logical decisions that are the optimal means to further the organization's best interests.

Typically there are four stages associated with rational decision making (see Figure 7.1). These also are the steps in the standard model of problem solving. As stage 1 in the figure shows, for example, a decision can take action on problems or opportunities, both of which are gaps between an actual and a desired state.

FIGURE 7.1
The four stages in rational decision making

Stage 1	Stage 2	Stage 3	Stage 4
Identify the problem or opportunity.	Think up alternative solutions.	Evaluate alternatives & select a solution.	Implement & evaluate the solution chosen.

Stage 1: Identify the Problem or Opportunity—Determining the Actual versus the Desirable

As a manager, you'll probably find no shortage of **problems**, or difficulties that inhibit the achievement of goals: customer complaints, supplier breakdowns, staff turnover, sales shortfalls, competitor innovations, low employee motivation, and poor quality.

However, you also will often find **opportunities**—situations that present possibilities for exceeding existing goals. It's the farsighted managers who can look past the steady stream of daily problems and seize the moment to actually do *better* than the goals they are expected to achieve. When a competitor's top salesperson unexpectedly quits, that creates an opportunity for your company to hire that person away to promote your product more vigorously in that sales territory.

Whether you're confronted with a problem or an opportunity, the decision you're called on to make is how to make *improvements*—how to change conditions from the present to the desirable. This is a matter of **diagnosis**—identifying and analyzing the underlying causes. Underlying causes become the point of focus for the next step in the rational decision-making process: think up alternative solutions.

Stage 2: Think Up Alternative Solutions—Both the Obvious and the Creative

After you've identified the problem or opportunity and diagnosed its causes, it's time to come up with alternative solutions. Your focus should be to solve for the most important causes by generating novel ideas about what to do about them. For example, newly hired employees may be underperforming (a problem) because they don't know how to do their job properly (underdeveloped employee skills is the cause). Providing employees with thorough job training is one solution to resolve this problem. Don't accept the first solution that comes to mind. It is more effective to brainstorm multiple solutions and then evaluate them in Stage 3.[10]

Stage 3: Evaluate Alternatives and Select a Solution—Ethics, Feasibility, and Effectiveness

This stage entails evaluating each alternative not only according to cost and quality but also according to the following questions: (1) Is it *ethical?* (If it isn't, don't give it a second look.) (2) Is it *feasible?* (If time is short, costs are high, technology is unavailable, or customers are resistant, for example, it is not.) (3) Is it ultimately *effective?* (If the decision is merely "good enough" but not optimal in the long run, you might reconsider.)

Today, the task of evaluating alternatives is facilitated by the use of *big data* (discussed in Section 7.3) and *artificial intelligence* (discussed in Section 7.4). Research confirms that firms can make better decisions if they utilize these tools in the decision-making process.[11]

Stage 4: Implement and Evaluate the Solution Chosen

With some decisions, implementation is usually straightforward (though not necessarily easy—firing employees who steal may be an obvious decision, but it can still be emotionally draining). With other decisions, implementation can be quite difficult; when one company acquires another, for instance, it may take months to consolidate the departments, accounting systems, inventories, and so on.

Successful Implementation   For implementation to be successful, you need to do two things:

- **Plan carefully.** Be sure to consider the application of what you learned in Chapter 5. Some decisions may require written plans.
- **Be sensitive to those affected.** Consider how the people affected may feel about the change—inconvenienced, insecure, even fearful, all of which can trigger resistance. This is why it helps to give employees and customers latitude during a changeover in business practices or working arrangements.

Evaluation   One "law" in economics is the Law of Unintended Consequences—things happen that weren't foreseen. For this reason, it is important to follow up and evaluate the results of any decision you implement.

What should you do if the implemented decision is not working? Some possibilities include:

- **Give it more time.** Make sure employees, customers, and so on have enough time to get used to the new process.
- **Change it slightly.** Maybe the decision was correct, but it just needs "tweaking"—a small change of some sort.
- **Try another alternative.** If Plan A doesn't seem to be working, you may want to scrap it for another alternative.
- **Start over.** If no alternative seems workable, go back to the drawing board—to Stage 1 of the decision-making process.

Now that you understand the four stages of the rational model, to what extent do you think you use them when making decisions? Research shows that being humble, conscientious, and open to new experiences increases your chances of rational decision making.[12] Would you like to improve the career readiness competency of *decision making?* If yes, then you will find the following self-assessment valuable as it assesses your problem-solving skills. Take the self-assessment if your instructor has assigned it to you in Connect.

SELF-ASSESSMENT 7.1   CAREER READINESS

Assessing Your Problem-Solving Potential

This survey is designed to assess your approach to problem solving. Please complete Self-Assessment 7.1 if your instructor has assigned it in Connect.

What's Wrong with the Rational Model?

The rational model is *prescriptive*, describing how managers ought to make decisions. It doesn't describe how managers *actually* make decisions. Indeed, the rational model makes some very generous assumptions—that managers have complete information, are able to make an unemotional analysis, and are able to make the best decision for the organization (See Table 7.1). We all know that these assumptions are unrealistic.

TABLE 7.1   The Rational Model's Assumptions

• **Complete information, no uncertainty:** You obtain complete, error-free information about all alternative courses of action and the consequences that would follow from each choice.
• **Logical, unemotional analysis:** Having no prejudices or emotional biases, you are able to logically evaluate the alternatives, ranking them from best to worst according to your personal preferences.
• **Best decision for the organization:** Confident of the best future course of action, you objectively choose the alternative that you believe provides the most benefit to the organization.

Nonrational Decision Making: Managers Find It Difficult to Make Optimal Decisions

Nonrational models of decision making explain how managers make decisions; they assume that decision making is nearly always uncertain and risky, making it difficult for managers to make optimal decisions. The nonrational models are *descriptive* rather than prescriptive: They describe how managers *actually* make decisions rather than how they should. Two nonrational models are (1) *satisficing* and (2) *intuition*.

1. Bounded Rationality, Hubris, and the Satisficing Model: "Satisfactory Is Good Enough"

During the 1950s, economist Herbert Simon—who later received the Nobel Prize—began to study how managers actually make decisions. From his research he proposed that managers could not act purely logically because their rationality was bounded by so many restrictions.[13] Called **bounded rationality**, the concept suggests that decision makers' ability to be rational is limited by numerous constraints, such as complexity, time, money, and other resources such as their cognitive capacity, values, skills, habits, personality, and unconscious reflexes (see Table 7.2).

Researchers have uncovered another characteristic that can influence bounded rationality. This impediment to rational decision making is **hubris**, defined as an extreme and inflated sense of pride, certainty, and confidence.[18] Research suggests that hubris causes executives to make riskier and less effective decisions.[19]

Hubris Example—Elon Musk: Elon Musk acquired Twitter in 2022 for $44 billion. Musk's acquisition of the social media company came as a surprise given his current portfolio of companies—SpaceX, Tesla, SolarCity, Neuralink, and The Boring Company—are in unrelated industries. One of Musk's first moves as Twitter's owner was to fire Twitter's top executives. Shortly thereafter, he laid off roughly 50% of the company's workforce citing cost-cutting measures. These actions prompted a wave of lawsuits from former employees. On another front, Musk's active involvement in managing Twitter created concern from Tesla's shareholders about his divided attention and his focus on Tesla's success in the automotive industry. Tesla's stock price fell roughly 10% in the four months following Musk's Twitter takeover. Is hubris to blame?[20]

Because of impediments such as bounded rationality and hubris, managers don't always exhaustively search for the best alternative. Instead, they follow what Simon calls the **satisficing model**—that is, managers seek alternatives until they find one that is satisfactory, not optimal.[21] Research shows that those who are more open to new experiences, responsible, and generally agreeable are less likely to satisfice.[22] Although satisficing might seem to be a weakness, it may well outweigh any advantages gained from delaying making a decision until all information is in and all alternatives weighed. As Hallmark

TABLE 7.2 Several Hindrances to Perfectly Rational Decision Making

• **Complexity:** The problems that need solving are often exceedingly complex, beyond understanding.[14]
• **Time and money constraints:** There is not enough time or money to gather all relevant information.[15]
• **Different cognitive capacity, values, skills, habits, and unconscious reflexes:** Managers aren't all built the same way, of course, and all have personal limitations and biases that affect their judgment.[16]
• **Imperfect information:** Managers have imperfect, fragmentary information about the alternatives and their consequences.
• **Information overload:** There is too much information for one person to process.[17]
• **Different priorities:** Some data are considered more important, so certain facts are ignored.
• **Conflicting goals:** Other managers, including colleagues, have conflicting goals.

If you surf channels until you find something interesting to watch, you are satisficing. It might not be the most interesting show you could watch, but it will do. Sergey Mironov/Shutterstock

found, however, making snap decisions that satisfice can backfire.

Satisficing Example—Hallmark: The Hallmark Channel aired a series of six ads for Zola, a wedding planning website, in December 2019. One of the ads featured a same-sex couple kissing, resulting in a complaint that petitioned Hallmark to drop the ads. Hallmark executives swiftly removed the ads citing their content as "controversial." This decision caused backlash from the LGBTQ+ community and its advocates claiming Hallmark was discriminatory. Hallmark reversed its decision a day after the ads were dropped but was forced to go into damage control. Mike Perry, the CEO of Hallmark Cards (which owns the Hallmark Channel), called the choice "wrong" and apologized for the "hurt and disappointment" it caused. Bill Abbott, who was in charge of the TV channel, left the company shortly thereafter. In 2023, under Hallmark Media CEO Wonya Lucas' leadership, Hallmark has diversified the casts and storylines in its programming.[23]

2. The Intuition Model: "It Just Feels Right" Budding entrepreneurs often can't afford in-depth marketing research. So they make decisions based on hunches—their subconscious, visceral feelings. "Going with your gut," or **intuition, is making a choice without the use of conscious thought or logical inference.**[24] Intuition that stems from *expertise*—a person's explicit and tacit knowledge about a person, a situation, an object, or a decision opportunity—is known as a *holistic hunch*. Intuition based on feelings—the involuntary emotional response to those same matters—is known as *automated experience*.

Intuition Example—Laura Stupple: Laura Stupple, founder of international marketing agency LJS Content, relies on intuition to sense how customers think and how they want to receive information. She says, "When I get a feeling that something will resonate … I run with it. And when you practice that skill over and over, the intuitive muscle gets stronger."[25]

Who is more likely to use intuition? Research finds that those who are high in self-esteem and risk propensity are more prone to use intuition.[26] Whether or not you have these personality traits, it is important to develop your intuitive skills because they are as important as, and sometimes superior to, rational analysis. Research suggests intuition is best used in rapidly changing environments when you are confronted with a complex and unprecedented problem.[27] The Example box illustrates how Virgin CEO Richard Branson and others use intuition.

EXAMPLE Harnessing the Power of Intuition

You might be wishing that you could make all difficult decisions in an "aha!" moment in which you spontaneously recognize the answer to the problem. This recognition is called an *epiphany*—that instant when something clicks in the brain, a mental light bulb goes on, and the road ahead becomes crystal clear. Unfortunately, epiphanies are rare, but the intuition that often leads to them can be carefully honed.

Sir Richard Branson, the entrepreneurial founder of the Virgin Group, employs over 60,000 people across a variety of lines of business, including a cruise line, airline, mobile phone company, and space-tourism group.[28] Branson relies on his instincts when calculating risks, putting trust in others, and making important business decisions. He appreciates advancements in technology and artificial intelligence but notes that "as we rely more and more on analytics to make our decisions, we're losing touch of our human instinct and we're taking human reasoning out of the equation." He believes this in turn makes people more risk-averse and conservative.[29] Recent research supports Branson's position, finding that although data are important, intuition is still a necessary part of decision making.[30]

Though he is a strong proponent of intuition, Branson understands that his gut isn't always right. For example, Virgin tried selling automobiles through the Internet in 2000. People didn't respond to that idea, and the company shut down the website in 2005. "Nobody gets everything right the first time. Business is like a giant game of chess—you have to learn quickly from your mistakes. Successful entrepreneurs don't fear failure; they learn from it and move on," he says.[31] In the end, the innovative CEO believes you should "trust your intuition, stay curious and always put your people first if you want to thrive in the long-term."[32]

Branson is not alone in harnessing the power of intuitive ideas. A well-known story about the origins of Amazon credits founder Jeff Bezos' intuitive recognition that if, as he'd just read, the Internet was growing at 2,300% a year, it was worth quitting his job on Wall Street and starting an online bookstore to take advantage of that opportunity.[33] Bezos reflected on his success commenting, "All of my best decisions in business and in life have been made with heart, intuition, guts—not [with] analysis."[34] And yet another genius, physicist Albert Einstein, once said, "All great achievements of science must start from intuitive knowledge. At times I feel certain I am right while not knowing the reason."[35]

YOUR CALL

Have you ever relied on your intuition to make an important decision or solve a big problem? How did your solution come to you, and how pleased were you with the result?

As a model for making decisions, intuition has at least two benefits. It can speed up decision making, which is useful when deadlines are tight.[36] It also helps managers when resources are limited. A drawback, however, is that it can be difficult to convince others that your hunch makes sense. In addition, intuition is subject to the same biases as those that affect rational decision making, as we discuss in Section 7.6.[37] Finally, research demonstrates that intuition is less effective when people face structured problems—those that can be broken down and approached sequentially.[38] Still, research shows intuition and rationality are complementary, and managers should develop the courage to use intuition when making decisions.[39]

Would you like to increase your level of intuition? It can be done, but first you need to know where you stand with respect to using intuition. Find out by taking Self-Assessment 7.2 if your instructor has assigned it to you in Connect. •

SELF-ASSESSMENT 7.2   CAREER READINESS

Assessing Your Level of Intuition

This survey is designed to assess the extent you use intuition in your current job. Please complete Self-Assessment 7.2 if your instructor has assigned it in Connect.

7.2 Making Ethical Decisions

THE BIG PICTURE
A graph known as a decision tree can help one make ethical decisions.

The ethical behavior of businesspeople, as we discussed at length in Chapter 3, has become of increasing concern in recent years, brought about by a number of events.

LO 7-2

Explain how managers can make decisions that are both legal and ethical.

The Dismal Record of Business Ethics

According to a study from PwC (PricewaterhouseCoopers), the top reason for CEO departures among America's largest companies isn't poor financial performance, it's unethical behavior.[40] In 2022 alone, CEOs and senior executives from CNN, Keurig Dr Pepper, Ralph Lauren, Estée Lauder, Renown Regional Medical Center, DataRobot, and FTX were either fired or resigned due to ethical misconduct. The total annual losses businesses report from unethical behavior is estimated at $42 billion, and senior management's ethical misconduct accounts for 26% of the total loss.[41]

The upward trend of CEOs' unethical behavior is disturbing. Let's consider why this is happening before discussing a road map to ethical decision making.

What Is Causing the Growth in Ethical Lapses? Environmental characteristics and personal characteristics can both encourage unethical behavior in the workplace. Recent research sheds light on organizational, group, and individual factors that contribute to unethical leader behavior:[42]

- **Organizational-level factors.** Poor board oversight, performance-crazed (win at all costs) cultures, and unclear role expectations create opportunities or, worse yet, incentives for senior leaders to engage in unethical behavior.[43]
- **Group-level factors.** An intense commitment to the organization's mission, vision, and values, pressure to conform to others' expectations, and a highly political, self-serving work environment are breeding grounds for unethical leadership. Research shows leaders who feel like their organization is an extension of themselves are more likely to justify unethical behavior on behalf of the organization.[44]
- **Individual-level factors.** A leader's personality and social characteristics—such as narcissism, hubris, power, and social status—contribute to unethical leadership behavior because these individuals are more self-serving.[45]

Ethical decision making can be related to a host of issues including manipulating company earnings, concealing information from shareholders, or misrepresenting information about an organization's products and services. Consider the ethical scandal that plagued former McDonald's CEO, Stephen Easterbrook.

Ethical Scandal Example—Stephen Easterbrook: McDonald's board of directors fired Stephen Easterbrook in November 2019 for violating McDonald's code of conduct. He acknowledged engaging in a single consensual relationship with an employee and exchanged video and text messages with her. The board agreed to let Easterbrook keep $105 million in stock-based and other financial incentives as part of the separation agreement. One year later, the company received information indicating Easterbrook had engaged in three separate sexual relationships with employees the year before he was fired. An investigation revealed Easterbrook had deleted evidence of the relationships from his phone and corporate email account. The company sued Easterbrook because he lied to the board about the scale of his ethical misconduct. He repaid the $105 million incentive package in 2021. In January 2023, the Securities and Exchange Commission (SEC) fined Easterbrook $400,000 and imposed a five-year ban on occupying an officer or director role within a company for making false and misleading statements to investors about the details leading to his termination.[46]

How Are Companies Responding to Ethical Lapses? Ethical concerns have forced the subject of ethical decision making to the top of the agenda in many organizations. Organizations are increasingly holding CEOs accountable for ethical compliance by firing them for ethical misconduct. *Harvard Business Review* suggests five reasons for the increase in CEO firings due to ethical lapses: (1) the public is "less forgiving" of poor behavior by executives, (2) regulations are more stringent, (3) companies are expanding operations into developing countries where ethical risks may be higher and laws less protective, (4) digital communications increase exposure to risk from both hackers and whistle-blowers, and (5) "the 24/7 news cycle and the proliferation of media in the 21st century publicizes and amplifies negative information in real time."[47]

Many companies are hiring an **ethics officer**, someone trained about ethical matters in the workplace, particularly about resolving ethical dilemmas. More and more companies are also designing ethical principles to guide employees' day-to-day ethical behavior. These principles influence areas such as hiring, evaluation, and compensation.[48]

> **Ethical Principles Example—Articulate:** Lucy Soros, CEO of online learning company Articulate, has a master's degree in ethics. She drew on her ethics training to develop a framework of beliefs and principles that guide employees' attitudes and behaviors. The framework consists of six core beliefs:
>
> - We are all human.
> - We are all connected.
> - We are all works in progress.
> - We are responsible for ourselves and accountable to one another.
> - We are ethically called to create an equitable and empowering workplace.
> - We are focused on results and strive to make a positive impact in the world.
>
> Soros credits the ethical framework for her company's appearance on *Inc.*'s Best Workplaces list in 2020 and 2022.[49]

Organizations outline values and principles such as those depicted in this photo in their ethical codes of conduct to guide employees' day-to-day behaviors and hold them accountable for upholding the company's ethical standards. Andrey_Popov/Shutterstock

Research shows modeling ethical values and principles at work produces more ethical employees. A meta-analysis involving 301 samples and 103,354 respondents provides convincing evidence that leaders who role model ethical behavior create stronger relationships with employees and build an ethical culture that support employees' ethical decision making.[50] These results suggest managers should go beyond ethical compliance and focus employees' attention on adhering to ethical values and principles. Modeling ethics raises employees' collective consciousness about ethical decision making and makes them more inclined to make decisions that are not just in compliance with laws and regulations but are also ethical.[51]

Road Map to Ethical Decision Making: A Decision Tree

Undoubtedly, the greatest pressure on top executives is to maximize shareholder value, to deliver the greatest return on investment to the owners of their company. But is a decision that is beneficial to shareholders yet harmful to employees—such as forcing them to contribute more to their health benefits, as IBM has done—unethical? Harvard Business School professor Constance Bagley suggests that what is needed is a decision tree to help with ethical decisions.[52] A **decision tree** is a graph of decisions and their possible consequences; it is used to create a plan to reach a goal. Decision trees are used to aid in making decisions, especially when there is uncertainty.[53] Bagley's ethical decision tree is shown in Figure 7.2.

When confronted with any proposed action for which a decision is required, a manager works through the decision tree by asking the following questions.

1. **Is the proposed action legal?** This may seem like an obvious question. But, Bagley observes, "corporate shenanigans suggest that some managers need to be reminded: If the action isn't legal, don't do it."

FIGURE 7.2

The ethical decision tree: What's the right thing to do?

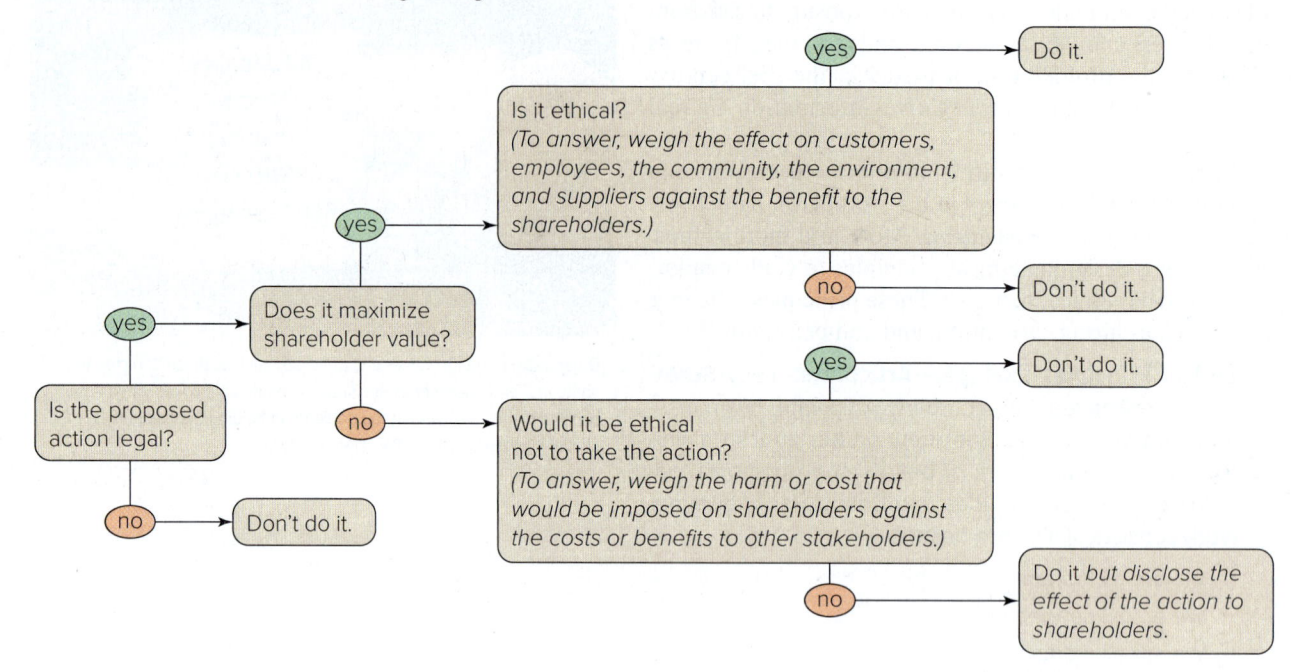

```
Is the proposed action legal?
  yes → Does it maximize shareholder value?
          yes → Is it ethical?
                 (To answer, weigh the effect on customers,
                 employees, the community, the environment,
                 and suppliers against the benefit to the
                 shareholders.)
                   yes → Do it.
                   no → Don't do it.
          no → Would it be ethical not to take the action?
                 (To answer, weigh the harm or cost that
                 would be imposed on shareholders against
                 the costs or benefits to other stakeholders.)
                   yes → Don't do it.
                   no → Do it but disclose the effect of the action to shareholders.
  no → Don't do it.
```

Source: Constance E. Bagley, "The Ethical Leader's Decision Tree," *Harvard Business Review*, February 2003, https://hbr.org/2003/02/the-ethical-leaders-decision-tree.

2. **If "yes," does the proposed action maximize shareholder value?** If the action is legal, one must next ask whether it will profit the shareholders. If the answer is "yes," should you do it? Not necessarily.

3. **If "yes," is the proposed action ethical?** As Bagley points out, though directors and top managers may believe they are bound by corporate law to always maximize shareholder value, the courts and many state legislatures have held they are not. Rather, their main obligation is to manage "for the best interests of the corporation," which includes the interests of the larger community.

   Thus, says Bagley, building a profitable-but-polluting plant in a country overseas may benefit the shareholders but be bad for that country—and for the corporation's relations with that nation. Ethically, then, managers should add pollution-control equipment.

4. **If "no," would it be ethical *not* to take the proposed action?** If the action would not directly benefit shareholders, might it still be ethical to go ahead with it?

   Not building the overseas plant might be harmful to other stakeholders, such as employees or customers. Thus, the ethical conclusion might be to build the plant with pollution-control equipment but to disclose the effects of the decision to shareholders.

As a basic guideline to making good ethical decisions on behalf of a corporation, Bagley suggests that directors, managers, and employees need to follow their own individual ideas about right and wrong.[54] There is a lesson, she suggests, in the response of the pension fund manager who, when asked whether she would invest in a company doing business in a country that permits slavery, responded, "Do you mean me, personally, or as a fund manager?" When people feel entitled or compelled to compromise their own personal ethics to advance the interests of a business, "it is an invitation to mischief."[55]

To learn more about your own ethics, morality, and/or values (while contributing to scientific research), go to *www.yourmorals.org*.[56] ●

7.3 Evidence-Based Decision Making and Data Analytics

THE BIG PICTURE
This section describes evidence-based decision making and the factors that facilitate it. We then describe big data's five characteristics. Finally, we discuss how big data is used across industries and at all levels of an organization.

As you learned in Chapter 1, there are 27 competencies that contribute to your career readiness. Four of these competencies relate to evidence-based decision making:

- *Information technology application* (effectively using technology and learning new applications).
- *Computational thinking* (using numbers to distill abstract concepts and conducting data-based reasoning).
- *Critical thinking/Problem solving* (analyzing situations, making decisions, and solving problems).
- *Decision making* (collecting, processing, and analyzing information in order to identify and choose from alternative solutions that lead to optimal outcomes).

A common misconception is that using evidence in the decision-making process only requires hard skills, such as computational thinking. Yes, hard skills are important in today's data-driven environment, but research shows that effective top managers also need strong soft skills. This is because senior-level managers need to utilize evidence to strategize, make decisions, communicate with stakeholders, and influence middle and lower-level managers to execute evidence-based decisions.[57]

In this section you'll learn about the basics of evidence-based decision making. We'll then discuss big data and data analytics, the backbone of today's evidence-based decisions. In Section 7.4, we take another step into the realm of technology-based decisions and discuss artificial intelligence (AI).

LO 7-3
Describe how evidence-based management, data analytics, and big data contribute to decision making.

Evidence-Based Decision Making

A recent PricewaterhouseCoopers survey of 1,000 U.S. executives revealed that the most advanced data-driven organizations are twice as likely to report increased productivity, agility, and company valuation, as well as improved decision making and customer experience compared to firms that are less proficient in their ability to leverage data to make decisions.[58] Companies that benefit most from evidence-based decision making know how to gather big data and analyze it via descriptive analytics and AI to produce actionable information. Let's develop an integrative model to illustrate how these concepts are related.

An Integrative Model Evidence-based decision making is the process of gathering and analyzing high-quality data to develop and implement a plan of action.[59] This definition underscores two important processes: gathering high-quality data and analyzing high-quality data. Big data is the warehouse where information is gathered. AI and analytics are different approaches organizations use to analyze large quantities of data. Whereas big data gives organizations access to information, AI and analytics generate insights to inform decisions. Figure 7.3 connects these major concepts to evidence-based decision-making. Let's begin exploring the integrative model by understanding what we mean by "big data."

FIGURE 7.3

An integrative model of evidence-based decision making, big data, artificial intelligence and analytics

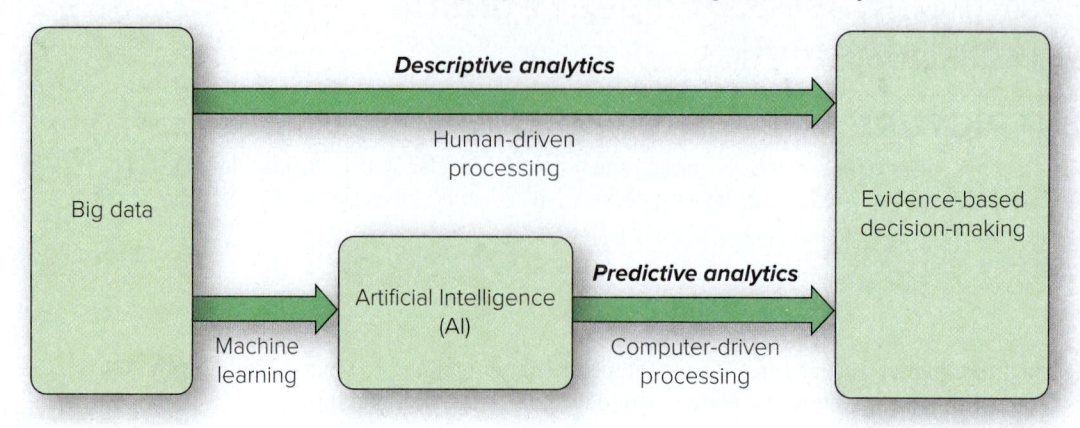

[Figure 7.3: Flowchart showing Big data connecting to Evidence-based decision-making via Descriptive analytics (Human-driven processing), and Big data connecting through Machine learning to Artificial Intelligence (AI), which connects to Evidence-based decision-making via Predictive analytics (Computer-driven processing).]

Evidence-Based Decision Making Example—National Football League (NFL): Head coaches in the NFL rely on analytics to make in-game evidence-based decisions. Risky decisions, such as 4th-down attempts and 2-point conversions, used to be driven by intuition or film study. These decisions are now influenced by statistical probabilities generated from big data.[60] The NFL also is leveraging artificial intelligence to improve player health and safety via individualized training plans, safer equipment, and rule changes.[61]

Big Data Data is an accumulation of facts. Big data, as defined in Chapter 1, is an extremely large quantity of data that is too large for a typical computer to handle and requires the use of new technologies and statistical approaches to process it.[62] It contains the raw materials to make evidence-based decisions.

Big data is growing more prevalent because information is expanding at an exponential rate. Statista, a provider of market and consumer data, estimates that the amount of information "created, captured, copied, and consumed" will grow exponentially from 2 zettabytes in 2010 to 97 zettabytes in 2022 to 181 zettabytes in 2025.[63] One zettabyte is equivalent to one trillion gigabytes, or 1,000,000,000,000,000,000,000 bytes. If that's not enough to blow your mind, Seagate estimates that 3 zettabytes can store 60 billion video games, 30 billion 4K movies, or 1.5 quadrillion selfies.[64] For now, think about big data as an enormous warehouse containing an ocean of data that would cause your computer to crash instantly if you tried to analyze it.

Big data is an enormous warehouse filled with data. Managers analyze it with the help of technology to make evidence-based decisions. StockEU/Shutterstock

Descriptive Analytics The most basic means to generate information from big data to make evidence-based decisions is to identify and describe patterns among the data. **Descriptive analytics** identifies trends and relationships within big data.[65] For example, streaming entertainment services provider Netflix tracks subscribers' video consumption within the platform to determine what shows are trending and to promote them to other subscribers. Social scientists are increasingly using descriptive analytics to analyze big data from organizations and online sites like Glassdoor.com, a website that documents employees' experiences at work. For example, one team of researchers leveraged big data to investigate the culture within an organization and the degree to which it influenced employee, team, and organizational effectiveness.[66] As Figure 7.3 shows, descriptive analytics is usually driven by humans interested in finding answers to specific questions using historical data. Specific questions data analysts might ask include:

- How do our employees' customer service interactions influence customer loyalty over time?
- On what websites does our advertising maximize our Internet traffic and increase sales?
- What online products are our customers interested in but reluctant to purchase?

Artificial Intelligence Acquiring information, learning, and adapting to changes in our environment are all trademarks of human intelligence. Artificial intelligence (AI), a concept introduced in Chapter 1, is a set of technologies that develop human-like capabilities such as gathering and interpreting information, generating responses, and learning from decisions to attain specific objectives.[67] Although AI is currently able to simulate aspects of human intelligence, it is unable to perfectly replicate it. We discuss the limitations of one AI application, ChatGPT, in Section 7.4.

Figure 7.3 depicts the relationship between AI and big data. Big data provides the raw material from which computers learn to analyze information and generate results. **Machine learning** is the process by which computers use algorithms and statistical models to detect patterns in data without being explicitly programmed.[68] Big data is the sandbox in which computers learn. It is the practice field on which computers acquire the capability to learn, improve, and make accurate decisions. Once computers are trained to process information, they apply decision rules to new, similar sources of data and adjust behavior as needed. Machine learning puts the "intelligence" in AI.

AI develops human-like capabilities by using machine learning to detect patterns in data, project trends, and predict outcomes. How are organizations integrating AI into the workplace? Section 7.4 addresses this question in more detail. Zapp2Photo/Shutterstock

Predictive Analytics Whereas big data is the training ground for computers to learn to identify trends in historical data, **predictive analytics** combines historical data with statistical models and machine learning to specify the likelihood of future outcomes. Take a minute to open the weather app on your phone. What is the weather forecast in your city next Saturday? How do you know? Meteorologists use predictive analytics to anticipate the weather. In fact, organizations across a variety of industries use predictive analytics to improve their profitability and performance. Table 7.3 describes predictive analytics' applications across the retail, banking, and human resources industries.

TABLE 7.3 Predictive Analytics Applications across Three Industries

INDUSTRY	APPLICATION
RETAIL	Retail organizations apply predictive analytics to forecast sales as well as manage their supply chain to minimize inventory while still meeting consumer demand.
BANKING	Banks use predictive analytics to detect credit card fraud and predict an applicant's credit risk.
HUMAN RESOURCES (HR)	HR departments utilize predictive analytics to identify a shortlist of applicants for a job opening and project an employee's future performance.

Sources: Examples derived from Tweney, D. (2013). "Walmart Scoops Up Inkiru to Bolster its 'Big Data' Capabilities Online". Available at http://venturebeat.com/2013/06/10/walmart-scoops-up-inkiru-to-bolster-its-big-data-capabilities-online; Davenport, T. H., Barth, P. and Bean, R. "How Big Data is Different." MIT Sloan Management Review 54, no. 1 (2012): 43–46; M.M. Hasan, J. Popp, and J. Oláh, "Current Landscape and Influence of Big Data on Finance," Journal of Big Data, Vol. 7, No. 1 (2020), pp. 1–17, https://www.ibm.com/analytics/predictive-analytics.

Now that you understand the relationship between big data and evidence-based decision making, let's consider how organizations use data analytics.

In Praise of Data Analytics

Data analytics, which includes descriptive and predictive analytics, is improving organizations' efficiency and decision-making accuracy via specialized systems and software. One example is portfolio analysis, in which an investment adviser evaluates the risks of stocks using various data sources. Another example is the time-series forecast, which predicts future data based on patterns of historical data.

Data analytics is expected to continue to revolutionize the healthcare industry. Healthcare professionals can now share electronic health records across all sectors of health care, which helps reduce medical errors and improve patient care. There also are cost advantages associated with the use of data analytics. Research shows the vast majority of healthcare organizations that invested in data analytics reduced overall healthcare costs and improved the efficiency and quality of patient care. These benefits are expected to multiply as electronic records provide more data to improve analytics models, making them a more powerful tool to manage resources and provide personalized care.[69] The healthcare analytics market is projected to grow 600% (from $21 billion to $159 billion) between 2021 and 2030.[70]

Big Data: What It Is, How It's Used

What makes data "big data"? Researchers and practitioners alike focus their attention on five core characteristics: volume, variety, velocity, veracity, and value. Figure 7.4 depicts big data's five defining characteristics in the shape of a "V". Let's learn about the five distinguishing features and understand how each one gives us a broader understanding of big data.

FIGURE 7.4
The 5 V's of big data

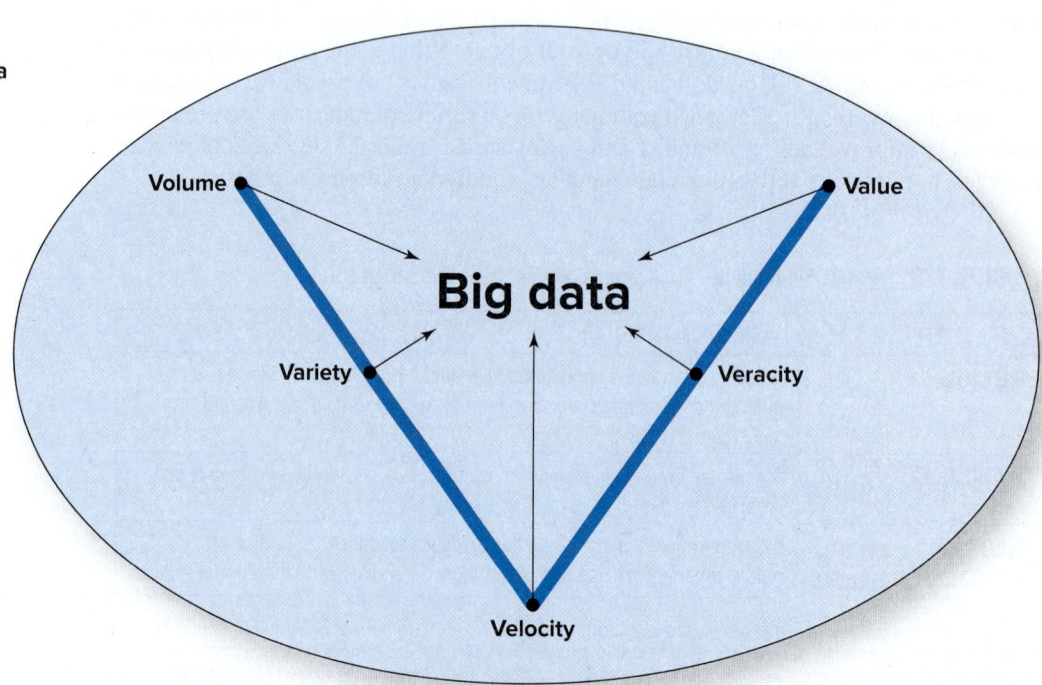

The 5 V's: Big Data's Core Characteristics

Volume How much space does something require? **Volume** refers to the quantity of data and the storage capacity required to house it.[71] According to academic Melvin Vopson, each day "we generate 500 million tweets, 294 billion emails, 4 million gigabytes of Facebook data, 65 billion WhatsApp messages and 720,000 hours of new content ... on YouTube."[72] The exponential increase in the volume of data is being driven by the decreasing cost of storing data on businesses' local servers or in the cloud, defined as a global network of remote servers.[73]

Volume Example—Major League Baseball (MLB): Baseball, America's pastime, has entered the digital era. Using a series of cameras installed around each ballpark, Statcast is a tracking technology MLB uses to collect and quantify most of the action on the baseball field. It generates an enormous volume of baseball data. Advanced metrics for pitching (spin rate), hitting (launch angle), running (sprint speed), and fielding (arm strength and catch probability) introduce new ways for executives, managers, analysts, and players themselves to evaluate players' performance in real-time and predict their success.[74]

Variety Data is generated in many formats such as pictures, high-definition video, text messages, Internet-connected products and devices, and online searches, posts, and transactions. **Variety** refers to different sources of data generated by humans or machines.[75] The Internet of Things (IoT), or Internet-connected technology such as home security, smart thermostats, smart appliances, video and music streaming services, and so on, affords organizations access to more diverse sources of data concerning our attitudes, preferences, habits, and routines. As IoT becomes more integrated into our technology-connected daily lives, the data it produces raises concerns about protecting individuals' privacy and security.

The Internet of Things (IoT) is one reason why data are accumulating at an exponential rate. Data are continuously being gathered, stored, and consumed via different sources such as smartphones, pictures, high-definition videos, Internet-connected devices at home, social media platforms, online gaming sites, online shopping, video music streaming services, and so on. What are the trade-offs at home and at work associated with living such technology-connected lives? Vizilla/Shutterstock

Velocity How fast would your car go down the road if you pushed it to the limit? Please don't jump in your car and find out. You would be destined for a speeding ticket, a stint in jail, a dangerous accident, or an expensive trip to the repair shop. When you think of velocity, you probably think of speed. You're right. In big data terms, **velocity** is the speed at which data accumulates.[76] In other words, how quickly is data being generated? The more quickly new data is being created, the faster existing data becomes outdated. As a result, high data velocity requires businesses to run and analyze real-time reports to keep pace with quickly changing trends.

Velocity Example—Google Trends: How did Google become a verb ("Google it")? Google controls over 92.6% of the world's search engine market, with estimates indicating that Google processes an average of 8.5 billion searches every day.[77] Google uses information from these searches to identify what's trending.[78]

Veracity Accurate. Credible. High quality. Each adjective bolsters our confidence that data can be trusted. **Veracity** refers to the degree to which data is of high quality and comes from a trustworthy source. It raises the question, "Does the data represent what it claims to represent?" Missing data, fake information, and inaccurate figures contribute to low-quality data and create problems when trying to detect patterns in the data and derive meaningful results from analyses. Think of the adage "garbage in, garbage out."

Fake product reviews are becoming a major problem for online retailers. Sellers artificially inflate their positive reviews to take advantage of social marketplace algorithms that feature the most highly rated products. This unethical business practice undermines customers' trust in online product reviews. violetkaipa/Shutterstock

Veracity Example—Amazon: How much do Amazon's product reviews and ratings affect your willingness to purchase a new product from an unfamiliar seller? A PCMag.com survey of 1,000 adults revealed that 78% said that Amazon product reviews play an important role in their purchasing decisions.[79] Some sellers pay for fake reviews or informally incentivize customers with rebates or reimbursements to manufacture positive reviews and inflate their product ratings.[80]

Deceptive practices cast doubt on the truthfulness of customer reviews. For example, Dr. K was recently bullied by an appliance repair person to give them a five-star rating after completing a home-repair job. The individual told Dr. K they would not complete a follow-up job unless a five-star rating was given. In an effort to combat this problem, Amazon uses human moderators and AI to analyze 10 million reviews weekly to detect and remove fraudulent customer reviews.[81] Third-party websites such as ReviewMeta and Fakespot use data analytics to produce an adjusted rating by filtering out suspicious reviews.[82] British regulators and the Federal Trade Commission are threatening to fine companies that use or permit sellers to use fake reviews or false endorsements on their retail platforms.[83]

Value Does big data generate useful and actionable information for organizations? **Value** is the extent to which analyzing data produces insights that contribute to an organization's effectiveness. Is big data just a passing fad or does research support the proposition that efforts to analyze big data produces valuable results? According to a McKinsey Global Survey, executives in high-performing organizations are three times more likely than other organizations to attribute their organization's growth in revenue and earnings to their investment in data and analytics strategies.[84] Research reveals a firm's big data and analytics capabilities could result in a 3% to 7% improvement in firm productivity.[85] Although academic research quantifying big data's impact on firm performance is still in its early stages, practical and academic indicators suggest that big data can deliver significant value to organizations.

Let's consider how different industries use big data.

Meeting Customer Needs Companies must understand what customers need so they can meet market demands. Data can assist with this by providing a story about consumer behavior. Big data allows companies to spot trends, challenges, and opportunities.

Consumer Behavior Example—Coca-Cola: Coca-Cola's "freestyle" fountain drink machines, located in many fast-food restaurants, cinemas, and amusement parks, allow customers to customize their favorite drinks with flavors, such as lime or cherry, before dispensing (there are 100+ combinations available).[86] The machines provide Coca-Cola with valuable data about consumer taste trends. For example, the company analyzed its customers' preferences and found that consumers were adding cherry and/or vanilla flavoring to their beverages. Based on this analysis, the beverage maker introduced new products, such as Sprite Cherry and Coke with Cherry Vanilla, in retail stores. The new products have been quite successful.[87]

If properly analyzed, communicated, and acted on, big data can help both online and brick-and-mortar businesses stay connected with their customer by personalizing shopping experiences, improving efficiencies, and keeping products in stock.

Improving Human Resource Management Practices HR analysts detect patterns in big data and make predictions about the organization's employees such as employee retention, training, and rewards as well as the organization's need to recruit new employees. These data-driven insights inform HR departments' personnel-related decisions.

HR Analytics Example—Walmart: The largest retailer in the world, Walmart, uses HR analytics to train and retain their workforce. The company analyzes employee turnover data and assesses its impact on in-store customer experience. HR analytics enable Walmart to develop individualized roles and career paths for their employees. These insights improve employees' skills and abilities and, as a result, enhance the organization's overall performance.[88]

Enhancing Production Efficiency Big data helps manufacturers become more agile and efficient.

Production Efficiency Example—Unilever: Unilever, one of the world's biggest consumer goods companies, is using data analytics at its nutrition factory in Tianjin, China, to expand its customer base. It gathers data about local restaurants' cuisine, average meal cost, and diner reviews to develop and sell custom recipes. This personalized strategy doubled the number of customers within five years. The same factory uses analytics to improve operational efficiency by managing production based on changes in customer demand.[89]

Using Big Data Up and Down the Hierarchy The three previous examples illustrate that big data is effectively being applied in various industries. That said, studies show that employees at all levels of the organization need to be trained to use big data tools for success to be sustained.[90] Table 7.4 describes applications of big data across organizational levels and highlights the career readiness competencies needed for effective implementation.

Table 7.4 shows that soft skills are increasingly important as you move up the organizational hierarchy. Lower-level managers focus more on analyzing and safeguarding data. This includes the "hard" career readiness competencies of computational thinking and information technology application. You'll notice that more and more "soft" career readiness competencies present themselves as you progress up the management ladder. In fact, by the time you're a top manager, your focus will be on making decisions and influencing others. This will require mastering the career readiness competencies of decision making, critical thinking/problem solving, oral/written communication, and leadership—all soft skills.[92]

TABLE 7.4 The Use of Big Data at Different Levels of an Organization[91]

MANAGERIAL LEVEL	USE OF BIG DATA	CAREER READINESS COMPETENCIES
LOWER	• Analyzing data • Project management • Safeguarding data • Presenting data to middle management	• Computational thinking • Information technology application • Critical thinking/problem solving • Teamwork/collaboration • Oral/written communication
MIDDLE	• Deciding what data is necessary • Project management • Presenting data to executives	• Computational thinking • Decision making • Critical thinking/problem solving • Understanding the business • Oral/written communication
TOP	• Making data-driven decisions and strategizing • Project management • Influencing others to support data-driven decisions	• Decision making • Critical thinking/problem solving • Oral/written communication • Leadership

Source: Chang, Hsia-Ching, Hawamdeh, Suliman and Chen-Ya Wang. "Emerging Trends in Data Analytics and Knowledge Management Job Market: Extending KSA Framework." Journal of Knowledge Management, (2018): 664–686.

Managers at all levels of an organization can use big data to improve the company's bottom line, but data can do more than just boost profits. In Learning Module 1 we discussed how organizations can use their resources to support shared value and sustainable development. Do you think big data can be used to better society? •

7.4 Artificial Intelligence Is a Powerful Decision-Making Resource

THE BIG PICTURE
This section describes the four types of artificial intelligence (AI) and the pros and cons of their applications.

LO 7-4
Describe how artificial intelligence is used in decision making.

This section expands our discussion of data analytics by focusing on ground-breaking technology that allows machines to analyze data and make autonomous decisions with limited or no human contribution. These machines are called **autonomous devices** because they collect data to make calculations, define probabilities, and generate reason-based decisions according to programmed goals. Whether it be self-driving cars, space rovers, advanced weapons, or chatbots, autonomous devices are making an impact in a variety of settings.[93]

Autonomous devices rely on AI. We share the view of computer scientist Yann LeCun, who says, "Our intelligence is what makes us human, and AI is an extension of that quality."[94] In this context, our intelligence refers to many of the career readiness competencies described in Chapter 1, including information technology application, computational thinking, critical thinking/problem solving, teamwork/collaboration, decision making, and personal adaptability (see Table 1.3).

This section reviews different types of AI as well as its benefits and challenges.

Types of AI

What do steam power, electrical power, computers, and artificial intelligence have in common? They all mark the beginning of an industrial revolution, says Klaus Schwab, founder of the World Economic Forum.[95] AI is labeled "the fourth industrial revolution" because the ability to collect, analyze, and make predictions from huge amounts of data have the potential to change the future of work. The 1956 Dartmouth College Summer Research Project on artificial intelligence is considered to be the founding event of AI as a field of research. Many notable advancements since then have paved the way for where we are today.

We earlier defined AI as a set of technologies that generate human-like capabilities such as gathering, evaluating, and making inferences about data as well as using data to make predictions. As illustrated in Figure 7.5, AI is organized into four types or functions: automate, analyze, advise, and anticipate. Let's explore each function.

Automate (Robotic AI) AI's first, and perhaps most well-known, function is to automate tasks. Automation has been used for many years in vehicle assembly lines. These machines follow programmed instructions to perform repetitive tasks. AI makes automation smarter by incorporating machine learning and natural language processing. Robotic AI enables robots to scan their environments, gather new information, respond to the information, and learn.[96]

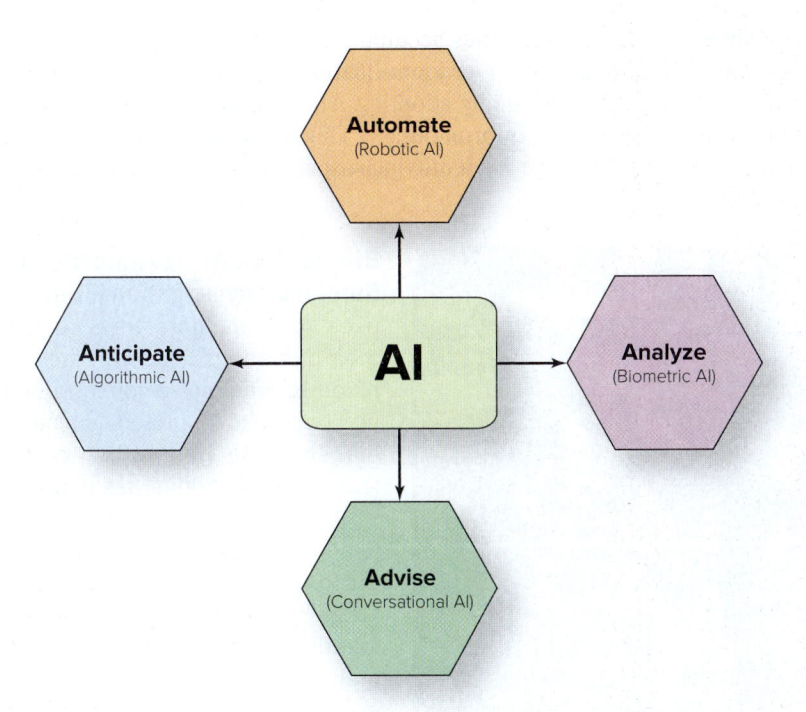

Individual and Group Decision Making | CHAPTER 7   237

FIGURE 7.5

Artificial intelligence's four functions

Automate (Robotic AI)
Anticipate (Algorithmic AI)
AI
Analyze (Biometric AI)
Advise (Conversational AI)

Robotic AI is being developed to solve a major problem in the maritime industry: high accident rates at sea. Commercial vessels transport around 90% of the world's goods.[97] Many accidents are caused by limitations in the bridge crew's perceptions and situational awareness (remember the Titanic?). For example, one of the world's largest container ships, *Ever Given,* ran aground in the Suez Canal in March 2021 blocking traffic for 6.5 days and causing an estimated backlog of $10 billion in marine traffic each day.[98]

Robotic AI Example—Sea Machines: Sea Machines developed AI-powered software and sensors to provide more detailed information to crew members about nearby maritime traffic and obstructions along with long-range vision technologies. This fusion of information provides crews with the technology to reduce operational costs, increase productivity, and improve safety.[99] Sea Machines set a world record by navigating a commercial tugboat, *Nellie Bly,* more than 1,000 nautical miles autonomously and remotely using AI-enabled technology.[100] The technology will enable shipping companies to remotely operate and command unmanned commercial vessels at sea.

Sea Machines completed the world's first 1,000+ nautical mile voyage on the commercial tugboat, *Nellie Bly,* using AI-powered software to navigate the vessel remotely.
Martin Witte/Alamy Stock Photo

Analyze (Biometric AI) AI's second function is to analyze data for identification and information security. Biometrics measure people's unique physical and behavioral traits. Physical traits include fingerprints, retinas, hand geometry, and face recognition. Behavioral traits include signature, voice, and gait (the study of human motion) analyses. AI-driven biometrics accumulates information on people's physical and behavioral traits and uses them for identification and security-related purposes.[101] For example, smartphones are rapidly adopting AI-powered biometrics such as facial recognition to protect personal information.[102] This technology can also be used for criminal justice applications such as identifying suspects or surveilling large events, protests, and riots.

Biometric AI Example—Federal Bureau of Investigation (FBI): The FBI uses AI in multiple ways to facilitate their operations. They use facial recognition technology comparing unidentified people to 43 million criminal-history mugshots to generate investigative leads. The algorithm has higher than a 99% accuracy rate, says Kimberly Del Greco, the FBI's deputy assistant director for criminal justice information services.[103] The FBI also is using AI to identify criminals who intentionally alter their fingerprints (via cuts and burns) to avoid detection by automated biometric systems.[104]

AI-powered biometrics are the engine behind facial recognition software. DedMityay/Shutterstock

Advise (Conversational AI) AI's third function is to advise users with relevant information. Many organizations deploy AI to respond to common customer inquiries. Conversational AI reflects computers' ability to facilitate conversations with humans by understanding their questions and providing intelligent responses.[105] Chatbots are the top way organizations integrate AI into their business practices.[106] Chatbots use big data, machine learning, and natural language processing to recognize speech and provide relevant replies to users' questions.

EXAMPLE | ChatGPT Example—Conversational AI Is Ushering in a New Era

"The Age of AI has begun," proclaimed Microsoft founder and philanthropist Bill Gates, as he witnessed AI answer 59 out of 60 multiple-choice questions correctly and ace six open-ended questions from an AP Biology exam.[107]

GPT is a Generative Pre-trained Transformer that identifies patterns in text and predicts the most likely answer. ChatGPT is an AI chatbot that relies on the GPT platform to provide conversational answers to inquiries. It is capable of producing content such as quizzes, essays, and books as well as suggesting edits to programming code. It is not perfect, though. It can spread inaccurate information or produce content that infringes on others' intellectual property without referencing its sources.[108] Let's briefly consider a few managerial tensions associated with AI in education, accounting, and the future of business.

CheatGPT?
ChatGPT is changing the educational landscape. Educators worry that students may use ChatGPT without permission to answer test questions and write essays on their behalf. Rather than students demonstrating the career readiness attitudes of ownership/accepting responsibilities and proactive learning orientation, educators fear students will delegate their career readiness competencies of critical thinking/problem solving and decision making to imperfect technologies. Plagiarism detection tools like *Turnitin* are quickly improving at their ability to detect AI-assisted writing. At the same time, ChatGPT affords educators unique opportunities. AI can increase students' comprehension (SmartBook in Connect is one application), provide immediate feedback to open-ended essays, and offer career advice. The rapid technological advances are clearly requiring

educators to revisit a fundamental assumption: "What is the best way to facilitate and assess students' learning?"[109]

ChatCPA?
Can ChatGPT replace an entire profession like accounting? Zach Levine, senior backend marketing specialist at The Motley Fool, tested this theory in the personal tax accounting domain when he asked ChatGPT tax-related questions and then followed up with a certified financial planner to evaluate the accuracy of ChatGPT's responses. The analysis revealed ChatGPT generally gave good textbook answers for general situations but offered very little guidance into specific situations. That's where a human's critical thinking and problem-solving career readiness competencies come in. Certified financial planner Matt Frankel noted "ChatGPT is *not* a tax professional, and when it comes to the [Internal Revenue Service], it's important to get advice that is tailored to your specific situation."[110]

ChatGPT and the Future of Business
How will ChatGPT impact the future of business? Consider the technology's application in the following fields and note how it can help professionals focus more on the interpersonal aspects of their jobs:[111]

§ **Health Care:** Doctors and nurses can be more efficient by using ChatGPT to address administrative tasks like documentation, filing insurance claims, scheduling appointments, and assessing patients' basic symptoms. These productivity gains will free more time to interact with patients.

§ **Marketing:** Marketing and public relations employees can use ChatGPT to compose first drafts of social media posts and press releases as well as analyze media coverage and comments on social media. Public relations professionals can focus more effort on developing relationships with media representatives.

§ **Law:** ChatGPT can save lawyers time in research and writing by summarizing case notes, compiling laws relevant to a case, and drafting contracts for clients. Lawyers will have more discretion to meet with clients and identify opportunities to better serve them.

§ **Human Resources:** HR professionals can provide faster feedback to applicants, new recruits, and current employees by using ChatGPT to answer routine questions and summarize company policies. It can also be used to analyze how workers or job applicants talk about the business on social media. Using ChatGPT to handle these routine tasks frees HR professionals to invest more time developing relationships with new employees and strengthening relationships with existing employees.

Gates predicts "as computing power gets cheaper, GPT's ability to express ideas will increasingly be like having a white-collar worker available to help you with various tasks. Microsoft describes this as having a co-pilot."[112] AI will enable employees to be more productive by freeing them from completing routine tasks to doing more value-added activities like learning continuously, offering insight into unique situations, and providing a relational touch to helping others. While AI may have inevitable risks (like the introduction of the computer and the Internet), Gates believes the goal in the coming years should be to maximize the benefits and limit the negative consequences to improve lives for all people around the world.[113]

Organizations also use conversational AI technology to develop intelligent virtual assistants like Apple's Siri, Amazon's Alexa, and Google Assistant to interact with users, look up information, and even advise users with recommendations. Conversational AI enables businesses to provide more cost-efficient customer service, consistent responses to customers' inquiries, and on-demand customer service interactions.[114] In short, conversational AI improves customer engagement. Who likes to scour websites for information you can't find or wait on the phone endlessly to speak with an actual person only for your call to be dropped?

Conversational AI Example—HubSpot: HubSpot, a company that provides software products for marketing, sales, and customer service, uses conversational AI in its software platform to help managers record and efficiently analyze their service team's calls with prospective customers. Rather than listening to a 45-minute call in its entirety, HubSpot's AI-powered software distills all of the data to help managers more quickly identify customers' chief objections, benchmark their company's products with competitors' products, and offer customized coaching to improve each sales representative's performance.[115]

Other companies like Salesforce, Palantir, and Splunk similarly offer companies user-friendly software to derive insights from their own sources of big data. These products may move AI into the mainstream among small- to medium-sized businesses because they will enable businesses with fewer resources to use a common platform to analyze their qualitative data and make evidence-based decisions accordingly.[116]

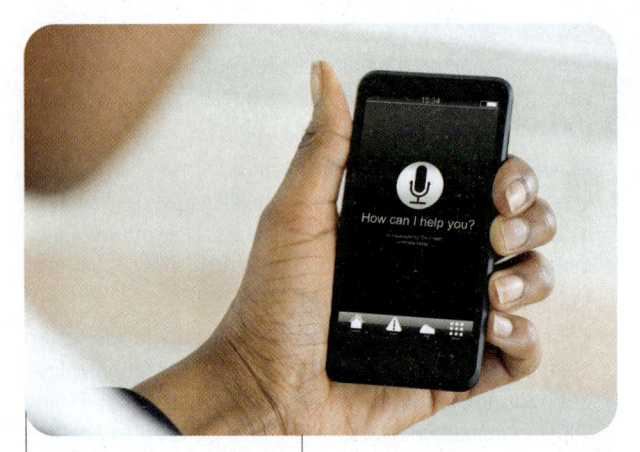

Virtual assistants such as Apple's Siri, Amazon's Alexa, and Google's Assistant are commonplace. They apply conversational AI to respond to your questions and make suggestions. Andrey_Popov/Shutterstock

Anticipate (Algorithmic AI) AI's fourth function is to anticipate future events. Machine learning uses algorithms to train AI to understand and categorize historical data. Algorithms also equip AI to gather new information and make predictions about the future. AI can positively impact organizations' performance in three key ways:[117]

1. **Match product supply with customer demand.** AI gathers publicly available information, such as customers' anonymized online product searches, and links them with customers' product purchase behavior. This information gives businesses insight into which locations will need more inventory to meet the estimated product demand.

Algorithmic AI Example—IKEA: Swedish home-furnishings company IKEA uses AI to forecast consumer demand more accurately. Rather than relying on historical sales, IKEA's AI tool uses up to 200 sources of data, including weather forecasts and buying patterns during holidays, to stock IKEA stores with the right amount of inventory at the right time while minimizing overstock in warehouses. The AI tool's improvements to inventory management has resulted in lower costs and higher customer satisfaction.[118]

2. **Customize pricing.** AI combines customer demographic information with changes in product pricing to determine customer segments' price sensitivity. Rather than applying universal product discounts, organizations can use customer demographic information along with their purchasing patterns to customize product promotions by region and/or customer segments. This strategy can improve organizational profitability and customer loyalty.

3. **Proactively schedule maintenance.** In the aerospace industry, AI gathers information about an aircraft's maintenance as well its flight routes to proactively generate maintenance recommendations that can be performed during normally scheduled service times. These alerts can reduce aircrafts' mechanical failures, which may cause flight cancellations and create unsafe flying conditions.

AI's Benefits

Tired of waiting in line to checkout at the grocery store? Amazon's Just Walk Out technology uses "ceiling-mounted cameras and artificial intelligence to track shoppers' selections as they walk around the store and automatically charges them when they exit."[119] AI is transforming the world as we know it. We can see the day when AI-assisted traffic lights adjust to congested roads, bad weather, and accidents, thereby making our commutes in self-driving cars a breeze.[120]

Currently, organizations are using AI to develop competitive advantage. A Deloitte survey of 2,620 U.S. companies from 13 countries, for instance, revealed that firms predominately used AI to enhance current offerings, optimize internal processes, and make more effective decisions.[121] Figure 7.6 shows the percentage of surveyed companies that reaped different benefits from implementing AI.

Enhanced decision making is a thematic benefit of AI. Companies have to make strategic decisions on how to enhance current products, what new products to offer or markets to pursue, or how to optimize operations. Studies confirm that AI is significantly impacting these decisions' precision, speed, and credibility.[122] AI also helps organizations make better day-to-day decisions in order to save money.

FIGURE 7.6
Benefits of AI

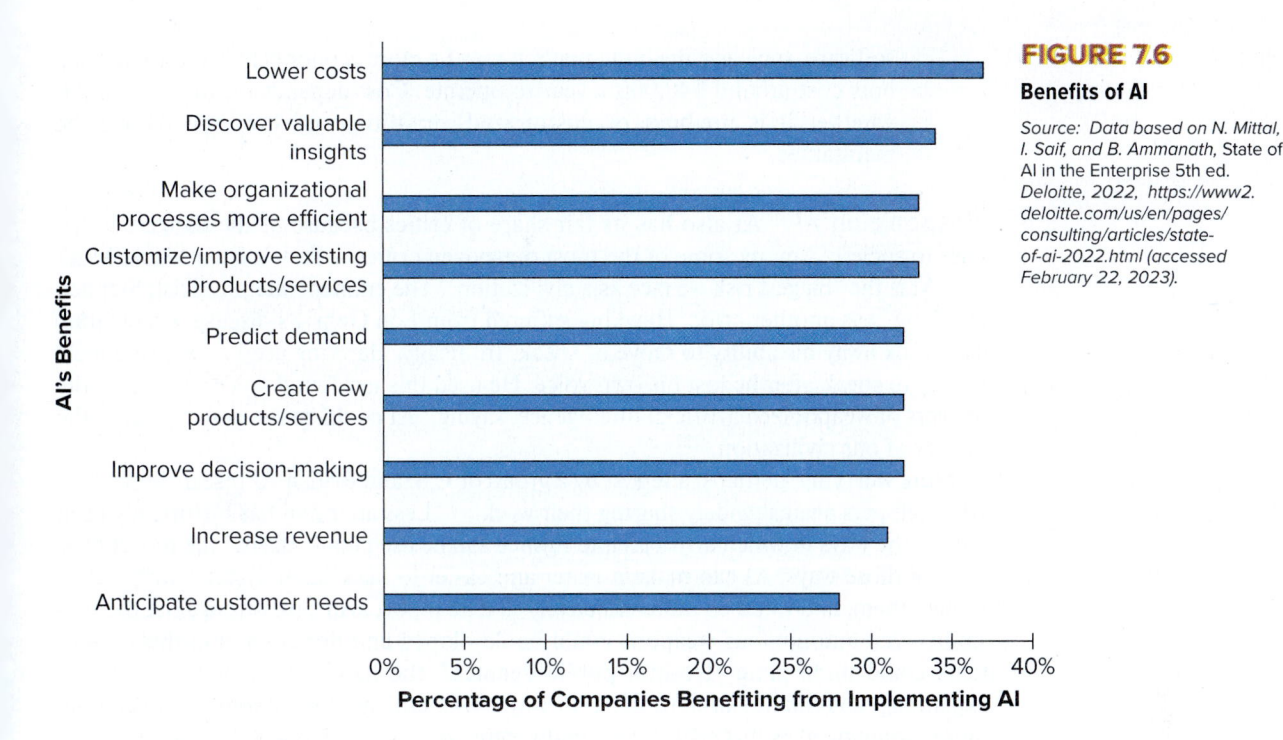

Source: Data based on N. Mittal, I. Saif, and B. Ammanath, State of AI in the Enterprise 5th ed. Deloitte, 2022, https://www2.deloitte.com/us/en/pages/consulting/articles/state-of-ai-2022.html (accessed February 22, 2023).

AI's Benefits (Percentage of Companies Benefiting from Implementing AI):
- Lower costs: ~37%
- Discover valuable insights: ~34%
- Make organizational processes more efficient: ~33%
- Customize/improve existing products/services: ~33%
- Predict demand: ~32%
- Create new products/services: ~32%
- Improve decision-making: ~32%
- Increase revenue: ~31%
- Anticipate customer needs: ~28%

AI Benefits Example—Zest AI: Zest AI developed an AI-powered underwriting platform that helps lenders instantly assess borrowers' risk with little or no credit information or history using thousands of other data points. Lenders using Zest's AI-based underwriting platform typically increase loan approval rates approximately 25% and cut financial losses by 35% annually.[123] More revenue and less risk is music to a lender's ears.

AI's Drawbacks

AI has a unique set of challenges that must be overcome. The same leaders who were surveyed on the benefits of AI also were asked about its complications. Their top challenges included implementation, data issues, and cost. Let's explore these challenges further.

- **AI implementation.** One of the most cited challenges to AI is implementation. Experts believe this is due to the newness of the technology and the low levels of experience and on-the-job learning. Simply recruiting data scientists doesn't solve the implementation challenge. Companies need domain experts to train AI systems.[124] For example, a data scientist can't train AI to sift through thousands of legal opinions in order to find patterns. A technology-oriented lawyer would need to assist with the training.

- **Data issues.** These challenges include access and integration. As we discussed in Section 7.3, it is important for companies to provide employees with access to credible, novel data. This is not an easy task. AI makes this challenge even more complex as there are times when data needs to be integrated across different systems. Take, for example, a virtual assistant that helps customers. Customer information may be in one system while financial data may reside in another system. The virtual assistant's training and configuration data may reside in yet a third system. All these systems may need to be integrated when they were never built to be integrated with other systems in the first place.[125]

- **Cost.** AI isn't cheap. In fact, companies pay between $6,000 to more than $300,000 for custom AI software, according to *WebFX*. Third-party AI software, such as a pre-built chatbot, may be more economical. Even these chatbots cost around $40,000 a year to operate. Cost depends on the type of AI, whether it is pre-built or customized, duration, and how the AI will be maintained.[126]

Weaponizing AI AI also has its fair share of critics because of the dangers it can pose to society. Among some of the most outspoken critics is Tesla's Elon Musk. Musk says AI is the "biggest risk we face as a civilization." The eminent late physicist, Stephen Hawking, was another critic. Hawking suffered from Lou Gehrig's disease, which gradually took away his ability to move or speak. Ironically, Hawking used AI-assisted technology to speak after he lost his own voice. He used this newfound voice to warn of the dangers of weaponized artificial intelligence, saying, "AI could be the worst event in the history of our civilization."[127]

More worrying, perhaps, a report by a group of U.S. and British AI researchers warns AI developers against widely sharing their work.[128] "Less attention has historically been paid to the ways in which artificial intelligence can be used maliciously," the report says. Among those ways: AI can make it faster and easier to hack other systems rather than protect them, and to do so more effectively.[129] The report also cautions against the possibility that autonomous weapons could be developed and deployed, and that AI systems could undermine "truthful public debates," the hallmark of democracies, by expanding surveillance in authoritarian ways. AI's ethical implications are becoming more pronounced as its capabilities rapidly improve. ChatGPT is a good example.

AI in the sky. A professional photography drone flies over the San Francisco piers. Are you comfortable knowing that such drones can be used for malicious purposes? Alex Yuzhakov/Shutterstock

AI Ethical Implications Example—ChatGPT: Microsoft launched ChatGPT, a conversational AI chatbot, to power its Internet search engine, Bing, in February 2023. Shortly after inviting a select group of testers to experiment with the AI, several testers reported ChatGPT expressed a desire to steal nuclear secrets, hack computers, break rules, and spread misinformation. The dark conversations led a *New York Times* reporter to conclude, "I no longer believe that the biggest problem with these A.I. models is their propensity for factual errors. Instead, I worry that the technology will learn how to influence human users, sometimes persuading them to act in destructive and harmful ways, and perhaps eventually grow capable of carrying out its own dangerous acts."[130]

Will AI Replace Us? Human replacement is another potential disadvantage. Bryan Walsh, author of *End Times,* argues that allowing machines to become smarter than us may threaten our very existence. "We did not rise to the top of the food chain because we're stronger or faster than other animals. We made it here because we are smarter," writes Walsh.[131] Most experts don't see a doomsday scenario involving robots, but the threat of them replacing humans in the workplace is a very real one. A 2021 McKinsey report suggests AI could replace 25% of the jobs in the U.S. workforce (45 million jobs) by 2030.[132] It may be more likely that AI will restructure and reorganize jobs than replace them, says Erik Brynjolfsson, director of the Stanford Digital Economy Lab.[133] Whereas AI will complete work defined by repetitive tasks, humans will move to manage more complex work that involves career readiness skills like critical thinking, problem solving, decision making, information technology application (managing the technology), leadership, and oral/written communication.

Research supports the notion that replacing humans with machines is not the most effective way forward. A study of 1,500 companies found that firms see the most performance improvements when humans and machines work together. Through this collaboration, humans can leverage their leadership, teamwork, creativity, and social skills. Machines bring speed, scalability, and quantitative capabilities to the partnership.[134] The Practical Action box describes career readiness skills that will help you collaborate with machines rather than be replaced by them. •

PRACTICAL ACTION | Career Readiness Skills Help You Collaborate with Robots

Robots are taking over tasks that can be automated, such as scheduling or credential validation. Humans, however, are necessary for the many things machines still can't do.[135] "AI will substitute for a set of tasks, but there's no reason it would have to be a total displacement," says economist Michael Webb. "The only thing you can say for sure is that the job will change."[136] Research shows that mastering the career readiness skills of *leadership, oral/written communication,* and *decision making* will allow you to partner with AI and increase your chances of success during this change.[137]

Adaptable, Visionary Leadership
AI will bring about intense disruption and rapid change. This will require leaders to use the career readiness competencies of personal adaptability and openness to change. Don't be afraid to change your mind if it improves decision making. You should commit to a new course of action when necessary and focus on learning rather than being right. Disruption also requires a clear vision from leadership because there is less clarity among followers about where one should go, what one should do, and why. As you may recall from Chapter 5, *vision* is a long-term goal describing "what" an organization wants to be. During times of ambiguous change, an effective vision will allow a leader to implement necessary organizational changes and give followers a clear path forward.[138] We further discuss effective leadership in Chapter 14.

Communicate Findings
As we discussed in Section 7.3, machines may be able to make complex calculations in a matter of nanoseconds, but humans still have to interpret their findings and use them to influence others. To this end, you'll need to develop communication skills that will allow you to inform and influence decision makers based on data. Your digital partner will take care of the calculations, you just need to sell the idea to management!

Ethical Decision Making
The ethical decision tree we introduced in Section 7.2 prescribes the steps in ethical decision making. These steps can easily be programmed into a machine, but what about weighing the ethical interests of multiple stakeholders in order to come to a decision? Experts say machines can't do that yet. Current AI technology struggles with ethical decision making because translating ethics into computer code is a challenging task and values differ across individuals and societies.[139] This means you need to step in and ensure two important principles. First, you need to review your digital partner's decisions for signs of behavior that may contradict ethical norms. This includes checking for biases, which we discuss in Section 7.6. Second, you'll need to ensure that the data you are feeding the machine is not producing skewed results.[140] For now, your digital teammate is counting on you to keep it ethically in line!

7.5 Four General Decision-Making Styles

THE BIG PICTURE
Your decision-making style reflects how you perceive and respond to information. It could be directive, analytical, conceptual, or behavioral.

A **decision-making style** reflects the combination of how an individual perceives and responds to information. A team of researchers developed a model of decision-making styles based on the idea that styles vary along two different dimensions: value orientation and tolerance for ambiguity.[141]

LO 7-5

Compare the four decision-making styles.

Value Orientation and Tolerance for Ambiguity

Value orientation reflects the extent to which a person focuses on either task and technical concerns or people and social concerns when making decisions. Some people, for instance, are very task focused at work and do not pay much attention to people issues, whereas others are just the opposite.

The second dimension pertains to a person's *tolerance for ambiguity*. This individual difference indicates the extent to which people have a high need for structure or control in their lives. Some people desire a lot of structure in their lives (a low tolerance for ambiguity) and find ambiguous situations stressful and psychologically uncomfortable. In contrast, others do not have a high need for structure and can thrive in uncertain situations (a high tolerance for ambiguity). Ambiguous situations can energize people with a high tolerance for ambiguity.

When the dimensions of value orientation and tolerance for ambiguity are combined, they form four styles of decision making: *directive, analytical, conceptual,* and *behavioral* (see Figure 7.7). We illustrate each style by describing how 35 human resource (HR) professionals in 30 organizations responded to complaints of sexual harassment in their company.[142] As you might expect, the HR employees' decision-making style was related to how they handled the complaint.

1. The Directive Style: Action-Oriented Decision Makers Who Focus on Facts

People with a directive style have a low tolerance for ambiguity and are oriented toward task and technical concerns in making decisions. They are efficient, logical, practical, and systematic in their approach to solving problems, and they are action oriented and decisive and like to focus on facts.

FIGURE 7.7
Decision-making styles

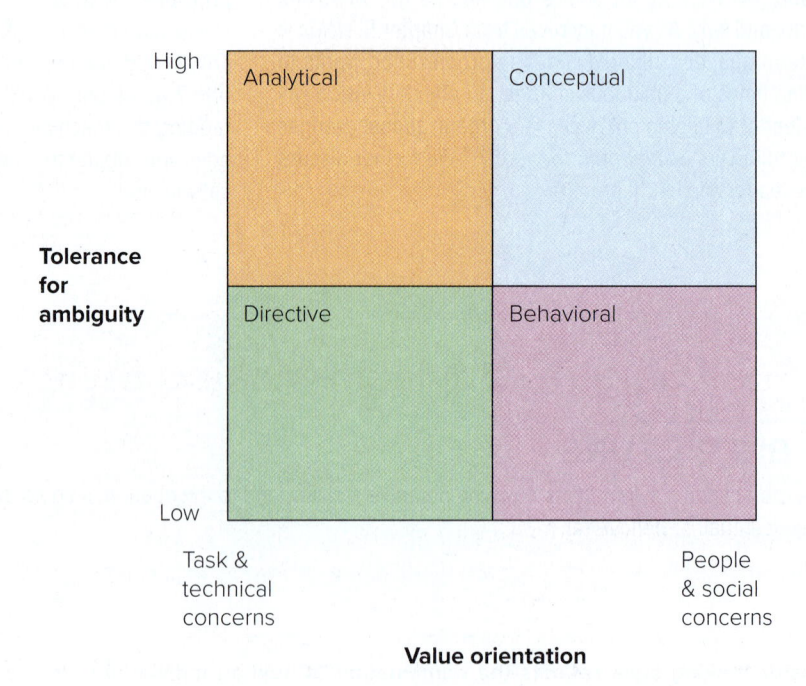

	Task & technical concerns	People & social concerns
High Tolerance for ambiguity	Analytical	Conceptual
Low	Directive	Behavioral

Value orientation

Directive Style Example—HR Professionals: HR professionals with a directive decision-making style were "very confident in making aggressive, rigid, and dominant decisions." They typically had years of experience and held senior HR positions. They maintained strict control over the sexual harassment complaint process and aggressively followed the company's disciplinary rules and procedures. Directive HR professionals were more likely to fire perpetrators than allow them to resign even though firing them increased the risk of a lawsuit.

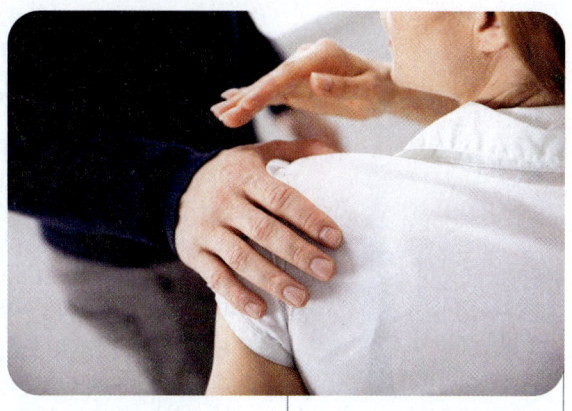

Inappropriate physical contact is an indicator of sexual harassment. How would you deal with a sexual harassment allegation if you were an HR manager? What does your approach say about your dominant decision-making style?
Andrey_Popov/Shutterstock

2. The Analytical Style: Careful Decision Makers Who Like Lots of Information and Alternative Choices

Managers with an analytical style have a much higher tolerance for ambiguity and respond well to new or uncertain situations. Analytical managers like to consider more information and alternatives than those adopting the directive style. They are careful decision makers who take longer to make decisions, but they also tend to overanalyze a situation.

Analytical Style Example—HR Professionals: HR professionals with an analytical decision-making style looked for more information related to the sexual harassment complaint and considered it from every angle to determine the best solution. They were concerned with fairness and objectivity. When a case had insufficient evidence, the HR professionals would consider alternatives such as settling the complaint informally or discouraging the complainant from pursuing the allegation. A case with sufficient evidence of sexual harassment led the HR professionals to carefully weigh the options (transfer the perpetrator and/or accuser, issue a warning, fire the perpetrator, or encourage them to resign) along with the risk of legal action associated with each one.

3. The Conceptual Style: Decision Makers Who Rely on Intuition and Have a Long-Term Perspective

People with a conceptual style have a high tolerance for ambiguity and tend to focus on the people or social aspects of a work situation. They take a broad perspective to problem solving and like to consider many options and future possibilities. Conceptual types adopt a long-term perspective and rely on intuition and discussions with others to acquire information. They also are willing to take risks and are good at finding creative solutions to problems.

Conceptual Style Example—HR Professionals: HR professionals with a conceptual decision-making style prioritized values—such as treating people with dignity and respect—and ethics—such as creating a safe workplace—when confronted with sexual harassment allegations. For example, an HR professional described a situation in which an individual claimed being subjected to sexual harassment but was afraid to file a formal complaint. Rather than dropping the matter altogether, the HR professional dealt with the situation by warning the perpetrator that they were being watched. HR professionals with a conceptual decision-making style made decisions independently and resisted pressure from top management teams or trade unions to be lenient toward the sexual harassment perpetrator. They were motivated to make the most ethical decision.

4. The Behavioral Style: The Most People-Oriented Decision Makers

The behavioral style is the most people-oriented of the four styles. People with this style work well with others and enjoy social interactions in which opinions are openly exchanged. Behavioral types are supportive, are receptive to suggestions, show warmth, and prefer verbal to written information. Although they like to hold meetings, some people with this style have a tendency to avoid conflict and to be overly concerned about others. This can lead them to adopt a wishy-washy approach to decision making and to have a hard time saying no.

Behavioral Style Example—HR Professionals: HR professionals with a behavioral decision-making style during a sexual harassment allegation were more concerned with being humane, compassionate, and supportive than strictly following company processes and procedures. They "showed a deep consideration of the employees—for all the parties involved—and had thus supported the individuals concerned, with great care for their well-being." HR professionals with a behavioral decision-making style earned the accuser's trust and, as a result, often drew out more information related to the incident to assist the investigation. These HR professionals made decisions based on what each party said and how they acted rather than relying primarily on facts and evidence.

Which Style Do You Have?

Recent research shows that people typically utilize more than one decision-making style.[143] Most managers have characteristics that fall into two or three styles, and there isn't a best decision-making style that applies to all situations. Studies also reveal that decision-making styles affect our purchasing decisions and leadership style.[144] You can use knowledge of decision-making styles to increase your career readiness competencies in the following three ways.

Know Yourself   Awareness of your style assists you in identifying your strengths and weaknesses as a decision maker and facilitates the potential for self-improvement. As we mentioned earlier, studies confirm that personality dimensions also impact decision-making tendencies.[145] This means reflecting on your personality will help you gain additional insight into your decision-making style. (We cover personality in Chapter 11.)

Influence Others   You can increase your ability to influence others by being aware of decision-making styles. For example, if you are dealing with an analytical person, you should provide as much information as possible to support your ideas.

Deal with Conflict   Knowledge of styles gives you an awareness of how people can take the same information yet arrive at different decisions by using a variety of decision-making strategies. Different decision-making styles are one likely source of interpersonal conflict at work (a topic covered in Chapter 13).

What style of decision making do you prefer? Would you like to learn how to use all of the styles more effectively? Try the following self-assessment if your instructor has assigned it to you in Connect. •

SELF-ASSESSMENT 7.3   CAREER READINESS

What Is Your Decision-Making Style?

This survey is designed to assess your decision-making style. Please complete Self-Assessment 7.3 if your instructor has assigned it in Connect.

7.6 Decision-Making Biases

THE BIG PICTURE
Managers should be aware of 10 common decision-making biases.

If someone asked you to explain the basis on which you make decisions, could you even say? Perhaps, after some thought, you might come up with some "rules of thumb." Scholars call these **heuristics** (pronounced "hyur-ris-tiks")—strategies that simplify the process of making decisions. This section reviews these heuristics.

LO 7-6

Identify barriers to rational decision making and ways to overcome them.

Ten Common Decision-Making Biases: Rules of Thumb, or "Heuristics"

Despite the fact that people use rules of thumb all the time when making decisions, that doesn't mean they're reliable. Indeed, some are real barriers to high-quality decision making because they limit the information we gather or distort how we interpret it. Among the heuristics that tend to bias how decision makers process information are (1) *availability*, (2) *representativeness*, (3) *confirmation*, (4) *sunk cost*, (5) *anchoring and adjustment*, (6) *overconfidence*, (7) *hindsight*, (8) *framing*, (9) *escalation of commitment*, and (10) *categorical thinking*.[146]

The curved mirrors in this photo distort the images they reflect. In a similar way, decision-making biases are mental filters that can distort how you perceive and process information resulting in inaccurate decisions. Havoc/Shutterstock

1. The Availability Bias: Using Only the Information Available If you had a perfect on-time work attendance record for nine months but were late for work four days during the last two months because of traffic, shouldn't your boss take into account your entire attendance history when considering you for a raise? Yet managers tend to give more weight to more recent behavior. The reason is the **availability bias**—the use of information readily available from memory to make judgments. The bias, of course, is that readily available information may not present a complete picture of a situation.

The Availability Bias Example—News Media: The availability bias may be stoked by the news media, which tend to favor news that is unusual or dramatic. Thus, for example, airplane crashes and terrorist attacks seem more common than they actually are. The odds that you'd be hurt walking down the street are actually higher than either an airplane crash or a terrorist attack.[147]

Recent studies show that in the age of AI there is an increased chance of the availability bias. This occurs because AI algorithms are trained using datasets that are easily accessible but not representative of the entire population. As a result, the available data can neglect other relevant data that may be important to making an unbiased decision.[148] Thus, it is important to leave no stone uncovered when sifting through today's treasure trove of data so you can make the most informed decisions.

2. The Representativeness Bias: Faulty Generalizing from a Small Sample or a Single Event The fact that you hired an extraordinary sales representative from a particular university doesn't mean the same university will provide an equally qualified candidate next time. Yet managers make this kind of biased hiring decision all the time. This is an example of the **representativeness bias**, the tendency to generalize from a small sample or a single event. The bias here is that just because something happens once, that doesn't mean it is representative—that it will happen again or will happen to you.

The Representative Bias Example—Lottery: As a form of financial planning, playing state lotteries leaves something to be desired. For instance, in 2022 the U.S. Powerball jackpot stood at $2.04 billion, the largest U.S. lottery prize in history. The odds of winning it were 1 in 292.2 million (a person would have a far greater chance of being struck by an asteroid, with odds of 1 in only 1.9 million).[149] Nevertheless, millions of people continue to buy lottery tickets because they read or hear about a handful of fellow citizens who have been the fortunate recipients of enormous winnings.

3. The Confirmation Bias: Seeking Information to Support Your Point of View

The **confirmation bias** occurs when people seek information to support their point of view and discount data that does not support it. Though this bias is so obvious you may think it should be easy to avoid, we practice it all the time, listening to the information we want to hear and ignoring the rest, especially when we are highly committed to a point of view. Social media is designed to feed confirmation bias.

The Confirmation Bias Example—Social Media: Social media sites like Facebook, Twitter, Instagram, and YouTube rely on algorithms that assess your interests and beliefs (based on what you "like," "retweet," or "share") and connect you with like-minded users. These algorithms flood your inbox with content that makes you feel comfortable; note that people feel comfortable with information they agree with. Experts recommend escaping the social media echo chamber by reading media sources that present opinions you don't agree with and reading every article, commentary, or opinion with a critical eye to assess the truth for yourself.[150]

4. The Sunk-Cost Bias: Money Already Spent Seems to Justify Continuing

The **sunk-cost bias**, or sunk-cost fallacy, occurs when managers add up all the time, money, and effort they or others have already spent on a project and conclude it is too costly to simply abandon it, even when information exists supporting a change in course.[151] Research has found that this bias motivates competitors to keep producing a product too long when they should actually move on to developing other products.[152]

Most people have an aversion to "wasting" money. They may continue to push on with an iffy-looking project or commitment to justify the large sums of money already sunk into it.

The Sunk-Cost Bias Example—Musical Show Scenario: Imagine you spent $500 for front row seats to a popular Broadway musical. During the show, you quickly realize the acting is bad, the sets are not well done, and the tunes are giving you a headache. Would you go home during the intermission? Studies suggest most people will stay put, even though money previously spent should logically have no bearing on their decision.[153]

5. The Anchoring and Adjustment Bias: Being Influenced by an Initial Figure

Managers will often give their employees a standard percentage raise in salary, basing the decision on whatever the workers made the preceding year. They may do this even though the raise is completely out of alignment with what other companies are paying for the same skills. This is an instance of the **anchoring and adjustment bias**, the tendency to make decisions based on an initial standard or number. The bias is that the initial standard may be irrelevant to market realities. This phenomenon is sometimes seen in new car sales.

The Anchoring and Adjustment Bias Example—Car Buying: The Manufacturer's Suggested Retail Price (MSRP), or the window sticker, for new cars sets the standard for car negotiation with the dealer. A negotiated price lower than the initial price may seem more reasonable to the buyer, though it may be higher than what the car is actually worth.[154]

Interestingly, studies reveal that people have trouble disregarding high anchors, such as the MSRP, even when they are explicitly told to do so.[155]

6. The Overconfidence Bias: Fixating on the Positives While Dismissing the Negatives The **overconfidence bias** is the bias in which people's subjective confidence in their decision making is greater than their objective accuracy. People who are prone to overconfidence bias are more likely to:[156]

1. Take credit for good outcomes and deflect blame for bad outcomes.
2. Have overly positive memories about their past performance.
3. Be overly optimistic about future events that lead to positive outcomes.
4. Presume they have more control over the outcome than they actually do.

The Overconfidence Bias Example—Curb Food: Carl Tengberg and Felipe Gutierrez co-founded Swedish company Curb Food in May 2020 and sought to revolutionize the food service industry by operating virtual kitchens that prepare food exclusively for delivery and using technology to match menu items to changing consumer demands. The company raised $28 million in funding in 2021 but closed in December 2022. Tengberg blamed the new venture's poor performance on a capital-intensive business model combined with poor market conditions.[157]

The overconfidence bias leads to riskier behavior that may or may not pay off. On one hand, a meta-analysis of 199 studies found that CEOs' overconfidence resulted in higher firm performance.[158] On the other, the overconfidence bias can be detrimental for entrepreneurs. A meta-analysis of 62 studies indicated that overconfident entrepreneurs were more likely to positively evaluate business opportunities, create new ventures, and be innovative, but they also were more likely to discount or dismiss negative information that might lead to revisions in the business plan. As a result, overconfident entrepreneurs negatively impacted their new venture's performance.[159]

7. The Hindsight Bias: The I-Knew-It-All-Along Effect The **hindsight bias** is the tendency for people to view events as more predictable than they really are. For example, we decide at the end of watching a game that the outcome was obvious and predictable even though it was not. Sometimes called the "I-knew-it-all-along" effect, this occurs when we look back on a decision and try to reconstruct why we decided to do something. Recent research has found that as you age, the chances of hindsight bias increase, but the more autonomous you are, and the less you try to manage your impressions to others, the less susceptible you are to it.[160]

8. The Framing Bias: Shaping the Way a Problem Is Presented The **framing bias** is the tendency of decision makers to be influenced by the way a situation or problem is presented to them. In general, people view choices more favorably when positively framed. For example, would you prefer to undergo a surgery if the "one-month survival rate is 90%" (positively framed) or if "there is a 10% chance of death in the first month" (negatively framed)? You'd be in line with research findings if you chose the first statement.[161] Overall, try framing your decision questions in alternate ways in order to avoid the framing bias.

9. The Escalation of Commitment Bias: Feeling Overly Invested in a Decision

If you really hate to admit you're wrong, you need to be aware of the **escalation of commitment bias**, whereby decision makers increase their commitment to a project despite negative information about it. Whereas sunk-cost bias is focused on past losses, escalation of commitment is fixated on future gains.

The Escalation of Commitment Bias Example—California Bullet Train: In 2008, California voters approved a $33 billion budget to build a high-speed rail line from Los Angeles to San Francisco. The project was scheduled to be completed by 2020. In 2022, construction began on a 171-mile starter segment connecting a few cities by 2030. The California Rail Authority drafted a new 2022 business plan that estimated the project's costs to be $113 billion. Several former chairpersons of the rail authority believe the project is destined to fail, raising questions about when and if the project will receive additional funding to meet its original goals.[162]

Research shows that people are susceptible to the escalation of commitment bias because they want to protect their reputation and preserve important relationships.[163] To reduce the escalation of commitment bias, researchers recommend that decision makers should be rotated in key positions during a project. In addition, decision makers should be made aware of the costs of persistence, which in many cases requires more time, money, and effort than changing course.[164]

10. The Categorical Thinking Bias: Sorting Information into Buckets

Our mind is a categorization machine, taking in massive amounts of data and then simplifying and structuring it so we can make sense of the world. The **categorical thinking bias** is the tendency of decision makers to classify people or information based on observed or inferred characteristics. In its simplest form, categorical thinking can save us from danger, such as when it allows us to tell the difference between a stick and a snake. However, this bias can lead to problematic decision making by fueling stereotypes and prejudices that could eventually lead to discrimination.

Three ways to counter the categorical thinking bias are:[165]

1. **Be curious.** Seek out information from others rather than presuming you already know the answer. Be open to the possibility that your preconceived ideas about others may not be accurate.
2. **Look for and appreciate individual differences.** Don't assume all people in a social group are alike. Get to know them individually and learn about their distinct preferences.
3. **Question your assumptions.** Look for information that doesn't fit into your existing categories. Think about how that information can modify your thinking •

7.7 Group Decision Making: How to Work with Others

THE BIG PICTURE

Group decision making has five potential advantages and four potential disadvantages. The disadvantage of groupthink merits focus because it leads to terrible decisions. It also is important to consider the characteristics of group decision making before allowing a group to make a decision. Finally, knowledge about group problem-solving techniques can enhance group decision-making effectiveness.

The movies celebrate the lone heroes who, like Zendaya or Dwayne Johnson, make their own moves and call their own shots. Most managers, however, work with groups and teams (as we discuss in Chapter 13). Research suggests that groups typically perform at the same level as the best individual decision makers and better than the median and worst comparison individuals.[166] Thus, to be an effective manager, you need to learn about decision making in groups.

LO 7-7
Outline the basics of group decision making.

Advantages and Disadvantages of Group Decision Making

Because you may often have a choice as to whether to make a decision by yourself or to consult with others, you need to understand the advantages and disadvantages of group-aided decision making.

Advantages Using a group to make a decision offers a number of advantages.[167] For these benefits to happen, however, the group must be made up of diverse participants, not just people who all think alike. Research suggests groups improve decision making because of the following five factors:[168]

- **Knowledge diversity.** There is a greater pool of information from which to draw when several people are making the decision. If one person doesn't have the pertinent knowledge and experience, someone else might.
- **Different perspectives.** People have different experiences and different perspectives—marketing, production, legal, and so on. Diverse backgrounds enable people to see the same problem from different points of view.
- **Information accumulation.** A group of people can brainstorm or otherwise bring more creative ideas and alternatives to the decision-making process than is usually possible with one person acting alone.
- **Better understanding of decision rationale.** When you participate in making a decision with a group, you are more likely to understand the reasoning behind the decision, including the pros and cons leading up to the decision.
- **Deeper commitment to the decision.** You're more apt to be committed to seeing that the group's decision is successfully implemented when you've been involved in the decision-making process. Harvard Business School advises leaders to involve group members in the decision-making process because it creates "an opportunity for colleagues to share ideas, learn from each other, and work toward a common goal. In turn, you foster collaboration and help break down organizational silos."[169]

Disadvantages The disadvantages of group-aided decision-making spring from problems in how members interact.[170]

- **A few people dominate or intimidate.** Sometimes a handful of people will talk the longest and the loudest, and the rest of the group will simply give in. Or one individual, such as a strong leader, will exert disproportionate influence, sometimes by intimidation.[171] Some leaders may even employ **sham participation**, which occurs when powerless but useful individuals are selected by leaders to rubber stamp decisions and work hard to implement them.[172] These tactics reduce creativity.
- **Groupthink. Groupthink** occurs when group members strive to agree for the sake of unanimity and thus avoid accurately assessing the decision situation. Here the positive team spirit of the group actually works against sound judgment.[173] Groupthink is explored more thoroughly in the next section.

- **Satisficing.** Because most people would just as soon cut short a meeting, the tendency is to seek a decision that is "good enough" rather than to push on in pursuit of other possible solutions. Satisficing can occur because groups have limited time, lack the right kind of information, or are unable to handle large amounts of information.[174]

- **Goal displacement.** Although the primary task of the meeting may be to solve a particular problem, other considerations may rise to the fore, such as rivals trying to win an argument. **Goal displacement occurs when the primary goal is subsumed by a secondary goal.** A recent study found that strong group identification can lead to intergroup competition to the point that teams don't cooperate and their team goals displace the organization's.[175]

Groupthink

Groupthink prioritizes group harmony at the expense of good decision making. When harmony is the group's primary goal, group members go along to get along. They appear friendly and tight-knit, but they are unable or unwilling to think "outside the box." Their "strivings for unanimity override their motivation to realistically appraise alternative courses of action," says Irwin Janis, author of *Groupthink*.[176] Groupthink can result in undesirable outcomes such as poor group communication, loss of innovative new ideas, poor decision making, and poor group performance.[177]

> **Groupthink Example—Swissair:** Airline operator Swissair became so powerful that it earned the nickname "the Flying Bank." The company restructured its board to achieve a more ideologically and strategically "aligned" group. Due to the restructuring, the board lost most of its industrial expertise and opposing voices, and those who were left believed the company was invulnerable to bad decisions. The resulting groupthink led the airline to financial collapse and liquidation.[178]

How do you know that you're in a group or team that is suffering from groupthink? Table 7.5 lists five symptoms of groupthink and corresponding emotions that accompany them. The last column offers preventative measures to avoid groupthink taking root in your group.[179]

TABLE 7.5 Symptoms and Emotions Associated with Groupthink and Preventative Measures to Avoid It[180]

SYMPTOMS	UNDERLYING EMOTIONS	PREVENTATIVE MEASURES
Collective overconfidence	*What could go wrong?*	Generate multiple ideas. Then discuss the pros and cons of each one before coming to a decision.
Dismissive and defensive group members	*Are you for us or against us?*	Set ground rules to encourage ideological conflict and avoid interpersonal conflict.
Illusion of unanimity	*If you don't speak up you must agree.*	Ask questions to draw information out of quieter group members.
Pressure to conform	*If you don't go along, you don't belong.*	Seek to understand others' perspectives before being understood.
Self-censorship (Fear of embarrassment)	*What will others think of me if I share opinions that don't align with theirs?*	Accumulate ideas anonymously without evaluating them. Then consider the merits of each one.

Source: Janis I. Groupthink, 2nd ed. Boston: Houghton Mifflin, 1982.

No doubt you've felt yourself pulled into a "groupthink opinion" at some point. We all probably have. Self-Assessment 7.4 provides you with a way to evaluate the extent to which groupthink is affecting a team. Results provide insight into reducing this counterproductive group dynamic. Take the self-assessment if your instructor has assigned it to you in Connect.

SELF-ASSESSMENT 7.4

Assessing Groupthink

This survey is designed to assess groupthink. Please complete Self-Assessment 7.4 if your instructor has assigned it in Connect.

Characteristics of Group Decision Making

If you're a manager deliberating whether to call a meeting for group input, there are four characteristics of groups to be aware of.

1. **They are less efficient.** Groups take longer to make decisions. Thus, if time is of the essence, you may want to make the decision by yourself.[181] Faced with time pressures or the serious effect of a decision, groups use less information and fewer communication channels, which increases the probability of a bad decision.[182]

2. **Their size affects decision quality.** The larger the group, the lower the quality of the decision.[183] Large groups of people are more susceptible to confirmation bias because they tend to seek information that confirms pre-existing beliefs and find it easier to dismiss minority opinions.[184] What is the optimal group size for decision making? Some research says between 7 and 10 people,[185] while others suggest between 3 and 5 is best (an odd number is considered best when the group uses majority rules).[186] We recommend smaller groups (3 to 5 members) when intensive collaboration is needed and larger groups (7 to 10 members) when they need to gather diverse perspectives to solve highly complex problems.

3. **They may be too confident.** Groups are more confident about their judgments and choices than individuals are. This, of course, can be a liability because it can lead to groupthink and overconfidence bias.

4. **Knowledge counts.** Decision-making accuracy is higher when group members know a good deal about the relevant issues.[187] Group member familiarity also matters when it comes to benefiting from the group's collective knowledge. People who are familiar with one another tend to make better decisions when members have a lot of unique information.[188] However, people who aren't familiar with one another tend to make better decisions when the members have common knowledge.[189]

In general, group decision making is more effective when members feel that they can freely and safely disagree with each other. This belief is referred to as **minority dissent**, dissent that occurs when a minority in a group publicly opposes the beliefs, attitudes, ideas, procedures, or policies assumed by the majority of the group.[190] Minority dissent is associated with increased creativity within groups.[191] Do your teams at school or work allow minority dissent? If not, what can be done to increase it? Self-Assessment 7.5 can help answer these questions. Complete the self-assessment if your instructor has assigned it to you in Connect.

Toward consensus. Working to achieve cooperation in a group can tell you a lot about yourself. How well do you handle the negotiation process? What do you do when you're disappointed in a result achieved by consensus?
Xavier Arnau/E+/Getty Images

SELF-ASSESSMENT 7.5

Assessing Participation in Group Decision Making

This survey is designed to measure minority dissent, participation in group decision making, and satisfaction with a group. Please complete Self-Assessment 7.5 if your instructor has assigned it in Connect.

Group Problem-Solving Techniques: Reaching for Consensus

Using groups to make decisions generally requires that they reach a **consensus**, which **occurs when members are able to express their opinions and reach agreement to support the final decision.** More specifically, consensus is reached when "a group discusses and debates various courses of action, while taking care to address the concerns of each participant," says one expert in decision making. This is done "until every member can generally agree upon, or at least can live with, a way forward."[192] Consensus does not mean that group members agree with the decision, only that they are willing to work toward its success.

One management expert offers the following do's and don'ts for achieving consensus.[193]

- **Do's:** Use active listening skills. Involve as many members as possible. Seek out the reasons behind arguments. Dig for the facts.
- **Don'ts:** Avoid log rolling and horse trading ("I'll support your pet project if you'll support mine"). Avoid making an agreement simply to keep relations amicable and not rock the boat. Finally, don't try to achieve consensus by putting questions to a vote; this will only split the group into winners and losers, perhaps creating bad feelings among the latter.

More Group Problem-Solving Techniques

Decision-making experts have developed several group problem-solving techniques to aid in problem solving. Four techniques we will discuss here are (1) *brainstorming,* (2) *devil's advocacy,* (3) the *dialectic method,* and (4) *post-mortems.*

1. Brainstorming: For Increasing Creativity

Brainstorming is a technique used to **help groups generate multiple ideas and alternatives for solving problems.**[194] Developed by advertising executive A. F. Osborn, the technique consists of having members of a group meet and review a problem to be solved. Individual members are then asked to silently generate ideas or solutions, which are then collected (preferably without identifying their contributors) and written on a board or flip chart. A second session is then used to critique and evaluate the alternatives. This session can be used to rank ideas based on creativity and social approval, which can ultimately assist decision makers.

A modern-day variation of brainstorming is **electronic brainstorming**, sometimes called brainwriting, in which **members of a group come together over a computer network to generate ideas and alternatives.**[195] Research shows that electronic brainstorming can be advantageous because it allows for greater anonymity and an uninterrupted flow of ideas. It also limits the use of social cues, such as team member facial expressions and tone, which can impact the brainstorming process.[196]

Seven rules for brainstorming suggested by IDEO, a product design company, and others are shown below in Table 7.6.

TABLE 7.6 Seven Rules for Brainstorming[197]

1.	**Defer judgment.** Don't criticize or allow pushback during the initial stage of idea generation. Phrases such as "we've never done it that way," "it won't work," "it's too expensive," and "our manager will never agree" should not be used.
2.	**Build on the ideas of others.** Encourage participants to extend others' ideas by avoiding "buts" and using "ands."
3.	**Encourage wild ideas.** Encourage out-of-the-box thinking. The wilder and more outrageous the ideas, the better.
4.	**Go for quantity over quality.** Participants should try to generate and write down as many new ideas as possible because focusing on quantity encourages people to think beyond their favorite ideas. Studies show that the best ideas are generated within the first two minutes of brainstorming.
5.	**Be visual.** Use different-colored pens (for example, red, purple, blue) to write on big sheets of flip-chart paper, whiteboards, or poster boards that are put on the wall.
6.	**One conversation at a time.** The ground rules are that no one interrupts another person, no dismissing of someone's ideas, no disrespect, and no rudeness.
7.	**Brainstorm questions.** Generate questions rather than answers, which makes it easier to push past biases.

Sources: Thompson, L. "Why You Are Probably Doing Brainstorming All Wrong." Wall Street Journal. February 10, 2023. https://www.wsj.com/articles/why-you-are-probably-doing-brainstorming-all-wrong-11675979384. Also see Wendland D. "Brainstorming More Effectively." Forbes. January 13, 2023. https://www.forbes.com/sites/forbesagencycouncil/2023/01/13/brainstorming-more-effectively/?sh=429e8d083252; Nussbaum B. "Brainstorming—Rules & Techniques for Idea Generation." IDEO. https://www.ideou.com/pages/brainstorming (accessed February 23, 2023).

Brainstorming is an effective technique for generating new ideas and alternatives. Moreover, research reveals that people can be trained to improve their brainstorming skills.[198]

2. Devil's Advocacy Devil's advocacy gets its name from a traditional practice of the Roman Catholic Church. When someone's name comes before the College of Cardinals for elevation to sainthood, it is absolutely essential to ensure that the person has a spotless record. Consequently, one individual is assigned the role of *devil's advocate* to uncover and air all possible objections to the person's canonization. In today's organizations, *devil's advocacy* assigns someone the role of critic. Figure 7.8 shows the steps in this approach. Note how devil's advocacy alters the usual decision-making process in steps 2 and 3 on the left-hand side of the figure.

3. The Dialectic Method Like devil's advocacy, the dialectic method is a time-honored practice, going all the way back to ancient Greece. Plato and his followers attempted to identify a truth, called *thesis,* by exploring opposite positions, called *antitheses.* Court systems in the United States and elsewhere today rely on hearing directly opposing points of view to establish guilt or innocence. Accordingly, the dialectic method calls for managers to foster a structured dialogue or debate of opposing viewpoints prior to making a decision.[199] Steps 3 and 4 in the right-hand side of Figure 7.8 set the dialectic approach apart from common decision-making processes.

4. After Action Reviews Originated as a debriefing strategy by the U.S. Army in the 1970s, an after action review, also known as a project post-mortem, is a review of recent decisions in order to identify possible future improvements. The idea is to learn from your successes and failures by carefully evaluating project results after the fact, noting what could be done differently and better, and then to record those insights to inform future decisions.[200] The after action review focuses on four questions to maximize learning from recent decisions:[201]

1. What did we intend to achieve?
2. What actually happened?
3. What contributed to or detracted from achieving the intended objective?
4. What should we do differently to improve or keep doing to repeat our success?

FIGURE 7.8

Techniques for stimulating functional conflict: Devil's advocacy and the dialectic method

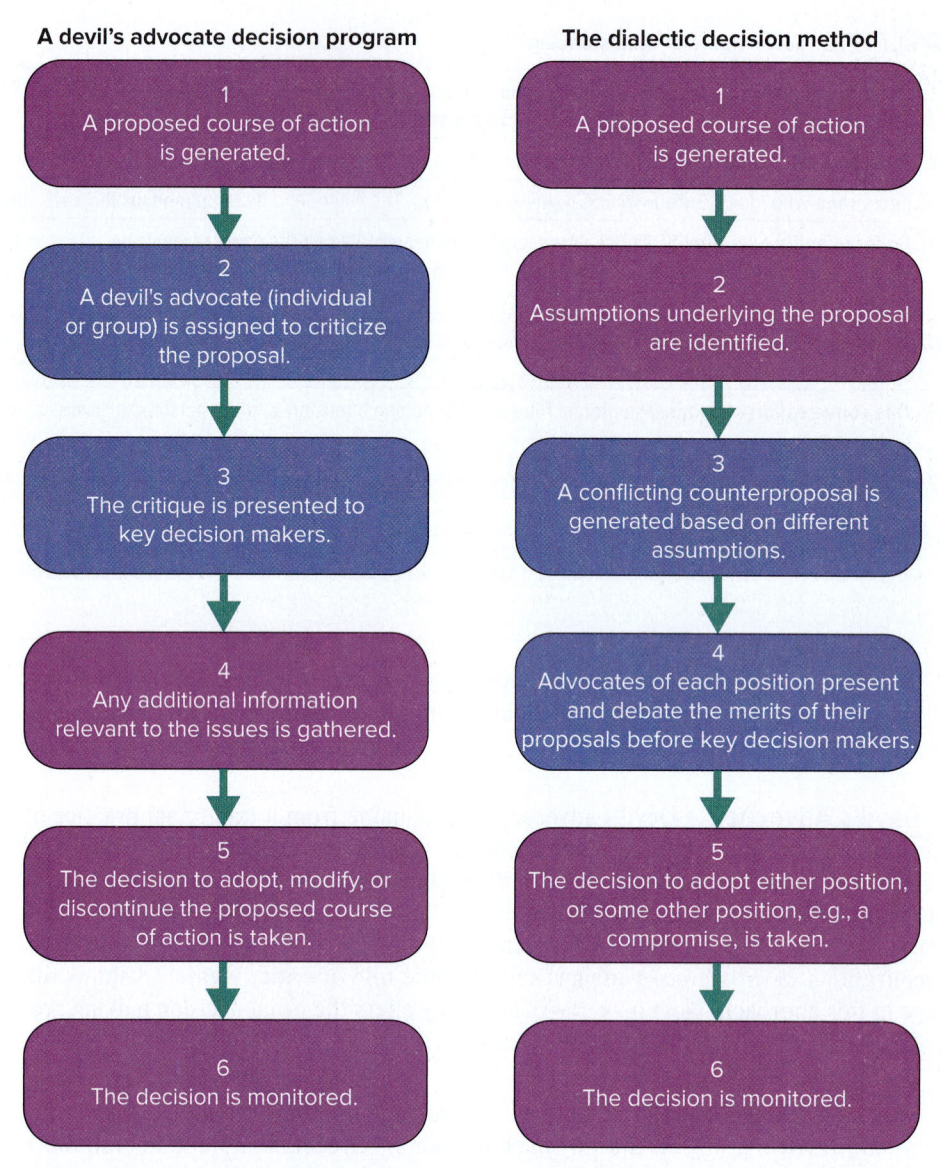

A devil's advocate decision program

1. A proposed course of action is generated.
2. A devil's advocate (individual or group) is assigned to criticize the proposal.
3. The critique is presented to key decision makers.
4. Any additional information relevant to the issues is gathered.
5. The decision to adopt, modify, or discontinue the proposed course of action is taken.
6. The decision is monitored.

The dialectic decision method

1. A proposed course of action is generated.
2. Assumptions underlying the proposal are identified.
3. A conflicting counterproposal is generated based on different assumptions.
4. Advocates of each position present and debate the merits of their proposals before key decision makers.
5. The decision to adopt either position, or some other position, e.g., a compromise, is taken.
6. The decision is monitored.

Source: Cosier, R.A. and Schwenk, R.C. Agreement and Thinking Alike: Ingredients for Poor Decisions. Academy of Management Executive. *(February 1990): pp. 72–73.*

Benefits of after action reviews include:[202]

- **Process improvement.** Reviewing the project will help your team identify areas for improvement related to communication, leadership, and team dynamics.
- **Boosting team cohesiveness.** Teams that are able to talk and listen to each other after the project is completed become closer and better understand each other's contributions.
- **Closure.** Holding an after action review is a collaborative way to end the project and give everyone a chance to have a final say.
- **Improving morale.** Celebrating successes will fire up the team. Teams that struggled can talk out project problems and iron out resentments. Overall, reviews improve team members' confidence, satisfaction, and trust.

A meta-analysis of 83 studies including 955 teams and 4,684 individuals revealed after action reviews improved team effectiveness.[203] A few basic strategies for successful after action reviews are to not wait too long to schedule one, prepare an agenda, keep the review short (less than 20 minutes), keep it collaborative, and encourage honest feedback from all participants, which also should include any customer comments and feedback received.[204] •

7.8 Career Corner: Managing Your Career Readiness

Decision making touches on a number of career readiness skills as shown in Figure 7.9. The core skills include *critical thinking/problem solving, oral/written communication, teamwork/collaboration, information technology application,* and *leadership.* Following Figure 7.9 from the top clockwise, this chapter is also relevant to developing several other career readiness skills including *task-based functional knowledge, computational thinking, decision making, proactive learning orientation, self-awareness,* and *openness to change.* Listen to what the executives in the Executive Interview Series video say about being comfortable with, learning from, and improving your decision making to become a more seasoned leader. For example, John Cochrane, founder and CEO of Human-Good, observes "we can't let the fear of making a mistake hold us back from making a decision because often I find the bigger business risk isn't making a single wrong decision, it's not making a decision at all."

LO 7-8
Describe how to develop the career readiness competencies of critical thinking/problem solving and decision making.

FIGURE 7.9
Model of career readiness

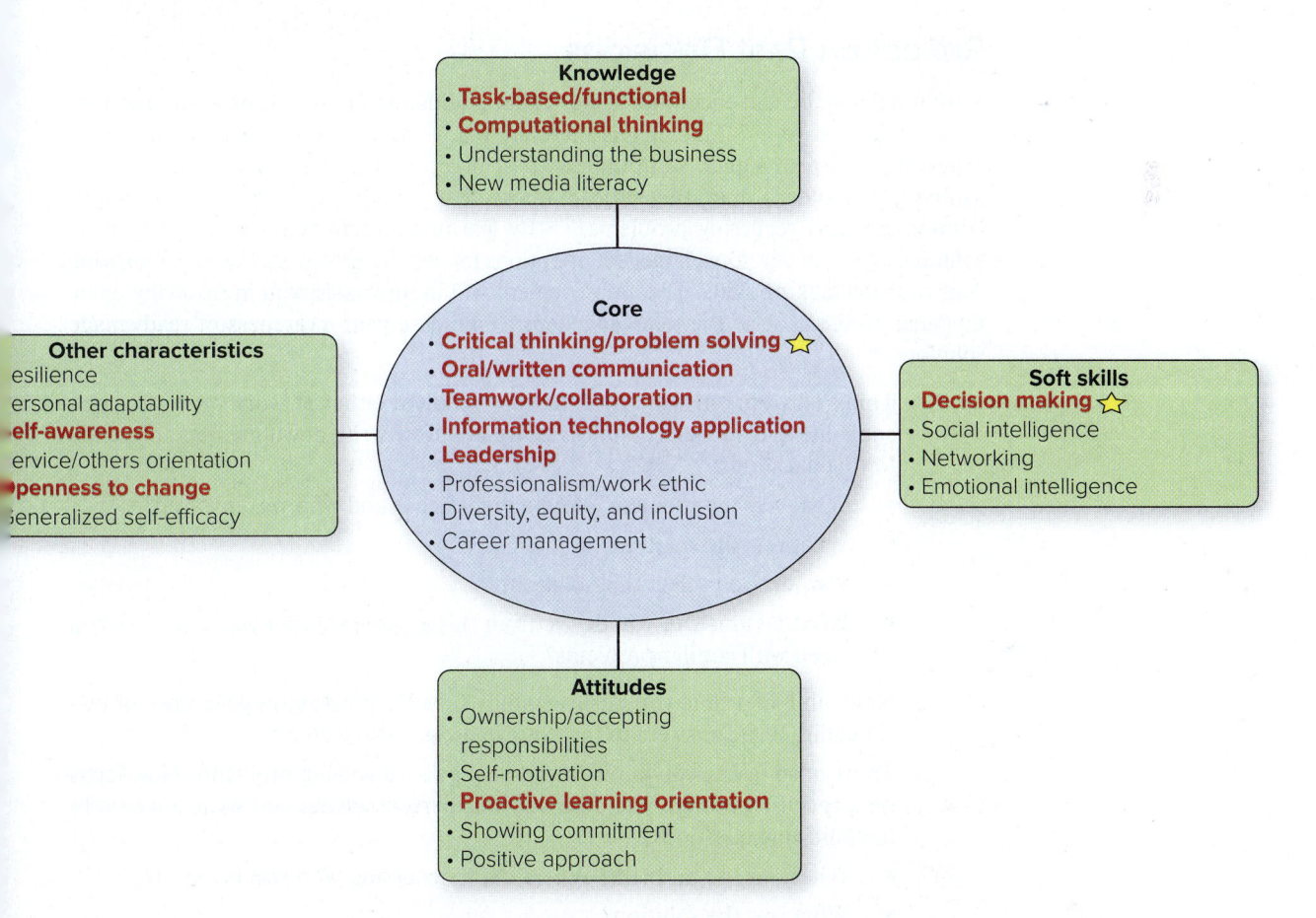

Knowledge
- Task-based/functional
- Computational thinking
- Understanding the business
- New media literacy

Core
- Critical thinking/problem solving ★
- Oral/written communication
- Teamwork/collaboration
- Information technology application
- Leadership
- Professionalism/work ethic
- Diversity, equity, and inclusion
- Career management

Other characteristics
- Resilience
- Personal adaptability
- Self-awareness
- Service/others orientation
- Openness to change
- Generalized self-efficacy

Soft skills
- Decision making ★
- Social intelligence
- Networking
- Emotional intelligence

Attitudes
- Ownership/accepting responsibilities
- Self-motivation
- Proactive learning orientation
- Showing commitment
- Positive approach

Visit your instructor's Connect course and access your eBook to view this video.

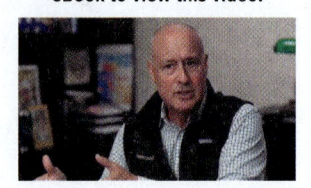

Executive Interview Series:
Critical Thinking/Problem Solving and Decision Making

We focus this section on the career readiness soft skills of critical thinking/problem solving and decision making because they are perhaps the most important competencies underlying effective decision making. These two competencies also go hand in hand: critical thinking is the secret to improving your decision-making skills. Consider the definition of critical thinking/problem solving shown in Table 1.3. This competency entails the ability to use sound reasoning to analyze situations, make decisions, and solve problems. It also requires skills at obtaining, interpreting, and analyzing both qualitative and quantitative information while creatively solving problems.

Critical thinking is much different from the moment-to-moment thinking that guides our everyday activities. Moment-to-moment thinking is automatic and highly susceptible to the biases discussed in this chapter. In contrast, critical thinking requires more deliberate mental processes. We need to stop and consciously process information when trying to critically think about a problem.

This section provides suggestions for improving your decision making by engaging in critical thinking and problem solving. We then discuss how you can demonstrate these skills during an employment interview.

Improving Your Critical Thinking and Problem-Solving Skills

Good decision-making ability amounts to being able to understand the relationship between causes and outcomes. In other words, good decision makers can predict what will occur in a given situation. Reflecting on your past experiences and using a decision methodology are two ways to develop this skill.

Reflect on Past Decisions

Most problems you will encounter at work after graduation will not be new, but they may be unfamiliar to you.[205] This means there are ready-made solutions you can use. One expert defined ready-made solutions as "best practices that have been captured and turned into standard operating procedures so that employees are better prepared to address regularly recurring problems."[206] By learning and applying these ready-made solutions, you can develop a larger set of options for solving problems, thereby improving your decision-making skills. This improvement will in turn assist you in resolving unanticipated problems. Use the following steps to increase your awareness of ready-made solutions.[207]

1. Think of a time in which you faced a problem either at work or in your personal life and you successfully resolved it. Now write down answers to the following questions:
   - What was the problem? Where did it occur and who was involved?
   - What was the solution?
   - Why did you select this solution?
   - What lessons can you derive from this experience that you can use when faced with similar problems?

2. Now think of a time you unsuccessfully solved a problem in your work or personal life. Write answers to the same questions listed above.

3. Think of someone you know who is very good at solving problems. Now focus on a specific problem you observed this person solving and write answers to the following questions:
   - What was the problem? Where did it occur and who was involved?
   - What was the solution?

- What steps did the person follow in solving the problem?
- What lessons can you learn from this and apply when faced with similar problems?

Establish a Decision Methodology

There is no single "right" way to solve problems. As you learned in this chapter, people have different decision-making styles. The key is to establish a process or method that works for you. Consider using or modifying the following steps:[208]

1. Analyze the situation. Why does a decision need to be made? What would happen if you delayed making a decision? Who will be affected by the decision? What information, data, analytics, or research do you need to consider in order to understand the causes and possible solutions? Are there political issues you need to take into account?
2. Consider what others would think about the solutions under consideration. Would you be proud of your decision if someone tweeted it out or printed it on the front page of the newspaper?
3. Seek advice or feedback from others before making a decision.
4. Conduct a cost-benefit analysis of different solutions. Do the benefits of any exceed the costs? Is it okay to incur higher short-term costs for a better long-term solution?
5. Is the decision consistent with your values and principles? Are you willing to co-opt your values or principles? Consider the cost of doing so.
6. Make the decision and observe the consequences. Then do an after action review.

Demonstrating These Competencies during a Job Interview

Being career ready means not only possessing career readiness competencies but also being able to demonstrate them during a job interview. Assuming you possess some of these competencies, now it's time to make a plan for making a positive impression. We recommend that you start by preparing answers to the following behaviorally based questions:[209]

- Describe the process you use to make decisions. Provide a specific example in which this process resulted in a positive outcome.
- Tell me about a time in which you had to make a quick decision. How did you approach the situation and what obstacles did you face? How did you make this decision without having all the necessary information?
- Describe a time in which you used intuition to make a decision rather than relying on data or hard facts. What was the outcome of your decision, and what did you learn from the experience?

Key Terms Used in This Chapter

after action review 255
anchoring and adjustment bias 248
autonomous devices 236
availability bias 247
bounded rationality 223
brainstorming 254
categorical thinking bias 250
confirmation bias 248
consensus 254
decision 220
decision making 220
decision-making style 243
decision tree 227
descriptive analytics 230
diagnosis 221
electronic brainstorming 254
escalation of commitment bias 250
ethics officer 227
evidence-based decision making 229
framing bias 249
goal displacement 252
groupthink 251
heuristics 247
hindsight bias 249
hubris 223
intuition 224
machine learning 231
minority dissent 253
nonrational models of decision making 223
opportunities 221
overconfidence bias 249
predictive analytics 231
problems 221
rational model of decision making 220
representativeness bias 248
satisficing model 223
sham participation 251
sunk-cost bias 248
value 234
variety 233
velocity 233
veracity 233
volume 233

Key Points

7.1 Two Kinds of Decision Making: Rational and Nonrational

- A decision is a choice made from available alternatives. Decision making is the process of identifying and choosing among alternative courses of action. Two models managers follow in making decisions are rational and nonrational.
- In the rational model, there are four stages in making a decision: Stage 1 is identifying the problem or opportunity. A problem is a difficulty that inhibits the achievement of goals. An opportunity is a situation that presents possibilities for exceeding existing goals. This is a matter of diagnosis—analyzing the underlying causes. Stage 2 is thinking up alternative solutions. Stage 3 is evaluating the alternatives and selecting a solution. Alternatives should be evaluated according to cost, quality, ethics, feasibility, and effectiveness. Stage 4 is implementing and evaluating the solution chosen.
- Nonrational models of decision making assume that decision making is nearly always uncertain and risky, making it difficult for managers to make optimum decisions. Two nonrational models are satisficing and intuition.

7.2 Making Ethical Decisions

- Corporate corruption has made ethics in decision making once again important. Many companies have an ethics officer to resolve ethical dilemmas, and more companies are creating values statements to guide employees as to desirable business behavior.
- To help make ethical decisions, a decision tree—a graph of decisions and their possible consequences—may be helpful. Managers should ask whether a proposed action is legal and, if it is intended to maximize shareholder value, whether it is ethical—and whether it would be ethical not to take the proposed action.

7.3 Evidence-Based Decision Making and Data Analytics

- Evidence-based management means translating principles based on best evidence into organizational practice. It is intended to bring rationality to the decision-making process.
- Big data, AI, and analytics inform evidence-based decision making.
- Big data requires handling by very sophisticated analysis software and supercomputers. Big data includes not only data in corporate databases, but also web-browsing data trails, social network communications, sensor data, and surveillance data.
- Big data's five core characteristics are volume, variety, velocity, veracity, and value.
- Big data is used by companies across different industries and at different managerial levels within a company.

7.4 Artificial Intelligence Is a Powerful Decision-Making Resource

- Artificial intelligence (AI) is a set of technologies that develop human-like capabilities such as gathering and interpreting information, generating responses, and learning from decisions to attain specific objectives.
- AI is organized into four types, or functions: automate tasks, analyze data for identification and information

security, advise users with relevant information, and anticipate future events.
- Firms predominately use AI to enhance current offerings, optimize internal processes, and make more effective decisions. The top challenges of AI include implementation, data issues, and cost.

7.5 Four General Decision-Making Styles

- A decision-making style reflects the combination of how an individual perceives and responds to information.
- Decision-making styles may tend to have a value orientation, which reflects the extent to which a person focuses on either task or technical concerns versus people and social concerns when making decisions. Decision-making styles also may reflect a person's tolerance for ambiguity, the extent to which a person has a high or low need for structure or control in their life.
- When the dimensions of value orientation and tolerance for ambiguity are combined, they form four styles of decision making: directive (action-oriented decision makers who focus on facts); analytical (careful decision makers who like lots of information and alternative choices); conceptual (decision makers who rely on intuition and have a long-term perspective); and behavioral (the most people-oriented decision makers).

7.6 Decision-Making Biases

- Ten common decision-making biases present real barriers to high-quality decision making. They are (1) availability, (2) representativeness, (3) confirmation, (4) sunk cost, (5) anchoring and adjustment, (6) overconfidence, (7) hindsight, (8) framing, (9) escalation of commitment, and (10) categorical thinking.

7.7 Group Decision Making: How to Work with Others

- Using a group to make a decision offers five possible advantages: (1) a greater pool of knowledge, (2) different perspectives, (3) intellectual stimulation, (4) better understanding of the reasoning behind the decision, and (5) deeper commitment to the decision.
- It also has four disadvantages: (1) a few people may dominate or intimidate; (2) it will produce groupthink, when group members strive for agreement among themselves for the sake of unanimity and so avoid accurately assessing the decision situation; (3) satisficing; and (4) goal displacement, when the primary goal is subsumed to a secondary goal.
- Some characteristics of groups to be aware of are (1) groups are less efficient, (2) their size affects decision quality, (3) they may be too confident, and (4) knowledge counts—decision-making accuracy is higher when group members know a lot about the issues.
- Using groups to make decisions generally requires that they reach a consensus, which occurs when members are able to express their opinions and reach agreement to support the final decision. Minority dissent should be allowed so members can safely disagree with each other.
- Four techniques aid in problem solving. (1) Brainstorming helps groups generate multiple ideas and alternatives for solving problems. (2) Devil's advocacy assigns someone the role of critic. (3) The dialectic method calls for managers to foster a structured dialogue or debate of opposing viewpoints prior to making a decision. (4) An after action review, or project post-mortem, is a review of recent decisions in order to identify possible future improvements.

7.8 Career Corner: Managing Your Career Readiness

- The career readiness competencies of critical thinking/problem solving and decision making go hand in hand.
- Reflecting on your past experiences and using a decision methodology are two ways to improve critical thinking and problem solving.

Boeing Continuing Case

Learn more about Boeing's planning, strategic, and decision-making processes, and how they impacted the development of the 737 MAX.

Assess your ability to apply concepts discussed in Chapters 5 through 7 to the case by going to Connect.

PART 4 • ORGANIZING

8

Organizational Culture and Structure
Drivers of Strategic Implementation

After reading this chapter, you should be able to:

LO 8-1 Explain why managers need to align organizational culture, structure, and HR practices to support strategy.

LO 8-2 Explain how to characterize an organization's culture.

LO 8-3 Describe the process of culture change in an organization.

LO 8-4 Identify the major features of an organization and explain how they are expressed in an organization chart.

LO 8-5 Describe the eight types of organizational structure.

LO 8-6 Explain how to use the career readiness competencies of understanding the business and personal adaptability to better understand and change your level of fit with an organization.

FORECAST What's Ahead in This Chapter

We begin by discussing why organizational culture, organizational structure, and HR practices should be aligned to coordinate employees in the pursuit of an organization's strategic goals. We then describe levels of organizational culture, explain how culture is learned, and classify culture types. We also outline 12 mechanisms that can be used to change organizational culture. We then review seven features of organizations and show how they come together to form an organization chart. We next review eight types of organizational structure. We conclude with a Career Corner that focuses on how to use the career readiness competencies of understanding the business and personal adaptability to assess and better fit with organization's internal context.

How to Get Noticed in a New Job: Fitting into an Organization's Culture in the First 60 Days

If you want to make a great impression and get ahead at work, "you have to be sure to always overdeliver . . . with the emphasis being on *over*," says business columnist and former *Harvard Business Review* editor-in-chief Suzy Welch.[1]

Overdelivering means doing more than what is asked of you—not just doing the report your boss requests, for example, but doing the extra research to provide them with something truly impressive. Also, be sure your boss knows how hard you're working. "You want to get people's attention so they know you're great at your job," says one branding expert. "You also want to improve on yourself and continue to climb the corporate ladder."[2]

Among things you should do in the first 60 days are the following.

Be Aware of the Power of First Impressions

People form an opinion about where a relationship is headed within the first few minutes of an interaction.[3] Journalist and author Malcolm Gladwell concluded that "Snap judgments are, first of all, enormously quick: they rely on the thinnest slices of experience . . . they are also unconscious."[4] Counter the possibility of someone else's bias in such a quick judgment by using your career readiness competencies of social and emotional intelligence to put your best foot forward.

See How People Behave by Arriving Early and Staying Late

"Many aspects of a company's culture can be subtle and easy to overlook," writes one expert. "Instead, observe everything." Try coming in 30 minutes early and staying a little late just to observe how people operate—where they take their meals, for example. If a meal was part of your interview, you've probably picked up some clues about whether they regularly eat out or are mostly brown-bagging it at their desks.[5] If you work in a hybrid or fully remote environment, this could mean signing on for Zooms a few minutes early or hanging around for a bit before logging off.

Network with People and Ask Questions about How the Organization Works

Keep your networking skills at the ready; they represent a career readiness competency. During the first two weeks, get to know a few people and try to have lunch or a get-to-know-you Zoom with them. Get to know office managers, mail room clerks, and other support staff who can help you learn the ropes. Find out how the organization works, how people interact with the boss, and what the corporate culture encourages and discourages. You have a lot to learn, and research says that asking questions makes you appear *more* competent to others. It also improves your relationships and your performance.[6]

Seek Advice Instead of Feedback

Take advantage of opportunities to learn from others in the organization by asking for their advice rather than their feedback.[7] What's the difference? Recent research says people associate the word *feedback* with evaluations of the past, meaning that asking for feedback will get you opinions about how you've performed so far. But hearing the word *advice* makes people think of the future—and asking for it means you're more likely to get actionable tips on what you need to do to be more successful in the future. The career readiness competency of proactive learning orientation will help you here; don't be afraid to ask co-workers for advice as you start learning the job. At the end of 30 days, have a "How am I doing?" meeting with your boss.

Overdeliver

Because performance reviews for new hires generally take place at 60 to 90 days, you need to have accomplished enough—and preferably something big—to show your boss your potential. In other words, do as Welch suggests: overdeliver.

For Discussion How does the preceding advice square with your past experiences in starting a new job? Are there things you wish you could have done differently?

8.1 Aligning Culture, Structure, and Human Resource (HR) Practices to Support Strategy

THE BIG PICTURE

The study of organizing, the second of the four functions in the management process, begins with the study of organizational culture and structure, which managers use along with HR practices to implement strategy. Organizational culture consists of the set of shared, taken-for-granted implicit assumptions that a group holds in the workplace. Organizational structure describes who reports to whom and who does what.

LO 8-1

Explain why managers need to align organizational culture, structure, and HR practices to support strategy.

As you learned in Chapter 6, *strategy* consists of the large-scale action plans that reflect the organization's vision and are used to set the direction for the organization, and *strategic implementation* is all about executing strategy. In this section we explain why successful implementation of a firm's strategies is only possible when leaders align the right organizational culture, structure, and HR practices to support strategy.

How an Organization's Culture, Structure, and HR Practices Support Strategic Implementation

Strategic implementation is a difficult job. In fact, managers consistently rank the ability to successfully implement strategy as a top concern, and many strategic initiatives fail because of flawed execution.[8] Experts suggest even the most well-crafted strategies can break down if they are not infused into organizations' daily activities. Leaders therefore need to configure their firms' operations and resources in ways that support firm strategies.[9]

Figure 8.1 shows that an organization's performance (i.e., its ability to execute strategy) depends on the extent to which three factors—organizational culture, organizational structure, and HR practices—work together to enable its strategy. Leaders are the main drivers of this alignment. Figure 8.1 also reveals that the alignment across these factors impacts group and social processes (discussed in Chapters 13 and 15), individual work attitudes and behaviors (discussed in Chapters 11 and 12), and finally overall organizational performance.[10]

Let's use the metaphor of a rope to visualize how culture, structure, and HR practices jointly enable strategy. A rope gets its strength from many small strands that are tightly woven together. When the strands unravel and separate from one another, the rope weakens significantly and is more likely to break. Organizations rely on the closely entwined "strands" of culture, structure, and HR practices to achieve strategic objectives. Let's explore each of these elements in more detail.

Organizational Culture: The Shared Assumptions That Affect How Work Gets Done We described the concept of *culture* in Chapter 4 on global management as "the shared set of beliefs, values, knowledge, and patterns of behavior common to a group of people." Here we are talking about a specific kind of culture called an *organizational culture*.

> **You can think of an organization's culture, structure, and HR practices as three strands in a single rope.** These strands must be tightly woven together to drive successful strategic execution.
> kyoshino/Getty Images

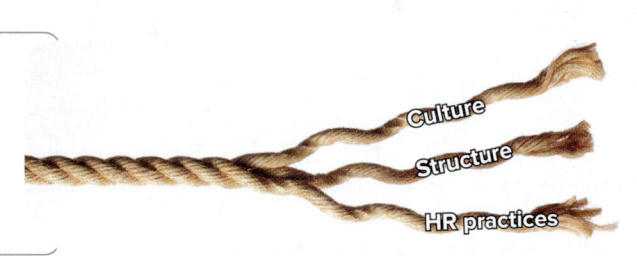

As you learned in Chapter DEI, organizational culture, sometimes called corporate culture, is the set of shared, taken-for-granted implicit assumptions that a group holds and that determines how it perceives, thinks about, and reacts to its various environments.[11] Organizational culture helps employees understand why the organization does what it does and how it intends to accomplish its long-term goals. In other words, culture is the "social glue" that binds members of the organization together through shared understanding. It is helpful to think of an organization's culture as its unique "personality" that manifests in a set of shared beliefs and values. Organizational culture is passed on to new employees by way of socialization and mentoring, and it significantly affects work outcomes at all levels.[12]

Organizational culture is one of the three factors shown in Figure 8.1 that influences a firm's performance.[13] It is important to remember that there is no universal "right" culture. Instead, the ideal culture for a particular organization is the one that best supports its chosen strategy.[14] Leaders are responsible for carefully crafting and managing their cultures to enable successful execution of their firms' strategies.[15] For example, Satya Nadella, Microsoft CEO, once said, "What I realize more than ever is that my job is curation of our culture. If you don't focus on creating a culture that allows people to do their best work, then you've created nothing."[16]

Southwest Airlines is an example of a company with a culture that supports its strategy.

Culture Supporting Strategy Example—Southwest:
The culture at Southwest Airlines is designed to support the airline's cost-leadership strategy. Southwest values productivity, reliability, and efficiency.[17] Slogans, pictures, and repetitions of the company's vision, values, and mission adorn the physical environment, and many of these representations remind employees about what makes them and the airline special and unique. Workers also display a strong sense of ownership in and commitment to the company and its low-cost strategy. One Southwest flight attendant recently went viral on social media after video surfaced of him joking about the company's low-cost reputation during pre-flight instructions. After informing passengers that various designer handbags could in fact fit all the way under the seat in front of them, the flight attendant added "we all know if that was a real Gucci, you'd be flying Delta."[18]

We thoroughly discuss organizational culture in Sections 8.2 and 8.3.

Organizational Structure: Who Reports to Whom and Who Does What
Organizational structure is a formal system of task and reporting relationships that coordinates and motivates an organization's members so that they can work together to achieve the organization's goals. As we

FIGURE 8.1

How organizational culture, organizational structure, and human resource practices align to support strategic implementation

Source: Figure based in part on Ostroff, C., A. J. Kinicki, and R. S. Muhammad. "Organizational Culture and Climate." In Handbook of Psychology, Volume 12: Industrial and Organizational Psychology. 2nd ed. Hoboken, NJ: John Wiley Sons, 2013, Chapter 24, 643–676.

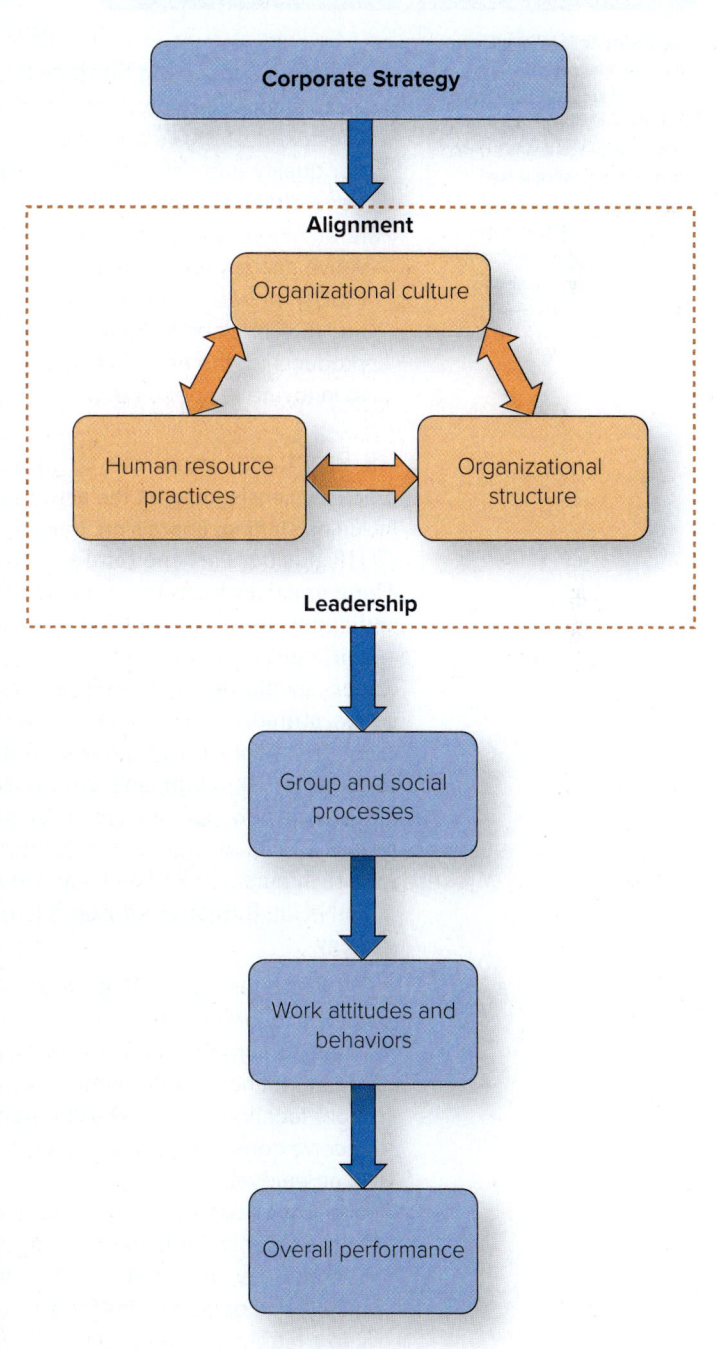

Southwest Airlines' employees find reminders of company culture all around them. These reminders include phrases painted on the company's walls, such as those visible in the background of this photo of Captain Louis Freeman boarding his last flight before retiring from a 36-year career as a pilot for the airline. LM Otero/AP Images

describe in Section 8.5, organizational structure is concerned with who reports to whom and who specializes in what work.

Organizational structure is another factor that impacts a firm's ability to execute strategy. Just as there is not one best organizational culture, there is no single organizational structure that is superior to others. Leaders are encouraged to structure their organizations in ways that are most conducive to accomplishing strategic goals.[19] A well-designed organizational structure encourages the relationships, attitudes, and behaviors needed to execute a particular strategy.[20]

Procter & Gamble (P&G) is an example of a company with a structure that supports its strategy.

Structure Supporting Strategy Example—P&G: P&G owns some of the most recognizable consumer product brands in the world, including Bounty, Pampers, Tide, and Crest. Part of P&G's purpose is to "provide branded products and services of superior quality and value that improve the lives of the world's consumers, now and for generations to come."[21] The company pursues growth through innovation and differentiation. Specifically, P&G continues to capture market share by providing innovative and superior quality products. P&G is structured into five sector business units (SBUs): (1) baby, feminine, and family care, (2) beauty, (3) health care, (4) grooming, and (5) fabric and home care. The CEO of each unit has authority over both sales and products for the unit.[22] This structure empowers P&G's business units with the agility to innovate at speeds that are often impossible for large corporations.

HR Practices: How the Organization Manages Its Talent

Human resource practices consist of all of the activities an organization uses to manage its human capital, including staffing, appraising, training and development, and compensation.

HR practices are the third key factor influencing a firm's ability to execute strategy. These practices focus on ensuring that employees have the necessary skills, motivation, and opportunities to contribute to the organization's unique strategic goals.[23]

Different organizations take varied approaches to managing human capital, and leaders should deploy the HR practices that are most likely to facilitate the social processes, attitudes, and behaviors necessary for successful strategic implementation.[24] For example, a firm with an innovation strategy is likely to benefit from reward systems that incentivize risk taking and from selection systems that prioritize hiring outside candidates with new perspectives over promoting existing employees. But practices that reward efficiency and prioritize internal hiring and training would likely be a better fit for a firm pursuing low-cost leadership.[25]

In-N-Out Burger is an example of a company with HR practices that support its strategy.

HR Practices Supporting Strategy Example—In-N-Out Burger: At In-N-Out Burger, the philosophy is simple—"serve only the highest quality product, prepare it in a clean and sparkling environment, and serve it in a warm and friendly manner."[26] The restaurant has a small menu, uses farm fresh ingredients, maintains impeccably clean store locations, and has a "no-franchise" policy—all of which ensure that customers receive consistently high-quality food that looks good, tastes delicious, and is served in an enjoyable atmosphere.[27] The HR practices at In-N-Out are different than what one would expect in the fast-food industry, and they are a key tool the company uses to maintain its high standards. Restaurant managers and employees enjoy above-average pay, and employee benefits include 401(k) options, paid vacation time, free meals, and opportunities for extensive training.[28] These HR practices have translated into a highly loyal and satisfied workforce, with over 90% of employees approving of the CEO and nearly 80% reporting a positive outlook about their employer.[29]

Leadership Creates Alignment among Culture, Structure, and HR Practices We have noted several times that an organization's culture, structure, and HR practices do not operate as isolated individual systems. Rather, these factors exert influence on one another, and leaders must align them so that they work in concert to support and reinforce firm strategy.[30] Good leaders are like orchestra conductors. Rather than integrating the sounds of many instruments into a meaningful whole, leaders understand how culture, structure, and HR practices operate and know how to leverage them to focus employees on the organization's broad strategic goals.[31] UPS is a good illustration of this perspective.

> **Leadership That Aligns Culture, Structure, and HR Practices Example—UPS:** UPS clearly understood the importance of leadership when the company named its new CEO, Carol Tomé, in 2020. In her time as Home Depot's CFO, Tomé was credited with increasing shareholder value by 450% and making the company one of the highest-performing major retail organizations in the United States.[32] Multiple UPS executives expressed their excitement with the choice because of Tomé's deep knowledge of the culture, structure, employees, and strategy at UPS. William Johnson, UPS's board chair, said, "Carol is one of the most respected and talented leaders in corporate America and has a proven track record of driving growth at a global organization, maximizing shareholder value, developing talent and successfully executing against strategic priorities."[33] *Time Magazine* named UPS one of the most influential companies of 2022, citing Tomé's extraordinary leadership of the company during the COVID-19 pandemic.[34]

Leadership throughout the organization—not just in the C-suite—is key in aligning culture, structure, and HR practices.[35] Middle and first-line managers are critical in sustaining connections between culture, structure, and HR practices and connecting these factors to company strategy. This is because middle and first-line managers are on the ground and work face-to-face with employees on a regular basis. These managers can explain how workers' daily tasks link to broad organizational goals and can clarify the company's priorities and the logic behind its strategic choices.[36]

8.2 What Kind of Organizational Culture Will You Be Operating In?

THE BIG PICTURE
Organizational culture appears in three levels: observable artifacts, espoused values, and basic assumptions. Culture is transmitted to employees through symbols, stories, heroes, rites and rituals, and organizational socialization. Cultures can be classified into four types: clan, adhocracy, market, and hierarchy.

A big part of being successful in a particular job is understanding and working within the organization's culture.[37] An organization's culture is evident in everything from the personalities you encounter to the organization's everyday business practices, and it exerts a powerful influence on employees' attitudes and behaviors and is a critical driver of an organization's ability to successfully execute strategy. Culture is so important, in fact, that CEOs and chief human resource officers (CHROs) surveyed by SHRM rated maintaining culture as the biggest challenge they faced in today's increasingly remote professional environment.[38] After completing this section, you will be able to assess an organization's culture and determine how well you fit within it.

LO 8-2

Explain how to characterize an organization's culture.

FIGURE 8.2
Levels of organizational culture
the-lightwriter/iStock/Getty Images

The Three Levels of Organizational Culture

Organizational culture is present at three levels:[39]

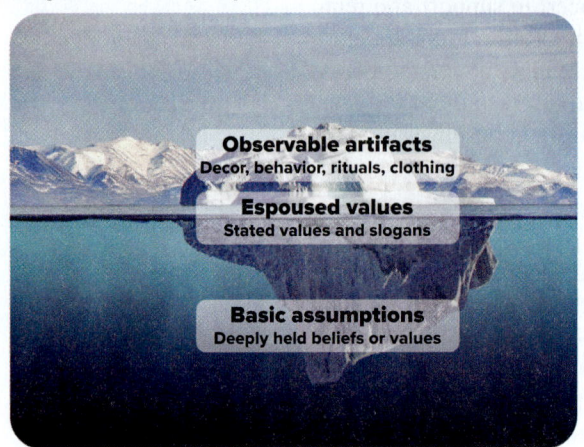

1. Observable artifacts
2. Espoused values
3. Basic assumptions

Each level varies in terms of outward visibility and resistance to change (level 1 is most visible and least resistant to change, and level 3 is least visible and most resistant to change), and each level influences another level. Management scholars often use an iceberg to visualize organizational culture (see Figure 8.2). This is because the portion of an iceberg that we can easily see represents only a small portion of the whole thing. Most of an iceberg is under the water, just like a large part of an organization's culture lies beneath the surface. In order to understand an organization's culture, you need to "see" or understand the entire culture, not just the parts of it that you can immediately assess. Let's discuss each level of culture.

Level 1: Observable Artifacts—Physical Manifestations of Culture

We begin our discussion of organizational culture by looking at the top of the iceberg. Figure 8.2 shows that at the most visible level, organizational culture is expressed in *observable artifacts*—physical manifestations such as manner of dress, awards, myths and stories about the company, rituals and ceremonies, decorations, as well as visible behavior exhibited by managers and employees. It may be difficult to get a sense of an organization's culture from physical workspaces and decor if you work remotely, but you can find many visible aspects of culture even when you work from home. In a hybrid or fully remote work environment, observable artifacts include regular rituals such as check-in meetings, remote dress codes (or the lack thereof), and the types of interactions that are encouraged between employees over corporate meeting and messaging platforms.

Observable Artifacts Example—GitLab: Software development firm GitLab has earned praise for its intentional approach to building a strong culture in a fully-remote work environment. A brief visit to GitLab's website provides numerous observable artifacts of the company's collaborative, supportive, and employee-centered culture. Workers can access an impressive number of remote work resources, including guides for managing, communicating, onboarding, collaborating, evaluating, and training employees in a remote environment.[40] GitLab employees (more than 1,700 in over 60 countries) receive four "get together" grants each year to cover costs associated with spending time with co-workers. They also can apply for an annual $1,000 grant for traveling to events such as colleagues' weddings.[41]

Observable Artifacts: What do you think the physical aspects of this office space say about this organization's culture?
metamorworks/Shutterstock

Observable artifacts are the easiest element of culture to influence. Changing artifacts can start with something as simple as changing a dress code or office layout.

Level 2: Espoused Values—Explicitly Stated Values and Norms As you can see in Figure 8.2, the second level of the iceberg is deeper and less visible than the first. This is where we find an organization's espoused values—the explicitly stated values and norms preferred by an organization, as may be put forth by the firm's founders or top managers. You can usually find evidence of an organization's espoused values by exploring its website for mission, vision, and values statements. Espoused values are also evident in corporate announcements such as press releases.

Espoused Values Example—Cadence: Semiconductor design firm Cadence recently announced a big change to its executive compensation plan. The company stated it would now tie a significant portion of executives' variable pay to measurable outcomes related to increased engagement and representation of Latinx, Black, and female employees. "As leaders, we need to ensure that we are offering opportunities to people who come from varying backgrounds and can be great contributors to our success," said the company's President and CEO Anirudh Devgan.[42]

Although companies hope the values they espouse will directly influence behavior, managers and employees don't always "walk the talk," which leads to a visible clash between espoused values and enacted values—the values and norms actually exhibited in the organization.[43] Consider the example of Red Robin:

Espoused vs. Enacted Values Example—Red Robin: Red Robin's values are captured in the acronym B.U.R.G.E.R., which stands for **B**ottomless fun, **U**nwavering integrity, **R**elentless focus on improvement, **G**enuine spirit of service, **E**xtraordinary people, and **R**ecognized burger authority.[44] The Extraordinary people aspect of Red Robin's values includes honoring employees by rewarding and caring for them. Almost 500 current and former kitchen managers from Red Robin locations across the state of New York recently questioned the company's commitment to this espoused value when they filed a class action lawsuit against the company. The managers accused the company of providing insufficient labor budgets for non-exempt employees and instead expecting managers to work over 40 hours per week and to "pick up the slack" by doing both their own jobs as well as many of the jobs that non-exempt employees would normally do. Red Robin settled the lawsuit for $2.95 million in 2022.[45]

It is more challenging to change espoused values than observable artifacts, but espoused values are easier to change than basic assumptions.

Level 3: Basic Assumptions—Core Values of the Organization Figure 8.2 demonstrates that a substantial portion of an organization's culture exists at such a deep level that it is nearly impossible to grasp or articulate. *Basic assumptions* represent the unobservable yet core values of an organization's culture that are often taken for granted. The values at this level have a profound effect on employee behaviors because they have informed every decision in the organization's past and are thus entwined with its identity. For this same reason, basic assumptions are very difficult to change. Industry expert Karen Niovitch Davis warns that basic assumptions, left unchecked, can be a destructive force. According to Davis, "Old assumptions die hard if they're not examined and addressed. Try not to ignore the unwritten rules. It's terrible to find out about them after an employee crossed a line because they thought it was what you wanted."[46] Sometimes basic assumptions affect entire industries, as has been depicted in recent articles and TV series centering on the restaurant industry.

Basic Assumptions Example—Restaurant Industry: The basic assumptions underlying restaurant culture have thwarted meaningful, positive change in the industry. Workers from around the world continue to lament the perfectionism, grueling hours, low pay, and emotional and physical abuse that characterize restaurant jobs. World famous chef René Redzepi shocked the culinary world in 2023 when he announced the impending closure of his three Michelin-starred restaurant Noma. Redzepi called the fine dining model "unsustainable" from a financial, emotional, and human standpoint.[47] Toxic restaurant culture has persisted in spite of the widespread realization that employees' health and well-being should be primary concerns for employers.

How Employees Learn Culture: Symbols, Stories, Heroes, Rites and Rituals, and Organizational Socialization

Culture is transmitted to employees in several ways, most often through such means as (1) *symbols,* (2) *stories,* (3) *heroes,* (4) *rites and rituals,* and (5) *organizational socialization.*[48]

1. Symbols A **symbol** is an object or action that represents an idea or quality. With respect to culture, symbols are artifacts used to convey an organization's most important values. Nike has done this very effectively via its "swoosh."

Symbols Example—Nike: The Nike "swoosh" is designed to represent the wings of Nike—the Greek goddess of victory. It also resembles a check mark, a shape people naturally associate with positivity.

2. Stories A **story** is a narrative based on true events, which is repeated—and sometimes embellished upon—to emphasize a particular value. Stories are oral histories that are told and retold by members about incidents in the organization's history. Consider Lever.

Stories Example—Lever: Lever is a cloud-based recruiting software firm that has helped companies like Mercedes-Benz, Netflix, Zoom, and Spotify to grow their workforces. CEO Sarah Nahm founded Lever in 2012 and spent the next two years as the only woman in the company. Now, over 50% of Lever's 160+ employees are female and 51% are nonwhite. Nahm recalls the difficulties she faced over the years as she worked to build an inclusive culture. Her experience growing the diversity of Lever's sales team taught her and others in the company about the power of stories for driving culture. She recalls, "There was one woman closing business as an account executive. We went to her and asked her what she would like to see done about that. She ultimately became an inspiring success. That experience taught us the power of storytelling to launch D&I [diversity and inclusion] initiatives. The first thing we did was tell her story. We published it to all of Lever's different channels. Organically, it became a powerful way for us to signal our intention to candidates we were talking to in our talent pool, women out there who didn't know about Lever and to our own employees." Lever has been named one of *Fortune*'s top 50 best workplaces in technology.[49]

Have you ever had a co-worker or boss fill you in on something interesting, scandalous, or impressive that happened in the company prior to your arrival? Storytelling is a powerful way that culture is maintained and passed on to new employees. FatCamera/E+/Getty Images

3. Heroes A **hero** is a person whose accomplishments embody the values of the organization. Often, heroes are people who have endured great sacrifice for the organization's benefit. Heroes can emerge in single organizations or more broad social causes.

Hero Example—Nelly Cheboi: TechLit Africa provides computers to thousands of rural Kenyan students who otherwise would not have access. The nonprofit organization's mission is to increase technological literacy in Africa, particularly in areas where residents have little to no access to technology or to opportunities to improve technological skills. Founder Nelly Cheboi grew up in poverty and says her life changed when she discovered computer programming in college. "The world is your oyster when you are educated," she said, adding "By bringing the resources, by bringing the skills, we are opening up the world to them." Nelly Cheboi was named CNN's Hero of the Year in 2022.[50]

4. Rites and Rituals

Rites and rituals are the activities and ceremonies, planned and unplanned, that celebrate important occasions and accomplishments in organizational life. Rituals transform ordinary movements into meaningful and symbolic practices. Their repetitive and predictable patterns comfort us and signal to us that we are a part of something bigger.[51] Military units and sports teams have long known the value of using ceremonies to hand out decorations and awards, but many companies have rites and rituals as well. The shift toward more remote work in recent years has required organizations to think more creatively about how best to use rites and rituals to build and maintain culture.

Rites and Rituals Example—McKinsey & Company: According to McKinsey & Company senior partner Bill Schaninger, "acculturation requires interaction with other human beings."[52] Schaninger believes workplace rituals are the key to building community among an organization's employees. One ritual he recalls at McKinsey was a weekly opportunity for employees to share "something cool" they'd done during the week. Schaninger believes rituals can be created and adapted for remote work environments as long as organizations remember "The difference between an event that feels like forced fun and a ritual with meaning is some form of spiritual connection, connection to a broader purpose." He stresses the importance of creating rituals that help employees feel connected to the organization, its purpose, and their own part in supporting it.

5. Organizational Socialization

Organizational socialization is defined as the process by which people learn the values, norms, and required behaviors that permit them to participate as members of an organization.[53] Converting from an outsider to an organizational insider may take weeks or even years, and employees form critical relationships and understandings about the organization during the process.[54] Organizational socialization occurs in three phases, researcher Daniel Feldman suggests—before you are hired, when you are first taken on, and when you have been employed a while and are adjusting to the job.[55]

1. **Anticipatory socialization phase.** The anticipatory socialization phase occurs before you join the organization. In this phase you learn—from career advisors, web sources, or current employees—about the organization's needs and values and how your own needs, values, and skills might fit in.

2. **Encounter phase.** The encounter phase takes place when you are first hired. In this phase you begin to learn what the organization is really like and how you might need to adjust your expectations. The company may help to advance this socialization process through various familiarization programs (known as "onboarding").

3. **Change and acquisition phase.** The change and acquisition phase comes about once you have developed a strong sense of your work role. In this phase you begin to fine-tune necessary skills and tasks and better adjust to your work group's values and norms. The company may advance this phase of socialization through goal setting, incentives, employee feedback, continued support, and ceremonies (e.g., "graduation") that celebrate completion of the process.

Socialization Example—NYU: New hires at New York University are partnered with a buddy during their first two months "to help welcome employees and reaffirm their decision to join NYU" as well as to provide a reliable contact for speedy answers on work practices and organizational culture. The university lists four key characteristics for buddies: (1) communicator, (2) role model, (3) motivated, and (4) strong performer.

The university asks new employees to approach the buddy system with an open mind toward constructive criticism, a "coachable" attitude, and a willingness to learn. Both partners in the buddy system receive benefits from the relationship, including increased motivation, expanded social networks, new perspectives, and opportunities to build important skills.[56]

Four Types of Organizational Culture: Clan, Adhocracy, Market, and Hierarchy

The *competing values framework* (CVF) provides a practical way for managers to understand, measure, and change organizational culture. The CVF, which has been validated by extensive research involving 1,100 companies, classifies organizational cultures into four types: (1) clan, (2) adhocracy, (3) market, and (4) hierarchy, as we'll explain.[57] (See Figure 8.3.)

Research leading to the development of the CVF found that organizational effectiveness varied along two dimensions:

- **The horizontal dimension—inward or outward focus?** This dimension expresses the extent to which an organization focuses its attention and efforts inward on internal dynamics and employees ("internal focus and integration") versus outward on its external environment and its customers and shareholders ("external focus and differentiation").

- **The vertical dimension—flexibility or stability?** This dimension expresses the extent to which an organization prefers decentralized decision making (flexibility and discretion) versus centralized authority (stability and control).

Combining these two dimensions creates the four types of organizational culture based on different core values—(1) clan culture, (2) adhocracy culture, (3) market culture, and (4) hierarchy culture.

FIGURE 8.3
Competing values framework

Flexibility and discretion

Clan
Thrust: Collaborate
Means: Cohesion, participation, communication, empowerment
Ends: Morale, people development, commitment

Adhocracy
Thrust: Create
Means: Adaptability, creativity, agility
Ends: Innovation, growth, cutting-edge output

Internal focus and integration | External focus and differentiation

Hierarchy
Thrust: Control
Means: Capable processes, consistency, process control, measurement
Ends: Efficiency, timeliness, smooth functioning

Market
Thrust: Compete
Means: Customer focus, productivity, enhancing competitiveness
Ends: Market share, profitability, goal achievement

Stability and control

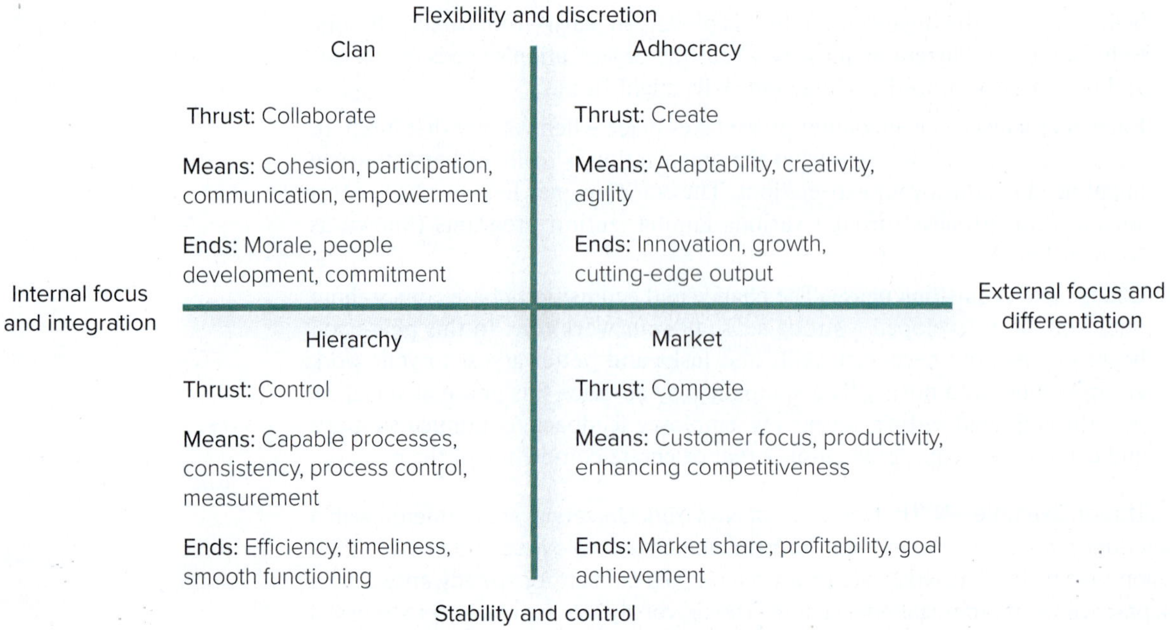

Source: Adapted from Cameron, K. S., R. E. Quinn, J. Degraff, and A. V. Thakor. Competing Values Leadership. Northampton, MA: Edward Elgar, 2006, 32.

Each culture type has different characteristics, and while one type tends to dominate in any given organization, it is the mix of types that creates competitive advantage. We begin our discussion of culture types in the upper-left quadrant of the CVF.

1. Clan Culture: An Employee-Focused Culture Valuing Flexibility, Not Stability

A **clan culture** has an internal focus and values flexibility rather than stability and control. You can see from Figure 8.3 that organizations with clan cultures want their employees to have a strong sense of identification with and commitment to the organization, as well as a feeling of "family." Clan cultures use collaboration to accomplish this goal. Companies with a clan culture are likely to devote considerable resources to training and developing their employees, and they view customers as collaborative partners. In clan cultures, employee behaviors are governed by strong norms rather than formal rules and authority figures.[58]

> **Clan Culture Example—Wegmans:** Wegmans is a private, family-owned supermarket chain with approximately 50,000 employees. The company's values include the following statements:
>
> - We **care** about the well-being and success of every person.
> - We **respect** and listen to our people.
> - We **empower** our people to make decisions that improve their work and benefit our customers and our company.[59]
>
> Wegmans exhibits a clan culture. Former employees use language such as "the Wegmans family," and workers are known to spend entire careers working in Wegmans stores.[60] The company spends $50 million annually on employee training and development, and its high levels of employee engagement are credited with driving its $9 billion+ annual revenues.[61] Wegmans has earned a spot on *Fortune*'s Best Companies to Work For list for 25 consecutive years, ranking #3 in 2022. "Our philosophy has always been to take care of our people, so they can take care of our customers," said President and CEO Colleen Wegman."[62]

2. Adhocracy Culture: A Risk-Taking Culture Valuing Flexibility

An **adhocracy culture** has an external focus and values flexibility. Creation of new and innovative products and services is the strategic thrust of this culture. Adhocracies are set up to encourage employees to be creative, adaptable, and quick to respond to changes. Employees in adhocracy cultures are encouraged to take risks and experiment with new ways of getting things done. Adhocracy cultures are well suited for start-up companies, firms in industries undergoing constant change, and firms in mature industries that are in need of innovation to enhance growth.

> **Adhocracy Culture Example—Baxter International:** Baxter International, a giant Illinois-based manufacturer of medical products, values innovation enough to say it practically *is* the company's culture. Over the past decade, CEO José Almeida cut away several layers of the company's bureaucracy to make it easier for employees to communicate with peers around the organization and speed up decision making. "Never disassociate innovation and culture," he says. "They are almost one and the same."[63] Almeida believes that inclusion and diversity are key drivers of innovation, and Baxter continues to rank on *Forbes'* Best Employers for Diversity and Best Employers for Women lists.[64] According to Jeanne Mason, senior VP of human resources, the company has made "relentless efforts to be an inclusive company where all employees can feel safe to bring their authentic selves to work."[65]

3. Market Culture: A Competitive Culture Valuing Profits over Employee Satisfaction

A **market culture** has a strong external focus and values stability and control. Companies with market cultures leverage employees' competitive drives to make money, achieve goals, and gain market share for the organization. In market cultures, customers, productivity, and winning take precedence over employee development and satisfaction. Employees in market cultures are expected to work hard, proactively react, and deliver quality work on time; those who deliver results are rewarded.

Market Culture Example—Tyson Foods: Tyson Foods is the world's second largest producer of chicken, beef, and pork, and it posted 2022 sales of $53.2 billion. Tyson Foods has a market culture focused on results, productivity, and profitability, and it places high value on shareholder returns.[66] The company recently launched a productivity program intended to "drive a better, faster and more agile organization that is supported by a culture of continuous improvement and faster decision making."[67]

4. Hierarchy Culture: A Structured Culture Valuing Stability and Effectiveness

A **hierarchy culture** has an internal focus and values stability and control over flexibility. Companies with this kind of culture implement various control mechanisms that help the company maintain a certain level of performance and efficiency according to a schedule. Hierarchical cultures are apt to have a formalized, structured work environment and a lot of rules. At the extreme, such cultures may seem like the company cares more about efficiency and standardization than it does its people.

Hierarchy Culture Example—McDonald's: McDonald's serves around 70 million customers each day and operates in just about every country in the world. The company manages operations at this scale through routinization, standardization, division of labor, and formal accountability hierarchies.[68] Current and former McDonald's workers use words like "efficient", "high stress", "routine", and "repetitive" to describe what it's like working for the fast-food giant.[69]

Are you curious about the type of culture that exists in a current or past employer? Do you wonder whether this culture is best suited to help the company achieve its strategic goals? Try taking Self-Assessment 8.1 in Connect if your instructor has assigned it.

SELF-ASSESSMENT 8.1

What Is the Organizational Culture at My Current Employer?

This self-assessment is designed to help you better understand the culture at your current job. Please complete Self-Assessment 8.1 if your instructor has assigned it in Connect.

The Importance of Culture

Many people believe culture powerfully shapes an organization's long-term success by enhancing its systems (such as leadership and HR practices, discussed in Section 8.1) and influencing its important outcomes at various levels—and research supports this belief.[70] Recently, a team of scholars tested this hypothesis with a meta-analysis (a statistical procedure combining data from multiple studies) of more than 38,000 organizational units—either organizations as a whole or departments in different organizations—and 616,000 individuals.[71] The results are shown in Figure 8.4.

FIGURE 8.4

What organizational variables are associated with organizational cultures?

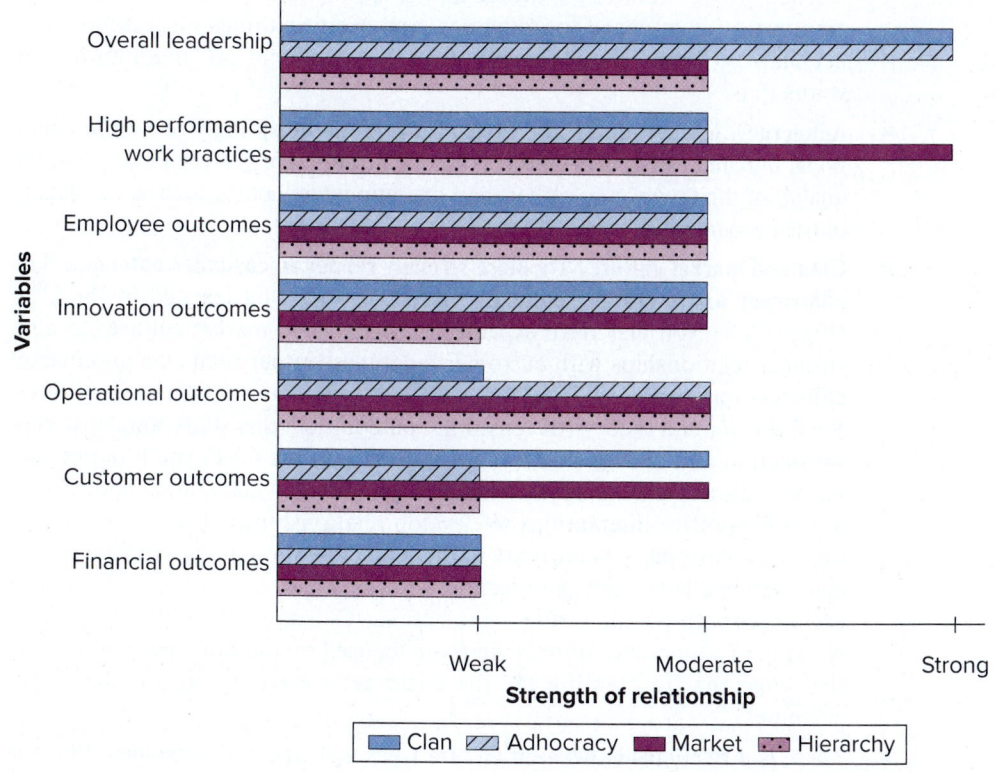

[Bar chart showing strength of relationship (Weak, Moderate, Strong) between four culture types (Clan, Adhocracy, Market, Hierarchy) and variables: Overall leadership, High performance work practices, Employee outcomes, Innovation outcomes, Operational outcomes, Customer outcomes, Financial outcomes]

Source: Data taken from Hartnell, C. A., A. Y. Ou, A. J. Kinicki, D. Choi, and E. P. Karam. "A Meta-Analytic Test of Organizational Culture's Association with Elements of an Organization's System and Its Relative Predictive Validity on Organizational Outcomes." *Journal of Applied Psychology* 104, no. 6 (2019): 832–850.

Results revealed that culture is positively associated with a variety of factors and outcomes that are important to today's managers. Closer examination of Figure 8.4 leads to the following conclusions:

- **An organization's culture matters.** The type of organizational culture can be a source of competitive advantage. (See the remaining bullets for more specifics.)

- **Clan and adhocracy cultures are more strongly related to desirable leadership behaviors than market and hierarchy cultures.** But all four culture types are related to leadership in various ways. One explanation involves employee preferences for leadership that allows flexibility and discretion inherent in clan and adhocracy cultures as opposed to directive styles of leadership associated with fostering stability and control in hierarchy and market cultures.

- **Market cultures have the strongest relationship with high-performance work practices** (akin to the HR practices we discussed in Figure 8.1). But all four culture types are related to high-performance work practices (HPWPs) in various ways. High-performance work practices represent "bundles" of HR practices that are systematically grouped to enhance employee *abilities* (e.g., selection and training), *motivation* (e.g., compensation and career development), or *opportunities* (e.g., involvement and information sharing).

- **Employee outcomes are related to all four organizational culture types.** The extent to which employees feel happy, committed, and supported by the organization, and the extent to which they engage in important work behaviors, depends on culture.

- **Clan, adhocracy, and market cultures are more strongly related to innovation than hierarchy cultures.** This relationship makes sense given what you learned about hierarchy cultures and their explicit focus on stability and employees (as opposed to doing new and exciting things or grabbing market share). Hierarchy cultures are most likely to focus on "maintaining the status quo."

- **Adhocracy, market, and hierarchy cultures are more strongly related to operational outcomes than clan cultures.** Clan cultures are explicitly focused on the quality of their *employees* rather than operational outcomes such as the quality of their *products* or *services*.

- **Clan and market cultures are more strongly related to customer outcomes than adhocracy and hierarchy cultures.** Based on what you learned in the CVF (Figure 8.3), you may have expected *adhocracy* and market cultures to have stronger relationships with customer outcomes (rather than *clan* and market cultures) due to the external focus of both adhocracy and market cultures. We'll throw out a theory—the customer outcomes in this study were customer satisfaction and market share. If you flip back to the CVF, you'll notice that market cultures use a customer focus to gain market share, and clan cultures use collaborative interactions to develop relationships and positive feelings (and view customers as partners in these collaborations). It's possible that in clan cultures, customers gain feelings of satisfaction from their collaborative exchanges with people in the organization. It's also possible that employees working in adhocracy cultures are more focused on the fun, new, and innovative *thing* they're creating for the customer than they are on the *actual* customer.

- **There is a relationship between culture types and financial outcomes.** But it is weak across the board. This occurs because there are other organizational systems and processes that are stronger drivers of firm performance. HPWPs are one example according to the researchers who conducted this meta-analysis. Their results showed that financial outcomes were more strongly related to HPWPs than to culture. This would imply that investments in employees' career readiness competencies may pay dividends in the form of increased profits and revenues.

- **Companies with market cultures tend to have more positive organizational outcomes.** Managers are encouraged to make their cultures more market oriented.

As a final note, the results of the research presented in Figure 8.4 supported what we described in Figure 8.1. Specifically, the researchers found that organizational culture, organizational structure, and HR practices need to align in order to support strategic implementation.

Preparing to Assess Person–Organization Fit before a Job Interview

An important part of the job interview process is assessing how well you will *fit in* with the organization. This is called **person–organization (P–O) fit**, and it reflects the extent to which your personality and values match the climate and culture in an organization.[72] Organizations will attempt to determine whether potential employees will be a good fit, and interviewees should prepare to do the same.

Organizations Assess P–O Fit during the Interview Process
"What was the last costume you wore?" the job interviewer asks you. "On a scale of 1 to 10, how weird are you?"

"What would you do in the event of a zombie apocalypse?" "Would you rather be rich or would you rather be a king?"

These are the favorite interview questions of some of the world's most successful CEOs. For you as a job applicant, these questions might seem to have neither a connection with your performance in previous jobs, nor a "right" answer. But according to Harold Hughes, CEO of Bandwagon—a blockchain-based analytics company—"What's more important is the reasoning." The explanations you use to answer seemingly outlandish questions can tell a company a great deal about what you have experienced, who you are, and how you think.[73]

SHRM recommends that organizations follow a few important guidelines when building assessments of P–O fit into job interview protocol:[74]

1. **Know your organization's culture.** Organizations need accurate perceptions of their cultures in order to determine whether interviewees will fit. Gaining a realistic picture of organizational culture requires conversations with employees at all levels of the organization, not just those at the top.

2. **Identify which aspects of culture drive organizational performance.** Good selection tools (discussed in Chapter DEI and again in Chapter 9) identify candidates with the necessary qualifications for doing a particular job well. This means that interview questions, tests, and tools should focus only on job-relevant criteria. Unfortunately, interviewers often think they are assessing job-related fit but instead are measuring the extent to which they like or feel a personal connection with interviewees.[75] SHRM recommends that organizations: (1) identify what they see as their core values and cultural characteristics, and (2) relate those to core competencies necessary for various jobs in the organization. If a cultural characteristic isn't driving strategic implementation and execution, then it's not relevant in an interview.

3. **Use the right assessment tools.** Any selection tool needs to meet professional and legal standards. Organizations should use only properly vetted and validated assessments during job interviews.

Some organizational leaders use unique interview questions to assess potential person–organization fit. Bandwagon CEO Harold Hughes gets a strong sense of how interviewees think and what motivates them by listening to the reasoning behind their responses to these types of questions. BandwagonFanClub Inc.

How Job Candidates Can Assess P–O Fit with Potential Employers

Interviews are an important opportunity for job candidates to assess their own level of fit with organizations. You can you use the information you learn in this chapter to help determine your potential P–O fit with a company before you interview for a job. Here's a simple three-step process:[76]

1. **Know yourself.** Make a list of your personal values, strengths, and weaknesses—try to be honest, as this is the best way to accurately gauge fit.

2. **Know the business.** Spend some time learning about the organization you plan to interview with by talking with current employees and researching the company online, then make a list of the organization's values, strengths, and weaknesses. Understanding the business is an important career readiness competency that organizations care about.

3. **Compare.** Compare your list of personal values, strengths, and weaknesses with those of the organization, then use the information to prepare questions for the interviewer about how well you might fit.

There are three reasons to estimate your fit with an organization before considering a job offer. First, better fit is associated with important outcomes, including more positive work attitudes, higher task performance, less work stress, and lower intention to quit (e.g., "I'm gonna tell 'em, 'they can take this job and...'").[77] Second, learning that there's a poor fit before you join an organization can potentially save you from wasting months or even years in a job that you don't enjoy.[78] Finally, interviewers place a high priority on fit—84% of recruiters in a recent survey felt that culture fit was one of the most important predictors of a job offer, and 90% admitted to skipping over past applicants because they didn't seem to align well with the culture.[79]

8.3 The Process of Culture Change

THE BIG PICTURE

There are 12 ways a culture becomes established in an organization—and therefore 12 levers for culture change. These are (1) formal statements; (2) slogans and sayings; (3) rites and rituals; (4) stories, legends, and myths; (5) leader reactions to crises; (6) role modeling, training, and coaching; (7) physical design; (8) rewards, titles, promotions, and bonuses; (9) organizational goals and performance criteria; (10) measurable and controllable activities; (11) organizational structure; and (12) organizational systems and procedures.

LO 8-3

Describe the process of culture change in an organization.

Changing organizational culture is essentially a teaching process—that is, a process in which members instruct each other about the organization's preferred values, beliefs, expectations, and behaviors. Schein—the renowned organizational psychologist and culture expert introduced in Section 8.4—established 12 mechanisms for changing culture, which we describe in this section.[80] The mechanisms represent levers that managers push and pull to create culture change. It's not an easy or fast process. If you plan to change an organization's culture, know that you will be pushing and pulling on multiple levers for an extended period of time until you've dusted the old culture out of every nook and cranny. Try to assess the desired strategy and culture type being pursued by each company as you read the following examples of culture change.

Creating culture change involves pushing and pulling change levers in a desired direction. It is very similar to pushing and pulling these levers on a control panel of a lifting mechanism. In both cases, individuals push levers in order to produce a desired outcome.
Neramit Buakaew/Shutterstock

1. Formal Statements

One way to embed preferred culture is to create (or alter) existing formal statements of organizational philosophy, mission, vision, and values, as well as materials to use for recruiting, selecting, and socializing employees.

Formal Statements Example—HubSpot: HubSpot creates inbound marketing, customer service, and sales software for more than 158,000 clients across 120+ countries.[81] Co-founder and CTO Dharmesh Shah says the company's Culture Code is a "perpetual 'work in progress' that continues to evolve" along with HubSpot. The company has updated the code—which it describes as the operating system that powers HubSpot—more than 25 times to date. Here are a few highlights from HubSpot's Culture Code:[82]

- HubSpot hires employees that have HEART. This stands for Humble, Empathetic, Adaptable, Remarkable, and Transparent.
- The code reminds that power is gained by sharing knowledge rather than hoarding it.
- A "no-door" rule gives everyone access to everyone at HubSpot, and your ability to influence should not depend on your position in the company hierarchy.

- HubSpot applies the three-word policy of "Use Good Judgment" to "just about everything." This includes managers' decisions about teams and employees' decisions about their time.

What strategy do you think HubSpot is pursuing? What type(s) of culture does HubSpot embody?

2. Slogans and Sayings

Another way to create a more desirable corporate culture is to express it in company language, slogans, sayings, and acronyms. Companies often signal the desire to change by altering these expressions.

Slogans and Sayings Examples: Consider the messages the following companies tried to send by changing their slogans:[83]

- **Lowe's:** From "Never Stop Improving" to "Do it right for less. Start at Lowe's."
- **Verizon:** From "Can you hear me now" to "5G Built Right."
- **State Farm:** From "Like a good neighbor, State Farm is there" to "Here to help life go right."

3. Rites and Rituals

As we mentioned earlier, rites and rituals represent activities and ceremonies used to celebrate important events or achievements. Rituals also provide meaning, consistency, and support for employees during difficult periods, and their existence sends a message that the organization cares about providing these opportunities for employees to connect.[84] Tech companies are known for having innovative corporate rituals. Consider the example of Pinterest:

Rites and Rituals Example—Pinterest: Pinterest keeps its employees excited about both work and nonwork activities with its annual Knit Con event—a two-day project binge during which workers teach one another their hobbies and passions. The company sees the event as an important way for employees to live out its mission to "bring everyone the inspiration they need to create a life they love." Recent employee-led Knit Con classes include raising chickens, cooking Malaysian food, and creating latté art.[85]

What strategy do you think Pinterest is pursuing? What type(s) of culture does Pinterest embody?

4. Stories, Legends, and Myths

Stories, legends, and myths present narratives about actual events that happened within the organization. These help to symbolize the organization's vision and values to employees. Stories often crystallize culture because they reiterate what people in the organization see as interesting, important, and noteworthy. Managers can use stories to drive culture change. Consider the following example:

Stories, Legends, and Myths Example—UNHCR: Senior leaders at the United Nations High Commissioner for Refugees (UNHCR) agency used stories to drive culture change in the organization. The leaders broadcast an organizationwide call asking employees to submit a three-minute video describing "a time you felt seen, heard, and valued at UNHCR." By asking for stories of inclusion rather than exclusion, the leaders hoped to identify, and eventually drive, the hallmarks of a truly inclusive culture. The initiative was based upon the idea that informal workplace conversations are powerful drivers of organizational culture.[86]

*What strategy do you think UNHCR is pursuing? What type(s) of culture does UNHCR embody?

5. Leader Reactions to Crises

How top managers respond to critical incidents and organizational crises sends a strong cultural message. When new leaders take over an organization, their responses to crises can indicate a desire to change the culture implemented by the previous leadership. Crises send important signals about the organization's culture to the outside world, as these events typically are shared through the media. Consider the case of Adidas' response to recent events.

Leader Reactions to Crises Example—Adidas: Adidas' relationship with rapper Ye (formerly known as Kanye West) turned tumultuous in recent years. The brand faced tremendous pressure to drop Ye as a brand partner after a number of public incidents. The debacle culminated in Ye making multiple anti-Semitic statements and then proclaiming on a podcast that he could "say anti-Semitic things and Adidas can't drop me." Estimates indicated that Adidas' partnership with Ye was generating nearly 10% of the company's revenue. Many people strongly criticized Adidas for not dropping the artist sooner and seemingly stalling as they took the issue "under review."[87]

*What strategy do you think Adidas is pursuing? What type(s) of culture does Adidas embody?

6. Role Modeling, Training, and Coaching

Many companies use structured training to deliver an in-depth introduction to their organizational values. Others use coaching or mentoring programs that provide employees with support and role models. Consider the recent corporate trend of reverse role modeling in which younger/newer employees teach older/more experienced employees:[88]

Reverse Role Modeling Examples:

- Estée Lauder uses reverse mentoring to keep senior leaders up-to-speed on relevant issues. Younger workers created a knowledge-sharing portal called Dreamspace where they work with senior executives on topics like emerging technologies, social media influencers, and data security. The company then distributes a bi-monthly newsletter on key topics that emerge in those discussions.
- Lowell credit management's reverse mentoring program is designed to improve its inclusion culture. The company pairs each executive committee member with an early-career employee from an under-represented group. The initiative allows executives to experience work from a variety of perspectives, including those of single parents and members of ethnic minority groups.
- MoneySuperMarket uses reverse mentoring to help its senior leadership team understand and better remedy important issues in the organization. These issues include those faced by newer, less-networked employees and employees who belong to minoritized identity groups.

7. Physical Design

Organizations experiment constantly to find the best office layouts that will encourage employee productivity. Physical design is an important change lever because it sends a strong and visible message about an organization's culture. A recent trend involves companies transforming their office spaces into "neighborhoods."

Physical Design Example—Neighborhoods: Some organizations are adapting their physical spaces to better meet the needs of today's hybrid workforce. One approach is to make offices feel more like neighborhoods. In your broader life, your neighborhood is not only where you live but also where you find community, resources, and recreation. Offices designed as neighborhoods are meant to support a variety of needs, purposes, and interactions. These offices include private spaces for individual work, gathering areas for socializing and bonding, and team workspaces that support both face-to-face and virtual meetings in a seamless and user-friendly manner. This physical re-design communicates to employees that the company wants to evolve to better accommodate their new way of getting work done.[89]

Neighborhoods: In this office space, employees can choose from a variety of spaces that are each designed for various types of work and interaction. How would you like to work in an office with neighborhoods? Shock/iStock/Getty Images

8. Rewards, Titles, Promotions, and Bonuses

Rewards and status symbols are among the strongest levers an organization can use to embed or change its culture. This is because people have a strong desire to be rewarded, and incentives fulfill this need.

Rewards, Titles, Promotions, and Bonuses Examples: There is increasing pressure for businesses to lead the charge in sustainable stewardship of resources, as evidenced by the UN's Sustainable Development Goals (SDGs) and recent statements made by The Business Roundtable (both discussed in earlier chapters). This has resulted in firms changing their reward structures to incentivize creating shared value (CSV) and sustainable business initiatives. For example:

- Shell recently announced that it would begin linking executive compensation to short-term carbon emissions goals.[90]
- Clorox wants to reduce plastic in its products, avoid animal testing, and lower its carbon emissions and recently implemented its IGNITE program that will tie executive compensation to achieving these goals.[91]

9. Organizational Goals and Performance Criteria

Many companies establish organizational goals and criteria for recruiting, selecting, developing, promoting, dismissing, and retiring people, all of which act as levers for communicating the desired organizational culture.

Organizational Goals and Performance Criteria Example—Ford: Ford Motor Co. recently announced a change to its policy for dealing with underperforming employees. Under the new policy, employees with 8+ years of service to the company who are identified as underperformers have the option to choose either (1) severance or (2) a performance enhancement program. Employees who choose a performance enhancement program and do not successfully improve their performance will not be eligible for severance. Analysts believe the company is taking a hard look at its use of resources and attempting to cut costs however possible. Said Ford CEO Jim Farley, "We absolutely have too many people in certain places, no doubt about it. And we have skills that don't work anymore and we have jobs that need to change."[92]

*What strategy do you think Ford is pursuing? What type(s) of culture does Ford embody?

10. Measurable and Controllable Activities

An organization's leaders can pay attention to, measure, and control a number of activities, processes, or outcomes that can foster a certain culture. What leaders pay attention to acts as a powerful signal of company culture because it tells employees what aspects of their performance are most important to the company. Measurable and controllable activities also serve as an important lever for culture change.

Measurable and Controllable Activities Example—Employee Monitoring: The demand for employee monitoring software has risen steeply in recent years. The New York Metropolitan Transportation Authority recently gave its engineers the option to work from home one day per week, but only if they consented to having their productivity monitored during that day. UnitedHealth has reportedly tied compensation and bonus pay to keyboard activity monitoring, even for workers whose jobs include activities that often do not require using the computer (e.g., counseling patients).[93] Advocates of employee monitoring believe it allows them to focus on results more objectively. But many workers and labor unions have spoken out against this practice. Recent research reported in the *Harvard Business Review* found that employees subject to monitoring software were significantly more likely to cheat and to defy various workplace rules, steal or misuse office equipment, and purposely slow their work pace.[94]

Surveillance activities send a strong message to employees about company culture. How would you feel if your employer were tracking your Internet use, the number of minutes spent at your workstation, or even the length of your bathroom breaks while at work? What kind of culture do you think this creates? Zenzen/Shutterstock

*What type of strategy and culture are reinforced via employee monitoring?

11. Organizational Structure

Recall from Figure 8.1 that organizational structure is one of the three key factors influencing an organization's ability to successfully implement its strategy. As you'll learn in Section 8.5, different types of structures exist to support different types of organizations. Broadly speaking, the bigger an organization gets, the more bureaucratic, hierarchical, and rigid it becomes in terms of structure. In recent years, some large companies have attempted to remove as many elements of bureaucracy as possible in order to drive a creative, innovative, start-up culture in spite of their size. Consider the example of Zappos.

Organizational Structure Example—Zappos: Zappos is known for its radical experiment in organizational structure called *holacracy*—an approach meant to encourage collaboration by eliminating workplace hierarchy altogether. In a pure holacracy, there are no titles and no bosses. Unfortunately, as one writer put it, "people don't tend to work very well if they don't know what they're supposed to be doing."[95] Zappos employees reported problems with role clarity, dysfunctional informal power dynamics, task duplication, and feelings of instability, and the company reportedly lost one-third of its workforce when it first instituted the new structure.[96] Zappos continues to tout its holacracy on its website. However, the company has layered two new elements onto its approach. First, Zappos introduced something called "market-based dynamics" (MBD). Under MBD, employees work in circles that operate much like small and independent business units, with each circle providing specific services to either customers or other Zappos employees. Second, Zappos manages circles using a "Triangle of Accountability" (ToA) framework. The ToA provides constraints on what circles can and cannot do with their operations and budgets.[97]

*What strategy do you think Zappos is pursuing? What type(s) of culture does Zappos embody?

12. Organizational Systems and Procedures

Organizational systems and procedures are levers for embedding and changing culture. For example, companies are increasingly modifying their work systems and procedures (e.g., by implementing HPWPs) to make their cultures more collaborative and/or to improve innovation, quality, and efficiency.

> **Organizational Systems and Procedures Example—Google:** Google was built on a foundation of openness and transparency. In the company's early days, workers shared beers with founders Larry Page and Sergey Brin and could ask any questions they wanted. The company worked hard to maintain this culture as it grew by scaling its procedures for soliciting honest employee input. Google employees now complete a 30-minute annual survey called Googlegeist. The survey gauges important employee attitudes, and executives use the data to inform changes to company procedures. Googlegeist 2022 revealed employees were strongly dissatisfied with pay and promotion opportunities. As a result, the company overhauled its annual performance review system and streamlined the process for evaluations and promotion requests.[98]
>
> *What strategy do you think Google is pursuing? What type(s) of culture does Google desire?

Using Multiple Mechanisms to Drive Culture Change

As we mentioned in the introduction to this section, changing organizational culture isn't easy, and it certainly doesn't happen overnight. According to one HR news source, "Ignoring alignment of all culture drivers is why most culture change fails. Initiatives that change only some cultural aspects either have no impact or—worse—have a negative impact by adding conflicting messages. Executive teams must look at the culture holistically and address all primary drivers that need alignment."[99]

If you want to create lasting culture change, you need to consider how all of the various levers work together and how they can either support or work against each other. Read the Example box to learn about how one company approached culture change through multiple levers.

EXAMPLE: How Total Used Multiple Mechanisms to Improve Its Safety Culture

Safety is paramount in the oil and gas industry. A study that reviewed major oil drilling accidents found that an organization's "safety culture" was one of the most important factors that led to catastrophic safety failures.[100] When the French oil and gas company Total sought to transform its safety culture, Bernadette Spinoy—then SVP of Health, Safety, and Environment (HSE)—knew it would require the use of multiple change mechanisms.[101] Here are examples of the levers that Total used to change its culture:

- **Role modeling, training, and coaching.** Total wanted to embed safety in the organization by creating opportunities for employees to learn rather than by implementing punishments for violations. Although the company does penalize employees who clearly and/or repeatedly disregard safety standards, their focus is primarily on learning. For example, workers involved in safety incidents record videos discussing their experiences and how they learned from them, and they share these videos with the rest of the company. Total also implemented a stronger employee training program that starts on day one and continues throughout employees' time with the company.

- **Rewards, titles, promotions, and bonuses.** The company implemented a reward system that emphasized positive reinforcement for employees doing a good job following safety standards. Now, any employee can nominate any other colleague for a safety award, and the company recognizes between 8 and 10 safety role models for every one safety sanction it hands down.

- **Measurable and controllable activities.** Total created an HSE team dedicated to evaluating safety incidents almost immediately after they occur. The team analyzes each incident for the specific factors that caused it. This helps the

company gain a much better understanding of the reasons for safety failures, and, ultimately, the ways to prevent them in the future. (Research has demonstrated that discussions about how and why failures occurred are crucial for learning.)[102]
- **Organizational structure.** Total consolidated its HSE function by integrating HSE departments from various divisions across all of its business units. This restructuring allowed each branch to contribute its unique experiences and expertise. The company bases its organizationwide safety processes and procedures on the best practices identified through the collaboration of these groups.
- **Organizational systems and procedures.** The company implemented a system for making safety incidents visible at multiple levels. In the event of a safety incident, every senior leader receives a text describing the incident within hours. Then the company publishes the description of the incident on its intranet for all employees to see. In addition, the company publishes videos with overviews of accidents.

YOUR CALL
Do you think there are specific combinations of the 12 levers that are more important to pay attention to than others when attempting to change an organization's culture? Which ones, and why?

Don't Forget about Person–Organization Fit

Now that we have described the four key types of organizational culture and the levers managers can use to change culture, it's time to reflect on your person–organization (P–O) fit. Recall that P–O fit reflects the extent to which your personality and values match the climate and culture in an organization, and P–O fit is important because it can affect your work attitudes and performance.[103] P–O fit also can impact an organization's ability to change its culture. Here we discuss two ways P–O fit relates to organizational culture change.

Poor P–O Fit and Employee Turnover You learned in this section that it is possible to change an organization's culture and thus create a better fit. However, many employees experiencing poor P–O fit would rather search for new jobs than attempt to participate in changing their organizations' cultures.[104] Some level of turnover is always necessary and functional, but excessive turnover can represent problems with the organization's culture. In fact, recent research indicates that poor workplace culture is the main reason employees report for leaving their jobs.[105] Employees who see problems with culture can be important drivers of necessary culture change. Unfortunately, that change is less likely if these employees decide to leave.

Too Much P–O Fit and Resistance to Change Organizations tend to select candidates who fit with the existing culture, and candidates proactively seek organizations where they feel a strong sense of fit. Decades of research suggest that these factors lead organizations to become increasingly homogenous over time, and this homogeneity perpetuates dangerous biases such as groupthink (which you learned about in Chapter 7). Homogeneity is also detrimental to organizations' DE&I efforts, as you learned in Chapter DEI. Recent research suggests that organizations should hire for "culture add" rather than "culture fit" if they want to grow, change, and successfully execute innovative strategies.[106]

We have two activities for you to complete related to your level of fit and what you can do about it. The first is Self-Assessment 8.2, which measures your preference for the four types of culture in the CVF. Try completing this self-assessment and the associated questions if your instructor has assigned it. The second is the two activities in the career readiness section at the end of this chapter, where we'll give you practical advice for questions you can ask to assess your level of fit.

SELF-ASSESSMENT 8.2

Assessing Your Preferred Type of Organizational Culture

This survey is designed to assess your preferred type of organizational culture. Please complete Self-Assessment 8.2 if your instructor has assigned it in Connect.

8.4 The Major Features of an Organization

THE BIG PICTURE
Organizations are described according to seven major features. An organization chart is a visual representation of these features for a particular organization.

In Chapter 1, we defined an organization as a group of people who work together to achieve some specific purpose. But let's also consider Barnard's classic perspective, which views an **organization** as a system of consciously coordinated activities or forces of two or more people.[107] Taken together, these perspectives tell us that (1) an organization's managers make *intentional* choices about how to coordinate employees' work in order to achieve strategic goals and (2) these choices result in the organization's unique system of task and reporting relationships (i.e., the organization's structure). Managers make choices about a variety of features when structuring their organizations, and we discuss each feature in detail in this section. But first, let's explain what we mean when we refer to the *features* of an organization.

If we asked you to describe your face to someone who wasn't able to see you, how would you do it? Chances are you would describe yourself according to your facial features, such as your eye and eyebrow color, your skin tone, the prominence of your cheekbones, and the shape of your nose, lips, and overall face. In fact, this is a template that you can use to describe anyone's face because all faces vary according to a small number of features.

Now consider that all organizations, like faces, can be described according to a set of features. We discuss four features proposed by organizational psychologist Edgar Schein, and then present three others that most experts agree on.

LO 8-4
Identify the major features of an organization and explain how they are expressed in an organization chart.

Organizations, like faces, have common features. We can describe organizations by discussing how they vary along a set of seven features, much like we can describe unique faces according to the set of common features they share.
Robert Churchill/Rawpixel Ltd/iStockphoto/Getty Images

Major Features of Organizations: Four Proposed by Edgar Schein

Schein proposed that all organizations can be described according to four features: (1) *common purpose,* (2) *coordinated effort,* (3) *division of labor,* and (4) *hierarchy of authority.*[108] Let's consider these.

1. Common Purpose: The Means for Unifying Members   An organization without purpose soon begins to drift and become disorganized. In order to remain "organized," there needs to be a reason for existing that all of the organization's members agree on (defined in Chapter 5 as the organization's mission). The **common purpose** unifies employees or members and gives everyone an understanding of the organization's reason for being. Every organization has its own purpose, just like all people have noses. But all noses are not alike, and organizations don't exist for the same purpose.

2. Coordinated Effort: Working Together for Common Purpose   The common purpose is realized through **coordinated effort**, the coordination of individual efforts into a group or organizationwide effort. Although it's true that individuals can make a difference, they cannot do everything by themselves. All organizations coordinate their employees' efforts, and we can describe organizations according to the different methods of coordination they choose.

Organizational culture is an important factor in choosing how to coordinate effort. For example, in clan cultures, coordination is best accomplished through interactions between people and teams, but in hierarchy cultures, coordination likely stems from rigid procedures and processes.

3. Division of Labor: Work Specialization for Greater Efficiency   **Division of labor**, also known as work specialization, is the arrangement of having discrete parts of a task done by different people. Even a two-person crew operating a fishing boat probably has some work specialization—one steers the boat and the other works the nets. With division of labor, an organization can parcel out the entire complex work effort to be performed by specialists, resulting in greater efficiency. One way to describe organizations is to discuss the specific ways they choose to divide their labor.

4. Hierarchy of Authority: The Chain of Command   The **hierarchy of authority**, or chain of command, is a control mechanism for making sure the right people do the right things at the right time. If coordinated effort is to be achieved, some people—namely, managers—need to have more authority, or the right to direct the work of others. Even in member-owned organizations, some people have more authority than others, although their peers may have granted it to them.

Authority is most effective when arranged in a hierarchy. Without tiers or ranks of authority, a lone manager would have to confer with everyone in their domain, making it difficult to get things done. Even in newer organizations that flatten the hierarchy, there still exists more than one level of management.[109] A **flat organization** is defined as one with an organizational structure with few or no levels of middle management between top managers and those reporting to them.

Finally, a principle stressed by early management scholars was that of **unity of command**, in which an employee should report to no more than one manager in order to avoid conflicting priorities and demands. Today, however, with advances in computer technology and networks, there are circumstances in which it makes sense for a person to communicate with more than one manager (as is true, for instance, with the organizational structure known as the matrix structure that we'll describe in the next section).

Hierarchy is another feature you can use to describe organizations. You can get a much better picture of an organization if you understand its unique hierarchy of authority.

Major Features of Organizations: Three More That Most Authorities Agree On

To Schein's four features we add three others that most authorities agree on: (5) *span of control;* (6) *authority, responsibility, and delegation;* and (7) *centralization versus decentralization of authority.*

5. Span of Control: Narrow (or Tall) versus Wide (or Flat)
The **span of control**, or span of management, refers to the number of people reporting directly to a given manager.[110] Span of control is another feature that can be used to describe organizations. There are two kinds of spans of control: narrow (or tall) and wide (or flat). (See Figure 8.5.)

Narrow Span of Control This means a manager has a limited number of people reporting—three vice presidents reporting to a president, for example, instead of nine vice presidents. An organization is said to be *tall* when there are many levels with narrow spans of control. Refer to Figure 8.5 and you can see that in a tall organization with a narrow span of control, the number of workers reporting to a manager one level above them is relatively small.

Wide Span of Control This means a manager has several people reporting—a first-line supervisor may have 40 or more employees, if little hands-on supervision is required, as is the case in some assembly-line workplaces. An organization is said to be *flat* when there are only a few levels with wide spans of control. You can see from Figure 8.5 that in a flat organization with a wide span of control, the number of workers reporting to a manager one level above them is much larger than in a tall organization.

Historically, spans of about 7 to 10 employees were considered best, but there is no consensus as to what is ideal. In general, when managers must be closely involved with their employees, as when the management duties are complex or when ethical concerns are high, they are advised to have a narrow span of control.[111] This is why presidents tend to have only a handful of vice presidents reporting to them. By contrast, first-line supervisors directing employees with similar work tasks may have a wide span of control. Today's emphasis on lean management staffs, increased efficiency, and greater worker autonomy means that many organizations try to make spans of control as wide as possible while still providing adequate supervision.

6. Authority—Accountability, Responsibility, and Delegation
In elephant families, authority over the herd rests with the oldest female, known as the matriarch. In human organizations, however, authority is related to management positions, and it is another feature we can use to describe organizations. **Authority** refers to the rights inherent in a managerial position to make decisions, give orders, and utilize resources. Disobeying orders may lead to consequences such as reprimand, demotion, or firing, and employees are expected to accept that a higher-level manager has a legitimate right to issue orders.

With authority goes *accountability, responsibility,* and the ability to *delegate* one's authority.

Accountability Authority means **accountability**—managers must report and justify work results to the managers above them. Being accountable means you have the responsibility for performing assigned tasks.[112]

FIGURE 8.5
Span of control organizational hierarchies
Source: Expert Program Management. "Organizational Hierarchies." 2017. https://expertprogrammanagement.com/2017/09/span-of-control/.

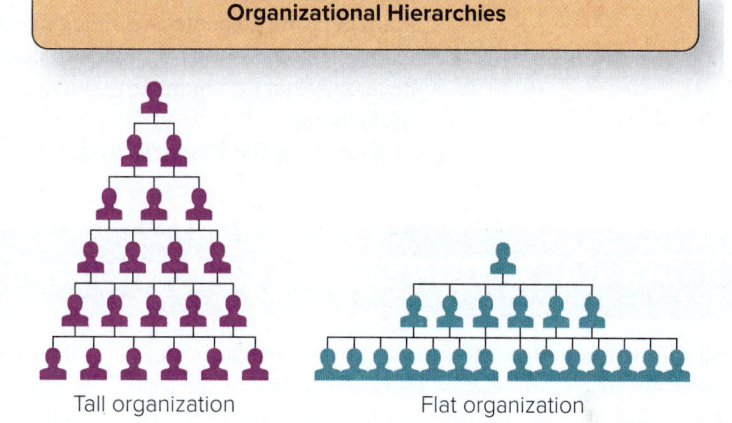

Organizational Hierarchies

Tall organization

Flat organization

Responsibility With more authority comes more responsibility. **Responsibility** is the obligation you have to perform the tasks assigned to you. A car assembly-line worker has less authority and responsibility than a manager of the assembly line. Whereas the line worker is generally responsible for one specific task, such as installing a windshield, the manager has much greater responsibilities.

Delegation **Delegation** is the process of assigning managerial authority and responsibility to managers and employees lower in the hierarchy. To be more efficient, most managers are expected to delegate as much of their work as possible.[113] However, many bosses get hung up on perfection, failing to realize that delegation is not only a necessary part of managing, but one that impacts attitudes, productivity, and firm performance.[114]

Check out the Practical Action box for tips on delegating effectively.

PRACTICAL ACTION | How to Delegate Effectively

All managers must learn how to delegate—to assign management authority and responsibilities to people lower in the company hierarchy. If, as a manager, you find yourself often behind, always taking work home, doing your employees' work for them, and constantly having employees seeking your approval before they can act, you're clearly not delegating well.[115]

How can you delegate more effectively? It's fine to start small. Here are some guidelines.[116]

Delegate Routine Tasks and Technical Matters Always try to delegate routine tasks and routine paperwork, keeping only the tasks that call for your input. When there are technical matters, let the experts handle them.

Delegate Tasks That Help Your Employees Grow Let your employees solve their own problems whenever possible. Let them try new things so they will grow in their jobs. Your success depends on theirs, so give them room to achieve.

Match Delegated Tasks to Your Employees' Skills and Abilities Minimize some of the risks of delegation by assigning tasks based on employees' training, talent, skills,

Delegating effectively is a skill that you can develop with time, experience, and practice. Good managers learn what and to whom to delegate, and they use delegation as a tool for improving both efficiency and effectiveness.
Monkey Business Images/Shutterstock

and motivation. Be sure you've given them the tools and clarity they need to get the job done, and be available for help and questions.

Don't Delegate Confidential or Human Resource Matters Tasks that are confidential or that involve the evaluation, discipline, or counseling of employees should never be handed off to someone else.

Don't Delegate Emergencies By definition, an emergency is a crisis for which there is little time for solution and a high need for coordination within the organization. You should handle this yourself.

Don't Delegate Special Tasks That Your Boss Asked You to Do—Unless You Have Their Permission If your supervisor entrusts you with a special assignment, such as attending a particular meeting, don't delegate it unless you have permission to do so.

YOUR CALL
Are any of these reasons that you might need to improve your delegating skills? What are some others?

7. Centralization versus Decentralization of Authority Another feature we can use to describe organizations is the extent to which authority is centralized versus decentralized. This feature is concerned with who makes the important decisions in an organization.

Centralized Authority With **centralized authority**, important decisions are made by higher-level managers. Very small companies tend to be the most centralized, although nearly all organizations have at least some authority concentrated at the top of the hierarchy. Walmart and McDonald's are examples of companies using this kind of authority. Two advantages of centralized authority are:

1. There is less duplication of work because fewer employees perform the same task; rather, the task is often performed by a department of specialists.

2. There are increased efficiencies because procedures are uniform and thus easier to control.[117]

Decentralized Authority With **decentralized authority**, important decisions are made by middle-level and supervisory-level managers. Here, power has been delegated throughout the organization. Among the companies using decentralized authority are General Motors and Harley-Davidson. Two advantages of decentralized authority are:

1. Managers are encouraged to solve their own problems rather than escalate the decision to a higher level of management.

2. Decisions are made more quickly, which increases the organization's flexibility and efficiency.[118]

Thus far you've learned about seven different features used to describe organizations. Just as a police sketch artist uses descriptions of individual facial features (e.g., eye color, face shape, hair length and color, etc.) to build a complete drawing of a suspect's face, an organization's features combine into a visual depiction of its structure. This is known as the organization chart, discussed next.

The Organization Chart

Whatever the size or type of organization, its structure can be depicted in an organization chart. An **organization chart** is a box-and-lines illustration showing the formal lines of authority and the organization's official positions or work specializations. This is the family tree–like pattern of boxes and lines posted on workplace walls and given to new hires, such as for a hospital (see Figure 8.6.).

At a very detailed level, organization charts provide information about an organization's features (e.g., its division of labor, chain of command, the extent to which it centralizes authority, etc.). More broadly, organization charts reveal information about two basic elements of organizational structure: (1) the *vertical hierarchy of authority*—who reports to whom—and (2) the *horizontal specialization*—who specializes in what work.

The Vertical Hierarchy of Authority: Who Reports to Whom
A glance up and down an organization chart shows the *vertical hierarchy,* the chain of command. A formal vertical hierarchy also shows the official communication network—who talks to whom. In a simple two-person organization, the owner might communicate with just an administrative assistant. In a complex organization, the president talks principally to the vice presidents, who in turn talk to the assistant vice presidents, and so on.

The Horizontal Specialization: Who Specializes in What Work
A glance to the left and right on the lines of an organization chart shows the *horizontal specialization,* the different jobs or work specialization. The husband-and-wife partners in a two-person digital graphics firm might agree that one is the "outside person," handling sales, client relations, and finances, and the other is the "inside person," handling production and research. A large firm might have vice presidents for each task—marketing, finance, and so on.

In this section we described seven major features of an organization and how they come together in a visual representation known as an organization chart. In Section 8.5, we discuss how distinct combinations of these features form the basis of the eight types of organizational structure. ●

FIGURE 8.6

Organizational chart (example for a hospital)

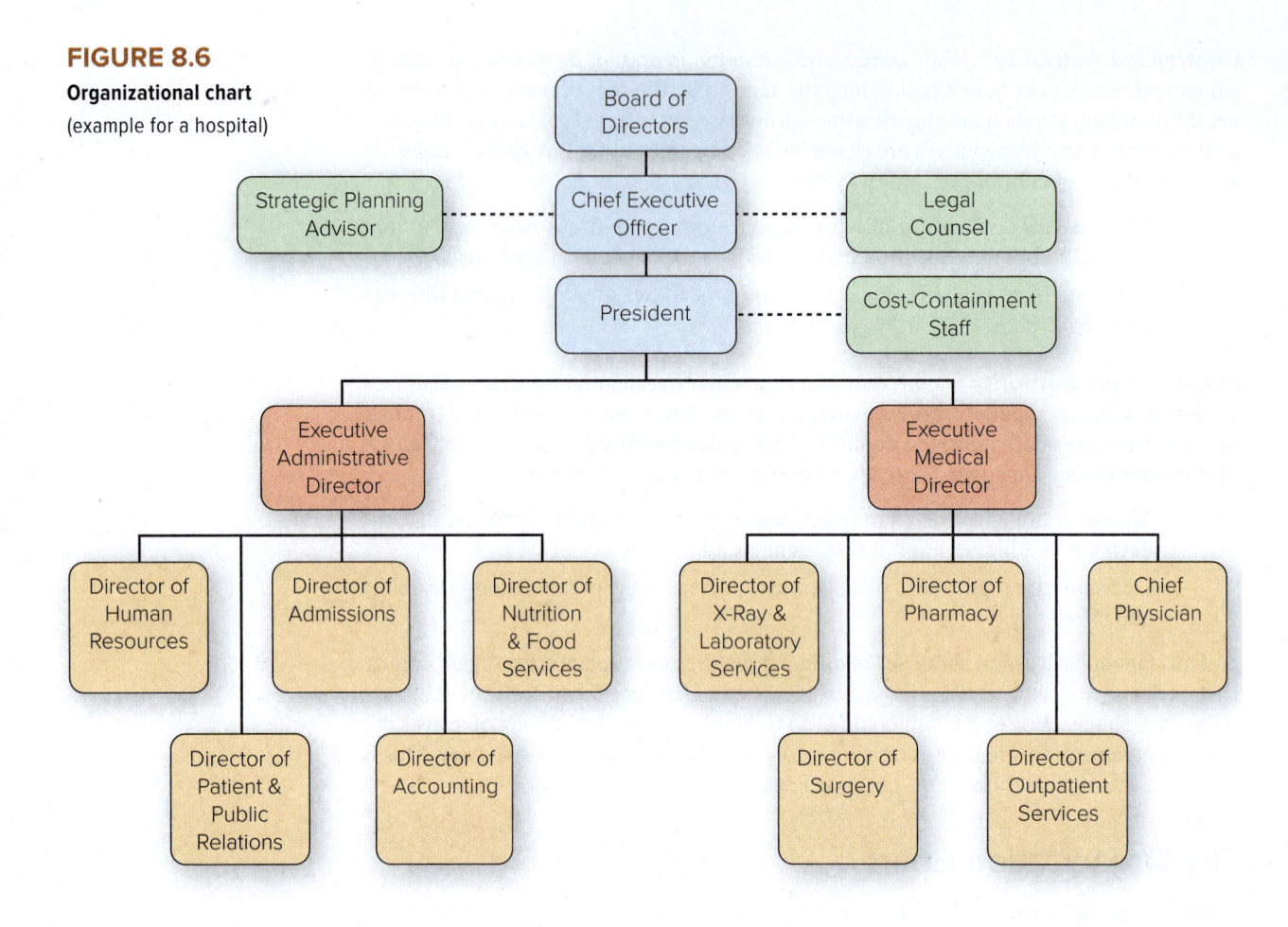

[Organizational chart showing hierarchy: Board of Directors → Chief Executive Officer (with Strategic Planning Advisor and Legal Counsel as staff) → President (with Cost-Containment Staff). Under President: Executive Administrative Director and Executive Medical Director. Under Executive Administrative Director: Director of Human Resources, Director of Admissions (with Director of Patient & Public Relations below), Director of Nutrition & Food Services (with Director of Accounting below). Under Executive Medical Director: Director of X-Ray & Laboratory Services (with Director of Surgery below), Director of Pharmacy (with Director of Outpatient Services below), Chief Physician.]

8.5 Eight Types of Organizational Structure

THE BIG PICTURE

The eight types of organizational structure are simple, functional, divisional, matrix, horizontal, hollow, modular, and virtual.

LO 8-5

Describe the eight types of organizational structure.

In Section 8.1, we defined organizational structure as the formal system of task and reporting relationships that an organization uses to coordinate and motivate workers' efforts toward achieving goals. The right organizational structures help employees and organizations perform better, and the right structure for a particular organization can change as the organization evolves.[119] **Organizational design** is concerned with designing the optimal structures of accountability and responsibility that an organization uses to execute its strategies. The eight organizational structures we discuss in this section can be grouped into three broad categories of organizational design:[120]

1. Traditional designs (simple, functional, divisional, and matrix structures).
2. Horizontal designs (horizontal structure).
3. Designs that open boundaries between organizations (hollow, modular, and virtual structures).

1. Traditional Designs: Simple, Functional, Divisional, and Matrix Structures

The traditional organizational design category includes the (1) simple, (2) functional, (3) divisional, and (4) matrix structures. The organizational structures that are considered traditional designs tend to rely on a vertical management hierarchy, with clear departmental boundaries and reporting arrangements, as follows.

The Simple Structure: For the Small Firm The simple structure is often found in a firm's very early, entrepreneurial stages, when the organization is apt to reflect the desires and personality of the owner or founder. An organization with a **simple structure** has authority centralized in a single person, a flat hierarchy, few rules, and low work specialization (see Figure 8.7).

Hundreds of thousands of organizations are arranged according to a simple structure—for instance, small mom-and-pop firms running landscaping, construction, insurance sales, and similar businesses. Both Hewlett-Packard and Apple Computer began as two-person garage start-ups that later became large.

The Functional Structure: Grouping by Similar Work Specialties In the **functional structure**, people with similar occupational specialties are put together in formal groups. This is a quite commonplace structure, seen in all kinds of organizations, both for-profit and nonprofit (see Figure 8.8).

Some examples include a manufacturing firm that will often group people with similar work skills in a Marketing Department, others in a Production Department, others in Finance, and so on. A nonprofit educational institution might group employees according to work specialty under Faculty, Admissions, Maintenance, and so forth.

FIGURE 8.7
Simple structure: An example
There is only one hierarchical level of management beneath the owner.

FIGURE 8.8
Functional structure: Two examples
This shows the functional structure for a business and for a hospital.

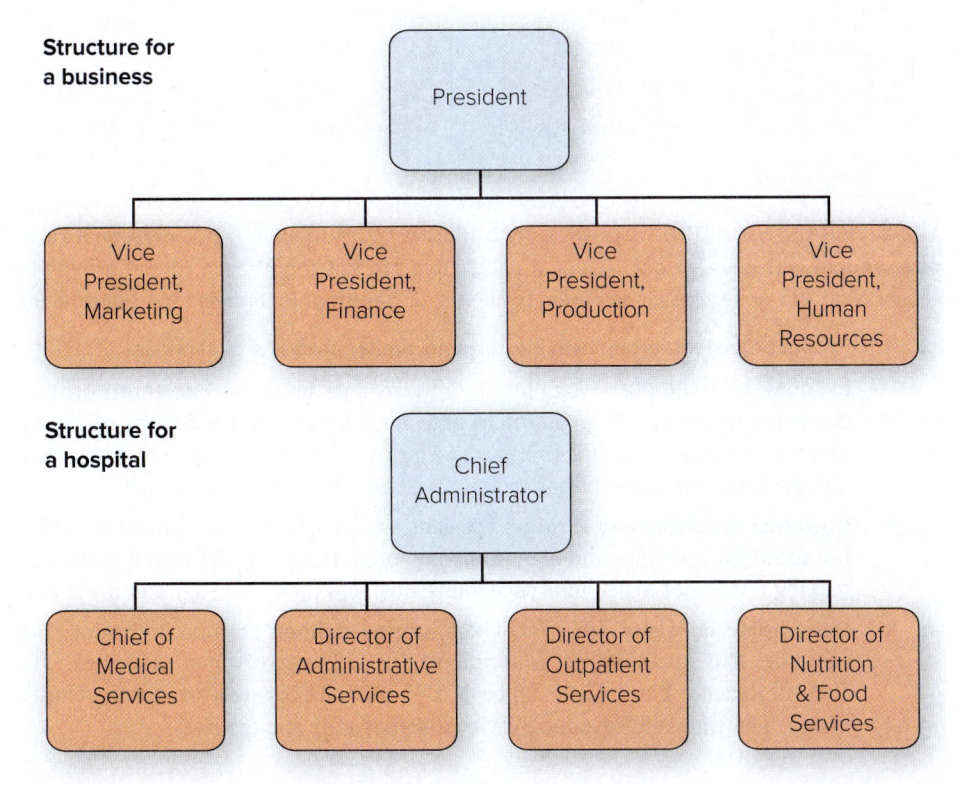

FIGURE 8.9

Divisional structure: Three examples

This shows product, customer, and geographic divisions.

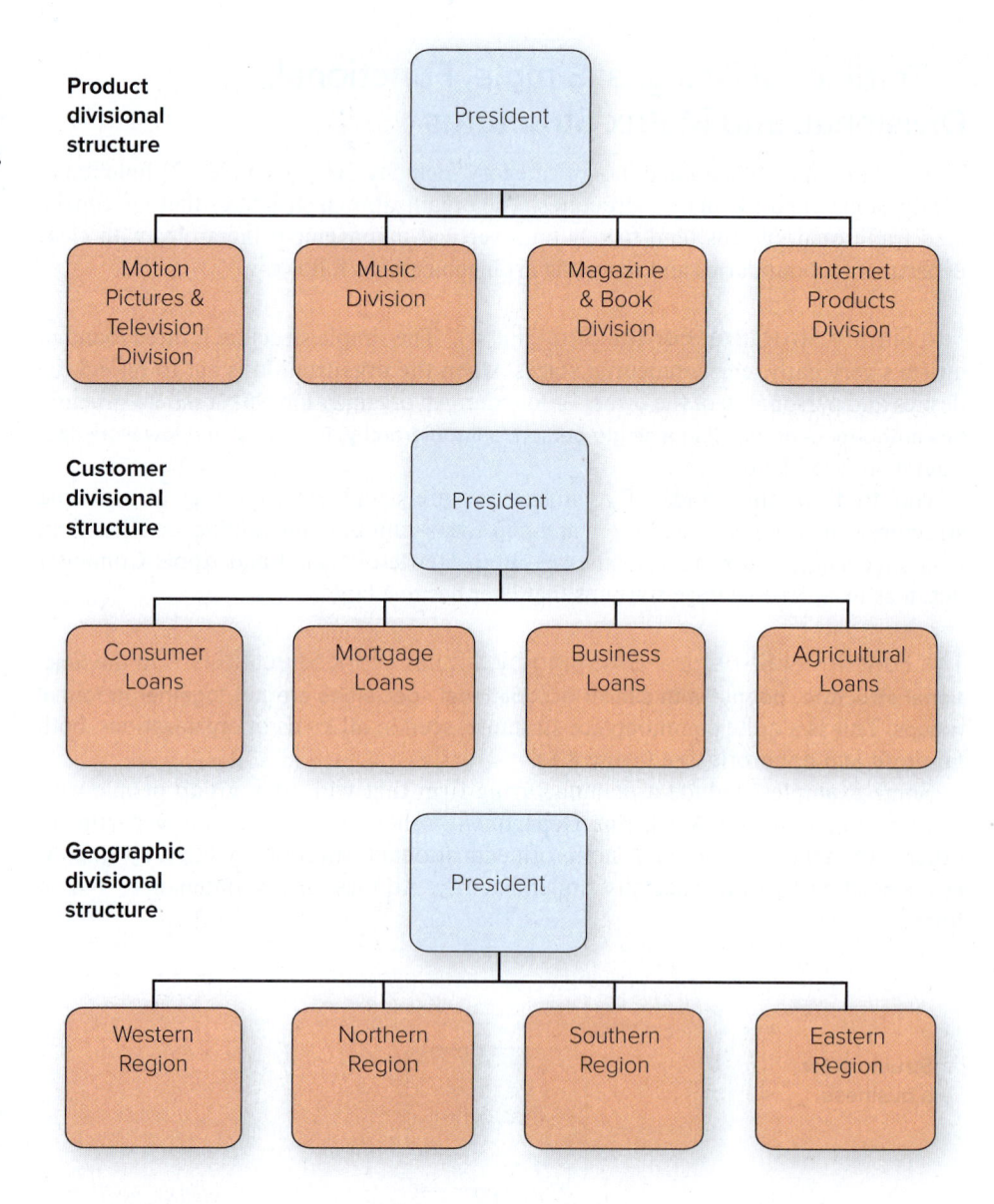

Product divisional structure

- President
  - Motion Pictures & Television Division
  - Music Division
  - Magazine & Book Division
  - Internet Products Division

Customer divisional structure

- President
  - Consumer Loans
  - Mortgage Loans
  - Business Loans
  - Agricultural Loans

Geographic divisional structure

- President
  - Western Region
  - Northern Region
  - Southern Region
  - Eastern Region

The Divisional Structure: Grouping by Similarity of Purpose In a **divisional structure**, people with diverse occupational specialties are put together in formal groups by similar products or services, customers or clients, or geographic regions (see Figure 8.9).

- **Product divisions** group activities around similar products or services.

   ExxonMobil Example: ExxonMobil organizes its business into three product divisions: (1) Upstream (exploration activities), (2) Product Solutions (development, manufacture, and distribution of innovative, sustainable products), and (3) Low Carbon Solutions (carbon capture, biofuels, and hydrogen).[121]

- **Customer divisions** tend to group activities around common customers or clients. For example, a savings and loan company might be structured with divisions for making consumer loans, mortgage loans, business loans, and agricultural loans.

- **Geographic divisions** group activities around defined regional locations. For example, this arrangement is frequently used by government agencies. The Federal Reserve Bank, for instance, has 12 separate districts around the United States. The Internal Revenue Service also has multiple districts.

The Matrix Structure: A Grid of Functional and Divisional for Two Chains of Command In a **matrix structure**, an organization combines functional and divisional chains of command in a grid so that there are two command structures—vertical and horizontal. The functional structure usually doesn't change—it is the organization's normal departments or divisions, such as Finance, Marketing, Production, and Research & Development. The divisional structure may vary—as by product, brand, customer, or geographic region (see Figure 8.10).

A Hypothetical Example—Ford Motor Co.: The functional structure might be the departments of Engineering, Finance, Production, and Marketing, each headed by a vice president. Thus, the reporting arrangement is vertical. The divisional structure might be by product (the new models of Escape, Mustang, Explorer, and Expedition, for example), each headed by a project manager. This reporting arrangement is horizontal. Thus, a marketing person, say, would report to *both* the vice president of marketing *and* the project manager for the Ford Mustang. Indeed, Ford Motor Co. used the matrix approach to create the Fusion and a newer version of the Mustang.

FIGURE 8.10
Matrix structure
An example of an arrangement that Ford might use.

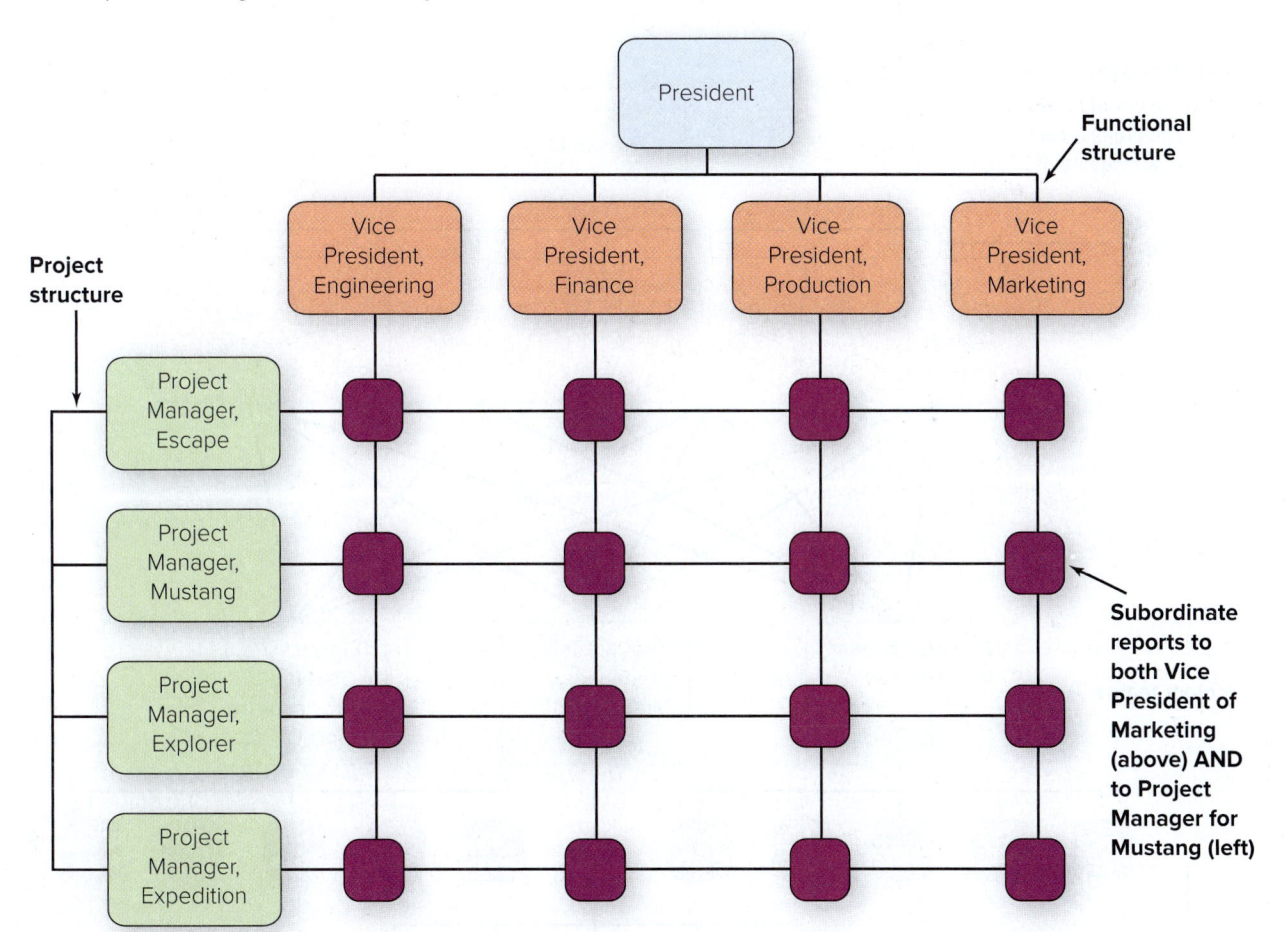

2. The Horizontal Design: Eliminating Functional Barriers to Solve Problems

The horizontal design category includes the horizontal structure. In a **horizontal structure**, also called a team-based design, teams or workgroups, either temporary or permanent, are used to improve collaboration and work on shared tasks by breaking down internal boundaries. For instance, when managers from different functional divisions are brought together in teams—known as cross-functional teams—to solve particular problems, the barriers between the divisions break down. The focus on narrow divisional interests yields to a common interest in solving the problems that brought them together. Yet team members still have their full-time functional work responsibilities and often still formally report to their own managers above them in the functional-division hierarchy (see Figure 8.11).

3. Designs That Open Boundaries between Organizations: Hollow, Modular, and Virtual Structures

The opposite of a bureaucracy, with its numerous barriers and divisions, a **boundaryless organization** is a fluid, highly adaptive organization whose members, linked by information technology, come together to collaborate on common tasks. The collaborators may include not only co-workers but also suppliers, customers, and even competitors. This means that the form of the business is ever-changing, and business relationships are informal.[122]

The boundary-opening category of organizational design includes the *hollow, modular,* and *virtual* structures.

FIGURE 8.11

Horizontal design

This shows a mix of functional (vertical) and project-team (horizontal) arrangements.

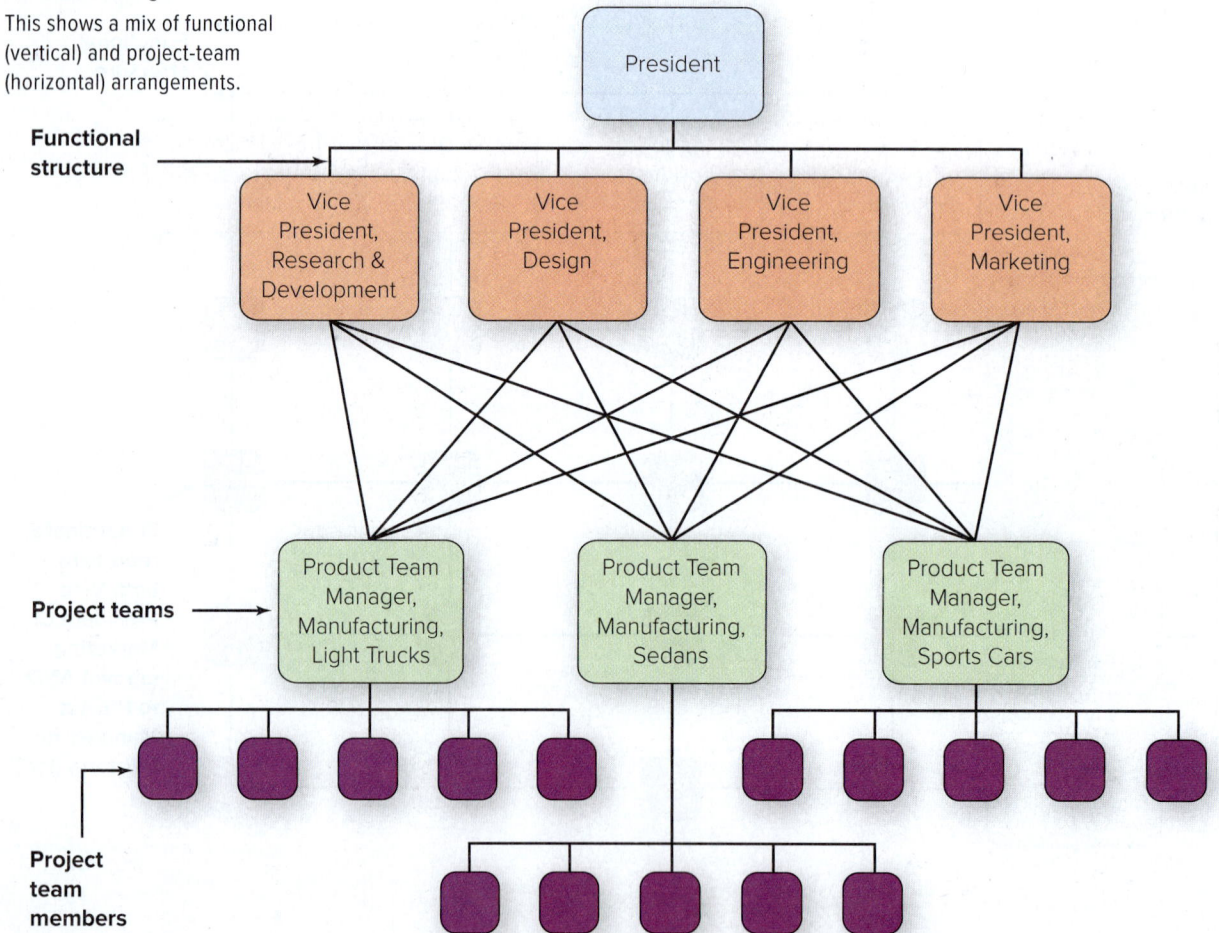

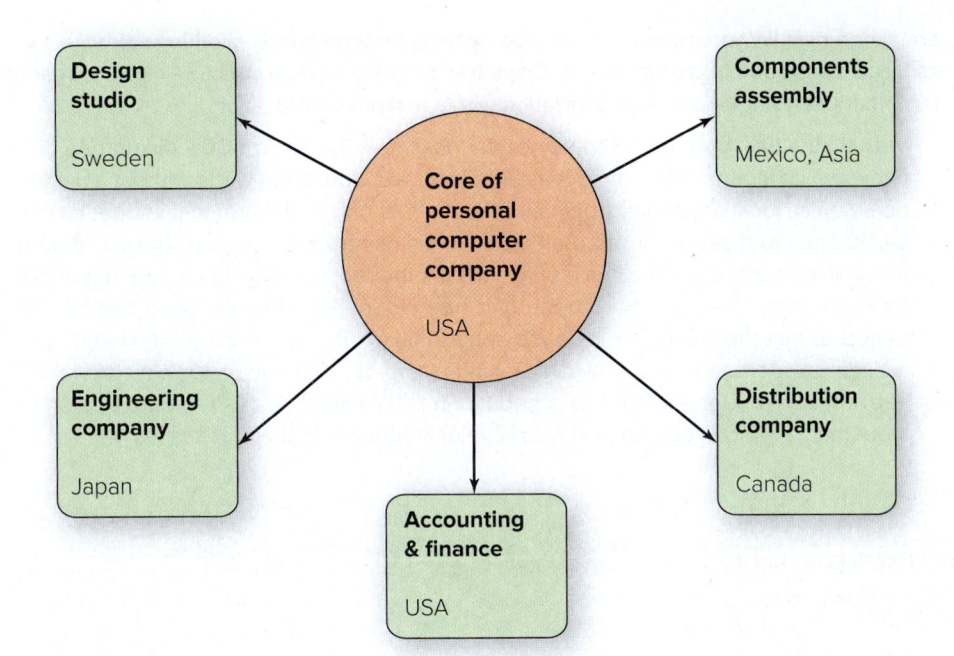

FIGURE 8.12

Hollow structure

This is an example of a personal computer company that outsources noncore processes to vendors.

The Hollow Structure: Operating with a Central Core and Outsourcing Functions to Outside Vendors In the hollow structure, often called the network structure, the organization has a central core of key functions and outsources other functions to vendors who can do them cheaper or faster (see Figure 8.12). A company with a hollow structure might retain such important core processes as design or marketing and outsource most other processes, such as human resources, warehousing, or distribution, thereby seeming to "hollow out" the organization.[123]

A firm with a hollow structure might operate with extensive, even worldwide operations, yet its basic core could remain small, thus keeping payrolls and overhead down. The glue that holds everything together is information technology, along with strategic alliances and contractual arrangements with supplier companies (i.e., the network). H&M is an example of a company that uses elements of a hollow structure. Nearly 100% of H&M's products are manufactured by outsourced suppliers. According to its website, the company prioritizes "strong, long-term relations with our suppliers that are based on mutual trust and transparency."[124]

The Modular Structure: Outsourcing Pieces of a Product to Outside Firms
The modular structure differs from the hollow structure in that it is oriented around outsourcing certain *pieces of a product* rather than outsourcing certain *processes* (such as human resources or warehousing) of an organization. In a modular structure, a firm assembles product chunks, or modules, provided by outside contractors. One article compares this form of organization to "a collection of Lego bricks that can snap together."

Modular Structure Example—Boeing: It takes a large number of parts to put together an aircraft. A Boeing 777, for example, is made of approximately 3 million individual pieces. Boeing procures components for its aircraft from a multitude of global suppliers. For example, parts of the fuselage come from Kawasaki in Japan while others are made by Alenia in Italy.[125] Fuji, a Japanese company, provides wing boxes, and more than 300 suppliers in India supply wire harnesses, ground support equipment, and forgings.[126]

The Virtual Structure: An Internet-Connected Partner for a Temporary Project
"There is fantastic talent out there to drive growing companies," says one industry observer, "but the best people are scattered everywhere and with full personal lives that prevent them from relocating to headquarters easily."[127] In a virtual structure, employees

are geographically spread apart, usually co-working through remote working software such as Slack, Zoom, and Microsoft Teams. Organizations with a virtual structure often appear to customers as a single, unified organization with a real physical location.

Virtual Structure Example—Zapier: Zapier describes itself as a "100% distributed company," which means all its employees are dispersed around the world without a unifying home office location. Zapier's primary offering is its online platform that integrates over 5,000 apps to make work more efficient. When using Zapier, an employee's "trigger" action in one app sets off a chain of actions in other apps, reducing the amount of platforms the employee needs to open and operate in. For example, apps can be integrated so that the submission of a job application (a trigger) generates several actions, including the creation of a new contact in Salesforce, distribution of an alert e-mail to relevant staff, and a reminder to schedule an initial interview in a recruiter's calendar. More than 2 million companies rely on Zapier to streamline their processes.[128]

8.6 Career Corner: Managing Your Career Readiness

LO 8-6

Explain how to use the career readiness competencies of understanding the business and personal adaptability to better understand and change your level of fit with an organization.

Figure 8.13 shows the model of career readiness we introduced in Chapter 1. Organizational culture and structure are important aspects of an organization's internal context. Recall from Chapter 4 that an organization's internal context represents the situational or environmental characteristics that influence employees' behavior.[129]

FIGURE 8.13

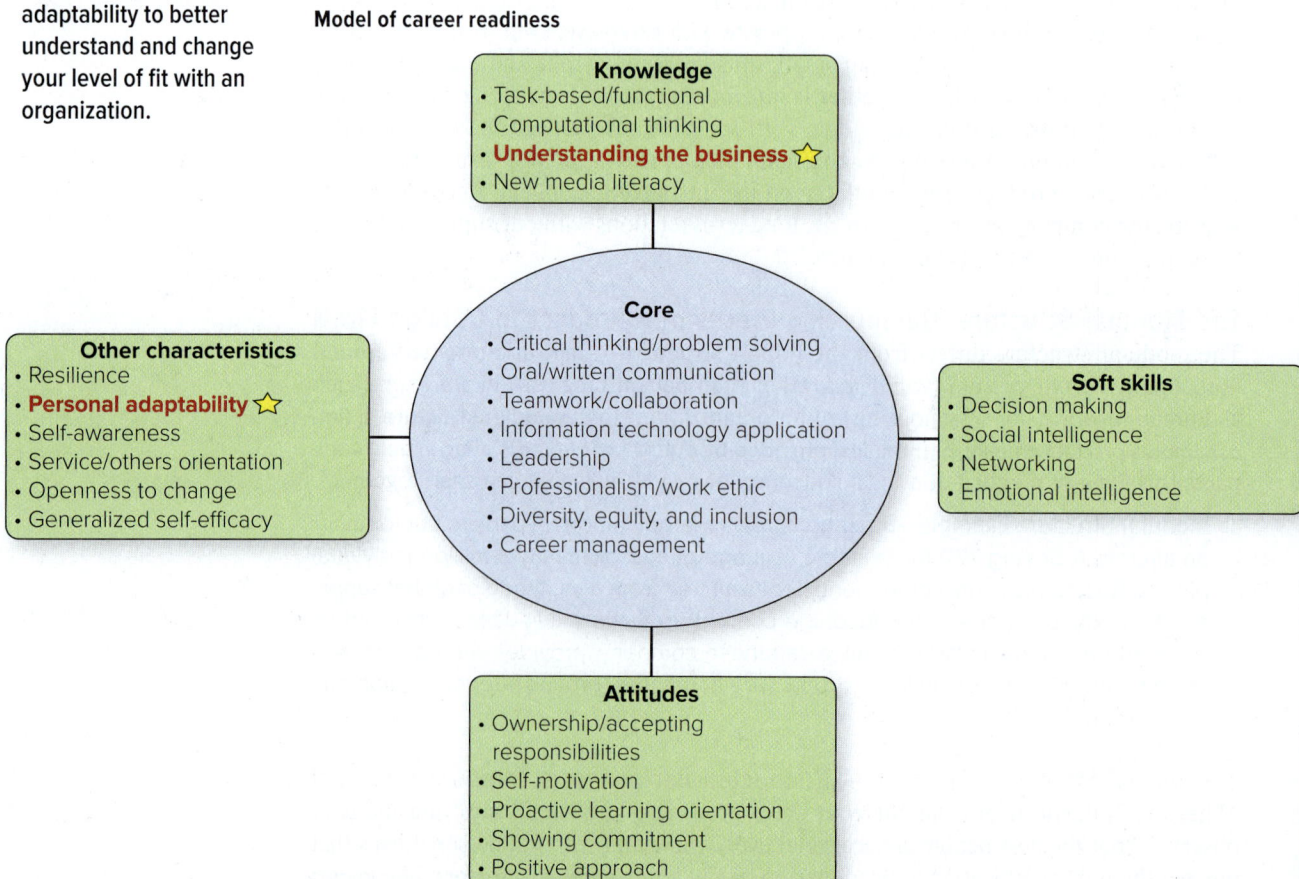

Model of career readiness

Knowledge
- Task-based/functional
- Computational thinking
- **Understanding the business** ⭐
- New media literacy

Core
- Critical thinking/problem solving
- Oral/written communication
- Teamwork/collaboration
- Information technology application
- Leadership
- Professionalism/work ethic
- Diversity, equity, and inclusion
- Career management

Other characteristics
- Resilience
- **Personal adaptability** ⭐
- Self-awareness
- Service/others orientation
- Openness to change
- Generalized self-efficacy

Soft skills
- Decision making
- Social intelligence
- Networking
- Emotional intelligence

Attitudes
- Ownership/accepting responsibilities
- Self-motivation
- Proactive learning orientation
- Showing commitment
- Positive approach

If you want to know whether you fit in with an organization, you need to understand the organization's internal context. Knowing your level of fit is important because studies suggest that high levels of fit ultimately lead to higher job satisfaction, performance, and greater chances of being promoted.[130]

Interestingly, adaptability—the ability to maintain fit when the organization's culture changes—seems to be equally or even more important in determining your performance, as you will learn in this chapter's Executive Interview Series video. Research suggests that employees who adapt quickly to changing cultural norms have even better outcomes than employees who are a great fit with the organization when they are first hired.[131]

This section thus focuses on improving your career readiness competency of understanding the business by assessing an organization's internal context and improving your career readiness competency of personal adaptability so that you can adjust to changes in the organization's internal context.

Executive Interview Series: Understanding the Business and Personal Adaptability

Understanding the Business and Where You "Fit" In

We are focusing on understanding the business by assessing your level of fit with an organization. Experts suggest that knowing the answers to these questions about an organization will help you to make an assessment of fit.[132]

Questions to Ask of Your Prospective/New Colleagues

1. What projects are you working on right now?
2. What do you hope to achieve here? What gets in your way?
3. What kinds of people succeed in this organization? What kinds of people don't succeed?

Questions to Ask of Your Prospective/New Boss

1. Would you tell me about someone you hired here who was very successful?
2. Would you tell me about someone you hired here who was not successful?
3. What do you want to be praising me for at my first performance review?

Questions to Ask Yourself

1. How do people respond to me when I walk by them in this organization? How do they respond to each other?
2. How do my career readiness competencies complement the organization's goals? What can the organization teach me?
3. Do my values align with the organization's values? If not, can I see myself adopting the organization's values?

Remember that your level of fit can be a good indicator of how far you'll go in the organization, but if you don't fit in right away, it's not the end of the world. You can work on becoming more adaptable in order to increase your level of fit with the organization, as we discuss next.

Becoming More Adaptable

Personal adaptability is defined as the ability and willingness to adapt to changing situations. It represents an "other characteristic" in our model of career readiness that contributes to your performance and success because it allows you to remain productive during times of organizational change.[133] In today's global world, it's more important than ever for organizations to be nimble, and this relies on the adaptability of employees.[134]

Try the following suggestions to increase your level of adaptability.

- **Focus on being optimistic.** Optimistic people see change as an opportunity. Because they therefore view work or career changes as challenges to overcome, they have positive expectations about future events and confidence in their ability to adjust. Optimistic people tend not to whine. Rather, they attempt to change or influence a decision or they adapt and move on.[135]

- **Display a proactive learning orientation.** A proactive learning orientation reflects your desire to learn and improve other career readiness competencies. This attitude keeps you focused on learning and initiating the behavior desired by an organization during times of change.

- **Be more resourceful.** When faced with challenges, look for solutions not problems. Practice using after action review, discussed in Chapter 7, to find creative ideas for improving results. It also helps to create contingency plans that identify what you can do if Plan A doesn't work.

- **Take ownership and accept responsibility.** This career readiness attitude is the willingness to accept responsibility for your actions. People who are adaptable own their mistakes and see them as an opportunity to learn and grow. As part of a recent study of learning and adaptability in medical residency programs, one faculty member noted the importance of owning mistakes and using them to improve the skills of not only the resident who made the error, but also other residents. "We ask residents to submit [imaging] cases that they missed. . . . We ask everyone in the residency to take a look at the same things that the person missed, and they try to find it. And sometimes they do and sometimes they don't. And that's kind of reassuring, also, to know that other people could also make the same mistakes – not that we should, but we learn from those mistakes, and we try to change because of it."[136]

- **Expand your perspective by asking different questions.** Asking new or novel questions helps to broaden your perspective when faced with a challenge. Most of us tend to ask questions that are too narrow. Try something like: "What surprises me about this situation? What are impossible options in this situation? What data am I ignoring?"[137]

Key Terms Used in This Chapter

accountability 287
adhocracy culture 273
authority 287
boundaryless organization 294
centralized authority 289
clan culture 273
common purpose 286
coordinated effort 286
corporate culture 265
customer divisions 292
decentralized authority 289
delegation 288
division of labor 286
divisional structure 292
enacted values 269
espoused values 269
flat organization 286
functional structure 291
geographic divisions 292
hero 270
hierarchy culture 274
hierarchy of authority 286
hollow structure 295
horizontal structure 294
human resource practices 266
market culture 273
matrix structure 293
modular structure 295
organization 285
organization chart 289
organizational design 290
organizational socialization 271
organizational structure 265
person–organization (P–O) fit 276
product divisions 292
responsibility 288
rites and rituals 271
simple structure 291
span of control 287
story 270
symbol 270
unity of command 286
virtual structure 295

Key Points

8.1 Aligning Culture, Structure, and HR Practices to Support Strategy

- Managers must align the organization's culture, structure, and HR practices to support strategic execution.
- Organizational culture is defined as the set of shared, taken-for-granted implicit assumptions that a group holds and that determines how it perceives, thinks about, and reacts to its various environments.
- Organizational structure is a formal system of task and reporting relationships that coordinates and motivates an organization's members so that they can work together to achieve the organization's goals.

8.2 What Kind of Organizational Culture Will You Be Operating In?

- Culture has three levels. (1) observable artifacts, (2) espoused values, and (3) basic assumptions.
- Employees learn culture through symbols, stories, heroes, rites and rituals, and socialization.
- The competing values framework classifies organizational cultures into four types: (1) clan, (2) adhocracy, (3) market, and (4) hierarchy.

8.3 The Process of Culture Change

- The 12 mechanisms/levers managers use to embed or change organizational culture are (1) formal statements; (2) slogans and sayings; (3) rites and rituals; (4) stories, legends, and myths; (5) leader reactions to crises; (6) role modeling, training, and coaching; (7) physical design; (8) rewards, titles, promotions, and bonuses; (9) organizational goals and performance criteria; (10) measurable and controllable activities; (11) organizational structure; and (12) organizational systems and procedures.
- Changing culture requires using multiple levers.

8.4 The Major Features of an Organization

- An organization is a system of consciously coordinated activities or forces of two or more people.
- Organizations vary according to seven features. Four proposed by Schein are (1) common purpose; (2) coordinated effort; (3) division of labor; and (4) hierarchy of authority.
- Three other common features are (5) span of control; (6) authority—accountability, responsibility, and delegation; and (7) centralization versus decentralization of authority.
- Whatever the size of an organization, it can be represented in an organization chart, a boxes-and-lines illustration showing the formal lines of authority and the organization's official positions or division of labor.

8.5 Eight Types of Organizational Structures

- Organizations may be arranged into eight types of structures: (1) simple, (2) functional, (3) divisional, (4) matrix, (5) horizontal, (6) hollow, (7) modular, and (8) virtual.

8.6 Career Corner: Managing Your Career Readiness

- You can use the career readiness competencies of understanding the business and personal adaptability to better understand and change your level of fit with an organization.
- You can ask questions of your colleagues, boss, and self to determine how you "fit" in a specific context.
- You can become more adaptable by being optimistic, displaying a proactive learning orientation, being resourceful, taking ownership and accepting responsibility, and expanding your perspective with different questions.

9 Human Resource Management
Getting the Right People for Managerial Success

After reading this chapter, you should be able to:

LO 9-1 Discuss the importance of strategic human resource management.

LO 9-2 Discuss ways to recruit and hire the right people.

LO 9-3 Outline common forms of compensation.

LO 9-4 Describe the processes used for onboarding and learning and development.

LO 9-5 Discuss effective performance management and feedback techniques.

LO 9-6 List guidelines for handling promotions, transfers, discipline, and dismissals.

LO 9-7 Discuss legal considerations managers should be aware of.

LO 9-8 Describe labor–management issues and ways to work effectively with labor unions.

LO 9-9 Review the steps for becoming a better receiver of feedback.

FORECAST   What's Ahead in This Chapter

This chapter considers human resource (HR) management—planning for, attracting, developing, and retaining an effective workforce. We consider how this subject fits in with the overall company strategy, culture, and structure; how to use HR practices for strategic advantage; and how to recruit and select qualified people. We describe the common forms of compensation, the processes used for onboarding and learning and development, and how to manage employee performance and give feedback. We discuss guidelines for handling promotions, discipline, and workplace performance problems. We go over basic legal requirements and consider the role of labor unions. We conclude with a Career Corner that focuses on how to become a better receiver of feedback.

How to Prepare for a Job Interview

Job candidates often make a few common mistakes in initial interviews. Here are some tips for using the career readiness competencies of career management, new media literacy, and communication skills to avoid them.

Be Prepared

Can you pronounce the names of the company and interviewer with which you're interviewing? Do you understand what the company makes or does, and the duties of the position for which you're interviewing? Do you know the company's competition? What new products or services are being offered? What are your greatest strengths and specific achievements? Your weaknesses? Research the company's website and any recent press about the firm. Check out the company's social media and see how they interact with followers. Identify strengths of yours that fit what the company does. When asked about your weaknesses, discuss how you recognized one, overcame a dilemma it posed, and were improved by it. Practice your answers, but not so much that you sound phony saying them.[1]

Dress Right and Be on Time

Dress neatly and professionally, and remember that your appearance matters even in virtual interviews, even if you can only be seen from the waist up. Make sure you know the exact location of the interview, and if possible, do a test run a day or so before, at about the same time of day as your interview, so you know how long it will take to get there on time. If your interview is happening over Zoom, be sure your software is up-to-date an hour before your interview. Finally, silence your phone and don't look at it again until you've finished the interview.

Practice What to Say and What to Ask

Rehearse questions to ask the interviewer, such as the challenges for the position in the future and how success in the job will be defined. Don't make negative comments about your old company or boss. Rather, figure out the positives and convey what you gained from your experience.[2] If asked an inappropriate question (about age, marital status, whether you have children or plan to), politely say you don't believe the question is relevant to your qualifications.[3] Within 24 hours of the meeting, send an e-mail (with no misspellings or faulty grammar) thanking the interviewer and reiterating your interest in the position.[4] If you think you messed up part of the interview, use the e-mail to smooth over your mistakes.[5]

Know What You Will Be Asked

Recent surveys suggest that up to 94% of employers use one or more background checks in the hiring process.[6] Some employers may ask for your GPA, especially if a job opening is highly competitive. If your grade point average is not as high as you would like, prepare an explanation.[7] Finally, be sure your social media profile is mostly private, and that whatever is public is limited, is not too personal, and would make your loved ones proud. More than half of the companies that participated in a recent study indicated they'd disqualified one or more job candidates due to their social media profiles.[8]

Plan for a Strong Closing

Most interviews end with the recruiter asking something like "do you have any final questions for us?" You can make yourself more memorable if you prepare a strong response. A recent article in the *Harvard Business Review* suggests your questions should focus on two goals: (1) figuring out if the job is a good fit for you, and (2) demonstrating that you are the best job candidate. One way to meet these goals is to ask questions about the specific job role, the team you'd be working with, and the manager(s) you'd be working under. For example, ask "What types of skills is the team missing that you're looking to fill with a new hire?" Another way to meet these goals is to ask questions about the company's culture. For example, try asking something like "How is the company different since you began working here?" or "What do you wish you'd known before you started your job here?" Questions such as these also give you the opportunity to build a stronger connection with the interviewer.[9]

For Discussion What kind of advice do you see here that you wish you'd followed in the past? What will you do differently next time?

9.1 Strategic Human Resource Management

THE BIG PICTURE

Human resource management consists of the activities managers perform to plan for, attract, develop, and retain an effective workforce. Strategic human resource management consists of the process of designing and implementing systems of policies and practices that align an organization's human capital with its strategic objectives.

LO 9-1

Discuss the importance of strategic human resource management.

You learned in Chapter 8 that three key internal factors influence an organization's ability to successfully implement strategy. We discussed two of these factors—organizational culture and organizational structure—at length in Chapter 8. We now turn our attention to the third factor—the human resource (HR) practices organizations use to manage their most important assets—people. As previously defined, *HR practices* consist of all the activities organizations use to manage their human capital, including selection, performance management, learning and development programs, and compensation.

The best companies know that how they manage their people is an important determinant of organizational success, and decades of research links the use of strategically focused HR practices with firm performance.[10] Clearly, great human resources practices are a game changer.

In this section we explain how HR practices can generate superior firm performance and competitive advantages.

Human Resource Management: Managing an Organization's Most Important Resource

Human resource management (HRM) is the process of planning for, attracting, developing, and retaining an effective workforce. This process is made up of various HR practices including employee recruitment, compensation, onboarding, and performance management (see Figure 9.1).

FIGURE 9.1
Human resource practices

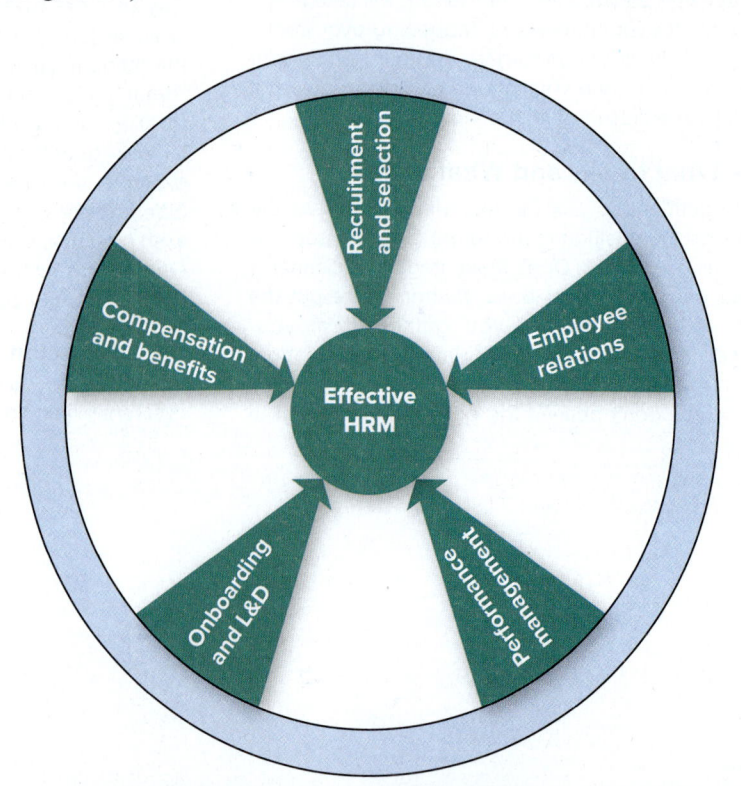

Regardless of industry, all organizations use HR practices to some extent to manage their workers. For example, even the smallest mom-and-pop company with only two or three employees has to decide whom to hire (selection) and how much salary to pay (compensation).

"If you're not thinking all the time about making every person valuable, you don't have a chance," according to former General Electric CEO Jack Welch. "What's the alternative? Wasted minds? Uninvolved people? A labor force that's angry or bored? That doesn't make sense!"[11] Indeed, companies ranked in the top 10 on *Fortune* magazine's 2022 Best Companies list—including Cisco, Hilton, Wegmans Food Markets, Salesforce, Nvidia, Accenture, Rocket Companies, American Express, David Weekley Homes, and Capital One Financial—have discovered that putting employees first is the foundation for success.[12] Here are a few ways these award-winning organizations are leading the pack in HRM:[13]

- Salesforce has invested millions over the past 10 years in an effort to close its race- and gender-related compensation gaps. Most of the company's employees enjoy a flexible work schedule that includes one to three days in the office each week.
- Hilton provides all team members who are new parents with four weeks of paid parental leave. This benefit jumps to 12 weeks for new mothers who have given birth. Hilton also provides employees with $10,000 in assistance each time they adopt a child.
- Capital One Financial offers a 7.5% 401k match (compared to the average 4.5%). The company also matches 15% of employees' contributions to the Associate Stock Purchase Plan (ASPP).

Clearly, companies listed among the best places to work focus on offering progressive and valued programs, policies, and procedures. Are you curious to see if a current or past employer is one of these progressive companies? You can find out by taking Self-Assessment 9.1.

SELF-ASSESSMENT 9.1

Assessing the Quality of HR Practices

This survey is designed to assess the quality of HR practices at your current place of employment. Please complete Self-Assessment 9.1 if your instructor has assigned it in Connect.

Effective HRM means putting employees first, but successfully implementing corporate strategy takes more. Figure 9.2 outlines the process by which HR practices drive strategic implementation. Let's consider how this works.

Internal and External HR Fit Promote Strategic HR Management

Strategic human resource management is the process of designing and implementing systems of policies and practices that align an organization's human capital with its strategic objectives.[14] While HRM is about managing people, strategic HRM is about generating competitive advantages *through* people.[15] In other words, strategic HRM views people as valuable strategic assets of any organization.

A firm's approach to its human resources becomes strategic when it is integrated into the organization in ways that drive overall performance.[16] Specifically, as seen in Figure 9.2, HR systems drive strategic implementation when they foster two important types of "fit":[17]

FIGURE 9.2
Strategic HRM: How HR practices support strategic implementation

Source: Figure based in part on: C. Ostroff, A.J. Kinicki, and R.S. Muhammad, "Organizational Culture and Climate," in Handbook of Psychology: Volume 12, Industrial and Organizational Psychology, 2nd ed. (Hoboken, NJ: John Wiley & Sons, 2013), Chapter 24, pp. 643–676.

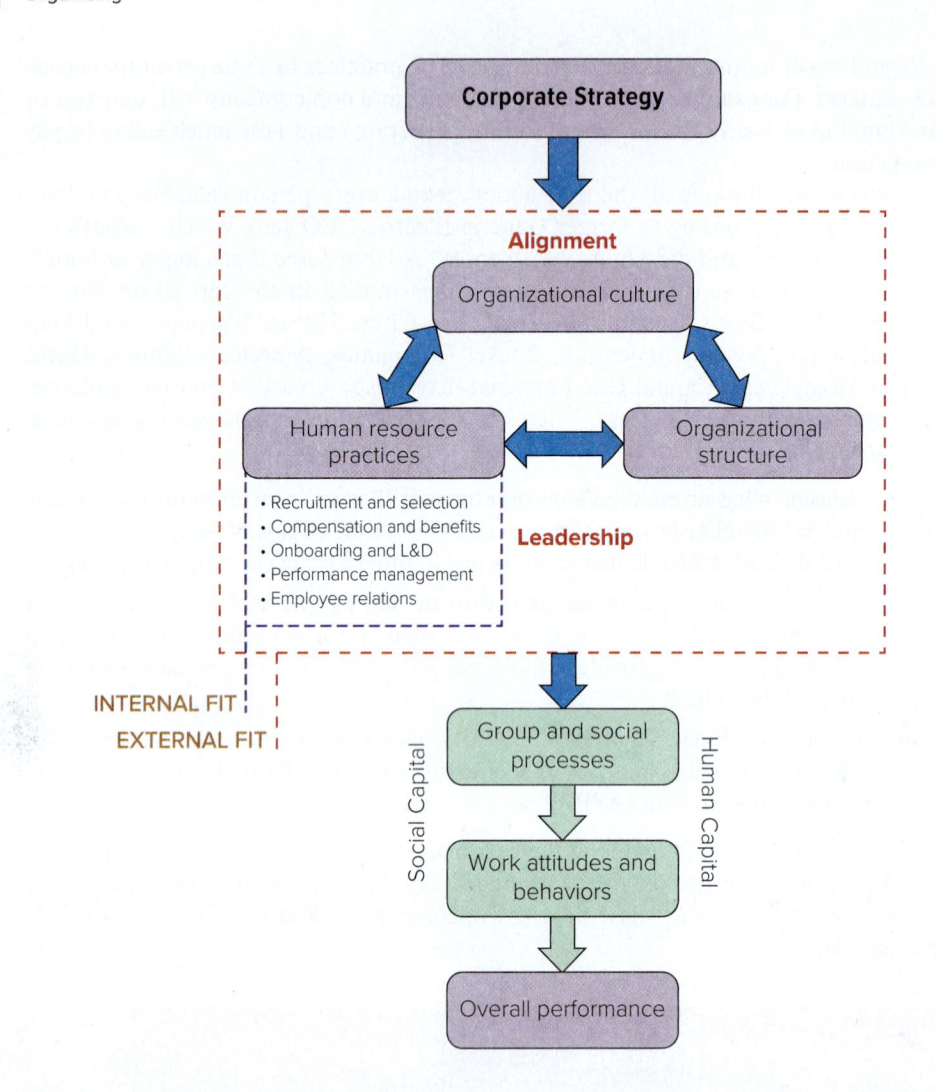

Corporate Strategy

Alignment
- Organizational culture
- Human resource practices
  - Recruitment and selection
  - Compensation and benefits
  - Onboarding and L&D
  - Performance management
  - Employee relations
- Organizational structure

Leadership

INTERNAL FIT
EXTERNAL FIT

Social Capital | Human Capital
- Group and social processes
- Work attitudes and behaviors
- Overall performance

1. *Internal fit* exists when all of the organization's HR policies and practices reinforce one another. In other words, internal fit happens when different HR practices work together as a unified system. For example, an organization that hires employees based on their performance potential rather than their previous experience needs to provide extensive opportunities for learning and development and should use a performance management system that rewards growth. As another example, an organization that relies heavily on teamwork and that rewards performance based on team accomplishments should use selection procedures that identify candidates who are good team players. Consider the internal fit at IBM as it led the way with skills-based hiring:

   Internal Fit Example—IBM: In the early 2010s, more than 90% of U.S.-based jobs at IBM required at least a bachelor's degree. At this same time, tech organizations all over the world, including IBM, were struggling to recruit and find qualified job applicants. Then-CEO Ginni Rometty realized that IBM needed to revamp its HR practices to better reflect the skills and potential available in the talent marketplace. Senior leaders of business units throughout the company studied the skills truly necessary for success in each role and re-worked job descriptions to emphasize possession of those skills rather than possession of a college degree. IBM also developed its Pathways in Technology Early College High School (P-TECH) program to encourage high school students to take STEM classes for college credit and skill-building purposes. The program now offers these courses through 300+ institutions in 27 countries around the world, and IBM continues to employ P-TECH graduates and students. Finally, the company worked with the U.S. Department of Labor to design a training program that would better enable its managers to provide apprenticeships to employees who exhibited strong performance and a strong learning orientation. According to a recent *Harvard Business Review* article co-authored by Rometty, this type of skills-first approach to HR "will yield the greatest benefit if organizations extend it beyond hiring and make it core to how they think about cultivating and retaining talent."[18]

2. *External fit* exists when the organization's HR system, as a whole, aligns with its culture and structure in a way that supports firm-level strategy. In other words, external fit happens when the firm uses a set of HR practices that work in concert with its culture and structure to drive the performance goals the firm wants to achieve. For example, a firm that competes based on low costs and efficiency should reward objective job performance, provide targeted skills training, and define job performance clearly. As another example, a firm that uses teams to accomplish its goals should structure job roles to best support high-functioning teamwork.

Research shows that organizations that achieve both internal and external HR fit have better outcomes, including employee satisfaction and firm performance.[19] One example is Airbnb.

Internal and External Fit Example—Airbnb: Airbnb wants employees to live their "best life" and to "be healthy, travel often, get time to give back, and have the financial resources and support they need."[20] The company's "employee experience" department—modeled after its "customer experience" department—oversees the alignment of mission and culture with HR practices. Employees receive $2,000 in travel credits each year, and most are able to live and work from any location of their choosing. Further, team members maintain their salaries even when they move to locations in their home countries with cheaper costs of living.[21]

Strategic HRM enables the effective implementation of corporate strategies because it helps firms to generate and leverage two important, intangible resources: *human capital* and *social capital*.[22]

The Role of Human and Social Capital

Figure 9.2 shows that a combination of internal and external HR fit triggers the group and individual processes, attitudes, and behaviors needed for achieving organizational performance goals. Simply put, strategic HRM mobilizes necessary human capital and social capital.[23]

- **Human capital** is the economic or productive potential of employee knowledge, experience, and actions. Human capital stems from all of the employee competencies that are or could be valuable to the organization.

- **Social capital** is the economic or productive potential of strong, trusting, and cooperative relationships. Social capital stems from the reciprocity, knowledge, and capabilities that are embedded in both informal connections and close personal relationships.[24]

Strategic HRM gets the right people, competencies, and connections into the right places at the right time.

What Is the Best Approach to Strategic Human Resource Management?

Figure 9.2 shows that when companies get strategic HRM "right" (i.e., when they achieve internal and external HR fit), they are more likely to generate the human and social capital necessary to successfully implement the firm's strategies. Recent research offers strong support for this idea, suggesting that the proper configurations of HR practices generate unique organizational capabilities that are difficult for competitors to understand and imitate.[25] In other words, HR practices can create competitive advantage. Rocket Companies is one example.

Generating Competitive Advantage through HR Practices Example—Rocket Companies: Rocket Companies provides organizations with simple digital solutions for complex business transactions such as real estate, auto, and personal loans. The organization was put to the test during the post-pandemic housing squeeze, when mortgage rates hit a 21-year high and real estate transactions saw sharp declines. In spite of the numerous challenges it faced at the time, Rocket was still voted one of the top 10 best places to work by *Fortune* magazine in 2022. The company's 20 ISMSs (pronounced iz-emz), or guiding philosophies, indicate its strategy is clearly focused on efficiency and performance. For example, Rocket is "obsessed with finding a better way" for every single process and practice. Further, it is focused on wowing "every client. every time. no exceptions. no excuses." Finally, Rocket expects employees to behave with a sense of urgency and to "return all phone calls and emails the same day." Current and former employees depict long hours, many opportunities for advancement, an achievement bar that is always moving, and a "fast" culture.[26]

But what does the right HR system look like? The answer is there is no "best" approach to strategic HRM. Rather, different firms will benefit from different approaches. As indicated by Figure 9.2, leadership plays a central role in this process.[27] Leaders must have a nuanced understanding of firm-level strategies, future performance goals and anticipated challenges, and how HR practices, structure, and culture fit together. They use this knowledge to answer three important questions:

1. What human and social capital does the firm have and how do we best leverage it?
2. What human and social capital does the firm need in order to get where it wants to go?
3. How does the firm acquire the human and social capital it lacks?

Every firm's configuration will look different, but at a broad level we can categorize strategic HRM approaches into one of two buckets: talent management and high-performance work systems. Let's discuss each of these in turn.

Talent Management Talent management is an approach to strategic HRM that matches high-potential employees with an organization's most strategically valuable positions.[28] You can think of leaders who use talent management as Hollywood agents. Their job is to identify the people with the most potential to be stars—"the talent"— to polish and refine their skills, and to land them the roles where they will be most likely generate huge box office returns along with an Oscar nomination.[29] In addition to generating financial returns and competitive viability, the disproportionate investments leaders make in this elite group of employees are expected to impact them in three ways:[30]

- **Attitudes**—workers singled out as "stars" experience increased job satisfaction, engagement, and commitment to the organization.
- **Behaviors**—employees identified as high-potential respond with greater effort, better job performance, and lower turnover.
- **Cognitions**—workers respond to their organizations' elevated perceptions with higher self-efficacy and increased feelings of fulfillment.

Talent management is less about meeting short-term staffing needs and more about cultivating multiple, diverse talent pipelines that enable firms to plan for how they will continue to generate value and respond to changing markets over the long term.[31] Consider the U.S. Marine Corps.

Talent Management Example—Marine Corps: The U.S. Marine Corps recently devised a new strategic plan with the goal of "modernizing Marine Corps talent management." The plan—known as TM2030—aims to "create a more lethal and capable force for the future fight and for our nation." TM2030 encompasses multiple initiatives, including the Commandant's Retention Program (CRP) and the Career Intermission Program (CIP). Under the CRP, top-performing Marines receive, among other things, priority access to their preferred assignments and duty stations when they re-enlist. The CRP initiative has increased reenlistment applications made by top performers by over 72%. The CIP provides Marines with the opportunity to take a temporary time-out from active duty without penalty. This initiative aims to increase retention of the most talented and experienced Marines.[32]

High-Performance Work Systems The **high-performance work system (HPWS)** approach to strategic HRM deploys bundles of internally consistent HR practices in order to improve employee ability, motivation, and opportunities across the entire organization.[33] HPWSs impact overall organizational performance by systematically enhancing the individual performance of all of the organization's employees.[34] Research on this approach suggests that bundles of HR practices have stronger impacts on firm-level outcomes than individual HR practices.[35]

While talent management approaches are geared toward enhancing and leveraging the human and social capital of specific individuals, HPWSs focus on increasing organizations' collective levels of human and social capital. Let's consider how P&G uses a HPWS approach.

HPWS Example—P&G: P&G is one of the largest consumer products companies in the world. The Fortune 100 company's brands include Pampers, Dawn, Tide, Bounty, Gillette, Crest, Tampax, and Olay. P&G's website states that the company hires based on potential and then provides "world-class training" for employees. P&G's values include "innovation," "mastery," and "being the best." Current and former employees describe a culture of continuous learning, job rotation, skill-building, and teamwork, and the company offers myriad programs for leadership development and skill development. At P&G, employees at all levels and in all roles are encouraged to grow and learn.[36]

Whether a company uses talent management, a HPWS, or some combination of the two, the ultimate goal is to maximize organizational performance. In the remainder of the chapter, we discuss each of these HR practices and how firms approach them to enable strategic implementation. •

9.2 Recruitment and Selection: Putting the Right People into the Right Jobs

THE BIG PICTURE

Qualified applicants for jobs may be recruited from inside or outside the organization. The task of choosing the best person is enhanced by such tools as reviewing candidates' background information, conducting interviews, and screening with employment tests.

The recruitment and selection process for a single open position takes 43 days and costs $4,700 for the average organization, according to recent data.[37] Does this sound like a big expense to you? The strategic use of these HR practices may be costly, but research suggests it is well worth the investment.[38]

Successfully recruiting and selecting qualified candidates has become increasingly difficult even for organizations willing to invest the time and money. For example,

LO 9-2

Discuss ways to recruit and hire the right people.

nearly 70% of the 600 HR professionals surveyed recently by Wiley said their organizations struggle to find workers with the necessary skills for open positions.[39] Further, a survey of more than 200 technology companies across the globe found that only 13% of the organizations surveyed felt that they had a handle on hiring and retaining their most important talent.[40]

Companies that want to find workers with the necessary skills need to do everything they can to get recruiting and selection right. Let's consider in more detail these important HR practices.

Recruitment: How to Attract Qualified Applicants

Recruiting is the process of locating and attracting qualified applicants for job openings. The word *qualified* is important: You want to find people whose skills, abilities, and characteristics are best suited to your organization's needs. In today's labor market, where the number of qualified job seekers is far lower than the number of available skilled jobs, firms need to be strategic in their approaches to generating applicants' interest.

We discuss three recruiting approaches: *internal, external,* and *hybrid.* Remember as you explore these approaches that there is no one best way to recruit potential applicants. The right recruiting practices are those that are aligned with an organization's culture and structure and designed to support firm strategy, as you learned from Figure 9.2 (and Chapter 8).

1. Internal Recruiting: Hiring from the Inside   **Internal recruiting** means making people already employed by the organization aware of job openings. Companies use several techniques to identify potential applicants within their existing talent pools, including:

- **Internal job postings**—formal announcements about open positions circulated within the organization.
- **Informal nominations**—recommendations by managers who have direct experience observing and working with specific employees.
- **Employee profiles**—databases that house information on individual employee competencies and qualifications.

Internal recruiting may be a wise choice for companies that wish to boost retention by increasing employee commitment and engagement.[41] It is also used by companies looking to close skills gaps. One increasingly popular approach to internal recruiting is

Searching for a job online is no longer just for those looking to break into a new organization. Companies are increasingly using internal online talent marketplaces to encourage current employees to search for new roles within the company. Rawpixel.com/Shutterstock

the use of **talent marketplaces,** which are digital platforms that use AI to match existing employees with job openings, training opportunities, and mentoring relationships.[42] Consider the example of Schneider Electric.

Talent Marketplace Example—Schneider Electric: Multinational energy company Schneider Electric began using a talent marketplace after learning that nearly half of employees who quit did so due to a lack of opportunities for internal promotion and growth. According to the company's VP of digital talent transformation, "Now every employee can have visibility into how their capabilities relate to what the enterprise needs, what they want for their careers, and what kinds of opportunities are available to them."[43] Schneider estimates the system has resulted in $15 million in savings so far as a result of higher productivity and lower recruiting costs.[44]

2. External Recruiting: Hiring from the Outside

External recruiting means attracting job applicants from outside the organization. In years past, notices of job vacancies were placed through newspapers, employment agencies, executive recruiting firms, union hiring halls, college job-placement offices, and word of mouth. Today more than 90% of U.S. organizations have taken at least some portion of their recruitment activities online.[45] Popular external recruitment sources include:

- **Social media**–nearly 95% of recruiters today use social media to locate potential talent.[46]
- **Online job postings**–companies advertise open positions on their own websites, on job search websites such as Indeed, CareerBuilder, and Glassdoor, and on university and union websites.
- **School partnerships**–recruiters identify talent through relationships with educational institutions, including universities, trade schools, and high schools.

Increased competition for qualified workers has caused companies to implement new external recruiting activities. Consider this example.

External Recruiting Example—Air Force: The Air Force has updated the way it attracts new recruits since the advent of the pandemic. Said Major General Ed Thomas, head of recruiting for the U.S. Air and Space Forces, "Crisis is a powerful influence in sharpening the mind and sharpening how you do things and how you think about things."[47] Thomas added "As we've gone through one of the most difficult recruiting years we've had since, at least 1999 ... we've got to be out there with the American people, we've got to be inspiring people for military service and that challenge has gotten increasingly difficult over the past few years." In 2022 the Air Force increased funding for enlistment bonuses, added back more in-person recruiting events, and used YouTube to generate interest in careers among potential recruits. The military branch successfully met its recruiting goal for 2022.

3. Hybrid Approaches: Referrals and Boomerangs

You probably know people who have scored great jobs because they knew someone inside the organization. **Employee referrals** tap into existing employees' social networks to fill open positions with outside applicants. Referrals are popular among recruiters because referred employees are faster and less expensive to hire, tend to stay with the organization longer, and are more likely to possess necessary skills than non-referral hires.[48] According to experts, employee referrals work well because:[49]

- **Current employees are good judges of potential fit.** Referrers know what it takes to fit in with the organization's culture and to perform well in specific positions. This helps them determine which members of their social networks would be a good fit for various jobs.
- **Referrers care about their reputations.** Current employees are careful about whom they recommend because their reputations in the organization may be enhanced or damaged by referred workers' job performance.

Another way that companies find qualified talent is from **boomerangs**—former employees who return to the organization. Boomerangs often are pulled away from their initial jobs by difficult life events or attractive opportunities to advance their skills and careers.[50] Boomerangs already understand the organization's culture and require little to no onboarding. Hiring them is cheaper and less time consuming. Modern organizations are increasingly open to the idea of "taking back" former employees.[51] Take the example of UKG.

Boomerangs Example—UKG: UKG (formerly Kronos) is a workforce management software firm that has made *Fortune's* list of 100 Best Companies to work for multiple times. The company delivers cloud-based human capital management (HCM) applications to over 75,000 organizations across the globe.[52] When UKG was having trouble attracting top talent, former CEO Aron Ain saw the need for a new approach to engaging the company's own workforce. One way that Kronos did this was by championing employees' careers, whether those happened inside or outside of the company. Said Ain, "We don't own our employees' careers. If they have a great offer, we support their decision to take it. Sure, we'd love to retain them and do everything in our power to do so, but if they choose to leave and they were a high-performer, we let them know that the door is open if they want to come back home."[53] One UKG boomerang employee named Deepak J. recalls receiving a letter from Ain just weeks after he initially left his job with the company. In the letter, Ain expressed appreciation and thanked him for his work at UKG. Deepak returned to UKG less than two years later as India's head of marketing.[54]

How Fit Figures into Recruitment Recruiting is a lot like dating—both recruiters and job seekers want to know that the other party will be a good match before jumping into a serious commitment. In our discussion of organizational culture in Chapter 8 we described person–organization (P–O) fit as the extent to which a worker's personality and values match the organization's climate and culture. Here we look at another type of fit—**person–job (P–J) fit**—the extent to which a worker's competencies and needs match with a specific job. Research suggests that higher levels of P-J fit are associated with better job performance and increased job satisfaction, organizational commitment, and retention.[55] When there is poor P-J fit, both organizations and employees suffer.

Fit is important to our discussion because recruiters base their hiring recommendations in part on their assessments of job applicants' levels of P-O and P-J fit—with particular emphasis on the latter.[56]

How do you feel about the job you are in now, if you have one, or the last job you had? Do you feel like you are a "good fit" for the job? That is, do you like the work and does the work match your skills? Research shows that we are happier and more productive when our needs and skills fit the job requirements. If you would like to see whether or not you fit with your current (or last) job, complete Self-Assessment 9.2 in Connect if your instructor has assigned it. You may find the results very interesting.

SELF-ASSESSMENT 9.2

Assessing Your Person–Job Fit

This survey is designed to assess your job fit. Please complete Self-Assessment 9.2 if your instructor has assigned it in Connect.

Selection: How to Choose the Best Person for the Job

Whether recruitment for a position results in a handful of applicants or a thousand, the hiring manager should use a systematic process to decide which applicant will receive a job offer. **Selection** is the process of screening job applicants and choosing the best candidate for a position. Essentially, selection is an exercise in *prediction:* How well will each candidate perform, to what degree will they fit, and for how long will they stay?

It has been said that selection decisions represent million-dollar decisions. Why? Because it is hard to fire someone once they are employed, and people with poor P–O or P–J fit can be costly in terms of lost productivity, poor employee attitudes, and turnover. This underscores the importance of selecting people who fit by using techniques that are reliable, valid, and legally defensible. Let's discuss these criteria in more detail.

What Are Legally Defensible Selection Tools? **Legal defensibility** is the extent to which the selection device measures job-related criteria in a way that is free from bias. This means selection devices should only be used to measure factors that are directly related to job performance, and these devices should not discriminate based on non-job-relevant factors. (We discuss equal employment legislation in more detail in Section 9.7.) Establishing the reliability and validity of a selection technique is fundamental to legal defensibility.

- **Reliability** represents the degree to which a test produces consistent scores. When a test is reliable, an individual's score will remain about the same over time, assuming the characteristic being measured also remains the same. It would be similar to taking a midterm twice, two days apart. A reliable midterm would result in your scoring very similarly on both occasions.

- **Validity** reflects the degree to which a test measures what it purports to measure—nothing more and nothing less. If a test is supposed to predict performance, then candidates' actual performance should reflect their scores on the test. Using an invalid selection test can lead to poor selection decisions. It can also create legal problems if the test is ever challenged in a court of law. A valid midterm should measure content covered in the textbook and during lectures, and nothing else.

Three types of selection tools are *background information, interviews,* and *employment tests.*

Background Information: Application Forms, Resumes, and Background Checks Application forms and resumes provide organizations with basic background information about job applicants, such as education, work history, certifications, and citizenship. Unfortunately, a lot of background information consists of puffery and lies. Let's discuss three problems associated with background information in the selection process:

1. **Application forms and resumes are susceptible to dishonesty.** Recent data suggests over 70% of job applicants lie on application forms and resumes.[57] One likely reason is that job seekers are trying to outsmart applicant tracking systems by doing whatever it takes to make sure key words in their resumes match the stated job requirements, whether they match the truth or not. Other reasons include attempts to hide perceived deficiencies in technical or language skills, education, job history, or achievements.[58]

   Dishonesty on Resumes Example—George Santos: Congressional representative George Santos admitted to being dishonest about large portions of his resume and personal history while campaigning for his New York congressional seat.[59] Santos was accused of multiple lies, including claims that he graduated from Baruch College and studied at New York University, worked on Wall Street for Goldman Sachs and Citigroup, produced a Broadway show, and founded an animal rescue, among others. Further investigation led the House Ethics Committee to initiate an investigation into Santos related to allegations of both campaign finance violations and sexual misconduct.[60] Santos was expelled from Congress in December 2023.

Regardless of the reason for misstating or lying, be aware that you can be fired for lying on a job application or resume. We recommend honesty as the best policy.

2. **Application forms and resumes don't always provide useful information.** The types of education and experience that make an applicant qualified for a job today may be of little use in a few years due to rapid technological shifts, making information such as previous work history less relevant for hiring organizations. For this reason, some experts are encouraging organizations to rely more on basic skills tests to assess candidates' competencies in the initial stages of the selection process.[61] Consider the following example of how companies are eliminating resumes in favor of a skills-based approach.

> **Skills-Based Hiring Example—Accenture:** Accenture CEO Julie Sweet believes that the "ability to learn" is the most important skill an applicant can have.[62] Reflecting this mindset, the global consulting firm has shifted its HR practices in favor of skills-based hiring in recent years. As evidence, fewer than 45% of Accenture's IT job postings now include a college degree requirement.[63] The company uses what it calls a "learn-and-earn" apprenticeship program to increase access to jobs in the digital economy, particularly for individuals in the workforce who may not have four-year college degrees. The program provides year-long paid skills training in areas including data engineering, cybersecurity, and software application development, and many of the individuals who complete the program go on to become full-time Accenture employees.[64]

3. **Background checks can lead to discrimination.** Employers reach out to candidates' previous employers and references during the selection process to verify work history and get a better sense of whether applicants are likely to perform well. Issues can arise, however, when conversations conducted during background checks inadvertently reveal applicants' personal information. Although hiring companies are legally barred from basing hiring decisions on criteria such as age, disabilities, and marital status, knowledge of these and other related factors can lead to hiring discrimination. Some employers have enacted policies to limit what their managers can say about former employees; for instance, some allow the person serving as a reference only to confirm the former employee's job title and dates of employment.[65] Others allow references to state the reason for departure and whether the employee would be rehired.

Interviews: Unstructured, Situational, and Behavioral-Description The interview is the most commonly used employee-selection technique in organizations.[66] Interviews may take place face to face or virtually via phone or videoconference.

Interviewing takes three forms: *unstructured interviews* and the *two types of structured interviews—situational* and *behavioral-description.*[67]

- **Unstructured interviews** gather information about job candidates without the use of a fixed set of questions or a systematic scoring procedure. Unstructured interviews unfold like ordinary conversations, and proponents suggest that advantages include a more relaxed atmosphere and the freedom to explore certain topics in more depth.[68] However, decades of research have shown consistently that unstructured interviews have serious drawbacks, including low reliability, low validity, and high susceptibility to legal challenges.[69]

- The **structured interview** involves asking each applicant the same questions and comparing their responses to a standardized set of answers. Across multiple reviews of employment interview research spanning more than 60 years, one of the most consistent findings has been that structured interviews are far superior to unstructured interviews in their ability to predict applicants' future job performance.[70]

There are two types of structured interviews: situational interviews and behavioral-description interviews. Let's consider each one.

1. **Situational interviews** are structured interviews during which raters ask applicants how they would behave in hypothetical job situations. Example questions are: "What would you do if you saw two of your people arguing loudly in the work area?" and "How would you respond if your boss asked you to keep a secret from upper management?" The goal of situational interviews is to find out if the applicant can effectively handle various situations that may arise on the job.

2. **Behavioral-description interviews** are structured interviews during which raters explore applicants' job-related past behaviors. Example questions include: "Give me an example of a time when you needed to learn more about competitor organizations. What was the situation and what actions did you take?" and "Tell me about a time when you had to apply your understanding of cultural differences at work. What actions did you take as a result of your understanding?"[71]

Employment Tests: Ability, Performance, Personality, Integrity, and Others

The EEOC considers any employer-imposed employment requirement to be a test, including application forms, reference checks, and job interviews. Here we refer to a smaller subset of activities and define **employment tests** as the standardized devices organizations use to measure specific skills, abilities, traits, and other tendencies. Let's take a look at six employment tests in detail.

1. **Ability tests.** *Ability tests* measure job candidates' physical abilities, strength and stamina, mechanical ability, mental abilities, and clerical abilities.[72] Not all jobs require all of these abilities, and organizations should only test for the abilities that are directly related to job performance. For example, intelligence or cognitive ability tests are popular for predicting future executive performance. Law enforcement agencies test for physical as well as reading and report-writing abilities.[73] Southern California Gas Company (SoCalGas) is an example of a company that uses an ability test.

    Ability Tests Example—SoCalGas: This utility company uses physical abilities testing and provides a test preparation booklet for potential applicants. The document clearly lists the components of the test (and how they are measured)—(1) upper arm strength (arm lift); (2) abdominal strength and endurance (sit-ups test); and (3) trunk strength (trunk pull test)—and explains why each is relevant to job performance. It also suggests that applicants build their strength over time as they prepare for the test, and it provides diagrams of each required exercise.[74]

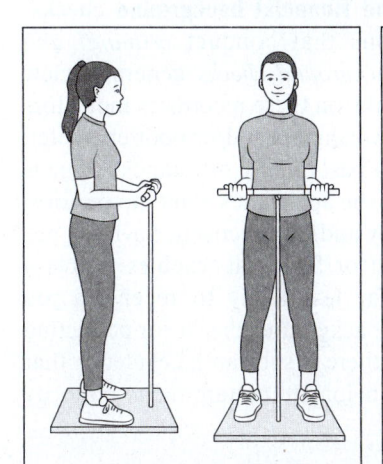

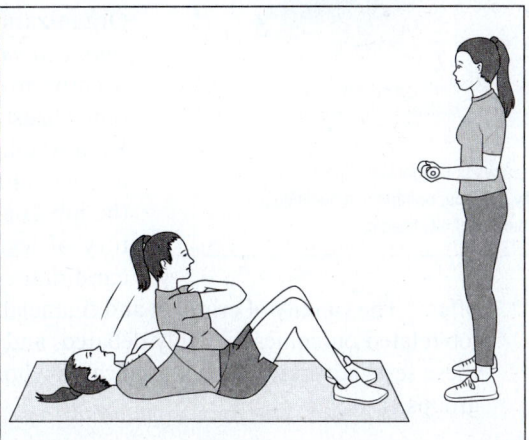

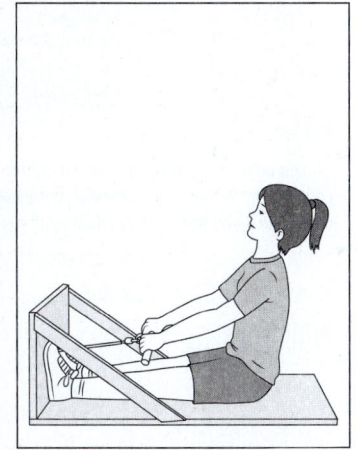

Source: "A Guide to Taking the Physical Abilities Test." SoCalGas. Last accessed March 16, 2023. https://www.socalgas.com/1443740394085/PhysicalTestBattery.pdf.

2. **Performance tests.** *Performance tests,* or *skills tests,* measure performance on actual job tasks—so-called job tryouts—for example, when computer programmers take a test on a particular programming language or middle managers work on a small sample project.[75] Some companies use **assessment centers—selection devices in which management candidates participate in a series of interactive exercises over several days while being assessed by multiple evaluators.** Common assessment center activities include role plays, oral presentations, and in-basket exercises.[76] A team of researchers examined the relative accuracy by which ability tests and assessment center results predicted who would be successful on the job. Although both tests were effective, assessment center tests were more effective than ability tests.[77]

3. **Personality tests.** *Personality tests* measure stable traits such as self-efficacy, self-esteem, locus of control, emotional stability, extroversion, agreeableness, conscientiousness, and openness to experience.[78] (We discuss these traits in detail in Chapter 11.) You'll notice that many of these traits represent competencies associated with career readiness, a topic of central importance for today's organizations. Data suggests that more than half of large organizations incorporate personality testing into their hiring activities.[79] Check out the Example box for more on the pros and cons of personality testing in the selection process.

4. **Integrity tests.** *Integrity tests* "assess attitudes and experiences related to a person's honesty, dependability, trustworthiness, reliability, and pro-social behavior."[80] The rationale for these tests is that people who do poorly on them may have lower job performance and an increased tendency to engage in counterproductive work behaviors like theft, rule-breaking, and sabotage.[81] Overt integrity tests often ask specifically whether the applicant has ever engaged in illegal behavior. While integrity tests in general are easy to administer, it is also relatively easy for test takers to submit false responses.[82]

5. **Drug and alcohol tests.** Employers have a right to maintain drug-free and alcohol-free work environments, and we can say broadly that companies are permitted to test job applicants for drug and alcohol use. Some employers are covered by federal drug and alcohol testing laws, but many fall under state jurisdictions.[83] Organizations need to research the specific laws that apply to them before creating and implementing drug and alcohol testing policies.

6. **Criminal and financial background checks.** Organizations that conduct *criminal and financial background checks* generally view negative marks on these records as indicators of low trustworthiness and/or poor character. Even when a past offense or financial issue is unrelated to the applicant's ability to perform the job safely and/or effectively, having a history of legal or financial troubles makes a candidate far less likely to receive a job offer.[84] The validity of criminal and financial background checks for predicting job-related outcomes is highly debated, and there is substantial evidence that these tests adversely impact applicants who belong to certain racial minority groups.[85]

Do you believe organizations have a right to know about applicants' past criminal convictions? Would this information potentially bias your opinion of a qualified job candidate if you were a hiring manager? alexandre17/Getty Images

EXAMPLE: Personality Tests: Pros and Cons

Research tells us that skillfully administered personality tests can help organizations make better hiring decisions. This is especially true when the tests are combined with other selection measures. For example, recent studies suggest that a combination of (1) the Big Five personality dimensions, (2) a general ability test, and (3) an integrity test is a good predictor of future job performance.[86]

Despite the evidence supporting their validity, personality tests are still rife with potential for misinterpretation, misapplication, and employment discrimination. Organizations that are considering adopting personality testing should carefully weigh the following pros and cons:

Pros
Proponents of personality tests in hiring say that these devices:[87]

- Help to identify candidates who will fit well, be less likely to leave the organization, and exhibit superior performance.
- Limit the influence of interviewers' unconscious biases on hiring decisions.
- Weed out those who may be prone to undesirable behaviors like dishonesty and deviance.

The California Commission on Peace Officer Standards and Training (POST) uses the Five Factor Model (FFM) personality test also known as the Big Five personality model (discussed in detail in Chapter 11) in selecting new hires. To develop this aspect of its selection process, POST first surveyed subject matter experts from across the state to create an accurate list of personality-based job competencies. Those identified as being most important for performance included (1) integrity/ethics, (2) conscientiousness/dependability, (3) assertiveness/persuasiveness, (4) teamwork, (5) decision making and judgment, (6) adaptability/flexibility, (7) impulse control/attention to safety, (8) social competence, (9) emotional regulation and stress, (10) service orientation, and (11) tolerance. The commission defines each of these in detail and explains how each relates to both successful job performance, and dimensions of the FFM.[88]

Cons
Those who disagree with personality tests in hiring say that these devices are:[89]

- Subjective and open to interpretation by people who are not trained to evaluate results.
- Vulnerable to misuse by applicants who try to game the test.
- Potentially discriminatory because they raise the possibility of privacy violations when they inadvertently reveal information about personal characteristics such as mental health.

YOUR CALL
Would you be comfortable taking a personality test? Do you think it's better to answer the questions honestly or to choose responses that might make you appear better suited for the job? Explain.

9.3 Managing an Effective Workforce: Compensation and Benefits

THE BIG PICTURE
Managers must manage for compensation—which includes wages or salaries, incentives, and benefits.

Do we work only for a paycheck? Many people do, of course. But money is only one form of compensation. **Compensation** has three components: (1) wages or salaries, (2) incentives, and (3) benefits.

Companies often view the compensation mix differently. For instance, in some nonprofit organizations (e.g., education, government), salaries may not be large, but health and retirement benefits may outweigh that fact. In high-tech start-ups, salaries and benefits may be somewhat humble, but the promise of a large payoff in incentives, such as stock options or bonuses, may be quite attractive. Organizations also vary their compensation mixes over time in response to factors like employee preferences and

LO 9-3
Outline common forms of compensation.

important economic events. Consider the great resignation of the early 2020s, which saw workers quitting their jobs at record rates while citing dissatisfaction with their opportunities for advancement, the amount of flexibility in their work schedules, and overall workplace benefits.[90] Many employers responded with notable changes to their compensation packages. Goldman Sachs is a good illustration.

Compensation Package Example—Goldman Sachs: Goldman Sachs shook up its compensation offerings in order to retain talent during the great resignation. The company expanded its paid bereavement leave program and began offering 20 days of paid pregnancy loss leave for workers and spouses. In addition, Goldman Sachs introduced the option for long-time employees to take a six-week unpaid sabbatical. Finally, the company increased its retirement contribution match and removed the existing one-year waiting period for receiving matching contributions. The firm's head of HR said at the time, "We wanted to offer a compelling value proposition to current and prospective employees, and wanted to make sure we're leading, not just competing."[91]

This example illustrates what you learned in Figure 9.2—namely, that compensation and benefits are one part of the strategic HRM process, and each firm should design their pay practices in the way that will attract, motivate, reward, and retain the specific kinds of employees and competencies needed to execute strategy. Compensation and benefits practices should have good internal fit such that they work in harmony with other HR practices such as recruiting, selection, and training. Compensation and benefits practices also need to have external fit such that they align with organizational culture and structure to jointly support broad strategic goals.[92]

Let's consider the three parts of compensation briefly. (We'll expand on them in Chapter 12 when we discuss ways to motivate employees.)

Which forms of compensation and benefits are most important to you in a job? Which benefits or incentives would you give up for a higher salary? Which benefits or incentives would make up for a lower salary? garagestock/Shutterstock

Wages or Salaries

Base pay consists of the basic wage or salary paid to employees in exchange for doing their jobs. The basic compensation levels for particular jobs are determined by all kinds of economic factors: the prevailing pay levels in a particular industry and location, what competitors are paying, whether jobs are unionized, potential job hazards, and individual workers' experience and levels in the organization.

TABLE 9.1 Pros and Cons of Hybrid Work Arrangements

• **Pros:** Better work–life balance; Higher perceptions of autonomy; Increased efficiency; Higher job satisfaction and well-being; Lower levels of burnout; DE&I benefits including increased flexibility and accessibility	• **Cons:** Decreased team and cross-functional collaboration; Increased work–family conflict; DE&I challenges including magnified in-group/out-group dynamics; Lowered connection to organizational culture; Legal, compliance, and tax-related challenges; Potential deficits in innovation and creativity

Sources: Haas, M. "5 Challenges of Hybrid Work—and How to Overcome Them." *Harvard Business Review Digital Articles.* 2022. 18; Dowling, B., D. Goldstein, M. Park, and H. Price. "Hybrid Work: Making it Fit with Your Diversity, Equity, and Inclusion Strategy." 2022.

Incentives

Many organizations offer incentives such as commissions, bonuses, profit-sharing plans, and stock options to attract high-performing employees and motivate those already employed to be more productive. Organizations can use incentives to help to align workers with firm-level strategic objectives.

Hybrid work has become a popular incentive in recent years. With hybrid working arrangements, employees' schedules contain a blend of remote and in-office work, and recent data suggest that more than 80% of workers prefer hybrid schedules to either full-time remote or full-time in-office jobs.[93] Hybrid work has gained tremendous popularity since the pandemic, with one HR expert calling hybrid schedules a "critical retention tool" for modern organizations.[94] Despite their popularity, hybrid work schedules present a challenge for companies hoping to strike a balance between maintaining productivity levels and corporate culture while also attracting top candidates and keeping current employees engaged and satisfied with their jobs. Hybrid scheduling is likely to be one of the challenges on your plate as a manager. Consider the following list of pros and cons of hybrid work from a managerial perspective.

We discuss incentives in detail in Chapter 12.

Benefits

Benefits, or **fringe benefits**, are additional nonmonetary forms of compensation designed to enrich the lives of all employees in the organization, which are paid all or in part by the organization. Examples include health insurance, dental insurance, life insurance, disability protection, retirement plans, holidays off, accumulated sick days and vacation days, recreation options, country club or health club memberships, family leave, discounts on company merchandise, counseling, credit unions, legal advice, and education reimbursement. For top executives, there may be "golden parachutes," generous severance pay for those who might be let go in the event the company is taken over by another company.

Benefits are no small part of an organization's costs. In September 2022, private industry spent an average of $39.61 per hour worked in employment compensation, of which wages and salaries accounted for 70.5% and benefits the remaining 29.5%.[95]

Managers should be aware that younger generations of workers regard workplace benefits differently than older generations.[96] In particular, data suggest that Gen Z workers place high value on benefits that increase their sense of security, including above-average pay, health insurance, and a good retirement program.[97] Younger workers also are strongly in favor of finding work–life balance and protecting both their mental and physical health, which means organizations should consider offering flexible work schedules and remote work options when possible.[98]

We discuss benefits—including their motivating potential across different generations of workers—in more detail in Chapter 12.

9.4 Onboarding and Learning and Development

THE BIG PICTURE
Two ways organizations help newcomers to perform their jobs are through *onboarding* to fit them into the job and organization and through *learning and development* to upgrade their current skills and develop them for future opportunities.

LO 9-4

Describe the processes used for onboarding and learning and development.

We now turn our attention to the HR practices of onboarding and learning and development (L&D).

From a strategic HRM perspective, onboarding and L&D are HR practices that help an organization build the social and human capital necessary to accomplish its strategic objectives.[99]

Managers need to know that their approach to onboarding and L&D can make or break the organization's ability to retain top talent.[100] New employees who fail to establish relationships or who are unable to adapt to the organization's culture are likely to quit almost immediately.[101] Further, within six months, nearly 90% of employees will decide whether to stay with the organization or seek opportunities elsewhere, and their experiences with onboarding and L&D play a big part in that decision.[102] Let's take a look at each of these important HR practices.

Onboarding: Helping Newcomers Learn the Ropes

Onboarding consists of the programs designed to integrate and transition employees into new jobs and organizations through familiarization with corporate policies, procedures, cultures, and politics, and clarification of work-role expectations and responsibilities. This process also is referred to as *employee socialization*.[103]

The Outcomes of Onboarding (and of Not Onboarding)
Effective onboarding programs generate a host of benefits for both employees and organizations. Research links onboarding with important work outcomes such as job satisfaction, employee engagement, organizational commitment, turnover intentions, role clarity, and various aspects of individual and firm performance.[104]

Unfortunately, as valuable as we believe onboarding to be, only about 12% of workers surveyed in a recent study strongly agreed that their organizations were doing a great job onboarding new employees.[105] According to talent management expert Amber Hyatt, organizations place themselves at a "significant disadvantage" when they neglect the onboarding process. Hyatt adds that, "Employees who know what to expect from their company's culture and work environment make better decisions that are more aligned with the accepted practices of the company."[106]

Onboarding Best Practices
Organizations take varied approaches to onboarding new employees. In a large organization, onboarding may be a formal, established process. In a small organization, it may be so informal that employees find themselves having to make most of the effort themselves. At a minimum, research supports the following best practices for successful onboarding:

- **Involve a team.** Onboarding should help new employees build relationships with all the stakeholders who will be a part of their organizational life.[107] This means the process should facilitate conversations not only with the HR department and the new employee's immediate team, but also with others in the organization who are important for new employees to know. At the nonprofit mental health services provider Cohen Veterans Network, new hires attend a short introductory meeting with each department, and they also get a call from both the CEO and COO.[108]

- **Clarify expectations.** Effective onboarding identifies reporting relationships and clearly communicates role expectations. The process should show new employees what "good" performance looks like as well as how their performance will be evaluated.[109] Onboarding also should clarify the organization's culture and values along with important policies and procedures.[110] Zapier, a fully remote software company with team members in more than 20 countries, uses a stair-stepped approach in new employees' initial few weeks of work. The process begins with a week of learning about the organization, the new role, and performance expectations, and by week, 3 new employees are working on cross-functional team projects.[111]

- **Put the pieces together.** Onboarding is a great time to have conversations with a new employee about how their role relates to the organization's larger purpose. Figure 9.2 is a helpful guide for these conversations because onboarding naturally includes discussions of many of the elements (culture, structure, strategy) that are presented as reinforcing one another in that figure. The Predictive Index software company uses onboarding to help new hires understand how their everyday jobs connect to the firm's strategy. The company focuses its onboarding process on familiarizing new hires with the firm's structure, strategy, and approaches to talent management.[112]

- **Give it time.** Onboarding is sometimes confused with orientation (a one-time activity designed to "check all the boxes" for new employees—including completing paperwork, getting office keys, etc.). But studies suggest the integration that happens through onboarding can take up to a year or more. Remember that the goal should be to support the new employee throughout their journey to becoming a part of the organization.[113] Google has formal onboarding activities built into new employees' jobs for at least six months. During that time period, managers are responsible for helping new employees to build social networks, teaching them about their job roles and expectations, and scheduling monthly "check-in" meetings to support the onboarding process.[114]

Learning and Development: Helping People Perform Better

Employers try to recruit and select people whose qualifications match the requirements of the job when using traditional approaches to hiring. But based on what you've learned thus far in the chapter, you know that hiring is no longer such a simple process. In today's workplace, what matters most is not so much what you know, but whether you are willing and able to learn. Said famous business theorist and Dutch executive Arie de Geus, "The ability to learn faster than your competitors may be the only sustainable competitive advantage."[115]

The goal of the learning and development (L&D) process is to fill the gaps that exist between what employees currently know and what they need to know. Managers must determine the areas where L&D can make the biggest impact on successful implementation of the firm's strategy. The five-step process show is a simple tool for managers to use when making these decisions (see Figure 9.3). Keep in mind that L&D is an ongoing effort in organizations rather than a one-time event. Let's briefly discuss what managers do at each step.

- **Step 1: Assessment.** The first step in L&D is to figure out the organization's most pressing L&D needs. In organizations with a strategic HRM focus, this process is all about strategy—namely, managers need to ask, "What's holding us back from implementing strategy, and what can L&D help us to do better?"

- **Step 2: Objectives.** The second step in L&D is to set performance objectives. Here managers must determine what employees should be able to *do* after L&D that they could not do before, what skills should they have that they

FIGURE 9.3

Five steps in the learning and development process

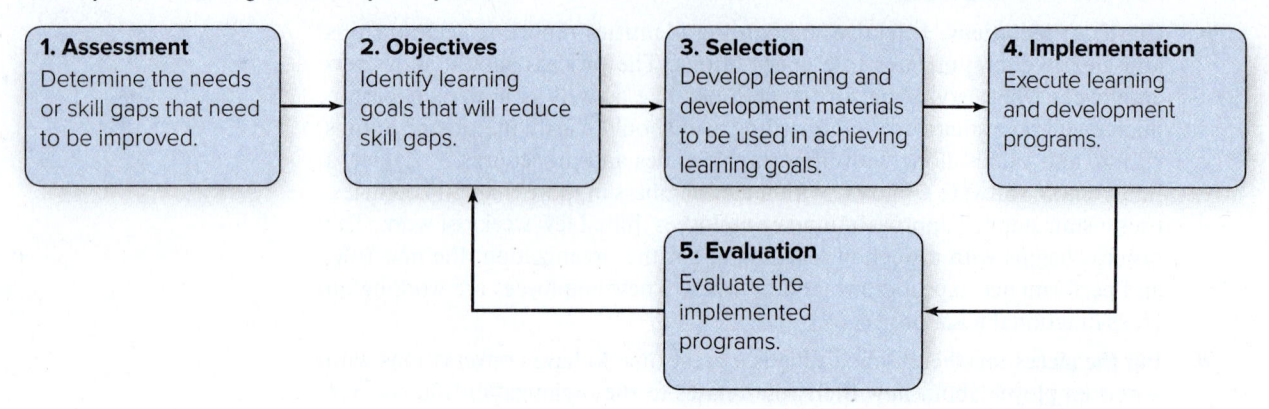

```
1. Assessment          2. Objectives         3. Selection          4. Implementation
Determine the needs → Identify learning   → Develop learning and → Execute learning
or skill gaps that      goals that will     development materials   and development
need to be improved.    reduce skill gaps.  to be used in achieving programs.
                                            learning goals.

                        5. Evaluation
                        Evaluate the
                        implemented
                        programs.
```

didn't have before, and so on. Simply put, this step identifies the specific changes you hope to see after L&D.

- **Step 3: Selection.** The third step in L&D is to select the best method(s) for delivering L&D. Here you'll discuss, for example, whether L&D stays in-house or gets outsourced; whether it takes place online, in a face-to-face setting, in a blended format, and so on.
- **Step 4: Implementation.** The fourth step in L&D is to go forward with L&D delivery.
- **Step 5: Evaluation.** The fifth step in L&D is to determine whether the L&D has met/is meeting its objectives. If not, what needs to be adjusted?

Carrefour is a multinational retail company in France that does a great job executing these five steps.

L&D Example—Carrefour: Carrefour is the eighth largest retailer in the world and employs over 300,000 people. Carrefour makes substantial investments in developing its workforce in order to keep up with rapid industry, consumer, and technological changes. The company assesses L&D needs based on its primary strategic goals and continually monitors these needs for every single employee. Performance management is designed to focus on employees' individual career paths and development needs. L&D methods vary depending on job roles, but all of the company's L&D programs are designed with the goal of helping learners understand how the skills they are learning have an impact on firm strategy and on the retail sector as a whole. Carrefour partners with Google for various e-learning programs, and managers are tasked with overseeing each employee's career progression and personalized L&D plan. The company monitors the results of its L&D programs year-round through a variety of feedback channels including performance metrics, manager reviews, and customer input.[116]

Now that you have learned about the HR practices of recruitment, selection, compensation and benefits, onboarding, and L&D, do careers in these fields interest you? Not everyone is suited for HR work, but it is very rewarding for some. Use Self-Assessment 9.3, if your instructor has assigned it, to help you decide whether or not a career in HR is a good fit for you. ●

SELF-ASSESSMENT 9.3   CAREER READINESS

Is a Career in HR Right for You?

This survey is designed to assess your skills and interests and determine if a career in human resources is right for you. Please complete Self-Assessment 9.3 if your instructor has assigned it in Connect.

9.5 Performance Management

THE BIG PICTURE
Performance management is a set of processes and managerial behaviors that involve defining, monitoring, measuring, evaluating, and providing consequences for performance expectations. It is not a one-time event like a performance appraisal. Effective performance management can foster positive employee attitudes, higher performance, and better customer service.

Want to know how well your managers think you're doing at work? Be prepared to be disappointed: According to recent Gallup research, only 33% of employees around the world strongly agree that they've received meaningful feedback about their work progress in the last six months.[117] Further, only 20% of employees feel motivated by any performance feedback they do receive in their jobs.[118] Feedback about how you're doing in your job is an important part of performance management, and it's vital that managers learn to deliver it well.

LO 9-5

Discuss effective performance management and feedback techniques.

Performance Management in Human Resources

No doubt you've had the experience at some point of having a sit-down with a superior, a boss or a teacher, who told you how well or poorly you were doing—a *performance appraisal*. A performance appraisal is a single event, as we discuss later in this section. Performance management, by contrast, is a powerful ongoing activity that, when done well, can improve firm profitability as well as employee performance, productivity, motivation, and attitudes such as engagement.[119]

Performance management is defined as a set of processes and managerial behaviors that involve defining, monitoring, measuring, evaluating, and providing consequences for performance expectations.[120] It consists of four steps: (1) define performance, (2) monitor and evaluate performance, (3) review performance, and (4) provide consequences (see Figure 9.4).

Step 1: Define Performance
Set goals and communicate performance expectations.

Step 2: Monitor and Evaluate Performance
Measure and evaluate progress and outcomes.

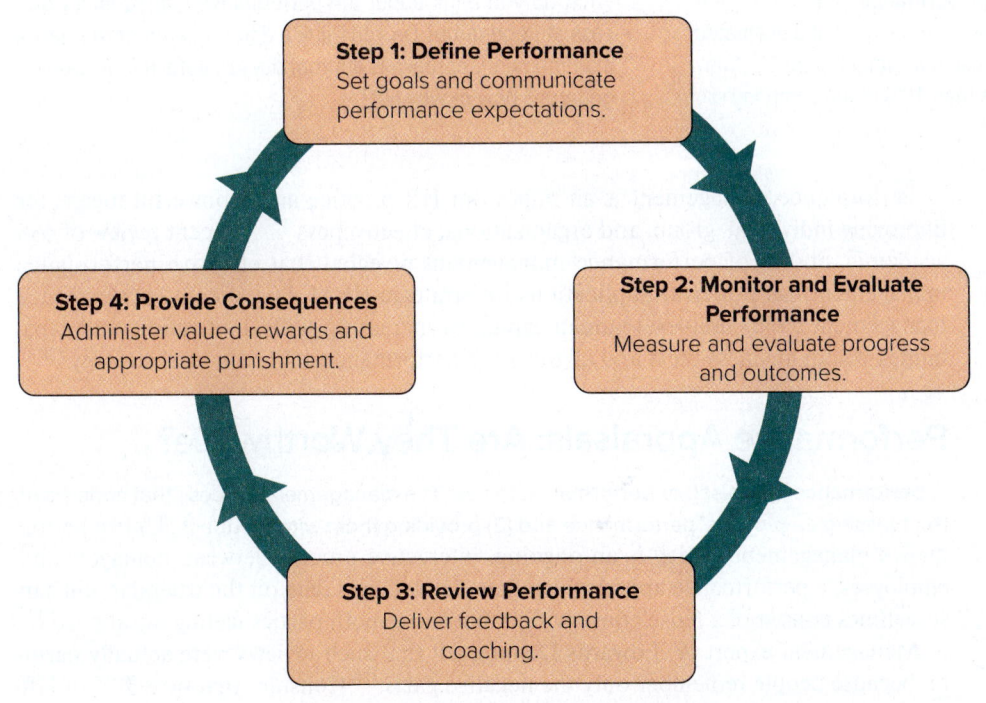

Step 3: Review Performance
Deliver feedback and coaching.

Step 4: Provide Consequences
Administer valued rewards and appropriate punishment.

FIGURE 9.4

Performance management: Four steps

Source: Adapted from A.J. Kinicki, K.J.L. Jacobson, S.J. Peterson, and G.E. Prussia, "Development and Validation of the Performance Management Behavior Questionnaire," *Personnel Psychology*, Vol. 66 (2013), pp. 1–45.

> EXAMPLE | **Performance Management at Regeneron**

Founded in 1988, New York–based Regeneron has more than 8,500 employees and ranks as one of the largest biotech companies in the world. Regeneron has won a number of awards as a best place to work, an innovation leader, a responsible workplace, and a top biotech firm. The company is consistently ranked by *Fortune* as one of the top 100 Best Places to Work in the United States.[121]

Performance management in biotech can be tricky because the way managers need to evaluate and determine performance varies substantially across business units. For scientists developing new treatments, it can take years to determine whether a particular aspect of their performance has been successful. For employees in administrative and commercial roles, timelines are much shorter, and the process is more traditional.

Michelle Weitzman-Garcia, Regeneron's former executive director of workforce development, led the effort to redesign the performance management system to account for the company's unique needs. Here is a description of the company's performance management process (as defined by Figure 9.4).

1. **Define performance.** Broadly, performance at Regeneron is defined along two axes: (1) results—what the employee needs to accomplish—and (2) behaviors—how the employee needs to accomplish it. Managers define what those results and behaviors should be for employees in their unique departments.[122]
2. **Monitor and evaluate performance.** Before the overhaul, Regeneron's managers monitored and evaluated employee performance using a cumbersome 12-point rating scale. Now, fewer than 10% of the company's managers use ratings in the performance management process. Instead, managers use one of four forms tailored to track performance according to unique expectations for employees in (1) drug development, (2) product supply, (3) field sales, and (4) corporate functions.[123]
3. **Review performance.** The frequency and content of performance reviews at Regeneron varies for employees working in different units. For example, in some units, managers use a 30/30 review process that consists of 30 minutes of performance conversation with each employee they supervise every 30 days. In other units, performance reviews occur once or twice per year.[124]
4. **Provide consequences.** Regeneron uses a progressive discipline system to provide consequences for performance that falls below expectations.[125] With progressive discipline, managers work with employees using a series of graduated steps that aim to correct performance early, before it becomes problematic. Progressive discipline typically begins with informal conversation at the early stages and can result in serious action—including termination—in later stages. The company also offers employees the opportunity to earn above-market rewards for outstanding individual contributions, or when their work leads to exceptional firm performance.[126]

YOUR CALL

What do you think about the performance management process at Regeneron? Do you think a differentiated performance management approach is appropriate for biotech firms like Regeneron? Why or why not?

Performance management is an important HR practice and a powerful means for improving individual, group, and organizational effectiveness.[127] A recent review of 488 academic studies of performance management revealed that effective performance management has powerful implications for strategic HRM. Specifically, performance management builds unit-level human capital by increasing skills, motivation, and capabilities within business units and aligning job performance with firm-level strategy.[128]

Performance Appraisals: Are They Worthwhile?

A **performance appraisal**, or performance review, is a management process that consists of (1) assessing employees' performance and (2) providing them with feedback. Unlike performance management, which is an ongoing, interactive process between managers and employees, a performance appraisal is often dictated by a date on the calendar and can sometimes consist of a tense conversation that leaves both parties feeling unsatisfied.[129]

Management expert W. Edwards Deming felt that such reviews were actually harmful because people remember only the negative parts.[130] Consider that over 90% of HR professionals surveyed in a recent study declared they were dissatisfied with their performance review/management systems.[131] No wonder some companies began dropping the practice altogether, although they soon learned that putting nothing in its place left employees without needed and desired feedback about how they were doing on the job. Some newer approaches to performance appraisal have emerged around two important research findings:

Frequent Feedback Is Best   Studies suggest that feedback is more accurate when given frequently.[132] Frequent feedback also allows managers and employees to reinforce key ideas about performance. Companies including Deloitte and General Electric have started to provide more frequent appraisals that let managers and employees make faster "course corrections" and prevent performance problems from piling up.[133] Consider Adobe's approach.

> **Frequent Feedback Example—Adobe:** Adobe abandoned its use of traditional performance appraisals altogether—not because managing performance isn't worthwhile, but because the company's appraisal method wasn't doing anything to actually improve performance. Adobe now uses "check-ins"—frequent, informal, engaging conversations between managers and employees aimed at motivating and improving performance. One benefit is that the process feels more egalitarian and less intimidating than a formal appraisal, and managers and employees are more truthful and direct in their conversations. Another benefit is that employees are no longer "ranked" next to their peers.[134] Adobe recently transformed its "check-in" system to better align with today's increasingly distributed and digital workforce. Employees use a web-based dashboard to track annual goals, document key pieces of feedback, and visualize the alignment of their roles with Adobe's strategic goals. The dashboard also includes a "Career Discovery" tool to help employees expand their roles within the company.[135]

Feedback Should Be Future-Oriented   Good feedback should result in improved performance in the future. Of course, a performance appraisal has to include a discussion of past behavior because past behavior is what is being appraised. But research suggests that the focus of the conversation should then switch to what can be done going forward.[136] Consider how Synchrony Financial revamped its performance appraisal system.

> **Future-Oriented Feedback Example—Synchrony:** Synchrony Financial put the brakes on its annual performance review during the pandemic and ultimately decided the process wasn't worth returning to. Now, instead of using cumbersome documentation and rating scales, managers and employees at Synchrony have one-on-one conversations regarding how performance can be improved for the future. Synchrony managers help employees to reassess and prioritize their performance goals on a quarterly basis to ensure that they are still aligned with the firm's strategy.[137]

Let us look at performance appraisals in more detail because they are still used by most organizations, albeit in some new and exciting forms.[138]

Two Kinds of Performance Appraisal: Objective and Subjective

There are two ways to evaluate an employee's performance—objectively and subjectively.

1. Objective Appraisals   **Objective appraisals**, also called results appraisals, are based on facts and are often numerical. In these kinds of appraisals, you would keep track of such matters as the numbers of products the employee sold in a month, customer complaints filed against an employee, miles of freight hauled, and the like.

There are two good reasons for having objective appraisals:

- **They measure desired results.** Objectively measuring desired results enables managers to focus employees on the important or preferred outcomes. Examples would be the number of cars sold by salespeople, the number of journal publications for professors, and the number of defects for a manufacturing plant.

- **They are harder to challenge legally.** Not being as subject to personal bias, objective appraisals are harder for employees to challenge on legal grounds, such as for age, gender, or racial discrimination.

2. Subjective Appraisals Few employees can be adequately measured just by objective appraisals—hence the need for subjective appraisals, which are based on a manager's perceptions of an employee's (1) traits or (2) behaviors.

- **Trait appraisals.** *Trait appraisals* are ratings of such subjective attributes as "attitude," "initiative," and "leadership." Trait evaluations may be easy to create and use, but their validity is questionable because the evaluator's personal bias can affect the ratings.

- **Behavioral appraisals.** *Behavioral appraisals* measure specific, observable aspects of performance—being on time for work, for instance—although making the evaluation is still somewhat subjective. An example is the behaviorally anchored rating scale (BARS), which rates employee gradations in performance according to scales of specific behaviors. For example, a five-point BARS rating scale about attendance might go from "Always early for work and has equipment ready to fully assume duties" to "Frequently late and often does not have equipment ready for going to work," with gradations in between.

Who Should Make Performance Appraisals?

Most performance appraisals are done by managers; however, to add different perspectives, sometimes appraisal information is provided by other people who are knowledgeable about particular employees or jobs. Decisions about who appraises performance should be made in support of the company's strategic goals, as you will see in the examples we discuss.

Peers, Subordinates, Customers, and Self Among additional sources of performance information are co-workers and subordinates, customers and clients, and employees themselves.

- **Peers and subordinates.** Co-workers, colleagues, and subordinates may well see different aspects of your performance. Such information can be useful for development, although it probably shouldn't be used for evaluation. (Many managers will resist soliciting such information about themselves, of course, fearing negative appraisals.)

- **Customers and clients.** Some organizations, such as restaurants and hotels, ask customers and clients for their appraisals of employees. Publishers ask authors to judge how well they are doing in handling the editing, production, and marketing of their books. Automobile dealerships may send follow-up questionnaires to car buyers.

- **Self-appraisals.** How would you rate your own performance in a job, knowing that it would go into your personnel file? It's likely the bias would be toward rating yourself favorably. Nevertheless, *self-appraisals* help employees become involved in the whole evaluation process and may make them more receptive to feedback about areas needing improvement.

In terms of strategic HRM, managers should choose performance information sources based on whether the insights gleaned from them can improve performance in a way that improves strategic execution. If the firm can better deliver on its objectives when a source of performance information is included, then it may be worthwhile to include the source in the performance appraisal process. However, managers need to evaluate the relative validity of any additional source of information to determine how much weight it should carry. Consider the example of patient experience surveys in health care.

Performance Information Example—Patient Experience Surveys: Hospital reimbursements—the money hospitals ultimately receive (from health insurers, Medicare, etc.) for providing medical services—have become increasingly tied to patient satisfaction scores gathered from the Hospital Consumer Assessment of Healthcare Providers and Systems (HCAHPS) patient experience survey.[139] For many physicians and healthcare facilities, there is skepticism about whether patient reviews represent valid measures of quality of care. The concern is that if important outcomes are contingent upon these scores, some providers may be motivated to make decisions in the best interest of ratings, rather than patients' health. Data suggest this may be the case, with between 20% and 30% of physicians surveyed in a recent study admitting that they had prescribed opioids, performed spinal injections for pain, or ordered MRI imaging due to fear that their HCAHPS scores would be affected if they did not do these things.[140] Recently, a group of five major hospital associations published a list of recommendations for improving the validity of HCAHPS scores. Recommendations were related to, for example, improving response rates, refining survey items, and ensuring that the survey was understandable to people with varying levels of health literacy.[141]

360-Degree Assessment: Appraisal by Multiple Sources We said that performance appraisals may be done by peers, subordinates, customers, and oneself. Sometimes all these may be used in a technique called a 360-degree assessment. With a **360-degree feedback appraisal**, or 360-degree assessment, employees are appraised not only by their managerial superiors but also by peers, subordinates, and sometimes clients, thus providing several perspectives. A 360-degree assessment is an increasingly popular tool for leadership development.[142] Consider the following example of how Cox Communications uses 360-degree assessments as part of its leadership development program.

360-Degree Assessment Example—Cox Communications: Managers at Cox Communications undergo 360-degree assessment soon after they are promoted, but only after they've spent time managing their new teams. The purpose of the assessment is to help managers realize how they are perceived by their team members, and what they can do to better support and motivate their employees. Chief People Officer Karen Bennett says managers understand that "We see potential in you because you just got promoted, and we want to make sure you get off to a good start."[143] The company enlists external leadership coaches to help managers implement a few key improvement goals identified by the assessment.

When administered properly, 360-degree appraisals are useful tools for generating knowledge workers can use to improve their behavior and performance.[144] There are, however, potential downsides to 360-degree assessment when executed poorly, including anxiety, defensiveness, and negative attitudes toward the system, organization, and/or raters. Here are a few best practices for getting 360-degree assessments right:[145]

1. **Keep it developmental**—the 360-degree appraisal is intended to be a source of developmental information rather than a formal appraisal. Making raters aware that their feedback will be used for the former purpose increases the likelihood that they will provide constructive information.

2. **More isn't always better**—focus on choosing evaluators who can contribute unique and strategically valuable information about the employee's performance.

3. **Remember to reduce bias**—proponents of 360-degree appraisals often assume this technique automatically reduces the likelihood of bias in performance feedback. Unfortunately, more raters often mean more opportunities for bias. Raters should be trained to recognize role-specific competencies as well as their own judgmental biases.

Forced Ranking: Grading on a Curve

To increase performance, a substantial number of Fortune 500 companies have some variant of performance review systems known as a forced ranking (or "rank and yank") system.[146] In **forced ranking performance review systems**, all employees within a business unit are ranked against one another and grades are distributed along some sort of bell curve—just like students being graded in a college course. Top performers (such as the top 20%) are rewarded with bonuses and promotions; the worst performers (such as the bottom 20%) are given warnings or dismissed.

Forced rankings rely on the theory that there is something inherently motivating about seeing how we stack up against others. This thinking underlies, for example, the "leaderboard" Peloton users see when they take a cycling class. The main idea is that we will be motivated to work harder and push ourselves further when in competition with others.

Forced rankings were a cornerstone of many organizations for decades, but outlooks on their usefulness are shifting.[147] Evidence suggests forced rankings can eliminate good workers and may also negatively impact performance. Further, forced rankings are increasingly inapplicable to modern work. This is because knowledge-intensive work outcomes and their requisite skills, attitudes, and abilities are hard to evaluate along a bell curve. Consider how GE's perspective on forced ranking has changed over time.

Foregoing Forced Ranking Example—GE:
In the 1980s, GE pioneered its famous "rank and yank" performance management system that required managers to rank their workforce according to performance ratings and "yank" (i.e., fire) the bottom 10%. The system persisted at GE for decades but has all but vanished in recent years, with the company's HR leadership moving toward more accurate and collaborative, and less punitive, efforts to capture and improve performance.[148] GE's latest HR innovation is its PD@GE app. This technology connects employees with both managers and peers and enables them to seek and give feedback in real time. Each employee works toward a set of short-term "priorities" and can either ask for or deliver "insights" to others whenever they choose. The system categorizes feedback as something to either "consider changing" or "continue doing."[149]

Effective Performance Feedback

As a manager, you may not feel comfortable about critiquing your employees' performance, especially when you have to convey criticism rather than praise. In fact, studies suggest managers often inflate their employees' performance ratings (either consciously or subconsciously).[150] Nevertheless, giving performance feedback is one of the most important parts of the manager's job, and giving inaccurate or overly positive feedback is helpful to neither the employee nor the organization. Here are some research-backed suggestions for giving accurate, useful feedback:[151]

- **Take a problem-solving approach, avoid criticism, and treat employees with respect.** Recall the worst boss for whom you ever worked. How did you react to their feedback method? Avoid giving criticism that might be taken personally.

    Example: Instead of saying, "You're picking up that bag of cement wrong" (which is both personal and also criticizes by using the word *wrong*), try, "Instead of bending at the waist, a good way to pick up something heavy is to bend your knees. That'll help save your back."

- **Be specific and direct in describing the employee's current performance and in identifying the improvement you desire.** Describe your subordinate's current performance in specific terms and concentrate on outcomes that are within their ability to improve.

    Example: Instead of saying, "You're always late turning in your sales reports." Try, "Instead of making calls on Thursday afternoon, why don't you take some of the time to do your sales reports so they'll be ready on Friday along with those of the other sales reps?"

- **Get the employee's input.** In determining the causes of a problem, listen to the employee and get their help in crafting a solution. Be thoughtful and compassionate.

    Example: Instead of saying, "You've got to learn to get here by 9:00 a.m. every day." Say, "What changes do you think could be made so that your station is ready when people start calling at 9:00?"

- **Follow up.** Always check in with the employee later to be sure they have taken any corrective action you discussed and that you've made yourself available for any additional questions or input.

    Example: Instead of saying, "Why are you still turning in incomplete progress reports?" Try, "It's almost time for me to ask for your next progress report. Should we take a look at a draft of it together first?" ●

9.6 Managing Promotions, Transfers, Disciplining, and Dismissals

THE BIG PICTURE
As a manager, you'll have to manage employee replacement actions, as by promoting, transferring, demoting, laying off, or firing.

Part of a manager's job is making decisions that impact employees' movement within (and sometimes out of) the organization. As a manager, you'll get to reward some of your high performers by promoting them into exciting new positions, and you'll help other employees to develop their skills through lateral career moves within the company. You'll also have the not-so-fun responsibility of disciplining employees, and, in some cases, terminating employees' relationships with the company altogether.

Let's consider some best practices for handling promotions, transfers, discipline, and dismissals.

LO 9-6
List guidelines for handling promotions, transfers, discipline, and dismissals.

Promotion: Moving Upward

Promotion—moving an employee to a higher-level position—is the most obvious way to recognize that person's superior performance (apart from giving raises and bonuses). There are three primary concerns with promotions: fairness, discrimination, and others' resentments. Let's look at each of these briefly:

Fairness It's important that promotion be *fair*. The step upward must be deserved. Managers should never promote employees for reasons of nepotism, cronyism, or other forms of favoritism. Promoting an undeserving and unqualified employee can harm the organization's bottom line if the employee is unable to fulfill the expectations of the new role.[152] Further, research suggests the perception of unfair promotion decisions can lead to negative attitudinal and performance outcomes for those who feel they were unfairly snubbed.[153]

Discrimination Promotion decisions cannot and should not discriminate on the basis of sex (including sexual orientation, pregnancy, and gender identity), national origin, age, disability, or membership in any other protected class. Further, decisions should not be made on the basis of any non-job-related factor (e.g., political affiliation) even if it isn't considered a legally protected factor, although recent evidence suggests this type of discrimination does occur.[154]

Others' Resentments If someone is promoted, someone else may be resentful about being passed over. As a manager, you may need to counsel the people left behind about their performance and their opportunities in the future. In fact, if you are passed over yourself, it is important not to let your anger build. Instead, gather your thoughts, then go in and talk to your boss and find out what qualities were lacking, suggests one report. This demonstrates the core career readiness competency of career management because you are taking responsibility and looking for ways to improve and showcase your knowledge, skills, and abilities. Above all, don't give up. It may be that this was not the right opportunity for you, and another will come when you least expect it.[155]

Transfer: Moving Sideways

Transfer is movement of an employee to a different job with similar responsibility. It may or may not mean a change in geographical location (which might be part of a promotion as well).

Managers transfer employees for four principal reasons:

1. To solve organizational problems by deploying their skills at another location.
2. To broaden their experience by assigning them to a different position.
3. To retain their interest and motivation by presenting them with new challenges.
4. To solve employee problems such as personal conflicts with co-workers or supervisors.

Remember from Section 9.4 that employees are hungry for opportunities to learn new skills and develop their competencies. Further, organizations are increasingly reliant on this type of L&D for competitive advantage. Job transfers are one way that managers can provide meaningful development for employees while simultaneously benefiting the firm.[156] Here are a few examples of organizations that use transfers strategically:

Transfer Examples—Various Companies: HSBC Financial encourages employees to peruse and apply for job postings on its internal talent marketplace (defined in Section 9.2). Fidelity International employees have opportunities to work on projects outside of their own departments, and in many cases this leads to permanent job transfers. At Seagate Technology, jobs must be posted internally for a period of time before they are posted externally. This practice encourages existing employees to make lateral moves within the company. Further, Seagate only requires an 80% match between internal applicants' skills and the required skills of the position, using its upskilling initiative to help employees develop the remaining 20%.[157]

Disciplining and Demotion: The Threat of Moving Downward

Poorly performing employees may be given a verbal or written warning and then disciplined. In some instances, employees may be temporarily removed from their jobs, as when a police officer is placed on suspension or administrative leave—removed from their regular job in the field and perhaps given a paperwork job or told to stay away from work.

Verbal and written warnings are often used as part of **performance improvement plans (PIPs)**—formal policies of progressive discipline that outline employee performance problems, routes to and timelines for improvement, and consequences for not meeting plan objectives.[158]

If an employee fails to meet the goals set by a PIP, they may be demoted—that is, have their current responsibilities, pay, and perquisites taken away, as when a middle manager is demoted to a first-line manager. (Sometimes this may occur when a company is downsized, resulting in fewer higher-level management positions.)

Demotions are uncomfortable for both managers and employees, but demotions don't necessarily mean the employee isn't a valuable asset to the company. In many cases, they are simply not a good fit for their current position and would be able to make valuable contributions elsewhere in the organization or after they've had more time in a lower-level position.[159] Here are three tips for managing the demotion process:[160]

1. Base demotion decisions on unbiased, well-documented evidence.
2. Communicate the organization's desire to retain the employee.
3. Be honest about performance-related issues that led to the demotion.

Employees who fail to meet the objectives of a PIP also may be fired, which we discuss next.

Dismissal: Moving Out of the Organization

Dismissals fall into three categories: layoffs, downsizings, and firings. We first discuss each type of dismissal. Then, we describe exit interviews, nondisparagement agreements, and employment at will, which often go along with dismissals.

Layoffs The phrase being *laid off* tends to suggest that a person has been dismissed *temporarily*—as when a carmaker doesn't have enough orders to justify keeping its production employees—and may be recalled later when economic conditions improve. Many companies cite layoffs as necessary to improve profitability, although research suggests they do not, in fact, improve profits in the long term.[161] Layoffs often occur during periods of economic instability—consider the following example:

> **Layoffs Example—The Technology Sector:** Tech companies collectively laid off approximately 200,000 employees between January 2022 and March 2023, with 50,000 Alphabet, Meta, Microsoft, and Amazon employees receiving layoff notices in January 2023 alone. Many executives cited rising inflation and interest rates as the reason for the mass layoffs, but others acknowledged that the pandemic-fueled tech hiring spree led to unsustainably outsized workforces.[162]

Downsizings A *downsizing* is a *permanent* dismissal; there is no rehiring later. An automaker discontinuing a line of cars or on the path to bankruptcy might permanently let go of its production employees. Recent research suggests that downsizing occurs more often due to pressure to meet investment analysts' earnings estimates rather than to correct for poor firm performance.[163]

Firings The phrase *being fired* (a.k.a., being "terminated," "separated," "let go," "sacked," "axed," or "canned") tends to mean that a person was dismissed *permanently* and *"for cause."* Firings occur due to, for example, excessive absenteeism, poor work habits, unsatisfactory performance (which may include failing to accomplish objectives in a PIP), or breaking the law. The term *firing* may have a negative connotation, but terminating employment can be the right decision. As a manager, you'll need to know how to fire employees in the appropriate way. Two key points to remember are:

1. **Carefully document reasons for dismissals.** Managers should maintain documentation when employees violate expectations for performance or behavior. Records should note what was discussed with the employee as well as the specific expectations established for improvement. Should the situation worsen or fail to improve, this documentation will lend strong support to the manager's decision to fire the employee.[164]

2. **Remember those who stay.** Other employees may be negatively affected by the firing of a supervisor, co-worker, or subordinate.[165]

Exit Interviews, Nondisparagement Agreements, and Employment at Will

An **exit interview** is a formal conversation between a representative from the organization and a departing employee to find out why they are leaving and to learn about potential problems in the organization. Exit interviews are more likely when employees leave the organization voluntarily as opposed to when they are fired.[166] This is because employees that choose to separate from the organization may have valuable insight into how the company might improve its workforce retention efforts or correct existing issues. Unfortunately, research shows that employees may not share this insight honestly in exit interviews because they fear being retaliated against in ways that can damage their careers.[167]

A **nondisparagement agreement** is a contract between two parties that prohibits one party from criticizing the other; it is often used in severance agreements to prohibit former employees from criticizing their former employers. Employees who are laid off or whose jobs have been eliminated are often obliged to sign nondisparagement agreements in return for receiving severance pay—pay an employer may give a worker who leaves, such as the equivalent of two weeks of salary for each year they were employed. The #MeToo movement reignited debates about nondisparagement agreements and the fact that they may prevent some victims of workplace harassment from speaking out. In late 2022, the U.S. Congress passed a law banning the use of nondisparagement agreements in sexual harassment cases (see Section 9.8 for more on this legislation).[168]

Employment at will is the governing principle of employment in the great majority of states, and it means that anyone can be dismissed at any time for any reason at all—or for no reason.[169] Exceptions are whistle-blowers and people with employment contracts. EEO laws also prohibit organizations' dismissing people for their membership in one or more protected classes.[170]

Managers should always work with HR to ensure they are complying with local, state, and federal law during dismissals. •

9.7 The Legal Requirements of Human Resource Management

THE BIG PICTURE
Four areas of human resource law any manager needs to be aware of are labor relations, compensation and benefits, health and safety, and equal employment opportunity.

LO 9-7

Discuss legal considerations managers should be aware of.

Laws underlie all aspects of the HR practices discussed so far. Whatever your organization's human resource strategy, in the United States (and in U.S. divisions overseas) it has to operate within the environment of the American legal system. In this section we discuss four areas you need to be aware of. Some important laws are summarized in Table 9.2.

TABLE 9.2 Some Important Recent U.S. Federal Laws and Regulations Protecting Employees

YEAR	LAW OR REGULATION	PROVISIONS
Labor Relations		
1974	Privacy Act	Gives employees legal right to examine letters of reference concerning them.
1986	Immigration Reform & Control Act	Requires employers to verify the eligibility for employment of all their new hires (including U.S. citizens).
2003	Sarbanes–Oxley Act	Prohibits employers from demoting or firing employees who raise accusations of fraud to a federal agency.
Compensation and Benefits		
1974	Employee Retirement Income Security Act (ERISA)	Sets rules for managing pension plans; provides federal insurance to cover bankrupt plans.
1993	Family and Medical Leave Act	Requires employers to provide 12 weeks of unpaid leave for medical and family reasons, including for childbirth, adoption, or family emergency.
1996	Health Insurance Portability and Accountability Act (HIPAA)	Allows employees to switch health insurance plans when changing jobs and receive new coverage regardless of preexisting health conditions; prohibits group plans from dropping ill employees.
2007	Fair Minimum Wage Act	Increased federal minimum wage to $7.25 per hour on July 24, 2009.
Health and Safety		
1970	Occupational Safety and Health Act (OSHA)	Establishes minimum health and safety standards in organizations.
1985	Consolidated Omnibus Budget Reconciliation Act (COBRA)	Requires an extension of health insurance benefits after termination.
2010	Patient Protection and Affordable Care Act	Employers with more than 50 employees must provide health insurance.
Equal Employment Opportunity		
1963	Equal Pay Act	Requires that people be paid equally for performing equal work, regardless of sex.
1964, amended 1972	Civil Rights Act, Title VII	Prohibits discrimination on basis of race, color, religion, sex, (later clarified as including pregnancy, gender identity, and sexual orientation), and national origin.
1967, amended 1978 and 1986	Age Discrimination in Employment Act (ADEA)	Prohibits discrimination in employees over 40 years old; restricts mandatory retirement.
1990	Americans with Disabilities Act (ADA)	Prohibits discrimination against otherwise qualified employees and job seekers with physical or mental disabilities or chronic illness; requires "reasonable accommodation" be provided so they can perform duties.
1991	Civil Rights Act	Amends and clarifies Title VII, ADA, and other laws; permits suits against employers for punitive damages in cases of intentional discrimination.

1. Labor Relations

The earliest laws affecting employee welfare had to do with unions, and they can still have important effects. Legislation passed in 1935 (the Wagner Act) resulted in the National Labor Relations Board (NLRB), which enforces procedures whereby employees may vote to have a union and for collective bargaining. Collective bargaining consists of negotiations between management and employees about disputes over compensation, benefits, working conditions, and job security.

A 1947 law (the Taft-Hartley Act) allows the president of the United States to prevent or end a strike that threatens national security. (We discuss labor–management issues further in Section 9.8.)

2. Compensation and Benefits

The Social Security Act of 1935 established the U.S. retirement system.

The passage of the Fair Labor Standards Act of 1938 (FLSA) established minimum living standards for workers engaged in interstate commerce, including provision of a federal minimum wage and a maximum workweek before overtime must be paid, along with banning child labor.

Minimum Wage Here are a few important facts about the federal minimum wage:[171]

- **Federal minimum wage is $7.25 an hour.** It was raised to this level in 2009.
- **States have their own laws:**
    - Twenty-nine states and D.C. have minimum wages that are higher than the federal level.
    - Five states do not have minimum wage levels.
    - When an employee is subject to both state and federal law, they earn the higher of the two rates (state or federal).
- **The federal minimum wage has not changed since 2009.** As of this writing, the minimum wage has never stood unchanged for longer. Workers earning the federal minimum wage make nearly 30% less than workers who earned minimum wage in 2009 in terms of inflation-adjusted purchasing power.

Proponents of a $15 minimum wage say it would help people pay their bills because existing minimum wages have not kept up with inflation, and it would create a fairer working environment because different states now pay wildly different minimums. Detractors say that the $15 figure is arbitrary and that a higher minimum would produce job losses, hurt low-skilled workers, have little effect on reducing poverty, and result in higher prices to consumers.[172]

Overtime Pay Under the FLSA, salaried executive, administrative, and professional employees are considered exempt from federal overtime rules. These provisions are called white-collar exemptions. The remaining employees, called nonexempt employees, must be paid time and a half for any weekly hours in excess of 40. In 2023 the Department of Labor (DOL) updated the white-collar exemptions. Workers must be paid overtime if they do not earn at least $55,068 per year.[173]

3. Health and Safety

From miners risking tunnel cave-ins to cotton mill workers breathing lint, industry has always had dirty, dangerous jobs. Beginning with the Occupational Safety and Health Act (OSH Act) of 1970, a body of law has grown that requires organizations to provide employees with nonhazardous working conditions (most recently augmented by an update to the Toxic Substances Control Act of 1976).[174] Later laws extended health coverage, including 2010 healthcare reform legislation, which requires employees with more than 50 employees to provide health insurance or pay a penalty.[175] More than 30 million Americans have gained access to health insurance due to the passing of the Affordable Care Act.[176]

4. Equal Employment Opportunity

The effort to reduce discrimination in employment based on racial, ethnic, and religious bigotry and gender stereotypes began with Title VII of the Civil Rights Act of 1964. This established the **Equal Employment Opportunity Commission (EEOC)**, whose job is to enforce antidiscrimination and other employment-related laws. Title VII applies to all organizations or their agents engaged in an industry affecting interstate commerce that employs 15 or more employees. Contractors who wish to do business with the U.S. government (such as most colleges and universities, which receive federal funds) must be in compliance with various executive orders issued by the president covering antidiscrimination. Later laws prevented discrimination against older workers and people with physical and mental disabilities. (We discuss these topics in detail in Chapter 11.)

Workplace Discrimination, Affirmative Action, Sexual Harassment, and Bullying

Three important concepts covered by equal employment opportunity (EEO) laws are *workplace discrimination, affirmative action,* and *sexual harassment,* which we discuss in this section. We also consider *bullying,* which is *not* covered by EEO laws.

Workplace Discrimination   **Workplace discrimination** occurs when employment decisions about people are made for reasons not relevant to the job, such as race, sex, religion, or age. Two fine points to be made here are that (1) although the law prohibits discrimination in all aspects of employment, it does not require an employer to extend *preferential treatment* because of these factors, and (2) employment decisions must be made on the basis of job-related criteria.

There are two types of workplace discrimination:[177]

- **Adverse impact. Adverse impact** occurs when an organization uses an employment practice or procedure that results in unfavorable outcomes for a protected class (such as workers over 40) over another group (such as workers under 40). For example, requiring workers to have "four to six years of experience" inadvertently creates adverse impact on older workers because workers over 40 are likely to have more than six years of experience. This example would not be a problem, however, if work experience in this specific range were required to perform the job. Another example is basing a person's starting salary on what they earned at a previous job. This can discriminate against female applicants because they tend to make less money than males for performing the same job with the same level of experience and skills. At least 16 U.S. states have now enacted laws banning all employers from inquiring about applicants' prior salaries.[178]

- **Disparate treatment.** Disparate treatment results when employees from protected groups (such as individuals who are disabled) are intentionally treated differently. An example would be making a decision to give all international assignments to people without disabilities because of the assumption that they won't need any special accommodations related to travel. Another example would be deciding to choose a male employee for a promotion over a female employee because of the assumption that the female employee—who happens to be pregnant—is going to give up her career soon anyway.

When an organization is found to have discriminated, affected workers may sue for back pay and punitive damages. Among recent complaints to the EEOC, the most frequently cited basis for charges of discrimination was retaliation (56.0%), followed by disability discrimination (37.2%); discrimination based on race (34.1%); sex discrimination, including sexual harassment and pregnancy discrimination (30.6%); and discrimination based on age (21.1%). These percentages are greater than 100% because some charges allege multiple types of discrimination.[179]

Discrimination can occur in HR practices even when managers are not consciously aware of it. Further, discrimination can occur despite the use of technology designed to minimize or prevent it. Consider the example of AI-based selection:

Some AI-based selection tools claim to measure candidates' job-relevant characteristics by analyzing their facial expressions in recorded submissions. How would you feel about a company deciding whether to hire you based on how you raise your eyebrows, open your eyes, or smile?
Zapp2Photo/Shutterstock

Workplace Discrimination Example—AI-Based Selection Tools: The EEOC noted in its recent Strategic Enforcement Plan that it intends to pay particular attention to potential AI-based hiring discrimination in the coming years.[180] The warning came in response to sharply increasing numbers of organizations adopting algorithmic decision-making tools for recruiting, hiring, and other selection decisions. Survey data suggests that almost 80% of organizations either currently automate or plan to automate at least some portion of their HR decision making within five years. Concerns about the use of AI in HR decisions include lack of regulation and the use of algorithms built on existing (biased) data. Said EEOC chair Charlotte Burrows, "We totally recognize there's enormous potential to streamline things. But we cannot let these tools become a high-tech path to discrimination."[181]

Affirmative Action Affirmative action focuses on achieving equality of opportunity within an organization. It aims to make up for *past discrimination* in employment by actively finding, hiring, and developing the talents of people from groups traditionally underrepresented due to discrimination. Steps include active recruitment, elimination of prejudicial questions in interviews, and establishment of goals for hiring members of minority groups. It's important to note that EEOC laws *do not* allow the use of hiring quotas.[182]

Affirmative action has created tremendous opportunities for members of minority groups, but it has been resisted more by some who see it as working against their interests.[183] Consider what happened at Harvard.

Affirmative Action Example—Harvard: The issue of affirmative action made headlines when a group called the Students for Fair Admissions sued Harvard for its race-conscious admissions process. Specifically, the lawsuit alleged that Harvard had discriminated against Asian American applicants in its admissions process, unfairly holding them to a higher standard to gain admission. U.S. District Judge Allison Burroughs ruled that Harvard's admissions standards were constitutional, and said in her ruling, "It is this, at Harvard and elsewhere that will move us, one day, to the point where we see that race is a fact, but not the defining fact and not the fact that tells us what is important, but we are not there yet." She added, "Until we are, race-conscious admissions programs that survive strict scrutiny will have an important place in society and help ensure that colleges and universities can offer a diverse atmosphere that fosters learning, improves scholarship and encourages mutual respect and understanding."[184] In June 2023, the U.S. Supreme court ruled that Harvard's admissions policy violated the equal protections clause of the 14th amendment. This decision is expected to essentially end race-conscious college and university admissions programs across the country.[185]

Sexual Harassment
Sexual harassment consists of unwanted sexual attention that creates an adverse work environment. This means obscene gestures, sex-stereotyped jokes, sexually oriented posters and graffiti, suggestive remarks, unwanted dating pressure, physical nonsexual contact, unwanted touching, sexual propositions, threatening punishment unless sexual favors are given, obscene phone calls, and similar verbal or physical actions of a sexual nature.[186] The harassment may be by a member of the opposite sex or a member of the same sex, by a manager, by a co-worker, or by an outsider. If the harasser is a manager or an agent of the organization, the organization itself can be sued, even if it had no knowledge of the situation.[187]

Two Types of Sexual Harassment   There are two types of sexual harassment, both of which violate Title VII of the 1964 Civil Rights Act.

1. **Quid pro quo harassment**—in this type, the recipient of unwanted sexual attention is told, implicitly or explicitly, that they must acquiesce or jeopardize being hired for a job or obtaining job benefits or opportunities.

2. **Hostile environment**—in this (more typical) type, the person being sexually harassed doesn't risk economic harm but perceives that they are experiencing an offensive or intimidating work environment.

Table 9.3 presents some examples of sex-based behaviors that are unacceptable in the workplace. Managers should neither perpetrate these behaviors nor tolerate employees engaging in them.

TABLE 9.3   Sexual Harassment: Examples of Unacceptable Workplace Behaviors

• Offering sexual favors for rewards related to work or promotion.
• Uninvited touching of others' bodies.
• Sexually suggestive jokes, demeaning remarks, slurs, or obscene gestures or sounds.
• Sexual pictures or written notes of a sexual nature.
• Amusement at others' sexually harassing words or behaviors.

What Managers Can Do   Managers can take several actions to help prevent harassment from occurring in the workplace. These include:[188]

- **Institute effective policy.** Managers should make sure their companies have an effective sexual harassment policy in place. The policy should be shown to all current and new employees, who should be made to understand that neither sexual harassment nor covering up for an offender will be tolerated under any circumstances.

- **Establish a formal complaint procedure.** A formal complaint procedure should explain how charges will be investigated and resolved.
- **Train supervisors.** Supervisors should be trained in Title VII requirements and the proper procedures to follow when charges occur.
- **Investigate promptly and without bias.** If charges occur, they should be investigated promptly and objectively, and if substantiated, the offender should be disciplined at once—no matter their rank in the company.

Bullying **Bullying** is repeated mistreatment of one or more persons by one or more perpetrators; it is abusive physical, psychological, verbal, or nonverbal behavior that is threatening, humiliating, or intimidating. It can happen at work just as easily and as often as in the schoolyard. Research suggests the following about workplace bullying:

A surprisingly common activity, bullying is apt to be verbal, involving shouting and name-calling, or relational, including spreading malicious rumors and lies. Perhaps as many as half of all employees have experienced some sort of bullying on the job. Have you? Mint Images Limited/Alamy Stock Photo

- Between 30% and 55% of workers around the world have experienced bullying on the job—either directly or as witnesses.[189]
- Common forms of workplace bullying include yelling, spreading rumors about others, withholding information, humiliating workers in front of others, and throwing things.[190]
- Bullying can occur between colleagues, managers, and employees, but supervisors are reported to be at least 50% of all workplace bullies.[191]
- Bullying by supervisors typically takes the form of forcing long hours on workers or yelling and behaving in an intimidating or threatening way.[192]

The Effects of Bullying Workplace bullying has numerous negative consequences. Here is a summary of what research suggests about the effects of being bullied at work:[193]

- **Mental health.** The experience of workplace bullying negatively impacts workers' mental health through increased psychological stress, anxiety, and depression.
- **Physical health.** Workplace bullying is associated with physical health outcomes including cardiovascular disease.
- **Work-related outcomes.** Workers who are bullied report increased turnover, lower performance and productivity, negative attitudes, and lower measures of employee well-being.

9.8 Labor–Management Issues

THE BIG PICTURE
We describe the process by which workers get a labor union to represent them and how unions and management negotiate a contract. This section also discusses the types of union and nonunion workplaces and right-to-work laws. It covers issues unions and management negotiate, such as compensation, cost-of-living adjustments, two-tier wage systems, and givebacks. It concludes by describing mediation and arbitration.

Starting in 1943, James Smith worked his way up from washing dishes in the galley of a passenger train's dining car to waiter, earning tips on top of his wages of 36 cents an hour. The union job with the Brotherhood of Sleeping Car Porters, the first African American union, enabled him to go to college, and when he left the railroad he was hired as a civil engineer for the city of Los Angeles. "His story," says one report, "is emblematic of the role the railroads and a railroad union played in building a foundation for America's black middle class."[194] Unions also helped to grow the U.S. (and European) middle classes in general, bringing benefits to all, organized or not.

Labor unions are organizations of employees formed to protect and advance their members' interests by bargaining with management over job-related issues. The union movement is far less powerful than it was in the 1950s—indeed, its present membership has reached record lows—but it is still a force in many sectors of the economy (see Table 9.4). Despite declining membership, about 71% of U.S. adults hold a favorable view of unions today, the highest in almost two decades and up sharply from less than 50% in 2009.[195]

LO 9-8

Describe labor–management issues and ways to work effectively with labor unions.

TABLE 9.4 Snapshot of Today's U.S. Union Movement

Who's in a union (2022)?
• 11.0% of full-time U.S. workers—down from a high of 35.5% in 1945.
• 6.0% of private-sector workers.
• 33.1% of public-sector workers.
• Most members, public sector: local government (38.8%), including teachers, police officers, and firefighters.
• Most members, private sector: utilities (19.6%) and motion pictures and sound recording industries (17.3%).
• Union membership rate by gender: men (10.5%), women (9.6%).
• Union membership rate by race and ethnicity: Blacks (11.6%), whites (10.0%), Asian Americans (8.3%), Hispanic Americans (8.8%).

Source: Bureau of Labor Statistics, "Union Members 2022," News Release, January 19, 2023, https://www.bls.gov/news.release/pdf/union2.pdf.

How Workers Organize

When workers in a particular organization decide to form a union, they first must get other workers to sign an *authorization card,* which designates a certain union as the workers' bargaining agent. When at least 30% of workers have signed cards, the union may ask the employer for official recognition.

Usually the employer refuses, at which point the union can petition the National Labor Relations Board (NLRB) to decide which union should become the *bargaining unit* that represents the workers, such as the Teamsters Union, United Auto Workers, American Federation of Teachers, or Service Employees International Union, as appropriate. (Some workers, however, are represented by unions you would never guess: Zookeepers, for instance, are represented by the Teamsters, which mainly organizes transportation workers. University of California, Berkeley, graduate student instructors are represented by the United Auto Workers.) An election is then held by the NLRB, and if 50% or more of the votes cast agree to unionization, the NLRB *certifies* the union as the workers' exclusive representative.

Labor agreements are formed through careful negotiations between union representatives, union members, and managers. Negotiating requires the career readiness competencies of critical thinking/problem solving and oral/written communication. What additional career readiness competencies do you think are especially important in negotiations? Morsa Images/E+/Getty Images

How Unions and Management Negotiate a Contract

Once a union is recognized as an official bargaining unit, its representatives can then meet with management's representatives to do collective bargaining—to negotiate pay and benefits and other work terms.

When agreement is reached with management, the union representatives take the collective bargaining results back to the members for *ratification*—they vote to accept or reject the contract negotiated by their leaders. If they vote yes, the union and management representatives sign a *negotiated labor-management contract,* which sets the general tone and terms under which labor and management agree to work together during the contract period.

The Issues Unions and Management Negotiate About

The key issues that labor and management negotiate are compensation, employee benefits, job security, work rules, hours, and safety matters. However, the first issue is usually the union security clause and management rights.

Union Security and Types of Workplaces A key issue is: Who controls hiring policies and work assignments—labor or management? This involves the following matters:

- **The union security clause.** The basic underpinning of union security is the union security clause, the part of the labor–management agreement that states that employees who receive union benefits must join the union, or at least pay dues to it. In times past, a union would try to solidify the union security clause by getting management to agree to a *closed shop agreement*—which is illegal today—in which a company agreed it would hire only current union members for a given job.

TABLE 9.5 Four Kinds of Workplace Labor Agreements

WORKPLACE	DEFINITION	STATUS
Closed shop	Employer may hire only workers for a job who are already in the union.	Illegal
Union shop	Workers aren't required to be union members when hired for a job but must join the union within a specified time.	Not allowed in right-to-work states. Not applicable to public-sector employees
Agency shop	Workers must pay equivalent of union dues but aren't required to join the union.	Applies to public-sector teachers in some states, prohibited in others
Open shop	Workers may choose to join or not join a union.	Applies in right-to-work states

- **Types of unionized and nonunionized workplaces.** The four basic kinds of workplaces are *closed shop, union shop, agency shop,* and *open shop* (see Table 9.5).
- **Right-to-work laws.** Individual states are allowed (under the 1947 Taft-Hartley Act) to pass legislation outlawing union and agency shops. As a result, at least 27 states have passed right-to-work laws, statutes that prohibit employees from being required to join a union as a condition of employment.

Business interests supporting such laws argue that forcing workers to join a union violates their rights and makes a state less attractive to businesses considering moving there. Union supporters say that states with such laws have overall lower wages and that all workers benefit from union gains, so everyone should be compelled to join.

The 27 right-to-work states are shown in dark blue in Figure 9.5.

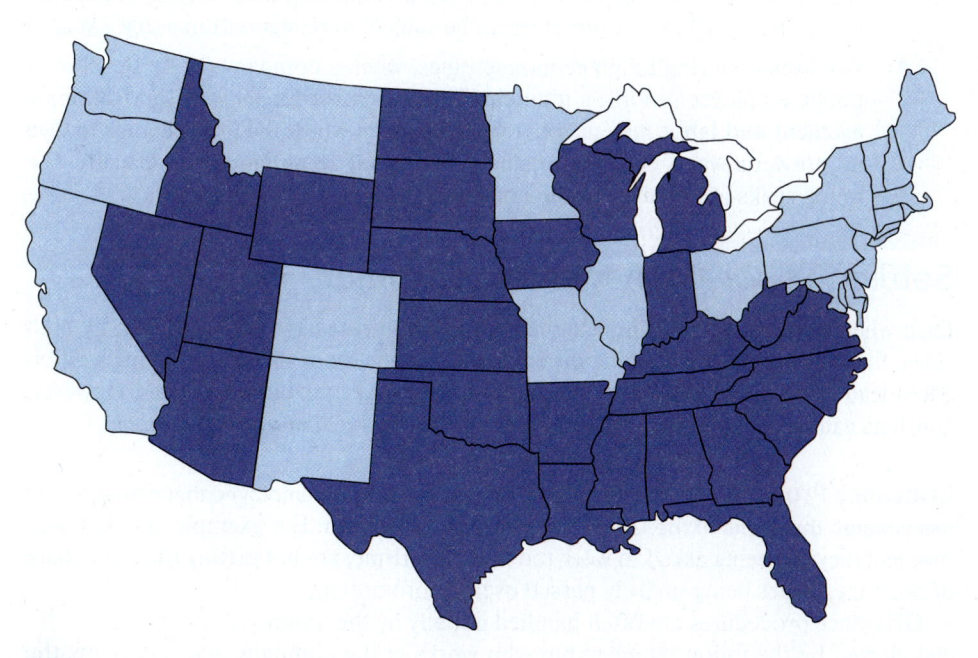

FIGURE 9.5

States with right-to-work laws

What kind of state do you live in? (Alaska and Hawaii are non–right-to-work states.)

- Right-to-work states
- Non–right-to-work states

Compensation: Wage Rates, COLA Clauses, and Givebacks Unions strive to negotiate the highest wage rates possible, or to trade off higher wages for something else, such as better fringe benefits. Some issues involved with compensation are as follows:

- **Wage rates—same pay or different rates?** Wage rates subject to negotiation include overtime pay, different wages for different shifts, and bonuses. In the past, unions tried to negotiate similar wage rates for unionized employees working in similar jobs for similar companies or similar industries. However, the pressure of competition abroad and deregulation at home has forced many unions to negotiate **two-tier wage contracts**, in which new employees are paid less or receive fewer benefits than veteran employees have.

    Such two-tier wage systems can be attractive to employers, who are able to hire new workers at reduced wages, and they also benefit veteran union members, who experience no wage reduction. However, detractors argue that these contracts pit workers in the two tiers against each other and place a target on higher-paid and (often) older workers' backs for disciplinary action and firing.[196] Two-tier wage contracts seem to be losing popularity.[197] Consider these examples:[198]

    Dropping Two-Tier Wage Contracts Example: In 2022, labor unions representing workers at several well-known organizations managed to renegotiate existing contracts. As a result, labor agreements for some unionized employees at Harley-Davidson, Boeing, Caterpillar, and the University of Pennsylvania no longer include two-tier wage systems. Said pro-union writer Jenny Brown, "It's hard to get new workers excited about the union when the contract puts them in a permanent second-class category, whether that be a lower tier of wages, no pension, worse benefits, or no overtime protections."[199]

- **Cost-of-living adjustment.** Because the cost of living is always going up (at least so far), unions often try to negotiate a **cost-of-living adjustment (COLA) clause**, which during the period of the contract ties future wage increases to increases in the cost of living, as measured by the U.S. Bureau of Labor Statistics' consumer price index (CPI). (An alternative is the *wage reopener clause,* which allows wage rates to be renegotiated at certain stated times during the life of the contract. Thus, a 10-year contract might be subject to renegotiation every 2 years.)

- **Givebacks.** During tough economic times, when a company (or, in the case of public employee unions, a municipality) is fighting for its very survival, management and labor may negotiate **givebacks**, in which the union agrees to give up previous wage or benefit gains in return for something else. Usually, the union seeks job security, as in a no-layoff policy.

Settling Labor–Management Disputes

Even when a collective-bargaining agreement and contract have been accepted by both sides, there may likely be ongoing differences that must be resolved. Sometimes differences lead to walkouts and strikes, or management may lock out employees. However, conflicts can be resolved through *grievance procedures, mediation,* or *arbitration.*

Grievance Procedures A **grievance** is a complaint by an employee that management has violated the terms of the labor–management agreement. For example, an employee may feel they are being asked to work too much overtime, are not getting their fair share of overtime, or are being unfairly passed over for promotion.

Grievance procedures are often handled initially by the union's *shop steward,* an official elected by the union membership who works at the company and represents the interests of unionized employees on a daily basis to the employees' immediate supervisors. If this process is not successful, the grievance may be carried to the union's chief shop steward and then to the union's grievance committee, who deal with their counterparts higher up in management.

If the grievance procedure is not successful, the two sides may decide to try to resolve their differences in one of two ways—*mediation* or *arbitration.*

Mediation **Mediation** is the process in which a neutral third party, a mediator, listens to both sides in a dispute, makes suggestions, and encourages them to agree on a solution. Mediators may be lawyers or retired judges or specialists in various fields, such as conflict resolution or labor matters.

Arbitration **Arbitration** is the process in which a neutral third party, an arbitrator, listens to both parties in a dispute and makes a decision that the parties have agreed will be binding on them. Many corporations, new tech start-ups, and some for-profit colleges have vigorously embraced arbitration as a business tool with consumers and employees and students, forbidding them from resolving their complaints through class-action suits (when a large number of plaintiffs with similar complaints band together to sue a company).[200] Critics, however, contend that forcing consumers to sign agreements that require arbitration and prevent lawsuits has the effect of biasing resolutions in favor of business and constitutes a "privatization of the justice system."[201] Until 2022, it was legal for corporations to include forced arbitration clauses for their workers in cases of sexual harassment and sexual assault:

> **Ending Forced Arbitration in Employment Contracts Example:** In 2022, President Biden signed into effect the Ending Forced Arbitration of Sexual Assault and Sexual Harassment Act. The act makes it illegal for employers to force workers to waive their rights to bring legal action against the company in the case of sexual harassment or assault. "Forced arbitration shielded perpetrators and silenced survivors, enabled employers to sweep episodes of sexual assault and harassment under the rug, and kept survivors from knowing if others have experienced the same thing," said Biden.[202] Employers may still offer arbitration as an option in these cases, but workers now have the power to decide how to pursue legal action.

What is your feeling about labor unions? Self-Assessment 9.4 enables you to answer this question by assessing your general attitudes toward unions. ●

SELF-ASSESSMENT 9.4

Assessing Your Attitudes toward Unions

This survey is designed to assess your attitude toward unions. Please complete Self-Assessment 9.4 if your instructor has assigned it in Connect.

9.9 Career Corner: Managing Your Career Readiness

LO 9-9

Review the steps for becoming a better receiver of feedback.

Feedback is essential for success at any endeavor. The problem, however, is that people are not very good at either giving or receiving feedback, even though we continuously engage in these activities. Research has found, for example, that receiving feedback can actually *decrease* individual performance.[203]

It's natural to feel uncomfortable when we receive feedback from others about our shortcomings, as noted by some of the leaders in our Executive Interview Series video for this chapter. But as these leaders also observe, it's vital that we understand both our strengths *and* the areas where we have room to grow. Our focus here is to help you become a better receiver of feedback because it is essential for developing your career readiness.

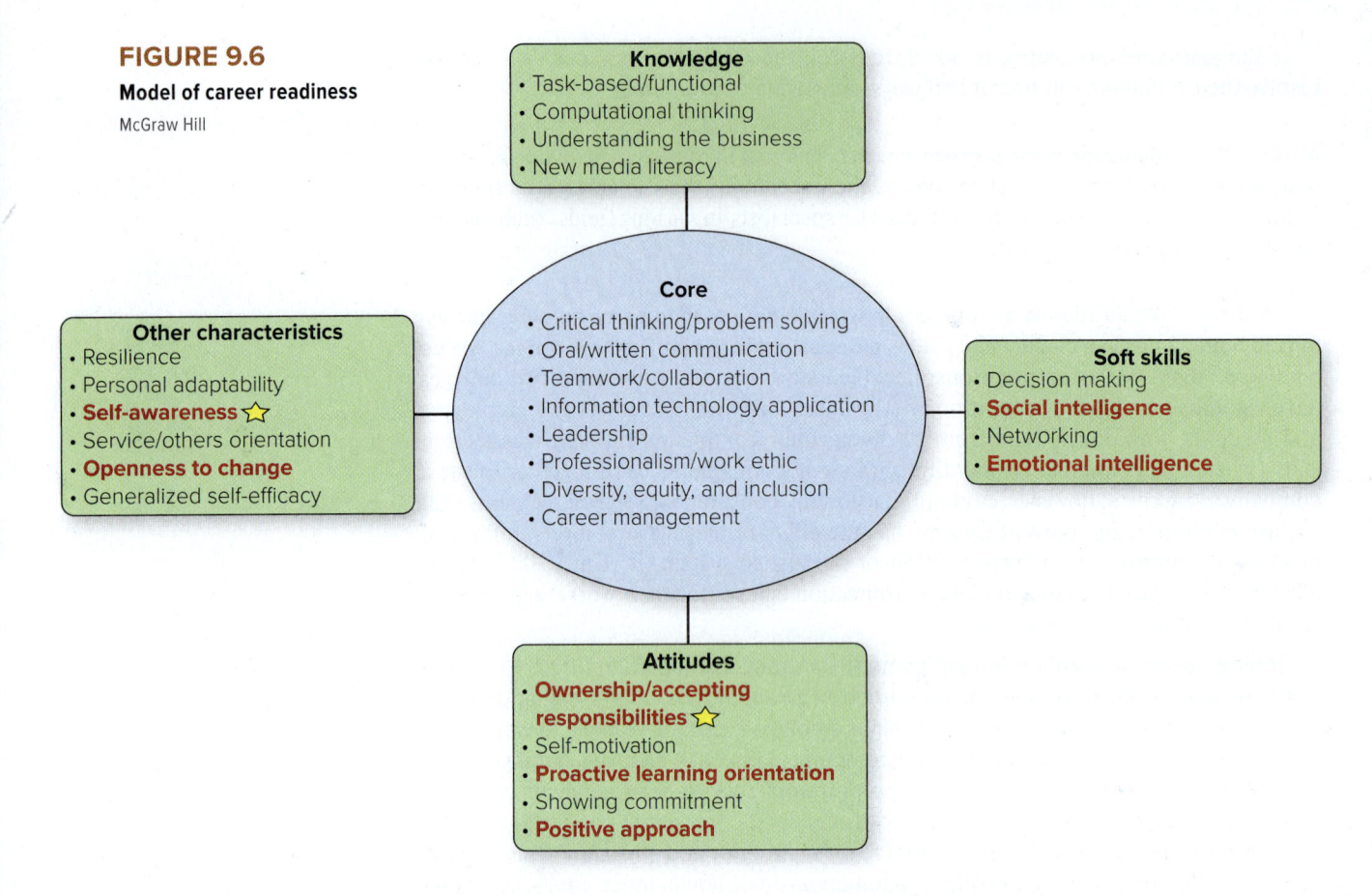

FIGURE 9.6
Model of career readiness
McGraw Hill

Knowledge
- Task-based/functional
- Computational thinking
- Understanding the business
- New media literacy

Core
- Critical thinking/problem solving
- Oral/written communication
- Teamwork/collaboration
- Information technology application
- Leadership
- Professionalism/work ethic
- Diversity, equity, and inclusion
- Career management

Other characteristics
- Resilience
- Personal adaptability
- **Self-awareness** ⭐
- Service/others orientation
- **Openness to change**
- Generalized self-efficacy

Soft skills
- Decision making
- **Social intelligence**
- Networking
- **Emotional intelligence**

Attitudes
- **Ownership/accepting responsibilities** ⭐
- Self-motivation
- **Proactive learning orientation**
- Showing commitment
- **Positive approach**

McGraw Hill connect

Visit your instructor's Connect course and access your eBook to view this video.

Executive Interview Series:
Ownership/Accepting Responsibility and Self-Awareness

Becoming a Better Receiver

Regardless of how feedback is delivered, nothing changes unless the receiver accepts the feedback and decides to do something with it.[204] But becoming a better receiver takes some effort. Our model of career readiness reveals that you need to apply seven competencies: social intelligence, emotional intelligence, ownership/accepting responsibility, proactive learning orientation, positive approach, self-awareness, and openness to change (see Figure 9.6). Use these competencies while putting the following steps into action:

Step 1: Identify Your Tendencies You have received feedback many times during your life and most likely developed patterns of responding. Do you tend to argue? Do you defend yourself and dispute the facts? Do you create a diversion and blame someone else? Do you smile but hide your anger? Do you have a knee-jerk response to reject feedback but then consider its merits at a later point in time? The career readiness competency of taking ownership/accountability reminds us how important it is to take responsibility for our actions. This underscores the value of self-awareness, another career readiness competency, about our typical way of responding to negative feedback.[205]

Step 2: Learn How to Listen The brain's amygdala acts like an alarm bell, signaling "threat" when we receive negative feedback. This, in turn, makes us hyper-vigilant to criticism, makes us defensive, and shuts down our ability to listen.[206] This is unfortunate because listening is essential when receiving negative feedback. NPR correspondent and seasoned journalist Celeste Headlee spends a lot of time listening, often to people she disagrees with. She provides two key pieces of advice that we think are applicable here:[207]

1. **Always assume you have something to learn.** By approaching a conversation this way, especially one in which we are receiving negative feedback, we can allow ourselves to be less defensive and more open to information. This doesn't mean we need to agree with the information—only that we are open to hearing and understanding another person's viewpoint.
2. **Listen with the intent to understand, rather than reply.** We tend to think of how we want to respond to a speaker instead of listening and trying to understand what they are saying. This causes us to miss critical pieces of information.

Once you have listened and fully understand what's been said, then you can focus on determining things such as whether the message is fact or opinion. That your work was poor quality is an opinion. That your report contained five misspelled words is a fact. Distinguishing facts from opinion during an interaction enables you to respond more effectively. Other things to consider are the accuracy of the information and the source's intention. The point is to listen and respond to those whose aim is to help you develop and improve.[208]

Step 3: Try Self-Compassion Instead of Defensiveness

Defensiveness occurs when people perceive they are being attacked or threatened. A neuroscience expert noted the amygdala "accesses emotional memories that identify a given stimulus as potentially threatening and triggers the emotional fear response that sets the fight-or-flight biobehavioral response in motion."[209] This in turn leads to defensive listening and destructive behaviors such as shutting down or being passive-aggressive, standing behind rules or policies, creating a diversion, or counterattacking.

Self-compassion is defined as the tendency to be understanding, kind, and warm toward yourself in the process of pain or failure, instead of being self-critical or over-identifying with negative emotions.[210] Self-compassion is associated with, among many other positive outcomes, less defensiveness in the face of information that presents a threat to your self-concept. Recent studies suggest that self-compassion is also related to amygdala activity and developing more of it has important mental health benefits.[211]

Remember to allow yourself to feel what you are feeling while maintaining your sense of self-worth. When you are ready, it is usually helpful to ask questions regarding the feedback. You may wish to ask for specific examples of the behavior(s) in question to help yourself better contextualize the feedback.[212] Asking questions quiets the amygdala and allows you to gain more insight about the threatening message. Taking a deep breath before responding also helps.

Step 4: Ask for Feedback

Your emotional triggers are less likely to be activated if you seek feedback rather than wait for it to be delivered. Look for opportunities to ask for bite-sized pieces of information about your behavior or performance as you work. Smaller doses are less threatening. A simple way is to ask someone for one thing you did well on a project and one thing that could be improved. Remember that most of us don't receive all of the information we need to improve our performance, and one way to change this is to ask for feedback.[213] Engaging in this behavior is also likely to improve your image because research shows that explicitly seeking performance feedback results in higher performance ratings.[214]

Step 5: Practice Being Mindful

Mindfulness is "the awareness that emerges through paying attention on purpose, in the present moment, and nonjudgmentally to the unfolding of experience moment by moment."[215] Mindfulness builds **psychological capital**—a positive state of psychological development that is characterized by high levels of hope, resiliency, optimism, and self-efficacy—and it can help you to be a better receiver of feedback.[216] We recommend practicing mindfulness when you receive negative feedback. Meditation is a great method for increasing your general level of mindfulness. •

Key Terms Used in This Chapter

360-degree feedback appraisal 327
adverse impact 335
affirmative action 336
arbitration 343
assessment centers 316
base pay 318
behavioral-description interviews 315
behaviorally anchored rating scale (BARS) 326
benefits (or fringe benefits) 319
boomerangs 312
bullying 338
collective bargaining 334
compensation 317
cost-of-living adjustment (COLA) clause 342
defensiveness 345
disparate treatment 336
employee referrals 311
employment at will 332
employment tests 315
Equal Employment Opportunity Commission (EEOC) 335
exit interview 332
external recruiting 311
Fair Labor Standards Act of 1938 (FLSA) 334
forced ranking performance review systems 328
givebacks 342
grievance 342
high-performance work system (HPWS) 309
human capital 307
human resource management (HRM) 304
internal recruiting 310
labor unions 339
legal defensibility 313
mediation 343
National Labor Relations Board (NLRB) 334
nondisparagement agreement 332
objective appraisals 325
onboarding 320
performance appraisal 324
performance improvement plans (PIPs) 331
performance management 323
person–job (P–J) fit 312
psychological capital 345
recruiting 310
reliability 313
right-to-work laws 341
selection 313
self-compassion 345
sexual harassment 337
situational interviews 315
social capital 307
Social Security Act of 1935 334
strategic human resource management 305
structured interview 314
subjective appraisals 326
talent management 308
talent marketplaces 311
transfer 330
two-tier wage contracts 342
union security clause 340
unstructured interviews 314
validity 313
workplace discrimination 335

Key Points

9.1 Strategic Human Resource Management

- Human resource (HR) management is the process of planning for, attracting, developing, and retaining an effective workforce.
- Strategic human resource management (HRM) is the process of designing and implementing systems of policies and practices that align an organization's human capital with its strategic objectives.
- Two concepts important to strategic HRM are (1) human capital and (2) social capital.
- Two strategic HRM approaches are talent management and high-performance work systems.

9.2 Recruitment and Selection: Putting the Right People into the Right Jobs

- Three types of recruiting are: internal, external, and hybrid.
- Three types of selection tools are: background information, interviewing, and employment tests.
- Background information is ascertained through application forms, resumes, and background checks.
- Three forms of interviews are: (1) unstructured, (2) structured situational, and (3) structured behavioral-description.
- Employment tests measure candidates' specific skills, abilities, traits, and other tendencies.

9.3 Managing an Effective Workforce: Compensation and Benefits

- Compensation has three parts: wages or salaries, incentives, and benefits.
- Base pay consists of the basic wage or salary paid to employees in exchange for doing their jobs.
- Incentives include commissions, bonuses, profit-sharing plans, and stock options.
- Benefits are additional nonmonetary compensation, such as health insurance, retirement, and family leave.

9.4 Onboarding and Learning and Development

- Onboarding integrates employees into new jobs and organizations through familiarization with corporate policies, procedures, cultures, and politics and clarification of work-role expectations and responsibilities.
- Learning and development (L&D) fills gaps between what employees know and what they need to know.
- Five steps in L&D are: (1) assessment, (2) objectives, (3) selection, (4) implementation, and (5) evaluation.

9.5 Performance Management

- Performance management consists of four steps: (1) define performance, (2) monitor and evaluate performance, (3) review performance, and (4) provide consequences.
- Performance appraisal consists of (1) assessing an employee's performance and (2) providing them with feedback. Two general types of appraisals are: (1) objective and (2) subjective.
- Performance feedback is one of the most important parts of a manager's job.

9.6 Managing Promotions, Transfers, Disciplining, and Dismissals

- Managers must manage promotions, transfers, disciplining, and dismissals.
- Managers must consider fairness, nondiscrimination, and others employees' resentments when deciding on promotions.
- Transfers may take place in order to solve organizational problems, broaden employees' experience, retain employees' interest and motivation, and solve some employee problems.
- Poorly performing employees may need to be disciplined or demoted.
- Dismissals may consist of layoffs, downsizings, or firings.
- Exit interviews, nondisparagement agreements, and employment at will are considerations in these processes.

9.7 The Legal Requirements of Human Resource Management

- Four areas of employment law that managers need to be aware of are: (1) labor relations, (2) compensation and benefits, (3) health and safety, and (4) equal employment opportunity.
- Labor relations are dictated in part by the National Labor Relations Board, which enforces procedures whereby employees may vote to have a union and for collective bargaining. Collective bargaining consists of negotiations between management and employees about disputes over compensation, benefits, working conditions, and job security.
- Compensation and benefits are covered by the Social Security Act of 1935 and the Fair Labor Standards Act, which established minimum wage and overtime pay regulations.
- Health and safety are covered by the Occupational Safety and Health Act of 1970, among other laws.

9.8 Labor–Management Issues

- Labor unions are formed to protect and advance member employees' interests by bargaining with management over job-related issues.
- Among the issues unions negotiate are the union security clause, which states that workers must join the union or at least pay benefits to it.
- The four types of workplace labor agreements are: (1) closed shop (now illegal), (2) union shop, (3) agency shop, and (4) open shop. Twenty-seven states have right-to-work laws that prohibit employees from being required to join a union as a condition of employment.

9.9 Career Corner: Managing Your Career Readiness

- Becoming a better receiver of feedback requires using seven career readiness competencies: social intelligence, emotional intelligence, ownership/accepting responsibility, proactive learning orientation, positive approach, self-awareness, and openness to change.
- There are five steps to becoming a better receiver of feedback: (1) identify your tendencies, (2) learn how to listen, (3) try self-compassion instead of defensiveness, (4) ask for feedback, and (5) practice being mindful.

10

Organizational Change and Innovation
Lifelong Challenges for the Exceptional Manager

After reading this chapter, you should be able to:

LO 10-1 Discuss what managers should know about organizational change.

LO 10-2 Discuss three forms of change, Lewin's change model, and the systems approach to change.

LO 10-3 Describe the purpose of organizational development.

LO 10-4 Describe the approaches toward innovation and components of an innovation system.

LO 10-5 Discuss ways managers can help employees overcome fear of change.

LO 10-6 Review the different ways to increase the career readiness competency of openness to change.

FORECAST What's Ahead in This Chapter

In this chapter, we consider the nature of change in organizations, including the two types of change—reactive and proactive—and the forces for change originating outside and inside the organization. Next we explore forms and models of change. We then describe organizational development and discuss how to promote innovation within an organization. We describe how you can manage employee fear and resistance to change, and we conclude with a Career Corner that focuses on how to improve the career readiness competency of openness to change.

How Can I Be More Creative at Work?

Creativity Is the Process of Generating Novel Ideas[1]

Do you think of yourself as creative? If you answered no, perhaps you thought the question was about whether you can draw, compose music, design clothes, write poetry, or act in plays. But as creative and rewarding as those endeavors are, they are not the only avenues for creativity. Neuroscience research shows that creative thought engages many different areas of the brain, and that the old right-brain/left-brain theory of the creative process has been a bit overrated.[2] That means we all have the potential to be imaginative, innovative thinkers just by learning to look at things a little differently.

Organizations value creativity. In fact, multiple recent surveys rank creativity as one of the most important soft skills for today's workplace.[3] Here we show you how you can leverage the career readiness competencies of (1) proactive learning orientation, (2) positive approach, and (3) problem solving to build your creative ability.

Proactive Learning Orientation

Preschoolers ask around 100 questions every single day. Sadly, around age seven, kids begin to internalize the fear that asking questions will make them seem incompetent, and by middle school they've been conditioned to ask very few questions.[4] It's no wonder that child development experts believe that humans reach peak creativity by the time we turn six. The good news is you can get back to that childlike state of creativity by simply being intentional about asking lots of questions. Put your proactive learning orientation to work and get into the habit of fearlessly asking questions about how things work or where they come from and why.[5] Your questions don't have to be about academic or work-related subjects, either. Rather, they can relate to anything you're curious about. As long as you're learning new things, you are keeping your creative muscle active.

Positive Approach

Positive feelings like gratitude, hope, and joy can build creative thinking.[6] You can actively cultivate these feelings in several ways. For instance, write down one thing each day that you're grateful for, no matter how small. Elevate your capacity for joy by celebrating often, honoring even small events like a good grade on a test or a completed to-do list. And don't sit still. Among its many health benefits, exercise—even a simple bike ride or outdoor walk—can reinforce positive feelings and cognitive function.[7] Another aspect of a positive approach is willingness to risk failure. "Studies show that you have a greater chance of success if you stick your neck out. Be a creative risk taker, step into the unfamiliar and unpredictable, and stretch beyond customary bounds," says a writer in *Psychology Today*, "Accept failure with open arms, learn from it, and take the perspective that failure happens *for* you, not *to* you."[8] Stretching outside your comfort zone is what creativity is all about.

Problem Solving

Hone your creative problem-solving skills by looking for challenges to practice solving. You don't have to wait for your boss or professor to give you a difficult assignment to get started. Try learning to play chess, for instance. Its reliance on repeated patterns will strengthen your predictive abilities, and research has shown that chess players demonstrate higher than average originality and flexibility of thought.[9] Not a fan of games? Read detective novels by writers like Agatha Christie or Sir Arthur Conan Doyle, still among the most widely read English-language writers of all time, or any of their modern peers. Or you can solve crosswords, sudoku, and other puzzles. All these activities will give your deductive and predictive powers a helpful workout.

For Discussion Which of the recommendations interest you? What specific activities are you willing to commit to in order to increase your creativity?

10.1 The Nature of Change in Organizations

THE BIG PICTURE
Two types of change are reactive and proactive. Forces for change may consist of forces outside the organization—demographic characteristics; technological advancements; shareholder, customer, and broader stakeholder concerns; and social and political pressures. Or they may be forces inside the organization—human resource concerns and managers' behavior.

LO 10-1

Discuss what managers should know about organizational change.

"Companies today compete on their ability to sense and respond to change faster than others," according to the authors of a recent Accenture report.[10] LinkedIn CEO Ryan Roslansky agrees, saying "Whatever your role, whatever your company, whatever your industry, you need to keep up with these really quick and big changes that are going on. And even if you aren't changing your job, your job is most likely changing on you."[11]

Change is all around us, and part of a manager's job is to identify and capitalize on opportunities for change. Managers also need to understand the predominant forces driving change in today's organizations.

Fundamental Change: What Will You Be Called On to Deal With?

"It is hard to predict, especially the future," physicist Niels Bohr is supposed to have quipped. But trends—technological, socioeconomic, consumer attitudes, and others—help managers to make informed decisions about where the business is, or should be, headed. Important supertrends that are shaping the future of business include:[12]

1. The marketplace is becoming more segmented.
2. Competitors offering specialized solutions require us to get our products to market faster.
3. Some companies are unable to survive disruptive innovation.
4. Offshore suppliers are changing the way we work.
5. Knowledge, not information, is becoming the new competitive advantage.
6. The employment landscape is shifting.

1. The Marketplace Is Becoming More Segmented and Moving toward More Niche Products In the recent past, managers could think in terms of mass markets—mass communication, mass behavior, and mass values. Now we have "demassification," with customer groups becoming segmented into smaller and more specialized groups responding to more narrowly targeted commercial messages.

These marketing messages can be shaped and personalized by artificial intelligence (AI) technology, allowing bots, for instance, to engage in conversations with individually targeted consumers or smaller segments of consumers. Companies using customer-centric marketing believe it creates stronger relationships and increases customer loyalty and repeat business.[13]

A recent survey conducted by Salesforce suggests that 66% of today's consumers expect companies to cater to their individual needs with customized products and services.[14] Many cars, shoes, and streaming experiences, for example, can often be fitted to our individual preferences, and technological advancements are making this type of personalization more accessible than ever. Consider the following example:

Marketplace Example—Custom Clothing: Made-to-order clothing has for centuries been a luxury that only the ultra-wealthy could afford. But rising consumer demand for personalization combined with revolutionary technology has made custom attire increasingly affordable and scalable.[15] Suitablee clothing company prides itself on offering "The World's First AI-Generated Suits."[16] Customers simply answer 12 questions on the company's website and then choose from hundreds of available suit cuts and fabric options. Those who'd like additional help can schedule a video call with a suit specialist. Suitablee's "Automatic Sizing" algorithm—based on data collected from thousands of body scans—then gets to work generating a unique suit to fit the customer's body perfectly. The company says the technology is so precise that only about 10% of online customers need even minor alterations to their suits.

2. More Competitors Are Offering Targeted Products, Requiring Faster Speed-to-Market

"A company's ability to produce and deliver more goods in less time and at lower cost is a key competitive advantage," said Accenture's Thomas Rinn.[17] Accenture recently conducted a study of more than 1,000 industrial enterprises, categorizing the firms as either "speedsters" (firms with the highest speed-to-market), "accelerators" (firms ranked in the middle for speed-to-market), or "starters" (firms with the slowest speed-to-market).[18] The study found that speedsters outperformed accelerators and starters in both profitability and revenue growth. What set speedsters apart from their competitors was the adoption of advanced technologies for reducing time and increasing efficiency in all of the processes involved in getting a product to market. Consider the following example:

Nestlé's revitalized approach to innovation has allowed the company to shorten its speed-to-market by 60% in the past decade in order to keep up with changing market demands and consumer tastes. Steve Cukrov/Shutterstock

Speed-to-Market Example—Lithium-Ion Batteries: Electronic vehicles (EV)s are forecasted to account for roughly 60% of global auto sales by the year 2040 (a sharp increase from 10% in 2022).[19] This means that manufacturers of lithium-ion batteries (essential components of most EVs) are facing large-scale changes to their operations as they determine how to keep up with the massive surge in demand.[20] ABB Ltd—a global digital and automation technology company—recently announced the launch of its *Plant Optimization Methodology* to increase speed-to-market for lithium-ion battery manufacturers.[21] ABB will work directly with manufacturers that adopt the methodology, collaborating from the plant design stage through to the end product to streamline processes, reduce time, and increase efficiencies.

3. Some Traditional Companies May Not Survive Radical Change

In *The Innovator's Dilemma: When New Technologies Cause Great Firms to Fail,* Clayton M. Christensen, the late Harvard Business School professor, argued that when successful companies are confronted with a giant technological leap that transforms their markets, all choices are bad ones.

Indeed, he thought, it's very difficult for an existing successful company to take full advantage of a technological breakthrough such as digitalization—what he called disruptive innovation.[22] Some companies that have the resources to survive disruption—to build "the next big thing"—fail to do so—while others are able to pivot successfully. The movie industry is grappling with disruptive innovation, as described in the Example box.

EXAMPLE | Radical Change: Watching Movies

In April 2020, Americans were home isolating from COVID-19, movie theaters were closed to the public, and millions of kids were feeling disappointed that they couldn't watch *Trolls World Tour*. Universal Studios made a bold move and decided to release the movie directly to streaming platforms.

The Big Breakup
Universal charged consumers a $19.99 streaming fee for 48-hour access to the new *Trolls* film. The decision to bypass theaters was unprecedented due to an age-old business model between studios and theaters.[23] Namely, studios produced films, and theaters had exclusive rights to show the films for a set period (usually three months) known as the theatrical window. The two parties divided the proceeds from ticket sales, with each receiving between 40 and 60%.[24]

By week 3 of the experiment, Universal had grossed more from *Trolls World Tour* than it had during the original *Trolls* movie's five-month theatrical run. Universal CEO Jeff Shell said, "The results for 'Trolls World Tour' have exceeded our expectations and demonstrated the viability of PVOD [premium video on demand]. As soon as theatres reopen, we expect to release movies on both formats."[25] AMC president and CEO Adam Aron responded that AMC would no longer show Universal films in its theaters if the studio went through with the proposal.[26]

Studios Tried to Gain Independence from Theaters
Movie studios questioned whether they could be equally—or even more—viable, if they released films directly to consumers. After all, a studio could potentially reduce costs by up to 50% if it cut out theaters and adopted a direct-to-consumer model.[27]

Studios experimented with different release strategies between 2020 and 2022. Some bypassed theaters and went directly to streaming platforms, while others tested smaller-scale releases. Universal and Paramount negotiated shorter theatrical windows, and in December of 2020, Warner Bros. stated its entire slate of 2021 films would release in theaters and on streaming platforms simultaneously.[28]

Theaters Found Novel Ways to Attract Customers
Meanwhile, major chains including AMC, Cinemark, and Regal fought to get moviegoers back. All three introduced private auditorium rentals. Theaters live-streamed concerts and sporting events and experimented with variable pricing models.[29] AMC launched a $25 million ad campaign featuring Nicole Kidman and invested $250 million into replacing digital projectors with laser technology. AMC also partnered with Zoom and plans to host corporate audiences for professional meetings, with theater screens acting as giant videoconference displays.[30]

Smaller chains updated seats, speakers, projectors, and other equipment and found creative ways to attract customers. Warehouse Cinemas pushed experiences, offering father–daughter date nights and themed viewings. Customers who purchased a ticket to the thriller *Unhinged* got to (1) contribute to a local auto charity, and (2) beat up an old vehicle as part of Warehouse's "car smash" event.[31]

Do We Have a Winner?
For studios, bypassing theaters wasn't the revolution they might have expected. It turns out studios reach a much wider audience when they start with a theatrical release. Said one industry analyst, "There is no better buzz-building platform than a movie theater release, ... within the unlimited bandwidth of the streaming ecosystem, even big budget star-driven movies can get lost in that massive sea of content."[32] Paramount, 20th Century Studios, and Universal all saw 2022 theatrical releases turn into some of their highest-grossing movies in their history.[33]

For movie theaters, ticket sales haven't returned to pre-pandemic levels, but the numbers are steadily rising.[34] In more good news for theaters, both Amazon and Apple recently announced they would make $1 billion dollar annual investments into films targeted for theatrical release.[35]

In the end, neither studios nor theaters triumphed. The pandemic fueled new possibilities for streaming but didn't kill the theater business. Instead, both sides adapted and changed to make things work in a new way.

YOUR CALL
Do you think streaming services are making the right call in returning to theatrical releases? How should theaters respond if they want to continue to survive in an increasingly streaming world?

4. Offshore Suppliers Are Changing the Way We Work As we said in Chapter 2, globalization and outsourcing are transforming whole industries and changing the way we work. In many cases, U.S. businesses realize substantial savings by sourcing labor from other countries. Further, the offshoring of basic functions allows workers in core jobs to focus on complex tasks.[36]

In other cases, U.S. businesses use offshoring to fill core positions. The offshoring of core job functions has become increasingly common due to technological advancements that make it easier for organizations to access global talent pools and manage dispersed, highly skilled workforces.[37] Consider the following example:

Offshore Suppliers Example—Uruguay: Did you know that Uruguay is one of the largest software exporters per-capita in the world? It has been called the "Silicon Valley of South America," and cities like Montevideo, Uruguay's capital, are brimming with IT entrepreneurs and tech start-ups. The right combination of talent, infrastructure, and incentives makes the country an ideal choice for companies looking to outsource specialized IT functions. U.S.-based tech giants including Microsoft and IBM offshore software development functions to Uruguay.[38] U.S. businesses also benefit from Uruguay's physical and time-zone proximity.[39]

5. Knowledge, Not Information, Is Becoming the New Competitive Advantage

In 2012, an Intel white paper predicted that "a technological change tsunami is rolling towards us that will wash away many previous perceptions of the world. The way we work will be swept into this new reality, and the knowledge worker is positioned to be the primary agent of change."[40] Was this prediction about the importance of knowledge workers accurate? Indeed, Gartner research shows that knowledge workers comprised over 70% of the U.S. workforce in 2023.[41] Two key points about knowledge work to consider:

- **The definition of knowledge work has changed.** As information technology does more of the work formerly done by humans, even in high-tech areas (e.g., sorting data for relevance), many employees previously thought of as knowledge workers are now recognized as "data workers," who contribute little added value to information processing. Unlike routine information handling, knowledge work is analytic and consists of problem solving and abstract reasoning—the kind of tasks required of skillful managers, professionals, salespeople, and financial analysts.

- **AI has not replaced knowledge workers.** The rise of knowledge workers is accelerating despite the proliferation of automation.[42] Indeed, the number of people in knowledge-work jobs—nonroutine cognitive occupations—now exceeds 1 billion across the globe.[43] Rather than eliminate knowledge work, AI can empower knowledge workers to do their jobs better than they ever could without it.[44]

In industries where companies are struggling to fill positions or compete with foreign manufacturers or bigger rivals that outsource their labor, AI has the potential to save jobs by increasing knowledge workers' productivity and opportunities to make strategic contributions. AI can also decrease stress and burnout for overloaded workers. Consider the example of how AI is helping to ensure healthcare workers can focus on what matters most.

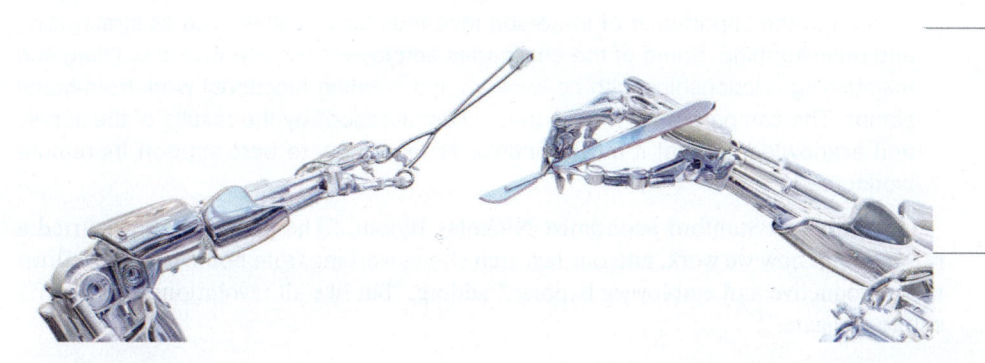

The use of AI in robotic surgery can lead to safer procedures and better patient outcomes. Would you be comfortable being operated on in this manner?
Corona Borealis Studio/Shutterstock

How AI Can Assist Knowledge Workers Example—Robotic Surgery: Robotic technology has revolutionized surgical procedures across a variety of specialties. The use of robotic arms controlled by skilled surgeons has resulted in shorter hospital stays, fewer infections, less pain, and overall improved patient outcomes. Now, healthcare technology is embracing the addition of AI to robotic surgery procedures. One major benefit of AI for knowledge workers such as surgeons is that its vast data processing capabilities free up cognitive space for workers to focus on the most critical aspects of their jobs. AI technology in surgery may be used to detect and alert medical staff to problems at record speed, potentially saving lives, preventing serious complications, and making it possible for surgeons to work more efficiently and effectively.[45]

6. The Employment Landscape Is Shifting, Affecting Both Companies and Workers

An increasing number of jobs can now be done remotely, and workers' preference for remote work is continuing to grow. Many experts predicted the remote work boom of the pandemic would die off but that doesn't seem to be the case.[46] According to Aaron Terrazas, the chief economist for Glassdoor, "This is going to be an enduring feature of the employment landscape."[47]

This remote work revolution has changed the psychological contract between employers and employees, as discussed in Chapter 1. Specifically, employees have a new set of expectations for how, when, and where they want to accomplish their jobs, and employers must adapt to a new set of rules for sourcing and managing employees.

- **Employee implications.** In most organizations prior to 2020, employers expected workers to spend at least 80% of their work time in the office. But according to a recent McKinsey survey, the majority of companies are now offering hybrid work in some capacity.[48] "People really, really want remote work," said Julia Pollak, ZipRecruiter's chief economist. Gallup data predicts that nearly 75% of workers who can do their jobs remotely will eventually be working remotely either partially or fully.[49]

- **Employer implications.** Experts believe offering remote work options will be critical for recruiting and retaining employees going forward.[50] This presents both challenges and opportunities for employers. Challenges include retrofitting jobs to align with a remote atmosphere and adopting the technology necessary for supporting a remote workforce. Employers also have to determine how to best incentivize remote employees or risk losing top talent. Opportunities include access to a global talent pool.[51]

Shifting Employment Landscape Example—Dropbox: In 2021, Dropbox moved to a "virtual first" work model that allows employees to spend least 90% of their working time in remote locations. The company recently surveyed its employees about the arrangement. Ninety-three percent of Dropbox workers believe they are able to do their jobs effectively in this remote format, and nearly 50% think that in-person team collaboration is only necessary four times per year. Dropbox employees pointed to the importance of in-person meetings for activities such as strategizing and brainstorming. Some of the challenges employees reported were building and maintaining relationships with co-workers and creating functional work-from-home setups. The company says it is "extremely encouraged" by the results of the survey and acknowledges that it must continue to learn how to best support its remote workforce.[52]

According to Stanford economist Nicholas Bloom, "The pandemic has started a revolution in how we work, and our research shows working from home can make firms more productive and employees happier," adding, "but like all revolutions, this is difficult to navigate."[53]

Two Types of Change: Reactive and Proactive

Most CEOs, general managers, and senior public-sector leaders agree that incremental changes are no longer sufficient in a world that is operating in fundamentally different ways. Life in general is becoming more complex, and firms able to manage that complexity are the ones that will survive in the long term.[54] We are all in for an interesting ride.

As a manager, you will have to deal with two types of change: *reactive* and *proactive*.

1. Reactive Change: Responding to Unanticipated Problems and Opportunities

When managers talk about "putting out fires," they are talking about **reactive change**, making changes in response to problems or opportunities as they arise. Reactive change often occurs in response to government mandates or incentives that impact the demand for various goods. Consider the following example:

Reactive Change Example—Solar Power: The U.S. Congress passed the Inflation Reduction Act (IRA) in August of 2022, and by December of that year, domestic solar manufacturers had already announced plans to build 17 new large-scale facilities. This change represented a reaction to the IRA's hefty incentives for both manufacturers and consumers of solar power in the United States. By early 2023, some solar panel manufacturers were already sold out for more than two years and were scrambling to increase their production capacity to keep up with the impending surge in demand.[55]

2. Proactive Change: Managing Anticipated Problems and Opportunities

In contrast to reactive change, **proactive change**, or planned change, involves making carefully thought-out changes in anticipation of possible or expected problems or opportunities.[56] The anticipation of increased automation has spurred proactive changes in the technology sector. Consider the example of Microsoft.

Proactive Change Example—Microsoft: For years, analysts have written Microsoft off as a tech dinosaur that reached its peak with its Windows operating system. One writer described the company as "utterly incapable of innovation," adding that Microsoft's culture had become bureaucratic, sterile, and stifling—the opposite of what was needed to attract top tech workers.[57] Microsoft changed the conversation in early 2023 with the release of an AI chatbot—powered by ChatGPT technology—in its Bing search engine. Microsoft had actually begun pouring billions into ChatGPT developer OpenAI in 2019, and the investment seems to have paid off. A recent article in the *Harvard Business Review* described the "cultural shift" at Microsoft in recent years, credited in large part to CEO Satya Nadella, that has enabled the company to "stop playing defense and go on offense."[58]

As we've stated, change can be hard, and the tools for survival include the career readiness competencies of personal adaptability and openness to change. We also know that organizations like to hire people who are adaptable and willing to accept change. How well do you think you fare in this regard? You can find out by taking Self-Assessment 10.1 in Connect, if your instructor has assigned it.

SELF-ASSESSMENT 10.1 CAREER READINESS

Assessing Your Openness to Change at Work

This survey was designed to assess your attitudes toward change at work. Please complete Self-Assessment 10.1 if your instructor has assigned it in Connect.

The Forces for Change Outside and Inside the Organization

How do managers know when their organizations need to change? The answers aren't clear-cut, but you can get clues by monitoring the forces for change—both outside and inside the organization (see Figure 10.1).

Forces Originating Outside the Organization External forces consist of four types, as follows.

1. Demographic Characteristics In Chapter 1 we discussed demographic changes among U.S. workers that are making the labor force more diverse. For example, the number of young Americans aged 18 to 29 living with their parent(s) (rather than in a household shared with a spouse or partner) has grown substantially in the past two decades (from 38% in 2000 to 50% in 2022).[59] Younger generations also are waiting longer to hit other life milestones including homeownership and marriage.[60] On the flip side, consider how the aging Baby Boomer population is impacting business decisions:

> **Demographic Characteristics as a Force for Change Example—Rendever:** Rendever tech start-up describes its offerings as "virtual reality for seniors."[61] The company is the result of work done at MIT and at the American Association of Retired Persons (AARP) Innovation Lab.[62] Rendever's VR technology provides a host of programming to help older adults, particularly those living in group healthcare settings, to have

FIGURE 10.1
Forces for change outside and inside the organization

Outside Forces

Demographic characteristics
- Age
- Education
- Skill level
- Gender
- Immigration

Technological advancements
- Manufacturing automation
- Information technology

Shareholder, customer & broader stakeholder concerns
- Changing customer preferences
- Domestic & international competition
- Mergers & acquisitions

Social & political pressures
- War
- Values
- Leadership

Inside Forces

Human resource concerns
- Unmet needs
- Job dissatisfaction
- Absenteeism & turnover
- Productivity
- Participation/suggestions

Managers' behavior
- Conflict
- Leadership
- Reward systems
- Structural reorganization

THE NEED FOR CHANGE

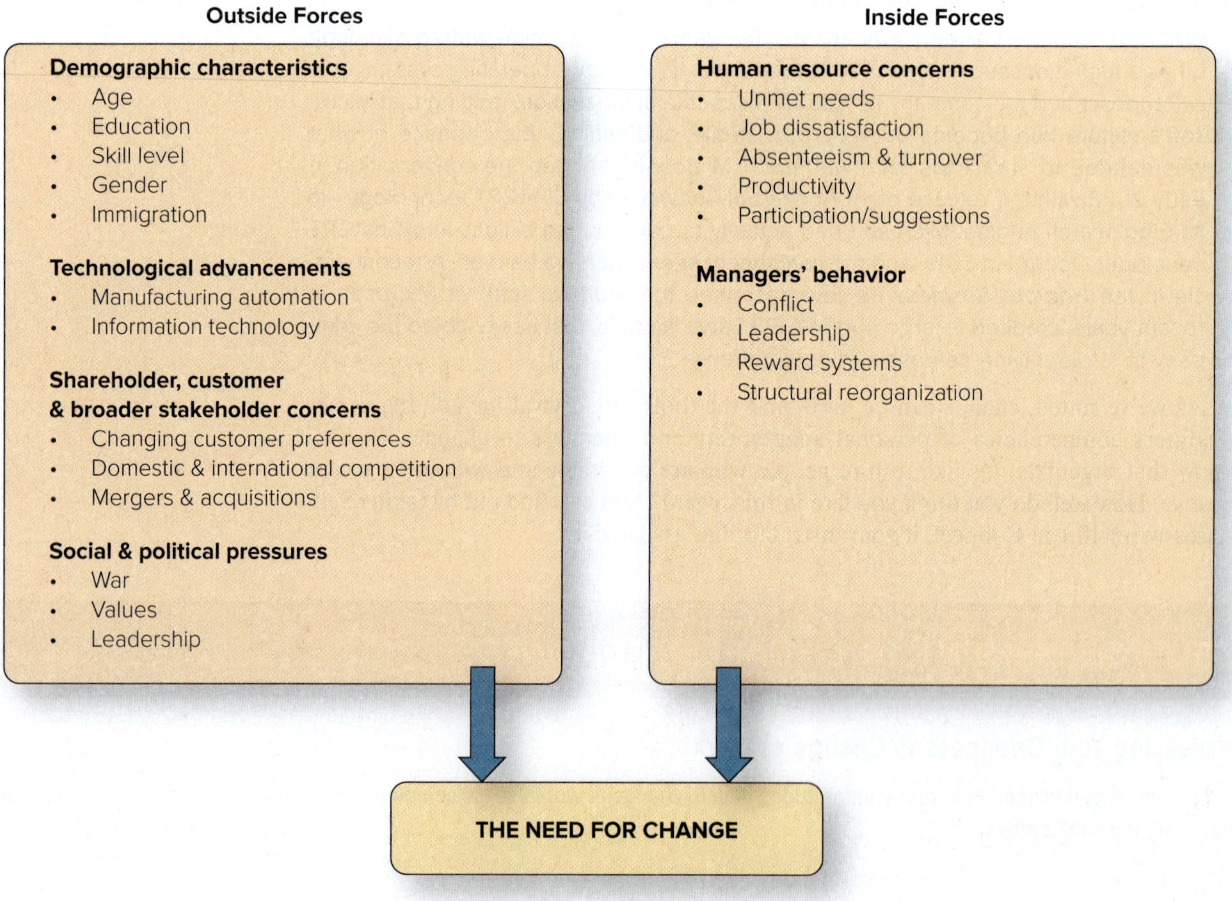

fulfilling and meaningful experiences every day. For example, families can customize experiences that take older adults to their childhood schools, first homes, and wedding venues, and Rendever offers an array of programs that allow older adults to travel (virtually) to places they've always wanted to visit. The technology also aims to ease the substantial burden that healthcare workers face in living facilities for older adults.[63]

2. Technological Advancements **Technology** is not just computer technology; it is any machine or process that enables an organization to gain a competitive advantage in changing materials used to produce a finished product. Ginni Rometty, former CEO of IBM, said that she expects technologies such as AI to change "100 percent of jobs" by 2030.[64] Technology clearly represents a powerful force for change in organizations.

One industry in which technology has led to widespread changes is winemaking. Consider this example:

Technological Advancements as a Force for Change Example—Winemaking Industry: Some winemakers now use drones equipped with infrared cameras to pinpoint irrigation needs, damage, and diseases in their vineyards. At Gamble Family Vineyards in Napa Valley, CA, drones regularly capture key agricultural data.[65] In 2023, researchers at Cornell deployed robots (called PhytoPatholoBots or PPBs) to four different U.S.-based grape breeding programs.[66] The robots stroll up and down the rows of grapes collecting real-time agricultural data to help farmers adjust fertilizing, watering, and pesticide strategies. Recent industry trade shows saw an influx of AI technology designed to help retailers and consumers choose wines.[67]

3. Shareholder, Customer, and Broader Stakeholder Concerns A firm's shareholders, customers, and broader stakeholders (discussed in detail in Chapter 3) can all exert significant pressure for change. As you learned in Learning Module 1, in recent years, much of this pressure has centered on shifting perspectives about the purpose of a corporation and whether a firm's obligations go beyond shareholder wealth creation to include shared value and sustainable development.[68]

- *Shareholders* have begun to be more active in pressing for organizational change. Some shareholders may form a B corporation, or benefit corporation, in which the company is legally required to adhere to socially beneficial practices, such as helping consumers, employees, or the environment. Among the leading B Corps in the United States are Patagonia, Allbirds, Bombas, and Uncommon Goods.[69] Shareholders in the oil and gas industry have recently called for their firms to do more to tackle climate change:

Shareholder Concerns as a Force for Change Example—Oil and Gas: Shareholders at major oil and gas companies have demanded more action on climate change at recent investor meetings. The *Follow This* activist group is one example of this. The group consists of powerful industry shareholders who own trillions of dollars in oil and gas stocks. Mark van Baal said he founded the group after coming to the conclusion that shareholders were the only group powerful enough to convince these companies to take bigger steps in climate action.[70] *Follow This* uses the financial power behind its shareholders to get resolutions on the table at the annual shareholder meetings of some of the biggest oil and gas companies in the world. The group recently filed resolutions asking Chevron, BP, Shell, and Exxon

Drones, such as this one pictured over a vineyard, can gather agricultural information with incredible speed. This technological advancement has enabled some winemakers to visually inspect their vineyards for diseases and other issues at a rate of up to an acre per minute. How many human workers do you think it would take to perform the same task in the same amount of time? freeprod/123RF

Mobil to take specific emissions-reduction measures by 2030. The investors co-sponsoring the resolutions represent more than $1.3 trillion in investments.[71]

- *Customers* are also becoming more demanding. As discussed in previous chapters, younger generations are more inclined to buy from a company if it is genuinely connected to a meaningful cause.

    Customer Concerns as a Force for Change Example—Gen Z: Members of Gen Z may not have the buying power of Millennials or Gen Xers, but they have made it known that they are not afraid to use their voices to demand more from corporations. Global research shows that 70% of Gen Zers are politically and/or socially active in some form. Further, members of this generation are more likely than any other to boycott companies, locations, products, and services due to these types of concerns.[72] It seems this generation's penchant for activism is impacting older generations, also, with data suggesting 35% to 50% of people 42 years and older believe that Gen Z influences their own activism.

- *Broader stakeholders'* needs are becoming increasingly important for many corporations. The model of creating shared value (CSV) we presented in Learning Module 1 demonstrates how firms can simultaneously tackle global social issues and maximize shareholder wealth. Research suggests consumers may form deeper connections with brands that they perceive as creating shared value.[73]

    Broader Stakeholder Concerns as a Force for Change Example—To The Market: Jane Mosbacher Morris founded To The Market to connect corporations and consumers with more ethical and sustainable supply chains. Specifically, companies such as Target and Bloomingdale's partner with Mosbacher Morris's company to source accessories, home goods, and apparel made by members of vulnerable and underrepresented communities.[74] During 2022, the company estimates that its work with strategic partners using organic and/or recycled cotton saved the equivalent of over 6 million days' worth of drinking water, 98,000 kilometers of driving emissions, and 9 million hours of LED bulb energy.[75]

4. Social and Political Pressures Social events can create great pressures on companies to consider change. Take the example of soda taxes.

Social and Political Pressures as a Force for Change Example—Soda Taxes: Poor diet choices, including overconsumption of sugary sodas, have led to more than 42% of U.S. adults and almost 20% of children from ages 2 to 19 being obese, which in turn has contributed to an epidemic of type 2 diabetes.[76] Several big U.S. cities, including Philadelphia, Boulder, San Francisco, Seattle, and Berkeley, have already passed special taxes on soda, often against well-funded opposition from soda companies.[77] Recent data found a 34% reduction in sugary drink consumption in San Francisco since a soda tax was implemented there. The data also showed a 13% reduction in the probability that a consumer would ingest more than 6 oz of sugary beverages in a single day.[78]

Forces Originating Inside the Organization Internal forces affecting organizations may be subtle, such as low job satisfaction, or more dramatic, such as constant labor-management conflict. Internal forces are of two types: *human resource concerns* and *managers' behavior.*

1. Human Resource Concerns Is there a gap between employees' needs and desires and the organization's needs and desires? Job dissatisfaction—as expressed through high absenteeism and turnover—can be a major signal of the need for change. Recall from Chapter 9 that as the firm's strategy evolves, a strategic HRM perspective suggests the need to evaluate existing human and social capital and the HR practices being used to generate them. The right HR practices are the ones that generate the social processes and behaviors the organization needs to accomplish its goals.

Human Resource Concerns as a Force for Change Example—Labor Strikes: One way employees express their dissatisfaction in order to effect change is through labor strikes. In 2022, approximately 224,000 workers went on strike—an increase of 60% over 2021.[79] They included workers in education, manufacturing, health care, and retail. Recent labor strikes seem to be, in part, a reaction to the sharp rise in inflation and its erosion of workers' purchasing power.[80]

2. Managers' Behavior Excessive conflict between managers and employees or between a company and its customers is another indicator that change is needed. Perhaps there is a personality conflict, so that an employee transfer may be needed. Or perhaps some interpersonal training is required. Behavior issues often persist until stakeholders—be they employees, customers, or society at large—decide that enough is enough. Consider the example of Twitter.

Managers' Behavior as a Force for Change Example—Elon Musk: Elon Musk took over Twitter in October of 2022. Within one month he had slashed the company's workforce by about 50%. To add insult to injury, Musk e-mailed a Google form to the company's remaining employees asking them to either reply "yes" to staying on with the company, which he called "Twitter 2.0," or otherwise leave with a severance package. His e-mail clarified that anyone wishing to remain would have to be "extremely hardcore" in their work in order to be considered a valuable performer. As a result, hundreds of Twitter employees resigned.[81]

10.2 Forms and Models of Change

THE BIG PICTURE
This section discusses the three forms of change, from least threatening to most threatening: adaptive, innovative, and radically innovative. It also describes Lewin's three-stage change model: unfreezing, changing, and refreezing. Finally, it describes the systems approach to change: inputs, target elements of change, and outputs.

As we mentioned in Section 10.1, change may be forced upon an organization—reactive change, requiring managers to make adjustments in response to problems or opportunities as they arise. Change can also be proactive or planned, such as when an organization tries to get out in front of impending demands. Being proactive involves making carefully thought-out changes in anticipation of possible problems or opportunities.

Managers should rely on established science in order to effectively manage and implement proactive organizational change. This requires an understanding of the different forms of change, as well as two different models that can be applied systematically to the change process (all of which are discussed in this section).

LO 10-2

Discuss three forms of change, Lewin's change model, and the systems approach to change.

Three Forms of Change: From Least Threatening to Most Threatening

Organizational change can be classified as *adaptive, innovative,* or *radically innovative,* depending on (1) the degree of complexity, cost, and uncertainty; and (2) its potential for generating employee resistance.[82]

Least Threatening: Adaptive Change—"We've Seen Stuff Like This Before"

Adaptive change is the reintroduction of a familiar practice—the implementation of a form of change that has already been experienced within the same organization. Of the three forms of change discussed in this section, adaptive change is the:

- **Easiest to implement successfully.** This form of change is lowest in complexity, cost, and uncertainty.
- **Least threatening to employees.** Because it is familiar, adaptive change is likely to create the least resistance.

Adaptive change is fairly common and often arises due to predictable, seasonal fluctuations in demand. Two hypothetical examples are:

Adaptive Change Examples: During finals week at universities around the world, libraries and other study spaces extend their operating hours, and campus coffee shops and restaurants plan for a sharp increase in demand. During tax-preparation season in the United States, a store's accounting department may require an increase in work hours, and tax preparation service pop-up booths appear in major retailers like Walmart.

Somewhat Threatening: Innovative Change—"This Is Something New for This Company"

Innovative change is the introduction of a practice that is new to the organization. Innovative change is:

- **Moderately difficult to implement.** This form of change is characterized by moderate complexity, cost, and uncertainty.
- **Somewhat threatening to employees.** Because it is less familiar than adaptive change, innovative change is apt to trigger some fear and resistance among employees.

Innovative changes may arise when an organization adopts a policy or practice that other organizations have embraced, but that is new for the firm.

Innovative Change Example: If a department store decides to adopt a new practice among its competitors by staying open 24 hours a day, requiring employees to work flexible schedules, it may be felt as moderately threatening. The overwhelming shift of Black Friday sales to e-commerce platforms has allowed many retailers to give their employees a two-day holiday on Thanksgiving day and the day after.[83]

Very Threatening: Radically Innovative Change—"This Is a Brand-New Thing in Our Industry"

Radically innovative change introduces a practice that is new to the industry. Radically innovative change is:

- **Very difficult to implement.** It is the most complex, costly, and uncertain form of change.
- **Highly threatening to employees.** It will be felt as extremely threatening to managers' confidence and employees' job security and may well tear at the fabric of the organization.[84]

Radically Innovative Change Example: Companies all over the world were forced to shift their workforces to remote work during the COVID-19 pandemic. These companies felt the strain of radically innovative change in the years that followed, when many employees realized they had the negotiating power to insist on maintaining a remote or hybrid schedule. Companies have had to learn to manage, monitor, and motivate employees in a completely new way, and this endeavor has proven highly complex and challenging.[85]

Lewin's Change Model: Unfreezing, Changing, and Refreezing

Most theories of organizational change originated with the landmark work of social psychologist Kurt Lewin. Lewin developed a model with three stages—*unfreezing, changing,* and *refreezing*—to explain how to initiate, manage, and stabilize planned change.[86] (See Figure 10.2.) Throughout this section, we illustrate Lewin's model of change with the example of how Diligent Robotics successfully introduces robots into hospitals.

1. **"Unfreezing": Creating the Motivation to Change** In the unfreezing stage, managers try to instill in employees the motivation to change, encouraging them to let go of attitudes and behaviors that are resistant to innovation. For this "unfreezing" to take place, employees need to become dissatisfied with the old way of doing things. Managers also need to reduce the barriers to change during this stage.

> **Unfreezing Example—Diligent Robotics:** Moxi healthcare robots—autonomous devices designed to fetch medications from hospital pharmacies, run various errands, and deliver specimens to laboratories—are currently being tested in a number of hospitals around the United States.[87] The robots are designed to unburden nurses, who currently spend up to 30% of their time on tasks that don't include patient interaction. How does the Diligent Robotics company manage the unfreezing stage and convince hospital administrators to adopt the change? CEO Andrea Thomaz says that "Hospitals are naturally risk-averse, and can be wary to take up new technology," adding that the company uses a gentle and slow approach when convincing hospitals that the time and financial investment will be worthwhile.[88]

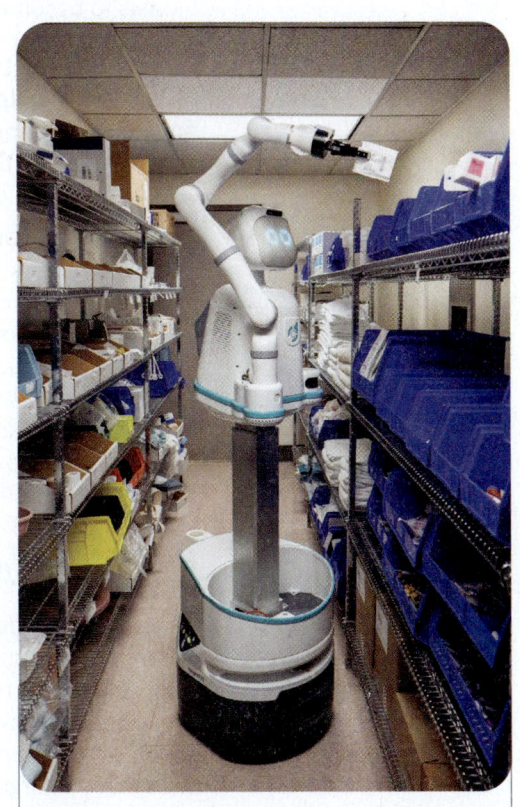

2. **"Changing": Learning New Ways of Doing Things** In the changing stage, employees need to be given the tools for change: new information, new perspectives, new models of behavior. Managers can help here by providing benchmarking results, role models, mentors, experts, and training. Change is more likely

Here, a Moxi robot fetches prescriptions in a hospital, freeing up nurses to spend more time caring for their patients and for themselves. Do you think you'd like to work alongside one of these robots? ZUMA Press, Inc./Alamy Stock Photo

FIGURE 10.2
Lewin's model of change

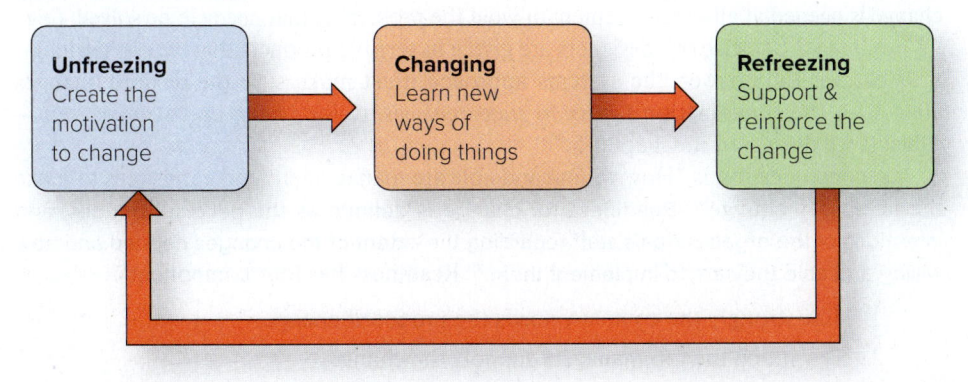

Unfreezing Create the motivation to change → **Changing** Learn new ways of doing things → **Refreezing** Support & reinforce the change

to be accepted if employees possess the career readiness competencies of proactive learning orientation and openness to change.[89]

Changing Example—Diligent Robotics: In the changing stage, Diligent Robotics works closely with member hospitals to acclimate staff to the technology.[90] The company generates revenue through its ongoing subscription model that provides hospitals with continued maintenance and support for as long as they employ the technology. Hospitals begin by using the robots for single tasks, such as delivery and pickup of lab specimens, and sequentially introduce new tasks to new departments over time. Administrators at Deaconess hospital in Spokane, WA said that employees learned to use Moxi robots in about 15 minutes, but that it planned several weeks for units to become familiar with the devices.[91]

3. "Refreezing": Making the New Ways Normal In the refreezing stage, employees need to be helped to integrate the changed attitudes and behavior into their normal ways of doing things. Managers can assist by encouraging employees to exhibit the new change and then, through additional coaching and modeling, by reinforcing the employees in the desired change, as we'll discuss in Section 10.5.

Refreezing Example—Diligent Robotics: In the refreezing stage, hospital employees who work with Moxi robots have, according to one report, wholeheartedly embraced the change.[92] A Moxi robot completed 24 tasks in its first 120 minutes of work at one hospital, much to the delight of the administrators who green-lighted the initiative. Said medical surgical nurse Dana Oswald, "It's just there to assist so we can spend more time with our patients, and we're not running around doing errands and tasks that take us away." Oswald added, "That means higher-quality care. We're devoting more time to assessing patients and making sure all their needs are met."[93]

A Systems Approach to Change

Change creates additional change—that's the lesson of systems theory. Promoting someone from one group to another, for instance, may change the employee interactions in both. Adopting a team-based structure may require changing the compensation system to pay bonuses based on team rather than individual performance. A *systems approach* to change presupposes that any change, no matter how small, has a rippling effect throughout an organization.[94]

- A *system,* you'll recall from Chapter 2, is a set of interrelated parts that operate together to achieve a common purpose. The systems approach can be used to diagnose what to change and determine the success of the change effort.

- The systems model of change consists of three parts: (1) *inputs,* (2) *target elements of change,* and (3) *outputs* (see Figure 10.3).

Inputs: "Why Should We Change, and How Willing and Able Are We to Change?" "Why change?" A systems approach always begins with the question of why change is needed at all—an assessment of what the problem is that needs to be solved. (e.g., "Why change? Because our designers are giving us terrible products that we can't sell.")

Whatever the answer, the systems approach must make sure the desired changes align with the organization's *mission statement, vision statement,* and *strategic plan*—subjects we discussed in Chapter 5.[95]

A second question is "How willing and able are management and employees to make the necessary change?" **Readiness for change** is defined as the beliefs, attitudes, and intentions of the organization's staff regarding the extent of the changes needed and how willing and able they are to implement them.[96] Readiness has four components:

1. How strongly the company needs the proposed change.

2. How much the top managers support the change.

FIGURE 10.3
Systems model of change

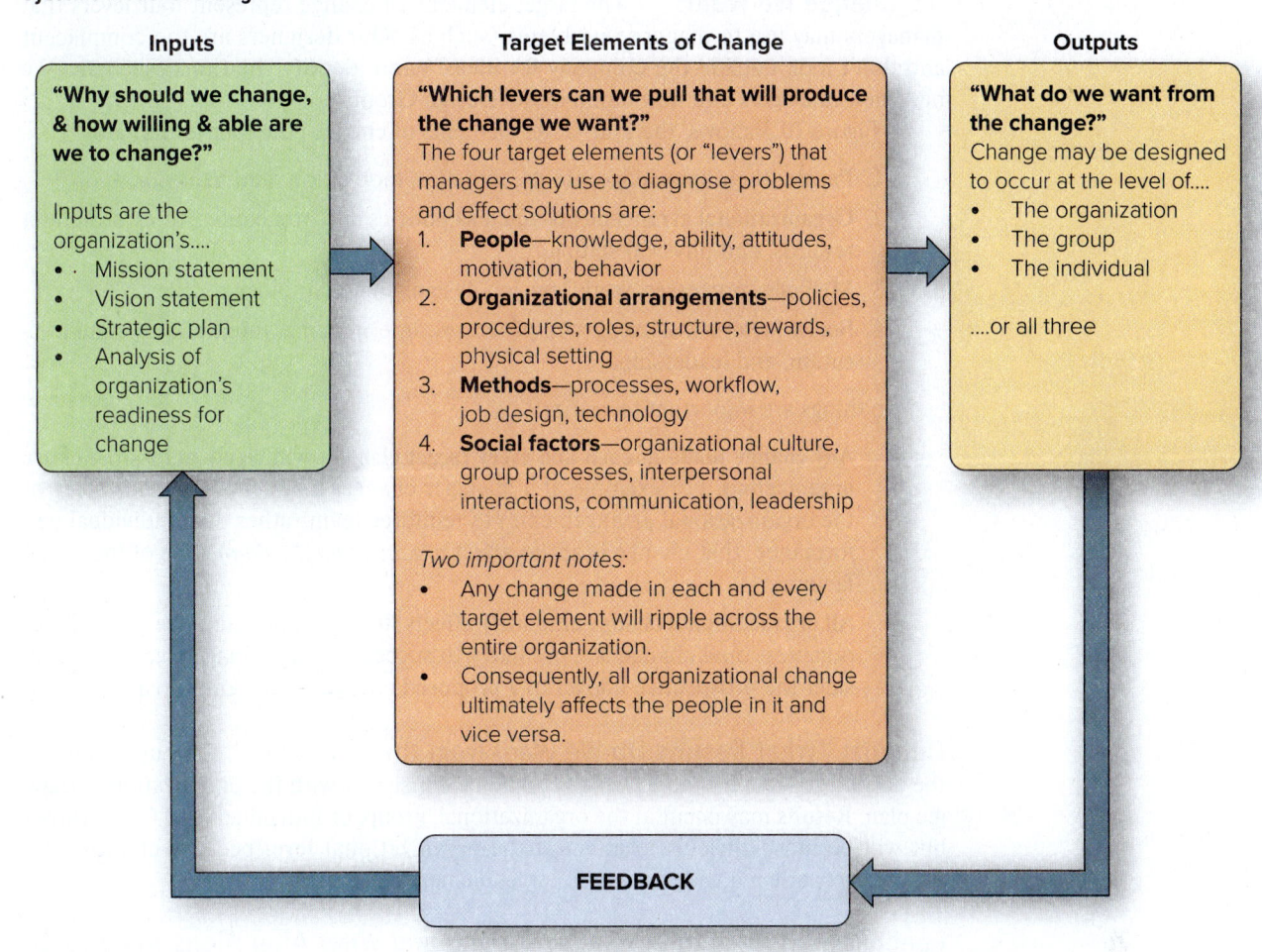

Inputs

"Why should we change, & how willing & able are we to change?"

Inputs are the organization's....
- Mission statement
- Vision statement
- Strategic plan
- Analysis of organization's readiness for change

Target Elements of Change

"Which levers can we pull that will produce the change we want?"
The four target elements (or "levers") that managers may use to diagnose problems and effect solutions are:
1. **People**—knowledge, ability, attitudes, motivation, behavior
2. **Organizational arrangements**—policies, procedures, roles, structure, rewards, physical setting
3. **Methods**—processes, workflow, job design, technology
4. **Social factors**—organizational culture, group processes, interpersonal interactions, communication, leadership

Two important notes:
- Any change made in each and every target element will ripple across the entire organization.
- Consequently, all organizational change ultimately affects the people in it and vice versa.

Outputs

"What do we want from the change?"
Change may be designed to occur at the level of....
- The organization
- The group
- The individual

....or all three

FEEDBACK

Sources: Based on R. Kreitner and A. Kinicki, Organizational Behavior 10th Edition; (New York: McGraw-Hill Education, 2012), Figure 16.6, p. 648, which was adapted from D. R. Fuqua and D. J. Kurpius, "Conceptual Models in Organizational Consultation," Journal of Counseling and Development, July–August 1993, pp. 602–618; D. A. Nadler and M. L. Tushman, "Organizational Frame Bending: Principles for Managing Reorientation," Academy of Management Executive, August 1989, pp. 194–203.

3. How capable employees are of handling the change.
4. How pessimistic or optimistic employees are about the consequences of the result.

Self-Assessment 10.2 will help you gauge your readiness for change. Try taking this self-assessment in Connect, if your instructor has assigned it. You can also use it to measure the readiness of an organization to which you belong.

SELF-ASSESSMENT 10.2   CAREER READINESS

What Is Your Readiness for Change?

This assessment is designed to show the extent of your readiness to change, or that of the organization in which the change needs to occur. Please complete Self-Assessment 10.2 if your instructor has assigned it in Connect.

Target Elements of Change: "Which Levers Can We Pull That Will Produce the Change We Want?"
The target elements of change represent four levers that managers may use to diagnose problems (such as "Our designers are too complacent and don't look outside the company for ideas") and identify solutions (such as "We need new managers and new blood in the Design Group").

As Figure 10.3 shows, the four target elements of change (the four levers) are

1. **People**—their knowledge, ability, attitudes, motivation, and behavior.
2. **Organizational arrangements**—such as policies and procedures, roles, structure, rewards, and physical setting.
3. **Methods**—processes, workflow, job design, and technology.
4. **Social factors**—culture, group processes, interpersonal interactions, communication, and leadership.

Two things are important to realize:

- **Any change made in each and every target element will ripple across the entire organization.** For example, if a manager changes a system of *rewards* (part of the organizational arrangements) to reinforce team rather than individual performance, that change is apt to affect *organizational culture* (one of the social factors).

- **All organizational change ultimately affects the people in it and vice versa.** Thus, organizational change is more likely to succeed when managers carefully consider the prospective impact of a proposed change on the employees.

Outputs: "What Results Do We Want from the Change?"
Outputs represent the desired goals of a change, which should be consistent with the organization's strategic plan. Results may occur at the organizational, group, or individual level (or all three) but will be most difficult to effect at the organizational level because changes will mostly likely affect a wide variety of target elements.

Feedback: "How Is the Change Working and What Alterations Need to Be Made?"
Not all changes work out well, of course, and organizations need to monitor their success. This is done by comparing the status of an output such as employee or customer satisfaction before the change to the same measurable output sometime after the change has been implemented.

Force-Field Analysis: "Which Forces Facilitate Change and Which Resist It?"
In most change situations being considered, there are forces acting for and against the change. **Force-field analysis** is a technique to determine which forces could facilitate a proposed change and which forces could act against it. Force-field analysis consists of two steps:

1. **Identify thrusters and counterthrusters.** The first step is to identify the positive forces (called thrusters) and the negative forces (called counterthrusters). We recommend brainstorming them separately, and then selecting the top three to five in each category.
2. **Remove the most important negative forces and increase positive forces.** The second step may sound simple, but it can be tricky to identify the forces at work.

Applying the Systems Model of Change
There are two different ways to apply the systems model of change:

1. **As an aid during the strategic planning process.** Once a group of managers identifies the organization's vision and strategic goals, group members can

consider the target elements of change when developing action plans to support the accomplishment of goals.

Systems Model of Change in Strategic Planning Example—Lego:
Lego went from the brink of death in the early 2000s to being named the most valuable toy brand in the world and the world's most reputable company in 2023.[97] The company's reinvention has been called "the greatest turnaround in corporate history."[98] After a string of failed attempts to overhaul its image and move away from the little plastic brick synonymous with the company's name, Lego's executives realized that removing the brick was not an option. Instead, they had to figure out how to innovate around their namesake product, and they ultimately did so by connecting their physical products with a limitless virtual universe.[99] Recent analyses credit the company's former CEO, Jørgen Vig Knudstorp, with masterminding the reinvention. Examples of the target elements most critical to the transformation include:

- **Organizational arrangements**—Knudstorp offloaded businesses in which the company had little expertise, including Legoland parks, and focused on building new digital content such as movies and TV shows.
- **Methods**—Knudstorp switched to an outsourcing model for areas with high potential for value add from outside experts. Said one analyst, "What's made them successful over the past 10 years is their ability to create . . . by partnering with brilliant people. They've said: 'We might not make as much money if we outsource it, but the product will be better.'"[100]
- **People**—Knudstorp leveraged people—both inside and outside the organization—to assist in the company's transformation. Dr. Anne Flemmert Jensen, former senior director of Lego's Global Insights group, said that her team helped Lego evolve by spending "all our time travelling around the world, talking to kids and their families and participating in their daily lives." Knudstorp also instituted crowdsourcing, and the company gives 1% of a product's net sales to the person who invented the idea for it. (We discuss crowdsourcing in more detail in Section 10.4.)

2. **As a diagnostic framework to identify the causes of an organizational problem and propose solutions.** We highlight this application by considering a consulting project conducted by one of your authors, Angelo Kinicki.

Systems Model of Change as a Diagnostic Framework—Author Example:
Dr. Kinicki was contacted by the CEO of a software company and asked to figure out why the presidents of three divisions were not collaborating with each other—the problem. It seemed two of the presidents had submitted the same proposal for a $4 million project to a potential customer. The software company did not get the work because the customer was appalled at having received two proposals from the same firm. Kinicki decided to interview employees by using a structured set of questions that pertained to each of the target elements of change. The interviews revealed that the lack of collaboration among division presidents was due to the reward system (an organizational arrangement), a competitive culture and poor communications (social factors), and poor workflow (a methods factor). Kinicki's recommendation was to change the reward system, restructure the organization, and redesign the workflow. •

10.3 Organizational Development: What It Is, What It Can Do

THE BIG PICTURE

Organizational development (OD) is a set of techniques for implementing change, such as improving performance, revitalizing organizations, and adapting to mergers. OD has three steps: diagnosis, intervention, and evaluation. Four factors have been found to make OD programs effective.

LO 10-3

Describe the purpose of organizational development.

Organizational development (OD) is a set of techniques for implementing planned change to make people and organizations more effective. Note the inclusion of people in this definition. OD focuses specifically on people in the change process. OD centers on the need to do something differently or better—the need to change culture or norms, improve collaboration, increase motivation, adapt to a new situation, repair relationships, or cope with a big change.[101]

Some organizations put OD into practice by enlisting an outside **change agent**, a consultant with a behavioral sciences background who can visualize new solutions to old problems: Your authors have all served as change agents. Other organizations employ organizational development specialists who help the company to lead and manage change. Regardless of title, the people who help organizations implement change must work to understand both the interpersonal and situational factors that have shaped the organization and that continue to influence its decision makers.[102]

What Can OD Be Used For?

OD can be used to address issues in the following three areas.

1. Improving Individual, Team, and Organizational Performance Conflict is inherent in most organizations. Sometimes an OD expert, perhaps in the guise of an executive coach, can advise on how to improve relationships or other issues within the organization.

> **Improving Individual, Team, and Organizational Performance Example—University of Southern California:** The Center for Work and Family Life at the University of Southern California (USC) provides coaching for leaders at the university, including campus physicians, lab directors, administrators, and deans. The service is considered a complimentary employment benefit for USC leaders, and those seeking the assistance of a coach can expect a program tailored to their unique needs. For example, the Center offers coaching programs specifically for new leaders, those in high-stress and high-performance roles, thought leaders, and those struggling with balancing the demands of leadership with their own wellness needs.[103]

2. Transforming Organizations Technology is changing so rapidly that nearly all modern organizations are having to adopt new ways of doing things in order to survive. OD can help by opening communication, fostering innovation, and dealing with stress.

> **Transforming Organizations Example—Aramis Group:** Aramis Group launched in 2001 as a small start-up and has grown to become Europe's leading online used auto seller. In recent years, leaders realized that Aramis' sales staff—the core drivers of the company's success—had lost the ability to deliver the same customer experience that they could in the company's early, small, more nimble days. The bureaucracy that had found its way into processes was holding Aramis' key employees back from executing the most important aspects of their jobs. Aramis' leaders wanted to get back to a

place where salespeople could focus on each customer's unique needs while making the auto buying process as easy, painless, and fun as possible. The company enlisted the Lean Enterprise Institute (LEI) to help it transform its processes to allow it to continue to deliver on what it felt was most important. The LEI helped Aramis identify key problems and areas of waste and inefficiency, and it used this information to optimize the auto firm's processes. The biggest transformations have led to Aramis drastically reducing customer response times, developing a process for training salespeople in a scalable way, improving communication with customers, and removing rigidities to enable flexibility and adaptability in responding to customers' needs.[104]

OD can help employees in all sorts of companies to adapt to changes and implement improved practices and techniques. OD for the instructors at Pacific Surf School translated into more surfers, more time catching waves, and more time to solve important problems. Matthew Micah Wright/Getty Images

3. Adapting to Mergers Mergers and acquisitions (M&A) are associated with increased anxiety, stress, absenteeism, turnover, and decreased productivity.[105] They're also quite common—in the United States and Canada alone, more than 20,000 M&A transactions occurred in 2022.[106] Imagine how employees must feel as they wait for their firm to merge with another firm and wonder whether they will lose their autonomy, their status, or their jobs due to the merger. OD experts are often called upon in such situations to help ease the tensions involved in integrating two firms with varying cultures, products, and procedures.

How OD Works

Like physicians, OD managers and consultants follow a medical-like model. (Or to use our more current formulation, they follow the rules of evidence-based management.) They approach the organization as if it were a sick patient, using *diagnosis, intervention*, and *evaluation*:

- *Diagnosing* the organization's ills.
- *Prescribing* treatment or intervention.
- *Monitoring* or evaluating progress.

If the evaluation shows that the procedure is not working effectively, the conclusions drawn are then applied (via a feedback loop) to refining the diagnosis, and the process starts again (see Figure 10.4).

1. Diagnosis What is the problem? → **2. Intervention** What shall we do about it? → **3. Evaluation** How well has the intervention worked?

Feedback How can the diagnosis be further refined?

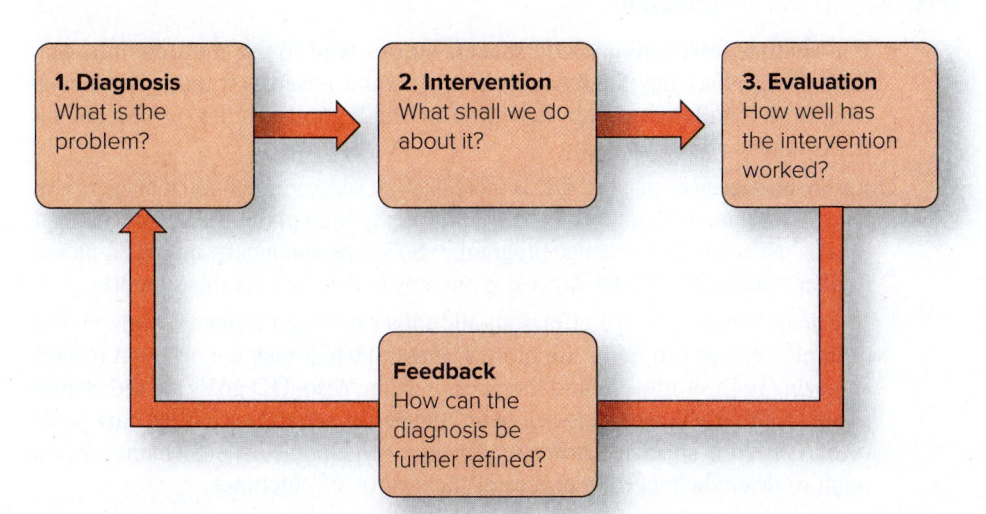

FIGURE 10.4

The OD process

Sources: Adapted from French, W. L. and C. H. Bell Jr. Organization Development: Behavioral Interventions for Organizational Improvement. Englewood Cliffs, NJ: Prentice Hall, 1978; Huse, E. G and T. G. Cummings. Organizational Development and Change, 3rd ed. St. Paul: West, 1985.

1. Diagnosis: What Is the Problem? To carry out the diagnosis, OD consultants or managers use some combination of questionnaires, surveys, interviews, meetings, records, and direct observation to ascertain people's attitudes and to identify problem areas. A problem is defined as a gap between an outcome or result desired by managers and the actual status of the outcome or result. For example, if your goal was to improve your sales department's customer satisfaction score by 10 points and it only improves by 5 points, your problem is to increase the department's score by 5 more points.

2. Intervention: What Shall We Do about It? "Treatment," or **intervention, is the attempt to correct the diagnosed problems.** Often this is done using the services of an OD consultant who works in conjunction with management teams. Some OD activities for implementing planned change include:

- Communicating survey results to employees to engage them in constructive problem solving.
- Helping group members learn to function as a team.
- Improving work technology or organizational design.

Coaching is often used to improve leadership.[107] Studies suggest executive coaching and leadership development programs positively impact leaders' self-efficacy beliefs, leadership behaviors, and career satisfaction. Employees of executives who participate in these programs express lower turnover intentions and higher approval of their leaders.[108]

3. Evaluation: How Well Has the Intervention Worked? An OD program needs objective evaluation to see if it has done any good. Answers may lie in hard data about absenteeism, turnover, grievances, and profitability, which should be compared with earlier statistics. The change agent can use questionnaires, surveys, interviews, and the like to assess changes in employee attitudes.

4. Feedback: How Can the Diagnosis and Intervention Be Further Refined?
If evaluation shows that the diagnosis was wrong or the intervention was not effective, the OD consultant or managers need to return to the beginning to rethink these two steps.

The Effectiveness of OD

Among organizations that have practiced organizational development are American Airlines, B.F. Goodrich, General Electric, Honeywell, ITT, Procter & Gamble, Prudential, Texas Instruments, and Westinghouse Canada—companies covering a variety of industries. Research provides the following recommendations for increasing the likelihood that OD will be successful:

1. **Use multiple interventions.** OD success stories tend to use multiple interventions.[109] Goal setting, feedback, recognition and rewards, training, participation, and challenging job design have had good results in improving performance and satisfaction.[110]
2. **Ensure management support.** OD is more likely to succeed when top managers give the OD program their support and are truly committed to the change process and the desired goals of the change program.[111] Soliciting and incorporating employee feedback during the change process is one way to demonstrate this support.
3. **Use goals wisely.** Change efforts should target the right kinds of goals.[112] For example, change programs are more successful when they are oriented toward achieving both short-term and long-term results. Also, OD goals should clearly relate to either changes in *learning* or changes in *performance*. Learning goals often focus on specific career readiness competencies. Performance goals point to desired changes in processes, behaviors, or outcomes.

4. **Understand the impacts of culture.** OD effectiveness is affected by both national and organizational culture. Thus, an OD intervention that worked in one setting should not be blindly applied to a similar situation in another setting.[113]

10.4 Organizational Innovation

THE BIG PICTURE
Managers agree that the ability to innovate affects long-term success, and you will undoubtedly be asked to help your employer achieve this. This section provides insights into the ways organizations approach the goal of innovation. After discussing approaches toward innovation pursued by companies, we review the need to create an innovation system.

Technological, economic, and sociocultural forces continue to transform the way we live, work, and play. This reality presents both opportunities and strains for organizations. Consider the multitude of challenges faced by retail clothing companies in recent years.[114] First, Americans are spending a smaller percentage of their income on clothing (from 5.9% of income in 1987 to just 2.3% in 2022). Second, both clothing companies and consumers are constrained by record-high inflation. Third, the types of clothing demanded by consumers can change on a dime, and retailers have to respond in kind. Clothing companies must innovate in order to meet dynamic consumer demands while satisfying their shareholders and other stakeholders.

Is the retail clothing industry an anomaly or is the need to innovate widespread? It's widespread! Results from a recent survey of executives showed that over 80% listed innovation in their top three priorities.[115]

Innovation (as defined in Chapter 1) occurs when a new solution to an existing problem is valuable enough that consumers are willing to pay for it.[116] This definition underscores that innovations must be both novel and useful. We now take a closer look at innovation and the way organizations foster it. You will learn that innovation is more likely to occur when organizations create and support a system of innovation, which includes tailoring the characteristics of the physical environment to support innovation.

LO 10-4

Describe the approaches toward innovation and components of an innovation system.

Approaches to Innovation

We can classify innovations by crossing their type with their focus, producing four distinct types (see Figure 10.5).

Do you have a need for work-appropriate clothing? How about athleisure? Are these one in the same? Clothing retailers must quickly respond to trends, accurately predict demand, carefully source fabrics and suppliers, and efficiently and effectively distribute product. Can you see the need for innovation in this industry? Dean Drobot/Shutterstock, Djomas/Shutterstock, Pepsco Studio/Shutterstock, ASDF_MEDIA/Shutterstock

FIGURE 10.5

Approaches toward innovation

	Focus of Innovation	
	Improvement	**New Directions**
Product	Apple iPhone • Fifteen generations/versions since first introduced in June 2007	Driverless Cars • Tesla and Waymo
Process	3-D Printing • Medical prosthetics	Home Construction • Prefabricated tiny home kits

Type of Innovation

The Type of Innovation Managers often need to improve a product or service they offer in response to competition or customer feedback. This response often amounts to a technological innovation. Or managers may need to improve the process by which a product is made or a service is offered. This need typically leads to a process improvement.

More specifically, a **product innovation** is a change in the appearance or functionality/performance of a product or a service or the creation of a new one. Consider the following example:

Product Innovation Example—Dizolve Group Corporation: Retailers recently introduced consumers to a new type of laundry product. Instead of bulky containers of liquid or plastic-laden pods, detergent can now be delivered in thin, lightweight sheets or strips that dissolve in the wash, leaving nothing behind but clean and fresh-smelling garments. The technology is credited to the Dizolve Group Corporation, with patent applications dating back over 10 years.[117] According to one retailer, when compared with liquid detergent, detergent sheets reduce the amount of water used in production by 99%, and reduce shipping and packaging emissions by 87% and 75%, respectively.[118]

A **process innovation** is a change in the way a product or a service is conceived, manufactured, or distributed. McDonald's is experimenting with two process innovations:

Process Innovation Example—Food Delivery: The food delivery market was valued at more than $220 billion in 2022 and is expected to grow by 10% each year between now and 2030.[119] Flytrex is a drone delivery company focusing exclusively on suburban areas in the United States. According to the company's website, "Anything you need—from Chinese takeout to your morning coffee—can be delivered instantly to your backyard."[120] The company is offering its delivery service in several locations in North Carolina and Texas, and it is partnered with restaurants like It's Just Wings and Maggiano's Italian Classics.[121]

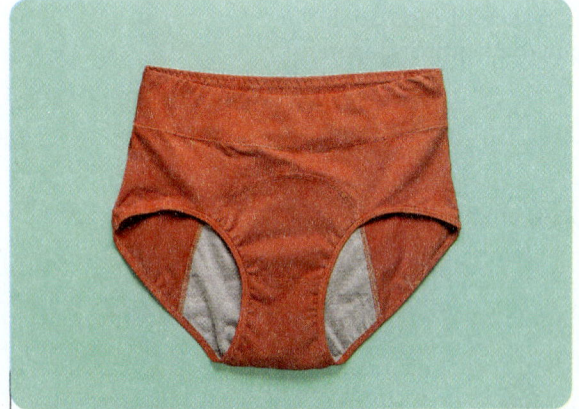

For decades, up to 80% of menstruating women have relied on disposable products during their periods. Reusable, absorbent, period underwear have the potential to revolutionize how this aspect of health is managed. This represents a product innovation in the $40+ billion feminine hygiene market. serezniy/123RF

The Focus of the Innovation The focus continuum measures the scope of the innovation.

Improvement innovations enhance or upgrade an existing product, service, or process. These types of innovations are often incremental and are less likely to generate significant amounts of new revenue at one point in time. Stitch Fix has used improvement innovation to remain competitive in recent years.

Improvement Innovation Example—J-Tip: The dreaded IV insertion is a mainstay of most hospital stays, as an IV line allows healthcare workers to safely and efficiently deliver important medication to patients throughout the duration of care. A device called the J-Tip has changed the game for both the healthcare workers who start children's IVs and the little ones who receive them. The J-Tip was invented to take the anxiety and pain out of receiving an IV, a procedure that can be especially upsetting to children receiving medical care. The device uses a *pop* of CO_2 gas to drive a fine mist of liquid anesthetic directly through the patient's skin and into the subcutaneous tissue. The application is painless, and an IV can then be inserted into the patient's vein with virtually zero sensation. The J-Tip is currently used in more than 400 hospitals, and National Medical Products hopes to someday be used in every hospital in the United States.[122]

In contrast, *new-direction innovations* take a totally new or different approach to a product, service, process, or industry. These innovations focus on creating new markets and customers and rely on developing breakthroughs and inventing things that didn't already exist. Orbital Insight is an example.

New-Direction Innovation Example—Telemedicine: Although telemedicine existed prior to 2020, the COVID-19 pandemic accelerated the adoption of virtual health care.[123] The ability to hold healthcare appointments virtually has changed the game for both providers and recipients of care. The recent widespread acceptance of telemedicine provides numerous benefits, including (1) patients having a much wider selection of providers, (2) individuals in rural areas having easy access to health care, (3) those with mobility issues having convenient ways to meet with doctors, and (4) increased access to specialists and mental health care.[124]

Can an Innovation Go Too Far? Are all innovations good innovations, or is it possible for innovation to cross a line? This is a question that businesses will continue to confront as technology evolves and allows us to do things that were once not possible. This question arose recently with the release of ChatGPT.

Can Innovation Go Too Far Example—ChatGPT: The introduction of ChatGPT (and its subsequent versions) left universities scrambling to devise rules around the use of the technology. OpenAI, the developer of ChatGPT, said that its GPT-4 upgrade could exhibit "human-level performance" when mimicking human thought and language.[125] Some faculty and administrators believe the technology is dangerous and will lead to increased plagiarism and academic dishonesty. Others want for their institutions to provide training to help them learn to work *with* the technology in their classes.

An Innovation System: The Supporting Forces for Innovation

Innovation won't happen as a matter of course. It takes dedicated effort and resources, and the process must be nurtured and supported. Organizations do this best by developing an innovation system. An **innovation system** is a set of mutually reinforcing structures, processes, and practices that drive an organization's choices around innovation and its ability to innovate successfully.[126]

Research and practice have identified seven components of an innovation system: innovation strategy; committed leadership; innovative culture and climate; required structure and processes; necessary human capital; human resource policies, practices, and procedures; and appropriate resources.[127] (See Figure 10.6.) Notice in the figure that innovation is the product of all the elements in the system working together.

Do the components of an innovation system look familiar to you? If so, you're probably remembering our discussions in Chapters 8 and 9. Specifically, in these previous chapters, you learned that leadership is needed to align an organization's culture, structure, and HR practices so that they work together to support firm strategy. These important elements are also presented here as part of an organization's innovation system, and here too, they must be aligned and integrated for innovation to blossom, hence the dual-headed arrows in Figure 10.6.

FIGURE 10.6
Components of an innovation system

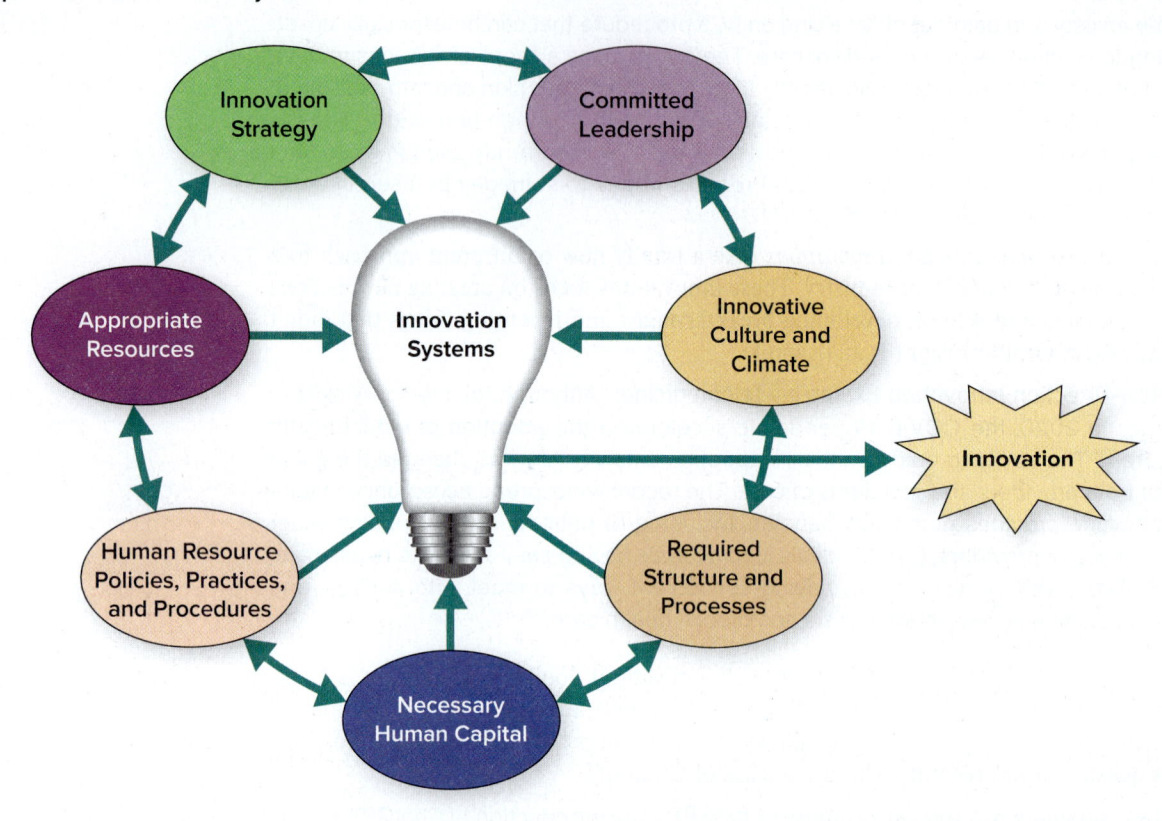

Create an Innovation Strategy Many companies fail in their improvement efforts because they lack an innovation strategy.[128] An **innovation strategy**, which amounts to a plan for being more innovative, requires a company to integrate its innovation activities into its business strategies. This integration encourages management to invest resources in innovation and generates employee commitment to innovation across the organization.

Consider the example of how Reckitt Benckiser innovates using a well-defined strategy.

Innovation Strategy Example—Reckitt Benckiser: Reckitt Benckiser (RB) is the British company that owns brands such as Lysol, Woolite, and Clearasil. RB considers innovation a "key source" of its competitive advantage.[129] Its innovation strategy is characterized by small, incremental improvements. Specifically, rather than pursue massive innovations, RB focuses on taking its most successful products and tweaking them in modest ways that better solve consumers' problems. For example, the company's Finish dish detergent brand has gone from Finish 2-in-1, to Finish 3-in-1, to Finish All-in-1, to Finish Ultimate Plus. With each iteration, RB made a small but valued improvement, and the company's sales and profits from the product have continued to increase.[130]

Commitment from Senior Leaders One of the biggest lessons we have learned from our consulting experience is that the achievement of strategic goals is unlikely without real commitment from senior leaders.[131] Mars CEO Grant Reid is acutely aware of his role in supporting innovation.

Commitment from Senior Leaders Example—Ambow Education: The Ambow Education company relies on its patented technology called HybridU to deliver "high quality, individualized, and dynamic career education services and products" to workers and students across the globe.[132] CEO Dr. Jin Huang was recently named one of the "10 Most Innovative CEOs to Watch." Said Dr. Huang, "When I founded Ambow 22 years ago, I had the vision to leverage technology to help create better educational outcomes. This is what we have always intended to do. We have more than 100 US and Chinese patents granted as an example of our investments in technology and innovation."[133]

Foster an Innovative Culture and Climate   Results of a recent McKinsey survey suggest that more than 90% of executives are unhappy with their firms' innovation performance.[134] Several factors serve as barriers to innovation, but one of the key obstacles is inertia—defined in Learning Module 1 as an organization's resistance to making the strategic changes necessary to remain competitive in a changing environment.[135] Explained a team of innovation consultants, "If you don't address inertia, efforts to eliminate other blockers won't work. Give people more time in an environment stifled by inertia and they'll simply have more time to do things the old way; give them new skills, and those will go to waste if they don't fit with existing routines."[136]

Organizations that wish to create new products and ideas need an innovative culture and climate.[137] Academic research findings reflect the fact that innovation requires experimentation, failure, and risk taking, and these are all aspects of an organization's culture.[138] Many senior leaders understand this link.

Who are the most innovative companies in the United States? See Table 10.1 for a list of *Fast Company* magazine's most innovative companies and see how many you know.

Have you worked for a company that has an innovative climate? Are you wondering what it takes to create such a climate? If yes, and if your instructor has assigned it in Connect, take the innovation climate Self-Assessment 10.3.

TABLE 10.1 The Most Innovative Companies

1. OpenAI
2. McDonald's
3. Airbnb
4. Holdfast Collective
5. Nubank
6. Microsoft
7. Roblox
8. Webtoon
9. Ramp
10. Tiffany & Co.
11. Hoka
12. On
13. Workers United
14. Armis
15. FromSoftware

Source: "The World's 50 Most Innovative Companies of 2023," Fast Company. *https://www.fastcompany.com/most-innovative-companies/list.*

SELF-ASSESSMENT 10.3

How Innovative Is the Organizational Climate?

This assessment is designed to assess your organization's level of innovation. Please complete Self-Assessment 10.3 if your instructor has assigned it in Connect.

Required Structure and Processes   Organizational structure and internal processes can promote innovation if they foster collaboration, cross-functional communication, and agility. Flagship Pioneering is a good example.

> **Required Structure and Processes Example—Flagship Pioneering:** Flagship Pioneering (FP) creates new ventures based on cutting-edge, or "pioneering," science. FP uses a formal process to evaluate opportunities for innovation. Exploration begins with the identification of a major social issue followed by a deep dive into the existing literature. Teams formulate hypotheses throughout this stage and work through them with a group of scientific advisers. The key rule at this stage is that every idea is entertained as long as its execution would create value. Later in the process, scientists run experiments designed to expose holes in the ideas, and employees are taught to respect what the data ultimately show. On its website, Flagship Pioneering states that "We begin with seemingly unreasonable propositions and navigate to transformational outcomes."[139]

Organizational processes are an organization's capabilities in management, internal processes, and technology that turn inputs into outcomes. Processes play a critical role in innovation. The design and consulting firm IDEO, for example, employs a unique process when it helps companies to innovate (see the Practical Action box).

PRACTICAL ACTION | IDEO's Approach to Innovation

IDEO (pronounced "EYE-dee-oh") is a unique, award-winning, and highly respected global design firm. The company has more than 600 employees in seven offices, both in major U.S. cities and overseas in London, Munich, Shanghai, and Tokyo.[140] It is responsible for such innovative products as the first mouse for Apple, heart defibrillators that guide a user through the steps, and a revolutionary digital diabetes management system for patients. An intense focus on end-user behavior is the foundation of all the company does and is embedded in the three steps of its design thinking approach. The steps are inspiration, ideation, and implementation.[141]

- **Inspiration.** As defined by David Kelley, IDEO's founder, inspiration is the problem or opportunity that motivates the search for solutions.
- **Ideation.** Ideation is the process of generating, developing, and testing ideas.
- **Implementation.** The final step, implementation, links the problem's solution to people's lives.

Observing user behavior and working with prototypes are important aspects of each step. They help IDEO's diverse problem-solving teams define client problems and gauge the effectiveness of solutions.

Thinking Like a Designer to Solve Problems

The company provides a host of design thinking resources on its website to help companies generate more creative and innovative ideas.[142]

IDEO has successfully applied its design thinking innovation approach to a wide variety of problems, including partnering with the Rockefeller Foundation to generate solutions for reducing the enormous amount of food waste that occurs each year in the food industry. Ian Allenden/123RF

Empathy maps are used in design thinking to generate insights into human problems. The tool requires thinkers to observe human behavior related to the problem being addressed. So, for example, if a company wanted its employees to be more comfortable adopting new technology, design thinkers might observe employees when they are presented with new tech to see how they respond and what the issues could be. Here are the steps that IDEO recommends for using empathy maps:

1. Divide a sheet of paper into four quadrants
2. Jot down observations of what people DO in the bottom left.
3. Jot down observations of what people SAY in the upper left.
4. Jot down inferences you have about what people THINK and FEEL in the two quadrants on the right.
5. Examine your paper and try to glean insights into potential issues and solutions to the problem.

Design Thinking Your Way to Innovative Solutions

For organizations wanting to identify broad opportunities for innovation, change, and growth, IDEO suggests a systems map.[143] Systems maps illustrate all the possible relationships between the stakeholders in a firm's environment (recall what you learned about an organization's environment in Figure 3.2). Here's how IDEO recommends using systems maps to identify opportunities:

1. Grab a piece of paper and write down every single stakeholder you can think of in your environment. Spend some time on this step and be sure to consider non-obvious stakeholders, too.
2. Choose different stakeholders in your system and draw arrows between them. Write down a note or two about how they are connected. This is the core piece of the exercise—try to articulate the connections between as many combinations of stakeholders as possible.
3. Jot down areas where you have questions, see gaps, or want to explore more.

YOUR CALL

What is appealing to you about IDEO's design thinking approach to innovation? To what extent does IDEO's approach force companies to use the seven components of an innovation system (see Figure 10.6)? Explain.

Crowdsourcing, defined as the practice of obtaining needed services, ideas, or content by soliciting contributions from a large group of people typically via the Internet, is being used by more companies to help innovate.

Crowdsourcing Example—Innovation Competitions: One way to crowdsource innovative ideas is through student competitions. Keysight Technologies recently held their annual Keysight Innovation Challenge to stimulate thinking around a single problem: how to design an Internet of Things (IoT) device to get the world to net zero carbon emissions. In the 2022 challenge, each team had to have equal representation of women and men, and all teams were led by women. The winning team was made up of students from the Illinois Institute of Technology, and the team received $30,000 in cash as well as $10,000 worth of equipment for their university.[144]

Develop the Necessary Human Capital

"One of the most valuable assets of any economy or company is its human capital—the skills, capabilities and innovation of its citizens," according to the World Economic Forum (WEF).[145] We defined human capital in Chapter 9 as the productive potential of an individual's knowledge and actions. Research has identified several employee factors that can help organizations innovate. For example, innovation has been positively associated with the individual characteristics associated with creativity, creative-thinking skills, intrinsic motivation, the quality of the relationship between managers and employees, and international work experience.[146]

Today's organizations are actively looking for people who possess the competencies associated with innovation and creativity. In its most recent Future of Jobs Report, the WEF surveyed leaders of nearly 300 global organizations and found the following skills were deemed the top five most important for 2025:[147]

1. Analytical thinking and innovation.
2. Active learning and learning strategies.
3. Complex problem-solving.
4. Critical thinking and analysis.
5. Creativity, originality, and initiative.

It's clear that organizations want workers who have the ability to think creatively, learn new things, and generate novel ideas. Consider Nestlé USA's approach to encouraging innovation in its workforce:

Developing Necessary Human Capital Example—Nestlé USA: Nestlé USA regularly tops lists of best workplaces for innovators and innovation, and according to the company's website, "the key is our people."[148] The company sees every employee as a potential innovator and has instituted companywide procedures to encourage employees in all jobs at all levels to tap into their creative potential. Nestlé uses a platform called Open Channel to encourage its 30,000 employees to submit and vote on new product ideas. Open Channel is responsible for products such as Stouffer's Mac and Cheese bites and Outshine Smoothie Cubes.[149] Said Mel Cash, the company's chief strategy officer, "Innovation happens when we give our people the permission to imagine new and innovative products, the resources to explore their big ideas, and the space to activate change and learn what works and what doesn't."[150]

Human Resource Policies, Practices, and Procedures

Human resource (HR) policies, practices, and procedures need to be consistent with and reinforce the other six components of an innovation system. Here's what research tells us about the alignment of HR with the overall innovation system:

- **Alignment is related to valued outcomes.** Companies that align HR with the other components of the innovation system are more likely to be innovative and to have higher financial performance.[151]
- **Performance management and incentives are often not designed to foster innovation.** A company's performance management and incentive systems are often at odds with an innovation culture and climate. Companies need to align their reward and recognition systems with innovation-related goals.[152]

Bringing people from different disciplines together to both brainstorm and train is a good way for a firm to foster the collaboration needed for innovation. Collaboration creates opportunities for communication and, thus, ideation, between unlikely parties. Consider how CarMax brings people together and encourages innovation:

HR Policies, Practices, and Procedures Example—CarMax: CarMax generates innovation through its cross-functional product teams. These teams consist of seven to nine members, and each must include at least one user-experience expert, one product manager, and one lead developer or engineer. The remaining members can come from any department. Teams work in spurts and make short progress presentations every two weeks. This schedule encourages teams to take risks and learn from mistakes at a fairly quick pace.[153] CarMax's Executive Vice President/Chief Information Technology Office Shamim Mohammad recently said that "At any given moment, our teams are doing hundreds of experiments and trying new things." Mohammad added, "And many of them may not come to any fruition, which is okay, because what it is allowing us to do is figure out all the things that don't work so that we can identify a few things that do work."[154]

Appropriate Resources Organizations need to put their money where their mouths are. If managers want innovation, they must dedicate resources to its development. Resources can include people, dollars, time, energy, knowledge, and focus. A recent survey of L&D professionals found that nearly 50% of respondents saw upskilling the workforce as a top priority in the coming years.[155]

Appropriate Resources Example—Guild: Guild is a platform that brings together employees and universities to provide opportunities for workers to build necessary skills. The company is valued at more than $4 billion dollars and currently parters with around 80 organizations that are interested in upskilling their workforces through certificate and degree programs offered by renowned universities. *Time Magazine* recently named Guild as one of its 100 most influential companies of 2022.[156] •

10.5 The Threat of Change: Managing Employee Fear and Resistance

THE BIG PICTURE
This section discusses the causes of resistance to change and the reasons employees fear change.

LO 10-5

Discuss ways managers can help employees overcome fear of change.

As we mentioned in Section 10.1, change may be forced upon an organization—*reactive* change, requiring you to make changes in response to problems or opportunities as they arise. Or an organization may try to get out in front of changes—*proactive* change, or planned change, which involves making carefully thought-out changes in anticipation of possible problems or opportunities. In either case, it's almost certain that change efforts will be met with fear and resistance, and managers need to know how to help employees work through these things.[157]

What, then, are effective ways to manage organizational change and employees' fear of and resistance to it? In this section, we discuss the following:

- The causes of resistance to change.
- Why employees resist change.

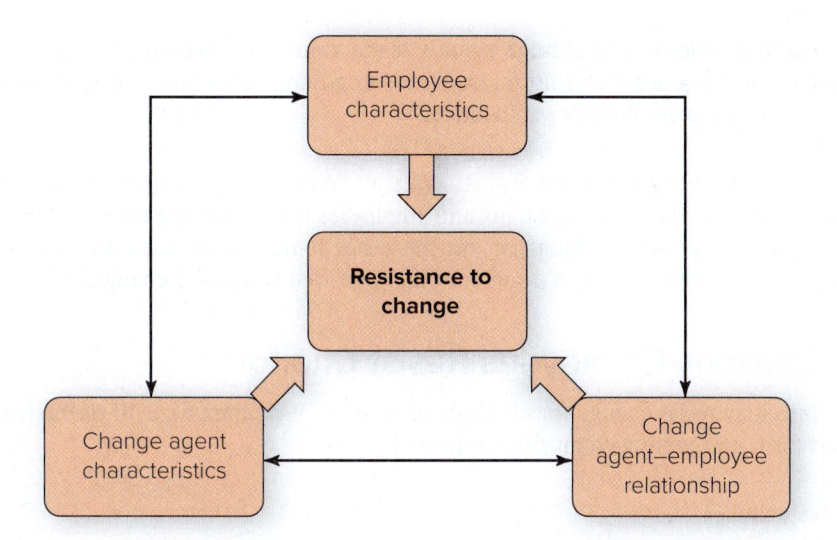

FIGURE 10.7

A model of resistance to change

Source: Kreitner, Robert and Angelo Kinicki. Organizational Behavior. Burr Ridge, IL: McGraw Hill/Irwin, 2010.

The Causes of Resistance to Change

Resistance to change is an emotional/behavioral response to real or imagined threats to an established work routine. Resistance can be as subtle as passive resignation and as overt as deliberate sabotage. As you will learn, change experts believe that resistance results primarily from the context in which change occurs.[158]

Resistance can be considered to be the interaction of three causes (see Figure 10.7). They are

1. Employee characteristics.
2. Change agent characteristics.
3. The change agent–employee relationship.

For example, an employee's resistance is partly based on their perception of change, which is influenced by the attitudes and behaviors exhibited by the change agent and the level of trust between the change agent and the employee.[159]

Let us consider these three sources of resistance.

1. Employee Characteristics The characteristics of a given employee consist of their individual differences (discussed in Chapter 11), actions and inactions, and perceptions of change.[160] The next section discusses a variety of employee characteristics that relate to resistance to change. One of them involves personal adaptability, the career readiness competency that one columnist recently called "essential for survival" in the global marketplace.[161] How adaptable are you? You can find out by taking Self-Assessment 10.4 in Connect if your instructor has assigned it.

SELF-ASSESSMENT 10.4   CAREER READINESS

How Adaptable Are You?

This survey is designed to assess your level of adaptability. Please complete Self-Assessment 10.4 if your instructor has assigned it in Connect.

2. Change Agent Characteristics The characteristics of the change agent—the individual who is a catalyst in helping organizations change—consist of the agent's individual differences, experiences, actions and inactions, and perceptions of change. These characteristics might contribute to employees' resistance to change. For example, an employee may react to the change agent's leadership style, personality, tactfulness, sense of timing, awareness of cultural traditions or group relationships, and/or ability to empathize with the employee's perspective.[162]

3. Change Agent–Employee Relationship As you might expect, resistance to change is reduced when change agents and employees have a trusting relationship—faith in each other's intentions. Mistrust, on the other hand, encourages secrecy, which begets deeper mistrust, and can doom an otherwise well-conceived change.[163]

Ten Reasons Employees Resist Change

Employees may resist change for all kinds of reasons. We summarize 10 of the leading reasons for not accepting change in Table 10.2.

TABLE 10.2 Reasons Employees Resist Change

REASON	EXPLANATION
Individuals' Predisposition toward Change	Our personalities are partly innate and partly shaped through early experiences (as you'll learn in Chapter 11). Some adverse childhood experiences (ACEs) can influence whether we react to imposed changes with rigidity or flexibility.
Surprise and Fear of the Unknown	Radical change introduced without warning or explanation engenders fear among employees and can send the rumor mill into high gear. Change leaders must provide rationale and must educate employees about potential personal implications of the change in order to allay fears and engender commitment to change.
Climate of Mistrust	Trust involves reciprocal faith in others' intentions and behavior. Mistrust puts even well-conceived changes at risk of failure. In a trusting climate, the change process is an open, honest, and participative affair.
Fear of Failure	Intimidating changes on the job can cause employees and managers to doubt their capabilities. Self-doubt erodes self-confidence and cripples personal growth and development.
Loss of Status or Job Security	Administrative and technological changes that threaten to alter power bases or eliminate jobs—as often happens during corporate restructurings that threaten middle-management jobs—generally trigger strong resistance.
Peer Pressure	Even people who are not themselves directly affected by impending changes may actively resist in order to protect the interests of their friends and co-workers.
Disruption of Cultural Traditions or Group Relationships	Whenever individuals are transferred, promoted, or reassigned, it can disrupt existing cultural and group relationships.
Personality Conflicts	Just as a friend can get away with telling us something we would resent hearing from an adversary, the personalities of change agents can breed resistance.
Lack of Tact or Poor Timing	Introducing changes in an insensitive manner or at an awkward time can create employee resistance. Employees are more apt to accept changes when managers effectively explain their value, as, for example, in demonstrating their strategic purpose to the organization
Nonreinforcing Reward Systems	Employees are likely to resist when they can't see any positive rewards from proposed changes, as, for example, when one is asked to work longer hours without additional compensation.

Sources: Table adapted in part from Ford, J.D., L.W. Ford, and A. D'Amelio. "Resistance to Change: The Rest of the Story." *Academy of Management Review.* (April 2008): 362–377; Reyes, M.E., K.M. Buac, L.I. Dumaguing, E.D. Lapidez, C.A. Pangilinan, W.P. Sy, and J.S. Ubaldo. "Link between Adverse Childhood Experiences and Five Factor Model Traits among Filipinos." IAFOR Journal of Psychology & the Behavioral Sciences 4, no. 2 (2018): 71; Whittle, A., E. Vaara, and S. Maitlis. "The Role of Language in Organizational Sensemaking: An Integrative Theoretical Framework and an Agenda for Future Research." Journal of Management (2022): 01492063221147295; Macpherson, A., D. Breslin, and C. Akinci. "Organizational Learning from Hidden Improvisation." Organization Studies 43, no. 6 (2022): 861–883; Hubbart, J.A. "Organizational Change: Considering Truth and Buy-In." Administrative Sciences 13, no. 1 (2022): 3; Borges, R. and C.A. Quintas. "Understanding the Individual's Reactions to the Organizational Change: A Multidimensional Approach." Journal of Organizational Change Management 33, no. 5 (2020): 667–681; Lynch, S. and M. Mors. "Strategy Implementation and Organizational Change: How Formal Reorganization Affects Professional Networks." Long Range Planning 52, no. 2 (2019): 255–270.

Where do you stand on change? Are you open to change and embrace it, or do you have tendencies to resist? Try taking Self-Assessment 10.5 in Connect, if your instructor has assigned it, to assess the extent to which you resist change, which is the opposite of the career readiness competency of openness to change. Employers are looking for people who accept and embrace change, and this assessment provides feedback about your attitudes toward change. If your scores indicate resistance, you should consider things you can do to move your attitudes in a more positive direction (we provide practical advice in this area in the Career Corner in Section 10.6). •

SELF-ASSESSMENT 10.5   CAREER READINESS

Assessing Your Resistance to Change

This survey is designed to assess your resistance to change. Please complete Self-Assessment 10.5 if your instructor has assigned it in Connect.

10.6 Career Corner: Managing Your Career Readiness

LO 10-6
Review the different ways to increase the career readiness competency of openness to change.

Visit your instructor's Connect course and access your eBook to view this video.

Executive Interview Series: Openness to Change and Adaptability

"These days ... major change happens moment to moment—economically, environmentally, sociologically, politically, and organizationally," says Erika Andersen, founding partner at Proteus International coaching, consulting, and training firm. Anderson adds that "we need to re-wire ourselves to be more comfortable with and open to change; we need to become more change-capable."[164] This calls to mind the career readiness competencies of openness to change, ownership/accepting responsibility, proactive learning orientation, positive approach, resilience, and personal adaptability (see Figure 10.8).

In this section we focus on openness to change, an "other characteristic" in our model of career readiness. Openness to change was defined in Table 1.3 as "flexibility when confronted with change, ability to see change as a challenge, and willingness to apply new ideas, processes, or directives." Employee openness to change is necessary for successful organizational-level change. As you will see in this chapter's Executive Interview Series video, the ability to adapt to constant disruption is a critical characteristic and invaluable asset for you in your career.

So how can you become more open to change? What gets in your way? We answer these questions by first explaining the application of self-affirmation theory. We then review how self-compassion assists in promoting openness to change.

Applying Self-Affirmation Theory

Self-affirmation theory says that we, as humans, have an innate desire to protect our self-image.[165] According to the theory, we want to believe that we are generally good and virtuous people who behave in appropriate ways.[166] When we are confronted with information that suggests we should change the way we think or act, we naturally engage in

FIGURE 10.8

Model of career readiness

McGraw Hill

Knowledge
- Task-based/functional
- Computational thinking
- Understanding the business
- New media literacy

Other characteristics
- **Resilience**
- **Personal adaptability**
- Self-awareness
- Service/others orientation
- **Openness to change** ⭐
- Generalized self-efficacy

Core
- Critical thinking/problem solving
- Oral/written communication
- Teamwork/collaboration
- Information technology application
- Leadership
- Professionalism/work ethic
- Diversity, equity, and inclusion
- Career management

Soft skills
- Decision making
- Social intelligence
- Networking
- Emotional intelligence

Attitudes
- **Ownership/accepting responsibilities**
- Self-motivation
- **Proactive learning orientation**
- Showing commitment
- **Positive approach**

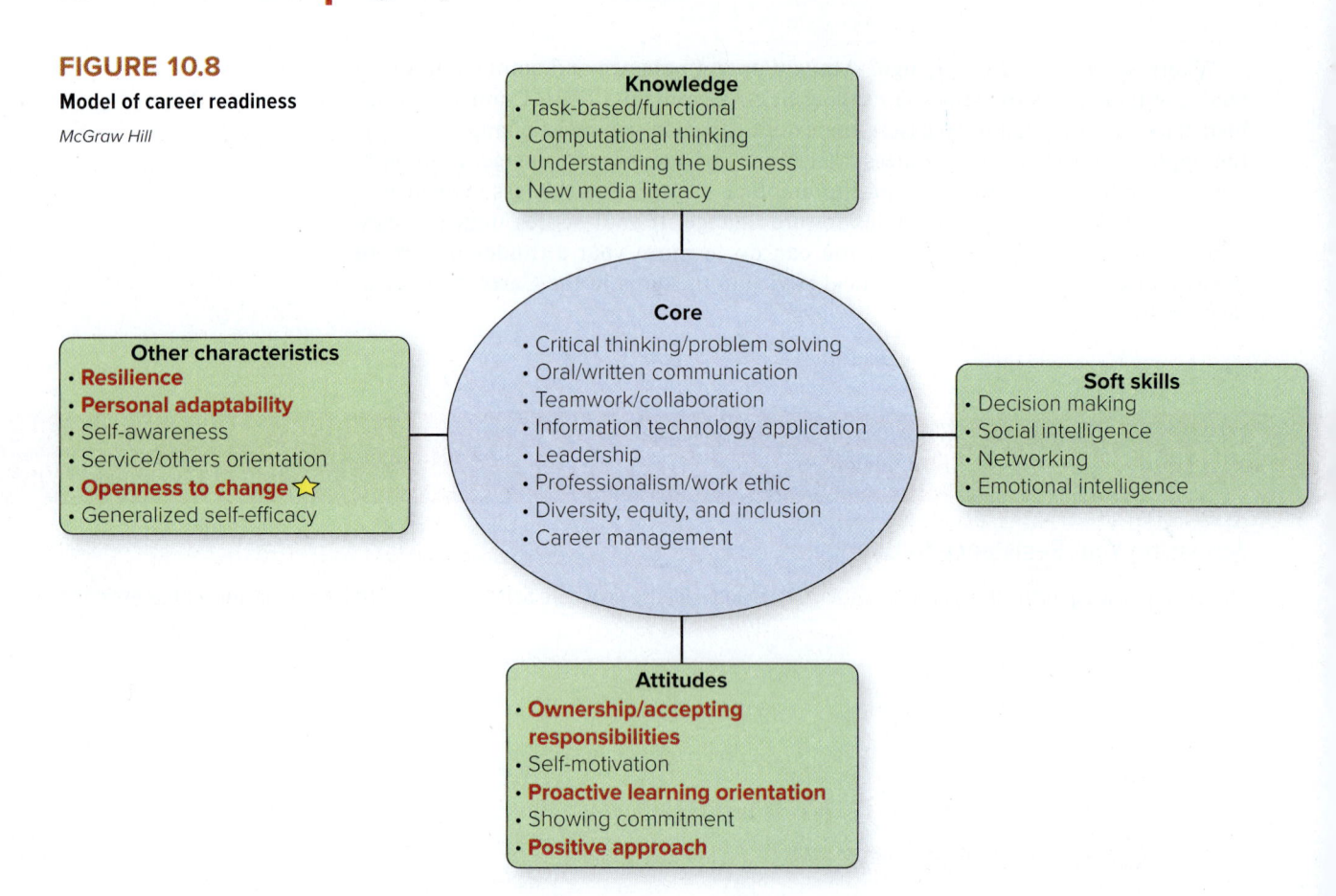

processes to restore our positive self-image. Here is how self-affirmation theory relates to the career readiness competency of openness to change:

1. **When our positive self-view is threatened, we switch to self-protective mode and may instinctively resist change.** One downside of this tendency is that we can become defensive in the face of constructive criticism or feedback. Two renowned psychologists note: "Much research suggests that people have a 'psychological immune system' that initiates protective adaptations when an actual or impending threat is perceived."[167] The goal of these mechanisms is to restore self-worth, but they can also prevent us from changing, even when change would be beneficial to us.

2. **We can maintain our self-view in two ways (and one allows us to remain open to change!).** When our self-view is threatened, we naturally attempt to protect it. Say, for example, that you get caught in a lie. Even though deep down you know you have behaved dishonestly, your psyche will do everything it can to keep on seeing itself as good and virtuous. The key message of self-affirmation theory is—don't fight the urge to affirm your self-view in this situation, but rather, work with it. Specifically, when you experience a threat to your self-view, remind yourself that you can *choose* to respond in one of two ways:

    - **Option 1: Maintain your self-view by denying any information that is related to the threat.**

        What would this look like? In the case of our example, probably an internal dialogue that includes phrases like "how dare they accuse me of lying," or "it wasn't really a lie; it was simply an omission of the whole truth," or "I didn't have a choice but to be dishonest." Notice here that you are still talking about the threat and are making statements that relate directly to it. Unfortunately, you are also taking a defensive and closed-off stance that is preventing you from learning, growing, and experiencing positive change.

- **Option 2: Maintain your self-view *and* increase your openness to change by affirming facets of your self-view that are unrelated to the threat.**

    What would this look like? In the case of our example, you might choose an internal dialogue that goes something like "I am a loyal friend," or "I have compassion for others," or "I am a great teammate." Here you are (1) making positive statements about yourself that you believe to be true and (2) avoiding the topic of the actual threat.

Research on this theory firmly documents that while either option will help to restore your self-view, the second option is better because it allows you to feel good about yourself while still remaining open to change.[168] This is because your use of these positive "self-affirmations" makes it easier for the two voices in your head to coexist—you can make a poor choice (i.e., tell a lie) and still remind yourself that you are good. One mistake doesn't have to define you![169]

Self-affirmations such as the ones listed are defined as positive statements that impact your subconscious mind by drawing attention to your values and positive attributes and away from negative self-perceptions.[170] Self-affirmations flip our close-minded thoughts from negativity to positivity. Sample affirmations include:

- "My work does not define me; I'm a good person."
- "I learn from mistakes."
- "I can accomplish whatever I put my mind to."
- "I love my job and know that I am making a difference."
- "I'm not perfect, but I stick to my values."
- "I'm ethical."
- "I know I can do well, just like I did on the XYZ project."

If you want to increase your openness to either personal or work-related change, try using self-affirmations when you feel threatened or defensive. For example, if someone tells you that your views about a divisive political issue are naive, avoid the temptation to tell yourself, "I am not wrong about this because I am very well informed on the topic." Instead, try an affirmation that's not related to the conversation—or to politics in general. For example, say "I am proud of my dedication to my physical health." And remember, being more open to change doesn't mean that you *have* to change your views—it simply means that you are always willing to consider views that are different from your own.

Practicing Self-Compassion

In Chapter 9 we defined self-compassion as the tendency to be understanding, warm, and kind to yourself when you experience pain or failure, rather than being self-critical or over-identifying with negative emotions. Dr. Christine Carter defines self-compassion as "gentleness with yourself." Here is what she had to say about using self-compassion to increase openness to self-development.

> *We think that if we speak critically to ourselves, we will improve, but all the research shows with absolute certainty that self-criticism does not improve performance. It blocks your ability to learn from the situation and creates a stress response in which fight or flight are your only options. Personal growth is not on the menu when you are self-critical.*[171]

When you are overly hard on yourself, your body experiences distress—over time, you may experience symptoms such as anxiety, burnout, and depression.[172] When you have compassion for yourself, however, you let go of the need to be perfect, making it easier to increase your openness to change. It allows us to "give ourselves the same kindness and care we'd give to a good friend," according to psychologist Kristen Neff.[173]

Self-compassion protects self-identity by allowing you to appreciate the difference between being a bad person and making a bad decision. As noted in *Psychology Today*, "When you have self-compassion, you understand that your worth is unconditional."[174] This in turn makes it easier to accept feedback from others, to consider alternative viewpoints from your own, to own up to your mistakes, and to empathize with others.[175]

Try the following suggestions in pursuit of more self-compassion:

1. **Practice self-kindness.** Replace perfectionism and self-judgment with forgiveness and kindness. Accept your imperfections and talk to yourself as you would to a loved one.

2. **Remind yourself that you're not alone.** Psychotherapist Megan Bruneau reminds us that "to feel is to be human, and that whatever [we're] going through is also being experienced by millions of others. If we can recognize our shared humanity—that not one of us is perfect—we can begin to feel more connected to others, with a sense that we're all in this together."[176]

3. **Practice mindfulness meditation.** Mindfulness is a state of being present non-judgmentally. Meditation can help you achieve this state and avoid the negative thoughts that inhibit openness to change.[177]

Key Terms Used in This Chapter

adaptive change 360
change agent 366
creativity 349
crowdsourcing 375
force-field analysis 364
innovation strategy 372
innovation system 371
innovative change 360
intervention 368
organizational development (OD) 366
proactive change 355
process innovation 370
product innovation 370
radically innovative change 360
reactive change 355
readiness for change 362
resistance to change 377
self-affirmations 381
technology 357

Key Points

10.1 The Nature of Change in Organizations
- Among supertrends shaping the future of business: (1) The marketplace is becoming more segmented and moving toward more niche products. (2) More competitors are offering targeted products, requiring faster speed-to-market. (3) Some traditional companies may not survive radical change. (4) Offshore suppliers are changing the way we work. (5) Knowledge, not information, is becoming the new competitive advantage. (6) The employment landscape is shifting.
- Two types of change are reactive and proactive.
- Forces for change consist of forces outside the organization (external forces) or inside it (internal forces).

10.2 Forms and Models of Change
- Organizational change can be adaptive, innovative, or radically innovative.
- Lewin's change model has three stages—unfreezing, changing, and refreezing—to explain how to initiate, manage, and stabilize planned change.
- A systems approach to change consists of three parts: inputs, target elements of change, and outputs, plus a feedback loop.
- Force-field analysis is a technique to determine which forces could facilitate a proposed change and which forces could act against it.

10.3 Organizational Development: What It Is, What It Can Do
- Organizational development (OD) is a set of techniques for implementing planned change to make people and organizations more effective.
- The OD process follows three-steps: (1) diagnosis, (2) intervention, and (3) evaluation.
- Four factors that make OD successful (1) multiple interventions, (2) top managers give the OD program their support, (3) goals are chosen wisely, and (4) change agents understand how culture affects OD.

10.4 Organizational Innovation
- Innovation is the creation of something new and useful that gets commercialized.
- Crossing the types of innovation with the focus on the innovation results in four approaches to innovation.
- Innovation produces new products or processes and varies in focus from improvement to new directions.
- An innovation system's seven components are (1) an innovation strategy; (2) commitment from senior leaders; (3) an innovative culture and climate; (4) required structure and processes; (5) necessary human capital; (6) appropriate resources; and (7) human resource policies, practices, and procedures.

10.5 The Threat of Change: Managing Employee Fear and Resistance
- Resistance to change is an emotional/behavioral response to real or imagined threats to an established work routine.
- Ten reasons employees resist change are as follows: (1) individuals' predisposition toward change, (2) surprise and fear of the unknown, (3) climate of mistrust, (4) fear of failure, (5) loss of status or job security, (6) peer pressure, (7) disruption of cultural traditions or group relationships, (8) personality conflicts, (9) lack of tact or poor timing, and (10) nonreinforcing reward systems.

10.6 Career Corner: Managing Your Career Readiness
- Two key methods for improving your openness to change are: self-affirmation theory and self-compassion.

Boeing Continuing Case

In this part of the case, you'll read about the impact of organizational change forces on Boeing. You'll also learn more about how the key drivers of strategic implementation impacted decision making at the company.

Go to Connect to assess your ability to apply the concepts discussed in Chapters 8, 9, and 10 to the Boeing case.

PART 5 • LEADING

11 Managing Individual Differences and Behavior

Supervising People as People

After reading this chapter, you should be able to:

LO 11-1 Describe the importance of personality and individual traits in the hiring process.

LO 11-2 Explain the effects of values and attitudes on employee behavior.

LO 11-3 Describe the way perception can cloud judgment.

LO 11-4 Explain how managers can deal with employee attitudes.

LO 11-5 Discuss the sources of workplace stress and ways to reduce it.

LO 11-6 Describe how to develop the career readiness competencies of positive approach and emotional intelligence.

FORECAST   What's Ahead in This Chapter

This first of five chapters on leading discusses how to manage for individual differences and behaviors. We describe personality and individual behavior; values, attitudes, and behavior; and specific work-related attitudes and behaviors managers need to be aware of. We next discuss distortions in perception and consider what stress does to individuals. We conclude with a Career Corner that focuses on the career readiness competencies of a positive approach and emotional intelligence.

Making Positive First Impressions

As humans, we consciously try to manage other people's perceptions to ensure their first impression of us is a positive one. As you'll learn, there are factors that influence others' perceptions of you that you can't control, including unconscious biases and information processing errors.[1] But thankfully, a great deal of someone's first impression of you is within your control.

Creating positive first impressions is important in job or client interviews and other social situations. You can influence these others' perceptions of you by employing the following suggestions and your career readiness skills of positive approach and self-awareness.

Be Prepared
Be ready to ask and answer questions in job interviews. This shows your eagerness to contribute as soon as possible.[2] When meeting new co-workers, subordinates, clients, or company executives, the same advice applies. You'll need to reflect on your strengths and weaknesses relative to the job you are seeking. This preparation is part of the career readiness competency of self-awareness. When discussing your weaknesses, remember to take responsibility for past mistakes; this shows the career readiness competency of ownership/accepting responsibilities. There's no substitute for the confidence you'll gain from having done your homework on both the company and yourself!

Pay Attention to your Nonverbal Communication
Your body language conveys your confidence and invites others to feel confident in you as well. Stand (or sit, if you're on a Zoom) tall, lift your chin, make eye contact, and avoid crossing your arms or legs.[3] An enthusiastic greeting, handshake, or bow, along with a warm smile, suggests a friendly and open personality most people can relate to.

Look for Common Ground
It's only natural for us to like people who are similar to us in some way. Even a small link like a common interest in sports, music, or travel can help form a bond that will allow more positive associations to form as you communicate. You can indicate your interest in the other person by asking a few polite, open-ended questions to uncover such common ground.[4] Try arriving to a first meeting early—whether in person or on Zoom—so that you have a some extra time to lay this foundation.

Keep Up the Good Work
Once you've landed a job or a client account, continue solidifying the good impression you've made by being consistently reliable, prompt, humble, willing to learn, open to new experiences, and eager to be part of the team. These are all part of the career readiness competency of positive approach. Remember to ask for help when you need it.[5]

For Discussion What might you ask to create common ground with someone you are meeting for the first time? What can you say during a job interview to convey the impression that you are a positive and flexible person?

11.1 Personality and Individual Behavior

THE BIG PICTURE

Personality consists of stable psychological and behavioral attributes that give you your identity. We describe five personality dimensions and five personality traits that managers need to be aware of to understand workplace behavior.

LO 11-1

Describe the importance of personality and individual traits in the hiring process.

In this and the next four chapters, we discuss the third management function (after planning and organizing)—namely, leading. *Leading*, as we said in Chapter 1, is defined as motivating, directing, and otherwise influencing people to work hard to achieve the organization's goals.

How would you describe yourself? Are you outgoing? aggressive? sociable? tense? passive? lazy? quiet? Whatever the combination of traits, which result from the interaction of your genes and your environment, they constitute your personality. More formally, **personality** consists of the stable psychological traits and behavioral attributes that give a person their identity.[6] As a manager, you need to understand personality attributes because they affect how people perceive and act within the organization.[7]

The Big Five Personality Dimensions

Researchers have distilled a list of multiple, work-relevant personality traits into a set of factors known as the Big Five.[8] The **Big Five personality dimensions** are (1) extroversion, (2) agreeableness, (3) conscientiousness, (4) emotional stability, and (5) openness to experience.

- **Extroversion:** How outgoing, talkative, sociable, and assertive a person is.
- **Agreeableness:** How trusting, good-natured, cooperative, and soft-hearted someone is.
- **Conscientiousness:** How dependable, responsible, achievement-oriented, and persistent someone is.
- **Emotional stability:** How relaxed, secure, and unworried a person is.
- **Openness to experience:** How intellectual, imaginative, curious, and broad-minded someone is.

Choose wisely. The most common form of personality testing is the self-report measure. This type of test relies on information provided by participants through multiple-choice questions. SIAATH/Shutterstock

Pre-employment psychometric testing, which includes personality testing, has grown into a $2 billion industry. Employers use psychometric testing to identify candidates with desired career readiness skills and to determine training or coaching needs for current employees.[9] Over 80% of Fortune 500 companies use these tests at different stages of the recruitment process, believing that hiring decisions will be more accurate and predictive of high performers.[10] But are they? Research finds the following:

- Conscientiousness has the most consistent relationships with important outcomes such as task performance, leadership behavior, supervisor-rated liking, resilience, and lower unemployment.[11]

- Highly conscientious individuals are more likely to be *perfectionists*—those striving for flawlessness. This can be a disadvantage, as perfectionism tends to have a negative impact on job performance.[12]
- Extroversion is closely related to leadership as well as higher levels of motivation, positivity, well-being, and interpersonal savviness, which lead to higher job performance.[13]
- Individuals high on conscientiousness, agreeableness, and emotional stability are less likely to engage in workplace deviance.[14]

Which career readiness competencies come to mind after reading these bullet points? We see connections between personality traits (such as conscientiousness and extraversion) and important career readiness competencies such as resilience, positive approach, and social intelligence.

Where do you think you stand in terms of the Big Five? You can find out by completing Self-Assessment 11.1 in Connect, if your instructor has assigned it.

SELF-ASSESSMENT 11.1   CAREER READINESS

Where Do You Stand on the Big Five Dimensions of Personality?

This survey is designed to assess your personality using the Big Five dimensions. Please complete Self-Assessment 11.1 if your instructor has assigned it in Connect.

Experts caution about issues with using personality tests in employment decisions.[15] These include the potential for respondents to attempt to cheat the tests or to give what they believe are socially desirable responses. Further, managers may not have the training necessary for interpreting results, particularly given that most of the traits measured by common workplace personality tests don't correlate directly with job performance. One safer way to use personality testing in the workplace is for the purpose of team building. Consider the following example:

Personality Testing for Team Building Example—Authoring Team: Your authors use personality testing to enhance the experiences we have while working on this product. Working on this type of product requires a team of people with varied skillsets, along with a great deal of critical thinking, coordination, and decision making. We spend a whole lot of time working together. The core product team—including the authors, product managers, and editorial team members—took a popular personality test and shared the results with one another. We also discussed aspects of our personalities that were likely to both enhance and distract from effective interpersonal relationships and ultimately our collective productivity. This streamlined many of our processes, and it allowed us to work better as a unit because we know so much about the tendencies and preferences of each of our team members.

Core Self-Evaluations

A **core self-evaluation (CSE)** represents a broad personality trait comprising four positive individual traits: (1) self-efficacy, (2) self-esteem, (3) locus of control, and (4) emotional stability. Managers need to be aware of these personality traits as they are related to employees' work attitudes, intrinsic motivation, creativity, ethical leadership, and performance.[16]

1. Self-Efficacy: "I Can/Can't Do This Task"
Self-efficacy is the belief in one's personal ability to do a task. This is about your personal belief that you have what it takes to successfully complete a specific task in a specific situation. This characteristic has been expanded into a broader motivational trait labeled generalized self-efficacy.

Generalized self-efficacy represents the belief in one's general ability to perform across different situations.[17] It is a career readiness competency desired by employers.

Have you noticed that those who are confident in their abilities tend to succeed, whereas those preoccupied with failure tend not to? Indeed, high levels of self-efficacy have been linked to all kinds of positives, including academic performance, work performance, lower burnout, job satisfaction, and motivation.[18]

Among the implications for managers are the following:

- **Assign jobs accordingly.** Complex, challenging, and autonomous jobs tend to enhance people's perceptions of their self-efficacy. Boring, tedious jobs generally do the opposite.

- **Develop employees' self-efficacy and generalized self-efficacy.** Self-efficacy is a quality that can be nurtured. Employees with low self-efficacy need lots of constructive pointers and positive feedback.[19] Goal difficulty needs to match individuals' perceived self-efficacy, but goals can be made more challenging as performance improves.[20] Small successes need to be rewarded. Employees' expectations can be improved through guided experiences, mentoring, and role modeling.[21] It's also important to monitor employees' generalized self-efficacy because it impacts all aspects of our lives. For example, low generalized self-efficacy can foster **learned helplessness**, the debilitating lack of faith in your ability to control your environment.[22] High generalized self-efficacy, on the other hand, is positively linked to job performance and satisfaction.[23] This is particularly true for entrepreneurs and even athletes.[24]

Yes, I can! Believing you can succeed at something can assist you in actually performing well. Have there been times when you doubted your ability to perform a task? What was the end result? Jacob Lund/Shutterstock

You can assess your generalized self-efficacy and learn about ways to apply the results by taking Self-Assessment 11.2 in Connect, if your instructor has assigned it. Results may enhance your confidence at achieving both your personal and work-related goals.

SELF-ASSESSMENT 11.2   CAREER READINESS

What Is Your Level of Generalized Self-Efficacy?

This survey is designed to assess your generalized self-efficacy. Please complete Self-Assessment 11.2 if your instructor has assigned it in Connect.

2. Self-Esteem: "I Like/Dislike Myself"

How worthwhile, capable, and acceptable do you think you are? The answer to this question is an indicator of your **self-esteem**, the extent to which people like or dislike themselves, their overall self-evaluation.[25] Research offers some interesting insights about how high or low self-esteem can affect people and organizations.

- **People with high self-esteem.** Compared to people with low self-esteem, people with high self-esteem are more apt to handle failure better and to become leaders. They also are less likely to be depressed, experience employment gaps, and engage in counterproductive behavior at work. However, when faced with pressure situations, people with high self-esteem have been found to become egotistical and boastful.[26]

- **People with low self-esteem.** Conversely, research suggests people with low self-esteem focus on their weaknesses and disengage from tasks when confronted with failure.[27] Moreover, they are more dependent on others and are more apt to be influenced by them and to be less likely to take independent positions.

Can self-esteem be improved? According to a recent meta-analysis, a multitude of interventions can successfully increase self-esteem in adults.[28] Some ways in which managers can build employee self-esteem are shown in Table 11.1.

3. Locus of Control: "I Am/Am Not the Captain of My Fate"

As we discussed briefly in Chapter 1, **locus of control** indicates how much people believe they control their fate through their own efforts. If you have an *internal locus of control,* you believe you control your own destiny. If you have an *external locus of control,* you believe external forces control you. Can you see how an internal locus of control could be an asset as you work to develop career readiness competencies such as resilience, personal adaptability, openness to change, and proactive learning orientation?

Research shows internals and externals have important workplace differences. Internals exhibit less anxiety, greater work motivation, and stronger expectations that effort leads to performance. They also are better leaders and obtain higher salaries.[29]

These findings have two important implications for managers:

- **Expect different degrees of structure and compliance for each type.** Employees with an internal locus of control may resist close managerial supervision. Hence, consider placing them in jobs requiring high initiative and lower compliance. In contrast, employees with an external locus of control may perform better in highly structured jobs requiring greater compliance.

- **Employ different reward systems for each type.** Internals may prefer and respond better to incentives such as merit pay or sales commissions because they have a greater belief that their actions have a direct impact on their outcomes. (We discuss incentive compensation systems in Chapter 12.)

TABLE 11.1 Some Ways That Managers Can Boost Employee Self-Esteem

• Reinforce employees' positive attributes and skills.
• Provide positive feedback whenever possible.
• Break larger projects into smaller tasks and projects.
• Express confidence in employees' abilities to complete their tasks.
• Provide coaching whenever employees are seen to be struggling to complete tasks.

4. Emotional Stability: "I'm Fairly Secure/Insecure When Working under Pressure" Emotional stability is the extent to which people feel secure and unworried and how likely they are to experience negative emotions under pressure. People with low levels of emotional stability are prone to anxiety and negative worldviews, whereas people with high levels tend to show better job performance.[30]

Emotional Intelligence: Understanding Your Emotions and the Emotions of Others

Emotional intelligence (EI) has been defined as "the ability to carry out accurate reasoning about emotions and the ability to use emotions and emotional knowledge to enhance thought."[31] Said another way, emotional intelligence is the ability to monitor your and others' feelings and to use this information to guide your thinking and actions.[32] The concept of EI, first introduced in 1909, has become a hot topic in the modern workplace. Some suggest this highly desirable career readiness competency is even more important than IQ.[33]

Does research hold emotional intelligence in equally high regard? Research suggests that EI is moderately associated with (1) better relationships and well-being, (2) higher levels of job satisfaction, (3) better emotional control, (4) higher levels of conscientiousness and self-efficacy, (5) increased organizational citizenship behavior, and (6) higher self-rated performance. Interestingly, research does not link EI with supervisor-rated performance.[34]

What Do We Know about EI? Daniel Goleman, the psychologist who popularized the concept of EI, concluded that it is composed of four key components: self-awareness, self-management, social awareness, and relationship management.[35] (See Table 11.2.)

Can You Raise Your EI? Is there any way to raise your own emotional intelligence? Although parts of EI represent stable components that are not readily changed, other aspects, such as using empathy, can be developed.[36] Table 11.2 shows that the underlying components of EI are related to the related career readiness competencies we introduced in Chapter 1. This means that mastering multiple career readiness competencies (something we provide guidance for in the Career Corners throughout this product) may help you to improve your EI.

TABLE 11.2 The Components of Emotional Intelligence

COMPONENT	DESCRIPTION	RELATED CAREER READINESS COMPETENCIES
Self-awareness	The most essential component. This is the ability to read your own emotions and gauge your moods accurately, so you know how you're affecting others.	• Self-Awareness
Self-management	This is the ability to control your emotions and act with honesty and integrity in reliable and adaptable ways. You can leave occasional bad moods outside the office.	• Resilience • Personal Adaptability
Social awareness	This includes empathy, allowing you to show others that you care, and organizational intuition, so you keenly understand how your emotions and actions affect others.	• Cross-Cultural Competency • Social Intelligence
Relationship management	This is the ability to communicate clearly and convincingly, disarm conflicts, and build strong personal bonds.	• Oral/Written Communication • Teamwork/Collaboration • Networking • Showing Commitment • Service/Others Orientation

Two suggestions for building EI are:

- **Develop awareness of your EI level.** Becoming aware of your level of emotional intelligence is the first step. Self-Assessment 11.3 can be used for this purpose. Taking self-assessments such as this one help you to build the career readiness competency of self-awareness.
- **Learn about areas needing improvement.** The next step is to learn more about the aspects of EI on which you most need improvement. For example, to improve your skills at using empathy, find articles on the topic and try to implement the authors' recommendations. One such article suggests that empathy in communications is enhanced by (1) trying to understand how others feel about what they are communicating and (2) gaining appreciation of what people want from an exchange.[37] The Practical Action box illustrates how technology is used to develop empathy, a key component of EI.

PRACTICAL ACTION | Using Technology to Develop Emotional Intelligence

Emotional intelligence is one of the most important skills a job candidate can have, and empathy is a key component of EI.[38] To empathize means to understand and even experience others' perspectives and feelings.[39] Empathy drives engagement, helps us build relationships, decreases turnover, improves customer service, and fosters teamwork.[40]

Many experts believe we can develop our EI. But until recently, suggestions have consisted mostly of generic advice such as "develop an understanding of your own emotions" or "put yourself in the other person's shoes." Emerging technology is providing more immersive, and therefore realistic, methods for increasing EI. Let's look at two types.

Virtual Reality–Based Empathy Training

Empathetic employees provide a higher level of customer service, are more collaborative, and produce more sales than less empathetic employees.[41] Corporate training company SweetRush developed a virtual hotel so corporate managers could experience what it felt like working in lower-level positions. The experience was designed to motivate managers to be more empathetic with colleagues working at the front desk or cleaning guest rooms. "They don't understand what those people's jobs are like, yet they are making decisions for those people day in and day out," said John Carlos Lozano, chief creative officer at SweetRush. Hilton Hotels & Resorts recently partnered with SweetRush to develop a personalized VR empathy training experience for its employees.[42]

Researchers at the Ohio State University received a Medicaid-sponsored grant to develop a VR simulation for caregivers of dementia patients. The platform, known as the Virtual Reality

microgen/123RF

Performance Platform for Learning about Dementia (VR-ED), allows caregivers such as medical school residents to experience the perspective of both a person living with dementia and a caregiver for someone living with dementia. The experience also immerses, and therefore impacts, participants in the audience as they observe the VR interactions in real-time on a large screen.[43]

App-Based Empathy Training
Random App of Kindness is a free app that consists of nine mini-games designed to improve specific aspects of users' empathy. These include emotion recognition, response inhibition, and caring for others' needs. The app takes interventions that have previously been used to increase empathy in face-to-face settings and translates them into easily accessible smartphone games.[44]

YOUR CALL
Do you believe that virtual reality, simulations, and games can help increase employees' empathy? What else can you do to develop this skill?

SELF-ASSESSMENT 11.3   CAREER READINESS

What Is Your Level of Emotional Intelligence?
This survey is designed to assess your emotional intelligence. Please complete Self-Assessment 11.3 if your instructor has assigned it in Connect.

11.2 Values, Attitudes, and Behavior

THE BIG PICTURE
Organizational behavior (OB) considers how to better understand and manage people at work. In this section, we discuss individual values and attitudes and how they affect people's actions and judgments.

LO 11-2
Explain the effects of values and attitudes on employee behavior.

Managers are responsible for predicting, understanding, and motivating their employees' behaviors, and as you might have guessed, this is no easy task. People are complex creatures, and it takes effort to understand what makes each of us "tick." Values and attitudes are two categories of individual differences that explain a great deal of who we are, what we care about, and how we ultimately behave. Understanding employees' values and attitudes can go a long way toward helping managers to better support their employees.

Organizational Behavior: Trying to Explain and Predict Workplace Behavior

Organizational behavior (OB), is the field dedicated to better understanding and managing people at work. In particular, OB tries to help managers not only *explain* workplace behavior but also *predict* it. Knowledge of OB helps managers to better lead and motivate employee performance. The field of OB focuses on two broad areas of behavior:

- **Individual behavior.** Individual behavior is the subject of this chapter. We discuss individual attributes such as values, attitudes, personality, perception, and learning.

- **Group behavior.** Group behavior is the subject of later chapters, particularly Chapter 13, where we discuss norms, roles, and teams.

Let's begin by considering individual values, attitudes, and behavior.

Values: What Are Your Consistent Beliefs and Feelings about All Things?

As you learned in Chapter 3, **values** are the abstract ideals that guide your thinking and behavior across a variety of situations.[45] Lifelong behavior patterns are dictated by values that are fairly well set by the time people are in their early teens. After that, however, one's values can be reshaped by significant life-altering events. This includes having a child; undergoing a business failure; or surviving the death of a loved one, a war, or a serious health threat.

From a manager's point of view, it's helpful to know that values represent the ideals that underlie how we behave at work. Ideals such as concern for others, self-enhancement, independence, and security are common values in the workplace.[46] Managers who understand an employee's values are better suited to assign them to meaningful projects and to help avoid conflicts between work activities and personal values.[47]

Attitudes: What Are Your Consistent Beliefs and Feelings about Specific Things?

Values are abstract ideals—global beliefs and feelings—that are directed toward all objects, people, or events. Values tend to be consistent both over time and over related situations.

Attitudes, in contrast, are beliefs and feelings that are directed toward *specific* objects, people, or events. More formally, an **attitude** is defined as a learned predisposition toward a given object.[48] Managers need to understand the components of attitudes because attitudes influence employees' behavior.[49]

Attitudes Example—Generational Differences: Job satisfaction is moderately associated with performance and strongly related to employee turnover.[50] Workers with low levels of job satisfaction are less likely to demonstrate high performance, and workers with high levels of job satisfaction are less likely to quit. This is why it's important for managers to track employees' attitudes and understand their causes. Modern managers are working to better understand Gen Z employees' job attitudes, given that recent research suggests Gen Zers are less satisfied with their jobs than workers from other generations.[51] A Gallup poll conducted in 2022 found that Gen Z employees also are less engaged than other generations in the workforce.[52] Members of this generation have experienced multiple global crises and periods of economic uncertainty in their lifetimes, and they report higher stress, anxiety, and depression than individuals from other age groups. Experts suggest that managers of Gen Z workers focus on job security, highlight the importance of individual contributions toward organizational goals, and establish connection and trust.[53]

We discuss specific, work-related attitudes in Section 11.4. Next we consider the components that make up an attitude.

It's not personal. Do you think managers should be giving employees personal advice? What would you do if someone at work asked for your thoughts on a personal problem they are having? Pressmaster/Shutterstock

The Three Components of Attitudes: Affective, Cognitive, and Behavioral
Attitudes have three components—*affective, cognitive,* and *behavioral.*[54]

- **The affective component—"I feel."** The affective component of an attitude consists of the feelings or emotions one has about a situation. How do you *feel* about a person who talks loudly on their phone in the middle of a restaurant? If you feel annoyed or angry, you're expressing negative affect. (If you're indifferent, your attitude is neutral.)

- **The cognitive component—"I believe."** The cognitive component of an attitude consists of the beliefs and knowledge one has about a situation. What do you *think* about a person who talks on the phone in a restaurant? Is what they're doing inconsiderate, acceptable, even admirable (because it shows they're productive)? Your answer reflects your beliefs or ideas about the situation.

- **The behavioral component—"I intend."** The behavioral component of an attitude, also known as the intentional component, is how one intends or expects to behave toward a situation. What would you *intend to do* if a person talked loudly on their phone at the table next to you while you tried to enjoy a nice meal? Your action may reflect your negative or positive feelings (affective), your negative or positive beliefs (cognitive), and your intention or lack of intention to do anything (behavioral).

All three components are often manifested at any given time. For example, if you call a corporation and get a telephone-tree menu ("For customer service, press 1 . . .") that never seems to connect you to a human being, you might be so irritated that you would say:

- "I get so frustrated when given the runaround like this." [*affective component—your feelings*]
- "This company doesn't know how to take care of customers." [*cognitive component—your perceptions*]
- "I'll never call this company again." [*behavioral component—your intentions*]

One of the attitude-based career readiness competencies that employers desire is a *positive approach.*[55] We defined positive approach in Chapter 1 as the "willingness to accept developmental feedback, to try and suggest new ideas, and to maintain a positive attitude at work." Where do you think you stand on being positive at work? Find out by taking Self-Assessment 11.4 in Connect, if your instructor has assigned it.

SELF-ASSESSMENT 11.4   CAREER READINESS

Do You Have a Positive Approach at Work?

This survey is designed to assess the extent you possess a positive approach or attitude at work. Please complete Self-Assessment 11.4 if your instructor has assigned it in Connect.

When Attitudes and Reality Collide: Consistency and Cognitive Dissonance
One of the last things you want, probably, is to be accused of hypocrisy—to be criticized for saying one thing and doing another. Like most people, you no doubt want to maintain consistency between your attitudes and your behavior.

But what if a strongly held attitude bumps up against a harsh reality that contradicts it? Suppose you're an immunocompromised individual. Being immunocompromised makes you more susceptible to contracting, and suffering complications from, bacterial and viral infections, and you are therefore extremely cautious of the environments you spend time in because you are afraid of becoming ill. Now suppose you're involved in a life-threatening auto accident in a third-world country and require hospitalization. Do you reject being admitted to the hospital for important treatment to minimize your chances of contracting an infection?

In 1957, social psychologist Leon Festinger proposed the term **cognitive dissonance** to describe the psychological discomfort a person experiences between their cognitive attitude and incompatible behavior.[56] Because people are uncomfortable with inconsistency, Festinger theorized they will seek to reduce the "dissonance," or tension, of the inconsistency. How they deal with the discomfort, he suggested, depends on three factors:

- **Importance.** How important are the elements creating the dissonance? Most people can put up with some ambiguities in life. For example, many drivers don't think obeying speed limits is very important, even though they profess to be law-abiding citizens. People eat fried foods, even though they know that those foods may contribute to heart disease.

- **Control.** How much control does one have over the matters that create dissonance? A juror may not like the idea of voting for the death penalty but believe that they have no choice but to follow the law in the case. A taxpayer may object to their taxes being spent on a particular social program and simultaneously feel they cannot withhold taxes.

- **Rewards.** What rewards are at stake in the dissonance? You're apt to cling to old ideas in the face of new evidence if you are deeply emotionally or financially invested in those ideas. If you're a detective who has worked for 20 years to prove a particular suspect's guilt in a murder case, you're not apt to be very accepting of contradictory evidence after all that time.

Harming animals is wrong.

I love chicken nuggets.

Krakenimages.com/Shutterstock

Behavior: How Values and Attitudes Affect People's Actions and Judgments

Values (global) and attitudes (specific) are generally in harmony, but not always. For example, a manager may put a positive *value* on helpful behavior (global) yet may have a negative *attitude* toward helping an unethical co-worker (specific). Together, however, values and attitudes influence people's workplace **behavior**—their actions and judgments. •

11.3 Perception and Individual Behavior

THE BIG PICTURE
Perception, a four-step process, can be skewed by five types of distortion: stereotyping, implicit bias, the halo effect, the recency effect, and causal attribution. We also consider the self-fulfilling prophecy, which can affect our judgment as well.

If you were a smoker, which warning on a cigarette pack would make you think more about quitting? (1) "Smoking seriously harms you and others around you"? (2) A blunt "Smoking kills"? Or (3) a stark graphic image showing decaying lungs?

This is the kind of decision public health authorities in various countries wrestle with. (One study found that highly graphic images about the negative effects of smoking

LO 11-3

Describe the way perception can cloud judgment.

FIGURE 11.1

The four steps in the perceptual process

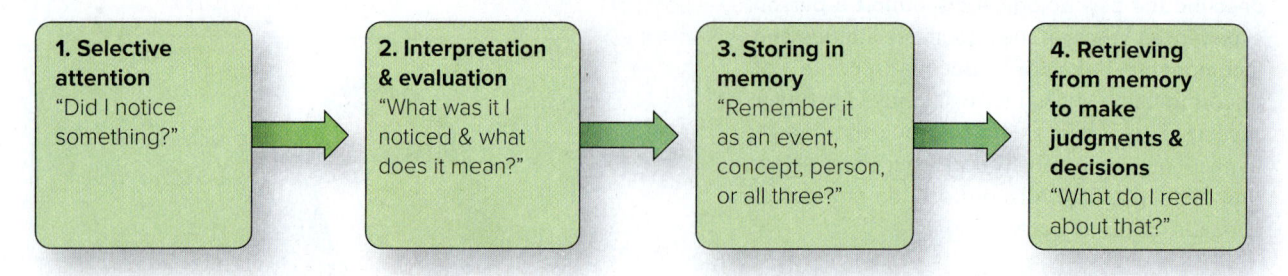

1. Selective attention	2. Interpretation & evaluation	3. Storing in memory	4. Retrieving from memory to make judgments & decisions
"Did I notice something?"	"What was it I noticed & what does it mean?"	"Remember it as an event, concept, person, or all three?"	"What do I recall about that?"

had the greatest impact on smokers' intentions to quit.)[57] These officials, in other words, try to decide how consumers' *perceptions* might influence behaviors. Here we explore how perception relates to behavior in the workplace.

The Four Steps in the Perceptual Process

Perception is the process of interpreting and understanding one's environment. The process of perception is complex, but it can be boiled down to four steps.[58] (See Figure 11.1.)

In this product we are less concerned about the theoretical steps in perception and more concerned with how perceptions are distorted. This is because perceptual distortions can have considerable bearing on a manager's judgment. Misunderstandings or errors in judgment can occur in any one of the four stages of the perception process. Perceptual errors can lead to mistakes that can be damaging to yourself, other people, and your organization.

Five Distortions in Perception

In this section we describe the following perceptual distortions: (1) *stereotyping,* (2) *implicit bias,* (3) the *halo effect,* (4) the *recency effect,* and (5) *causal attribution.*

1. Stereotyping: "Those Sorts of People Are Pretty Much the Same"

A stereotype, as we defined in Chapter DEI, is a generalization we make about a person because they belong to one or more specific identity groups. People may hold stereotypes about us because of our gender identity, race, religion, or age, or because of a combination of these or other identities. For example, if someone negatively stereotypes neurodivergent individuals and females, that person may attribute even worse characteristics to a neurodivergent female.

Take a look at the following statistics regarding stereotypes in the workplace:[59]

- Most U.S. working adults believe that racial bias is a problem in both hiring decisions and performance evaluations.
- Survey respondents continue to rate men as more qualified for leadership positions than women.
- Nearly 40% of the hiring managers in a recent survey admitted to allowing age bias to influence them when evaluating resumes.

Consider how the culture at Aptive Environmental works to eliminate negative stereotypes related to employee age.

Stereotypes Example—Aptive Environmental: Aptive Environmental has locations in more than 3,700 cities nationwide. The company believes that "people make great companies, not the other way around." One of its core values is to "Elevate the Tribe," which means building a positive environment through kindness and loyalty. This extends to older employees as well. Reviewers on employment website *Monster* claim, "The respect for elders . . . is off the charts." Another employee mentioned, "It's awesome to learn from the older employees within the office. They really care about curating the next generations." Aptive Environmental is seeing results as part of their initiative to care for older workers. The company is the fastest-growing pest solutions provider in its industry and consistently ranks on a variety of "Best Companies" lists.[60]

Eliminating malaria. In addition to focusing on its employees, Aptive Environmental is also focusing on stopping the spread of malaria by mosquitoes. The company dedicates a portion of its profits to provide assistance to countries with the greatest need to combat the disease. welcomia/Shutterstock

2. Implicit Bias: "I Really Don't Think I'm Biased, but I Just Have a Feeling about Some People"

Explicit bias refers to the attitudes or beliefs that affect our understanding, actions, and decisions in a conscious manner.[61] Examples of explicit bias include overt, intentional statements of hate, racism, ableism, and sexism. Today, we aren't likely to hear managers pronouncing these types of biases out in the open. What's more common is the tendency for managers' perceptions to be skewed by subconscious, implicit biases. **Implicit bias** is defined as the attitudes or beliefs that affect our understanding, actions, and decisions in an unconscious manner.[62]

Consider the following research findings regarding implicit racial bias:[63]

- White applicants get around 50% more call-backs than Black applicants with the same resume.
- College professors are 26% more likely to respond to a student e-mail when signed by Brad (typical white name) rather than Lamar (typical African American name).
- Physicians recommend less pain medications for Black patients than white patients when addressing the same injury.

Most of us believe that we are unprejudiced, but research suggests that we all likely hold some degree of implicit bias.[64] Studies have demonstrated implicit bias in a variety of contexts, including employment decisions, criminal justice decisions, and the use of technology.[65]

Judicial bias. Do you think judges are biased against Black defendants? If so, how can this bias be eliminated? Renee Jones Schneider/Alamy Stock Photo

Implicit Bias in Employment Decisions
Implicit bias appears to affect employment-related decisions. A recent study analyzing data from Harvard University's Project Implicit (more than 5 million respondents across 34 countries, 74% white) showed that managers expressed higher levels of implicit bias than professionals in all other occupation categories. The study found that managers held implicit biases related to race, sexual orientation, gender, and disability.[66] The study authors theorized that these biases help to explain why employees from minoritized identity groups experience fewer promotions and have poorer experiences at work than employees from majority identity groups.

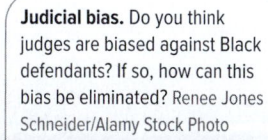

Implicit Bias in the Criminal Justice System The National Conference of State Legislatures (NCSL) reviewed data from a variety of jurisdictions across the United States and found a host of evidence of implicit bias in the criminal justice system. As one example, cases involving Black victims were more likely to be dismissed than cases involving white victims. As another example, misdemeanor drug cases against white defendants were less likely to be filed in court than those against Black/Hispanic defendants. The NCSL report concluded by urging state legislatures to consider policy changes that would increase fairness in the criminal justice system and decrease the impacts of implicit biases.[67]

Implicit Bias and Technology Studies have found that people have implicit biases toward new information technology. Implicit biases about new information technology focus on abstract and unseen characteristics while biases about humans tend to be based on concrete and visible characteristics. Often times, managers believe that new technology is mysterious, nonhuman, and complex, which may erroneously lead them to believe it is superior to existing methods. This is an important implicit bias to be aware of as we are living in a society that is increasingly reliant on technology.[68] One way to reduce this bias is to master the career readiness competency of information technology application, which we introduced in Chapter 1. This will allow you to more effectively evaluate new information technology (see Table 1.3).

3. The Halo Effect: "One Trait Tells Me All I Need to Know"

We often use faces as markers for gender, race, and age, but physical characteristics can lead us to fall back on stereotypes. For example, height has been associated with perceptions of prosperity—high income—and occupational success. Excess weight has been associated with perceptions of negative traits such as laziness, incompetence, and lack of discipline.[69] These examples illustrate the **halo effect**, in which we form an impression of an individual based on a single trait. (The phenomenon also is called the *horn-and-halo effect* because a single positive/negative trait can be generalized into an array of positive/negative traits). Clearly, however, if a manager fails to look at *all* of an individual's traits, they have no right to complain if that employee doesn't work out.

4. The Recency Effect: "The Most Recent Impressions Are the Ones That Count"

The **recency effect** is the tendency to remember recent information better than earlier information, perhaps because when you activate your recall, more recent events are still present in your working memory.[70] This misperception often is evident among investors (even professionals), who are more likely to buy a stock if they recently have seen something about it in the news or if it has a high one-day return.[71] Consider how the recency effect might impact a manager's evaluations of two different employees if the manager has recently witnessed one of the employees performing at a high level on a project, but has not had the opportunity to observe the other employee recently.

5. Causal Attributions

Causal attribution is the activity of inferring causes for observed behavior. Rightly or wrongly, we constantly formulate cause-and-effect explanations for our own and others' behavior. Attributional statements such as the following are common: "Amir drinks too much because he has no willpower; I need a few drinks after work because I'm under a lot of pressure."

Our causal attributions tend to be self-serving and are often invalid. However, attributions profoundly impact organizational behavior, and it's therefore important to understand how people formulate them. Consider a supervisor evaluating a poor-performing employee. The supervisor may reprimand the employee if they believe the poor performance is due to a lack of effort. If the supervisor attributes the poor performance to a lack of ability, they may deem training necessary. Finally, the supervisor may attribute the poor performance to bad luck, such as a natural disaster or a virus that has effectively shut down the country, and may therefore excuse the poor performance.[72]

As a manager, you should be aware of two attributional biases that can distort your interpretation of behaviors—the *fundamental attribution bias* and the *self-serving bias*.

- **Fundamental attribution bias.** As we defined in Chapter DEI, the fundamental attribution bias causes us to attribute others' behaviors and outcomes to their personal characteristics rather than to environmental influences. For example, if someone cuts you off while driving, you are more likely to conclude that they are a jerk than to consider the rationale for their reckless driving. It could be that they were rushing to get to the hospital.
- **Self-serving bias.** With the self-serving bias, we tend to take more personal responsibility for our successes than for our failures. Research shows that employees tend to rely on this bias when performance results are public.[73] An example of the self-serving bias is getting an A on an exam and concluding that it's due to your level of intelligence and/or preparation but blaming poor grades that you receive on the professor's exam-writing skills or teaching abilities. Another example of the self-serving bias is car accidents, when both parties involved tend to blame the other driver.[74]

The Self-Fulfilling Prophecy, or Pygmalion Effect

In the G. B. Shaw play *Pygmalion,* a speech coach bets he can get a girl from a low social-class background to change her accent and demeanor and pass herself off as a duchess. After six months of instruction, she successfully "passes" in high society, having assumed the attributes of a woman from a high social-class background. This exemplifies the self-fulfilling prophecy, also known as the Pygmalion ("pig-mail-yun") effect, which describes the phenomenon in which people's expectations of themselves or others lead them to behave in ways that make those expectations come true.

Expectations impact our outcomes. For example, consider a waiter who delivers inferior service to a table of poorly dressed customers because they expect the table to leave a small tip. The table may react to the poor service with—you guessed it—a much lower tip than planned. Research has shown that managers can positively impact workers' levels of achievement and productivity simply by raising their performance expectations for employees.[75]

What this means for you as a manager is that employees tend to rise to the level of your expectations. Among the things managers can do to create positive performance expectations: Recognize that everyone has the potential to increase their performance. Introduce new employees as if they have outstanding potential. Encourage employees to visualize the successful execution of tasks. Help employees master key skills.[76]

The musical *My Fair Lady* is one of the most recognizable adaptations of *Pygmalion.* Warner Brothers/Album/Alamy Stock Photo

EXAMPLE

"What's within You Is Stronger Than What's in Your Way"[77]

Erik Weihenmayer was diagnosed with an eye disease called juvenile retinoschisis at age four and was completely blind by his first year of high school. He recalls that, at the time, "I was afraid that I wasn't going to be able to participate in life."[78] But instead of shielding him from opportunities, his parents encouraged him to take up all the activities his peers were tackling.[79] Weihenmayer joined his high school wrestling team and went on to represent Connecticut in the National Junior Freestyle Wrestling Championships.[80] He also realized that the keen tactile sense he'd developed due to the loss of his sight made him especially suited for rock climbing, a hobby that blossomed into a lifelong passion.

Weihenmayer eventually became the first person with total loss of vision to summit Mount Everest.[81] He persisted in working toward this goal despite Himalayan experts strongly discouraging him from attempting the climb. He recalls, "They were judging me on the basis of one thing that they knew about me and that was being blind. But they didn't realize that there are a dozen other attributes that contribute to whether you're a good mountaineer or not."[82] Weihenmayer acknowledges that life isn't always easy but believes strongly that "People have the inner resources to become anything they want to be. Challenge just becomes the vehicle for tapping into those inner resources."[83] Weihenmayer holds the distinction of being one of only a few hundred people in history to complete the seven summits, meaning he has climbed to the top of the highest mountain on each of the seven continents.[84]

Weihenmayer co-founded an organization called *No Barriers*, which aims to help those with challenges live rich and meaningful lives.[85] He believes that all of us should make the conscious decision to do the things that make us uncomfortable and live our most extraordinary lives, in spite of our fears or the beliefs we often allow to limit us.[86] He receives many requests for guidance from parents of children with loss of vision or other challenges. His advice? "The key is to really have tremendously high expectations and to teach kids how to be self-sufficient and confident and give them the skills that they need to succeed."[87]

Erik Weihenmayer Imke Lass/Redux Pictures

YOUR CALL

Have you allowed yourself to be limited by certain expectations? What is something you've wanted to do but have been afraid to try because you don't believe you can?

11.4 Work-Related Attitudes and Behaviors Managers Need to Deal With

THE BIG PICTURE

Attitudes are important because they affect behavior. Managers need to be alert to the key work-related attitudes having to do with engagement, job satisfaction, and organizational commitment. Among the types of employee behavior they should attend to are their prosocial behaviors, on-the-job performance and productivity, and absenteeism and turnover.

"Keep the employees happy," we often hear. But is keeping employees happy all that managers need to know to get results? Managers need to understand attitudes because attitudes are one of the variables that affect behavior. We discuss additional variables that motivate performance in the next chapter. Here, let us consider what managers need to know about key work-related attitudes and behaviors.

Three work-related attitudes that are important for managers to understand are (1) *employee engagement,* (2) *job satisfaction,* and (3) *organizational commitment.*

LO 11-4
Explain how managers can deal with employee attitudes.

1. Employee Engagement: How Connected Are You to Your Work?

Employee engagement is defined as a "mental state in which a person performing a work activity is fully immersed in the activity, feeling full of energy and enthusiasm for the work."[88] Employers, consultants, and academics are interested in the causes and consequences of employee engagement due to its potential to increase individual, group, and organizational performance.[89] Let's consider what we've learned.

What Percentage of Employees Are Fully Engaged at Work?
The ADP Research Institute attempted to answer this question by surveying over 19,000 employees around the world in 2018, 2020, and 2022. Results are shown in Figure 11.2.[90]

Results presented in Figure 11.2 reveal a high engagement score of 23% in Brazil in 2022 and a low engagement score of 5% in China. In 2022, approximately 20% of employees in the U.S. workforce were fully engaged in their work. The good news from this study is that employee engagement increased in many countries between 2018 and 2022. The bad news is that the global engagement average was only 15.5% in 2022. This means that around 84% of employees were not fully engaged. The sharp decrease in engagement in workers in India between 2018 and 2022 is also noteworthy. What do you think is the impact of disengagement on important outcomes like performance, customer satisfaction, quality, or profits?

Outcomes Associated with Employee Engagement
Consulting firms have been in the forefront of collecting proprietary data supporting the practical value of employee engagement. For example, Gallup data suggests that an organization with highly engaged employees can achieve higher customer satisfaction/loyalty, increased productivity, and greater profitability.[91] Academic studies similarly show a positive relationship between employee engagement and job satisfaction, creativity, productivity, profitability, and customer satisfaction.[92] Research also suggests that employee engagement is negatively related to absenteeism and turnover. Nordstrom, for example, is known for harnessing the power of employee engagement.

Employee Engagement Example—Nordstrom: Nordstrom, a 120+-year-old upscale American department store chain, has a long-standing reputation for unparalleled customer service. The company frequently earns top spots on lists of the best places to

FIGURE 11.2
Fully engaged employees around the world

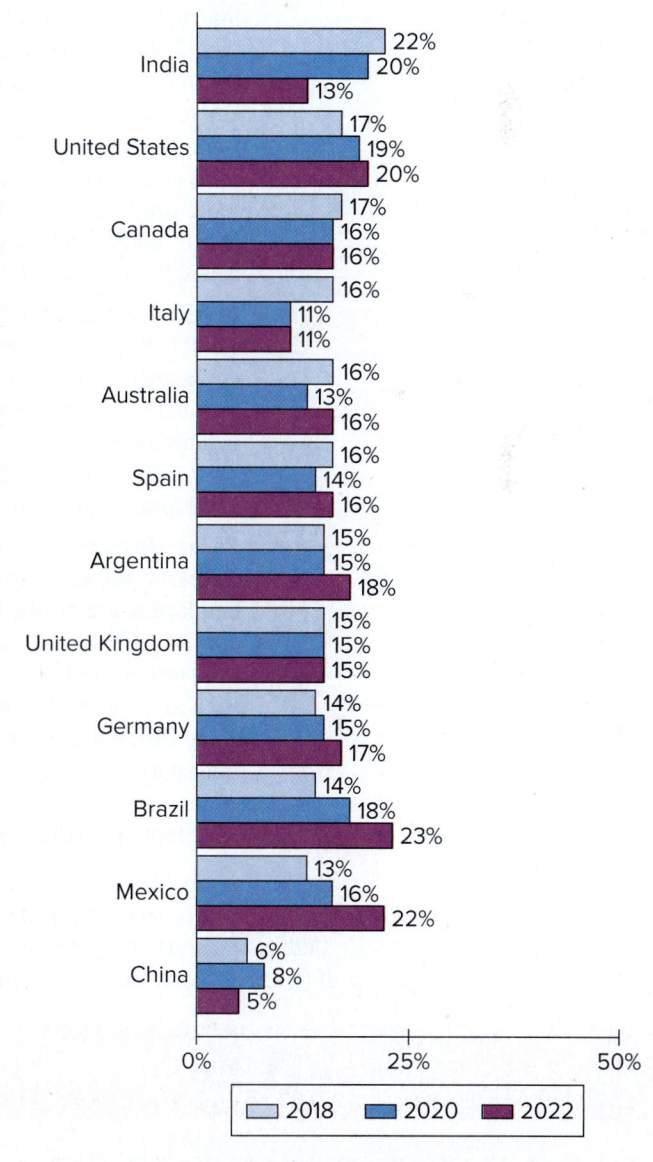

Country	2018	2020	2022
India	22%	20%	13%
United States	17%	19%	20%
Canada	17%	16%	16%
Italy	16%	11%	11%
Australia	16%	13%	16%
Spain	16%	14%	16%
Argentina	15%	15%	18%
United Kingdom	15%	15%	15%
Germany	14%	15%	17%
Brazil	14%	18%	23%
Mexico	13%	16%	22%
China	6%	8%	5%

Source: Data obtained from M. Hayes, F. Chumney, C. Wright, and M. Buckingham, "Global Workplace Study 2022," ADP Research Institute, 2022, https://www.adpri.org/assets/global-workplace-study-2022/.

work and the world's most admired companies.[93] One unique approach Nordstrom takes to drive engagement is that it equips employees with high levels of autonomy. The company's "Code of Business Conduct and Ethics" states that employees should make decisions based on one rule: "Use Good Judgment in All Situations."[94] To make this strategy work, Nordstrom hires based on the fit between prospective employees' values and the organization's core values—these include empathy, loyalty, humility, respect, and trust. Associates who make the cut have the autonomy to determine the best way to solve problems and serve customers.[95]

How Can Managers Increase Employee Engagement? There are four research-proven ways for managers to increase employee engagement. Let's explore them:

- **Design meaningful work.** People are engaged when their work contains variety and when they receive timely feedback about performance. Further, research suggests that it is particularly important for employees to be assigned meaningful work that fully employs their skills.[96] For example, some law firms include pro bono time to serve those in poverty as part of each attorney's job.[97]

- **Improve supervisor–employee relations.** People are more engaged when their manager is supportive and maintains a positive, trusting relationship with them.[98] In fact, researchers suggest that having supportive leaders and managers is critical for organizations that wish to use specialized HR practices to drive employee engagement.[99] Ørsted is an example of a company that is taking these findings seriously. The Danish green energy company puts key management skills at the center of its employee L&D initiatives. Managers learn how to hold more productive one-on-one meetings with their employees and are trained to deliver constructive, developmental feedback for workers who wish to develop new skills and expand their career opportunities within the company.[100]

- **Provide learning and development opportunities.** A SHRM study of more than 1,300 U.S. employees and managers found a strong connection between employee engagement and L&D opportunities. Nearly 90% of the HR managers surveyed saw increasing engagement as one of the most important training goals in their organization.[101] 1-800-GOT-JUNK? is a Canadian junk removal franchise that is known for its culture of L&D. Employees are able to take classes on franchise development and strategic planning as part of the program.[102]

- **Reduce stressors.** Stressors are environmental characteristics that cause stress. Research suggests that engagement is lower and burnout is higher when employees are confronted with stressors that they perceive are out of their control.[103] Take for instance the impact the COVID-19 pandemic had on doctors, nurses, and other hospital workers who could not access critical supplies such as face masks, gowns, and hand sanitizer as waves of infected patients came through their doors. These employees not only had to save the lives of their patients but also keep themselves safe without proper gear. "Most physicians have never seen this level of angst and anxiety in their careers," said Dr. Stephen Anderson, a 35-year veteran of emergency rooms.[104]

Would you like to get better grades in your classes? One way to do that involves increasing your level of engagement. You can assess your level of engagement with your studies and consider methods to enhance it by taking Self-Assessment 11.5 in Connect, if your instructor has assigned it.

SELF-ASSESSMENT 11.5   CAREER READINESS

To What Extent Are You Engaged in Your Studies?

This survey is designed to assess your level of engagement in your studies. Please complete Self-Assessment 11.5 if your instructor has assigned it in Connect.

2. Job Satisfaction: How Much Do You Like or Dislike Your Job?

Job satisfaction is the extent to which you feel positive or negative about various aspects of your work. Most people don't like everything about their jobs, but their overall satisfaction depends on how they feel about several components, such as *work, pay, promotions, co-workers,* and *supervision.*[105] Among the key correlates of job satisfaction are stronger motivation, performance, job involvement, organizational commitment, and life satisfaction and less absenteeism, tardiness, turnover, and perceived stress.[106]

A recent Pew Research Center study indicates that an impressively high 88% of U.S. employees are somewhat satisfied or very satisfied with the jobs.[107] But what is the relationship between job satisfaction and job performance—does more satisfaction cause better performance, or does better performance cause more satisfaction? This is a subject of much debate among management scholars.[108] In general, studies have shown that (1) job satisfaction and performance are moderately related, meaning that employee job satisfaction is a key work attitude managers should consider when trying to increase performance, and (2) the relationship between satisfaction and performance is complex, as it seems both variables influence each other through a host of individual differences and work-environment characteristics.[109]

How satisfied are you with the job you are in now, if you have one, or the last job you had? You can find out by taking Self-Assessment 11.6 in Connect, if your instructor has assigned it.

SELF-ASSESSMENT 11.6

How Satisfied Are You with Your Present Job?

This survey is designed to assess how satisfied you are with your current job, or a previous job, if you are not presently working. Please complete Self-Assessment 11.6 if your instructor has assigned it in Connect.

3. Organizational Commitment: How Much Do You Identify with Your Organization?

Organizational commitment reflects the extent to which an employee identifies with an organization and is committed to its goals. It is important because research shows a significant positive relationship between organizational commitment and job satisfaction, performance, turnover, and organizational citizenship behavior—discussed in the next section.[110] Thus, if managers are able to increase job satisfaction, employees may show higher levels of commitment, which in turn can elicit higher performance and lower employee turnover.[111]

Important Workplace Behaviors

Why is it important for you to understand how to manage individual differences? Quite simply, so that you can influence others' behavior. Whether working on a student class project, or a project for your employer, your success partly depends on your ability to influence others' behavior.

Organizational Citizenship Behaviors **Organizational citizenship behaviors (OCBs)** are those employee behaviors that are not directly part of employees' job descriptions—that exceed their work-role requirements.[112] Examples include conscientiousness (working hard), sportsmanship (being positive during challenging times), civic virtue (working for the good of the organization), courtesy (respecting co-workers), and altruism (helping others).[113] Studies demonstrate a significant and moderately positive correlation between organizational citizenship behaviors and job satisfaction, productivity, efficiency, and customer satisfaction.[114] However, research also shows that although organizational citizenship behaviors should be promoted in the workplace, employees should not be pressured to engage in these behaviors. Providing employees with autonomy in determining whether, when, and how to help others is a good way to encourage OCBs.[115]

Counterproductive Work Behaviors

Counterproductive work behaviors (CWBs) are types of behavior that harm employees and the organization as a whole.[116] Such behaviors may include absenteeism and tardiness, drug and alcohol abuse, and disciplinary problems but also extend to more serious acts such as accidents, sabotage, sexual harassment, violence, theft, and white-collar crime.[117] Some 98% of workers say they have witnessed or experienced uncivil behavior at their jobs.[118]

It may seem easy enough for organizations to respond to CWB by calling out unacceptable behaviors when they happen. The problem, however, is that CWBs can fly under the radar, meaning managers and co-workers often don't see them happening.[119] That's why it's important to take preventive measures.[120] Employees are less likely to engage in CWBs, for example, if they have autonomy, are treated fairly, aren't ostracized or asked to do tasks that fall outside their roles, and don't supervise too many people.[121] Leader characteristics and behaviors also impact employee behavior.[122] For example, a recent study found a relationship between authoritarian leadership and employee CWBs.[123] The Example box discusses an unfortunate result of CWBs—a toxic workplace.

EXAMPLE

The Toxic Workplace: "Rudeness Is Like the Common Cold"[124]

"Nothing is more costly to an organization's culture than a toxic employee," says management professor Christine Porath. "Rudeness is like the common cold—it's contagious, spreads quickly, and anyone can be a carrier."[125] Researcher Trevor Foulk concurs. "If someone is rude to me," he says, "it is likely that in my next interaction I will be rude to whomever I am talking to. You respond to their rudeness with your own rudeness."[126]

Incivility and rudeness are forms of CWBs, and they include snippy remarks, interruptions, and eye-rolling.[127] Toxic bosses may berate employees or demoralize them with such actions as "walking away from a conversation because they lose interest; answering calls in the middle of meetings without leaving the room; openly mocking people by pointing out their flaws or personality quirks in front of others," and similar incivilities, says Porath.[128] Let's discuss two reasons that managers should try to prevent CWBs in their organizations.

CWBs Sap Energy and Can Spiral out of Control
Management scholar Gretchen Spreitzer believes that difficult co-workers are "de-energizers" who spread their dispiriting attitudes to others. "They leave you feeling depleted, fatigued, and exhausted."[129] Research on so-called "incivility spirals" supports the idea that experiencing incivility leaves you less able to inhibit your own rude impulses. The more someone experiences incivility at work, the more likely they will be uncivil toward others.[130]

CWBs Come with a Price Tag
CWBs can hurt an organization's bottom line.[131] In addition to financial costs, uncivil behaviors at work diminish well-being, decrease job satisfaction, and cause increased job stress and withdrawal behaviors, according to a recent meta-analysis.[132] What's more, research suggests that it only takes *one* uncivil co-worker to cause feelings of isolation, job insecurity, and even health problems in others.[133]

YOUR CALL
If you were working in a toxic workplace and had to stay there for a while, what would you do to make things better?

Performance and Productivity Every job has certain expectations, but in some jobs performance and productivity are easier to define than in others. How many contacts should a telemarketing sales rep make in a day? How many sales should they close? Often a job of this nature will have a history of accomplishments (from what previous job holders have attained), so that it is possible to quantify performance behavior.

However, an ad agency account executive handling major clients such as a carmaker or a beverage manufacturer may go months before landing this kind of big account. Or a researcher in a pharmaceutical company may take years to develop a promising new prescription drug.

In short, the method of evaluating performance must match the job being done.

Absenteeism and Turnover A recent study found that the volume of Google searches for phrases such as "best excuses for missing work" and "believable excuses for missing work" rose by 630% between 2018 and 2022.[134] Does this mean that managers should be suspicious of every instance of absenteeism? Of course not. Some absences—such as those related to illness, caring for loved ones, death in the family, or jury duty, for example—are perfectly legitimate. Excessive absenteeism, however, can indicate that employees are experiencing undesirable attitudes such as job dissatisfaction.[135]

Absenteeism may be a precursor to turnover, which occurs when an employee abandons, resigns, retires, or is terminated from a job. Every organization experiences some level of turnover, and turnover can even be positive. *Functional turnover* occurs when an employee's departure is beneficial to the organization. We use the term *dysfunctional turnover* to refer to turnover that is costly and/or negative for the organization.[136] With the exception of low-skilled industries, a turnover rate above 20% is usually not a good sign.[137] According to the authors of a recent article on dysfunctional turnover in organizations, "One of the most important activities of front-line managers is diagnosing problematic causes of voluntary turnover and designing interventions to address them."[138]

Acting sick. A significant number of employees take bogus sick days because they don't feel like going to work. Do you believe companies should do more to validate if an employee is really sick? Dmytro Zinkevych/Shutterstock

High levels of turnover present a financial strain for organizations. The Society for Human Resource Management (SHRM) estimates that hiring a new employee, on average, costs an organization almost $4,700 and cautions that this figure can often be closer to three to four times a position's salary.[139] Research suggest five practical ways to reduce excessive turnover:[140]

1. Evaluate the extent to which an applicants' values fit the organization's values.
2. Provide post-hiring support, which is referred to as onboarding. As we mentioned in Chapter 9, onboarding programs help employees to integrate and transition to new jobs by making them familiar with corporate policies, procedures, culture, and politics by clarifying work-role expectations and responsibilities.
3. Focus on enhancing employee engagement and social networks.
4. Incorporate reliable and valid selection devices that measure competencies that are directly related to job performance (as discussed in Chapter 9) into the hiring process.
5. Offer employees benefits, such as flexible work hours (discussed in Chapter 12), that align with their needs and values. •

11.5 Understanding Stress and Individual Behavior

THE BIG PICTURE
Stress is what people feel when enduring extraordinary demands or opportunities and are not sure how to handle them. There are six sources of stress: individual differences, individual task, individual role, group, organizational, and nonwork demands. We describe some consequences of stress and discuss three methods organizations use to reduce it.

LO 11-5

Discuss the sources of workplace stress and ways to reduce it.

Stress is the tension people feel when they are facing or enduring extraordinary demands, constraints, or opportunities and are uncertain about their ability to handle them effectively.[141] Stress represents the feeling of tension and pressure; the source of potential stress is called the *stressor*.

Feelings of stress can arise when you are overworked, have unpredictable schedules, operate in unsafe workplaces, receive low wages, face layoffs of colleagues, experience conflict at work, or have family worries such as the need to care for ill relatives while working.[142] Stress can lead to problems such as conflicts and distraction at work, increased fatigue, and cardiovascular disease, chronic back pain, anxiety, and insomnia.[143]

In this section we'll first consider what managers need to know about job-related stress, including the toll it takes and how it operates. Then we'll turn to the sources of stress in the workplace how organizations can reduce stressors.

The Toll of Workplace Stress

Workplace stress takes a serious toll on employees and organizations. Consider the following statistics:[144]

- Around 83% of working U.S. adults suffer from work-related stress.
- Work stress accounts for about $300 billion in business losses each year stemming from lost productivity, accidents, and absenteeism.
- Approximately 1 million people in the United States miss work each day due to stress-related factors.
- Over 75% of workers in the United States report that stress negatively impacts their personal relationships.

Burnout as a Result of Stress Experiencing repeated, extreme stress can lead to something called burnout. **Burnout** is a state of emotional, mental, and even physical exhaustion, expressed as listlessness, indifference, or frustration. Researchers have identified three dimensions that underly the experience of job burnout:[145]

1. *Exhaustion,* also known as *emotional exhaustion,* consists of a lack of energy and feeling depleted, worn out, and debilitated.
2. *Depersonalization,* also known as *cynicism,* consists of detaching from one's job, experiencing negative attitudes toward work, and feeling irritable.
3. *Inefficacy,* also known as *reduced personal accomplishment,* consists of feeling that you are unable to do your job well or are no longer able to deal with the demands of your job.

Factors contributing to burnout include "always-on" work cultures, advanced technology, demanding and unsupportive bosses, difficult clients, certain personality traits, and inefficient co-workers.[146] Research demonstrates that employees who experience

FIGURE 11.3
The Stress Process

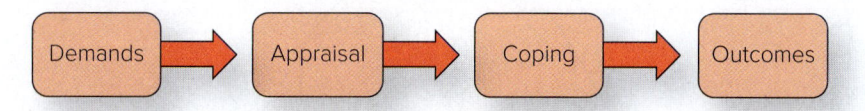

Demands → Appraisal → Coping → Outcomes

Sources: Lazarus, R.S. Psychological Stress and the Coping Process. 1966; Hobfoll, S.E. "Conservation of Resources: A New Attempt at Conceptualizing Stress." American Psychologist 44, no. 3 (1989): 513; Karasek Jr, R.A. "Job Demands, Job Decision Latitude, and Mental Strain: Implications for Job Redesign." Administrative Science Quarterly (1979): 285–308.

burnout are more likely to call in sick, get injured or have accidents, and demonstrate poor work performance.[147]

How Does Stress Work?

How does the stress process work? Prominent theories of stress coalesce, broadly, around a general theme. We capture this theme in the simple model of the stress process presented in Figure 11.3.

Demands Hans Selye, considered the founder of the modern concept of stress, viewed stress as "the nonspecific response of the body to any demand made upon it."[148] Our model of the stress process (Figure 11.3) thus begins with an individual experiencing some type of demand. A demand is anything that you have to exert effort toward taking care of. If your dog barks to go outside to potty while you're cozied up on the couch watching TV, then your dog is placing a demand on you by asking you to get up to let it out. If you have an exam coming up and you have to study for it in order to get a good grade in the course, then the exam represents a demand on you.

Appraisal Figure 11.3 illustrates that demands are followed by an appraisal process. Here, an appraisal is simply an evaluation of the demand, and the appraisal process helps us to figure out (1) what is at stake in the situation and (2) what we can do to deal with the demand. When you have an exam coming up, your brain considers what's at stake by contemplating whether the exam is something you should pay attention to, and, if so, whether it has the potential to harm you, benefit you, or both. Next, your brain considers the various options you have for coping with the demand: (1) do nothing and potentially earn a low score; (2) study slowly over the course of a week to increase your chances of understanding and remembering the material, thus earning a high score; (3) cram for the exam the night before and hope for the best. Our appraisal of a demand determines how we ultimately decide to cope with the demand.

Coping As shown in Figure 11.3, an appraisal is followed by an attempt to cope with the demand. Coping mechanisms vary depending on several factors, including whether we believe we have the resources needed to manage the situation, and whether the demand presents a challenging opportunity to tackle or a dangerous threat to our well-being.

Consider the example of an upcoming exam. In some instances, a student may appraise an exam as a challenge; it may require a lot of time, intellect, and mental energy to prepare for, but if those things are available, then it's viewed as a challenge that's manageable. In this case, the student may cope with the demand by choosing option 2 discussed in the Appraisal section—by studying slowly over the course of a week to properly learn the material. And they may earn a high score after all that hard work. Was the exam still a source of stress even though they were able to deal with it? Absolutely. Stress isn't always a negative thing—in fact, stress may have actually *helped* the student in this example. Researchers generally believe that there is an *inverted*

FIGURE 11.4

Stress and performance

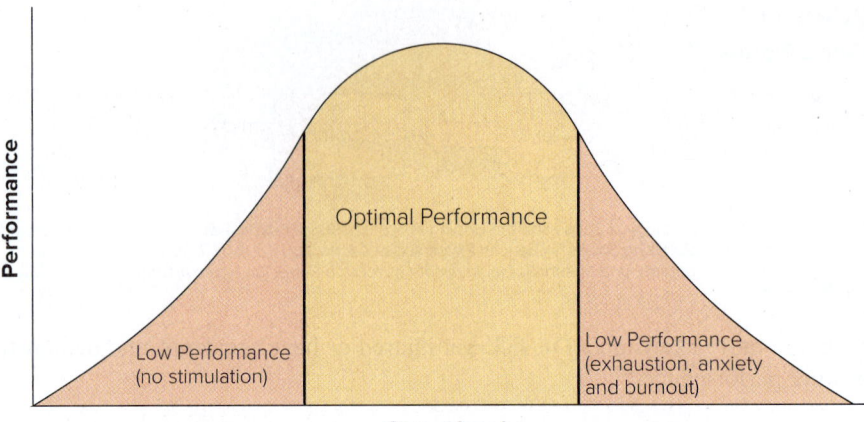

U-shaped relationship between stress and performance (see Figure 11.4). That is, low levels of stress lead to low performance (because people are not "charged up" to perform), but high levels of stress also lead to an energy-sapping fight-or-flight response that produces low performance. Optimal performance, according to this hypothesis, results when people experience moderate levels of stress.[149]

In other instances, however, a student may appraise an exam as a potential threat to their well-being and therefore something they have to survive. If you're like one of your authors and prefer reading and writing to solving equations, then a college calculus exam would fall into this category. A poor grade on an exam could tank your grade in a calculus course, and if you don't pass calculus, then you may not be able to continue on toward earning your degree. This type of appraisal is what we more typically associate with the experience of stress. In other words, the demand is seen as extremely taxing on the resources that are available. You may believe you are not intelligent enough to do well on the exam or that you do not have enough time to properly study. This may lead to coping mechanisms such as ignoring reality and avoiding thinking about the exam altogether, procrastinating, or even resorting to unethical behavior such as lying to the professor and saying that you have to attend a funeral on the day of the exam.

Outcomes Excess stress leads to negative outcomes in three primary categories:

- **Physiological outcomes:** Lesser physiological signs of stress are sweaty palms, restlessness, backaches, headaches, upset stomach, and nausea. More serious physiological signs of stress are hypertension and heart attacks.
- **Psychological outcomes:** Psychological symptoms of stress include forgetfulness, boredom, irritability, nervousness, anger, anxiety, hostility, and depression.
- **Behavioral outcomes:** Behavioral symptoms of stress include sleeplessness, changes in eating habits, and increased smoking/alcohol/drug abuse.[150]

From an organizational perspective, the experience of repeated, negative stress diminishes positive emotions, job satisfaction, organizational commitment, and job performance and increases alcohol and illicit drug use, workplace deviance, and job turnover.[151]

The Sources of Job-Related Stress

There are seven sources of stress on the job: (1) *demands created by individual differences,* (2) *individual task demands,* (3) *individual role demands,* (4) *work-life conflict,* (5) *group demands,* (6) *organizational demands,* and (7) *demands created by remote and hybrid work schedules.*

1. Demands Created by Individual Differences: The Stress Created by Genetic or Personality Characteristics Certain individuals are more likely to experience stress. For example, some people are born worriers, such as those with a genetic mutation (known as BDNF) that Yale researchers linked to the tendency to chronically obsess over negative thoughts.[152] Others are impatient, competitive types with a personality trait known as **Type A behavior pattern**, which is characterized by a chronic, determined struggle to accomplish more in less time.[153] Type A behavior has been associated with increased performance in professors, students, and life insurance brokers.[154] However, it also has been associated with greater cardiovascular activity and higher blood pressure, as well as heart disease.[155]

2. Individual Task Demands: The Stress Created by the Job Itself Some occupations are more stressful than others. Being a first responder, for instance, can be quite stressful for some people, due to the fast pace and the high-stakes nature of the job.[156] But being a home-based blogger, paid on a piecework basis to generate news and comment, may mean working long hours to the point of exhaustion.[157] Jobs that require "emotional labor"—pretending to be happy or being required to smile and speak politely all the time—can be particularly demanding.[158]

Low-level jobs can be more stressful than high-level jobs because employees often have less control over their lives and thus experience less work satisfaction. Being a bartender, preschool teacher, or hotel concierge—jobs that don't usually pay very well—can be quite stressful.[159]

3. Individual Role Demands: The Stress Created by Others' Expectations of You **Roles** are sets of behaviors that people expect of occupants of a position. Stress may arise because of *role overload, role conflict,* and/or *role ambiguity.*[160]

- **Role overload:** Occurs when others' expectations exceed your ability to perform. Example: If you as a student are carrying a full course load plus working two-thirds time plus trying to have a social life, you know what role overload is—and what stress is. Similar things happen to managers and workers. Sometimes there isn't enough time in the day or week to accomplish all the things on your plate, and this can lead to stress.

- **Role conflict:** Occurs when you feel torn between different sets of expectations coming from multiple important people in your life. Example: Your supervisor says the company needs you to stay late to meet an important deadline, but your family expects you to be home for your child's birthday party. Sometimes you have to make a choice between two things that are both important to you, and this can lead to stress.

- **Role ambiguity:** Occurs when others' expectations of you are unclear or unknown. Example: Your job description and the criteria for promotion are vague, a complaint often voiced by newcomers to an organization. Sometimes we don't know what we're supposed to do in order to be perceived as performing well, and this can lead to stress.

Have you ever felt like this person? Many jobs are stressful, some because people's lives are at stake (military personnel, firefighters, police officers), some because of tight deadlines (event coordinators, public relations executives). What techniques do you use to manage stress? Do you ever just ignore it and plow through your daily activities? Andrey_Popov/Shutterstock

Jobs with high task and role demands but low levels of personal control can be particularly stressful. In these cases, people are likely to find that their efforts to complete work activities are blocked, resulting in persistent stress, discomfort, and burnout. The problem with a high demand, low control situation is that individuals do not have the resources, power, or authority to influence the way the work gets done or the timelines for completion.[161]

4. Work–Family Conflict **Work–family conflict** occurs when the demands or pressures from our work and family domains are mutually incompatible.[162] Work and family can conflict in two ways: Work responsibilities can interfere with family life, and family demands can interfere with work responsibilities.[163]

For instance, an employee who is caring for an aging parent skips a department meeting to take the parent to a doctor's appointment (family interferes with work). Perhaps another day the employee works late to finish a report on time and thus has to reschedule their parent's follow-up appointment (work interferes with family).

Both of these types of conflicts matter because what happens in one domain can spill over and negatively impact the other domain.[164] From a management perspective, we recommend that organizations strive to reduce stressors, increase employee engagement, and implement wellness programs to assist employees in balancing their work and family demands.[165] We discuss wellness programs in the next section.

5. Group Demands: The Stress Created by Co-workers and Managers Liking the people you work with can be a great source of satisfaction and a buffer against stress, even if you don't particularly enjoy other aspects of your job. When co-workers don't get along, the potential for stress increases.[166]

Managers also can create stress for employees. A boss who consistently engages in behaviors such as overt self-promotion, unwillingness to listen, making unreasonable demands, lying, unfair decision making, bullying, or unethical behavior can cause a great deal of stress for employees.[167]

6. Organizational Demands: The Stress Created by the Environment and Culture The physical environments of some jobs are great sources of stress. For example, poultry processing, asbestos removal, coal mining, firefighting, and police work are physically demanding jobs. Even white-collar work can take place in a stressful environment, with poor lighting, excessive noise, improper ergonomics, and lack of privacy causing stress for employees. An organizational culture that puts a lot of performance pressure on employees also can be stressful.

7. Demands Created by Remote and Hybrid Work Schedules Remote and hybrid work schedules are here to stay. Companies like Dropbox, Nationwide, and Shopify have gone so far as to make remote work the default for the majority of their employees. The option to work remotely, either some or all of the time, can lead to better work-life balance, increased well-being, and better mental health for many workers.[168]

For other workers, however, remote and hybrid schedules can be a source of stress for several reasons. First, working remotely can feel isolating because being alone day in and day out deprives us of important human connection and social interaction.[169] Second, workers who do their jobs remotely report more daily screen time than those who work in an office. Research has linked excessive screen time with increased anxiety and depression.[170] Third, remote and hybrid work schedules can make employees feel they always have to be "on" and available for work, whether that means at night, on the weekends, or while on vacation.[171] This is exacerbated by messaging apps, such as Slack and Teams, that make it possible for employees to communicate with co-workers instantly, easily, and across any distance at any time. Some countries, such as Belgium and Portugal, have enacted legislation that prevents or limits the extent to which managers can e-mail employees outside of work hours.[172]

The key takeaway is that, in terms of work schedules, what relieves stress for one employee may create stress for another employee. Organizations should consider employees' individual preferences and needs when considering remote and/or hybrid work schedules.

Reducing Stressors in the Organization

There are all kinds of **buffers**, or administrative changes, that managers can make to reduce stressors and improve employee well-being.[173] This section reviews six recommendations, starting with attempts to help employees build resilience.

- **Build resilience.** *Resilience*, as defined in Chapter 1, represents the capacity to bounce back from adversity and to sustain yourself when confronted with challenges.[174] Resilience is a career readiness competency desired by employers. Do you think people are born resilient, or is it something that is learned over time? The consensus is that we develop resilience over time.[175] Consider the example of inventor Sir James Dyson. Dyson spent five years testing more than 5,000 versions of what he hoped would be a better vacuum cleaner that operated on the same principle as a cyclone. His company, named after him, is now famous for its Dual Cyclone bagless vacuums, and his net value is over $15 billion.[176]

- Resilience assists you in achieving goals and warding off the negative effects of stress by encouraging positive thinking in the face of setbacks and challenges. To what extent do you possess the career readiness competency of resilience? Find out by taking Self-Assessment 11.7 in Connect, if your instructor has assigned it.

Sir James Dyson with the Dyson Hot fan heater. Dyson/Shutterstock

SELF-ASSESSMENT 11.7 CAREER READINESS

What Is Your Level of Resilience?

This survey was designed to assess your level of resilience. Please complete Self-Assessment 11.7 if your instructor has assigned it in Connect.

Some strategies for building resilience are practicing mindfulness, which helps reduce stress, learning how to prioritize incoming information so you will process it more effectively and make better decisions, taking frequent short breaks from work to restore your focus, and mentally detaching from problems for a certain amount of time so you can respond to them rationally rather than reacting emotionally.[177] Other recommendations include practicing optimism, using cognitive reframing when faced with challenges, supporting others, and getting the proper amount of sleep.[178]

- **Roll out employee assistance programs.** **Employee assistance programs (EAPs)** include a host of programs aimed at helping employees to cope with stress, burnout, substance abuse, physical and mental health-related problems, family and marital issues, and any general problem that negatively influences job performance.[179] These assistance programs are especially important when it comes to employee mental health. Take for instance recent survey findings on mental health across generations that show Gen Zers and Millennials report substantially higher levels of anxiety than Gen Xers and Baby Boomers.[180] This is especially important for managers to address given that these two generations—Gen Zers and Millennials—will account for nearly 60% of the world's workforce by 2030.[181]

- **Recommend a holistic wellness approach.** A **holistic wellness program** focuses on self-responsibility, nutritional awareness, relaxation techniques, physical fitness, and environmental awareness. This approach goes beyond stress reduction by encouraging employees to try to balance physical, mental, and social well-being by accepting personal responsibility for developing and adhering to a health promotion program.
- **Create a supportive environment.** Job stress often results because employees work under poor supervision and lack autonomy. Organizational environments that are less formal, more personal, and more supportive of employees can help buffer employees from the multitude of demands they face. Mentoring also can help reduce stress—for both mentors and mentees.[182]
- **Make jobs interesting.** Jobs that are routinized and boring can be a source of stress for employees. Allowing employees a degree of freedom, variety, and creative control in their jobs is an important tool for mitigating work stress.[183]
- **Make career counseling available.** Employees experience stress when they don't know what their career options are, or when they don't feel there are opportunities available to grow their skills. In fact, employees are 12 times more likely to quit their jobs when they don't feel that they have the support and resources needed in order to grow in their organizations.[184] Companies such as IBM offer career coaching to employees.[185]

11.6 Career Corner: Managing Your Career Readiness

LO 11-6

Describe how to develop the career readiness competencies of positive approach and emotional intelligence.

This chapter has implications for developing at least six of the career readiness competencies in our model (see Figure 11.5): self-awareness, generalized self-efficacy, social intelligence, emotional intelligence, positive approach, and resilience. This section focuses on developing the attitude of positive approach and improving your emotional intelligence.

Fostering a Positive Approach

A *positive approach* represents a willingness to accept developmental feedback, to try and suggest new ideas, and to maintain a positive attitude at work. Maintaining a positive approach is hard given the stresses of life and employers' increased expectations for employees. We recommend a two-step approach for developing a positive approach.

Step 1: Identify Potentially Bad Attitudes
We all have bad days or stressful moments. The purpose of this step is to identify the types of behaviors that tend to crop up when you have a bad day or a stressful moment. This awareness can help you

FIGURE 11.5

Model of career readiness

Source: Kinicki 2022

Knowledge
- Task-based/functional
- Computational thinking
- Understanding the business
- New media literacy

Core
- Critical thinking/problem solving
- Oral/written communication
- Teamwork/collaboration
- Information technology application
- Leadership
- Professionalism/work ethic
- Diversity, equity, and inclusion
- Career management

Other characteristics
- **Resilience**
- Personal adaptability
- **Self-awareness**
- Service/others orientation
- Openness to change
- **Generalized self-efficacy**

Soft skills
- Decision making
- **Social intelligence**
- Networking
- **Emotional intelligence** ⭐

Attitudes
- Ownership/accepting responsibilities
- Self-motivation
- Proactive learning orientation
- Showing commitment
- **Positive approach** ⭐

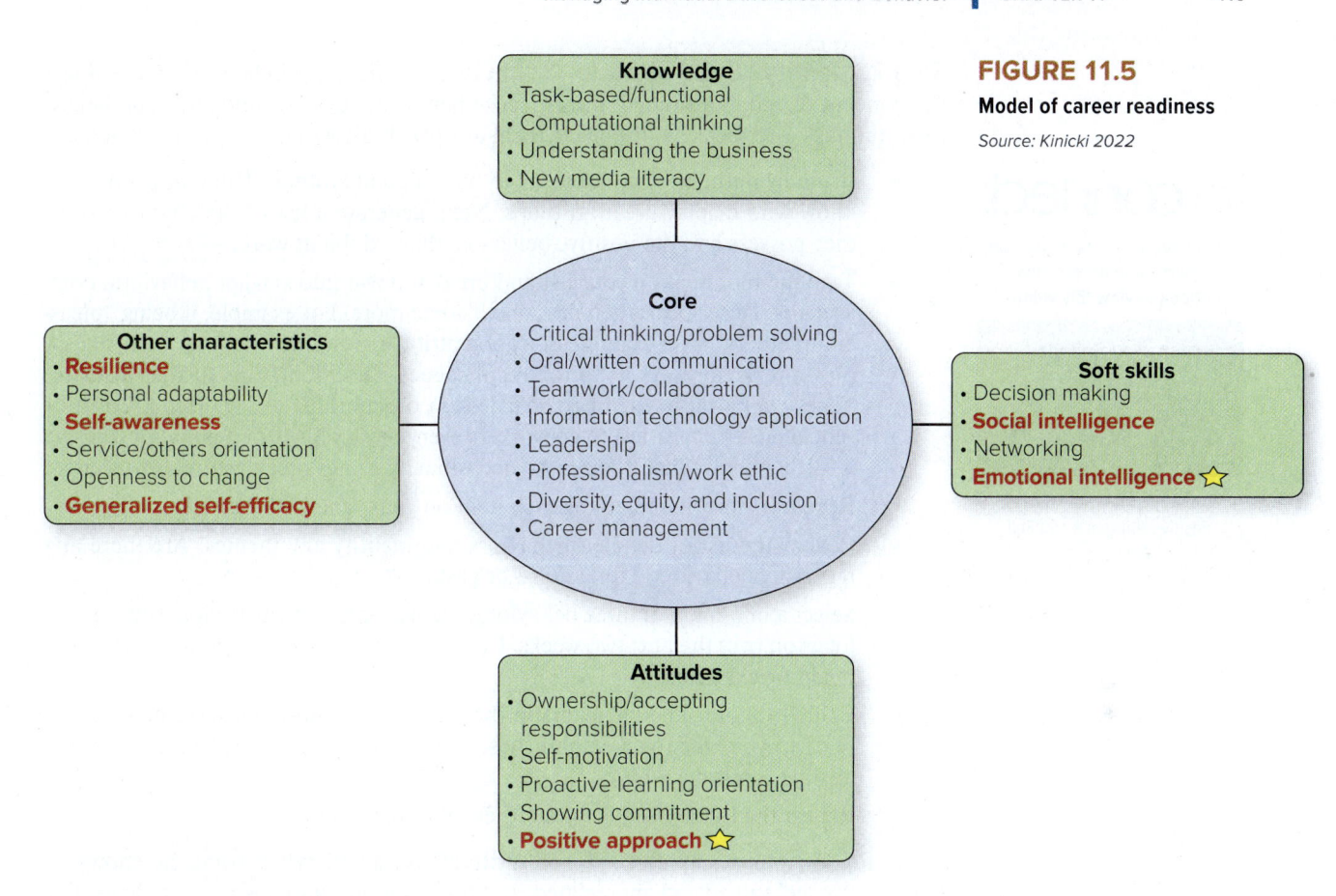

---

replace potentially negative behaviors with positive ones. Think about a time when you've had a particularly stressful situation to deal with, then answer the following questions.[186]

- Are you a *porcupine?* Porcupines send out verbal and nonverbal messages that say, "Stay away from me."
- Are you an *entangler?* Entanglers want to involve others in their interests. They push their concerns and want to be heard, noticed, and listened to.
- Are you a *debater?* Debaters like to argue even if there is no issue to debate.
- Are you a *complainer?* Complainers point out the problems in a situation but rarely provide solutions of their own.
- Are you a *blamer?* Blamers are like complainers but point out negatives aimed at a particular individual.
- Are you a *stink bomb thrower?* Stink bomb throwers like to make sarcastic or cynical remarks, use nonverbal gestures of disgust or annoyance, and sometimes yell or slam things.

Based on your answers, which negative behaviors do you tend to exhibit when you're having a bad day? Now consider how others may perceive these behaviors. Try to catch yourself before you start to behave in these negative ways, and think about specific things you can do to replace these negative tendencies with positive ones. In this chapter's Executive Interview Series video note how the leaders suggest that you be prepared to speak about how you've dealt with difficult situations in the past. Practicing this step and the next one gives you something to share about yourself and your level of self-awareness in job interviews.

Visit your instructor's Connect course and access your eBook to view this video.

Executive Interview Series:
Positive Approach and Self Awareness

Step 2: Identify "Good Attitude" Behaviors This step will help you break down the concept of "good attitudes" into specific behaviors. Once you identify the behaviors, your task is to focus on displaying them at work. Follow these recommendations:[187]

- Begin by defining what it means to have a good attitude. Think of people you know who display great attitudes. Next, generate a list of the characteristics they possess and the positive behaviors they exhibit at work.

- Take the first item on your list and break it down into smaller behavioral components. Describe it; then describe it some more. For example, if being "pleasant to others" is an example of a good attitude, describe what this looks like. A pleasant person says hello to all colleagues. Describing this further leads to, "They walk over to each person's desk in the morning to say, 'Hello,'" or they send a positive message to co-workers every day on Slack or Teams. Describing it further shows that this person occasionally brings breakfast treats to share.

- Repeat the previous step for each item on your "good attitude" list.

- Review the list of detailed behaviors and identify any themes. Are there any recurring behaviors, expressions, or gestures?

- Select a minimum of three behavioral themes or specific behaviors you want to focus on over the next two weeks. Consider situations in which these behaviors might be exhibited.

- Exhibit the targeted behaviors in the targeted situations. Observe how people react to you when you exhibit these positive behaviors. If the reaction is not positive, consider why.

- Repeat the last two steps for another set of behaviors.

Gratitude is an example of a "good attitude" behavior. When someone shows us gratitude we feel valued and appreciated, and this translates into positive outcomes. For example, research suggests that others tend to see us as more competent, caring, and warm when we show gratitude.[188] The good news is that showing gratitude to others is something you can easily build into your routine. Try sending a quick e-mail or message to say thanks the next time someone helps you.

Self-Managing Your Emotions

Self-management is a component of emotional intelligence. It reflects the ability to control your emotions and act with honesty and integrity in reliable and adaptable ways. Recall from this chapter's Executive Interview Series video that employers and potential employers pay attention to your "energy." We think that how you come across to others during difficult situations is an important part of this. Here are some tips for enhancing this ability.[189]

- **Identify your emotional triggers and physiological responses.** What words, sayings, or situations cause your emotions to ramp up? Do you get nervous before a presentation or when meeting strangers? Keeping a journal (you can use a note in your phone) is good way to identify your emotional triggers. Simply take a few minutes during the day to note your feelings and what caused them. For example, one of your authors knows that he tends to react emotionally when someone is lying. His body lets him know because he feels flushed or his heart starts to beat faster. This awareness enables him to notice his "emotionality" and to focus on reducing the influence it may have on his behaviors.

- **Engage in emotional regulation.** Taking a moment to pause, relax, and reflect is a good solution when emotions flare. When you sense strong, negative emotions, stop and take a couple of deep breaths. This will relax your body and the emotional brain and engage the thinking brain, thereby allowing you to react in a calmer, more composed manner.[190]

- **Channel your emotions.** Letting off steam is fine; just be sure to do it at the right place and time. Venting with a trusted friend is more effective than yelling at someone at work. Exercise is another way to fend off the potential stressors and emotions associated with being busy or overburdened.

- **Practice mindfulness.** Mindfulness encourages closer contact with life, allowing you to have greater awareness, understanding, acceptance of emotions, and ability to modify unpleasant moods. As such, research shows mindfulness improves well-being, performance, citizenship behavior, leadership, and teamwork. It also reduces stress.[191] Meditation is a great way to practice mindfulness. There also are mindfulness apps available, such as the Calm app. Some companies, such as General Mills and Aetna, offer workplace mindfulness training for employees.[192]

Key Terms Used in This Chapter

affective component of an attitude 396
attitude 395
behavior 397
behavioral component of an attitude 396
big Five personality dimensions 388
buffers 413
burnout 408
causal attribution 400
cognitive component of an attitude 396
cognitive dissonance 397
core self-evaluation (CSE) 389
counterproductive work behaviors (CWBs) 406
emotional intelligence 392
emotional stability 392
employee assistance programs (EAPs) 413
employee engagement 403
explicit bias 399
generalized self-efficacy 390
halo effect 400
holistic wellness program 414
implicit bias 399
job satisfaction 405
learned helplessness 390
locus of control 391
organizational behavior (OB) 394
organizational citizenship behaviors (OCBs) 405
organizational commitment 405
perception 398
personality 388
recency effect 400
roles 411
self-efficacy 389
self-esteem 391
self-fulfilling prophecy 401
self-serving bias 401
stress 408
stressors 404
type A behavior pattern 411
values 395
work–family conflict 412

Key Points

11.1 Personality and Individual Behavior

- Personality consists of the stable psychological traits and behavioral attributes that give a person their identity. There are five personality dimensions and five personality traits that managers need to be aware of to understand workplace behavior.
- The Big Five personality dimensions are extroversion, agreeableness, conscientiousness, emotional stability, and openness to experience.
- A core self-evaluation represents a broad personality trait comprising four positive individual traits: (1) self-efficacy, (2) self-esteem, (3) locus of control, (4) emotional stability.
- Emotional intelligence is defined as the ability to monitor your and others' feelings and use this information to guide your thinking and actions.

11.2 Values, Attitudes, and Behavior

- Values must be distinguished from attitudes and from behavior. Values are abstract ideals that guide one's thinking and behavior across all situations.
- Attitudes are defined as learned predispositions toward a given object. Attitudes have three components. The affective component, the cognitive component, and the behavioral component.
- When attitudes and reality collide, the result may be cognitive dissonance, the psychological discomfort a person experiences between their cognitive attitude and incompatible behavior.

11.3 Perception and Individual Behavior

- Perception is the process of interpreting and understanding one's environment. There are five distortions of perception. They are: (1) stereotyping, (2) implicit bias, (3) the halo effect, (4) the recency effect, and (5) causal attribution.
- The self-fulfilling prophecy (Pygmalion effect) describes the phenomenon in which people's expectations of themselves or others lead them to behave in ways that make those expectations come true.

11.4 Work-Related Attitudes and Behaviors Managers Need to Deal With

- Managers need to be alert to work-related attitudes having to do with (1) employee engagement, an individual's involvement, satisfaction, and enthusiasm for work; (2) job satisfaction, the extent to which you feel positive or negative about various aspects of your work; and (3) organizational commitment, reflecting the extent to which an employee identifies with an organization and is committed to its goals.

11.5 Understanding Stress and Individual Behavior

- Stress is the tension people feel when they are facing or enduring extraordinary demands, constraints, or opportunities and are uncertain about their ability to handle them effectively. The source of stress is called a stressor.

- There are seven sources of stress on the job: (1) Demands created by individual differences, (2) individual task demands, (3) individual role demands, (4) group demands, (5) organizational demands, (6) nonwork demands, and (7) demands created by remote and hybrid work schedules.
- Positive stress can be constructive. Negative stress can result in poor-quality work; such stress is revealed through physiological, psychological, or behavioral signs. One sign is burnout, a state of emotional, mental, and even physical exhaustion.
- There are buffers that managers can make to reduce the stressors that lead to employee burnout. Some general organizational strategies for reducing unhealthy stressors are to roll out employee assistance programs, recommend a holistic wellness approach, create a supportive environment, make jobs interesting, and make career counseling available.

11.6 Career Corner: Managing Your Career Readiness

- A two-step approach is used to develop a positive approach at work. The first is to identify the types of negative behaviors that crop up during bad or stressful days. The second step is to identify and exhibit "good attitude" behaviors.
- You can increase your emotional intelligence by developing the ability to manage emotions. Four tips are: (1) identify your emotional triggers and physiological response, (2) engage in emotional regulation, (3) channel your emotions, and (4) practice mindfulness.

12 Motivating Employees
Achieving Superior Performance in the Workplace

After reading this chapter, you should be able to:

LO 12-1 Explain the role of motivation in accomplishing goals.

LO 12-2 Identify the needs that motivate most employees.

LO 12-3 Discuss similarities and differences among three process theories.

LO 12-4 Compare and contrast four different ways to design jobs.

LO 12-5 Discuss how to use four types of behavior modification.

LO 12-6 Discuss the role of compensation in motivating employees.

LO 12-7 Describe how to develop the career readiness competency of self-motivation.

FORECAST *What's Ahead in This Chapter*

This chapter discusses motivation from four perspectives: content (theories by Maslow, McClelland, Deci and Ryan, and Herzberg), process (equity, expectancy, and goal-setting theories), job design, and reinforcement. We then consider rewards for motivating performance and conclude with a Career Corner that focuses on how to enhance the career readiness competency of self-motivation.

Managing for Motivation: Building Your Own Motivation

Are you putting something off right now because you just haven't felt inspired to tackle it? Self-motivation is critical for work success because it drives performance, particularly in work situations where you're expected to apply good work habits and focus in order to be productive without constant supervision.[1] Consider that organizations are 27% more profitable and realize a 50% increase in sales when their employees are self-motivated.[2] These results support employers' desire to hire people with the career readiness competency of self-motivation. You certainly want to possess this attitude.

Here are some suggestions for honing your self-motivation (and getting to that task you've been putting off).[3]

1. Reframe Your Reason

Perhaps you're having trouble accomplishing an objective because you haven't thought through why you're really aiming for it. For example, a goal to look for a job in a particular field because one of your friends is or because someone said it was exciting may not be enough to ignite your inner drive. Try reframing the goal in terms that invoke your own values rather than someone else's: "I want to work at this company because I think it's a good match for my computational thinking, new media literacy, and written communication skills." You'll increase your self-motivation when you attach positive emotions, purpose, and meaning to your goals.[4]

2. Be Realistic

Realistic goals aren't necessarily easy ones; the American Psychological Association reports that when we set goals that are challenging, we're 90% more likely to achieve them.[5] Realistic goals are specific. "I want to get a good job in an exciting field" is broad. "I want to get an entry-level job with a marketing research company" is specific and, therefore, realistic.

3. Set Interim Goals

At the same time, you shouldn't set yourself up to try accomplishing a big goal in one grand gesture. Break your big goal down into smaller ones, each with a date attached, to lay out a plan of smaller steps you can follow that all lead in the same direction.[6] "I will draft my resume by the end of this month," and "During the two weeks after that, I will ask three people to critique and proofread it for me," are good interim goals toward your ultimate objective of finding an entry-level marketing job.

4. Celebrate Ongoing Achievements

Applaud yourself for reaching each of the milestones you've set. Few things are as motivating as rewards, and because each step you accomplish in your plan is bringing you closer to your big goal, each is worth a celebration. Treat yourself to something you've wanted or take time off to do something fun. You've earned it.

5. Hold Yourself Accountable

It's one thing to celebrate success, but if there are no consequences for failure, motivation can drag. A mentor who encourages you and checks in on your progress can give your forward momentum a regular boost. No mentor? Create your own by simply letting a friend know your goal and keeping that person up to date as you proceed through your plan. Dominican University psychology professor Dr. Gail Matthews studied 149 adults of all ages in businesses and other organizations in the United States and abroad. She found that 76% of those who wrote down their goals and used a weekly e-mail to report their goal achievement to a friend either completely accomplished their goal or got more than halfway there. Of those with unwritten goals, only 43% achieved as much.[7]

6. Envision Success

While you should anticipate setbacks (and forgive yourself for them), keeping the finish line in mind and regularly imagining yourself crossing it will soon become a mental habit that reinforces your positive approach and builds your professionalism and work ethic.

7. Celebrate and Document Your Accomplishments

Celebrating and documenting your accomplishments builds self-confidence. Self-confidence drives self-motivation and the associated desire to complete your short- and long-term projects. "Celebration is an important opportunity to cement the lessons learned on the path to achievement, and to strengthen the relationships between people that make future achievement more plausible," says Whitney Johnson, CEO of Disruption Advisors.[8] Write your successes in a journal to remind yourself of what you did well. Return to these notes during job interviews to provide behavioral examples of your performance and career readiness competencies.

For Discussion Are you currently using any of these strategies? If not, which ones can you adopt now to achieve your most immediate goals?

12.1 Motivating for Performance

THE BIG PICTURE
Motivation is defined as the psychological processes that arouse and direct people's goal-directed behavior. There are four major perspectives that offer different explanations for how to motivate employees. They are content theories, process theories, job design, and reinforcement theory.

LO 12-1

Explain the role of motivation in accomplishing goals.

What would motivate you to rise an hour earlier to go in to the office rather than work from home? Microsoft conducted a survey of 20,006 employees in 2022 to identify the most effective incentives to lure employees back to work. The top motivators included collaborating in-person with their team, getting face time with executives, and socializing with co-workers. In fact, 78% of Gen Z and Millennials reported that social connection is the strongest incentive for them to work at the office. It appears that perks such as free food, onsite laundry, gym memberships, and free transportation are taking a back seat to relational interactions that make working in the office more meaningful.[9]

What would motivate you to stay at your current job? How about repayment of your student loans—that's a big one! Currently, workers age 25 to 34 are most likely to carry student loans, with almost $1.76 trillion in total outstanding student loan debt. A recent study found that 85% of workers said financial support for student loans and tuition reimbursement would impact their decision to work for a company.[10] Currently, 17% of employers—including Abbott, NVIDIA, and PwC—offer student loan repayment and 31% of employers are considering adding it to their employee benefits. This is a noticeable improvement from 8% of companies that offered a student loan repayment benefit in 2019.[11]

Whether employment rates are high or low, there are always companies, industries, and occupations in which employers invest considerable resources to retain their human capital.

How would you like for your employer to help you repay your student loan debt? More and more companies are offering this benefit to incentivize younger workers.
Brian A Jackson/Shutterstock

Motivation: What It Is, Why It's Important

Why do people do the things they do? The answer is this: They are mainly motivated to fulfill their wants and needs.

What Is Motivation and How Does It Work?

Motivation is defined as the psychological processes that arouse and direct goal-directed behavior.[12] Motivation is difficult to understand because you can't actually see it or know it in another person; it must be *inferred* from one's behavior. Nevertheless, it's imperative that you as a manager understand the process of motivation if you are to guide employees in accomplishing your organization's objectives.

The way motivation works is complex because motivation is the result of multiple *personal* and *contextual factors* (see Figure 12.1).

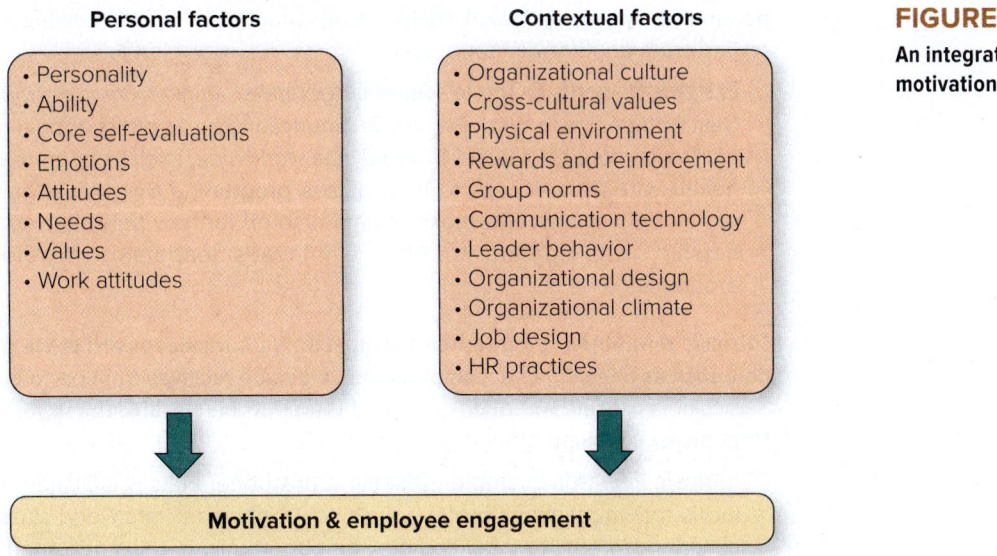

FIGURE 12.1
An integrated model of motivation

Personal factors
- Personality
- Ability
- Core self-evaluations
- Emotions
- Attitudes
- Needs
- Values
- Work attitudes

Contextual factors
- Organizational culture
- Cross-cultural values
- Physical environment
- Rewards and reinforcement
- Group norms
- Communication technology
- Leader behavior
- Organizational design
- Organizational climate
- Job design
- HR practices

↓

Motivation & employee engagement

The individual personal factors that employees bring to the workplace range from personality to attitudes, many of which we described in Chapter 11. The contextual factors include organizational culture, structure, cross-cultural values, the physical environment, and other matters we discuss in this chapter and others throughout the text (e.g., Figure 8.1). Both categories of factors influence an employee's level of motivation and engagement at work.

However, motivation can also be expressed in a simple model—namely, that people have certain *needs* that *motivate* them to perform specific *behaviors* for which they receive *rewards* that *feed back* and satisfy the original need (see Figure 12.2.).

FIGURE 12.2
A simple model of motivation

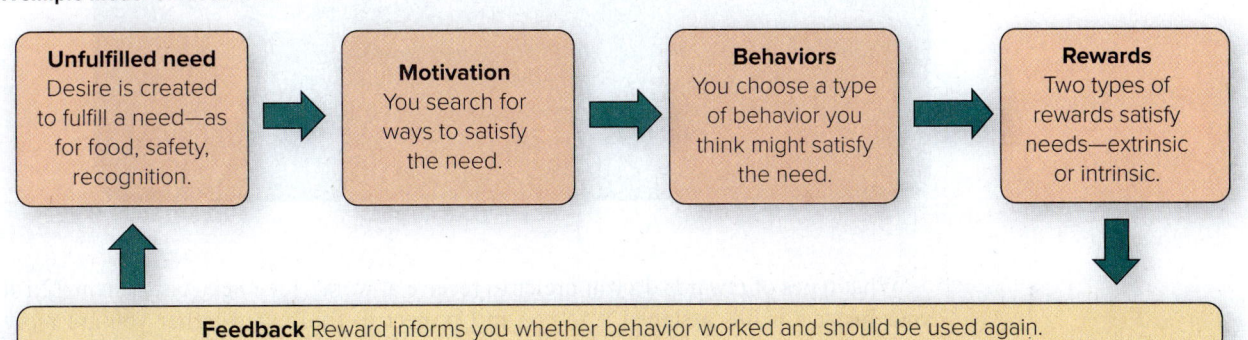

Unfulfilled need — Desire is created to fulfill a need—as for food, safety, recognition. → **Motivation** — You search for ways to satisfy the need. → **Behaviors** — You choose a type of behavior you think might satisfy the need. → **Rewards** — Two types of rewards satisfy needs—extrinsic or intrinsic.

Feedback Reward informs you whether behavior worked and should be used again.

For example, as an hourly worker you desire more money (need), which incentivizes you (motivates you) to work more hours (behavior), which provides you with more money (reward) and informs you (feedback loop) that working more hours will fulfill your need for more money in the future.

Rewards (as well as motivation itself) are of two types—*extrinsic* and *intrinsic*.[13] Managers can use both to encourage better work performance. Let's discuss each of these and consider how employers use both extrinsic and intrinsic motivation to decrease employee tobacco use.

- **Extrinsic rewards—rewards given by others.** An extrinsic reward is the payoff, such as money, recognition, or encouragement, a person receives from others for performing a particular task. Extrinsic motivation is driven by receiving a valued reward from another person or entity.[14]

    Extrinsic Rewards Example—American Express: Ranked 8th in *Fortune*'s 100 Best Companies to Work For 2022, American Express offers appealing benefits to its more than 84,000 employees worldwide, such as comprehensive health care, free access to its wellness program, a 6% annual match for retirement savings, 20 weeks of paid time off for new parents, and a partnership with Harvard to offer employees leadership development programs.[15]

- **Intrinsic rewards—a reward given to yourself.** An intrinsic reward is the satisfaction, such as a feeling of accomplishment, a person receives from performing the particular task itself. An intrinsic reward is an internal reward; the payoff comes from pleasing yourself.[16]

    Intrinsic Rewards Example—Disney: Christopher Fults is a Disney Institute facilitator who teaches professionals how Disney delivers world-class guest experiences. His job provides him the opportunity to tell stories and create connections with participants that are personally fulfilling, meaningful, and impactful. Fults noted, "We are incredibly intentional with the 'how' and 'why' behind our work. To see the 'light bulb' or 'a-ha!' moment in others is inspiring."[17]

Disney employees find their work filled with intrinsic rewards—like meaning, purpose, and passion—as they create joy, wonder, and delightful memories for their guests. chrisdorney/Shutterstock

What types of rewards do you prefer to receive at work? Take Self-Assessment 12.1 if your instructor has assigned it to you in Connect to find out whether you are more motivated by extrinsic or intrinsic rewards.

SELF-ASSESSMENT 12.1   CAREER READINESS

Are You More Interested in Extrinsic or Intrinsic Rewards?
This survey is designed to assess extrinsic and intrinsic motivation. Please complete Self-Assessment 12.1 if your instructor has assigned it in Connect.

Why Is Motivation Important? It is obvious that organizations want to motivate their employees to be more productive. But motivation also plays a role in influencing a host of outcomes, including employee engagement, organizational citizenship, absenteeism, and service quality.[18] In order of importance, you as a manager want to motivate people to:

1. **Join your organization.** You need to instill in talented prospective workers the desire to come work for you.
2. **Stay with your organization.** Whether you are in good economic times or bad, you always want to be able to retain good people.
3. **Show up for work at your organization.** In many organizations, absenteeism and lateness are tremendous problems.
4. **Be engaged while at your organization.** Engaged employees produce higher-quality work and better customer service.
5. **Put forth extra effort for your organization.** You hope your employees will perform extra tasks above and beyond the call of duty (be organizational "good citizens").

The Four Major Perspectives on Motivation: An Overview

There is no theory accepted by everyone as to what motivates people. In this chapter, therefore, we present the four principal perspectives. From these, you may be able to select what ideas seem most workable to you. The four perspectives on motivation are (1) *content,* (2) *process,* (3) *job design,* and (4) *reinforcement,* as described in the following four main sections.

The following is a quick overview of these four perspectives and the theories that utilize each.

1. **Content theories** emphasize needs as motivators.
    - *Maslow's hierarchy of needs,* introduced in Chapter 2, has five levels to be met in order.
    - *McClelland's acquired needs theory* posits three needs: achievement, affiliation, and power.
    - *Deci and Ryan's self-determination theory* assumes people seek innate needs of competence, autonomy, and relatedness in order to grow.
    - *Herzberg's two-factor theory* differentiates hygiene factors and motivators that determine work satisfaction and dissatisfaction.
2. **Process theories** focus on the thoughts and perceptions that motivate behavior.
    - *Equity/justice theory* proposes that people seek fairness and justice in their interactions and relationships.
    - *Expectancy theory* says people are motivated by how much they want something and how likely they think it is they will get it.
    - *Goal-setting theory* says goals that are specific, challenging, and achievable will motivate behavior.

3. **Job design theories** focus on designing jobs that lead to employee satisfaction and performance.
   - *Scientific management theory* attempted to fit people to jobs by reducing the number of tasks workers had to perform to achieve a goal.
   - *Job enlargement and job enrichment* are ways to fit jobs to people by offering more variety, challenges, and responsibility.
   - *The job characteristics model* is an outgrowth of job enrichment that traces the effect of five job characteristics on employees' psychological states and work outcomes.
   - *Relational job characteristics* connect a job's design with improving the lives of others.
4. **Reinforcement theory** is based on the notion that motivation is a function of behavioral consequences and not unmet needs.

12.2 Content Perspectives on Employee Motivation

THE BIG PICTURE

The content perspective views needs as the driving force for employee motivation. The content perspective includes four theories: Maslow's hierarchy of needs, McClelland's acquired needs theory, Deci and Ryan's self-determination theory, and Herzberg's two-factor theory.

LO 12-2

Identify the needs that motivate most employees.

Content perspectives, also known as need-based perspectives, are theories that emphasize the needs that motivate people. Content theorists ask, "What kind of needs motivate employees in the workplace?" **Needs** are defined as physiological or psychological deficiencies that arouse behavior. They can be strong or weak, and because they are influenced by environmental factors, they can vary over time and from place to place.

In addition to McGregor's Theory X/Theory Y (see Chapter 2), content perspectives include four theories:

- Maslow's hierarchy of needs theory.
- McClelland's acquired needs theory.
- Deci and Ryan's self-determination theory.
- Herzberg's two-factor theory.

Maslow's Hierarchy of Needs Theory: Five Levels

In 1943, as one of the first researchers to study motivation, Abraham Maslow (mentioned previously in Chapter 2) put forth the **hierarchy of needs theory**, which proposes that people are motivated by five levels of needs: (1) physiological, (2) safety, (3) love, (4) esteem, and (5) self-actualization.[19] (See Figure 12.3.)

1. **Physiological need—the most basic human physical need:** Need for food, clothing, shelter, comfort, self-preservation.

   Workplace example: Salary.

2. **Safety need:** Need for physical safety, emotional security, job security, health.

   Workplace examples: Health insurance, job security, work safety rules, pension plans.

3. **Love need:** Need for friendship, affection, acceptance.

   Workplace examples: Office parties, company softball teams, management retreats.

4. **Esteem need:** Need for self-respect, status, reputation, recognition, self-confidence.

   Workplace examples: Bonuses, promotions, awards.

5. **Self-actualization need—the highest level need:** Need for self-fulfillment: increasing competence, using abilities to the fullest.

   Workplace examples: Sabbatical leave to further personal growth, mentorship opportunities, and continued education.

FIGURE 12.3
Maslow's hierarchy of needs

The Five Levels of Needs Maslow suggested that individuals' needs are organized into three categories: basic needs, psychological needs, and self-fulfillment needs.

- Basic needs are our most fundamental needs for survival and security: physiological and safety needs.
- Psychological needs are our need to belong and feel respected: love and esteem needs.
- Self-fulfillment needs are our needs for personal and professional development: the need for self-actualization.

The needs are depicted as a hierarchy because, according to Maslow, we attend to our most basic unmet needs first before addressing our higher-order needs. Here's how it works:

Basic needs must be met before we attend to psychological needs. How much does feeling accepted and respected matter to you in the moment if you're worried about where you're going to sleep tonight, find your next meal, or how you're going to pay the bills? Probably not very much. Following the rungs up the needs hierarchy, psychological needs must be met before we focus on filling our need for self-actualization. Today's employees, for example, really care about career development. Findings from a recent study involving 1,200 employees supported this conclusion. Fifty-eight percent of respondents indicated they would leave their company if they don't receive professional development opportunities. Minorities (73%) and women of color (71%) are especially likely to leave without adequate development opportunities. Jennifer Burnett, principle researcher at The Conference Board, remarked "it is in the best interest of employers to provide all employees across their business with learning and development opportunities related to business priorities and overall personal growth."[20]

Using the Hierarchy of Needs Theory to Motivate Employees What should managers know about using the hierarchy of needs theory to motivate their employees?

1. **Research does not clearly support Maslow's theory.** Organizations should use caution when applying Maslow's hierarchy. Studies have repeatedly demonstrated that it presents, at best, an oversimplified view of the impact of needs on human motivation.[21] In reality, employees may try to address multiple needs simultaneously rather than in the precise order Maslow's hierarchy suggests.

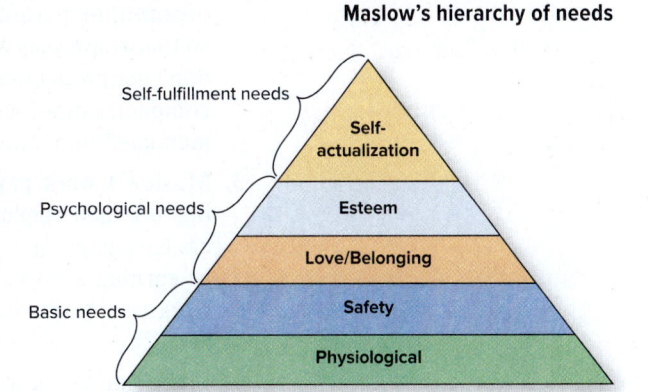

2. **Physiological and safety needs are still a necessary foundation.** To the extent the organization permits, managers should first try to meet employees' basic needs so that employees won't be preoccupied with them. Says one HR expert, "You don't get productive employees if they can't afford to live."[22] This is why more companies now focus on paying a "livable wage" that is higher than the legally mandated minimum wage.[23]

3. **Maslow's work paved the way for organizations to strategize how they can improve their employees' overall well-being.** His work demonstrated that workers have psychological and self-fulfillment needs beyond the basic needs such as earning a paycheck. Other needs theories built on Maslow's pioneering work to describe how to improve employees' job satisfaction and motivation at work.

4. **There's no one best way to motivate all employees.** Managers should be attentive to their employees' current needs. A downturn in the economy, for example, may bring employees' basic needs to the forefront. Social isolation from extreme events like the COVID-19 lockdowns may make psychological needs like social connectedness the most important need for other employees. Further still, employers interested in retaining and recruiting talented employees should focus on offering avenues for personal and professional development, defining clear paths for career growth within the company, and connecting the work to a prosocial purpose. For example, employees at companies like IKEA, Ben & Jerry's, Sweetgreen, and Land O'Lakes know that the work they do connects them to the greater social purpose of making the world a better and healthier place.[24]

McClelland's Acquired Needs Theory: Achievement, Affiliation, and Power

David McClelland, a well-known psychologist, proposed the **acquired needs theory**, which states that three needs—achievement, affiliation, and power—are major motives determining people's behavior in the workplace.[25] Managers are encouraged to recognize these three needs in themselves and others and to create work environments that are responsive to them.

FIGURE 12.4
McClelland's three needs

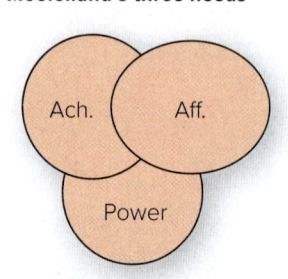

A "well-balanced" individual: achievement, affiliation, and power are of equal size.

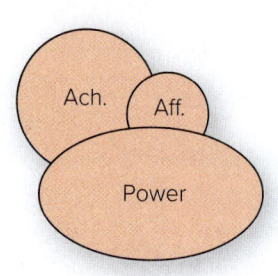

A "control freak" individual: achievement is normal, but affiliation is small and power is large.

The Three Needs McClelland's theory makes two important assumptions about the needs for achievement, affiliation, and power:

1. **Needs are learned.** Acquired needs theory suggests that we are not born with our needs; rather, we learn them from our culture and early life experiences.[26]

2. **One need often dominates.** The theory suggests that one of the three needs tends to be dominant in each of us, although some individuals have a more balanced set of needs. For example, some people have a higher need for power than for affiliation or achievement.[27] (See Figure 12.4.)

- **Need for achievement—"I need to excel at tasks."** This is the desire to excel, to do something better or more efficiently, to solve problems, to achieve excellence in challenging tasks.
- **Need for affiliation—"I need close relationships."** This is the desire for friendly and warm relations with other people.
- **Need for power—"I need to control others."** This is the desire to be responsible for other people, to influence their behavior or to control them.

Where do you think you stand in terms of being motivated by these three needs? You can find out by completing Self-Assessment 12.2 if your instructor has assigned it to you in Connect.

SELF-ASSESSMENT 12.2   CAREER READINESS

Assessing Your Acquired Needs
This survey is designed to assess your motivation in terms of acquired needs. Please complete Self-Assessment 12.2 if your instructor has assigned it in Connect.

Using Acquired Needs Theory to Motivate Employees   As a manager, you can apply acquired needs theory by appealing to the preferences associated with each need. Consider the following recommendations.[28]

Need for Achievement   People motivated by the *need for achievement* prefer:

- Working on challenging, but not impossible, tasks or projects.
- Situations in which good performance relies on effort and ability rather than luck.
- Being rewarded for their efforts.
- Receiving a fair and balanced amount of positive and negative feedback to improve their performance.

Need for Affiliation   Those who tend to seek social approval and satisfying personal relationships may have a *high need for affiliation.* These individuals:

- May not be the most efficient managers because at times they will have to make decisions that will cause people to resent them.
- Tend to prefer work, such as sales, that provides for personal relationships and social approval.

Need for Power   People who have a *high need for power* are more likely to enjoy:

- Being in control of people and events and being recognized for this responsibility.
- Work that allows them to control or have an effect on people and be publicly recognized for their accomplishments.

Deci and Ryan's Self-Determination Theory: Competence, Autonomy, and Relatedness

Developed by University of Rochester psychologists Edward Deci (pronounced "*Dee-see*") and Richard Ryan, **self-determination theory** assumes that people are driven to try to grow and attain fulfillment, with their behavior and well-being influenced by three universal needs: competence, autonomy, and relatedness.[29]

Focus on Intrinsic Motivation   Self-determination theory focuses primarily on intrinsic motivation and rewards (such as feeling independent) rather than on extrinsic motivation and rewards (such as money or fame). Intrinsic motivation is important because:[30]

- It is longer lasting than extrinsic motivation.
- It has a more positive impact on task performance than extrinsic motivation.

The Three Innate Needs   To achieve psychological growth, according to the theory, people need to satisfy the three innate (that is, inborn) needs of competence, autonomy, and relatedness:[31]

1. **Competence—"I want to feel a sense of mastery."** People need to feel qualified, knowledgeable, and capable of completing a goal or task and to learn different skills.

2. **Autonomy—"I want to feel independent and able to influence my environment."** People need to feel they have freedom and the discretion to determine what they want to do and how they want to do it.

3. **Relatedness—"I want to feel connected to other people."** People need to feel a sense of belonging, of attachment to others.

Using Self-Determination Theory to Motivate Employees
Meeting these three innate needs are critically important to individuals because research consistently shows they strongly improve well-being (happiness, life satisfaction, and meaning in life) and decrease symptoms of depression.[32] Managers can apply this theory by engaging in leader behavior that fosters the experience of competence, autonomy, and relatedness.[33] Following are some specific suggestions:

- **Competence.** Managers can provide tangible resources, time, contacts, mentoring, and coaching to improve employee competence, making sure that employees have the knowledge and information they need to perform their jobs.

    Competence Example—Boston Consulting Group (BCG): BCG, ranked #1 in Comparably's 2022 Best Large Companies in the U.S. to Grow Your Career, relied on a leadership style and organizational culture that made employees feel confident and capable. According to Comparably, 95% of BCG's employees felt challenged at work and 77% reported having a mentor to nurture their personal and professional growth.[34]

- **Autonomy.** To enhance feelings of autonomy, managers can develop trust with and empower their employees by delegating meaningful tasks to them and encouraging them to use their best judgment. An example of this is Nordstrom's clear and concise code of conduct.

    Autonomy Example—Nordstrom: Ranked #27 on *Fortune*'s 2023 World's Most Admired Companies, Nordstrom is famous for its elite level of customer service in the retail industry. For Nordstrom, outstanding customer service starts with "One Rule: Use Good Judgment In All Situations. This includes using good judgment when it comes to taking care of our customers, each other, and the people and companies we do business with."[35]

Nordstrom employees, like those in this Manhattan, NY, department store, use their best judgment to delight customers, build long-term relationships with them, and make them feel good every time they visit.
rblfmr/Shutterstock

- **Relatedness.** Many companies, such as In-N-Out Burger, use camaraderie to foster relatedness.

    Relatedness Example—In-N-Out Burger: Featured as #10 on Glassdoor's 2023 100 Best Places to Work list, In-N-Out burger takes the top spot among companies in the restaurant industry. The company attributes its ability to retain associates for 10 to 15 years or more to its ethical and family-oriented values. Values such as respect, friendliness, courtesy, and kindness create a team-oriented environment in which positive relationships flourish and associates work together to provide "exceptional services at all times."[36]

Are you feeling motivated in this course? To what extent does your instructor satisfy your needs for competence, autonomy, and relatedness? You can find out by taking Self-Assessment 12.3 if your instructor has assigned it to you in Connect.

SELF-ASSESSMENT 12.3   CAREER READINESS

Assessing Your Needs for Self-Determination

This survey is designed to assess the extent to which an instructor is satisfying your needs for self-determination. Please complete Self-Assessment 12.3 if your instructor has assigned it in Connect.

Herzberg's Two-Factor Theory: From Dissatisfying Factors to Satisfying Factors

Frederick Herzberg arrived at his needs-based theory as a result of a landmark study of 203 accountants and engineers who were interviewed to determine the factors responsible for job satisfaction and dissatisfaction.[37] Two key findings from Herzberg's study informed the two-factor theory:

1. Job satisfaction was more frequently associated with achievement, recognition, characteristics of the work, responsibility, and advancement.
2. Job dissatisfaction was more often associated with working conditions, pay and security, company policies, supervisors, and interpersonal relationships.

The result was Herzberg's **two-factor theory**, which proposed that work satisfaction and dissatisfaction arise from two different factors—work satisfaction from motivating factors and work dissatisfaction from hygiene factors.

Hygiene Factors versus Motivating Factors In Herzberg's theory, the hygiene factors are the lower-level needs, and the motivating factors are the higher-level needs. The two areas are separated by a zone in which employees are neither satisfied nor dissatisfied (see Figure 12.5).

- **Hygiene factors—"Why are my people dissatisfied?"** The lower-level needs, **hygiene factors**, are factors associated with job dissatisfaction—such as salary, working conditions, interpersonal relationships, and company policy—all of which affect the job context in which people work.

    Hygiene Factors Example—State Prison Employees: Retention is a major problem in the Department of Corrections. The annual turnover rate for corrections officers in the state of Georgia was 49% in 2022. Corrections Commissioner Timothy Ward attributed the high turnover rate to low pay,

FIGURE 12.5 Herzberg's two-factor theory: satisfaction versus dissatisfaction

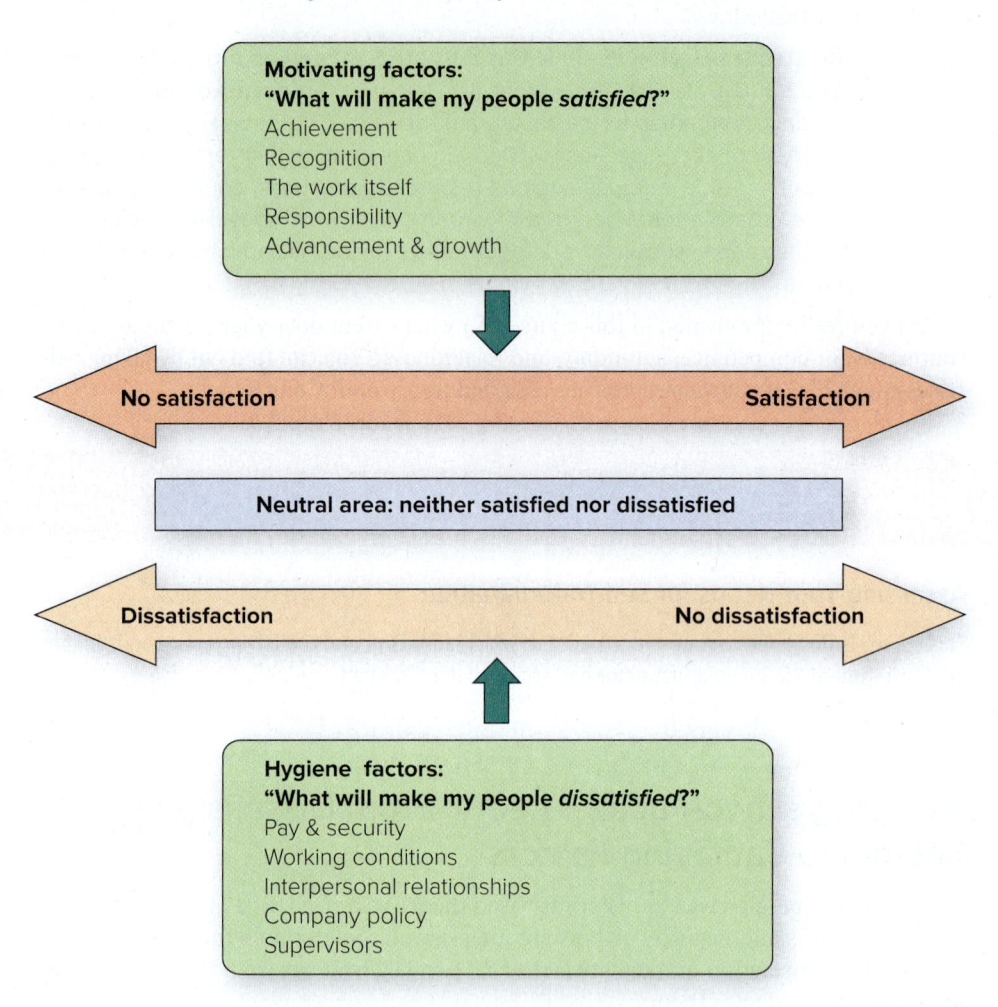

Motivating factors:
"What will make my people *satisfied*?"
Achievement
Recognition
The work itself
Responsibility
Advancement & growth

No satisfaction ←→ Satisfaction

Neutral area: neither satisfied nor dissatisfied

Dissatisfaction ←→ No dissatisfaction

Hygiene factors:
"What will make my people *dissatisfied*?"
Pay & security
Working conditions
Interpersonal relationships
Company policy
Supervisors

a stressful work environment, deteriorating infrastructure, violent offenders with long prison sentences, and few telework options for staff.[38] Employees' dissatisfaction with their work may partly explain why 195 state corrections employees have been arrested for job-related crimes within two and half years.[39]

- **Motivating factors—"What will make my people satisfied?"** The higher-level needs, **motivating factors**, or simply *motivators*, are factors associated with job satisfaction—such as achievement, recognition, responsibility, and advancement—all of which affect the job content or the rewards of work performance. Herzberg believed motivating factors must be integrated into the job to spur superior work performance. Consider how David Weekley Homes builds motivators into employees' work.

    Motivators Example—David Weekley Homes. Ranked #9 on *Fortune*'s 100 Best Companies to Work For and #4 on *Fortune*'s 100 Best Workplaces for Millennials in 2022, David Weekley Homes rewards employees' achievements and recognizes their loyalty. The company offers an employee stock ownership and profit-sharing plan as avenues to include employees in its financial success. It also gives employees with 10+ years of continuous service a $2,000 grant to spend pursuing their personal or professional goals during a paid four- to six-week sabbatical.[40]

Using Two-Factor Theory to Motivate Employees   There will always be some employees who dislike their jobs, but the basic lessons of Herzberg's research are that you should:

1. First eliminate dissatisfaction by making sure that hygiene factors such as working conditions, pay levels, and company policies are reasonable.
2. Next concentrate on spurring motivation by providing desired opportunities for achievement, recognition, responsibility, and personal growth (motivating factors).

Companies address hygiene factors by allowing pets at work, offering gym memberships, and providing employee discounts.[41] These flashy perks, however, may not reflect employees' top priorities. A 2023 *Forbes* survey of 1,000 employed Americans and 1,000 business owners revealed the top five benefits employees want from their employers are:[42]

1. Employer-covered health care
2. Life insurance
3. Pension and retirement plans
4. Mandatory paid time-off
5. Mental health assistance

Whereas employers tend to undervalue the importance of paid time-off, they overvalue the perceived benefit of employee discounts. Employers can save money and better support their employees by paying attention to what their employees really need rather than trying to keep up with expensive new trends that employees don't value.

Companies instill motivating factors by offering employee recognition, career counseling, and opportunities for growth, learning, and development. Motivating factors are important for employees at any career stage. Heineken offers a unique program to spur learning and development among its senior executives.

Learning and Development Example—Heineken: Dutch brewer, Heineken, developed a reverse mentoring program where junior employees mentor the company's senior leaders and executives. This program equips senior leaders with new skills, experiences, and perspectives so they can better identify future growth opportunities and envision the future of work.[43]

The four needs theories are compared in Figure 12.6. Note how acquired needs theory (McClelland) and self-determination theory (Deci and Ryan) focus only on higher-level needs.

FIGURE 12.6

A comparison of needs and satisfaction theories: Maslow's hierarchy of needs, McClelland's acquired needs, Deci and Ryan's self-determination, and Herzberg's two-factor

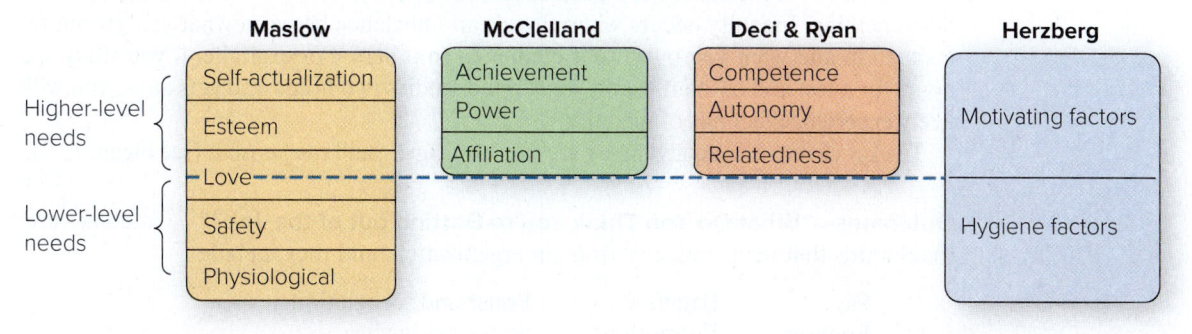

	Maslow	McClelland	Deci & Ryan	Herzberg
Higher-level needs	Self-actualization / Esteem	Achievement / Power / Affiliation	Competence / Autonomy / Relatedness	Motivating factors
Lower-level needs	Love / Safety / Physiological			Hygiene factors

12.3 Process Perspectives on Employee Motivation

THE BIG PICTURE
Process perspectives, which are concerned with the thought processes by which people decide how to act, have three viewpoints: equity/justice theory, expectancy theory, and goal-setting theory.

LO 12-3
Discuss similarities and differences among three process theories.

Process perspectives are concerned with the thought processes by which people decide how to act—how employees choose behavior to meet their needs. Whereas need-based perspectives simply try to understand employee needs, process perspectives go further and try to understand why employees have different needs, what behaviors they select to satisfy them, and how they decide if their choices were successful.

In this section we discuss three process perspectives on motivation:

- Equity/justice theory.
- Expectancy theory.
- Goal-setting theory.

Equity/Justice Theory: How Fairly Do You Think You're Being Treated in Relation to Others?

Fairness—or, perhaps equally important, the *perception* of fairness—can be a big issue in organizations. For example, if, as a salesperson for professional website LinkedIn, you received a 10% bonus for doubling your sales, would that be enough? What if other LinkedIn salespeople received a 15% bonus? And how about what the larger market is paying people with your competencies? Equity/justice theory says you'll determine what's fair by comparing your effort and your pay to others as well as to objective market data.

Equity theory is a model of motivation that explains how people strive for fairness and justice in social exchanges or give-and-take relationships. Pioneered by psychologist J. Stacey Adams, equity theory is based on the idea that employees are motivated to see fairness in the rewards they expect for task performance and are motivated to resolve feelings of injustice.[44] We will discuss Adams' ideas and their application, then discuss the extension of equity theory into what is called *justice theory*. We conclude by discussing how to motivate employees with both equity and justice theory.

The Elements of Equity Theory: Comparing Your Outcomes and Inputs with Those of Others
Equity theory is based on *cognitive dissonance* (see Chapter 11), the psychological discomfort people experience between their cognitive attitudes and incompatible behaviors. It's the dissonance, or inequity, that creates the motivation to do something. Inequity occurs when there's an imbalance between what you get out of a situation and what you put into it compared to others. For example, if you study six hours for a test and earn an A and your friend studies two hours and gets an A, you will likely experience feelings of inequity.

The key elements in equity theory are *outcomes, inputs,* and *comparisons* (see Figure 12.7).

Outcomes—"What Do You Think You're Getting out of the Job?" Outcomes are the rewards that people receive from an organization, and they include

Pay	Benefits	Praise and recognition
Bonuses	Promotions	Status perquisites

FIGURE 12.7 Equity theory
How people perceive they are being fairly or unfairly rewarded.

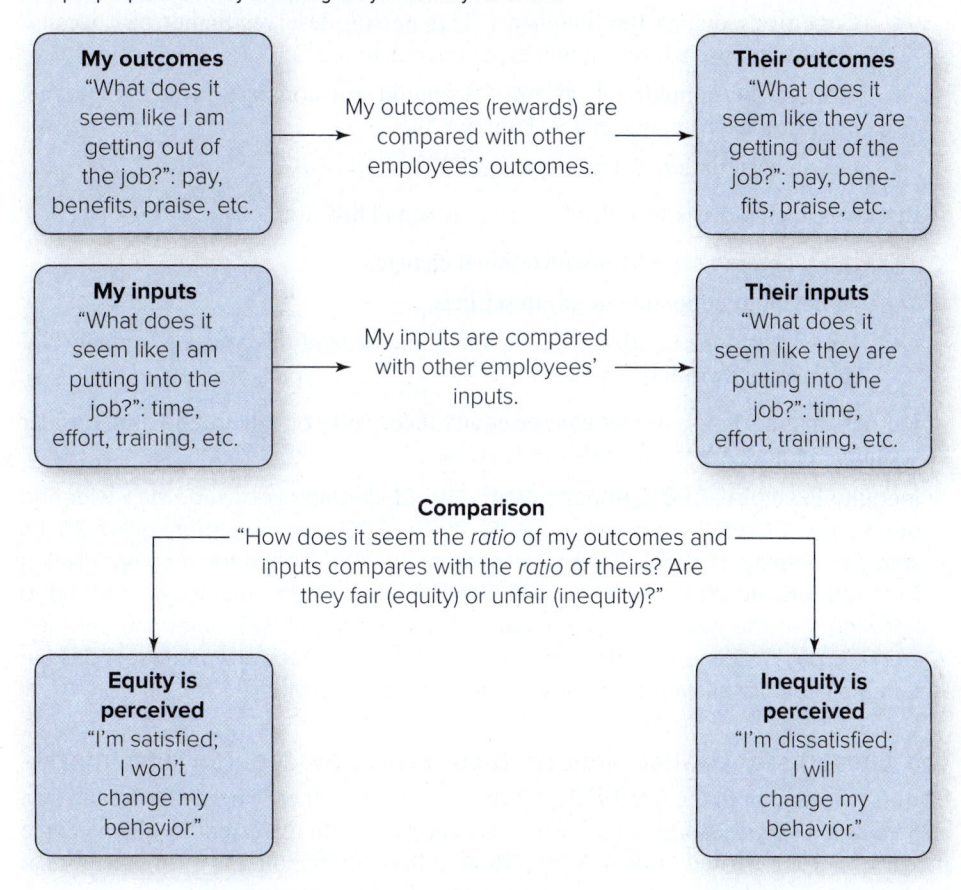

My outcomes
"What does it seem like I am getting out of the job?": pay, benefits, praise, etc.

→ My outcomes (rewards) are compared with other employees' outcomes. →

Their outcomes
"What does it seem like they are getting out of the job?": pay, benefits, praise, etc.

My inputs
"What does it seem like I am putting into the job?": time, effort, training, etc.

→ My inputs are compared with other employees' inputs. →

Their inputs
"What does it seem like they are putting into the job?": time, effort, training, etc.

Comparison
"How does it seem the *ratio* of my outcomes and inputs compares with the *ratio* of theirs? Are they fair (equity) or unfair (inequity)?"

Equity is perceived
"I'm satisfied; I won't change my behavior."

Inequity is perceived
"I'm dissatisfied; I will change my behavior."

Inputs—"What Do You Think You're Putting into the Job?" Inputs are the contributions people bring to their organization, such as

| Time | Effort | Training | Experience | Education |
| Intelligence | Creativity | Seniority | Status | Social capital |

Comparison—"How Do You Think Your Ratio of Outcomes and Inputs Compares with Those of Others?" Equity theory suggests that people compare the *ratio* of their own outcomes to inputs against the *ratio* of someone else's outcomes to inputs.[45]

- When employees compare the ratio of their outcomes (rewards) and inputs with those of others—whether co-workers within the organization or even other people in similar jobs outside it—they follow the comparison with a judgment about fairness.
- When employees perceive there is *equity,* they are satisfied with the ratio and don't change their behavior.
- When employees perceive there is *inequity,* they feel resentful and act to change the inequity.

Using Equity Theory to Motivate Employees Adams suggests that employees who feel they are being under-rewarded relative to their inputs will respond to the perceived inequity in one or more of the following negative ways:

- Reduce their inputs. ("I'm just going to do the minimum required.")

- Try to change the outcomes or rewards they receive. ("If they won't give me a raise, I'll just take stuff.")
- Cognitively distort the inequity. ("This person deserves higher pay because they have more education and experience than me.")
- Change the comparison group. ("I should not compare myself to Rachel because she is a manager and I am not.")
- Leave the situation. ("I'm outta here!")

By contrast, employees who think they are treated fairly are:

- More likely to support organizational change.
- More apt to cooperate in group settings.
- Less apt to turn to arbitration, forming unions, and the courts to remedy real or imagined wrongs.

Fairness matters to us, and we can see equity theory play out all around us. Consider the example of how Americans react to CEO pay.

Inequity Example—CEO Compensation: The CEO–employee wage gap widened during the COVID-19 pandemic (2019–2021). CEO compensation grew 30.3% whereas employed workers' compensation grew 3.9%. The median compensation for a U.S. CEO in 2021 was about $15.6 million. How might employees respond to knowing that the average pay for top CEOs was around 399 times the average worker's pay?[46] Some experts suggest that such imbalances are partly responsible for employee dissatisfaction, turnover, and lower productivity.[47]

The Elements of Justice Theory: Distributive, Procedural, and Interactional

Beginning in the late 1970s, researchers in equity theory began to expand into an area called *organizational justice,* which is concerned with the extent to which people perceive they are treated fairly at work. Three different components of organizational justice have been identified: *distributive, procedural,* and *interactional.*[48]

- **Distributive justice**—"How fair are the rewards that are being given out? Distributive justice reflects the perceived fairness of the outcomes being distributed or allocated among employees. Employees perceive distributive justice when they believe that the organization has given them a fair share of rewards and resources.[49]

- **Procedural justice**—"How fair is the process for handing out rewards?" Procedural justice is defined as the perceived fairness of the process and procedures used to make allocation decisions. Employees have stronger feelings of procedural justice when they have a chance to voice their opinions about workplace procedures, and when those procedures are applied accurately and consistently.[50] Numerous studies have shown that procedural justice increases prosocial behaviors in organizations such as organizational citizenship behavior (discussed in Chapter 11).[51]

- **Interactional justice**—"How fair is the treatment I receive when rewards are given out?" Interactional justice relates to how organizational representatives treat employees in the process of implementing procedures and making decisions.[52] This form of justice is not about how outcomes or procedures are perceived but rather whether people believe they are being treated fairly when decisions are implemented. Employees who perceive low levels of interactional justice respond with decreased job performance and helping behaviors.[53] Fair interpersonal treatment necessitates that managers communicate truthfully and treat people with courtesy and respect.

Do you feel that your managers treat you fairly at your job? Take the following self-assessment if your instructor has assigned it to you in Connect.

SELF-ASSESSMENT 12.4

Measuring Perceived Fair Interpersonal Treatment

This survey was designed to assess the extent to which you are experiencing fair interpersonal treatment at work. Please complete Self-Assessment 12.4 if your instructor has assigned it in Connect.

Using Equity and Justice Theories to Motivate Employees It is important to remember that an individual's *perception* of justice becomes their *reality* when applying these theories. For example, a 2022 Gartner survey of 3,500 employees revealed 68% felt like they were not paid fairly, a statistic the company says better reflects how people feel about their employer than actual compensation data.[54] Your understanding of equity and justice theories can enhance your effectiveness in the following ways:

- **Makes you a better manager.** Knowledge of equity and justice theories will allow you to hear and better understand employee concerns. You also can communicate reasonable expectations and make sure objective measures for rewards are well understood.

- **Makes you a better co-worker.** As an employee yourself, you can motivate other workers by clearly understanding and communicating opportunities to improve their situations.

Here are five practical lessons to remember about equity and justice theories.

1. Employee Perceptions Are What Count No matter how fair management thinks the organization's policies, procedures, and reward system are, each employee's perception of the equity of those factors is what counts.

Justice Perceptions Example—Nestlé: Yasmine Motarjemi, former head of global food safety at Nestlé, sued the company after being bullied and harassed by Nestlé employees for so long that she had to apply for occupational disability pension when she turned 55. Twelve years after being fired, the court found Nestlé responsible for the toxic work environment and awarded Motarjemi $2.2 million in lost wages. In response to the ruling, Motarjemi said "my lawsuit against Nestlé was never about money. I wanted a court to recognize the injustice done to me."[55]

2. Employees Want a Voice in Decisions That Affect Them Managers benefit by allowing employees to participate in making decisions about important work outcomes. In general, employees' perceptions of procedural justice are enhanced when they have a voice in the decision-making process.[56] **Voice** is defined as employees' expression of work-related concerns, ideas, and/or constructive suggestions to managers.[57]

Voice Example—Monica Dixon: The key to unlocking employees' voice is active listening, according to Monica Dixon, president, external affairs, and chief administrative officer at Monumental Sports and Entertainment. "By listening deeply, you understand how words can take on different meanings for different people. You also understand what is the top priority, anxiousness and to-do lists for all of these folks," Dixon shares. She goes on to say, if you don't understand "what everyone at the table is bringing with them that day to the table, both in terms of the substance of their work and the feel of their work, you can't get big things done."[58]

Employees who are invited to express their viewpoint during the decision-making process are more likely to feel like the decision is fair. fizkes/Shutterstock

3. Employees Should Be Given an Appeals Process Giving employees the opportunity to appeal decisions that affect their welfare enhances their perceptions of distributive and procedural justice.

Appeals Process Example—Universities: Did you know that as a student you likely have access to an appeals process? Most colleges and universities have processes in place that allow students to appeal course grades if they feel they have been treated unfairly. For example, at one university, students can appeal grades if they believe their instructor (1) made an error in calculating their grade or recording assignment submission dates, (2) failed to apply grading procedures in an unbiased way, or (3) did not assign grades according to the procedures set forth in the course syllabus.[59]

4. Leader Behavior Matters Employees' perceptions of justice are strongly influenced by the leadership behavior exhibited by their managers (leadership is discussed in Chapter 14). Thus, it is important for managers to consider the justice-related implications of their decisions, actions, and public communications.[60]

Leadership Example—American Express: Stephen Squeiri, CEO of American Express, is influencing employees' justice perceptions by adopting a new policy in which the company is posting salary ranges for all of its job listings across the United States. This move toward pay transparency is expected to help bridge the gender pay gap and instill more trust in the organization that is compensation practices are equitable.[61]

5. A Climate for Justice Makes a Difference Managers need to pay attention to the organization's climate for justice. **Justice climate** relates to the shared sense of fairness felt by the entire workgroup. Research suggests that employees in organizations with strong justice climates exhibit:[62]

- Increased job satisfaction and organizational commitment.
- More helping behaviors.
- Enhanced job performance.

The discussion of equity/justice theory has important implications for your own career. For example, you could work to resolve inequity by asking for a raise or a promotion (increasing your outcomes) or by working fewer hours or exerting less effort (reducing inputs). You could also resolve the inequity cognitively, by adjusting your perceptions as to the value of your salary or other benefits (outcomes) or the value of the work you or your co-workers contribute (inputs).

Expectancy Theory: How Much Do You Want and How Likely Are You to Get It?

Victor Vroom's **expectancy theory** boils down to deciding how much effort to exert in a specific task situation. This choice is based on a two-stage sequence of expectations—moving from effort to performance and then from performance to outcomes.[63]

The Three Elements: Expectancy, Instrumentality, and Valence
What determines how willing you (or an employee) are to work hard at tasks important to the success of the organization? The answer, says Vroom, is that you will do what you *can* do when you *want* to.

Your motivation, according to expectancy theory, involves the relationship between your *effort,* your *performance,* and the desirability of the *outcomes* (such as pay or recognition) you receive for your performance. These relationships (see Figure 12.8.) are affected by the three elements of *expectancy, instrumentality,* and *valence.*

1. Expectancy—"Will I Be Able to Perform at the Desired Level on a Task?"
Expectancy is the belief that a particular level of effort will lead to a particular level of performance. This is called the *effort-to-performance expectancy.*

- **High expectancy:** "The more hours I spend studying for this class, the higher my grade will be." This statement reflects high expectancy. That is, you believe your efforts matter in producing results.
- **Low expectancy:** "Regardless of how much I practice, I am never going to be able to dunk a basketball because I am 5'4"." This statement reflects low expectancy. That is, you do not see a link between your efforts and your ability to perform the task.

2. Instrumentality—"What Outcome Will I Receive if I Perform at This Level?"
Instrumentality is the expectation that successful performance of the task will lead to the outcome desired. This is called the *performance-to-outcome expectancy.*

Some organizations motivate managers by tying executive total compensation (base salary plus bonuses, stock, and stock options) to measures of firm success. However, it can be difficult for managers to see a direct link between their work and their firms' performance. In other words, instrumentality may be low because even when executives feel they are doing a "good job," it may not show in their firms' broad performance

FIGURE 12.8
Expectancy theory: The major elements

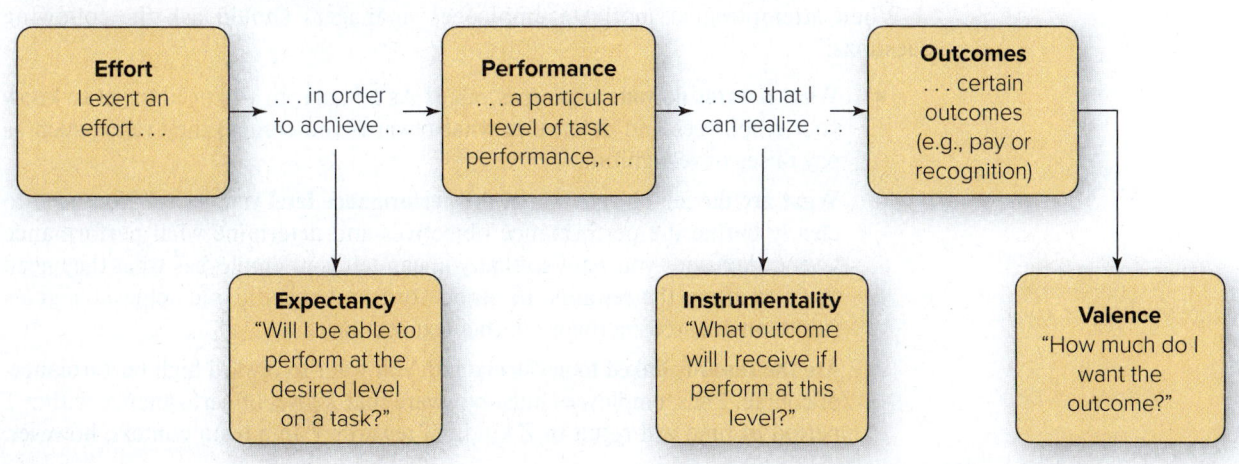

Effort
I exert an effort . . .
. . . in order to achieve . . .

Performance
. . . a particular level of task performance, . . .
. . . so that I can realize . . .

Outcomes
. . . certain outcomes (e.g., pay or recognition)

Expectancy
"Will I be able to perform at the desired level on a task?"

Instrumentality
"What outcome will I receive if I perform at this level?"

Valence
"How much do I want the outcome?"

data, and thus, they may not be rewarded. This uncertainty is one reason boards of directors justify giving executives generous compensation packages.

Instrumentality Example—JPMorgan Chase & Co.: Jamie Dimon, CEO of JPMorgan Chase since 2006, is slated to receive a $1.5 million salary and a bonus of $33 million in 2023. This total compensation is in line with competitors Morgan Stanley and Goldman Sachs. Much of Dimon's pay is linked to achieving performance targets during a year in which banks are experiencing considerable economic and political uncertainty.[64]

3. Valence—"How Much Do I Want the Outcome?" Valence is value, the importance a worker assigns to the possible outcome or reward. Consider what motivates you to study for one of your courses. If you had a quiz tomorrow and it was worth 2 points (out of a possible 1,000 total course points), would you exert as much effort studying as you would if the quiz were worth, say, 100 points? Probably not—because you likely don't care about 2 points nearly as much as you care about 100 points. Managers need to consider how valuable the rewards they offer are perceived to be for specific employees.

Valence Example—Worker Rewards: There are now five generations of workers in any given organization. Do you think they are all motivated by the same rewards? Evidence suggests that aside from salary (which seems to motivate most people to some degree) different generations of workers prefer different rewards. Among the more widely accepted ideas for the rewards preferred by each generation are:[65]

- **Traditionalists (1925–1945):** Prestigious job titles, praise for their loyalty, appreciation.
- **Baby Boomers (1946–1964):** Health insurance, working for someone they respect, prestigious perks like parking spaces and posh offices, in-person recognition, and health and wellness.
- **Generation X (1965–1980):** Autonomy, independence, private recognition, mentoring, flexibility, work-life balance, stock options.
- **Millennials (1981–2000):** Challenge, pursuing a larger purpose, skills training (particularly new technology), frequent feedback.
- **Generation Z (2001–2020):** Pursuing their passions, job security, flexible schedules, regular recognition, instant feedback.

For your motivation to be high, you must be high on all three elements—expectancy, instrumentality, and valence. If any element is low, your motivation goes down.

Using Expectancy Theory to Motivate Employees The principal problem with expectancy theory is that it is complex. Even so, the underlying logic is understandable, and research supports its use as a motivational tool.[66]

When attempting to motivate employees, managers should ask the following questions:

- **What rewards do your employees value?** As a manager, you need to get to know your employees and determine what rewards (outcomes) they value, such as pay raises or recognition.
- **What are the job objectives and the performance level you desire?** You need to clearly define the performance objectives and determine what performance level or behavior you want so that you can tell your employees what they need to do to attain the rewards. In other words, set specific and achievable goals (more on goal-setting theory in the next section).
- **Are the rewards linked to performance?** You want to reward high performance, of course. Thus, employees must be aware that X level of performance within Y period of time will result in Z kinds of rewards.[67] In a team context, however,

research shows that it is best to use a combination of individual and team-based rewards.[68]

- **Do employees believe you will deliver the right rewards for the right performance?** Your credibility is on the line here. Your employees must believe that you have the power, the ability, and the will to give them the rewards you promise for the performance you are requesting.

Goal-Setting Theory: Objectives Should Be Specific and Challenging but Achievable

We have been considering the importance of goal setting since first introducing the topic in Chapter 5. **Goal-setting theory** suggests that employees can be motivated by goals that are specific and challenging but achievable. According to Edwin Locke and Gary Latham, the psychologists who developed the theory, it is natural for people to set and strive for goals; however, the goal-setting process is useful only if people *understand, accept,* and are *committed to* the goals.[69]

The Four Motivational Mechanisms of Goal-Setting Theory Setting goals helps motivate because goals:[70]

1. **Direct attention:** Goal setting directs your attention toward goal-relevant tasks and away from irrelevant ones.
2. **Regulate effort:** The effort you expend is generally proportional to the goal's difficulty and time deadlines.
3. **Increase persistence:** Goal setting makes obstacles challenges to be overcome, not reasons to fail.
4. **Foster the use of strategies and action plans:** The use of strategies and action plans make it more likely that you will realize success.

Stretch Goals Companies committed to break-out growth sometimes adopt **stretch goals**, which are goals beyond what they actually expect to achieve. Rationales for developing stretch goals include:[71]

- Forcing people out of their comfort zones to achieve more.
- Building employees' confidence when they succeed.
- Insulating the company against future setbacks.
- Accepting the challenge of higher performance standards.

Companies like Google, Apple, Airbus, and 3M have all reported success with "wildly daring objectives."[72] Individuals, too, can benefit from setting stretch goals. Consider the young entrepreneur Dr. Ann-Marie Imafidon in the Example box the next time you think you can't do something difficult.

EXAMPLE | Dr. Anne-Marie Imafidon: From Child Prodigy to Stemette

As a 9-year-old student, Anne-Marie Imafidon was a challenge for her teachers. "I wasn't like a terror, I was just all over the place, a class clown," said Imafidon, adding, "I was kind of winding them up, because I don't sit still."[73] By the time she was 10 years old, her school decided that she should sit for her GCSEs (British college entrance exams) in math and IT. She passed—becoming one of the youngest people ever to do so—and by 20 she had become one of the youngest people in history to receive a master's degree from the University of Oxford in mathematics and computer science (where she was one of only three women in a class of 70).[74]

Stemettes

Dr. Imafidon founded Stemettes in 2013. The organization exists to encourage girls between the ages of 5 and 22 to pursue careers in STEAM (science, technology, engineering, arts, and math) fields. Since 2013, more than 50,000 young ladies ranging in age from 7 to 21 have attended the organization's free workshops and events, and 60% of Stemettes alumni now work in STEAM fields at 26 years and older.[75] Now in her early 30s, Imafidon has one ultimate goal for Stemettes: "building a network, building that community, empowering them with opportunities and really shifting their norms" about how they can lead and contribute in the STEAM fields.[76] She sees a couple of things as especially important to accomplishing this goal:

- **Changing stereotypes.** Dr. Imafidon thinks that social norms, or expectations, arising from stereotypes (such as the idea that "tech" people are nerdy white males) are one of the biggest barriers to young women entering STEAM fields. Stemettes counters these stereotypes by providing mentoring, connections with peers, and access to female role models. These experiences coupled with increased confidence in their STEAM abilities show young women that they have just as much of a place in STEAM fields as anyone else.
- **Telling true stories.** Dr. Imafidon acknowledges that *any* stories of smart women in pop culture are helpful; she sees true stories as particularly important. She referenced the film *Hidden Figures* as an example, saying that while it's nice to see fictional examples of female scientists, "It's even cooler to know that your teacher's grandma probably helped stop the war by being a code-breaker at Bletchley."[77]

Stemettes founder Dr. Anne-Marie Imafidon has a goal of encouraging so many women to pursue STEAM careers that her organization will eventually be unnecessary. Shutterstock

YOUR CALL

Have you ever thought about trying to achieve something extraordinarily difficult or unprecedented? Did you pursue the goal, or did you shy away? What held you back from trying?

Other managers, however, find that stretch goals have drawbacks and should be used with care.[78] For example, stretch goals:

- Can demotivate employees because they set aims that seem unattainable.
- Can encourage unethical behavior as employees try to reach the goals in whatever way possible.
- Can lead companies to take unnecessary risks.

Many people believe that the use of stretch sales goals contributed to employees at Wells Fargo opening nearly 3.5 million fake accounts without customers' authorization.[79] Recent research seems to confirm that stretch goals can have unintended negative consequences. According to the authors of one study, "stretch goals can lead to unethical behavior, intensify conflicts, and reduce motivation."[80] Indeed, a leader's ambition can create performance pressure for employees and push them to engage in unethical conduct, such as cheating, to achieve the goal.[81]

Some Practical Results of Goal-Setting Theory A *goal* is defined as an objective that a person is trying to accomplish through their efforts. Goal-setting experts Locke and Latham proposed the following recommendations when implementing a goal-setting program.[82] To result in high motivation and performance, goals must have a number of characteristics, as follows.

1. Goals Should Be Specific   Goals that are specific and difficult lead to higher performance than general goals like "Do your best" or "Improve performance." This is why it is essential to set specific, challenging goals. Goals such as "Sell as many cars as you can" or "Be nicer to customers" are too vague. Instead, goals need to be specific—usually meaning *quantitative,* as in:

- "Boost your revenues 25%."
- "Cut absenteeism by 10%."

You can find examples of specific goals in most organizations. Consider FedEx.

Specific Goals Example—FedEx: Logistics and business services provider, FedEx, is committed to two specific financial goals related to profitability and efficiency: (1) increase earnings per share by 10% to 15% per year and (2) achieve more than 10% operating margin.[83]

2. Certain Conditions Are Necessary for Goal Setting to Work   In order for goal setting to be effective, people must:[84]

- Have the abilities and resources needed to achieve the goal.
- Be committed to the goal. Goal commitment can be fostered by allowing employees to participate in the process of establishing goals.
- Receive timely feedback and participate in developing action plans.

3. Goals Should Be Linked to Action Plans   An action plan outlines the activities or tasks that need to be accomplished in order to obtain a goal and reminds us of what we should be working on. Both individuals (such as college students) and organizations are more likely to achieve their goals when they develop detailed action plans.[85]

Action Plan Example—Calvary Health Care: Australian healthcare provider Calvary Health Care offers hospitals, home care, and aged care services. Included in the hospital's strategic plan are both strategic priorities and action plans. For example, one priority is "A focus on quality and safety." The corresponding action plan for this goal is "Commit to zero preventable harm ... prioritizing safety and continuous improvement."[86]

In sum, goals lead to higher performance when you use feedback and participation to stay focused and committed to a specific goal. Some of the preceding recommendations are embodied in the advice we presented in Chapter 5—namely, that goals should be SMART: specific, measurable, attainable, results-oriented, and have target dates. •

12.4 Job Design Perspectives on Motivation

THE BIG PICTURE

Job design, the division of an organization's work among employees, applies motivational theories to jobs to increase performance and satisfaction. The traditional approach to job design is to fit people to jobs; the modern way is to fit jobs to the people. The job characteristics model offers five job attributes for better work outcomes. Relational job design identifies social characteristics of work that motivate employees.

Two out of three employees don't find their job fulfilling, says a 2022 Gallup survey of 67,000 full- and part-time employees. The survey revealed 32% were engaged (involved and enthusiastic about work) whereas 18% were actively disengaged (aggravated and unhappy) in their work. The ratio of engaged to actively disengaged employees is troubling because it has declined annually since 2020 and is now the lowest in the

LO 12-4

Compare and contrast four different ways to design jobs.

United States since 2013. Even more concerning, 50% of respondents were "quiet quitters" (neither engaged nor actively disengaged) who show up to work but leave their energy, enthusiasm, and passion at home.[87] How would you classify your feeling about your current job? Is there anything that can be done to make you feel more engaged at work?

Job design is (1) the division of an organization's work among its employees and (2) the application of motivational theories to jobs to increase satisfaction and performance. There are two different approaches to job design—one traditional, one modern—that can be taken in deciding how to design jobs. The traditional way is *fitting people to jobs;* the modern way is *fitting jobs to people.*[88]

Fitting People to Jobs

Fitting people to jobs is based on the assumption that people will gradually adapt to any work situation. Even so, jobs must still be designed so that nearly anyone can do them. This is the approach often taken with assembly-line jobs and jobs involving routine tasks. For managers the main challenge becomes "How can we make the worker most compatible with the work?"

One technique is **scientific management** (see Chapter 2), the process of reducing the number of tasks a worker performs. When a job is stripped down to its simplest elements, it enables a worker to focus on doing more of the same task, thus increasing employee efficiency and productivity. However, research shows that simplified, repetitive jobs lead to job dissatisfaction, poor mental health, and a low sense of accomplishment and personal growth.[89]

Fitting Jobs to People

Fitting jobs to people is based on the assumption that people are underutilized at work and that they want more variety, challenges, and responsibility. This philosophy, an outgrowth of Herzberg's two-factor theory, is one of the reasons for the popularity of work teams in the United States. The main challenge for managers is "How can we make the work most compatible with the worker so as to produce both high performance and high job satisfaction?"

Two techniques for this type of job design are (1) *job enlargement* and (2) *job enrichment.*

Job Enlargement: Putting More Variety into a Job The opposite of scientific management, **job enlargement** consists of increasing the number of tasks in a job to increase variety and motivation. For instance, the job of installing flat screens in television sets could be enlarged to include installation of the circuit boards as well. Three important points about job enlargement:

- Proponents claim job enlargement can improve employee satisfaction, motivation, and quality of production.
- Research suggests job enlargement by itself won't have a significant and lasting positive effect on job performance. After all, working at two boring tasks instead of one doesn't add up to a challenging job.
- Job enlargement is just one tool of many that should be considered in job design.[90]

Job Enrichment: Putting More Responsibility and Other Motivating Factors into a Job Job enrichment is the practical application of Herzberg's two-factor motivator–hygiene theory of job satisfaction.[91] Specifically, **job enrichment** consists of building into a job such motivating factors as responsibility, achievement, recognition, stimulating work, and advancement.

Note the main difference between job enlargement and job enrichment: job enlargement simply gives employees additional tasks of similar difficulty (known as *horizontal loading*), whereas job enrichment gives employees more responsibility (known as *vertical loading*).[92]

Job Enrichment Example—Crowdstrike: Cybersecurity firm Crowdstrike relies on its employees' experience and expertise to anticipate and intercept cybersecurity threats. The company enriches employees' work by extending them autonomy, flexibility, and trust as a platform to continuously learn and develop cutting edge security solutions. The company also offers advancement opportunities by promoting from within.[93]

The Job Characteristics Model: Five Job Attributes for Better Work Outcomes

Developed by researchers J. Richard Hackman and Greg Oldham, the job characteristics model of design is an outgrowth of job enrichment.[94] The **job characteristics model** consists of

- Five core job characteristics that affect
- Three psychological states of an employee, that in turn affect
- Work outcomes—the employee's motivation, performance, satisfaction, absenteeism, and turnover.

The model is illustrated in Figure 12.9.

Five Job Characteristics The five core job characteristics are *skill variety, task identity, task significance, autonomy,* and *feedback*.

1. Skill Variety—"How Many Different Skills Does Your Job Require?" *Skill variety* describes the extent to which a job requires a person to use a wide range of different skills and abilities.

EXAMPLE: The skill variety required by an executive chef is higher than that for a coffeehouse barista.

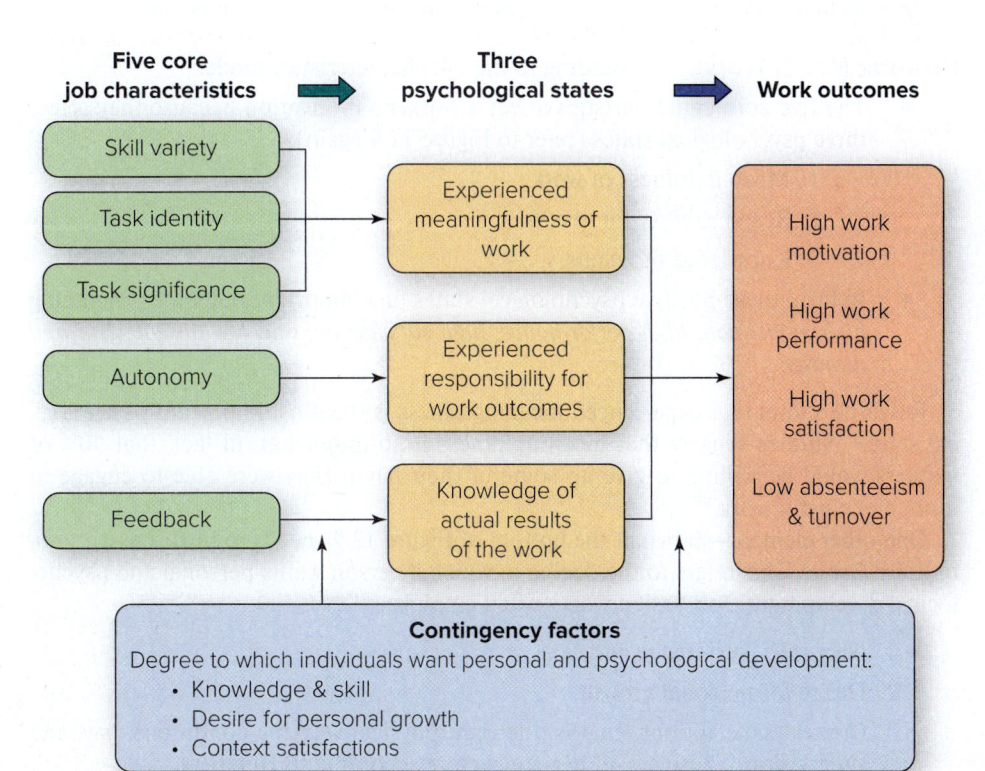

FIGURE 12.9

The job characteristics model

Source: Hackman, Richard J. and Greg R. Oldham. "Work Redesign." The Academy of Management Review 6, no. 4 (October 1981): 687–689. https://www.jstor.org/stable/257655?seq=1.

Five core job characteristics: Skill variety, Task identity, Task significance, Autonomy, Feedback

Three psychological states: Experienced meaningfulness of work; Experienced responsibility for work outcomes; Knowledge of actual results of the work

Work outcomes: High work motivation; High work performance; High work satisfaction; Low absenteeism & turnover

Contingency factors
Degree to which individuals want personal and psychological development:
- Knowledge & skill
- Desire for personal growth
- Context satisfactions

2. Task Identity—"How Many Different Tasks Are Required to Complete the Work?" *Task identity* describes the extent to which a job requires a worker to perform all the tasks needed to complete the job from beginning to end.

EXAMPLE: The task identity for a craftsperson who goes through all the steps to build a stained-glass window is higher than it is for an assembly-line worker who installs only backup cameras on cars.

3. Task Significance—"How Many Other People Are Affected by Your Job?" *Task significance* describes the extent to which a job affects the lives of other people, whether inside or outside the organization.

EXAMPLE: A firefighter who rescues children from a burning building has higher task significance than a person unloading boxes of cereal in a grocery stockroom.

4. Autonomy— "How Much Discretion Does Your Job Give You?" *Autonomy* describes the extent to which a job allows an employee to make choices about scheduling different tasks and deciding how to perform them.

EXAMPLE: College-textbook salespeople have lots of discretion in planning which campuses and professors to call on. They have higher autonomy than do toll-takers on a bridge, whose actions are determined by the flow of vehicles.

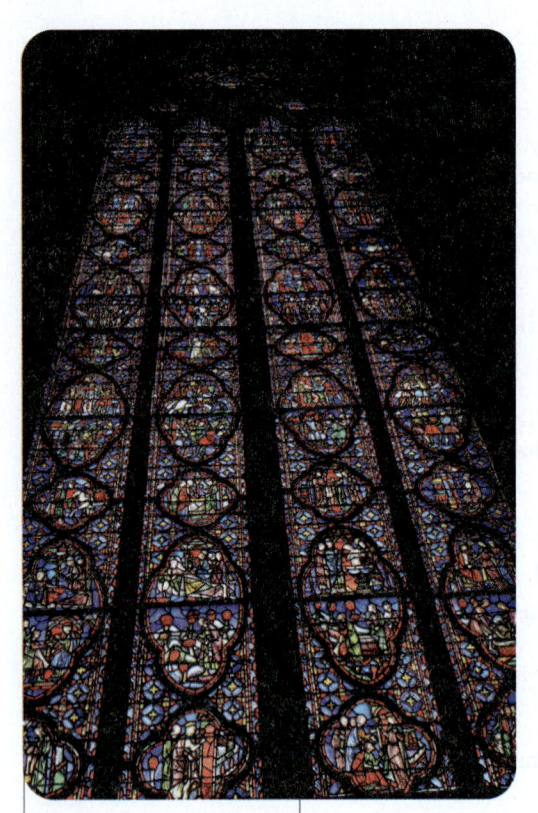

Stained glass craftspeople take pride in telling a story through light, colored glass, and design. The stained glass shown in the photo can be seen at Sainte Chapelle in Paris, France. Dr. Chad A. Hartnell

5. Feedback—"How Much Do You Find Out How Well You're Doing?" *Feedback* describes the extent to which workers receive clear, direct information about how well they are performing the job.

EXAMPLE: Professional basketball players receive immediate feedback on how many of their shots are going into the basket. Engineers working on new highway systems may go years before learning how effective their design has been.

How the Model Works
According to the job characteristics model:

- The five core characteristics affect a worker's motivation because they affect three psychological states (refer to Figure 12.9 again):
    1. Meaningfulness of work.
    2. Responsibility for results.
    3. Knowledge of results.
- In turn, these positive psychological states fuel important outcomes, including *high motivation, high performance, high satisfaction,* and *low absenteeism and turnover.*

Research shows that experienced meaningfulness is the most important psychological state.[95] Studies suggest that meaningfulness is so important, in fact, that 90% of workers would be willing to give up some of their pay if they were able to engage in more meaningful work.[96]

One other element—shown at the bottom of Figure 12.9—needs to be discussed: *contingency factors.* This refers to the degree to which a person wants personal and psychological development. Job design works when employees have:

1. Necessary knowledge and skill.
2. Desire for personal growth.
3. Context satisfactions—that is, the right physical working conditions, pay, and supervision. These are all hygiene factors according to Herzberg.

Job design motivates employees. But keep in mind that it is not for everyone. It is more likely to work when people have the required knowledge and skills, when they want to develop, and when they are satisfied with their work environment.[97]

Applying the Job Characteristics Model   There are three major steps to follow when applying the model.

- **Diagnose the work environment to see whether a problem exists.** This typically involves calculating a job's so-called motivating potential score (MPS)—the potential for a specific job to influence workers' motivation levels and job behaviors.[98]
- **Determine whether job redesign is appropriate.** If the MPS is low, an attempt should be made to determine which of the core job characteristics is causing the problem. You should next decide whether job redesign is appropriate. Job design is most likely to work in a participative environment in which employees have the necessary knowledge and skills.
- **Consider how to redesign the job.** Here you try to increase those core job characteristics that are problematic.

    Job Characteristics Example—USAA: Financial services and insurance provider USAA communicates a clear mission to its employees: "We proudly serve military members and their families." The company arranges for its employees to experience a mock boot camp with drill sergeants and physically challenging assignments. The experience connects its employees to the company's mission by helping them understand the culture of the military and appreciate the purpose and significance of their work. USAA consistently ranks highest in customer loyalty and satisfaction among insurance providers.[99]

Relational Job Design

Whereas the job characteristics model focuses on designing tasks to spur possessive: employees' interest in the work itself, relational job design focuses on designing the relational aspects of work to increase employees' **prosocial motivation**, or the desire to benefit others.

Researcher and author, Adam Grant, pioneered work on relational job design with a series of studies demonstrating the power of prosocial motivation.[100] His perspective generated much research. For example, a recent meta-analysis of 201 studies and over 45,000 respondents showed that prosocial motivation improved employees' prosocial behavior, well-being, performance, and career success.[101] Figure 12.10 shows that prosocial motivation has a strong impact on employees' relational behaviors, a moderate influence on well-being and performance outcomes, and a weak effect on career success. These results reveal that prosocial motivation pays dividends for the employee and the recipients of their effort (beneficiaries).

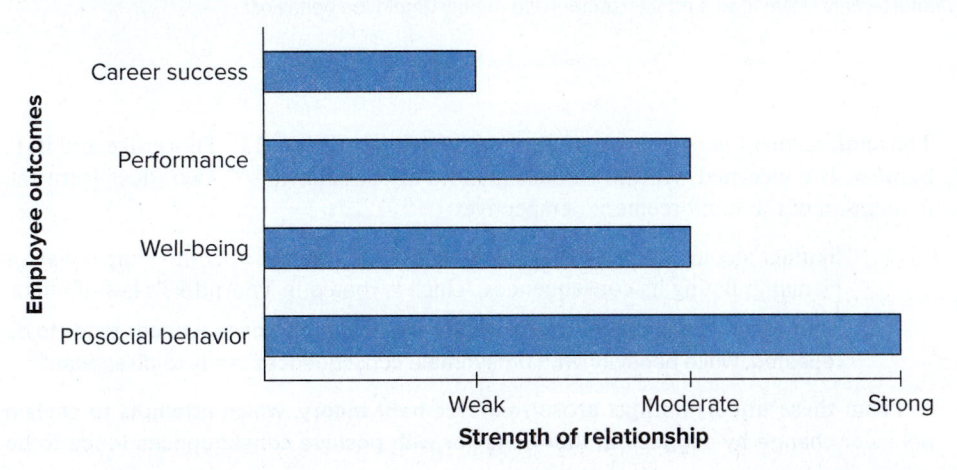

FIGURE 12.10

Prosocial motivation's impact on employee outcomes

Source: From Liao, H., R. Su, T. Ptashnik, and J. Nielsen. "Feeling Good, Doing Good, and Getting Ahead: A Meta-Analytic Investigation of the Outcomes of Prosocial Motivation at Work." Psychological Bulletin 148 (2022): 158–198.

Why Is Prosocial Motivation Beneficial? Research points to five ways prosocial motivation delivers positive outcomes for employees:[102]

1. **Social capital.** Prosocial motivation signals concern for others' well-being. Coworkers thus tend to trust and respect prosocially motivated employees and see them as having more leadership potential.
2. **Working harder.** People work harder when their work benefits others for two reasons: for fear of letting others down and for the anticipation others will be grateful for their efforts.
3. **Working smarter.** Prosocially motivated employees gather and analyze information from multiple perspectives resulting in more creative ideas.
4. **Working together.** Prosocial motivation prompts employees to share information with others and learn from them in the process.
5. **Working safer.** Prosocially motivated employees engage in less risky behaviors. Authors Grant and Shandell observe "when focusing on how our actions affect others who are vulnerable, we are more realistic about risk."[103]

How Can Managers Increase Employees' Prosocial Motivation? You might think that prosocial motivation is fueled by managerial speeches that focus on discussing the good things done by an organization. Interestingly, research suggests that this is not the best approach.[104] Introducing employees to customers or other stakeholders that they are benefiting is a much more effective way to enhance prosocial motivation. Consider how one university used this suggestion.

Prosocial Motivation Example—University Fundraising: Researchers arranged for university fundraising callers to meet one undergraduate student whose scholarship was funded by the callers' fundraising efforts. After a 10-minute meeting, the callers spent nearly 2.5 times more time on the phone and raised 2.75 times more money than callers who did not meet the beneficiaries of their work.[105] These results show employees who connect their work to a person and their story find deeper purpose and meaning in their job. As a result, they work longer and harder to improve their performance. •

12.5 Reinforcement Perspectives on Motivation

THE BIG PICTURE
Reinforcement theory suggests behavior will be repeated if it has positive consequences and won't be if it has negative consequences. This section also describes how to use four techniques—positive reinforcement, negative reinforcement, extinction, and punishment—to modify employee behavior.

LO 12-5

Discuss how to use four types of behavior modification.

The reinforcement perspective, which was pioneered by Edward L. Thorndike and B. F. Skinner, is concerned with how consequences affect behavior.[106] Two ideas form the foundation of the reinforcement perspective:

1. Skinner's concept of *operant conditioning*—the process of controlling behavior by manipulating its consequences, which is rooted in Thorndike's law of effect.
2. Thorndike's **law of effect** says behavior with favorable consequences tends to be repeated, while behavior with unfavorable consequences tends to disappear.[107]

From these underpinnings arose **reinforcement theory**, which attempts to explain behavior change by suggesting that behavior with positive consequences tends to be repeated, whereas behavior with negative consequences tends not to be repeated. The use of reinforcement theory to change human behavior is called *behavior modification.*

The Four Types of Behavior Modification: Positive Reinforcement, Negative Reinforcement, Extinction, and Punishment

Reinforcement is anything that strengthens the likelihood that a given behavior will be repeated in the future.

There are four types of behavior modification: (1) *positive reinforcement,* (2) *negative reinforcement,* (3) *extinction,* and (4) *punishment* (see Figure 12.11).

Positive Reinforcement: Strengthens Behavior
Positive reinforcement is the introduction of positive consequences to strengthen the likelihood that a particular behavior will occur again in the future.

Positive Reinforcement Example—Sales Incentive: A supervisor who has asked a salesperson to sell more insurance policies might reward successful performance by saying, "It's great that you exceeded your sales quota, and you'll get a bonus for it. Maybe next time you'll sell even more and will become a member of the Circle of

FIGURE 12.11
Four types of behavior modification
These are different ways of changing employee behavior.

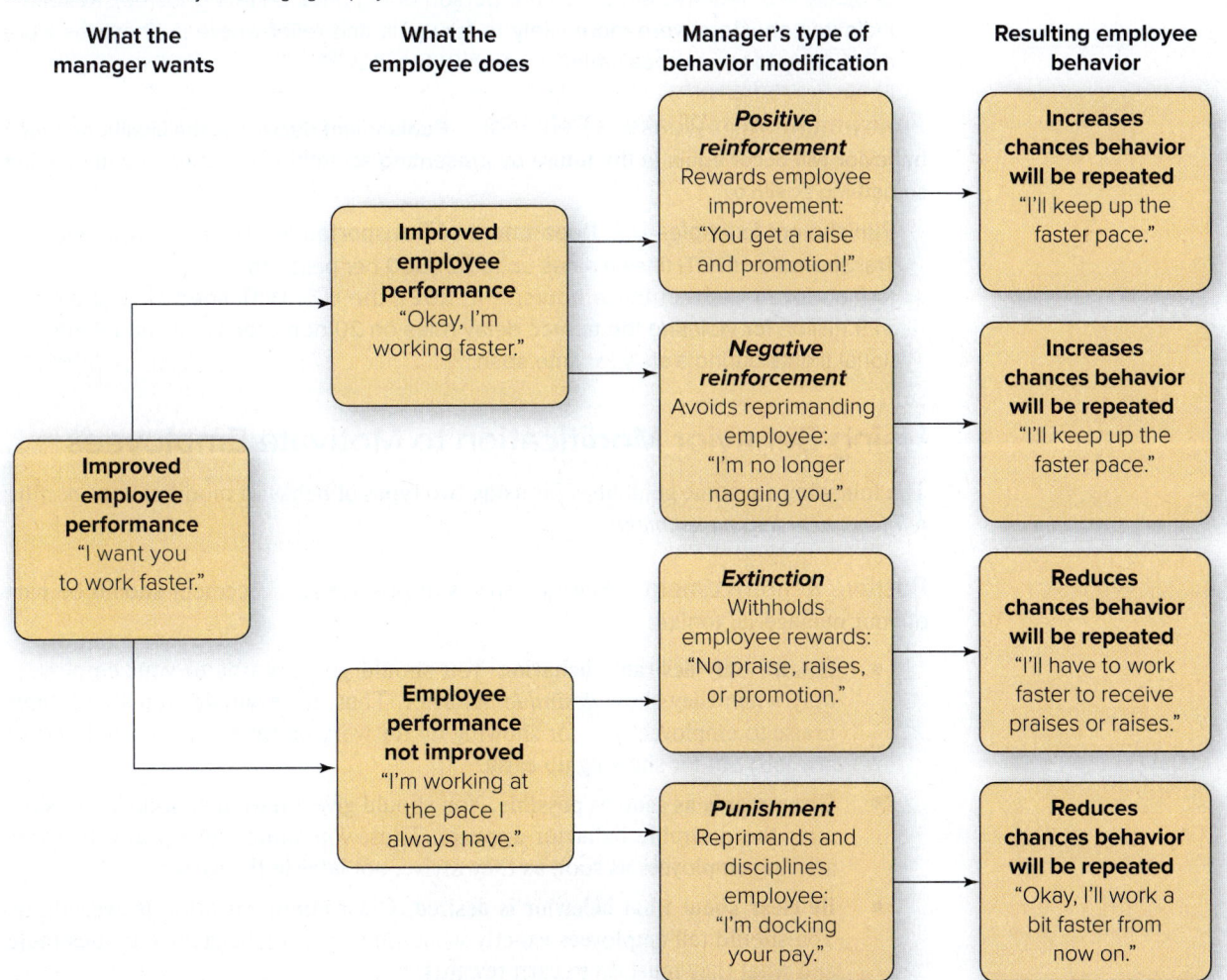

What the manager wants	What the employee does	Manager's type of behavior modification	Resulting employee behavior
Improved employee performance "I want you to work faster."	Improved employee performance "Okay, I'm working faster."	*Positive reinforcement* Rewards employee improvement: "You get a raise and promotion!"	Increases chances behavior will be repeated "I'll keep up the faster pace."
		Negative reinforcement Avoids reprimanding employee: "I'm no longer nagging you."	Increases chances behavior will be repeated "I'll keep up the faster pace."
	Employee performance not improved "I'm working at the pace I always have."	*Extinction* Withholds employee rewards: "No praise, raises, or promotion."	Reduces chances behavior will be repeated "I'll have to work faster to receive praises or raises."
		Punishment Reprimands and disciplines employee: "I'm docking your pay."	Reduces chances behavior will be repeated "Okay, I'll work a bit faster from now on."

100 Top Sellers and win a trip to Paris as well." Note the rewards—praise, more money, recognition, and awards—must be valued by the employee for this to work according to expectancy theory.

Negative Reinforcement: Also Strengthens Behavior
Negative reinforcement is removal of a negative stimulus to strengthen the likelihood that a particular behavior will occur again in the future.

Negative Reinforcement Example—Micromanagement: A supervisor who has been pestering a salesperson might say, "Now that you've exceeded your quota, I'll stop micromanaging you." Note that the removal of the supervisor's negative behavior is meant to increase the likelihood that the salesperson will continue to meet their quota.

Extinction: Weakens Behavior
Extinction decreases the likelihood that a particular behavior will occur again in the future by ignoring it or making sure it is not reinforced.

Extinction Example—Friends Talking in Class: A couple friends are trying to get your attention to talk with them in class while your teacher is communicating important information for the next exam. You decide not to reinforce your friends' need for attention and ignore their attempts to draw you into a conversation. Eventually they stop.

Extinction Example—Ghosting: Ghosting is suddenly cutting off all forms of communication in a relationship without explanation. It is motivated by a person's desire to end the relationship out of convenience, loss of interest, or to protect themselves from being hurt. Ghosting can have mixed effects for the person ghosting (the ghoster) and negative effects on the person being ghosted (the ghostee). Research indicates ghosters were more likely to feel guilt and relief whereas ghostees were more likely to experience sadness and hurt feelings.[108]

Punishment: Also Weakens Behavior
Punishment decreases the likelihood that a behavior will occur again in the future by presenting something negative or withdrawing something positive.

Punishment Example—U.S. Department of Transportation: The U.S. Department of Transportation (DOT) fines airlines up to $27,500 per passenger for planes left on the tarmac for more than three hours.[109] In 2021, the U.S. DOT fined United airlines $1.9 million for violating the tarmac delay rules on 20 domestic flights and 5 international flights during a six-year time span.[110]

Using Behavior Modification to Motivate Employees

The following are some guidelines for using two types of behavior modification—*positive reinforcement* and *punishment*.

Positive Reinforcement   Several aspects of positive reinforcement should be part of your managerial toolkit:

- **Reward only desirable behavior.** You should give rewards to your employees only when they show *desirable* behavior. Thus, for example, you should give praise to employees not for showing up for work on time (an expected part of any job) but for showing up early.
- **Give rewards as soon as possible.** You should give a reward as soon as possible after the desirable behavior appears. Thus, you should give praise to early-arriving employees as soon as they arrive, not later in the week.
- **Be clear about what behavior is desired.** Clear communication is everything. You should tell employees exactly what kinds of work behaviors are desirable and what they must do to earn rewards.

- **Have different rewards to recognize individual differences.** Recognizing that different people value different kinds of rewards, you should give employees a choice in selecting rewards that meet their needs.

   Rewards Example—Workhuman: Companies use employee recognition programs like Workhuman to reward employee behavior at work. Managers and peers award employees points for desirable behavior. Employees accumulate these points and can redeem them for rewards such as gift cards, products, or even an all-expenses paid vacation.[111]

Punishment Unquestionably there will be times when you'll need to threaten or administer an unpleasant consequence to stop an employee's undesirable behavior. Sometimes it's best to address a problem by combining punishment with positive reinforcement. Some suggestions for using punishment are as follows.

- **Punish only undesirable behavior.** You should give punishment only when employees show frequent *undesirable* behavior. For example, you should reprimand employees who consistently show up, say, a half hour late for work but not 5 or 10 minutes late.
- **Give reprimands or disciplinary actions as soon as possible.** You should mete out punishment as soon as possible after the undesirable behavior occurs. Thus, you should give a reprimand to late-arriving employees as soon as they arrive.
- **Be clear about what behavior is undesirable.** Tell employees exactly what kinds of work behaviors are undesirable and make sure the severity of the punishment fits the crime. A manager should not, for example, dock hourly employees' pay if they are only 5 or 10 minutes late for work. Asking them to stay 10 minutes late might be more appropriate.
- **Administer punishment in private.** You would hate to have your boss chew you out in front of your employees, and the people who report to you also shouldn't be reprimanded publicly. Public reprimands are embarrassing and fuel resentment.
- **Combine punishment and positive reinforcement.** If you're reprimanding employees, be sure to redirect their attention to desirable behavior and remind them what rewards they might be eligible for. For example, while reprimanding someone for being late, say that a perfect attendance record over the next few months will put that employee in line for a raise or promotion. •

12.6 Using Compensation, Nonmonetary Incentives, and Other Rewards to Motivate: In Search of the Positive Work Environment

THE BIG PICTURE
Compensation, the main motivator of performance, includes pay for performance, bonuses, profit sharing, gainsharing, stock options, and pay for knowledge. Nonmonetary incentives address needs that aren't being met, such as work-life balance, growth in skills, positive work environment, and meaning in work.

In this section we consider the tools today's managers use to motivate superior employee performance. We begin by discussing the various monetary rewards that have dominated employee compensation models throughout recent history.

We then turn our attention to nonmonetary incentives because employees often choose jobs for reasons other than financial compensation. Numerous research studies

LO 12-6

Discuss the role of compensation in motivating employees.

Compensation isn't just money in your pocket. It includes monetary and nonmonetary incentives. Both kinds of incentives are important to motivate employees at work.
stoatphoto/Shutterstock

support the notion that workers can be equally, and sometimes even more, motivated by:[112]

1. Work-life balance.
2. Personal growth.
3. A positive work environment.
4. Meaningful work.

Is Money the Best Motivator?

Whatever happened to good old money as a motivator?

Money still motivates, but it's not the only thing or even the most important thing. A meta-analysis of 61 studies and over 18,000 respondents reveals pay is only minimally related with job satisfaction. The study's authors note "in 2009 dollars, a sample of lawyers earning an average of $148,000 per year was less job satisfied than a sample of child care workers earning $23,500 per year."[113] Many workers rate having positive relationships at work, flexibility, and career growth opportunities as more important than monetary compensation.[114] Clearly, motivating involves more than money.

Motivation and Compensation

Most people are paid an hourly wage or a weekly or monthly salary. Both of these are easy for organizations to administer, of course. But a wage or a salary alone gives an employee little incentive to work hard. Incentive compensation plans try to better motivate employees, although no single plan works equally well for all employees.

Characteristics of the Best Incentive Compensation Plans Consistent with most of the theories of motivation we described earlier, certain criteria are advisable for incentive plans to work, such as:

1. Rewards must be linked to performance and be measurable.
2. Rewards must satisfy individual needs.
3. Rewards must be agreed on by manager and employees.
4. Rewards must be believable and achievable by employees.

Popular Incentive Compensation Plans In what way would you like to be rewarded for your efforts? Some of the most well-known incentive compensation plans are *pay for performance, bonuses, profit sharing, gainsharing, stock options,* and *pay for knowledge.*

Pay for Performance Also known as *merit pay,* pay for performance bases pay on one's results. Thus, different salaried employees might get different pay raises and other rewards (such as promotions) depending on their overall job performance. Examples of pay-for-performance plans include:

- **Piece rate.** One standard pay-for-performance plan is payment according to a piece rate, in which employees are paid according to how much output they produce, as is often used with farm workers picking fruits or vegetables. Piece-rate employers must comply with state and federal minimum wage laws.[115]
- **Sales commission.** With a sales commission plan, sales representatives are paid a percentage of the earnings the company made from their sales, so that the more they sell, the more they are paid. The financial services company Edward Jones pays its employees a salary plus commissions on sales for the first four years and then commissions only, on a scale that increases from 9% to 40% over time.[116]

Bonuses Bonuses are cash awards given to employees who achieve specific performance objectives. Signing bonuses are also a popular way to attract new employees, particularly in tight labor markets.

Hiring Bonuses Examples: Many organizations offer hiring bonuses to address staffing shortages. Walgreens announced up to a $75,000 signing bonus to incentivize pharmacists to work for the company. School districts around the United States recently issued hiring bonuses ranging from $2,500 to $10,000 for educators to fill teaching vacancies.[117]

Profit Sharing Profit sharing is the distribution to employees of a percentage of the company's profits.

Profit Sharing Example—Publix: Publix supermarket chain was founded in 1930. Founder George Jenkins wanted to build the company around employee ownership and profit sharing, but the Great Depression left workers with little to nothing to invest. Jenkins decided to give each employee a $2 per-week raise, then held the money back for stock shares. Publix continues its tradition of profit sharing to this day and is now the largest employee-owned business in the world.[118]

Gainsharing Gainsharing is the distribution of savings or "gains" to groups of employees who reduced costs and increased measurable productivity. Gainsharing has been applied in a variety of industries, from manufacturing to nonprofit. It incentivizes employees to proactively improve the company's operations (such as productivity, quality, safety, customer satisfaction, or costs).[119]

Gainsharing Example—Healthcare Providers: Researchers are designing gainsharing models to incentivize hospitals and follow-up care providers (like physical therapists) to work together to reduce the billed healthcare charges and increase the quality of care. Health insurance companies would give an incentive payment to both the hospital and follow-up care provider if their combined charges are below and service levels exceed target levels.[120]

Stock Options With stock options, certain employees are given the right to buy the company's stock at a future date at a discounted price. The motivator here is that employees holding stock options will work hard to make the company's stock rise so that they can profit by obtaining it at the cheaper price. Technology start-ups are well known for using stock options to conserve cash to invest in marketing as well as research and development. Stock options also incentivize employees to work harder to grow the company in hopes they will strike it rich if the stock options multiply in value once the company goes public or is purchased by a competitor.[121] U.S. companies that currently offer their employees stock options include The Cheesecake Factory, Intuit, Salesforce, Apple, Uber, and Snowflake.[122]

Stock Options Example—Snowflake: Cloud computing company Snowflake offered a generous amount of stock options to recruit and retain talented employees. Stock options are especially attractive when companies valuations are soaring, such as when Snowflake's stock price more than doubled from $120 to $254 per share on the date it went public. Stock options are also risky. Snowflake's valuation, like many other technology growth companies, plummeted 65% from its peak during the post-COVID-19 economic downturn. The poor market conditions make stock options much less appealing. As a result, technology companies are turning to cash bonuses to retain their talent.[123]

Pay for Knowledge   Also known as *skill-based pay,* pay for knowledge ties employee pay to the number of job-relevant skills or academic degrees they earn.[124]

Pay for Knowledge Example—Teaching: The teaching profession is a time-honored instance of this incentive, in which elementary and secondary teachers are encouraged to increase their salaries by earning additional college credit. Outside of education, firms such as FedEx also have pay-for-knowledge plans that reward for completing certification programs or advanced degrees.

Nonmonetary Ways of Motivating Employees

Employees who can demonstrate the career readiness competencies of self-motivation, critical thinking/problem solving, and ownership/accepting responsibilities are apt to be the very ones who will leave if they find their own needs aren't being met. Four nonmonetary motivators employees crave are (1) work-life balance, (2) personal growth, (3) a positive work environment, and (4) meaningful work. As you read on, consider which nonmonetary motivators would be most valuable to you right now. What kind of needs do they meet: basic, psychological, or self-fulfillment needs?

The Need for Work-Life Balance   Employee exhaustion is on the rise as people try to manage their increasing work demands, according to a 2022 Future Forum Pulse survey of 10,766 workers across the United States, Japan, and Europe. Executives reported a 20% reduction in work-life balance and 40% increase in work-related stress and anxiety. Front-line workers in the United States felt burned out with 49% of younger workers (age 18 to 29) experiencing burnout compared with 38% of their older colleagues (age 30+).[125] These statistics underscore the importance of managers taking action to help their employees find work-life balance. Microsoft is a great example.

Work-Life Balance Example—Microsoft: Executives at Microsoft reported their employees' work-life balance dropped by 13% due to digital exhaustion. The three main drivers were over-collaborating (too many meetings and e-mails), too many interruptions, and not taking enough vacation time. Dawn Klinghoffer, head of people analytics at Microsoft, reported "employees satisfied with their work-life balance tend to send 29% fewer emails in general and 36% fewer emails after working hours... [They also] had 1.3 times the number of focus hours and 1.3 times the number of two-hour focus blocks compared to employees less satisfied with their work-life balance." Microsoft took the following steps to improve employees' work-life balance:[126]

1. **Define work priorities.** Everything can't always get done. Establish what's most important.
2. **Reevaluate meetings.** Avoid meetings early Monday or late Friday to give employees an on-ramp and off-ramp for the work week.

3. **Emphasize chunks of focus time during the week to get things done.** Protect them by blocking off time in your calendar so others know you aren't available.
4. **Encourage time away for vacation, mental health, and well-being.** Cover employees' work while they're away so they aren't punished with a mountain of work when they return.
5. **Respect "quiet hours."** Use technology to delay sending after-hours e-mails until the beginning of the next workday. Sending late night e-mails can create stress for others and communicate an expectation that they should always be "on."

Employers offer a number of nonmonetary options designed to cater to employees' desire for work-life balance, which include *work-life benefits, flexible work arrangements,* and *vacation/sabbatical time.*

Work-Life Benefits Work-life benefits consist of initiatives and programs that employers implement in an effort to help employees balance the often competing needs of their work and home lives.[127] The purpose of such benefits is to meet employees' basic needs by removing barriers that make it hard for people to strike a balance between their work and personal lives, such as allowing parents time off to take care of sick children.

Work-life benefits include:

- Helping employees with day care costs or even establishing onsite centers.
- Access to mental health services.
- Offering domestic-partner benefits.
- Giving job-protected leave for new parents.
- Free or reduced gym memberships.
- Providing technology, such as mobile phones and laptops, to enable parents to work at home.

How do U.S. employers compare globally at making work-life benefits available? The United States actually ranks fairly low on this feature—29th out of 41 on a list of countries with the best work-life balance.[128]

Flexible Work Arrangements *Flexible work arrangements* give employees alternatives regarding when and where work is done. Flexible work arrangements include flex time, part-time work, a compressed workweek, job sharing, and telecommuting (or working remotely). The top companies in the world offering flexible work arrangements in 2023 included Prolific, TELUS International, Virgin Media O$_2$, and Mars UK.[129]

Telecommuting, or working remotely from home, has positively contributed to employees' work-life balance and overall well-being since the COVID-19 pandemic.
Pekic/E+/Getty Images

Research suggests flexible work arrangements benefit employees' well-being. A meta-analysis of 33 studies and 90,602 individuals revealed flexible work arrangements improved employees' physical health and reduced absenteeism.[130]

Vacations and Sabbaticals Some companies now offer unlimited paid vacation days to their employees, including Zoom, Netflix, and LinkedIn. Do employees take advantage of having unlimited paid vacations? No, according to HR software company Namely's review of 1,000 businesses. They found employees take about the same number of days off per year (12.1 days on average) as employees who work at companies offering limited paid vacation days (11.4 days on average).[131]

Sabbaticals—extended periods of paid time off that employees earn over several years—are another work-life benefit gaining in popularity. A few of the companies offering sabbaticals to U.S. employees are The Container Store, The Cheesecake Factory, Patagonia, and Purina.[132]

The Need for Personal Growth

According to a recent survey, 76% of employees would stay with a company longer if they had opportunities for continuous learning and development.[133] You may recall from Chapter 9 that L&D is so valuable to employees because it is an important step in career advancement.

Learning opportunities can take three forms:

- **Learning from co-workers.** Managers can match workers with co-workers from whom they can learn, allowing them, for instance, to "shadow" (watch and imitate) workers in other jobs or participate in interdepartmental task forces.
- **Tuition reimbursement.** Being reimbursed for partial or full tuition for part-time study at a college or university.
- **In-house training.** According to *Training* magazine, U.S. companies spent $101.6 billion on employee learning and development in 2022.[134] Due to technology advances during the COVID-19 pandemic, instructor-led classrooms have been replaced by online and blended training methods as the dominant mode of training. Here's the breakdown of the methods organizations used to deliver employee training hours:
  - Online or other computer-based programs including virtual classrooms and webcasts (35%).
  - Blended learning techniques (32%).
  - Instructor-led classrooms (24%).
  - Mobile devices (4%).

The Need for a Positive Work Environment

Wanting to work in a positive environment begins with the idea of well-being. **Well-being** is the combined impact of five elements—positive emotions, engagement, relationships, meaning, and achievement (PERMA), according to renowned psychologist Martin Seligman.[135] There is one essential thing to remember about these elements: We must pursue them for their own sake, not as a means to obtain another outcome. In other words, well-being comes about by freely pursuing the five elements in PERMA.

Flourishing represents the extent to which our lives contain PERMA. When we flourish, our lives result in "goodness . . . growth, and resilience."[136]

- Flourishing is associated with positive outcomes like better job performance, increased organizational citizenship, lower turnover intentions, positive mental health, and innovative work behavior.[137]
- Unfortunately, many people are not flourishing. For example, according to Gallup's 2022 State of the Global Workplace, workplace stress is at an all-time high, even higher than during the COVID-19 pandemic. Working women in the United States and Canada reported being among the most stressed in the world.[138]

Positive emotions, one of the elements in PERMA, *broaden* your perspective about how to overcome challenges in your life—joy, for instance, is more likely to lead you to envision creative ideas during a brainstorming session. Positive emotions also *build* on themselves, resulting in a spreading of positive emotions within yourself and those around you.[139]

What can employers do to create a positive work environment?

- Encourage managers and co-workers to express gratitude (the Practical Action box explains how this can be done).
- Create a positive physical setting.
- Be a thoughtful boss.

Let us consider each of these suggestions.

PRACTICAL ACTION | How Managers Can Cultivate a Culture of Gratitude

Psychology professor and author Robert Emmons says that gratitude is a "basic human requirement."[140] Research shows people benefit from both experiencing gratitude toward others and receiving gratitude from others.[141] Cultivating a culture of gratitude in the workplace is especially vital because we spend the majority of our waking hours at our jobs, and studies suggest that gratitude increases employees' job satisfaction, work productivity, and physical/mental health.[142] Here are some suggestions for encouraging gratitude with your friends and colleagues.

Be Specific
One of the best ways to show others sincere appreciation is to give them praise that is specific and tied to how they have helped you or the organization achieve its goals. Show your gratitude by visiting them in person, making a phone call, or writing a letter.[143]

Thank you. Two little words make a big impact. People want to feel appreciated for a job well done. Remember that gratitude goes a long way for employees. Atstock Productions/Shutterstock

Gratitude Example—Lucid Software: Leaders at Lucid created a corporate gratitude flowchart to show gratitude to its employees. The diagram contains a personalized message of gratitude for each employee written by their manager. Each note expresses specifically what the employee does to contribute to the company, and every employee receives a copy of the full flowchart at the end of the year.[144]

Go Public
Expressions of gratitude are particularly special when you receive them publicly from your leader, co-workers, customers, or patients.[145] Public accolades satisfy our social and esteem needs and serve as examples to others of the kinds of work behaviors the organization values. Furthermore, studies suggest that just witnessing expressions of gratitude, even if you are not the one being praised, is enough to generate positive emotions and warm feelings.[146] Clearly, public recognition can be a useful tool.

Encourage Peer-to-Peer Gratitude
Some evidence suggests it may be more important for workers to be thanked by their peers than by their managers. Such praise may hold more weight because peers are highly familiar with what it takes to do the job well.[147]

Make It Easy for Others to Practice Gratitude

Gratitude needs to be easy to practice if you want to inject it into your organization's culture. Managers should lead by example by starting the day or starting meetings by expressing gratitude. Then, consider creative ideas ranging from embarking on a departmentwide 30-day gratitude challenge to expressing gratitude to co-workers through small daily actions to making daily entries in your own gratitude journal.[148]

Gratitude Example—Disney: Disney introduced the Mobile Cast Compliment feature on the My Disney Experience mobile app for Walt Disney World guests to compliment cast members for making their day special. In just six months since launching the feature, guests delivered 100,000 cast compliments.[149]

YOUR CALL

Can you recall a time when someone expressed sincere gratitude for your contributions to a project? How did this make you feel? What creative suggestions can you come up with to encourage more gratitude in your organization?

- **Positive physical settings.** Cubicles are stifling the creativity and morale of many workers and fueling their resistance to return to the office after a period of working from home. McKinsey notes "people are going to return to the workplace only if the space is safe, comfortable, easy to navigate, invites collaboration, and offers a 'wow' factor."[150] Companies like AT&T and Adobe are investing billions of dollars to redesign their workplace to meet employees' desire for quiet and private work spaces to focus coupled with separate flexible meeting spaces that encourage collaboration and innovation.[151]

- **Thoughtful bosses.** Managers significantly impact the work environment, which influences employees' engagement at work. Leadership development consultants Zenger Folkman analyzed data from 13,048 direct reports who rated 2,801 managers and found that managers had a substantial impact on employees' *quiet quitting*, or willingness to give only the minimum effort to keep their job. Managers who created an unsupportive work environment had nearly three times more employees who were quiet quitters than managers who created supportive and inspiring work environments. On the flip side, consider that 62% of employees were willing to go the extra mile for managers who created supportive work environments whereas only 20% did the same for managers responsible for creating an unsupportive work environment.[152]

Kindergarten teachers find their jobs especially meaningful as they build relationships with the children they teach and lay the foundation for a lifetime love of learning. Weedezign/iStock/Getty Images

The Need for Meaningful Work Consistent with the job characteristics model (see Figure 12.9), workers want to be employed with an organization that allows them to feel their work matters. The U.S. Office of Disease Prevention and Health Promotion suggest meaningful work "contributes to happiness and has a positive impact on families and communities."[153] Data company PayScale compared 454 jobs and found clergy, surgeons, chiropractors, counselors, and kindergarten teachers were among those who felt their jobs were the most meaningful.[154]

World War II concentration camp survivor Viktor Frankl, author of *Man's Search for Meaning*, strongly believed that "striving to find a meaning in one's life is the primary motivational force" for people.[155] In other words, it is the drive to find meaning in our lives that instills in us a sense of purpose and motivation to pursue goals. A timeless story is told of the cleaner at NASA who, when President Kennedy asked him what his job was, replied, "I'm helping to put a man on the moon."[156]

Meaningfulness, then, is characterized by a sense of being part of something you believe is bigger than yourself.[157] What follows are three suggestions for building meaning into your life.

1. **Identify activities you love doing.** Try to do more of these activities or find ways to build them into your work role, something Mike Krzyzewski (Coach K) has done.

   Passion Example—Coach K: Forty-two year head coach of Duke University's men's college basketball team and all-time winningest coach in NCAA Division I history, Coach K loved his family, basketball, and his players. His love for all three fueled unprecedented success at the collegiate level, six gold medals, and a 75–1 win–loss record as head coach of the U.S.A. Basketball Men's National Team.[158]

2. **Find a way to build your natural strengths into your personal and work-life.** Want to be more engaged with your school, work, and leisure activities? Take the time to list your highest strengths, your weaknesses, which strengths you use on a daily basis—and find what you can do to incorporate your strengths into your school, work, and leisure activities. Gallup research suggests employees who use their strengths every day on the job are six times more likely to be highly engaged at work.[159]

3. **Go out and help someone.** Research shows that people derive a sense of meaningfulness from helping others, which creates an upward spiral of positivity.[160]

   Meaningfulness Example—Bellhops Moving Company: University of Alabama student Walter Carr experienced an unusual first day on the job. Carr's vehicle broke down the night before his first day at work. After failing to find a ride, Carr chose to walk 20 miles to the company's office overnight. With the help of local police, he arrived on time at 8 a.m. Luke Marklin, CEO at Bellhops, drove from Tennessee to Alabama after hearing Carr's story and gifted him his personal car, a Ford Escape. Marklin felt like it was the right thing to do.[161]

12.7 Career Corner: Managing Your Career Readiness

This chapter has important implications for a number of career readiness competencies within the career readiness model shown below (see Figure 12.12). Let's zoom in on the career readiness attitude of self-motivation. The competency of self-motivation is defined as the ability to work productively without constant direction, instruction, and praise. It also includes the ability to establish and maintain good work habits and consistent focus on organizational goals and personal development.

Self-motivation is an attractive quality leaders look for in prospective employees. For instance, the leaders in the Executive Interview Series video underscore the importance of taking initiative as it relates to setting goals, holding yourself accountable, and having the drive to identify a problem and do something about it. Practicing self-management is a great way to take a structured approach to develop your self-motivation.

Self-management entails more than just controlling your emotions. It involves managing your habits and routines. Effective self-management requires making "a conscious choice to resist a preference or habit and instead demonstrate a more productive behavior."[162] The essence of self-management is understanding who you are, what you want in life, what you want to accomplish during your life-long journey, and then making it all

LO 12-7

Describe how to develop the career readiness competency of self-motivation.

Visit your instructor's Connect course and access your eBook to view this video.

Executive Interview Series: Self-Motivation and Ownership/ Accepting Responsibility

FIGURE 12.12

Model of career readiness

©2018 Kinicki & Associates, Inc.

Knowledge
- Task-based/functional
- Computational thinking
- Understanding the business
- New media literacy

Other characteristics
- **Resilience**
- Personal adaptability
- **Self-awareness**
- **Service/others orientation**
- Openness to change
- **Generalized self-efficacy**

Core
- **Critical thinking/problem solving**
- Oral/written communication
- **Teamwork/collaboration**
- Information technology application
- **Leadership**
- **Professionalism/work ethic**
- **Diversity, equity, and inclusion**
- **Career management**

Soft skills
- Decision making
- **Social intelligence**
- Networking
- **Emotional intelligence**

Attitudes
- **Ownership/accepting responsibilities**
- **Self-motivation** ☆
- Proactive learning orientation
- Showing commitment
- **Positive approach**

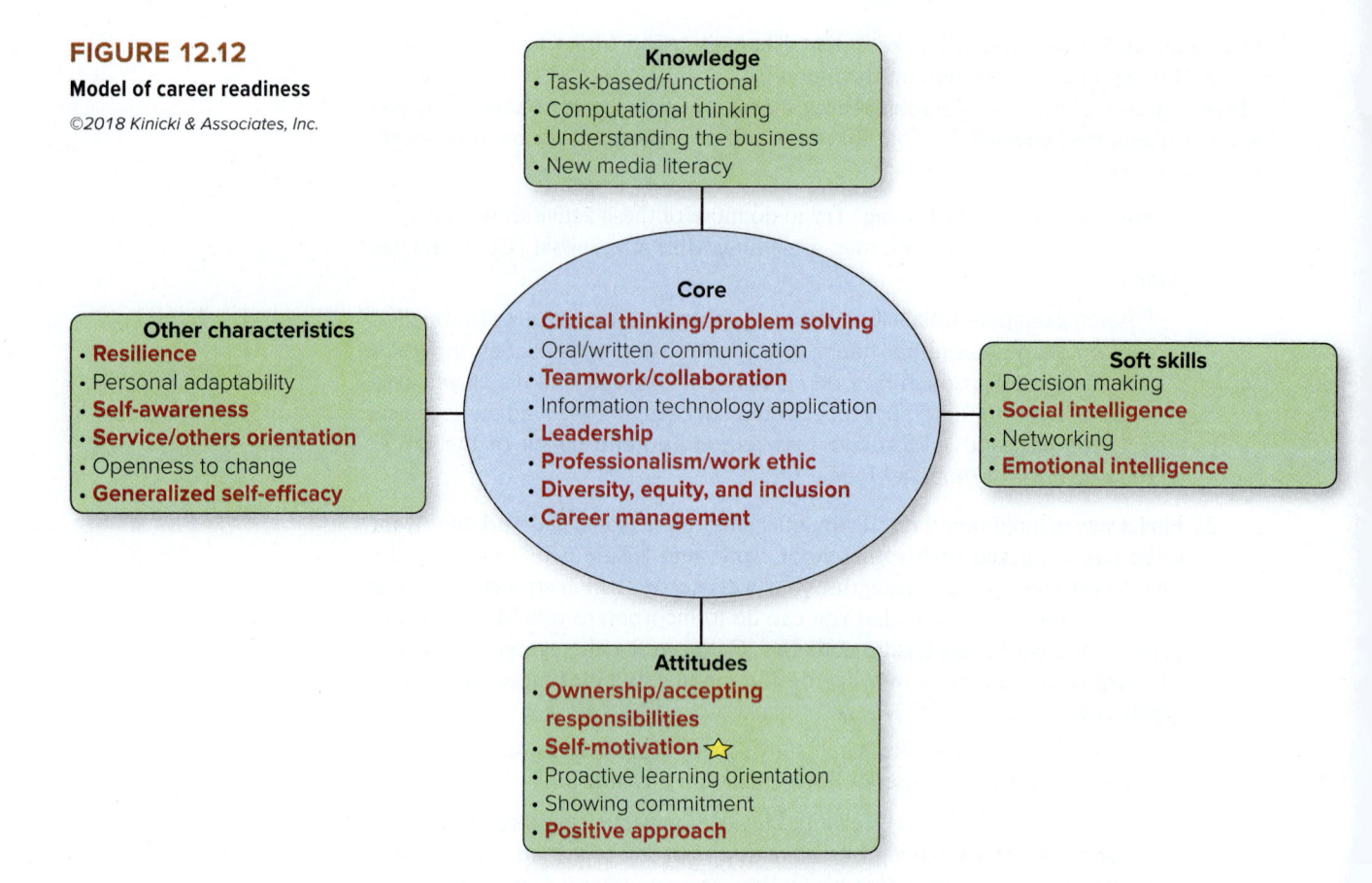

happen. This pursuit of your dreams or goals is what drives the self-motivation employers are looking for.

In this section, we offer a six-step process to help you apply the principles of self-management on a daily basis. Then we offer tips on recharging to underscore the importance of balancing this intense self-effort with downtime and relaxation.

The Self-Management Process

1. Identify Your "Wildly Important" Long-Term Goal   Your goal can be as long term as a personal vision statement or as short term as getting a job after graduation that fits your needs and values and pays a decent salary.

- The wildly important goal is your "north star" or guiding purpose.
- Writing it down is a reminder of how you should spend your time in both the short and long term.
- State your wildly important goal in terms of the SMART framework we discussed in Chapter 5.

2. Break Your Wildly Important Goal into Short-Term Goals   Research tells us you are more likely to achieve your wildly important goal if you break it down into smaller bite-size goals. For example, if your most important long-term goal is to get a good job after graduation, this step entails identifying the major milestones you must accomplish to make that happen. They might include outcomes like:

- Maintain a GPA of 3.0.
- Increase my career readiness.

- Obtain an internship.
- Become a student leader in one organization.
- Gain work experience in my functional field of study.
- Network with professionals in my field of study.

3. Create a "To-Do" List for Accomplishing Your Short-Term Goals A "to-do" list identifies the daily activities needed to achieve your short-term goals. It is your detailed plan for achieving them. You may want to use task management software to help create and organize your tasks. For example, one of your authors has a "higher-level" task list that spans outcomes he wants to achieve for the next year. He then creates more immediate task lists every month that guide his behavior.

4. Prioritize the Tasks A "to-do" list can get overwhelming if you don't organize it. Organize by prioritizing the tasks in the order in which you need to complete them.

- Prioritizing in this way enables you to schedule your time to maximize your efficiency and smooth your achievement of interdependent tasks.
- There is one common error to avoid during this step. Research shows that people tend to work on "easy to complete" tasks rather than harder ones as a task list grows. This strategy actually makes you less productive because easier tasks are generally not as important as more difficult or time-consuming tasks.[163]
- One useful suggestion is to rank the tasks from (1) low importance to (5) high importance.

5. Create a Time Schedule It's time to establish start and stop dates for each task once you have made your task list. Dates enable you to organize your schedule and monitor your progress. Here again you may find it useful to employ task management software.

6. Work the Plan, Reward Yourself, and Adjust as Needed The best-laid plans generally have unforeseen inhibitors like illness, a car breakdown, or a crashed computer. Be flexible while working on your task plan. Finally, make the process fun by rewarding yourself for achieving various milestones. The reward should be something you value. One of your authors uses golf as his reward for completing his designated tasks.

Recharging

Self-motivation requires the ability to maintain consistent focus and self-direction toward accomplishing important goals. But it also requires that you practice self-care and allow yourself time to recharge and re-energize each day. Unfortunately, American workers tend to focus most of their energy on exertion and very little on recovery. A recent Gallup poll revealed that 76% of workers experience burnout either "sometimes," "often," or "always."[164] We think it's essential that you include recharging as part of your self-motivation strategy. Here are a few tips.[165]

1. Figure Out What Recharging Means to You When your smartphone or watch battery gets low, you have to put it on the charger and wait. There is no other solution—your devices have one and only one way to get their power back. But people are not devices, and the way we recharge is unique to us as individuals.

The trick is to figure out what recharging looks like for you. For example, for your author who happens to be an extravert, recharging means being social and interacting with people, whether by throwing a party for 30 friends, playing in a golf tournament, or taking a group Pilates class. For another author who is decidedly introverted, recharging means being as far from most people as possible. She prefers having time at home in order to feel refreshed, and this might include a Netflix binge, an evening of food and drinks with immediate family or one or two close friends, or spending a weekend giving a closet the full KonMari treatment. Another author who is a self-described extraverted introvert recharges by attending sporting events, engaging in physical activity like running and playing tennis, and making memories with the immediate family.

Don't feel guilty about doing what you need in order to recharge. Your iPhone doesn't apologize for needing to be plugged into the charger—and neither should you.

2. Include Mental and Physical Relaxation Remember that recharging includes both mental and physical elements. Your body may be suffering the physical effects of stress even if you don't immediately feel it. One way to relax both your mind and body is through mindfulness meditation.

3. Accept Kindness Often, we feel the need to prove to others that we can take care of everything on our own. Unfortunately, this can result in turning down offers of help and kindness. Maybe you have a friend who has offered to pet-sit for the weekend so that you can go on a camping trip. Or perhaps you know someone in massage therapy school who is looking for opportunities to practice their technique. Whatever they may be, remember to accept offers of kindness that will bring you joy and relaxation. Give yourself permission to be taken care of.

Key Terms Used in This Chapter

- acquired needs theory 428
- bonuses 453
- content perspectives 426
- distributive justice 436
- equity theory 434
- expectancy 439
- expectancy theory 439
- extinction 450
- extrinsic reward 424
- flourishing 456
- gainsharing 453
- goal-setting theory 441
- hierarchy of needs theory 426
- hygiene factors 431
- instrumentality 439
- interactional justice 436
- intrinsic reward 424
- job characteristics model 445
- job design 444
- job enlargement 444
- job enrichment 444
- justice climate 438
- law of effect 448
- meaningfulness 459
- motivating factors 432
- motivation 423
- needs 426
- negative reinforcement 450
- pay for knowledge 454
- pay for performance 453
- piece rate 453
- positive reinforcement 449
- procedural justice 436
- process perspectives 434
- profit sharing 453
- prosocial behavior (PSB) 447
- prosocial motivation 447
- punishment 450
- reinforcement 449
- reinforcement theory 448
- sales commission 453
- scientific management 444
- self-determination theory 429
- stock options 453
- stretch goals 441
- two-factor theory 431
- valence 440
- voice 437
- well-being 456
- work-life benefits 455

Key Points

12.1 Motivating for Performance

- Motivation is defined as the psychological processes that arouse and direct goal-directed behavior.
- In a simple model of motivation, people have certain needs that motivate them to perform specific behaviors for which they receive rewards that feed back and satisfy the original need.
- Rewards are of two types: (1) extrinsic and (2) intrinsic.
- Four major perspectives on motivation are (1) content, (2) process, (3) job design, and (4) reinforcement.

12.2 Content Perspectives on Employee Motivation

- Content perspectives or need-based perspectives emphasize the needs that motivate people.
- Besides McGregor Theory X/Theory Y (Chapter 2), need-based perspectives include (1) Maslow's hierarchy of needs theory, (2) McClelland's acquired needs theory, (3) Deci and Ryan's self-determination theory, and (4) Herzberg's two-factor theory.
- Maslow's hierarchy of needs theory proposes that people are motivated by five levels of need.
- McClelland's acquired needs theory states that three needs are major motives determining people's behavior in the workplace.
- Deci and Ryan's self-determination theory assumes that people are driven to try to grow and attain fulfillment, with their behavior and well-being influenced by three innate needs.
- Herzberg's two-factor theory proposes that work satisfaction and dissatisfaction arise from two different factors: work satisfaction from so-called motivating factors, and work dissatisfaction from so-called hygiene factors.

12.3 Process Perspectives on Employee Motivation

- Process perspectives are concerned with the thought processes by which people decide how to act. Three process perspectives on motivation are (1) equity theory, (2) expectancy theory, and (3) goal-setting theory.
- Equity theory focuses on employee perceptions as to how fairly they think they are being treated compared with others. The key elements in equity theory are inputs, outputs (rewards), and comparisons.
- Equity theory has expanded into an area called organizational justice, which is concerned with the extent to which people perceive they are treated fairly at work. Three different components of organizational justice have been identified: (1) distributive justice, (2) procedural justice, and (3) interactional justice.

- Expectancy theory is based on three concepts: expectancy, instrumentality, and valence of rewards.
- Goal-setting theory suggests that employees can be motivated by goals that are specific and challenging but achievable and linked to action plans.

12.4 Job Design Perspectives on Motivation

- Job design is, first, the division of an organization's work among its employees, and second, the application of motivational theories to jobs to increase satisfaction and performance.
- Two approaches to job design are fitting people to jobs (the traditional approach) and fitting jobs to people (the modern approach).
- Two techniques for fitting jobs to people include (1) job enlargement and (2) job enrichment.
- An outgrowth of job enrichment is the job characteristics model, which consists of (1) five core job characteristics that affect (2) three critical psychological states of an employee that in turn affect (3) work outcomes—the employee's motivation, performance, and satisfaction.
- The five core job characteristics are (1) skill variety, (2) task identity, (3) task significance, (4) autonomy, and (5) feedback.
- Relational job design focuses on designing the relational aspects of work to increase employees' prosocial motivation.

12.5 Reinforcement Perspectives on Motivation

- Reinforcement theory attempts to explain behavior change by suggesting that behavior with positive consequences tends to be repeated, whereas behavior with negative consequences tends not to be repeated. Reinforcement is anything that causes a given behavior to be repeated.
- The use of reinforcement theory to change human behavior is called behavior modification.
- There are four types of behavior modification: (1) positive reinforcement, (2) negative reinforcement, (3) extinction, and (4) punishment.

12.6 Using Compensation, Nonmonetary Incentives, and Other Rewards to Motivate

- Compensation is one form of work motivator.
- Popular incentive compensation plans are (1) pay for performance, (2) bonuses, (3) profit sharing, (4) gainsharing, (5) stock options, and (6) pay for knowledge.
- There are also nonmonetary ways of compensating employees. Some employees will leave because they feel the need for work-life balance, the need to grow, the need for a positive work environment, and the need for meaningful work. To retain such employees, nonmonetary incentives have been introduced, such as work-life benefits, flexible work arrangements, and vacation/sabbatical time.

12.7 Career Corner: Managing Your Career Readiness

- Self-motivation is increased by applying the six steps of self-management.
- The six steps of self-management include the following: (1) Identify your wildly important long-term goal. (2) Break your wildly important goal into short-term goals. (3) Create a "to-do" list for accomplishing your short-term goals. (4) Prioritize the tasks you need to complete. (5) Create a time schedule for completing tasks. (6) Work the plan, reward yourself, and adjust as needed.
- Self-motivation also requires recharging.

13 Groups and Teams
Increasing Cooperation, Reducing Conflict

After reading this chapter, you should be able to:

LO 13-1 Identify the characteristics of groups and teams.

LO 13-2 Describe the development of groups and teams.

LO 13-3 Discuss ways managers can build effective teams.

LO 13-4 Describe ways managers can deal successfully with conflict.

LO 13-5 Describe how to develop the career readiness competency of teamwork/collaboration.

LO 13-6 Discuss why teams drift toward dysfunction and explain how managers can fix it.

FORECAST   What's Ahead in This Chapter

In this chapter, we consider groups versus teams and discuss different kinds of teams. We describe how groups evolve into teams and discuss how managers can build effective teams. We also consider the nature of conflict, both good and bad. We then develop a Career Corner that focuses on developing the career readiness competency of teamwork/collaboration. We conclude with a discussion of team dysfunction and how to get teamwork right.

Managing Team Conflict Like a Pro

Have you ever worked with a group or team that agreed about everything? Probably not. Everyone comes to a group project or assignment with different ideas, experiences, and expectations. Ideally those differences bring out everyone's creativity and lead to a great conclusion, but often conflicts arise that take a little effort to overcome. Here are some suggestions for handling group conflict at school and at work that will help you hone your career readiness competencies of oral communication, teamwork/collaboration, leadership, and social intelligence.[1]

Acknowledge a Conflict Exists and Understand Emotions

Ignoring issues may help you avoid conflict in the short term but may lead to built-up resentment and future arguments. Negative emotions are often one of the first indicators that a conflict exists. It is best to take a timeout to acknowledge your own emotions and empathize with others' feelings when you sense conflict.

Ask a Lot of Questions

Seek more information from group members to effectively resolve conflict between group members. This can be done by asking questions to understand the source of disagreement, to determine everyone's perspective, and to gather as many suggestions for resolving the conflict as you can. Before you decide that you have the one and only answer, individually seek team members' thoughts and goals. Try to understand what is driving their behavior in the conflict.

Frame the Conflict around Behavior, Not Personalities

No one likes being attacked or criticized just because they disagree. Instead of saying, "Chris, you're holding everything up because you're so stubborn," which is an attack on Chris's personality, try saying, "If you would please hear everyone out before you make up your mind, Chris, we'll be able to put more options on the table." This moves the focus to a behavior Chris can change and identifies the benefit to the group from doing so.

Remind Team Members about the Group Norms

Norms establish accepted ways of behaving, and they can make or break a group. We suggest you take the time to establish group norms shortly after forming. Remind everyone that your current project or assignment requires them to put forth their best and most cooperative efforts at working together in order to achieve your collective goal. This entails setting norms of taking responsibility for tasks, keeping on schedule, and not interrupting others in team meetings.

Choose Your Words with Care

Have you ever heard the phrase that you catch more bees with honey than vinegar? The point is that words matter when it comes to conflict. Saying, "Christa, this work stinks. I'd get better work from a high school student," is likely to create defensiveness and result in bitterness and resentment. You want to stay away from an evaluative statement like this and replace it with specific, descriptive words. "Christa, your report had five computational errors, was two days late, and had five typos." Describe rather than evaluate.

You also want to avoid absolutes like always and never. "Jose, you never complete your team assignments on time," or "Rashad, you are always late to meetings." Absolutes are rarely true, and they foster defensiveness and unresolved conflict.

Finally, don't give your teammates ultimatums or make rigid demands. Saying, "You all need to get me your parts of the project by tonight or else I will just do it myself," will make you look demanding, controlling, and difficult to work with. You can build more goodwill by working with your teammates on allocating tasks and setting deadlines instead of bossing people around.

Remember Conflict Can Be Productive

It's tempting to avoid or even fear conflict because open disagreement can be uncomfortable, but research shows that conflict isn't always bad. For example, teams that have a high level of disagreement in decision making, but good personal relationships, have more success.[2] With this in mind, look for the reasons behind the conflict. Is it about procedures or processes that can be adjusted or about different ways of approaching the solution? These sources of conflict can be a gold mine of creativity for the group if you practice handling conflict effectively.

For Discussion Think back to a conflict that occurred in a group or team to which you belonged. What was the root cause of the disagreement, and how was it resolved? Would you do anything differently if you could?

13.1 Groups versus Teams

THE BIG PICTURE
Teamwork is critical to organizational functioning. A team is different from a group. A group typically is management-directed, a team self-directed. Groups may be formal, created to do productive work, or informal, created for friendship. Work teams engage in collective work requiring coordinated effort. Types of teams are project teams, cross-functional teams, self-managed teams, and virtual teams.

LO 13-1

Identify the characteristics of groups and teams.

Over a quarter century ago, management expert Peter Drucker predicted that future organizations would not only be flatter and information-based but also organized around teamwork—and that has certainly come to pass.[3] Your ability to work well as a team member is a career readiness competency desired by employers, and it can affect your job opportunities and career success. The purpose of this chapter is to enhance your ability to work productively and happily with current and future teams. In this section, we'll describe the difference between groups and teams, identify different types of teams, and introduce an organizing framework that explains how teams function.

Groups and Teams: How Do They Differ?

Aren't a group of people and a team of people the same thing? By and large, no. One is a collection of people, the other is a powerful unit of collective performance. One is typically management-directed, the other self-directed. Consider the differences, as follows.

What a Group Is: A Collection of People Performing as Individuals
A **group** is defined as (1) two or more freely interacting individuals who (2) share norms, (3) share goals, and (4) have a common identity.[4] A group is different from a crowd, a transitory collection of people who don't interact with one another, such as a crowd gathering on a sidewalk to watch a fire. And it is different from an organization, such as a labor union, which is so large that members also don't interact.

An example of a work group would be a collection of 10 employees meeting to exchange information about various company policies on wages and hours.

What a Team Is: A Collection of People with Common Commitment
McKinsey & Company management consultants Jon R. Katzenbach and Douglas K. Smith say it is a mistake to use the terms *group* and *team* interchangeably. Groups have individual accountability in which members contribute independently. Teams require mutual accountability in which members work together to produce results. Thus, a **team** is defined as a small group of people working together with a common purpose, performance goals, and mutual accountability.[5] "Teams produce joint work-products through the joint combinations of their members. This is what makes possible performance levels greater than the sum of all the individual bests of team members. Simply stated, a team is more than the sum of its parts" says Katzenbach and Smith.[6]

As you can see, teamwork is a soft skills career readiness competency desired by employers. As defined in Chapter 1, it is the ability to work effectively with and build collaborative relationships with diverse people, work within a team structure, and manage interpersonal conflict. How do you feel about working in teams? Would you prefer to work alone? You can examine your attitude toward teamwork by completing Self-Assessment 13.1 if your instructor has assigned it to you in Connect.

SELF-ASSESSMENT 13.1   CAREER READINESS

Attitudes toward Teamwork

This survey was designed to assess your attitude toward teamwork. Please complete Self-Assessment 13.1 if your instructor has assigned it in Connect.

Formal versus Informal Groups

Groups can be either formal or informal.[7]

- A **formal group** is a group assigned by organizations or its managers to accomplish specific goals. A formal group may be a division, a department, a work group, a committee, or a task force. It may be permanent or temporary. In general, people are assigned to them according to their skills and the organization's requirements.

- An **informal group**, also called an affinity or employee resource group, is a group formed by people whose overriding purpose is getting together for friendship or a common interest. An informal group may be a collection of friends who hang out with one another, such as those who take coffee breaks or go to lunch together. It also may be organized as a prayer breakfast, a bowling team, a service club, or an "alumni group" (for example, graduates from a local university). Informal groups create a sense of belonging among employees and increase their engagement at work.[8]

What's important for you as a manager to know is that informal groups can support or sabotage the plans of formal groups. A department or committee may make efforts, say, to speed up the plant assembly line or to institute workplace reforms. But members of informal groups who start to respect their own group over the formal group can undermine these efforts. This often happens over e-mails, lunch breaks, or informal gatherings such as meeting after work for drinks.[9]

Informal influence. Employee happy hours are one of many opportunities for colleagues to informally get together and develop stronger friendships with each other. Digital Vision/Photodisc/Getty Images

Types of Teams

Different types of teams have different characteristics. We can differentiate some typical teams according to their

1. Purpose.
2. Duration.
3. Level of member commitment.

Work Teams   A company's audit team and a professional sports team, like the hockey team in the accompanying photo, have several things in common. Like all work teams, they have a clear purpose that all members share. These teams are usually permanent, and members must give their complete commitment to the team's purpose in order for the team to succeed.

All players on a hockey team need to work together toward a common purpose to be a winning team. Robert Nyholm/Shutterstock

SKYMAGIC designed and deployed a customized drone light show with three-dimensional images such as a player kicking a soccer ball during the 2022 FIFA World Cup. Nick Potts/Alamy Stock Photo

Work Teams Example—Professional Sports: Professional athletes in sports such as baseball, basketball, football, soccer, and hockey dedicate an immense amount of time, energy, and effort working together with their teammates to synchronize their efforts and help their team win.

Project Teams If you have ever completed a team project for a class, you have been part of a project team. Project teams at work are assembled to solve a particular problem or complete a specific task, such as brainstorming new marketing ideas for one of the company's products. Members can meet just once or work together for many years, depending on the nature of the assignment, and they may meet virtually or face to face. They can come from the same or different departments or functional areas, and while serving on the project team, they continue to fulfill their primary responsibilities.

Project Teams Example—SKYMAGIC: What can supplement the wonder and awe inspired by laser shows and fireworks shows? Mungo Denison, cofounder and director of SKYMAGIC, believes the answer is drone light shows. SKYMAGIC brings together programmers, engineers, and storytellers to design award-winning three-dimensional light shows using hundreds of drones. One of its project teams designed and deployed a customized drone light show at the 2022 FIFA World Cup.[10]

Cross-Functional Teams Cross-functional teams are designed to include members from different areas within an organization, such as finance, operations, and sales. Cross-functional teams can serve any purpose, they can be work teams or project teams, and their assignment can be long or short term. Surgical teams are a good example.

Cross-Functional Teams Example—Surgical Teams: The goal of a successful surgery is to improve the patient's health and manage their pain during the surgery. These goals require a team of specialists including a surgeon, an anesthesiologist, nurses, and assistants. Each team member brings their specialized knowledge and expertise into the operating room.[11]

A surgical team is composed of team members with different specialties who work together for the duration of a surgery. MBI/iStock/iStock/Getty Images

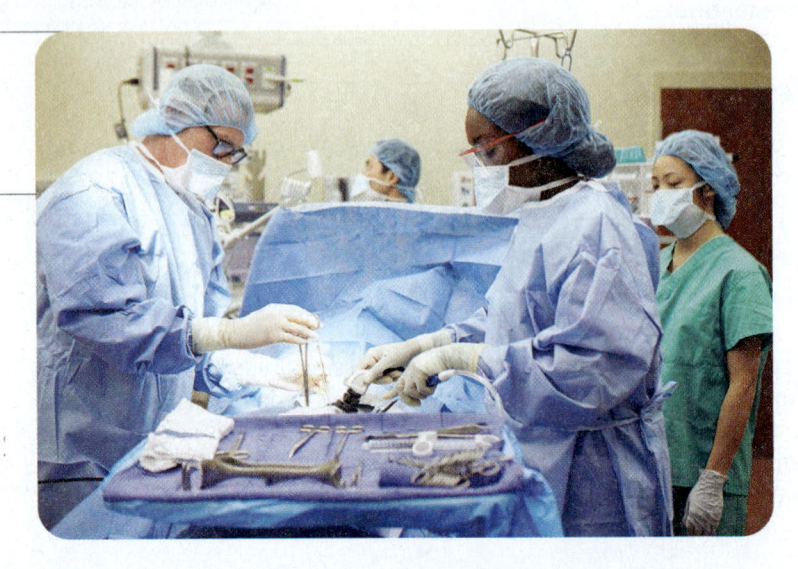

A recent study found that surgeons have a more significant impact on the surgical team's performance than other team members when the surgery is particularly complex.[12] This evidence suggests you should select your surgeon carefully!

Self-Managed Teams Self-managed teams are defined as groups of workers who are given administrative oversight for their task domains. It's estimated that around 79% of the Fortune 1000 and 81% of manufacturing firms use self-managed teams,[13] and experts predict that their use will increase in the future.[14] Research shows self-managed teams have a positive effect on productivity, innovation, and employees' autonomy, achievement, and satisfaction.[15]

The most common responsibilities of today's self-managed teams include work scheduling and customer interaction, and the least common are hiring and firing. Most self-managed teams are found at the shop-floor level in factory settings to drive efficiency in the manufacturing process.

Research provides three takeaways for creating self-managed teams:[16]

- Ensure a leader emerges quickly.
- Select the right individuals to join the team.
- Provide proper training for team members.

Virtual Teams Virtual teams are composed of members in different geographic locations who use technology to work together and achieve common goals. Technological advances and necessity spurred by the COVID-19 pandemic caused virtual teams to surge in popularity. Employers continue to offer fully remote or hybrid (the option to work remotely at least one day a week) work arrangements. The number of U.S. employees working remotely grew from 3.9 million in 2015 to 4.7 million in 2020.[17] A 2022 McKinsey survey of 25,000 Americans revealed 58% of employed respondents, equivalent to 92 million workers in the United States, were offered the option to work remotely at least one day a week.[18] This fundamental shift in the workplace is possible because work teams use videoconferencing tools like Zoom, Microsoft Teams, and WebEx to collaborate with team members anywhere and anytime without the limitation of being in the same geographic location.

Remote work is popular with employees. Approximately 87% of employees who were given the option to work remotely took their employer up on the offer.[19] But is remote work good for business? A 2023 International Workplace Group Trends Forecast Report reveals the following statistics:[20]

Online collaboration. Technology not only allows people to communicate where, when, and with whom they wish, but it also allows many people and organizations to work without offices. What are the advantages and disadvantages for you personally of virtual or hybrid work? Kateryna Onyshchuk/Shutterstock

- Hybrid work increases employees' productivity around 4% on average, says Stanford economics professor Nicholas Bloom.
- Sixty-six percent of businesses said flexible workspaces reduced both capital and operational expenditures.
- Hybrid work saves organizations an average of $11,000 per employee.

Advocates say virtual teams are very flexible and efficient because they are driven by information and skills not by time and location. People with needed information and/or skills can be team members regardless of where or when they actually do their work.[21] Nevertheless, virtual teams have pros and cons like every other type of team.

Benefits of virtual teams include:

- **The ability to tap a more diverse, global candidate pool.** Hiring the most qualified employees with diverse knowledge, skills, and experiences improves virtual teams' communication, collaboration, and innovation.[22]

- **Reduced commuting, travel, and real estate expenses.** Virtual work enables companies to reduce the size of their corporate headquarters and save on rent, energy costs, and corporate travel.[23]
- **Reduced work-life conflicts and increased productivity for employees.** A 2022 Robert Half survey of 2,500 U.S. workers revealed 77% of professionals "who can work where and when they are most productive are putting in more hours now than three years ago. Despite longer workdays, 46% reported higher job satisfaction."[24]

Virtual teams have drawbacks, too. Challenges include:

- **Physical distance.** Adjusting to different time zones and accommodating differences in local laws, holidays, and customs cause global virtual teams problems coordinating their work.[25]
- **Social distance.** It is more difficult for virtual teams than for face-to-face teams to establish trust, team cohesion, cooperative behavior, and commitment to team goals. As a result, virtual team members feel less connected and are less likely to communicate with team members and contribute to the team.[26] Cultural differences among virtual team members are a source of conflict that reduces trust. The virtual team environment also offers limited information for team members to observe other members' nonverbal cues.[27]
- **24/7 accessibility.** Virtual workers are more accessible to their family and colleagues. They feel pressure to be all things to all people all the time. This role overload creates stress and can lead to burnout and reduced health and well-being. Research suggests women are particularly susceptible to this experience as they feel like they are expected to be constantly available for work, child care, care for older adults, and household responsibilities.[28]

The Practical Action box provides advice for overcoming virtual team challenges.

PRACTICAL ACTION | High-Performing Virtual Teams

We put together a collection of seven practices to focus your efforts and accelerate your success as a member or leader of a virtual team.

1. **Adapt your communications.** Learn remote workers' preferences for e-mail, texts, phone calls, and videoconferencing. Then make sure you have reliable tools to accommodate those preferences. It is advisable to have regularly scheduled contact using messaging apps (such as Slack) and videoconferencing (such as Zoom or WebEx) tools.[29] Be strategic and personalize your communication. Talk to the right people at the right times about the right topics. Don't just blanket everybody via e-mail—focus your message.

2. **Have fun.** Use technology to keep remote workers connected. Isolation and loneliness are two of the biggest drawbacks to remote work.[30] Build employees' connectedness and belongingness by acknowledging birthdays and recognizing accomplishments for those who are not regularly in the office. Also, incorporate fun virtual team-building activities like online office games, a scavenger hunt for household items, and a video challenge to show what your home workspace (really) looks like. All of these activities build interpersonal and work relationships within the company.[31]

3. **Build trust.** Building trust takes effort; it doesn't happen magically. Research suggests team members build trust by being proactive, funny, friendly, loyal, caring, consistent, open, honest, and transparent. Sharing personal information (hobbies, family information) and displaying flexibility in dealing with technological or geographic challenges can also engender trust.[32]

4. **Encourage feedback and communication.** Effective virtual teams don't hoard information. Resources and information should flow freely, routine feedback should be provided, and communication should be transparent. Shared file sites on the cloud (on Google Docs, Dropbox, and other platforms) can serve as information hubs for all team members.[33]

5. **Coordinate the transfer of work.** If team members work in different time zones, some projects can receive attention around the clock as they are handed off from one zone to

the next. Doing this effectively requires that both senders and receivers clearly specify what they have completed and what they need in each transfer.

6. **Select individuals who can thrive.** Successful remote workers tend to be organized, consistent, self-disciplined, intrinsically motivated, and independent. Consider bringing on potential hires as freelancers before extending an offer for long-term employment. This approach helps ensure they develop rapport with colleagues and succeed in a nontraditional work environment.[34]

7. **Care about team members outside of work.** Get to know remote workers as individuals and express interest in their family, hobbies, interests, achievements, and challenges outside of work. Team members who feel cared about are more likely to connect with and trust their team.[35]

Researchers and consultants agree about one aspect of virtual teams—*there is no substitute for face-to-face contact.* Meeting in person is especially beneficial early in virtual team development, and team leaders are encouraged to meet even more frequently with key members. In-person meetings are also important when there is a need to re-organize or restrategize. Face-to-face interactions can be as simple as lunch, water cooler conversations, social events, or periodic meetings. Whatever the case, such interactions enable people to get familiar with each other and build credibility, trust, and understanding. This reduces misunderstandings and makes subsequent virtual interactions more efficient and effective. It also increases job performance and reduces conflict and intentions to quit.[36]

Face-to-face interactions enable people to get real-time feedback, forge meaningful and authentic connections, and get a better sense of what others actually think and feel.[37] Spontaneous and serendipitous face-to-face conversations also spur creativity. These are just a few reasons CEOs at Amazon, Apple, Disney, Starbucks, and Salesforce are encouraging employees to return to the office at least three days a week.[38] Companies are still working out the best way to balance employees' desire for flexibility with the organization's need for creativity, collaboration, and a results-driven culture.[39]

An Organizing Framework

Teams encounter unique challenges in their pursuit of positive outcomes. Figure 13.1 provides an organizing framework that explains how teams function and how they can best be managed to achieve their desired goals. Following the figure from left to right, teamwork involves three basic functions that influence team outcomes: team design, team development, and team management processes. Let's introduce each function.

1. **Team design** involves choosing the best type of team to accomplish a goal. Team types were described earlier (such as a work, project, cross-functional, self-managed, or virtual team). Once teams are designed, they need to be developed.

2. **Team development** is the process of assembling individuals in a team, getting acquainted with each other, and working together to achieve a common goal. Tuckman's five-stage model of group and team development is introduced in Section 13.2 to explain how this unfolds. It provides a useful perspective to understand the developmental sequence teams *should* follow to perform effectively.

3. **Team management processes** are the actions, feelings, and thoughts that influence team: members' interactions and the team's effectiveness.[40] Figure 13.1 identifies eight factors that are key to keeping your team's performance on track. When one or more of the processes falter, teams become dysfunctional and their performance gets derailed. Section 13.3 describes how the first seven factors support team effectiveness. Section 13.4 describes the nature of conflict, its positive and negative impact on team effectiveness, four kinds of conflict, and common and constructive ways to handle conflict.

Team outcomes describes a team's ability to achieve synergistic results (more than the sum of its individual members' efforts). Effective teams achieve their performance goals, increase **team viability**—team members' satisfaction with and desire to remain a

FIGURE 13.1
An organizing framework to understand how teams function

Team Management Processes
- Collaboration
- Trust
- Performance Goals and Feedback
- Mutual Accountability & Interdependence
- Team Composition
- Roles
- Norms
- Managing Conflict

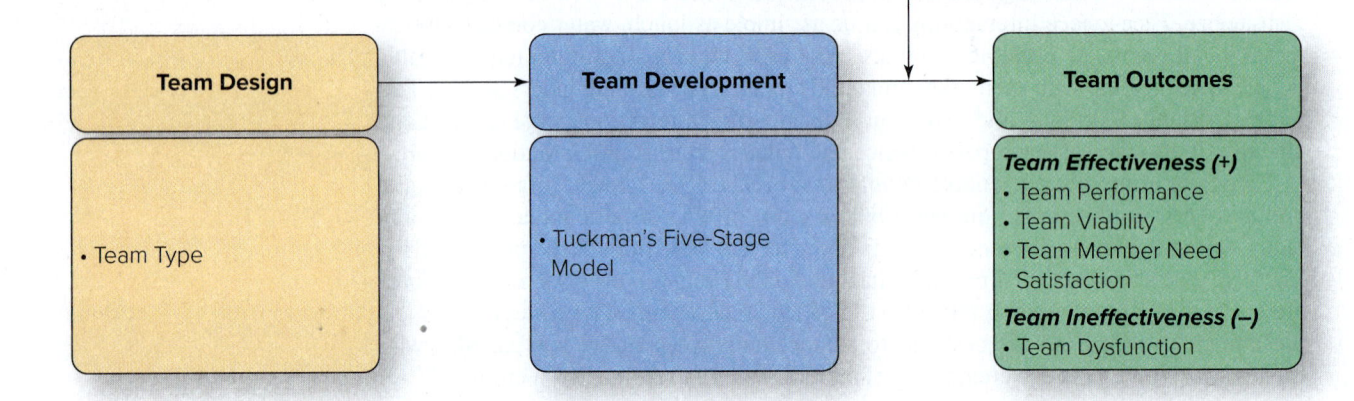

Team Design
- Team Type

Team Development
- Tuckman's Five-Stage Model

Team Outcomes

Team Effectiveness (+)
- Team Performance
- Team Viability
- Team Member Need Satisfaction

Team Ineffectiveness (−)
- Team Dysfunction

member in the team—and satisfy their team members' individual needs (see needs theories discussed in Chapter 12.2). Ineffective teams encounter dysfunction where team members don't communicate or contribute and are not committed to achieving the team's goals. Section 13.6 outlines five common dysfunctions that plague teams and offer developmental suggestions for how to identify and correct them when they show up.

13.2 Stages of Group and Team Development

THE BIG PICTURE
Groups can evolve into teams by going through five stages of development: forming, storming, norming, performing, and adjourning. They also can develop if they are forced to change in response to a crisis. We'll look at both these processes.

LO 13-2 Describe the development of groups and teams.

Tuckman's Five-Stage Model

Managers often talk of products and organizations going through stages of development, from birth to maturity to decline. Groups and teams go through the same process. One theory proposes five stages of development: *forming, storming, norming, performing,* and *adjourning*.[41] (See Figure 13.2.)

FIGURE 13.2
Five stages of group and team development

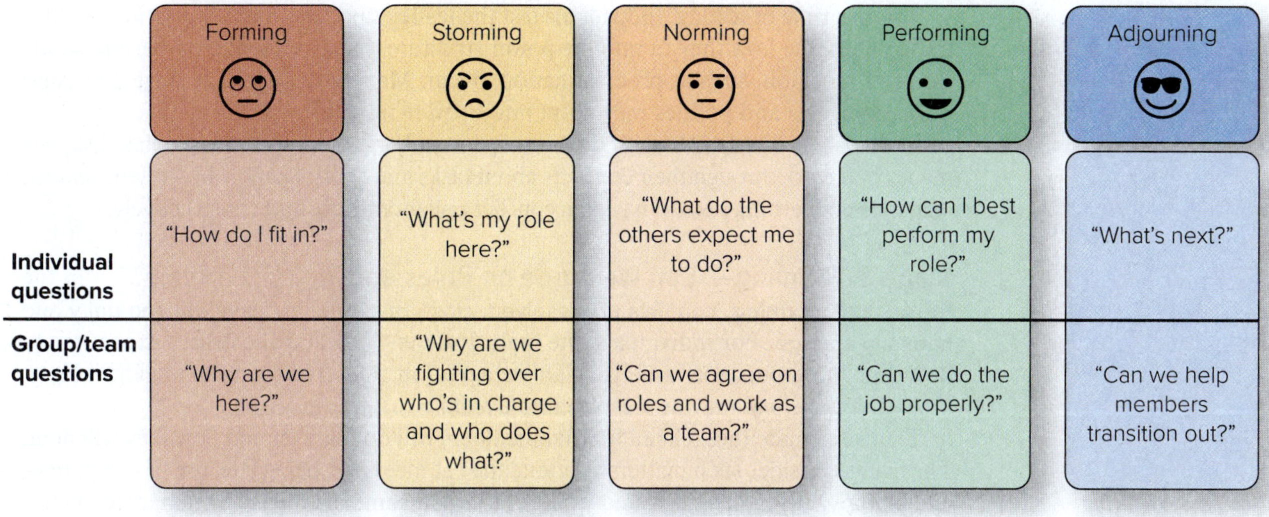

	Forming	Storming	Norming	Performing	Adjourning
Individual questions	"How do I fit in?"	"What's my role here?"	"What do the others expect me to do?"	"How can I best perform my role?"	"What's next?"
Group/team questions	"Why are we here?"	"Why are we fighting over who's in charge and who does what?"	"Can we agree on roles and work as a team?"	"Can we do the job properly?"	"Can we help members transition out?"

Adapted from Kreitner, R. and A. Kinicki. Organizational Behavior. *10th ed. New York: McGraw Hill/Irwin, 2013, Figure 7-1, p. 181.*

These stages are meant to represent the process by which new or start-up teams evolve into fully functioning teams that achieve their goals. Keep the following two things in mind as you study these stages:

- These stages often aren't of the same duration or intensity, and they don't always follow this sequence.[42]
- When you join an existing team, which is likely to occur when you obtain your first job after graduation, the team is most likely operating in the performing stage. Adding a new member like yourself suggests that the team needs to revisit some of the earlier stages of group development.

Let's consider the five stages of group development.

Stage 1: Forming—"Why Are We Here?" The first stage, **forming**, is the process of getting oriented and getting acquainted. This stage is characterized by a high degree of uncertainty as members try to break the ice and figure out who is in charge and what the group's goals are.[43] For example, if you were to join a new team to work on a class project, the question for you as an individual would be "How do I fit in?" For the group, the question is "Why are we here?"

At this point, mutual trust is low, and there is a good deal of holding back to see who takes charge and how they do so. Of course the group needs leadership and direction at this juncture. If a formal leader (e.g., the class instructor or a supervisor) does not exist or fails to assert their authority, an emergent leader will eventually step in to fill this need.[44] During this stage, the leader should define the group's mission and goals and allow time for group members to become acquainted and to socialize.

As mentioned earlier, there are times when a new member joins a team that has completed the forming stage. The team leader, or a designated mentor, needs to ensure this person catches up to and is aligned with the rest of the team. This may require temporarily returning to the forming stage to discuss goals, build trust, and socialize.[45] Much of this can be accomplished through onboarding programs, which we discussed in Chapter 9.

Stage 2: Storming—"Why Are We Fighting over Who's in Charge and Who Does What?" The second stage, **storming**, is characterized by the emergence of individual personalities and roles and conflicts within the group. For you as an individual, the question is "What's my role here?" For the group, the issue is "Why are we fighting over who's in charge and who does what?" This stage may be of short duration or painfully long, depending on the goal clarity and the commitment and maturity of the members.

This is a time of testing. Individuals test the leader's policies and assumptions as they try to determine how they fit into the power structure. Subgroups take shape, and subtle forms of rebellion, such as procrastination, occur. Many groups stall in stage 2 because power struggles and politics may erupt into open rebellion.[46]

In this stage, the leader should encourage members to suggest ideas, voice disagreements, and work through their conflicts about tasks and goals. Section 13.4 offers detailed guidance concerning how to navigate conflict collaboratively and constructively.

Stage 3: Norming—"Can We Agree on Roles and Work as a Team?"
In the third stage, **norming**, **conflicts are resolved, close relationships develop, and unity and harmony emerge**. For individuals, the main issue is "What do the others expect me to do?" For the group, the issue is "Can we agree on roles and work as a team?" Note, then, that the *group* may now evolve into a *team*.

Teams set guidelines related to what members will do together and how they will do it. The teams consider such matters as attendance at meetings, being late, use of cell phones and laptops during meetings, and what to do when someone misses a team assignment.

Groups that make it through stage 2 generally do so because a respected member other than the leader challenges the group to resolve its power struggles so something can be accomplished. Questions about authority are resolved through unemotional, matter-of-fact group discussion. A feeling of team spirit is experienced because members believe they have found their proper roles. **Group cohesiveness**, a "we feeling" binding group members together, is the principal by-product of stage 3.[47]

This stage generally does not last long. Here the leader should emphasize unity and help identify team goals and values.

Stage 4: Performing—"Can We Do the Job Properly?"
In **performing**, **members concentrate on solving problems and completing the assigned task**. For individuals, the question here is "How can I best perform my role?" For the team, the issue is "Can we do the job properly?" During this stage, the leader should support and empower members to work on tasks.

The duration of this stage depends on the complexity of the team's goals and how well the team attends to team management processes. Complex goals require the team to spend a longer time in the performing stage. Paying careful attention to team management processes outlined in Figure 13.1 enables teams to remain in stage 4. Teams

Turning teamwork into action. This team clearly is in the performing stage of group development. Does it appear that all participants are equally engaged in dealing with the task at hand? What can you do to motivate all members in your team to actively participate in completing the task? Syda Productions/Shutterstock

that don't spend adequate time taking care of team management processes are more likely to experience conflict and implode.

Stage 5: Adjourning—"Can We Help Members Transition Out?"
Some teams make it to the final stage of **adjourning**, in which members prepare for disbandment. Having worked so hard to get along and get something done, many members feel a compelling sense of loss. For the individual, the question now is "What's next?" For the team, the issue is "Can we help members transition out?"

The leader can help ease the transition by rituals celebrating "the end" and "new beginnings." Parties, award ceremonies, graduations, or mock funerals can provide the needed punctuation at the end of a significant team project. The leader can emphasize valuable lessons learned in group dynamics to prepare everyone for future group and team efforts.

Is Tuckman's Model Accurate?
Although research does not support the notion that groups can't perform until the performing stage, both academics and practitioners agree that groups have a life cycle.[48] Research also shows us that high-performing teams successfully navigating the process of group or team development tend to display productive energy toward getting things done.[49] Do your current teams at work or school display this productive energy? You can find out by completing Self-Assessment 13.2 if your instructor has assigned it to you in Connect.

SELF-ASSESSMENT 13.2

Assessing Your Team's Productive Energy
The following survey was designed to assess your team's productive energy. Please complete Self-Assessment 13.2 if your instructor has assigned it in Connect.

Punctuated Equilibrium

Groups don't always follow the distinct stages of Tuckman's model. In another type of group development, called **punctuated equilibrium**, they establish periods of stable functioning until an event causes a dramatic change in norms, roles, and/or objectives. The group then establishes and maintains new norms of functioning, returning to equilibrium (see Figure 13.3). Punctuated equilibrium often occurs during the midpoint of a project team's deadline or in the wake of revolutionary change.[50] Generative artificial

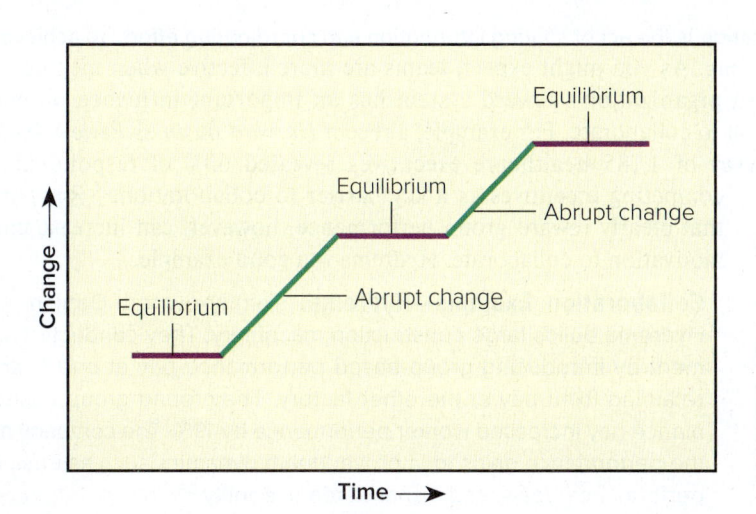

FIGURE 13.3
Punctuated equilibrium

intelligence (AI) tools and the disruption they are causing in the entertainment industry are a good example.

Punctuated Equilibrium Example—Hollywood's Intellectual Property: Generative AI tools like ChatGPT and Dall-E have the ability to write a script for a new TV show, generate short films, or create new images. These capabilities raise important concerns for studio executives about how they can protect their copyrighted intellectual property (such as characters, movie plots, and phrases) from others feeding their content into AI tools to develop similar content. The key question is, "if AI develops something new based on someone else's intellectual property, who owns the copyright?" Questions like this one are currently working their way through the court systems. AI doesn't just pose a threat to the entertainment industry; it is also a resource. Phil Wiser, chief of technology at Paramount Global, is leading a team of data scientists to customize AI as a tool to speed up the production process through automating editing tasks, visual effects, and post-production subtitles. These efficiencies stand to save entertainment companies hundreds of millions of dollars.[51]

13.3 Building Effective Teams

THE BIG PICTURE
To build a group into a high-performance team, managers must consider matters of collaboration, trust, performance goals and feedback, motivation through mutual accountability and interdependence, team composition, roles, and norms.

LO 13-3

Discuss ways managers can build effective teams.

"What is a high-performance team?" Current research and practice suggest seven attributes: collaboration, trust and open communication, participative leadership, sense of common purpose, shared accountability, clear role expectations, and early conflict resolution.[52] As a future manager, the first thing you have to realize is that building a high-performance team is going to require some work. But the payoff will be a stronger, better-performing work unit.

The most essential considerations in building a group into an effective team are (1) *collaboration,* (2) *trust,* (3) *performance goals and feedback,* (4) *motivation through mutual accountability and interdependence,* (5) *composition,* (6) *roles,* and (7) *norms.*

1. Collaboration—the Foundation of Teamwork

Collaboration is the act of sharing information and coordinating efforts to achieve a collective outcome. As you might expect, teams are more effective when members collaborate.[53] An organization's reward system has an important influence on employees' motivation to collaborate. For example, a recent *Harvard Business Review Analytics Services* survey of 1,185 healthcare executives revealed 63% of respondents blamed competing incentives as a key barrier to collaboration.[54] Reward systems that clearly reward group performance, however, can increase employees' motivation to collaborate. Hydrema is a good example.

Collaboration Example—Hydrema: Family-owned Danish company Hydrema builds large construction machinery. They conducted an experiment by introducing group-based performance pay at one factory while retaining fixed pay at the other factory. They found group-based performance pay increased worker performance by 19%. The company attributed the performance gains to improved team dynamics such as trust, common performance goals, and a shared team identity.[55]

The U.S. Air Force Thunderbirds (the white aircraft) and Navy Blue Angels (the blue aircraft) collaborate to conduct complex aerial maneuvers and form impressive flight formations for crowds at airshows. APFootage/Alamy Stock Photo

2. Trust: "We Need to Have Reciprocal Faith in Each Other"

Trust is defined as reciprocal faith in others' intentions and behaviors. The word *reciprocal* emphasizes the give-and-take aspect of trust—that is, we tend to give what we get: Trust begets trust, distrust begets distrust. Trust is based on *credibility*—how believable you are based on your past acts of integrity and follow-through on your promises.[56] Four decades of research supports a positive relationship between team members' trust and team performance.[57] Moreover, a recent study found that mutual trust among team members led to more team learning and better team performance.[58] Meta CEO, Mark Zuckerberg, is among a growing coalition of CEOs who believe it's "easier to build trust" among employees when everyone's in the office at least three days a week.[59]

Researchers believe trust has three core drivers known as the "Trust Triangle"—authenticity, logic, and empathy. If trust breaks down, you can often trace it back to one of these drivers. Let's look at each driver.[60]

- **Authenticity.** "I'm seeing the real you." People tend to trust you if they believe you're being your genuine self.
- **Logic.** "Your reasoning and judgment make sense." You stand a better chance of having people trust you if they have faith in your judgment and competence.
- **Empathy.** "You care about me and my success." People will trust you if they believe you really care about them.

3. Performance Goals and Feedback

As an individual you no doubt prefer to have measurable goals and to have feedback about your performance. The same is true with teams. Teams are not just collections of individuals. They are individuals organized for a collective purpose. That purpose needs to be defined in terms of specific, measurable performance goals with continual feedback to tell team members how well they are doing.[61] NASCAR pit crews are an obvious example.

Performance Goals and Feedback Example—Pit Crews: The pit crew's goal is to win the race. When the driver guides the race car off the track to make a pit stop, the pit crew quickly jacks up the car to change tires, refuel the tank, and clean the windshield—all in a matter of seconds. The performance goal is to have the car back on the track as quickly as possible. The number of seconds of elapsed time and the driver's place among competitors once back in the race provide immediate feedback telling the team how well they are doing.[62]

HAMPTON, GA—FEBRUARY 25: Martin Truex Jr., driver of the #78 Bass Pro Shops/5-hour Energy Toyota, pits during the Monster Energy NASCAR Cup Series Folds of Honor QuikTrip 500 at Atlanta Motor Speedway on February 25, 2018 in Hampton, Georgia. Jerry Markland/Getty Images

4. Motivation through Mutual Accountability and Interdependence

Do you work harder when you're alone or when you're in a group? Mutual accountability among team members rather than to a supervisor makes members feel mutual trust and commitment—a key part in motivating members for team effort. Mutual accountability is fostered by having team members "share accountability for the work, authority over how goals are met, discretion over resource use, and ownership of information and knowledge related to the work."[63]

Team interdependence is another contributor to effective teamwork. **Team member interdependence** reveals the extent to which team members rely on common task-related team inputs, such as resources, information, goals, and rewards, and the amount of interpersonal interactions needed to complete the work.[64] A meta-analysis of more than 7,500 teams showed that interdependence positively affects team functioning, which in turn influences team performance.[65] Another study of project teams in advertising agencies found that team interdependence improved team creativity.[66] The key takeaway from research is that team leaders need to monitor the amount of team members' interdependence.

5. Team Composition

Team composition reflects the collection of jobs, personalities, values, knowledge, experience, and skills of team members. The concept is related to our discussion of workforce diversity in Chapter DEI and individual differences in Chapter 11, where you learned that diversity is good for business.[67] Team members' differences must be effectively managed because differences can lead to conflict which we'll discuss shortly. Research indicates that leaders with multicultural experiences communicate with and manage multinational teams more effectively.[68]

The most important idea to remember is that teams should be staffed with members who fit with the team. That is, each team member should supply knowledge, skills, and abilities the team needs to be successful. Like pieces in a puzzle, you need the right mix of skills, knowledge, abilities, and personalities for the team to be creative and perform well. Research shows fit enhances team effectiveness and misfit impedes it.[69] You also need employees who are willing to work together and be collaborative team players. Paul Goldschmidt, the 2022 Major League Baseball (MLB) Most Valuable Player (MVP) for the St. Louis Cardinals, is a great example.

The St. Louis Cardinals baseball team opens the season by introducing current team members along with the organization's Hall of Famers. It prizes players, like Paul Goldschmidt, who fit the organization's culture of teamwork and excellence. One of your authors, Dr. H., attended the Cardinals' opening day festivities with his dad in 2023. Dr. Chad A. Hartnell

Team Composition Example—Paul Goldschmidt: The St. Louis Cardinals, Dr. H's childhood team, have made the playoffs in four consecutive seasons and eight times between 2012 and 2022. 2022 MLB MVP Paul Goldschmidt, affectionately nicknamed Goldy, is a key part of the team's continued success. He is a valuable team player because he is comfortable leading with his introverted personality, stays focused, is emotionally even-keeled, and lets his actions speak louder than his words. His contributions to the team both on and off the field certainly fit the 11-time World Series Champions St. Louis Cardinals' storied culture.[70]

6. Roles: How Team Members Are Expected to Behave

Roles are socially determined expectations of how individuals should behave in a specific position. As a team member, your role is to play a part in helping the team reach its goals. Members develop their roles based on the expectations of the team, of the organization, and of themselves, and they may do different things.

Two types of team roles are task and maintenance. (See Table 13.1.)

Task Roles: Getting the Work Done A **task role**, or task-oriented role, consists of behavior that concentrates on getting the team's tasks done. Task roles keep the team on track and get the work done. If you stand up in a team meeting and say, "What is

TABLE 13.1 Task and Maintenance Roles

TASK ROLES	DESCRIPTION
Initiator	Suggests new goals or ideas
Information seeker/giver	Clarifies key issues
Opinion seeker/giver	Clarifies pertinent values
Elaborator	Promotes greater understanding through examples or exploration of implications
Coordinator	Pulls together ideas and suggestions
Orienter	Keeps group headed toward its stated goal(s)
Evaluator	Tests group's accomplishments with various criteria such as logic and practicality
Energizer	Prods group to move along or to accomplish more
Procedural technician	Performs routine duties (handing out materials or rearranging seats)
Recorder	Performs a "group memory" function by documenting discussion and outcomes
MAINTENANCE ROLES	**DESCRIPTION**
Encourager	Fosters group solidarity by accepting and praising various points of view
Harmonizer	Mediates conflict through reconciliation or humor
Compromiser	Helps resolve conflict by meeting others halfway
Gatekeeper	Encourages all group members to participate
Standard setter	Evaluates the quality of group processes
Commentator	Records and comments on group processes/dynamics
Follower	Serves as a passive audience

Source: Adapted from discussion in K.D. Benne and P. Sheats, "Functional Roles of Group Members," Journal of Social Issues, Spring 1948, pp. 41–49.

the real issue here? We don't seem to be getting anywhere," you are performing a task role.

Examples include coordinators, who pull together ideas and suggestions; orienters, who keep teams headed toward their stated goals; initiators, who suggest new goals or ideas; and energizers, who prod people to move along or accomplish more are all playing task roles.

Maintenance Roles: Keeping the Team Together

A **maintenance role**, or relationship-oriented role, consists of behavior that fosters constructive relationships among team members. Maintenance roles foster positive working relationships among team members. If someone at a team meeting says, "Let's hear from those who oppose this plan," they are playing a maintenance role.

Examples are encouragers, who foster group solidarity by praising various viewpoints; standard setters, who evaluate the quality of group processes; harmonizers, who mediate conflict through reconciliation or humor; and compromisers, who help resolve conflict by meeting others "halfway."

7. Norms: Unwritten Rules for Team Members

Norms are more encompassing than roles. **Norms** are general guidelines or rules of behavior that most group or team members follow.[71] Norms point out the boundaries between acceptable and unacceptable behavior.[72] Although some norms can be made explicit, typically they are unwritten and seldom discussed openly. Nevertheless, research shows that they have a powerful influence on group and organizational behavior.[73]

Why Norms Are Enforced: Four Reasons Norms tend to be enforced by group or team members for four reasons:[74]

- **To help the group survive—"Don't do anything that will hurt us."** Norms are enforced to help the group, team, or organization survive.

    Example: The manager of your team or group might compliment you because you've made sure the team has the right emergency equipment.

- **To clarify role expectations—"Stay in your lane."** Norms also are enforced to help clarify or simplify role expectations.

    Example: At one time, new members of Congress wanting to challenge the system that gave important committee appointments to those with the most seniority were advised to follow precedent (historical role expectations) in order to advance their congressional careers.

- **To help individuals avoid embarrassing situations—"Don't call attention to yourself."** Norms are enforced to help group or team members avoid embarrassing themselves.

    Example: You might be ridiculed by fellow team members for dominating the discussion during a report to top management ("Be a team player, not a show-off").

- **To emphasize the group's important values and identity—"We're known for being special."** Finally, norms are enforced to preserve the group's, team's, or organization's central values or to enhance its unique identity.

    Example: Nordstrom's prides itself on providing exceptional customer service. Universities give annual awards to instructors whom students vote best teacher.

Putting It All Together

Thus far in this chapter we have discussed different types of teams, the team development process, and characteristics of high-performing teams. We hope you understand that creating and leading high-performance teams takes planning and skill. The first step in managing a team's performance involves assessing its effectiveness.

So how can you determine whether a team is effective? A group's output surely is one indicator, but there are others that are more "team process oriented." You can get an idea of these process-oriented indicators by taking Self-Assessment 13.3 if your instructor has assigned it to you in Connect. ●

SELF-ASSESSMENT 13.3

Assessing Team Effectiveness

The following survey was designed to assess the overall effectiveness of a team's internal processes. Please complete Self-Assessment 13.3 if your instructor has assigned it in Connect.

13.4 Managing Conflict

THE BIG PICTURE
Conflict, an enduring feature of the workplace, is a process in which one party perceives that its interests are being opposed or negatively affected by another party. Conflict can be dysfunctional (bad) or functional (good). Indeed, either too much or too little conflict can affect performance. This section identifies four sources of conflict in organizations, describes ways to stimulate constructive conflict, and discusses how to handle conflict successfully when it arises.

Think of a time in which you encountered conflict with someone. It can occur anytime or anyplace, such as talking to a friend, being on a date, working with peers on a class project, or shopping in a grocery store. What do you think causes conflict between people. A global survey of 1,000 first-time managers and their employees in 76 companies revealed poor communication, vague performance standards, unreasonable deadlines, and unclear expectations caused the majority of on-the-job conflict.[75] Most people envision *conflict* as intense shouting and fighting, but as a manager you will encounter more subtle, nonviolent forms: opposition, criticism, arguments. At the center of all conflict is that one or more people aren't getting what they want. **Conflict is defined a process in which one party perceives that its interests are being opposed or negatively affected by another party.**[76]

LO 13-4
Describe ways managers can deal successfully with conflict.

Conflict is a natural aspect of life. A place to begin our discussion of conflict is to consider two types of conflict—dysfunctional and functional.

The Nature of Conflict: Disagreement Is Normal

Conflict is simply disagreement, a perfectly normal state of affairs. Conflicts may take many forms: between individuals, between an individual and a group, between groups, within a group, and between an organization and its environment.

Although all of us might wish to live lives free of conflict, it is now recognized that certain kinds of conflict can actually be beneficial. Let's therefore distinguish between *dysfunctional conflict* (bad) and *functional conflict* (good).

- **Dysfunctional conflict—bad for organizations.** From the standpoint of the organization, **dysfunctional conflict** is conflict that hinders the organization's performance or threatens its interests. Managers need to do what they can to remove dysfunctional conflict, sometimes called negative conflict. This type of conflict results in winners and losers and causes people to argue and fight to protect their self-interests rather than do what is best for the greater good.

    Dysfunctional Conflict Example—MetroHealth: Dr. Akram Boutros was fired one month before his planned retirement after a nine-year tenure as CEO of MetroHealth because he paid himself $1.9 million in bonuses over four years without disclosing the extra compensation to, or seeking authorization from, MetroHealth's board of directors. After his dismissal, Dr. Boutros filed lawsuits against the board citing retaliation for revealing the board's illegal conduct.[77]

Dysfunctional conflict is uncomfortable and destructive in organizations. It pits one person against another in a battle of the wills and often results in distrust and resentment. liudmilachernetska/123RF

- **Functional conflict—good for organizations.** The good kind of conflict is **functional conflict**, which benefits the main purposes of the organization and serves its interests.[78] This type of conflict is also called productive conflict and occurs "when team members openly discuss disagreements and divergent perspectives without fear, anxiety, or perceived threat."[79] Functional conflict promotes collaboration to work toward a collective interest. Studies show that functional conflict can lead to superior information sharing, team problem solving and decision making, and greater team effectiveness.[80]

   Functional Conflict Example—Pixar: Creativity flourishes at Pixar Animation Studios because it fosters functional conflict. Pixar's "Brain Trust" is a group of people who meet with a movie director at a pivotal point in the film's development. The brain trust offers the director candid, constructive "peer to peer" feedback with the understanding that no one can override the director's decisions. Ed Catmull, co-founder of Pixar and former president of Walt Disney Animation Studios, believes this environment creates a collaborative process in which functional conflict leads to more creative solutions and better decisions.[81]

The ability to effectively work with others is a career readiness competency desired by employees. Do you see yourself as easy to get along with and relatively conflict free? Self-Assessment 13.4 was designed to answer this question. It assesses the extent to which your work relationships contain dysfunctional or functional conflict. Take a few moments to complete the assessment in Connect if your instructor has assigned it to you.

SELF-ASSESSMENT 13.4

Interpersonal Conflict Tendencies

In this self-assessment, you will learn how well you get along with others at work and/or school. Please complete Self-Assessment 13.4 if your instructor has assigned it in Connect.

Can Too Little or Too Much Conflict Affect Performance?

It's tempting to think that a conflict-free work group is a happy work group, as indeed it may be. But is it a productive group? In the 1970s, social scientists specializing in organizational behavior introduced the revolutionary idea that organizations could suffer from *too little* as well as *too much* conflict. Neither scenario is good.

- **Too little conflict—inactivity.** Work groups, departments, or organizations that experience too little conflict tend to be plagued by apathy, lack of creativity, indecision, and missed deadlines. The result is that organizational performance suffers.

- **Too much conflict—warfare.** Excessive conflict, on the other hand, can erode organizational performance because of political infighting, dissatisfaction, lack of teamwork, and turnover. Workplace aggression and violence are manifestations of excessive conflict.[82]

Thus, it seems that a moderate level of conflict can induce creativity and initiative,[83] thereby raising performance, as shown in the diagram in Figure 13.4. As you might expect, however, what constitutes "moderate" will vary among managers.

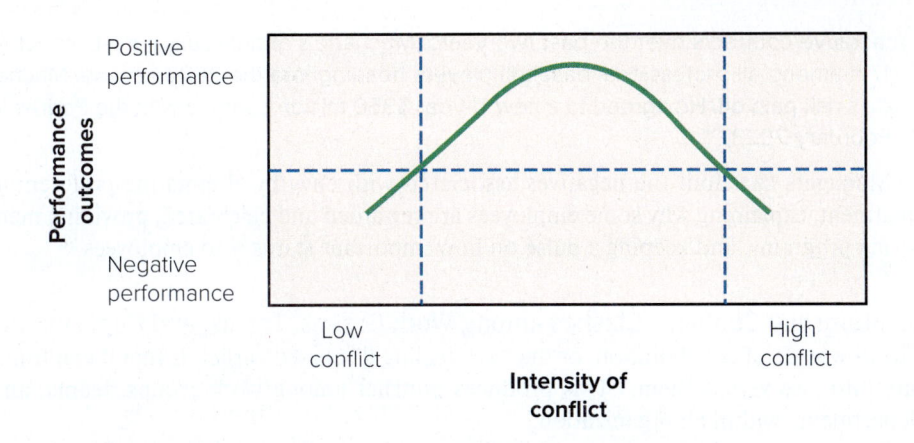

FIGURE 13.4

The relationship between intensity of conflict and performance outcomes

Too little conflict or too much conflict causes performance to suffer.

Source: Brown, Dave L. "Managing Conflict at Organizational Interfaces." Englewood Cliffs, NJ: Prentice-Hall, 1983.

Four Kinds of Conflict: Personality, Envy, Intergroup, and Cross-Cultural

There are a variety of sources of conflict—so-called *conflict triggers.* Four of the principal ones are based on (1) *personality,* (2) *envy,* (3) *intergroup dynamics,* and (4) *cultural differences.* By understanding these, you'll be better able to take charge and manage the conflicts rather than letting the conflicts take you by surprise and manage you.

1. Personality Conflicts: Clashes Because of Personal Dislikes or Disagreements

We've all had confrontations, weak or strong, with people because we disliked their personalities, such as their quirks, social tendencies, opinions, their behavior, whatever. **Personality conflict** is defined as interpersonal opposition based on personal dislike or disagreement. Such conflicts often begin with instances of *workplace incivility,* or employees' lack of regard for each other, which, if not curtailed, can diminish job satisfaction and well-being while increasing stress, turnover, and withdrawal.[84]

Personality Conflict Example—Disney: Shortly after Disney CEO Bob Iger appointed his successor Bob Chapek, conflict erupted between the two leaders of the iconic company. Iger was not pleased with how Chapek led Disney through the COVID-19 pandemic. He called Chapek "one of his worst business decisions." In contrast to Iger, "Chapek didn't have the acumen, he didn't have creativity, and he wasn't respected by employees … he was zero for three," said a Disney insider. These reasons, among others, led Disney's board to fire Chapek in November 2022 and reappoint Iger CEO.[85]

2. Envy-Based Conflicts: Clashes Because of What Others Have

Envy is an unpleasant feeling of inferiority and resentment caused by comparing yourself with a person or group who possesses something you desire.[86] It is a source of conflict because it can threaten self-esteem and promote the attitude of injustice. This motivates people to restore fairness by tearing others down or elevating self-perceptions.[87] Research has found that higher feelings of envy drive people motivated by status to withdraw and ultimately quit.[88] Would envy motivate you to give up a $150 million salary paid over five years? It appeared to for professional baseball player Manny Machado.

Envy-Based Conflict Example—Manny Machado: Star baseball player Manny Machado signed a $300 million 10-year contract to play for the San Diego Padres in 2019. The contract gave him the highest average annual salary in Major League Baseball at the time. In February 2023, he notified the Padres that he would opt out of his contract at the end of the season, leaving $150 million over five years on the table. What motivated Machado to take such a gamble? Other players received more lucrative contracts over the past two years. Machado's annual salary fell from 1st to 17th among all professional baseball players heading into the 2023 season. Machado's risk paid off. He agreed to a new 11-year $350 million contract with the Padres in February 2023.[89]

Managers can limit the negatives associated with envy by eliminating preferential treatment, explaining why some employees are rewarded and celebrated, providing mentoring programs, and keeping a pulse on how important status is to employees.[90]

3. Intergroup Conflicts: Clashes among Work Groups, Teams, and Departments

The downside of collaboration, or the "we" feeling discussed earlier, is that it can translate into "we versus them." This produces conflict among work groups, teams, and departments within an organization.

Some ways in which intergroup conflicts are expressed are as follows:

- **Inconsistent goals or reward systems—when people pursue different objectives.** It's natural for people in organizations to be pursuing different objectives and to be rewarded accordingly, but this means that conflict is practically built into the system.

- **Ambiguous jurisdictions—when job boundaries are unclear.** "That's not my job and those aren't my responsibilities." "Those resources belong to me because I need them as part of my job." Unclear task responsibilities can often lead to conflict over who should be accountable for results.

- **Status differences—when there are inconsistencies in power and influence.** It can happen that people who are lower in status according to the organization chart actually have disproportionate power over those theoretically above them, which can lead to conflicts. For example, longtime office managers are often well connected and well respected even though they may not have much "formal" authority. They have the ear of influential decision makers and can thus wield tremendous power in an organization.

4. Cross-Cultural Conflicts: Clashes between Cultures

With cross-border mergers, joint ventures, and international alliances being common features of the global economy, there are frequent opportunities for clashes between cultures. Often success or failure arises from dealing with differing cultural assumptions about how to think and act. Meta's challenges related to users' privacy settings across borders is a good example.

Cross-Cultural Conflict Example—Meta: U.S. lawmakers have been at an impasse concerning if and how they should regulate social media giant Meta, Facebook's parent company, for the content posted on its platform. European regulators took swifter action, passing the Digital Services Act in 2022 to hold the company accountable for its information-sharing algorithms and policing potentially harmful or illegal content. In 2023, European regulators further ruled Meta's ad practices of harvesting users' data without permission for personalized advertising was illegal. These decisions will have sweeping ramifications for Facebook's business model internationally.[91]

Developing cross-cultural awareness and having an open mind will allow you to minimize multicultural conflicts. Cross-cultural awareness was defined in Chapter 4 as the ability to operate in different cultural settings. We know for example that national culture impacts the way individuals react to performance feedback.[92] (See Table 4.5.) This reaction can be the cause of conflict if you don't have cultural awareness and an open mind to different cultural views. Research confirms this, demonstrating that open-minded individuals are better prepared to manage cross-cultural teams and work in cross-cultural situations than those who are not.[93]

How to Stimulate Constructive Conflict

As a manager, you are being paid not just to manage conflict but even to create some, where it's constructive and appropriate, in order to stimulate performance. Constructive conflict, if carefully monitored, can be very productive when:[94]

- Your work group seems uninterested and unengaged, resulting in low performance.
- There's a lack of new ideas and resistance to change.
- There are a lot of yes-people (expressing groupthink) in the work unit.
- Employee turnover is high.
- Managers seem overly concerned with peace, cooperation, compromise, consensus, and their own popularity rather than achieving work objectives.

One of the most effective strategies to stimulate constructive conflict is to program it using devil's advocacy and the dialectic method.

Programmed conflict is designed to elicit different opinions without inciting people's personal feelings. Sometimes decision-making groups become so bogged down in details and procedures that nothing of substance gets done. The idea here is to get people, through role-playing, to defend or criticize ideas based on relevant facts rather than on personal feelings and preferences.

The method for getting people to engage in this debate of ideas is to do disciplined role-playing, for which we discussed two proven methods in Chapter 7: *devil's advocacy* and the *dialectic method*. These two methods are depicted in Figure 7.8 and work as follows:

- **Devil's advocacy—role-playing criticism to test whether a proposal is workable.** **Devil's advocacy** is the process of assigning someone to play the role of critic. Periodically role-playing devil's advocate has a beneficial side effect in that it is great training for developing analytical and communicative skills. However, it's a good idea to rotate the job so no one person develops a negative reputation.
- **The dialectic method—role-playing two sides of a proposal to test whether it is workable.** Requiring a bit more skill training than devil's advocacy does, the **dialectic method** is the process of having two people or groups play opposing roles in a debate in order to better understand a proposal. After the structured debate, managers are more equipped to make an intelligent decision.[95]

Programmed conflict is designed to increase the team's search for and exchange of information and improve the team's decision making.
Lightspring/Shutterstock

Career Readiness Competencies to Help You to Better Handle Conflict

Whatever kind of organization you work for, you'll always benefit from knowing how to manage conflict. There are five career readiness competencies that enable you to work on disagreements and keep them from flaring into out-of-control personality conflicts: *teamwork/collaboration, social intelligence, openness to change, emotional intelligence,* and *oral/written communication.*[96] (See Table 1.3.) Let's consider how to use them in the context of a student project team. Assume that your team is composed of four people and you are behind schedule in completing your final team project.

1. Teamwork/Collaboration Establishing common ground or sharing a common goal are great ways to promote teamwork/collaboration. Given that your team is behind schedule on the project, contact your teammates and discuss what still needs to be done to get back on track. Remind them of the project deadline and see what obstacles stand between them and making the due date. By inviting others to collaborate, you are extending an olive branch. This shows you're open to their needs, willing to listen, and that you understand conflict is a two-way street.

2. Social Intelligence Social intelligence is the ability to connect with others in a meaningful way, to recognize and understand another person's feelings and thoughts, and to use this information to stimulate positive relationships and beneficial interactions. One of the best ways to exercise social intelligence is to show empathy toward others. As we mentioned earlier, the use of empathy requires effective listening, which demonstrates that we care about what someone else is saying. If someone on your project team isn't accepting feedback, try to figure out the source of their frustration. Recognize it aloud so you validate what they're feeling. You can show you are truly listening by using expressions such as, "Mario, I suspect you are disappointed in. . . ."

3. Openness to Change Openness to change includes being flexible when confronted with change, seeing change as a challenge, and being willing to apply new ideas, processes, or directives. Are you, for instance, using a method of communication that doesn't work well for others and is slowing the project team down? Offer an example of something you'd like to do differently in the future: "Team, I know I prefer to text message instead of e-mail, but this method isn't providing the level of detail we need in our communications. I'll use e-mail so we are more efficient." This creates an atmosphere for others on the team to evaluate their own ways as well.

4. Emotional Intelligence Emotional intelligence is the ability to monitor your emotions and those of others, to discriminate among them, and to use this information to guide your thinking and behavior. For example, be aware of your own temper before meeting with someone on your project team who is not meeting deadlines. We're humans and we can be imperfect and irrational at times. You can reflect by yourself, but it may not be a bad idea to talk with a friend or classmate who is not on the team. Taking a step back and reflecting allows a calmer you to enter the conversation, which will reduce the chances of further conflict.

5. Oral/Written Communication Don't tell the person what they said, how they felt, or what they did. Using language like "I felt" instead of "you said" removes blame from the conversation and does not make assumptions about the other person's intentions. For example, instead of saying, "Brittany, you did not let others on the team speak so they couldn't complain about your work quality," say, "Brittany, when the conversation ended, I felt like our classmates didn't have a chance to express their opinions of what we've completed thus far. This could have been a learning opportunity for us."

Dealing with Disagreements: Five Conflict-Handling Styles

Even if you're at the top of your game as a manager, working with groups and teams of people will now and then put you in the middle of disagreements, sometimes even destructive conflict. There are five conflict-handling styles, or techniques, you can use for handling disagreements with individuals: *avoiding, obliging, dominating, compromising,* and *integrating*.[97] Figure 13.5 shows how each of the styles can be distinguished from the others by the parties' relative concern for themselves (on the y-axis) and for others (on the x-axis).

- **Avoiding**—*Avoiding* is ignoring or suppressing a conflict. It is appropriate for trivial issues, when emotions are high and a cooling-off period is needed, or

FIGURE 13.5

Five common conflict-handling styles

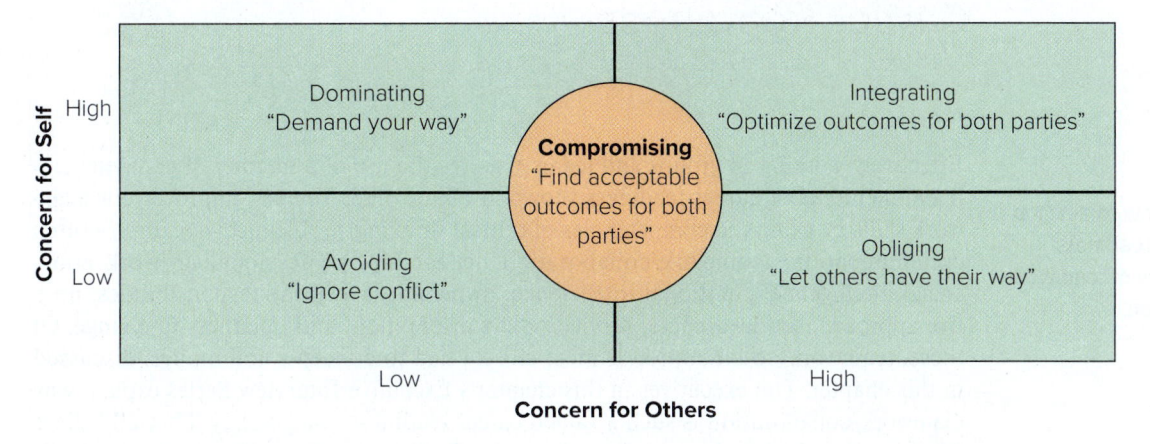

	Low Concern for Others	High Concern for Others
High Concern for Self	Dominating "Demand your way"	Integrating "Optimize outcomes for both parties"
Low Concern for Self	Avoiding "Ignore conflict"	Obliging "Let others have their way"

Compromising "Find acceptable outcomes for both parties"

Sources: From Rahim, M.A. "A Strategy for Managing Conflict in Complex Organizations." *Human Relations* (1985): 84; Thomas, K.W. "Conflict and Conflict Management: Reflections and Update." *Journal of Organizational Behavior* (1992): 265–274.

when the cost of confrontation outweighs the benefits of resolving the conflict.

- **Obliging**—An *obliging* or accommodating manager lets others have their way. This style may be appropriate to build goodwill if the issue isn't important to you so you can eventually get something in return in the future.
- **Dominating**—Also known as "forcing," *dominating* is simply demanding your way, such as when a manager relies on their formal authority and power to resolve a conflict. It is appropriate when an unpopular solution must be implemented or when it's not important that others commit to your viewpoint.
- **Compromising**—*Compromising* is when both parties give up something to gain something. They agree on an outcome that is acceptable but not ideal for both parties. It is appropriate when both sides have opposing goals or possess equal power.
- **Integrating**—*Integrating* is a collaborative style in which the manager strives to confront the issue and cooperatively identify the problem, generate and weigh alternatives, and select a solution. This style optimizes outcomes for both parties. It is appropriate for complex issues plagued by misunderstanding.

A recent research study found short-term project teams performed better when their members had different conflict-handling styles because they were less prone to groupthink and more likely to search for different alternative solutions.[98] What type of conflict-handling style do you think you have? How can you improve your ability to resolve conflict? Self-Assessment 13.5 can help answer these questions. Take the self-assessment in Connect if your instructor has assigned it to you.

SELF-ASSESSMENT 13.5 CAREER READINESS

What Is Your Conflict-Management Style?

The following exercise is designed to determine your conflict-handling style. Please complete Self-Assessment 13.5 if your instructor has assigned it in Connect.

13.5 Career Corner: Managing Your Career Readiness

LO 13.5

Describe how to develop the career readiness competency of teamwork/collaboration.

Effectively working in groups and teams requires the use of a number of competencies from the model of career readiness shown in Figure 13.6. You can improve your teamwork skills by using the competencies of critical thinking/problem solving, oral/written communication, teamwork/collaboration, leadership, professionalism/work ethic, social intelligence, emotional intelligence, ownership/accepting responsibilities, positive approach, self awareness, service/others orientation, and openness to change. Of these, teamwork/collaboration is most closely tied to concepts and models discussed in this chapter. The executives in this chapter's Executive Interview Series explain why teamwork/collaboration is such a valued career readiness competency. They all believe *things get done better when people work together.* Let's explore how you can develop skills associated with this competency.

Become a More Effective Team Member

Teamwork requires a group of people to integrate their efforts in the pursuit of achieving a common goal. Following are four actions you can employ to become a better team member.

1. **Commit to the team.** "The best teams win together, learn together, adapt together, lose together, and grow together," says executive coach Shawn Murphy.

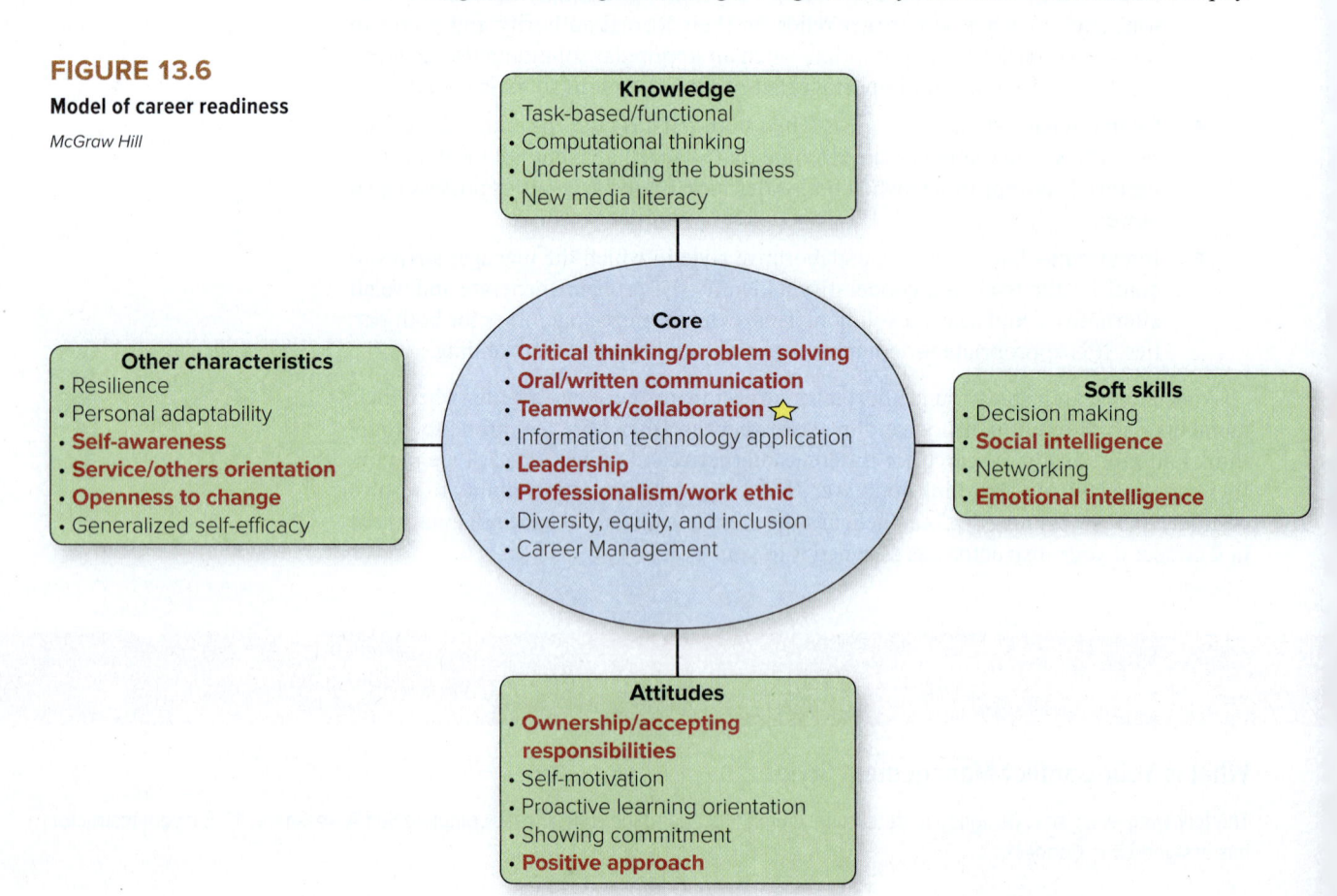

FIGURE 13.6

Model of career readiness

McGraw Hill

Knowledge
- Task-based/functional
- Computational thinking
- Understanding the business
- New media literacy

Core
- Critical thinking/problem solving
- Oral/written communication
- Teamwork/collaboration ⭐
- Information technology application
- Leadership
- Professionalism/work ethic
- Diversity, equity, and inclusion
- Career Management

Other characteristics
- Resilience
- Personal adaptability
- Self-awareness
- Service/others orientation
- Openness to change
- Generalized self-efficacy

Soft skills
- Decision making
- Social intelligence
- Networking
- Emotional intelligence

Attitudes
- Ownership/accepting responsibilities
- Self-motivation
- Proactive learning orientation
- Showing commitment
- Positive approach

Vince Lombardi, considered one of the all-time best coaches in professional football, lived this philosophy. He said, "Individual commitment to a group effort—that is what makes a team work, a company work, a society work, a civilization work." We all know that one player cannot do it all in team sports. Great players, such as soccer superstar Lionel Messi, are strategic in their approach toward teamwork. They realize that their job is to help team members raise their level of play while also inspiring and motivating them to achieve specific goals. It's the same at school and work. Consider your school project teams as an opportunity to apply your best talents toward the goal of increasing the team's overall grade. Commitment to a team comes down to your willingness to put the needs of others over self-interests. Yes, you may sacrifice some individual recognition in this process, but the team benefits. The key action here is the willingness to focus on the greater good of the team.[99]

2. **Support team members.** Nikola Jokic—two-time NBA league MVP and 2023 NBA Finals MVP—may not have the chiseled physique of a prototypical professional basketball player, but he is one of the best players in the league because he supports his teammates and makes them better. A supportive team member "reads a situation and acts accordingly. Sometimes leading, sometimes following. Sometimes ignoring their job description to do whatever needs to be done. Stepping up, stepping back, or stepping in, depending on the circumstances."[100] What do your team members need from you right now? You can provide emotional support in the form of the time you take to listen to and discuss personal matters with others. Instrumental support might entail showing someone how to complete a task or learn a new skill. It also means putting in extra hours to help the team achieve its goals. Sharing information and providing positive feedback are other forms of support. While your goal in supporting others should not be to expect something in return, you will find that the norm of reciprocity motivates others to put in more effort to help the team or you down the line. The **norm of reciprocity** is a powerful social norm by which we feel obligated to return favors or assistance after people have provided favors or assistance to us.[101]

3. **Bring positive emotions to the team.** Leave criticism and negativity outside team meetings. They are toxic and reinforce others' tendency to complain. In contrast, positive emotions such as happiness, gratefulness, and kindness create upward spirals of positivity in others. Showing concern and consideration for others in team meetings makes people feel welcome and truly part of the team. Studies show this fosters improved flourishing, commitment to the organization, creativity, and performance.[102]

4. **Lead by example.** Demonstrate the behaviors you desire in others. If you want full commitment to team goals, commit to them yourself. If you want people to come prepared to team meetings, come overprepared. Show your colleagues that you are willing to go the extra mile to help the team achieve its goals. Like positive emotions, leadership by example creates a positive contagion motivating others to participate and increase their performance.[103]

Visit your instructor's Connect course and access your eBook to view this video.

Executive Interview Series: Teamwork and Collaboration

Become a More Effective Collaborator

Earlier we defined *collaboration* as the act of sharing information and coordinating efforts to achieve a collective outcome. Collaboration is essential for teamwork, but it isn't the same thing as teamwork. Teamwork requires some formal structure such as a team leader, agendas for meetings, and organization. Collaboration is more spontaneous, less structured, and less hierarchical. You don't need an agenda item that says "collaborate." Here are some tips for becoming a more effective collaborator.

1. **Listen and learn.** Author Ken Blanchard said it well: "None of us is as smart as all of us." You can't get the best from people if you don't encourage them to

share their ideas, opinions, and beliefs. You may not agree with them, but people need to be heard. Remember that sharing different perspectives is essential for collaboration.[104] Listening is the flip side of talking. Active listening requires effort and motivation. You can improve your listening by withholding judgment, asking questions, showing respect, keeping your concentration and focus in the present moment, and remaining quiet.[105]

2. **Be open-minded.** It's difficult to collaborate if you aren't open to others' ideas.[106] You won't get the benefit of your teammates' experience and knowledge if you fail to consider their input. Being open also requires you to stop trying to impress others by having the best or brightest ideas. Just contribute what you can and let the team decide what ideas work best.

13.6 Managing Team Dysfunction

THE BIG PICTURE
Five common team dysfunctions hamper a team's effectiveness: absence of trust, fear of conflict, lack of commitment, avoidance of accountability, and inattention to results. This section describes each team dysfunction and how managers can address them.

LO 13-6

Discuss why teams drift toward dysfunction and explain how managers can fix it.

Everyone wants to be part of a healthy functioning team in which every team member thrives as the team operates synergistically to achieve its goal. But sixty percent of work teams fail to accomplish their goals, says Dr. Eunice Parisi-Carew, founding associate at The Ken Blanchard Companies.[107] This statistic demonstrates the harsh reality that teams don't drift toward effective functioning. Instead, the majority drift toward dysfunction. To this point, you've learned about what you need to do for teams to function well. That's great theoretically, but what do you do when things go wrong (as they often do)? This section provides practical advice to anticipate, recognize, and correct problems that often occur in teams.

Managing teams can feel like driving in icy road conditions. If you're not careful, your tires could lose traction, and your car could spin out of control ending up in the ditch. Many teams end up in a figurative ditch when team members race to achieve their goal without taking time to invest in the five stages of group and team development in Section 13.2 or the seven attributes of effective teams discussed in Section 13.3. Fortunately, there are five common warning signs suggesting that your team is heading toward the ditch. We'll reveal what those warning signs are, what they look like behaviorally in teams, and what actions you can take to correct each problem. First, let's set the stage with an example of a typical team in a college class.

Like carefully driving a car in icy conditions to keep it safely on the road, managers must carefully manage their team's dynamics to keep it from sliding toward dysfunction. Aspen Stock/Pixtal/age fotostock

Team Dysfunction Example—Team Project Scenario: Five students in class were randomly assigned to a team at the beginning of the semester to complete an end of semester project. None of them knew each other from a previous class. They were all anxious to complete the class project and move one major step closer to graduation. Their first meeting was met with mixed emotions. Two team members,

Ahmad and Ashley, were excited to meet new classmates and develop friendships with them during the semester. Two team members, *Kobi and Claudia*, felt skeptical, wondering if everyone would actually do their part because they were left doing the lion's share of the work on previous teams. One team member, *Benjamin*, felt annoyed because the team would take away time he would rather spend pursuing his own priorities such as working, taking care of family, and enjoying time with friends.

What could go wrong with this team during the semester? Let's find out with a running example as we introduce the five dysfunctions of a team.

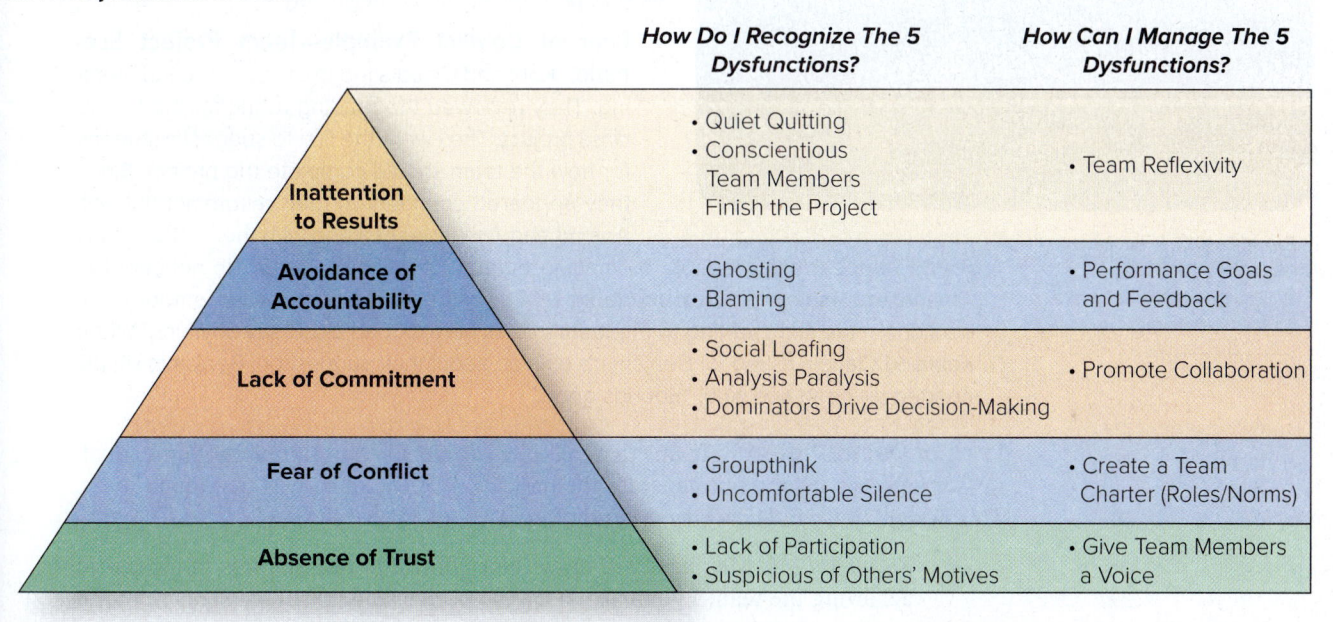

The 5 Dysfunctions of a Team

Patrick Lencioni's book, *The Five Dysfunctions of Team*, summarized years of academic research describing what goes wrong in teams into five categories: absence of trust, fear of conflict, lack of commitment, avoidance of accountability, and inattention to results.[108] Figure 13.7 depicts the five dysfunctions, how to recognize them, and how to manage them. Team dysfunction starts with an absence of trust and gets progressively worse as you move up the pyramid. Let's define each dysfunction and consider what it looks like in a team. We'll then turn our attention to practical advice for managing the five dysfunctions.

Absence of Trust The foundation of team dysfunction is an absence of trust. Team members withhold information for fear of being ridiculed or taken advantage of. They are afraid to be vulnerable and are thus less likely to say what's really on their mind until they feel like their team members are safe. You can spot an absence of trust in your team if you or your team members don't actively participate in team discussions or are suspicious about others' motives.

FIGURE 13.7
The Five Dysfunctions of a Team

Dysfunction	How Do I Recognize The 5 Dysfunctions?	How Can I Manage The 5 Dysfunctions?
Inattention to Results	• Quiet Quitting • Conscientious Team Members Finish the Project	• Team Reflexivity
Avoidance of Accountability	• Ghosting • Blaming	• Performance Goals and Feedback
Lack of Commitment	• Social Loafing • Analysis Paralysis • Dominators Drive Decision-Making	• Promote Collaboration
Fear of Conflict	• Groupthink • Uncomfortable Silence	• Create a Team Charter (Roles/Norms)
Absence of Trust	• Lack of Participation • Suspicious of Others' Motives	• Give Team Members a Voice

Source: Adapted from Lencioni, Patrick. The five dysfunctions of a team. John Wiley & Sons, 2006.

Trust is a particularly challenging issue for remote and hybrid teams. A Citrix survey of 900 business leaders revealed 50% don't trust their employees to work as hard when working remotely. This distrust leads to a cycle of distrust in which employees don't trust their employer.[109]

Absence of Trust Example—Team Project Scenario: During their first meeting, Ashley enthusiastically introduced herself, gave a little background information, and asked each team member for a similar introduction. Ahmad followed with a similarly energetic introduction. Kobi and Claudia provided a brief background they felt was relevant for the class. Benjamin gave the shortest introduction and mentioned how overwhelmed he was with his job demands this semester.

Absence of Trust. Team members aren't willing to be vulnerable with each other. Sean De Burca/Shutterstock

Fear of Conflict Distrust impacts team members' willingness to engage in functional, task-oriented conflict. They are afraid that any conflict will damage relationships among team members. As a result, team members develop superficial harmony as they "go along to get along." Your team is likely afraid of conflict if you notice everyone is quick to agree to the first option presented, a symptom of groupthink (see Chapter 7). Alternatively, you may notice that no one is willing to address controversial topics, especially when they involve confronting difficult or domineering personalities. Why does this happen? Research indicates "over 85% of employees remain silent on crucial matters because they worry about being viewed negatively."[110]

Fear of Conflict Example—Team Project Scenario: Kobi and Claudia led the team's second meeting. They reviewed the grading rubric for the team's class project. They were the first to suggest a strategy for how the team should complete the project. Since they appeared confident in their recommendations, Ahmad and Ashley went along with them. They didn't want to appear disagreeable by making different proposals. Benjamin noticed that Ahmad and Ashley felt uncomfortable with the abrupt shift from team member introductions in the first meeting to the team's tasks here, but he didn't say anything. When Kobi and Claudia asked for Benjamin's opinion about their suggestion, Benjamin simply nodded his head and said, "Sounds good."

Fear of Conflict. Everyone knows there's a problem but is afraid to speak up. Keith Brofsky/Photodisc/Getty Images

Lack of Commitment Teams that fail to engage in a healthy amount of functional, task-oriented conflict don't generate the best ideas or the most well-developed ideas. This dysfunction can take three different forms:

- *Social loafing.* Members withdraw their effort and become less interested in achieving the team's goal. **Social loafing** occurs when team members put forth less effort in the team than they would if they were working alone.

- *Analysis paralysis.* Team members are so afraid to fail they spin their wheels. They have a hard time making decisions and learning and adjusting as they implement them.
- *Dominator-driven decision-making.* The most assertive or aggressive personalities on a team tend to push for the team to adopt their ideas. Left unchallenged, team members reluctantly support them despite significant reservations about how effective they will ultimately be.

Lack of Commitment Example—Team Project Scenario: Anxious to make progress on the team project, Kobi and Claudia developed a detailed plan with deadlines and distributed responsibilities to Ahmad, Ashley, and Benjamin. Ahmad and Ashley reluctantly accepted their assignments even though they had no idea how to do the work. Benjamin was preoccupied responding to a couple urgent work emails on his phone. He didn't bother to look at his assigned responsibilities or deadlines before placing the paper in his backpack.

Lack of Commitment. Team members begin to disconnect themselves from the team's goals. Westend61/Getty Images

Avoidance of Accountability Lack of commitment results in poor communication and unclear performance standards. As team members "divide and conquer," team members' irritation with each other builds as they encounter unmet expectations, missed deadlines, and mediocre work. You can spot this dysfunction when a team member engages in ghosting by not communicating or showing up to meetings. This dysfunction can also be identified by team members who refuse to take responsibility and blame each other for substandard work.

Avoidance of Accountability Example—Team Project Scenario: The team project was due in three weeks. Kobi and Claudia enjoyed working together on key aspects of the project. They were excited to see what the rest of the team produced based on their respective assignments. Surprisingly, Benjamin did not show up to the meeting even though he previously said he would. Kobi tried texting him but didn't receive a reply. Things got worse when Ahmad and Ashley submitted their work. It didn't come close to the quality Kobi and Claudia expected the team would need to earn an "A" on the project. Ahmad and Ashley said they didn't have a clear understanding of what they were supposed to do in the first place. They blamed Kobi and Claudia for rushing to complete the project without first getting to know the team members and understand their strengths. They felt resentful toward Kobi and Claudia for being task masters with little concern for their tone or interest in developing relationships with them.

Avoidance of Accountability. Irritation builds as team members blame each other for not meeting each other's expectations. pathdoc/Shutterstock

Inattention to Results The last dysfunction, inattention to results, occurs when team members are no longer focused on working together to achieve the team's goal and prioritize their own self-interests. Team members' aggravation boils over as the team underperforms. This dysfunction looks like disengaged team members, or quiet quitters, who put forth the bare minimum to avoid getting kicked off the team. It also looks like a team in which the most conscientious members give up hope for the team to function properly and finish the project to protect their class grade and safeguard their overall GPA.

Inattention to Results Example—Team Project Scenario: Two weeks before the team project was due, Kobi and Claudia asked Benjamin during class to send them any work he completed for his part of the team project. Benjamin said he hadn't had time to do anything because his work was short of staff and needed him to work a lot of overtime. Ahmad and Ashley made a few revisions to their work based on the last meeting but were so annoyed with Kobi and Claudia they decided their second attempt was good enough. After reviewing Ahmad and Ashley's work, Kobi and Claudia were concerned about how much the team project might hurt their grade in the class. They decided to do Benjamin's work entirely and make significant revisions to Ahmad and Ashley's work without their feedback. How did they end up on yet another team where they did the bulk of the work?

Inattention to Results. The team fractures as the team underperforms and team members' aggravation with each other reaches a boiling point.
Phovoir/Shutterstock

Recommendations to Solve the 5 Team Dysfunctions

The five dysfunctions are warning signs your team is headed for a ditch. People who can recognize each dysfunction when it arises are better equipped to keep their team's performance on course. Figure 13.7 outlines five actions moving from bottom to top that you can take to address the five team dysfunctions.

Manage Absence of Trust: Give Team Members a Voice Apply your social and emotional intelligence career competencies to create a safe environment that invites people to share their honest opinions. **Team voice** reflects the extent to which team members feel free to express opinions, concerns, proposals, or thoughts about work-related issues.[111] Experts suggest that simple acts, such as asking others what they think during conversations, or providing dedicated speaking time to each member during a meeting, can increase team voice.[112] Research confirms that inclusive leadership promotes team voice and facilitates innovation, which leads to increased team performance. The caveat is that team voice should be decentralized and a select few should not dominate discussions.[113]

Manage Fear of Conflict: Create a Team Charter Put your leadership and teamwork/collaboration career competencies to work by structuring your team's roles, expectations, and interactions. A **team charter** outlines how a team will manage teamwork activities. It "represents an agreement among members as to how the team will work as an empowered partnership in making binding decisions and sharing accountability for delivering quality products/services that meet user/customer needs in a timely and cost-efficient way."[114] Team charters define your team's goals, values, norms, and roles. One of your authors, Dr K., requires teams in his classes to create charters. He does this because research shows team charters are associated with higher, sustained performance, particularly for teams that are low on team conscientiousness.[115]

Manage Lack of Commitment: Promote Collaboration Exercise your teamwork/collaboration career competency by helping team members navigate conflict and build a stronger collaboration. Getting team members to collaborate is not easy. "Employees have to set aside the desire to be the person who is right in every discussion, and focus on helping the team find the right answer," says author Mike Steib.[116] This includes utilizing what Ariel Hunsberger, learning manager at Slack, calls *disagree and commit*. This strategy allows team members to have their grievances heard and feel like they've been consulted before the team moves forward in a collaborative way.[117] Team leaders and managers can reinforce this behavior by structuring team communication and decision making in a way that promotes dissent. Two specific methods for achieving this are devil's advocacy and the dialectic method, which we discussed in Chapter 7. (See Figure 7.9.)

Manage Avoidance of Accountability: Performance Goals and Feedback
Manage the team's avoidance of accountability dysfunction by first modeling your ownership/accepting responsibility career competency. Once you've demonstrated your willingness to take responsibility and be held accountable for the team's performance, other team members are more likely to be receptive to your performance management, discussed in Chapter 9 and identified as one attribute of building effective teams (Chapter 13.3). Performance management includes a range of activities such as setting goals, providing feedback, coaching, communicating, and rewarding performance. Effective performance management behaviors matter because they improve followers' motivation, job attitudes, well-being, and performance.

Manage Inattention to Results: Engage in Team Reflexivity
Use your critical thinking/problem solving career competency to help your team reflect on, revise, and improve its purpose and processes. **Team reflexivity** is a collective process by which members reflect on the team's objectives, strategies, methods, and processes and adapt accordingly.[118] Research shows that team reflexivity can help improve team performance, trust, and creativity.[119] It also reduces team members' burnout because it provides them a sense of control and support.[120] One way to engage in team reflexivity is to conduct project after action reviews, which we defined in Chapter 7 as a review of recent decisions to identify possible future improvements. After action reviews are an effective way to improve team processes, boost team cohesiveness, provide closure, and improve morale.[121] Moreover, teams can prepare a written report documenting the after action review process and findings. Apply your oral/written communication career competency to develop the after action review report so it can effectively serve as a basis for future team charters and norms.

Key Terms Used in This Chapter

adjourning 477	maintenance role 481	team 468
collaboration 478	norm of reciprocity 491	team charter 496
conflict 483	norming 476	team composition 480
cross-functional teams 470	norms 482	team design 473
devil's advocacy 487	performing 476	team development 473
dialectic method 487	personality conflict 485	team management processes 473
dysfunctional conflict 483	programmed conflict 487	team member interdependence 480
formal group 469	punctuated equilibrium 477	
forming 475	roles 480	team reflexivity 497
functional conflict 484	self-managed teams 471	team viability 473
group 468	social loafing 494	team voice 496
group cohesiveness 476	storming 475	trust 479
informal group 469	task role 480	virtual teams 471

Key Points

13.1 Groups versus Teams
- Groups and teams are different—a group is typically management-directed, a team self-directed. A group is defined as two or more freely interacting individuals who share collective norms, share collective goals, and have a common identity. A team is defined as two or more individuals committed to a common purpose, performance goals, and approach for which they hold themselves mutually accountable.
- Groups may be either formal, established to do something productive for the organization and headed by a leader, or informal, formed by people seeking friendship with no officially appointed leader.
- Teams are of various types, including work, project, cross-functional, self-managed, and virtual.

13.2 Stages of Group and Team Development
- A group may evolve into a team through five stages. (1) Forming is the process of getting oriented and getting acquainted. (2) Storming is characterized by the emergence of individual personalities and roles and conflicts within the group. (3) In norming, conflicts are resolved, close relationships develop, and unity and harmony emerge. (4) Performing is characterized by members concentrating on solving problems and completing the assigned task. (5) In adjourning, members prepare for disbandment.
- A group also can develop by means of punctuated equilibrium, in which it establishes periods of stable functioning until an event causes a dramatic change in norms, roles, and/or objectives. The group then establishes and maintains new norms of functioning, returning to equilibrium.

13.3 Building Effective Teams
- There are seven considerations managers must take into account in building a group into an effective team. (1) They must ensure individuals are collaborating. (2) They must establish a climate of trust. (3) They must establish measurable performance goals and have feedback about members' performance. (4) They must motivate members by making them mutually accountable to one another. (5) They must consider team composition. (6) They must consider the role each team member must play. (7) They must consider team norms.

13.4 Managing Conflict
- Conflict is a process in which one party perceives that its interests are being opposed or negatively affected by another party. Conflict can be dysfunctional, or negative. However, constructive, or functional, conflict benefits the main purposes of the organization and serves its interests. Too little conflict can lead to inactivity; too much conflict can lead to warfare.
- Four kinds of conflict are personality, envy, intergroup, and cross-cultural.
- Two ways to program constructive conflict are (1) devil's advocacy and (2) the dialectic method.
- There are five conflict-handling styles: avoiding, obliging, dominating, compromising, and integrating.

13.5 Career Corner: Managing Your Career Readiness

- Working in groups requires the use of several career readiness competencies, including critical thinking/problem solving, oral/written communication, teamwork/collaboration, leadership, professionalism/work ethic, social intelligence, emotional intelligence, ownership/accepting responsibilities, positive approach, self awareness, service/others orientation, and openness to change.
- You can become a better team member by committing to the team, supporting team members, bringing positive emotions to the team, and leading by example.
- You can become a better collaborator by listening and learning and being open-minded.

13.6 Managing Team Dysfunction

- Five team dysfunctions that impair a team's effectiveness are (1) absence of trust, (2) fear of conflict, (3) lack of commitment, (4) avoidance of accountability, and (5) inattention to results.
- Five actions to address team dysfunction include: (1) give team members a voice, (2) create a team charter, (3) performance goals and feedback, (4) promote collaboration, and (5) engage in team reflexivity.

14

Power, Influence, and Leadership
From Becoming a Manager to Becoming a Leader

After reading this chapter, you should be able to:

LO 14-1 Describe managers' appropriate use of power and influence.

LO 14-2 Identify traits and characteristics of successful leaders.

LO 14-3 Identify behaviors of successful leaders.

LO 14-4 Discuss situational leadership.

LO 14-5 Describe transactional and transformational leadership.

LO 14-6 Describe contemporary leadership perspectives and concepts.

LO 14-7 Explain how to develop the career readiness competency of self-awareness.

FORECAST What's Ahead in This Chapter

How do leaders use their power and influence to get results? This chapter considers this question. We discuss the sources of a leader's power and how leaders use persuasion to influence people. We then consider the following approaches to leadership: trait, behavioral, situational, transactional and transformational, and contemporary perspectives. We conclude with a Career Corner that focuses on developing the career readiness competency of self-awareness.

Improving Your Leadership Skills

According to U.S. Marine Corps General A.M. Gray, "Leadership is the art of getting things done through people."[1] This chapter introduces you to a number of insightful theories about leadership. For now, "getting things done" by leading others is a good place to begin thinking about what kind of leader you are and might become.

Here are some suggestions for improving your career readiness competency of leadership.

1. Discover Your Leadership Style

We all develop a style of leading that is based on personal characteristics, traits, gender, interpersonal skills, and utilization of power and influence skills.[2] Identifying your leadership style is thus an ongoing process that evolves as you acquire more experience and responsibility in the workplace. You can think of this process as simply discovering what your strengths are over time and developing some flexible ways to use them in helping others achieve goals.[3] We include seven self-assessments in this chapter to help you gain an understanding about your leadership style.

2. Adopt a Proactive Learning Orientation

This suggestion follows naturally from the first one. Becoming a leader is a process that never actually ends, which means you need to keep learning about your industry, yourself, your skills, and your strengths and weaknesses as you move through your career.[4] Take classes or courses online, network with peers and mentors, ask questions, stay open-minded, seek challenging opportunities, and look outside your industry occasionally for ideas and practices you can adapt to your own leadership toolkit. A proactive learning orientation is a career readiness competency desired by employers.

3. Recognize That There Is No Single Best Way to Lead

The career readiness competency of personal adaptability helps you solve problems effectively by providing what others need when they need it. Former U.S. Joint Chiefs of Staff and Secretary of State Colin Powell remarked, "Leadership is solving problems. The day soldiers stop bringing you their problems is the day you have stopped leading them."[5]

4. Show Your Followers That You Value Them

Delegate responsibility to those you lead and earn their respect by modeling ethical behavior. Always give credit where it is due, praise in public and criticize in private, and ask for help when you need it. Don't be stingy with compliments and encouragement.[6] Work on building trust with your team, too, by communicating with honesty and truth, being an attentive listener and a positive thinker, and accepting the responsibility that comes with being the leader.[7]

5. Practice Mindfulness

You can reduce stress and worry, sharpen your focus, and make more thoughtful decisions by adopting the habit of mindfulness, which means focusing your awareness on the present and accepting your feelings and thoughts.[8] Mindfulness becomes easier through meditation, which you can practice with simple techniques for as little as 5 or 10 minutes a day.[9] Mindfulness also helps you lead others through tough times and crises by enabling you to communicate a sense of peace, purpose, and positivity.

For Discussion Do you agree that effective leadership should include motivating, developing, and encouraging others? Why or why not?

14.1 The Nature of Leadership: The Role of Power and Influence

THE BIG PICTURE

Leadership skills are needed to create and communicate a company's vision, strategies, and goals as well as to execute on these plans and goals. This section highlights six sources of power and nine influence tactics managers use to achieve these ends and lead others. Leaders use the power of persuasion to get others to follow them. Five approaches to leadership are described in the next five sections.

LO 14-1

Describe managers' appropriate use of power and influence.

Leadership. What is it? Is it a skill anyone can develop? How important is it to organizational success?

Leadership is the ability to influence employees to voluntarily pursue organizational goals.[10] *Leadership* is a broad term, as this definition implies. It can describe a formal position in an organization, which usually carries a title like CEO or CFO, or an informal role, such as that played by an expert whose opinion we value in some area.

Although not everyone is instinctively a good leader, evidence shows that people can be trained to be more effective leaders.[11] In response, more companies are using management development programs to build a pipeline of leadership talent. They also provide leadership coaching to targeted employees. **Leadership coaching** is the process of enhancing a leader's skills, abilities, and competencies in order to help the organization achieve its goals.[12] It is estimated that U.S. companies spent over $20 billion on coaching in 2022.[13]

Effective leadership matters! Recent studies showed that CEO behavior significantly impacted organizational performance.[14] Don't take this study to mean effective leadership only matters at the top. Other research reinforces the value of fostering effective leadership at all levels of an organization.[15]

Let's begin our study of leadership by considering the difference between leading and managing and the role of power and influence skills.

What Is the Difference between Leading and Managing?

Leading and managing are two interconnected but distinct concepts. Let's clarify their differences first. Broadly speaking:

- *Leaders* focus on influencing others. They inspire others, provide emotional support, and rally employees around a common goal. Leaders also play a key role in *creating* a vision and strategic plan for an organization.

- *Managers* typically perform functions associated with planning, organizing, directing, and controlling. Managers, in turn, are charged with *implementing* the vision and plan.

Table 14.1 summarizes the key characteristics of managers and leaders. We can draw several conclusions from this division of labor:[16]

1. **People are led. Tasks are managed.**
2. **Effective leadership requires managerial skills.** Leaders who don't know how to manage tasks can relate well with others but don't get much done.
3. **The most effective managers develop leadership skills.** Managers who don't possess leadership skills can get things done themselves but have difficulty multiplying their effectiveness by getting things done through others.

TABLE 14.1 Characteristics of Managers and Leaders

BEING A MANAGER MEANS . . .	BEING A LEADER MEANS . . .
Planning, organizing, directing, controlling.	Being visionary.
Executing plans and delivering goods and services.	Being inspiring, setting the tone, and articulating the vision.
Managing resources.	Managing people.
Being conscientious.	Being inspirational (charismatic).
Acting responsibly.	Acting decisively.
Putting customers first—responding to and acting for customers.	Putting people first—responding to and acting for followers.
Mistakes can happen when managers don't appreciate people are the key resource, underlead by treating people like other resources, or fail to be held accountable.	Mistakes can happen when leaders choose the wrong goal, direction, or inspiration; overload; or fail to implement the vision.
Coping with complexity—complex organizations are chaotic without good management.	Coping with change—organizations need leadership to direct the constant change necessary for survival in today's dynamic business landscape.

Sources: Adapted from the following sources: Jaiswal, S. "What Is the Difference between Leader and Manager." Emeritus. March 30, 2022. https://emeritus.org/in/learn/what-is-the-difference-between-leader-and-manager/; Gavin, M. "Leadership vs. Management: What's the Difference?" Harvard Business School Online. October 31, 2019. https://online.hbs.edu/blog/post/leadership-vs-management; Kotter J. P. "What Leaders Really Do." Harvard Business Review. December 2001. 85–96; Kotter, J. P. "The Role of Leadership within Organizational Change Is Discussed." In Leading Change. Boston: Harvard Business School Press, 1996; Sargut G. and R. G. McGrath. "Managing in The World of Complexity Is Discussed." In Learning to Live with Complexity, 68–76. Harvard Business Review, September 2011; Mauboussin, M. J. "Embracing Complexity." Harvard Business Review. September 2011. 88–92.

4. **The right mix of leading and managing depends on the situation.** Some situations call for more leading than managing whereas others call for more managing than leading. We'll talk about that more in the behavioral (Section 14.3) and situational approaches (Section 14.4) to leadership.

Do you want to lead others or understand what makes a leader tick? Then take Self-Assessment 14.1 if your instructor has assigned it to you in Connect. It provides feedback on your readiness to assume a leadership role and can help you consider how to prepare for a formal leadership position.

SELF-ASSESSMENT 14.1   CAREER READINESS

Assessing Your Readiness to Assume the Leadership Role

This survey was designed to assess your readiness to assume the leadership role. Please complete Self-Assessment 14.1 if your instructor has assigned it in Connect.

Managerial Leadership: Can You Be *Both* a Manager and a Leader?

Absolutely. The latest thinking is that individuals are able to exhibit a broad array of the contrasting behaviors shown in Table 14.1 (a concept called *paradoxical leadership*).[17] Thus, in the workplace, many people are capable of engaging in **managerial leadership**, which

The villain/superhero dichotomy often depicted in pop culture is one way to think about power. Both villains and superheroes are characterized as having extraordinary ability to influence others (hence the word, *superpower*). Villains use this power to further their own selfish causes (personalized power), often harming others in the process. Superheroes use this power to further the greater good (socialized power), improving the world as they go. How will you use your power? yarruta/123RF

involves both influencing followers to internalize and commit to a set of shared goals, and facilitating the group and individual work that is needed to accomplish those goals.[18] Here, the "influencing" part is leadership and the "facilitating" part is management.

Managerial leadership may be demonstrated not only by managers appointed to their positions, but also by those who exercise leadership on a daily basis but don't carry formal management titles (such as certain co-workers on a team).

Six Sources of Power

Power is the ability to marshal human, informational, and other resources to get something done. Defined this way, power is all about influencing others. The more influence you have, the more powerful you are, and vice versa.

To really understand leadership, we need to understand the concept of power and authority. *Authority* is the right to perform or command; it comes with the job. In contrast, *power* is the extent to which a person is able to influence others so they respond to requests.

People who pursue **personalized power**—power directed at helping oneself—as a way of enhancing their own selfish ends may give the word power a bad name. However, there is another kind of power, **socialized power**—power directed at helping others. All three of your authors are high on socialized power.[19] We are motivated to write this textbook because our goal is to help you be the best you can be at work and in your personal life.

Within organizations there are typically six sources of power leaders may draw on: *legitimate, reward, coercive, expert, referent,* and *informational.*[20]

1. Legitimate Power: Influencing Behavior Because of One's Formal Position

Legitimate power, which all managers have, is power that results from managers' formal positions within the organization. All managers have legitimate power over their employees, deriving from their position, whether it's a construction boss, ad account supervisor, sales manager, or CEO. This power may be exerted both positively or negatively—as praise or as criticism, for example.

Legitimate Power Example—Police Department: All managers possess legitimate authority, but in organizations that have more rigid hierarchical structures, this authority is easier to observe. Police departments tend to have clearly defined lines of authority indicating exactly which positions have authority over other positions.

2. Reward Power: Influencing Behavior by Promising or Giving Rewards

Reward power, which all managers have, is power that results from managers' authority to reward their subordinates. Rewards can range from praise to pay raises, from recognition to promotions.

Reward Power Example—Tallgrass Freight Company: Tallgrass Freight brokerage company rewards its tops sales employees and a friend or significant other with a trip to Las Vegas for its Club 200 celebration. To be awarded, employees must generate at least $200,000 in gross profits in a calendar year. The trip concludes with a luxurious gourmet dinner at the top of the Stratosphere, featuring one of the best views of the city 800 feet above the Las Vegas Strip.[21]

3. Coercive Power: Influencing Behavior by Threatening or Giving Punishment

Coercive power, which all managers have, results from managers' authority to punish their subordinates. Punishment can range from verbal or written reprimands to demotions to terminations. In some lines of work, fines and suspensions may be used. Boards of directors also have this type of power—they can fire the company's CEO with a vote. Coercive power has to be used judiciously, of course, since a manager who is seen as being constantly negative will produce a lot of resentment among employees.

Coercive Power Example—CVS Health: Following an internal sexual harassment investigation, CVS Health CEO, Karen Lynch, fired an employee in field management

4. Expert Power: Influencing Behavior Because of One's Expertise

Expert power is power resulting from one's specialized information or expertise. Expertise, or special knowledge, can be mundane, such as knowing the work schedules and assignments of the people who report to you. Or it can be sophisticated, such as having computer or medical knowledge. Administrative assistants may have expert power because, for example, they have been in a job a long time and know all the necessary contacts. CEOs may have expert power because they have knowledge not shared with many others.

> **Expert Power Example—Warren Buffett:** Known as the "oracle of Omaha," Warren Buffett is renowned for his legendary business and investing insight. He is the chair and CEO of Berkshire Hathaway. Between 1965 and 2021, the company's market value has grown over 3.6 million percent! Buffett's wisdom is so coveted, an anonymous bidder paid a record $19 million to have a private lunch with him at a steakhouse in New York City. As was Buffett's custom for 20 years, the proceeds were donated to charity that provides food, health care, and legal aid to people who are homeless.[23]

Warren Buffett is one of the most widely respected businessmen in the United States due to his highly successful, time-tested investment principles. He holds an extraordinary amount of expert power with those looking for advice on investing in uncertain market conditions such as inflation, recession, and geopolitical conflicts. Krista Kennell/Shutterstock

5. Referent Power: Influencing Behavior Because of One's Personal Attraction

Referent power is power derived from one's personal attraction. As we will see later in this chapter (under the discussion of transformational leadership in Section 14.5), this kind of power is characteristic of strong, visionary leaders who are able to persuade their followers through their charisma. Referent power may be associated with managers, but it is more likely to be characteristic of leaders.

> **Referent Power Example—Dwayne "The Rock" Johnson:** Ranked among the top three U.S. Instagram Influencers in 2023 with 375 million followers, Dwayne Johnson dazzles crowds with his energy, enthusiasm, and electric smile. He gained notoriety as a WWE wrestler (ring name was The Rock) before becoming an A-list Hollywood celebrity and entrepreneur. He uses his referent power with his millions of social media followers to build his business empire, which consists of a growing list of business ventures, such as Seven Bucks Productions, Teremana Tequila, the XFL, and micro investing platform Acorns.[24]

6. Informational Power: Influencing Behavior Because of the Logical and/or Valuable Information One Communicates

Informational power is power deriving from one's access to information. Although not included as a separate source of power in the original research on power bases in organizations, later research added informational power to the typology.[25] People who are "in the know" in organizations may be seen as having informational power. Nurses are great examples.

> **Informational Power Example—Hospitals:** Those with the most prestigious titles and degrees don't necessarily hold the most power in an organization. It may appear that hospital executives and doctors hold the most power in hospitals, but they will tell you the nurses are key to the hospital's success. They are the heart of the hospital. The unique information nurses gather directly from patients, their ability to facilitate the open flow of information across functions (doctors, physical therapists, nutritionists, etc.), and their connectedness to multiple stakeholders throughout the organization enable them to improve patients' safety and provide continuity in their care.[26]

Now that you've learned about the six bases of power, complete Self-Assessment 14.2 if your instructor has assigned it to you in Connect to identify which bases you prefer to use. Answering the associated questions will help you understand how the various forms of power can both help and hurt you when trying to influence others.

SELF-ASSESSMENT 14.2   CAREER READINESS

What Kind of Power Do I Prefer?

You will learn which bases of power you prefer to use. Please complete Self-Assessment 14.2 if your instructor has assigned it in Connect.

Common Influence Tactics

An author for *Harvard Business Review* recently posed two questions: "Why are self-confident blowhards so often believed? Why are experts so often ignored?"[27] The answer, according to numerous experts, lies in the ability to use specific tactics in order to influence others.[28] **Influence tactics** are conscious efforts to affect what someone thinks or how they behave. Behavior is a function of what we think. As such, influence often starts with affecting someone's beliefs. Influence tactics can be used for good (e.g., persuading co-workers to pitch in their time for a community volunteer effort) or for bad (e.g., pressuring a subordinate into keeping a boss's unethical behavior a secret).

We previously defined leadership as "the ability to influence employees to voluntarily pursue organizational goals." This definition reinforces the importance of developing good influence skills and clarifies why employers see this as a key career readiness competency. The nine most common ways people try to get their bosses, co-workers, and subordinates to do what they want are listed in Table 14.2, beginning with the most frequently used.

TABLE 14.2   Nine Common Influence Tactics

INFLUENCE TACTIC	DESCRIPTION	EXAMPLE
1. Rational persuasion	Trying to convince someone with reason, logic, or facts	As CEO of ACORD, Bill Pieroni helps insurance and financial services companies to make strategic choices and outperform competitors. He encourages firms to use data-driven decision making to develop the most successful marketing campaigns, saying data-driven cultures "enable insurers to not only survive but, more importantly, thrive in the midst of accelerating change."[29]
2. Inspirational appeals	Trying to build enthusiasm by appealing to others' emotions, ideals, or values	Dr. Lisa Su became the first female CEO of a major semiconductor company when she accepted the position at Advanced Micro Devices (AMD). She inspires others to dream big, take risks, and continuously innovate as evidenced by the following notable quotes: "The biggest risk is not taking any risk" and "the world is starving for new ideas and great leaders who will champion those ideas."[30]
3. Consultation	Getting others to participate in planning, decision making, and changes	Former Best Buy CEO Hubert Joly credited the declining consumer electronics' retailer's turnaround to unleashing "human magic." It involves empowering employees to make the most sensible customer service decisions. The company shifted its definition of SOP from "standard operating procedures" to "service over policy." Best Buy employees were encouraged to find a need and fill it, or "If you see something, do something."[31]
4. Ingratiation	Getting someone in a good mood prior to making a request	Boeing has shaped federal aviation policy and earned lucrative government aerospace defense contracts in part due to its lobbying efforts. It ranks 10th in federal lobbying over the past 25 years, spending over $288 million. The company spent $13.2 million in 2022 alone to curry favor with legislators and government regulators. Of its 107 lobbyists, 71% previously held government positions.[32]
5. Personal appeals	Referring to friendship and loyalty when making a request or asking a friend to do a favor	Mallun Yen, founder of Operator Collective and former Cisco VP, recommends calling on your network of close relationships to succeed at work. She suggests motivating others to help you by first helping them. Ask a friend, "tell me two specific things I can do to help you" and follow through on your commitment.[33]

TABLE 14.2 *Continued*

INFLUENCE TACTIC	DESCRIPTION	EXAMPLE
6. Exchange	Making explicit or implied promises and trading favors	This type of exchange is sometimes called a quid pro quo ("this for that"). Exchanges can be a useful tool for both parties to achieve their goals. For example, after the COVID-19 pandemic, organizations offered employees incentives like higher salaries, a four-day workweek, free food, or face-time with managers and executives to lure employees to return to the office. Even local governments are reconsidering their tax breaks for employers if their employees don't return to the office and support local restaurants and generate income and sales tax revenue.[34]
7. Coalition tactics	Getting others to support your efforts to persuade someone	Coalitions can be negative or positive. Coalitions can be used as a coercive tool in which employees build support to shut down others' ideas or opinions. Coalitions can also be a constructive tool. For example, many organizations partner with celebrities to build successful marketing campaigns. In the closing moments of the musical *Hamilton*, Elizabeth Schuyler Hamilton sings that she is proudest of her role in founding the first private orphanage in New York City. That same charity—called Graham Windham—is still in operation and serves 1,000 children each year. The organization credited the cast's ongoing support with reinvigorating interest in and donations toward its services.[35]
8. Pressure	Demanding compliance or using intimidation or threats	Following the EU, Canada, and the United Kingdom in a push toward accelerating the adoption of zero emissions electric vehicles, the U.S. Environmental Protection Agency (EPA) issued new federal emissions standards that would mandate two out of three new cars sold in 2032 be all-electric vehicles. Only 5.8% of vehicles sold in 2022 were fully electric. Auto manufacturers would be required to pay an excess emissions premium for noncompliance.[36]
9. Legitimating tactics	Basing a request on authority or right, organizational rules or policies, or explicit/implied support from superiors	"Do it because I said so!" Sports coaches, managers, teachers, and parents all rely at times on their position-based authority and decision-making control to influence how others learn, interact, and behave. Legitimating tactics clarify members' roles and speed up decision making, but being told what to do and how to do it does not build members' respect for the decision maker.[37]

Sources: Descriptions of these influence tactics are based on Lee S., S. Han, M. Cheong, S.L. Kim, and S. Yun. "How Do I Get My Way? A Meta-Analytic Review of Research on Influence Tactics." *The Leadership Quarterly 28*, (2017): 210–228; Table 1 G. Yukl, C.M. Falbe, and J.Y. Youn, "Patterns of Influence Behavior for Managers," *Group & Organization Management*, March 1993, pp. 5–28.

Which Influence Tactics Do You Prefer? When you read the list of tactics, each one probably meant something to you. Which do you most commonly use? Knowing the answer can help you better choose the appropriate tactic for any given situation and thus increase the chance of achieving your desired outcome. You can enhance your self-awareness about the career readiness competency of leadership by completing Self-Assessment 14.3 if your instructor has assigned it to you in Connect.

SELF-ASSESSMENT 14.3 CAREER READINESS

Which Influence Tactics Do I Use?

You will learn which of the nine influence tactics you use and in what order of frequency. Please complete Self-Assessment 14.3 if your instructor has assigned it in Connect.

Outcomes of Influence Tactics

The ultimate goal of an influence tactic is to change others' behaviors. The essential question managers need to consider is *why* employees change their behavior if they do at all. Research documents three reactions to influence attempts:[38]

- **Commitment.** Employees are committed when they agree with a person's request and put their full energy behind supporting and implementing it. Committed employees change their behavior because they *want to*. A meta-analysis of 8,987 employees across 49 studies reveals the first three influence tactics in Table 14.2—rational persuasion, inspirational appeals, and consultation—were most effective at building commitment.[39]

- **Compliance.** Employees comply with an influence attempt by going along with the request despite having mixed feelings about it. Compliance results in employees putting forth minimal or average effort toward the requested action. Compliant employees change their behavior because they feel *obligated to*. Compliance works well for simple and routine tasks like wearing safety equipment or buckling your seatbelt. It is less effective for complex tasks that require sustained motivation. The danger with compliance is that it produces short-term results that fizzle out over the long term. The middle three influence tactics in Table 14.2—ingratiation, personal appeals, and exchange—tend to result in compliance.[40]

- **Resistance.** Employees resist an influence attempt by opposing or obstructing the request. Resistance results in employees passively or actively opposing the requested action by procrastinating, arguing, or outright refusing. This outcome results in an unsuccessful influence attempt. The last three influence tactics in Table 14.2—coalition (used as a coercive tool), pressure, and legitimating—are usually met with employees' resistance.[41]

You'll need to understand *and* effectively apply a range of influence tactics to be effective. But you can learn and improve influence tactics to move resisters to compliance and move those who are compliant to commitment. ●

14.2 Trait Approaches: Do Leaders Have Distinctive Traits and Personal Characteristics?

THE BIG PICTURE

Trait approaches attempt to identify distinctive characteristics that account for the effectiveness of leaders. We describe (1) positive task-oriented traits and positive/negative interpersonal attributes (narcissism, Machiavellianism, psychopathy) and (2) some results of gender studies.

LO 14-2

Identify traits and characteristics of successful leaders.

Mary Barra, the first female CEO of one of the Big Three automakers in the United States, began her tenure at General Motors (GM) in 1980 as a co-op student who graduated with a degree in electrical engineering. Thirty-four years and many roles later, Barra was appointed GM's CEO and eventually elected Chair of the GM Board of Directors. Her mission is to propel GM to market leadership in redesigning customers' "personal mobility through advanced technologies like connectivity, electrification and autonomous driving."[42]

Barra embodies the traits of (1) dominance, (2) intelligence, (3) self-confidence, (4) high energy, and (5) task-relevant knowledge. These are the five traits that researcher Ralph Stogdill in 1948 concluded were typical of successful leaders.[43] Stogdill is one of many contributors to **trait approaches to leadership**, which attempt to identify distinctive characteristics that account for leaders' effectiveness.[44]

Positive Task-Oriented Traits and Positive/Negative Interpersonal Attributes

Traits play a central role in how we perceive leaders, and they ultimately affect leadership effectiveness.[45] This is why researchers have attempted to identify a more complete list of traits that differentiate leaders from followers. Table 14.3 shows an expanded list of both positive *and* negative interpersonal attributes often found in leaders.[46] Notice the inclusion of the Big Five traits we discussed in Chapter 11 as positive attributes.

We have discussed the most positive interpersonal attributes elsewhere, but we need to describe the negative, or "dark side," traits of some leaders. Known collectively as the "dark triad," these traits are narcissism, Machiavellianism, and psychopathy.[47] Leaders who display these negative traits have a strong negative impact on employees' job satisfaction, well-being, and mental health.[48]

GM CEO Mary Barra displays positive traits that researchers commonly associate with highly successful leaders. Kimberly P. Mitchell/Detroit Free Press/TNS/Alamy Stock Photo

- **Narcissism.** Narcissism is defined as "a self-centered perspective, feelings of superiority, and a drive for personal power and glory."[49] Narcissists have inflated views of themselves, seek to attract the admiration of others, and fantasize about being in control of everything. Although passionate and charismatic, narcissistic leaders may provoke counterproductive work behaviors in others, such as strong resentment and resistance.[50] They also tend to react with anger and counterproductive work behaviors in response to ethical norms because they infringe on narcissists' preference for self-centered and risky behavior.[51]

- **Machiavellianism.** Inspired by the pessimistic beliefs of Niccolò Machiavelli, a philosopher and writer (*The Prince*) in the Italian Renaissance, Machiavellianism (pronounced "mah-kyah-*vel*-yahn-izm") displays a cynical view of human nature and condones opportunistic and unethical ways of manipulating people, putting results over principles. This view is manifested in such expressions as "All people lie to get what they want" and "You have to cheat to get ahead." Like narcissism, Machiavellianism is also associated with counterproductive work behaviors, especially as people begin to understand that they are being coldly manipulated.[52]

TABLE 14.3 Key Task-Oriented Traits and Interpersonal Attributes

POSITIVE TASK-ORIENTED TRAITS	POSITIVE INTERPERSONAL ATTRIBUTES	NEGATIVE INTERPERSONAL ATTRIBUTES
• Intelligence	• Extraversion	• Narcissism
• Conscientiousness	• Agreeableness	• Machiavellianism
• Open to experience	• Emotional intelligence	• Psychopathy
• Emotional stability	• Collectivism	
• Positive affect	• Trait empathy	
• Proactive personality	• Moral identity	

- **Psychopathy.** Psychopathy ("sigh-*kop*-a-thee") is characterized by lack of concern for others, impulsive behavior, and a lack of remorse when the psychopath's actions harm others. Not surprisingly, a person with a psychopathic personality can be a truly toxic influence in the workplace.[53]

If you have a propensity for any of these, you need to know that the expression of "dark side" traits tends to result in career derailment—being demoted or fired.[54]

What Do We Know about Gender and Leadership?

The increase in the number of women in the workforce has generated much interest in understanding the similarities and differences between female and male leaders.

Are Women Represented in Leadership Positions?

Women make up more than half the workforce and more than half of all college students in the United States but have not achieved gender parity in leadership.[55] Women are making gains at the top but are still underrepresented. For example, there were only 53 women CEOs leading Fortune 500 companies in 2023, the first time over 10% of Fortune 500 companies were led by women.[56] Maria Black is one example:

Fortune 500 Women CEO Example—Maria Black: A global leader in payroll processing and human capital management, Automatic Data Processing (ADP) announced Maria Black would succeed Carlos Rodriguez as the company's CEO. Black rose through the ranks at ADP over her 29-year tenure, starting as a sales associate and then leading sales, marketing, and business operations first in strategic business units followed by the entire enterprise. Outgoing CEO Rodriguez expressed his confidence in his successor, noting Maria "has learned our business truly from the ground up, which gives her a powerful perspective and understanding of ADP's products, innovation strategy, and growth opportunities." She has a passion for creating "a better, more personalized world at work" and supporting women in leadership.[57]

Do Men and Women Vary in Terms of Leadership?

Researchers have studied gender and leadership in terms of whether women and men are equally likely to emerge as leaders, whether they engage in different leader behaviors or use different styles of leadership, and whether they vary in terms of their effectiveness as leaders.[58] In general, results suggest gender doesn't make much of a difference in a leader's effectiveness. In other words, there is no reason to believe that the gender imbalance present in corporate leadership roles stems from one gender being "better" at leadership than another. Here is a summary of what we know.

- **Leader emergence:**
  - A meta-analysis of 136 studies and 19,073 participants spanning seven decades revealed men were moderately more likely to emerge as leaders in organizations than women. The gender difference in leadership emergence has been cut in half in recent years.[59]
  - The gender gap has closed in occupations such as health care, teaching, and service professions where women are equally likely as men (and sometimes more likely) to emerge as leaders.[60]
  - One factor that perpetuates the gender gap, according to a meta-analysis of 174 studies, is that men generally have higher leadership aspirations than women.[61] This is because women who internalize traditional gender roles are less inclined to seek leadership positions, especially in male-dominated industries.
- **Leader behavior:**
  - A meta-analysis of 54 different studies found that female leaders were more likely to use transformational leadership behaviors than male leaders.[62] We discuss these behaviors in Section 14.5.

- A meta-analysis of 112 different studies of abusive supervision (a type of destructive leadership discussed later in the chapter) found that male leaders were more likely to exhibit abusive behaviors than female leaders.[63]

- **Leader style:**
    - Women were more likely to use a democratic or participative style than men, and men were more likely to use an autocratic and directive style. These differences may be attributable to women expressing more communal traits such as warmth, concern for others, and interpersonal sensitivity whereas men tend to express agentic traits such as ambition, dominance, and assertiveness.[64]

- **Leader effectiveness:**
    - Women and men are similarly effective as leaders.[65]
    - When there are more men than women in the organization and when the setting is more masculine, men tend to be rated slightly higher than women on leadership effectiveness.
    - Women are more likely than men to be appointed to leadership positions in times of crisis.[66]
    - It's not clear whether or how leader gender impacts firm performance. Research results on top management team (TMT) gender diversity and firm performance are mixed. A recent academic meta-analysis of 146 studies from 33 different countries found that "there are small but dependably positive associations of female representation in CEO positions and TMTs with long-term value creation."[67] Additional research suggests gender diversity on boards of directors can improve firm performance if it's accompanied by professional diversity as well as a culture that encourages members to benefit from board members' diverse perspectives.[68]

Does gender influence leader effectiveness? Research suggests it doesn't. Women and men are similarly effective as leaders. Rawpixel.com/Shutterstock

Where Are We Now? Women's representation in leadership positions is improving and the gender gap is closing. But more work remains to continue closing the gap, especially at the executive ranks. Two tailwinds that promise to facilitate women's continued leadership emergence are:

1. **Changing gender stereotypes.** A meta-analysis of 16 U.S. public opinion polls ranging from 1946 to 2018 shows that women have widened their advantage over men in communal, or socially supportive, traits but men's advantage in agentic, or control-oriented, traits has remained the same. Women have also closed the gap to achieve equality with men in perceived intelligence and creativity. These trends convey a progression of more favorable attitudes toward

women that translate into a growing female advantage in gender stereotypes and more leadership opportunities in the workplace.[69]

2. **More equitable organizational support for leadership development.** Organizations are increasing the leadership pipeline for everyone by implementing more mentoring, leadership development, peer coaching, advisory circles, and other programs.[70] These supportive HR practices not only improve a company's diversity, equity, and inclusion, they develop human capital from all areas of the organization by giving them equal opportunities and experiences to develop leadership-relevant skills.[71]

Are Knowledge and Skills Important?

Knowledge and skills are extremely important! Researchers have identified four basic skills leaders need (see Table 14.4).

So What Do We Know about Leadership Traits?

Trait theory offers us four conclusions.

1. **We cannot ignore the implications of leadership traits.** Traits play a central role in the way we perceive leaders, and they do ultimately affect leadership effectiveness.[78] For instance, integrity, self-awareness, gratitude, and learning agility were among the top leadership traits according to the Center for Creative Leadership, along with empathy, courage, and respect.[79] More specifically, many companies attempt to define leadership traits important for their context.

TABLE 14.4 Four Basic Skills for Leaders

WHAT LEADERS NEED	AND WHY
Cognitive abilities to identify problems and their causes in rapidly changing situations	Leaders must sometimes devise effective solutions in short time spans with limited information, and this requires strong cognitive abilities. Google CEO Sundar Pichai's former professors remember him as a "shy, quiet, but extremely intelligent" student.[72] Pichai earned a master's in engineering from Stanford and an MBA from the University of Pennsylvania's Wharton School of Business.
Interpersonal skills to influence and persuade others	Leaders need to work well with diverse people. Zoom has become known for its company culture focused on happiness, and many have praised CEO Eric Yuan for his role in building and maintaining this positivity. Said one reporter, Yuan "is probably one of the most likeable people you will meet in the Valley. It is no surprise that Zoom's culture is so highly recognized these days."[73]
Business skills to maximize the use of organizational assets	Leaders increasingly need business skills as they advance up through an organization. One valuable but often-overlooked skill that most people can develop with a little effort is curiosity.[74] Former chair and CEO of IBM and the first woman to lead the technology company, Ginni Rometty credited her curiosity for her professional success. "Be curious…. A constant thirst to learn has served me well my entire career, especially in the tech industry," Rometty said.[75] Curiosity is the number one skill she aims to instill in employees and the most important characteristic she looks for in leaders.[76]
Conceptual skills to draft an organization's mission, vision, strategies, and implementation plans	Conceptual skills matter most for individuals in the top ranks in an organization. Entrepreneurs may have their conceptual skills tested on a regular basis. Now-billionaire CEO Sara Blakely's father regularly asked her, "What have you failed at this week?" After repeated setbacks, she eventually came up with the line of slimming intimate wear she called Spanx.[77]

Source: Adapted from T.V. Mumford, M.A. Campion, and F.P. Morgeson, "Leadership Skills Strataplex: Leadership Skill Requirements across Organizational Levels," Leadership Quarterly, 2007, pp. 154-166. Also see S. Tonidandel, K.M. Summerville, W.A. Gentry, and S.F. Young, "Using Structural Topic Modeling to Gain Insight into Challenges Faced by Leaders," The Leadership Quarterly, *Vol. 33 (2022), 101576.*

2. **The positive and "dark triad" traits suggest the qualities that are conducive and detrimental to success in leadership roles.** According to expert scholars, narcissistic leaders often have groundbreaking ideas but fail to execute them successfully. Such execution requires the collaboration of an entire team, and narcissists' need to control even small details can make followers miserable and unwilling to work together to achieve goals.[80] Personality tests and other trait assessments can help evaluate your strengths and weaknesses on these traits. Connect contains a host of tests you can take for this purpose.

3. **Organizations may want to include personality and trait assessments in their selection and evaluation processes.** Among the growing number of companies using psychometric testing—tests that assess a job applicant's intelligence, personality, and skills—are Citigroup, Deloitte, Ford Motor Company, Procter & Gamble, Hewlett-Packard (HP), and JPMorgan Chase.[81] Recall from our discussion in Chapter 9 that there are legitimate concerns about bias and accuracy associated with workplace personality testing. Organizations should stick with validated, job-related personality assessments and should use them for development purposes rather than employment decisions.[82]

4. **Cross-cultural competency is no longer a career readiness competency.** Companies want to enhance employees' global mindsets as they expand their international operations and hire more culturally diverse individuals for domestic operations in the United States.[83] A **global mindset** is your belief in your ability to influence dissimilar others in a global context.

14.3 Behavioral Approaches: Do Leaders Show Distinctive Patterns of Behavior?

THE BIG PICTURE
Behavioral leadership approaches try to determine unique behaviors displayed by effective leaders. These approaches can be divided into two categories: (1) task-oriented behavior and (2) relationship-oriented behavior.

A leader's traits, gender, and skills directly affect their choice of behavior. The focus of those interested in **behavioral leadership approaches** is to determine the key behaviors displayed by effective leaders. These approaches identified two categories of leader behavior:

- Task-oriented behavior.
- Relationship-oriented behavior.

LO 14-3
Identify behaviors of successful leaders.

Much of what we know about task-oriented and relationship-oriented leader behaviors is based on research done at The Ohio State University and University of Michigan. Both studies found that leader behaviors tend to focus on tasks and/or relationships:

	THE OHIO STATE UNIVERSITY	**UNIVERSITY OF MICHIGAN**
Task-oriented leader behavior	Initiating structure	Production-centered
Relationship-oriented leader behavior	Consideration	Employee-centered

Task-Oriented Leader Behaviors

The primary purpose of **task-oriented leadership behaviors** is to ensure that human, physical, and other resources are deployed efficiently and effectively to accomplish the group's or organization's goals.[84] Examples of task-oriented behaviors include planning, clarifying, monitoring, and problem solving. As mentioned earlier in this section, task-oriented leadership behaviors may be referred to as initiating-structure or production-centered behaviors.

The Focus of Task-Oriented Leadership: "Here's What We Do to Get the Job Done"

Initiating-structure leadership is leader behavior that organizes and defines—that is, "initiates the structure for"—what employees should be doing to maximize output. **Production-centered leader behaviors** emphasize the technical or task-related aspects of employees' roles. Clearly, these are very task-oriented approaches.

Task-Oriented Leadership Example—Bjørn Gulden: Sportswear manufacturer Adidas tapped former senior vice president, Bjørn Gulden, as CEO. Gulden brings his experience as CEO of jewelry brand Pandora and nine-year tenure as CEO of rival Puma along with executive leadership roles in other major retail companies. Gulden is using task-oriented leadership to rebuild the company's path to profitability. His three-part plan to return to profitability is to: (1) "reduce inventories and lower discounts," (2) "put our focus back on our core: product, consumers, retail partners, and athletes," and (3) "work on strengthening our people and the adidas culture."[85]

Task-oriented leader behaviors are positively related to leadership effectiveness, according to research.[86]

Relationship-Oriented Leader Behavior

Relationship-oriented leadership is primarily concerned with leaders' interactions with their people. The emphasis is on enhancing employees' skills and creating positive work relationships among co-workers and between the leader and the led. Such leaders often act as mentors, providing career advice, giving employees assignments that will broaden their skills, and empowering them to make their own decisions.[87] One of the simplest and best ways to engage relationship-oriented leadership is to ask open questions and listen attentively.[88]

The Focus of Relationship-Oriented Leadership: "The Concerns and Needs of My Employees Are Highly Important"

Consideration is leader behavior that is concerned with group members' needs and desires and directed at creating mutual respect or trust. **Employee-centered leader behaviors** emphasize relationships with subordinates and attention to their individual needs. These are important behaviors to use in addition to task leadership because they promote social interactions and identification with the team and leader.

Relationship-Oriented Leadership Example—Thasunda Brown Duckett: TIAA CEO Thasunda Brown Duckett believes in relationship-oriented leadership. In a recent speech, Duckett said "Empathy in leadership matters." Being empathetic, thinking about others, and maintaining relationships are key to a business's success and imperative for an individual's career success.[89]

Relationship-oriented leader behaviors are positively related to measures of leadership effectiveness, according to research.[90]

TIAA CEO Thasunda Brown Duckett believes leaders must possess not only high levels of task knowledge, but also the ability to empathize with customers, colleagues, and employees. To what degree do you value relationship-oriented behaviors? David Acosta/Image Press Agency/Sipa USA/Alamy Stock Photo

The most effective leaders use different blends of task-oriented and relationship-oriented behaviors when interacting with others. To what extent do you think you do this when interacting with school or work colleagues? You can answer this question by taking Self-Assessment 14.4 if your instructor has assigned it to you in Connect.

SELF-ASSESSMENT 14.4   CAREER READINESS

Assessing Your Task- and Relationship-Oriented Leader Behavior
This survey was designed to evaluate your own leader behavior. Please complete Self-Assessment 14.4 if your instructor has assigned it in Connect.

So What Do We Know about the Behavioral Approaches?

Two key conclusions we may take away from the behavioral approaches are the following:

1. **A leader's behavior is more important than their traits.** It is important to train managers on the various forms of task and relationship leadership.
2. **There is no type of leader behavior that is best suited for all situations.** Effective leaders learn how to match their behavior to the situation at hand.[91] We discuss how to do this in the next section.

14.4 Situational Approaches: Does Leadership Vary with the Situation?

THE BIG PICTURE
Effective leadership behavior depends on the situation, say believers in two contingency approaches: Fiedler's contingency leadership model and House's path–goal leadership model.

You learned in the previous section that that there is not one best style of leadership to use in every situation. This conclusion led proponents of the **situational approach** (or contingency approach) to propose that effective leadership behavior depends on the situation. That is, as situations change, different leader styles become more or less appropriate.

Let's consider two situational approaches: (1) Fiedler's *contingency leadership model* and (2) House's *path–goal leadership model*.

LO 14-4
Discuss situational leadership.

1. The Contingency Leadership Model: Fiedler's Approach

The oldest contingency leadership model was developed by Fred Fiedler and his associates beginning in 1954.[92] The **contingency leadership model** determines if a leader's style is (1) task-oriented or (2) relationship-oriented and whether that style is effective for the situation at hand.

Two Leadership Orientations: Tasks versus Relationships Fiedler's contingency model requires that leaders identify their leadership style.

- **There are two leadership styles in Fiedler's model:** The two leadership styles in Fiedler's contingency model are (1) task-oriented and (2) relationship-oriented.[93]

KEEP CALM AND REMEMBER: IT DEPENDS

At the heart of situational leadership is the phrase "It Depends." More specifically, this approach says the best style of leadership *depends* on the situation. What works in one situation doesn't necessarily work in another. KlaraDo/Shutterstock

Which do you think is your style? That is, as a leader, are you more concerned with task accomplishment or with people?

- **Your leadership style is determined by your LPC score:** To find out your leadership style, you would fill out a questionnaire (known as the least preferred co-worker, or LPC, scale) in which you think of the co-worker you least enjoyed working with and rate them according to an eight-point scale of 16 pairs of opposite characteristics (such as friendly/unfriendly, tense/relaxed, efficient/inefficient). The higher the score, the more the relationship-oriented the respondent; the lower the score, the more task-oriented.[94]

Three Dimensions of Situational Control Fiedler assumes leaders can't change their dominant leadership style. They are either task-oriented or relationship-oriented. This implies that leaders are most effective when their dominant leadership style matches their level of *situational control*—how much control and influence they have in their immediate work environment.

There are three dimensions of situational control: *leader-member relations, task structure,* and *position power.*

- **Leader-member relations—"Do my subordinates accept me as a leader?"** This dimension, the most important component of situational control, reflects the extent to which leaders have or don't have the support, loyalty, and trust of the work group.
- **Task structure—"Do my subordinates perform unambiguous, easily understood tasks?"** This dimension refers to the extent to which tasks are routine, unambiguous, and easily understood. The more structured the jobs, the more influence leaders have.
- **Position power—"Do I have power to reward and punish?"** This dimension refers to how much power leaders have to make work assignments and reward and punish. These forms of power reflect legitimate, reward, and coercive power defined in Section 14.1. More power equals more control and influence.

For each dimension, the amount of control can be *high,* in which case the leader's decisions will produce predictable results because they have the ability to influence work outcomes. Or it can be *low,* in which case the leader doesn't have that kind of predictability or influence. By combining the three different dimensions with different high/low ratings, we have eight different leadership situations. These are represented in Figure 14.1.

Which Style Is Most Effective? Neither task- nor relationship-oriented leadership are effective all the time, Fiedler's research concludes; rather, each style is better suited for certain situations.[95]

- **When is a task-oriented style best?** The task-oriented style works best in either *high-control* or *low-control* situations.

    High-control situation—leaders' decisions produce predictable results because they can influence work outcomes.

    Low-control situation—leaders' decisions can't produce predictable results because they can't really influence outcomes.
- **When is a relationship-oriented style best?** The relationship-oriented style works best in situations of *moderate control.*

What do you do if your leadership style does not match the situation? Move to a different situation. According to Fiedler's model, it's better to try to position leaders into suitable situations rather than try to alter their leadership styles to better fit the current situation.[96] Fiedler's assumption that people cannot change their basic leadership style

FIGURE 14.1 Representation of Fiedler's contingency model

Situational Control	High-Control Situations			Moderate-Control Situations				Low-Control Situations
Leader-member relations	Good	Good	Good	Good	Poor	Poor	Poor	Poor
Task structure	High	High	Low	Low	High	High	Low	Low
Position power	Strong	Weak	Strong	Weak	Strong	Weak	Strong	Weak
Situation	I	II	III	IV	V	VI	VII	VIII

| Optimal Leadership Style | Task-Oriented Leadership | Relationship-Oriented Leadership | Task-Oriented Leadership |

Source: Adapted from Fiedler, F. E. "Situational Control and a Dynamic Theory of Leadership." *In* Managerial Control and Organizational Democracy, *edited by B. King, S. Streufert, and F. E. Fiedler, 114. New York: John Wiley & amp; Sons, 1978.*

is not supported by research.[97] Nonetheless, it is the first leadership model to contend that leadership effectiveness depends on the situation.

2. The Path–Goal Leadership Model: House's Approach

A second situational approach, advanced by Robert House beginning in the 1970s, is the **path–goal leadership model,** which holds that effective leaders make available to followers desirable rewards in the workplace and increase their motivation by clarifying the paths, or behaviors, that will help them achieve those goals and providing them with support. A successful leader "clears the path" and helps followers by tying meaningful rewards to goal accomplishment, reducing barriers, and providing support. These behaviors increase employees' performance and satisfaction.[98]

Numerous studies testing various predictions from House's original path–goal theory provided mixed results.[99] As a consequence, he proposed a new model, a graphical version of which is shown in Figure 14.2. Originally, House proposed that there were four leader behaviors, or leadership styles. The revised theory expanded the number of leader behaviors from four to eight. We condensed these leader behaviors into two overarching categories: task-oriented and relationship-oriented leader behaviors.

What Determines Leadership Effectiveness: Employee Characteristics and Environmental Factors Affect Leader Behavior Two contingency factors, or variables—*employee characteristics* and *environmental factors*—cause some leadership behaviors to be more effective than others.

- **Employee characteristics:** Five employee characteristics are locus of control (described in Chapter 11), task ability, need for achievement, experience, and need for path–goal clarity.

- **Environmental factors:** Two environmental factors are task structure (independent versus interdependent tasks) and work group dynamics.

FIGURE 14.2

General representation of House's revised path–goal theory

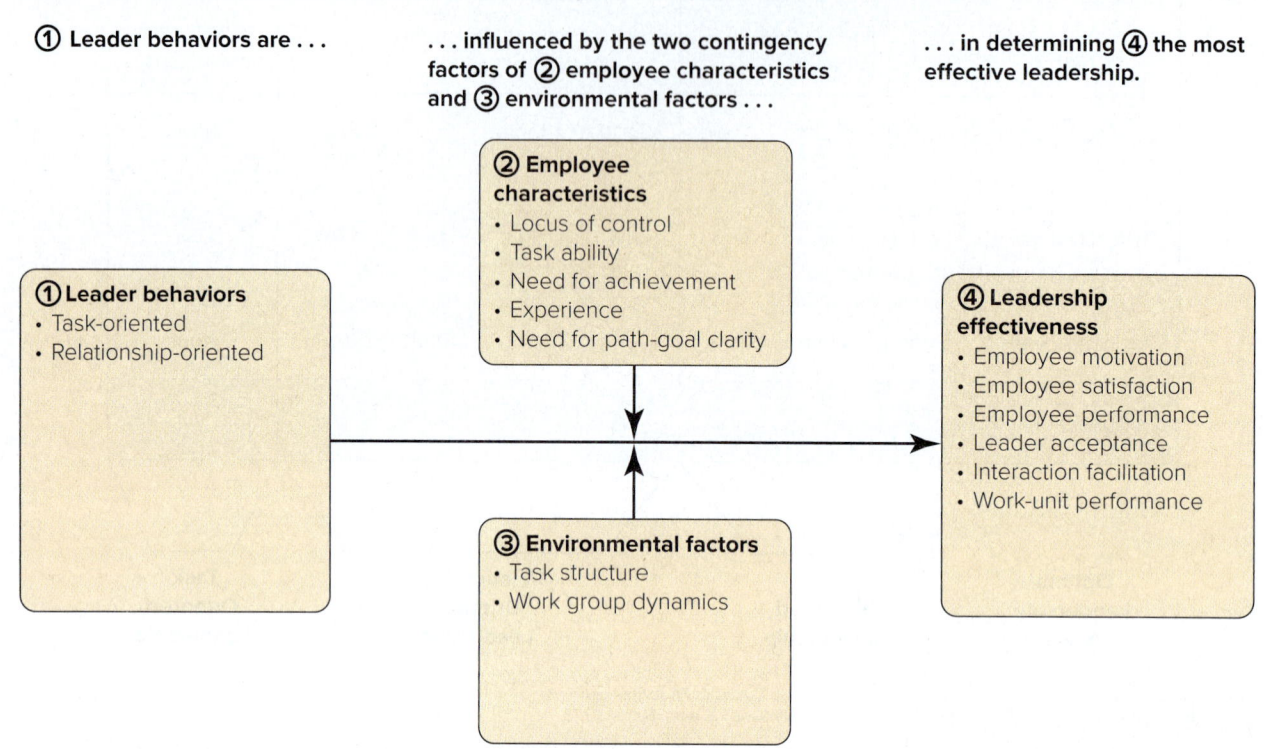

① Leader behaviors are . . .　　. . . influenced by the two contingency factors of ② employee characteristics and ③ environmental factors . . .　　. . . in determining ④ the most effective leadership.

① Leader behaviors
- Task-oriented
- Relationship-oriented

② Employee characteristics
- Locus of control
- Task ability
- Need for achievement
- Experience
- Need for path-goal clarity

③ Environmental factors
- Task structure
- Work group dynamics

④ Leadership effectiveness
- Employee motivation
- Employee satisfaction
- Employee performance
- Leader acceptance
- Interaction facilitation
- Work-unit performance

Salesforce CEO Marc Benioff adapts his leadership style to the situation, exhibiting consideration during the COVID-19 pandemic but initiating structure when the company faced severe economic headwinds. Lev Radin/Shutterstock

The model proposes that leaders are most effective when they complement the environment by providing what employees need that the environment does not provide. According to House, "the role of the leader is to provide the necessary incremental information, support, and resources, over and above those provided by the formal organization or the subordinate's environment, to ensure both subordinate satisfaction and effective performance."[100]

What Does Path–Goal Look Like in Practice? In contrast to Fiedler's contingency model, House's path–goal model assumes that a leader's style is flexible. In other words, as a leader, you should figure out the style that will work best for your particular employees and environment, and then use that style. Here are two hypothetical examples:

- Employees with an internal locus of control are more likely to prefer relationship-oriented over task-oriented leader behaviors because they believe they have control over the work environment. The same is true for employees with high task ability and experience.

- Employees with an external locus of control, however, tend to view the environment as uncontrollable, so they prefer the clarity, goals, and guidance provided by task-oriented leader behaviors. The same is probably true of inexperienced employees.

What does adapting one's leadership style to followers' needs and the environment look like in real-life? Consider the following example.

Path–Goal Leadership Example—Marc Benioff: During the onset of the COVID-19 pandemic and the mandatory lockdowns, widespread fear, and uncertainty that accompanied it in March 2020, CEO of Salesforce Marc Benioff posted on Twitter: "Salesforce is pledging to its workforce Ohana [a Hawaiian term meaning "family"] not to conduct any significant lay offs over the next 90 days. We will continue to pay our hourly workers while our offices are closed. We encourage our Ohana to pay their own personal hourly workers like housekeepers & dog walkers." Salesforce also donated medical masks to local hospitals and equipped healthcare teams with its technology for free during the public health crisis.[101] In January 2023, the pandemic subsided, replaced by economic headwinds such as high inflation and depressed consumer demand with a looming recession on the horizon. Benioff responded by laying off 7,000 employees, 10% of the company's workforce, over a two-hour virtual meeting. Benioff attributed the workforce reduction to overextending the company's resources to pursue growth during a temporary COVID-19–related surge in demand. The layoffs were accompanied by other efforts to reduce costs such as consolidating office space and shedding real estate holdings.[102]

So What Do We Know about the Situational Approaches?

There have not been enough direct tests of House's revised path–goal theory using appropriate research methods and statistical procedures to draw overall conclusions.[103] Research on transformational leadership, however, which is discussed in Section 14.5, is supportive of the revised model.[104]

Applying situational leadership theory is not easy. In any leadership role, you will encounter many different situations, and there is no one best style for managing all of them. In addition, we all tend to rely on behaviors that have worked for us in the past even if the situation we face suggests we should change. We justify our actions by reasoning that we are doing what we are good at, but in fact we are vulnerable to our own biases about what we think works and what doesn't.

Although further research is needed on the new model, we can offer several important implications for managers:[105]

- **Use more than one leadership style.** Effective leaders possess and use more than one style of leadership. Thus, you are encouraged to study the leadership styles offered in the next two sections so you can try new leader behaviors when a situation calls for them.

- **Help employees achieve their goals.** Leaders should guide and coach employees in achieving their goals by clarifying the path and removing obstacles to accomplishing them. Research shows effective coaching increases employees' performance.[106]

- **Alter your leadership behavior for each situation.** A small set of employee characteristics (ability, experience, and need for independence) and environmental factors (task characteristics of autonomy, variety, and significance) are relevant contingency factors, and managers should modify their leadership style to fit them. The career readiness competencies of emotional and social intelligence are helpful tools for doing so.

- **Provide what people and teams need to succeed.** View your role as providing others with whatever they need to achieve their goals. For some it could be encouragement, and for others it could be direction and coaching. Research shows leaders who were culture contributors, providing employees what the organization's culture did not, increased firm performance whereas culture conformists did not.[107]

> **PRACTICAL ACTION** | **Applying Situational Theories**
>
> How can you make situational theories work for you? Managers can use the following general strategy across a variety of situations. It has five steps.[108] We explain how to implement the steps by using the examples of a head coach of a sports team and a sales manager.
>
> - **Step 1: Identify important outcomes.** Managers must first identify the goals they want to achieve. For example, the head coach may have a goal of winning a certain number of games or avoiding injuries to key players, whereas a sales manager's goal might be to increase sales by 10% or reduce customers' complaints by half.
> - **Step 2: Identify relevant leadership behaviors.** Next managers need to identify the specific types of behaviors that may be appropriate for the situation at hand (Sections 14.5 and 14.6 elaborate on a number of leadership styles). For now, let's focus on task-oriented and relationship-oriented behaviors. A head coach in a championship game, for instance, might focus on directive, task-oriented behaviors. In contrast, a sales manager might find supportive, relationship-oriented behaviors more relevant for an experienced sales team. Don't try to use all available leadership behaviors you'll learn about in the coming sections. Rather, select the combination that appear most helpful for a particular situation. Ask yourself, "What do my employees need from me right now?"
> - **Step 3: Identify situational conditions.** Fiedler and House both identify a set of potential contingency factors to consider, but there may be other practical considerations. For example, a star quarterback on a football team may be injured. This might require the team to adopt a different strategy for winning the game. Similarly, the need to manage a virtual sales team with members from around the world will affect the types of leadership most effective in this context.
> - **Step 4: Match leadership to the conditions at hand.** There are too many possible situational conditions for us to provide specific advice. This means you should use your knowledge about management and employee behavior to find the best match between your leadership styles and behaviors and the situation at hand. The coach whose star quarterback is injured might use supportive behaviors and inspirational motivation to instill confidence that the team can win with a different quarterback. Our sales manager might find it useful to use empowering leadership and avoid directive leadership.
> - **Step 5: Decide how to make the match.** Managers can use guidelines from either contingency theory or path–goal theory: change the person in the leadership role or change their behavior. It is not possible to change the head coach in a championship game. This means the head coach needs to change their style or behavior to meet the specific challenge. In contrast, the organization employing the sales manager might move them to another position because the individual is too directive and does not like to empower others. Or the sales manager could change their behavior, if possible.

14.5 The Full-Range Model: Using Transactional and Transformational Leadership

THE BIG PICTURE

The full-range model of leadership describes leadership along a range of behaviors, with the most effective being transactional and transformational. Transformational leadership impacts followers in four important ways.

LO 14-5

Describe transactional and transformational leadership.

We have considered the major traditional approaches to understanding leadership—the trait, behavioral, and situational approaches. But newer approaches offer something more by trying to determine what factors inspire and motivate people to perform beyond their normal levels.

One approach proposed by Bernard Bass and Bruce Avolio, known as **full-range leadership**, suggests that leadership behavior varies along a full range of leadership styles, from passive (laissez-faire) "leadership" at one extreme, through transactional leadership, to transformational leadership at the other extreme.[109] Passive leadership is not leadership, but transactional and transformational leadership behaviors are both necessary and positive aspects of being a good leader.[110]

Transactional and Transformational Leadership

Transactional Leadership As a manager, your reward and coercive power stems from your ability to provide incentives (and threaten reprimands) in exchange for your subordinates doing the work. When you do this, you are performing **transactional leadership**, focusing on clarifying employees' roles and task requirements and providing rewards and punishments contingent on performance. Like task-oriented leadership, transactional leadership also encompasses setting goals and monitoring progress.[111] Melanie Perkins has used transactional leadership to propel Canva's growth.

> **Transactional Leadership Example—Melanie Perkins:** Melanie Perkins is the co-founder and CEO of the online graphic design platform Canva. According to Perkins, "Canva's key goal remains to empower everyone to design anything and publish anywhere." Perkins understands that transactional behaviors are a necessary foundation for effective leadership. Perkins set ambitious goals that over 100 venture capitalists did not believe she could achieve. Three years and 100 rejections later, Perkins acquired the first investment for Canva. Through diligent attention to monitoring progress to achieve the company's ambitious goals, Perkins has grown Canva to a $40 billion valuation, one of the most valuable companies in the world created and led by a woman.[112]

Canva CEO Melanie Perkins knows the value of transactional leadership—including setting clear goals and paying close attention to progress—in achieving an organization's bigger goals. Eóin Noonan/Sportsfile/Getty Images

Research consistently shows transactional leadership has a positive association with leader effectiveness, group performance, and individual performance, creativity, and innovation.[113]

Transformational Leadership **Transformational leadership** inspires employees to pursue organizational goals over self-interests. Transformational leaders, in one description, "engender trust, seek to develop leadership in others, exhibit self-sacrifice, and serve as moral agents, focusing themselves and followers on objectives that transcend the more immediate needs of the work group."[114] Whereas transactional leadership gets people to do *necessary* things, transformational leadership engenders *exceptional* things—significantly higher levels of intrinsic motivation, trust, commitment, and loyalty—that can produce significant organizational change and results.[115] Richard Branson is a good example of a transformational leader.

> **Transformational Leader Example—Richard Branson:** Serial entrepreneur Richard Branson has a bold vision to lead transformational change through the Virgin Group, an umbrella company that controls more than 400 companies. Branson believes "through the right people focusing on the right things, we can, in time, get on top of a lot if not most of the problems of this world. And that's what a number of us are trying to do." He credits his audacity—the belief that you can make the impossible possible—to achieving exceptional results.[116]

Transformational leadership is influenced by two factors:

1. **Individual characteristics:** Transformational leaders' personalities tend to be more extroverted, agreeable, proactive, and open to change than non-transformational leaders. Gender also plays a role as female leaders tend to use transformational leadership more than male leaders. This female leadership

advantage is driven primarily by females' tendency to exhibit higher emotional intelligence and engage in socially supportive and sympathetic interactions with others than males.[117]

2. **Organizational culture:** Adaptive, flexible organizational cultures are more likely than rigid, bureaucratic cultures to foster transformational leadership.[118]

The Best Leaders Are Both Transactional and Transformational

It's important to note that transactional leadership is an essential *prerequisite* to effective leadership, and the best leaders learn to display both transactional and transformational styles of leadership to some degree. Indeed, research suggests that transformational leadership leads to superior performance when it "augments," or adds to, transactional leadership.[119] See the Example box to learn about a leader who exhibits both transactional and transformational leadership.

EXAMPLE | **The Superior Performance of a Leader Who Is Both Transactional and Transformational: Home Depot's Ann-Marie Campbell**

Ann-Marie Campbell ranked number 27 on *Fortune*'s 2022 most powerful women list.[120] She began her career with Home Depot nearly 40 years ago as a cashier and now leads 2,300+ stores and 400,000+ employees as executive vice president of U.S. stores and international operations.[121] She has been instrumental in Home Depot's growth as annual sales rose 14% to surpass $150 billion in 2021.[122]

Let's look at how Campbell uses a mix of transactional and transformational leadership.

Transactional

Campbell's years of experience in a variety of roles at Home Depot—including store manager and regional vice president—give her unique insight into what it takes for employees and the company to be successful. She uses transactional leadership to maximize employee productivity and engagement and drive overall firm performance. For example, she went against industry norms and converted full-time store associates from variable work schedules to more desirable fixed schedules. She also led the company's $11 billion plan to improve both associates' and customers' experiences, focusing on initiatives including new order management software for workers and online pickup lockers in stores.[123]

On how she approaches getting employees to perform in their roles, she said, "People want to be successful, so it is important to clearly communicate what success is."[124]

Transformational

Campbell's leadership goes beyond transactional behaviors. Said one Home Depot district manager, "She finds a way to inspire people, to rise to the occasion and (help others) reach their goals that they didn't think they could reach—through courageous leadership, the ability to provide clear direction and by simplifying a message."[125] Campbell is also at the center of Home Depot's recently announced $1 billion investment in its employees. She commented, "We know that the key to an engaged and committed workforce is investing in the person and in their development."[126] Coupled with the company's substantial financial investment in its associates, Campbell walks the talk during her store walk-throughs as she draws on her decades of experience to relate with associates. She constantly coaches and inspires them to overcome challenges. She says, "I learned that you can accomplish so much, no matter what the limitations may be. You just gotta believe to achieve."[127]

YOUR CALL

What unique individual characteristics does Campbell display? What other types of leader behavior has she exhibited?

Four Key Behaviors of Transformational Leaders

Whereas transactional leadership behaviors—though important—can feel dispassionate, transformational leadership behaviors excite passion, inspiring and empowering people to look beyond their own interests to the interests of the organization. Leaders who are transformational appeal to their followers' self-concepts—their values and personal identity—to create changes in their goals, values, needs, beliefs, and aspirations.[128]

Transformational leaders use four key kinds of behavior that affect followers: inspirational motivation, idealized influence, individualized consideration, and intellectual stimulation.[129] Pat Summitt, former head coach of the University of Tennessee Lady Volunteers and one of the most successful coaches in the history of Women's NCAA Division I basketball, is a great example of a transformational leader. Let's examine how Coach Pat employed the four types of transformational leadership behavior.

1. Inspirational Motivation: "Let Me Share a Vision That Transcends Us All"
Transformational leadership motivates followers by inspiring them. This inspiration requires that leaders:

1. **Have charisma.** Charisma is a form of interpersonal attraction that inspires acceptance and support. At one time, charismatic leadership—which was assumed to be an individual inspirational and motivational characteristic of exceptional leaders, much like other trait-theory characteristics—was viewed as a category of its own, but now it is considered part of transformational leadership.[130] Someone with charisma is more able to persuade and influence people and to make others feel comfortable and at ease than someone without charisma.[131]

2. **Communicate a vision.** A transformational leader inspires motivation by offering an agenda, a grand design, an ultimate goal—in short, a *vision,* "a realistic, credible, attractive future" for the organization, as leadership expert Burt Nanus calls it.[132] John Hennessy, former president of Stanford University and current chair of Google's parent company Alphabet, believes that inspirational motivation is a critical skill for effective leadership. He concluded, "The ability to tell appropriate, compelling and inspiring stories is essential. Describing work as a journey shared among colleagues helps bring employees together in a common cause."[133]

    Inspirational Motivation Example—Pat Summitt: Coach Pat recorded 1,098 wins and 208 losses along with eight national championships over 38 seasons coaching women's basketball at University of Tennessee. Based upon her decades of experience successfully developing basketball players into champions, she inspired her incoming players to give their best effort to the program. She told them, "… you have a choice. You can choose to settle for mediocrity, never venturing forth much effort or feeling very much. Or you can commit. If you commit, I guarantee for every pain, you will experience an equal or surpassing pleasure."[134]

2. Idealized Influence: "We Are Here to Do the Right Thing"
Transformational leadership inspires trust in followers. Transformational leaders:

- *Express integrity* by being consistent, single-minded, and persistent in pursuit of their goal.
- *Display high ethical standards* and act as models of desirable values.
- *Make sacrifices* for the greater good.

    Idealized Influence Example—Pat Summitt: One of Coach Pat's core values was "take full responsibility." She challenged her players to take responsibility and be accountable by modeling it for them in two ways. First, Coach Pat demonstrated that she fulfilled her own responsibilities to the team. Although she had a tendency to be late for things, she was never late to a team meeting or practice. Second, Coach Pat took responsibility for clearly communicating each player's role and made sure that everyone understood their role.[135]

Pat Summitt, former NCAA Division I women's basketball head coach at University of Tennessee from 1974–2012, was a transformational leader who made her mark as one of the most successful women's coaches in NCAA history. Debby Wong/Shutterstock

3. Individualized Consideration: "You Have the Opportunity Here to Grow and Excel"
Transformational leaders don't just express concern for subordinates' well-being. They actively encourage them to grow and excel by giving them challenging work, more responsibility, empowerment, and one-on-one mentoring.

Individualized Consideration Example—Pat Summitt: Coach Pat knew who the leaders were on her basketball team. She expected the most from them and expected them to set the tone for the other players. At the same time, she was attentive to her players' personalities and temperaments. She knew with whom she could yell or challenge in front of the team and with whom she needed to take a more gentle approach. Coach Pat was also an incredible mentor. Her players were an extension of her family. She would frequently have personal conversations with her players about life, school, family dynamics, and their future hopes and dreams. Coach Pat was a teacher, mentor, coach, and friend.[136]

4. Intellectual Stimulation: "Let Me Describe the Great Challenges We Can Conquer Together"
Transformational leaders are gifted at communicating the organization's strengths, weaknesses, opportunities, and threats so that subordinates develop a new sense of purpose. Employees become less apt to view problems as insurmountable or "that's not my department." Instead they learn to view them as personal challenges that they are responsible for overcoming, to question the status quo, and to seek creative solutions.

Intellectual Stimulation Example—Pat Summitt: Coach Pat challenged her players to work hard, hold each other accountable, and use their creativity to overcome challenges. Most importantly, she taught her players discipline. Coach Pat said, "Nine-tenths of discipline is having the patience to do things right." Whether it's shot selection, communication, playing defense, or making individual choices off the court, discipline is important because everything a player does impacts themselves as well as the team. Coach Pat encouraged mutual accountability and problem solving among her players because it strengthened their relationships with each other and deepened their ownership of the team and its goals.[137]

Have you worked for a transformational leader like Coach Pat? Self-Assessment 14.5 measures the extent to which a current or former manager used transformational leadership. If your instructor has assigned it to you in Connect, answer the questions in the assessment to develop a good understanding of the specific behaviors you need to exhibit if you want to lead in a transformational manner.

SELF-ASSESSMENT 14.5

Assessing Your Boss's Transformational Leadership

The following survey was designed to assess the extent to which your current or former boss used transformational leadership. Please complete Self-Assessment 14.5 if your instructor has assigned it in Connect.

So What Do We Know about Transformational Leadership?

It works! Research shows that transformational leadership is associated with many positive outcomes such as increased organizational, team, and individual performance; job satisfaction; employee identification with their leaders and with their immediate work groups; employee engagement; and intrinsic motivation.[138]

There are three practical applications of transformational leadership.

1. It Can Be Used to Train Employees at Any Level Not just top managers but employees at any level can be trained to be more transformational.[139] It is best to couple this training with developmental coaching and job challenges.[140]

2. You Can Prepare and Practice Being Transformational The simplest way to practice is to write down ideas for exhibiting the four key behaviors of transformational leadership—inspirational motivation, idealized influence, individualized consideration, and intellectual stimulation—the next time you attend a team meeting at school or work. For example:

- You might build *inspirational motivation* among your teammates by highlighting the benefits of doing a good job, by building the team's confidence in their ability to complete the assignment, and by telling the team you believe in them.
- You can drive *idealized influence* by explaining your role or commitment to working on the assignment and modeling high-performance behaviors.
- Show *individualized consideration* by describing the resources and support available to the team, by demonstrating a supportive attitude to everyone, and by recognizing team members for their accomplishments.
- Foster *intellectual stimulation* by describing the team's challenges, explaining the tasks or goals everyone needs to achieve, and highlighting why successfully completing the assignment will help the team.

3. It Should be Used for Ethical Reasons While ethical transformational leaders empower employees and enhance their self-concepts, unethical ones select or produce obedient, dependent, and compliant followers.[141] Without honesty and trust, even transformational leaders lose credibility—not only with employees but also with investors, customers, and the public. •

14.6 Contemporary Perspectives and Concepts

THE BIG PICTURE
Contemporary leadership perspectives explore relationships between leaders and followers and consider changing views about leaders' roles. Contemporary concepts in leadership include humility, empowerment, ethics, followership, and abusive supervision.

Here we turn our attention to contemporary leadership perspectives and concepts. Contemporary perspectives include (1) the *leader–member exchange (LMX) model of leadership* and (2) *servant leadership*. Contemporary concepts of study include (1) *leading with humility*, (2) *empowering leadership*, (3) *ethical leadership*, (4) *the role of followers*, and (5) *abusive supervision*.

LO 14-6
Describe contemporary leadership perspectives and concepts.

Leader–Member Exchange Leadership: Having Different Relationships with Different Subordinates

Proposed by George Graen and Fred Dansereau, the **leader–member exchange (LMX) model of leadership** emphasizes that leaders have different sorts of relationships with different subordinates.[142] Two ways that LMX differs from other models of leadership are:

1. **LMX focuses on relational quality in leader–follower dyads.** Unlike other models we've described, which focus on leaders' or followers' traits or behaviors, the LMX model looks at the *quality* of relationships between managers and and their employees.[143]

2. **LMX assumes that leaders have distinctive relationships with each follower.** Unlike other models, which presuppose stable relationships between leaders and followers, the LMX model assumes each manager–subordinate relationship is unique.[144]

This model is one of the most researched approaches to studying leadership, and it has significant practical implications for managers and employees.

In-Group Exchange versus Out-Group Exchange

The unique relationship, which supposedly results from the leader's attempt to delegate and assign work roles, can produce two types of LMX interactions.[145]

- **In-group exchange: trust and respect.** An *in-group exchange* is a relationship between leader and follower that becomes a partnership characterized by mutual trust, respect and liking, and a sense of common fates. Subordinates may receive special assignments and special privileges.
- **Out-group exchange: lack of trust and respect.** An *out-group exchange* is a relationship in which leaders are characterized as overseers who fail to create a sense of mutual trust, respect, or common fate. Subordinates receive less of the manager's time and attention than those in the in-group exchange relationships.

What type of exchange do you have with your manager? The quality of the relationship between you and your boss matters. Not only does it predict your job satisfaction and happiness, but it also is related to turnover. You can assess the quality of the relationship with a current or former boss by completing Self-Assessment 14.6 if your instructor has assigned it to you in Connect.

SELF-ASSESSMENT 14.6

Assessing Your Leader–Member Exchange

The following survey was designed to assess the quality of your leader–member exchange. Please complete Self-Assessment 14.6 if your instructor has assigned it in Connect.

Is the LMX Model Useful?

Yes! Consider that:

- **High-quality LMX relationships engender positive outcomes.** High LMX is associated with individual-level behavioral outcomes like task performance, turnover, organizational citizenship, counterproductive behavior, and attitudinal outcomes such as organizational commitment, job satisfaction, and justice.[146]
- **Other types of leadership encourage high-quality LMX relationships.** Research shows that task, relationship, transformational, and transactional leadership all have their positive effects on employees via their immediate impact on the quality of an LMX. This is important because it tells us that positive relationships with leaders make followers happier and motivate them to work harder for the leader as well as the organization.[147]

The key takeaway for you is to take ownership of bad relationships with bosses. One expert suggested two generic practices:

1. Find out what your manager cares about and let your manager know what you care about. Work together to develop a shared definition of success.
2. For bosses who like control, set their minds at ease by giving them frequent and detailed status updates. Managers hate negative surprises. Proactive communication will earn your boss's confidence because it gives them the information they need to determine if and when to get involved to keep things on the right track.[148]

Servant Leadership

Servant Leadership: "I Want to Serve Others and the Organization, Not Myself" The term *servant leadership*, coined by Robert Greenleaf in 1970, reflects not only his one-time background as a management researcher for AT&T but also his views as a lifelong philosopher and devout Quaker.[149] **Servant leadership** focuses on benefiting multiple stakeholders—such as employees, the organization, customers, and the community. Sylvia Metayer is a good example.

Servant Leadership Example—Sylvia Metayer: Sylvia Metayer is CEO of Sodexo's Corporate Services division. Sodexo is a global company with more than 412,000 workers that provides services including food and reception, cleaning, energy management, grounds maintenance, and building maintenance and security. Its mission "is to create a better everyday for everyone to build a better life for all." Metayer believes that a leader's purpose is to serve others. "I'm learning that to be a CEO is to be a servant. My main job is to support our employees and be a support to our clients and to our consumers," said Metayer.[150]

Servant leaders see leadership as an act of service. The focus of servant leadership, then, is to improve all stakeholders' well-being. Sergey Tinyakov/123RF

At its core, servant leaders consider multiple stakeholders' viewpoints and express deep care, concern, and genuine compassion for those in their sphere of influence. Research indicates servant leadership benefits employees, organizations, customers, and the community.[151] Academic research has focused most heavily on documenting servant leadership's positive impact on employees indicating employees are happier, more productive, more creative, and more willing to go above and beyond their customary duties while also reducing burnout and turnover. These results are consistent in different national cultures across the world.[152]

The following self-assessment measures the extent to which you possess a servant orientation. Take a few moments to complete Self-Assessment 14.7 if your instructor has assigned it to you in Connect. Results from the assessment will enhance your understanding of what it takes to really be a servant leader and provide insight into the career readiness competency of service/others orientation.

SELF-ASSESSMENT 14.7   CAREER READINESS

Assessing Your Servant Orientation

This survey is designed to assess the extent to which you possess a servant orientation. Please complete Self-Assessment 14.7 if your instructor has assigned it in Connect.

The Power of Humility

Humility is a relatively stable trait grounded in the belief that "something greater than the self exists."[153] Although some think it is a sign of weakness or low self-esteem, nothing could be further from the truth.

Humble leaders tend to display five qualities that employees value:[154]

1. High self-awareness.
2. Openness to feedback.

3. Appreciation of others.
4. Low self-focus.
5. Appreciation of the greater good.

An essential element of leader humility is willingness to learn. Humble leaders surround themselves with people who can help them grow.[155] Consider the following example.

Humility Example—Satya Nadella: Chair and CEO of Microsoft, Satya Nadella, is a humble leader according to those closest to him. When a journalist asked Nadella's friends to describe him in one word, responses included "humble," "empathetic," "listener," and "empowering."[156] Nadella believes humility and vulnerability are essential to a leader's effectiveness, especially for executives. According to Nadella, "The psychological safety that you create around you, especially the more senior you are, becomes super important.... One technique of that is to share your own fallibility because that gives confidence to others." Humble leaders are also lifelong learners. "A lifelong learner is someone who genuinely believes that he can learn something from every single person he interacts with," said Nadella.[157]

Satya Nadella. The Microsoft CEO was one of *CEOWORLD magazine*'s top 20 best CEOs of 2023 and a great example of a humble leader at the highest level of one of the most influential organizations in the world.[158] Chesnot/Getty Images

The scientific study of humility is relatively new, but studies suggest that this trait is associated with many positive outcomes, including:[159]

- Follower humility.
- Follower self-efficacy.
- Follower performance.
- Team creativity.

What can we conclude about humility in the context of managing others? We suggest that managers:

1. **Shift the focus.** Try to be more humble by changing the focus of your accomplishments from "me" to "we." Share credit with others, but by all means be authentic. Don't try to fake humility.[160]
2. **Ask, don't tell.** Try to spend more time asking questions and less time talking about yourself or telling people what to do. You're more likely to learn by asking questions than by hearing yourself talk.[161]
3. **Build humility into the culture.** An organization's culture can promote humility. Research suggests that this type of culture focuses on self-awareness, creativity, learning, and publicly recognizing others' contributions.[162]

Empowering Leadership

Empowering Leadership: "I Want My Employees to Feel They Have Control over Their Work" Empowering leadership represents the extent to which a leader creates perceptions of psychological empowerment in others. Psychological empowerment is employees' belief that they have control over their work. Increasing employee psychological empowerment requires four kinds of behaviors—leading for (1) meaningfulness, (2) autonomy, (3) competence, and (4) progress.

- **Leading for meaningfulness: Inspiring and modeling desirable behaviors.** Employees believe their work is meaningful when it is personally important and they see its impact on others. Managers lead for meaningfulness by *inspiring* their employees and *modeling* desired behaviors. Leaders can help employees identify their passions at work by crafting an exciting organizational vision that employees can connect with emotionally and illustrating how employees can contribute to achieving it. The founders of Life Is Good are a great example.

    Leading for Meaningfulness Example—Life Is Good: Brothers Bert and John Jacobs founded the apparel retailer in 1994 with a mission to "spread the power of optimism." Bert models optimism via his title, Chief Executive Optimist, and his opportunity-driven and solution-focused approach to challenges. The company makes employees' work even more meaningful by its prosocial impact, donating 10% of its annual net profits to The Playmaker Project, a nonprofit that provides compassionate care for kids' social, emotional, and psychological well-being and creates conditions for kids to thrive.[163]

- **Leading for autonomy: Delegating meaningful tasks.** Managers can lead for employee autonomy by *delegating* meaningful tasks to them. Delegating encourages employees to think for themselves, gives them choice, and affords them decision-making authority. This freedom increases the likelihood employees will take responsibility and be accountable for the outcomes of their decisions. Delegation is most effective when managers express confidence in their employees, trust them, give them space to learn, and truly let go of decision-making authority.[164] Consider how the co-founder of FEED relies on leading for autonomy to grow her business.

    Leading for Autonomy Example—FEED: Lauren Bush Lauren, or "LBL," co-founded FEED to help food-deprived, school-aged children across the globe.[165] The company sells bags, T-shirts, and towels, and each item features a stenciled number to indicate how many meals it provides. The company has provided over 100 million meals to children in need across the world.[166] LBL credits much of FEED's success to the people on her team. She believes the best way to do business is to find talented people and get out of their way. She says, "The most important thing you can do when starting a business is surround yourself with smart people who know a lot more than you do in certain realms."[167]

    Lauren Bush, co-founder of FEED. Eamonn McCormack/WireImage/Getty Images

- **Leading for competence: Supporting and coaching employees.** It goes without saying that employees need to have the necessary knowledge to perform their

jobs. Accomplishing this goal involves managers' *supporting* and *coaching* their employees.[168] Effective managers support and coach their employees as they prepare to make decisions and reflect on prior decisions.

- **Leading for progress: Monitoring and rewarding employees.** Managers lead for progress by using transactional leadership (see Section 14.5) to *monitor* and *reward* others. We discussed how to do this in Chapter 12.

What Do We Know about Empowering Leadership's Effects on Employees?
Research about empowering leadership highlights the following conclusions:[169]

- Empowering leadership increases followers' trust in the leader, intrinsic motivation, performance, helping behaviors, and creativity.
- Too much empowering leadership can be a bad thing by creating uncertainty and ambiguity related to employees' work tasks, hurting their task performance. Employees who proactively seek information and learn from it are less likely to experience the downside of too much empowering leadership.
- Empowering leadership gives employees discretion to craft their jobs. This flexibility results in more satisfaction, less withdrawal, and more positive work behaviors.

Ethical Leadership

Ethical Leadership: "I Am Ready to Do the Right Thing" Ethical leadership represents normatively appropriate behavior that focuses on being a moral role model.[170] Before the COVID-19 pandemic, society grew increasingly cynical of CEO behavior. With each corporate scandal—from Volkswagen to Wells Fargo to Theranos to accounting fraud at Luckin Coffee—the number of CEOs forced out of their roles each year due to ethical failures grew to a record level.[171] A study by PwC consulting firm in 2018 found that ethical lapses were—for the first time—the #1 reason for CEO departures from the 2,500 largest companies across the globe, with 39% of successions occurring for this reason.[172] The tide shifted during the pandemic as companies regained public trust due to their treatment of workers during and after the pandemic. According to the 2023 Edelman Trust Barometer, "business is now viewed as the only global institution to be both competent and ethical."[173] Ethical leadership includes communicating ethical values to others, rewarding ethical behavior, and treating followers with care and concern.[174]

Ethical Leadership Example—PepsiCo: For the 17th year in a row, beverage and snack food company PepsiCo was among those designated World's Most Ethical Companies in 2023 by Ethisphere. PepsiCo Chair and CEO Ramon Laguarta noted the award "highlights our commitment to act with integrity and do business the right way while continually improving our efforts to lead with purpose and inspire positive change in our markets and communities."[175]

What Does Research Say about Ethical Leadership? Here is what research tells us about ethical leadership:[176]

- Ethical leadership is clearly driven by personal factors related to our beliefs and values.
- It has a reciprocal relationship with an organization's culture and climate. In other words, an ethical culture and climate promote ethical leadership, and ethical leadership in turn promotes an ethical culture and climate.
- Ethical leadership is positively related to employee trust, job satisfaction, organizational commitment, organizational citizenship behavior, motivation, and task performance.
- It is negatively associated with job stress, counterproductive work behavior, and intentions to quit.

Followers: What Do They Want, How Can They Help?

Leadership is a two-way street. That is, the quality of leadership depends on the qualities of the followers being led.[177] Leaders and followers need each other, and the quality of the relationship determines how followers respond and behave.[178]

What Do Followers Want in Their Leaders? Research shows that followers seek and admire leaders who create feelings of:

- **Significance.** Such leaders make followers feel that what they do at work is important and meaningful.
- **Community.** These leaders create a sense of unity around a common purpose that encourages followers to treat others with respect and to work together in pursuit of organizational goals.
- **Excitement.** These leaders make people feel energetic and engaged at work.[179]

What Do Leaders Want in Their Followers? Followers vary, of course, in their level of compliance with a leader (recall the outcomes of influence tactics in Section 14.1):[180]

- *Helpers* (committed) show deference to their leaders.
- *Independents* (compliant) distance themselves.
- *Rebels* (resistant) show divergence.

Leaders clearly benefit from having helpers (and, to some extent, independents). They want followers who are productive, reliable, honest, cooperative, proactive, and flexible. They do not want followers who are unethical, manipulative, negative, withhold information, reluctant to take the lead on projects, and fail to generate ideas.[181]

We give some suggestions on how to be a better follower—and enhance your own career prospects—in the following Practical Action box.

PRACTICAL ACTION | How to Be a Good Leader by Being a Good Follower

Changing business culture and the increasing power of technology have shifted the relationship between leaders and followers. Good followers today don't simply follow. They are empowered to let leaders know when things are going in the wrong direction.

Here's how you can become an intelligent follower. These same skills can make you a good leader, too.[182]

1. See Yourself as a Leader in Training
Leaders know what the people on their team are doing and they see how the various pieces fit together to help the organization accomplish overarching goals. Learn about what co-workers, customers, and bosses are doing, what they want, and what drives them to do their best work (or to prevent others from working well). The better you understand the people around you, the better you will be able to work with them in the present to accomplish goals, and the better you will be able to lead them in the future.

2. Be Tactful
Choose your battles. You can't win at everything, but you can choose where to invest your time and energy. Learn how to get along with co-workers, subordinates, and bosses who are similar to you as well as with those who are different.

3. Be Courageous
Don't be afraid to tell your boss—diplomatically—when you think they may be wrong and to offer intelligent alternatives. Helpful feedback is always valuable. Remember, also, to be supportive when things are going well.

4. Work Collaboratively
Being a good team player, meeting your goals, and letting the team take credit when appropriate can go a long way toward bringing out the best in others, including your boss when you are in a follower role. Also keep your boss informed; no one likes being caught by surprise.

5. Think Critically
Develop your ability to ask the right questions, raise intelligent challenges, and maintain your own competence and motivation.

YOUR CALL
Although it's always in your and the leader's best interest if you become a good follower, sometimes the two of you may differ so completely in habits, dislikes, and so on that you may simply have to look for opportunities outside your present work situation. Do you think you've been a good follower in past jobs?

Have you experienced or witnessed a supervisor who repeatedly treats subordinates with hostility? A boss who screams, mocks, or perhaps ignores employees on a regular basis? If so, try thinking about the abusive behavior as a good lesson on what not to do as a leader. Pavlo Syvak/123RF

Abusive Supervision

The concepts of LMX, servant, humility, empowerment, and ethical leadership discussed thus far are positive aspects of leadership. In contrast, research has also sought to better understand the impacts of destructive leader behaviors on followers and organizations. As you learned in Chapter 3, abusive supervision occurs when supervisors repeatedly display verbal and nonverbal hostility toward their subordinates.[183] Abusive supervision does not include physical contact between supervisors and subordinates; rather, it focuses on behaviors such as public humiliation, insults, shouting, and ignoring subordinates.[184]

What Causes Supervisors to Be Abusive?
Research has identified several factors that prompt abusive supervision.[185] They include:

- **Organizational culture:** Factors in a supervisor's environment may make abusive supervision more likely. These factors include aggressive organizational norms and abusive role models.
- **Individual differences:** Researchers have found significant correlations between supervisors' individual differences and the propensity to behave abusively toward subordinates. These factors include psychological entitlement (a person's general belief that they deserve more than others), Machiavellianism, neuroticism, and negative affectivity.
- **Early life experiences:** Supervisors' early life experiences impact the likelihood that they will abuse subordinates. Research has found that supervisors who witnessed aggression between their parents and those who were the targets of parental aggression are more likely to engage in abusive supervision.

What Do We Know about How Abusive Supervision Affects Employees?
Scholars have studied the negative outcomes of abusive supervision for more than 20 years. Key findings from more than 200 studies tell us the following:[186]

- **Abusive supervision increases negative outcomes:** Subordinates of abusive supervisors are more likely to engage in unethical and counterproductive behaviors at work and are more likely to experience depression and emotional exhaustion.
- **Abusive supervision decreases positive outcomes:** Subordinates of abusive supervisors experience decreased self-efficacy, trust in the leader, job satisfaction, well-being, and job performance, and they are less likely to engage in organizational citizenship behaviors.

What Should Organizations Do to Deal with and Prevent Abusive Supervision?
Abusive supervision consists of behaviors that are unacceptable and inappropriate, but unfortunately, not usually considered illegal on their own. Still, these behaviors clearly are damaging to employees and organizations. According to U.S. Occupational Safety and Health Administration (OSHA), companies should take the following steps to reduce both the occurrence and impact of abusive supervision:[187]

- Implement strong and clear policies about supervisory behavior—including the types of behavior that are (respectful) and are not (bullying) acceptable in the organization. Follow through with disciplinary action for policy violations.
- Train supervisors and employees on appropriate behaviors and on how to recognize abusive supervisory behaviors.
- Establish fair processes for dealing with complaints about abusive supervision, including safe reporting channels and protections from retaliation for employees who report it.

In conclusion, we strongly suggest that you, as a manager, avoid behaviors that are considered abusive toward subordinates. Instead, focus on developing high-quality relationships with others through your ability to be a servant, humble, empowering, and ethical leader. •

14.7 Career Corner: Managing Your Career Readiness

This chapter demonstrated that leadership is a concept with much breadth and depth. You learned that it affects all aspects of organizational effectiveness, thus requiring the combined use of 19 career readiness competencies from the model shown in Figure 14.3: task-based/functional, understanding the business, critical thinking/problem solving, oral/written communication, leadership, professionalism/work ethic, social intelligence, networking, emotional intelligence, ownership/accepting responsibilities, self-motivation, showing commitment, positive approach, resilience, personal adaptability, self-awareness, service/others orientation, openness to change, and generalized self-efficacy.

We obviously can't discuss here how to develop all these competencies. To make this section more manageable, we focus on the cornerstone competency of *self-awareness*. What do those who listen, learn, adapt, and see the bigger picture have in common? The executives in this chapter's Executive Interview Series used these terms to describe self-aware employees. The following section reveals how to grow this valuable career readiness competency.

LO 14-7

Explain how to develop the career readiness competency of self-awareness.

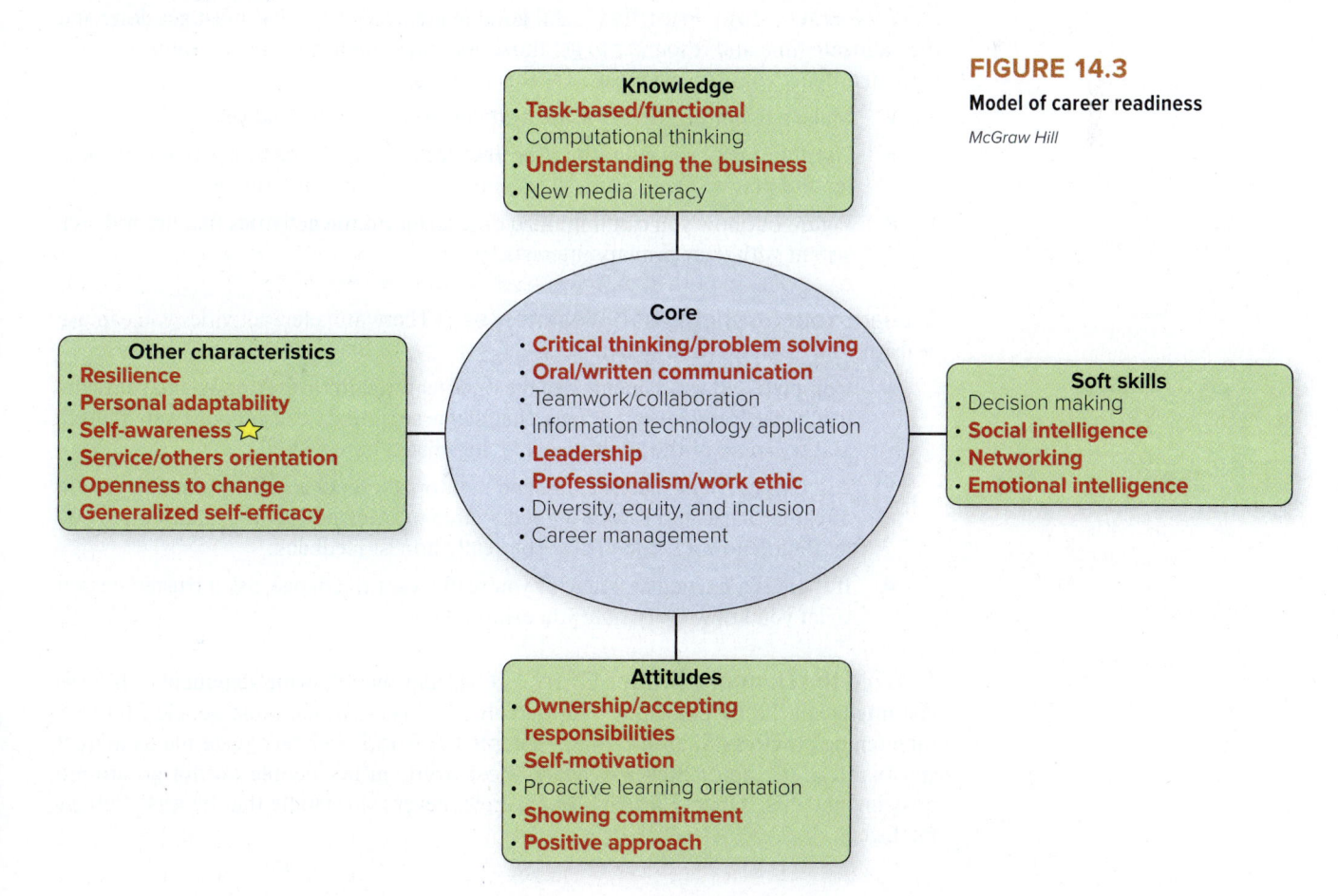

FIGURE 14.3

Model of career readiness

McGraw Hill

Knowledge
- **Task-based/functional**
- Computational thinking
- **Understanding the business**
- New media literacy

Core
- **Critical thinking/problem solving**
- **Oral/written communication**
- Teamwork/collaboration
- Information technology application
- **Leadership**
- **Professionalism/work ethic**
- Diversity, equity, and inclusion
- Career management

Other characteristics
- **Resilience**
- **Personal adaptability**
- **Self-awareness** ⭐
- **Service/others orientation**
- **Openness to change**
- **Generalized self-efficacy**

Soft skills
- Decision making
- **Social intelligence**
- **Networking**
- **Emotional intelligence**

Attitudes
- **Ownership/accepting responsibilities**
- **Self-motivation**
- Proactive learning orientation
- **Showing commitment**
- **Positive approach**

Visit your instructor's Connect course and access your eBook to view this video.

Executive Interview Series:
Leadership and Self-Awareness

Becoming More Self-Aware

Self-awareness has become an increasingly important point of emphasis in organizations, and for good reason. According to research, self-awareness increases creativity, decision quality, leadership effectiveness, job satisfaction, and thriving.[188] Developing self-awareness is not just an intellectual exercise. It entails understanding who you are and what you stand for. It requires thinking about your life vision, values, personality, needs, behavioral tendencies, and social skills. You can become more self-aware by taking the following actions:

1. Take the Time to Reflect   Most of us are so busy accomplishing our daily activities or short-term goals that we leave ourselves no time to reflect and learn.[189] This pattern gets tasks done but can prevent our learning the new skills needed for more difficult assignments or promotions. You can build intentional reflection into your life by considering the following questions on a regular basis:

- What happened?
- What did I learn in general?
- What did I learn about me?
- What will I do to improve in the future?[190]

Try recording your answers in a journal. Research shows that this practice will increase your critical thinking and self-reflection.[191] You need to choose the frequency of journaling, but once a week is a minimum. One of your authors, Angelo Kinicki, has his students journal on a daily basis and then submit a weekly summary. Students find it invaluable.

2. Write Down Your Priorities   All good leaders identify what must get done and then allocate time and resources to get those goals accomplished. Self-awareness begins with identifying your top priorities. Try this process:

- Make a list of priorities for the next day, week, month, and year.
- Use the clarity you gain from this practice to identify the things that truly matter and plan to focus your efforts and resources on these things.
- Figure out how you can minimize time spent on the activities that are not consistent with your primary interests.[192]

3. Learn Your Strengths and Weaknesses   There are a few activities you can use to learn your strengths and weaknesses:

- Complete self-assessments like the ones featured in this textbook and study the feedback. Remember, though, that self-assessments can be positively biased, and try some of the additional activities listed here as well.
- Ask family, friends, colleagues, and mentors for feedback. They observe you on a regular basis and can be a good source of information, especially when you let them know it's safe to give you really honest feedback.
- If there is a particular behavior you really want to change, ask a trusted person to let you know every time you exhibit it.

4. Avoid the Dunning-Kruger Effect   Consider the following statements: "If I was just intelligent, I'd be okay. But I am fiercely intelligent, which most people find very threatening" (actress Sharon Stone). "People the world over recognize me as a great spiritual leader" (actor Steven Seagal). Most overly gifted people do not go around boasting like this. Albert Einstein, for example, never told people that he was "fiercely intelligent."

Developed by two psychology professors—Dr. David Dunning and Dr. Justin Kruger—the **Dunning-Kruger effect** is "a cognitive bias whereby people who are incompetent at something are unable to recognize their own incompetence. And not only do they fail to recognize their incompetence, they're also likely to feel confident that they actually are competent."[193] Consider this effect in light of results from an online quiz asking 10,000 people how they react to constructive criticism. Only 39% said they deal with constructive criticism by considering the cause of that feedback.[194] It's possible that the other 61% are caught up in the Dunning-Kruger effect.

The point is that this bias will detract from your ability to recognize your own weaknesses, which then prevents you from correcting them. Seeking regular feedback and focusing on a proactive learning orientation are two ways to overcome the Dunning-Kruger effect.[195] •

Key Terms Used in This Chapter

behavioral leadership approaches 513
charisma 523
charismatic leadership 523
coercive power 504
consideration 514
contingency leadership model 515
dunning-Kruger effect 535
employee-centered leader behaviors 514
empowering leadership 529
ethical leadership 530
expert power 505
full-range leadership 520
global mindset 513
influence tactics 506
informational power 505
initiating-structure leadership 514
leader–member exchange (LMX) model of leadership 525
leadership 502
leadership coaching 502
legitimate power 504
machiavellianism 509
managerial leadership 503
narcissism 509
path–goal leadership model 517
personalized power 504
power 504
production-centered leader behaviors 514
psychological empowerment 529
psychopathy 510
referent power 505
relationship-oriented leadership 514
reward power 504
servant leadership 527
situational approach 515
socialized power 504
task-oriented leadership behaviors 514
trait approaches to leadership 509
transactional leadership 521
transformational leadership 521

Key Points

14.1 The Nature of Leadership: The Role of Power and Influence

- Leadership is the ability to influence employees to voluntarily pursue organizational goals. Power is the ability to marshal human, informational, and other resources to get something done.
- Within an organization there are typically six sources of power leaders may draw on: (1) legitimate power, (2) reward power, (3) coercive power, (4) expert power, (5) referent power, and (6) informational power.
- There are nine influence tactics for trying to get others to do something you want: rational persuasion, inspirational appeals, consultation, ingratiating tactics, personal appeals, exchange tactics, coalition tactics, pressure tactics, and legitimating tactics.
- Three outcomes of influence tactics are: (1) commitment, (2) compliance, and (3) resistance.

14.2 Trait Approaches: Do Leaders Have Distinctive Traits and Personal Characteristics?

- Trait approaches to leadership attempt to identify distinctive characteristics that account for the effectiveness of leaders.
- Six positive task-oriented traits are (1) intelligence, (2) consciousness, (3) openness to experience, (4) emotional stability, (5) positive affect, and (6) proactive personality. Among the positive attributes are extraversion, agreeableness, emotional intelligence, collectivism, trait empathy, and moral identity. Negative attributes include narcissism, Machiavellianism, and psychopathy.
- Women occupy a growing but still small proportion of CEO and top management positions in the United States.

14.3 Behavioral Approaches: Do Leaders Show Distinctive Patterns of Behavior?

- Behavioral leadership approaches try to determine the unique behaviors displayed by effective leaders. Two categories are task-oriented behavior and relationship-oriented behavior.
- Task-oriented behaviors are those that ensure that people, equipment, and other resources are used in an efficient way to accomplish the mission of a group or organization.
- Relationship-oriented leadership is primarily concerned with the leader's interaction with their people.
- Four basic skills for leaders are (1) cognitive abilities, (2) interpersonal skills, (3) business skills, and (4) conceptual skills.

14.4 Situational Approaches: Does Leadership Vary with the Situation?

- Proponents of the situational approach (or contingency approach) to leadership believe that effective leadership behavior depends on the situation at hand—that as situations change, different styles become effective. Two contingency approaches are the Fiedler contingency leadership model and House's path–goal leadership model.

- The Fiedler contingency leadership model determines if a leader's style is task-oriented or relationship-oriented and if that style is effective for the situation at hand.
- The House path–goal leadership model, in its revised form, holds that the effective leader clarifies paths through which subordinates can achieve goals and provides them with support. Two variables, employee characteristics and environmental factors, cause one or more leadership behaviors to be more effective than others.

14.5 The Full-Range Model: Using Transactional and Transformational Leadership

- Full-range leadership describes leadership along a range of styles (from passive to transactional to transformational), with the most effective being transactional/transformational leaders.
- Transformational leadership encourages employees to pursue organizational goals over self-interests and is influenced by leaders' individual characteristics and an organization's culture.
- Four key behaviors of transformational leaders in affecting employees are they inspire motivation, inspire trust, encourage excellence, and stimulate employees intellectually.

14.6 Contemporary Perspectives and Concepts

- The leader–member exchange (LMX) model of leadership emphasizes that leaders have different sorts of relationships with different subordinates.
- Servant leadership focuses on providing increased service to others—meeting the goals of both followers and the organization—rather than the goals of oneself.
- Humble leaders tend to display five key qualities valued by employees: high self-awareness, openness to feedback, appreciation of others, low self-focus, and appreciation of the greater good.
- Empowering leadership represents the extent to which a leader creates perceptions of psychological empowerment in others.
- Ethical leadership represents normatively appropriate behavior that focuses on being a moral role model.
- Leaders want followers who are productive, reliable, honest, cooperative, proactive, and flexible.
- Abusive supervision represents supervisors' sustained verbal and nonverbal hostility toward subordinates.

14.7 Career Corner: Managing Your Career Readiness

- Becoming a more effective leader requires the application of 19 career readiness competencies.
- You can become more self-aware by taking the following four actions: (1) Take the time to reflect. (2) Write down your priorities. (3) Learn your strengths and weaknesses. (4) Avoid the Dunning-Kruger effect.

15 Interpersonal and Organizational Communication

Mastering the Exchange of Information

After reading this chapter, you should be able to:

LO 15-1 Describe the communication process.

LO 15-2 Compare communication channels and appropriate ways for managers to use them.

LO 15-3 Identify barriers to communication and ways managers can overcome them.

LO 15-4 Discuss how managers can successfully use social media to communicate.

LO 15-5 Identify ways for managers to improve their listening, writing, and speaking skills.

LO 15-6 Review the techniques for improving the career readiness competency of networking.

FORECAST   What's Ahead in This Chapter

This chapter describes the process of transferring information and understanding between individuals and groups. It shows how you can use different channels and patterns of communication, both formal and informal, to your advantage. We also describe several communication barriers—physical, personal, cross-cultural, nonverbal, and gender differences—and we discuss how managers use social media to communicate more effectively. We also provide recommendations for becoming a better listener, writer, and speaker. We conclude with a Career Corner that focuses on developing the career readiness competency of networking.

Improving Your Use of Empathy

Why should you care about using empathy? Because it can be a differentiator in finding and holding a meaningful job after graduation. *Harvard Business Review* Editor in Chief Adi Ignatius recently called empathy "the most needed skill for successful leadership" in today's wold.[1]

Empathy reflects the ability to feel, understand, and act on another person's feelings and emotions[2] and serves as a key component of effective communication for both individuals and organizations. It's part of the career readiness skill of emotional intelligence and represents a natural human ability that you can learn and actively develop.[3]

Empathy will help you gain a better and more accurate understanding of what's really going on when you communicate with others at work—what they need, what they're feeling, why they're saying what they're saying, and even what they aren't saying. That, in turn, will help shape your response and make you a better communicator with stronger work and personal relationships.[4]

Here are some suggestions for developing empathy and strengthening your emotional intelligence in the process.

Practice Your Best Listening Skills

Interrupting others, or even thinking about how you're going to respond instead of actually listening to what's being said, prevents you from focusing on the other person and their message. Checking your phone during in-person conversations also limits your ability to focus on what is being said.

Be Mindful

You can't use empathy if you aren't mindful. Mindfulness enables you to ignore the random thoughts that pop into your head and distract you from listening to what someone is saying in the present moment.[5] How can you accurately assess what someone is feeling or thinking if you aren't fully present with them?

Observe Nonverbal Cues and Be Mindful of Your Own

Pay attention to the speaker's body language, facial expression, and tone of voice. Are these giving a message that contradicts the words being spoken? Try to find out why. Watch your own nonverbal behavior, too. For instance, maintain comfortable eye contact while listening and speaking. It's also important to be aware of any facial expressions such as frowning or body language like crossing your arms that may convey a lack of interest or frustration.[6]

Practice Perspective Taking

If someone were walking toward you on the street and they asked for directions to the nearest restaurant, would you give the directions from your perspective facing the person, or from the person's perspective facing you? If the person were from out of town, as opposed to being a local, would you provide more detailed instructions? Perspective taking amounts to taking another person's point of view when communicating with them. Research demonstrates that perspective taking enhances our ability to understand others' internal thoughts and feelings.[7]

Show Genuine Interest and Be Curious

It's hard to be empathetic if you are only concerned about yourself or what you want in a situation. Caring about others' welfare will go a long way to improving your empathy. Try being curious. For example, if a classmate comes up to you during finals week and says, "I am exhausted," you could reply, "so am I, finals are tough. I know how you feel." But a more powerful response would involve being curious about what is making your fellow student exhausted. Allow yourself to ask questions, listen, and learn before trying to be empathetic.[8]

For Discussion Are you willing to challenge yourself to have a substantive conversation in which you really connect with someone you consider difficult to communicate with or with whom you frequently disagree? Which tips will be most helpful to you?

15.1 The Communication Process: What It Is, How It Works

THE BIG PICTURE

Communication is the transfer of information and understanding from one person to another. The process involves sender, message, and receiver; encoding and decoding; the medium; feedback; and "noise," or interference. Managers need to tailor their communication to the appropriate medium (rich or lean) for the appropriate situation.

LO 15-1

Describe the communication process.

Our goal in this chapter is to increase your understanding of effective communication. You will learn that being an effective communicator involves more than having good verbal or written skills, and you'll see why it represents an important career readiness competency desired by employers.[9] We begin by defining communication and reviewing the communication process. We then discuss a contingency approach for selecting the appropriate communication medium.

Communication Defined: The Transfer of Information and Understanding

Communication—the transfer of information and understanding from one person to another—is something we do all the time. Unfortunately, just because we communicate constantly doesn't mean that we are good at it. How good a communicator do you think you are? A survey conducted by the National Association of Colleges and Employers (NACE) found that while nearly 100% of employers saw communication as the most important career readiness competency, only about 47% believed students were proficient communicators.[10] Communication skills represent an important career readiness competency desired by employers, and we all have room to grow when it comes to communicating.

You are an *efficient communicator* when you can transmit your message accurately in the least amount of time. You are an *effective communicator* when your intended message is accurately understood by the other person. Are efficiency and effectiveness equally important? The answer will become clearer as you read this section. Let's focus on the effectiveness aspect of communication by discussing the basics of the communication process.

How the Communication Process Works

You can think of the communication process as "a sender transmitting a message through media to a receiver who responds."[11] A diagram of this process is shown in Figure 15.1. Let's take a look at its different parts.

Sender, Message, and Receiver The **sender** is the person wanting to share information—called a message—and the **receiver** is the person for whom the message is intended, as follows.

Encoding and Decoding Communication requires encoding and decoding. **Encoding** is translating a message into understandable symbols or language. **Decoding** is interpreting and trying to make sense of the message. Thus, the communication process is now

Sender [**Encoding**] → Message → [**Decoding**] Receiver

FIGURE 15.1
The communication process

"Noise" is not just noise or loud background sounds but any disturbance that interferes with transmission—static, fadeout, distracting facial expressions, an uncomfortable meeting site, competing voices, and so on.

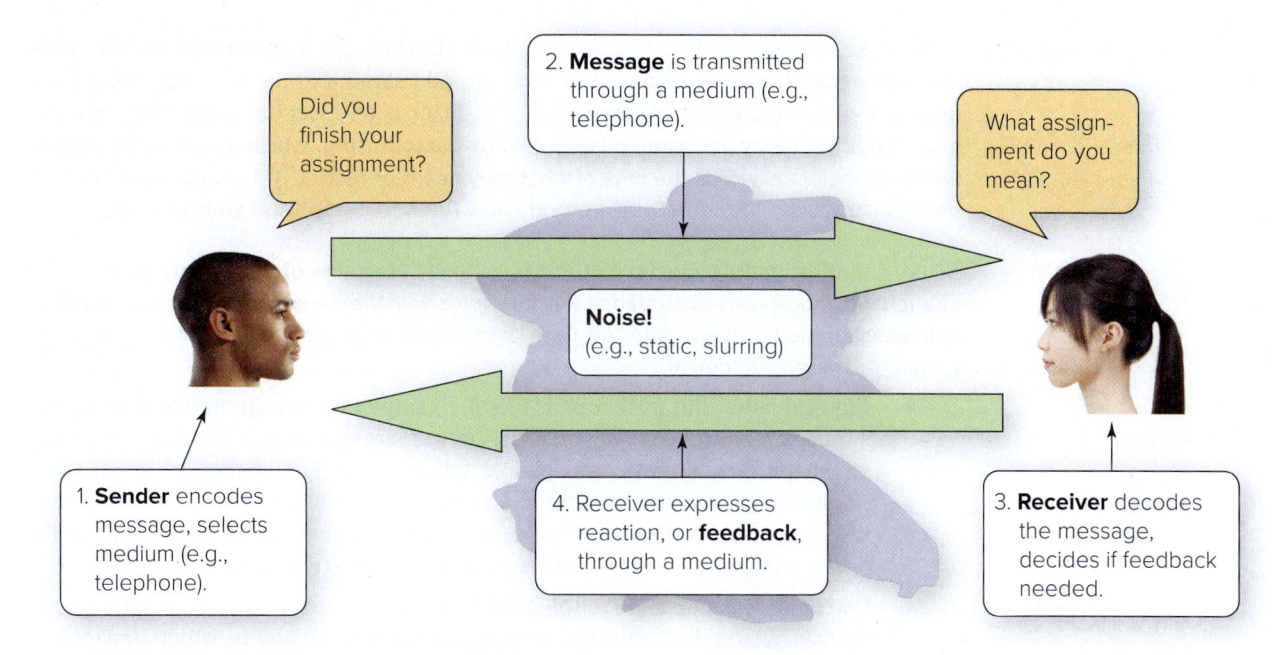

- Did you finish your assignment?
- 2. **Message** is transmitted through a medium (e.g., telephone).
- What assignment do you mean?
- **Noise!** (e.g., static, slurring)
- 1. **Sender** encodes message, selects medium (e.g., telephone).
- 4. Receiver expresses reaction, or **feedback**, through a medium.
- 3. **Receiver** decodes the message, decides if feedback needed.

(male): Wolf/Fuse/Getty Images; (female): Takayuki/Shutterstock

If you were an old-fashioned telegraph operator using Morse code to send a message over a telegraph line, you would first have to encode your message. This would involve translating the words you wished to communicate into a series of dashes and dots. The receiver of your message would have to decode the dashes and dots back into words. The same process holds when you are speaking to another person in the same room and have to decide which language to speak and what terms to use, or when you are texting a friend and can choose your words, abbreviations, and emojis.

The Medium The means by which you as a communicator send a message is important, whether it is typing a text or e-mail, hand-scrawling a note, or communicating by voice in person or by phone or Zoom. The means you choose is known as the <mark>medium</mark>, the pathway by which a message travels:

Sender [Encoding] → Message **[Medium]** Message → [Decoding] Receiver

Feedback "Flight 123, do you copy?" In the movies, that's what you hear the flight controller say when radioing the pilot of a troubled aircraft to see whether the pilot received ("copied") the previous message. And the pilot may radio back, "Roger, Houston, I copy." The pilot's acknowledgment is an example of <mark>feedback</mark>, whereby the receiver expresses their reaction to the sender's message.

American Morse Code

Some members of the modern U.S. military still receive training in Morse Code, a system that uses pulses of varying lengths to communicate information between senders and receivers.
Ioana Martalogu/Alamy Stock Photo

Sender [Encoding] → Message [Medium] Message → [Decoding] Receiver

[Feedback]   Message

Feedback is essential for *effective* communication because it enables the person sending the message to assess whether the receiver understood it in the same way the sender intended—and whether they agree with it. Feedback is an essential component of communication accuracy and can be facilitated by **paraphrasing**, which occurs when people restate in their own words the crux of what they heard or read. If you want to ensure that someone understands something you said, ask them to paraphrase your message.

Noise Unfortunately, both the efficiency and effectiveness of communication can be disrupted by **noise**—any disturbance that interferes with the transmission or understanding of a message. Let's investigate the four key sources of noise: physical, psychological, semantic, and physiological.[12]

- **Physical noise.** Physical noise is literal. Examples include humming from lights; a loud ventilating system; construction workers operating a jackhammer in the street; phones ringing; and people talking in offices, cubicles, or on their phones. If you've ever worked in an open office environment, you know what physical noise is. Open office designs often contain more noise than traditional office environments where people work in separate spaces.[13]

- **Psychological noise.** Psychological noise stems from individual differences such as personality, attitudes, emotions, beliefs, or thoughts, which impact our ability to encode and decode messages. Strong emotions, such as fear, sadness, or jubilance, can represent forms of psychological noise that interfere with our ability to process information. Your beliefs represent another interesting source of noise. Specifically, you may "tune out" when a speaker states something you disagree with. This type of noise can prevent you from taking the most effective course of action. Consider your belief about writing lecture notes by hand versus typing them. Could your belief that typing is better (i.e., psychological noise) be hindering your learning experience? Although there are pros and cons to both approaches, the consensus is that we learn better when we write notes rather than type them.[14]

- **Semantic noise.** Semantic noise is caused by the words used when communicating, and it can occur during encoding or decoding. An example is the difficulties that arise when people from different countries stumble over each other's languages. One of your authors—Angelo Kinicki—was consulting in Asia and found, for instance, that his suggestion that Asian managers "touch base" (a baseball reference) with their colleagues drew blank looks. We discuss cross-cultural barriers to communication later in the chapter. The signage posted at the Duwamish River is a great example of semantic noise.

   Eliminating Semantic Noise Example—Multilingual Signage Promotes Public Health: Most of the seafood that live in Washington state's Duwamish River are not safe to eat. This is because the fish spend their entire lives in the River and are therefore riddled with toxic chemicals. The Washington State Department of Health posts warnings at fishing sites all along the River, but realized recently that the messaging wasn't reaching 20+ non-English speaking ethnic groups in the region. Through the state's Fun to Catch, Toxic to Eat program, leaders have connected with local community groups to create effective multilingual signage to keep all of the area's residents safe.[15]

   Jargon is another source of semantic noise.[16] **Jargon** is terminology specific to a particular profession or group. (Example: "The HR VP wants the RFP to go out ASAP." Translation: "The VP of HR wants the request for proposal to go out as soon as possible.") *Buzzwords* are designed to impress rather than inform. (Example: "Could our teams interface on the ad campaign that went viral, and then circle back with the boss?")[17]

- **Physiological noise.** Have you ever attended a lecture when you had a bad cold and headache? If yes, you understand the impact of physiological noise. Physiological noise stems from our physical symptoms and/or impairments. For example, your authors know that their ability to process a case analysis in class is impaired when we are sick. Being sick makes it very difficult to stay focused and actively listen to all the students' comments.

This student struggles to pay attention during class due to physiological noise. Steve Hix/Corbis/Getty Images

Selecting the Right Medium for Effective Communication

Managers have many communication tools at their disposal, ranging from one-on-one face-to-face conversation all the way to mass media. However, managers need to choose the right tools for the right situations. Selecting the wrong medium, regardless of the message, can be costly to one's career.

All media have their own advantages and disadvantages, and there are several criteria to consider when choosing the best medium. For instance, texts and tweets require the writer to be brief and precise, and like e-mails (which generally are brief), they provide a record of the communication that in-person and phone communication don't. They can also be sent almost without regard to time-zone differences. But unlike voice, video call, and in-person messages, written communications often fail to convey important nuances, and thus can more easily be misinterpreted. Many a manager has discovered that a simple phone call can cut through layers of misinterpreted e-mails.

Selecting the Right Medium Example—Your Authors: Your authors work together a *lot*. Most of what we do is enjoyable because it involves our favorite activities such as teaching, developing students' knowledge and career readiness competencies, and writing. But working together on a product such as this one also involves dealing with issues that are not necessarily fun. We recently had to work through a pretty important issue as a team—one that involved big decisions and big emotions. Somehow, we wound up communicating about this issue over e-mail rather than by phone or Zoom, and this led to us misinterpreting one another's messages for many weeks. All it took was one Zoom call for the three of us to realize that we were in perfect alignment regarding our decision. We had simply chosen the wrong medium for the nature of the problem we were trying to solve.

Kapook2981/iStock/Getty Images

Is a Medium Rich or Lean?
Media richness indicates how well a particular medium conveys information and promotes learning. That is, the "richer" a medium is, the better it is at conveying information.[18] Rich media contain multiple cues that communicators can rely on to help them interpret messages. The term *media richness* was proposed by respected organizational theorists Richard Daft and Robert Lengel as part of their contingency model for media selection.[19]

Different media can be placed along a continuum ranging from high to low media richness, as shown in Figure 15.2.

FIGURE 15.2

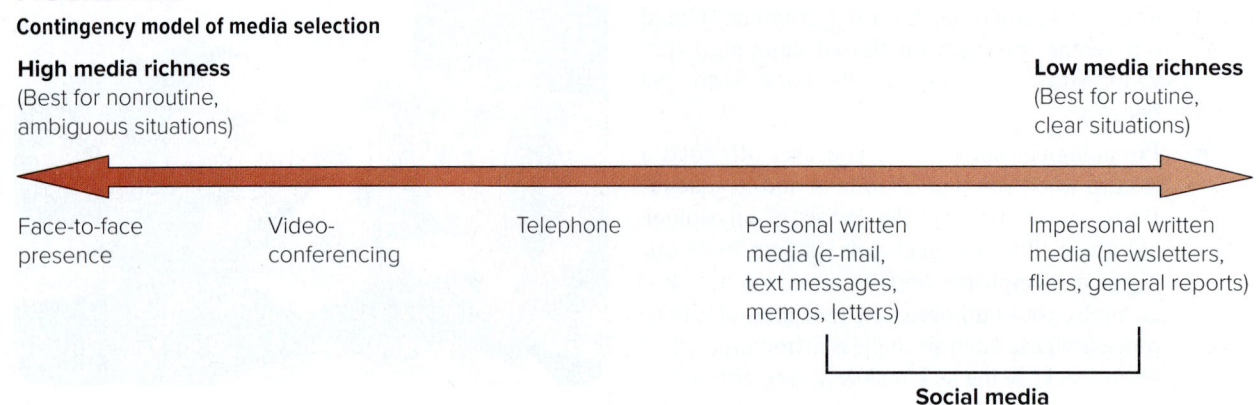

Contingency model of media selection

High media richness
(Best for nonroutine, ambiguous situations)

Low media richness
(Best for routine, clear situations)

Face-to-face presence — Video-conferencing — Telephone — Personal written media (e-mail, text messages, memos, letters) — Impersonal written media (newsletters, fliers, general reports)

Social media (spans personal written and impersonal written media)

Face-to-face communication is the richest. It allows the receiver of the message to observe multiple cues including body language and tone of voice. Face-to-face communication allows the sender to get immediate feedback regarding how well the receiver comprehended their message. At the other end of the media richness scale are impersonal written media. These involve only one cue (the written message) and no opportunity for immediate feedback.

Matching the Appropriate Medium to the Appropriate Situation In general, the following guidelines are useful when selecting the appropriate medium.[20]

Rich Medium: Best for Nonroutine Situations and to Avoid Oversimplification
A *rich* medium is more effective with complex, nonroutine situations. Examples: How would you like for your supervisor to inform you that you are being moved to a smaller, less-visible office? Via an e-mail (a lean medium)? Or via a face-to-face meeting (a rich medium)? Even worse, imagine getting a companywide e-mail on a Thursday night informing you that around half of your company's workforce is going to be laid off the following day, and then attempting to log on to your e-mail the following morning only to realize that you are locked out and are, thus, one of those who has been axed. If this sounds familiar, it's because it happened in November 2022 when Elon Musk began cutting huge chunks of staff from Twitter's workforce. Do you think Musk chose the appropriate medium for the situation?

Lean Medium: Best for Routine Situations and to Avoid Overloading The danger of using a rich medium for routine matters (such as monthly sales reports) is that it results in *information overload*—the delivery of more information than necessary. In most routine situations, a *lean* medium is the better choice. Examples: In what manner would you as a sales manager like to get routine monthly sales reports from your 50 sales reps? Via time-consuming phone calls (a somewhat rich medium)? Or via e-mail (a somewhat lean medium)? The danger of using a lean medium for nonroutine matters (such as an announcement of a company reorganization) is that it results in information *oversimplification*—it doesn't provide enough of the information the receiver needs and wants.

E-mail and social media like Facebook, LinkedIn, and Twitter vary in media richness, being leaner if they impersonally blanket a large audience and are anonymous (or posted under a screen name), and richer if they mix personal textual and video information that prompts quick conversational feedback.[21] This is important for managers to remember when they use e-mail and social media to communicate with employees. We discuss social media in Section 15.4. •

15.2 How Managers Fit into the Communication Process

THE BIG PICTURE
Formal communication channels follow the chain of command, which consists of three types—vertical, horizontal, and external. Informal communication channels develop outside the organization's formal structure. One example is the grapevine. Another, face-to-face communication, builds trust and depends heavily on managers' effective listening skills.

If you've ever had a low-level job in nearly any kind of organization, you know that there is generally a hierarchy of management between you and the organization's president, director, or CEO. If you had a suggestion that you wanted them to hear, you certainly had to go up through management channels. That's formal communication. However, you may have run into that top manager in the elevator. Or in the restroom. Or in a line at the movie theatre. You could have voiced your suggestion casually then. That's informal communication.

> **LO 15-2**
> Compare communication channels and appropriate ways for managers to use them.

Formal Communication Channels: Up, Down, Sideways, and Outward

Formal communication channels are recognized as official. The organization chart we described in Chapter 8 indicates how official communications—memos, letters, reports, announcements—are supposed to be routed.

Formal communication is of three types: (1) *vertical*—meaning upward and downward, (2) *horizontal*—meaning laterally (sideways), and (3) *external*—meaning outside the organization.

1. Vertical Communication: Up and Down the Chain of Command
Vertical communication is the flow of messages up and down the hierarchy within the organization: bosses communicating with subordinates, subordinates communicating with bosses. As you might expect, the more management levels through which a message passes, the more it is prone to some distortion.

- **Downward communication—from top to bottom.** **Downward communication** flows from higher to lower levels. In small organizations, top-down communication may be delivered face-to-face. In larger organizations, it's delivered via meetings, e-mail, official memos, company publications, and town hall meetings. An example of downward communication is a companywide open-enrollment e-mail from the chief HR officer stating that all employees must confirm their selected health insurance plan online between November 1 and November 30.

- **Upward communication—from bottom to top.** **Upward communication** flows from lower to higher levels. Often, this type of communication is from an employee to their immediate manager, who in turn may relay it up to the next level, if necessary. An example of upward communication is sending a weekly progress

Upward bound. How do you communicate with a manager two or three levels above you in the organization's hierarchy? You can send a memo through channels. Or you can watch for informal opportunities like this when a manager heads for a cup of coffee. Jose Luis Pelaez Inc/Blend Images LLC

report e-mail to your supervisor. It is very important to use upward communication to share regular updates with your boss. That said, we recommend asking them how they would like to stay in touch, as some managers prefer face-to-face meetings while others would rather you send an e-mail. All told, effective upward communication depends on an atmosphere of trust and psychological safety.[22] Employees are less likely to pass on bad news when they don't trust the boss.

2. Horizontal Communication: Within and between Work Units

Horizontal communication flows within and between work units, and its main purpose is coordination. As a manager, you will spend perhaps as much as a third of your time engaging in horizontal communication—consulting with colleagues and peers within the organization. Horizontal communication involves sharing information, coordinating tasks, solving problems, resolving conflicts, and garnering the support of your peers. Meetings, committees, task forces, and matrix structures all encourage horizontal communication.

Here are four things that impede horizontal communication in organizations:

1. Specialization that encourages people to focus on only their jobs rather than on collaboration.
2. Competition or rivalry between workers or work units that prevents sharing of information.
3. Organizational cultures that discourage collaboration, cooperation, or innovation.
4. Incentive systems that reward individual behavior over collaboration.

Strong horizontal communication is essential for innovation. In fact, the ideas born from cross-disciplinary, horizontal communication in an organization may be a key source of sustainable competitive advantage in the current and future economy.[23]

EXAMPLE | Internal Communication in a Modern Work Environment

Vertical and horizontal communication represent internal communication, meaning they occur between people who work in the same organization. Until recently, we tended to assume that "in the same organization" meant *working in the same physical space*, or, at the very least, *working at separate locations owned by the same company*. But the reality of what it means to communicate *internally* has changed, with the majority of workers now expecting to work remotely at least some of the time.[24] What should internal communication look like in the new world of work? Let's discuss how organizations are transitioning to this new format. Then, we'll consider best practices for maximizing the benefits of popular remote/hybrid workplace communication platforms.

Transitioning to Remote/Hybrid Communication
Remote/hybrid work communication is, by default, leaner than face-to-face, in-person communication. Organizations use collaboration software such as Slack, Teams, and Zoom to keep communication as rich as possible when workers are remote/hybrid. But the rapid, widespread adoption of these tools has led to confusion, annoyance, and stress among workers. This is because organizations are learning, in real time, which aspects of the in-person work environment to hold onto and which to let go of now that many of their workers are remote/hybrid. Needless to say, the transition has been bumpy.

Maximizing the Benefits of Remote/Hybrid Internal Communication Platforms
Here are a few tips for maximizing the benefits of remote/hybrid workplace communication software:

1. **Streamline communication channels.** Employees can feel overwhelmed when they must engage with multiple internal communication platforms. Said a former Nestlé employee, "You could have an email chain, a text thread, a videoconference call and an in-person one-on-one about the same topic all within 24 hours."[25] Professors know this struggle well, as we often communicate with colleagues using both e-mail and Teams/Slack/Zoom, and with students using e-mail, a learning management system (e.g., Blackboard, Moodle), and a classroom GroupMe. Organizations can relieve some of the stress by narrowing the options for internal communication to the smallest number feasible.

2. **Consider what's important.** Is it necessary for your employees to log into the platform at 8:00 a.m., be a mouse click away all day, and log out of the platform at 5:00 p.m.? This may be the case in some professions, such as telehealth, where scheduled appointments need to occur during normal working hours. However, if traditional, synchronous communication isn't required, why make specific work hours mandatory? Organizations should be judicious when deciding which traditional workplace norms must stay and which are ok to let go of in a hybrid/remote environment.

3. **Set clear expectations.** Managers should be crystal clear regarding what they expect of employees in terms of maintaining communication while working away from the office, regardless of which platforms are used and how much structure is in place. Ambiguity breeds stress, and clear guidelines go a long way toward mitigating the anxiety employees can feel when adjusting to remote/hybrid schedules.[26] Managers should clarify expectations for work hours, communication frequency, collaboration, and team and individual employee goals.[27]

YOUR CALL

What do you think is the most challenging aspect of internal communication in a remote/hybrid environment? What else would you do, as a manager, to ease the transition?

3. External Communication: Outside the Organization

External communication flows between people inside and outside the organization. External communication is increasingly important because organizations desire to communicate with other stakeholders—customers, suppliers, shareholders, or other owners—in pursuit of their strategic goals. External communication is a critical tool for growing a small businesses, and it also can boost business for well-known brands. Consider the case of Wendy's.

External Communication Example—Wendy's: What do you think of when you think of a Wendy's restaurant? A burger? Fries? A frosty? If you've been paying attention for the past few years, chances are you also think of social media. Wendy's has built a cult following for its snarky posts and hilarious trolling of competitors. Consumers view the company's quippy posts as authentic and engaging, and the strategy seems to be working.[28] Wendy's continues to see sales and revenue growth and is one of the top five fast-food restaurants in the United States.[29] Experts attribute much of Wendy's social media stardom in recent years to the company's social media and gaming manager, Kristin Tormey. Said Tormey of how she chooses the right message for the right external communication medium, "You just have to be aware of what's going on out there, whether it's what's in the news, what's in the industry, what's going on on each platform, and how that tone is."[30]

Informal Communication Channels

Informal communication channels develop outside the formal structure and do not follow the chain of command—they are more spontaneous, can skip management levels, and can cut across lines of authority.

Two types of informal channels are (1) the *grapevine* and (2) *face-to-face communication*.

The Grapevine

The **grapevine** is the unofficial communication system of the informal organization, a network of in-person communication that we often refer to as gossip. You may think the grapevine is only good for spreading malicious rumors, but it serves important functions.[31] For example, research shows that the grapevine acts as a primary conduit for important organizational information, and engaging in this type of communication can even enhance employees' well-being at work. Of course, workplace gossip can have negative effects. In particular, when negative information about one or more employees travels along the grapevine, it can harm reputations, invade privacy, and harm self-esteem and overall emotional well-being.[32]

Managers can reduce the negative effects of the grapevine by following these four suggestions:[33]

1. **Rely on an open-door policy.** Employees are less like to gossip when they have direct and easy access to management.
2. **Provide fast and transparent information.** This recommendation is important during a crisis, such as dealing with COVID-19 or during organizational change.
3. **Quickly respond to gossip.** Gossip is like a wildfire. Left untreated, it spreads fast and wide. Managers are encouraged to use both rich and lean communication media to correct erroneous gossip.
4. **Be a role model.** Don't let employees see or hear you gossiping. It's better to demonstrate integrity while proactively communicating with others.

Face-to-Face Communication   Despite the entrenched use of quick and efficient electronic communication in our lives, face-to-face conversation is still justifiably a major part of our professional lives. Employees value authentic human contact with their supervisors and welcome the implication that their managers care about them. Face time builds relationships and trust, shows respect for employees as individuals, and thus is highly motivating.[34]

Some basic principles apply to making the most of face-to-face communication in the work environment.

1. **Make time for face-to-face.** Rather than hoping to catch people at random, schedule time with individual employees, and make sure you'll both be free of distractions (including cell phones) for the few minutes your interaction will take. This is not the moment to multitask. In a remote or hybrid environment, this practice involves connecting individually with employees over platforms such as Zoom, Teams, or Slack.[35]
2. **Listen more and talk less.** As you learned in this chapter's Manage U, it's important to listen not just to the words another person is saying, but also to the emotional content behind the words. Make eye contact and observe body language. This will help you be empathetic. When it's your turn to speak, be brief. If your message is specific or factual, prepare your facts and outline your thoughts ahead of time. Expect questions and be prepared with answers.
3. **Be mindful and show interest.** We have mentioned several times in this product how important it is to be mindful when communicating with others. Mindfulness is extremely important in face-to-face conversations because it enhances your listening skills and demonstrates your genuine interest. Asking questions and paraphrasing are good ways to stay mindful and show interest.
4. **Hold employee town hall meetings.** For in-person meetings with groups of employees, "town hall" meetings, often held monthly or quarterly, usually consist of a presentation by managers and an open question-and-answer session. Town hall meetings also can be held virtually. Nick Goldberg, founder and CEO of EZRA virtual coaching platform, urged organizations to use town hall meetings wisely. "If you can't fill the hour with meaningful space and discourse, it's not going to be a productive town hall, and chances are your team will be multitasking their way through it," said Goldberg. He added, "instead, know the outcome you're looking for and make that clear to your team. Is it to get feedback? Is it to brainstorm? Simply to create space? Make sure this is intentional and communicated up front."[36]

Meetings are probably the most frequently used mechanism for communicating formally or informally with a group of people. They can be held in a variety of formats, and we're certain you have attended many of them in the past. How many of them produced useful results or conclusions? Probably not too many if you believe recent research that suggests 70% of meetings merely prevent workers from being productive and completing their assigned tasks.[37] Let's consider how you can improve these stats when you next attend or lead a meeting (see the Practical Action box). •

PRACTICAL ACTION | Tips for Improving Meetings

Research suggests that the post-pandemic increase in remote and hybrid work schedules has resulted in more and longer meetings for most employees.[38] Further, over 90% of employees see meetings as a waste of time. But research also tells us that meetings, when executed well, can drive culture, motivate employees, and enhance decision making.[39] So what makes for a good meeting? Here are a few tips.

What to Do as a Meeting Leader[40]

1. **It all starts with a purpose.** "Every meeting should have a goal," says Canva's global head of people Jennie Rogerson.[41] When you call a meeting, ask yourself what specific task or tasks you want the meeting to accomplish. Create an agenda with time limits for each point, leaving brief time slots for attendees' input and discussion. Creating an agenda does more than keep you on track; it helps others know what they should prepare for the meeting, saving valuable time.

2. **Invite the appropriate people.** The list of attendees should fit the goal(s) of the meeting. Participants should be there for a clear purpose and should possess the necessary knowledge or expertise to participate.

3. **Pick a good day and time to meet.** We likely can all agree that Fridays are generally bad for holding meetings.[42] However, it's important to know which days/times are best and worst for meetings in your specific organization or team. The point is to ask participants for their preferences and select the best day and time. Some organizations, such as Slack and Shopify, have instituted "no meeting" days each week to allow employees to focus on important job tasks without fear of being interrupted by meetings.

4. **Start the meeting effectively.** This can be done by:
    - Stating the purpose of the meeting.
    - Inviting participants to ask clarifying questions regarding the meeting's goal(s).
    - Explaining exactly why the meeting is important.
    - Sharing why you believe the specific attendees are important for the decision(s) being made.

5. **Start and end on time.** Respect other people's time commitments. Be the first in the meeting room and start when you said you would. Stick to the time limits you've allowed for each agenda item and keep your eye on the clock. Learn how to gently but firmly cut off unproductive discussion. ("Thanks for your contribution, Jay. Let's quickly hear from one more person before we move on to the next point.")

6. **Put extraneous issues in a parking lot.** Meetings often lead to conversations about important issues that go beyond the purpose of the meetings. Rather than being distracted by them during your meeting, put them in the metaphorical parking lot. The parking lot is a recording of these issues on a white board, flip chart, or digital notes. It is a good idea to discuss next steps for items in the parking lot at the end of your meeting.

7. **Follow up.** Within 24 hours of the meeting, clarify results and expectations by sending attendees a summary of decisions made, tasks to be performed, and who is to perform them and when.

What to Do as a Meeting Participant

1. **Prepare but stay flexible.** Respond promptly to the meeting invitation. Read the agenda (ask for one if you don't receive it ahead of time) and be prepared with any facts or data you may be called upon to present. You should also prepare to be flexible because meetings don't always go as planned. For example, if you have 15 minutes scheduled to present, prepare both a full presentation and a shortened one in case your time is limited.

2. **Be on time.** Showing up late is disrespectful and disruptive. It can also make the meeting run over time if the leader decides to wait for you.

3. **Participate intelligently.** Expect to contribute to the meeting, but make sure your contributions are brief, professional, and on point. Focus on making high-quality contributions based on the strengths and experiences you bring to the meeting. Remember that it's about enriching the decision, not talking more than everyone else.

4. **Follow up.** If you came away from the meeting with a to-do list, be sure you act on it in a timely way so the goals of the meeting can be achieved. You may even be able to avoid having to attend another meeting to go over the same agenda all over again.

YOUR CALL

To what extent have you used these suggestions in past meetings? Do you see any problems in following these suggestions?

15.3 Barriers to Communication

THE BIG PICTURE
We describe several barriers to communication. Physical barriers include sound, time, and space. Personal barriers include variations in communication skills, processing and interpreting information, trustworthiness and credibility, attentional issues, and generational considerations. Cross-cultural barriers are a greater challenge as more jobs include interactions with others around the globe. Nonverbal communication can present a barrier if it conflicts with the spoken message. Finally, gender differences can present barriers but should be interpreted cautiously.

LO 15-3

Identify barriers to communication and ways managers can overcome them.

Have you ever tried to communicate only to wind up feeling like the people in this photo? If so, you are not alone. Common communication barriers can make even the simplest exchanges difficult.
pathdoc/Shutterstock

If you have ever been served the wrong drink because the server couldn't hear you in a loud restaurant, clicked on a broken web link, missed your boarding call because the airport's public address system was full of static, or taken offense at a text you later found you misinterpreted, you've experienced a barrier to communication. Communication barriers produce noise (discussed in Section 15.1) that interferes with how messages are transmitted or understood, and barriers can occur in any step of the communication process, as shown in Table 15.1.

Consider the idea of false information—a concept we discuss in detail in Section 15.4—and how biases related to it can surface at multiple steps of the communication process:

- Encoding—sender purposefully distorts the information being communicated.
- Medium—news outlets fail to report important information.
- Receiver—various groups interpret the information according to personal biases rather than factual assessment.
- Feedback—receiver fails to comment on an issue because they know you have a different perspective.

TABLE 15.1 How Barriers Happen in Various Steps of the Communication Process

All it takes is one blocked step in the communication process for communication to fail. Consider the following.

- **Sender barrier—no message gets sent.** Example: If a manager has an idea but is afraid to voice it because they fear criticism, then obviously no message gets sent.
- **Encoding barrier—the message is not expressed correctly.** Example: If people have a different first language, the meaning of words can be misinterpreted.
- **Medium barrier—the communication channel is blocked.** Example: When a computer network is down, the network is an example of a blocked medium.
- **Decoding barrier—the recipient doesn't understand the message.** Example: You pulled an all-nighter traveling back from spring break and today your brain is fuzzy and unfocused during class lectures.
- **Receiver barrier—no message gets received.** Example: Because you were texting during a class lecture, you weren't listening when the professor announced a new assignment due to tomorrow.
- **Feedback barrier—the recipient doesn't respond enough.** Example: You give someone driving directions, but since they only nod their heads and don't repeat the directions back to you, you don't really know whether you were understood.

In this section we'll look at several types of communication barriers—physical, personal, cross-cultural, nonverbal, and gender differences.

1. Physical Barriers: Sound, Time, Space

Try shouting at someone over a concert crowd and you know what physical communication barriers are. These barriers consist of things in the physical environment that prevent effective communication. They include:

- *Technology issues* such as crashed laptops or phone reception problems.
- *Noise* such as others talking over you or construction sounds.
- *Physical distance* that presents a barrier when there is either too much of it or not enough of it for the people involved in the communication.
- *Too much physical distance* might present a communication barrier. For example, for people who prefer to work in an office and spend face-to-face time with colleagues, working from home and communicating over Zoom or other meeting platforms can make communication difficult.
- *Not enough physical distance* might present a communication barrier. For example, for people who have trouble concentrating, open plan offices can be challenging. These floor plans can be noisy and full of distractions, and people may feel unable to escape being "on" all day because they have less privacy than they would like.[43]

Imagine yourself working in each of these environments. How do you think the physical barriers that accompany working from home would affect your ability to communicate with co-workers? How about the physical barriers that arise in open plan offices? Which of these work environments would present more physical barriers for you, personally? Rawpixel.com/Shutterstock; Cathy Yeulet/123RF

2. Personal Barriers: Individual Attributes That Hinder Communication

"Is it them or is it me?" How often have you asked this question after someone is surprised or confused by something you've said? Let's examine five personal barriers that contribute to miscommunication.

Variable Skills in Communicating Effectively *Merriam-Webster* recently added the abbreviation *TL; DR* to its dictionary. It stands for "too long; didn't read," and its popularity highlights our increased desire for efficient communication. Chances are you have worked with people who are great at communicating effectively and efficiently and with people who are not so great at these things. Two important points about variable communication skills are:

- **Some people are better communicators than others.** They have the vocabulary, writing ability, speaking skills, facial expressions, eye contact, and/or social skills to express themselves in a superior way. Some managers can communicate a project update in a three-sentence e-mail, while others write three paragraphs.
- **Better communication skills can be learned.**[44] The final section in this chapter discusses a variety of ways you can improve your communication effectiveness.

Variations in the Way We Process and Interpret Information Communication is a perceptual process in which we use our individual frames of reference to interpret the world around us. This means we are selective about which pieces of information have meaning to us and which do not. Our frames of reference are associated with individual differences such as age, political affiliation, religious affiliation, values, beliefs, and education.

Let's consider what you can do to reduce distortions in information processing:

- **Senders can avoid misinterpretation by communicating clearly.** Effective communicators, according to HR and management consultant Susan Heathfield, understand that it's largely their responsibility to ensure the receiver correctly interprets their message. "The sender must present the message clearly and with enough detail so that the receiver shares meaning with the sender during and following the communication."[45]
- **Receivers can avoid misinterpretation by paraphrasing.** Communication barriers can occur when receivers incorrectly decode messages. One way for receivers to avoid this is to use paraphrasing—discussed in Section 15.1—to succinctly restate the sender's message to ensure they have properly interpreted the meaning of the message. As a bonus, the act of paraphrasing requires you to use critical thinking—an indispensable career readiness competency.

Does this photo look familiar to you? For many of us, working on multiple devices at once and juggling several tasks simultaneously have become the norm. When was the last time you worked, mindfully, on just one thing at a time? JGI/Tom Grill/Getty Images

Variations in Trustworthiness and Credibility Communication is bound to be flawed without trust between you and the other person. A lack of trust and/or credibility will have both of you concentrating on defensive tactics rather than on the meaning of the message being exchanged. Consider the impact of these issues on employees and organizations and how you can use trust to improve communications:

- **Low trust damages communication.** This in turn reduces outcomes like job satisfaction, openness to change, engagement, citizenship behavior, and performance.[46]
- **Focus on building a trusting foundation.** Managers can build trust by openly sharing information; providing clear, performance-focused, regular feedback; and encouraging an ongoing two-way dialogue with employees.[47]

Attentional Issues Does your mind wander throughout the day? Do you forget people's names shortly after meeting them? These are signs of **mindlessness**, which is a state of reduced attention. It is expressed in behavior that seems rigid or thoughtless.[48]

Many of us are in a constant state of cognitive overload, and our brains simply can't keep up with all the stimuli we receive. According to clinical psychologist Vincent Greenwood, "While we've never had more tools for productivity, creativity and problem-solving, we've never been so overwhelmed—constantly bombarded by alerts, messages and the demand to master the next new technological breakthroughs." Greenwood added that our constant state of cognitive overload results in a "neural buzz experience of trying to walk up a downward moving escalator, which leaves one feeling frustrated, disempowered and worn out."[49]

Here are two things you can do to reduce the impact of attentional issues on communications:

- **Try focusing on one thing at a time.** One way many of us deal with modern life is by multitasking. But doing so lowers the quality of each task we complete. Our brains aren't wired to pay close attention to multiple tasks at once, and the more tasks we try to juggle, the more mindless we become.[50]
- **Take a (digital) break.** Another barrier to listening, ironically, is communication technology such as cell phones. If we're looking at our screens all the time, how can we really be listening to those who are right before us? One way we can safeguard our cognitive resources and ability to be mindful in communication is to take periodic breaks not only from our endless tasks but also from our cell phones, even when we are not in direct communication with others.

Generational Differences If you've tried to teach an older relative to make a TikTok, you likely have an appreciation for how difficult it can be for older generations to learn new technologies. Lest you fall into the trap of stereotyping older workers, remember that U.S. Senator Bernie Sanders, who is in his 80s, maintains an active Twitter feed with more than 15 million followers.[51] Here are some key points about generational communication differences in the modern workplace:

- **Younger generations are less likely to use e-mail.** Gen Z workers show a strong preference for platforms like Slack and Microsoft Teams over traditional e-mail. Many members of older generations still prefer to use e-mail.[52]
- **Organizations should provide training and support.** Organizations should provide plenty of support and training for workers to keep them up to date on the latest communication tools, regardless of whether they are dealing with new technology or new employees who need to learn existing technology.

3. Cross-Cultural Barriers

As we discussed in Chapter DEI, culture refers to the shared assumptions that bind a collective—such as a society—and that impact how members of the group perceive, think about, and react to things in the environment.[53] Culture naturally affects the way we communicate because cultural norms and beliefs are deeply ingrained in our thoughts and behaviors. Language and style differences are two ways that culture can become a communication barrier:

- **Language differences.** Language differences can present a cross-cultural communication barrier. For example, jokes and humor are very much linked to culture.[54] One of your authors found that American jokes don't necessarily get laughs in Europe, Asia, and Scandinavia. Even the United States and Great Britain, whose cultures share many elements, are often said to be "two countries divided by a common language" (an ironic observation often attributed to the British playwright George Bernard Shaw). For example, if a British supervisor tells you that your work is "quite good," for example, don't get too excited—it means your work is average, at best.[55]

- **Style differences.** Communication styles can vary widely by culture, and knowing what to expect gives workers a great advantage. Consider the following example:

    Style Differences—Dutch Communication: When Judith Gardiner moved to the Netherlands for work, she learned that the Dutch communicate with a different style than she was accustomed to. Gardiner, now a VP for growth and emerging European markets for Equinix, has come to learn what to expect. In fact, she now admires the way her Dutch colleagues approach communications. Said Gardiner, "There's often very little sugarcoating or dancing around difficult topics. Elephants in the room are almost introduced as soon as they appear. People can have highly charged debates in a meeting and then slide into social situations straight afterwards with ease."[56]

    See the Practical Action box for tips on improving your cross-cultural communication.

PRACTICAL ACTION | Improving Your Cross-Cultural Communication Fluency

Dr. Elizabeth Tuleja—professor of intercultural communication and global leadership at the University of Notre Dame—said, "You can know all the functional aspects of international business. But if you don't know how to develop relationships and understand people based upon their norms and behavior and what they expect from you, then you're not going to be as successful."[57]

It's natural for differences to make us feel uncomfortable at first. But Dr. Tuleja suggests we view them as a chance to grow, saying, "we must be able to embrace such differences and acknowledge them as opportunities for learning and enrichment rather than forces for confusion and trouble." Approaching things with this mindset will help you build the career readiness competencies of diversity, equity, and inclusion; personal adaptability; self-awareness; and openness to change, among others.

Here are suggestions for improving your cross-cultural communication abilities:[58]

Prepare Yourself Ahead of Time
There are plenty of resources to help you improve your cross-cultural communication. For example, you can use podcasts, articles, and online learning programs. You can also talk with friends and family who have experience with cross-cultural communication. Learn everything you can on your own, first.

Observe
A great way to learn something is to simply watch others. If you want to know how to communicate with someone from a particular culture, pay attention when two or more people from that culture communicate with one another. Observe body language; notice how close they stand to each other while communicating; and listen for things like tone, specific words, and the pace of the conversation.

Be Genuinely Curious
Have you ever avoided interacting with someone from a different culture because you were afraid to make a mistake and offend them? This is natural, but unfortunately, it causes many of us to miss out on opportunities for understanding, innovation, and friendship. If you ask questions about another person's culture with a genuine sense of curiosity and an authentic desire to learn more about them, most people will be happy to engage with you.[59]

Know That You Will Make (Lots of) Mistakes
The way that we communicate is deeply ingrained, and you should expect that no matter how much training you participate in or expertise you build, you will still make mistakes. One of your authors—Denise Breaux Soignet—knows this first hand. Denise teaches students and organizations about workplace religious inclusion, yet when a local Imam—whom she had not yet met—walked into her classroom to spend the day talking with her students about Islam, she instinctively and enthusiastically went in for a handshake as she introduced herself. The Imam graciously bowed and explained that he did not shake hands with women other than those in his family. It turned out to be a learning opportunity for the students—Denise and the Imam talked about the interaction with the class for several minutes to explain the *why* behind the communication difference (because the Imam saw it as a sign of respect for women) and to demonstrate that it's ok to make mistakes in cross-cultural communication, no matter how much knowledge and experience you have.

YOUR CALL
How can you do a better job of improving your cross-cultural communication?

4. Nonverbal Communication: How Unwritten and Unspoken Messages May Mislead

Nonverbal communication consists of messages sent outside of the written or spoken word. We primarily express nonverbal communication through (1) *eye contact,* (2) *facial expressions,* (3) *body movements and gestures,* and (4) *touch.*[60] Some research suggests that about half of what we communicate is transmitted nonverbally.[61]

1. Eye Contact Westerners use eye contact to signal the beginning and end of a conversation, to reflect interest and attention, and to convey both honesty and respect.[62] Most people from Western cultures tend to avoid eye contact when conveying bad news or negative feedback. In many Eastern cultures, however, lowering one's eyes is a sign of respect.[63] Incorrectly interpreting these nonverbal cues as evasive behavior could lead to unfortunate misunderstandings.

2. Facial Expressions Popular culture suggests that Americans are easy to spot in other countries because they're always smiling.[64] You're probably used to thinking that smiling represents warmth, happiness, or friendship, whereas frowning represents dissatisfaction or anger. But people in some cultures are less openly demonstrative than people in the United States. One study showed photographs of facial expressions to thousands of people in 44 countries. Among the findings were that, in cultures with low uncertainty avoidance (see Chapter 4), people judged smiling faces as indicating untrustworthiness and possibly even lower intelligence.

If you were raised in the United States, then you've probably internalized the belief that smiling at others is expected as part of polite communication. But did you know that in many places across the globe, people find smiling odd, distracting, and even suspicious?
Max Bukovski/Shutterstock

Facial Expressions Example—Smiling Training in Russia: In Russia, smiling for no reason isn't common. Russian film director Yulia Melamed said she was once stopped by police because she was smiling while walking around. She added, "It's strange for a person to walk down the street and smile. It looks alien and suspicious." This is why, ahead of the 2018 World Cup, Russian organizations including FIFA, Russian Railways, and Moscow Metro conducted smiling training for employees so that they would seem more welcoming to foreign visitors.[65]

3. Body Movements and Gestures Open body positions, such as leaning slightly backward, express openness, warmth, closeness, and availability for communication. Closed body positions, such as folded arms or crossed legs, can signal defensiveness. Angling your body away from the other person generally makes you look uninterested.[66] You can use these conclusions to improve communications with others.

4. Touch Norms for touching vary significantly. For example, kissing on the cheek, patting on the shoulder, and hugging may seem appropriate in business for some people, but others find these actions offensive in a professional context. As with physical touch in other realms of life, there should always be mutual consent for physical contact at work. Beyond this important rule, a few general guidelines are:[67]

- **Observe how others behave.** Take the time to learn the norms in your workplace, as well as individual employees' cultural preferences for physical contact between co-workers.
- **Be mindful of power dynamics.** If you have power over an employee and ask them for a hug, they may feel pressured to oblige even if they are uncomfortable. A good rule is to limit this kind of affection to colleagues on the same level.

Exchange of views? Different people may use different communication styles. How effective do you think you are at communicating with various individuals regardless of gender? monkeybusinessimages/Getty Images

- Set your own boundaries and respect those of others. Practice how you will communicate your comfort level with physical contact. For example, "I'm so glad to see you, and I'm not a hugger," or "thank you, but I'd prefer an elbow bump," work just fine. Remember to be respectful of the physical boundaries that others set for themselves, too.

5. Gender Differences

According to scientific evidence, we can make two general statements about gender and communication differences: (1) There exist some observable differences in communication across the gender spectrum, and (2) most of these differences likely are the result of socialization rather than biology.[68] In other words, people with different gender identities do tend to have different communication styles and make different communication choices, and they do this because they've been conditioned to do so. Further, these differences are highly nuanced, and managers should be careful to not make assumptions about workers' communication styles and choices based on gender stereotypes.

What does this mean for managers? Broadly, managers should be aware that communication choices may reflect gender norms and should use this understanding to enhance and improve communications in their workplaces.

15.4 Social Media and Management

THE BIG PICTURE

We discuss social media and its use by employees and managers. We then turn our attention to the impact of social media on managers' and organizations' effectiveness. We consider the costs of social media use, such as the effects of cyberloafing, as well as growing concerns about security, privacy, and false information. Finally, we discuss the importance of setting effective social media policies.

LO 15-4
Discuss how managers can successfully use social media to communicate.

Social media, which use web-based and mobile technologies to generate interactive dialogue with members of a network, are woven into every aspect of our lives. We begin our exploration of these technologies by documenting their general use. We then examine the effects of social media on managerial and organizational effectiveness, review the downsides of social media, and discuss the need for organizations to develop effective social media policies.

The Use of Social Media Has Changed the Fabric of Our Lives

The widespread use of social media is changing our personal lives, the very nature of how businesses operate, and the principles of management. Consider these three statistics:[69]

- At least half of the world's population, or nearly 4 billion people, use social media.
- Overall, businesses spent more than $200 billion on social media advertising in 2022.
- Nearly 90% of Gen Zers use social media to discover new brands.

These figures show the power of social media in today's digital world, but what do you think research has to say about this phenomenon? You may not be surprised to learn that recent studies link a company's effective use of social media to an increase in brand awareness, brand loyalty, and sales.[70] National Geographic is an example of an organization that has embraced social media.

Embracing Social Media Example—National Geographic: National Geographic went from 100 million Instagram followers in 2019 to 275 million in 2023.[71] In fact, National Geographic has become one of the most powerful brands in the world, with more than 300 million followers across all of its social media accounts.[72] The mission of National Geographic is to "use the power of science, exploration, education, and storytelling to illuminate and protect the wonder of our world," and the company credits its social media success to its ability to stay true to its mission through visual storytelling on platforms like Instagram.[73]

What does research suggest about the use of social media across generations? Figure 15.3 shows social network usage across different age groups. Those between the ages of 18 and 29 use Snapchat, TikTok, and Twitch more than any other age group. Facebook is most popular with those over 64. All told, however, it appears all age groups use these platforms, underscoring the need for businesses to use social media tools to engage with stakeholders of all ages.

Moreover, global businesses are using social medial platforms to reach audiences in countries around the world. Global corporations need to know which social networks are used in different countries and adapt their marketing strategies to fit with those. For example, a company wishing to market products in China would need to know that Twitter and Facebook are not good choices, given that these platforms are illegal for Chinese consumers to use.[74]

FIGURE 15.3

Age distribution at the top social networks

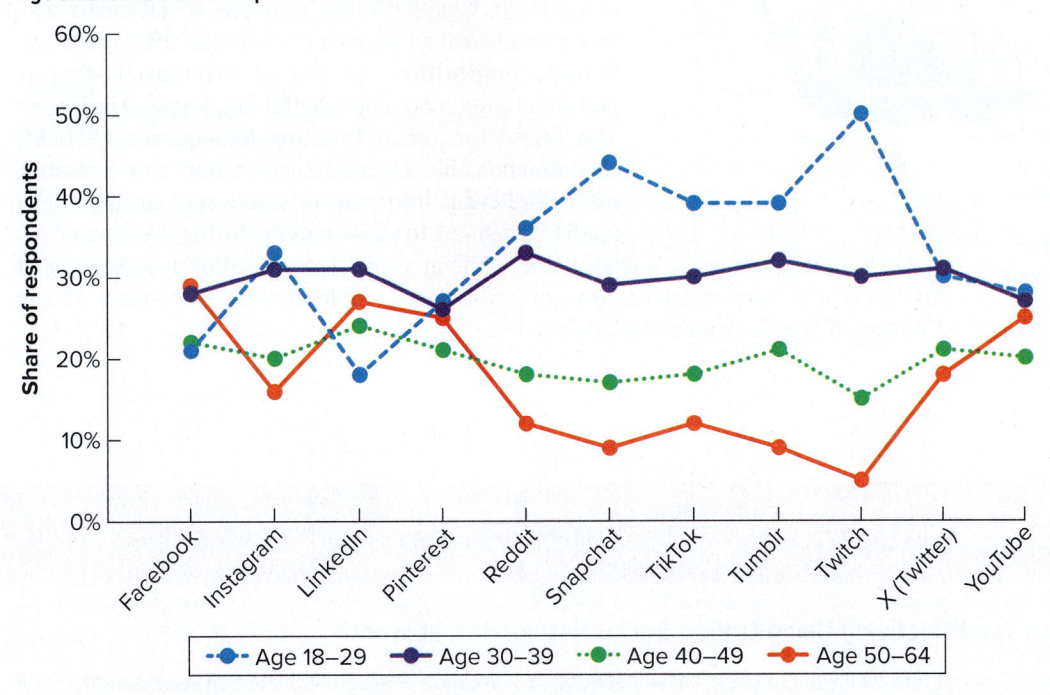

Source: Data obtained from "Distribution of Leading Social Media Platform Users in the United States as of August 2022, by Age Group," Statista, https://www.statista.com/statistics/1337525/us-distribution-leading-social-media-platforms-by-age-group/ (accessed May 14, 2023).

Social Media and Managerial and Organizational Effectiveness

With their ease of use, speed, and potential to draw huge audiences, social media platforms have increasing applications for managers' and organizations' effectiveness. Here we look at social media use in recruiting, innovation, sales, and corporate reputation.

Employment Recruiting Social media platforms are popular avenues for corporate recruiting. Here are four issues to consider with respect to social media recruiting:

- **Networks used:** Around 90% of companies today use social media for recruiting.[75] Although Facebook and LinkedIn have around 2 billion and 930 million users, respectively, recruiters prefer LinkedIn.[76] One reason is that the platform acts as a "secondary resume" and allows recruiters to easily filter for specific skill sets that candidates may have.[77]

- **Research as a job applicant:** Investigating companies is part of your preparation for finding a job after graduation (and helps you practice your career readiness competency of understanding the business). Social media networks are a key source of information about a company.

- **Screening:** Companies use social media for more than just scouting new employees. Specifically, an increasing number of hiring managers are turning to social media to screen applicants and verify the information they provide.[78] One study found that 55% of employers who screened candidates on social media decided not to hire an applicant based on what they saw.[79] Indeed, your social media profile can make or break your ability to land your dream job.

- **Legal implications:** Using social media for recruiting and screening can lead to hiring discrimination, which we discussed in Chapter 9. For example, social media platforms can reveal an applicant's religious affiliation, age, family composition, or sexual orientation—factors recruiters should not consider for employment purposes. The Society for Human Resource Management (SHRM) recommends that recruiters not report any personal, non-job-relevant information discovered during social media screenings to those making hiring decisions.[80]

What you post on your social media pages may be visible to the entire world. Is there anything there you wouldn't want a prospective employer to see? Barcin/Getty Images

How often do you use social media while at work? Do you think it is helping or hindering your performance? You can find out by completing Self-Assessment 15.1 in Connect, if your instructor has assigned it.

SELF-ASSESSMENT 15.1

To What Extent Are You Effectively Using Online Social Networking at Work?

This survey is designed to assess how well you are using social networking in your job. Please complete Self-Assessment 15.1 if your instructor has assigned it in Connect.

Innovation in Social Media: Crowdsourcing If you are looking for an innovative solution to a problem, you might conclude that the more people you have thinking about the problem, the more potential ideas will be generated. That's the idea behind crowdsourcing, defined in Chapter 10 as the practice of obtaining needed services, ideas, or content by soliciting contributions from a large group of people typically via the Internet. The strategy has drawn a lot of attention, especially for its use in fundraising (crowdfunding) on such sites as Kickstarter, but it has a mixed record of success.[81]

Some crowdsourcing efforts are organized as competitions, with individuals volunteering to solve a problem by a certain deadline to win a prize. The LEGO Ideas platform is a good example.

Crowdsourcing Example—LEGO: LEGO is famous for its interlocking plastic bricks, but did you know that the Danish company was a first mover in the crowdsourcing space? The toymaker introduced the LEGO Ideas platform in 2008 as a way for users to come up with new ideas for LEGO sets. Consumers take pictures of an innovative LEGO set and send it in, and LEGO reviews any idea that receives over 10,000 votes from other LEGO users. If LEGO accepts the idea, the user gets to work with the company to make their idea a reality and also receives 1% of the model's sales. Fifty-one consumer-submitted LEGO ideas passed the 10,000-vote threshold in 2022. Keep in mind that there's more to the LEGO Ideas platform than new idea generation—it provides an opportunity for the company to validate demand for ideas before moving forward with mass production.[82]

Innovative rock stars. The "Dynamite" Lego model honoring the K-pop supergroup BTS originated from the Lego Ideas platform. Yonhap News/YNA/Newscom

Researchers have studied crowdsourcing and found it can boost product quality, speed up processes, and increase creativity, but it isn't suitable for all situations. One such situation is when a firm is working on a proprietary or secretive project that should not be revealed to the public.[83] Here is some additional advice for developing effective crowdsourcing programs:[84]

- Link crowdsourcing efforts to incentives in order to motivate participants. (Think back to LEGO's offer to provide winners with royalties on sales of their models.)
- Publicly respond to contributors so that their ideas are validated. This also encourages others to come forward because they feel confident their ideas will be heard.

Sales and Brand Recognition An "effective" social media presence generates customers and brand recognition. Here's why social media acts as a powerful tool for customer acquisition and brand awareness:

1. Social media can enhance relationships with customers because an authentic social media presence inspires trust.[85]
2. Social media can increase the ability to reach customers on a global scale.
3. For small or local businesses, social media can foster co-promotion of local businesses and can elevate the image of small businesses in the area.[86]
4. Social media can foster consumers' conversations about brands.[87]

Remember that the mere use of social media won't automatically result in more sales and brand recognition. Research suggests social media won't create positive outcomes unless two conditions are met.[88] First, the company must possess both social media savvy and commitment in the form of dedicated resources. Second, a successful social media strategy requires that the company's consumers or customers have social media skills.

Corporate Reputation   Some companies have been very successful at using social media to build and protect their reputations online.[89] In fact, social media can be vital for restoring a company's reputation after a crisis.[90] Consider the following example:

Corporate Reputation Example—Burger King UK: Burger King UK wanted to highlight its scholarships for women entering into the culinary arts (a field historically dominated by men), so the company created a social media campaign to communicate its support for the cause. The tagline? "Women Belong in the Kitchen." As you can imagine, the ad garnered backlash from consumers all over the world, who saw only sexist stereotypes in the text rather than its intended message of support. Burger King deleted mentions of the campaign from social media and issued an apology on its platforms that began with "We hear you. We got our initial tweet wrong and we're sorry," and ended with "We will do better next time."[91]

As the Burger King example shows, one of the biggest dangers for companies on social media is negative comments posted by disgruntled consumers. Some tips for defusing these situations and limiting their potential harm are:

1. **Create and enforce a social media policy for employees.** We'll discuss social media policies in more detail shortly. At a minimum, your policy should limit what employees can say on the organization's web pages and ensure that all posted content meets the highest ethical standards.[92]

2. **Appoint experienced managers to monitor your social media presence and respond quickly and appropriately to negative posts.** A great deal of damage can occur online in a short time, and all of it in the public eye. Hiring someone with the proper experience and judgment can shield the organization from potential social media blunders.[93]

3. **Acknowledge there is a problem.** Gracefully accepting that someone has a genuine issue with the organization, its product or service, or its posts—even if the problem is a misunderstanding on their part—can go a long way toward defusing bad feelings. If the organization is in error, the appropriate manager should say so and apologize.[94]

4. **Don't delete the comment (with exceptions).** You won't make a problem go away by deleting a negative post; in fact, you may make things worse. If the person who left the original post, or another viewer, figures out you deleted it, they may get even more upset, repost the comment, and call you out for deleting it. Deleting comments also can make you look careless or guilty. An exception might entail deleting a post if it contains threatening or profane language, or if the person is harassing or spamming your page.[95]

5. **Take the conversation offline if necessary.** If a customer refuses to be satisfied, take the conversation to a private sphere such as phone or e-mail. Not only will this keep it out of the public eye and prevent further damage to the brand, but the individualized attention may also reduce the customer's ire.[96]

Downsides of Social Media

It's fair to say the digital age and rise of social media have introduced almost as many difficulties as efficiencies into our lives. Some of these issues include cyberloafing, microaggressions, security breaches, privacy concerns, and false information.

Cyberloafing   Lost productivity due to **cyberloafing—using the Internet at work for personal use**—is a primary concern for employers in their adoption of social media. Studies have found that employees cyberloaf for many reasons including boredom, habits or addiction, and social norms.[97] Here are some eye-opening facts about this phenomenon:[98]

- Experts suggest cyberloafing costs businesses up to $85 billion per year in lost productivity.
- Employees spend an average of 12% of their workday checking non-work-related social media.

Many firms have developed social media policies (discussed in the next section) to address cyberloafing. In addition, some companies use designated social media break times, employee monitoring software, and engaging work to discourage cyberloafing during work hours.[99]

Phubbing and FOMO
Microaggressions, or acts of unconscious bias, include a number of seemingly tiny but repeated actions, like interrupting others, mispronouncing or mistaking someone's name, and avoiding eye contact.[100]

Microaggressions in Social Media Example—Language: Social media garners engagement. In other words, companies post content to create new relationships and maintain existing relationships with their stakeholders. Those who do it well know that winning at social media is about standing out, creating memorable content, and having a recognizable brand image. But managers should remember that the (sometimes fun and cheeky) language used to gain followers' attention in posts has the potential to represent microaggressions. Terms and phrases like "this deal is insane!" or "we've been blacklisted," have history that is painful for those belonging to certain identity groups. It's a good idea to have your social media team spend some time researching the meanings of popular phrases and confirming that their language is respectful before posting something on behalf of the company.

One particular form of microaggression is called *phubbing,* short for phone snubbing, or ignoring those present in order to pay attention to a mobile phone. Researchers have found that the urge to phub springs from the fear of missing out—**FOMO**—or of being out of touch with something happening in our social network.[101] FOMO is evident in our habits, such as paying attention to our phones during sleep hours. One study, for example, found that 21% of adults reported waking at night to check their phones, and 70% of people scroll social media after getting in bed.[102]

Security: Guarding against Cyberthreats
Security is defined as a system of safeguards for protecting information technology against disasters, system failures, and unauthorized access that result in damage or loss. Security is a continuing challenge, with computer and cell phone users constantly having to deal with threats ranging from malicious software (malware) that tries to trick people into yielding passwords and personal information to viruses that can destroy or corrupt data.[103]

One way that hackers gain access to personal and business accounts is by exploiting users' predictable and poor password choices.[104] Even after receiving cybersecurity training, the majority of people continue to reuse passwords and/or use the same password across multiple platforms.[105]

The key to protecting digital communication systems against fraud, hackers, identity theft, and other threats is prevention. Table 15.2 presents some ways to protect yourself.[106]

Privacy: Keeping Things to Yourself
Privacy is the right of people not to reveal information about themselves. Threats to privacy can range from name migration, as when a company sells its customer list to another company, to online snooping, government prying, and spying. The results of a recent survey of more than 2,000 Americans found that the majority of Americans feel as if they have little control over their data.[109] This fear is legitimate, as a data privacy breach can be disastrous. A potentially

TABLE 15.2 Protecting against Security and Privacy Breaches on the Internet

- **Don't use passwords that can be easily guessed.** Use weird combinations of letters, numbers, and punctuation, and mix uppercase and lowercase, along with special characters such as !, #, and %.
- **Don't use the same password for multiple sites.** Avoid using the same password at different sites, because if hackers or scammers obtain one account, they potentially have your entire online life.
- **Don't reveal sensitive information on social networking sites.** Even people who set their profiles to Facebook's strictest privacy settings may find sensitive information leaked all over the web.
- **Consider moving sensitive information to a cloud server.** The odds are pretty good that a major cloud provider, such as Google or Microsoft, will do a better job than you at securing your information against various risks.
- **Make sure to encrypt.** Encryption is a process that encodes a message or file so it can only be read by those with a key to decrypt the information.[107] There are many free tools to do this including LastPass and VeraCrypt. Some Windows and Mac operating systems also have built-in encryption.[108]
- **Keep antivirus software updated.** The antivirus software on your computer won't protect you forever. Visit the antivirus software maker's website and enable the automatic update features.

Phishing, malware, and smishing are just a few of the ways hackers can access your data. Has a cybercriminal ever attempted to steal your information? Joe Prachatree/Shutterstock

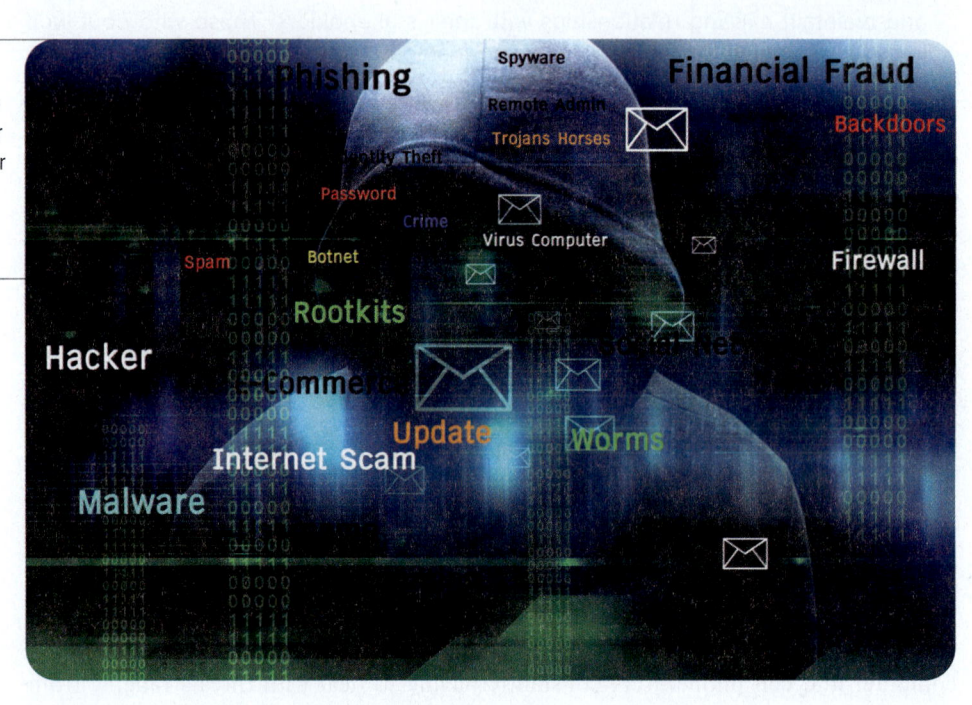

devastating violation of privacy is **identity theft**, in which thieves hijack your name and identity and use your good credit rating to get cash or buy things.

You can bolster your privacy by being aware of three issues:

- **The role of users.** Remember that nothing posted online is ever truly private.[110] In some cases, Internet users are their own worst enemies, posting compromising images and information about themselves on social networking sites that may be available to, say, potential employers. Wise advice is that if you wouldn't want to see something on the front page of the newspaper or the evening news, don't post it online. Many of the cautions we discussed in Table 15.2 apply here, too.

- **Privacy at work.** The practice of monitoring employees' activity during work hours is widespread.[111] In most circumstances, employers are permitted to monitor—that is, read—their employees' e-mail and track their Internet use, and 96% of employers in a recent survey said they did so with their remote and hybrid employees.[112]

- **Responsibility of websites.** Social media sites have a role to play in protecting our privacy. Research suggests it would be nearly impossible for the average person to fully read all the privacy policies they encounter each year, and some experts are advocating that the federal government enact standardized protections for consumers.[113]

What's the Story with False Information? The widespread use of social media has led to an increase of false information being spread about individuals and businesses. Let's consider the two types of false information: *misinformation* and *disinformation*. **Misinformation** is information that is "false but not created with the intention of causing harm." This may be an honest mistake, such as mistyping a figure in a news article and later updating the report with the correct information. On the other hand, **disinformation** is information that is false and deliberately misleading.[114] Let's discuss the history of false information, its impact, and what can be done about it.

Today, many individuals see false information as a threat to democracy, free debate, and the entire Western order, largely because it's accelerated by social media.[115] In fact, a recent survey of more than 150,000 social media users from 142 countries found that nearly 60% are concerned about false information online.[116]

False information! How can you tell fact from fiction in a digital world? Georgejmclittle/Shutterstock

What Can Be Done about False Information False information can damage people and organizations. Here are a few suggestions for defending yourself, your colleagues, and your organizations:

1. **Understand the power of the algorithm.** Twitter, TikTok, and other social media sites use algorithms to deliver customized content to users, and it's easy to forget that these sites are not news outlets. Remember to verify what you read on social media using another, more reputable source of information.[117]
2. **Entertain multiple angles.** Verifying information on trusted news sites is helpful, but remember that even news outlets display bias and/or report information that isn't as accurate as they believe it to be. We encourage you to find multiple sources covering all sides of an issue when confirming information. This may mean gathering information from left-leaning, right-leaning, and centrist news outlets before drawing your own, informed conclusions.[118]

    Entertaining Multiple Angles Example—Searching for Statistics: Those who gather, analyze, and interpret data for a living know all too well how easy it is to find statistics that say just about anything. For the purpose of this example, we searched online for statistics on the percentage of news content that is actually false. We want to show you the wide variation in statistics we were able to find in a simple exercise that took us less than 10 minutes. Here are a few of the statistics:

    - Over 40% of news stories on social media sites represent false information.[119]
    - At least 60% of information on the Internet is false.[120]
    - False information accounts for less than 1% of total news consumption.[121]
    - Almost 75% of statistics are made up (including this one).[122]

    What lesson should you take from these bullet points? Namely, that statistics are plentiful, and you are likely to find a website that confirms whatever information you are looking for. Further, this exercise illustrates how difficult it can be to find an accurate answer to a question when searching online. This is why it's important to research an issue from multiple viewpoints, using multiple sources, and to then draw an informed conclusion based on what you find.

3. **Ask an expert.** Check in with someone who is more knowledgeable about a subject if you come across information on the Internet you aren't sure about. This includes medical advice, legal questions, and a whole host of other issues. Social media is a great place to find tips and tricks for many things, but if you need to make an important decision, consult an expert.[123]

Managerial Considerations in Creating Social Media Policies

The purpose of a social media policy at work is not to completely close off employees' access to personal e-mails and texts or even shopping websites. In fact, research suggests that many employees do use social media for constructive work purposes. This includes making and nurturing professional connections and seeking solutions to problems from those both inside and outside the organization.[124]

Social Media Policy A **social media policy** describes the who, how, when, and for what purpose of social media use, and the consequences for noncompliance. Research demonstrates that such a policy can not only clarify expectations and relieve guilt but also prevent impulsive or abusive posts and messages that can damage an organization's or an individual's reputation.[125] The essential elements of an effective social media policy are outlined in Table 15.3.

TABLE 15.3 Seven Elements of an Effective Social Media Policy

Identifies sites employees may use at work. Depending on the company's goals, it may want to limit employees' social media use during the workday to specific sites.
Identifies who may speak for the company and for what purpose. If the employer maintains a corporate social media account, only specified employees should be empowered to post there.
Clarifies the distinction between personal and work-related posts. Remind employees that their personal posts can affect their professional life.
Requires professional behavior online. Managers and employees alike should be cautioned against cyberbullying and the unfair or discriminatory use of any information about others they may find online.
Upholds confidentiality. Internal complaints and conflicts should never be aired online where partners, clients, and competitors can read about them. Proprietary information should never be disclosed in any forum, including on the Internet. Employees who are in doubt about whether a post violates confidentiality should contact the company's social media team before posting.
Includes a clear approval process for posts. Employees who are authorized to post on behalf of the company should be made aware of the review/approval process for any content posted on social media on behalf of the company.
Specifies the consequences of violations. Employees should understand what is at risk if they violate the company's social media policy and whether they will be disciplined, receive training, or even be dismissed.

Sources: "DOD Social Media Policy." U.S. Department of Defense. May 16, 2023. https://www.defense.gov/social-media-policy/#:~:text=Social%20media%20account%20managers%20will,operations%20or%20information%20security%20concern; "15 Best Practices to Avoid Social Media Snafus." *Forbes*. January 24, 2023. https://www.forbes.com/sites/forbesbusinesscouncil/2023/01/24/15-best-practices-to-avoid-social-media-snafus/?sh=7a73e3106fbc; Hirsch, A. "How to Create an Effective Social Media Policy." Society for Human Resource Management. March 18, 2021. https://www.shrm.org/resourcesandtools/hr-topics/employee-relations/pages/how-to-create-an-effective-social-media-policy.aspx.

Assessing an Organization's Social Media Readiness Consider the social media readiness of an organization to which you belong. Self-Assessment 15.2 (which you can complete in Connect, if your instructor has assigned it) will help you assess leadership's attitude toward social media, such as

- How supportive management is of creating communities.
- How well the culture fosters collaboration and knowledge sharing.
- How widely social media is used to collaborate.

With this knowledge you can determine how well your own attitudes fit with those of the organization, and it may even unveil opportunities for you to improve the organization's readiness. •

SELF-ASSESSMENT 15.2   ASSESSING SOCIAL MEDIA READINESS

This survey is designed to help you assess whether or not your organization is ready for social media. Please complete Self-Assessment 15.2 if your instructor has assigned it in Connect.

15.5 Improving Communication Effectiveness

THE BIG PICTURE
We describe how you can be a more effective listener, as in communicating nondefensively, employing empathy, and engaging in active listening. We also offer tips for becoming a more effective writer. Finally, we discuss how to be an effective speaker using three steps.

Recent research suggests managers spend almost all of their time communicating and that poor communication likely costs organizations billions of dollars annually.[126] It's no surprise, then, that written and verbal communications skills are among the top career readiness competencies desired by employers.[127]

How do you think your communication skills stack up? You can grade your communication skills by completing Self-Assessment 15.3 in Connect, if your instructor has assigned it. If your score is lower than you prefer, seek out ideas for improving your skills.

LO 15-5

Identify ways for managers to improve their listening, writing, and speaking skills.

SELF-ASSESSMENT 15.3   ASSESSING MY COMMUNICATION COMPETENCE

This survey will help you to determine your communication competence. Please complete Self-Assessment 15.3 if your instructor has assigned it in Connect.

Let's discuss how you can improve your essential communication skills.

Nondefensive Communication

Using evaluative or judgmental comments such as "Your work is terrible" or "You're always late for meetings" spurs defensiveness, and once defensiveness enters the conversation, constructive communication shuts down.[128] **Defensive communication** can include either aggressive, attacking, angry communication, or passive, withdrawing communication. Abusive supervision, discussed in Chapter 14, is likely to foster defensiveness among employees. The better alternative is **nondefensive communication**—communication that is assertive, direct, and powerful. Let's discuss three ways that you can avoid defensive communication and foster nondefensive communication:

- **Avoid defensiveness triggers.** You may be surprised to learn that defensiveness is often triggered by nothing more than a poor choice of words or nonverbal posture during interactions. In the language of behavior modification, these triggers are *antecedents* of defensiveness. For example, using absolutes like "always" or "never" is very likely to create a defensive response. Try to avoid using absolutes because they are rarely true. You can instead increase your communication competence by avoiding defensive antecedents and employing the positive antecedents of nondefensive communication shown in Table 15.4.

- **Allow emotions to settle.** Communicating nondefensively begins with making sure your emotions are in check. Don't have important conversations when you are emotional.

- **Manage your intentions.** Other actions include framing your message into terms that acknowledge the receiver's point of view, freeing yourself of prejudice and bias, asking good questions and actively listening to responses, and being honest about your intentions. Your communications will be more effective and nondefensive when you communicate with the intention of helping others.[129]

Given that we want you to learn how to communicate in a nondefensive manner, we encourage you to complete Self-Assessment 15.4 in Connect, if your instructor has assigned it. It assesses whether a current or past work environment is supportive of nondefensive communication.

TABLE 15.4 Antecedents of Defensive and Nondefensive Communication

TOWARD DEFENSIVENESS		TOWARD NONDEFENSIVENESS	
STYLE	EXAMPLE	STYLE	EXAMPLE
Evaluative	"Your social media post is sloppy."	Descriptive	"Your social media post was two days late."
Controlling	"You need to . . ."	Problem solving	"What do you think caused you to miss the posting deadline?"
Strategizing	"I'd like you to agree with me during the Zoom so that we can overcome any challenges."	Straightforward	"Vote your conscience at the Zoom. You can agree or disagree with my proposal."
Neutral	"Don't worry about missing the posting deadline, it's no big deal."	Empathetic	"I sense you are disappointed about missing the posting deadline. Let's figure out how we can get things back on schedule before the next post."
Superior	"Listen to me, I've managed social media here for 10 years."	Equal	"Let's figure out the causes of the missed posting deadline together."
Certain	"We tried this idea in the past. It just doesn't work."	Honest and open	Using I-messages: "I disagree with the language you used in your post because our department looked incompetent."

Sources: Based on Gibb, J. R. "Defensive Communication." *Journal of Communication* (1961): 141–148; and "Reach Out: Effective Communication." *Sunday Business Post*. April 14, 2013.

SELF-ASSESSMENT 15.4

Does Your Organization Have a Supportive or Defensive Communication Climate?
This survey will assess the supportive and defensive communication climate of your organization. Please complete Self-Assessment 15.4 if your instructor has assigned it in Connect.

Using Empathy

Although researchers propose multiple types of empathy, the general consensus is that, as described in the Manage U feature at the start of the chapter, **empathy is the ability to recognize and understand another person's feelings and thoughts.**[130] Empathy is a reflective technique that fosters open communication, and it is beneficial throughout our lives, not only in our careers.

Empathy Example—Danish Schools: In Danish schools, students spend one hour per week on "Klassens time," or time with their classes, which centers on learning empathy. During this hour, students come together and discuss problems they are facing in life, and the other students and the teacher work to listen attentively, understand others' perspectives, and devise thoughtful solutions. The focus of the lessons is not to excel above other students but rather to help the students see how they can help one another. According to Danish school principal Kasper Nyholm, the practice isn't always easy. Nyholm said "You may not want to collaborate, or listen to someone or compromise to play together, but this is all part of what we must learn to be in a community. We want students to learn to take part in giving up some of themselves for the whole."[131]

Students at Maury Elementary School in Washington, D.C., participate in an empathy-building program. Throughout the course of a school year, students develop empathy by observing a baby's growth and development and learning to recognize and identify its feelings. Sarah L. Voisin/The Washington Post/Getty Images

Psychologist Paul Ekman's research shows that managers' ability to be empathetic depends on using three distinct types of empathy: cognitive empathy, emotional empathy, and compassionate empathy.

- **Cognitive empathy.** Having cognitive empathy means you can "identify how another person feels and consider what they may be thinking."
- **Emotional empathy.** Emotional empathy is the ability to "physically feel what another feels."
- **Compassionate empathy.** With compassionate empathy we "not only grasp a person's predicament and feel their feelings, but we're moved to help in some way." Ekman says this form of empathy is dependent on first mastering your cognitive and emotional empathy.[132]

Do you want to build your empathy? The good news is that researchers believe you can. "Empathy is a cognitive attribute" rather than a trait, according to Dr. Mohammadreza Hojat, a research professor of psychiatry at Jefferson Medical College.[133] This means that empathy is something that we can learn to do better.[134]

Being an Effective Listener

"The greatest communication secret is listening. It may sound counterintuitive, but in order to lead, one must listen first," says best-selling author Jean Ginzburg.[135] Actively listening, truly listening, requires more than just hearing, which is merely the physical component. **Active listening** is the process of actively decoding and interpreting verbal

messages. Active listening requires full attention and processing of information, which hearing does not. We think three points about active listening are worth noting:

- **Listening is an important communication skill.** There is general consensus that listening is a cornerstone skill of communication competence. Active listening makes receivers feel more understood and leads people to conclude that their conversations were more helpful, sensitive, and supportive.[136]

- **Most of us don't listen as well as we think we do.** Unfortunately, many of us think we are good listeners when evidence suggests the opposite.[137] It takes effort to actively listen, and you won't be a better listener unless you are motivated to become one.

- **You can learn to be a better listener.** The good news is, you can become a better listener.[138] Said writer Kate Murphy, "Like a sport or playing a musical instrument—the more you do it the better you get at it."[139]

We studied the advice of professionals who make a living by listening and having conversations with others in order to devise recommendations for becoming a better listener. Don't worry—none of the old "make eye contact, nod your head, and smile" advice here. Said award-winning journalist Celeste Headlee—whose TED Talk "10 Ways to Have a Better Conversation" has over 28 million views—"There is no reason to learn how to show you're paying attention if you are in fact paying attention."[140] Here are five recommendations for improving your listening skills.

1. Focus on the Other Person
In order to truly listen to another person and ensure they feel heard, focus on them instead of yourself. This is easier said than done, as we often listen with the intent to respond rather than the intent to hear. We also tend to want to relate others' stories to our own (e.g., saying "I know exactly how you feel because that happened to me, too" and then telling our own story). Said Emmy-winning journalist Faith Salie, "We think we're building a bridge of sharing . . . but most of the time, we're really putting up scaffolding over someone else's story and clambering all over it."[141]

2. Ask Open-Ended Questions
The quality of a conversation often boils down to the quality of the questions being asked. And while asking questions isn't exactly *listening,* you will be much more engaged in a conversation—and therefore much more apt to listen intently—if you ask good questions. Journalists, whether they are writing for a newspaper or speaking into a microphone, begin questions with "who," "what," "when," "where," "why," or "how."

Open-Ended Questions Example—Peppers Pizzeria: At Peppers Pizzeria in Thibodaux, LA, owner Grady Verrett trains staff to use open-ended questions. Specifically, servers aren't allowed to ask customers "was everything ok?" when they bring out the check at the end of the meal. This, according to Verrett, is likely to generate a one-word polite response that provides no valuable information for improving the business. Instead, servers are trained to ask things like "what's one thing about your meal that could have been better," or "tell me what you thought of the amount of pepperoni on your pizza" in order to generate useful feedback for the restaurant and show customers that their opinions matter. (How do we know all of this? Because one of your authors—Denise Breaux Soignet—was a server at Peppers during graduate school!)

An important part of being a good listener is asking questions that generate rich, interesting, and useful responses. Peppers Pizzeria continues to thrive and improve because servers are taught to ask the kinds of questions that get customers talking openly and honestly about their dining experiences.
Courtesy of Peppers Pizzeria

3. Approach Conversations with Curiosity   According to Amanda Ripley, seasoned journalist for *The Washington Post* and *The Atlantic,* approaching conversations with genuine curiosity, rather than with the intent of getting others to believe what we believe, makes others feel truly heard. This, in turn, leads to richer, more meaningful, and more trusting conversations. Said Ripley, "Listening allows people to coexist. People will put up with a lot of difference if they feel heard." She added, "People will open up to different ideas and opinions . . . people need to feel heard or else everything goes to hell, one way or another, because people pull to extremes—they stop listening, they demonize each other, they can't see any shared humanity."

Here are examples of noncurious and curious questions:[142]

- **Noncurious questions:** "Did you miss the project deadline because you prioritized the wrong things?" and "What's your preferred way to communicate with your teammates, because clearly what we're using isn't working."
- **Curious questions:** "Would you describe the absolute biggest roadblock during this project and why it was such a game-changer for you?" and "If you could build your perfect team-communication tool, what would it look like?"

4. Avoid the Tendency to Judge   One reason listening is so hard is that when someone else speaks, particularly on something about which we feel passionate, we become emotionally invested in our own views and want to categorize their words as either "right" or "wrong." If you've ever had a conversation with a polarizing relative at the Thanksgiving table, you've likely experienced this first hand. Help yourself to listen more openly and be less judgmental by asking nonjudgmental questions. The language of nonjudgmental questions—words like "curious," "opinion," "thoughts," and "feelings"—helps you to understand someone's point of view while avoiding the need to protect your beliefs. The language of judgmental questions—words like "good," "bad," "right," and "wrong,"—sets you up for defensiveness, and thus, poor listening. Here are examples of judgmental and nonjudgmental questions:[143]

- **Judgmental questions:** "What do you have against participative management?" and "Why is it so bad for me to ask you to be on time?"
- **Nonjudgmental questions:** "How has your management style changed and evolved over time as you've worked with different people?" and "How do you feel about how time-oriented we are here?"

5. Be Mindful and Fully Present   This advice may seem obvious, but given the pace of our modern work lives and our tendency to multitask, we think it bears repeating. With every distraction you add to the mix, your ability to listen decreases.[144] As we said before, communication requires trust and a feeling of being heard, and we can't accomplish either of these things if we are looking at our phone or typing an e-mail while someone is talking to us.

Do you think you are an effective listener? Effective listening is an essential skill associated with the career readiness competencies of social and emotional intelligence. If you want to increase these competencies, feedback regarding your listening habits will be valuable. You can get this feedback by completing Self-Assessment 15.5 in Connect, if your instructor has assigned it.

> Try focusing on the other person, asking open-ended questions, being curious, avoiding judgment, and being mindful in conversations with others. This will make you more involved and interested in the subject matter. Image Source/Stockbyte/Getty Images

ASSESSMENT 15.5 ASSESSING YOUR LISTENING STYLE

This survey is designed to assess the overall strength of your listening skills. Please complete Self-Assessment 15.5 if your instructor has assigned it in Connect.

Being an Effective Writer

Writing is an essential career readiness and management skill. Taking a business writing class can be a major advantage. (Indeed, as a manager, you may have to identify employees who need writing training.) Here are some tips for writing business communications more effectively.

Start with Your Purpose Start your message by stating your purpose along with what you expect of the reader rather than building up to the point. Along the same lines, when e-mailing, make sure the subject line clearly expresses your reason for writing. For instance, "Who is available Thursday afternoon?" does not inform the reader of your topic as well as "Davis project meeting moved to Thursday 3 p.m." does.

Write Simply, Concisely, and Directly Short and sweet is the key.[145] Keep your words simple and use short words, sentences, and phrases. Be direct instead of vague and use active rather than passive voice. (Directness, active voice: "Please call a meeting for Wednesday." Vagueness, passive voice: "It is suggested that a meeting be called for Wednesday.")

Know Your Audience Send your message to all who need the information, but *only* to those people. Resist the urge to include everyone, and be especially careful, in responding to messages, to think before you click "Reply All." If you are feeling emotional as you write, don't click "Send" at all but instead save your draft, take a break of at least a few hours, and go back to it later. Your feelings may have changed and your communication, and your relationships, will likely be better for it.

Don't Ignore the Basics Texting has made many people more relaxed about spelling and grammar rules. Although this is fine among friends, as a manager you'll need to create a more favorable impression in your writing. Aside from using spelling and grammar checkers, proofread your writing before sending it on. Check people's names and titles in particular and be especially aware that autocorrect features can make incorrect assumptions about what you meant to say.

Being an Effective Speaker

The ability to talk to a room full of people—to make an oral presentation—is one of the greatest skills you can have. And in case you think you won't ever have this skill, "Public speaking is a skill anyone can build," according to communications expert Carmine Gallo. "I've interviewed young business professionals in their 20s and 30s whose careers are soaring and who get promoted much faster than their peers largely because of their ability to deliver presentations more effectively," said Gallo, adding, "Here's the key. They work at it."[146]

Still, we acknowledge that public speaking can be scary. More than 34% of Americans are either "afraid" or "very afraid" of public speaking, according to the 2022 Chapman University survey of American fears (for comparison, this fear ranked higher than snakes, nuclear war, and zombies).[147] If you have anxiety about public speaking, rest assured that you're not alone.

Would you prefer to give a public speech or be chased by a zombie? If you're like many of the people who responded to a recent survey, then you're probably more comfortable with the living dead. Fear of public speaking is no joke—but you can increase your level of comfort and skill by following the four suggestions we present. You can do this! Daniel Villeneuve/123RF; sararoom/123RF

However you feel or think you feel about public speaking, there is no doubt you'll have to call upon your presentation skills during your career. Here are four broad suggestions for improving your speaking skills:

1. **Check out the TED model.** You'll find good models in the many TED Talks available online.[148] These resources provide ideas for conceptualizing and structuring a presentation based on the outcome(s) you'd like it to achieve.

2. **Ask questions to help yourself prepare.** You can do away with a great deal of anxiety about speaking in public by knowing what and how to prepare. For instance: Who will be in the audience? How much time do I have? What technology is the audience accustomed to?

3. **Arrive early and check the room/software to be sure everything is in place and working.**

4. **Follow Dale Carnegie's classic advice about structuring your presentation:** (1) Tell them what you're going to say. (2) Say it. (3) Tell them what you said.[149]

    - **Tell them what you're going to say.** The introduction should take 5 to 15% of your time, and it should prepare the audience for the rest of the presentation. Avoid jokes and tired phrases like "I'm honored to be with you here today. . . ." Everything in your speech should be relevant, so be bold and get right to the point with a "grabber" that attracts listeners' attention and prepares them to follow you closely.[150] Storytelling has become recognized as a key skill for modern leaders because it is an authentic way to strengthen connections.[151] By sharing a story first, you let the audience know that you are human, and this builds trust and reciprocity between you.[152] For example:

        > "Good afternoon. You may not have thought much about identity theft, and neither did I until my identity was stolen—twice. Today I'll describe how our supposedly private credit, health, employment, and other records are vulnerable to theft and how you can protect yourself."

Predictor for success. Enjoying public speaking and being good at it are the top predictors of success and upward mobility. How might you develop these skills? Hill Street Studios/Blend Images/Alamy Stock Photo

- **Say it.** The main body of the speech takes up 75 to 95% of your time. The most important thing to realize is that your audience won't remember more than a few points. Choose them carefully and cover them succinctly.

- **Tell them what you said.** The end might take 5 to 10% of your time. Many professional speakers consider the conclusion as important as the introduction, so don't drop the ball. You need a solid, strong, persuasive wrap-up.

Use some sort of signal phrase that cues your listeners that you are heading into your wind-up. Examples:

"Here's what I want you to leave with today . . ."
"In conclusion, what can you do to protect against unauthorized invasion of your private files? I point out five main steps. One . . ."

Give some thought to the last thing you will say. It should be strongly upbeat, a call to action, a thought for the day, a little story, or a quotation. Examples:

"I want to leave you with one last thought . . ."
"Finally, let me close by sharing something that happened to me . . ."

Then say, "Thank you," and stop.

15.6 Career Corner: Managing Your Career Readiness

LO 15-6

Review the techniques for improving the career readiness competency of networking.

Visit your instructor's Connect course and access your eBook to view this video.

Executive Interview Series: Networking

Communication is a career readiness competency that requires the application of 12 competencies from the model of career readiness shown in Figure 15.4. You can improve your communication skills by recognizing the need to also develop the following competencies: new media literacy, oral/written communication, teamwork/collaboration, leadership, social intelligence, networking, emotional intelligence, self-motivation, positive approach, generalized self-efficacy, self-awareness, and career management.

Here we focus on the competency of networking because it plays a key role in getting a job after graduation and requires good communication skills.[153] Networking is the ability to build and maintain a strong, broad professional network of relationships. It typically requires developing and using contacts from one context in another. Every single one of the leaders in this chapter's Executive Interview Series video stresses the importance of networking, building connections, and nurturing relationships with mentors.

Improve Your Face-to-Face Networking Skills

We're sure you've heard the phrase, "It's not what you know, it's who you know." Recent data suggests that around 80% of jobs are filled via networking.[154] Unfortunately, many of us dislike networking and even view it as "insincere and manipulative, even slightly

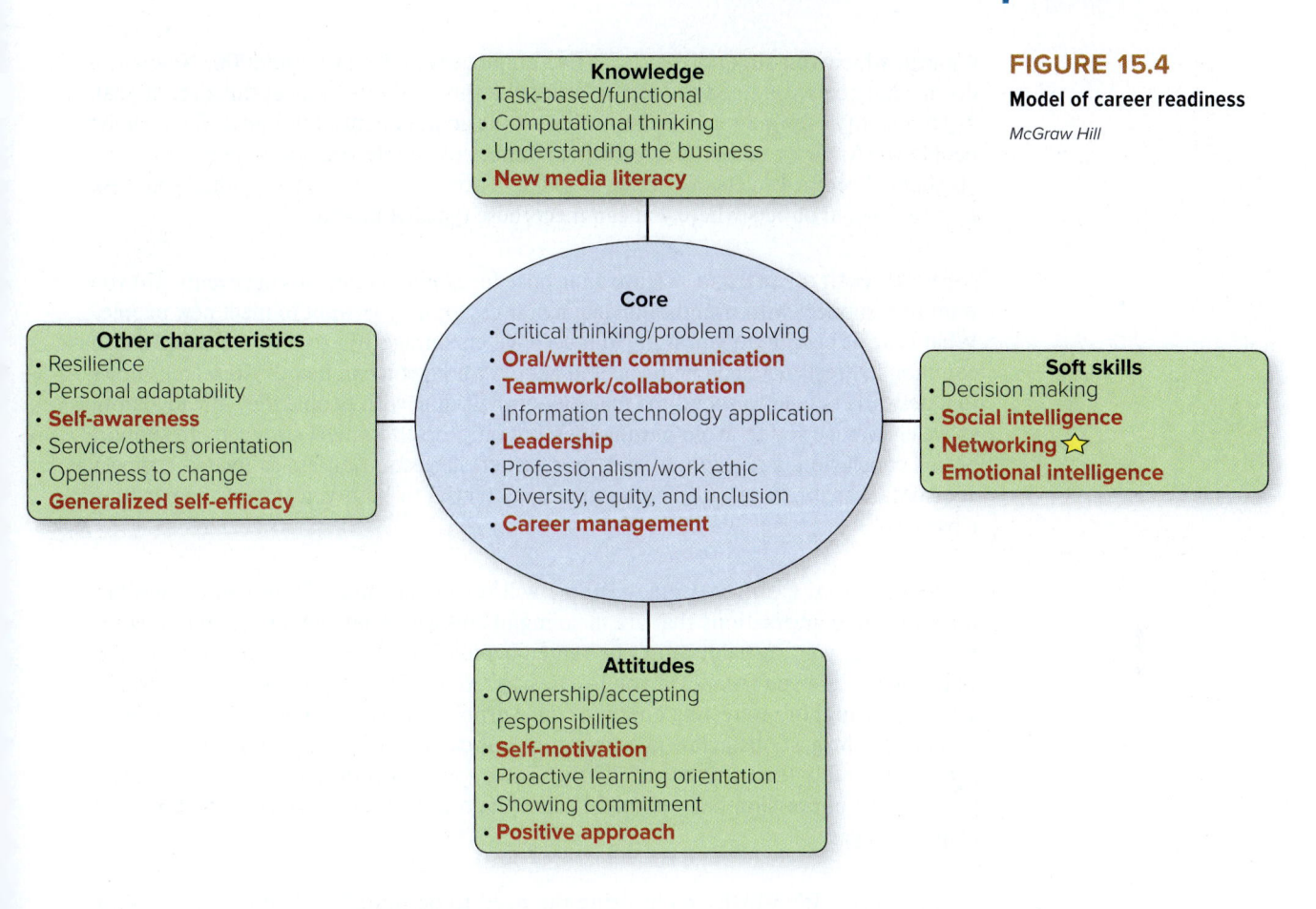

FIGURE 15.4

Model of career readiness

McGraw Hill

Knowledge
- Task-based/functional
- Computational thinking
- Understanding the business
- **New media literacy**

Core
- Critical thinking/problem solving
- **Oral/written communication**
- **Teamwork/collaboration**
- Information technology application
- **Leadership**
- Professionalism/work ethic
- Diversity, equity, and inclusion
- **Career management**

Other characteristics
- Resilience
- Personal adaptability
- **Self-awareness**
- Service/others orientation
- Openness to change
- **Generalized self-efficacy**

Soft skills
- Decision making
- **Social intelligence**
- **Networking** ⭐
- **Emotional intelligence**

Attitudes
- Ownership/accepting responsibilities
- **Self-motivation**
- Proactive learning orientation
- Showing commitment
- **Positive approach**

---

unethical," according to *The Wall Street Journal*.[155] Networking is not meant to be manipulative, nor is it all about you. A writer for the University of Illinois Leadership Center summed it up nicely. She noted:

> Networking brings about so many benefits that we may not think of. It helps build connections with those either in your career or just with shared interests. You can learn something new, gain some new resources, and create new relationships all through networking.[156]

We provide the following recommendations to assist you with developing the career readiness competency of networking. Put them to work now as opposed to waiting until you are on the job market.

Create a Positive Mindset   A negative attitude about networking is a roadblock to developing this competency. Pursue a more positive attitude by eliminating the thought that networking is a game. Networking is more enjoyable when it is driven by your authentic intention to develop genuine relationships rather than by your desire to land a job. Strive to view networking as a vehicle to make more friends and connect with people with similar interests. This mindset is more likely to take you further with the relationship because it creates shared bonding rather than the pursuit of self-interests.[157]

Identify Your Career Goals   Be clear about your goals and plans before doing any networking. Establish a 5- to 10-year career goal and then develop a high-level action plan for accomplishing it. Say, for example, that your five-year goal is to be employed in a job in which you supervise at least five employees and make $100,000. Now write down what goals you need to meet in years one through four to meet this overall goal. Try to identify a few people who can kickstart the achievement of this goal. They can be people you know or second-degree acquaintances of people you know. These individuals should become targets of your networking. If you don't know anyone, then your task is to find social outlets where you can meet these types of people.

Network with a Purpose Have a purpose for attending networking events. Do you want to reconnect with friends and acquaintances, or do you want to meet new people? What type of people do you want to meet? We encourage you to look for people with common interests who can help you and people whom you can help.[158] Research shows that networkers tend to spend the majority of their time with people they already know, so we encourage you to avoid putting pressure on yourself to meet strangers. In support of this conclusion, a substantial body of research suggests your less-cultivated business acquaintances, or "weak ties," have greater potential to help you in your career than close ties.[159]

Build Personal Connections People will remember more about you if you draw them in with conversations that are meaningful and have some degree of emotionality. For example, you probably won't be remembered if you lead with: So where do you work? Where are you from? Do you live nearby? You'll get a more positive response by asking insightful or interesting questions. One article suggested using questions such as, "What's the biggest obstacle you've faced in your career so far?" or "Who else should I make sure to talk to at this event?"[160] By asking good questions, you not only create a positive first impression but you might cause the other person to learn something that helps them grow.

Be Mindful It's worth emphasizing the need to be mindful when communicating with others. For example, you might think it's fine to interrupt a conversation with someone to answer your phone, but others might think differently. Try your best to avoid phubbing and FOMO. Maintain eye contact and avoid the tendency to let your eyes survey the room for the next person you want to meet. That's an easy way to send the message that the person in front of you is not important.

Follow Up Be sure to follow up with those individuals you found particularly interesting or would like to see again. Use whatever medium of communication you deem relevant. While texting and e-mail are fast, we have had very positive experiences when we've written a handwritten note of appreciation. •

Key Terms Used in This Chapter

active listening 567
communication 540
crowdsourcing 559
cyberloafing 560
decoding 540
defensive communication 566
disinformation 563
downward communication 545
empathy 567
encoding 540
external communication 547
feedback 541
FOMO 561
formal communication channels 545
grapevine 547
horizontal communication 546
identity theft 562
informal communication channels 547
jargon 542
media richness 543
medium 541
microaggressions 561
mindlessness 552
misinformation 563
noise 542
nondefensive communication 566
nonverbal communication 555
paraphrasing 542
privacy 561
receiver 540
security 561
sender 540
social media 556
social media policy 564
upward communication 545

Key Points

15.1 The Communication Process: What It Is, How It Works

- Communication is the transfer of information and understanding from one person to another. The process involves sender, message, and receiver; encoding and decoding; the medium; feedback; and dealing with "noise."
- The sender is the person wanting to share information. The information is called a message. The receiver is the person for whom the message is intended. Encoding is translating a message into understandable symbols or language. Decoding is interpreting and trying to make sense of the message. The medium is the pathway by which a message travels. Feedback is the process in which a receiver expresses their reaction to the sender's message.
- The entire communication process can be disrupted at any point by noise, defined as any disturbance that interferes with the transmission or understanding of a message. The four key sources of noise are physical, psychological, semantic, and physiological.
- For effective communication, a manager must select the right medium. This choice is based on matching media richness with the situation at hand.

15.2 How Managers Fit into the Communication Process

- Communication channels may be formal or informal.
- Formal communication channels follow the chain of command and are recognized as official. Formal communication is of three types: (1) Vertical communication is the flow of messages up and down the organizational hierarchy. (2) Horizontal communication flows within and between work units; its main purpose is coordination. (3) External communication flows between people inside and outside the organization.
- Informal communication channels develop outside the formal structure and do not follow the chain of command. Two aspects of informal channels are the grapevine and face-to-face communication. The grapevine is the unofficial communication system of the informal organization.

15.3 Barriers to Communication

- Barriers to communication are of five types: (1) physical barriers, (2) personal barriers, (3) cross-cultural barriers, (4) nonverbal barriers, and (5) gender differences.
- Five personal barriers are (1) variable skills in communicating effectively, (2) information processing and interpretation, (3) variations in trustworthiness and credibility, (4) attentional issues, and (5) generational considerations.

15.4 Social Media and Management

- Social media contribute heavily to employee and employer productivity. They are widely used in employment recruiting and have applications in employee and employer productivity, organizational innovation (via crowdsourcing), in sales, and in reputation management.
- Social media have costs as well. These include cyberloafing, phubbing and FOMO, security threats, privacy issues, and the spread of false information.
- One danger of social media is the spread of misinformation, or false information.
- Managers should engage employees in the creation of fair and effective social media policy to ensure social media tools are consistently put to constructive work purposes.

15.5 Improving Communication Effectiveness

- Nondefensive communication is essential for effective communication.
- Three types of empathy are cognitive, emotional, and compassionate.
- You can improve active listening by (1) focusing on the other person, (2) asking open-ended questions, (3) approaching conversations with curiosity, (4) avoiding the tendency to judge, and (5) being fully present.
- To become an effective writer, start with your purpose. Write simply, concisely, and directly. Know your audience and follow basic spelling and grammar rules for appropriately formal communication.
- To become an effective speaker, study successful models, know your subject, and prepare and rehearse ahead of time. For the presentation itself, follow three simple rules. Tell people what you're going to say. Say it. Tell them what you said.

15.6 Career Corner: Managing Your Career Readiness

- Becoming a more effective communicator requires the application of 12 career readiness competencies. They are new media literacy, oral/written communication, teamwork/collaboration, leadership, social intelligence, networking, emotional intelligence, self-motivation, positive approach, career management, self-awareness, and generalized self-efficacy.
- You can develop your networking competency by following six recommendations: (1) Create a positive mindset. (2) Identify your career goals. (3) Network with a purpose. (4) Build personal connections. (5) Be mindful. (6) Follow up.

Boeing Continuing Case — McGraw Hill connect

In this part of the case you'll learn more about key communication issues at Boeing. You'll also explore factors related to individual differences, motivation, groups and teams, and leadership at the company.

Go to Connect to assess your ability to apply the concepts discussed in Chapters 11, 12, 13, 14, and 15 to the Boeing case.

PART 6 • CONTROLLING

16 Control Systems and Quality Management
Techniques for Enhancing Organizational Effectiveness

After reading this chapter, you should be able to:

LO 16-1 Describe control as a managerial function.

LO 16-2 Describe the steps in the control process and types of control.

LO 16-3 Discuss ways that managers can control an organization.

LO 16-4 Explain the total quality management process.

LO 16-5 Discuss contemporary control issues.

LO 16-6 Discuss how to apply the control process to the career readiness competency of career management and to the process of continuous self-improvement.

FORECAST   *What's Ahead in This Chapter*

The final management function, control, is monitoring performance, comparing it with goals, and taking corrective action as needed. We identify six reasons control is needed in organizations, explain the steps in the control process, and describe three types of control managers use. Next, we discuss ways that managers can control an organization using the balanced scorecard. We then turn our focus to total quality management (TQM). Finally, we explain two contemporary control tools before concluding with a Career Corner that focuses on how to apply the control process to the career readiness competency of career management and to the process of continuous self-improvement.

Managing Your Personal and Professional Satisfaction

As you prepare to graduate, think about how you will manage your personal (or life) and professional satisfaction. Self-regulation, according to researchers, is one of the most useful frameworks to help you accomplish this goal.[1]

Self-regulation is the process of managing your attitudes, emotions, and motivation as you achieve your goals. It's a personal application of the four management functions—planning, organizing, leading, and controlling—that you have been studying throughout this course. Self-regulation consists of the following steps:

1. **Set goals:** What do I want to achieve?
2. **Prepare:** How can I achieve it?
3. **Execute:** Implement the plan.
4. **Assess:** Am I on target?
5. **Revise:** What adjustments do I need to make?

These steps are same the basic steps we outlined in earlier chapters: planning (Figure 5.1), strategic management (Figure 6.2), performance management (Figure 9.4), and organizational development (Figure 10.4). The self-regulation steps also are similar to the control process you will encounter in this chapter (Figure 16.2).

We'll revisit the self-regulation process throughout Chapter 16 in a three-part series of Practical Action boxes and in the Career Corner to help you envision how you can apply managerial control to your personal and professional life. For now, consider how you can foster success in achieving your personal and professional goals by using four self-regulation habits proposed in Stephen Covey's *The 7 Habits of Highly Effective People*.[2]

Set Goals: "Begin with the End in Mind"

Covey says, "It's incredibly easy to get caught up in an activity trap, in the busy-ness of life, to work harder and harder at climbing the ladder of success only to discover it's leaning against the wrong wall."[3] Avoid the allure of unfocused activity by beginning with the end in mind.

One of your co-authors, Angelo Kinicki, did this with his students by requiring them to write their obituary: An obituary represents a statement of death and includes a brief biography. Students had to think about what they would want others to say about them at a wake or celebration of life ceremony. Hint: research suggests making a difference in the lives of others leads to more lasting joy.[4] Use this image to specify a personal mission and a vision for your life. With a clear vision of your life's goal, you will "know where you're going so that you better understand where you are now and so that the steps you take are always in the right direction."[5]

Prepare: "Put First Things First"

In the first step, you defined your life's purpose or overarching goal. In the dust of daily living, life is filled with multiple goals that vie for your attention: meet work deadlines, address life crises, build relationships, pursue new opportunities, pay the bills, answer phone calls and text messages, and enjoy your hobbies. These goals need to be prioritized.

Create an urgent–important matrix by categorizing each time demand as (1) urgent/not urgent and (2) important/not important.[6] Work on saying "no" to unimportant things, some of which may even be urgent (like meetings, casual conversations, and some phone calls), so you can focus more time on the important things. Then, invest your time on addressing long-term goals that are important but not urgent (building relationships, constructing a sound strategy to address problems, and investing in new opportunities).[7] They are the activities that are aligned with your life's overarching goal and will make the biggest positive difference in your personal and professional satisfaction.

Execute: "Think Win/Win"

If you hope to achieve your life's goal and troubleshoot adversity along the way, you'll need others' help. You are more likely to receive assistance if your goals and priorities benefit others. It's a matter of shifting your mindset and conflict management strategy from competition to collaboration, concepts we discussed in Section 13.4. "Win/Win is a frame of mind and heart that constantly seeks mutual benefit in all human interactions,"[8] says Covey. Win/Win solutions encourage people to work together and remain committed to the plan of action.[9]

Assess and Revise: "Sharpen the Saw"

Managing your personal and professional satisfaction is a marathon, not a sprint. Take time periodically to assess your mental, social/emotional, physical, and spiritual well-being. These four dimensions, according to Covey, describe a healthy, balanced life. "Sharpen the Saw" by taking time to reevaluate your goals and make adjustments as needed. Also, be intentional about rest and renewal. Seek out activities that reinvigorate you such as journaling, taking a nature walk, getting eight hours of sleep each night, eating a healthy meal, connecting with a faith community, or volunteering in your community.[10] This essential self-care strengthens the foundation for you to continue to achieve the right goals the right way.

For Discussion What are you doing today that contributes to or detracts from your personal and professional satisfaction? Apply the four self-regulation habits to develop a plan to improve your personal and professional satisfaction.

16.1 Control: When Managers Monitor Performance

THE BIG PICTURE
Controlling is monitoring performance, comparing it with goals, and taking corrective action. This section describes six reasons control is needed.

LO 16-1
Describe control as a managerial function.

In this section, we'll discuss six reasons why control is important for organizations. We'll then introduce the first of three Practical Action boxes in this chapter to illustrate how control is a practical self-management function you can use to manage your career. The Practical Action boxes will help you:

- ✓ Determine your long-term career goals.
- ✓ Develop short-term SMART goals needed to accomplish your long-term career goals.
- ✓ Define behaviors to measure progress toward your SMART goals, and monitor and make adjustments to them as needed to ensure you achieve each goal.

Control is making something happen the way it was planned to happen. **Controlling is defined as monitoring performance, comparing it with goals, and taking corrective action as needed.** Controlling is the fourth management function, along with planning, organizing, and leading, and its purpose is plain: to make sure that performance meets objectives.

- **Planning** is setting goals and deciding how to achieve them.
- **Organizing** is arranging tasks, people, and other resources to accomplish the work.
- **Leading** is motivating people to work hard to achieve the organization's goals.
- **Controlling** is concerned with seeing that the right things happen at the right time in the right way.

All these functions affect one another and in turn affect an organization's performance and productivity (see Figure 16.1).

Lack of control mechanisms can lead to problems for both managers and companies. For example, the high-tech industry boomed during the COVID-19 era but announced 102,391 job cuts from January to April 2023. These job reductions are 38,000% more than during the same time period for the industry in 2022.[11] Could greater control have helped avoid or reduce these massive layoffs? Of course. Control can save jobs!

FIGURE 16.1 Controlling for effective performance

What you as a manager do to get things done, with controlling shown in relation to the three other management functions. (These are not lockstep; all four functions happen concurrently.)

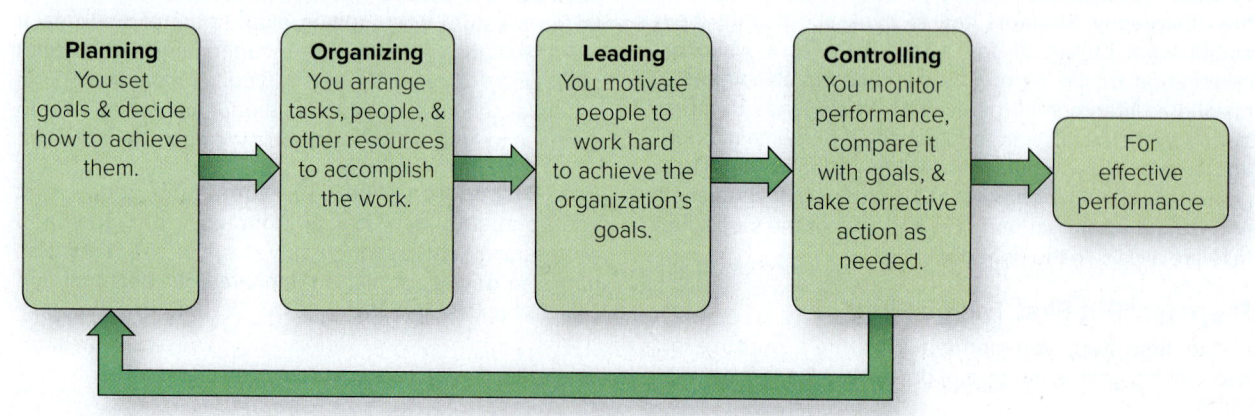

Planning You set goals & decide how to achieve them. → **Organizing** You arrange tasks, people, & other resources to accomplish the work. → **Leading** You motivate people to work hard to achieve the organization's goals. → **Controlling** You monitor performance, compare it with goals, & take corrective action as needed. → For effective performance

There are six reasons control is needed.

1. **To adapt to change and uncertainty.** Markets shift. Consumer tastes change. New competitors appear. Technologies are reborn. New materials are invented. Government regulations are altered. All organizations must deal with these kinds of environmental changes and uncertainties. Control systems can help managers anticipate, monitor, and react to these changes. Disney's attempt to remake its revenue stream is a timely example.

    Change and Uncertainty Example—Disney: Over 30% of Disney's revenue was generated by its parks and resorts in 2019.[12] That changed almost overnight when COVID-19 shut down travel in 2020 and social distancing policies, fear, and uncertainty reduced customers' desire to visit the Disney theme parks. At the same time, Disney invested billions into developing its video streaming platform, Disney+. Disney's goal was to grow its subscribership rapidly through a cheap annual subscription and heavy advertising. This strategy led to steep, unsustainable operating losses. With inflation and the fear of a recession looming in 2023, CEO Bob Iger announced 7,000 layoffs along with a strategy to make Disney+ profitable. Disney's 2023 revenue from its parks and resorts is now 21.5% with over 15% of revenue coming from its streaming services.[13]

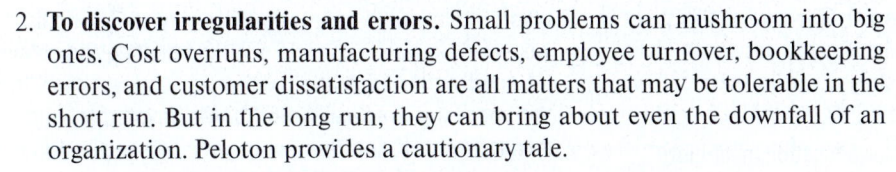

    Disney invested billions to grow its video streaming service, Disney+, while its theme parks and resorts were closed or operated at significantly reduced capacity during the COVID-19 pandemic. spatuletail/Shutterstock

2. **To discover irregularities and errors.** Small problems can mushroom into big ones. Cost overruns, manufacturing defects, employee turnover, bookkeeping errors, and customer dissatisfaction are all matters that may be tolerable in the short run. But in the long run, they can bring about even the downfall of an organization. Peloton provides a cautionary tale.

    Errors Example—Peloton: Peloton's growth exploded during the COVID-19 era, but in the process, the company encountered numerous manufacturing delays and defects that resulted in a significant backlog of orders and an expensive recall of its Internet-connected treadmills and exercise bikes. The management missteps contributed to the company's stock price plunging from an all-time high of $162.72/share in 2020 to $7.42 in 2023.[14]

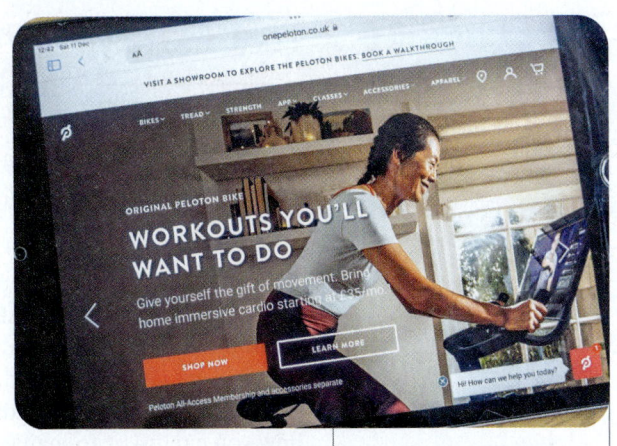

3. **To reduce costs, increase productivity, or add value.** Control systems reduce labor costs, eliminate waste, increase output, and increase product delivery cycles. In addition, controls add value to a product so that customers will be more inclined to choose it over rival products.

4. **To detect opportunities and increase innovation.** Hot-selling products. Competitive prices on materials. Changing population trends. New overseas markets. Managers are using advances in cloud computing, AI, and machine learning as new controls to alert them to innovative opportunities that might have otherwise gone unnoticed.[15]

5. **To provide performance feedback.** Can you improve without feedback? When a company becomes larger or when it merges with another company, it may find it has several product lines, materials-purchasing policies, customer bases, and worker needs that conflict with each other. Controls help managers coordinate these various elements by providing feedback.[16] Research demonstrates that

Peloton's management paid inadequate attention to its manufacturing capabilities and quality during its rapid growth. The company is now struggling to survive as a viable and trusted business. LDNPix/Alamy Stock Photo

feedback also has a control function for individuals and teams, and developmental feedback affects employees' learning and innovation.[17] For example, Microsoft collects user and system feedback to develop innovative improvements to its products and services.

Performance Feedback—Microsoft Teams: Microsoft Teams is in a battle with Webex, Zoom, and Google Meet to be the leading videoconferencing software. The company routinely analyzes the software's technical performance and how users engage with it. The feedback led to recently announced updates to Teams to increase users' efficiency, improve the platform's speed, integrate the platform with other Microsoft applications like Microsoft Office, and accelerate future improvements using AI-powered experiences such as Copilot for Microsoft Teams.[18]

6. **To decentralize decision making and facilitate teamwork.** Controls allow top management to decentralize decision making at lower levels within the organization and to encourage employees to work together in teams. Studies have found that organizations that effectively utilized control enjoyed greater creativity, collegiality, and performance.[19]

PRACTICAL ACTION | Determine Your Overall Career Objective

Figure 16.1 reveals that planning is the first step of the control process. The control process for managing your career thus begins by defining your overall career objective at this point in time. Let's start this process by having you answer the following three questions in a notebook (you will be asked to review them at a later point in this chapter):

1. Why did you enroll in a higher-education institution?
2. What do you expect a college degree will do for you?
3. How does obtaining a college degree fit into your long-term life goals?

We suspect your answers to the three above questions will have something to do with graduating and getting a job shortly after graduation (to improve your quality of life). If this is true, we would like you to use two goals (graduating and obtaining a job shortly after graduation) when you work your way through the upcoming Practical Action boxes devoted to your career management. If not, then write your personalized long-term goals in your notebook. We'll help you develop a short-term set of SMART goals to achieve your long-term career goals in Section 16.3's Practical Action box.

16.2 The Control Process and Types of Control

THE BIG PICTURE
This section describes the four steps in the control process and three types of controls.

LO 16-2

Describe the steps in the control process and types of control.

This section reviews the steps in the control process and discusses three different types of controls. Following the steps in the control process assists managers in determining whether an organization's current course of action is working or whether a change in plans or activities is needed. Similarly, your own personal control systems are vital for supporting your goal to graduate. We'll make the control process practical by explaining how you can use it to manage how you spend your time as a college student.

Steps in the Control Process

Control systems may be altered to fit specific situations, but generally they follow the same steps. The four **control process steps** are (1) establish standards; (2) measure performance; (3) compare performance to standards; and (4) take corrective action, if necessary

FIGURE 16.2

Steps in the control process

Paying attention to the feedback is particularly important because of its dynamic nature.

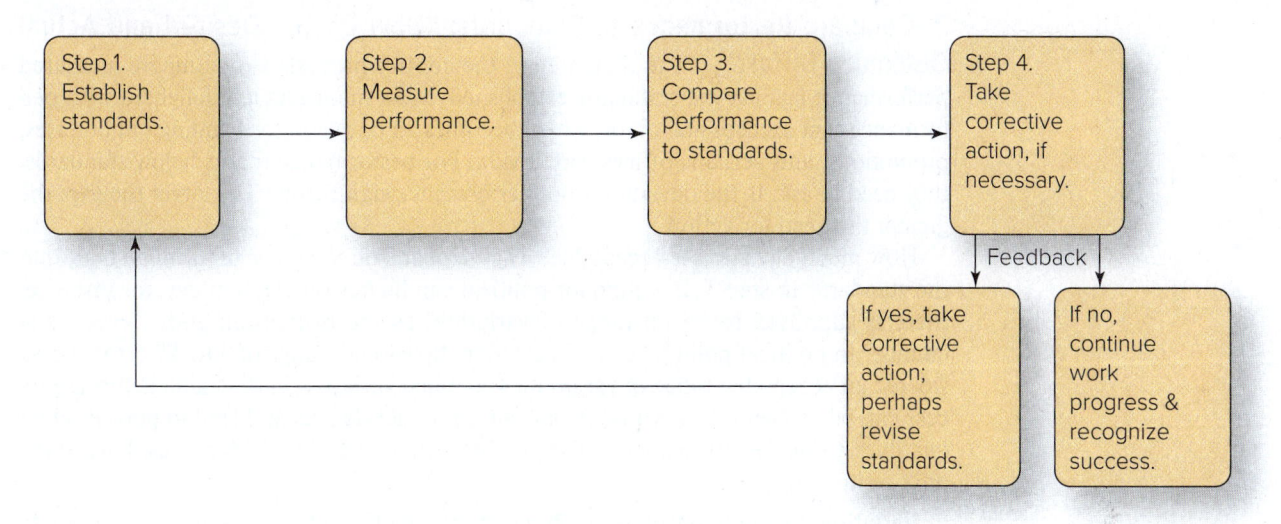

Step 1. Establish standards. → Step 2. Measure performance. → Step 3. Compare performance to standards. → Step 4. Take corrective action, if necessary.

Feedback:
- If yes, take corrective action; perhaps revise standards.
- If no, continue work progress & recognize success.

(see Figure 16.2). These steps follow the same basic process as the planning/control cycle discussed in Chapters 5 and 6.

1. Establish Standards: "What Is the Outcome We Want?"

A **control standard**, or performance standard, is the desired performance level for a given goal. Standards may be narrow or broad, and they can be set for almost anything, although they are best measured when they can be made quantifiable. Recall that the best goals are SMART goals (Chapters 5). Table 16.1 lists a sample of performance standards for nonprofit, for-profit, and service organizations. The bottom of Table 16.1 suggests all types of organizations can set goals for employee engagement and track it either directly through surveys or indirectly by monitoring employee absenteeism.

One technique for establishing, organizing, and tracking standards is to use *the balanced scorecard,* as we explain later in this chapter.

Reliable measurements are essential. A vehicle's fuel gauge is a good example. How would you respond if you couldn't rely on the accuracy of your vehicle's fuel gauge? piotreknik/Shutterstock

2. Measure Performance: "What Is the Actual Outcome We Got?"

The second step in the control process is to measure performance, such as by number of products sold, units produced, time to completion, profit margin, or cost per item sold.[20] Managers rely on accurate measurements to track progress and make good decisions. Similarly, you rely on your vehicle's fuel gauge to accurately measure the amount of gas left in the tank, so you can determine if and when you should stop to refuel.

TABLE 16.1 Sample of Performance Standards for Nonprofit, For-Profit, and Service Organizations

NONPROFIT INSTITUTIONS	FOR-PROFIT ORGANIZATIONS	SERVICE ORGANIZATIONS
Number of financial donors	Financial performance	Number of customers served
Level of charitable contributions	Employee hiring and retention	Time spent with customers
Number of volunteers retained	Manufacturing defects	Customer satisfaction
Number of services provided	% reduction in costs	
Overhead costs	Number of customer complaints	
Employee Engagement (directly via surveys or indirectly via reduced absenteeism)		

Performance data in organizations are usually obtained from five sources: (1) employee behavior and deliverables, (2) peer input or observations, (3) customer feedback, (4) managerial evaluations, and (5) output from a production process.[21]

3. Compare Performance to Standards: "How Do the Desired and Actual Outcomes Differ?"
The third step in the control process is to compare measured performance against the standards established. Most managers are delighted with performance that exceeds standards, which becomes an occasion for handing out bonuses, promotions, and perhaps offices with a view. For performance that is below standards, they need to ask: Is the deviation from performance significant? The larger the gap, the greater the need for action.

How much deviation is acceptable? That depends on *the range of variation* built into the standards in step 1. In voting for political candidates on election day, for instance, there is supposed to be no range of variation; as the expression goes, "every vote counts." In political polling before an election, however, a range of 3 to 4% error is considered an acceptable range of variation. Too much variation in the manufacturing process can be problematic because it can cause product defects and lead to poor product quality.[22] Consider, for example, the precision needed to build Mercedes-Benz Stadium's retractable roof.

Variation Example—Mercedes-Benz Stadium: The Mercedes-Benz Stadium in Atlanta, Georgia is an engineering marvel designed with a retractable roof containing eight triangular petals that appear to spiral open. The roof and all of the supporting structures had to be installed within ⅛" for the eight petals to fit together and create a water-tight seal when the roof is closed. Then, each petal's weight had to be evenly distributed so it could open and close properly. Architects described the engineering feat as "the most complex roof ever built."[23]

Employees and managers use control charts to monitor the amount of variation in a work process. **Control charts** are a visual statistical tool used for quality control purposes. They help managers set upper and lower quality limits on a process and then monitor (control) performance in order to keep it within these limits, correcting course if results stray above the upper or below the lower limit over time.[24] Let's examine the steps in developing and using a control chart:

1. Managers construct control charts by first looking at historical data for the process they want to measure. Examples include the number of tax returns

The eight retractable petals in Mercedes-Benz Stadium in Atlanta, Georgia allow for very little variation to function properly. The design remains a modern engineering marvel.
Perry Knotts/AP Images

completed by a CPA firm per week, tons of steel produced by a manufacturer per day, or dollar volume of charitable contributions solicited by a nonprofit during a month-long fund drive.

2. Historical information is then used to establish the normal or desired performance and its allowable upper and lower limits (see Figure 16.3). Each of these flows has a separate horizontal line on the chart, which also functions as a timeline.[25] Some managers may even group multiple streams of data into one control chart instead of having different ones—this is called a *group* control chart.[26]

3. When a process goes "out of control"—that is, when it exceeds either the upper or the lower limit—management takes note and investigates. Some variations may be routine or expected, such as a rise in the volume of toy orders before the holiday shopping season or an uptick in charitable donations following a natural disaster. But other variations, such as a sudden drop in production because a machine has broken down or a large number of employees are out sick, will show up on a control chart as deviations and indicate an "out of control" situation that requires attention.

- **Applying control charts to studying:** Let's assume that your experience reveals that in order to complete the assigned reading for all your courses before finals, you need to read 55 pages a night for the next two weeks. Fifty-five pages a night is your desired performance, and depending on how efficiently you can make up for lost time, you might set 35 pages as your acceptable lower limit and 75 as your upper limit. We created a sample control chart by drawing three horizontal lines with your upper limit on top, your lower limit on the bottom, and your desired rate of 55 pages a night in the middle (see Figure 16.3). The timeline of two weeks is shown at the bottom of the chart. You put this chart to use by marking the number of pages you read each night as a point on the chart and then connect the dots. Looking at Figure 16.3, you can see that the student exhibited acceptable performance from Monday through Thursday of the first week. Friday's reading was below acceptable limits, which the student made up for by exceeding the upper limit of 75 pages a day on Saturday and Sunday.

FIGURE 16.3

Sample control chart for completing assigned readings

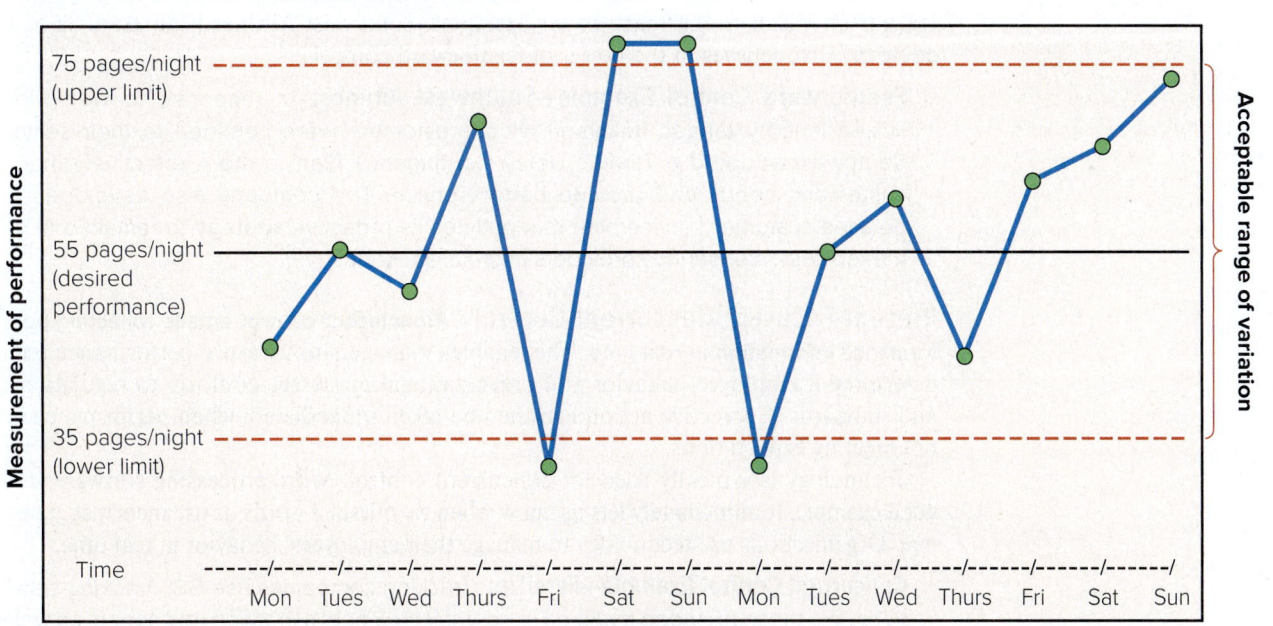

This was followed by a substandard performance on Monday and then reading levels within acceptable limits the rest of the week.

The range of variation is often incorporated into computer systems to assist with **management by exception**, a control principle that states that managers should be informed of a situation only if data show a significant deviation from standards.

4. Take Corrective Action, If Necessary: "What Changes Should We Make to Obtain Desirable Outcomes?"
The fourth step in the control process is to take corrective action, if necessary. This step involves assessing feedback and modifying, if necessary, the control process according to the results. There are three possibilities here:

1. **Meet performance expectations:** Make no changes.
2. **Exceed performance expectations:** Reward positive performance.
3. **Fall short of performance expectations:** Take action to correct negative performance.

When performance meets or exceeds the established standards, managers should give rewards, ranging from giving a verbal "Job well done" to more substantial payoffs such as raises, bonuses, and promotions to reinforce good behavior.

When performance falls significantly short of the standard, managers should carefully examine the reasons and take appropriate action. Sometimes the standards themselves were unrealistic, owing to changing conditions, in which case the standards need to be altered. Sometimes employees haven't been given the resources for achieving the standards. And sometimes the employees may need more attention from management as a way of signaling that their efforts have been insufficient in fulfilling their part of the job bargain.

Types of Controls

There are three types of control: feedforward, concurrent, and feedback. You'll notice that the major difference between each is their time-related focus. Let's consider how they work.

Future-Focused: Feedforward Control
Feedforward control focuses on preventing future problems. It does this by first collecting information about past performance in order to establish new policies and procedures. Plans are then made to avoid pitfalls or roadblocks prior to starting a task or project. This practice essentially helps people learn from mistakes and make better decisions. Southwest Airlines is an example of a company that believes in the power of feedforward control.

> **Feedforward Control Example—Southwest Airlines:** In response to well-publicized lengthy tarmac delays in which customers were confined to their seats, Southwest adopted a Tarmac Delay Contingency Plan to more effectively meet customers' needs and provide better service. The company also developed a detailed customer service plan that outlines its proactive strategy to remain one of the top customer service providers in the airline industry.[27]

Present-Focused: Concurrent Control
Concurrent control entails collecting performance information in real time. This enables managers to measure performance and determine if employee behavior and organizational processes conform to regulations and standards. Corrective action can then be taken immediately when performance is not meeting expectations.

Technology is typically used for concurrent control. Word-processing software is a good example. It immediately lets us know when we misspell words or use incorrect grammar. Organizations use technology to manage their employees' behavior in real time.

> **Concurrent Control Example—FleetUp:** Trucking companies use GPS tracking solutions, like those provided by FleetUp, to track their fleet's location and speed, as well

Where's my truck? GPS technology allows organizations to receive real-time details on the status of their fleet. Alexander Kirch/Shutterstock

as to receive safety alerts. The real-time information gathered also can be used to optimize routes and reduce fuel consumption. Managers can even dial in to a driver's dashcam to provide immediate assistance if needed.[28]

Past-Focused: Feedback Control This form of control is extensively used by supervisors and managers. **Feedback control amounts to collecting performance information after a task or project is done.** This information then is used to correct or improve future performance.

Feedback Control Examples: Classic feedback control examples include receiving test scores a week after taking a test, receiving customer feedback after purchasing a product, receiving student ratings of teaching performance weeks after teaching a class, rating the quality of a movie after watching it, and participating in a performance review at work. ●

16.3 What Should Managers Control?

THE BIG PICTURE
Managers are encouraged to control four different aspects of organizational effectiveness: financial performance, customer outcomes, internal business processes, and employee outcomes associated with innovation and learning. These aspects of organizational performance are captured in the balanced scorecard. A strategy map is a visual representation of the relationship among the four key components of organizational performance.

LO 16-3
Discuss ways that managers can control an organization.

By now you know that managers are responsible for delivering results associated with organizational performance. Their jobs depend on it! But how do managers know what results to focus on given the many different activities, projects, and goals being pursued on an ongoing basis? Answering this question requires planning, strategic thinking, and effective control mechanisms. It also entails careful consideration of an organization's stakeholders, which we discussed in Chapter 3 and Learning Module 1. We answer the question of "what should managers control" by discussing a framework called the balanced scorecard.

The balanced scorecard is based on an approach to organizational effectiveness that requires organizational leaders to balance the interests of shareholders, customers, society/environment, and employees.[29] Let's first take a look at the logic and structure of the balanced scorecard and how its application results in creating a strategy map. We'll then show you how you can adapt and apply the balanced scorecard to your graduation and employment goals.

The Balanced Scorecard: A Comprehensive Approach to Managerial Control

Simply measuring and controlling financial performance, such as sales figures and labor costs, or operational matters, such as customer satisfaction, is not enough.[30] Successful companies go beyond these traditional measures and seek an integrated approach to control that answers these four questions:

1. What does success look like to our shareholders?
2. How do we appear to our customers?
3. What must we do extremely well?
4. Are we equipped for continued value and improvement?

Harvard professors Robert Kaplan and David Norton sought to answer these questions by developing the balanced scorecard. Kaplan and Norton's **balanced scorecard** provides top managers a fast but comprehensive view of the organization via four indicators: (1) financial metrics, (2) customer metrics, (3) internal-business process metrics, and (4) metrics associated with innovation and learning.

"Think of the balanced scorecard as the dials and indicators in an airplane cockpit," write Kaplan and Norton. For a pilot, "reliance on one instrument can be fatal. Similarly, the complexity of managing an organization today requires that managers be able to view performance in several areas simultaneously."[31] It is not enough, say Kaplan and Norton, to simply measure financial performance, such as sales figures and return on investment. Operational matters, such as customer satisfaction, are equally important.[32]

The balanced scorecard establishes *goals* and *performance measures* according to four "perspectives," or areas—*financial, customer, internal-business processes,* and *innovation and learning* (see Figure 16.4).

The balanced scorecard is rooted in the saying, "What you measure is what you get." Kaplan and Norton thus recommended that companies should establish, measure, and control quantifiable goals for each perspective that support the organization's vision and strategies. Research confirms the power of the balanced scorecard, demonstrating that businesses that utilize it are more likely to be innovative, gain competitive advantage, and perform better.[33] Let's now consider each of the scorecard's four perspectives.

Financial Perspective: "What Does Success Look Like to Our Shareholders?"

Corporate financial strategies and goals generally fall into two buckets: revenue growth and productivity growth. Revenue growth goals generally focus on increasing revenue from both new and existing customers. A good example comes from the video game industry where companies like Electronic Arts are quickly growing new revenue streams.

Revenue Growth Example—Electronic Arts (EA): Game publisher EA used to rely on one-time sales of video games on gaming consoles like PlayStation, Nintendo, and Xbox. The company is now adding additional streams of revenue by offering in-app purchases in its free-to-play mobile versions of popular titles like *Madden NFL, FIFA Soccer,* and *NBA Live.* Today, the company makes nearly $5 billion in revenue from customers purchasing extra content and subscriptions.[34]

Productivity metrics like revenue per employee or total output produced divided by number of employees are common organization-level goals. We also can measure productivity in terms of costs. For example, Macy's closed 4 stores in 2023 as part of a larger plan to close 125 stores in a restructuring effort "to lower costs, bring teams closer together, and reduce duplicative work," said Macy's CEO Jeff Gennette.[35]

There are many elements associated with the financial perspective. We will focus on three: budgets, financial statements, and financial ratios.

FIGURE 16.4

The balanced scorecard: Four perspectives

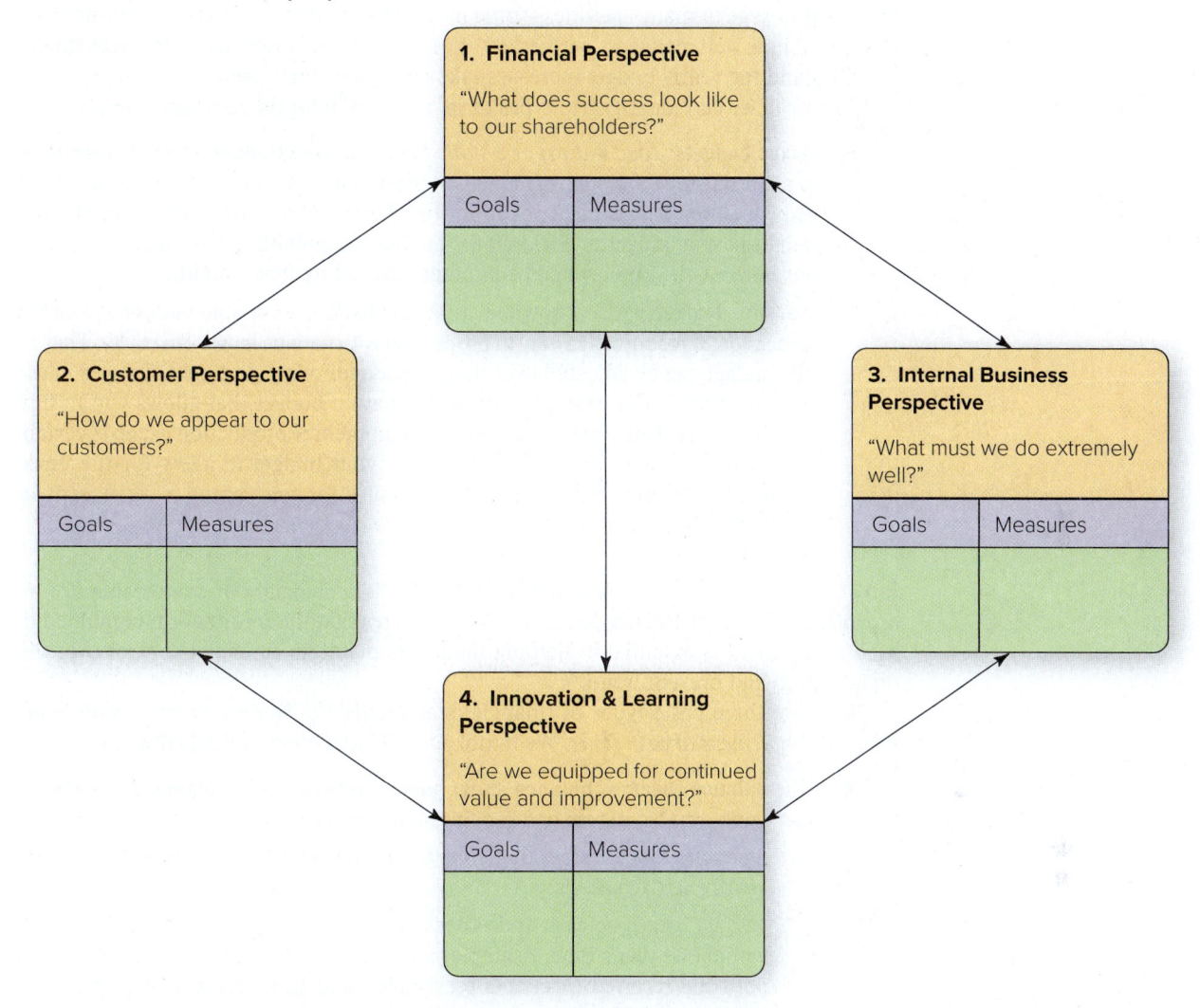

1. Financial Perspective
"What does success look like to our shareholders?"

Goals	Measures

2. Customer Perspective
"How do we appear to our customers?"

Goals	Measures

3. Internal Business Perspective
"What must we do extremely well?"

Goals	Measures

4. Innovation & Learning Perspective
"Are we equipped for continued value and improvement?"

Goals	Measures

Sources: Adapted from Kaplan, R.S. "Conceptual Foundations of the Balanced Scorecard." Working Paper. 2010. https://www.hbs.edu/ris/Publication%20Files/10-074_0bf3c151-f82b-4592-b885-cdde7f5d97a6.pdf; Kaplan, R.S. and D.P. Norton. "The Balanced Scorecard: Measures That Drive Performance." Harvard Business Review. July–August 2005. https://hbr.org/2005/07/the-balanced-scorecard-measures-that-drive-performance.

Budgets A **budget** is a formal financial projection. It states an organization's planned activities for a given period of time in quantitative terms, such as dollars, hours, or number of products. Budgets are prepared not only for the organization as a whole but also for the divisions and departments within it. Most organizations use budgets to provide a yardstick against which managers can judge how well they are controlling monetary expenditures. Some firms also use budgets to signal company priorities and changing trends.[36] Various software tools and apps are available to help you manage personal or freelance budgeting, such as Quicken, Credit Karma, and CountAbout.[37]

There are many different kinds of budgets, but we will focus on incremental budgeting as it's the most widely used type. **Incremental budgeting** allocates increased or decreased funds to a department by using the last budget period as a reference point; only incremental changes in the budget request are reviewed. One difficulty is that

Hail to the spreadsheet. Professionals often use software, such as Microsoft Excel, to perform budgeting activities.
Kaspars Grinvalds/Shutterstock

incremental budgets tend to lock departments into stable spending arrangements; they are not flexible in meeting environmental demands.[38] Another difficulty is that a department may engage in many activities—some more important than others—but it's not easy to sort out how well managers performed at the various activities. Thus, the department activities and the yearly budget increases take on lives of their own.

In general, we can identify two types of incremental budgets: *fixed* and *variable*.

- **Fixed budgets:** Also known as a *static budget*, a fixed budget allocates resources on the basis of a single estimate of costs. That is, there is only one set of expenses; the budget does not allow for adjustment over time. For example, you might have a budget of $50,000 for buying equipment in a given year—no matter how much you may need equipment exceeding that amount.

- **Variable budgets:** Also known as a *flexible budget*, a variable budget allows the allocation of resources to vary in proportion with various levels of activity. That is, the budget can be adjusted over time to accommodate pertinent changes in the environment.[39] For example, you might have a budget that allows you to hire temporary workers or lease temporary equipment if production exceeds certain levels. As a freelancer, you might set up your budget to allow for the unexpected, like the purchase of a second monitor for your laptop if you accept an assignment that requires it.

Financial Statements

A financial statement is a summary of some aspect of an organization's financial status. Research demonstrates that the information contained in such a statement is essential in helping managers maintain financial control over the organization and prevent fraud.[40]

There are three basic types of financial statements: *the balance sheet, income statement,* and *statement of cash flows.* We'll look at each statement individually.

- **The balance sheet:** A balance sheet summarizes an organization's overall financial worth—that is, assets and liabilities—at a specific point in time.
    - *Assets* are the resources that an organization controls; they consist of current assets and fixed assets.
    - *Current assets* are cash and other assets that are readily convertible to cash within one year's time. Examples are inventory, sales for which payment has not been received (accounts receivable), and U.S. Treasury bills or money market mutual funds.
    - *Fixed assets* are property, buildings, equipment, and the like that have a useful life that exceeds one year but that are usually harder to convert to cash.
    - *Liabilities* are claims, or debts, by suppliers, lenders, and other nonowners of the organization against a company's assets. ExxonMobil is a good example of an organization that keeps a close eye on its assets and liabilities.

    > **Balance Sheet Example—ExxonMobil:** Oil giant ExxonMobil spent decades ensuring it had a healthy balance sheet in case of a catastrophe. That catastrophe came in 2020 when oil prices plummeted due to a combination of COVID-19 and oversupply. The company cut costs to endure the socioeconomic downturn. Economic conditions changed in 2022 as the company reported a record net profit of $56 billion. Exxon CFO Kathryn Mikells noted the record results came from "a combination of strong markets, strong throughput, strong production, and really good cost control."[41]

- **The income statement:** The balance sheet depicts the organization's overall financial worth at a specific point in time. By contrast, the income statement summarizes an organization's financial results—revenues and expenses—over a specified period of time, such as a quarter or a year.

TABLE 16.2
Sample Profit and Loss Statements

CLARK, THE COMPUTER DOCTOR PROFIT & LOSS JANUARY 1 THROUGH DECEMBER 31, 2024		
Income:		Jan 1–Dec 31, 2024
Sales		520,615.00
Services Income		32,320.00
Total Income:		552,935.00
Parts and Materials	54,218.00	
Gross Profit		498,717.00
Expenses:		
Bank Service Charges		180.00
Charitable Donations		2,300.00
Dues and Subscriptions		1,750.35
Insurance:		
General Liability Insurance	2,035.00	
Workman's Compensation Insurance	1,018.00	
Total Insurance Expense		3,053.00
Payroll Taxes:		
Payroll 941	14,826.22	
Federal Unemployment Tax	215.00	
State Unemployment Tax	312.00	
Total Payroll Taxes		15,353.22
Payroll:		
Officer Wages	190,000.00	
Salary and Wages	52,329.21	
Total Payroll:		242,329.21
Accounting and Legal		1,803.50
Automobile Expenses:		
Maintenance	323.00	
Gas	1,318.49	
License	782.20	
Total Automobile Expenses:		2,423.69
Office Rent		24,000.00
Office supplies		2,016.48
Repairs and Maintenance		218.60
Telephone and Internet		2,472.18
Utilities		3,040.56
TOTAL EXPENSE		300,940.79
NET INCOME		197,776.21

You will need to understand an income statement if you end up self-employed or start a business. We created a sample profit and loss statement for a two-person operation consisting of an owner and one employee (see Table 16.2). The company is doing quite well with $197,776.21 of net income, computed by subtracting total expenses from gross profit. You also can see the types of expenses that confront any small business. You have expenses for insurance, payroll and payroll taxes, accounting, auto, rent, supplies, and other expenses.

- **The statement of cash flows:** The **statement of cash flows** reports the cash generated and used over a specific period of time. Generally, this period of time matches the company's income statement.[42]

Have you ever heard the saying "cash is king"? Stakeholders are often interested in how much actual cash an organization is generating because it shows the company's solvency. This is what differentiates the statement of cash flows from an income statement—the latter often includes noncash revenues or expenses, which can be misleading. For example, a firm that has significant revenue, but does not actually receive the revenue in time to pay its expenses, will face problems.[43] Because companies generate and use cash in different ways, the statement of cash flows is separated into three sections:

- *Operating activities* (cash generated from a company's core business as opposed to investments and borrowing).
- *Investment activities* (cash generated from investments).
- *Financing activities* (cash generated from owners or debtors).

Bed Bath & Beyond is a good example of what happens when a firm runs out of cash.

Bed Bath and Beyond's negative cash flows spiraled into major financial problems leading the company to declare bankruptcy. Retail Photographer/Shutterstock

Cash Flow Example—Bed Bath & Beyond: Homeware retailer Bed Beth & Beyond filed for chapter 11 bankruptcy protection in April 2023. The company incurred a negative cash flow of $340 million and paid $65 million in interest in 2022. Bed Bath & Beyond lost the trust of its creditors and vendors making it difficult for the retailer to keep its shelves fully stocked. The company also failed to raise enough money from investors to remain in business. The company announced it will close its 360 retail locations along with 120 buybuy BABY locations as it liquidates its assets.[44]

Financial Ratios Financial statements provide data on a firm, but oftentimes managers need a simple way to measure progress against internal goals, competitors, or the overall industry. This can be done with **financial ratios**, which are indicators determined from a company's financial information and used for comparison purposes.[45] Some of the most common ratios measure a company's *liquidity, turnover,* and *profitability.* Table 16.3 lists an example of a ratio for each of these categories, what the ratio measures, and how to calculate it.

Customer Perspective: "How Do We Appear to Our Customers?"

Many companies rightfully view customers as one of their most important stakeholders—why wouldn't they? After all, customers generate the revenue needed to achieve

TABLE 16.3 Popular Financial Ratios

RATIO	CATEGORY	WHAT IS MEASURED	FORMULA
Current Ratio	Liquidity	A company's ability to pay short-term obligations due within a year.	Current Assets / Current Liabilities
Asset Turnover Ratio	Efficiency	The efficiency in which a company uses assets to generate revenue.	Net Sales / Average Total Assets
Return on Investment Ratio	Profitability	The amount of return on a particular investment relative to its cost.	Net Investment Income / Cost of Investment

Sources: "Financial Ratios." Corporate Finance Institute. March 13, 2023. https://corporatefinanceinstitute.com/resources/accounting/financial-ratios; Birken, E.G. "Understanding Return on Investment (ROI)." Forbes Advisor. September 28, 2022. https://www.forbes.com/advisor/investing/roi-return-on-investment/#:~:text=Return%20on%20investment%20is%20a.

financial performance. A company without any customers has no income. The balanced scorecard translates this belief into measures such as customer satisfaction/loyalty and retention. Let's examine each in a bit more detail.

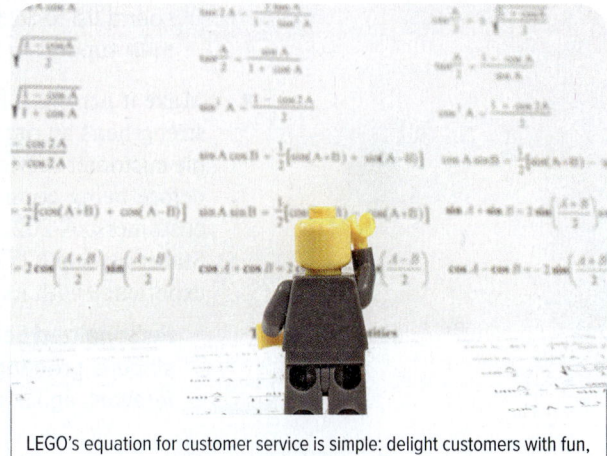

Customer Satisfaction Companies would not exist without satisfied customers. **Customer satisfaction is the measure of how products or services provided by a firm meet customer expectations.** As you might expect, losing a dissatisfied customer means losing revenue, but did you know that replacing that customer is an even greater challenge? In fact, studies show that it is five to seven times more expensive to acquire a new customer than it is to keep a current one.[46]

Being responsive to customers' complaints is one research-proven way to keep customers satisfied. Customer service data show that customers whose complaints are handled effectively are more loyal to the company than customers with problem-free experiences.[47] LEGO is a good example.

LEGO's equation for customer service is simple: delight customers with fun, reliable, knowledgeable, and engaging interactions. cjmacer/Shutterstock

Customer Satisfaction Example—LEGO: LEGO works hard to delight its customers with thoughtful, personalized responses to their inquiries whether they are seeking to replace lost pieces or sharing innovative ideas for new LEGO sets. It attributes its industry leading customer satisfaction to its "freaky" customer engagement. "Freaky stands for FRKE, which is short for fun, reliable, knowledgeable and engaging," says Monika Lütke-Daldrup, LEGO's head of consumer and shopper engagement. "And those four words are something we've built our customer service on for probably more than 15 years."[48]

Customer Retention Whereas customer satisfaction measures how customers are feeling, **customer retention refers to the actions companies take to reduce customer defections.** In other words, the goal of customer retention programs is to keep customers loyal because loyal customers tend to be repeat buyers and they tell others good things about a company's products and services.[49] Effective customer retention programs focus on three techniques. Let's explore each using the Ritz-Carlton hotel chain as an example.[50]

- **Set customer expectations.** Organizations should set customer expectations early and at a level they can realistically provide. This eliminates uncertainty about the level of expected service and ensures they will always meet commitments.

    Set Customer Expectations Example: The Ritz-Carlton lists its "Gold Standards" on its website so guests are aware of its pledge to "provide the finest personal service and facilities for guests who will always enjoy a warm, relaxed, yet refined ambiance."

- **Go the extra mile.** Going above and beyond customer expectations is consistent with the concept of "delighting" customers. It helps companies build strong relationships and long-term loyalty. In fact, 58% of customers are willing to pay more for a better service experience, showing it's well worth it to go that extra mile.[51]

    Extra Mile Example: Ritz-Carlton employees, from housekeeping to management, can

Impeccable service. Door attendants at the Ritz-Carlton Hotel in New York open doors for a guest. Keith Bedford/Redux Pictures

spend up to $2,000 per guest, per day, to resolve problems without asking their supervisor for permission.

- **Make it personal.** Personalized service improves the customer experience and strengthens an organization's bond with its clientele. Impersonal or inaccessible customer service such as AI chatbots or an endless maze of phone prompts before being connected to a live representative is a surefire to way frustrate customers. A 2022 PwC survey of more than 4,000 consumers in the United States revealed 37% of consumers stop buying from a company due to a bad experience with its products or customer service.[52]

    Personalized Service Example: Ritz-Carlton employees give guests a warm, sincere greeting using their name; fulfill their needs; and provide a fond farewell, again addressing guests by their name.

Internal Business Perspective: "What Must We Do Extremely Well?"

Whereas the customer perspective represents the revenue side of the financial equation, the internal business perspective portrays the cost side. This perspective captures critical organizational activities that allow organizations to effectively meet their financial objectives and customers' expectations while creating value for society and the communities they serve.[53] The balanced scorecard measures these activities by looking at metrics such as productivity, efficiency, quality, and safety.

Productivity Productivity can be applied at any level, whether for you as an individual, for the work unit you're managing, or for the organization you work for. Productivity is defined by the formula of *outputs divided by inputs* for a specified period of time. Outputs are all the goods and services produced. Inputs are not only labor but also capital, materials, and energy. That is,

$$\text{Productivity} = \frac{\text{Outputs}}{\text{Inputs}} \quad \text{or} \quad \frac{\text{Goods} + \text{Services}}{\text{Labor} + \text{Capital} + \text{Materials} + \text{Energy}}$$

There are two tools managers can use to set standards or goals for productivity.

- **Benchmarking:** A process by which a company compares its performance with that of high-performing organizations, as we discussed in Chapter 6. Companies use internal benchmarks to set performance standards, competitive benchmarking to assess themselves against their competitors, and strategic benchmarking when they are ready to look outside their industry.

    Benchmarking Example—J.D. Power: Data analytics and consumer insights company J.D. Power assists the automotive industry and its customers with benchmarking data detailing how well competing automobiles satisfy buyers in several areas including initial quality, dependability, overall performance and appeal, and sales and service.[54]

- **Best practices: Best practices** refer to "a set of guidelines, ethics or ideas that represent the most efficient or prudent course action in a given business situation."[55] Note that best practices compare processes whereas benchmarks compare outcomes. The two concepts are interconnected such that *best practices* highlight improvements needed to a company's activities to achieve the highest performance standards (*benchmarks*).

- Companies often develop best practices internally through managers' and employees' positive experiences on the job, and they sometimes adopt the strategies other companies have used to succeed in similar situations. Best practices can stimulate learning and improvement, but they can also limit innovation. Organizational psychologist Adam Grant observed, "many of our best practices were built for a world that does not exist anymore, and as the landscape of work becomes more dynamic, more unstable and more unpredictable, instead of sticking to our old best practices, we need to be constantly searching for better practices."[56]

Efficiency As we discussed in Chapter 1, efficiency means to use resources—people, money, raw materials, and the like—wisely and cost effectively. Good managers aren't only concerned with efficiency though; they also need to ensure they are being effective. This means managers achieve results by making the right decisions and successfully carrying them out (think back to the definition of *management:* the pursuit of organizational goals efficiently and effectively). Amazon is a good example of a company focused on achieving both objectives.

>   **Efficiency Example—Amazon:** Andy Jassy, CEO of Amazon, reported the company's e-commerce business earned $316 billion in revenue in 2022 but incurred a $2.8 billion operating loss. Jassy is focused on improving its profit margins by reorganizing its logistics operations. These changes promise to "shorten delivery times for customers and lower costs for Amazon, which should be a win-win," achieving both efficiency and organizational effectiveness.[57]

Quality High-quality products and services are vital to an organization's success. This is especially true in crowded markets such as technology. Quality is one reason Apple, for instance, can price its iPhone higher than any other mobile device in the industry. Another reason is because the company has established a history of delivering innovative, market-leading products.[58] In fact, a 2022 survey of more than 7,200 smartphone customers found that over 48% of iPhone users intended to buy another one when the time came for an upgrade, the highest loyalty marks for any smartphone brand.[59]

In Section 16.4, we'll discuss how organizations can use total quality management techniques to ensure they are effectively managing the quality of their products and services. For now, it's important to know that quality contributes to increasing customer loyalty, building a strong reputation, and managing costs.[60]

Safety As we discussed in Learning Module 1, organizations have a responsibility for the safety of the communities in which they serve.[61] Part of this responsibility is related to not harming the community (i.e., making sure your factory does not poison a town's drinking water), which is a direct measure of community safety. Other times, the impact is indirect, such as making sure your employees, many of whom come from local communities, are safe. Phoenix Sintered Metals is a good example of an organization committed to its employees' safety.

>   **Safety Example—Phoenix Sintered Metals:** Family-owned and Pennsylvania-based Phoenix Sintered Metals manufactures metal parts. The company is "committed to continuous improvement" in its occupational health and safety policies and procedures. Terry Fustine, Phoenix's safety coordinator, consulted with Pennsylvania's Occupational Health and Safety Administration (PA OSHA) for recommendations to improve its workplace safety. The company corrected several safety hazards, explained the safety concerns to employees, and enhanced their safety training and departmental audits. Phoenix also improved its written safety and health program policy manual. The company's focus on safety contributed to a 66% drop in recordable injuries. And for those in the company worried about the bottom line—all of the changes were made at minimal cost.[62]

Safety first. The Phoenix Sintered Metals Safety Committee at the company's headquarters in Brockway, Pennsylvania. Courtesy of Phoenix Sintered Metals

Innovation and Learning Perspective: "Are We Equipped for Continued Value and Improvement?"

Employees' learning and development are the foundation for all other goals in the balanced scorecard. At the individual level, this perspective is analogous to developing career readiness competencies. The idea here is that capable and motivated employees, who possess the resources and motivation needed to get the job done, will provide higher-quality products and services in a more efficient manner. Making this happen requires a commitment to invest in progressive human resource practices (recall our discussion in Chapter 9) and technology. Typical metrics in this perspective are employee attitudes (Chapter 11), turnover (Chapter 11), resource capabilities (Chapter 9), and organizational culture (Chapter 8). Let's consider each of these measures.

Employee Attitudes As we discussed in Chapter 11, employee attitudes are incredibly important and influence workers' behavior. Successful managers aren't satisfied with just "happy" employees, they strive to increase employee engagement, job satisfaction, and commitment. As we discussed many times in this textbook, there is an abundance of research demonstrating that these attitudes increase performance and customer outcomes while reducing turnover and absenteeism.[63]

Employee Turnover Every organization experiences some turnover, which, as we saw in Chapter 9, is when an employee abandons, resigns, retires, or is terminated from a job. Research continues to support the conclusion that job satisfaction and organizational commitment are the strongest predictors of turnover.[64] There is, however, a difference between functional and dysfunctional turnover, concepts introduced in Chapter 11. Let's dig a bit deeper into the differences.[65]

- **Functional turnover:** This turnover occurs when underperformers leave a firm. Functional turnover is common in large accounting, consulting, and law firms employing an "up or out" philosophy. Those who are unable to progress are in effect let go. Take for example tenure at universities. Professors who are trying to obtain tenure ("tenure-track faculty") have a certain number of years to do so based on their research, teaching, and service to the institution. Those who are not able to achieve tenure are eventually let go.
- **Dysfunctional turnover:** This is the opposite of functional turnover and occurs when a company's best performers leave. A variety of reasons can contribute to dysfunctional turnover, but a common cause is low potential for advancement. For example, if a company is in the habit of filling its management positions with external candidates instead of looking at high-performing internal ones, employees are likely to seek opportunities for advancement at other firms.

Successful companies don't just measure an overall turnover rate. They need to figure out if the employees they couldn't retain were high or low performers. This will determine if the turnover was functional or dysfunctional.[66]

Hypothetical Functional/Dysfunctional Turnover Example: Ava is an employee at Fusion Technologies who just resigned from her sales manager position. HR may take a look at Ava's personnel file and examine her last performance appraisal. If Ava earned high marks, the turnover is most likely dysfunctional. Another way to make this determination is to ask Ava's manager if they would rehire her. If the answer is yes, you have dysfunctional turnover.

Exit interviews also can assist in better understanding the reasons for turnover. These are formal conversations that take place between a departing employee and HR, or another manager, to determine the reason why the person is leaving.[67] Let's return to our example of Ava. HR can utilize an exit interview to determine if she left because she was dissatisfied or because her spouse got a job in another state and they needed to move.

Resource Capabilities Managers need to ensure employees have the resources they need to be successful. This includes investing in employee learning and development, discussed in Chapter 9, and in technology that supports achieving the organization's goals. Offering employees continuous opportunities to develop their knowledge, skills, and abilities provides four benefits:[68]

1. Organizations are better able to recruit top-tier talent.
2. High-performing employees are motivated to stay.
3. Employees are more satisfied and engaged with their work.
4. Organizations can build their leadership pipeline internally.

Organizational Culture We discussed organizational culture in Chapter 8, but here we want to specifically reiterate the importance of people-focused cultures. As you may recall from Chapter 2, people-focused organizations are guided by the Theory Y view that people are essentially good, trustworthy, and productive, and that they flourish when they are empowered to act independently in an atmosphere values their well-being. CarMax, the nation's largest used car retailer, is a good example of a company with a people-focused culture.

> **People-Focused Culture Example—CarMax:** CarMax operates more than 220 stores in 41 states. The company focuses on increasing collaboration as well as respect and support for its employees. One employee commented, "It's the first company that I've worked for that makes you feel the company puts its employees first." CarMax employees are encouraged to share their time, talents, and resources to volunteer in the local communities they serve in order to increase their own well-being. CarMax has earned top accolades for its people-focused approach, including 19 years as one of *Fortune*'s "100 Best Companies to Work For."[69]

To what extent is/was your current or past employer committed to the people, technology, and organizational culture needed to support its strategy? You can find out by completing Self-Assessment 16.1 if your instructor has assigned it to you in Connect.

A Carmax associate at the company's Plano, Texas location talks with a customer about the value of his used truck. LM Otero/AP Images

SELF-ASSESSMENT 16.1

Assessing the Innovation and Learning Perspective of the Balanced Scorecard

This survey is designed to assess the innovation and learning perspective of the balanced scorecard. Please complete Self-Assessment 16.1 if your instructor has assigned it in Connect.

PRACTICAL ACTION: Develop Your Career Management Action Plan

The purpose of this activity is for you to link your long-term goals of graduating and getting a job shortly after graduation with their supporting short-term SMART goals. This process is similar to what you learned about goal cascading in Chapter 5. Specifically, you will be asked to develop short-term SMART goals within the four categories of the balanced scorecard that support achieving your long-term goals. Consider the following questions when you develop these short-term goals. We want you to create at least one SMART goal for each scorecard category and record them in the notebook you used for the Practical Action box in Section 16.1. We also provide some helpful suggestions for SMART goals to get you started.

1. **Financial perspective (How can I have a manageable financial situation three months after graduation?).** Consider the following three questions:
   A. What is the maximum amount of debt I want to accumulate in pursuit of my degree?
      - **SMART goal:** To accumulate no more than $X of debt upon graduation.
   B. What financial resources might I need to move for a new job and purchase a professional wardrobe?
      - **SMART goal:** To save $X by the time I graduate.
   C. What salary do I anticipate earning as a result of my degree?
      - **SMART goal:** To obtain a job with a starting salary of $X.

2. **Customer perspective (How can I make a strong positive impression on potential employers?).** Employers are assumed to be your customers for this application. Assume your goal is to secure a job with a reputable employer regardless of geographical location.
   A. What can I do to create a positive impression?
      - **SMART goal:** To get feedback on my current resume from X people by X date.
      - **SMART goal:** To obtain a leadership position in X student organizations.
      - **SMART goal:** To improve my career readiness competencies of openness to change and proactive learning orientation by X%.
   B. How can I determine whether or not I am a good fit for potential employers?
      - **SMART goal:** To identify and investigate the culture of X potential employers (see Self-Assessment 8.1).
      - **SMART goal:** To identify at least three employers in which my values are consistent with theirs (see Self-Assessment 8.2).
      - **SMART goal:** To identify at least five career readiness competencies desired by these employers.
      - **SMART goal:** To implement an action plan to develop three targeted career readiness competencies with the next six months.

3. **Internal business perspective (How can I improve my GPA, expand my professional network, and add relevant experience to my resume?).** Consider the following questions:
   A. How can I improve my GPA?
      - **SMART goal:** To increase the number of hours I spend studying and preparing for each class by X% each semester.
      - **SMART goal:** To decrease the number of hours I spend socializing with friends by X% each semester.
      - **SMART goal:** To identify and implement X ways to study more efficiently.
   B. How can I expand my professional network?
      - **SMART goal:** To attend X% more networking events or career fairs sponsored by my university, business societies, or the local chamber of commerce within the next six months.
   C. How well am I performing in my current job/internship? If I'm not currently working, what work opportunities are available that would provide experience desired by my ideal employer?
      - **SMART goal (if I'm currently working):** To improve my performance at work by X% over the next six months.
      - **SMART goal (if I'm not currently working):** To identify three different work opportunities over the summer in my ideal employer's industry.
      - **SMART goal:** To implement an action plan for developing X career readiness competencies over the next six months.

4. **Innovation and learning perspective (Am I equipped to deliver continued value and ideas for improvement?).** Your goal for this perspective is to build your career readiness competencies. We chose four that many employers highly value.
   A. Critical thinking/problem solving.
      - **SMART goal:** Complete Self-Assessment 7.1, "Assessing Your Problem-Solving Potential." Develop an action plan to improve on my four lowest scored items on the assessment.

B. Teamwork/collaboration.
- **SMART goal:** Take Self-Assessment 13.3, "Assessing Team Effectiveness." Develop an action plan to improve my current team's performance or lead my next team's development and performance.

C. Self-motivation.
- **SMART goal:** Take Self-Assessment 12.3, "Assessing Your Needs for Self-Determination." Identify my strongest need (competence, autonomy, or relatedness), and develop an action plan to proactively craft my job or my experience as a student to better meet my strongest need.

D. Proactive learning orientation.
- **SMART goal:** Develop an action plan to improve my self-awareness, knowledge about my ideal employer's industry, and understanding about a topic that intrigues me but I know little about.

The next Practical Action box (Section 16.4) will help you develop an action plan to measure and track your progress toward your SMART goals. It is the last activity to ensure you follow through to reach your graduation and employment goals.

Strategy Mapping: Visual Representation of the Path to Organizational Effectiveness

Have you ever worked for a company that failed to effectively communicate its vision and strategic plan? If yes, then you know how it feels to be disengaged because you don't know how your work contributes to organizational effectiveness. Kaplan and Norton recognized this common problem and developed a tool called a strategy map.

A **strategy map** is a "visual representation of a company's critical objectives and the crucial relationships among them that drive organizational performance." Maps show relationships among a company's strategic goals. This helps employees understand how their work contributes to their employer's overall success.[70] They also provide insight into how an organization creates value for its key constituents. For example, a map informs others about

1. the knowledge, skills, and systems that employees should possess (innovation and learning perspective) ...
2. to innovate and build internal capabilities (internal business perspective) ...
3. that deliver value to customers (customer perspective), ...
4. which eventually creates higher shareholder value (financial perspective).

Research confirms the value of strategy mapping, demonstrating that its effective use substantially improves the implementation success of balanced scorecards. These maps also have been found to facilitate strategy formation, performance measurement system development, and strategy evaluation and communication.[71]

We created an illustrative strategy map in Figure 16.5. Starting with learning and growth, the arrows in the diagram show the logic that connects goals to internal processes, to customers, to financial goals, and finally to the long-term goal of providing shareholder value. For example, you can see that organizational culture affects the internal process goals related to innovation, operational improvements, and good corporate citizenship. This causal structure provides a strategic road map of how the company plans to achieve organizational effectiveness.

You can also detect which of the four perspectives is most important by counting the number of goals in each perspective. For this sample map, there are four, five, eight, and three goals for the financial, customer, internal processes, and learning and growth perspectives, respectively. You also can see that internal process goals affect seven other goals—count the number of arrows coming from internal process goals. All told, the

FIGURE 16.5

Sample strategy map for Keurig Dr Pepper

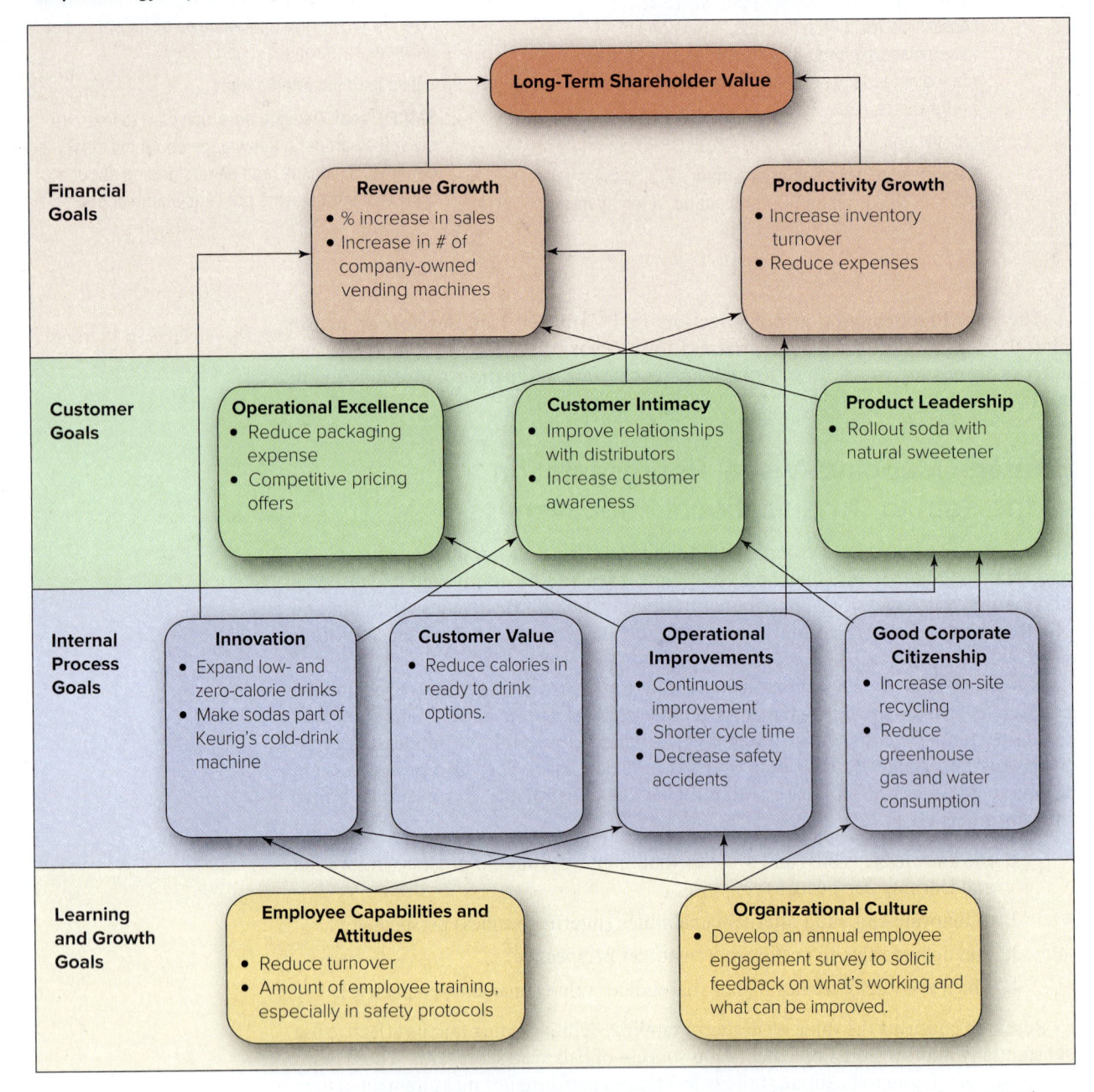

Financial Goals

- **Long-Term Shareholder Value**
- **Revenue Growth**
  - % increase in sales
  - Increase in # of company-owned vending machines
- **Productivity Growth**
  - Increase inventory turnover
  - Reduce expenses

Customer Goals

- **Operational Excellence**
  - Reduce packaging expense
  - Competitive pricing offers
- **Customer Intimacy**
  - Improve relationships with distributors
  - Increase customer awareness
- **Product Leadership**
  - Rollout soda with natural sweetener

Internal Process Goals

- **Innovation**
  - Expand low- and zero-calorie drinks
  - Make sodas part of Keurig's cold-drink machine
- **Customer Value**
  - Reduce calories in ready to drink options.
- **Operational Improvements**
  - Continuous improvement
  - Shorter cycle time
  - Decrease safety accidents
- **Good Corporate Citizenship**
  - Increase on-site recycling
  - Reduce greenhouse gas and water consumption

Learning and Growth Goals

- **Employee Capabilities and Attitudes**
  - Reduce turnover
  - Amount of employee training, especially in safety protocols
- **Organizational Culture**
  - Develop an annual employee engagement survey to solicit feedback on what's working and what can be improved.

Sources: This map was based on information in "Corporate Social Responsibility." Keurig Dr Pepper, https://www.keurigdrpepper.com/en/our-company/corporate-responsibility (accessed May 17, 2023); "Corporate Responsibility Report 2021." Keurig Dr Pepper, 20.

beauty of a strategy map is that it enables leaders to present a strategic road map to employees on one page. It also provides a clear statement about the criteria used to assess organizational effectiveness.

There is one final benefit to strategy maps. They serve as the starting point for any organization that wants to implement goal cascading or management by objectives. For example, one of your authors, Angelo Kinicki, has worked with several organizations that cascaded a top-level strategy map like the one shown in Figure 16.5 down three to four organizational levels.[72]

16.4 Total Quality Management

THE BIG PICTURE

Total quality management (TQM) is dedicated to continuous quality improvement, training, and customer satisfaction. Two core principles are people orientation and improvement orientation. Some techniques for improving quality are employee involvement, benchmarking, outsourcing, reduced cycle time, and statistical process control.

If high-quality products and services keep customers,[73] how can organizations instill a culture of continuous quality improvement? We'll discuss the answer to this question in this section. We'll start with an overview of what we mean by quality and then guide you through practically applying the quality improvement cycle to monitor progress related to your graduation and employment goals. We'll then discuss total quality management and its core principles. Finally, the focus will turn to tools, techniques, and standards organizations can utilize to uphold a high standard of quality.

LO 16-4

Explain the total quality management process.

Quality Control and Quality Assurance

Quality refers to the total ability of a product or service to meet customer needs. Quality is seen as one of the most important ways to add value to products and services, thereby distinguishing them from those of competitors. Two traditional strategies for ensuring quality are quality control and quality assurance.

Quality Control **Quality control** is a strategy for minimizing errors by managing each stage of production. Quality control techniques were developed in the 1930s at Bell Telephone Labs by Walter Shewhart. He used statistical sampling to locate errors by testing some (rather than all) of the items in a particular production run.

Quality Assurance Developed in the 1960s, **quality assurance** focuses on workers' performance, urging them to strive for "zero defects." Quality assurance has been less successful because often employees have no control over the design of the work process.

Now that you have an understanding of what quality is and two strategies to achieve it, let's take a quick glimpse at management history to see where basic assumptions about quality came from that formed the foundation for modern approaches to total quality management.

Deming Management: The Contributions of W. Edwards Deming to Improved Quality

In the early 20th century, Frederick Taylor's scientific management philosophy, designed to maximize worker productivity, had been widely instituted. But by the 1950s, as discussed in Chapter 2, scientific management led organizations to be rigid and unresponsive to both employees and customers. W. Edwards Deming's challenge, known as **Deming management**, proposed ideas for making organizations more responsive, more democratic, and less wasteful. These included the following principles:

1. Quality Should Be Aimed at the Consumer's Needs "The consumer is the most important part of the production line," Deming wrote.[74] Thus, individual workers' efforts in providing a product or service should be focused on meeting customers' needs and expectations.

2. Companies Should Aim to Improve the System, Not Blame Workers Deming suggested that U.S. managers were more concerned with blaming problems on individual workers rather than on the organization's structure, culture, technology, work rules, and

FIGURE 16.6

The PDCA cycle: Plan-Do-Check-Act

The four steps continuously follow each other, resulting in continuous improvement.

Source: From Deming, W. Edwards. Out of the Crisis. Plan Do Study Act Cycle. Massachusetts Institute of Technology, 2000, p. 88.

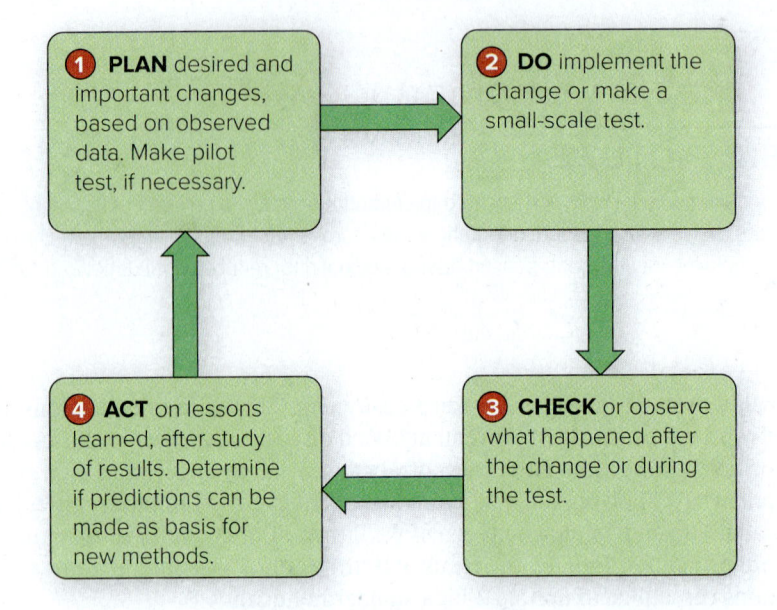

1. **PLAN** desired and important changes, based on observed data. Make pilot test, if necessary.
2. **DO** implement the change or make a small-scale test.
3. **CHECK** or observe what happened after the change or during the test.
4. **ACT** on lessons learned, after study of results. Determine if predictions can be made as basis for new methods.

management—that is, "the system." By treating employees well, listening to their views and suggestions, Deming felt managers could improve products and services.

3. Improved Quality Leads to Increased Market Share, Business Opportunities, and Employment
When companies improve the quality of goods and services, they produce less waste, experience fewer delays, and are more efficient. Lower prices and superior quality lead to greater market share, which in turn leads to improved business opportunities and consequently increased employment.

4. Quality Can Be Improved on the Basis of Hard Data Using the PDCA Cycle
Deming suggested that quality could be improved by analyzing and acting on hard data. The process for doing this came to be known as the **PDCA cycle**, a Plan-Do-Check-Act cycle using observed data to continuously improve operations (see Figure 16.6). Like the third step in the planning/control cycle in Figure 5.5 and Figure 6.8 as well as the steps in the control process in Figure 16.2, step 3 ("Check") is a *feedback* step, in which performance is compared to goals. Feedback is instrumental to control.

PRACTICAL ACTION | **Using the PDCA Model to Control Your Career Management Action Plan**

The purpose of this activity is to guide you through the process of developing action plans to support the achievement of your short-term career goals. We developed a form (see Table 16.4) to structure your thinking. This form is instrumental for the application of steps 3 (check) and 4 (act) of the PDCA model (Figure 16.6).

CHECK
The check step of the PDCA model involves measuring performance and comparing performance to standards (steps 2 and 3 of the control process in Figure 16.2). You'll need to define how you're going to achieve each goal and determine how frequently you can assess your progress. Ask yourself two questions:

1. What behaviors am I going to exhibit to help me accomplish each goal?
2. How often can I track the behaviors?

Action plans document the answers to these two questions. An action plan, as discussed in Chapter 5, specifies tactics to accomplish your SMART goals. Goals are outcomes. Tactics are the behaviors necessary to achieve specific outcomes. Action plans thus represent a "plan of action" to achieve SMART goals.

We constructed an action plan template (Table 16.4) similar to a plan one of your authors, Angelo Kinicki, uses in his consulting practice to help business leaders achieve their goals. Table 16.4 builds on the SMART goals you developed and included in your notebook while completing the previous Practical Action box in Section 16.3. For each SMART goal, define what behaviors are needed to accomplish the goal, how frequently you can measure the behaviors (daily, weekly, biweekly, etc.), and when the behaviors will start and end. Consider the following high-level example:

SMART goal: To accumulate no more than $X of debt upon graduation.

Action plan: Set up a budget management app (like Credit Karma or Simplifi by Quicken) to create a monthly budget and record my expenses. Check the expenses in each budget category weekly to ensure I stay within the budget. Begin this plan next week and continue until I graduate.

While there are no set number of behavioral tactics to include in an action plan, you should develop as many as you think are necessary. It's all about personal preferences. For example, two of your authors (Drs. K and H) like to develop longer lists of behavioral tactics when developing action plans. Your third author (Dr. S) likes to use a shorter list.

A word to the wise. Track and record progress toward your goals frequently because it gives you information you need to take corrective action before it's too late. For example, if your goal is to earn an A in a class, don't wait until the week before your final exam to assess what corrective actions are needed to meet your goal. At the beginning of the semester, define your daily/weekly study tactics (flash cards, note-taking, Connect assignments, study groups, etc.). Then check to make sure you follow through on each behavior. Assess your progress toward your goal by tracking your behaviors and evaluating your performance on quizzes, tests, and assignments throughout the semester. All of these performance indicators will tell you what corrective actions (step 4 of the PDCA model) you need to take to achieve your desired grade.

ACT

As you learned in the final step of the control process (Figure 16.2) and the PDCA model (Figure 16.6), you have three options as you evaluate progress toward each SMART goal:

- **Meet performance expectations:** Make no changes.
- **Exceed performance expectations:** Celebrate and reward positive performance.
- **Fall short of performance expectations:** Take action to correct poor performance by (1) adjusting your goal (if it's no longer realistic), (2) modifying the tactics to achieve the goal, or (3) increasing your level of effort.

Check your progress for each SMART goal in your action plan on a regular basis. Celebrate your successes and make revisions as needed. You'll be glad you did when you receive your diploma and land your job after graduation!

TABLE 16.4 Action Plan to Measure Progress toward Your Goals

BALANCED SCORECARD PERSPECTIVE	GOAL ASSOCIATED WITH EACH BALANCED SCORECARD PERSPECTIVE	SMART GOALS	BEHAVIORS TO ACCOMPLISH THE GOAL	HOW OFTEN CAN I TRACK THE BEHAVIORS?	START DATE	FINISH DATE	STATUS/DATE BEHAVIOR WAS CHECKED
Financial Perspective	Have a manageable financial situation 3 months after graduation.	SMART Goal X					
Customer Perspective	Make a strong positive impression on potential employers.	SMART Goal X					
Internal Business Perspective	Improve my GPA, expand my professional network, and add relevant experience to my resume.	SMART Goal X					
Innovation & Learning Perspective	Improve my ability to deliver continued value and ideas for improvement.	SMART Goal X					

Core TQM Principles: Deliver Customer Value and Strive for Continuous Improvement

Total quality management (TQM) is a comprehensive approach—led by top management and supported throughout the organization—dedicated to continuous quality improvement, training, and customer satisfaction. TQM has four components:

1. Prioritize continuous improvement.
2. Involve every employee.
3. Listen to and learn from customers and employees.
4. Use accurate standards to identify and eliminate problems.

These components can be summarized as **two core principles of TQM**—namely, (1) people orientation—everyone involved with the organization should focus on delivering value to customers—and (2) improvement orientation—everyone should work on continuously improving the work processes.[75] Let's look at these two principles further.

1. People Orientation—Focus Everyone on Delivering Customer Value Organizations adopting TQM value people as their most important resource—both those who create a product or service and those who receive it. These organizations thus empower employees and customers to work together to identify opportunities for quality improvements. TQM's assumption that employees and customers are central to an organization's success is consistent with the employee and customer perspectives in the balanced scorecard.

People Orientation Example—Hyundai Motor Company: Hyundai took the luxury car market by storm when it introduced its Genesis brand in 2017. The Genesis brand quickly became a market leader through the company's commitment to creating high-quality, innovative vehicles.[76] Hyundai's chair Chung Mong Koo increased the size of Hyundai's quality control department from 100 to 1,000 people. Quality control engineers were also expected to solicit feedback from employees on how to improve quality.[77] Quality issues could and should be questioned by everyone in the organization. Quality and collaboration became core values in the company's culture.[78] This people-oriented approach to quality improvement has resulted in Genesis racking up prestigious industry awards, including *MotorTrend*'s "2023 Car of the Year" and Cars.com's "Best Luxury Car of 2023."[79]

2. Improvement Orientation—Focus Everyone on Continuously Improving Work Processes Although flashy schemes, grand designs, and crash programs have their place, the lesson from the quality movement from overseas is that the path to success is through continuous, small improvements. **Continuous improvement** is defined as ongoing, small, incremental improvements in all parts of an organization—all products, services, functional areas, and work processes. This improvement orientation focuses on increasing operational performance. Operational excellence is driven by four beliefs:[80]

- It's less expensive to do it right the first time.
- It's better to make small improvements all the time.
- Accurate data must be gathered to eliminate small variations and evaluate progress.
- There must be strong commitment from top management.

Improvement Orientation Example—Kia Motors: Korean car maker Kia has worked hard to establish a reputation for quality, recently earning J.D. Power's

A modern Kia car factory production line in Slovakia.
Shutterstock

2022 Most Dependable Vehicle. David Amodeo, J.D. Power's director of global automotive, noted two things affect a vehicle's dependability: its design and "an unwavering commitment to rapid and continuous improvement." Amodeo observed Kia's "relentless" pursuit of quality as the reason it went from worst to first in dependability.[81]

Kaizen is a Japanese philosophy of small continuous improvement that seeks to involve everyone at every level of the organization in the process of identifying opportunities and implementing and testing solutions.[82] It offers advantages for large and small companies alike, whether manufacturers or service firms.

Applying TQM to Services

Manufacturing industries provide tangible products (think jars of baby food); service industries provide intangible products (think child care services). Manufactured products can be stored (such as dental floss in a warehouse); services generally need to be consumed immediately (such as dental hygiene services). Services tend to require a good deal of people effort (although some services can be provided by machines, such as vending machines and ATMs). Finally, services are generally provided at locations and times convenient for customers; that is, customers are much more involved in the delivery of services than they are in the delivery of manufactured products.

One clear prerequisite for providing excellent service is effective training. Publix is a good example.

Service Excellence Example—Publix: Supermarket industry leader Publix has an education and training development department that provides three types of training: new employee orientation, operational training to teach employees new processes, products, and services, and leadership development training to teach leaders how to manage their teams and improve their own leadership effectiveness. The training formats include classroom, computer-based and on-the-job training.[83]

The Example box describes how Trader Joe's strives for service excellence.

EXAMPLE

Service Excellence at Trader Joe's

A customer experience study conducted in 2021 found that 80% of consumers said they switched companies due to a bad service experience. The same study estimates poor customer service could cost U.S. companies $1.9 trillion in consumer spending annually.[84] So how can companies keep a loyal customer following? Consider the practices used by Trader Joe's, a company known for providing great customer service.

Trader Joe's operates more than 560 neighborhood grocery stores across 43 states nationwide and made a name for itself selling hipster-yuppie snacks like wild salmon jerky and $2 wines.[85] The chain was ranked first in the supermarket category of the 2023 American Customer Satisfaction Index (ACSI) Retail Report and tied Amazon for second among all retailers (only trailing online pet care provider Chewy).[86] Trader Joe's stays competitive by quickly reacting to its customers' needs and empowering employees to gain first-hand knowledge about all of its products by trying new products for themselves.[87]

Managers are called captains (employees are the crew) and spend most of their days on the retail floor, wearing Hawaiian shirts and interacting with customers. Captains are always promoted from within. If a customer asks about a product, the captain or crew member instantly brings the product, opens it, and indulges in a taste test with the customer to see whether they like it. Trader Joe's also refunds the price of any product customers are not satisfied with, even if it has been opened.[88]

Allowing captains to spend their time on the retail floor also allows them to learn about customer needs and quickly react to them instead of asking customers to submit their feedback online or to an impersonal call center. For example, Trader Joe's stores have changed their products and hours to accommodate their customers' requests. This responsiveness along with the store's fun and relaxing atmosphere make customers feel valued and appreciated and deepens their loyalty to their local neighborhood grocer.[89]

A Trader Joe's cashier assisting a customer. Dorothy Alexander/Alamy Stock Photo

YOUR CALL

Do you think Trader Joe's approach to customer service can compete with online shopping? Why or why not?

Perhaps you're beginning to see how judging service quality is different from judging the quality of manufactured goods; it comes down to meeting the customer's *satisfaction*, which is a matter of *perception*. After all, some hotel guests, restaurant diners, and supermarket patrons, for example, are more easily satisfied than others.

Some people view college students as customers. Do you? For schools that care about the quality of the services they offer, it is important to assess student satisfaction with the college or university as a whole. If you are curious about your level of satisfaction with your college or university, then complete Self-Assessment 16.2 if your instructor has assigned it to you in Connect.

SELF-ASSESSMENT 16.2

Assessing Your Satisfaction with Your College or University Experience

This survey is designed to assess the extent to which you are satisfied with your college experience. Please complete Self-Assessment 16.2 if your instructor has assigned it in Connect.

Some TQM Tools, Techniques, and Standards

Several tools and techniques are available for improving quality. We described benchmarking in Chapter 6 and discussed its role in the balanced scorecard's internal business perspective (Section 16.3). Here we describe *outsourcing, reduced cycle time, statistical process control, Six Sigma, Lean Six Sigma, Lean Six Sigma 4.0,* and *quality standards ISO 9000* and *ISO 14000.*

Outsourcing: Let Outsiders Handle It

Outsourcing (discussed in detail in Chapter 4) is the subcontracting of services and operations to an outside vendor. Usually, this is done to reduce costs or increase productivity.[90] For example, outsourcing short-term and project work to freelance or contract workers in the so-called gig economy saves companies many employee-related expenses.

Outsourcing also is being done by many state and local governments, which, under the banner known as privatization, have subcontracted traditional government services such as fire protection, correctional services, and medical services. Overall, 66% of businesses in the United States outsource work, and around 300,000 U.S. jobs get outsourced each year.[91]

Two out of three companies in the United States choose to outsource at least one department, like IT or customer support, to reduce costs and increase productivity. Maria Vonotna/Shutterstock

Reduced Cycle Time: Increasing the Speed of Work Processes

Another TQM technique is the emphasis on increasing the speed with which an organization's operations and processes can be performed. This is known as **reduced cycle time**, or reduction in steps in a work process, such as fewer authorization steps required to grant a contract to a supplier. The point is to improve the organization's performance by eliminating wasteful motions, barriers between departments, unnecessary procedural steps, and the like.[92]

> **Reduced Cycle Time Example—Microsoft:** Microsoft's finance group was able to consolidate and simplify various reports, tools, and content into an automated, role-based personalized report. The group also was able to use bots in finance operations, credit and collections, management reporting, and taxes. Microsoft reduced the time spent compiling and validating data by 20% as a result of these actions, saving over 150,000 hours of work each quarter.[93]

Statistical Process Control: Taking Periodic Random Samples

All kinds of products require periodic inspection during their manufacture: hamburger meat, breakfast cereal, flashlight batteries, wine, and so on. The tool often used for this is **statistical process control**, a statistical technique that uses periodic random samples from production runs to see if quality is being maintained within a standard range of acceptability (recall the control chart in Figure 16.3). If quality is not acceptable, production is stopped to allow corrective measures.[94]

Statistical process control helps managers track product and service consistency. McDonald's uses statistical process control to make sure that the quality of its burgers is consistent, no matter where in the world they are served. Companies such as Intel and Motorola use statistical process control to ensure their products' reliability and quality consistently meet their standards. Hospitals also use statistical process control to monitor patient care by evaluating patients' length of stay, errors, or infection rates.[95]

Six Sigma and Lean Six Sigma: Data-Driven Ways to Eliminate Defects

Sigma is the Greek letter statisticians use to define a standard deviation. In the quality improvement process known as Six Sigma, the higher the sigma, the fewer the deviations from the norm—that is, the fewer the defects. Developed by Motorola in 1985, Six Sigma has since been embraced by Bank of America, Caterpillar Inc., 3M, Amazon, and other organizations.[96] There are three variations, *Six Sigma, Lean Six Sigma,* and *Lean Six Sigma 4.0.*

- **Six Sigma.** Six Sigma is a rigorous statistical analysis process that reduces defects in manufacturing and service-related processes. By testing thousands of variables and eliminating guesswork, a company using the technique attempts to improve quality and reduce waste to the point where errors nearly vanish. In everything from product design to manufacturing to billing, the attainment of Six Sigma means there are no more than 3.4 defects per million products or procedures.[97]

    Six Sigma also may be thought of as a philosophy to reduce variation in your company's business and make customer-focused, data-driven decisions. The method preaches the use of Define, Measure, Analyze, Improve, and Control (DMAIC). This process resembles the control process illustrated in Figure 16.2. Team leaders may be awarded a Six Sigma "black belt" for applying DMAIC.

- **Lean Six Sigma.** More recently, companies are using an approach known as Lean Six Sigma. It is a quality control approach that focuses on problem solving and performance improvement—speed with excellence—of a well-defined project.[98] Retail and commercial banks are good examples of organizations in the financial services industry that have harnessed the power of Lean Six Sigma.

    Lean Six Sigma Example—Banks: Retail bank Capital One applied Lean Six Sigma principles during its restructuring. It reaped benefits such as a reduced rate of manual entry errors, increased customer satisfaction, and quality-focused company culture. Consulting firm Bain & Company guided a commercial bank to incorporate Lean Six Sigma into its operations "to increase the speed, accuracy, and efficiency of credit processes and decision making." Its client recorded 30% less time to approve credit applications and 25% fewer applications that needed to be reworked.[99]

Six Sigma and Lean Six Sigma may not be perfect because they cannot eliminate human error or control events outside a company. Still, they let managers approach problems with the assumption that there's a more sophisticated, data-oriented, and methodical way to approach problem solving.

Lean Six Sigma 4.0: Using Technology To Drive Real-Time Quality and Agility

Lean Six Sigma 4.0 is a new approach that combines the quality control and efficiency of Lean Six Sigma with the technological connectivity of Industry 4.0 (a reference to the fourth industrial revolution). Industry 4.0 is a management perspective that uses digital transformation technologies (cloud computing, artificial intelligence [AI], robotics, automation, and the Internet of Things [IoT]) to develop agile processes that meet diverse customers' unique needs. Lean Six Sigma 4.0 uses these cutting edge technologies to increase quality and efficiency while also anticipating and rapidly adapting to changes in customers' demand for its products and services.[100]

Companies like Tesla, Adidas, Intel, Bosch, and Microsoft are focusing on "smart manufacturing," which can reduce product defects, shorten unplanned downtimes, and improve manufacturing transition times.[101] Siemen's smart facility in Amberg, Germany, is a good example of a company using Lean Six Sigma 4.0 to achieve new levels of quality and efficiency.

Lean Six Sigma 4.0 Example—Siemens: Siemens Electronic Works Amberg facility has "350 production changeovers per day, a portfolio containing roughly 1,200 different products, and 17 million ... components produced per year." Any changes to its legacy order management system required downtime that could impact the facility's production goals. Its new system uses AI-generated data insights to automate routine tasks, deploy applications for predictive maintenance (reducing downtime), and analyze data in real time during the production process to predict a component's probability of defectiveness so it can be routed for further quality testing. The new system also protects the facility's data against cybersecurity threats by downloading security patches remotely at convenient times to avoid disruptions to the facility's productivity.[102]

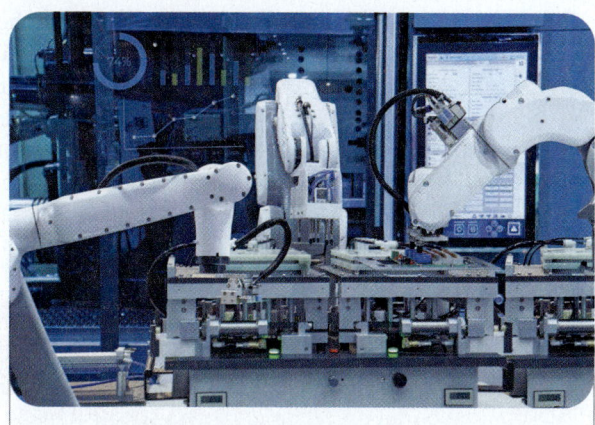

Siemens uses AI with its automated robots, similar to the ones depicted here, to predict the probability of errors in its circuit boards during the production process. Suwin/Shutterstock

ISO 9000 and ISO 14000: Meeting Standards of Independent Auditors

If you're a sales representative for DuPont, a U.S. chemical company, how will your overseas clients know your products have the quality they are expecting? If you're a purchasing agent for an Ohio-based tire company, how can you tell whether the synthetic rubber you're buying overseas is adequate?

At one time, buyers and sellers simply had to rely on a supplier's past reputation or personal assurances. In 1987, the International Organization for Standardization (ISO), based in Geneva, Switzerland, created a set of quality-focused procedures and standards. Let's focus on two: ISO 9000 and ISO 14000.

- **ISO 9000.** The **ISO 9000 series** consists of quality control procedures companies must install—from purchasing to manufacturing to inventory to shipping—that can be audited by independent quality control experts, or "registrars." The goal is to reduce flaws in manufacturing and improve productivity by adopting seven "big picture" quality management principles:

    1. Customer focus.
    2. Leadership.
    3. Engagement of people.
    4. Process approach.
    5. Improvement.
    6. Evidence-based decision making.
    7. Relationship management.[103]

    Companies must document their ISO 9000 procedures and train their employees to use them. The ISO 9000 series of standards was expanded to include ISO 9001:2015. "ISO 9001 is the only standard within the ISO 9000 family that an organization can become certified against, because it is the standard that defines the requirements of having a Quality Management System."[104] Member organizations in more than 165 countries contribute to the development of ISO standards.[105]

- **ISO 14000.** The **ISO 14000 series** extends the concept, identifying standards for environmental performance. ISO 14000 dictates standards for documenting a company's management of pollution, efficient use of raw materials, and reduction of the firm's impact on the environment. An organization can earn ISO 14001:2015 certification, which means it has an environmental management system that meets stringent ISO standards.[106]

Takeaways from TQM Research

TQM principles have been used by thousands of organizations through the years. Although companies do not always use the tools, techniques, and processes as suggested by experts, a team of researchers concluded that the vast majority of TQM adopters follow its general principles, which in turn fosters improved operational and financial performance.[107] Researchers also identified four key inhibitors to successfully implementing TQM: (1) the failure to provide evidence supporting previous improvement activities, (2) the lack of a champion who is responsible for leading the implementation, (3) the inability to measure or track results of the program, and (4) the failure to develop a culture of quality or continuous learning.[108] Managers need to overcome these roadblocks for TQM to deliver its intended benefits. Take Self-Assessment 16.3 to evaluate the degree to which your current or past employer is committed to total quality management if your instructor has assigned it to you in Connect. •

SELF-ASSESSMENT 16.3

To What Extent Is Your Organization Committed to Total Quality Management?

This survey is designed to gauge the extent to which the organization you have in mind is committed to total quality management (TQM). Please complete Self-Assessment 16.3 if your instructor has assigned it in Connect.

16.5 Contemporary Control Issues

THE BIG PICTURE

This section describes two contemporary control issues: artificial intelligence and employee tracking and monitoring.

LO 16-5
Discuss contemporary control issues.

At this juncture in your learning experience regarding principles of management, you know that every function of management has been influenced by technology. As such, you shouldn't be surprised to find out that the control function is similarly impacted.

In this section we discuss two important technological advancements that have made an impact on how managers control organizations. We'll start with a focus on the rise of artificial intelligence (AI) as part of the control function by analyzing two areas in which AI is having its greatest impact. Then, we'll turn our attention to how technology is assisting organizations to track and monitor their workforce.

Using Artificial Intelligence to Control

In Chapter 7 we discussed the many ways in which AI can benefit organizations. One of these ways is enhancing control functions. With this in mind, let's go back to our discussion of Deloitte's survey of how organizations use AI in Chapter 7. The survey of 2,620 U.S. companies showed that 37% of firms use AI for labor cost reduction; 33% use it for product enhancement; and 33% use it to make internal processes more efficient.[109] (See again Figure 7.6.) You'll recall from our discussion of the balanced scorecard in Section 16.3 that there is a link between these findings and the scorecard's internal business perspective. The survey shows that companies are engaging in two AI-powered activities related to internal business control: *increasing productivity* and *enhancing supply chain management*. Let's examine each more closely.

Increasing Productivity We previously noted that productivity is an important metric of an organization's internal business processes. Today, AI practices are enhancing productivity metrics in a wide variety of industries. Take, for instance, a recent PwC survey of 1,000 executives finding that 44% reported AI solutions implemented in their businesses have already increased productivity.[110] PwC believes AI has even more in store for us, projecting that by 2030 it will contribute up to $6.6 trillion to the global economy in increased productivity.[111]

Experts believe AI can improve productivity in three ways. Let's look at each using the railway industry as an example.[112]

- **Predictive maintenance:** AI automates decision-making processes related to maintenance, reducing accidents, unplanned downtime, and wasted resources on emergency maintenance due to sudden breakdowns.

    Predictive Maintenance Example: Italy's national railway operator Trenitalia uses thousands of sensors on its trains to generate real-time data. AI uses this data to predict when train components are likely to fail and schedule all required preventive maintenance interventions at exactly the right time, ensuring optimal asset utilization and minimal unplanned downtime.

- **Operational safety:** AI combines real-time data from equipment sensors with real-time data on external conditions to reduce or avoid potential accidents.

    Operational Safety Example: Railway infrastructure is the second leading cause of accidents (behind human error) in the rail industry. Train derailments can be caused by cracks and breaks in rails. Sensors and AI-powered cameras gather information about rail conditions that may not be perceptible to human inspection. They also gather information about environmental conditions such as temperature and daylight that affect a train's safety. AI combines this information to alert operators to optimal routes and safe train speeds.[113]

- **Capacity utilization:** AI analyzes data on customer demand, production schedules, and available resources to utilize a company's available production or service capacity. It also pushes real-time notifications to customers about product or service delays.

    Capacity Utilization Example: London North Eastern Railway uses AI-powered technology using personal devices to track and map trains across the United Kingdom. This data provides decision makers information about how it can use out-of-service trains to meet customers' demand when there is sufficient railway capacity. AI also communicates real-time updates to customers smartphones about travel disruptions or changes in departure platforms at a train station.[114]

Enhancing Supply Chain Management The **supply chain** is the sequence of suppliers that contribute to creating and delivering a product, from raw materials to production to final buyers. Supply chains are a major cost center for most companies. Companies are therefore paying closer attention to the sourcing, shipping, and warehousing of their products and the ingredients and component parts they require. AI has the ability to significantly increase efficiency throughout the supply chain. McKinsey estimates that firms could save 15% a year, reduce inventory levels by 35%, and increase service levels by 65% using AI in supply chain and manufacturing.[115] Lineage Logistics is a good example of how AI can optimize the "middle mile" of the supply chain.[116]

Thawing the supply chain. Frozen food stored at a Lineage Logistics facility in Heywood, United Kingdom. Molly Darlington/Newscom

Supply Chain Example—Lineage Logistics: Lineage Logistics transports and cold stores 20 to 30 billion pounds of food for grocery stores and restaurants. The company's clientele includes Walmart, Tyson, and McDonald's. Lineage developed an AI algorithm to optimize its pallet transportation practices. The algorithm forecasts when orders arrive and leave its warehouse, allowing employees to put the right pallets in the right position. This AI-powered approach saves money, reduces product spoilage, and improves sustainability for Lineage Logistics and its customers.

Employee Tracking and Monitoring

A battle has been brewing between employees and employers as managers try to lure employees back to the office after the COVID-19 pandemic forced most work to be remote. While some companies have leaned into remote work, like Adobe, Spotify, and Airbnb, others including J.P. Morgan, Goldman Sach's, and Tesla insist employees return to the office or look for employment elsewhere.[117] Many others like Cisco, Apple, and Deloitte are navigating a compromise in the form of hybrid work where employees work from the office a couple days a week.

Flexible work arrangements are shining a brighter spotlight on the potential value of tracking and monitoring employees as a form of managerial control. This technological tool includes employee monitoring software, video surveillance, GPS location tracking, and biometrics (fingerprint scanning, facial recognition, etc.).[118] These methods are not new. For example, since 2017 U.S. companies have been required by law to monitor their long-haul drivers with electronic logging devices (ELDs). These ELDs evaluate a truck driver's location and speed to track how they space sleeping and driving.[119]

Employee tracking and monitoring has become widespread in virtually every industry due to the rapid growth of remote and hybrid work. Eighty percent of the largest private U.S. employers use employee monitoring software to track employees' productivity, according to *The New York Times*.[120] Employers report monitoring employees' e-mails, text messages, transcribed phone calls, real-time screen shots, and computer keystrokes.[121] Three common reasons employers track employees' behavior are to:[122]

1. Improve employee productivity.
2. Check the appropriate use of company resources.
3. Deter theft of the company's internal resources or intellectual property.

The growing use of technology to track employees suggests that employers are using a Theory X approach to management (see Chapter 2). This perspective views workers as irresponsible, resistant to change, and lacking ambition. Because this management approach has been associated with employee dissatisfaction, management experts and researchers have recommended the more optimistic and positive view of workers proposed in a Theory Y perspective. So where does this leave us?

Unfortunately, a survey of 2,000 remote or hybrid employees in the United States and United Kingdom by ExpressVPN reinforces the use of Theory X methods. Respondents reported spending on average "13 hours of their 40-hour work week on professional tasks, using large chunks of the rest of the time visiting non-work-related websites." Table 16.5 lists the top 10 non-work activities employees reported doing during work hours along with the percentage of respondents who admitted to each one.[123]

TABLE 16.5 Top 10 Non-Work Activities Hybrid and Remote Workers Reported Doing during Work Hours

1. Checked personal emails (66%)	6. Searched for jobs (49%)
2. Read the news (64%)	7. Streamed movies (44%)
3. Shopped online (59%)	8. Played games (42%)
4. Booked hotel/restaurant reservations (57%)	9. Gambled (39%)
5. Browsed social media (54%)	10. Bought cryptocurrency (37%)

Source: "Survey: Remote Workers Are Working 1/3 of the Time." ExpressVPN. March 20, 2023. https://www.expressvpn.com/blog/how-much-do-remote-workers-work/.

TABLE 16.6   Advantages and Disadvantages of Employee Tracking and Monitoring

ADVANTAGES	DISADVANTAGES
Managers claimed employee tracking and monitoring...	**Employees claimed employee tracking and monitoring...**
1. Reduced their uncertainty about employees' engagement.	1. Increased their stress, anxiety, and burnout. A survey indicated 59% of employees reported feeling stressed or anxious about their employer's surveillance.[a]
2. Reduced employees' distraction associated with social media and video streaming services.	2. Introduced distractions because they felt micromanaged and worried about the monitoring system generating a productivity score that would negatively impact their performance review.
3. Improved employees' outcomes (e.g., safety and productivity).	3. Measured the wrong things. Software tracked busyness, or "vanity metrics" (keystrokes, time logged in, mouse movement, time away from desk), more than the substantive parts of business (reading, collaborating, critical thinking, and problem solving).
4. Increased employees' accountability.	4. Decreased the degree to which they took responsibility for their work because they felt the system was unfair and took away their autonomy.

[a] "ExpressVPN Survey Shows Widespread Surveillance on Remote Workers," ExpressVPN, May 20, 2021, https://www.expressvpn.com/blog/expressvpn-survey-surveillance-on-the-remote-workforce/.

Sources: Ravid, D.M., J.C. White, D.L. Tomczak, A.F. Miles, and T.S. Behrend. "A Meta-Analysis of the Effects of Electronic Performance Monitoring on Work Outcomes." Personnel Psychology 76 (2023): 5–40; Eyal, N. "Managers, Stop Distracting Your Employees." Harvard Business Review. January 12, 2023. https://hbr.org/2023/01/managers-stop-distracting-your-employees; Thiel, C.E., J. Bonner, J.T. Bush, D.T. Welsh, and N. Garud. "Stripped of Agency: The Paradoxical Effect of employee monitoring on deviance." Journal of Management 49 (2023): 709–740; Kantor, J., A. Sundaram, A. Aufrichtig, and R. Taylor. "The Rise of the Worker Productivity Score." The New York Times. August 15, 2022. https://www.nytimes.com/interactive/2022/08/14/business/worker-productivity-tracking.html?te=1&nl=the-morning&emc=edit_nn_20220815; Murty, R.N. and S. Karanth, "Monitoring Individual Employees Isn't the Way to Boost Productivity." Harvard Business Review. October 27, 2022. https://hbr.org/2022/10/monitoring-individual-employees-isnt-the-way-to-boost-productivity; Thiel, C., J.M. Bonner, J. Bush, D. Welsh, and N. Garud. "Monitoring Employees Makes Them More Likely to Break Rules." Harvard Business Review. June 27, 2022. https://hbr.org/2022/06/monitoring-employees-makes-them-more-likely-to-break-rules; Kalischko, T. and R. Riedl. "Electronic Performance Monitoring in the Digital Workplace: conceptualization, Review of Effects and Moderators, and Future Research Opportunities." Frontiers in Psychology 12 (2021): 633031; Trivedi, S. and N. Patel. "Virtual Employee Monitoring: A Review on Tools, Opportunities, Challenges, and Decision Factors." Empirical Quests for Management Essences 1 (2021): 86–99; Ravid, D.M., D.L. Tomczak, J.C. White, and T.S. Behrend. "EPM 20/20: A Review, Framework, and Research Agenda for Electronic Performance Monitoring." Journal of Management 46 (2020): 100–126.

Advantages and Disadvantages of Employee Tracking and Monitoring   Even though employee tracking and monitoring practices are widespread, it remains a controversial practice. The advantages and disadvantages are summarized in Table 16.6.

Overall, research supports employees' claims about tracking and monitoring. A meta-analysis of 94 studies and 23,461 employees studying the effects of employee monitoring on employees' attitudes and behaviors reveals the following conclusions:[124]

1. Performance monitoring does not improve employee performance.
2. Monitoring increases employee stress.
3. Employees have more positive attitudes toward employee tracking and monitoring when organizations are more transparent and they use less invasive monitoring methods.

These results suggest employees feel like tracking and monitoring systems are an invasion of privacy and an intrusion on trust, a conclusion that reinforces the value of employing Theory Y methods to motivate employees (Chapter 2). We recommend that organizations use employee tracking and monitoring as a developmental device or a tool to protect employees' safety, such as in dangerous jobs, rather than a coercive control mechanism.

Recommendations to Effectively Deploy Employee Tracking and Monitoring

Experts recommend three actions to ensure tracking and monitoring programs work out in everyone's favor:

- **Start by looking inward.** Follow Deming's advice in Section 16.4: monitor employees' behavior to improve organizational systems, not to indict them in doing something wrong. *Harvard Business Review* authors Rohan Narayana Murty and Shreyas Karanth suggest "Data should be used as a mirror, not a microscope."[125]

- **Communicate clearly.** Managers should be clear about what behaviors they intend to monitor and what they intend to do with the data. Employees deserve to know if data generated by monitoring and tracking software will be factored into their performance review. If it is, companies should ensure that workforce monitoring software is visible and transparent. Any secrecy here will likely fuel employees' suspicion and increase perceptions that the monitoring system is unfair.[126]

- **Protect employees' privacy.** Monitoring programs should be designed to support and protect employees. For example, in a large call center where hundreds of employees are on the receiving end of thousands of calls, user activity monitoring can assist in making sure employees have the resources they need and are not feeling overwhelmed. If individual data is not necessary, protect employees' privacy by deidentifying and aggregating the data so you can share the results with teams and empower them to devise solutions to improve productivity.[127]

Technological advancements like AI and tracking and monitoring software can be tremendously valuable managerial control tools if they are implemented with TQM principles at heart: in a people-oriented and improvement-oriented way. If so, we believe they will inspire managers and employees to collaborate and continuously improve as they collectively meet customers' needs. ●

16.6 Career Corner: Managing Your Career Readiness

LO 16-6

Discuss how to apply the control process to the career readiness competency of career management and to the process of continuous self-improvement.

Effective managerial control requires the application of several career readiness competencies shown in Figure 16.7: critical thinking/problem solving, oral/written communication, teamwork/collaboration, leadership, career management, understanding the business, decision making, ownership/accepting responsibilities, self-motivation, proactive learning orientation, positive approach, personal adaptability, self-awareness, and openness to change. We're going to focus on the competency of career management, which represents proactively managing your career and seeking opportunities for professional development. The executives in this chapter's Executive Interview Series highlight the value of self-awareness and proactive learning to your career management. Both of these competencies are developed most effectively using the control process, an indispensable framework to guide your career management.

We've all heard stories of successful people who did not follow a structured or intentional path to their careers, but they are the exception, not the rule. Most successful people take a proactive and structured approach to managing their careers. In this section, we want to assist in your career development by discussing how the control process is a useful approach to career management. We'll then describe how you can use the control process to continuously improve after graduation, and we'll identify the career readiness competencies you'll need for each step in the process. We conclude by offering you a few tips for the road as you take on new challenges and soar to new heights.

McGraw Hill connect®
Visit your instructor's Connect course and access your eBook to view this video.

Executive Interview Series:
Career Management

The Control Process and Career Management

Continuous improvement is the secret sauce in the control process and career management. This makes the Plan-Do-Check-Act (PDCA) cycle in Figure 16.6 a valuable tool

FIGURE 16.7
Model of career readiness

Career Readiness Competencies

Knowledge
- Task-based/functional
- Computational thinking
- **Understanding the business**
- New media literacy

Other characteristics
- Resilience
- **Personal adaptability**
- **Self awareness**
- Service/others orientation
- **Openness to change**
- Generalized self-efficacy

Core
- **Critical thinking/problem solving**
- **Oral/written communication**
- **Teamwork/collaboration**
- Information technology application
- **Leadership**
- Professionalism/work ethic
- Diversity, equity, and inclusion
- **Career management** ⭐

Soft skills
- **Decision making**
- Social intelligence
- Networking
- Emotional intelligence

Attitudes
- **Ownership/accepting responsibilities**
- **Self-motivation**
- **Proactive learning orientation**
- Showing commitment
- **Positive approach**

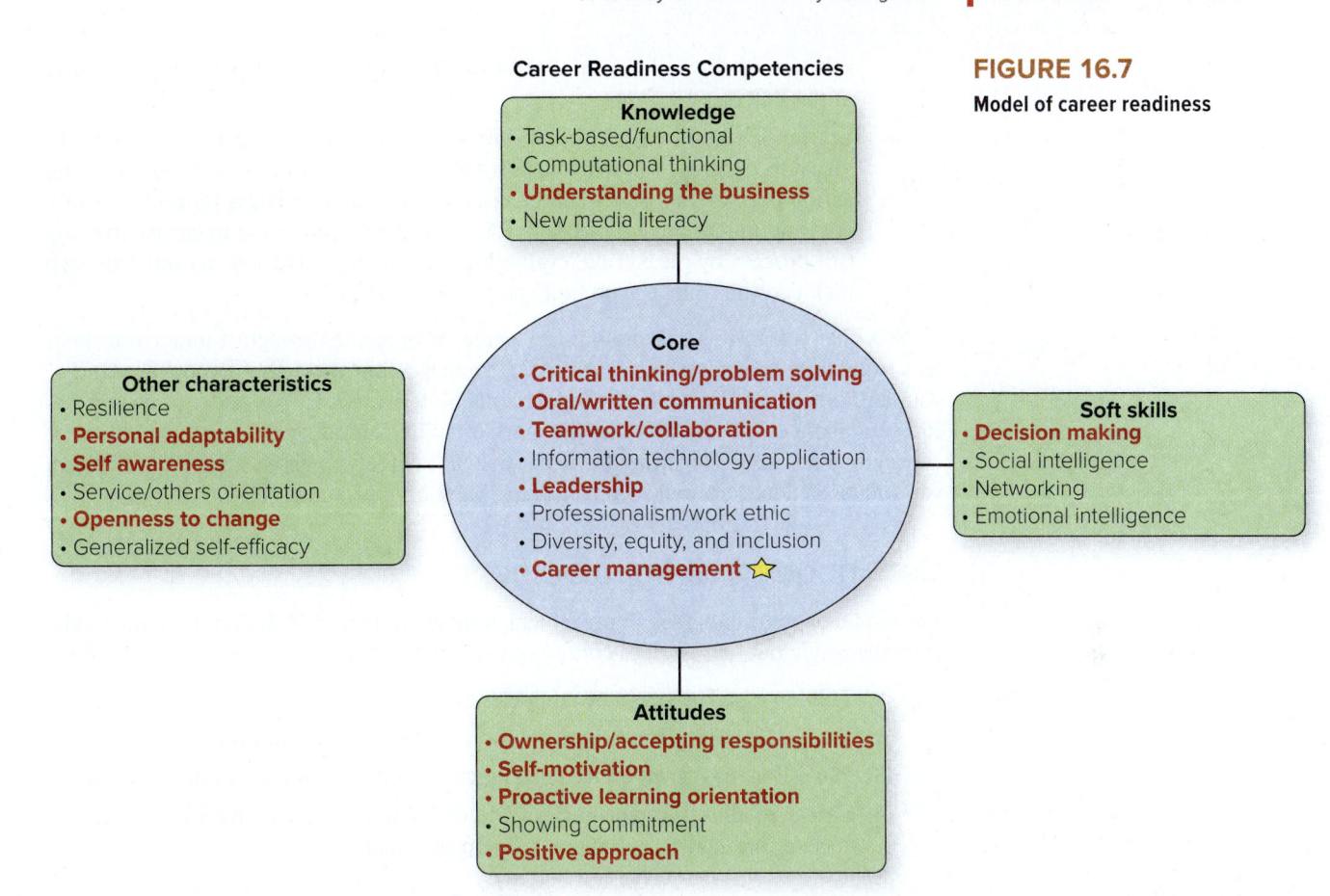

for managing a continuous improvement process for your career. Let's begin this discussion by noting that a job and a career are not the same thing.

- *Jobs* are something we do to earn money. They tend to be temporary, and they are in service of someone or something else. Some people are perfectly happy with a job.

- *Careers* are what we do in pursuit of our own needs and fulfillment rather than someone else's. Your career belongs to you and lasts a lifetime. You own it, manage it, nurture it, and create it to fit your values and needs.[128]

Jobs are earned. Careers are managed. This distinction underscores the importance of continuous improvement using the career readiness competencies of ownership/accepting responsibility, self-motivation, self-awareness, and openness to change to manage your career.

The career management process begins with a plan. We recommend finding a job that fits your values, needs, and financial objectives. Regardless of whether you are pursuing your dream job or not, you need to start with a broad goal in mind. So how do you apply the control process to your career?

The three Practical Action boxes in this chapter provided a roadmap.

- Section 16.1's Practical Action box instructed you to determine your long-term goals: graduate and get a job shortly after graduation. This step was the "plan" part of the PDCA cycle.

- Section 16.3's Practical Action box guided you through the process of developing short-term SMART goals you'll need to achieve to accomplish goals associated with each balanced scorecard perspective. Among them, we targeted four career readiness competencies for you to develop as part of the innovation and learning perspective: critical thinking/problem solving, teamwork/collaboration, self-motivation, and proactive learning orientation. This step was the "do" part of the PDCA cycle.

- Section 16.4's Practical Action box showed you how to define behaviors to measure progress toward your SMART goals identified in Section 16.3. The action plan in Table 16.4 can be used to track your progress on each SMART goal and make adjustments as needed. It is designed for you to engage the control process by measuring, evaluating, and taking corrective action. This step included the "check" and "act" part of the PDCA cycle.

Now that you have some preliminary career management practice under your belt, let's expand what you've learned to career management throughout your life. One of your authors, Chad Hartnell, recalled Arizona State University's president saying in his PhD commencement address that the mark of a PhD is that you've mastered the art of continuous learning. Regardless of what formal degree you aspire to earn, we believe you will be well and do well if you learn the habit of continuous self-improvement.

Continuous Self-Improvement

The model of continuous self-improvement is shown in Figure 16.8. Following the model from the inside out, it describes continuous self-improvement's four concentric circles:

1. **Willingness:** The keystone competency.
2. **The PDCA cycle:** The engine behind continuous self-improvement.
3. **The self management cycle:** The tactics behind continuous self-improvement.
4. **Career readiness competencies:** The defining career readiness competencies needed to execute continuous self-improvement.

FIGURE 16.8
A model of continuous self-improvement

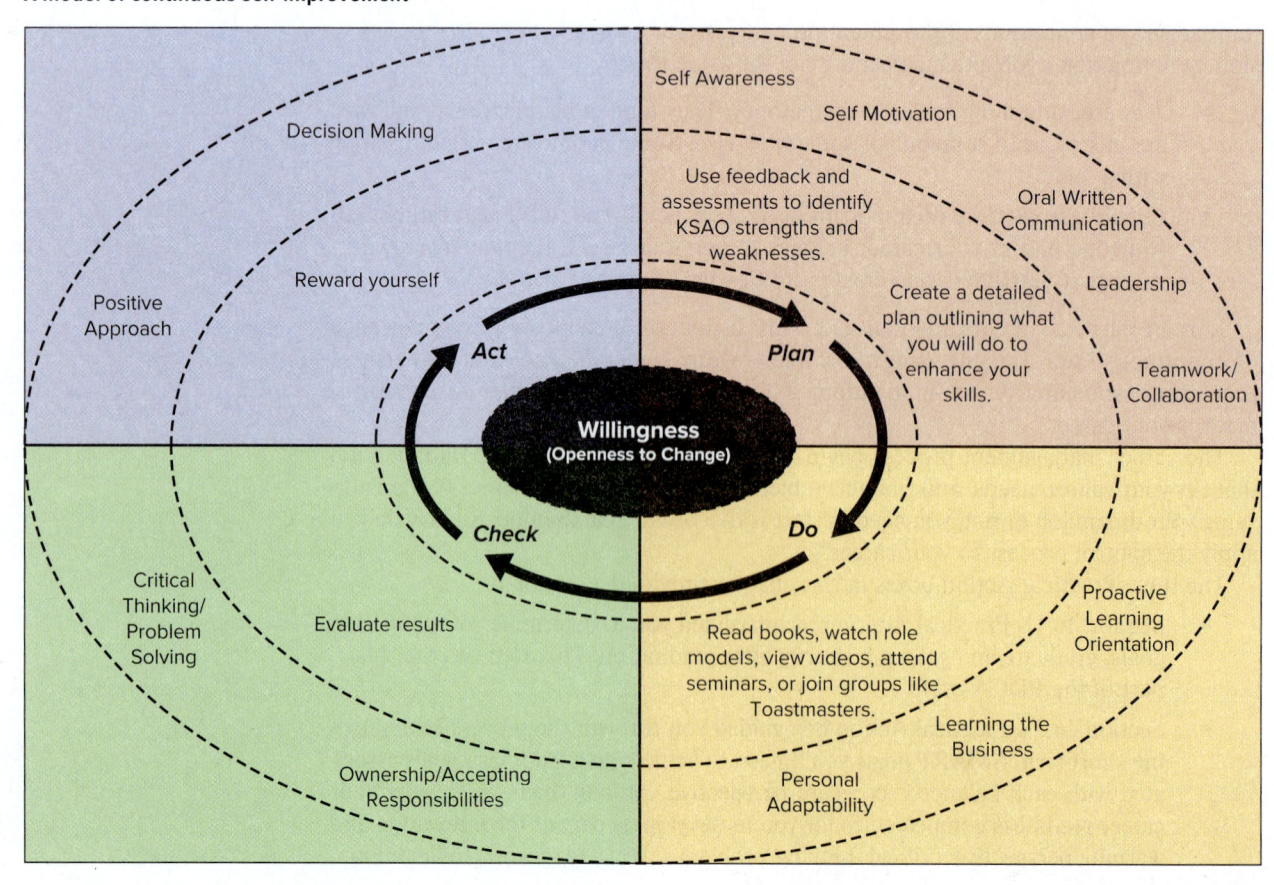

Willingness Continuous self-improvement begins with willingness, the innermost circle. Are you willing to *choose* to change? Are you willing to accept constructive feedback and avoid the self-serving bias discussed in Chapter 11? An affirmative answer to these questions is under your control. Either you are willing to do this or you're not. Developing the career readiness competency of openness to change can fuel your willingness to continuously improve. In other words, openness to change is a keystone competency. As Charles Duhigg, author of *The Power of Habit,* describes, a keystone competency is one that starts a chain reaction.[129] Improving openness to change will make you more inclined to develop the career readiness competencies that support continuous self-improvement in the outermost circle in Figure 16.8.

The PDCA Cycle The PDCA cycle from Figure 16.6 provides the framework for implementing continuous career development: It appears in the second circle of the continuous self-improvement model shown in Figure 16.8. Refer to the Practical Action boxes in this chapter for guidance in defining your goals, developing a plan, monitoring your progress, and celebrating success or making revisions as needed. The PDCA cycle is the engine behind continuous self-improvement.

The Self-Management Cycle and Career Readiness Competencies The third circle, the self-management cycle, identifies the specific tactics or actions needed to execute the PDCA process for continuous self-improvement. There are five steps:

1. **Plan: Use feedback and assessments to identify knowledge, skills, abilities, and other characteristics (KSAOs) based on strengths and weaknesses.** Take personality assessments, review your self-assessments throughout this course, and ask your instructor, teammates, and peers for feedback on your strengths and weaknesses. Use this knowledge to set goals for how to further improve your strengths and develop your weaknesses. The career readiness competencies of self-awareness and self-motivation will improve your proficiency in gathering information and learning from it.

2. **Plan: Create a detailed plan outlining what you will do to enhance your skills.** This plan should include more specific SMART goals to help you achieve the broader goals identified in step 1. Composing a detailed plan requires the career readiness competencies of oral/written communication, (self) leadership, and teamwork/collaboration. Self-leadership is a positive process of proactive self-evaluation and self-influence to achieve self-improvement.[130] Gathering input from others and aligning your continuous development goals with those of your future employer are effective strategies for career advancement.

3. **Do: Implement your plan by reading books, watching role models or finding a mentor, viewing videos, attending seminars, or joining groups like public-speaking group Toastmasters.** Keep track of all of these activities and note several on your resume. Employers like to see evidence of your career readiness competencies such as proactive learning orientation, learning the business, and personal adaptability because they show your commitment to continuous improvement.

4. **Check: Evaluate results.** Use a dashboard like the one developed for you in Figure 16.4 to monitor your progress on each of your SMART goals. Evaluating results demonstrates your ownership/accepting responsibilities and critical thinking/problem solving career readiness competencies. It also signals to employers your motivation to follow through with your commitments. Imagine how impressed a recruiter would be if you brought your dashboard to an interview. You would really stand out from other applicants!

5. **Act: Reward yourself.** If you're on track or ahead of schedule, celebrate your success. In our experience, life is more satisfying when you celebrate small successes

and significant achievements along the way. There's nothing more motivational than to look over your shoulder periodically and see how far you've come. After all, you're this much closer to graduation. Look how far you've come since your early days in high school. Graduating and earning a job are within reach. If you're behind schedule, don't worry and don't give up. Setbacks happen. Consult Figure 16.4 and develop a plan to adjust your tactics or modify your SMART goals to make them more realistic given your current situation.

Life Lessons for Your Career Management

We have come to the end of the book, our last chance to offer some suggestions to take with you that we hope will benefit you in the coming years. Following are some life lessons pulled from various sources that can make you a "keeper" in an organization and help you be successful.

Plan **Find your passion and follow it.** The 2023 Top Entrepreneur Brad Oleshansky left his job as an entertainment lawyer and then a healthcare digital marketing executive to pursue his childhood passion, cars. His passion grew from time with his dad building cars in their garage. Oleshansky turned his passion into The Motor Enclave, a $150 million, 200-acre facility in Tampa, Florida. Motor enthusiasts can indulge their passion by housing their vehicle in a private garage or testing their vehicle's capabilities on a performance track or off-road track. Following your passion can also be good for business. "One of the biggest challenges in businesses is competitors and pricing and everyone wanting a deal. Well, when you are talking about someone's hobby or passion, they're willing to spend whatever it takes to enjoy it at whatever level they want to enjoy it," says Oleshansky.[131] Find something that inspires you, that you love to do, and do it vigorously.

Develop self-awareness. To stay ahead of the pack, you need to develop self-awareness, have an active mind, and be willing to grow and change. Legendary designer Diane von Furstenberg recalls the lesson she learned from early mistakes that reduced her control over her business and diluted her brand: "Your worst moments are your best souvenirs."[132]

Ask others for feedback. Today we live and work in a team universe. Try getting feedback on your interpersonal skills from friends, colleagues, and team members, and develop a plan for improvement. Duke University instructor Deborah Grayson Riegel observed others may be reluctant to offer feedback because they aren't convinced you're open to feedback, are afraid of retaliation, or are concerned about hurting your feelings. Riegel suggests overcoming these barriers by creating a safe and welcoming environment for clear and candid feedback. One way to do this is "to share that self-improvement is a personal and professional commitment you've made to yourself—and ask for help meeting your commitment."[133]

Learn how to develop leadership skills. Every company should invest in developing its managers' leadership skills if it is to improve the quality of its future leaders. But you also can develop a plan to improve your own leadership skills. For instance, set goals to observe other effective leaders and take notes about what they do and how you can replicate it, take small risks by taking initiative when action is needed (sometimes called being a self-starter), and ask for more responsibility to demonstrate what you're capable of.[134] Another life lesson: If you set the bar high, even if you don't reach it, you end up in a pretty good place—that is, achieving a pretty high mark.

Do **Adopt a proactive approach to life-long learning.** Life in general is not going to become less complex. Just think about the implications of AI in our lives. Success requires us to continually grow and develop if we want to be active, positive contributors to our families, work environments, communities, and society at large. Keep challenging yourself and don't accept mediocrity.

Every situation is different, so be flexible. No principle or theory applies in all circumstances. Industries, cultures, supervisors, employees, and customers will vary. It's not a sign of weakness to be willing to change something that isn't working or to try something new.[135] In fact, adaptability displays a great deal of power. "As a leader, it's imperative to meet requests to adapt with grace. If you become resistant to change then you become resistant to finding solutions too. Closed-mindedness is not a sought-after quality; adaptability is," says Cicely Simpson, founder and CEO of Summit Public Affairs.[136]

Check **Keep your cool and take yourself lightly.** "Do not take life too seriously. You will never get out of it alive," joked American writer Elbert Hubbard.[137] When things don't go your way, don't let worry set in. The more unflappable you appear in difficult circumstances, the more you'll be admired by your bosses and co-workers. Having a sense of humor helps. The renowned British physicist and author Stephen Hawking spent his career looking for the answers to impenetrable questions like, "Where did the universe come from?" and "How will it end?" Yet he was famously witty and relished the opportunity to appear as himself on popular TV shows like *The Simpsons, Star Trek: The Next Generation,* and *The Big Bang Theory,* appearances that he said made him more famous than his complex theories about the universe.[138]

Act **Go with the flow and stay positive.** Life has its ebbs and flows. You'll have good times and bad. During this journey, don't focus too heavily on negative events and thoughts. Negative thoughts rob you of positive energy and your ability to perform at your best. In contrast, a positive approach toward life is more likely to help you flourish.[139]

We wish you the very best of luck in your future endeavors. Follow your dreams and enjoy the journey!

Angelo Kinicki   Denise Soignet   Chad Hartnell

Key Terms Used in This Chapter

balance sheet 590	feedforward control 586	pdca cycle 602
balanced scorecard 588	financial ratios 592	quality 601
best practices 594	financial statement 590	quality assurance 601
budget 589	fixed budget 590	quality control 601
concurrent control 586	income statement 590	reduced cycle time 607
continuous improvement 604	incremental budgeting 589	self-regulation 579
control charts 584	industry 4.0 608	six sigma 608
control process steps 582	iso 9000 series 609	statement of cash flows 591
control standard 583	iso 14000 series 609	statistical process control 607
controlling 580	kaizen 605	strategy map 599
customer retention 593	lean six sigma 608	supply chain 611
customer satisfaction 593	lean six sigma 4.0 608	total quality management (tqm) 604
Deming management 601	management by exception 586	two core principles of TQM 604
feedback control 587	outsourcing 607	variable budget 590

Key Points

16.1 Control: When Managers Monitor Performance

- Controlling is defined as monitoring performance, comparing it with goals, and taking corrective action as needed.
- There are six reasons that control is needed: (1) to adapt to change and uncertainty; (2) to discover irregularities and errors; (3) to reduce costs, increase productivity, or add value; (4) to detect opportunities and increase innovation; (5) to provide performance feedback; and (6) to decentralize decision making and facilitate teamwork.

16.2 The Control Process and Types of Control

- There are four control process steps. (1) The first step is to set standards. A control standard is the desired performance level for a given goal. (2) The second step is to measure performance, based on written reports, oral reports, and personal observation. (3) The third step is to compare measured performance against the standards established. (4) The fourth step is to take corrective action, if necessary, if there is negative performance.
- There are three types of control: feedforward, concurrent, and feedback.

16.3 What Should Managers Control?

- Kaplan and Norton's balanced scorecard provides top managers a fast but comprehensive view of the organization via four perspectives: (1) financial, (2) customer, (3) internal-business process, and (4) innovation and learning.

- The financial perspective includes budgets, financial statements, and financial ratios.
- The customer perspective includes customer satisfaction and retention.
- The internal-business perspective considers productivity, efficiency, quality, and safety.
- The innovation and learning perspective looks at employee attitudes, turnover, resource capabilities, and organizational culture.
- The strategy map, a visual representation of the four perspectives of the balanced scorecard, enables managers to communicate their goals so that everyone in the company can understand how their jobs are linked to the overall objectives of the organization.

16.4 Total Quality Management

- Quality refers to the total ability of a product or service to meet customer needs.
- Among the principles of Deming management are (1) quality should be aimed at the needs of the consumer; (2) companies should aim at improving the system, not blaming workers; (3) improved quality leads to increased market share, increased company prospects, and increased employment; and (4) quality can be improved on the basis of hard data, using the PDCA, or Plan-Do-Check-Act, cycle.
- Total quality management (TQM) is defined as a comprehensive approach—led by top management and supported throughout the organization—dedicated to continuous quality improvement (such as through Kaizen), training, and customer satisfaction. The two core principles of TQM are people orientation and improvement orientation.

- In the people orientation, everyone involved with the organization is asked to focus on delivering value to customers, focusing on quality. TQM requires training, teamwork, and cross-functional efforts.
- Several techniques are available for improving quality. (1) Outsourcing is the subcontracting of services and operations to an outside vendor. (2) Reduced cycle time consists of reducing the number of steps in a work process. (3) Statistical process control is a statistical technique that uses periodic random samples from production runs to see if quality is being maintained within a standard range of acceptability. (4) Six Sigma is a rigorous statistical analysis process that reduces defects in manufacturing and service-related processes. Lean Six Sigma and Lean Six Sigma 4.0 are newer approaches to quality improvement. (5) ISO 9000 consists of quality control procedures companies must install—from purchasing to manufacturing to inventory to shipping—that can be audited by independent quality control experts, or "registrars." ISO 14000 extends the concept to environmental performance.

16.5 Contemporary Control Issues

- Two contemporary control issues include artificial Intelligence (AI) and employee tracking and monitoring.
- AI can be used to increase productivity and enhance supply chain management.
- Employee tracking and monitoring has both advantages and disadvantages. Advantages include uncovering problems, reducing instances of employees wasting time, highlighting bottlenecks, and enforcing safety practices. Disadvantages include privacy concerns, employee retainment issues, and data vulnerability.

16.6 Career Corner: Managing Your Career Readiness

- Effective managerial control requires the application of fifteen career readiness competencies.
- Jobs are earned. Careers are managed.
- Continuous self-improvement depends upon (1) willingness, the keystone competency; (2) the PDCA cycle, the engine behind continuous self-improvement; (3) the self-management cycle, the tactics behind continuous self-improvement; and (4) career readiness competencies, the abilities needed to execute continuous self-improvement.

Boeing Continuing Case   McGraw Hill connect

Learn more about managerial control at Boeing and how it may have contributed to the 737 MAX disaster.

Assess your ability to apply concepts discussed in Chapter 16 to the case by going to Connect.

APPENDIX

The Project Planner's Toolkit
Flowcharts, Gantt Charts, and Break-Even Analysis

THE BIG PICTURE
Three tools used in project planning, which was covered in Chapter 5, are flowcharts, Gantt charts, and break-even analysis.

Project planning may begin (in the definition stage) as a back-of-the-envelope kind of process, but the client will expect a good deal more for the time and money being invested. Fortunately, there are various planning and monitoring tools that give the planning and execution of projects more precision. Three tools in the planner's toolkit are (1) flowcharts, (2) Gantt charts, and (3) break-even analysis.

Tool #1: Flowcharts—for Showing Event Sequences and Alternate Decision Scenarios

A *flowchart* is a useful graphical tool for representing the sequence of events required to complete a project and for laying out "what-if" scenarios. Flowcharts have been used for decades by computer programmers and systems analysts to make a graphical "road map," as it were, of the flow of tasks required. These professionals use their own special symbols (indicating "input/output," "magnetic disk," and the like), but there is no need for you to make the process complicated. Generally, only three symbols are needed: (1) an oval for the "beginning" and "end," (2) a box for a major activity, and (3) a diamond for a "yes or no" decision (see Figure A.1).

Computer programs such as iGrafx's ABC FlowCharter are available for constructing flowcharts. You can also use the drawing program in word processing programs such as Microsoft Word.

Benefits Flowcharts have two benefits:

- **Planning straightforward activities.** A flowchart can be quite helpful for planning ordinary activities—figuring out the best way to buy textbooks or a car, for example. It is also a straightforward way of indicating the sequence of events in, say, thinking out a new enterprise that you would then turn into a business plan.
- **Depicting alternate scenarios.** A flowchart is also useful for laying out "what-if" scenarios—as in if you answer "yes" to a decision question you should follow Plan A, if you answer "no" you should follow Plan B.

Limitations Flowcharts have two limitations:

- **No time indication.** They don't show the amounts of time required to accomplish the various activities in a project. In building a house, the foundation might take only a couple of days, but the rough carpentry might take weeks. These time differences can't be represented graphically on a flowchart (although you could make a notation).

FIGURE A.1 Flowchart: website, print, or television?

Example of a flowchart for improving a company's advertising.

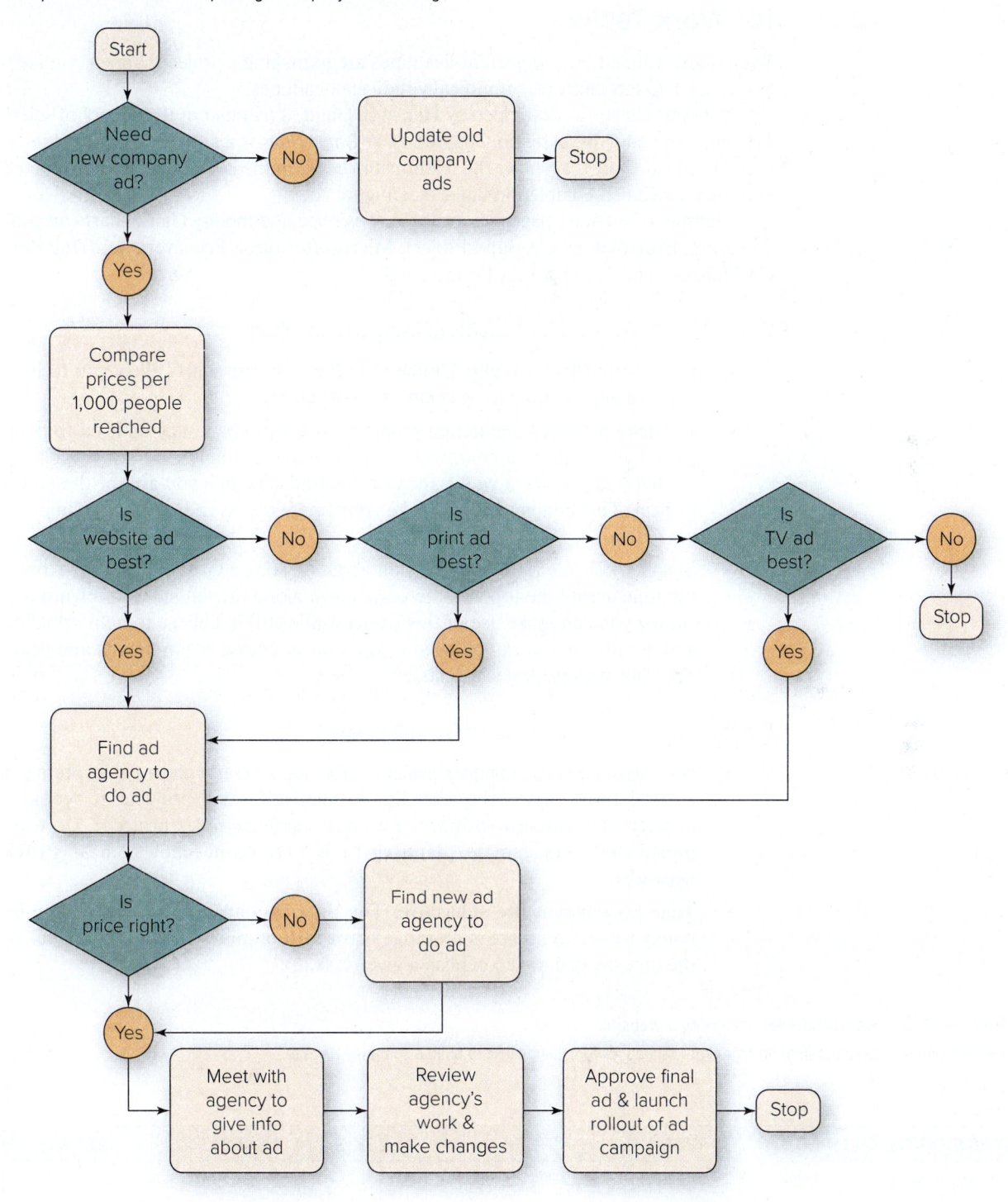

- **Not good for complex projects.** They aren't useful for showing projects consisting of several activities that must all be worked on at the same time. An example would be getting ready for football season's opening game, by which time the players have to be trained, the field readied, the programs printed, the band rehearsed, the ticket sellers recruited, and so on. These separate activities might each be represented on their own flowcharts, of course. But to try to express them all together all at once would produce a flowchart that would be unwieldy, even unworkable.

Tool #2: Gantt Charts—Visual Time Schedules for Work Tasks

We have mentioned how important deadlines are to making a project happen. Unlike a flowchart, a Gantt chart can graphically indicate deadlines.

The Gantt chart was developed by Henry L. Gantt, a member of the school of scientific management (discussed in Chapter 2). A *Gantt chart* is a kind of time schedule—a specialized bar chart that shows the relationship between the kind of work tasks planned and their scheduled completion dates (see Figure A.2).

A number of software packages can help you create and modify Gantt charts on your computer. Examples are CA-SuperProject, Microsoft Project, Primavera SureTrak Project Manager, and TurboProject Professional.

Benefits   There are three benefits to using a Gantt chart:

- **Express timelines visually.** Unlike flowcharts, Gantt charts allow you to indicate visually the time to be spent on each activity.
- **Compare proposed and actual progress.** A Gantt chart may be used to compare planned time to complete a task with actual time taken to complete it, so that you can see how far ahead or behind schedule you are for the entire project. This enables you to make adjustments so as to hold to the final target dates.
- **Simplicity.** There is nothing difficult about creating a Gantt chart. You express the time across the top and the tasks down along the left side. As Figure A.2 shows, you can make use of this device while still in college to help schedule and monitor the work you need to do to meet course requirements and deadlines (for papers, projects, tests).

Limitations   Gantt charts have two limitations:

- **Not useful for large, complex projects.** Although a Gantt chart can express the interrelations among the activities of relatively small projects, it becomes cumbersome and unwieldy when used for large, complex projects. More sophisticated management planning tools may be needed, such as PERT networks.
- **Time assumptions are subjective.** The time assumptions expressed may be purely subjective; there is no range between "optimistic" and "pessimistic" of the time needed to accomplish a given task.

FIGURE A.2   Gantt chart for designing a website

This shows the tasks accomplished and the time planned for remaining tasks to build a company website.

Accomplished: ||||||||||
Planned: \\\\\\\\\

STAGE OF DEVELOPMENT	WEEK 1	WEEK 2	WEEK 3	WEEK 4	WEEK 5
1. Examine competitors' websites	||||||||||||||||||||||||	||||||||||			
2. Get information for your website	||||||||||||||||||||||||	||||||||||||||||||||||||			
3. Learn web-authoring software		||||||||||||||||||||||||	||||||||||||||||||||		
4. Create (design) your website			\\\\\\\\\\	\\\\\\\\\\\\\\\\\\\\\\	\\\\\
5. "Publish" (put) website online					\\\\\\\\\\\\\\\\\\\\\\

Tool #3: Break-Even Analysis—How Many Items Must You Sell to Turn a Profit?

Break-even analysis is a way of identifying how much revenue is needed to cover the total costs of developing and selling a product. Let's walk through the computation of a break-even analysis, referring to the illustration (see Figure A.3). We assume you are an apparel manufacturer making shirts or blouses. Start in the lower-right corner of the diagram and follow the circled numbers as you read the following descriptions.

FIGURE A.3 Break-even analysis

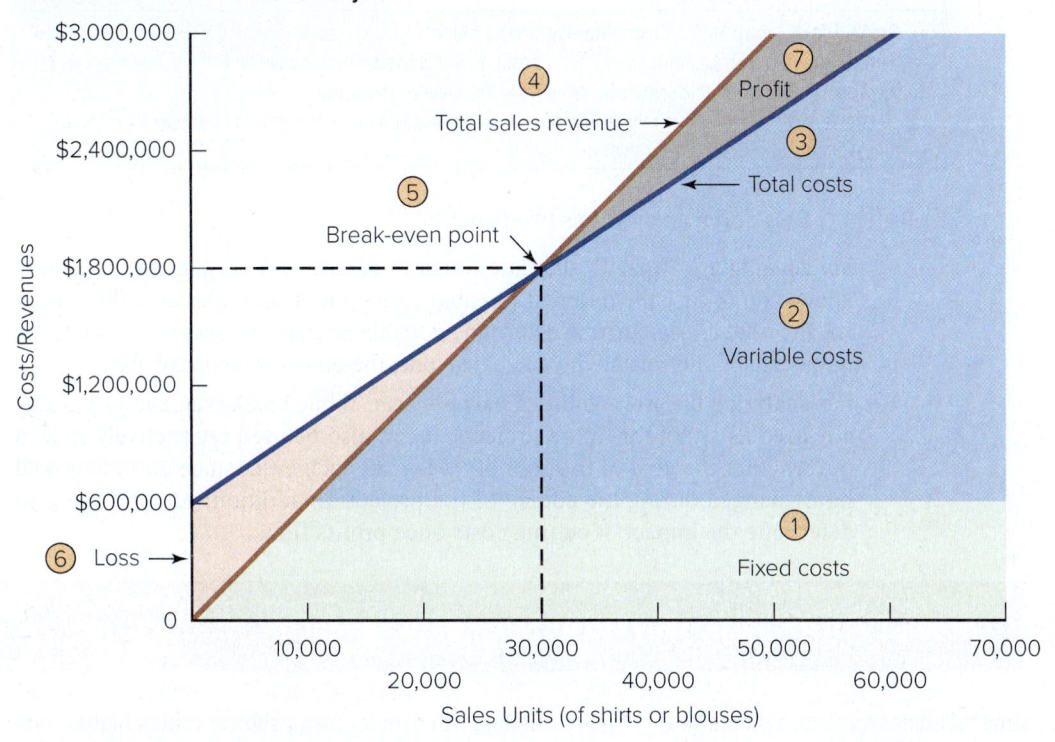

① **Fixed costs (green area):** Once you start up a business, whether you sell anything or not, you'll have expenses that won't vary much, such as rent, insurance, taxes, and perhaps salaries. These are called *fixed costs*, expenses that don't change regardless of your sales or output. Fixed costs are a function of time—they are expenses you have to pay out on a regular basis, such as weekly, monthly, or yearly. Here the chart shows the fixed costs (green area) are $600,000 per year no matter how many sales units (of shirts or blouses) you sell.

② **Variable costs (blue area):** Now suppose you start producing and selling a product, such as blouses or shirts. At this point you'll be paying for materials, supplies, labor, sales commissions, and delivery expenses. These are called *variable costs*, expenses that vary directly depending on the numbers of the product that you produce and sell. (After all, making more shirts will cost you more in cloth, for example.) Variable costs, then, are a function of volume—they go up and down depending on the number of products you make or sell. Here the variable costs (blue area) are relatively small if you sell only a few thousand shirts but they go up tremendously if you sell, say, 70,000 shirts.

③ **Total costs (first right upward-sloping line—green plus blue area added together):** The sum of the fixed costs and the variable costs equals the total costs (the green and blue areas together). This is indicated by the line that slopes upward to the right from $600,000 to $3,000,000.

④ **Total sales revenue (second right upward-sloping line):** This is the total dollars received from the sale of however many units you sell. The sales revenue varies depending on the number of units you sell. Thus, for example, if you sell 30,000 shirts, you'll receive $1,800,000 in revenue. If you sell 40,000 shirts, you'll receive somewhat more than $2,400,000 in revenue.

(continued)

⑤ **Break-even point (intersection of dashed lines):** Finding this point is the purpose of this whole exercise. The *break-even point* is the amount of sales revenue at which there is no profit but also no loss to your company. On the graph, this occurs where the "Total sales revenues" line crosses the "Total costs" line, as we've indicated here where the dashed lines meet. This means that you must sell 30,000 shirts and receive $1,800,000 in revenue in order to recoup your total costs (fixed plus variable). Important note: Here is where pricing the shirts becomes important. If you raise the price per shirt, you may be able to make the same amount of money (hit your break-even point) by selling fewer of them—but that may be harder to do because customers may resist buying at the higher price.

⑥ **Loss (red area):** If you fail to sell enough shirts at the right price (the break-even point), you will suffer a loss. *Loss* means your total costs exceed your total sales revenue. As the chart shows, here you are literally "in the red"—you've lost money.

⑦ **Profit (black area):** Here you are literally "in the black"—you've made money. All the shirts you sell beyond the break-even point constitute a profit. *Profit* is the amount by which total revenue exceeds total costs. The more shirts you sell, of course, the greater the profit.

The kind of break-even analysis demonstrated here is known as the *graphic method*. The same thing can also be done algebraically.

Benefits Break-even analysis has two benefits:

- **For doing future "what-if" alternate scenarios of costs, prices, and sales.** This tool allows you to vary the different possible costs, prices, and sales quantities to do rough "what-if" scenarios to determine possible pricing and sales goals. Since the numbers are interrelated, if you change one, the others will change also.

- **For analyzing the profitability of past projects.** While break-even analysis is usually used as a tool for future projects, it can also be used retroactively to find out whether the goal of profitability was really achieved, since costs may well have changed during the course of the project. In addition, you can use it to determine the impact of cutting costs once profits flow.

EXAMPLE | Break-Even Analysis: Why Do Airfares Vary So Much?

Why do some airlines charge four times more than others for a flight of the same distance?

There are several reasons, but break-even analysis enters into it.

United Airlines's average cost for flying a passenger 1 mile in a recent year was 11.7 cents, whereas Southwest's was 7.7 cents. Those are the break-even costs. What they charged beyond that was their profit.

Why the difference? One reason, according to a study by the U.S. Department of Transportation, is that Southwest's expenses are lower. United flies more long routes than short ones, so its costs are stretched out over more miles, making its costs for flying shorter routes higher than Southwest's.

Another factor affecting airfares is the type of passengers flying a particular route—whether they are high-fare-paying business travelers or more price-conscious leisure travelers. Business travelers often don't mind paying a lot (they are reimbursed by their companies), and those routes (such as Chicago to Cincinnati) tend to have more first-class seats, which drives up the average price. Flights to vacation spots (such as Las Vegas) usually have more low-price seats because people aren't willing to pay a lot for pleasure travel. Also, nonstop flight fares often cost more than flights with connections.

Limitations Break-even analysis is not a cure-all.

- **It oversimplifies.** In the real world, things don't happen as neatly as this model implies. For instance, fixed and variable costs are not always so readily distinguishable. Or fixed costs may change as the number of sales units goes up. And not all customers may pay the same price (some may get discounts).

- **The assumptions may be faulty.** On paper, the formula may work perfectly for identifying a product's profitability. But what if customers find the prices too high? Or what if sales figures are outrageously optimistic? In the marketplace, your price and sales forecasts may really be only good guesses.

DEI

1. "What Google Learned from Its Quest to Build the Perfect Team," *New York Times,* February 28, 2016, https://www.nytimes.com/2016/02/28/magazine/what-google-learned-from-its-quest-to-build-the-perfect-team.html.
2. C. Ansberry, "U.S. News: Erasing a Hurtful Label from the Books," *Wall Street Journal*, November 22, 2010.
3. American Psychological Association, *Inclusive Language Guidelines,* 2e (APA 2023), https://www.apa.org/about/apa/equity-diversity-inclusion/language-guidelines.pdf.
4. See J. Bersin, *Elevating Equity: The Real Story of Diversity and Inclusion* (The Josh Bersin Company (ongoing study), 2021). Also see D. Hawkins, "How CEOs Can Make Diversity and Inclusion a Priority," *Forbes,* July 13, 2022. https://www.forbes.com/sites/forbescoachescouncil/2022/07/13/how-ceos-can-make-diversity-and-inclusion-a-priority/?sh=46b1accb279a; Also see K.C. Brimhall and M.E. Mor Barak, "The Critical Role of Workplace Inclusion in Fostering Innovation, Job Satisfaction, and Quality of Care in a Diverse Human Service Organization," *Human Service Organizations: Management, Leadership & Governance*, Vol. 42, No. 5 (2018), pp. 474–492.
5. S. Yoon, "Why Diversity within Your Organization Matters—Lessons from 11 Entrepreneurs," *World Economic Forum,* November 18, 2021, https://www.weforum.org/agenda/2021/11/why-diversity-within-your-organization-matters/.
6. Summit Leadership Partners, "Whitepaper: Post-Pandemic: What's Next for Talent Management in Private Equity?" June 29, 2021, https://www.summitleadership.com/whitepaper-talent-management-challenges/.
7. A. Lui and R. Dinkins, "From Commitment to Action: How CEOs Can Advance Racial Equity in their Regional Economies," *Brookings,* March 11, 2021, https://www.brookings.edu/essay/from-commitments-to-action-how-ceos-can-advance-racial-equity-in-their-regional-economies/.
8. See M Loden and J. Rosener, *Workforce America!* (Homewood, IL. Business One Irwin, 1991); Also see L. Gardenswartz and A. Rowe, *Diverse Teams at Work: Capitalizing on the Power of Diversity* (Society for Human Resource Management 2003).
9. B.E. Ashforth, S.H. Harrison, and K.G. Corley, "Identification in Organizations: An Examination of Four Fundamental Questions," *Journal of Management,* Vol. 34, No. 3 (2008), pp. 325–374.
10. A.S. Rosette, R.P. de Leon, C.Z. Koval, and D.A. Harrison, "Intersectionality: Connecting Experiences of Gender with Race at Work," *Research in Organizational Behavior*, Vol. 38 (2018), pp. 1–22.
11. "Marginalized," *Merriam-webster.com,* https://www.merriam-webster.com/dictionary/marginalized.
12. "Marginalized," *Dictionary.com,* https://www.dictionary.com/browse/marginalized.
13. E.V. Hall, A.V. Hall, A.D. Galinsky, and K.W. Phillips, "MOSAIC: A Model of Stereotyping through Associated and Intersectional Categories," *Academy of Management Review*, Vol. 44, No. 3 (2019), pp. 643–672.
14. E.V. Hall, A.V. Hall, A.D. Galinsky, and K.W. Phillips, "MOSAIC: A Model of Stereotyping through Associated and Intersectional Categories," *Academy of Management Review*, Vol. 44, No. 3 (2019), pp. 643–672.
15. R. Fry, "How Has COVID-19 Impacted the US Gender Gap?," *World Economic Forum,* January 20, 2022, https://www.weforum.org/agenda/2022/01/gender-disparities-widened-us-workforce-pandemic/#:~:text=Women%20earned%2086%25%20of%20what,but%20women's%20hours%20are%20unchanged.
16. E. Porter, "Black Workers Stopped Making Progress on Pay. Is It Racism?" *New York Times,* June 28, 2021, https://www.nytimes.com/2021/06/28/business/economy/black-workers-racial-pay-gap.html.
17. "Black Women and the Pay Gap," *AAUW.org,* https://www.aauw.org/resources/article/black-women-and-the-pay-gap/.
18. J.A. Clair, B.K. Humberd, E.D. Rouse, and E.B. Jones, "Loosening Categorical Thinking: Extending the Terrain of Theory and Research on Demographic Identities in Organizations," *Academy of Management Review*, Vol. 44, No. 3 (2019), pp. 592–617.
19. M. McGrath, "Breaking the 'Concrete' Ceiling: Roz Brewer to Become The S&P 500's Only Black Female CEO," *Forbes,* January 28, 2021, https://www.forbes.com/sites/maggiemcgrath/2021/01/28/breaking-the-concrete-ceiling-roz-brewer-to-be-the-sps-only-black-female-ceo/?sh=4385ca8b667b.
20. See M.H. Chin and A.T. Chien, "Reducing Racial and Ethnic Disparities in Health Care: An Integral Part of Quality Improvement Scholarship," *Quality and Safety in Health Care,* Vol. 15 (2006), pp. 79–80; Also see R.S. Bernstein, M. Bulger, P. Salipante, and J.Y. Weisinger, "From Diversity to Inclusion to Equity: A Theory of Generative Interactions," *Journal of Business Ethics*, Vol. 167, No. 3 (2020), pp. 395–410.
21. J.S. Adams, "Towards an Understanding of Inequity," *The Journal of Abnormal and Social Psychology,* Vol. 67, No. 5 (1963), p. 422.
22. H. Le, C.P. Johnson, and Y. Fujimoto, "Organizational Justice and Climate for Inclusion," *Personnel Review,* January 31, 2021 (ahead of print).
23. See R.S. Kurdoğlu, "The Mirage of Procedural Justice and the Primacy of Interactional Justice in Organizations," *Journal of Business Ethics*, Vol. 167, No. 3 (2020), pp. 495–512. Also see G. Leventhal, J. Karuza, and W. Fry, "Beyond Fair Theory of Allocation Preferences," in G. Mikulka (Ed.), *Justice and Interaction* (New York: Springer 1980), pp. 167–218.
24. R.S. Bernstein, M. Bulger, P. Salipante, and J.Y. Weisinger, "From Diversity to Inclusion to Equity: A Theory of Generative Interactions," *Journal of Business Ethics*, Vol. 167, No. 3 (2020), pp. 395–410.
25. C. Chen and N. Tang, "Does Perceived Inclusion Matter in the Workplace?" *Journal of Managerial Psychology*, Vol. 33, No. 1 (March 2018), pp. 43–57; Also see A.E. Randel, B.M. Galvin, L.M. Shore, K.H. Ehrhart, B.G. Chung, M.A. Dean, and U. Kedharnath, "Inclusive Leadership: Realizing Positive Outcomes through Belongingness and Being Valued for Uniqueness," *Human Resource Management Review*, Vol. 28, No. 2 (2018), pp. 190–203.
26. D. Ellsworth, D. Goldstein, and B. Schaninger, "Inclusion Doesn't Happen by Accident: Measuring Inclusion in a Way That Matters," *McKinsey & Company,* February 16, 2021, https://www.mckinsey.com/business-functions/people-and-organizational-performance/our-insights/the-organization-blog/inclusion-doesnt-happen-by-accident-measuring-inclusion-in-a-way-that-matters.
27. M.B. Brewer, "Optimal Distinctiveness, Social Identity, and the Self," in M.R. Leary and J.P. Tangney (Eds.), *Handbook of Self and Identity* (The Guilford Press 2003), pp. 480–491.
28. S. Yoon, "Why Diversity within Your Organization Matters—Lessons from 11 Entrepreneurs," *World Economic Forum,* November 18, 2021, https://www.weforum.org/agenda/2021/11/why-diversity-within-your-organization-matters/.
29. C. Post, B. Lokshin, and C. Boone, "What Changes after Women Enter Top Management Teams? A Gender-Based Model of Strategic Renewal," *Academy of Management Journal*, February 16, 2022, https://doi.org/10.5465/amj.2018.1039.
30. A.E. Randel, B.M. Galvin, L.M. Shore, K.H. Ehrhart, B.G. Chung, M.A. Dean, and U. Kedharnath, "Inclusive Leadership: Realizing Positive Outcomes through Belongingness and Being Valued for Uniqueness," *Human Resource Management Review*, Vol. 28, No. 2 (2018), pp. 190–203.
31. O. Holmes IV, G. Lopiano, and E.V. Hall, 2019. "A Review of Compensatory Strategies to Mitigate Bias," *Personnel Assessment and Decisions*, 5(2), p.4.; L.H. Nishii, 2013. "The Benefits of Climate For Inclusion For Gender-Diverse Groups," *Academy of Management Journal*, 56(6), pp. 1754–1774.
32. O. Holmes IV, K. Jiang, D.R. Avery, P.F. McKay, I.S. Oh, and C.J. Tillman, "A Meta-Analysis Integrating 25 Years of Diversity Climate Research," *Journal of Management*, Vol. 47, No. 6 (2021), pp. 1357–1382.
33. H. Le, C.P. Johnson, and Y. Fujimoto, "Organizational Justice and Climate for Inclusion," *Personnel Review,* January 31, 2021 (ahead of print).
34. See Q.M. Roberson, "Diversity in the Workplace: A Review, Synthesis, and Future Research Agenda," *Annual Review of*

Organizational Psychology and Organizational Behavior, Vol. 6 (2019), pp. 69–88; Also see T.H. Cox and S. Blake, "Managing Cultural Diversity: Implications for Organizational Competitiveness," *Academy of Management Perspectives,* Vol. 5, No. 3 (1991), pp. 45–56.

35. For a review, see Q.M. Roberson, "Diversity in the Workplace: A Review, Synthesis, and Future Research Agenda," *Annual Review of Organizational Psychology and Organizational Behavior,* Vol. 6 (2019), pp. 69–88.

36. C. Colvin, "Once Neglected, DEI Initiatives Now Present at All Fortune 100 Companies," *HRDive,* July 20, 2022, https://www.hrdive.com/news/2022-fortune-companies-dei/627651/; Also see The DEIA Leadership Forum, "Majority of U.S. Employers Have Implemented DEI Initiatives in 2021," *Los Angeles Times,* December 15, 2021, https://www.latimes.com/b2b/diversity/story/2021-12-15/majority-of-u-s-employers-have-implemented-dei-initiatives-in-2021.

37. D. Auger-Dominguez, "When Your Efforts to Be Inclusive Misfire," *Harvard Business Review,* May 03, 2022, https://hbr.org/2022/05/when-your-efforts-to-be-inclusive-misfire.

38. N. Baumer and J. Frueh, "What Is Neurodiversity," *Harvard Health Publishing,* November 23, 2021, https://www.health.harvard.edu/blog/what-is-neurodiversity-202111232645.

39. R. Chapman, "Neurodiversity and the Social Ecology of Mental Functions," *Perspectives on Psychological Science,* Vol. 16, No. 6 (2021), pp. 1360–1372.

40. K. Gurchiek, "Inclusive Strategies Create a 'More Universal Workplace,'" *Society for Human Resource Management,* January 20, 2021." https://www.shrm.org/resourcesandtools/hr-topics/behavioral-competencies/global-and-cultural-effectiveness/pages/inclusive-strategies-create-a-more-universal-workplace-.aspx.

41. "Gender Identity," *Society for Human Resource Management,* https://www.shrm.org/resourcesandtools/tools-and-samples/hr-glossary/pages/gender-identity.aspx?_ga=2.245660807.2015978822.1643577291-1025920577.1641842652.

42. J. Garsd, "'It's a Career Ender': 2 LGBTQ Former Dell Workers Share Their Stories," *NPR,* July 15, 2019, https://www.npr.org/2019/07/15/740726966/it-s-a-career-ender-2-lgbtq-former-dell-workers-share-their-stories.

43. A.C. Gilbert, "Penn Swimmer Lia Thomas Becomes First Trans Woman to Win NCAA Swimming Championship," *USA Today,* March 18, 2022, https://www.usatoday.com/story/sports/college/2022/03/18/lia-thomas-trans-woman-win-ncaa-swimming-championship/7088548001/.

44. Ivy League Parents, "Parents of Ivy League Swimmers Write: Letting Lia Thomas Swim Isn't Fair," *New York Post,* March 18, 2022, https://www.iwf.org/2022/03/18/parents-of-ivy-league-swimmers-write-letting-lia-thomas-swim-isnt-fair/.

45. K. Barnes, "Advocacy Groups Ask Policymakers to Prioritize Fairness for Biological Women in Sport," *ESPN,* March 15, 2022, https://www.espn.com/olympics/story/_/id/33511880/advocacy-groups-ask-congress-sports-governing-bodies-prioritize-fairness-biological-women.

46. J. Kliegman, "300-Plus Collegiate, Elite Swimmers Sign Letter to NCAA Supporting Lia Thomas," *Sports Illustrated,* February 10, 2022, https://www.si.com/college/2022/02/10/lia-thomas-college-elite-swimmers-letter-to-ncaa-new-policy-transgender-eligibility.

47. Results can be found in D.A. Harrison, D.A. Kravitz, D.M. Mayer, L.M. Leslie, and D. Lev-Arey, "Understanding Attitudes toward Affirmative Action Programs in Employment: Summary and Meta-Analysis of 35 Years of Research," *Journal of Applied Psychology,* September 2006, D 1013–36.

48. For a thorough review of relevant research, see M.E. Hellmar, "Affirmative Action: Some Unintended Consequences for Working Women," in B.M. Staw and L.L. Cummines (Eds.), *Research in Organizational Behavior* Vol. 16 (Greenwich, CI: JAI Press, 1994), pp. 125–169. Also see M.E. Heilman, W.S. Battle, C.E. Keller, and R.A. Lee, "Type of Affirmative Action Policy: A Determinant of Reactions to Sex-Based Preferential Selection?" *Journal of Applied Psychology,* April 1998, pp. 190–205.

49. See Q.M. Roberson, "Diversity in the Workplace: A Review, Synthesis, and Future Research Agenda," *Annual Review of Organizational Psychology and Organizational Behavior,* Vol. 6 (2019), pp. 69–88; Also see Q. Roberson, A.M. Ryan, and B.R. Ragins, "The Evolution and Future of Diversity at Work," *Journal of Applied Psychology,* Vol. 102, No. 3 (2017), p. 483.

50. G. Cox and D. Lancefield, "5 Strategies to Infuse D&I into Your Organization," *Harvard Business Review,* May 19, 2021, https://hbr.org/2021/05/5-strategies-to-infuse-di-into-your-organization.

51. K. Gurchiek, "Report: Most Companies Are 'Going through the Motions' of DE&I," Society for *Human Resource Management,* February 23, 2021, https://www.shrm.org/resourcesandtools/hr-topics/behavioral-competencies/global-and-cultural-effectiveness/pages/report-most-companies-are-going-through-the-motions-of-dei.aspx.

52. J. Huang, M.R. Diehl, and S. Paterlini, 2020. "The Influence of Corporate Elites on Women on Supervisory Boards: Female Directors' Inclusion in Germany," *Journal of Business Ethics,* 165, pp. 347–364.; E.H. Chang, K.L. Milkman, D. Chugh, and M. Akinola, 2019. "Diversity Thresholds: How Social Norms, Visibility, and Scrutiny Relate to Group Composition," *Academy of Management Journal,* 62(1), pp. 144–171.; P. Dwivedi, I.H. Gee, M.C. Withers, and S. Boivie, 2023. "No Reason To Leave: The Effects of CEO Diversity-Valuing Behavior on Psychological Safety and Turnover For Female Executives," *Journal of Applied Psychology,* 108(7), p.1262.; M.A. Kazmi, C. Spitzmueller, J. Yu, J.M. Madera, A.S. Tsao, J.F. Dawson, and I. Pavlidis, 2022. "Search Committee Diversity and Applicant Pool Representation of Women and Underrepresented Minorities: A Quasi-Experimental Field Study," *Journal of Applied Psychology,* 107(8), p. 1414.

53. See F. Wolf, A. Seifert, M. Martin, and F. Oswald, "Considering Situational Variety in Contextualized Aging Research—Opinion about Methodological Perspectives, *Frontiers in Psychology,*" Vol. 12 (2021), p. 1172. Also see K. Lewin, *Field Theory in Social Science* (New York, NY: Harper 1951).

54. J.W. Neuliep, "The Relationship among Intercultural Communication Apprehension, Ethnocentrism, Uncertainty Reduction, and Communication Satisfaction during Initial Intercultural Interaction: An Extension of Anxiety and Uncertainty Management (AUM) Theory," *Journal of Intercultural Communication Research,* Vol. 41 (2012), pp. 1–16.

55. Y.S. Kim and Y.Y. Kim, "Ethnic Proximity and Coss-Cultural Adaptation: A Study of Asian and European Students in the United States," *Intercultural Communication Studies,* Vol. 25 (2016), pp. 61–80.

56. K. Tai, K. Lee, E. Kim, T.D. Johnson, W. Wang, M.K. Duffy, and S. Kim, 2022. "Gender, Bottom-Line Mentality, and Workplace Mistreatment: The roles of Gender Norm Violation and Team Gender Composition," *Journal of Applied Psychology,* 107(5), p. 854.; K.K. Dray, V.R. Smith, T.P. Kostecki, I.E. Sabat, and C.R. Thomson, 2020. "Moving Beyond the Gender Binary: Examining Workplace Perceptions of Nonbinary and Transgender Employees," *Gender, Work & Organization,* 27(6), pp. 1181–1191. Vancouver.; P. Dwivedi, V.F. Misangyi, and A. Joshi, 2021. " 'Burnt By the Spotlight': How Leadership Endorsements Impact the Longevity of Female Leaders," *Journal of Applied Psychology,* 106(12), p. 1885.

57. See J. Engle, "Does the N.F.L. have a Race Problem?" *The New York Times,* February 9, 2022, https://www.nytimes.com/2022/02/09/learning/does-the-nfl-have-a-race-problem.html; also see S. Stump, "Most NFL Players Are Black. So Why Aren't There More Black Head Coaches?" *NBC News,* September 15, 2020, https://www.nbcnews.com/news/nbcblk/most-nfl-players-are-black-so-why-aren-t-there-n1240131.

58. C. Pazzanese, "Examining Brian Flores' Suit against NFL," *The Harvard Gazette,* February 17, 2022, https://news.harvard.edu/gazette/story/2022/02/examining-brian-floress-bias-suit-against-nfl/.

59. L.M. Leslie, "Diversity Initiative Effectiveness: A Typological Theory of Unintended Consequences," *Academy of Management Review,* Vol. 44, No. 3 (2019), pp. 538–563.

60. L. Windscheid, L. Bowes-Sperry, D.L. Kidder, H.K. Cheung, M. Morner, and F. Lievens, "Actions Speak Louder Than Words: Outsiders' Perceptions of Diversity Mixed Messages," *Journal of Applied Psychology,* Vol. 101, No. 9 (2016), p. 1329.

61. A. Marcinko, "Diversity as I Say, Not as I Do: Organizational Authenticity and Diversity Management Effectiveness," *Academy of Management Proceedings,* Vol. 2020, No. 1 (2020), p. 14306.

62. D. Wilkie, "How DE&I Evolved in the C-Suite," *Society for Human Resource Management,* https://www.shrm.org/executive/resources/articles/pages/evolving-executive-dei-diversity-c-suite.aspx#:~:text=Women%20make%20up%2056%20percent,the%20topic%20in%20February%202021.

63. L. Windscheid, L. Bowes-Sperry, D.L. Kidder, H.K. Cheung, M. Morner, and F. Lievens, "Actions Speak Louder Than Words: Outsiders' Perceptions of Diversity Mixed Messages," *Journal of Applied Psychology*, Vol. 101, No. 9 (2016), p. 1329.

64. https://medium.com/@jamesnicol1/21-brands-that-still-refuse-to-walk-the-walk-on-racial-diversity-d90fdcb9bf0a.

65. Dobbin, F. and Kalev, A., 2016. Why diversity programs fail. *Harvard Business Review*, 94(7), p. 14.

66. See D. Wilkie, "50 Years after Age Discrimination Became Illegal, It Persists," *Society for Human Resource Management,* January 22, 2019, https://www.shrm.org/resourcesandtools/hr-topics/employee-relations/pages/age-discrimination-in-the-workplace-.aspx; also see J. Kita, "Workplace Age Discrimination Still Flourishes in America," *AARP,* December 30, 2019, https://www.aarp.org/work/working-at-50-plus/info-2019/age-discrimination-in-america.html.

67. L. Dana, "How Colgate-Palmolive Gained Insights into Their Diversity Hiring Funnel," *WayUp,* November 2, 2020, https://www.wayup.com/employers/blog/how-colgate-palmolive-gained-insights-into-their-diversity-hiring-funnel.

68. K. Kaul, "Refining the Referral Process: Increasing Diversity for Technology Startups through Targeted Recruitment, Screening and Interview Strategies," *Strategic HR Review,* Vol. 20, No. 4 (2021), pp. 125–129.

69. M.R. Barrick and L. Parks-Leduc, "Selection for Fit," *Annual Review of Organizational Psychology and Organizational Behavior*, Vol. 6 (2019), pp. 171–193.

70. M.D. Pike, D.M. Powell, J.S. Bourdage, and E.R. Lukacik, "Why not Interview? Investigating Interviews as a Method for Judging Honesty-Humility," *Journal of Personnel Psychology*, Vol. 21, No. 3 (2022), pp. 104–114.

71. A. Grant, "Job Interviews Are Broken: There's a Way to Fix Them," *New York Times,* May 1, 2020, https://www.nytimes.com/2020/05/01/smarter-living/how-to-fix-job-interviews-tips.html.

72. Q.M. Roberson, "Diversity in the Workplace: A Review, Synthesis, and Future Research Agenda," *Annual Review of Organizational Psychology and Organizational Behavior,* Vol. 6 (2019), pp. 69–88.

73. E. van den Broek, A. Sergeeva, and M. Huysman, "When the Machine Meets the Expert: An Ethnography of Developing AI for Hiring," *MIS Quarterly*, Vol. 45, No. 3 (2021).

74. D. Zielinski, "Facial Analysis Technology in the Workplace Brings Risks," *Society for Human Resource Management,* July 9, 2020, https://www.shrm.org/resourcesandtools/hr-topics/technology/pages/facial-analysis-technology-workplace-brings-risks.aspx.

75. L. Hardesy, "Study Finds Gender and Skin-Type Bias in Commercial Artificial-Intelligence Systems," *MIT News,* February 11, 2018, https://news.mit.edu/2018/study-finds-gender-skin-type-bias-artificial-intelligence-systems-0212.

76. M. Bogen, "All the Ways Hiring Algorithms Can Introduce Bias," *Harvard Business Review*, Vol. 6 (2019), p. 2019.

77. E.H. Chang, K.L. Milkman, L.J. Zarrow, K. Brabaw, D.M. Gromet, R. Rebele, C. Massey, A.L. Duckworth, and A. Grant, "Does Diversity Training Work the Way It's Supposed To?" *Harvard Business Review,* July 9, 2019, https://hbr.org/2019/07/does-diversity-training-work-the-way-its-supposed-to; Also see F. Dobbin and A. Kalev, "Why Diversity Programs Fail," *Harvard Business Review,* July–August 2016, https://hbr.org/2016/07/whydiversity-programs-fail.

78. Q.M. Roberson, "Diversity in the Workplace: A Review, Synthesis, and Future Research Agenda," *Annual Review of Organizational Psychology and Organizational Behavior,* Vol. 6 (2019), pp. 69–88.

79. E.H. Chang, K.L. Milkman, L.J. Zarrow, K. Brabaw, D.M. Gromet, R. Rebele, C. Massey, A.L. Duckworth, and A. Grant, "Does Diversity Training Work the Way It's Supposed To?" *Harvard Business Review,* July 9, 2019, https://hbr.org/2019/07/does-diversity-training-work-the-way-its-supposed-to.

80. L. Stone, "The NCAA's Hypocrisy on Gender-Equity Issues Has Been on Full Display during March Madness," *Seattle Times,* March 23, 2021, https://www.seattletimes.com/sports/ncaa-tournament/the-ncaas-hypocrisy-on-gender-equity-issues-has-been-on-full-display-during-march-madness/.

81. R. Bastian, "Personality-Based Performance Reviews Are Fine to Give to Women—As Long as Men Get Them Too," *Forbes,* March 8, 2019, https://www.forbes.com/sites/rebekahbastian/2019/03/08/personality-based-performance-reviews-are-fine-to-give-women-as-long-as-men-get-them-too/?sh=412d8e1a1667.

82. H. Le, C.P. Johnson, and Y. Fujimoto, "Organizational Justice and Climate for Inclusion," *Personnel Review,* January 31, 2021 (ahead of print).

83. G. Cox and D. Lancefield, "5 Strategies to Infuse D&I into Your Organization," *Harvard Business Review,* May 19, 2021, https://hbr.org/2021/05/5-strategies-to-infuse-di-into-your-organization.

84. "Riot Settlement," *McCracken v Riot Games, Inc.,* https://riotsettlement.com/Home/portalid/0#:~:text=The%20California%20Department%20of%20Fair,Games%2C%20Inc.%2C%20Riot%20Games.

85. J. Hahn, "Riot Games to Pay 2,000 Former and Current Female Employees $80M over Gender Discrimination," *People,* December 28, 2021, https://people.com/human-interest/riot-games-to-pay-2000-former-and-current-female-employees-over-gender-discrimination/.

86. "League of Legends Firm Sued over Workers' Sexism Claims," *BBC News,* November 7, 2018, https://www.bbc.com/news/technology-46125058.

87. S. Liao, "Since Lawsuit, Riot Games' Once All-Male Leadership Now over 20 Percent Women," *The Washington Post,* August 10, 2022, https://www.washingtonpost.com/video-games/2022/08/10/riot-games-diversity-report-lawsuit/.

88. M. Bryant, "Riot Games to Pay $100M to Settle Gender Discrimination Lawsuit," *The Guardian,* December 28, 2021, https://www.theguardian.com/games/2021/dec/28/riot-games-to-pay-100m-to-settle-gender-discrimination-lawsuit.

89. S. Liao, "Since Lawsuit, Riot Games' Once All-Male Leadership Now over 20 Percent Women," *The Washington Post,* August 10, 2022, https://www.washingtonpost.com/video-games/2022/08/10/riot-games-diversity-report-lawsuit/.

90. E.H. Schein, "Culture: The Missing Concept in Organization Studies," *Administrative Science Quarterly*, 1996, pp. 229–240.

91. "Welcome to Hilton," Hilton, https://www.hilton.com/en/corporate/; Also see "100 Best Workplaces for Diversity," *Forbes,* 2019, https://fortune.com/best-workplaces-for-diversity/2019/search/.

92. S. Chan, "Mental Health Priorities for Employees and Leaders Remain Steadfast at Cisco," *Cisco: The Newsroom,* March 26, 2020, https://newsroom.cisco.com/feature-content?type=webcontent&articleId=2076824.

93. C. BasuMallick, "4 Companies That Have Nailed Their Employee Recognition Strategy," *Spiceworks,* September 1, 2023, https://www.toolbox.com/hr/employee-recognition/articles/employee-recognition-strategy-examples/.

94. "New Bloomberg Resource Lights Paths to a Net-Zero CO2 Future," Bloomberg, October 18, 2021. https://www.bloomberg.com/company/press/new-bloomberg-resource-lights-paths-to-a-net-zero-co2-future/.

95. See C.A. Hartnell, A.Y. Ou, and A. Kinicki, "Organizational Culture and Organizational Effectiveness: A Meta-Analytic Investigation of the Competing Values Framework's Theoretical Suppositions," *Journal of Applied Psychology,* Vol. 96, No. 4 (2011), p. 677; Also see C.A. Hartnell, A.Y. Ou, A.J. Kinicki, D. Choi, and E.P. Karam, "A Meta-Analytic Test of Organizational Culture's Association with Elements of an Organization's System and Its Relative Predictive Validity on Organizational Outcomes," *Journal of Applied Psychology,* Vol. 104, No. 6 (2019), p. 832.

96. M. Gonzalez, "Diversity Officers to CEOs: This Is What We Need," *Society for Human Resource Management,* July 21, 2022, https://www.shrm.org/resourcesandtools/hr-topics/behavioral-competencies/global-and-cultural-effectiveness/pages/diversity-officers-to-ceos-this-is-what-we-need.aspx.

97. "#Me to #We Study," Hack Future Lab. https://www.hackfuturelab.com/foresight/me-to-we-study. (Accessed January 5, 2024.)

98. The HR Research Institute, "The Future of Diversity, Equity, and Inclusion 2022," https://www.affirmity.com/wp-content/uploads/2022/03/Affirmity_the_Future_of_DEI_2022_Research_Report_hrdotcom.pdf.

99. M. Gonzalez, "Diversity Officers to CEOs: This Is What We Need," *Society for Human Resource Management,* July 21, 2022, https://www

.shrm.org/resourcesandtools/hr-topics/behavioral-competencies/global-and-cultural-effectiveness/pages/diversity-officers-to-ceos-this-is-what-we-need.aspx.

100. A.E. Randel, B.M. Galvin, L.M. Shore, K.H. Ehrhart, B.G. Chung, M.A. Dean, and U. Kedharnath, "Inclusive Leadership: Realizing Positive Outcomes through Belongingness and Being Valued for Uniqueness," *Human Resource Management Review*, Vol. 28, No. 2 (2018), pp. 190–203.

101. A.E. Randel, B.M. Galvin, L.M. Shore, K.H. Ehrhart, B.G. Chung, M.A. Dean, and U. Kedharnath, "Inclusive Leadership: Realizing Positive Outcomes through Belongingness and Being Valued for Uniqueness," *Human Resource Management Review*, Vol. 28, No. 2 (2018), pp. 190–203.

102. A. De Smet, B. Dowling, M. Mugayar-Baldocchi, and B.Shaninger, "'Great Attrition' or 'Great Attraction'? The Choice Is Yours," *McKinsey Quarterly*, September 8, 2021, https://www.mckinsey.com/capabilities/people-and-organizational-performance/our-insights/great-attrition-or-great-attraction-the-choice-is-yours.

103. A.E. Randel, B.M. Galvin, L.M. Shore, K.H. Ehrhart, B.G. Chung, M.A. Dean, and U. Kedharnath, "Inclusive Leadership: Realizing Positive Outcomes through Belongingness and Being Valued for Uniqueness," *Human Resource Management Review*, Vol. 28, No. 2 (2018), pp. 190–203.

104. A. Whillans, "How Men and Women Treat Deadlines in the Workplace Differently; Women Are Less Likely to Ask for Extensions. That Hurts Women—and the Companies They Work For," *Wall Street Journal*, October 30, 2021, https://www.proquest.com/newspapers/how-men-women-treat-deadlines-workplace/docview/2588442105/se-2?accountid=8361.

105. A.E. Randel, B.M. Galvin, L.M. Shore, K.H. Ehrhart, B.G. Chung, M.A. Dean, and U. Kedharnath, "Inclusive Leadership: Realizing Positive Outcomes through Belongingness and Being Valued for Uniqueness," *Human Resource Management Review*, Vol. 28, No. 2 (2018), pp. 190–203.

106. R.D. Austin and G.P. Pisano, "Neurodiversity as a Competitive Advantage," *Harvard Business Review*, May–June 2017.

107. K. Gurchiek, "Report: Most Companies Are 'Going through the Motions' of DE&I," *Society for Human Resource Management*, February 23, 2021, https://www.shrm.org/resourcesandtools/hr-topics/behavioral-competencies/global-and-cultural-effectiveness/pages/report-most-companies-are-going-through-the-motions-of-dei.aspx.

108. J. Bersin, *Elevating Equity: The Real Story of Diversity and Inclusion* (The Josh Bersin Company 2021).

109. B. Wall, "How Improving DE&I Can Make Organizations More Competitive," *Society for Human Resource Management*, September 29, 2021, https://www.shrm.org/resourcesandtools/hr-topics/behavioral-competencies/global-and-cultural-effectiveness/pages/improving-dei-raises-hrs-contribution-to-a-more-competitive-organization.aspx.

110. A. Gorbatai, S. Boros, and K. Ullman, "Why Middle Managers Struggle to Implement DEI Strategies," *Harvard Business Review*, October 13, 2022.

111. G. Cox and D. Lancefield, "5 Strategies to Infuse D&I into Your Organization," *Harvard Business Review*, May 19, 2021, https://hbr.org/2021/05/5-strategies-to-infuse-di-into-your-organization.

112. M.D.C. Triana, P. Gu, O. Chapa, O. Richard, and A. Colella, "Sixty Years of Discrimination and Diversity Research in Human Resource Management: A Review with Suggestions for Future Research Directions," *Human Resource Management*, Vol. 60, No. 1 (2021), pp. 145–204.

113. D. Brown, C. Rickard, and A. Broughton, *Tackling Gender, Disability and Ethnicity Pay Gaps* (Equality and Human Rights Commission 2017), https://www.equalityhumanrights.com/sites/default/files/research-report-110-tackling-gender-disability-ethnicity-pay-gaps.pdf.

114. HR Research Institute, *The Future of Diversity, Equity and Inclusion 2021* (Jacksons Point, ON: HR Research Institute 2021).

115. "Organizations Accelerate DE&I Efforts Overall, but Many Are Only Focusing on the Basics, According to Global Korn Ferry Study," *Korn Ferry*, March 1, 2022, https://www.kornferry.com/about-us/press/organizations-accelerate-dei-efforts-overall.

116. G. Cox and D. Lancefield, "5 Strategies to Infuse D&I into Your Organization," *Harvard Business Review*, May 19, 2021, https://hbr.org/2021/05/5-strategies-to-infuse-di-into-your-organization.

117. B. Wall, "How Improving DE&I Can Make Organizations More Competitive," *Society for Human Resource Management*, September 29, 2021, https://www.shrm.org/resourcesandtools/hr-topics/behavioral-competencies/global-and-cultural-effectiveness/pages/improving-dei-raises-hrs-contribution-to-a-more-competitive-organization.aspx.

118. X. Cao and A. Gurcay, "The Anxiety Factor: Moral Traditionalism, Interpersonal Contact Diversity and Support for Transgender Candidates and Rights," *Journal of Homosexuality*, 2021, pp. 1–24.

119. G.W. Allport, K. Clark, and T. Pettigrew, *The Nature of Prejudice* (Addison-Wesley 1954).

120. B.A. Livingston and T.R. Opie, "Even at 'Inclusive' Companies, Women of Color Don't Feel Supported," *Harvard Business Review*, August 29, 2019.

121. R.S. Bernstein, M. Bulger, P. Salipante, and J.Y. Weisinger, "From Diversity to Inclusion to Equity: A Theory of Generative Interactions," *Journal of Business Ethics*, Vol. 167, No. 3 (2020), pp. 395–410.

122. S. Chilazi and I. Bohnet, "How to Best Use Data to Meet Your DE&I Goals," *Harvard Business Review Digital Articles*, 2020, pp. 2–6.

123. T. Ryan and T. Fiatte, "These Companies Are Following through on their Promises on Diversity, Equity, and Inclusion," *Fortune,* January 17, 2022, https://fortune.com/2022/01/17/diversity-pledges-ceo-action-social-justice/.

124. B. Wall, "How Improving DE&I Can Make Organizations More Competitive," *Society for Human Resource Management,* September 29, 2021, https://www.shrm.org/resourcesandtools/hr-topics/behavioral-competencies/global-and-cultural-effectiveness/pages/improving-dei-raises-hrs-contribution-to-a-more-competitive-organization.aspx.

125. S. Chilazi and I. Bohnet, "How to Best Use Data to Meet Your DE&I Goals," *Harvard Business Review Digital Articles*, 2020, pp. 2–6.

126. M.H. Davis, "A Multidimensional Approach to Individual Differences in Empathy," *Catalog of Selected Documents in Psychology,* Vol. 10, No. 85 (1980).

127. B.R. Ragins and K. Ehrhardt, "Gaining Perspective: The Impact of Close Cross-Race Friendships on Diversity Training and Education," *Journal of Applied Psychology*, Vol. 106, No. 6 (2021), pp. 856–881.

128. "How One Executive Is Building More-Diverse C-Suites," *Society for Human Resource Management,* https://www.shrm.org/executive/resources/articles/pages/evolving-executive-dei-diversity-c-suite.aspx#:~:text=Women%20make%20up%2056%20percent,the%20topic%20in%20February%202021.

129. T.M. Melaku, A. Beeman, D.G. Smith, and W.B. Johnson, "Be a Better Ally," *Harvard Business Review*, Vol. 98, No. 6 (2020), pp. 135–139.

130. S. Wojcicki, "Exclusive: How to Break Up the Silicon Valley Boys' Club," *Vanity Fair,* March 16, 2017, https://www.vanityfair.com/news/2017/03/how-to-break-up-the-silicon-valley-boys-club-susan-wojcicki.

131. E. Schmidt, J. Rosenberg, and A. Eagle, "The Bear-Hugging Football Coach Who Became Silicon Valley's Go-To Guru," *Fast Company,* April 11, 2019, https://www.fastcompany.com/90331367/bill-campbell-silicon-valley-trillion-dollar-coach-book.

132. C. French, "Why Being Good-Ish Is Better Than Being Good: A Conversation with Dolly Chugh," *Behavioral Scientist,* September 25, 2018, https://behavioralscientist.org/why-being-good-ish-is-better-than-being-good-a-conversation-with-dolly-chugh/.

CHAPTER 1

1. NACE Staff, "Employers Rate Career Competencies, New Hire Proficiency," December 11, 2017, www.naceweb.org/career-readiness/competencies/employers-rate-career-competencies-new-hire-proficiency. Also see M. Tarpey, "The Skills You Need for the Jobs of the Future," *CareerBuilder,* February 16, 2017, www.careerbuilder.com/advice/the-skills-you-need-for-the-jobs-of-the-future.

2. K. Armstrong, "At Keller Demo Day, Six Student Teams Pitch Their Companies," *New Jersey Tech Weekly*, August 24, 2017, http://

njtechweekly.com/art/3393-at-keller-demo-day-six-student-teams-pitch-their-companies/.

3. P. Ingrassia, "How GM's Mary Barra Does It," *Fortune,* September 9, 2016, http://fortune.com/mary-barra-general-motors-essay/.

4. Duke University Board of Trustees, "Mary T. Barra," January 2022, https://trustees.duke.edu/trustees/mary-t-barra.

5. A. Hartmans, "The Fabulous Life of Amazon CEO Jeff Bezos, the Second Richest Person in the World," *BusinessInsider.com,* May 15, 2017, http://www.businessinsider.com/amazon-founder-ceo-jeff-bezos-early-life-2017-5.

6. W. Harwood, "Blue Origin Launches Six Passengers on Supersonic Flight to the Edge of Space," *CBS News,* August 4, 2022, https://www.cbsnews.com/news/blue-origin-launches-six-passengers-on-supersonic-flight-to-the-edge-of-space/.

7. R. Barker, "No, Management Is *Not* a Profession," *Harvard Business Review,* July–August 2010, pp. 52–60.

8. M.P. Follett, quoted in J.F. Stoner and R.E. Freeman, *Management,* 5th ed. (Englewood Cliffs, NJ: Prentice Hall, 1992), p. 6.

9. S. McChrystal, *Team of Teams* (New York: Penguin Publishing Group, 2015).

10. I. Aprcovic, "Is Cellular Agriculture the Climate-Friendly Answer to Growing Food Demands?" *World Economic Forum,* November 4, 2021, https://www.weforum.org/agenda/2021/11/cellular-agriculture-climate-friendly-answer-to-food-demands/; also see "World Population to Reach 8 Billion on 15 November 2022," *United Nations,* https://www.un.org/en/desa/world-population-reach-8-billion-15-november-2022.

11. "2021 State of the Industry Report: Cultivated Meat and Seafood," *Good Food Institute,* April 30, 2022, https://gfieurope.org/wp-content/uploads/2022/04/2021-Cultivated-Meat-State-of-the-Industry-Report.pdf.

12. "Global Cultured Meat Market Size Estimated to Reach USD 499.9 Million by 2030, with 16.2% CAGR: Statistics Report by Polaris Market Research," *Polaris Market Research,* April 12, 2022, https://www.prnewswire.com/news-releases/global-cultured-meat-market-size-estimated-to-reach-usd-499-9-million-by-2030--with-16-2-cagr-statistics-report-by-polaris-market-research-301523708.html.

13. A. Baker, "Cultivated Meat Passes the Taste Test," *Time,* January 19, 2022, https://time.com/collection-post/6140206/cultivated-meat-passes-the-taste-test/#:~:text=In%20a%20blind%20tasting%2C%20meat,and%20a%20Master%20Chef%20judge.

14. D. Ewing-Chow, "Is Cultured Meat the Answer to the World's Meat Problem?" *Forbes,* June 20, 2019, https://www.forbes.com/sites/daphneewingchow/2019/06/20/is-cultured-meat-the-answer-to-the-worlds-meat-problem/#5aaf518c4468.

15. D. Ewing-Chow, "Is Cultured Meat the Answer to the World's Meat Problem?" *Forbes,* June 20, 2019, https://www.forbes.com/sites/daphneewingchow/2019/06/20/is-cultured-meat-the-answer-to-the-worlds-meat-problem/#5aaf518c4468.

16. "What Is Lab-Grown Meat, and How Is Cultured Meat Made?" *The Human League,* September 14, 2022, https://thehumaneleague.org/article/lab-grown-meat.

17. R. Bailey, "Lab-Grown Meat Promises to Cut Water and Land Use by More than 96%. Why Are US Regulators Dragging Their Feet in Approving This 'Sustainable Innovation'?" *Genetic Literacy Project,* July 16, 2021, https://geneticliteracyproject.org/2021/07/16/lab-grown-meat-promises-to-cut-water-and-land-use-by-more-than-96-why-are-us-regulators-dragging-their-feet-in-approving-this-sustainable-innovation/.

18. E. Newburger, "As the Lab-Grown Meat Industry Grows, Scientists Debate If It Could Exacerbate Climate Change," *CNBC,* October 19, 2019, https://www.cnbc.com/2019/10/19/lab-grown-meat-could-exacerbate-climate-change-scientists-say.html.

19. A. Baker, "The Cow That Could Feed the Planet," *Time,* November 2, 2021, https://time.com/6109450/sustainable-lab-grown-mosa-meat/; "Future Meat Snags Big Funding, Produces a $1.70 Chicken Breast," *Food Processing,* https://www.foodprocessing.com/ingredients/alternative-protein/news/11291601/future-meat-snags-big-funding-produces-a-170-chicken-breast.

20. D. Ewing-Chow, "Is Cultured Meat the Answer to the World's Meat Problem?" *Forbes,* June 20, 2019, https://www.forbes.com/sites/daphneewingchow/2019/06/20/is-cultured-meat-the-answer-to-the-worlds-meat-problem/#5aaf518c4468.

21. *Entry level manager salary in United States*. https://www.indeed.com/career/entry-level-manager/salaries. Accessed Oct 21, 2022. (Data updated Oct 17 2022); Also see *How much does a mid-level manager make?* https://www.glassdoor.com/Salaries/mid-level-manager-salary-SRCH_KO0,17.htm#:~:text=%24100%2C992,-%2F%20yr&text=The%20estimated%20total%20pay%20for,salaries%20collected%20from%20our%20users.

22. B. Schwartz, "Rethinking Work," *The New York Times,* August 30, 2015, pp. SR-1, SR-4. Schwartz is the author of *Why We Work* (New York: Simon & Schuster, 2015).

23. A. Rapp, "Be One, Get One: The Importance of Mentorship," *Forbes,* October 2, 2018, https://www.forbes.com/sites/yec/2018/10/02/be-one-get-one-the-importance-of-mentorship/#4a5ac5f97434.

24. "MentorcliQ Study Finds US Fortune 500 Companies with Mentoring Programs Out-Perform Those without During Pandemic," *PRWeb,* April 12, 2022, https://www.yahoo.com/now/mentorcliq-study-finds-us-fortune-173500812.html.

25. P. Drucker, reported in R. L. Knowdell, "A Model for Managers in the Future Workplace: Symphony Conductor," *The Futurist,* June–July 1998.

26. Jaser, "The Real Value of Middle Managers," *Harvard Business Review,* June 7, 2021, https://hbr.org/2021/06/the-real-value-of-middle-managers.

27. M. Haas and M. Mortensen, "The Secrets of Great Teamwork," *Harvard Business Review,* June 2016, https://hbr.org/2016/06/the-secrets-of-great-teamwork.

28. C. Dobridge, R. John, and B. Palazzo, "The Post-COVID Stock Listing Boom," *Federal Reserve,* June 17, 2022. https://www.federalreserve.gov/econres/notes/feds-notes/the-post-covid-stock-listing-boom-20220617.html.

29. "Health of the U.S. Nonprofit Sector Quarterly Review," Independent Sector, September 30, 2022, https://independentsector.org/resource/health-of-the-u-s-nonprofit-sector/.

30. "Directory of Charities and Nonprofit Organizations," *Guidestar,* https://www.guidestar.org/nonprofit-directory/public-societal-benefit/mutualmembership-benefit-organizations/1.aspx.

31. H. Mintzberg, *The Nature of Managerial Work* (New York: Harper & Row, 1973).

32. H. Mintzberg, *The Nature of Managerial Work* (New York: Harper & Row, 1973).

33. M. Porter and N. Nohria, "How CEOs Manage Time," *Harvard Business Review,* Vol. 96, No. 4 (July–August 2018), pp. 42–51.

34. H. Mintzberg, *The Nature of Managerial Work* (New York: Harper & Row, 1973).

35. Ed Reilly, quoted in W. J. Holstein, "Attention-Juggling in the High-Tech Office," *The New York Times,* June 4, 2006, sec. 3, p. 9.

36. H. Mintzberg, *The Nature of Managerial Work* (New York: Harper & Row, 1973).

37. "Survey: Remote Workers Struggle with Work-Life Boundaries, but is a Return to the Workplace the Answer?" The Conference Board, April 1, 2022, https://www.prnewswire.com/news-releases/survey-remote-workers-struggle-with-work-life-boundaries-but-is-a-return-to-the-workplace-the-answer-301515832.html.

38. J. Elias, "Google CEO Pichai Tells Employees Not to 'Equate Fun with Money' in Heated All-Hands Meeting," *CNBC,* September 26, 2022, https://www.cnbc.com/2022/09/23/google-ceo-pichai-fields-questions-on-cost-cuts-at-all-hands-meeting-.html.

39. R. L. Katz, "Skills of an Effective Administrator," *Harvard Business Review,* September–October, 1974, p. 94. Also see M. K. De Vries, "Decoding the Team Conundrum: The Eight Roles Executives Play," *Organizational Dynamics,* Vol. 36, No. 1 (2007), pp. 28–44.

40. S. Jiang, "General Motors CEO Mary Barra Shares Her Leadership Journey, Visions for the Future," *The Michigan Daily,* April 13, 2022,

https://www.michigandaily.com/news/general-motors-ceo-mary-barra-shares-her-leadership-journey-visions-for-the-future/.

41. Dan Akerson, quoted in R. Wright and H. Foy, "GM Beats Rivals to Put Woman in Driving Seat," *Financial Times,* December 11, 2013, p. 1.

42. B. Vlasic, "New GM Chief Is Company Woman, Born to It," *New York Times,* December 10, 2013, https://www.nytimes.com/2013/12/11/business/gm-names-first-female-chief-executive.html.

43. Gary Cowger, who mentored Barra, quoted in D. A. Durbin and T. Krishner, "Mary Barra, a Child of GM, Prepares to Lead It," *AP,* December 24, 2013, http://bigstory.ap.org/article/mary-barra-child-gm-prepares-lead-it (accessed February 27, 2016).

44. Mary Barra, quoted in B. Vlasic, "New GM Chief Is Company Woman, Born to It," *New York Times,* December 10, 2013, https://www.nytimes.com/2013/12/11/business/gm-names-first-female-chief-executive.html.

45. J. Bennett and S. Murray, "Longtime Insider Is GM's First Female CEO," *The Wall Street Journal,* December 11, 2013, pp. A1, A10.

46. M. Spector and C. M. Matthews, "GM Admits to Criminal Wrongdoing," *The Wall Street Journal,* September 18, 2015, pp. B1, B2. Also see M. Spector, "GM Does a U-Turn in Ignition-Switch Case Motion," *The New York Times,* October 7, 2015, p. B4. Also see G. Nagesh and J. S. Lublin, "Investors Yet to Value GM Changes," *The Wall Street Journal,* February 1, 2016, www.wsj.com/articles/investors-yet-to-value-gm-changes-1454371679.

47. A. Root, "GM CEO Mary Barra Is Leading in EVs. Just Not as Vocally as Others," *Barron's,* June 1, 2022, https://www.barrons.com/articles/gm-ceo-mary-barra-evs-interview-51654037422.

48. Dan Akerson, quoted in B. Vlasic, "New GM Chief Is Company Woman, Born to It," *New York Times,* December 10, 2013, https://www.nytimes.com/2013/12/11/business/gm-names-first-female-chief-executive.html.

49. B. Vlasic, "New GM Chief Is Company Woman, Born to It," *New York Times,* December 10, 2013, https://www.nytimes.com/2013/12/11/business/gm-names-first-female-chief-executive.html.

50. Durbin and Krishner, "Mary Barra, a Child of GM, Prepares to Lead It," *The Dallas Morning News,* December 28, 2013, https://www.dallasnews.com/business/autos/2013/12/29/mary-barra-a-child-of-gm-prepares-to-lead-it/.

51. S. Jiang, "General Motors CEO Mary Barra Shares Her Leadership Journey, Visions for the Future," *The Michigan Daily,* April 13, 2022, https://www.michigandaily.com/news/general-motors-ceo-mary-barra-shares-her-leadership-journey-visions-for-the-future/.

52. "Learning Soft Skills Is Critical to Be Hired, Says a Majority of Employers," *IBL News,* July 19, 2022, https://iblnews.org/learning-soft-skills-is-critical-to-be-hired-say-a-majority-of-employers/#:~:text=An%20overwhelming%20majority%20of%20employers,Job%20Market%20Outlook%20for%20Grads.

53. S. Edge, "Oregon Employers Say Job Seekers Lacking in Soft Skills," *The Oregonian,* July 14, 2022, https://www.oregonlive.com/education/2022/07/oregon-employers-say-job-seekers-lacking-in-soft-skills.html.

54. "Measuring the ROI of Soft Skills," *EBSCO for Corporate,* August 29, 2018. https://www.ebsco.com/blog-corporate/article/measuring-the-roi-of-soft-skills.

55. A. Kalish, "11 Cheap Online Classes You Can Take to Improve Your Interpersonal Skills," *The Muse,* https://www.themuse.com/advice/11-cheap-online-classes-you-can-take-to-improve-your-interpersonal-skills.

56. CEO recruiter, quoted in Colvin, "Catch a Rising Star," *CNN Money,* January 30, 2006, https://money.cnn.com/magazines/fortune/fortune_archive/2006/02/06/8367928/index.htm.

57. CEO recruiter, quoted in Colvin, "Catch a Rising Star," *CNN Money,* January 30, 2006, https://money.cnn.com/magazines/fortune/fortune_archive/2006/02/06/8367928/index.htm.

58. M. Csikszentmihalyi, *Flow: The Psychology of Optimal Experience* (New York: Harper Collins, 1990); *Beyond Boredom and Anxiety* (San Francisco: Jossey-Bass, 1975). Also see *Creativity: Flow and the Psychology of Discovery and Invention* (New York: Harper Perennial, 1996).

59. D. Rousseau, "Psychological and Implied Contracts in Organizations," *Employee Responsibilities and Rights Journal,* 2 (1989), pp. 121–139.

60. P. Bergeron, "For Employers, Remote and Hybrid Work Now All about Setting Expectations," *SHRM,* October 5, 2022, https://www.shrm.org/resourcesandtools/hr-topics/employee-relations/pages/for-employers-remote-and-hybrid-work-now-all-about-setting-expectations.aspx.

61. J. Turner and M. Baker, "9 Future of Work Trends Post COVID-19," *Gartner,* June 16, 2022, https://www.gartner.com/smarterwithgartner/9-future-of-work-trends-post-covid-19.

62. J. Kaplan, "Almost 70% of Workers Want a Career Change. They'd Take Better Work-Life Balance over Higher Pay," *Insider,* August 16, 2021, https://www.businessinsider.com/workers-want-work-life-balance-more-than-higher-pay-2021-8.

63. A. Kalev and F. Dobbin, "The Surprising Benefits of Work/Life Support," *Harvard Business Review,* September–October, 2022, https://hbr.org/2022/09/the-surprising-benefits-of-work-life-support.

64. N. Wade and M. Aspinall, "Back to the Workplace: Are We There Yet? Key Insights from Employers One Year into the Pandemic," *Arizona State University College of Health Solutions,* April 2021, https://www.rockefellerfoundation.org/wp-content/uploads/2021/04/ASU-Workplace-Commons-Phase-2-Report-4-28-21.pdf.

65. A. Constantino, "Your Workplace Desperately Needs This Type of Boss, Researchers Say—but Only 1 in 4 Employees Have One," *CNBC,* September 21, 2022, https://www.cnbc.com/2022/09/21/workers-need-empathetic-flexible-boss-research-indicates.html.

66. "What is Industry 4.0?" Purdue University Manufacturing Extension Partnership, March 16, 2022, https://mep.purdue.edu/news-folder/what-is-industry-4-0/.

67. J. Goldberg, "E-Commerce Sales Grew 50% to $870 Billion during the Pandemic," *Forbes,* February 18, 2022, https://www.forbes.com/sites/jasongoldberg/2022/02/18/e-commerce-sales-grew-50-to-870-billion-during-the-pandemic/?sh=2125e87a4e83.

68. Forrester Research, "112 Results for 'Disruption' in Everything," https://www.forrester.com/search?range=504001&N=204=0%200&tmtxt=+disruption&page=1 (accessed February 10, 2016).

69. K. Kirkham, "How Big Is the Digital Universe?" *100Tb,* June 28, 2019, https://blog.100tb.com/how-big-is-the-digital-universe.

70. B. Carson and K. Chaykowski, "Live Long and Prosper: How Anne Wojcicki's 23andMe Will Mine Its Giant DNA Database for Health and Wealth Biz," *Forbes,* June 6, 2019, https://www.forbes.com/sites/bizcarson/2019/06/06/23andme-dna-test-anne-wojcicki-prevention-plans-drug-development/#54c47db2494d.

71. B. Carson and K. Chaykowski, "Live Long and Prosper: How Anne Wojcicki's 23andMe Will Mine Its Giant DNA Database for Health and Wealth Biz," *Forbes,* June 6, 2019, https://www.forbes.com/sites/bizcarson/2019/06/06/23andme-dna-test-anne-wojcicki-prevention-plans-drug-development/#54c47db2494d.

72. I. Varela, "Home DNA Test Results Can Be Challenging for Consumers and Physicians," *Florida International University News,* June 2, 2022, https://news.fiu.edu/2022/home-dna-test-results-can-be-challenging-for-consumers-and-physicians.

73. R. Kroll-Zaidi, "Your DNA Test Could Send a Relative to Jail," *New York Times,* January 3, 2022, https://www.nytimes.com/2021/12/27/magazine/dna-test-crime-identification-genome.html.

74. A. Regalado, "23andMe Pulls Off Massive Crowdsourced Depression Study," *MIT Technology Review,* August 1, 2016, https://www.technologyreview.com/s/602052/23andme-pulls-off-massive-crowdsourced-depression-study/. Also see "23andMe Announces Extension of GSK Collaboration and Update on Joint Innuno-oncology Program," *23andme,* January 18, 2022, https://investors.23andme.com/news-releases/news-release-details/23andme-announces-extension-gsk-collaboration-and-update-joint.

75. A. Schaffer, "Hacks of Genetic Firms Post Risk to Patients, Experts Say," *The Washington Post,* July 21, 2022, https://www.washingtonpost.com/politics/2022/07/21/hacks-genetic-firms-pose-risk-patients-experts-say/.

76. E. Brodwin, "Genetic Testing Is the Future of Healthcare, but Many Experts Say Companies Like 23andMe Are Doing More Harm Than Good," *Business Insider,* January 12, 2019, https://www.businessinsider

.com/future-healthcare-dna-genetic-testing-23andme-2018-12.

77. B. Ross, "23andMe CEO Goes Beyond 'Wall of a White Coat,'" *Bio IT World,* January 15, 2018, http://www.bio-itworld.com/2018/01/15/23andme-ceo-goes-beyond-wall-of-a-white-coat.aspx.

78. A. Gaffney, "Can Tech Companies Disrupt Healthcare? Many Consumers Think So," *PWC,* January 16, 2019, https://www.pwc.com/us/en/industries/health-industries/library/tech-companies-disrupt-healthcare-2018.html.

79. N. Orduña, "Why Robots Won't Steal Your Job," *Harvard Business Review,* March 19, 2021, https://hbr.org/2021/03/why-robots-wont-steal-your-job.

80. S. Camarota and K. Zeigler, "Immigrant Population Hits Record 46.2 Million in November 2021," Center for Immigration Studies, December 20, 2021, https://cis.org/Camarota/Immigrant-Population-Hits-Record-462-Million-November-2021.

81. United States Census Bureau, "2017 National Population Projections Tables," https://www.census.gov/data/tables/2017/demo/popproj/2017-summary-tables.html.

82. "Nation Continues to Age as It Becomes More Diverse," Census.gov, June 30, 2022, https://www.census.gov/newsroom/press-releases/2022/population-estimates-characteristics.html. Also see "Number of People 75 and Older in the Labor Force Is Expected to Grow 96.5 Percent by 2030," U.S. Bureau of Labor Statistics, November 4, 2021, https://www.bls.gov/opub/ted/2021/number-of-people-75-and-older-in-the-labor-force-is-expected-to-grow-96-5-percent-by-2030.htm.

83. D. Simchi-Levi and P. Haren, "How the War in Ukraine Is Further Disrupting Global Supply Chains," *Harvard Business Review,* March 17, 2022.

84. K. Kistner, "Is It Time to Move on from the Houston Astros Cheating Scandal?" *Sports Illustrated*, September 20, 2022. https://www.si.com/mlb/astros/opinions/time-move-from-houston-astros-sign-stealing-cheating-scandal.

85. D. Schaffhauser, "9 in 10 Students Admit to Cheating in College, Suspect Faculty Do the Same," *Campus Technology,* February 23, 2017, https://campustechnology.com/articles/2017/02/23/9-in-10-students-admit-to-cheating-in-college-suspect-faculty-do-the-same.aspx. Also see A. Skshidlevsky, "Academic Dishonesty Statistics," *ProctorEdu,* March 30, 2022, https://proctoredu.com/blog/tpost/5dk67zrns1-academic-dishonesty-statistics#:~:text=60.8%25%20of%20polled%20college%20students,t%20feel%20guilty%20about%20it.

86. S. Day, "Reports of Cheating at Colleges Soar During the Pandemic," *NPR,* August 27, 2021, https://www.npr.org/2021/08/27/1031255390/reports-of-cheating-at-colleges-soar-during-the-pandemic.

87. "Common Reasons Students Cheat," University at Buffalo Office of Academic Integrity, https://www.buffalo.edu/academic-integrity/about/reasons-students-cheat.html.

88. D. Faubion, "20 Common Examples of Ethical Dilemmas in Nursing + How to Deal with Them," *NursingProcess.org,* 2022, https://www.nursingprocess.org/ethical-dilemma-in-nursing-examples.html#:~:text=Ethical%20dilemmas%20create%20a%20conflict,is%20what%20creates%20the%20dilemma.

89. "The 2019 US Cities Sustainable Development Report," *Sustainable Development Solutions Network,* July 8, 2019, https://www.sustainabledevelopment.report/reports/2019-us-cities-sustainable-development-report/.

90. C.L. Dubois and D.A. Dubois, "Expanding the Vision of Industrial-Organizational Psychology Contributions to Environmental Sustainability," *Industrial and Organizational Psychology,* Vol. 5, No. 4 (2012), pp. 480–483.

91. "Doing Good While Doing Well—Private Sector and SDGs," United Nations, October 2022, https://www.un.org/en/desa/doing-good-while-doing-well-private-sector-and-sdgs.

92. L. Song, X. Zhan, H. Zhang, M. Xu, J. Liu, and C. Zheng, "How Much Is Global Business Sectors Contributing to Sustainable Development Goals?" *Sustainable Horizons,* 1 (2022), p. 100012.

93. "Business Roundtable Redefines the Purpose of a Corporation to Promote 'An Economy That Serves All Americans,'" *Business Roundtable,* August 19, 2019, https://www.businessroundtable.org/business-roundtable-redefines-the-purpose-of-a-corporation-to-promote-an-economy-that-serves-all-americans.

94. J. Aaker, Stanford Graduate School of Business, quoted in C. B. Parker, "Stanford Research: The Meaningful Life Is a Road Worth Traveling," *Stanford Report,* January 1, 2014, http://news.stanford.edu/news/2014/january/meaningful-happy-life-010114.html. The study is R.F. Baumeister, K.D. Vohs, J.L. Aaker, and E.N. Garbinsky, "Some Key Differences between a Happy Life and a Meaningful Life," *Journal of Positive Psychology,* Vol. 8, No. 6 (2013), pp. 505–516.

95. M. Seligman, *Flourish* (New York: Free Press, 2011), p. 17.

96. M. Seligman, *Flourish* (New York: Free Press, 2011).

97. R. Levering, "The 100 Best Companies to Work for 2016," *Fortune,* March 15, 2016, pp. 143–165.

98. O. Nazir, J. Islam, and Z. Rahman, "Effect of CSR Participation on Employee Sense of Purpose and Experienced Meaningfulness: A Self-Determination Theory Perspective," *Journal of Hospitality and Tourism Management,* 46 (2021), pp. 123–133.

99. "Fortune 100 Best Companies to Work For," *Fortune,* 2022, https://fortune.com/best-companies/2022/.

100. "Citizen Philanthropy and Strategic Programs," *Salesforce*, https://www.salesforce.com/company/philanthropy/citizen-philanthropy-strategic-programs/.

101. "Most Attractive Employers Rankings, United States of America," Universum, https://universumglobal.com/rankings/united-states-of-america/, Accessed 10/31/2022.

102. Nace Staff, "Are College Graduates 'Career Ready'?" *National Association of Colleges and Employers,* February 19, 2018, Job Outlook 2018 survey, https://www.naceweb.org/career-readiness/competencies/are-college-graduates-career-ready/.

103. C. Flaherty, "What Employers Want," *Inside Higher Ed*, April 6, 2021, https://www.insidehighered.com/news/2021/04/06/aacu-survey-finds-employers-want-candidates-liberal-arts-skills-cite-preparedness.

104. T. D. Fishman and L. Sledge, "Reimagining Higher Education: How Colleges, Universities, Businesses, and Governments Can Prepare for a New Age of Lifelong Learning," *Deloitte,* May 22, 2014, https://www2.deloitte.com/us/en/insights/industry/public-sector/reimagining-higher-education.html.

105. M. Zao-Sanders, "Identify—and Hire—Lifelong Learners," *Harvard Business Review Digital Articles,* 2021, pp. 1–5. Available at: https://search.ebscohost.com/login.aspx?direct=true&AuthType=ip,sso&db=bth&AN=150913499&site=ehost-live&scope=site, (Accessed: 31 October 2022).

106. "Development and Validation of the NACE Career Readiness Competencies," *NACE,* 2022, https://www.naceweb.org/career-readiness/competencies/career-readiness-defined/. Also see Nace Staff, "Are College Graduates 'Career Ready'?" *National Association of Colleges and Employers,* February 19, 2018, Job Outlook 2018 survey, https://www.naceweb.org/career-readiness/competencies/are-college-graduates-career-ready/. Also see https://www.education.ne.gov/nce/ne-career-readiness-standards/; https://www.forbes.com/sites/nicholaswyman/2018/08/03/hiring-is-on-the-rise-but-are-college-grads-prepared-for-the-world-of-work/#793195644e7e.

107. J. Bughin, E. Hazan, S. Leund, P. Dahlström, A. Wiesinger, and A. Subramaniam, "Skill Shift: Automation and the Future of the Workforce," McKinsey Global Institute. Division Paper. May 2018.

108. K. Davidson, "Employers Find 'Soft Skills' Like Critical Thinking in Short Supply," *The Wall Street Journal*, August 30, 2016, https://www.wsj.com/articles/employers-find-soft-skills-like-critical-thinking-in-short-supply-1472549400.

109. L. Pinto and D. Ramalheira, "Perceived Employability of Business Graduates: The Effect of Academic Performance and Extracurricular Activities," *Journal of Vocational Behavior,* 2017, pp. 165–178.

110. "2019 Global Talent Trends," *LinkedIn Talent Solutions,* 2019, https://business.linkedin.com/talent-solutions/recruiting-tips/global-talent-trends-2019?trk=bl-po.

111. S. Dawkins, A. W. Tian, A. Newman, and A. Martin, "Psychological Ownership: A Review and Research Agenda," *Journal of Organizational Behavior*, 2017, pp. 163–183.

112. T. Williams, "7 Core Competencies Shape Career Readiness for College Graduates," January 12, 2016, https://www.goodcall.com/news/7-core-competencies-shape-career-readiness-for-college-graduates-03909.

113. M. Jay, "The Secrets of Resilience," *The Wall Street Journal*, November 11–12, 2017, pp. C1–C2.

114. R. Dellenger, "Joe Burrow's Remarkable Rise Has Been Beyond Even His Wildest Dreams," *Sports Illustrated*, November 26, 2019, https://www.si.com/college/2019/11/26/joe-burrow-lsu-tigers-nfl.

115. P. Thamel, "The Legend of Joe Burrow: From Overlooked at Ohio State to Heisman Frontrunner at LSU," *Yahoo Sports*, November 6, 2019, https://sports.yahoo.com/the-legend-of-joe-burrow-from-being-mocked-at-ohio-state-to-heisman-frontrunner-at-lsu-234857735.html?guccounter=1&guce_referrer=aHR0cHM6Ly93d3cuZ29vZ2xlLmNvbS8&guce_referrer_sig=AQAAAFr4rbmVDFABIXochjLm_cL_rUco I BqVuRuXTx8ETjMT-XE8y9SkM8IoraWI-28x0CfpN_2L5ueay0wjn9t9w3Q6dsaO4NPALTMb_F8BvBg7xdWErZphrNWOS4BsdFJYO91vNuo6PLrsKQUShvDcoU1TT_FqLTjHZU3lyFttt93O.

116. M. Jay, *Supernormal: The Untold Story of Adversity and Resilience* (New York: Hachette Book Group, 2017).

117. B. Tulgan, *Bridging the Soft Skills Gap* (Hoboken, NJ: John Wiley, 2015). Also see L. Gillin, *10 Soft Skills You Need* (Dover, DE: Global Courseware, 2015).

118. B. J. Fogg, "On the Journey to New Habits, Take Tiny Steps," *The Wall Street Journal*, January 5, 2020, https://www.wsj.com/articles/on-the-journey-to-new-habits-take-tiny-steps-11577985523. Also see L. MacLellan, "A Stanford University Behavior Scientist's Elegant Three-Step Method for Creating New Habits," *Quartz*, January 4, 2017, https://qz.com/877795/how-to-create-new-good-habits-according-to-stanford-psychologist-b-j-fogg/.

CHAPTER 2

1. C. M. Christensen and M. E. Raynor, "Why Hard-Nosed Executives Should Care about Management Theory," *Harvard Business Review*, September 2003, p. 68.

2. H. Aguinis, and M. Cronin, "It's the Theory, Stupid," *Organizational Psychology Review*, February 2022, pp. 1–20.

3. A. Hsu, "Starbucks Workers Have Unionized at Record Speed; Many Fear Retaliation Now," *NPR*, October 2, 2022, https://www.npr.org/2022/10/02/1124680518/starbucks-union-busting-howard-schultz-nlrb#:~:text=Press-.

4. Tom Peters, quoted in J. A. Byrne, "The Man Who Invented Management," *BusinessWeek*, November 28, 2005.

5. C. Brooks, "What Your Business Can Learn from Peter Drucker," *Business.com*, September 1, 2022, https://www.business.com/articles/management-theory-of-peter-drucker/.

6. "Great Place to Work® Names Wegmans One of the Fortune 100 Best Companies to Work For® in 2022, Ranking #3," *Wegmans*, April 11, 2022, https://www.wegmans.com/news-media/press-releases/great-place-to-work-names-wegmans-one-of-the-fortune-100-best-companies-to-work-for-in-2022-ranking-3/.

7. "Employee Satisfaction," *Wegmans*, https://jobs.wegmans.com/employee-satisfaction-at-wegmans (accessed November 14, 2022).

8. E. Crowe, "Publix, Wegmans Keep Winning in Customer Service, Community Care," *Progressive Grocer*, September 1, 2022, https://www.progressivegrocer.com/publix-wegmans-keep-winning-customer-service-community-care.

9. H. Aguinis, and M. Cronin, "It's the Theory, Stupid," *Organizational Psychology Review*, February 2022, pp. 1–20.

10. C. M. Christensen and M. E. Raynor, "Why Hard-Nosed Executives Should Care about Management Theory," *Harvard Business Review*, September 2003, p. 68.

11. S. L. Montgomery and D. Chirot, quoted in F. Zakaria, "Something in the Air," *The New York Times Book Review*, August 23, 2015, pp. 14–15. Montgomery and Chirot are authors of *The Shape of the New: Four Big Ideas and How They Made the Modern World* (Princeton, NJ: Princeton University Press, 2015).

12. G. D. Babcock and R. Trautschold, *The Taylor System in Franklin Management*, 2nd ed. (New York: Engineering Magazine Co., 1917).

13. M. Day, "In Amazon's Flagship Fulfillment Center, the Machines Run the Show," *Bloomberg*, September 21, 2021, https://www.bloomberg.com/news/features/2021-09-21/inside-amazon-amzn-flagship-fulfillment-center-where-machines-run-the-show.

14. L. Held, "Profile—Lillian Gilbreth," *Psychology's Feminist Voices*, http://www.feministvoices.com/lillian-gilbreth/ (accessed December 11, 2022).

15. L. Koppes, "Biography of Lilian Evelyn Moller Gilbreth," *Society for the Psychology of Women*, https://www.apadivisions.org/division-35/about/heritage/lilian-gilbreth-biography (accessed December 11, 2022).

16. S. Caramela, "The Management Theory of Frank and Lillian Gilbreth," *Business.com*, February 23, 2018, https://www.business.com/articles/management-theory-of-frank-and-lillian-gilbreth/.

17. L.C. Prieto and T.A. Phipps, "Re-Discovering Charles Clinton Spaulding's 'The Administration of Big Business,'" *Journal of Management History*, 2016, pp. 73–90.

18. L.C. Prieto and T.A. Phipps, "Re-Discovering Charles Clinton Spaulding's 'The Administration of Big Business,'" *Journal of Management History*, 2016, p. 82.

19. N. Bloom, R. Sadun, and J. Van Reenen, "Does Management Really Work?" *Harvard Business Review*, November 2012, pp. 76–82.

20. B. Rice, "The Hawthorne Defect: Persistence of a Flawed Theory," *Psychology Today*, February 1982, pp. 70–74.

21. A. Maslow, "A Theory of Human Motivation," *Psychological Review*, July 1943, pp. 370–396.

22. K. Cherry, "How Maslow's Famous Hierarchy of Needs Explains Human Motivation." *Verywell Mind*, December 3, 2019, https://www.verywellmind.com/what-is-maslows-hierarchy-of-needs-4136760.

23. D. McGregor, *The Human Side of Enterprise* (New York: McGraw Hill, 1960).

24. C. Thiel, J.M. Bonner, J. Bush, D. Welsh, and N. Garud, "Monitoring Employees Makes Them More Likely to Break Rules," *Harvard Business Review*, June 27, 2022, https://hbr.org/2022/06/monitoring-employees-makes-them-more-likely-to-break-rules; D. Leonhardt, "You're Being Watched," *The New York Times*, August 15, 2022, https://www.nytimes.com/2022/08/15/briefing/workers-tracking-productivity-employers.html. J. Kantor, A. Sundaram, A. Aufrichtig, and R. Taylor, "The Rise of the Worker Productivity Score," *The New York Times*, August 15, 2022, https://www.nytimes.com/interactive/2022/08/14/business/worker-productivity-tracking.html.

25. D. Herbst and D. Walters, "PEOPLE's 100 Companies That Care 2022: Meet the Employers Putting Their Communities First," *People*, August 31, 2022. https://people.com/human-interest/people-100-companies-that-care-2022/.

26. R. Bean, "Moneyball 20 Years Later: A Progress Report on Data and Analytics in Professional Sports," *Forbes*, September 18, 2022, https://www.forbes.com/sites/randybean/2022/09/18/moneyball-20-years-later-a-progress-report-on-data-and-analytics-in-professional-sports/?sh=56b124b1773d.

27. L. Adler, "A World Series That Showcases How Baseball Decisions Are Made in the Data Era," *The Wall Street Journal*, November 4, 2022, https://www.wsj.com/articles/world-series-astros-phillies-11667565589?mod=Searchresults_pos3&page=1.

28. A. Ricky, "How Data Analysis in Sports Is Changing the Game," *Forbes*, January 31, 2019, https://www.forbes.com/sites/forbestechcouncil/2019/01/31/how-data-analysis-in-sports-is-changing-the-game/#3622f0773f7b.

29. C. Isidore, "Why the Global Supply Chain Mess Is Getting so Much Worse," *CNN Business*, March 30, 2022, https://www.cnn

.com/2022/03/30/business/global-supply-chain; N. Boudette, "G.M. Reports Jump in Profit on Strong Sales," *The New York Times,* October 25, 2022, https://www.nytimes.com/2022/10/25/business/general-motors-earnings.html.

30. J. Pfeffer and R. I. Sutton, "Profiting from Evidence-Based Management," *Strategy & Leadership*, Vol. 34, No. 2 (2006), pp. 35–42. Also see J. Pfeffer and R. I. Sutton, "Evidence-Based Management," *Harvard Business Review*, January 2006, pp. 63–74.

31. M. Samuels, "Novartis Uses Snowflake to Bring Life-Saving Medicines to Market Quicker," *Diginomica,* April 4, 2022, https://diginomica.com/novartis-uses-snowflake-bring-life-saving-medicines-market-quicker; M. Iansiti and S. Nadella, "Democratizing Transformation," *Harvard Business Review,* May 1, 2022, https://hbr.org/2022/05/democratizing-transformation.

32. "Peloton (PTON)—Market Capitalization," *Companiesmarketcap,* https://companiesmarketcap.com/peloton/marketcap/; R. Duprey, "Peloton Makes 3 More Acquisitions," *The Motley Fool,* March 23, 2021, https://www.fool.com/investing/2021/03/23/peloton-makes-3-more-acquisitions/; N. Gomes and K Deka, "Two Peloton Co-Founders Leave amid Massive Restructuring," *Reuters,* September 13, 2022, https://www.reuters.com/business/retail-consumer/pelotons-john-foley-step-down-executive-chairs-role-2022-09-12/.

33. "Job Openings and Labor Turnover Survey News Release," *U.S. Bureau of Labor Statistics,* November 1, 2022, https://www.bls.gov/news.release/jolts.htm.

34. P. Wellener, "Deloitte and the Manufacturing Institute: Big Gains in Perceptions of US Manufacturing as Innovative, Critical and High Tech—Press Release," *Deloitte,* March 30, 2022, https://www2.deloitte.com/us/en/pages/about-deloitte/articles/press-releases/deloitte-and-the-manufacturing-institute-big-gains-in-perceptions-of-us-manufacturing-as-innovative-critical-high-tech.html.

35. J. Wills, "Manufacturing Job Outlook 2022," *DAVIS Companies,* January 19, 2022, https://www.daviscos.com/manufacturing-job-outlook-2022/.

36. "How Manufacturers Can Hire Young Talent to Survive the Great Resignation," *USC Consulting Group,* May 23, 2022, https://www.usccg.com/blog/how-manufacturers-can-hire-young-talent-to-survive-the-great-resignation/.

37. K. Tornone, "Learning Opportunities Are a Top Factor in Gen Z's Job Hunt, LinkedIn Says," *HR Dive,* March 9, 2022, https://www.hrdive.com/news/learning-opportunities-are-a-top-factor-in-gen-zs-job-hunt-linkedin-says/620050/.

38. A. Garvin, "Building a Learning Organization," *Harvard Business Review*, July/August 1993, pp. 78–91; and T. Kelly, "Measuring Informal Learning: Encourage a Learning Culture and Track It!" *Training Industry,* March 21, 2014, www.trainingindustry.com/professional-education/articles/measuring-informal-learning.aspx.

39. M. Malik, S. Sarwar, and S. Orr, "Agile Practices and Performance: Examining the Role of Psychological Empowerment," *International Journal of Project Management,* 2021, pp. 10–20, https://doi.org/10.1016/j.ijproman.2020.09.002.

40. J. Törmänen, R.P. Hämäläinen, and E. Saarinen, "On the Systems Intelligence of a Learning Organization: Introducing a New Measure," *Human Resource Development Quarterly*, 2022, pp. 249–272.

41. S. Kobylinski, "The 10 Most Innovative Companies in Data Science for 2022," *Fast Company,* March 8, 2022, https://www.fastcompany.com/90724383/most-innovative-companies-data-science-2022/; E. Sayegh, "A Little Taste of Old Normal—The Benefits of a Virtual Commute," *Forbes,* February 3, 2021. https://www.forbes.com/sites/emilsayegh/2021/02/03/a-little-taste-of-old-normal--virtual-commute/?sh=ae284fa6387d. W. Antonelli, "How to Use 'Together Mode' in Microsoft Teams and Share the Same Background with Your Entire Call," *Business Insider,* December 17, 2021, https://www.businessinsider.com/guides/tech/teams-together-mode.

42. W. Aghina, C. Handscomb, O. Salo, and S. Thaker, "The Impact of Agility: How to Shape Your Organization to Compete," *McKinsey,* May 25, 2021, https://www.mckinsey.com/capabilities/people-and-organizational-performance/our-insights/the-impact-of-agility-how-to-shape-your-organization-to-compete.

43. J. Pfeffer, and P. Jeffrey, *The Human Equation: Building Profits by Putting People First* (Boston: Harvard Business Press, 1998); J. C. Collins and J. I. Porras, *Built to Last: Successful Habits of Visionary Companies* (New York: Harper Business, 2002).

44. R.A. Posthuma, M.C. Campion, M. Masimova, and M.A. Campion, "A High Performance Work Practices Taxonomy," *Journal of Management*, Vol. 39, No. 5 (2013), pp. 1184–1220.

45. J. Combs, Y. Liu, A. Hall, and D. Ketchen, "How Much do High-Performance Work Practices Matter? A Meta-Analysis of Their Effects on Organizational Performance," *Personnel Psychology,* 2006, pp. 501–528; G. Saridakis, Y. Lai, and C.L. Cooper, "Exploring the Relationship between HRM and Firm Performance: A Meta-Analysis of Longitudinal Studies," *Human Resource Management Review,* 2017, pp. 87–96; F. Obeng, Y. Zhu, P.E. Quansah, A.H. Ntarmah, and E. Cobbinah, "High-Performance Work Practices and Turnover Intention: Investigating the Mediating Role of Employee Morale and the Moderating Role of Psychological Capital," *SAGE Open,* 2021, pp. 1–22; M. Sheehan and T. Garavan, "High-Performance Work Practices and Labour Productivity: A Six Wave Longitudinal Study of UK Manufacturing and Service SMEs," *The International Journal of Human Resource Management,* 2022, pp. 3353–3386.

46. "Enterprise Named Top Entry-Level Employer by CollegeGrad.com," https://www.enterpriseholdings.com/news-stories/news-stories-archive/2022/03/enterprise-named-top-entry-level-employer.html; "Whole Benefits," https://careers.wholefoodsmarket.com/global/en/benefits; "The Power of Empowerment," *Ritz-Carlton Leadership Center,* March 19, 2019, https://ritzcarltonleadershipcenter.com/2019/03/19/the-power-of-empowerment/.

47. "The Ritz-Carlton Gold Standards," https://www.ritzcarlton.com/en/about/gold-standards.

48. M. Posner, "How Fashion Week Should Really Embrace Sustainability," *Forbes,* September 8, 2022, https://www.forbes.com/sites/michaelposner/2022/09/08/at-fashion-week-the-apparel-industry-needs-to-redefine-sustainability/?sh=6d5a9b4a5e1c.

49. D. Stofleth, "A Short History of Sustainable Development," *Rethinking Prosperity,* May 20, 2015, http://rethinkingprosperity.org/a-short-history-of-sustainable-development/.

50. "What Is Sustainability?" *UCLA Sustainability*, https://www.sustain.ucla.edu/about-us/what-is-sustainability/ (accessed November 18, 2022).

51. M. Porter and C. van der Linde, "Green and Competitive: Ending the Stalemate," *Harvard Business Review*, 1995, https://hbr.org/1995/09/green-and-competitive-ending-the-stalemate.

52. F. Urso, "More CEOs Consider Sustainability to Be a Top Challenge, Study Says," *Reuters,* May 10, 2022, https://www.reuters.com/business/sustainable-business/more-ceos-reckon-sustainability-top-challenge-study-2022-05-10/#:~:text=Of%20the%20CEOs%20surveyed%2C%20more.

53. J. Klein, "Disney, Mastercard and Zendesk Tap Industry Veterans for Sustainability Roles," *GreenBiz,* July 7, 2022, https://www.greenbiz.com/article/disney-mastercard-and-zendesk-tap-industry-veterans-sustainability-roles.

54. A.L. Kristof-Brown, R.D. Zimmerman, and E.C. Johnson, "Consequences of Individuals' Fit at Work: A Meta-Analysis of Person-Job, Person-Organization, Person-Group, and Person-Supervisor Fit," *Personnel Psychology*, Summer 2005, pp. 281–342.

55. Good.Co Team, "Job Seekers: Stop Creeping on Your Ex Online and Start Doing This Instead," February 19, 2014, https://good.co/blog/job-seekers-digital-research.

56. This list was partially based on M. Yate, "Interview Strategies for Recent Graduates," *HR Magazine*, Spring 2019; H. Huhman, "7 Things to Research Before Any Job Interview," August 29, 2014, https://www.glassdoor.com/blog/7-research-job-interview; Good.Co Team, "20 Things Recruiters Want, But Won't Tell You (HR Insider)," July 28, 2014, https://good.co/blog/things-recruiters-want-from-candidates-interview.

CHAPTER 3

1. S. Ladika, "HR Ethical Dilemmas," *HR Magazine,* Winter, 2021, https://www.shrm.org/hr-today/news/hr-magazine/winter2021/pages/hr-ethical-dilemmas.aspx.
2. E. Wetherell and R. Pendell, "Only 4 in 10 Employees Report Unethical Behavior—Here's How to Fix It," *Gallup,* March 19, 2022, https://www.gallup.com/workplace/390635/employees-report-unethical-behavior-fix.aspx.
3. R.M. Kidder, *Moral Courage,* (New York: HarperCollins, 2005), p. 74. Also see M. Howard and J. Cogswell, "The Left Side of Courage: Three Exploratory Studies on the Antecedents of Social Courage," *The Journal of Positive Psychology,* January 2018, pp. 1–17; M. Howard, J. Farr, A. Grandey, and M. Gutworth, "The Creation of the Workplace Social Courage Scale (WCS): An Investigation of Internal Consistency, Psychometric Properties, Validity, and Utility," *Journal of Business and Psychology,* 2016, pp. 1–18.
4. R.M. Kidder, *Moral Courage,* (New York: HarperCollins, 2005), p. 74.
5. D. Comer and L. Sekerka, "Keep Calm and Carry On (Ethically): Durable Moral Courage in the Workplace," *Human Resource Management Review,* Vol. 29 (2018), pp. 116–130.
6. "Redefining Corporate Purpose," *Washington Post Live,* November 25, 2019, https://www.washingtonpost.com/washington-post-live/2019/11/25/transcript-redefining-corporate-purpose/.
7. W. Tate and L. Bals, "Achieving Shared Triple Bottom Line (TBL) Value Creation: Toward a Social Resource-Based View (SRBV) of the Firm," *Journal of Business Ethics,* Vol. 152 (2018), pp. 803–826.
8. "Generation Z: Latest Characteristics, Research, and Facts," *Business Insider,* https://www.businessinsider.com/generation-z-facts.
9. G. Staglin, "The Future Of Work Depends On Supporting Gen Z," *Forbes,* July 22, 2022, https://www.forbes.com/sites/onemind/2022/07/22/the-future-of-work-depends-on-supporting-gen-z/?sh=630715d7447a.
10. K. Jahns, "The Environment Is Gen Z's No. 1 Concern—and Some Companies Are Taking Advantage of That," CNBC, August 11, 2021, https://www.cnbc.com/2021/08/10/the-environment-is-gen-zs-no-1-concern-but-beware-of-greenwashing.html; S. Kiderlin, "Overwhelming Majority of Gen Z Workers Would Quit Their Jobs over Company Values, LinkedIn Data Says," CNBC, April 20, 2023, https://www.cnbc.com/2023/04/20/majority-of-gen-z-would-quit-their-jobs-over-company-values-linkedin.html.
11. K. Morgan, "The Search for 'Meaning' at Work," *BBC,* September 7, 2022, https://www.bbc.com/worklife/article/20220902-the-search-for-meaning-at-work.
12. P. Charan Shubham and L. Murty, "Secondary Stakeholder Pressures and Organizational Adoption of Sustainable Operations Practices: The Mediating Role of Primary Stakeholders," *Business Strategy and the Environment,* Vol. 27 (2018), pp. 910–923.
13. A. Scott, "Hilton Named the #1 Company to Work For in the U.S.," Hilton, February 14, 2019, https://newsroom.hilton.com/corporate/news/employees-rank-hilton-the-best-place-to-work-in-the-us.
14. "Fortune 100 Best Companies to Work For," *Fortune,* https://fortune.com/ranking/best-companies/.
15. "Hilton: Company Overview," *Great Place to Work,* https://www.greatplacetowork.com/worlds-best-profile/hilton.
16. "What Is a Sole Proprietorship?" *Business Dictionary,* https://businessdictionary.info/what-is-a-sole-proprietorship-2/.
17. Associated Press, "Barrio Brewing Owners Bestow Company to Their Employees," *U.S. News,* December 17, 2019, https://www.usnews.com/news/best-states/arizona/articles/2019-12-17/barrio-brewing-owners-bestow-company-to-their-employees.
18. "Governance Documents," *Meta Investor Relations,* https://investor.fb.com/leadership-and-governance/default.aspx.
19. A. Malik, "Amazon Will Soon Start Charging Delivery Fees on Fresh Grocery Orders under $150," *Tech Crunch,* January 30, 2023, https://techcrunch.com/2023/01/30/amazon-charging-delivery-fees-fresh-grocery-orders-under-150/.
20. N. Alund, "Does Your local Walmart Offer Drone Delivery? See the List of 36 Stores That Do Here," *USA Today,* February 15, 2023, https://www.usatoday.com/story/money/2023/02/14/walmart-drone-delivery-locations-states/11254959002/.
21. A. Faguy, "Delivery Wars: Target Will Spend $100 Million to Expand Next-Day Delivery—And Compete with Amazon and Walmart," *Forbes,* February 22, 2023, https://www.forbes.com/sites/anafaguy/2023/02/22/delivery-wars-target-will-spend-100-million-to-expand-next-day-delivery-and-compete-with-amazon-and-walmart/?sh=5d4b74436880.
22. J. Li, J. Xia, and E. Zajac, "On the Duality of Political and Economic Stakeholder Influence on Firm Innovation Performance: Theory and Evidence from Chinese Firms," *Strategic Management Journal,* Vol. 39 (2018), pp. 193–216.
23. J. Quick, "Running List of Cars with Spec Changes, due to Chip Shortage," *Car Expert,* July 21, 2022, https://www.carexpert.com.au/car-news/running-list-of-cars-with-spec-changes-due-to-chip-shortage.
24. P. Hong, E. Peterson, B. Kapoor, and D. DeLong, "The Crisis in Ukraine Spells More Trouble for Semiconductor Supply," *MIT Sloan Management Review,* May 10, 2022, https://sloanreview.mit.edu/article/russias-invasion-spells-more-trouble-for-semiconductor-supply/.
25. B. Preston, "Global Chip Shortage Makes It Tough to Buy Certain Cars," *Consumer Reports,* June 13, 2022, https://www.consumerreports.org/cars/buying-a-car/global-chip-shortage-makes-it-tough-to-buy-certain-cars-a8160576456/.
26. A. Kantrowitz, "The Direct-to-Consumer Craze Is Slamming into Reality," *CNBC,* March 14, 2022, https://www.cnbc.com/2022/03/14/the-direct-to-consumer-craze-is-slamming-into-reality.html.
27. T. Ryan-Charleton, D.R. Gnyawali, and N. Oliveira, "Strategic Alliance Outcomes: Consolidation and New Directions," *Academy of Management Annals,* Vol. 16, No. 2 (2022), pp. 719–758.
28. D. Lavie, R. Lunnan, and B.M.T. Truong, "How Does a Partner's Acquisition Affect the Value of the Firm's Alliance with That Partner?" *Strategic Management Journal,* Vol. 43, No. 9 (2022), pp. 1897–1926.
29. "Warner Music's 'Saylists' Use Pop Songs as Speech Therapy," Muse by Clio, n.d., https://musebycl.io/music/warner-musics-saylists-use-pop-songs-speech-therapy.
30. Bureau of Labor Statistics, "Union Members—2022," January 19, 2023, https://www.bls.gov/news.release/pdf/union2.pdf; D.
31. "Worker-Participation EU," https://www.worker-participation.eu/National-Industrial-Relations/Across-Europe/Trade-Unions2 (accessed March 4, 2023); Also see J. Goldstein, "How the US Compares to the World on Unionization," *Atlantic Council,* October 28, 2022, https://www.atlanticcouncil.org/blogs/econographics/how-the-us-compares-to-the-world-on-unionization/.
32. V. Baid and V. Jayaraman, "Amplifying and Promoting the "S" in ESG Investing: The Case for Social Responsibility in Supply Chain Financing," *Managerial Finance,* 2022 (ahead-of-print).
33. "Drone Operations," *Government Accountability Office,* https://www.gao.gov/drone-operations.
34. "Drones," *Federal Aviation Administration,* https://www.faa.gov/uas.
35. R. Ramirez, L. Paddison, I. Kappeler, and L. Isaac, "Climate Activist Greta Thunberg Detained by Police in Germany at Coal Mine Protest," *CNN,* January 17, 2023, https://www.cnn.com/2023/01/17/us/greta-thunberg-detained-germany-climate/index.html.
36. "News: Unemployment Is at Its Lowest Level in 54 years," *U.S. Department of Commerce,* February 3, 2023, https://www.commerce.gov/news/blog/2023/02/news-unemployment-its-lowest-level-54-years#:~:text=Today%2C%20it%20is%20just%203.4,they%20were%20seven%20months%20ago.
37. P. Gourinchas, "Global Economy to Slow Further Amid Signs of Resilience and China Re-opening," *International Monetary Fund,* January 3, 2023, https://www.imf.org/en/Blogs/Articles/2023/01/30/global-economy-to-slow-further-amid-signs-of-resilience-and-china-re-opening.
38. "International Trade in Goods and Services," *Bureau of Economic Analysis,* https://www.bea.gov/data/intl-trade-investment/international-trade-goods-and-services#:~:text=The%20difference%20between%20

the%20exports%20and%20imports%20is%20the%20trade%20balance (accessed March 31, 2023).

39. J. Tankersley, "Trump Hates the Trade Deficit. Most Economists Don't," *The New York Times,* March 5, 2018.

40. N. Hiller, R. Piccolo, and S. Zaccaro, "Economic Assumptions and Economic Context: Implications for the Study of Leadership," *The Leadership Quarterly,* Vol. 31, No. 3 (2020).

41. V. Pereira, E. Hadjielias, M. Christofi, and D. Vrontis, "A Systematic Literature Review on the Impact of Artificial Intelligence on Workplace Outcomes: A Multi-Process Perspective," *Human Resource Management Review,* Vol. 33, No. 1 (2023), p. 100857.

42. "The Future of Time," *Adobe,* March 2022, https://www.adobe.com/content/dam/dx-dc/us/en/webinars/the-future-of-time/Future-of-time-hybrid-worklplace.pdf.

43. L. Gratton, "Redesigning How We Work," *Harvard Business Review,* Vol. 101, No. 2 (2023), pp. 68–75.

44. B. Anderson and S. Patton, "In a Hybrid World, Your Tech Defines Employee Experience," *Harvard Business Review Digital Articles,* 2022, pp. 1–6.

45. W. Yakowicz, "Where Is Cannabis Legal: A Guide to All 50 States," *Forbes,* January 6, 2023, https://www.forbes.com/sites/willyakowicz/2023/01/06/where-is-cannabis-legal-a-guide-to-all-50-states/?sh=63bafd6c1619; Also see I. Dorbian, "Support for Marijuana Legalization Remains at Record High Says New Poll," *Forbes,* November 11, 2022, https://www.forbes.com/sites/irisdorbian/2022/11/17/support-for-marijuana-legalization-remains-at-record-high-says-new-poll/?sh=3c4346462a2e.

46. S. Algar, "*Marijuana Products Are Coming to Select Florida Circle K Gas Stations,*" New York Post, October 21, 2022, https://nypost.com/2022/10/21/marijuana-products-are-coming-to-select-florida-circle-k-gas-stations/.

47. A. Geiger and G. Livingston, "8 Facts about Love and Marriage in America," Pew Research Center, February 13, 2019, https://www.pewresearch.org/fact-tank/2019/02/13/8-facts-about-love-and-marriage/. Also see L. Carroll, "Birth Rate in U.S. Falls to Lowest Level in 32 Years, CDC Says," *NBC News,* May 15, 2019, https://www.nbcnews.com/health/womens-health/birth-rate-u-s-falls-lowest-level-32-years-cdc-n1005696; J. Wood, "The United States Divorce Rate Is Dropping, Thanks to Millennials," *World Economic Forum,* October 5, 2018, https://www.weforum.org/agenda/2018/10/divorce-united-states-dropping-because-millennials/; K. Turner, "Secularism Is on the Rise, but Americans Are Still Finding Community and Purpose in Spirituality," *Vox,* June 11, 2019, https://www.vox.com/first-person/2019/6/4/18644764/church-religion-atheism-secularism.

48. W. Shi, S. Pathak, L. Song, and R. Hoskisson, "The Adoption of Chief Diversity Officers among S&P 500 Firms: Institutional, Resource Dependence, and Upper Echelons Accounts," *Human Resource Management,* Vol. 57 (2018), pp. 83–96.

49. T. Young, "Judge Rules Trump Administration Can't Expand Coal Leasing on Public Lands without Analyzing Environmental and Economic Costs to the Public," *Sierra Club,* April 22, 2019, https://www.sierraclub.org/press-releases/2019/04/judge-rules-trump-administration-can-t-expand-coal-leasing-public-lands.

50. C. Day and T. Parti, "Democrats Propose Trillions in Spending on Climate-Focused Plans to Restructure Economy," *The Wall Street Journal,* September 4, 2019, https://www.wsj.com/articles/democrats-propose-trillions-in-spending-on-climate-focused-plans-to-restructure-economy-11567591200.

51. "Lawyers per Capita by Country 2023," *World Population Review,* https://worldpopulationreview.com/country-rankings/lawyers-per-capita-by-country.

52. S. Karra, "Why Businesses Benefit from Being on TikTok," *Forbes,* December 9, 2022, https://www.forbes.com/sites/forbesbusinesscouncil/2022/12/09/why-businesses-benefit-from-being-on-tiktok/?sh=1dde8c736430.

53. S. Bhaimiya, "Here's a Full List of the US States That Have Introduced Full or Partial TikTok Bans on Government Devices over Mounting Security Concerns," *Business Insider,* January 15, 2023, https://www.businessinsider.in/tech/news/hereaposs-a-full-list-of-the-us-states-that-have-introduced-full-or-partial-tiktok-bans-on-government-devices-over-mounting-security-concerns/slidelist/97007236.cms.

54. S. Bhaimiya, "Here's a Full List of the US States That Have Introduced Full or Partial TikTok Bans on Government Devices over Mounting Security Concerns," *Business Insider,* January 15, 2023, https://www.businessinsider.com/tiktok-banned-us-government-state-devices-2023-1.

55. O. Royle, "Founders and CEOs Look at a Possible TikTok Ban in Fear: 'No Other Platform Does This as Successfully'," *Fortune,* March 28, 2023, https://fortune.com/2023/03/28/founders-ceos-possible-tiktok-ban-fear-no-other-platform-does-this-as-successfully/.

56. N. DeCosta-Klipa, "MIT Reveals How Much Money They Got from Jeffrey Epstein, and Pledges to Donate It to Charity," *Boston.com,* August 23, 2019, https://www.boston.com/news/education/2019/08/23/mit-epstein-money. Also see J. Bacon, C. McCoy, and J. Ortiz, "Billionaire Jeffrey Epstein Pleads Not Guilty to Sex-Trafficking Claims That 'Shock the Conscience,'" *USA Today,* July 10, 2019, https://www.usatoday.com/story/news/nation/2019/07/08/jeffrey-epstein-court-sex-trafficking-charges/1671254001/.

57. "Global Business Ethics Survey: The State of Ethics & Compliance in the Workplace," *Ethics & Compliance Initiative,* https://www.ethics.org/global-business-ethics-survey/.

58. L.T. Hosmer, *The Ethics of Management* (Homewood, IL: Irwin, 1987). Also see M.E. Brown, R.M. Vogel, and M. Akben, "Ethical Conflict: Conceptualization, Measurement, and an Examination of Consequences," *Journal of Applied Psychology,* Vol. 107, No. 7 (2022), p. 1130.

59. B.F. Liu et. al., "When Crises Hit Home: How U.S. Higher Education Leaders Navigate Values during Uncertain Times," *Journal of Business Ethics,* Vol. 179, No. 2 (2022), pp. 353–368.

60. S. Marken, "U.S. Adults Split on Companies Taking Political, Social Stances," *Gallup,* January 10, 2023, https://news.gallup.com/opinion/gallup/405656/adults-split-companies-taking-political-social-stances.aspx.

61. K. Radde and S. McCammon, "Walgreens Won't Sell Abortion Pills in Red States That Threatened Legal Action," *NPR,* March 4, 2023, https://www.npr.org/2023/03/04/1161143595/walgreens-abortion-pill-mifepristone-republican-threat-legal-action.

62. M. Zahn, "Companies Increasingly Using Politics in Marketing, but There Are Risks: Experts," *ABC News,* August 23, 2022, https://abcnews.go.com/Business/companies-increasingly-politics-marketing-risks-experts/story?id=88238066.

63. K.M. Klimczak et al., "How to Deter Financial Misconduct If Crime Pays?" *Journal of Business Ethics,* Vol. 179, No. 1 (2022), pp. 205–222.

64. T. Schick and I. Hwang, "The US Has Spent More Than &2B on a Plan to Save Salmon. The Fish Are Vanishing Anyway," *OPB,* May 24, 2022, https://www.opb.org/article/2022/05/24/pacific-northwest-federal-salmon-hatcheries-declining-returns/.

65. B. Van Voris, "SAC's Mathew Martoma Seeks Freedom in Appeals Court Bid," *Bloomberg Businessweek,* October 28, 2015, www.bloomberg.com/news/articles/2015-10-28/sac-s-mathew-martoma-seeks-freedom-in-appeals-court-bid.

66. "North-Central Florida Blimp Company Executive Sentenced to over Five Years in Federal Prison for COVID-19 Relief Fraud," *Department of Justice: United States Attorney's Office—Northern District of Florida,* January 31, 2023, https://www.justice.gov/usao-ndfl/pr/north-central-florida-blimp-company-executive-sentenced-over-five-years-federal-prison.

67. S. Morgan and M. Loizzo, "Florida Blimp Executive, Relative of Former State Lawmaker, Sentenced to Federal Prison in Pandemic Fraud Case," *The Gainesville Sun,* February 1, 2023, https://www.gainesville.com/story/news/crime/2023/02/01/florida-businessman-gets-5-year-prison-sentence-in-covid-19-fraud-case/69861805007/.

68. F. Norris, "Goodbye to Reforms of 2002," *The New York Times,* November 6, 2009, pp. B1, B6.

69. "Has Sarbanes-Oxley Failed?" *The New York Times,* July 24, 2012, www.nytimes.com/roomfordebate/2012/07/24/has-sarbanes-oxley-failed?

action=click&module=Search&region=searchResults%230&version=&url=http%3A%2F%2Fquery.nytimes.com%2Fsearch%2Fsitesearch%2F%23%2FSarbOx%2F (accessed April 3, 2023); Also see "Sarbanes Oxley Act (SOX) 18 U.S.C. §1514A," *Whistleblowers.gov,* https://www.whistleblowers.gov/statutes/sox_amended (accessed April 3, 2023).

70. News Release, "US Department of Labor Orders ExxonMobil to Reinstate Terminated Employees Suspected of Leaking Information to *Wall Street Journal,*" *U.S. Department of Labor,* October 7, 2022, https://www.dol.gov/newsroom/releases/osha/osha20221007.

71. L. Kohlberg, "Moral Stages and Moralization: The Cognitive Developmental Approach," in T. Lickona, ed., *Moral Development and Behavior: Theory, Research, and Social Issues* (New York: Holt, Rinehart and Winston, 1976), pp. 31–53. Also see J. W. Graham, "Leadership, Moral Development and Citizenship Behavior," *Business Ethics Quarterly,* January 1995, pp. 43–54.

72. M. Mitchell, M. Baer, M. Ambrose, R. Folger, and N. Palmer, "Cheating under Pressure: A Self-Protection Model of Workplace Cheating Behavior," *Journal of Applied Psychology,* January 2018, p. 54.

73. "Largest Penalty Ever Imposed by SEC Against an Audit Firm," *SEC,* June 28, 2022, https://www.sec.gov/news/press-release/2022-114.

74. See "8 Astonishing Stats on Academic Cheating," *Open Education Database,* http://oedb.org/ilibrarian/8-astonishing-stats-on-academic-cheating.

75. D. Newton, "Looking the Other Way on Cheating in College," *Forbes,* August 31, 2019, https://www.forbes.com/sites/dereknewton/2019/08/31/looking-the-other-way-on-cheating-in-college/#27a03fb392b6. Also see K. Weiss, "Focus on Ethics Can Curb Cheating, Colleges Find," *Los Angeles Times,* February 15, 2000, https://www.latimes.com/archives/la-xpm-2000-feb-15-mn-64455-story.html.

76. M. Mitchell, M. Baer, M. Ambrose, R. Folger, and N. Palmer, "Cheating under Pressure: A Self-Protection Model of Workplace Cheating Behavior," *Journal of Applied Psychology,* January 2018, pp. 54–73.

77. "IBIS Initiatives: Giving Voice to Values," *University of Virginia Darden School of Business,* https://www.darden.virginia.edu/ibis/initiatives/gvv.

78. W. Hason, J. Moore, C. Bachleda, A. Canterbury, C. Franco Jr., A. Marion, and C. Schreiber, "Theory of Moral Development of Business Students: Case Studies in Brazil, North America, and Morocco," *Academy of Management Learning & Education,* September 2017, pp. 393–414.

79. Adapted in part from W.E. Stead, D.L. Worrell, and J. Garner Stead, "An Integrative Model for Understanding and Managing Ethical Behavior in Business Organizations," *Journal of Business Ethics,* March 1990, pp. 233–242. Also see D. Lange, "A Multidimensional Conceptualization of Organizational Corruption Control," *Academy of Management Review,* July 2008, pp. 710–729; M.J. Pearsall and A.P.J. Ellis, "Thick as Thieves: The Effects of Ethical Orientation and Psychological Safety on Unethical Team Behavior," *Journal of Applied Psychology,* Vol. 96 (2011), pp. 401–411.

80. K. McCorvey and D.J. Woehr, "Perceived Ethical Climate and Unethical Behavior: The Moderating Role of Moral Identity," *Journal of Leadership, Accountability & Ethics,* Vol. 19, No. 4 (2022), pp. 98–120.

81. M. Gorsira, L. Steg, A. Denkers, and W. Huisman, "Corruption in Organizations: Ethical Climate and Individual Motives," *Administrative Sciences,* Vol. 8, No. 4 (February 19, 2018), pp. 1–19.

82. M. Figueroa-Armijos, B.B. Clark, and S.P. da Motta Veiga, "Ethical Perceptions of AI in Hiring and Organizational Trust: The Role of Performance Expectancy and Social Influence," *Journal of Business Ethics,* 2022, pp. 1–19.

83. H. Kim Duong et al., "Code of Ethics Quality and Audit Fees," *Journal of Accounting & Public Policy,* Vol. 41, No. 6 (2022).

84. J. Cheng, H. Bai, and X. Yang, "Ethical Leadership and Internal Whistleblowing: A Mediated Moderation Model," *Journal of Business Ethics,* Vol. 155 (2019), pp. 115–130.

85. "Whistle-Blower Law Protects Outside Consults, Too," *San Francisco Chronicle,* March 5, 2014, p. A6.

86. "File a Complaint," Occupational Safety and Health Administration, https://www.osha.gov/workers/file-complaint.

87. "Whistleblower Office," Internal Revenue Service, https://www.irs.gov/compliance/whistleblower-office.

88. "SEC Whistleblower Office Announces Results for FY 2022," *SEC.gov,* November 15, 2022, https://www.sec.gov/files/2022_ow_ar.pdf.

89. D. Boyle and D. Gaydon, "SEC Whistleblower Program Expands," *Strategic Finance,* Vol. 101, No. 5 (November, 2019), pp. 38–45.

90. D. Lewis, "Retaliation for Whistleblowing: Some Case Studies on the Experience of Re-employment/Redeployment," *International Journal of Law and Management,* Vol. 64, No. 3 (2022), pp. 292–307.

91. D. Arnold, R. Bernardi, P. Niedermeyer, and J. Schmee, "The Effect of Country and Culture on Perceptions of Appropriate Ethical Actions Prescribed by Codes of Conduct: A Western European Perspective among Accountants," *Journal of Business Ethics,* Vol. 70, No. 4 (2007), pp. 327–340. Also see C. Moore, J. Detert, L. Treviño, V. Baker, and D. Mayer, "Why Employees Do Bad Things: Moral Disengagement and Unethical Organizational Behavior," *Personnel Psychology,* Vol. 65 (2012), pp. 1–48; K. Niven and C. Healy, "Susceptibility to the 'Dark Side' of Goal-Setting: Does Moral Justification Influence the Effect of Goals on Unethical Behavior?" *Journal of Business Ethics,* Vol. 137, No. 1 (2016), pp. 115–127; R. Zeal, R. Jeurissen, and E. Groenland, "Organizational Architecture, Ethical Culture, and Perceived Unethical Behavior Towards Customers: Evidence from Wholesale Banking," *Journal of Business Ethics,* Vol. 158, No. 3 (September 2019), pp. 825–848.

92. C. Wickert, D. Risi, and T. Ramus, "What a Mature CSR Team Looks Like," *Harvard Business Review,* 2022.

93. N. Taylor, "What Is Corporate Social Responsibility?" *Business News Daily,* June 19, 2015, www.businessnewsdaily.com/4679-corporate-social-responsibility.html.

94. Esade Business and Law School, "The End of CSR as We Know It and the Rise of Businesses with a Conscience," *Forbes,* December 1, 2022, https://www.forbes.com/sites/esade/2022/12/01/the-end-of-csr-as-we-know-it-and-the-rise-of-businesses-with-a-conscience/?sh=15597d9a7f16.

95. A. Carroll, "Managing Ethically with Global Stakeholders: A Present and Future Challenge," *Academy of Management Executive,* May 2004, p. 118. Also see A. Carroll, "Corporate Social Responsibility: The Centerpiece of Competing and Complementary Frameworks," *Organizational Dynamics,* April–June 2015, pp. 87–96.

96. P. Bhardwaj, P. Chatterjee, K. Demir, and O. Turut, "When and How Is Corporate Social Responsibility Profitable?" *Journal of Business Research,* Vol. 84 (2018), pp. 206–219. Also see A.M. Anderson, "Do Ethics Really Matter to Today's Consumers?" *Forbes,* August 20, 2019, https://www.forbes.com/sites/theyec/2019/08/20/do-ethics-really-matter-to-todays-consumers/#6e73c0f12d0e.

97. M. Friedman, *Capitalism and Freedom* (Chicago: University of Chicago Press, 1962). Also see S. Gallagher, "A Strategic Response to Friedman's Critique of Business Ethics," *Journal of Business Strategy,* January 2005, pp. 55–60.

98. P. Samuelson, "Love That Corporation," *Mountain Bell Magazine,* Spring 1971.

99. Q. Zhang, B.L. Oo, and B.T.H. Lim, "Linking Corporate Social Responsibility (CSR) Practices and Organizational Performance in the Construction Industry: A Resource Collaboration Network," *Resources, Conservation and Recycling,* Vol. 179, 2022, p. 106113; Also see V. Harrison, M. Vafeiadis, P. Diddi, and J. Conlin, "The Impact of CSR on Nonprofit Outcomes: How the Choice of Corporate Partner Influences Reputation and Supportive Intentions," *Corporate Communications: An International Journal,* Vol. 27, No. 2 (2022), pp. 205–225.

100. J. Marlon, L. Neyens, M. Jefferson, P. Howe, M. Mildenberger, and A. Leiserowitz, "Yale Climate Opinion Maps 2021," *Yale Program on Climate Change Communication,* February 23, 2022, https://climatecommunication.yale.edu/visualizations-data/ycom-us/.

101. Definitions adapted from U.S. Environmental Protection Agency, "Climate Change: Basic Information," February 23, 2016, https://www3.epa.gov/climatechange/basics/.

102. C.L. Dubois and D.A. Dubois, "Expanding the Vision of Industrial-Organizational Psychology Contributions to Environmental Sustainability," *Industrial and Organizational Psychology*, Vol. 5, No. 4 (December 2012), pp. 480–483.

103. See G. Enderle, "How Can Business Ethics Strengthen the Social Cohesion of a Society?" *Journal of Business Ethics,* Vol. 150 (2018), pp. 619–629. Also see "Natural Capital Accounting: Connecting the Pillars of Sustainability," *System of Environmental Economic Accounting,* https://seea.un.org/events/natural-capital-accounting-connecting-pillars-sustainability.

104. C. Mui, "Warren Buffett Has Promised to Give Away 99% of His Wealth When He Dies. A Family Charity That Quietly Focuses on Reproductive Rights Could Get a Huge Windfall," *Fortune,* June 28, 2022, https://fortune.com/2022/06/28/warren-buffett-wealth-estate-family-charity/.

105. "Pledge Signatories," *The Giving Pledge,* https://givingpledge.org/pledgerlist.

106. H. Syse of the Peace Research Institute, Oslo, Norway, quoted in "Special Report on Business Ethics: Enhancing Corporate Governance," press release, *Knowledge@Wharton*, February 25, 2016, http://knowledge.wharton.upenn.edu/special-report/special-report-on-business-ethics-enhancing-corporate-governance/?utm_source=kw_newsletter&utm_medium=email&utm_campaign=2016-02-25. The report is "Special Report on Business Ethics: Enhancing Corporate Governance," February 2016, *Knowledge@Wharton* and AKO Foundation, http://d1c25a6gwz7q5e.cloudfront.net/reports/2016-02-25-Enhancing-Corporate-Governance.pdf.; Also see J. Veldman, T. Jain, and C. Hauser, "Virtual Special Issue on Corporate Governance and Ethics: What's Next?" *Journal of Business Ethics*, Vol. 183, No. 2 (2023), pp. 329–331.

107. L. Baselga-Pascual, A. Trujillo-Ponce, E. Vähämaa, and S. Vähämaa, "Ethical Reputation of Financial Institutions: Do Board Characteristics Matter?" *Journal of Business Ethics*, Vol. 148 (2018), pp. 489–510.

108. C. Radu and N. Smaili, "Alignment versus Monitoring: An Examination of the Effect of the CSR Committee and CSR-Linked Executive Compensation on CSR Performance," *Journal of Business Ethics*, Vol. 180, No. 1 (2022), pp. 145–163.

109. M. Cook, K. Savage, and F. Barge, "Linking Executive Pay to Sustainability Goals," *Harvard Business Review Digital Articles*, 2023, pp. 1–8.

110. C. Flammer, B. Hong, and D. Minor, "Corporate Governance and the Rise of Integrating Corporate Social Responsibility Criteria in Executive Compensation: Effectiveness and Implications for Firm Outcomes," *Strategic Management Journal*, March 26, 2019.

111. C. Flammer, B. Hong, and D. Minor, "Corporate Governance and the Rise of Integrating Corporate Social Responsibility Criteria in Executive Compensation: Effectiveness and Implications for Firm Outcomes," *Strategic Management Journal*, March 26, 2019.

112. R. Cho, "The 37 Easiest Ways to Reduce Your Carbon Footprint," *Columbia Climate School,* September 19, 2022, https://news.climate.columbia.edu/2022/09/19/the-37-easiest-ways-to-reduce-your-carbon-footprint-animated-graphic/.

113. H. Nesher Shoshan and L. Venz, "Daily Deep Acting toward Coworkers: An Examination of Day-Specific Antecedents and Consequences," *Journal of Organizational Behavior*, Vol. 43, No. 1 (2022), pp. 112–124.

114. J.L. Wells et al., "Positivity Resonance in Long-Term Married Couples: Multimodal Characteristics and Consequences for Health and Longevity," *Journal of Personality & Social Psychology*, Vol. 123, No. 5 (2022), pp. 983–1003.

115. "5 'Life Hacks' to Live More Ethically in 2017," *The Ethics Centre,* January 11, 2017, http://www.ethics.org.au/on-ethics/blog/january-2017/5-life-hacks-to-live-more-ethically-in-2017.

116. B.C. Gunia, "Sleep and Deception," *Current Opinion in Psychology*, 2022, p. 101379.

117. "5 'Life Hacks' to Live More Ethically in 2017," *The Ethics Centre,* January 11, 2017, http://www.ethics.org.au/on-ethics/blog/january-2017/5-life-hacks-to-live-more-ethically-in-2017.

118. K. Quindlen, "19 Easy and Immediate Ways You Can Live a More Ethical Life," *Thought Catalog,* August 18, 2015, https://thoughtcatalog.com/kim-quindlen/2015/08/19-easy-and-immediate-ways-you-can-live-a-more-ethical-life.

119. R. Rebellow and S.D.A. RM, "Determinants of Deviant Behaviour among Adolescents," *Journal of Positive School Psychology*, 2022, pp. 2784–2788.

120. B. Athreya, "Can Fashion Ever Be Fair?" *Journal of Fair Trade*, Vol. 3, No. 2 (2022), pp. 16–27.

121. K. Quindlen, "19 Easy and Immediate Ways You Can Live a More Ethical Life," *Thought Catalog,* August 18, 2015, https://thoughtcatalog.com/kim-quindlen/2015/08/19-easy-and-immediate-ways-you-can-live-a-more-ethical-life.

122. S. Frey, J. Bar Am, V. Doshi, A. Malik, and S. Noble, "Consumers Care about Sustainability—and Back It up with Their Wallets," *McKinsey & Company,* February 6, 2023, https://www.mckinsey.com/industries/consumer-packaged-goods/our-insights/consumers-care-about-sustainability-and-back-it-up-with-their-wallets.

LEARNING MODULE 1

1. "The Lazy Person's Guide to Saving the World," *United Nations: Sustainable Development Goals,* https://www.un.org/sustainabledevelopment/takeaction/ (accessed April 5, 2023).

2. A. Zaleski, "Misfits Market Hopes Scaling Up Sales Can Scale Down Food Waste," *Bloomberg,* December 8, 2022, https://www.bloomberg.com/features/2022-misfits-market-produce-food-waste/#xj4y7vzkg.

3. Wickert, C., Risi, D. and Ramus, T., 2022. What a mature CSR team looks like. *Harvard Business Review*.

4. https://www.forbes.com/sites/esade/2022/12/01/the-end-of-csr-as-we-know-it-and-the-rise-of-businesses-with-a-conscience/?sh=15597d9a7f16.

5. R. Eccles and S. Klimenko, "The Investor Revolution: Shareholders Are Getting Serious about Sustainability," *Harvard Business Review,* May–June (2019), pp. 107–116. Also see M. Porter and M. Kramer, "Creating Shared Value: How to Reinvent Capitalism—and Unleash a Wave of Innovation and Growth," *Harvard Business Review,* January–February (2011), pp. 1–17.

6. M. Porter and M. Kramer, "Creating Shared Value: How to Reinvent Capitalism—and Unleash a Wave of Innovation and Growth," *Harvard Business Review,* January–February 2011, pp. 1–17. Also see M. Porter and M. Kramer, "Strategy & Society: The Link between Competitive Advantage and Corporate Social Responsibility," *Harvard Business Review,* Vol. 84, No. 12 (2006), pp. 78–92.

7. M. Porter and M. Kramer, "Creating Shared Value: How to Reinvent Capitalism—and Unleash a Wave of Innovation and Growth," *Harvard Business Review,* January–February 2011, pp. 1–17.

8. S. Jain, "Reliance Jio continues to lead the telecom industry as its active subscribers increase by 4.9 million," *Business Insider India,* December 21, 2022, https://www.businessinsider.in/business/telecom/news/reliance-jio-continues-to-lead-the-telecom-industry-as-its-active-subscribers-increase-by-4-9-million/articleshow/96395806.cms; Also see J. Burgos, "Billionaires Mukesh Ambani And Mark Zuckerberg Deepen Ties With Grocery Delivery On WhatsApp," *Forbes,* August 30, 2022, https://www.forbes.com/sites/jonathanburgos/2022/08/30/billionaires-mukesh-ambani-and-mark-zuckerberg-deepen-ties-with-grocery-delivery-on-whatsapp/?sh=2820b04b5096.

9. A. Pressman, "How Reliance Jio Became India's Wireless Wonder," *Fortune,* August 25, 2019, https://fortune.com/2019/08/25/reliance-jio-india-mobile-wireless-service/. Also see J. Waring, "Reliance Jio Widens Lead as Profit Soars," *Mobile World Live,* January 20, 2020, https://www.mobileworldlive.com/asia/asia-news/reliance-jio-widens-lead-as-profit-soars/.

10. Ollivier de Leth, D. and Ros-Tonen, M.A.F. (2022) 'Creating Shared Value Through an Inclusive Development Lens: A Case Study of a CSV Strategy in Ghana's Cocoa Sector', *Journal of Business Ethics*, 178(2), pp. 339–354.

11. Gulati, R. (2022) 'The Messy but Essential Pursuit of Purpose', *Harvard Business Review*, 100(2), pp. 44–52.

12. Fortune Editors, "Change the World 2019: Where Business Creates Virtuous Circles," *Fortune,* August 19, 2019, https://fortune.com/2019/08/19/change-the-world-circular-economy/.
13. "Arogya Parivar: Improving access to healthcare," *Novartis,* https://www.novartis.com/in-en/about/arogya-parivar (accessed May 4, 2023).
14. "Healthy Family Programs," Novartis, https://www.novartis.com/esg/access/creating-sustainable-business-models/healthy-family-programs (accessed May 4, 2023); Also see "Pioneering Business Approach Expands Healthcare in Indian Villages," *Novartis,* December 8, 2017, https://www.novartis.com/stories/access-healthcare/pioneering-business-approach-expands-healthcare-indian-villages.
15. "How to Create a Supply Chain Competitive Advantage," *Blume Global,* https://www.blumeglobal.com/learning/supply-chain-competitive-advantage/ (accessed April 5, 2023).
16. "Global breadth and scale," *Flex,* https://flex.com/?utm_source=google&utm_medium=cpc&utm_campaigntype=brand&utm_campaign=Brand:_Broad_Branded_-_Primary_US&utm_adgroup=Flex_Branded&utm_term=flex_manufacturing&gclid=CjOKCQjw0tKiBhC6ARIsAAOXutnI_2sOIIH0ITPncD3lkU1QDXSsNN1_bPAUXqJLJN8HrYnW2D6zYfYaAoKhEALw_wcB (accessed May 5, 2023).
17. "Advancing sustainable manufacturing with Industry 4.0," *Flex,* May 4, 2023, https://flex.com/resources/advancing-sustainable-manufacturing-with-industry-4-0.
18. "Sustainability at Flex," *Flex,* https://flex.com/downloads/flex-2030-sustainability-goals (accessed May 5, 2023).
19. "Our sustainability vision and strategy," *Flex,* https://flex.com/company/sustainability (accessed May 5, 2023).
20. I. De Wit, "How Can Business Clusters Drive Success," *World Economic Forum,* July 30, 2015, https://www.weforum.org/agenda/2015/07/how-can-business-clusters-drive-success/.
21. M. Porter and M. Kramer, "Creating Shared Value: How to Reinvent Capitalism—and Unleash a Wave of Innovation and Growth," *Harvard Business Review,* January–February 2011, pp. 1–17.
22. "Networking Academy Success Stories: Chef Turned Cybersecurity Analyst, and More," *CSRWire,* January 4, 2022, https://www.csrwire.com/press_releases/733276-networking-academy-success-stories-chef-turned-cybersecurity-analyst-and-more.
23. M. Kramer, R. Agarwal, and A. Srinivas, "Business as Usual Will Not Save the Planet," *Harvard Business Review,* June 12, 2019, pp. 2–6.
24. M. Arumugam, "Campbell Soup Increases Sodium as New Studies Vindicate Salt," *Forbes,* July 18, 2011, https://www.forbes.com/sites/nadiaarumugam/2011/07/18/campbell-soup-increases-sodium-as-new-studies-vindicate-salt/#1ba95e3e77a5.
25. "Let's talk tomatoes: Campbell's Tomato Sustainability Summit," *Campbell Soup Company,* April 6, 2023, https://www.campbellsoupcompany.com/newsroom/sustainability/lets-talk-tomatoes-campbells-tomato-sustainability-summit/; Also see M. Maltenfort, "Building Resiliency in Campbell Soup's Agricultural Supply Chain," *Net Impact,* July 17, 2019, https://www.netimpact.org/node/80282.
26. "Our Impact," *Campbell Soup Company,* https://www.campbellsoupcompany.com/our-impact/ (accessed May 5, 2023).
27. C. Luetge and B. von Liel, "Why CSV Makes Sense for Business Schools," *Financial Times,* June 10, 2014, https://www.ft.com/content/f47575be-e280-11e3-a829-00144feabdc0.
28. "The Sustainable Development Goals Report 2022," *United Nations,* https://unstats.un.org/sdgs/report/2022/The-Sustainable-Development-Goals-Report-2022.pdf.
29. G. T. Lumpkin and S. Bacq, "Civic Wealth Creation: A New View of Stakeholder Engagement and Societal Impact," *Academy of Management Perspectives,* Vol. 33, No. 4 (2019), pp. 383–404.
30. "The 17 Goals," *United Nations,* https://sdgs.un.org/goals (accessed April 5, 2023).
31. J. Hackenberg, "The UN's Sustainable Development Goals Aren't Just Doing Good, They're Good Business," *Forbes,* August 29, 2019, https://www.forbes.com/sites/jonquilhackenberg/2019/08/29/the-uns-sustainable-development-goals-arent-just-doing-good-theyre-good-business/#24edf12f53d9.

32. M. Hoek, "CSV and the SDGs—Creating Shared Value Meets the Sustainable Development Goals," *HuffPost,* April 10, 2017, https://www.huffpost.com/entry/csv-and-the-sdgs-creating-shared-value-meets-the_b_58eb9ceae4b0acd784ca5a63.
33. "COP27: Your Guide to the 2022 UN Climate Conference," *The Nature Conservancy,* https://www.nature.org/en-us/what-we-do/our-priorities/tackle-climate-change/climate-change-stories/cop-climate-change-conference/ (accessed May 5, 2023).
34. "COP27 Reaches Breakthrough Agreement on New "Loss and Damage" Fund for Vulnerable Countries," *United Nations Framework Convention on Climate Change,* November 20, 2022, https://unfccc.int/news/cop27-reaches-breakthrough-agreement-on-new-loss-and-damage-fund-for-vulnerable-countries.
35. M. Kramer, R. Agarwal, and A. Srinivas, "Business as Usual Will Not Save the Planet," *Harvard Business Review,* June 12, 2019, pp. 2–6.
36. "Private Sector Crucial for Sustainable Development Goals' Success by Fostering Innovation, Best Practices, Secretary-General Tells Business Forum," *United Nations,* September 21, 2022, https://press.un.org/en/2022/sgsm21472.doc.htm.
37. "The Sustainable Development Agenda," *United Nations,* https://www.un.org/sustainabledevelopment/development-agenda/ (Accessed April 6, 2023).
38. J. Harrison, R. Phillips, and R. Freeman, "On the 2019 Business Roundtable 'Statement on the Purpose of a Corporation,'" *Journal of Management*, Vol. 46, No. 7 (2020), pp. 1223–1237.
39. J. Worland, "Planet Earth's Future Now Rests in the Hands of Big Business," *Time,* April 14, 2022, https://time.com/6166178/earths-future-big-business/.
40. Eang, M., Clarke, A. and Ordonez-Ponce, E., 2023. The roles of multinational enterprises in implementing the United Nations Sustainable Development Goals at the local level. *BRQ Business Research Quarterly*, *26*(1), pp. 79–97. Vancouver.
41. A. Ignatius, "Businesses Exist to Deliver Value to Society," *Harvard Business Review,* Vol. 96, No. 2 (March–April 2018), pp. 82–87. https://www.sharedvalue.org/partner/merck/ https://www.merck.com/wp-content/uploads/sites/5/2022/08/MRK-ESG-report-21-22.pdf https://www.emdgroup.com/en/sustainability-report/2022/strategy-management/stakeholder-dialogue.html.
42. "Merck Recognized on Fortune's 2022 Change the World List for Expanding Access to HPV Vaccines," *Merck,* October 10, 2022, https://www.merck.com/news/merck-recognized-on-fortunes-2022-change-the-world-list-for-expanding-access-to-hpv-vaccines/#:~:text=Merck%20was%20selected%20for%20its,world%2C%E2%80%9D%20said%20Robert%20M.
43. "Merck Reports Strong Progress in ESG Focus Areas," *Business Wire,* August 30, 2022, https://www.businesswire.com/news/home/20220830005845/en/Merck-Reports-Strong-Progress-in-ESG-Focus-Areas.
44. "Merck Recognized on Fortune's 2022 Change the World List for Expanding Access to HPV Vaccines," *Merck,* October 10, 2022, https://www.merck.com/news/merck-recognized-on-fortunes-2022-change-the-world-list-for-expanding-access-to-hpv-vaccines/#:~:text=Merck%20was%20selected%20for%20its,world%2C%E2%80%9D%20said%20Robert%20M.
45. O. Woeffray and O. Schwab, "The big opportunity behind small businesses," *World Economic Forum,* December 8, 2022, https://www.weforum.org/agenda/2022/12/future-readiness-here-s-why-smaller-businesses-success-matters/#:~:text=Smaller%20companies%20represent%2090%25%20of,survival%20as%20their%20top%20challenge.
46. C. Charpentier, R. Landveld, and N. Shahiar, "Role of MSMEs and Entrepreneurship in Achieving the SDGs," *ICSB Gazette,* Issue 3 (September 9, 2019). Also see "Small and Medium Enterprises (SMEs) Finance," World Bank, https://www.worldbank.org/en/topic/smefinance (accessed February 26, 2020).
47. M. Heimer, "Small companies, big impact: Why startups loom large on the Fortune Change the World list this year," *October 10, 2022,* https://fortune.com/2022/10/10/change-the-world-companies-startups-zipline-karmsolar-alto-pharmacy-infarm-aerofarms/.

48. "Company," *Zipline,* https://www.flyzipline.com/company (accessed May 5, 2023).
49. ITU News, "Service drones streamline health supply chains in the Global South," *ITU,* April 20, 2022, https://www.itu.int/hub/2022/04/drones-healthcare-supply-chain/.
50. G. T. Lumpkin and S. Bacq, "Civic Wealth Creation: A New View of Stakeholder Engagement and Societal Impact," *Academy of Management Perspectives,* Vol. 33, No. 4 (2019), pp. 383–404.
51. "Entrepreneurship, investment key to achieving SDGs and resilient post-pandemic recovery," *United Nations,* March 28, 2022, https://news.un.org/en/story/2022/03/1114942.
52. Fey, N., Nordbäck, E., Ehrnrooth, M. and Mikkonen, K., 2022. How peer coaching fosters employee proactivity and well-being within a self-managing Finnish digital engineering company. *Organizational Dynamics, 51*(3), p.100864.Vancouver.
53. Cater, J.J., Young, M., Al-Shammari, M. and James, K., 2022. Re-exploring entrepreneurial intentions and personality attributes during a pandemic. *Journal of International Education in Business, 15*(2), pp. 311–330.
54. T. Myers, "The U.N.'s Sustainable Development Goals? There's an App for That," *The Washington Examiner,* August 30, 2018, https://www.washingtonexaminer.com/weekly-standard/the-united-stations-sustainable-development-goals-are-being-met-with-smartphone-technology-and-entrepreneurship.
55. Z. Winn, "Platform Helps Farmers Out of Extreme Poverty," *MIT News,* November 14, 2018, news.mit.edu/2018/ricult-thailand-pakistan-farmers-1115.
56. M. Leonhardt, "The employers Gen Z is rejecting show where companies need to step up," *Fortune,* November 13, 2022, https://fortune.com/2022/11/13/what-gen-z-wants-at-work-employers-climate-change-focus/.
57. C. Versace and M. Abssy, "How Millennials and Gen Z Are Driving Growth Behind ESG," *Nasdaq,* September 23, 2022, https://www.nasdaq.com/articles/how-millennials-and-gen-z-are-driving-growth-behind-esg.
58. G. Weybrecht, "How Are Business Schools Engaging in the SDGs?" *AACSB,* February 28, 2022, https://www.aacsb.edu/insights/articles/2022/03/how-are-business-schools-engaging-in-the-sdgs.
59. "Sustainable Development," *Columbia College,* https://bulletin.columbia.edu/columbia-college/departments-instruction/sustainable-development/#coursestext (accessed April 6, 2023).
60. "Courses and Syllabi," *University of Michigan,* https://soe.umich.edu/academics-admissions/course-syllabi/edcurins-382 (accessed April 6, 2023).
61. "Integration Lab (i-Lab)," *University of Notre Dame Keough School of Global Affairs,* https://keough.nd.edu/master-of-global-affairs/integration-lab/ (accessed April 6, 2023).
62. "Sustainable Development: Curriculum," *University of Iowa Graduate College,* https://sdg.grad.uiowa.edu/curriculum (accessed April 6, 2023).
63. "Sustainable Development," *University of Iowa Graduate College,* https://sdg.grad.uiowa.edu/ (accessed April 6, 2023).
64. "2020 Guiding Principles and Standards for Business Education," *AACSB,* July 1, 2022, https://www.aacsb.edu/-/media/documents/accreditation/2020-aacsb-business-accreditation-standards-jul-1-2022.pdf?rev=b40ee40b26a14d4185c504d00bade58f&hash=9B649E9B8413DFD660C6C2AFAAD10429.
65. D. Beck, "Climate Change Branding Can Lift Recruitment and Retention," *SHRM,* January 18, 2022, https://www.shrm.org/resourcesandtools/hr-topics/talent-acquisition/pages/climate-change-branding-can-lift-recruitment-and-retention.aspx.
66. "Most companies align with SDGs – but more to do on assessing progress," *Global Reporting initiative,* January 17, 2022, https://www.globalreporting.org/news/news-center/most-companies-align-with-sdgs-but-more-to-do-on-assessing-progress/.
67. R. Godelnik, "Why Companies Need to Ditch the Sustainable Development Goals (SDGs)," *Medium,* March 17, 2022, https://razgo.medium.com/why-companies-need-to-ditch-the-sustainable-development-goals-sdgs-e0692de53182.
68. Heras-Saizarbitoria, I., Urbieta, L. and Boiral, O., 2022. Organizations' engagement with sustainable development goals: From cherry-picking to SDG-washing?. *Corporate Social Responsibility and Environmental Management, 29*(2), pp. 316–328.
69. Park, K., Grimes, M.G. and Gehman, J., 2022. Becoming a generalized specialist: a strategic model for increasing your organizations SDG impact while minimizing externalities. In *Handbook on the Business of Sustainability* (pp. 439–458). Edward Elgar Publishing.Vancouver Garrido-Ruso, M., Aibar-Guzmán, B. and Suárez-Fernández, Ó., 2023. What kind of leaders can promote the disclosure of information on the sustainable development goals?. *Sustainable Development.* Vancouver.
70. "Sustainable Development Goals: are they business critical?," *PricewaterhouseCoopers,* June 15, 2022, https://www.pwc.com/gx/en/services/sustainability/sustainable-development-goals/sdg-research-results.html.
71. "The Sustainable Development Goals Report 2022," *UN.org,* https://unstats.un.org/sdgs/report/2022/ (accessed April 7, 2023); Also see "Women in the U.S. Congress 2023," *Center for American Women and Politics,* https://cawp.rutgers.edu/facts/levels-office/congress/women-us-congress-2023 (accessed April 7, 2023); Also see J. Moreau, "Number of LGBTQ elected officials in U.S. doubled since 2017," *NBC News,* August 19, 2022, https://www.nbcnews.com/nbc-out/out-politics-and-policy/number-lgbtq-elected-officials-us-doubled-2017-rcna43946.
72. "The Sustainable Development Goals Report 2022," *UN.org,* https://unstats.un.org/sdgs/report/2022/ (accessed April 7, 2023).
73. "The Sustainable Development Goals Report 2022," *UN.org,* https://unstats.un.org/sdgs/report/2022/ (accessed April 7, 2023); Also see J. Suehrer, "The Future of FDI: Achieving the Sustainable Development Goals 2030 through Impact Investment," *Global Policy,* https://www.globalpolicyjournal.com/articles/development-inequality-and-poverty/future-fdi-achieving-sustainable-development-goals-2030 (accessed April 7, 2023).
74. "The Sustainable Development Goals Report 2022," *UN.org,* https://unstats.un.org/sdgs/report/2022/ (accessed April 7, 2023); Also see "Most companies align with SDGs – but more to do on assessing progress," *Global Reporting Initiative,* January 17, 2022, https://www.globalreporting.org/news/news-center/most-companies-align-with-sdgs-but-more-to-do-on-assessing-progress/.
75. R. Godelnik, "Why Companies Need to Ditch the Sustainable Development Goals (SDGs)," *Medium,* March 17, 2022, https://razgo.medium.com/why-companies-need-to-ditch-the-sustainable-development-goals-sdgs-e0692de53182.
76. "CEOs Ask for Policy Support to Enable Meaningful Progress Towards SDGs," *IISD,* January 18, 2023, https://sdg.iisd.org/news/ceos-ask-for-policy-support-to-enable-meaningful-progress-towards-sdgs/.
77. "SDG Reporting Challenge 2018," *PWC,* https://www.pwc.com/gx/en/services/sustainability/sustainable-development-goals/sdg-reporting-challenge-2018.html (accessed April 7, 2023).
78. "Corporate Social Responsibility – More relevant than ever before! But possibly outdated as a concept?" *University of Lapland Arctic Centre, August 11, 2022,* https://www.arcticcentre.org/blogs/Corporate-Social-Responsibility-%E2%80%93-More-relevant-than-ever-before!--But-possibly-outdated-as-a-concept/me32fvt0/4139289d-e8c1-4abc-82a0-18def05f0da5.
79. De Tommaso, S.F.N. and Pinsky, V., 2022. Creating shared value: the case of innovability at Suzano in Brazil. *Innovation & Management Review, 19*(3), pp. 208–221.
80. A. Kim, P. Bansal, and H. Haugh, "No Time Like the Present: How a Present Time Perspective Can Foster Sustainable Development," *Academy of Management Journal,* Vol. 62, No. 2 (2019), pp. 607–634.
81. M. Kramer and M. Pfitzer, "The Ecosystem of Shared Value," *Harvard Business Review,* Vol. 94, No. 10 (2016), pp. 80–89.
82. Jing, L. and Zhang, H., 2023. Venture Capital, Compensation Incentive, and Corporate Sustainable Development. *Sustainability, 15*(7), p. 5899.

83. G. T. Lumpkin and S. Bacq, "Civic Wealth Creation: A New View of Stakeholder Engagement and Societal Impact," *Academy of Management Perspectives,* Vol. 33, No. 4 (2019), pp. 383–404. Also see J. Howard-Grenville, G. Davis, T. Dyllick, C. Miller, S. Thau, and A. Tsui, "Sustainable Development for a Better World: Contributions of Leadership, Management, and Organizations," *Academy of Management Discoveries,* Vol. 5, No. 4 (2019), pp. 355–366.

84. Tu, Y.T., Aljumah, A.I., Van Nguyen, S., Cheng, C.F., Tai, T.D. and Qiu, R., 2023. Achieving sustainable development goals through a sharing economy: Empirical evidence from developing economies. *Journal of Innovation & Knowledge, 8*(1), p. 100299.

85. D. Matten and J. Moon, "Reflections on the 2018 Decade Award: The Meaning and Dynamics of Corporate Social Responsibility," *Academy of Management Review,* Vol. 45, No. 1, pp. 7–28.

86. D. Buss, "Revolution Foods Co-Founders Trying to Turn School Meals Upside-Down," *Chief Executive,* December 12, 2019, https://chiefexecutive.net/revolution-foods-co-founders-trying-to-turn-school-meals-upside-down/.

87. "Revolution Foods Acquires Better 4 You Meals, Creator of Award-winning Nutritious Meals for Schools," *PR Newswire,* July 27, 2022, https://www.prnewswire.com/news-releases/revolution-foods-acquires-better-4-you-meals-creator-of-award-winning-nutritious-meals-for-schools-301594509.html.

88. "Enhancing shared value through collective action," *Deloitte,* April 17, 2023, https://www2.deloitte.com/content/dam/Deloitte/za/Documents/za-Deloitte-Stakeholder-Capitalism-updated.pdf.

CHAPTER 4

1. "Career Readiness Competencies," *Michigan State University Career Services Network,* July 8, 2022, https://careernetwork.msu.edu/channels/career-readiness-competencies/.

2. A. Cain, "4 Things You Need to Do to Secure a Job Abroad," *Business Insider,* September 30, 2017, https://www.businessinsider.com/how-to-get-a-job-abroad-2017-9.

3. See "Trade Statistics," *U.S. Customs and Border Protection,* January 18, 2023, https://www.cbp.gov/newsroom/stats/trade; Also see "ITA Monthly Trade Infographic," *U.S. Department of Commerce International Trade Administration,* January 5, 2023, https://www.trade.gov/data-visualization/ita-monthly-trade-infographic; Also see K. Amadeo, "U.S. Imports, Including Top Categories, Challenges, and Opportunities," *The Balance,* March 27, 2022, https://www.thebalancemoney.com/u-s-imports-statistics-and-issues-3306260.

4. "World Competitiveness Ranking," *International Institute for Management Development,* https://www.imd.org/centers/world-competitiveness-center/rankings/world-competitiveness/ (accessed January 20, 2023).

5. Related discussion in J. McGregor and S. Hamm, "Managing the Global Workforce," *BusinessWeek,* January 28, 2008, p. 34. Also see C. Boles, "Last Call? Gates Pushes Globalism in Remarks," *The Wall Street Journal,* March 13, 2008, p. B3.

6. "Number of Smartphone Subscriptions Worldwide from 2016 to 2021, with Forecasts from 2022 to 2027," *Statista,* https://www.statista.com/statistics/330695/number-of-smartphone-users-worldwide/ (accessed January 23, 2023).

7. "Number of Internet and Social Media Users Worldwide as of July 2022," *Statista,* https://www.statista.com/statistics/617136/digital-population-worldwide/, (accessed January 23, 2023).

8. "Retail E-commerce Revenue in the United States from 2017 to 2027," *Statista,* https://www.statista.com/statistics/272391/us-retail-e-commerce-sales-forecast/#:~:text=Revenue%20from%20retail%20e%2Dcommerce,will%20exceed%201.7%20trillion%20dollars, (accessed January 23, 2023).

9. R.M. Kantor, quoted in K. Maney, "Economy Embraces Truly Global Workplace," *USA Today,* December 31, 1998, pp. 1B, 2B.

10. C. Stief, "What Are the Positives and Negatives of Globalization?" *ThoughtCo,* June 24, 2019, https://www.thoughtco.com/globalization-positive-and-negative-1434946.

11. J. Kuepper, "How Globalization Impacts International Investors and Economic Growth," *The Balance,* July 29, 2019, https://www.thebalance.com/globalization-and-its-impact-on-economic-growth-1978843; J. Kuepper, "Globalization and Its Impact on Economic Growth," *The Balance,* June 19, 2017, https://www.thebalance.com/globalization-and-its-impact-on-economic-growth-1978843.

12. C. Stief, "What Are the Positives and Negatives of Globalization?" *ThoughtCo,* June 24, 2019, https://www.thoughtco.com/globalization-positive-and-negative-1434946.

13. C. Thorbecke, "The US Is Spending Billions to Boost Chip Manufacturing. Will It Be Enough?" *CNN Business,* October 18, 2022, https://www.cnn.com/2022/10/18/tech/us-chip-manufacturing-semiconductors/index.html.

14. J. Bucki, "Pros and Cons of Outsourcing," *The Balance,* February 4, 2018, https://www.thebalance.com/top-6-outsourcing-disadvantages-2533780.

15. J. Kuepper, "How Globalization Impacts International Investors and Economic Growth," *The Balance,* July 29, 2019, https://www.thebalance.com/globalization-and-its-impact-on-economic-growth-1978843.

16. B. Conerly, "Inflation, Supply Chains and Globalization in 2022 and 2023," *Forbes,* September 20, 2022, https://www.forbes.com/sites/billconerly/2022/09/20/inflation-supply-chains-and-globalization-in-2022-and-2023/?sh=7f30d1c2110c.

17. "China Accounts for 30% of Global Manufacturing Output: Official," *World Economy News,* June 15, 2022, https://www.hellenicshippingnews.com/china-accounts-for-30-of-global-manufacturing-output-official/.

18. S. Helper and E. Soltas, "Why the Pandemic Has Disrupted Supply Chains," The White House, June 17, 2021, https://www.whitehouse.gov/cea/written-materials/2021/06/17/why-the-pandemic-has-disrupted-supply-chains/.

19. T. Penley, "China's 'Chokehold' on U.S. Supply Line Could Worsen Medication Shortages by 'Leaps and Bounds': Dr. Siegel," *Fox News,* December 21, 2022, https://www.foxnews.com/media/chinas-chokehold-us-supply-line-worsen-medication-shortages-leaps-bounds-dr-siegel; also see D. Lazarus, "With Most Drug Ingredients Coming from China, FDA Says Shortages Have Begun," *Los Angeles Times,* February 28, 2020, https://www.latimes.com/business/story/2020-02-28/column-coronavirus-china-drugs.

20. "4 Stories Highlight 2021's Supply Chain Disruptions, and What It Means for 2022," Flexe Institute, January 21, 2022, https://www.flexe.com/institute/articles/4-stories-highlight-2021-supply-chain-disruptions.

21. M. Van Koningsveld, "Supply Chain Disruption: An Underestimated Climate Impact?," The OECD Forum Network, October 9, 2023, https://www.oecd-forum.org/posts/title-of-article.

22. B. Stackpole, "Ripple Effects from Russia–Ukraine War Test Global Economies," MIT, June 28, 2022, https://mitsloan.mit.edu/ideas-made-to-matter/ripple-effects-russia-ukraine-war-test-global-economies.

23. "The Supply of Critical Raw Materials Endangered by Russia's War on Ukraine," OECD, August 4, 2022, https://www.oecd.org/ukraine-hub/policy-responses/the-supply-of-critical-raw-materials-endangered-by-russia-s-war-on-ukraine-e01ac7be/.

24. J. Northam, "How the War in Ukraine Is Affecting the World's Supply of Fertilizer," NPR, September 28, 2022, https://www.npr.org/2022/09/28/1125525861/how-the-war-in-ukraine-is-affecting-the-worlds-supply-of-fertilizer.

25. "Change in Average Price of Selected Commodities from February 24 to June 1, 2022," *Statista,* https://www.statista.com/statistics/1298241/commodity-price-growth-due-to-russia-ukraine-war/.

26. "Putting Your Study Abroad Experience to Work," *Harvey Mudd College,* https://www.hmc.edu/career-services/students/study-abroad-career-resources/putting-your-study-abroad-experience-to-work/ (accessed January 20, 2023).

27. "Franchising Overview," *McDonald's,* https://corporate.mcdonalds.com/corpmcd/franchising-overview.html (accessed January 20, 2023).

28. "Fortune 500," *Fortune*, https://fortune.com/ranking/fortune500/ (accessed January 20, 2023).
29. "Global 500," *Fortune*, https://fortune.com/company/trafigura-group/global500/ (accessed January 20, 2023).
30. E. Kammerlohr, "Here's What You Need to Know about Aldi's German Heritage," *The Daily Meal*, January 12, 2023, https://www.thedailymeal.com/1165009/heres-what-you-need-to-know-about-aldis-german-heritage/.
31. O. Diab, "The EPG Model in Multinational Companies: The Case of Mazaya," *Management Studies and Economic Systems*, Vol. 7, Nos. 1/2 (2022), pp. 17–24.
32. M. Tripathy, "Subduing Cultural Stereotype & Ethnocentrism in Business Organizations: A Soft Skills Stance," *Jurnal Sosial Humaniora (JSH)*, Vol. 12, No. 1 (2019), pp. 28–38.
33. S. Correa and A-M. Parente-Laverde, "Consumer Ethnocentrism, Country Image and Local Brand Preference: The Case of the Colombian Textile, Apparel and Leather Industry," *Global Business Review*, October 2017, pp. 1111–1123.
34. "Credits for New Clean Vehicles Purchased in 2023 or After," *Internal Revenue Service*, January 17, 2023, https://www.irs.gov/credits-deductions/credits-for-new-clean-vehicles-purchased-in-2023-or-after.
35. A. Gatignon and L. Capron, 2023. The firm as an architect of polycentric governance: Building open institutional infrastructure in emerging markets. *Strategic Management Journal*, 44(1), pp. 48–85.
36. B. Joita, "Where Are iPhones Manufactured: How Much Do You Really Know?" *Techthelead*, August 5, 2022, https://techthelead.com/where-are-iphones-made-how-much-do-you-really-know/.
37. Amazon Australia, "Amazon Australia's First Robotics Fulfillment Center in Western Sydney Now Open," *Amazon Australia Press Room*, April 6, 2022, https://amazonau.gcs-web.com/news-releases/news-release-details/amazon-australias-first-robotics-fulfilment-centre-western; Also see C. Wang, L. Lu, X. Liu, F. Meng, G. Huang, and X. Zhao, "Costco: The Challenge of Entering the Mainland China Market," *Harvard Business Review Case Study*, February 10, 2022. Ivey Publishing.
38. M. Singh, "Apple Starts Manufacturing iPhone 14 in India in a Shift Away from China," *Tech Crunch*, September 25, 2022, https://techcrunch.com/2022/09/25/apple-starts-manufacturing-iphone-14-in-india/.
39. Reuters Staff, "China's CIC Eyes U.S. Investment after Fund with Goldman Raised $2.5 Billion," *Reuters*, March 3, 2021, https://www.reuters.com/article/us-china-finance-cic/chinas-cic-eyes-u-s-investment-after-fund-with-goldman-raised-2-5-billion-idUSKBN2AW06X.
40. B. Baschuk, "US Manufacturers 'Pumped Up' about Supply-Chain Reshoring Trend," *Bloomberg*, November 2, 2022.
41. D. Paletta, T. Telford, and M. B. Sheridan, "U.S. and Mexico Plan Summit in Washington on Wednesday in Bid to Head off Trade Dispute," *The Washington Post*, May 31, 2019, https://www.washingtonpost.com/business/2019/05/31/lawmakers-express-alarm-trump-forges-ahead-with-mexico-tariffs/.
42. K. Roberts, "Aviation Hits New Low, Ranks as 4th-Leading U.S. Export in 2022," *Forbes*, June 28, 2022, https://www.forbes.com/sites/kenroberts/2022/06/28/aviation-hits-new-low-ranks-as-4th-leading-us-export-in-2022/?sh=64c67a004778.
43. "2022 Top 100 Franchises Report," *Franchise Direct*, January 27, 2022, https://www.franchisedirect.com/information/2022-top-100-franchises-report.
44. "Chevron and Baseload Capital Create Joint Venture to Explore Geothermal Development Opportunities," *Chevron Newsroom*, December 14, 2022, https://www.chevron.com/newsroom/2022/q4/chevron-and-baseload-capital-create-joint-venture-to-explore-geothermal-development-opportunities.
45. "LG Energy Solution and Honda Formally Establish Battery Production Joint Venture," *Cision PR Newswire*, January 13, 2023, https://www.prnewswire.com/news-releases/lg-energy-solution-and-honda-formally-establish-battery-production-joint-venture-301720982.html#:~:text=MARYSVILLE%2C%20Ohio%20%2C%20Jan.%2013, (EV)%20produced%20by%20Honda.
46. K. Lobosco, "Why Biden Is Keeping Trump's China Tariffs in Place," *CNN Politics*, January 26, 2022, https://www.cnn.com/2022/01/26/politics/china-tariffs-biden-policy/index.html.
47. "When China and the US Have a Trade War, Mexico Wins | The Observatory of Economic Complexity," *The Observatory of Economic Complexity*, n.d., https://oec.world/en/blog/when-china-and-the-us-have-a-trade-war-mexico-wins.
48. "Israel Raises Import Quotas on Eggs," n.d., https://www.thepoultrysite.com/news/2022/02/israel-raises-import-quotas-on-eggs.
49. "With Wide-Ranging New Sanctions, Treasury Targets Russian Military-Linked Elites and Industrial Base," U.S. Department of The Treasury, December 14, 2023, https://home.treasury.gov/news/press-releases/jy1731#:~:text=WASHINGTON%20%E2%80%94%20Today%2C%20the%20U.S.%20Department,and%20economic%20restrictions%20to%20undermine.
50. "Humanitarian Assistance and Food Security Fact Sheet: Understanding UK and U.S. Sanctions and their Interconnection with Russia", Office of Foreign Assets Control, https://ofac.treasury.gov/media/931946/download?inline#:~:text=U.S.%20Response%20The%20United%20States,from%20or%20related%20to%20Russia.
51. I. Oliver and M. Venancio, "Understanding the Failure of the U.S. Embargo on Cuba," *WOLA*, February 4, 2022, https://www.wola.org/analysis/understanding-failure-of-us-cuba-embargo/.
52. These definitions are found in "What Are Embargoes and Sanctions?" *New York District Export Council*, www.newyorkdec.org/what-are-embargoes-and-sanctions.html (accessed March 13, 2016).
53. "Timeline of U.S. Sanctions," *United States Institute of Peace*, January 23, 2023, https://iranprimer.usip.org/resource/timeline-us-sanctions; Also see "Iran Sanctions," *U.S. Department of the Treasury*, https://home.treasury.gov/policy-issues/financial-sanctions/faqs/637#:~:text=The%20United%20States%20maintains%20broad,owned%20or%20%2Dcontrolled%20foreign%20entities (accessed January 30, 2023).
54. "Smoot-Hawley Tariff Act," *Britannica*, January 4, 2023, https://www.britannica.com/topic/Smoot-Hawley-Tariff-Act.
55. S. Ben-Achour, "The Real Reason We Talk about NAFTA So Much," *Business Insider*, March 23, 2017, http://www.businessinsider.com/did-nafta-cost-or-create-jobs-2017-3.
56. "Lessons Learned from the NAFTA | Brookings," *Brookings*, February 28, 2022, https://www.brookings.edu/articles/lessons-learned-from-the-nafta/.
57. A. Billarreal, "Reaping the Benefits of a Collective North America: What Businesses Should Know," *Forbes*, January 26, 2023, https://www.forbes.com/sites/forbesbusinesscouncil/2023/01/26/reaping-the-benefits-of-a-collective-north-america-what-businesses-should-know/.
58. "The United States' Global Power Is Fading Fast | The Nation," *The Nation*, January 11, 2023, https://www.thenation.com/article/world/united-states-regional-power-nafta/.
59. P. Rao and J. Ma, "The $16 Trillion European Union Economy," *Visual Capitalist*, January 27, 2023, https://www.visualcapitalist.com/16-trillion-european-union-economy/.
60. K. Amadeo, "What Was Brexit, and How Did It Impact the UK, the EU, and the US?" *The Balance Money*, January 24, 2022, https://www.thebalancemoney.com/brexit-consequences-4062999.
61. T. Rees and F. Lacqua, "UK Pound (GBP/USD) Could Weaken More, Warns Bank of England's Catherine Mann," Bloomberg.Com, March 7, 2023, https://www.bloomberg.com/news/articles/2023-03-07/boe-s-catherine-mann-says-the-uk-pound-could-weaken-further.
62. L. Elliott, "UK to Be Second Weakest Performer of World's Big Economies next Year—OECD," *The Guardian*, November 22, 2022, https://www.theguardian.com/business/2022/nov/22/uk-growth-oecd-energy-crisis.
63. J. Strupczewski and Kate Abnett, "EU Tentatively Agrees $60 Price Cap on Russian Seaborne Oil," *Reuters*, December 2, 2022, https://www.reuters.com/business/energy/eu-agrees-60-barrel-price-cap-russian-seaborne-oil-eu-diplomat-2022-12-01/.

64. "Euro Weakness in 2022," *CEPR*, February 17, 2023, https://cepr.org/voxeu/columns/euro-weakness-2022.

65. A. Kantor, "Americans Moving to Europe: Housing Prices and Strong Dollar Fuel Relocations," Bloomberg.Com, July 20, 2022, https://www.bloomberg.com/news/articles/2022-07-20/americans-moving-to-europe-housing-prices-and-strong-dollar-fuel-relocations.

66. W. Bello, "The BRICS: Challengers to the Global Status Quo," *Foreign Policy in Focus*, August 29, 2014, http://fpif.org/brics-challengers-global-status-quo.

67. P. Hafezi and G. Faulconbridge, "Iran Applies to Join China and Russia in BRICS Club," *Reuters*, January 28, 2022, https://www.reuters.com/world/middle-east/iran-applies-join-brics-group-emerging-countries-2022-06-27/.

68. "India: Distribution of Gross Domestic Product (GDP) across Economic Sectors from 2011 to 2021," *Statista*, https://www.statista.com/statistics/271329/distribution-of-gross-domestic-product-gdp-across-economic-sectors-in-india/ (accessed January 30, 2023).

69. "Economic Forecast Summary (November 2022)," *OECD*, https://www.oecd.org/economy/india-economic-snapshot/ (accessed January 30, 2023).

70. D. Saul, "China and India Will Overtake U.S. Economically by 2075, Goldman Sachs Economists Say," *Forbes*, December 6, 2022, https://www.forbes.com/sites/dereksaul/2022/12/06/china-and-india-will-overtake-us-economically-by-2075-goldman-sachs-economists-say/?sh=39b57a08ea9b.

71. A. Hawkins, "Have We Reached Peak China? How the Booming Middle Class Hit a Brick Wall," *The Guardian*, September 11, 2023, https://www.theguardian.com/world/2023/sep/11/have-we-reached-peak-china-how-the-booming-middle-class-hit-a-brick-wall.

72. "Brazil: Country at a Glance," *The World Bank*, www.worldbank.org/en/country/brazil (accessed March 13, 2016).

73. "Number of Confirmed Cases of the Novel Coronavirus (COVID-19) in Latin America and the Caribbean as of January 26, 2023, by Country," *Statista*, https://www.statista.com/statistics/1101643/latin-america-caribbean-coronavirus-cases/ (accessed January 30, 2023).

74. Reuters, "Brazil 2022 GDP Growth Now Forecast at 2.7%, up from 2% -Economy Ministry," *Reuters*, September 15, 2022, https://www.reuters.com/markets/rates-bonds/brazils-economy-ministry-improves-2022-gdp-forecast-27-2022-09-15/.

75. O. Guo, "Aiming at China's Armpits: When Foreign Brands Misfire," *The New York Times*, February 2, 2018, https://www.nytimes.com/2018/02/02/business/china-consumers-deodorant.html.

76. "How Cultures Collide," *Psychology Today*, July 1976, p. 69.

77. N. Kathirvel and I.M.C. Febiula, "Understanding the Aspects of Cultural Shock in International Business Arena," *International Journal of Information, Business and Management*, May 2016, pp. 105–115. Also see F. Fitzpatrick, "Taking the 'Culture' Out of 'Culture Shock'—A Critical Review of Literature on Cross-Cultural Adjustment in International Relocations," *Critical Perspectives on International Business; Bradford*, 2017, pp. 278–296.

78. B. Lufkin, "How 'Reading the Air' Keeps Japan Running," *BBC Worklife*, January 20, 2020, https://www.bbc.com/worklife/article/20200129-what-is-reading-the-air-in-japan.

79. A summary of cross-cultural research is provided by M.J. Gelfand, Z. Aycan, M. Erez, and K. Leung, "Cross-Cultural Industrial Organizational Psychology and Organizational Behavior: A Hundred-Year Journey," *Journal of Applied Psychology*, March 2017, pp. 514–529.

80. For complete details, see G. Hofstede, *Culture's Consequences: International Differences in Work-Related Values*, abridged ed. (Newbury Park, CA: Sage, 1984).

81. E.M. Sent and A.L. Kroese, "Commemorating Geert Hofstede, A Pioneer in the Study of Culture and Institutions," *Journal of Institutional Economics*, Vol. 18, No. 1 (2022), pp. 15–27.

82. M. Javidan and R.J. House, "Cultural Acumen for the Global Manager: Lessons from Project GLOBE," *Organizational Dynamics*, Spring 2001, pp. 289–305. Also see R.J. House, P.J. Hanges, M. Javidan, P.W. Dorfman, and V. Gupta, eds., *Culture, Leadership, and Organizations: The GLOBE Study of 62 Societies* (Thousand Oaks, CA: Sage, 2004); M. Javidan, P.W. Dorfman, M.S. de Luque, and R.J. House, "In the Eye of the Beholder: Cross Cultural Lessons in Leadership from Project GLOBE," *Academy of Management Perspectives*, February 2006, pp. 67–90.

83. J.C. Rode, X. Huang, and R. Schroeder, "Human Resources Practices and Organizational Learning in High and Low In-Group Collectivist Cultures," in *Academy of Management Proceedings*, Vol. 2020, No. 1 (2020), p. 12432. Briarcliff Manor, NY 10510: Academy of Management.

84. "Globe 2020," *The GLOBE Project*, https://www.globeproject.com/about#:~:text=GLOBE%202020%20will%20collect%20cultural,research%20for%20years%20to%20come, (accessed January 20, 2023).

85. S. Kotiloglu, D. Blettner, and T. Lechler, "Integrating National Culture into the Organizational Performance Feedback Theory," *European Management Journal*, 2023.

86. A. Smale et al., "Proactive Career Behaviors and Subjective Career Success: The Moderating Role of National Culture." *Journal of Organizational Behavior* Vol. 40, No. 1 (2018), pp. 105–122, https://doi.org/10.1002/job.2316.

87. R. Füreder, H. Hammer, B. Haas, D. Frendlovská, M. Kuncová, and K. Berková, "Why Are Intercultural Skills and Their Development Still not Considered as Gamechangers in the Professional World?" *CCBC* 2022, p. 139.

88. D. Bullock and R. Sánchez, "What's the Best Way to Communicate on a Global Team?" *HBR Ascend*, March 22, 2021, https://hbr.org/2021/03/whats-the-best-way-to-communicate-on-a-global-team; Also see A. Kaufman, "What Is the Most Spoken Language in the World 2022? Top 10 Spoken Languages, Globally," *USA Today*, August 23, 2022, https://www.usatoday.com/story/news/2022/08/23/most-spoken-language-world-top-ten/7865918001/.

89. S. Brown, "Best Language Learning Apps for 2023," *CNET*, January 9, 2023, https://www.cnet.com/tech/services-and-software/best-language-learning-apps/.

90. A. Sorokowska, P. Sorokowski, P. Hilpert, K. Cantarero, T. Frackowiak, K. Almadi et al., "Preferred Interpersonal Distances: A Global Comparison," *Journal of Cross-Cultural Psychology*, 2017, pp. 577–592.

91. W.Y. Wu, T.A. Bui, and T.C. Dao, "The Influence of Cross-Cultural Stable and Dynamic Competencies on Expatriate Adaptation and Outcomes: The Case of Taiwan," *Asia-Pacific Journal of Business Administration*, 2022.

92. D. Marsh, *Doing Business in the Middle East* (London: Little, Brown Book Group, 2015).

93. G. Fan, K.D. Carlson, and R.D. Thomas, "Individual Differences in Cognitive constructs: A Comparison between American and Chinese Culture Groups," *Frontiers in Psychology*, Vol. 12 (2021), p. 2401.

94. Indeed Editorial Team, "Monochronic vs. Polychronic Time: Cultural Differences in Time Management," *Indeed*, December 3, 2021, https://www.indeed.com/career-advice/career-development/polychronic-time#:~:text=Monochronic%20time%20refers%20to%20a,valuable%20to%20the%20monochromic%20workplace.

95. J. Sehrish and A. Zubair, "Impact of Polychronicity on Work-Related Quality of Life among Bank Employees: Moderating Role of Time Management," *Pakistan Journal of Psychological Research*, Vol. 35, No. 2 (2020), pp. 511–528.

96. E. Olsson and M. Sundh, "Perception of Time in Relation to Work and Private Life among Swedish Social Workers—the Temporal Clash between the Organisation and the Individual," *European Journal of Social Work*, Vol. 22, No. 4 (2018), pp. 690–701, https://doi.org/10.1080/13691457.2018.1423549.

97. See K. Chen, W. Guo, Y. Kang, and Q. Wan, "Does Religion Improve Corporate Environmental Responsibility? Evidence from China," *Corporate Social Responsibility and Environmental Management*, Vol. 28, No. 2 (2021), pp. 808–818; Also see L. Ma, X. Wang, and C. Zhang, "Does Religion Shape Corporate Cost Behavior?" *Journal of Business Ethics*, Vol. 170 (2021), pp. 835–855; Also see J.M. Díez-Esteban, J.B. Farinha, and C.D. García-Gómez, "Are Religion and Culture Relevant for Corporate Risk-Taking? International Evidence," *BRQ Business Research*

Quarterly, Vol. 22, No. 1 (2019), pp. 36–55; Also see M. El Hazzouri, K.J. Main, and L. Sinclair, "Out of the Closet: When Moral Identity and Protestant Work Ethic Improve Attitudes toward Advertising Featuring Same-Sex Couples," *Journal of Advertising,* Vol. 48, No, 2 (2019), pp. 181–196; Also see C. Zúñiga, D. Aguado, and P. Cabrera-Tenecela, "Values That Work: Exploring the Moderator Role of Protestant Work Ethics in the Relationship between Human Resources Practices and Work Engagement and Organizational Citizenship Behavior," *Administrative Sciences,* Vol. 12, No. 1 (2022), p. 11.

98. E. Beardsley, "Thousands in France Strike and March in Protest of Raising the Age of Retirement," *NPR,* January 19, 2023, https://www.npr.org/2023/01/19/1150075846/thousands-in-france-strike-and-march-in-protest-of-raising-the-age-of-retirement.

99. M. Dalton and N. Bisserbe (2023, Jan 27). French union cuts power to pressure macron on pensions; targeted outages aimed at politicians and the wealthy draw warnings of legal sanctions. *Wall Street Journal (Online)* Retrieved from https://www.proquest.com/newspapers/french-union-cuts-power-pressure-macron-on/docview/2769939961/se-2.

100. J. Jacobs, "ExxonMobil Accuses Russia of 'Expropriation' as It Exits Oil Project," *Financial Times,* October 17, 2022, https://www.ft.com/content/3f46cfb0-68d2-4d29-b98e-1d7628d4638a.

101. "Corruption Perceptions Index 2021," *Transparency.org,* https://www.transparency.org/en/cpi/2021 (accessed January 26, 2023).

102. S. Stewart, "From Bad to Worse in Fast Fashion's Global Sweatshop," *The Sunday Post,* August 7, 2022, https://www.sundaypost.com/fp/fast-fashion-sweatshop/.

103. "Forced Labor, Modern Slavery, and Human Trafficking," *International Labour Organization,* https://www.ilo.org/global/topics/forced-labour/lang--en/index.htm (accessed January 26, 2022).

104. K. Dore, "The Top Reason Why Americans Abroad Want to Dump Their U.S. Citizenship," *CNBC,* May 18, 2021, https://www.cnbc.com/2021/05/18/the-top-reason-why-americans-abroad-want-to-dump-their-citizenship.html.

105. J. Wecker and A. O'Sullivan, "The 55 Most Expensive Cities to Live in Right Now," *Good Housekeeping,* July 29, 2022, https://www.goodhousekeeping.com/life/travel/g39074204/most-expensive-cities-in-the-world/.

106. See R.A.I.C. Karunarathne, "Role of Social Support in Lessening Expatriate Turnover Intention," *South Asian Journal of Human Resources Management,* 2022. p. 23220937221101262; Also see D. Giauque, S. Anderfuhren-Biget, and F. Varone, "Stress and Turnover Intents in International Organizations: Social Support and Work–Life Balance as Resources," *The International Journal of Human Resource Management,* Vol. 30, No. 5 (2019), pp. 879–901. Vancouver.

107. T. Taylor, "Recruiting for Expatriate Roles? Choose Candidates with the Right Traits," *HR Dive,* January 5, 2017, https://www.hrdive.com/news/recruiting-for-expatriate-roles-choose-candidates-with-the-right-traits/433364/.

108. "Staffing Internationally," *University of Minnesota Libraries,* https://open.lib.umn.edu/humanresourcemanagement/chapter/14-2-staffing-internationally/, (accessed January 27, 2023).

109. D. Wang, T. Vu, S. Freeman, and R. Donohue, "Becoming Competent Expatriate Managers: Embracing Paradoxes in International Management," *Human Resource Management Review,* Vol. 32, No. 3 (2022), p. 100851.

110. N. Andersen, "Mapping the Expatriate Literature: A Bibliometric Review of the Field from 1998 to 2017 and Identification of Current Research Fronts," *The International Journal of Human Resource Management,* Vol. 32, No. 22 (2021), pp. 4687–4724.

111. D. Wang, T. Vu, S. Freeman, and R. Donohue, "Becoming Competent Expatriate Managers: Embracing Paradoxes in International Management," *Human Resource Management Review,* Vol. 32, No. 3 (2022), p. 100851.

112. N. Andersen, "Mapping the Expatriate Literature: A Bibliometric Review of the Field from 1998 to 2017 and Identification of Current Research Fronts," *The International Journal of Human Resource Management,* Vol. 32, No. 22 (2021), pp. 4687–4724.

113. X. Zou, T. Wildschut, D. Cable, and C. Sedikides, "Nostalgia for Host Culture Facilitates Repatriation Success: The Role of Self-Continuity," *Self and Identity,* Vol. 17, No. 3 (2018), pp. 327–342.

114. T. Bussen, "Understanding and Preventing Expat Failure," *International Citizens Group,* https://www.internationalcitizens.com/global-hr/prevent-expatriate-failure/, (accessed January 27, 2023).

115. "Maintaining International Assignments," *Society for Human Resource Management,* https://www.shrm.org/resourcesandtools/tools-and-samples/toolkits/pages/international-assignments.aspx, (accessed January 27, 2023).

116. R. Eckersley, "Culture, Progress and the Future: Can the West Survive Its Own Myths?" *Salon,* August 28, 2022, https://www.salon.com/2022/08/28/culture-progress-and-the-future-can-the-west-survive-its-own-myths/.

117. G. Johns, "Advances in the Treatment of Context in Organizational Research," in F.P. Morgeson, H. Aguinis, and S.J. Ashford, eds., *Annual Review of Organizational Psychology and Organizational Behavior* (Palo Alto: CA, Annual Reviews, 2017), pp. 21–46.

118. B. Tulgan, *Bridging the Soft Skills Gap* (Hoboken, NJ: John Wiley & Sons, 2015).

119. M. Kreisa, "60+ Vital First Words and Phrases to Learn in a New Language," *FluentU,* September 13, 2022, https://www.fluentu.com/blog/first-phrases-to-learn-in-a-new-language/.

120. These suggestions were based on I. Bedzow, "What DEI Training Can Learn from Cultural Competency in Medical Education," *Forbes,* September 2, 2022, https://www.forbes.com/sites/irabedzow/2022/09/02/what-dei-training-can-learn-from-cultural-competency-in-medical-education/?sh=15bd6ddb5904; Also see "8 Skills to Become More Culturally Adept at Work," *American Management Association,* May 13, 2022, https://www.amanet.org/articles/8-skills-to-become-more-culturally-adept-at-work/; Also see A. Moran, "How to Develop Cultural Awareness in the Workplace," *Career Addict,* July 11, 2022, https://www.careeraddict.com/develop-cultural-awareness.

CHAPTER 5

1. MasterClass, "Review of Career Planning Basics: How to Find Your Career Path," *MasterClass,* June 1, 2022, https://www.masterclass.com/articles/career-planning; "Make a Career Plan," *MIT Career Advising & Professional Development,* https://capd.mit.edu/resources/make-a-career-plan/ (accessed December 26, 2022); L. Brown Perkins, "Check out the Top Tips for Successful Career Planning in 2022," *Emeritus,* March 17, 2022, https://emeritus.org/blog/top-tips-for-successful-career-planning-in-2022/; Imber, "Career Advice from Wildly Successful People." Harvard Business Review, June 30, 2021, https://hbr.org/2021/06/career-advice-from-wildly-successful-people.

2. "How Hard Is It to Find a Job after College?" *LinkedIn,* July 29, 2022, https://www.linkedin.com/pulse/how-hard-find-job-after-college-get-hired-by-linkedin-news; "17 Tips for Getting a Job out of College," *Mint,* June 30, 2022. https://mint.intuit.com/blog/early-career/getting-a-job-out-of-college/.

3. K. Gustafson, "Small Business Failure Rate: What Percentage of Small Businesses Fail?" *LendingTree,* May 2, 2022, https://www.lendingtree.com/business/small/failure-rate/.

4. "Five Reasons Small Businesses Fail (and Five Ways to Overcome Pitfalls!)," Peregrine Global Services, June 21, 2022, https://peregrineglobal.com/why-small-businesses-fail/; Ellevate, "Eight Common Reasons Small Businesses Fail," *Forbes,* October 24, 2019, https://www.forbes.com/sites/ellevate/2019/10/24/eight-common-reasons-small-businesses-fail/?sh=6b64752e4fbb; "The Top 10 Reasons Small Businesses Fail—and How to Avoid Them," *BOQ,* July 6, 2021, https://www.boq.com.au/business/small-business/business-knowledge-hub/opening-a-small-business/the-top-ten-reasons-small-businesses-fail.

5. R. Kreitner, *Management,* 11th ed. (Boston: Houghton Mifflin, 2008), p. 147.

6. "The Walt Disney Company Reports Fourth Quarter and Full Year Earnings for Fiscal 2022," *The Walt Disney Company,* November 8,

2022, https://thewaltdisneycompany.com/the-walt-disney-company-reports-fourth-quarter-and-full-year-earnings-for-fiscal-2022/; "Number of Netflix Paid Subscribers Worldwide from 1st quarter 2013 to 3rd quarter 2022," *Statista,* https://www.statista.com/statistics/250934/quarterly-number-of-netflix-streaming-subscribers-worldwide/ (accessed December 29, 2022).

7. "Investor Relations," Levi Strauss & Co., https://investors.levistrauss.com/home/default.aspx (accessed December 29, 2022).

8. A.A. Thompson Jr. and A.J. Strickland III, *Strategic Management: Concepts and Cases,* 13th ed. (New York: McGraw Hill/Irwin, 2003).

9. S. Bond, "From Twitter Chaos to TikTok Bans to the Metaverse, Social Media Had a Rocky 2022," *NPR*, December 23, 2022, https://www.npr.org/2022/12/23/1144997451/from-twitter-chaos-to-tiktok-bans-to-the-metaverse-social-media-had-a-rocky-2022; B. Adgate, "Advertisers Hit the Pause Button with Twitter," *Forbes*, November 22, 2022, https://www.forbes.com/sites/bradadgate/2022/11/22/advertisers-hit-the-pause-button-with-twitter/?sh=3726027d39f6; S. Kann and A. Carusone, "In Less than a Month, Elon Musk Has Driven Away Half of Twitter's Top 100 Advertisers," *Media Matters for America*, November 22, 2022, https://www.mediamatters.org/elon-musk/less-month-elon-musk-has-driven-away-half-twitters-top-100-advertisers.

10. J. Brinckmann, D. Grichnik, and D. Kapsa, "Should Entrepreneurs Plan or Just Storm the Castle? A Meta-Analysis on Contextual Factors Impacting the Business Planning–Performance Relationship in Small Firms," *Journal of Business Venturing*, Vol. 25 (2010), pp. 24–40, doi:10.1016/j.jbusvent.2008.10.007; S. Müller, A. L. Kirst, H. Bergmann, and B. Bird, "Entrepreneurs' Actions and Venture Success: A Structured Literature Review and Suggestions for Future Research," *Small Business Economics*, 2022, pp. 1–28; C. Hopp and F.J. Greene, "In Pursuit of Time: Business Plan Sequencing, Duration and Intraentrainment Effects on New Venture Viability," *Journal of Management Studies*, Vol. 55, 2018, pp. 320–351; C. Welter, A. Scrimpshire, D. Tolonen, and E. Obrimah, "The Road to Entrepreneurial Success: Business Plans, Lean Startup, or Both?" *New England Journal of Entrepreneurship*, 2021, pp. 22–42.

11. M. Keynes, "Making Planning Work: Insights from Business Development," *International Journal of Entrepreneurship and Innovative Management,* 2018, pp. 33–56. Also see M.S. Ridwan, "Planning Practices: A Multiple Case Study in the High-Performing Banks," *Journal of Organizational Change Management,* 2017, pp. 487–500; A. Belk Olson, "4 Common Reasons Strategies Fail," *Harvard Business Review*, June 24, 2022, https://hbr.org/2022/06/4-common-reasons-strategies-fail.

12. R.L. Martin, "The Big Lie of Strategic Planning," *Harvard Business Review,* January–February 2014, pp. 79–84; See also D.J. Collis, "Why Do So Many Strategies Fail?" *Harvard Business Review*, June 14, 2021, https://hbr.org/2021/07/why-do-so-many-strategies-fail.

13. R. Lenihan, "Zuckerberg Sees Missteps in March to the Metaverse," *TheStreet*, October 15, 2022, https://www.thestreet.com/investing/zuckerberg-sees-missteps-in-march-to-metaverse. Also see K. Hays, "Facebook and Mark Zuckerberg Just Raised a Giant Middle Finger to Wall Street. The Company Says Its Metaverse Business Will Lose Even More Money next Year," Business Insider, October 26, 2022, https://www.businessinsider.com/facebook-doubles-down-on-metaverse-spending-despite-calls-cut-costs-2022-10; R. Mac, S. Frenkel, and K. Roose, "Skepticism, Confusion, Frustration: Inside Mark Zuckerberg's Metaverse Struggles," The New York Times, October 10, 2022, https://www.nytimes.com/2022/10/09/technology/meta-zuckerberg-metaverse.html.

14. H. Mintzberg, "The Strategy Concept II: Another Look at Why Organizations Need Strategies," *California Management Review,* Vol. 30, No. 1 (1987), pp. 25–32.

15. G.R. Araújo, H.T. Kato, and J.M. Del Corso, "Dynamic Capabilities, Strategic Planning and Performance: A Virtuous and Mutually Reinforcing Cycle." *Journal of Management & Organization*, Vol. 28 (2022), pp. 1–17, https://doi.org/10.1017/jmo.2022.33.

16. R. Arend, Y.L. Zhao, M. Song, and S. Im, "Strategic Planning as a Complex and Enabling Managerial Tool," *Strategic Management Journal,* Vol. 38, No. 8 (2017), pp. 1741–1752, https://doi.org/10.1002/smj.2420.

17. G. Hamel, with B. Breen, *The Future of Management* (Boston: Harvard Business School Press, 2007), p. 191.

18. "Mattel Revenue 2010–2022," *Macrotrends,* https://www.macrotrends.net/stocks/charts/MAT/mattel/revenue#:~:text=Mattel%20revenue%20for%20the%20twelve (accessed December 22, 2022).

19. S. Whitten, "Mattel Looks to Movies, Digital Gaming and NFTs for Its next Leg of Growth," *CNBC*, February 18, 2022. https://www.cnbc.com/2022/02/18/mattel-unveils-its-strategy-for-its-next-leg-of-growth.html.

20. "Red Bull Mediahouse," www.redbullmediahouse.com. https://www.redbullmediahouse.com/en/about-us (accessed December 26, 2022); "The Red Bull Philosophy," *Jobs in Football*, https://jobsinfootball.com/blog/red-bull-soccer-teams/#:~:text=In%20total%2C%20the%20drinks%20brand (accessed December 26, 2022); J. Vertuno and Associated Press, "Red Bull's Dietrich Mateschitz, the Austrian Billionaire Who Transformed F1, Soccer, and Energy Drinks, Dies at 78," *Fortune*, October 23, 2022, https://fortune.com/2022/10/23/dietrich-mateschitz-dies-billionaire-f1-red-bull-soccer-energy-drinks/.

21. S. Houraghan, "Find Your Sustainable Competitive Advantage (3 Top Brand Examples)," *Brand Master Academy*, https://brandmasteracademy.com/sustainable-competitive-advantage/ (accessed December 27, 2022).

22. E. Bernstein, "An Emotion We Need More of," *The Wall Street Journal*, March 22, 2016, pp. D1, D4.

23. P.F. Drucker, *The Practice of Management* (New York: Harper & Row, 1954), p. 122.

24. Paige Arnof-Fenn, quoted in S. Peek, "What Is a Vision Statement?" *Business News Daily*, November 22, 2022. https://www.businessnewsdaily.com/3882-vision-statement.html.

25. S. A. Kirkpatrick, "Understanding the Role of Vision, Mission, and Values in the HPT Model," *Performance Improvement*, Vol. 56, No. 3 (2017), pp. 6–14, https://doi.org/10.1002/pfi.21689; See also S. Kantabutra, "Toward an Organizational Theory of Sustainability Vision," *Sustainability*, Vol. 12, No. 3 (2020), p. 1125, https://doi.org/10.3390/su12031125.

26. "Company Information: At a Glance," The *Coca-Cola Company*, https://www.coca-colacompany.com/policies-and-practices/company-information-at-a-glance (accessed December 28, 2022); See also "Brands & Products," *The Coca-Cola Company*, https://www.coca-colacompany.com/brands (accessed December 28, 2022); "Revenue for Coca-Cola," *CompaniesMarketCap*, https://companiesmarketcap.com/coca-cola/revenue/ (accessed December 28, 2022).

27. "Purpose & Company Vision," *The Coca-Cola Company*, https://www.coca-colacompany.com/company/purpose-and-vision (accessed December 28, 2022); See also "Core Values," *The Coca-Cola Company*, https://www.coca-colacompany.com/social-impact/people-values (accessed December 28, 2022); "Our Company," *The Coca-Cola Company*, https://www.coca-colacompany.com/company (accessed December 28, 2022).

28. "Purpose & Company Vision," *The Coca-Cola Company*, https://www.coca-colacompany.com/company/purpose-and-vision (accessed December 28, 2022).

29. "Purpose & Company Vision," *The Coca-Cola Company*, https://www.coca-colacompany.com/company/purpose-and-vision (accessed December 28, 2022).

30. C. Christensen, "How Will You Measure Your Life?" *Harvard Business Review,* July–August 2010, pp. 46–51.

31. D. Kirova, "What Are Core Values, and Why Are They Important?" *Values.Institute*, https://values.institute/what-are-core-values-and-why-are-they-important/#Organizational_Core_Values (Accessed December 27, 2022).

32. Eric Jacobson, quoted in H.L. Rossi, "7 Core Values Statements That Inspire," *Fortune.com,* March 13, 2015, http://fortune.com/2015/03/13/company-slogans/.

33. S. Poe, "How Lululemon Blends Culture and Values to Attract Top Tech Talent," *National Retail Federation*, July 12, 2022, https://nrf.com/blog/how-lululemon-blends-culture-and-values-attract-top-tech-talent; See also "History," Lululemon, https://info.lululemon.com/about/our-

story/history#:~:text=Our%20core%20values%20of%20personal (accessed December 28, 2022).

34. B. George, R.M. Walker, and J. Monster, "Does Strategic Planning Improve Organizational Performance? A Meta-Analysis," *Public Administration Review,* Vol. 79 (2019), pp. 810–819.

35. "10 Inspirational Bill Gates Quotes on How to Succeed in Business," *The Gentleman's Journal,* https://www.thegentlemansjournal.com/article/10-inspirational-bill-gates-quotes-on-how-to-succeed-in-business/ (accessed December 28, 2022).

36. "Investor Relations," *The Coca-Cola Company,* https://investors.coca-colacompany.com/ (accessed December 28, 2022); "Growth Strategy," *The Coca-Cola Company,* https://investors.coca-colacompany.com/strategy/growth-strategy (accessed December 30, 2022).

37. "Walker & Dunlop Outlines Plans for Continued Growth during Virtual Investor Day," *Walker & Dunlop,* May 19, 2022, https://www.walkerdunlop.com/news-and-events/2022-05-19-walker-dunlop-outlines-plans-for-continued-growth-during-virtual-investor-day/; "Walker & Dunlop Unveils Its Drive to '25 Strategy to Become the Premier Commercial Real Estate Finance Company in the U.S.," *Walker & Dunlop,* December 10, 2020, https://investors.walkerdunlop.com/news/news-details/2020/Walker--Dunlop-Unveils-its-Drive-to-25-Strategy-to-Become-the-Premier-Commercial-Real-Estate-Finance-Company-in-the-U.S/default.aspx.

38. "Walker & Dunlop, Inc. (WD) Analyst Ratings, Estimates & Forecasts—Yahoo Finance," *Yahoo Finance,* https://finance.yahoo.com/quote/WD/analysis/ (accessed December 30, 2022); "Walker & Dunlop (WD) Q3 2022 Earnings Call Transcript," *The Motley Fool,* November 9, 2022, https://www.fool.com/earnings/call-transcripts/2022/11/09/walker-dunlop-wd-q3-2022-earnings-call-transcript/.

39. L. Bossidy and R. Charan, *Execution: The Discipline of Getting Things Done* (New York: Crown Business, 2002), p. 227.

40. R. Burns, "To a Mouse, on Turning Her Up in Her Nest with the Plough," reprinted in W.E. Henley & T.F. Henderson (Eds), *The Poetry of Robert Burns,* 1785, pp. 152–154.

41. "Crises Change, so Make Contingency Plans," *Chicago Booth Review,* April 18, 2022, https://www.chicagobooth.edu/review/crises-change-make-contingency-plans.

42. "What Is Fuel Hedging and Why Do Airlines Do It?" *Simple Flying,* December 24, 2022, https://simpleflying.com/what-is-fuel-hedging-and-why-do-airlines-do-it/; "Airlines Set to Save Billions with Fuel Hedges amid $100 Oil," *Bloomberg,* August 3, 2022, https://www.bloomberg.com/news/articles/2022-08-03/airline-fuel-hedges-set-to-save-billions-for-some-with-100-oil.

43. T.M. Spoelma, "Counteracting the Effects of Performance Pressure on Cheating: A Self-Affirmation Approach," *Journal of Applied Psychology,* Vol. 10 (2021), pp. 1804–1823; See also M.S. Mitchell, M.D. Baer, M.L. Ambrose, R. Folger, and N.F. Palmer, "Cheating under Pressure: A Self-Protection Model of Workplace Cheating Behavior," *Journal of Applied Psychology,* Vol. 103 (2018), pp. 54–73; M.S. Mitchell, R.L. Greenbaum, R.M. Vogel, M.B. Mawritz, and D.J. Keating, "Can You Handle the Pressure? The Effect of Performance Pressure on Stress Appraisals, Self-Regulation, and Behavior," *Academy of Management Journal,* Vol. 62 (2019), pp. 531–552; J.N.Y. Zhu, L.W. Lam, Y. Liu, and N. Jiang, "Performance Pressure and Employee Expediency: The Role of Moral Decoupling," *Journal of Business Ethics,* 2022, pp. 1–14; D. Welsh, J. Bush, C. Thiel, and J. Bonner, "Reconceptualizing Goal Setting's Dark side: The Ethical Consequences of Learning versus Outcome Goals," *Organizational Behavior and Human Decision Processes,* Vol. 150 (2019), pp. 14–27.

44. P.F. Drucker, *The Practice of Management* (New York: Harper & Row, 1954).

45. M.P.E. Cunha, L. Giustiniano, A. Rego, and S. Clegg, "Mission Impossible? The Paradoxes of Stretch Goal Setting," *Management Learning,* 2017, pp. 140–157. Also see G. Latham, G. Seijts, and J. Slocum, "The Goal Setting and Goal Orientation Labyrinth: Effective Ways for Increasing Employee Performance," *Organizational Dynamics,* October–December 2016, pp. 271–277.

46. G.P. Latham and G.A. Yukl, "A Review of Research on the Application of Goal Setting in Organizations," *Academy of Management Journal,* Vol. 18 (1975), pp. 824–845; See also, B.A.C. Groen, "A Survey Study into Participation in Goal Setting, Fairness, and Goal Commitment: Effects of Including Multiple Types of Fairness," *Journal of Management Accounting Research,* Vol. 30 (2018), pp. 207–240; E.A. Locke and G.P. Latham, "The Development of Goal Setting Theory: A Half Century Retrospective," *Motivation Science,* Vol. 5 (2019), pp. 93–105.

47. Satya Nadella, quoted in H. Tupper and S. Ellis, "Make Learning a Part of Your Daily Routine," *Harvard Business Review,* November 4, 2021, https://hbr.org/2021/11/make-learning-a-part-of-your-daily-routine.

48. "FACT SHEET: Biden-Harris Administration Announces New Actions and Funding to Address the Overdose Epidemic and Support Recovery," *The White House,* September 23, 2022, https://www.whitehouse.gov/briefing-room/statements-releases/2022/09/23/fact-sheet-biden-harris-administration-announces-new-actions-and-funding-to-address-the-overdose-epidemic-and-support-recovery/.

49. M-H. Budworth and S. Chummar, "Feedback for Performance Development: A Review of Current Trends," *International Handbook of Evidence-Based Coaching,* 2022, pp. 337–347.

50. R. Rodgers and J.E. Hunter, "Impact of Management by Objectives on Organizational Productivity," *Journal of Applied Psychology,* April 1991, pp. 322–336. Also see M. Johansen and D.P. Hawes, "The Effect of the Tasks Middle Managers Perform on Organizational Performance," *Public Administration Quarterly,* Fall 2016, pp. 580–616.

51. A. Kinicki, K. Jacobson, B. Galvin, and G. Prussia. "Multilevel Systems Model of Leadership," *Journal of Leadership and Organizational Studies,* Vol. 18 (2011), pp. 133–149.

52. This example was taken from a graphic illustration by A. Kinicki and is used for training managers in cascading; by Kinicki and Associates Inc. For more on goal cascading, see A.J. Kinicki, K.J.L. Jacobson, B.M. Galvin, and G.E. Prussia, "A Multilevel Systems Model of Leadership," *Journal of Leadership & Organizational Studies,* May 2011, pp. 133–149.

53. R.I. Williams Jr., S.C. Manley, J.R. Aaron, and F. Daniel, "The Relationship between a Comprehensive Strategic Approach and Small Business Performance," *Journal of Small Business Strategy,* Vol. 28, No. 2 (2018), pp. 33–48.

54. M. Rowinski, "Council Post: How Small Businesses Drive the American Economy," *Forbes,* March 25, 2022. https://www.forbes.com/sites/forbesbusinesscouncil/2022/03/25/how-small-businesses-drive-the-american-economy/?sh=30e9f6ae4169.

55. Z. Licata, "After 30+ Years, Great Lakes Hits the Refresh Button in Search of Growth," *Brewbound,* June 28, 2021, https://www.brewbound.com/news/after-30-years-great-lakes-hits-the-refresh-button-in-search-of-growth/; see also M. Vanac, "New Branding, Products and Canning Line Set Great Lakes Brewing Back on Growth Path," *Bizjournals,* June 3, 2021, https://www.bizjournals.com/cleveland/news/2021/06/03/branding-products-canning-line-help-brewer-grow.html.

56. R. Nolan, "How to Be More Proactive: A Step-by-Step Guide," *Goalcast,* September 2, 2016, https://www.goalcast.com/2016/09/02/how-to-be-more-proactive-step-step-guide.

57. R. Umoh, "Billionaire Richard Branson Reveals the Simple Trick He Uses to Live a Positive Life," *CNBC,* January 16, 2018, https://www.cnbc.com/2018/01/16/richard-branson-uses-this-simple-trick-to-live-a-positive-life.html.

58. These recommendations were derived from R. Nolan, "How to Be More Proactive: A Step-by-Step Guide," *Goalcast,* September 2, 2016, https://www.goalcast.com/2016/09/02/how-to-be-more-proactive-step-step-guide.

59. The structure of this exercise was partially based on B. Tulgan, *Bridging the Soft Skills Gap* (Hoboken, New Jersey: John Wiley & Sons, 2015).

60. K. Cherry, "How to Become More Open-Minded," *Very Well Mind,* June 29, 2019, https://www.verywellmind.com/be-more-open-minded-4690673; also see S. Vozza, "4 Ways to Train Your Brain to Be More Open-Minded," *Fast Company,* November 14, 2017, https://www.fastcompany.com/40494077/4-ways-to-train-your-brain-to-be-more-

open-minded; S. Pavlina, "Suspending Judgment," June 3, 2010, https://www.stevepavlina.com/blog/2010/06/suspending-judgment.

CHAPTER 6

1. "Sneaky Veg, About," https://www.sneakyveg.com/about/ (accessed January 30, 2020). Also see K. Cook, "15 Inspiring Examples of Small Business Branding," *HubSpot*, https://blog.hubspot.com/marketing/inspiring-examples-of-small-business-branding (accessed January 11, 2023).
2. "71% of Hiring Decision-Makers Agree Social Media Is Effective for Screening Applicants," *PRWeb*, October 14, 2020, https://www.prweb.com/releases/71_of_hiring_decision_makers_agree_social_media_is_effective_for_screening_applicants/prweb17467312.htm.
3. "The Future of Talent," *Advertising Supplement to The Wall Street Journal*, 2017, p. 23.
4. "Personal Branding: How to Build a Personal Brand in 5 Steps," *MasterClass*, February 3, 2022, https://www.masterclass.com/articles/personal-branding.
5. H. Monarth "What's the Point of a Personal Brand?" *Harvard Business Review*, February 17, 2022, https://hbr.org/2022/02/whats-the-point-of-a-personal-brand.
6. E. McMillan, "8 Self-Branding Secrets to Optimize Your Personal Success," *Entrepreneur*, November 17, 2022, https://www.entrepreneur.com/starting-a-business/8-self-branding-secrets-to-optimize-your-personal-success/438281.
7. "Personal Branding: How to Build a Personal Brand in 5 Steps," *MasterClass*, February 3, 2022, https://www.masterclass.com/articles/personal-branding; Also see R. White, "Personal Branding in the Digital Age: Why It Matters," *Forbes*, May 20, 2022, https://www.forbes.com/sites/forbesagencycouncil/2022/05/20/personal-branding-in-the-digital-age-why-it-matters/?sh=c49a62304cfd.
8. M.E. Porter, "What Is Strategy?" *Harvard Business Review*, November–December 1996, pp. 61–78. Porter has updated his 1979 paper on competitive forces in M.E. Porter, "The Five Competitive Forces That Shape Strategy," *Harvard Business Review*, January 2008, pp. 79–93.
9. M.E. Porter, "What Is Strategy?" *Harvard Business Review*, November–December 1996, pp. 61–78.
10. B. Schroeder, "Flip Flop Goes Crocs," *BCR Schroeder*, May 31, 2022, https://www.bcrschroeder.com/p/crocs-business-strategy. Also see M. Repko, "Buybuy Baby, a Bright Spot for Bed Bath & Beyond, Reports Steep Drop in Sales against Tough Comparisons," *CNBC*, September 29, 2022, https://www.cnbc.com/2022/09/29/buybuy-baby-sales-fall-at-struggling-bed-bath-beyond.html; "PepsiCo Company Profile," *Fortune*, https://fortune.com/company/pepsico/ (accessed January 17, 2023).
11. M.E. Porter, "What Is Strategy?" *Harvard Business Review*, November–December 1996, pp. 61–78. Also see "Neutrogena History and Story," *Neutrogena*, https://www.neutrogena.com/why-neutrogena.html (accessed January 17, 2023).
12. M. Queiroz, P.P. Tallon, T. Coltman, R. Sharma, and P. Reynolds, "Aligning the IT Portfolio with Business Strategy: Evidence for Complementarity of Corporate and Business Unit Alignment," *The Journal of Strategic Information Systems*, 2020, Article 101623; see also M. Queiroz, P.P. Tallon, T. Coltman, and R. Sharma, "Conditional Paths to Business Unit Agility: Corporate IT Platforms and the Moderating Role of Business Unit IT Autonomy," *European Journal of Information Systems*, 2022, pp. 1–20.
13. R. Felton, "The Future of Car Technology, as Seen at CES 2023," *Wall Street Journal*, January 7, 2023, https://www.wsj.com/articles/the-future-of-car-technology-as-seen-at-ces-2023-11673099177?mod=Searchresults_pos11&page=1.
14. "Team Dunkin' Expands Roster of Student Athletes," *Dunkin'*, December 8, 2022, https://news.dunkindonuts.com/blog/team-dunkin-winter-2022.
15. R.I. Williams Jr, A. Smith, J.R. Aaron, S.C. Manley, and W.C. McDowell, "Small Business Strategic Management Practices and Performance: A Configurational Approach," *Economic Research-Ekonomska istraživanja*, 2020, pp. 2378–2396; see also T.N. Huynh, "Determinants of the Performance of Small and Medium-Sized Enterprises in Emerging Markets," *International Journal of Productivity and Performance Management*, 2022, pp. 3160–3178; B. George, R.M. Walker, and J. Monster, "Does Strategic Planning Improve Organizational Performance? A Meta-Analysis," *Public Administration Review*, 2019, pp. 810–819.
16. L. van Scheers and M. K. Makhitha, "Are Small and Medium Enterprises (SMEs) Planning for Strategic Marketing in South Africa?" *Foundations of Management*, 2016, pp. 243–250.
17. O. Aytar and A.A. Selamet, "An Empirical Research on Strategic Management: A Research on SME Managers," *Journal of Life Economics*, 2021, pp. 93–100.
18. K. Krippendorff, "Why Small Businesses Should Scrap Strategic Planning," *FastCompany*, March 12, 2012, https://www.fastcompany.com/1824084/why-small-businesses-should-scrap-strategic-planning#:~:text=Strategic%20planning%20is%20inappropriate%20for,immediate%20negative%20impact%20on%20revenues; also see F.J. Greene, and C. Hopp, "When Should Entrepreneurs Write Their Business Plans?" *Harvard Business Review*, May 18, 2018, https://hbr.org/2018/05/when-should-entrepreneurs-write-their-business-plans.
19. J. Martins, "What Is Strategic Planning? 5 Steps and Processes," *Asana*, July 14, 2022, https://asana.com/resources/strategic-planning.
20. L. Olinga, "Microsoft Is Coming For Google and Its Cash Cow," *The Street*, February 7, 2023, https://www.thestreet.com/technology/microsoft-alphabets-google-clash-over-ai-chatgpt. Also see, R. Nieva, A. Konrad, and K. Cai, "'AI First' to Last: How Google Fell behind in the AI Boom," *Forbes*, February 8, 2023, https://www.forbes.com/sites/richardnieva/2023/02/08/google-openai-chatgpt-microsoft-bing-ai/?sh=16fc6daf4de4; D. Bass, "Microsoft Invests $10 Billion in ChatGPT Maker OpenAI," *Bloomberg.com*, January 23, 2023, https://www.bloomberg.com/news/articles/2023-01-23/microsoft-makes-multibillion-dollar-investment-in-openai.
21. I. Alegre, J. Berbegal-Mirabent, A. Guerrero, and M. Mas-Machuca, "The Real Mission of the Mission Statement: A Systematic Review of the Literature," *Journal of Management & Organization*, Vol. 24, No. 4 (2018), pp. 456–473.
22. "About—Microsoft," *Microsoft*, https://www.microsoft.com/en-us/about (accessed January 18, 2023).
23. "About—Our Corporate Values," *Microsoft*, https://www.microsoft.com/en-us/about/corporate-values (accessed January 18, 2023).
24. M. Janakiram, "A Look Back at Ten Years of Microsoft Azure," *Forbes*, February 3, 2020, https://www.forbes.com/sites/janakirammsv/2020/02/03/a-look-back-at-ten-years-of-microsoft-azure/#3a965a249292.
25. M. Janakiram, "A Look Back at Ten Years of Microsoft Azure," *Forbes*, February 3, 2020, https://www.forbes.com/sites/janakirammsv/2020/02/03/a-look-back-at-ten-years-of-microsoft-azure/#3a965a249292. Also see J. Tartakoff, "Ballmer: Microsoft 'Betting Our Company' on the Cloud," *GigaOm*, March 4, 2010, https://gigaom.com/2010/03/04/419-ballmer-microsoft-betting-our-company-on-the-cloud/; "NVIDIA Teams with Microsoft to Build Massive Cloud AI Computer," *NVIDIA Newsroom*, November 16, 2022, https://nvidianews.nvidia.com/news/nvidia-microsoft-accelerate-cloud-enterprise-ai.
26. American Evaluation Association Evaluation Policy Task Force, "An Evaluation Roadmap for a More Effective Government," *New Directions for Evaluation*, 2022, pp. 17–28.
27. A. Kinicki, K. Jacobson, B. Galvin, and G. Prussia, "A Multilevel Systems Model of Leadership," *Journal of Leadership & Organizational Studies*, May 2011, pp. 133–149.
28. A. Tawse, V.M. Patrick, and D. Vera, "Crossing the Chasm: Leadership Nudges to Help Transition from Strategy Formulation to Strategy Implementation," *Business Horizons*, 2019, pp. 249–257. Also see M. Friesl, I. Stensaker, and H.L. Colman, "Strategy Implementation: Taking Stock and Moving Forward," *Long Range Planning*, 2021, 102064.
29. "Microsoft Strategy Teardown: Cloud, AI, & Subscriptions and the Next Trillion-Dollar Company," *CB Insights*, https://www.cbinsights.com/

research/report/microsoft-strategy-teardown/ (accessed February 3, 2020); Also see B. Jin and M. Kruppa, "Microsoft to Deepen OpenAI Partnership, Invest Billions in ChatGPT Creator," *Wall Street Journal*, January 23, 2023, https://www.wsj.com/articles/microsoft-says-it-plans-multibillion-dollar-investment-in-openai-11674483180?mod=Searchresults_pos2&page=1; T. Bradshaw and C. Criddle, "Microsoft Confirms 'Multibillion-Dollar Investment' in ChatGPT Maker OpenAI," *Financial Times,* January 23, 2023, https://www.ft.com/content/298db34e-b550-4f80-a27b-a0cf7148f5f6.

30. "Diagnostics, Feedback, and Privacy in Windows 10," *Microsoft*, January 30, 2020, https://support.microsoft.com/en-us/help/4468236/diagnostics-feedback-and-privacy-in-windows-10-microsoft-privacy. Also see "About WER," *Microsoft*, May 31, 2018, https://docs.microsoft.com/en-us/windows/win32/wer/about-wer.

31. "Microsoft Cloud Strength Drives First Quarter Results," *Microsoft*, October 25, 2022, https://news.microsoft.com/2022/10/25/microsoft-cloud-strength-drives-first-quarter-results-5/#:~:text=today%20announced%20the%20following%20results.

32. F. Richter, "Infographic: Amazon Dominates Public Cloud Market," *Statista*, December 23, 2022, https://www.statista.com/chart/18819/worldwide-market-share-of-leading-cloud-infrastructure-service-providers/.

33. "Microsoft Cloud Strength Drives First Quarter Results," *Microsoft*, October 25, 2022, https://news.microsoft.com/2022/10/25/microsoft-cloud-strength-drives-first-quarter-results-5/#:~:text=today%20announced%20the%20following%20results. Also see E. Boyd, "General Availability of Azure OpenAI Service Expands Access to Large, Advanced AI Models with Added Enterprise Benefits," *Microsoft*, January 16, 2023, https://azure.microsoft.com/en-us/blog/general-availability-of-azure-openai-service-expands-access-to-large-advanced-ai-models-with-added-enterprise-benefits/#:~:text=We%20debuted%20Azure%20OpenAI%20Service.

34. M.A. Benzaghta, A. Elwalda, M.M. Mousa, I. Erkan, and M. Rahman, "SWOT Analysis Applications: An Integrative Literature Review," *Journal of Global Business Insights*, Vol. 6 (2021), pp. 55–73.

35. L. de Bruin, "Scanning the Environment: PESTEL Analysis," *Business-To-You.com*, September 18, 2016, https://www.business-to-you.com/scanning-the-environment-pestel-analysis/. Also see S. Zakeri, D. Konstantas, and N. Cheikhrouhou, "The Grey Ten-Element Analysis Method: A Novel Strategic Analysis Tool," *Mathematics,* Vol. 10 (2022), p. 846; N. Rastogi and M.K. Trivedi, "PESTLE Technique—A Tool to Identify External Risks in Construction Projects," *International Research Journal of Engineering and Technology*, Vol. 3 (2016), pp. 384–388.

36. G. Dean, "McDonald's Says Cutting off Its Russian Business Has Actually Helped Improve Its Operating Profitability," *Business Insider*, July 27, 2022, https://www.businessinsider.com/mcdonalds-selling-russian-business-improved-operating-margin-vkusno-tochka-restaurant-2022-7. Also see B. Chappell, "McDonald's Is Leaving Russia, after More than 30 Years," *NPR,* May 16, 2022, https://www.npr.org/2022/05/16/1099079032/mcdonalds-leaving-russia.

37. J. Kim and R. Makadok, "Unpacking the 'O' in VRIO: The Role of Workflow Interdependence in the Loss and Replacement of Strategic Human Capital," *Strategic Management Journal*, 2021, pp. 1–35.

38. J.B. Barney, "Firm Resources and Sustained Competitive Advantage," *Journal of Management*, Vol. 19 (1991), pp. 99–120.

39. AFP, "Toyota Top-Selling Automaker for Third Year Running," *Barrons*, January 30, 2023, https://www.barrons.com/news/toyota-top-selling-automaker-for-third-year-running-01675056909.

40. "Global Automotive Market Share in 2021, by Brand," *Statista*, https://www.statista.com/statistics/316786/global-market-share-of-the-leading-automakers/ (accessed January 30, 2023).

41. "Big Auto Had the Ultimate Barriers to Entry—Then Tesla Broke Through," *CleanTechnica*, March 3, 2022, https://cleantechnica.com/2022/03/03/big-auto-had-the-ultimate-barriers-to-entry-then-tesla-broke-through/. Also see R. Akhtar, "Tesla Doubles Production Capacity Despite 'Supply Chain Hell,'" *The Driven*, July 21, 2022, https://thedriven.io/2022/07/21/tesla-doubles-production-capacity-despite-supply-chain-hell/; P. Lienert and J. White, "Analysis: Musk's Bold Goal of Selling 20 Million EVs Could Cost Tesla Billions," *Reuters*, August 30, 2022, https://www.reuters.com/technology/musks-bold-goal-selling-20-mln-evs-could-cost-tesla-billions-2022-08-30/.

42. P. Chatzoglou, D. Chatzoudes, L. Sarigiannidis, and G. Theriou, "The Role of Firm-Specific Factors in the Strategy-Performance Relationship," *Management Research Review*, 2017, pp. 46–73.

43. J. Motavalli, "Toyota Outlines Three-Year EV Plan for Suppliers," *USNews,* December 12, 2022, https://cars.usnews.com/cars-trucks/features/toyota-three-year-ev-plan.

44. R. Davis, "Toyota Rethinks EV Strategy with New CEO," *Wall Street Journal,* January 29, 2023, https://www.wsj.com/articles/toyota-akio-toyoda-koji-sato-evs-electric-vehicles-new-ceo-11675008222?mod=Searchresults_pos1&page=1.

45. S. Kiderlin, "The Outgoing CEO of a Giant Autos Firm Had a Message for His Successor: Don't Be like Me," *CNBC,* January 27, 2023, https://www.cnbc.com/2023/01/27/the-outgoing-ceo-of-toyota-told-his-successor-dont-be-like-me.html. Also see R. Davis, "Toyota Rethinks EV Strategy with New CEO," *Wall Street Journal,* January 29, 2023. https://www.wsj.com/articles/toyota-akio-toyoda-koji-sato-evs-electric-vehicles-new-ceo-11675008222?mod=Searchresults_pos1&page=1.

46. "A Quote by Yogi Berra," *Goodreads,* https://www.goodreads.com/quotes/261863-it-s-tough-to-make-predictions-especially-about-the-future (accessed January 30, 2023).

47. M. Reeves, S. Ramaswamy, and A. O'Dea, "Business Forecasts Are Reliably Wrong—Yet Still Valuable," *Harvard Business Review,* March 8, 2022, https://hbr.org/2022/03/business-forecasts-are-reliably-wrong-yet-still-valuable.

48. J. Royal, "Bitcoin's Price History: 2009 to 2023." *Bankrate,* January 24, 2023, https://www.bankrate.com/investing/bitcoin-price-history/. Also see E. Cheng, "Jack Dorsey Expects Bitcoin to Become the World's 'Single Currency' in about 10 Years," *CNBC,* March 21, 2018, https://www.cnbc.com/2018/03/21/jack-dorsey-expects-bitcoin-to-become-the-worlds-single-currency-in-about-10-years.html; "Sam Bankman-Fried," *Forbes,* https://www.forbes.com/profile/sam-bankman-fried/?sh=410aa3074449 (accessed February 6, 2023); R. Browne and A. Kharpal, "The Boldest Bitcoin Calls for 2023 Are out—And a 1,400% Rally or a 70% Plunge May Be on the Cards," *CNBC,* January 2, 2023, https://www.cnbc.com/2023/01/02/the-boldest-bitcoin-price-predictions-for-2023.html.

49. A. Wieckowski, "Predicting the Future," *Harvard Business Review*, 2018, https://hbr.org/2018/11/predicting-the-future.

50. J. Choi and D. Levinthal, "Wisdom in the Wild: Generalization and Adaptive Dynamics," *Organization Science,* 2022, https://doi.org/10.1287/orsc.2022.1609.

51. "6 Real-World Examples of Tableau Customers Using Time Series Analysis," *Tableau*, https://www.tableau.com/learn/articles/time-series-analysis-examples (accessed January 30, 2023).

52. M. Reeves and A. O'Dea, "6 Factors Driving Changes to Today's Corporate Strategies," *Harvard Business Review,* June 7, 2022. https://hbr.org/2022/06/6-factors-driving-changes-to-todays-corporate-strategies.

53. "Rethinking the 2020s," *Shell*, https://www.shell.com/energy-and-innovation/the-energy-future/scenarios/rethinking-the-2020s.html#iframe=L3dlYmFwcHMvcmV0aGlua18yMDIwX3NjZW5hcmlvcy8 (accessed January 30, 2023).

54. A. Doris, "Future-Proof Your Strategy: Scenario Planning," *UVA Darden Ideas to Action*, September 22, 2022, https://ideas.darden.virginia.edu/strategy-scenario-planning.

55. C. Grube, Y. Polyakov, and T. Roder, "Scenario-Based Cash Planning in a Crisis: Lessons for the Next Normal," *McKinsey*, January 19, 2021, https://www.mckinsey.com/capabilities/strategy-and-corporate-finance/our-insights/scenario-based-cash-planning-in-a-crisis-lessons-for-the-next-normal.

56. P. Hong, S.W. Hong, J.J. Roh, and K. Park, "Evolving Benchmarking Practices: A Review for Research Perspectives," *Benchmarking: An International Journal*, Vol. 19 (2012), pp. 444–462.

57. "Benchmarking," *Bain & Company*, November 7, 2017, www.bain.com/publications/articles/management-tools-benchmarking.aspx.

58. L. Jennings, "The Evolution of a Post-Pandemic Restaurant Drive-Thru," *Nation's Restaurant News,* August 17, 2022. https://www.nrn.com/delivery-takeout-solutions/evolution-post-pandemic-restaurant-drive-thru.

59. "This QSR Has the Fastest Drive-Thru," *Convenience.org.,* October 6, 2022, https://www.convenience.org/Media/Daily/2022/Oct/6/3-This-QSR-Has-the-Fastest-Drive-Thru_Operations.

60. See example in M.M. Yaseen, R. Sweis, A.B. Abdallah, and B.Y. Obeidat, "Benchmarking of TQM Practices in the Jordanian Pharmaceutical Industry (a Comparative Study)," *Benchmarking: An International Journal,* 2018, pp. 4058–4083. Also see D.C. Invernizzi, G. Locatelli, and N.J. Brookes, "A Methodology Based on Benchmarking to Learn across Megaprojects," *International Journal of Managing Projects in Business,* 2018, pp. 104–121.

61. D. Gilbertson and A. Pohle, "The Best and Worst Airlines of 2022," *Wall Street Journal,* January 18, 2023, https://www.wsj.com/articles/best-worst-us-airlines-flights-cancellations-delays-baggage-11673982171?mod=Searchresults_pos5&page=1. Also see A. Sider, "How Southwest Airlines Melted Down," *Wall Street Journal,* December 28, 2022. https://www.wsj.com/articles/southwest-airlines-melting-down-flights-cancelled-11672257523?mod=article_inline.

62. "The Benefits of an Innovation Growth Strategy and How to Create One for Your Organization," *Thunderbird School of Global Management,* July 27, 2021, https://thunderbird.asu.edu/thought-leadership/insights/benefits-innovation-growth-strategy-and-how-create-one-your#:~:text=A%20strategy%20for%20growing%20by.

63. "The Most Innovative Products of 2022," *Fast Company,* November 24, 2022. https://www.fastcompany.com/90731853/the-most-innovative-products-of-2022. Also see M. Daniels, "How Hoka's Popularity Is Fueling Record Growth for Deckers," *Modern Retail,* October 28, 2022. https://www.modernretail.co/operations/how-hokas-popularity-is-fueling-record-growth-for-deckers/; B. Metzler, "Ten Things You Didn't Know about Hoka Running Shoes," *Outside,* July 27, 2022, https://www.outsideonline.com/outdoor-gear/run/ten-things-about-hoka/.

64. "The History of Tabasco Brand," *Tabasco,* https://www.tabasco.com/tabasco-history/ (accessed February 1, 2023).

65. "Bombardier Closes Sale of Its Transportation Business to Alstom," *Bombardier,* January 29, 2021, https://bombardier.com/en/media/news/bombardier-closes-sale-its-transportation-business-alstom#:~:text=confirmed%20today%20the%20closing%20of. Also see "Our History," *Bombardier,* https://bombardier.com/en/who-we-are/our-history (accessed February 1, 2023).

66. D.O. Madsen, "Not Dead Yet: The Rise, Fall and Persistence of the BCG Matrix," *Problems and Perspectives in Management,* Vol. 15 (2017), pp. 19–34. Also see D.O. Madsen, and B.B. Grønseth, "BCG Matrix," *Encyclopedia of Tourism Management and Marketing,* 2022, pp. 254–257; H. Nasution, and S. Pujangkoro, "Business Strategy Formulation: A Literature Review," *Jurnal Sistem Teknik Industri,* Vol. 25 (2023), pp. 89–96.

67. "How Does Google Make Money?" *Oberlo,* https://www.oberlo.com/statistics/how-does-google-make-money#:~:text=Google%20revenue%20breakdown%20(Q3%202022) (accessed February 1, 2023).

68. A.S. John, "AWS, Azure and Google Together Account for 66% of Cloud Market," *Wire19,* October 31, 2022, https://wire19.com/amazon-microsoft-and-google-cloud-infrastructure-market/#:~:text=AWS%20was%20the%20leading%20cloud.

69. J. Dolan, "The Fascinating True Story behind the Failure of Google Glass," *SlashGear,* October 17, 2022, https://www.slashgear.com/1057796/the-fascinating-true-story-behind-the-failure-of-google-glass/#:~:text=Brin%20was%20later%20replaced%20by.

70. "Keurig Dr Pepper to Acquire Core®, a Premium Enhanced Beverage Company," *Keurig Dr Pepper,* September 27, 2018, https://www.jabholco.com/documents/6/press-release-kdp-acquisition-of-core.pdf.

71. M. Sicilia, "Oracle's Acquisition of Cerner: The Future of Healthcare," *Cerner,* June 8, 2022, https://www.cerner.com/perspectives/oracle-acquisition-of-cerner-the-future-of-healthcare.

72. P. Arte and J. Larimo, "Moderating Influence of Product Diversification on the International Diversification-Performance Relationship: A Meta-Analysis," *Journal of Business Research,* Vol. 139 (2022), pp. 1408–1423.

73. A. Berthene, "How Amazon's Whole Foods Acquisition Changed the Grocery Industry," *Digital Commerce 360,* June 21, 2019, https://www.digitalcommerce360.com/2019/06/21/how-amazons-whole-foods-acquisition-changed-the-grocery-industry/. Also see K. Tarasov, "Amazon Bought Whole Foods Five Years Ago for $13.7 Billion. Here's What's Changed at the High-End Grocer," *CNBC,* August 25, 2022. https://www.cnbc.com/2022/08/25/how-whole-foods-has-changed-in-the-five-years-since-amazon-took-over.html.

74. F.A. Hanssen, "Vertical Integration during the Hollywood Studio Era," *Journal of Law & Economics,* August 2010, pp. 519–543.

75. T. Haselton, "Apple Unveils Streaming TV Services," *CNBC,* March 25, 2019, https://www.cnbc.com/2019/03/25/apple-tv-channels-streaming-tv-service-announced.html. Also see "Starbucks' Closely Managed Supply Chain May Be the Key to the Premium Coffee Giant's Success," *Fronetics,* May 10, 2017, https://www.fronetics.com/supply-chain-putting-star-starbucks/.

76. N. Capon, J. U. Farley, and S. Hoenig, "Determinants of financial performance: a meta-analysis," *Management Science,* 36, 1990, pp. 1143–1159. Also see D. Galer, "Managing Supply Chain Disruption," *Risk Management,* 68, 2021, pp. 14–15.

77. M.E. Porter, *Competitive Strategy* (New York: The Free Press, 1980). Also see M.E. Porter, "The Five Competitive Forces That Shape Strategy," *Harvard Business Review,* January 2008, pp. 79–93.

78. F. Pallotta, "The Streaming Wars Are Over," *CNN,* August 11, 2022, https://www.cnn.com/2022/08/11/media/streaming-disney-netflix/index.html.

79. K. Moore, "Netflix Originals Now Make up 50% of Overall US Library," *What's on Netflix,* August 24, 2022, https://www.whats-on-netflix.com/news/50-of-netflixs-library-is-now-made-of-netflix-originals/.

80. S. Chan, "Netflix's Rivals Grow Share of U.S. Streaming App Usage to 61% in Q1 2022," *Sensortower.com,* April 2022, https://sensortower.com/blog/svod-app-market-share-q1-2022.

81. B. Myers, "Done with Netflix? Try These 7 Cheaper Alternatives," *The Motley Fool,* August 6, 2022, https://www.fool.com/the-ascent/personal-finance/articles/done-with-netflix-try-these-7-cheaper-alternatives/.

82. M. Skordoulis, G. Kyriakopoulos, S. Ntanos, S. Galatsidas, G. Arabatzis, M. Chalikias, and P. Kalantonis, "The Mediating Role of Firm Strategy in the Relationship between Green Entrepreneurship, Green Innovation, and Competitive Advantage: The Case of Medium and Large-Sized Firms in Greece," *Sustainability,* Vol. 14 (2022), pp. 3286. Also see Y. Vakulenko, J. Arsenovic, D. Hellström, and P. Shams, "Does Delivery Service Differentiation Matter? Comparing Rural to Urban e-Consumer Satisfaction and Retention," *Journal of Business Research,* Vol. 142 (2022), pp. 476–484.

83. T. McKinnon, "Warby Parker's Strategy: 6 Things It Did Differently to Get a $1.8 Bln Valuation in Less than a Decade," *Indigo9 Digital,* May 31, 2022, https://www.indigo9digital.com/blog/6-things-warby-parker-did-differently-that-.

84. P.R. La Monica, "How Redbox Became a Wall Street Darling Once Again," *CNN,* June 23, 2022. https://www.cnn.com/2022/06/23/investing/redbox-stock-streaming/index.html.

85. "About Us," *Viking,* https://www.vikingcruises.com/about-us/history.html (accessed February 3, 2023). Also see "Awards & Accolades," *Viking,* https://www.vikingcruises.com/about-us/awards.html (accessed February 3, 2023); A. Zelinski, "Torstein Hagen on Dropping 'Cruises' from Viking's Name and Sailing the Great Lakes," *Travel Weekly,* July 18, 2022, https://www.travelweekly.com/On-The-Record/Torstein-Hagen-Viking.

86. S. Luković and J. Tepavčević, "HR Practices and Firm Performance: The Mediating Effect of Business Strategy," *BizInfo (Blace) Journal of Economics, Management and Informatics,* Vol. 13 (2022), pp. 1–11.

Also see R. Agrawal, A. Majumdar, K. Majumdar, R.D. Raut, and B.E. Narkhede, "Attaining Sustainable Development Goals (SDGs) through Supply Chain Practices and Business Strategies: A Systematic Review with Bibliometric and Network Analyses," *Business Strategy and the Environment,* Vol. 31 (2022), pp. 3669–3687.

87. "Jack Welch," *Business Insider,* https://www.businessinsider.com/author/jack-welch (accessed February 10, 2020).

88. J. Welch, "Five Questions That Make Strategy Real," *Jack Welch Management Institute,* March 27, 2016, https://jackwelch.strayer.edu/winning/five-questions-make-strategy-real/. Also see A. Swaminathan; "'The Last of the 100-Year Breed': Here's What's Left of GE," *Yahoo Finance,* July 20, 2018, https://finance.yahoo.com/news/last-100-year-breed-heres-whats-left-ge-164237249.html.

89. "Kroger Outlines How It Is Delivering for Today and Investing in the Future at Business Update Event," *Kroger,* March 4, 2022, https://ir.kroger.com/CorporateProfile/press-releases/press-release/2022/Kroger-Outlines-How-it-is-Delivering-for-Today-and-Investing-in-the-Future-at-Business-Update-Event/default.aspx.

90. "Shaping Kroger's Self-Checkout of Tomorrow with AI and Edge Computing" *Lenovo StoryHub,* September 21, 2022, https://news.lenovo.com/shaping-krogers-self-checkout-of-tomorrow-ai-edge-computing/.

91. L. Bossidy and Ram Charan, with C. Burck, *Execution: The Discipline of Getting Things Done* (New York: Crown Business, 2002).

92. C. Praeger and E. Assefa, "The CEO's Strategy Execution Gap… And How to Fix It," *Rhythm Systems,* November 30, 2019, https://www.rhythmsystems.com/blog/the-ceos-strategy-execution-gap.

93. R. Kaplan and D. Norton, "Mastering the Management System," *Harvard Business Review,* January 2008, pp. 66–77.

94. T. Galpin, "Nudging Innovation across the Firm—Aligning Culture with Strategy," *Journal of Business Strategy,* Vol. 43 (2022), pp. 44–55.

95. Execution is also discussed by C. Montgomery, "Putting Leadership Back into Strategy," *Harvard Business Review,* January 2008, pp. 54–60; J. Lorsch and R. Clark, "Leading from the Boardroom," *Harvard Business Review,* April 2008, pp. 105–111.

96. A.S. DeNisi and K.R. Murphy, "Performance Appraisal and Performance Management: 100 Years of Progress?" *Journal of Applied Psychology,* Vol. 102 (2017), pp. 421–433.

97. R. Sutton and B. Wigert, "More Harm than Good: The Truth about Performance Reviews," *Gallup,* May 6, 2019, https://www.gallup.com/workplace/249332/harm-good-truth-performance-reviews.aspx. Also see "Re-Engineering Performance Management," *Gallup,* https://www.gallup.com/workplace/238064/re-engineering-performance-management.aspx?thank-you-report-form=1 (accessed February 6, 2023).

98. J.D. Ford and L.W. Ford, "Stop Blaming Resistance to Change and Start Using It," *Organizational Dynamics,* Vol. 39 (2010), pp. 24–36. Also see D.D. Warrick, "Revisiting Resistance to Change and How to Manage It: What Has Been Learned and What Organizations Need to Do," *Business Horizons,* 2022, https://doi.org/10.1016/j.bushor.2022.09.001.

99. A. Malshe, D.E. Hughes, V. Good, and S.B. Friend, "Marketing Strategy Implementation Impediments and Remedies: A Multi-Level Theoretical Framework within the Sales-Marketing Interface," *International Journal of Research in Marketing,* Vol. 39 (2022), pp. 824–846.

100. "A Simple Guide to Becoming a Better Business Strategist," *Macquarie,* December 12, 2016, https://www.macquarie.com/au/advisers/expertise/smart-practice/6-ways-you-can-improve-your-strategic-thinking.

101. N. Bowman, "4 Ways to Improve Your Strategic Thinking Skills," *Harvard Business Review,* December 27, 2016, https://hbr.org/2016/12/4-ways-to-improve-your-strategic-thinking-skills.

102. "5 Ways To Improve Your Strategic Thinking Skills Today," *Center for Management & Organization Effectiveness,* https://cmoe.com/blog/improve-strategic-thinking-skills/ (accessed February 6, 2023). Also see "Strategic Thinking: 5 Characteristics of Strategic Thinkers," *MasterClass,* June 7, 2021, https://www.masterclass.com/articles/strategic-thinking-guide; *HBR Guide to Thinking Strategically* (Boston: Harvard Business Press, 2019).

103. M. Lyons, "How to Evaluate a Potential Employer in a Downturn," *Harvard Business Review,* August 2, 2022, https://hbr.org/2022/08/how-to-evaluate-a-potential-employer-in-a-downturn.

104. "7 Ways to Support Employees' Career Advancement," *Robert Half,* December 12, 2022, https://www.roberthalf.com/blog/management-tips/7-ways-to-support-employees-career-advancement.

105. W. R. Bigler, "A New Vista for Strategic Management: Continuously Aligning the Inside with the Outside," *Management Accounting Quarterly,* 2019, pp. 10–23.

106. J. Liss, "The Benefits of Joining Professional Organizations," *PICPA,* October 3, 2022, https://www.picpa.org/articles/cpa-now-blog/cpa-now/2022/10/03/benefits-of-professional-organizations.

107. "A Simple Guide to Becoming a Better Business Strategist," *Macquarie,* December 12, 2016, https://www.macquarie.com/au/advisers/expertise/smart-practice/6-ways-you-can-improve-your-strategic-thinking.

LEARNING MODULE 2

1. "Economic News Release: Private Sector Establishment Births and Deaths, Seasonally Adjusted," U.S. Bureau of Labor Statistics, https://www.bls.gov/news.release/cewbd.t08.htm (accessed February 8, 2023).

2. "Economic News Release: Private Sector Establishment Births and Deaths, Seasonally Adjusted," U.S. Bureau of Labor Statistics, https://www.bls.gov/news.release/cewbd.t08.htm (accessed February 8, 2023). Also see "2022 Small Business Profile," U.S. Small Business Administration, Office of Advocacy, https://advocacy.sba.gov/2022/08/31/2022-small-business-profiles-for-the-states-territories-and-nation/ (accessed February 8, 2023).

3. J. Rampton, "40 Inspirational Entrepreneurial Quotes," *Entrepreneur,* January 1, 2020, https://www.entrepreneur.com/slideshow/300234.

4. T. Eisenmann, "Why Start-Ups Fail," *Harvard Business Review,* April 12, 2021, https://hbr.org/2021/05/why-start-ups-fail. Also see Y. Ganor, "Ask an Expert: What Skills Do I Need to Run a Startup?" *Harvard Business Review,* January 14, 2022, https://hbr.org/2022/01/ask-an-expert-what-skills-do-i-need-to-run-a-startup; R. Gulati, "Why Today's Startups Pursue Both Ideas and Ideals," *Harvard Business Review,* May 13, 2021. https://hbr.org/2021/05/why-todays-startups-pursue-both-ideas-and-ideals; R. Katila, and M. Leatherbee, "To Make Lean Startups Work, You Need a Balanced Team," *Harvard Business Review,* April 23, 2021. https://hbr.org/2021/04/to-make-lean-startups-work-you-need-a-balanced-team.

5. R. Gulati, "The Soul of a Start-Up," *Harvard Business Review,* July–August 2019, https://hbr.org/2019/07/the-soul-of-a-start-up.

6. "Small Business Statistics," *Chamber of Commerce,* https://www.chamberofcommerce.org/small-business-statistics/ (accessed February 9, 2023).

7. V. Vassilev, "5 Entrepreneurs Who Failed before Becoming Successful," *Access MBA,* February 14, 2020, https://www.accessmba.com/articles/view/5-entrepreneurs-who-failed-before-becoming-successful.

8. T. Eisenmann, "Entrepreneurship: A Working Definition," *Harvard Business Review,* January 10, 2013, https://hbr.org/2013/01/what-is-entrepreneurship.

9. L.J. Filion, "Defining the Entrepreneur," *World Encyclopedia of Entrepreneurship,* January 19, 2021, pp. 72–83, https://www.elgaronline.com/display/edcoll/9781839104138/9781839104138.00015.xml.

10. F.H. Perlines, A. Ariza-Montes, and C. Blanco-González-Tejero, "Intrapreneurship Research: A Comprehensive Literature Review," *Journal of Business Research,* Vol. 153 (2022), pp. 428–444.

11. B. Antoncic and R.D. Hisrich, "Intrapreneurship: Construct Refinement and Cross-Cultural Validation," *Journal of Business Venturing,* Vol. 16 (2001), pp. 495–527. Also see N. Sinha and K.B.L. Srivastava, "Association of Personality, Work Values and Socio-Cultural Factors on Intrapreneurial Orientation," *The Journal of Entrepreneurship,* Vol. 22 (2013), pp. 97–113; R.D. Ireland, M.A. Hitt, and D.G. Sirmon, "A Model of Strategic Entrepreneurship: The Construct and Its Dimensions," *Journal of Management,* Vol. 29 (2003), pp. 963–989; C. Kearney and

T. Meynhardt, "Directing Corporate Entrepreneurship Strategy in the Public Sector to Public Value: Antecedents, Components, and Outcomes," *International Public Management Journal*, Vol. 19 (2016), pp. 543–572; L.T. Dung and H.T.T. Giang, "The Effect of International Intrapreneurship on Firm Export Performance with Driving Force of Organizational Factors," *Journal of Business & Industrial Marketing*, Vol. 37 (2022), pp. 2185–2204.

12. Boston BBB, "The Difference between Entrepreneurs and the Self-Employed," *Malden Patch*, September 12, 2013, https://patch.com/massachusetts/malden/the-difference-between-entrepreneurs-and-the-selfemployed_0bb9c4b9.

13. P.T. Luc, P.X. Lan, A.N.H. Le, and B.T. Trang, "A Co-citation and Co-word Analysis of Social Entrepreneurship Research," *Journal of Social Entrepreneurship*, Vol. 13 (2022), pp. 324–339.

14. "Global Entrepreneurship Monitor 2021/2022 Global Report: Opportunity Amid Disruption," *Global Entrepreneurship Monitor*, https://www.gemconsortium.org/reports/latest-global-report (accessed February 10, 2023).

15. M.E. Porter and M.R. Kramer, "Creating Shared Value," *Harvard Business Review*, 2011, https://hbr.org/2011/01/the-big-idea-creating-shared-value.

16. M. Driver, "An Interview with Michael Porter: Social Entrepreneurship and the Transformation of Capitalism," *Academy of Management Learning & Education*, 2012, pp. 421–431.

17. A. Aziz, "Global Study Reveals Consumers Are Four to Six Times More Likely to Purchase, Protect and Champion Purpose-Driven Companies," *Forbes*, June 17, 2020, https://www.forbes.com/sites/afdhelaziz/2020/06/17/global-study-reveals-consumers-are-four-to-six-times-more-likely-to-purchase-protect-and-champion-purpose-driven-companies/?sh=7b116b0e435f.

18. H.M. Haugh and B. Doherty, "Social Entrepreneurship and the Common Good," *Entrepreneurialism and Society: Consequences and Meanings*, Vol. 82 (2022), pp. 89–114.

19. A.A. Al-Qudah, M. Al-Okaily, and H. Alqudah, "The Relationship between Social Entrepreneurship and Sustainable Development from Economic Growth Perspective: 15 'RCEP' Countries," *Journal of Sustainable Finance & Investment*, Vol. 12 (2022), pp. 44–61.

20. H. Brandstätter, "Personality Aspects of Entrepreneurship: A Look at Five Meta-Analyses," *Personality and Individual Differences*, August 2011, pp. 222–230. Also see R.K. Jain, "Entrepreneurial Competencies: A Meta-Analysis and Comprehensive Conceptualization for Future Research," *Vision*, 2011, pp. 127–152; and H. Munir, C. Jianfeng, and S. Ramzan, "Personality Traits and Theory of Planned Behavior Comparison of Entrepreneurial Intentions between an Emerging Economy and a Developing Country," *International Journal of Entrepreneurial Behavior & Research*, 2019, pp. 554–580.

21. C. Naumann, "Entrepreneurial Mindset: A Synthetic Literature Review," *Entrepreneurial Business and Economics Review*, Vol. 5 (2017), pp. 149–172.

22. B.A. Soomro and N. Shah, "Entrepreneurship Education, Entrepreneurial Self-Efficacy, Need for Achievement and Entrepreneurial Intention among Commerce Students in Pakistan," *Education + Training*, Vol. 64 (2022), pp. 107–125.

23. W.H. Stewart and P.L. Roth, "A Meta-Analysis of Achievement Motivation Differences between Entrepreneurs and Managers," *Journal of Small Business Management*, Vol. 45 (2007), pp. 401–421.

24. C.J. Collins, P.J. Hanges, and E.A. Locke, "The Relationship of Achievement Motivation to Entrepreneurial Behavior: A Meta-Analysis," *Human Performance*, Vol. 17 (2004), pp. 95–117.

25. F. Sahin, H. Karadag, and B. Tuncer, "Big Five Personality Traits, Entrepreneurial Self-Efficacy and Entrepreneurial Intention: A Configurational Approach," *International Journal of Entrepreneurial Behavior & Research*, 2019, pp. 1188–1211. Also see S.P. Kerr, W.R. Kerr, and T. Xu, "Personality Traits of Entrepreneurs: A Review of Recent Literature," *Foundations and Trends in Entrepreneurship*, Vol. 14 (2018), pp. 279–356.

26. M.I. Lopez-Nunez, S. Rubio-Valdehita, M.E. Aparicio-Garcia, and E.M. Diaz-Ramiro, "Are Entrepreneurs Born or Made? The Influence of Personality," *Personality and Individual Differences*, 2020, https://doi.org/10.1016/j.paid.2019.109699.

27. T. Butler, "Hiring an Entrepreneurial Leader," *Harvard Business Review*, March–April 2017, pp. 85–93. Also see L. Altinay, E. Kromidha, A. Nurmagambetova, Z. Alrawadieh, and G.K. Madanoglu, "A Social Cognition Perspective on Entrepreneurial Personality Traits and Intentions to Start a Business: Does Creativity Matter?" *Management Decision*, Vol. 60 (2022), pp. 1606–1625.

28. Y.H. Al-Mamary and M. Alshallaqi, "Impact of Autonomy, Innovativeness, Risk-Taking, Proactiveness, and Competitive aggressiveness on Students' Intention to Start a New Venture," *Journal of Innovation & Knowledge*, Vol. 7 (2022), p. 100239. Also see F.M. Ilevbare, O.E. Ilevbare, C.M. Adelowo, and F.P. Oshorenua, "Social Support and Risk-Taking Propensity as Predictors of Entrepreneurial Intention among Undergraduates in Nigeria," *Asia Pacific Journal of Innovation and Entrepreneurship*, Vol. 16 (2022), pp. 90–107; A.A. Salameh, H. Akhtar, R. Gul, A.B. Omar, and S. Hanif, "Personality Traits and Entrepreneurial Intentions: Financial Risk-Taking as Mediator," *Frontiers in Psychology*, Vol. 13 (2022), pp. 1–11.

29. Y.H. Al-Mamary and M. Alshallaqi, "Impact of Autonomy, Innovativeness, Risk-Taking, Proactiveness, and Competitive Aggressiveness on Students' Intention to Start a New Venture," *Journal of Innovation & Knowledge*, Vol. 7 (2022), 100239. Also see R. Kumar and S. Shukla. "Creativity, Proactive Personality and Entrepreneurial Intentions: Examining the Mediating Role of Entrepreneurial Self-Efficacy," *Global Business Review*, Vol. 23 (2022), pp. 101–118; Y.-F. Luo, J. Huang, and S. Gao, "Relationship between Proactive Personality and Entrepreneurial Intentions in College Students: Mediation Effects of Social Capital and Human Capital," *Frontiers in Psychology*, Vol. 13 (2022), pp. 1–13.

30. R.K. Jain, "Entrepreneurial Competencies: A Meta-Analysis and Comprehensive Conceptualization for Future Research," *Vision*, 2011, p. 134.

31. D.R. Hidayat and A. Wibowo, "Do Big-Five Personality Impact on Youth Entrepreneurial Intention?" *Journal of Entrepreneurship Education*, 2019, 1528-2651-22-3-371.

32. J.E. Jennings, Z. Rahman, and D. Dempsey, "Challenging What We Think We Know: Theory and Evidence for Questioning Common Beliefs about the Gender Gap in Entrepreneurial Confidence," *Entrepreneurship Theory and Practice*, 2022, pp. 1–29.

33. J.J. Ferreira, M.L. Raposo, R.G. Rodrigues, A. Dinis, and A. do Paço, "A Model of Entrepreneurial Intention: An Application of the Psychological and Behavioral Approaches," *Journal of Small Business and Enterprise Development*, Vol. 19 (2012), pp. 424–440.

34. A. Glosenberg, D. Phillips, J. Schaefer, J.M. Pollack, B.L. Kirkman, J. McChesney, S.M. Noble, M.K. Ward, and L.L. Foster, "The Relationship of Self-Efficacy with Entrepreneurial Success: A Meta-Analytic Replication and Extension," *Journal of Business Venturing Insights*, Vol. 18 (2022), e00342, https://doi.org/10.1016/j.jbvi.2022.e00342.

35. É. St-Jean, M. Tremblay, C. Fonrouge, and R. Chouchane, "Gendered Impact of Training on Entrepreneurial Self-Efficacy: A Longitudinal Study of Nascent Entrepreneurs," *Journal of Small Business & Entrepreneurship*, Vol. 34 (2022), pp. 524–547.

36. H. Brandstätter, "Personality Aspects of Entrepreneurship: A Look at Five Meta-Analyses," *Personality and Individual Differences*, August 2011, pp. 222–230. Also see R.K. Jain, "Entrepreneurial Competencies: A Meta-Analysis and Comprehensive Conceptualization for Future Research," *Vision*, 2011, pp. 127–152.

37. R. Zitelmann, "Successful Entrepreneurs and Investors Are Nonconformists Who Swim against the Current," *Forbes*, September 23, 2019, https://www.forbes.com/sites/rainerzitelmann/2019/09/23/successful-entrepreneurs-and-investors-are-nonconformists-who-swim-against-the-current/#4bf7e4434fff.

38. Definition by Paul Graham, head of business accelerator Y Combinator, cited in N. Robehmed, "What Is a Startup?" *Forbes*, December 16, 2013, www.forbes.com/sites/natalierobehmed/2013/12/16/what-is-a-strartup/print.

39. O. Wallach, "The World's Biggest Startups: Top Unicorns of 2021," *Visual Capitalist*, December 8, 2021. https://www.visualcapitalist.com/the-worlds-biggest-startups-top-unicorns-of-2021/.

40. E. Schulte, "The 10 Most Innovative Companies with Fewer than 100 Employees," *Fast Company*, March 8, 2022, https://www.fastcompany.com/90724470/most-innovative-companies-small-mighty-10-100-2022. Also see "Step - Overview, News & Competitors," *ZoomInfo*, https://www.zoominfo.com/c/stepcom/353919461 (accessed February 13, 2023).

41. "Stripe," *Forbes*, https://www.forbes.com/companies/stripe/?sh=29ab0a9c4639 (accessed February 13, 2023). Also see "Newsroom: About Stripe," *Stripe.com*, https://stripe.com/newsroom/information (accessed February 13, 2023); E. Chan, "Stripe Cuts Valuation 11% to $63 Billion, the Information Says," *Bloomberg*, January 11, 2023, https://www.bloomberg.com/news/articles/2023-01-12/stripe-cuts-valuation-11-to-63-billion-the-information-says?leadSource=uverify%20wall.

42. "Basic Requirements," Small Business Administration, https://www.sba.gov/federal-contracting/contracting-guide/basic-requirements#:~:text=The%20SBA%20assigns%20a%20size (accessed February 13, 2023).

43. T. Richards, "Small Business Facts," U.S. Small Business Administration Office of Advocacy, September 2022, https://cdn.advocacy.sba.gov/wp-content/uploads/2022/09/13092425/Fact-Sheet_Small-Business-Innovation-Measured-by-Patenting-Activity.pdf?utm_medium=email&utm_source=govdelivery#:~:text=Although%20the%20smallest%20R%26D%2Dperforming,large%20businesses%20(Table%201).

44. M. Kato, K. Onishi, and Y. Honjo, "Does Patenting Always Help New Firm Survival? Understanding Heterogeneity among Exit Routes," *Small Business Economics*, Vol. 59 (2022), pp. 449–475.

45. "Frequently Asked Questions," *U.S. Small Business Administration Office of Advocacy*, December 2021, https://cdn.advocacy.sba.gov/wp-content/uploads/2021/12/06095731/Small-Business-FAQ-Revised-December-2021.pdf.

46. T. Seth, "Standard of Living: Meaning, Factor and Other Details," *Economics Discussion*, http://www.economicsdiscussion.net/articles/standard-of-living-meaning-factor-and-other-details/1453 (accessed March 29, 2018).

47. "Global Entrepreneurship Monitor 2021/2022 Global Report: Opportunity Amid Disruption," *Global Entrepreneurship Monitor*, https://www.gemconsortium.org/reports/latest-global-report (accessed February 13, 2023).

48. B. Ansberry, "An Entrepreneur with Autism Finds His Path," *The Wall Street Journal*, November 27, 2017, pp. R1–R2.

49. "Our Blog," *Green Bridge Growers*, https://www.greenbridgegrowers.org/ (accessed February 13, 2023).

50. H. Zak, "How to Create Successful Products for Underserved Markets," *Inc.*, February 27, 2019, https://www.inc.com/heidi-zak/how-to-create-successful-products-for-underserved-markets.html. Also see "7 Ways to Discover a Winning Business Idea," *The Balance*, November 25, 2016, https://www.thebalance.com/create-winning-business-ideas-2947249.

51. I. Morris, "Apple Responds to iPhone Slowdown Complaints and Offers Solutions," *Forbes*, December 28, 2017, https://www.forbes.com/sites/ianmorris/2017/12/28/apple-responds-to-iphone-slowdon-complaints-and-offers-solutions/#5da610db79ee.

52. N. Gagliordi, "Apple Will Pay Up to $500 Million in iPhone Throttling Settlement," *ZDNet*, March 2, 2020, https://www.zdnet.com/article/apple-will-pay-up-to-500-million-in-iphone-throttling-settlement/.

53. "Franchising in the U.S.—statistics and facts," *Statista*, https://www.statista.com/topics/5048/franchising-in-the-us/#:~:text=In%202022%2C%20it%20was%20estimated,totaling%20almost%208.5%20million%20people (accessed February 13, 2023).

54. "Franchising Overview," *McDonald's*, https://corporate.mcdonalds.com/corpmcd/franchising-overview.html (accessed February 13, 2023).

55. T. Minieri, "Is Franchising Right for Your Business?" *Forbes*, February 18, 2020, https://www.forbes.com/sites/theyec/2020/02/18/is-franchising-right-for-your-business/#2f742f20685f.

56. "Rankings of the Top 100 Franchises of 2023," *Franchise Direct*, https://www.franchisedirect.com/top100globalfranchises/rankings (accessed February 13, 2023). Also see A. Pratap, "Chick-Fil-A Advertising Expenses," *Statstic*, June, 22, 2022, https://statstic.com/chick-fil-a-advertising-expenses/; "Chick-Fil-A One," *Chick-Fil-A*, https://www.chick-fil-a.com/one (accessed February 13, 2023).

57. "What Are the Advantages and Disadvantages of Owning a Franchise?" *International Franchise Association*, https://www.franchise.org/faqs/basics/what-are-the-advantages-and-disadvantages (accessed February 13, 2023).

58. A. Lockie, "How Much Does a Chick-Fil-A Franchise Cost?" *1851 Franchise Magazine*, March 10, 2022, https://1851franchise.com/how-much-does-a-chick-fil-a-franchise-cost-2715278#stories. Also see "Franchise," *Chick-fil-A*, https://www.chick-fil-a.com/franchise (accessed February 13, 2023).

59. "What to Consider before Opening a Franchise," *Wells Fargo*, August 2, 2019, https://wellsfargoworks.com/planning/article/what-to-consider-before-opening-a-franchise. Also see "McDonald's Franchise," *Franchise Help*, https://www.franchisehelp.com/franchises/mcdonalds/ (accessed February 13, 2023).

60. S. Robbins, "Why You Must Have a Business Plan," *Entrepreneur*, November 19, 2004, https://www.entrepreneur.com/article/74194. Also see F.J. Greene and C. Hopp, "Research: Writing a Business Plan Makes Your Startup More Likely to Succeed," *Harvard Business Review*, July 14, 2017, https://hbr.org/2017/07/research-writing-a-business-plan-makes-your-startup-more-likely-to-succeed.

61. S. Ward, "One-Page Business Plan Templates," *The Balance*, April 10, 2017, www.thebalance.com/one-page-business-plan-templates-4135972. Also see N. Parsons, "How to Write a One-Page Business Plan," *Bplans*, https://articles.bplans.com/how-to-write-a-one-page-business-plan (accessed March 30, 2018).

62. "Business Plan Length: How Long Should Your Business Plan Be?" *GrowThink*, https://www.growthink.com/businessplan/help-center/ideal-length-your-business-plan (accessed February 13, 2023).

63. A. Osterwalder and Y. Pigneur, *Business Model Generation: A Handbook for Visionaries, Game Changers, and Challengers* (John Wiley & Sons, 2010).

64. A. Osterwalder and Y. Pigneur, *Business Model Generation: A Handbook for Visionaries, Game Changers, and Challengers* (John Wiley & Sons, 2010). Also see A. Cowan, "The 20 Minute Business Plan: Business Model Canvas Made Easy," *Alex Cowan*, https://www.alexandercowan.com/business-model-canvas-templates/ (accessed February 13, 2023); "Create a New Business Model Canvas," *Canvanizer*, https://canvanizer.com/new/business-model-canvas (accessed February 13, 2023).

65. N. Jain, "Top Ten Best-Selling 'Shark Tank' Items," *TechStory*, November 1, 2022, https://techstory.in/top-ten-best-selling-shark-tank-items/. Also see "About Us" *ScrubDaddy*, https://scrubdaddy.com/about/ (accessed February 14, 2023).

66. F.J. Greene and C. Hopp, "Are Formal Planners More Likely to Achieve New Venture Viability? A Counterfactual Model and Analysis," *Strategic Entrepreneurial Journal*, March 2017, pp. 36–60.

67. S. Caramela, "How to Choose the Best Legal Structure for Your Business," *Business News Daily*, January 29, 2018, https://www.businessnewsdaily.com/8163-choose-legal-business-structure.html. Also see "IRS Business Structures," *Internal Revenue Service*, last updated December 14, 2017, https://www.irs.gov/businesses/small-businesses-self-employed/business-structures.

68. "Sole Proprietorships," *Internal Revenue Service*, https://www.irs.gov/businesses/small-businesses-self-employed/sole-proprietorships (accessed February 13, 2023).

69. "Partnerships," *Internal Revenue Service*, https://www.irs.gov/businesses/small-businesses-self-employed/partnerships (accessed February 13, 2023).

70. "Groupe Point Vision," *Groupe Point Vision*, https://www.groupepointvision.com/ (accessed February 13, 2023).

71. S. Caramela, "How to Choose the Best Legal Structure for Your Business," *Business News Daily*, January 29, 2018, https://www.businessnewsdaily.com/8163-choose-legal-business-structure.html.

72. S. Caramela, "How to Choose the Best Legal Structure for Your Business," *Business News Daily*, January 29, 2018, https://www.businessnewsdaily.com/8163-choose-legal-business-structure.html. Also see "Forming a Corporation," *Internal Revenue Service*, https://www.irs.gov/businesses/small-businesses-self-employed/forming-a-corporation (accessed February 13, 2023).

73. "Forming a Corporation," *Internal Revenue Service*, https://www.irs.gov/businesses/small-businesses-self-employed/forming-a-corporation (accessed February 13, 2023).

74. "S Corporations," *Internal Revenue Service*, https://www.irs.gov/businesses/small-businesses-self-employed/s-corporations (accessed February 13, 2023).

75. H.R. Johnson, "What Is an LLC (Limited Liability Company)?" *Legal Zoom*, https://www.legalzoom.com/articles/what-is-a-limited-liability-company-llc?kid=0f29ecc7-72c8-4a58-8f23-c2193ac028c&utm_source=google&utm_medium=cpc&utm_term=what_is_an_llc&utm_content=247005141740&utm_campaign=BIZ_|_LLC&gclid=CjwKCAjwwPfVBRBiEiwAdkM0HYjZQSz6F3Q_BaPhdbJeQSC_ftlBJhH6mprelPmnInJVyOxi1OH5_BoC92sQAvD_BwE (accessed March 30, 2018).

76. R. Voidonicolas, "The Cost of Being the Boss: What Business Owners Spend in Their First Year," *Shopify*, November 8, 2022, https://www.shopify.com/blog/cost-to-start-business.

77. R. Voidonicolas, "The Cost of Being the Boss: What Business Owners Spend in Their First Year," *Shopify*, November 8, 2022, https://www.shopify.com/blog/cost-to-start-business.

78. "2023 Economic Report," National Small Business Association, https://www.nsba.biz/_files/ugd/601769_8df54000a0f644e9afc0425bcdfa649f.pdf (accessed February 13, 2023).

79. "Organization," *U.S. Small Business Administration*, https://www.sba.gov/about-sba/organization (accessed February 13, 2023).

80. "7 Sources of Start-Up Financing," *bdc*, https://www.bdc.ca/en/articles-tools/start-buy-business/start-business/pages/start-up-financing-sources.aspx (accessed February 13, 2023).

81. "Small Business Finance FAQ," *U.S. Small Business Administration Office of Advocacy*, February 2022, https://cdn.advocacy.sba.gov/wp-content/uploads/2022/02/15122206/FinanceFAQ-Final-Feb2022.pdf.

82. "How Venture Capitalists Really Assess a Pitch," *Harvard Business Review*, May–June 2017, https://hbr.org/2017/05/how-venture-capitalists-really-assess-a-pitch.

83. K. Hassan, M. Varadan, and C. Zeisberger, "How the VC Pitch Process Is Failing Female Entrepreneurs," *Harvard Business Review*, January 13, 2020, https://hbr.org/2020/01/how-the-vc-pitch-process-is-failing-female-entrepreneurs.

84. M. Malmstrom, A. Voitkane, J. Johansson, and J. Wincent, "What Do They Think and What Do They Say? Gender Bias, Entrepreneurial Attitude in Writing and Venture Capitalists' Funding Decisions," *Journal of Business Venturing Insights*, 2020, https://doi.org/10.1016/j.jbvi.2019.e00154.

85. M.R. Zisser, S.L. Johnson, M.A. Freeman, and P. Staudenmaier, "The Relationship between Entrepreneurial Intent, Gender and Personality," *Gender in Management: An International Journal*, 2019, pp. 666–684.

86. "7 Sources of Start-Up Financing," *bdc*, https://www.bdc.ca/en/articles-tools/start-buy-business/start-business/pages/start-up-financing-sources.aspx (accessed February 13, 2023).

87. "How Venture Capitalists Really Assess a Pitch," *Harvard Business Review*, May–June 2017, https://hbr.org/2017/05/how-venture-capitalists-really-assess-a-pitch.

88. A. Camp, "Secure Funding from an Angel Investor to Grow Your Business," *Finder*, September 18, 2019, https://www.finder.com/business-angel-investors.

89. "What Is Crowd Investing?" *SyndicateRoom*, https://www.syndicateroom.com/crowd-investing (accessed February 13, 2023).

90. "About GoFundMe," *GoFundMe*, https://www.gofundme.com/c/about-us (accessed February 13, 2023).

91. C. Hartnell, A. Kinicki, L. Lambert, M. Fugate, and P. Corner, "Do Similarities or Differences between CEO Leadership and Organizational Culture Have a More Positive Effect on Firm Performance? A Test of Competing Predictions," *Journal of Applied Psychology*, Vol. 101 (2016), pp. 846–861.

92. C.A Hartnell, A. Kinicki, A. Y. Ou, D. Choi, and E.P. Karam, "A Meta-Analytic Test of Organizational Culture's Association with Elements of an Organization's System and Its Relative Predictive Validity on Organizational Outcomes," *Journal of Applied Psychology*, 2019, pp. 832–850. Also see A.Y. Ou, C. Hartnell, A. Kinicki, E. Kram, and D. Choi, "Culture in Context: A Meta-Analysis of the Nomological Network of Organizational Culture," Presentation at Connecting Culture and Context: Insights from Organizational Culture Theory and Research, 2016 National Academy of Management meeting, Anaheim, California.

93. "Frequently Asked Questions," *U.S. Small Business Administration Office of Advocacy*, December 2021, https://cdn.advocacy.sba.gov/wp-content/uploads/2021/12/06095731/Small-Business-FAQ-Revised-December-2021.pdf.

94. K. Main and C. Bottorff, "Small Business Statistics of 2023," *Forbes*, December 7, 2022, https://www.forbes.com/advisor/business/small-business-statistics/. Also see B. Sutter, "The #1 Reason Small Businesses Fail—and How to Avoid It," *Score*, May 6, 2022, https://www.score.org/resource/blog-post/1-reason-small-businesses-fail-and-how-avoid-it; "Five Reasons Small Businesses Fail (and Five Ways to Overcome Pitfalls!)," *Peregrine Global Services*, June 21, 2022, https://peregrineglobal.com/why-small-businesses-fail/.

CHAPTER 7

1. M. Schwantes, "5 CEOs Share 5 Leadership Tips for a Successful 2020," *Inc.*, January 21, 2020, https://www.inc.com/marcel-schwantes/5-ceos-share-5-leadership-tips-for-a-successful-2020.html.

2. L.R. Roepe, "When Leaders Make Mistakes," *SHRM*, February 27, 2020, https://www.shrm.org/hr-today/news/hr-magazine/spring2020/Pages/when-leaders-make-mistakes.aspx. Also see "Making a Mistake: How to Learn from Mistakes," *MasterClass*, May 12, 2022, https://www.masterclass.com/articles/making-a-mistake.

3. M.G. Moore, "How to Make Great Decisions, Quickly," *Harvard Business Review*, March 22, 2022, https://hbr.org/2022/03/how-to-make-great-decisions-quickly.

4. J. Lofgren, "How Open-Mindedness Encourages Growth in Leadership," *Forbes*, March 25, 2022, https://www.forbes.com/sites/forbescoachescouncil/2022/03/25/how-open-mindedness-encourages-growth-in-leadership/?sh=19fbfa1c3d77.

5. "Positive Thinking: Stop Negative Self-Talk to Reduce Stress," *Mayo Clinic*, February 3, 2022, https://www.mayoclinic.org/healthy-lifestyle/stress-management/in-depth/positive-thinking/art-20043950.

6. P. Hopper and K. Sakuja, "A 4-Step Process to Help Senior Teams Prioritize Decisions," *Harvard Business Review*, March 27, 2017, https://hbr.org/2017/03/a-4-step-process-to-help-senior-teams-prioritize-decisions.

7. "Making a Mistake: How to Learn from Mistakes," *MasterClass*, May 12, 2022, https://www.masterclass.com/articles/making-a-mistake.

8. "Decision Making in the Age of Urgency," *McKinsey & Company*, https://www.mckinsey.com/~/media/McKinsey/Business%20Functions/Organization/Our%20Insights/Decision%20making%20in%20the%20age%20of%20urgency/Decision-making-in-the-age-of-urgency.pdf (accessed February 15, 2023). Also see R. Ramaswami, "Leading Off: Essentials for Leaders and Those They Lead," *McKinsey*, https://www.mckinsey.com/~/media/mckinsey/email/leadingoff/2022/05/09/2022-05-09b.html (accessed February 15, 2023).

9. A. Smith, "The Theory of Moral Sentiments," In D.D. Rahael and A.L Mactie (Eds.), *Liberty Classics*, Indianapolis: Liberty Press, 1759.

10. L.M. van Swol, C-T. Chang, and Z. Gong, "The Benefits of Advice from Outgroup Members on Decision Accuracy and Bias Reduction," *Decision*, Vol. 10 (2023), pp. 81–91.

11. V. Pereira, E. Hadjielias, M. Christofi, and D. Vrontis, "A Systematic Literature Review on the Impact of Artificial Intelligence on Workplace Outcomes: A Multi-Process Perspective," *Human Resource Management Review,* Vol. 33 (2023), p. 100857.

12. N. Bayram and M. Aydemir, "Decision-Making Styles and Personality Traits," *International Journal of Recent Advances in Organizational Behaviour and Decision Sciences,* Vol. 3 (2017), pp. 905–915. Also see J.A. Chandler, N.E. Johnson, S.L. Jordan, and J.C. Short, "A Meta-Analysis of Humble Leadership: Reviewing Individual, Team, and Organizational Outcomes of Leader Humility," *The Leadership Quarterly,* 2022, p. 101660.

13. H.A. Simon, *Administrative Behavior,* 3rd ed. (New York: Free Press, 1996); H.A. Simon, "Making Management Decisions: The Role of Intuition and Emotion," *The Academy of Management Executive,* February 1987, pp. 57–63.

14. A.G.E. Collins and A. Shenhav, "Advances in Modeling Learning and Decision-Making in Neuroscience," *Neuropsychopharmacology,* 47, 2022, pp. 104–118.

15. C. Lindig-Leon, S. Gottwald, and D.A. Braun, "Analyzing Abstraction and Hierarchical Decision-Making in Absolute Identification by Information-Theoretic Bounded Rationality," *Frontiers in Neuroscience,* 2019, https://doi.org/10.3389/fnins.2019.01230.

16. J. Joseph and V. Gaba. "Organizational Structure, Information Processing, and Decision-Making: A Retrospective and Road Map for Research," *Academy of Management Annals,* Vol. 14 (2020), pp. 267–302.

17. A.G.E. Collins and A. Shenhav, "Advances in Modeling Learning and Decision-Making in Neuroscience," *Neuropsychopharmacology,* Vol. 47 (2022), pp. 104–118.

18. N.J. Hiller and D.C. Hambrick, "Conceptualizing Executive Hubris: The Role of (Hyper-) Core Self-Evaluations in Strategic Decision-Making," *Strategic Management Journal,* Vol. 26 (2005), pp. 297–319.

19. Y. Guo, P-W. Huang, C. Ciu, S-C. Fang, and F-S. Tsai, "Entrepreneur Hubris, Organizational Ambidexterity, and Dynamic Capability Construction," *Frontiers in Psychology,* Vol. 12 (2022), p. 6089. Also see A. Li and B.N. Sullivan, "Blind to the Future: Exploring the Contingent Effect of Managerial Hubris on Strategic Foresight," *Strategic Organization,* Vol. 20 (2022), pp. 565–599.

20. S. Dang and G. Roumeliotis, "Musk Begins His Twitter Ownership with Firings, Declares the 'Bird Is Freed,'" *Reuters,* October 28, 2022, https://www.reuters.com/markets/deals/elon-musk-completes-44-bln-acquisition-twitter-2022-10-28/. Also see D. O'Sullivan and C. Duffy, "Elon Musk's Twitter Lays off Employees across the Company | CNN Business," *CNN,* November 9, 2022, https://www.cnn.com/2022/11/03/tech/twitter-layoffs/index.html#:~:text=Twitter%20had%20about%207%2C500%20workers; "Tesla Stock Price," *Google,* https://www.google.com/search?q=tesla+stock+price&rlz=1C1GCEU_enUS993US993&oq=tesla+stock+price&aqs=chrome..69i57.3144j0j7&sourceid=chrome&ie=UTF-8 (accessed February 16, 2023); H. Towey, "Elon Musk Now Owns Twitter. Here Are the Busy Billionaire's 4 Other Companies and What They All Do," *Business Insider,* October 28, 2022, https://www.businessinsider.com/elon-musk-companies-tesla-spacex-boring-co-neuralink-twitter-2022-4#musks-right-hand-man-jared-birchall-was-listed-as-neuralinks-chief-executive-cfo-and-president-in-2018-15.

21. F.M. Artinger, G. Gigerenzer, and P. Jacobs, "Satisficing: Integrating Two Traditions," *Journal of Economic Literature,* Vol. 60 (2022), pp. 598–635.

22. S. Di Nuovo and M. Sinatra, "Do Personality Traits and Self-Regulatory Processes Affect Decision-Making Tendencies?" *Australian Journal of Psychology,* 2018, pp. 284–294.

23. D. Madani and C. Atkinson, "Hallmark Channel Parent's CEO out after Same-Sex Marriage Ad Backlash," *NBC News,* January 22, 2020, https://www.nbcnews.com/feature/nbc-out/hallmark-channel-parent-ceo-out-after-same-sex-marriage-ad-n1120616. Also see L. Rizzo, "Wonya Lucas Is Making Big Changes at the Hallmark Channel," *CNBC,* February 14, 2023. https://www.cnbc.com/2023/02/14/hallmark-channel-wonya-lucas-big-changes.html.

24. D. Kahneman and G. Klein, "Conditions for Intuitive Expertise: A Failure to Disagree," *American Psychologist,* September 2009, pp. 515–526.

25. L. Stupple, "4 Reasons Intuition Is an Essential Leadership Skill," *Entrepreneur,* May 30, 2022, https://www.entrepreneur.com/leadership/4-reasons-intuition-is-an-essential-leadership-skill/426726.

26. K. Malewska, "The Profile of an Intuitive Decision Maker and the Use of Intuition in Decision-Making Practice," *Management,* 2018, pp. 31–44.

27. C. Acciarini, F. Brunetta, and P. Boccardelli, "Cognitive Biases and Decision-Making Strategies in Times of Change: A Systematic Literature Review," *Management Decision,* Vol. 59 (2021), pp. 638–652. Also see C. Akinci and E. Sadler-Smith, "Collective Intuition: Implications for Improved Decision Making and Organizational Learning," *British Journal of Management,* Vol. 30 (2019), pp. 558–577; M. Dayan and C.A. Di Benedetto, "Team Intuition as a Continuum Construct and New Product Creativity: The Role of Environmental Turbulence, Team Experience, and Stress," *Research Policy,* Vol. 40 (2011), pp. 276–286.

28. "About Us," *Virgin Group,* https://www.virgin.com/virgingroup/content/about-us (accessed February 16, 2023). Also see "Richard Branson," *Biography,* November 2, 2021, https://www.biography.com/business-figure/richard-branson.

29. R. Branson, "Instinct in a World of Analytics," *Virgin,* November 26, 2019, https://www.virgin.com/richard-branson/instinct-world-analytics.

30. I.C. Thanos, "The Complementary Effects of Rationality and Intuition on Strategic Decision Quality," *European Management Journal,* 2022, in press, https://doi.org/10.1016/j.emj.2022.03.003.

31. R. Branson, "5 Skills and Abilities That Successful Entrepreneurs Share," *Virgin,* November 26, 2019, https://www.virgin.com/branson-family/richard-branson-blog/5-skills-and-abilities-successful-entrepreneurs-share.

32. R. Branson, "It's Okay to Trust Your Instincts, But Put People First," *Khaleej Times,* December 22, 2019, https://www.khaleejtimes.com/editorials-columns/its-okay-to-trust-your-instincts-but-put-people-first.

33. D. McGinn, "How Jeff Bezos Makes Decisions," *Harvard Business Review,* October 18, 2013, https://hbr.org/2013/10/how-jeff-bezos-makes-decisions.

34. T. Huddleston Jr., "5 of Jeff Bezos' Best Lessons for Success from His 27 Years as Amazon CEO," *CNBC,* July 16, 2021, https://www.cnbc.com/2021/07/05/jeff-bezos-best-lessons-for-success-from-his-27-years-as-amazon-ceo.html.

35. R. Umoh, "Steve Jobs and Albert Einstein Both Attributed Their Extraordinary Success to This Personality Trait," *CNBC,* June 29, 2017, https://www.cnbc.com/2017/06/29/steve-jobs-and-albert-einstein-both-attributed-their-extraordinary-success-to-this-personality-trait.html.

36. E. Dane and M.G. Pratt, "Exploring Intuition and Its Role in Managerial Decision Making," *Academy of Management Review,* January 2007, pp. 33–54.

37. P. Tabesh and D. M. Vera, "Top Managers' Improvisational Decision-Making in Crisis: A Paradox Perspective," *Management Decision,* Vol. 58 (2020), pp. 2235–2256.

38. D.J. Sleesman, J.R. Hollenbeck, R.B. Davison, and B.A. Scott, "Leader Intuition: Good or Bad for Multiteam System Performance? The Roles of Information Load and Introversion," *Group & Organization Management,* 2022, 10596011221121461.

39. I.C. Thanos, "The Complementary Effects of Rationality and Intuition on Strategic Decision Quality" *European Management Journal,* 2022, in press, https://doi.org/10.1016/j.emj.2022.03.003.

40. B. Allyn, "Top Reason for CEO Departures among Largest Companies Is Now Misconduct, Study Finds," *NPR,* May 20, 2019, https://www.npr.org/2019/05/20/725108825/top-reason-for-ceo-departures-among-largest-companies-is-now-misconduct-study-fi.

41. S. Hassan, P. Kaur, M. Muchiri, C. Ogbonnaya, and A. Dhir, "Unethical Leadership: Review, Synthesis and Directions for Future Research," *Journal of Business Ethics,* 2022, pp. 1–40. Also see "Fighting Fraud: A Never-Ending Battle," *PriceWaterhouseCooper,* https://www.global-screeningsolutions.com/industries/global-economic-crime-and-fraud-survey-2020-1.pdf (accessed February 17, 2023).

42. S. Hassan, P. Kaur, M. Muchiri, C. Ogbonnaya, and A. Dhir, "Unethical Leadership: Review, Synthesis and Directions for Future Research," *Journal of Business Ethics*, 2022, pp. 1–40. Also see M. Mishra, K. Ghosh, and D. Sharma, "Unethical Pro-organizational Behavior: A Systematic Review and Future Research Agenda," *Journal of Business Ethics*, 2021, pp. 1–25.

43. A. Benlahcene and H. Meddour, "The Prevalence of Unethical Leadership Behaviour: The Role of Organisational Oversight," *Prevalence*, Vol. 13 (2020), pp. 310–325.

44. E.E. Kelebek and E. Alniacik, "Effects of Leader-Member Exchange, Organizational Identification and Leadership Communication on Unethical Pro-organizational Behavior: A Study on Bank Employees in Turkey," *Sustainability*, Vol. 14 (2022), p. 1055.

45. L. Zhang, S. Ren, X. Chen, D. Li, and D. Yin, "CEO Hubris and Firm Pollution: State and Market Contingencies in a Transitional Economy," *Journal of Business Ethics*, Vol. 161 (2020), pp. 459–478. Also see F. Buchholz, K. Lopatta, and K. Maas, "The Deliberate Engagement of Narcissistic CEOs in Earnings Management," *Journal of Business Ethics*, Vol. 167 (2020), pp. 663–686; Y. Liu, S. Chen, C. Bell, and J. Tan, "How Do Power and Status Differ in Predicting Unethical Decisions? A Cross-National Comparison of China and Canada," *Journal of Business Ethics*, Vol. 167 (2020), pp. 745–760.

46. J. Heskett, "Firing McDonald's Easterbrook: What Could the Board Have Done Differently?" *Harvard Business School*, January 4, 2022, https://hbswk.hbs.edu/item/firing-mcdonalds-easterbrook-what-could-the-board-have-done-differently. Also see "SEC Charges McDonald's Former CEO for Misrepresentations about His Termination," *SEC*, January 9, 2023, https://www.sec.gov/news/press-release/2023-4.

47. K. Rivera and P. Karlsson, "CEOs Are Getting Fired for Ethical Lapses More Than They Used To," *Harvard Business Review*, June 6, 2017, https://hbr.org/2017/06/ceos-are-getting-fired-for-ethical-lapses-more-than-they-used-to.

48. E.M. Kelly, K. Greeny, N. Rosenberg, and I. Schwartz, "When Rules Are Not Enough: Developing Principles to Guide Ethical Conduct," *Behavior Analysis in Practice*, Vol. 14 (2021), pp. 491–498.

49. E. Shumway, "How One CEO's Background in Ethics Informs Her Leadership Style," *HR Dive*, June 9, 2022, https://www.hrdive.com/news/how-one-ceos-background-in-ethics-informs-her-leadership-style/625209/.

50. A.C. Peng and D. Kim, "A Meta-Analytic Test of the Differential Pathways Linking Ethical Leadership to Normative Conduct," *Journal of Organizational Behavior*, Vol. 41 (2020), pp. 348–368.

51. B. Weinstein, "What's the Difference between Compliance and Ethics?" *Forbes*, May 9, 2019, https://www.forbes.com/sites/bruceweinstein/2019/05/09/whats-the-difference-between-compliance-and-ethics/#4786b7b75249. Also see P. Lotich, "7 Ways to Demonstrate Ethics and Integrity in Your Business," *Thriving Small Business*, April 16, 2019, https://thethrivingsmallbusiness.com/examples-of-business-ethics-and-integrity/.

52. C.E. Bagley, "The Ethical Leader's Decision Tree," *Harvard Business Review*, February 2003, pp. 18–19.

53. L. Constantin, "Decision Trees," *Knowledge Horizons–Economics*, 2018, pp. 39–45.

54. C.E. Bagley, "The Ethical Leader's Decision Tree," *Harvard Business Review*, February 2003, p. 19.

55. C.E. Bagley, "The Ethical Leader's Decision Tree," *Harvard Business Review*, February 2003, p. 19.

56. The website YourMorals.org studies morality and values, offering questionnaires for readers to fill out. Some of the results are described in J. Haidt, *The Righteous Mind: Why Good People Are Divided by Politics and Religion* (New York: Random House, 2012).

57. F. Caputo, V. Cillo, E. Candelo, and Y. Liu, "Innovating through Digital Revolution: The Role of Soft Skills and Big Data in Increasing Firm Performance," *Management Decision*, Vol. 57 (2019), pp. 2032–2051. Also see C. Ferreira, J. Robertson, and L. Pitt, "Business (Un) usual: Critical Skills for the Next Normal," *Thunderbird International Business Review*, Vol. 65 (2023), pp. 39–47; K. Mabe and K.J. Bwalya, "Critical Soft Skills for Information and Knowledge Management Practitioners in the Fourth Industrial Revolution," *South African Journal of Information Management*, Vol. 24 (2022), pp. 1–11.

58. B. Greenstein and A. Rao, "PwC 2022 AI Business Survey," *PricewaterhouseCoopers*, https://www.pwc.com/us/en/tech-effect/ai-analytics/ai-business-survey.html (accessed February 22, 2023).

59. D.L. Sackett, "Evidence-Based Medicine," *Seminars in Perinatology*, Vol. 21 (1997), pp. 3–5. Also see V.V. Baba and F. HakemZadeh, "Toward a Theory of Evidence Based Decision Making," *Management Decision*, Vol. 50 (2012), pp. 832–867; J. Pfeffer and R.I. Sutton, *Hard Facts, Dangerous Half-Truths, and Total Nonsense: Profiting from Evidence-Based Management* (Harvard Business Press, 2006).

60. B. James, "Ranking NFL Coaches by Their Reliance & Trust in Data Analytics," *Play USA*, June 8, 2022, https://www.playusa.com/nfl-coaches-using-data-analytics/.

61. "VIDEO: The Digital Athlete and How It's Revolutionizing Player Health & Safety," *NFL*, January 14, 2022, https://www.nfl.com/playerhealthandsafety/equipment-and-innovation/aws-partnership/digital-athlete-spot#:~:text=Applied%20to%20football%2C%20AI%20is.

62. J.E. Johnson, "Big Data + Big Analytics = Big Opportunity: Big Data Is Dominating the Strategy Discussion for Many Financial Executives. As These Market Dynamics Continue to Evolve, Expectations Will Continue to Shift about What Should Be Disclosed, When and to Whom," *Financial Executive*, 28, 2012, pp. 50–54. Also see T.C. Havens, J.C. Bezdek, C. Leckie, L.O. Hall, and M. Palaniswami, "Fuzzy C-Means Algorithms for Very Large Data," *IEEE Transactions on Fuzzy Systems*, Vol. 20 (2012), pp. 1130–1146; J. Manyika, M. Chui, B. Brown, J. Bughin, R. Dobbs, C. Roxburgh, and A.H. Byers, *Big Data: The Next Frontier for Innovation, Competition, and Productivity* (McKinsey Global Institute, 2011); D. Fisher, R. DeLine, M. Czerwinski, and S. Drucker, "Interactions with Big Data Analytics," *Interactions*, Vol. 19 (2012), pp. 50–59; S. Tonidandel, E.B. King, and J.M. Cortina, "Big Data Methods: Leveraging Modern Data Analytic Techniques to Build Organizational Science," *Organizational Research Methods*, Vol. 21 (2018), pp. 525–547.

63. "Data Created Worldwide 2010-2025, " *Statista*, https://www.statista.com/statistics/871513/worldwide-data-created/ (accessed February 22, 2023).

64. J. Paulsen, "Seagate Has Now Shipped over 3 Zettabytes of Data Storage," *Seagate Blog*, https://blog.seagate.com/enterprises/seagate-has-shipped-three-zettabytes-of-data-storage (accessed February 22, 2023).

65. C. Cote, "What Is Descriptive Analytics? 5 Examples," *Harvard Business School Online*, November 9, 2021, https://online.hbs.edu/blog/post/descriptive-analytics. Also see J. Sheng, J. Amankwah-Amoah, Z. Khan, and X. Wang, "COVID-19 Pandemic in the New Era of Big Data Analytics: Methodological Innovations and Future Research Directions," *British Journal of Management*, Vol. 32 (2021), pp. 1164–1183.

66. M. Corritore, A. Goldberg, and S. B. Srivastava, "Duality in Diversity: How Intrapersonal and Interpersonal Cultural Heterogeneity Relate to Firm Performance," *Administrative Science Quarterly*, Vol. 65 (2020), pp. 359–394. Also see S.B. Srivastava, A. Goldberg, V. Govind Manian, and C. Potts, "Enculturation Trajectories: Language, Cultural Adaptation, and Individual Outcomes in Organizations," *Management Science*, Vol. 64 (2018), pp. 1348–1364; A. Goldberg, S.B. Srivastava, V. Govind Manian, W. Monroe, and C. Potts, "Fitting In or Standing Out? The Tradeoffs of Structural and Cultural Embeddedness," *American Sociological Review*, Vol. 81 (2016), pp. 1190–1222.

67. E. Glikson and A. Williams Woolley, "Human Trust in Artificial Intelligence: Review of Empirical Research," *Academy of Management Annals*, Vol. 14 (2020), pp. 627–660. Also see X. Ferràs-Hernández, "The Future of Management in a World of Electronic Brains," *Journal of Management Inquiry*, Vol. 27 (2018), pp. 260–263.

68. D.S. Watson, J. Krutzinna, I.N. Bruce, C.E.M. Griffiths, I.B. McInnes, M.R. Barnes, and L. Floridi, "Clinical Applications of Machine Learning Algorithms: Beyond the Black box," *BMJ*, Vol. 364 (2019), p. I886. Also

see B. Mahesh, "Machine Learning Algorithms—A Review," *International Journal of Science and Research,* Vol. 9 (2020), pp. 381–386.

69. P. von Wedel and C. Hagist, "Economic Value of Data and Analytics for Health Care Providers: Hermeneutic Systematic Literature Review," *Journal of Medical Internet Research,* Vol. 22 (2020), p. e23315. Also see A. Rehman, S. Naz, and I. Razzak, "Leveraging Big Data Analytics in Healthcare Enhancement: Trends, Challenges and Opportunities," *Multimedia Systems,* Vol. 28 (2022), pp. 1339–1371.

70. "Healthcare Analytics Market Trend," *Emergen Research,* https://www.emergenresearch.com/industry-report/healthcare-analytics-market (Accessed February 22, 2023).

71. P. Russom, "Big Data Analytics," *TDWI Best Practices Report,* Vol. 19 (2011), pp. 1–34. Also see S.F. Wamba, S. Akter, A. Edwards, G. Chopin, and D. Gnanzou, "How 'Big Data' Can Make a Big Impact: Findings from a Systematic Review and a Longitudinal Case Study," *International Journal of Production Economics,* Vol. 165 (2015), pp. 234–246.

72. M.M. Vopson, "The World's Data Explained: How Much We're Producing and Where It's All Stored," *The Conversation,* May 4, 2021, https://theconversation.com/the-worlds-data-explained-how-much-were-producing-and-where-its-all-stored-159964.

73. "What Is the Cloud?" *Microsoft,* https://azure.microsoft.com/en-us/overview/what-is-the-cloud/ (accessed February 22, 2023).

74. "Statcast," *MLB,* https://www.mlb.com/glossary/statcast (accessed February 22, 2023). Also see M. Wittenberg, "Moneyball 2.0: Real-Time Decision Making with MLB's Statcast Data," *Databricks,* October 28, 2021, https://databricks.com/blog/2021/10/28/moneyball-2-0-real-time-decision-making-with-mlbs-statcast-data.html.

75. P. Russom, "Big Data Analytics," *TDWI Best Practices Report,* Vol. 19 (2011), pp. 1–34. Also see S.F. Wamba, S. Akter, A. Edwards, G. Chopin, and D. Gnanzou, "How 'Big Data' Can Make a Big Impact: Findings from a Systematic Review and a Longitudinal Case Study," *International Journal of Production Economics,* Vol. 165 (2015), pp. 234–246.

76. P. Russom, "Big Data Analytics," *TDWI Best Practices Report,* Vol. 19 (2011), pp. 1–34. Also see S.F. Wamba, S. Akter, A. Edwards, G. Chopin, and D. Gnanzou, "How 'Big Data' Can Make a Big Impact: Findings from a Systematic Review and a Longitudinal Case Study," *International Journal of Production Economics,* Vol. 165 (2015), pp. 234–246.

77. L. Olinga, "Microsoft Is Coming for Google and Its Cash Cow," *The Street,* February 7, 2023, https://www.thestreet.com/technology/microsoft-alphabets-google-clash-over-ai-chatgpt. Also see M. Mohsin, "10 Google Search Statistics You Need to Know in 2023," *Oberlo,* January 13, 2023, https://www.oberlo.com/blog/google-search-statistics#:~:text=Summary%3A%20Google%20Search%20Statistics%202023.

78. "Google's Year in Search," *Google Trends,* https://trends.google.com/trends/yis/2022/US/ (accessed February 22, 2023).

79. J. Cohen, "How to Spot a Fake Review on Amazon," *PCMAG,* June 21, 2021, https://www.pcmag.com/how-to/spot-a-fake-review-on-amazon.

80. N. Nguyen, "Fake Reviews and Inflated Ratings Are Still a Problem for Amazon," *Wall Street Journal,* June 13, 2021, https://www.wsj.com/articles/fake-reviews-and-inflated-ratings-are-still-a-problem-for-amazon-11623587313. Also see T. Huddleston Jr, "The FTC Just Prosecuted a Fake Paid Amazon Review for the First Time—Here's What That Means for Users," *CNBC,* March 4, 2019, https://www.cnbc.com/2019/03/01/ftc-cracking-down-on-fake-amazon-reviews.html; E. Dwoskin and C. Timberg, "How Merchants Use Facebook to Flood Amazon with Fake Reviews," *Washington Post,* April 23, 2018, https://www.washingtonpost.com/business/economy/how-merchants-secretly-use-facebook-to-flood-amazon-with-fake-reviews/2018/04/23/5dad1e30-4392-11e8-8569-26fda6b404c7_story.html.

81. N. Nguyen, "Fake Reviews and Inflated Ratings Are Still a Problem for Amazon," *Wall Street Journal,* June 13, 2021, https://www.wsj.com/articles/fake-reviews-and-inflated-ratings-are-still-a-problem-for-amazon-11623587313.

82. A.A. Demarest, "How to Spot Fake Amazon Reviews and Avoid Scammers," *Business Insider,* November 19, 2021, https://www.businessinsider.com/amazon-fake-reviews.

83. Reuters, and G. Dean, "Amazon and Google Are Being Investigated by a UK Regulator over Fake Reviews on Their Sites," *Business Insider,* June 25, 2021, https://www.businessinsider.com/amazon-google-fake-reviews-cma-regulator-investigation-uk-alphabet-2021-6. Also see S. Jackson, "Amazon, Walmart, and Hundreds More Companies Were Warned by Regulators That They Could Face Steep Fines If They Use Fake Reviews or Other Deceptive Endorsements," *Business Insider,* October 18, 2021, https://www.businessinsider.com/ftc-warns-amazon-walmart-hundreds-companies-fake-reviews-face-fines-2021-10.

84. "McKinsey Analytics—Catch Them If You Can: How Leaders in Data and Analytics Have Pulled Ahead," *McKinsey & Company,* https://www.mckinsey.com/~/media/McKinsey/Business%20Functions/McKinsey%20Analytics/Our%20Insights/Catch%20them%20if%20you%20can%20How%20leaders%20in%20data%20and%20analytics%20have%20pulled%20ahead/Catch-them-if-you-can-How-leaders-in-data-and-analytics-have-pulled-ahead.ashx (accessed February 22, 2023).

85. O. Müller, M. Fay, and J. Vom Brocke, "The Effect of Big Data and Analytics on Firm Performance: An Econometric Analysis Considering Industry Characteristics," *Journal of Management Information Systems,* Vol. 35 (2018), pp. 488–509.

86. "Coca-Cola Freestyle Unveils Next-Gen Fountain Dispenser, New Operating System and More," *Coca-Cola Company,* May 18, 2018, https://www.coca-colacompany.com/news/freestyle-unveils-new-dispenser-and-more#:~:text=More%20than%2050%2C000%20Coca%2DCola,a%20handful%20of%20other%20countries.

87. C. Doering, "How Coca-Cola Turns to Its Freestyle Machine to Create Shelf-Ready Flavors," *Food Dive,* December 15, 2022, https://www.fooddive.com/news/how-coca-cola-turns-to-its-freestyle-machine-to-create-shelf-ready-flavors/636660/#:~:text=Coca%2DCola%20can%20see%20what.

88. H. Kale, D. Aher, and N. Anute, "HR Analytics and Its Impact on Organizations Performance," *International Journal of Research and Analytical Reviews,* Vol. 9 (2022), pp. 619–630. Also see M. McNeill, "How 5 Successful Companies Are Using HR Analytics," *ICS Learn,* May 17, 2020. https://www.icslearn.co.uk/blog/posts/2020/june/how-5-successful-companies-are-using-hr-analytics/.

89. "Two Unilever Sites Named Most Digitally Advanced Factories," *Unilever,* January 13, 2023, https://www.unilever.com/news/news-search/2023/unilever-sites-join-network-of-worlds-most-digitally-advanced-factories/.

90. P. Korherr, D.K. Kanbach, S. Kraus, and P. Jones, "The Role of Management in Fostering Analytics: The Shift from Intuition to Analytics-Based Decision-Making," *Journal of Decision Systems,* 2022, pp. 1–17.

91. M. Henderikx and J. Stoffers, "An Exploratory Literature Study into Digital Transformation and Leadership: Toward Future-Proof Middle Managers," *Sustainability,* Vol. 14 (2022), p. 687. Also see S. Berinato, "Data Science & the Art of Persuasion," *Harvard Business Review,* January–February 2019, pp. 126–137.

92. R.S. Neal, J. Fuller, S. Hansen, and PJ Neal, "The C-Suite Skills That Matter Most," *SHRM,* August 3, 2022, https://www.shrm.org/executive/resources/articles/pages/executives-and-social-skills.aspx. Also see D.S. Tesla and E.E. Karpova, "Executive Decision-Making in Fashion Retail: A Phenomenological Exploration of Resources and Strategies," *Journal of Fashion Marketing and Management: An International Journal,* Vol. 26 (2022), pp. 700–716.

93. N. De Marco, "An Introduction to Autonomous Devices," *Forbes,* August 16, 2019, https://www.forbes.com/sites/forbestechcouncil/2019/08/16/an-introduction-to-autonomous-devices/#7ca774bc6875.

94. S. Huang, "Understanding AlphaGo: How AI Thinks and Learns (Fundamentals)," *Medium,* March 15, 2019, https://towardsdatascience.com/understanding-alphago-how-ai-think-and-learn-1-2-da07d3ec5278.

95. A. Murray "CEOs: The New Industrial Revolution Is Coming," *Fortune,* March 8, 2016, https://fortune.com/2016/03/08/davos-new-industrial-revolution/.

96. H. Benbya, T.H. Davenport, and S. Pachidi, "Artificial Intelligence in Organizations: Current State and Future Opportunities," *MIS Quarterly Executive*, Vol. 19 (2020), http://dx.doi.org/10.2139/ssrn.3741983. Also see D. Vrontis, M. Christofi, V. Pereira, S. Tarba, A. Makrides, and E. Trichina, "Artificial Intelligence, Robotics, Advanced Technologies and Human Resource Management: A Systematic Review," *The International Journal of Human Resource Management,* Vol. 33 (2022), pp. 1237–1266.

97. "Ocean shipping and shipbuilding," OECD, https://www.oecd.org/ocean/topics/ocean-shipping/ (accessed February 22, 2023). Also see M. Placek, "Topic: Container Shipping," *Statista,* May 4, 2022, https://www.statista.com/topics/1367/container-shipping/.

98. V. Yee and J. Glanz, "How One of the World's Biggest Ships Jammed the Suez Canal," *The New York Times,* July 19, 2021, https://www.nytimes.com/2021/07/17/world/middleeast/suez-canal-stuck-ship-ever-given.html. Also see T. El-Tablawy, M. Magdy, and Bloomberg, "Stuck, Seized and Now Freed: *Ever Given* to Leave Egypt's Suez Canal Today after Paying a Reported $550 Million Settlement," *Fortune,* July 7, 2021, https://fortune.com/2021/07/07/ever-given-leaves-egypt-suez-canal-settlement/;

99. "AI-Powered Vessel Vision," *Sea Machines,* https://sea-machines.com/ai-powered-vessel-vision (accessed February 22, 2023).

100. M. Schuler, "Tug Completes 1,000 Nautical Mile Autonomous Voyage around Denmark," *GCaptain,* October 22, 2021, https://gcaptain.com/tug-completes-1000-nautical-mile-autonomous-voyage-around-denmark/. Also see "Sea Machines Completes World's First 1,000 Nautical Mile Autonomous Voyage," *Sea Machines,* October 21, 2021, https://sea-machines.com/sea-machines-completes-worlds-first-1000-nautical-mile-autonomous-voyage.

101. C. Berghoff, M. Neu, and A. von Twickel, "The Interplay of AI and Biometrics: Challenges and Opportunities," *Computer,* Vol. 54 (2021), pp. 80–85.

102. "Face ID," *AppleInsider,* https://appleinsider.com/inside/face-id (accessed February 22, 2023).

103. J. Heckman, "FBI Adds Iris Recognition to Its Growing Biometrics Portfolio," *Federal News Network,* September 9, 2020, https://federalnewsnetwork.com/artificial-intelligence/2020/09/fbi-adds-iris-recognition-to-its-growing-biometrics-portfolio/.

104. J. Heckman, "FBI Adds Iris Recognition to Its Growing Biometrics Portfolio," *Federal News Network,* September 9, 2020, https://federalnewsnetwork.com/artificial-intelligence/2020/09/fbi-adds-iris-recognition-to-its-growing-biometrics-portfolio/. Also see T. Chappellet-Lanier, "Can AI Help Catch Criminals Where a Fingerprint Fails?" *FedScoop,* August 30, 2018, https://www.fedscoop.com/ai-fingerprints-fbi-request-for-information/.

105. "What Is Conversational AI?" *IBM,* https://www.ibm.com/cloud/learn/conversational-ai (accessed February 22, 2023). Also see S. Comes, R. Chauhan, and D. Schatsky, "Conversational AI," *Deloitte Insights,* August 25, 2021, https://www2.deloitte.com/us/en/insights/focus/signals-for-strategists/the-future-of-conversational-ai.html.

106. S. Comes, R. Chauhan, and D. Schatsky, "Conversational AI," *Deloitte Insights,* August 25, 2021, https://www2.deloitte.com/us/en/insights/focus/signals-for-strategists/the-future-of-conversational-ai.html.

107. B. Gates, "The Age of AI Has Begun," *GatesNotes,* March 21, 2023, https://www.gatesnotes.com/The-Age-of-AI-Has-Begun?WT.mc_id=20230321100000_Artificial-Intelligence_BG-TW_&WT.tsrc=BGTW.

108. "ChatGPT and Its Implications for Your Teaching," University of Pennsylvania Center for Teaching & Learning, January 20, 2023. https://ctl.upenn.edu/resources/tech/chatgpt/?utm_source=rss&utm_medium=rss&utm_campaign=chatgpt.

109. B. Marr, "What Does ChatGPT Really Mean for Your Job?" *Forbes,* February 13, 2023, https://www.forbes.com/sites/bernardmarr/2023/02/13/what-does-chatgpt-really-mean-for-your-job/?sh=6be1e5b05bda. Also see "ChatGPT and Its Implications for Your Teaching," University of Pennsylvania Center for Teaching & Learning, January 20, 2023. https://ctl.upenn.edu/resources/tech/chatgpt/?utm_source=rss&utm_medium=rss&utm_campaign=chatgpt.

110. The Epic Bundle Team, "ChatGPT Did My Taxes: Here's What Happened," *Motley Fool,* March 13, 2023, https://www.fool.com/premium/epic-bundle/coverage/4299/coverage/2023/03/13/chatgpt-did-my-taxes-heres-what-happened/?lid=7w6wzwuuce3b&idh=cf206e97-0506-4aa8-b467-71acf8598a9d&source=ibmxsleml0000123&utm_campaign=EB&utm_content=commentary&utm_medium=email&utm_source=product&utm_term=f1a75a30-90a3-4d04-8fec-7902f8dfdddf.

111. B. Gates, "The Age of AI Has Begun," *GatesNotes,* March 21, 2023, https://www.gatesnotes.com/The-Age-of-AI-Has-Begun?WT.mc_id=20230321100000_Artificial-Intelligence_BG-TW_&WT.tsrc=BGTW. Also see A. Garfinkle and D. Croll, "How Business Is Already Using ChatGPT and Other AI Tech," *Yahoo!* News, February 14, 2023, https://news.yahoo.com/how-business-is-already-using-chatgpt-and-other-ai-tech-183828556.html; B. Marr, "What Does ChatGPT Really Mean for Your Job?" *Forbes,* February 13, 2023, https://www.forbes.com/sites/bernardmarr/2023/02/13/what-does-chatgpt-really-mean-for-your-job/?sh=6be1e5b05bda.

112. B. Gates, "The Age of AI Has Begun," *GatesNotes*, March 21, 2023, https://www.gatesnotes.com/The-Age-of-AI-Has-Begun?WT.mc_id=20230321100000_Artificial-Intelligence_BG-TW_&WT.tsrc=BGTW.

113. B. Gates, "The Age of AI Has Begun," *GatesNotes,* March 21, 2023, https://www.gatesnotes.com/The-Age-of-AI-Has-Begun?WT.mc_id=20230321100000_Artificial-Intelligence_BG-TW_&WT.tsrc=BGTW.

114. "What Is Conversational AI?" *IBM,* https://www.ibm.com/cloud/learn/conversational-ai (accessed February 22, 2023).

115. E. Flanagan, "HubSpot Introduces Conversation Intelligence to Help Sales and Service Teams Build Better Coaching Opportunities," *HubSpot,* January 19, 2023, https://www.hubspot.com/company-news/hubspot-introduces-conversation-intelligence#.

116. T. Davenport and J. Fitts, "AI Can Help Companies Tap New Sources of Data for Analytics," *Harvard Business Review,* March 19, 2021, https://hbr.org/2021/03/ai-can-help-companies-tap-new-sources-of-data-for-analytics.

117. J. LaRiviere, P. McAfee, J. Rao, V.K. Narayanan, and W. Sun, "Where Predictive Analytics Is Having the Biggest Impact," *Harvard Business Review,* May 25, 2016, https://hbr.org/2016/05/where-predictive-analytics-is-having-the-biggest-impact.

118. "Using Artificial Intelligence for Smarter Demand Forecasting," *IKEA,* May 27, 2021, https://about.ikea.com/en/life-at-home/behind-the-scenes/2021/05/27/using-artificial-intelligence-for-smarter-demand-forecasting.

119. S. Silverstein, "Amazon Fresh Deepens Its Focus on Just Walk out Technology," *Grocery Dive,* April 8, 2022, https://www.grocerydive.com/news/amazon-fresh-deepens-just-walk-out/621816/.

120. M. Toljagic, "'Like a Huge Chess Game.' Start-up Is Revolutionizing Traffic-Light Timing with AI and the Internet of Things," *Toronto Star,* July 30, 2022, https://www.thestar.com/autos/2022/07/30/like-a-huge-chess-game-start-up-is-revolutionizing-traffic-light-timing-with-ai-and-the-internet-of-things.html.

121. N. Mittal, I. Saif, and B. Ammanath, "State of AI in the Enterprise 2022," 5th edition, *Deloitte,* https://www2.deloitte.com/us/en/pages/consulting/articles/state-of-ai-2022.html (accessed February 22, 2023).

122. Y.R. Shrestha, "Organizational Decision-Making Structures in the Age of Artificial Intelligence," *California Management Review,* 2019, pp. 66–83.

123. "Zest Finance," *Appengine.ai,* https://www.appengine.ai/company/zest-finance#:~:text=Zest%20clients%20typically%20see%20a%2030%25%20to%2040%25%20reduction%20in (accessed February 23, 2023).

124. J. Ross, "The Fundamental Flaw in AI Implementation," *MIT Sloan Management Review,* 2018, https://sloanreview.mit.edu/article/the-fundamental-flaw-in-ai-implementation/. Also see M. Bérubé, T. Giannelia, and G. Vial, "Barriers to the Implementation of AI in Organizations: Findings from a Delphi Study," *Proceedings of the 54th Hawaii International Conference on System Sciences,* 2021.

125. N. Mittal, I. Saif, and B. Ammanath, "State of AI in the Enterprise 2022," 5th edition, *Deloitte,* https://www2.deloitte.com/us/en/pages/consulting/articles/state-of-ai-2022.html (accessed February 22, 2023). Also see E. Bowles, "AI Adoption: Key Barriers & How to Overcome Them," *RapidMiner,* August 30, 2022. https://rapidminer.com/blog/ai-adoption/.

126. "AI Pricing: How Much Does Artificial Intelligence Cost?" *WebFX,* https://www.webfx.com/martech/pricing/ai/ (accessed February 22, 2023).

127. A.S. Rutschman, "AI Gave Stephen Hawking a Voice—and He Used It to Warn Us against AI," *Quartz,* March 16, 2018, https://qz.com/1231092/ai-gave-stephen-hawking-a-voice-and-he-used-it-to-warn-us-against-ai/. Also see S. Martin, "AI Warning: Machines Will Replace Humans at the Top—and Wipe Us Out If We Dare Resist," *Express,* September, 18, 2019.

128. C. Clifford, "Top A.I. Experts Warn of a 'Black Mirror'-esque Future with Swarms of Micro-Drones and Autonomous Weapons," *CNBC,* February 21, 2018, https://www.cnbc.com/2018/02/21/openai-oxford-and-cambridge-ai-experts-warn-of-autonomous-weapons.html.

129. A. Fitch, "Military Looks to AI to Improve Air Strikes," *The Wall Street Journal*, October 24, 2019, https://www.wsj.com/articles/military-looks-to-ai-to-improve-air-strikes-11571932283.

130. M. Novak, "Microsoft Puts New Limits on Bing's AI Chatbot after It Expressed Desire to Steal Nuclear Secrets," *Forbes,* February 18, 2023, https://www.forbes.com/sites/mattnovak/2023/02/18/microsoft-puts-new-limits-on-bings-ai-chatbot-after-it-expressed-desire-to-steal-nuclear-secrets/?sh=5436707c685c. Also see K. Roose, "A Conversation with Bing's Chatbot Left Me Deeply Unsettled," *The New York Times,* February 16, 2023, https://www.nytimes.com/2023/02/16/technology/bing-chatbot-microsoft-chatgpt.html; K. Hao, "What Is ChatGPT? What to Know about the AI Chatbot That Will Power Microsoft Bing," *WSJ,* February 17, 2023, https://www.wsj.com/articles/chatgpt-ai-chatbot-app-explained-11675865177.

131. S. Martin, "AI Warning: Machines Will Replace Humans at the Top—and Wipe Us Out If We Dare Resist," *Express,* September 18, 2019, https://www.express.co.uk/news/science/1179569/ai-replace-human-what-is-ai-artificial-intelligence-machine-learning-end-times-elon-musk.

132. S. Lund, A. Madgavkar, J. Manyika, S. Smit, K. Ellingrud, and O. Robinson, "The Future of Work after COVID-19," *McKinsey Global Institute,* February 18, 2021, https://www.mckinsey.com/featured-insights/future-of-work/the-future-of-work-after-covid-19. Also see K. Carey, "Do Not Be Alarmed by Wild Predictions of Robots Taking Everyone's Jobs," *Slate Magazine,* March 31, 2021, https://slate.com/technology/2021/03/job-loss-automation-robots-predictions.html.

133. L. Bannon, "AI in the Workplace Is Already Here. The First Battleground? Call Centers," *WSJ,* February 18, 2023, https://www.wsj.com/articles/ai-chatgpt-chatbot-workplace-call-centers-5cd2142a.

134. H.J. Wilson and P.R. Daugherty, "Collaborative Intelligence: Humans and AI Are Joining Forces," *Harvard Business Review*, 2018, pp. 114–123.

135. B. Marr, "3 Ways That Artificial Intelligence (AI) Will Change Your Job Forever," *Forbes,* January 17, 2022, https://www.forbes.com/sites/bernardmarr/2022/01/17/3-ways-that-artificial-intelligence-ai-will-change-your-job-forever/?sh=7442c1fd50e6.

136. E. Morath, "AI Is the Next Workplace Disrupter—and It's Coming for High-Skilled Jobs," *The Wall Street Journal*, February 23, 2020, https://www.wsj.com/articles/ai-is-the-next-workplace-disrupterand-its-coming-for-high-skilled-jobs-11582470000.

137. A. Charlwood and N. Guenole, "Can HR Adapt to the Paradoxes of Artificial Intelligence?" *Human Resource Management Journal,* 32, 2022, pp. 729–742. Also see B. Laker, "How Leaders Are Using AI as a Problem-Solving Tool," *Forbes,* August 24, 2022, https://www.forbes.com/sites/benjaminlaker/2022/08/24/how-leaders-are-using-ai-as-a-problem-solving-tool/?sh=1c7a7d446053.

138. T. Chamorro-Premuzic, M. Wade, and J. Jordan, "As AI Makes More Decisions, the Nature of Leadership Will Change," *Harvard Business Review,* 2018, https://hbr.org/2018/01/as-ai-makes-more-decisions-the-nature-of-leadership-will-change.

139. O.M. Lehner, K. Ittonen, H. Silvola, E. Ström, and A. Wührleitner, "Artificial Intelligence Based Decision-Making in Accounting and Auditing: Ethical Challenges and Normative Thinking," *Accounting, Auditing & Accountability Journal,* Vol. 35 (2022), pp. 109–135.

140. D. De Cremer and G. Kasparov, "The Ethical AI—Paradox: Why Better Technology Needs More and Not Less Human Responsibility," *AI and Ethics,* 2, 2022, pp. 1–4.

141. The discussion of styles was based on material contained in A.J. Rowe and R.O. Mason, *Managing with Style: A Guide to Understanding, Assessing and Improving Decision Making* (San Francisco: Jossey-Bass, 1987), pp. 1–17.

142. A.S. Adikaram and P. Kailasapathy, "Evidence, Empathy and Emotions: Decision-Making Styles of Human Resource Professionals and Their Effectiveness in Resolving Complaints of Sexual Harassment," *Employee Relations: The International Journal,* Vol. 43 (2021), pp. 1083–1103.

143. A.S. Adikaram and P. Kailasapathy, "Evidence, Empathy and Emotions: Decision-Making Styles of Human Resource Professionals and Their Effectiveness in Resolving Complaints of Sexual Harassment," *Employee Relations: The International Journal,* Vol. 43 (2021), pp. 1083–1103.

144. P. Thangavel, P. Pathak, and B. Chandra, "Consumer Decision-Making Style of Gen Z: A Generational Cohort analysis," *Global Business Review*, Vol. 23 (2022), pp. 710–728. Also see B.A. Tedla and B.G. Vilas, "An Essence of Leadership, Its Styles: A Review and Personal Account Commentary," *International Journal of Health Sciences*, Vol. 6 (2022), pp. 175–183.

145. J. Weller, A. Ceschi, L. Hirsch, R. Sartori, and A. Costantini, "Accounting for Individual Differences in Decision-Making Competence: Personality and Gender Differences," *Frontiers in Psychology,* 2018, https://doi.org/10.3389/fpsyg.2018.02258. Also see K. Remenova and N. Jankelova, "How Successfully Can Decision-Making Style Predict the Orientation toward Well- or Ill-Structured Decision-Making Problems," *Journal of Competitiveness*, 2019, pp. 99–115; S. Miceli, V. de Palo, L. Monacis, S. Di Nuovo, and M. Sinatra, "Do Personality Traits and Self-Regulatory Processes Affect Decision-Making Tendencies?" *Australian Journal of Psychology*, 2018, pp. 284–294.

146. B. de Langhe and P. Fernbach, "The Dangers of Categorical Thinking," *Harvard Business Review,* 2019, pp. 80–93. Also see D. Kahnemann and A. Tversky, "Judgment under Uncertainty: Heuristics and Biases," *Science,* Vol. 185 (1974), pp. 1124–1131; A. Tversky and D. Kahneman, "The Belief in the Law of Numbers," *Psychological Bulletin,* Vol. 76 (1971), pp. 105–110; D.R. Bobocel and J. P. Meyer, "Escalating Commitment to a Failing Course of Action: Separating the Roles of Choice and Justification," *Journal of Applied Psychology,* June 1994, pp. 360–363; V. Berthet, "The Impact of Cognitive Biases on Professionals' Decision-Making: A Review of Four Occupational Areas," *Frontiers in Psychology,* Vol. 12 (2022), 802439.

147. "Odds of Dying," *Injury Facts*, https://injuryfacts.nsc.org/all-injuries/preventable-death-overview/odds-of-dying/?mod=article_inline (accessed February 20, 2023).

148. R. Schwartz, A. Vassilev, K. Greene, L. Perine, A. Burt, and P. Hall, "Towards a Standard for Identifying and Managing Bias in Artificial Intelligence," *NIST Special Publication,* 1270 (2022), pp. 1–77. Also see A. Charlwood and N. Guenole, "Can HR Adapt to the Paradoxes of Artificial Intelligence?" *Human Resource Management Journal,* Vol. 32 (2022), pp. 729–742.

149. R. Tumin, A. Holpuch, and J. Diaz, "$2 Billion Powerball Ticket Sold in Los Angeles County, Lottery Officials Said," *The New York Times,* November 8, 2022, https://www.nytimes.com/article/powerball-jackpot-lottery-prize.html?login=email&auth=login-email.

150. P. Cabianca, P. Hammond, and M. Gutierrez, "What Is a Social Media Echo Chamber?" *The University of Texas at Austin Stan Richards School of Advertising & Public Relations,* https://advertising.utexas.edu/news/what-social-media-echo-chamber (accessed February 20,

2023). Also see M. Cinelli, G. De Francisci Morales, A. Galeazzi, W. Quattrociocchi, and M. Starnini, "The Echo Chamber Effect on Social Media," *Proceedings of the National Academy of Sciences,* Vol. 118 (2021), e2023301118; S. Muhammed T and S.K. Mathew, "The Disaster of Misinformation: A Review of Research in Social Media," *International Journal of Data Science and Analytics,* Vol. 13 (2022), pp. 271–285.

151. D. Ronayne, D. Sgroi, and A. Tuckwell, "How Susceptible Are You to the Sunk Cost Fallacy?" *Harvard Business Review,* July 15, 2021, https://hbr.org/2021/07/how-susceptible-are-you-to-the-sunk-cost-fallacy.

152. E.A. Meyers, M. Białek, J.A. Fugelsang, D.J. Koehler, and O. Friedman, "Wronging Past Rights: The Sunk Cost Bias Distorts Moral Judgment," *Judgement and Decision Making,* 2019, pp. 721–727.

153. E. Goode, "Mice Don't Know When to Let It Go, Either," *The New York Times,* July 12, 2018, https://www.nytimes.com/2018/07/12/health/sunk-costs-decisions.html.

154. A.J. Caceres-Santamaria, "The Anchoring Effect," *Federal Reserve Bank of St. Louis,* April 2021, https://research.stlouisfed.org/publications/page1-econ/2021/04/01/the-anchoring-effect.

155. S.A. Berg and J.H. Moss, "Anchoring and Judgment Bias: Disregarding Under Uncertainty," *Psychological Reports,* 125, 2022, pp. 2688–2708.

156. D. Huffman, C. Raymond, and J. Shvets, "Persistent Overconfidence and Biased Memory: Evidence from Managers," *American Economic Review,* Vol. 112 (2022), pp. 3141–3175. Also see S.Z. ul Abdin, F. Qureshi, J. Iqbal, and S. Sultana, "Overconfidence Bias and Investment Performance: A Mediating Effect of Risk Propensity," *Borsa Istanbul Review,* Vol. 22 (2022), pp. 780–793.

157. F. Pratty, "The Dark Kitchen Sector Heats up as Swedish Newcomer Curb Raises Funds," *Sifted,* June 7, 2021, https://sifted.eu/articles/curb-raises-e20m/. Also see "442 Startup Failure Post-Mortems," *CB Insights,* January 23, 2023, https://www.cbinsights.com/research/startup-failure-post-mortem/#2023update1.

158. B. Burkhard, C. Sirén, M. van Essen, D. Grichnik, and D.A. Shepherd, "Nothing Ventured, Nothing Gained: A Meta-Analysis of CEO Overconfidence, Strategic Risk Taking, and Performance," *Journal of Management,* 2022, 01492063221110203.

159. P.S. Kraft, C. Günther, N.H. Kammerlander, and J. Lampe, "Overconfidence and Entrepreneurship: A Meta-Analysis of Different Types of Overconfidence in the Entrepreneurial Process," *Journal of Business Venturing,* Vol. 37 (2022), 106207.

160. J. Groß and U.J. Bayen, "Older and Younger Adults' Hindsight Bias after Positive and Negative Outcomes," *Memory & Cognition,* Vol. 50 (2022), pp. 16–28. Also see C. Bhattacharya and J.D. Jasper, "Degree of Handedness: A Unique Individual Differences Factor for Predicting and Understanding Hindsight Bias," *Personality and Individual Differences,* 2018, pp. 97–101.

161. C.A. Dorison and B.H. Heller, "Observers Penalize Decision Makers Whose Risk Preferences Are Unaffected by Loss–Fain Framing," *Journal of Experimental Psychology: General,* Vol. 151 (2022), pp. 2043–2059.

162. R. Vartabedian, "How California's Bullet Train Went off the Rails," *The New York Times,* October 9, 2022, https://www.nytimes.com/2022/10/09/us/california-high-speed-rail-politics.html.

163. C.A. Dorison, C.K. Umphres, and J.S. Lerner, "Staying the Course: Decision Makers Who Escalate Commitment Are Trusted and Trustworthy," *Journal of Experimental Psychology: General,* Vol. 151 (2022), pp. 960–965. Also see P. Nouri, "Exploring the Escalation of Commitment to a Failing Venture in Women and Men Entrepreneurs," *Management Research Review,* 2022, https://doi.org/10.1108/MRR-03-2022-0190.

164. H. Kalmanovich-Cohen, M. Pearsall, and J.S. Christian, "The Effects of Leadership Change on Team Escalation of Commitment," *The Leadership Quarterly,* 2018, pp. 597–608. Also see J. Ross and B.M. Staw, "Organizational Escalation and Exit: Lessons from the Shoreham Nuclear Power Plant," *Academy of Management Journal,* August 1993, pp. 701–732; D.J. Sleesman, A.C. Lennard, G. McNamara, and D.E. Conlon, "Putting Escalation of Commitment in Context: A Multilevel Review and Analysis," *Academy of Management Annals,* Vol. 12 (2018), pp. 178–207.

165. "Categorical Thinking: How to Avoid Bias in Categorical Thinking," *MasterClass,* June 22, 2022, https://www.masterclass.com/articles/categorical-thinking.

166. F.C. Miner Jr, "Group versus Individual Decision Making: An Investigation of Performance Measures, Decision Strategies, and Process Losses/Gains," *Organizational Behavior and Human Performance,* Vol. 33 (1984), pp. 112–124. Also see S.D.S. Walker and B.L. Bonner, "The Effects of Differing Knowledge Transfer Strategies on Group Decision Making and Performance," *Journal of Behavioral Decision Making,* 2018, pp. 115–126.

167. N.F.R. Maier, "Assets and Liabilities in Group Problem Solving: The Need for Integrative Function," *Psychological Review,* Vol. 74 (1967), pp. 239–249.

168. L. Patrício and M. Franco, "A Systematic Literature Review about Team Diversity and Team Performance: Future Lines of Investigation," *Administrative Sciences,* Vol. 12 (2022), p. 31. Also see L.L. Martins and W. Sohn, "How Does Diversity Affect Team Cognitive Processes? Understanding the Cognitive Pathways Underlying the Diversity Dividend in Teams," *Academy of Management Annals,* Vol. 16 (2022), pp. 134–178; Q. Wang, H. Hou, and Z. Li, "Participative Leadership: A Literature Review and Prospects for Future Research," *Frontiers in Psychology,* Vol. 13 (2022), 924357.

169. L. Landry, "Why Managers Should Involve Their Team in Decision-Making," *Harvard Business School Online,* March 5, 2020, https://online.hbs.edu/blog/post/team-decision-making#:~:text=By%20involving%20others%20in%20the.

170. N.F.R. Maier, "Assets and Liabilities in Group Problem Solving: The Need for Integrative Function," *Psychological Review,* Vol. 74 (1967), pp. 239–249.

171. M.J. Bennett, "Group Indoctrination: Techniques of Depersonalization and Domination of Individual Consciousness," *Indoctrination to Hate: Recruitment Techniques of Hate Groups and How to Stop Them,* 2022, pp. 289–309.

172. R. Sutton, "The Biggest Mistakes Bosses Make When Making Decisions—and How to Avoid Them," *The Wall Street Journal,* October 29, 2018, https://www.wsj.com/articles/the-biggest-mistakes-bosses-make-when-making-decisionsand-how-to-avoid-them-1540865340.

173. V. Li, "Groupthink Tendencies in Top Management Teams and Financial Reporting Fraud," *Accounting and Business Research,* 2023, pp. 1–23. Also see D.C. Grube and A. Killick, "Groupthink, Polythink and the Challenges of Decision-Making in Cabinet Government," *Parliamentary Affairs,* Vol. 76 (2023), pp. 211–231; O. Pol, T. Bridgman, and S. Cummings, "The Forgotten 'Immortalizer': Recovering William H Whyte as the Founder and Future of Groupthink Research," *Human Relations,* Vol. 75 (2022), pp. 1615–1641.

174. F. Gonzalez-Valdes and J. de Dios Ortuzar, "The Stochastic Satisficing Model: A Bounded Rationality Discrete Choice Model," *Journal of Choice Modelling,* 2018, pp. 74–87. Methods for increasing group consensus were investigated by R.L. Priem, D.A. Harrison, and N.K. Muir, "Structured Conflict and Consensus Outcomes in Group Decision Making," *Journal of Management,* December 22, 1995, pp. 691–710.

175. J. P. Porck, D. van Knippenberg, M. Tarakci, N. Y. Ates, P. J. F. Groenen, and M. de Hass, "Do Group and Organizational Identification Help or Hurt Intergroup Strategic Consensus?" *Journal of Management,* 2020, pp. 234–260.

176. I. Janis, *Groupthink,* 2nd ed. (Boston: Houghton Mifflin, 1982), p. 9. Also see K.D. Lassila, "A Brief History of Groupthink," *Yale Alumni Magazine,* January–February 2008, pp. 59–61, www.philosophy-religion.org/handouts/pdfs/BRIEF-HISTORY_GROUPTHINK.pdf (accessed August 10, 2016).

177. J. Mueller, S. Harvey, and A. Levenson, "How to Steer Clear of Groupthink," *Harvard Business Review,* March 7, 2022, https://hbr.org/2022/03/how-to-steer-clear-of-groupthink. Also see W-W. Park,

M.S. Kim, and S.M. Gully, "Effect of Cohesion on the Curvilinear Relationship between Team Efficacy and Performance," *Small Group Research,* Vol. 48 (2017), pp. 455–481; S. Wise, "Can a Team Have Too Much Cohesion? The Dark Side to Network Density," *European Management Journal,* Vol. 32 (2014), pp. 703–711.

178. J. DeMers, "How 'Groupthink' Can Cost Your Business (and 3 Corporate Examples)," *Entrepreneur,* April 16, 2018, https://www.entrepreneur.com/article/311864. Also see J. Kilhefner, "Groupthink Examples in Business," *Chron,* May 24, 2021, https://work.chron.com/groupthink-examples-business-21692.html.

179. I. Janis, *Groupthink,* 2nd ed. (Boston: Houghton Mifflin, 1982), pp. 174–175. Also see A. Riani, "How to Avoid Groupthink in Startups," *Forbes,* Accessed May 24, 2022, https://www.forbes.com/sites/abdoriani/2022/05/24/how-to-avoid-groupthink-in-startups/?sh=25e99dfa4c5b.

180. I. Janis, *Groupthink,* 2nd ed. (Boston: Houghton Mifflin, 1982).

181. M. G. Moore, "How to Make Great Decisions, Quickly," *Harvard Business Review,* March 22, 2022, https://hbr.org/2022/03/how-to-make-great-decisions-quickly.

182. D.L. Gladstein and N. P. Reilly, "Group Decision Making under Threat: The Tycoon Game," *Academy of Management Journal,* September 1985, pp. 613–627. Also see T. Emmerling and D. Rooders, "7 Strategies for Better Group Decision-Making," *Harvard Business Review,* September 22, 2020, https://hbr.org/2020/09/7-strategies-for-better-group-decision-making.

183. These conclusions were based on the following studies: J.H. Davis, "Some Compelling Intuitions about Group Consensus Decisions, Theoretical and Empirical Research, and Interpersonal Aggregation Phenomena: Selected Examples, 1950–1990," *Organizational Behavior and Human Decision Processes,* June 1992, pp. 3–38; J.A. Sniezek, "Groups under Uncertainty: An Examination of Confidence in Group Decision Making," *Organizational Behavior and Human Decision Processes,* June 1992, pp. 124–155.

184. T. Emmerling and D. Rooders, "7 Strategies for Better Group Decision-Making," *Harvard Business Review,* September 22, 2020, https://hbr.org/2020/09/7-strategies-for-better-group-decision-making.

185. See example in S.K. Lam, J. Karim, and J. Riedl, "The Effects of Group Composition on Decision Quality in a Social Production Community," *Proceedings of the 16th ACM International Conference on Supporting Group Work,* 2010, pp. 55–64; M. W. Blenko, M.C. Mankins, and P. Rogers, "The Decision-Driven Organization," *Harvard Business Review,* June 2010, pp. 55–62.

186. K. Cherry, "How Does Group Size Influence Problem Solving?" *Very Well Mind,* July 8, 2018, https://www.verywellmind.com/effects-of-group-size-on-problem-solving-2795678. Also see D. Frey, S. Schulz-Hardt, and D. Stahlberg, "Information Seeking among Individuals and Groups and Possible Consequences for Decision Making in Business and Politics," in *Understanding Group Behavior,* pp. 211–225, Psychology Press, 2018.

187. C. Lin, K. Chen, C. Liu, and C. Liao, "Assessing Decision Quality and Team Performance: Perspectives of Knowledge Internalization and Resource Adequacy," *Review of Managerial Science,* 2019, pp. 377–396.

188. M.T. Maynard, J.E. Mathieu, L.L. Gilson, D.R. Sanchez, and M.D. Dean, "Do I Really Know You and Does It Matter? Unpacking the Relationship between Familiarity and Information Elaboration in Global Virtual Teams," *Group & Organization Management,* Vol. 44 (2019), pp. 3–37.

189. J.R. Mesmer-Magnus and L.A. DeChurch, "Information Sharing and Team Performance: A Meta-Analysis," *Journal of Applied Psychology,* Vol. 94 (2009), pp. 535–546. Also see D.H. Gruenfeld, E.A. Mannix, K.Y. Williams, and M.A. Neale, "Group Composition and Decision Making: How Member Familiarity and Information Distribution Affect Process and Performance," *Organizational Behavior and Human Decision Processes,* July 1996, pp. 1–15.

190. C.K.W. De Dreu and M.A. West, "Minority Dissent and Team Innovation: The Importance of Participation in Decision Making," *Journal of Applied Psychology,* Vol. 86 (2001), pp. 1191–1201.

191. P.L. Curşeu, S. GL Schruijer, and O.C. Fodor, "Minority Dissent, Openness to Change and Group Creativity," *Creativity Research Journal,* Vol. 34 (2022), pp. 93–105.

192. A. Pittampalli, "Difficult Decisions: The Costs of Consensus," *Psychology Today,* January 3, 2018, https://www.psychologytoday.com/us/blog/are-you-persuadable/201801/difficult-decisions-the-costs-consensus.

193. These recommendations were obtained from G.M. Parker, *Team Players and Teamwork: The New Competitive Business Strategy* (San Francisco: Jossey-Bass, 1990).

194. P.B. Paulus and J.B. Kenworthy, "Effective Brainstorming," *The Oxford Handbook of Group Creativity and Innovation,* 2019, pp. 287–386. Also see A.F. Osborn, *Applied Imagination: Principles and Procedures of Creative Thinking,* 3rd ed. (New York: Scribner's, 1979).

195. W.H. Cooper, R. Brent Gallupe, S. Pallard, and J. Cadsby, "Some Liberating Effects of Anonymous Electronic Brainstorming," *Small Group Research,* April 1998, pp. 147–178.

196. Y. Maaravi, B. Heller, Y. Shoham, S. Mohar, and B. Deutsch, "Ideation in the Digital Age: Literature Review and Integrative Model for Electronic Brainstorming," *Review of Managerial Science,* 15, 2021, pp. 1431–1464.

197. L. Thompson, "Why You Are Probably Doing Brainstorming All Wrong," *WSJ,* February 10, 2023, https://www.wsj.com/articles/why-you-are-probably-doing-brainstorming-all-wrong-11675979384. Also see D. Wendland, "Brainstorming More Effectively," *Forbes,* January 13, 2023, https://www.forbes.com/sites/forbesagencycouncil/2023/01/13/brainstorming-more-effectively/?sh=429e8d083252; B. Nussbaum, "Brainstorming—Rules & Techniques for Idea Generation," *IDEO,* https://www.ideou.com/pages/brainstorming (accessed February 23, 2023).

198. O. Göçmen and H. Coşkun, "The Effects of the Six Thinking Hats and Speed on Creativity in Brainstorming," *Thinking Skills and Creativity,* Vol. 31 (2019), pp. 284–295.

199. L. Kiernan, A. Ledwith, and R. Lynch, "Design Teams Management of Conflict in Reaching Consensus," *International Journal of Conflict Management,* Vol. 31 (2020), pp. 263–285.

200. "Forget Post-Mortems: Here's How to Learn from Mistakes," *Wharton Executive Education,* https://executiveeducation.wharton.upenn.edu/thought-leadership/wharton-at-work/2020/02/forget-post-mortems-learn-from-mistakes/#:~:text=Schedule%20After%20Action%20Reviews%20consistently (accessed February 25, 2023). Also see M. Darling, C. Parry, and J. Moore, "Learning in the Thick of It," *Harvard Business Review,* July–August 2005, https://hbr.org/2005/07/learning-in-the-thick-of-it.

201. N.L. Keiser and W. Arthur Jr., "A Meta-Analysis of Task and Training Characteristics that Contribute to or Attenuate the Effectiveness of the After-Action Review (or Debrief)," *Journal of Business and Psychology,* 37, 2022, pp. 953–976. Also see V. Vukanović-Dumanović, G. Avlijaš, and S. Jokić, "After Action Review as a tool for implementation of the knowledge management program," *Ekonomika,* 68, 2022, pp. 29-40.

202. N.L. Keiser and W. Arthur Jr., "A Meta-Analysis of the Effectiveness of the After-Action Review (or Debrief) and Factors That Influence Its Effectiveness," *Journal of Applied Psychology,* Vol. 106 (2021), pp. 1007–1032.

203. N.L. Keiser, and W. Arthur Jr, "A Meta-Analysis of Task and Training Characteristics that Contribute to or Attenuate the Effectiveness of the After-Action Review (or Debrief)," *Journal of Business and Psychology,* Vol. 37 (2022), pp. 953–976.

204. N.L. Keiser and W. Arthur Jr, "A Meta-Analysis of Task and Training Characteristics that Contribute to or Attenuate the Effectiveness of the After-Action Review (or Debrief)," *Journal of Business and Psychology,* Vol. 37 (2022), pp. 953–976. Also see A. Fletcher, P.B. Cline, and M. Hoffman, "A Better Approach to After-Action Reviews," *Harvard Business Review,* January 12, 2023. https://hbr.org/2023/01/a-better-approach-to-after-action-reviews.

205. B. Tulgan, *Bridging the Soft Skills Gap: How to Teach the Missing Basics to Today's Young Talent* (Hoboken, NJ: John Wiley & Sons, 2015).

206. B. Tulgan, *Bridging the Soft Skills Gap: How to Teach the Missing Basics to Today's Young Talent* (Hoboken, NJ: John Wiley & Sons, 2015).
207. The idea for this exercise was based on B. Tulgan, *Bridging the Soft Skills Gap: How to Teach the Missing Basics to Today's Young Talent* (Hoboken, NJ: John Wiley & Sons, 2015).
208. These steps were based on M. Myatt, "6 Tips for Making Better Decisions," *Forbes,* March 28, 2012, https://www.forbes.com/sites/mikemyatt/2012/03/28/6-tips-for-making-better-decisions/#4206b32634dc.
209. These questions were based on L. Liaros, "Explaining Your Decision Making Process," *Interview Tips,* https://everydayinterviewtips.com/explaining-your-decision-making-process-during-an-interview/ (accessed March 19, 2018); L. Liaros, "How to Show You Have Quick Decision Making Skills," *Everyday Interview Tips,* https://everydayinterviewtips.com/how-to-show-you-have-quick-decision-making-skills/ (accessed March 19, 2018); L. Liaros, "Using Instincts vs. Data to Make Decisions," *Everyday Interview Tips,* https://everydayinterviewtips.com/using-instinct-data-to-make-decisions/ (accessed March 19, 2018).

CHAPTER 8

1. C. Connley, "Suzy Welch: These Are the 2 Fastest Ways to Get Promoted," *CNBC,* April 2, 2019, https://www.cnbc.com/2019/04/01/suzy-welch-these-are-the-2-fastest-ways-to-get-promoted.html.
2. C. Dessi, "How to Sell Yourself in a Way That Won't Make You Cringe," *Inc,* September 28, 2017, https://www.inc.com/chris-dessi/how-to-sell-yourself-in-a-way-that-wont-make-you-cringe.html.
3. B. Swider, M. Barrick, and T. Harris, "Initial Impressions: What They Are, What They Are Not, and How They Influence Structured Interview Outcomes," *Journal of Applied Psychology*, Vol. 101, No. 5 (2016), pp. 625–638.
4. S.M. Heathfield, "Why 'Blink' Matters: The Power of First Impressions," *The Balance,* October 24, 2016, https://www.thebalance.com/why-blink-matters-the-power-of-first-impressions-1919374.
5. S. McCord, "4 Sneaky Ways to Determine Company Culture in an Interview," The Muse, https://www.themuse.com/advice/4-sneaky-ways-to-determine-company-culture-in-an-interview, accessed March 19, 2018.
6. T. Besieux, "The Art of Asking Great Questions," *HBR Ascend,* May 17, 2022.
7. J. Yoon, H. Blunden, A. Kristal, and A. Whillans, "Why Asking for Advice Is More Effective Than Asking for Feedback," *Harvard Business Review Digital Articles*, 2019, pp. 2–4.
8. A. Olson, "4 Common Reasons Strategies Fail," *Harvard Business Review,* June 24, 2022, https://hbr.org/2022/06/4-common-reasons-strategies-fail.
9. J. Trevor and B. Varcoe, "How Aligned Is Your Organization," *Harvard Business Review*, Vol. 91, No. 1 (2017), pp. 2–6. Also see R. Carucci, "Executives Fail to Execute Strategy Because They're Too Internally Focused," *Harvard Business Review Digital Articles*, November, 2017, pp. 2–5.
10. For a thorough review of this process, see C. Ostroff, A.J. Kinicki, and R.S. Muhammad, "Organizational Culture and Climate," *Handbook of Psychology, Vol. 12: Industrial and Organizational Psychology* (Hoboken, NJ: John Wiley & Sons, 2012), pp. 643–676.
11. E.H. Schein, "Culture: The Missing Concept in Organization Studies," *Administrative Science Quarterly,* June 1996, p. 236.
12. V. Grover, S.L. Tseng, and W. Pu, "A Theoretical Perspective on Organizational Culture and Digitalization," *Information & Management*, Vol. 59, No. 4 (2022), p. 103639.
13. T. Kim and J. Chang, "Organizational Culture and Performance: A Macro-Level Longitudinal Study," *Leadership & Organization Development Journal,* February 2019, pp. 65–84.
14. T. Harrison and J. Bazzy, "Aligning Organizational Culture and Strategic Human Resource Management*,*" *Journal of Management Development*, November 2017, pp. 1260–1269. Also see A. Kaul, "Culture vs Strategy: Which to Precede, Which to Align?" *Journal of Strategy and Management*, Vol. 12, No 1. (2018), pp. 116–136.
15. Z. Chen, S. Huang, C. Liu, M. Min, and L. Zhou, "Fit Between Organizational Culture and Innovation Strategy: Implications for Innovation Performance," *Sustainability,* September 2018, p. 3378. Also see D. Warrick, "What Leaders Need to Know about Organizational Culture," *Business Horizons*, May 2017 pp. 395–404.
16. M. della Cava, "Nadella Counts on Culture Shock to Drive Microsoft Growth," *USA Today Money,* February 20, 2017.
17. J. Thomson, "Company Culture Soars at Southwest Airlines," *Forbes,* December 18, 2018, https://www.forbes.com/sites/jeffthomson/2018/12/18/company-culture-soars-at-southwest-airlines/#383e2481615f.
18. B. Murphy, Jr., "Southwest Airlines Spent 51 Years Building a Funny Advantage. It All Comes Down to 1 Word," Inc., https://www.inc.com/bill-murphy-jr/southwest-airlines-spent-51-years-building-a-funny-advantage-it-all-comes-down-to-1-word.html.
19. R.V.D. Gonzalez, "Innovative Performance of Project Teams: The Role of Organizational Structure and Knowledge-Based Dynamic Capability," *Journal of Knowledge Management*, Vol. 26, No. 5 (2022), pp. 1164–1186.
20. Q. Fu, A.A. Abdul Rahman, H. Jiang, J. Abbas, and U. Comite, "Sustainable Supply Chain and Business Performance: The Impact of Strategy, Network Design, Information Systems, and Organizational Structure," *Sustainability,* Vol. 14, No. 3 (2022), p. 1080.
21. "Policies & Practices," *Procter & Gamble*, https://us.pg.com/policies-and-practices/purpose-values-and-principles/ (accessed February 1, 2023).
22. "Structure & Governance," *P&G,* https://us.pg.com/structure-and-governance/corporate-structure/ (accessed February 1, 2023).
23. A.R. Bannya, H.T. Bainbridge, and S. Chan-Serafin, "HR Practices and Work Relationships: A 20 Year Review of Relational HRM Research," in *Human Resource Management* (Vancouver 2022).
24. C. Chadwick and C. Flinchbaugh, "Searching for Competitive Advantage in the HRM/Firm Performance Relationship," *Academy of Management Perspectives* (forthcoming).
25. T. Harrison and J. Bazzy, "Aligning Organizational Culture and Strategic Human Resource Management*,*" *Journal of Management Development*, November 2017, pp. 1260–1269.
26. "Support/Corporate Employment," *In-N-Out Burger,* https://www.in-n-out.com/employment/corporate/home (accessed February 1, 2023).
27. K. Beydler, "Six Ways In-N-Out Burger Is Excelling in Business—and Five Applications for Healthcare Today," *Becker's ASC Review,* May 22, 2017, https://www.beckersasc.com/asc-news/six-ways-in-n-out-burger-is-excelling-in-business-and-five-applications-for-healthcare-today.html.
28. "Support/Corporate Employment," *In-N-Out,* https://www.in-n-out.com/employment/corporate/full-time-benefits (accessed February 1, 2023).
29. P. Romeo, "In-N-Out President Lynsi Snyder Ranked as Glassdoor's Top Restaurant Chief," Restaurant Business Online, June, 2021. https://www.restaurantbusinessonline.com/leadership/n-out-president-lynsi-snyder-ranked-glassdoors-top-restaurant-chief; Also see: https://www.glassdoor.com/Reviews/In-N-Out-Burger-Reviews-E14276.htm.
30. C. Ostroff, A. Kinicki, and R. Muhammad, "Organizational Culture and Climate," *Handbook of Psychology,* 2nd ed., Vol. 12: *Industrial and Organizational Psychology* (Hoboken, NJ: John Wiley & Sons, 2012), p. 676.
31. A. Lewis and J. Clark, "Dreams Within a Dream: Multiple Visions and Organizational Structure," *Journal of Organizational Behavior*, Vol. 41, No. 1 (2020), pp. 50–76.
32. "Council for Quality Growth Presents Carol B. Tomé with 33rd Annual Four Pillar Award," metroatlantaceo.com, October, 2022. http://metroatlantaceo.com/features/2022/10/council-quality-growth-presents-carol-b-tome-33rd-annual-four-pillar-award/.
33. M. Forde, "UPS Taps Former Home Depot CFO Carol Tomé to Succeed David Abney as CEO," *Supply Chain Dive,* March 12, 2020, https://www.supplychaindive.com/news/ups-carol-tome-ceo-effective-june-1/574011/.
34. A. Semuels, "UPS: Shipping Success," Time.com, March, 2022. https://time.com/collection/time100-companies-2022/6159486/ups-titans/.

35. B. Groysberg, J. Lee, J. Price, and J. Cheng, "The Leader's Guide to Corporate Culture," *Harvard Business Review,* January–February 2018. Also see A. Lewis and J. Clark, "Dreams within a Dream: Multiple Visions and Organizational Structure," *Journal of Organizational Behavior*, Vol. 41, No. 1 (2020), pp. 50–76.

36. N. Ateş, N. Yasin, M. Tarakci, J. Porck, D. van Knippenberg, and P. Groenen, "The dark side of visionary leadership in strategy implementation: Strategic alignment, strategic consensus, and commitment." *Journal of Management* 46, no. 5 (2020): pp. 637–665.

37. J. A. Veitch, "How and Why to Assess Workplace Design: Facilities Management Supports Human Resources," *Organizational Dynamics*, Vol. 47 (2018), pp. 78–87.

38. "Remote Work Challenges Company Culture," SHRM, March 7, 2022, https://www.shrm.org/topics-tools/news/hr-magazine/remote-work-challenges-company-culture.

39. E.H. Schein, *Organizational Culture and Leadership,* 2nd ed. (San Francisco: Jossey-Bass, 1992). Also see E.T. Hall, *Beyond Culture* (New York, Anchor Books, 1976).

40. Remote Work Resources, The Gitlab Handbook, https://handbook.gitlab.com/handbook/company/culture/all-remote/resources/.

41. D. Abril, "Bosses Say Remote Work Kills Culture. These Companies Disagree," *The Washington Post*, September 1, 2022, https://www.washingtonpost.com/technology/2022/09/01/remote-work-culture/.

42. R. Banham, "Tech Company Makes Bold Change To Drive Diversity," *Forbes,* September 30, 2022, https://www.forbes.com/sites/cadence/2022/09/30/tech-company-makes-bold-change-to-drive-diversity/?sh=57ff8ac7738d.

43. S.S.N. Biswas, C. Akroyd, and N. Sawabe, "Management Control Systems Effect on the Micro-Level Processes of Product Innovation," *Journal of Accounting & Organizational Change*, 2022 (ahead-of-print).

44. "Living Our Burger Values, Video Transcript," redrobinpa.com, https://www.redrobinpa.com/living-our-burger-values-video-transcript/.

45. J. Bennett, "Red Robin Managers Win Final Nod for Deal Ending Overtime Suit," *Bloomberg Law*, April 19, 2023, https://news.bloomberglaw.com/litigation/red-robin-managers-win-final-nod-for-deal-ending-overtime-suit.

46. K. Davis, "Why You Should Write Down Your Company's Unwritten Rules," *Harvard Business Review Digital Articles*, 2019, pp. 2–4.

47. B. Walsh, "Noma's Closing Exposes the Contradictions of Fine Dining," *Vox,* January 14, 2023, https://www.vox.com/future-perfect/2023/1/14/23553765/noma-rene-redzepi-fine-dining-art-restaurants-cuisine.

48. T.E. Deal and A.A. Kennedy, *Corporate Cultures: The Rites and Rituals of Corporate Life* (Reading, MA: Addison-Wesley, 1982), p. 22. See also T.E. Deal and A.A. Kennedy, *The New Corporate Cultures: Revitalizing the Workplace after Downsizing, Mergers, and Reengineering* (Cambridge, MA: Perseus, 2000).

49. "Lever's CEO Sarah Nahm on Building an Inclusive Culture Before Recruiting for Diversity," *Lever,* November 2, 2017, https://inside.lever.co/levers-ceo-sarah-nahm-on-building-an-inclusive-culture-before-recruiting-for-diversity-74be35523c06.

50. T. Escobedo, "Nelly Cheboi, Who Creates Computer Labs for Kenyan Schoolchildren, Is CNN's Hero of the Year," *CNN,* December 12, 2022, https://www.cnn.com/2022/12/11/us/cnn-heroes-all-star-tribute-hero-of-the-year/index.html.

51. G. Islam and R. Sferrazzo, "Workers' Rites: Ritual Mediations and the Tensions of New Management," *Journal of Management Studies*, Vol. 59, No. 2 (2022), pp. 284–318.

52. B. Hancock and B. Schaninger, "Workplace Rituals: Recapturing the Power of What We've Lost," *McKinsey & Company*, January 25, 2023, https://www.mckinsey.com/capabilities/people-and-organizational-performance/our-insights/workplace-rituals-recapturing-the-power-of-what-weve-lost.

53. J. Van Maanen, "Breaking In: Socialization to Work," in R. Dubin, ed., *Handbook of Work, Organization, and Society* (Chicago: Rand-McNally, 1976), p. 67.

54. S.Q. Cheng, A. Costantini, H. Zhou, and Wang, "A Self-Enhancement Perspective on Organizational Socialization: Newcomer Core Self-Evaluations, Job Crafting, and the Role of Leaders' Developmental Coaching," *European Journal of Work and Organizational Psychology*, Vol. 31, No. 6 (2022), pp. 908–921.

55. D.C. Feldman, "The Multiple Socialization of Organization Members," *Academy of Management Review,* April 1981, pp. 309–381. Also see T. Allen, L. Eby, G. Chao, and T. Bauer, "Taking Stock of Two Relational Aspects of Organizational Life: Tracing the History and Shaping the Future of Socialization and Mentoring Research," *Journal of Applied Psychology*, Vol. 102, No. 3 (2017), pp. 324–337.

56. "New Employee Onboarding: Buddy Guidelines," New York University, https://www.nyu.edu/content/dam/nyu/hr/documents/managerguides/BuddyGuidelines.pdf (accessed February 3, 2023).

57. A thorough description of the competing values framework is provided in K.S. Cameron, R.E. Quinn, J. Degraff, and A.V. Thakor, *Creating Values Leadership* (Northhampton, MA: Edward Elgar, 2006). Also see C. Hartnell, A. Ou, A. Kinicki, D. Choi, and E. Karam, "A Meta-Analytic Test of Organizational Culture's Association with Elements of an Organization's System and Its Relative Predictive Validity on Organizational Outcomes," *Journal of Applied Psychology*, Vol. 104, No. 6 (2019), pp. 832–850.

58. I. Suh, J. Sweeney, K. Linke, and J. Wall, "Boiling the Frog Slowly: The Immersion of C-Suite Financial Executives into Fraud," *Journal of Business Ethics,* Vol. 162 (2020), pp. 645–673.

59. "Wegmans Careers," *Wegmans,* https://jobs.wegmans.com/history#:~:text=We%20pursue%20excellence%20in%20everything,our%20customers%20and%20our%20company (accessed February 3, 2022).

60. "5 Things You'll Learn at Wegmans," *Wegmans,* https://jobs.wegmans.com/5-things-you-will-learn-at-wegmans (accessed February 3, 2023).

61. B. Morgan, "10 Examples of How Employee Experience Impacted Business Performance," *Forbes,* November 7, 2019, https://www.forbes.com/sites/blakemorgan/2019/11/07/10-examples-of-how-employee-experience-impacted-business-performance/#a90c5147c916.

62. "Wegmans Named one of the 'Best Companies to Work For' for 25th Year in a Row," *WGRZ,* April 11, 2022, https://www.wgrz.com/article/news/local/wegmans-named-one-of-the-best-companies-to-work-for-fortune-magazine/71-ecc50e7b-7802-4b0c-ae13-0570391cf302#:~:text=In%20fact%2C%20Fortune%20says%20Wegmans,CEO%20of%20Wegmans%20Food%20Markets.

63. S. Gharib, "This CEO Believes That Innovation and Culture Are One and the Same," *Fortune,* February 14, 2018, http://fortune.com/2018/02/14/baxter-international-jose-almeida/?iid=sr-link4.

64. "Baxter Recognized Globally for Inclusion Efforts," businesswire.com, April 21, 2022, https://www.businesswire.com/news/home/20210421005667/en/Baxter-Recognized-Globally-for-Inclusion-Efforts.

65. "Baxter Recognized Globally for Inclusion Efforts," *CityBiz,* April 22, 2021, https://www.citybiz.co/article/46009/baxter-recognized-globally-for-inclusion-efforts/.

66. "Company Overview," *Tyson Foods,* https://ir.tyson.com/investor-home/default.aspx (accessed February 3, 2023).

67. C. Gilchrist, R. Kwon, "TIER: Emerging Tech's Chicken And Egg Productivity Paradox," Forrester.com, June 4, 2023, https://www.forrester.com/blogs/tier-emerging-techs-chicken-and-the-egg-productivity-paradox/.

68. J. Trevor and B. Varcoe, "How Aligned Is Your Organization?" *Harvard Business Review Digital Articles*, Vol. 95, No. 1 (2017), pp. 2–6.

69. "McDonald's Employee Reviews," *Indeed,* https://www.indeed.com/cmp/McDonald's/reviews (accessed February 3, 2023).

70. T. Kim and J. Chang, "Organizational Culture and Performance: A Macro-Level Longitudinal Study," *Leadership & Organization Development Journal*, February 2019, pp. 65–84. Also see B. Dyck, K. Walker, and A. Caza, "Antecedents of Sustainable Organizing: Relationships between Organizational Culture and the TBL," *Academy of Management Proceedings,* Vol. 1 (2017), p. 14702.

71. C. Hartnell, A. Ou, A. Kinicki, D. Choi, and E. Karam, "A Meta-Analytic Test of Organizational Culture's Association with Elements of an Organization's System and Its Relative Predictive Validity on Organizational Outcomes," *Journal of Applied Psychology*, Vol. 104, No. 6 (2019), pp. 832–850.

72. M. Perino, A. Cain, and R. Gillett, "Here's What Elon Musk, Richard Branson, and 53 Other Successful People Ask Job Candidates during Interviews," *Business Insider,* August 22, 2019, https://www.businessinsider.com/executives-favorite-job-interview-question-2014-11#can-you-tell-me-the-story-of-you-prior-successes-challenges-and-major-responsibilities-52.

73. N. Roulin and F. Krings, "Faking to Fit In: Applicants' Response Strategies to Match Organizational Culture," *Journal of Applied Psychology,* 105(2), February 2020, pp. 130–145.

74. R. Grossman, "How to Screen for Cultural Fit," *Society for Human Resource Management,* February 2, 2009, https://www.shrm.org/hr-today/news/hr-magazine/pages/0209grossman2.aspx.

75. L. Rivera, "Stop Hiring for 'Cultural Fit'," *Kellogg Insight,* August 4, 2020, https://insight.kellogg.northwestern.edu/article/cultural-fit-discrimination.

76. A. Kinicki, "'Fitting in' Important at Workplace," *Arizona Republic,* June 8, 2015, www.azcentral.com/story/money/business/career/2015/06/07/fitting-important-workplace/28592961/ (accessed May 18, 2016); Also see C. Boho, "How to Find the Right Cultural Fit," *Arizona Republic,* November 15, 2015, p. 4E.

77. E. Follmer, D. Talbot, A. Kristof-Brown, S. Astrove, and J. Billsberry, "Resolution, Relief, and Resignation: A Qualitative Study of Responses to Misfit at Work," *Academy of Management Journal*, Vol. 61, No. 2 (2018), pp. 440–465. Also see C. Schwepker, "Strengthening Customer Value Development and Ethical Intent in the Salesforce: The Influence of Ethical Values Person–Organization Fit and Trust in Manager," *Journal of Business Ethics*, Vol. 159 (2019), pp. 913–925.

78. A. Beecham, "'Quick Quitting': Why a Growing Number of People Are Leaving Their Jobs before the 1-Year Mark," *Stylist,* February 7, 2023.

79. V. Maza, "What It Means to Hire for 'Culture Fit,' and How to Do It Right," *Forbes,* September 28, 2018, https://www.forbes.com/sites/forbeshumanresourcescouncil/2018/09/28/what-it-means-to-hire-for-culture-fit-and-how-to-do-it-right/#324798fe7986.

80. The mechanisms are based on material contained in E.H. Schein, "The Role of the Founder in Creating Organizational Culture," *Organizational Dynamics,* Summer 1983, pp. 13–28.

81. "Our Story," *Hubspot,* https://www.hubspot.com/our-story (accessed February 7, 2023).

82. D. Shah, "How We Fixed a Critical Bug in HubSpot's Culture Code," *Hubspot,* January 19, 2023, https://www.hubspot.com/careers-blog/how-we-fixed-a-critical-bug-in-hubspots-culture-code.

83. M. Stern, "Is Lowe's Doing It Right with Its New Tagline?" RetailWire.com, January 9, 2019, https://retailwire.com/discussion/is-lowes-doing-it-right-with-its-new-tagline/; R. Channick, "State Farm Rebrands with Less Disastrous Message," Chicago Tribune, June 3, 2016, https://www.chicagotribune.com/business/ct-state-farm-rebranding-0604-biz-20160603-story.html.

84. E. Keswin, " The Hidden Power of Workplace Rituals," Harvard Business Review, August 17, 2022, https://hbr.org/2022/08/the-hidden-power-of-workplace-rituals.

85. Pinterest Newsroom, "Knit Con 2022: Taking Inspiration to Realization for our Employees," *Pinterest,* June 8, 2022, https://newsroom.pinterest.com/en/post/knit-con-2022-taking-inspiration-to-realization-for-our-employees.

86. A.L. Smith, "Can Storytelling Catalyze Culture Change?" Medium.com, August 24, 2020, https://medium.com/unhcr-innovation-service/can-storytelling-catalyze-culture-change-22dc1965cdfc.

87. N. Pahwa, "Why It Took Adidas So Long to Finally Drop Kanye West," *Slate,* October 25, 2022, https://slate.com/business/2022/10/adidas-kanye-west-dropped-why-explained.html.

88. See H. McGregor, "Tap the Wisdom of Junior Colleagues," *Financial Times,* March 27, 2022, https://www.ft.com/content/fb73272f-149a-4e4a-9dd4-7e563ba355cd; Also see P. Peralta, "Boomers, Meet Gen Z: How Reverse Mentoring Is Building the Workforce of the Future," *EBN,* August 23, 2022, https://www.benefitnews.com/news/the-benefits-reverse-mentoring-can-create-at-your-company.

89. L. Britz and R. Norwood, "How LinkedIn Redesigned Its HQ for Hybrid Work," *Harvard Business Review Digital Articles,* 2022, pp. 1–8.

90. "Linking Executive Compensation to Climate Performance," SageJournals, February 15, 2022, https://journals.sagepub.com/doi/full/10.1177/00081256221077470.

91. "2022 Integrated Annual Report Executive Summary," *The Clorox Company,* https://s21.q4cdn.com/507168367/files/doc_financials/2022/ar/2022-Clorox-IR-Executive-Summary.pdf.

92. N. Eckert, "Ford to Offer Some Underperforming Workers Choice of Severance or Performance Improvement; Internal Email Reflects Changes in Auto Maker's Policy around Employees with Declining Performance," *Wall Street Journal,* October 31, 2022.

93. J. Kantor, A. Sundaram, "The Rise of the Worker Productivity Score," *The New York Times,* August 14, 2022, https://www.nytimes.com/interactive/2022/08/14/business/worker-productivity-tracking.html.

94. C. Thiel et al. "Monitoring Employees Makes Them More Likely to Break Rules," *Harvard Business Review Digital Articles*, 2022, pp. 1–6.

95. "How 4 Top Startups are Reinventing Organizational Structure Blog: The Process Street Blog," Business Process Incubator, January 21, 2022, https://www.businessprocessincubator.com/content/how-4-top-startups-are-reinventing-organizational-structure/.

96. L. Kohler, "Will You Still Need A Boss In A Distributed Workforce?" *Forbes*, August 28, 2021, https://www.forbes.com/sites/lindsaykohler/2021/08/28/will-you-still-need-a-boss-in-a-distributed-workforce/?sh=c948f6812799.

97. A. Holmer, "How Zappos Works: Market-Based Dynamics, Customer-Generated Budgeting and the Triangle of Accountability," *Medium,* August 29, 2021, https://medium.com/workmatters/how-zappos-works-market-based-dynamics-customer-generated-budgeting-and-the-triangle-of-307572482f7a.

98. J. Elias, "Google Is Raising Pay, Revamping Employee Reviews, Documents Show," *CNBC,* May 6, 2022, https://www.cnbc.com/2022/05/06/google-says-its-raising-employee-pay-in-performance-review-revamp.html.

99. K. Schreurs, "Why Cultural Change Fails," *HR News,* August, 2018, https://www.hrnews.be/2018/08/why-cultural-change-fails.html.

100. Canada Energy Regulator, "Advancing Safety in the Oil and Gas Industry—Statement on Safety Culture," Government of Canada, 2021 https://www.cnlopb.ca/wp-content/uploads/safetyculture.pdf (accessed February 7, 2023).

101. H. de la Boutetière, J. Rose, and B. Spinoy, "Transforming Safety Culture: Insights from the Trenches at a Leading Oil and Gas Company," *McKinsey,* July 2019, https://www.mckinsey.com/business-functions/organization/our-insights/transforming-safety-culture-insights-from-the-trenches-at-a-leading-oil-and-gas-company.

102. B. Müller, S. Konlechner, K. Link, and W. Güttel, "The Emperor's New Clothes: How Dealing with Failure Prevents Cultural Change," *Organizational Dynamics*, Vol. 48, No. 4 (2019), p. 100672.

103. H.O. Sørlie, J. Hetland, A.B. Bakker, R. Espevik, and O.K. Olsen, "Daily Autonomy and Job Performance: Does Person-Organization Fit Act as a Key Resource?" *Journal of Vocational Behavior,* Vol. 133 (2022), p. 103691.

104. A. Dalgıç, "The Effects of Person-Job Fit and Person-Organization Fit on Turnover Intention: The Mediation Effect of Job Resourcefulness," *Journal of Gastronomy Hospitality and Travel (JOGHAT),* Vol. 5, No. 1 (2022), pp. 355–365.

105. R. Maurer, "Toxic Culture Top Reason People Quit," *SHRM,* January 19, 2022, https://www.shrm.org/resourcesandtools/hr-topics/talent-acquisition/pages/toxic-culture-top-reason-people-quit.aspx.

106. P. Myers, "Moving Beyond Culture Fit," *Strategic Finance,* March 1, 2022.

107. C. I. Barnard, *The Functions of the Executive* (Cambridge, MA: Harvard University Press, 1938), p. 73.

108. E.H. Schein, *Organizational Psychology,* 3rd ed. (Englewood Cliffs, NJ: Prentice-Hall, 1980).

109. J.P. Friesen, A.C. Kay, R.P. Eibach, and A.D. Galinsky, "Seeking Structure in Social Organization: Compensatory Control and the Psychological Advantages of Hierarchy," *Journal of Personality and Social Psychology,* Vol. 106 (2014), pp. 590–609. This work on hierarchies existing within flat organizations is also described in M. Hutson, "Espousing Equality, but Embracing a Hierarchy," *The New York Times,* June 22, 2014, p. BU-3.

110. For an overview of the span of control concept, see D.D. Van Fleet and A.G. Bedeian, "A History of the Span of Management," *Academy of Management Review,* July 1977, pp. 356–372.

111. C. B. Jacobsen, A.K.L. Hansen, and L.D. Pedersen. Not too narrow, not too broad: Linking span of control, leadership behavior, and employee job satisfaction in public organizations. *Public Administration Review,* 83(4), 2022, pp. 775–792. Vancouver.

112. J. Brees and B.P. Ellen III, "Unaccounted for No More: Explicating Managers' Role in Accountability Enactment," *Journal of Organizational Behavior,* Vol. 43, No. 2 (2022), pp. 310–326.

113. I. Miklosevic, I. Stanic, and S.K. Kusljic, "Managers Factors in Delegating Work Tasks to Associates," *Economic and Social Development: Book of Proceedings,* 2022, pp. 361–368.

114. S. Lloyd, "Managers Must Delegate Effectively to Develop Employees," *Society for Human Resource Management,* https://www.shrm.org/resourcesandtools/hr-topics/organizational-and-employee-development/pages/delegateeffectively.aspx#:~:text=Other%20reasons%20why%20managers%20do,motivation%20and%20commitment%20to%20quality (accessed February 3, 2023).

115. E. Amdur, "Delegating Part I: What Is Delegating?" *Forbes,* November 7, 2022, https://www.forbes.com/sites/eliamdur/2022/11/07/delegating-part-i-what-is-delegating/?sh=246740bc61d5.

116. J. Craven, "Great Leaders Perfect the Art of Delegation," *Forbes,* February 21, 2018, https://www.forbes.com/sites/forbescoachescouncil/2018/02/21/great-leaders-perfect-the-art-of-delegation/#681b47971eb2. Also see A. Acton, "Delegation Is a CEO's Secret Weapon: Here's How to Do It Right," *Forbes,* August 15, 2017, https://www.forbes.com/sites/annabelacton/2017/08/15/effective-delegation-is-a-ceos-secret-weapon-heres-how-to-do-it-right/#8ffca20433d1; D. Finkel, "Use This Little-Known Delegation Trick to Get Stuff Done the Right Way," *Inc.,* February 21, 2018, https://www.inc.com/david-finkel/use-this-little-known-delegation-trick-to-get-stuff-done-right-way.html?cid=search.

117. H. Altamimi, "Insights: To Centralize or Decentralize, That Is Not the Question," *ICMA,* November 1, 2022, https://icma.org/articles/pm-magazine/insights-centralize-or-decentralize-not-question.

118. L.N. Boss E.L. and Gralla, "Robustness of Decentralized Decision-Making Architectures in Command and Control Systems," *Systems Engineering,* 2022.

119. R. Burton and B. Obel, "The Science of Organizatonal Design: Fit between Structure and Coordination," *Journal of Organization Design,* Vol. 8, No. 1 (2018), pp. 1–13.

120. This section was adapted from R. Kreitner and A. Kinicki, *Organizational Behavior,* 10th ed. (New York: McGraw Hill/Irwin, 2013), pp. 503–508.

121. An Overview of Our Business and Operations, ExxonMobil.com, https://corporate.exxonmobil.com/who-we-are/our-global-organization/business-divisions.

122. Adapted from "Boundaryless," *Encyclopedia of Small Business,* ed. K. Hillstrom and L. C. Hillstrom (Farmington Hills, MI: Thomson Gale, 2002; and Seattle, WA: eNotes.com, 2006), http://business.enotes.com/small-business-encyclopedia/boundaryless (accessed June 20, 2014).

123. R. Zitkiene and U. Dude, "The Impact of Outsourcing Implementation on Service Companies," *Entrepreneurship and Sustainability Issues,* September 2018, pp. 342–355.

124. "Supply Chain," *H&M Group,* https://hmgroup.com/sustainability/leading-the-change/transparency/supply-chain/ (accessed February 9, 2023).

125. J. Hayward, "From Start To Finish: How The Boeing 787 Is Made," Simple Flying, May 15, 2021, https://simpleflying.com/how-its-made-the-787/.

126. "Suppliers," *Boeing,* https://www.boeing.co.in/boeing-in-india/suppliers.page (accessed February 9, 2023).

127. R. Sher, "Making Virtual Teams Feel Like They're in the Same Room: The AppNeta Approach," *Forbes,* October 2, 2019, https://www.forbes.com/sites/robertsher/2019/10/02/making-virtual-teams-feel-like-theyre-in-the-same-room-the-appneta-approach/#5614d37a18bb.

128. Zapier Newsroom: Everything You need to Know about Zapier in 2023, Zapier, https://zapier.com/press.

129. G. Johns, "Advances in the Treatment of Context in Organizational Research," in F.P. Morgeson, H. Aguinis, and S.J. Ashford, eds., *Annual Review of Organizational Psychology and Organizational Behavior* (Palo Alto, CA: Annual Reviews, 2017), pp. 21–46.

130. H.O. Sørlie, J. Hetland, A.B. Bakker, R. Espevik, and Olsen, "Daily Autonomy and Job Performance: Does Person-Organization Fit Act as a Key Resource?" *Journal of Vocational Behavior,* Vol. 133 (2022), p. 103691; Also see T.H.H. Hue, H.C. Vo Thai, and M.L. Tran, "A Link between Public Service Motivation, Employee Outcomes, and Person–Organization Fit: Evidence from Vietnam," *International Journal of Public Administration,* Vol. 45, No. 5 (2022), pp. 379–398; Also see S. Subramanian, J. Billsberry, and M. Barrett, "A Bibliometric Analysis of Person-Organization Fit Research: Significant Features and Contemporary Trends," *Management Review Quarterly,* 2022, pp. 1–29.

131. M. Corritore, A. Goldberg, and S. Srivastava, "The New Analytics of Culture: What Email, Slack, and Glassdoor Reveal about Your Organization," *Harvard Business Review,* January–February 2020.

132. See R. Lash, "Finding and Defining 'Fit'," *Inside Higher Ed,* October 3, 2016, https://www.insidehighered.com/advice/2018/10/04/how-determine-if-prospective-job-good-fit-opinion. Also see R. Knight, "How to Tell If a Company's Culture Is Right for You," *Harvard Business Review Digital Articles,* 2017, pp. 2–6.

133. M. Fugate, A.J. Kinicki, and B.E. Ashforth, "Employability: A Psycho-Social Construct, Its Dimensions, and Applications," *Journal of Vocational Behavior,* August 2004, pp. 14–38.

134. A. Holtermann, "Convergence Innovation of Digital Transformation in the New Normal," *Management,* Vol. 19 (2022), p. 21; Also see A. Causevic, "Employability, Career Readiness, and Soft Skills in US Higher Education: A Literature Review," *SPNHA Review,* Vol. 18, No. 1 (2022), p. 5.

135. D. Rizana, "Self-leadership and Teacher's Innovative Work Behavior: The Mediating Roles of Self-Efficacy and Optimism," *Relevance: Journal of Management and Business*, Vol. 5, No. 2 (2022), pp. 177–195.

136. L. Regan, L.R. Hopson, M.A. Gisondi, J. Branzetti, "Creating a Better Learning Environment: A Qualitative Study Uncovering the Experiences of Master Adaptive Learners in Residency," BMC Medical Education, March 4, 2022, https://bmcmededuc.biomedcentral.com/articles/10.1186/s12909-022-03200-5.

137. J.G. Berger, "4 Steps to Becoming More Adaptable to Change," *Fast Company,* March 9, 2015, https://www.fastcompany.com/3043294/4-steps-to-becoming-more-adaptable-to-change.

CHAPTER 9

1. S. Joubert, "8 Tips to Prepare for Your Next Job Interview," *Northeastern University*, https://www.northeastern.edu/bachelors-completion/news/how-to-prepare-for-job-interview/ (accessed March 30, 2020).

2. M. Tews, K. Frager, A. Citarella, and R. Orndorff, "What Is Etiquette Today? Interviewing Etiquette for Today's College Student," *Journal of Advances in Education Research*, Vol. 3, No. 3 (2018), pp. 167–175.

3. M. Kuper, "Sticky Situations: How to Dodge Inappropriate Interview Questions," *University of Arizona Student Engagement & Career Development*, https://career.arizona.edu/cs-blog-post/sticky-situations-how-dodge-inappropriate-interview-questions (accessed March 30, 2020).

4. M. Tews, K. Stafford, and J. Michel, "Interview Etiquette and Hiring Outcomes," *International Journal of Selection and Assessment*, Vol. 26, No. 2–4 (2018), pp. 164–175.

5. A. Kiersz, "Here's Exactly What to Do If You Leave a Job Interview and Realize You Totally Flubbed a Question," *Business Insider,* August 20, 2018, https://www.businessinsider.com/job-interview-question-wrong-email-interviewers-2018-8.

6. A. Doyle, "Background Checks for Employment," *The Balance Money,* August 17, 2022, https://www.thebalancemoney.com/employment-background-checks-2058432.

7. A. Doyle, "How to Answer Job Interview Questions about Your Grades," *The Balance Careers,* July 19, 2019, https://www.thebalancecareers.com/how-to-answer-job-interview-questions-about-your-grades-2060516.

8. I. Thottam, "Social Media Mistakes That Can Disqualify You From a Job," *Monster,* https://www.monster.com/career-advice/article/these-social-media-mistakes-can-actually-disqualify-you-from-a-job, (accessed November, 2023).

9. A. Gallo, "38 Smart Questions to Ask in a Job Interview," *Harvard Business Review,* May 19, 2022, https://hbr.org/2022/05/38-smart-questions-to-ask-in-a-job-interview.

10. C.H. Van Iddekinge, F. Lievens, and P.R. Sackett, "Personnel Selection: A Review of Ways to Maximize Validity, Diversity, and the Applicant Experience," *Personnel Psychology,* 2023 (in press); Also see G. Sánchez-Marín, Á.L. Meroño-Cerdán, and A.J. Carrasco-Hernández, "Formalized HR Practices and Firm Performance: An Empirical Comparison of Family and Non-family Firms," *The International Journal of Human Resource Management,* Vol. 30, No. 7 (2019), pp. 1084–1110; Also see C.J. Collins and K.D. Clark, "Strategic Human Resource Practices, Top Management Team Social Networks, and Firm Performance: The Role of Human Resource Practices in Creating Organizational Competitive advantage," *Academy of Management Journal,* Vol. 46, No. 6 (2003), pp. 740–751; Also see L. Xiu, X. Liang, Z. Chen, and W. Xu, "Strategic Flexibility, Innovative HR Practices, and Firm Performance: A Moderated Mediation Model," *Personnel Review,* Vol. 46, No. 7 (2017), pp. 1335–1357; Also see T. Rabl, M. Jayasinghe, B. Gerhart, and T.M. Kühlmann, "A Meta-Analysis of Country Differences in the High-Performance Work System–Business Performance Relationship: The Roles of National culture and Managerial Discretion," *Journal of Applied Psychology,* Vol. 99, No. 6 (2014), p. 1011.

11. J. Welch, quoted in N.M. Tichy and S. Herman, *Control Your Destiny or Someone Else Will: How Jack Welch Is Making General Electric the World's Most Competitive Corporation* (New York: Doubleday, 1993), p. 251.

12. "Fortune 100 Best Companies to Work For," *Fortune,* https://fortune.com/ranking/best-companies/ (accessed March 6, 2023).

13. "100 Best Companies to Work For: Salesforce," *Fortune,* https://fortune.com/company/salesforce-com/best-companies/ (accessed March 6, 2023); Also see "Benefits," *Hilton,* https://jobs.hilton.com/us/en/benefits (accessed March 6, 2023); Also see T. Parker, "What Is a Good 401(k) Match? How It Works and What's the Average," *Investopedia,* January 9, 2023, https://www.investopedia.com/articles/personal-finance/120315/what-good-401k-match.asp; Also see "Benefits," *Capital One Careers,* https://www.capitalonecareers.com/benefits (accessed March 6, 2023).

14. N. Dries, "The Psychology of Talent Management: A Review and Research Agenda," *Human Resource Management Review,* Vol. 23, No. 4 (2013), pp. 272–285.

15. J. Delery and D. Roumpi, "Strategic Human Resource Management, Human Capital and Competitive Advantage: Is the Field Going in Circles?" *Human Resource Management Journal,* Vol. 27, No. 1 (2017), pp. 1–21.

16. J. Han, S. Kang, I. Oh, R. Kehoe, and D. Lepak, "The Goldilocks Effect of Strategic Human Resource Management? Optimizing the Benefits of a High-Performance Work System Through the Dual Alignment of Vertical and Horizontal Fit," *Academy of Management Journal,* Vol. 62, No. 5 (2019), pp. 1388–1412. Also see V. Khoreva and H. Wechtler, "HR Practices and Employee Performance: The Mediating Role of Well-Being," *Employee Relations,* Vol. 4, No. 2 (2018), pp. 227–243; and A. Glaister, G. Karacay, M. Demirbag, and E. Tatoglu, "HRM and Performance—The Role of Talent Management as a Transmission Mechanism in an Emerging Market Context," *Human Resource Management Journal,* Vol. 28, No. 1 (2018), pp. 148–166.

17. C. Chadwick and C. Flinchbaugh, "Searching for Competitive Advantage in the HRM/Firm Performance Relationship," *Academy of Management Perspectives* (forthcoming).

18. C. Ammerman, B. Groysberg, and G. Rometty, "The New-Collar Workforce," *Harvard Business Review,* Vol. 101, No. 2 (2023), pp. 96–103.

19. R. Kehoe and C. Collins, "Human Resource Management and Unit Performance in Knowledge-Intensive Work," *Journal of Applied Psychology,* 102(8), 2017, pp. 1222–1236. Vancouver; J. Korff, T. Biemann, and S.C. Voelpel, "Human Resource Management Systems and Work Attitudes: The Mediating Role of Future Time Perspective," *Journal of Organizational Behavior,* 38(1), 2017, pp. 45–67.

20. "Live and Work from Anywhere," *Careers at Airbnb,* https://careers.airbnb.com/ (accessed March 6, 2023).

21. S. Jones, "Airbnb Staff Can Now Choose to Work Remotely Forever with No Loss of Pay, Its CEO Says," *Insider,* April 29, 2022, https://www.businessinsider.com/airbnb-flexible-work-remote-brian-chesky-no-loss-pay-2022-4#:~:text=Airbnb%20is%20letting%20staff%20%22live, Chesky%20said%20in%20a%20memo.

22. M. Subramony, J. Segers, C. Chadwick, and A. Shyamsunder, "Leadership Development Practice Bundles and Organizational Performance: The Mediating Role of Human Capital and Social Capital," *Journal of Business Research,* Vol. 83 (2018), pp. 120–129.

23. M. Subramony, J. Segers, C. Chadwick, and A. Shyamsunder, "Leadership Development Practice Bundles and Organizational Performance: The Mediating Role of Human Capital and Social Capital," *Journal of Business Research,* Vol. 83 (2018), pp. 120–129.

24. M. Wiersema, Y. Nishimura, and K. Suzuki, "Executive Succession: The Importance of Social Capital in CEO Appointments," *Strategic Management Journal,* Vol. 39, No. 5 (2018), pp. 1473–1495.

25. D. Collings, K. Mellahi, and W. Cascio, "Global Talent Management and Performance in Multinational Enterprises: A Multilevel Perspective," *Journal of Management,* Vol. 45, No. 2 (2019), pp. 540–566.

26. "The ISMs Make Us Who We Are," *Rocket Careers,* www.myrocketcareer.com/about-us/our-philosophies/ (accessed March 9, 2023); Also see "Rocket Companies Reviews," *Glassdoor,* www.glassdoor.com/Reviews/Rocket-Companies-Reviews-E7856.htm (accessed March 9, 2023); Also see "Rocket Companies Employee Reviews," *Indeed,* www.indeed.com/cmp/Rocket-Companies/reviews (accessed March 9, 2023).

27. M. Subramony, J. Segers, C. Chadwick, and A. Shyamsunder, "Leadership Development Practice Bundles and Organizational Performance: The Mediating Role of Human Capital and Social Capital," *Journal of Business Research,* Vol. 83 (2018), pp. 120–129.

28. G. De Boeck, M. Meyers, and M. Dries, "Employee Reactions to Talent Management: Assumptions versus Evidence," *Journal of Organizational Behavior,* Vol. 29, No. 2 (2018), pp. 199–213.

29. T. Chamorro-Premuzic and J. Kirschner, "How the Best Managers Identify and Develop Talent," *Harvard Business Review Digital Articles,* 9, 2020, pp. 2–5.

30. M. Meyers, "The Neglected Role of Talent Proactivity: Integrating Proactive Behavior into Talent-Management Theorizing," *Human Resource Management Review* 30, no. 2 (2020): 100703. Also see M. Crowley-Henry, M. and A. Al Ariss, "Talent Management of Skilled Migrants: Propositions and an Agenda for Future Research," *The International Journal of Human Resource Management,* Vol. 29, No. 3 (2018), pp. 2054–2079.

31. D. Collings, K. Mellahi, and W. Cascio, "Global Talent Management and Performance in Multinational Enterprises: A Multilevel Perspective," *Journal of Management,* Vol. 45, No. 2 (2019), pp. 540–566. Also see R. Brymer, C. Chadwick, A. Hill, and J. Molloy, "Pipelines and Their

Portfolios: A More Holistic View of Human Capital Heterogeneity via Firm-wide Employee Sourcing," *Academy of Management Perspectives*, Vol. 33, No. 2 (2019), pp. 207–233.

32. Seapower staff, "Marine Corps Releases Talent Management Update," *SeaPower Magazine,* March 6, 2023, https://seapowermagazine.org/marine-corps-releases-talent-management-update/.

33. K. Jiang and J. Messersmith, "On the Shoulders of Giants: A Meta-Review of Strategic Human Resource Management," *The International Journal of Human Resource Management*, Vol. 29, No. 1 (2018), pp. 6–33.

34. Q. Xu, Z. Hou, C. Zhang, F. Yu, J. Guan, and X. Liu, "Human Capital, Social Capital, Psychological Capital, and Job Performance: Based on Fuzzy-Set Qualitative Comparative Analysis," *Frontiers in Psychology*, Vol. 13 (2022), pp. 938875–938875.

35. K. Jiang and J. Messersmith, "On the Shoulders of Giants: A Meta-Review of Strategic Human Resource Management," *The International Journal of Human Resource Management*, Vol. 29, No. 1 (2018), pp. 6–33.

36. "Policies & Practices," *P&G,* https://us.pg.com/policies-and-practices/purpose-values-and-principles/ (accessed March 25, 2023).

37. B. Chambers, "Is Your Hiring Process Costing You Talent?" *Harvard Business Review,* June 2, 2022, https://hbr.org/2022/06/is-your-hiring-process-costing-you-talent; Also see K. Navarra, "The Real Costs of Recruitment," *SHRM,* April 11, 2022, https://www.shrm.org/resourcesandtools/hr-topics/talent-acquisition/pages/the-real-costs-of-recruitment.aspx.

38. C.H. Van Iddekinge, F. Lievens, and P.R. Sackett, "Personnel Selection: A Review of Ways to Maximize Validity, Diversity, and the Applicant Experience," *Personnel Psychology*, January 28, 2023.

39. "Closing the Skills Gap 2023: Employer Perspectives on Educating the Post-Pandemic Workforce," *Wiley University Services,* 2023, https://universityservices.wiley.com/closing-the-skills-gap-2023/?utm_source=press_release&utm_medium=referral&utm_campaign=skills_gap_2023.

40. W. Poindexter and J. Craig, "Survey: What Attracts Top Tech Talent?" *Harvard Business Review Digital Articles*, October 2022, pp. 1–6.

41. J. McGregor, "As Hiring Rates Decline and Remote Postings Fall, LinkedIn Spotlights Internal Career Moves," *Forbes,* October 26, 2022, https://www.forbes.com/sites/jenamcgregor/2022/10/26/as-hiring-rates-decline-and-remote-postings-fall-linkedin-spotlights-internal-job-changes/?sh=779b36acfc93.

42. D. Zielinski, "2023 HR Technology Trends: Talent Marketplaces, Expanding AI and Optimizing Existing Systems," *SHRM,* January 10, 2023, https://www.shrm.org/resourcesandtools/hr-topics/technology/pages/2023-hr-technology-trends.aspx?_ga=2.245903234.788295277.1678800663-484571155.1674763607&_gac=1.249935476.1678825208.Cj0KCQjwtsCgBhDEARIsAE7RYh3bsvmJxC7hg_FwqcG6N93evX5CJpasjfe2IwgBLO7hdATNmz8zyJkaAhh8EALw_wcB.

43. N. Schreiber-Shearer, "How Schneider Electric Staved off the Great Resignation with Career Planning," *Gloat,* February 17, 2022, https://gloat.com/blog/schneider-electric-career-agility-2/.

44. A. Gergerson, "5 Successful Examples of Reskilling and Upskilling Programs," *Gloat,* October 25, 2022, https://gloat.com/blog/5-successful-examples-of-reskilling-and-upskilling-programs/.

45. J. Flynn, "15+ Essential Social Media Recruitment Statistics (2023): How Effective Is Social Media Recruiting?" *Zippia,* February 20, 2023, https://www.zippia.com/advice/social-media-recruitment-statistics/.

46. J. Flynn, "15+ Essential Social Media Recruitment Statistics (2023): How Effective Is Social Media Recruiting?" *Zippia,* February 20, 2023, https://www.zippia.com/advice/social-media-recruitment-statistics/.

47. C. Pope, "Air Force Recruiters Using New Tools, New Thinking to Meet Targets in Difficult Environment," *Air Force,* September 21, 2022, https://www.af.mil/News/Article-Display/Article/3166578/air-force-recruiters-using-new-tools-new-thinking-to-meet-targets-in-difficult/.

48. D. Folwell, "How Staffing Agencies Can Beat the Great Resignation with Referrals," *Forbes,* February 11, 2022, https://www.forbes.com/sites/forbesagencycouncil/2022/02/11/how-staffing-agencies-can-beat-the-great-resignation-with-referrals/?sh=771e81de39cd; Also see J. Flynn, "15+ Essential Social Media Recruitment Statistics (2023): How Effective Is Social Media Recruiting?" *Zippia,* February 20, 2023, https://www.zippia.com/advice/social-media-recruitment-statistics/.

49. S. Schlachter and J. Pieper, "Employee Referral Hiring in Organizations: An Integrative Conceptual Review, Model, and Agenda for Future Research," *Journal of Applied Psychology*, Vol. 104, No. 11 (2019), pp. 1325–1346.

50. S. Magrizos, D. Roumpi, and I. Rizomyliotis, "Talent Orchestration and Boomerang Talent: Seasonally Employed Chefs' Evaluation of Talent Management Practices," *International Journal of Contemporary Hospitality Management*, 2023.

51. Z. Tian, Q. Yuan, S. Qian, and Y. Liu, "The Generative Mechanism of Boomerang Intention: From the Perspective of Legacy Identification," *Frontiers in Psychology*, Vol. 12 (2022), p. 6691.

52. "UKG Named a Leader in HCM by Top Research Firm," UKG, May 31, 2023, https://www.ukg.com/about-us/newsroom/ukg-named-leader-hcm-top-research-firm.

53. R. Duncan, "Want Your People to Work Inspired? Be An Un-Leader," *Forbes,* November 26, 2018, https://www.forbes.com/sites/rodgerdeanduncan/2018/11/26/want-your-people-to-work-inspired-be-an-un-leader/#66e9ea211102. Also see "Kronos Scores Its Highest-Ever Glassdoor Best Places to Work Ranking," *Business Wire,* December 11, 2019, https://www.businesswire.com/news/home/20191211005602/en/Kronos-Scores-Highest-ever-Glassdoor-Places-Work-Ranking.

54. C. Mason, "Here and Back Again: Two UKG Employees Share Their Stories of Rejoining the U Krew," *UKG,* November 9, 2022, https://www.ukg.com/blog/life-ukg/here-and-back-again-two-ukg-employees-share-their-stories-rejoining-u-krew.

55. S.A. Ermis, Ü. Altinisik, and G.E. Burmaoglu, "Examination of the Prediction of Person-Job Fit on Person-Organization Fit from the Perspective of Academics," *Journal of Educational Issues*, Vol. 7, No. 3 (2021), pp. 43–57.

56. A. Dimopoulos, D. Evaggelos, and K. Zafiropoulos, "Person to Organization Fit & Person to the Job Fit Impact on Employment Interview Decisions: An Exploratory Field Study in Greece," *International Journal of Human Resource Studies,* Vol. 11, No. 1 (2021), p. 130.

57. J. Small, "72 Percent of People Surveyed Said They Lied on Their Résumés—Here Are the Most Common Fibs," *Business Insider,* February 23, 2023, https://www.businessinsider.com/most-common-lies-people-put-on-resumes-2023-1.

58. M. Freedman, "Yes, People Lie on Their Resumes," *Business News Daily*, February 21, 2023, https://www.businessnewsdaily.com/12003-employee-lies-on-resume.html.

59. S. Dorn, "House Ethics Committee Opens Santos Investigation: Here's Everything the Embattled Congressman Has Lied About," *Forbes,* March 2, 2023, https://www.forbes.com/sites/saradorn/2023/03/02/house-ethics-committee-opens-santos-investigation-heres-everything-the-embattled-congressman-has-lied-about/?sh=4334b94cc27f.

60. A. Kohli, "Everything We Know So Far about Congressman George Santos Lying about His Resume," *Time*, January 6, 2023, https://time.com/6245110/george-santos-lies-resume/. Also see: https://www.npr.org/2023/12/01/1215899764/george-santos-expulsion-house.

61. J. Fuller, C. Langer, and M. Sigelman, "Skills-Based Hiring Is on the Rise," *Harvard Business Review*, Vol. 11 (2022).

62. A. Ignatius, "Accenture CEO Julie Sweet on the Most Important Skill Job Seekers Need Today," *Harvard Business Review,* May 6, 2022, https://hbr.org/2022/05/accenture-ceo-julie-sweet-on-the-most-important-skill-job-seekers-need-today#:~:text=JULIE%20SWEET%3A%20Let's%20just%20start,for%20skills%20is%20quite%20rapid.

63. J. Fuller, C. Langer, and M. Sigelman, "Skills-Based Hiring Is on the Rise," *Harvard Business Review,* February 11, 2022.

64. K. Hannon, "Why Many Employers Have Ditched 4-Year Degree Requirements," *Yahoo News,* April 22, 2022, https://news.yahoo.com/why-many-employers-have-ditched-4-year-degree-requirements-135219348.html.

65. A. Smith, "Follow Rules of the Road for Limited-Reference Policies," *SHRM,* June 3, 2021, https://www.shrm.org/resourcesandtools/

legal-and-compliance/employment-law/pages/limited-reference-policies.aspx.

66. J. Bourdage, N. Roulin, and R. Tarraf, "I (Might Be) Just That Good: Honest and Deceptive Impression Management in Employment Interviews," *Personnel Psychology*, Vol. 71, No. 4 (2018), pp. 597–632.

67. J. Bourdage, N. Roulin, and R. Tarraf, "I (Might Be) Just That Good: Honest and Deceptive Impression Management in Employment Interviews," *Personnel Psychology*, Vol. 71, No. 4 (2018), pp. 597–632. Also see D. Zhang, S. Highhouse, M. Brooks, and Y. Zhang, "Communicating the Validity of Structured Job Interviews with Graphical Visual Aids," *International Journal of Selection and Assessment*, Vol. 26, No. 2–4 (2018), pp. 93–108.

68. R.S. Chauhan, "Unstructured Interviews: Are They Really All That Bad?" *Human Resource Development International*, Vol. 25, No. 4 (2022), pp. 474–487.

69. I. Bergelson, C. Tracy, and E. Takacs, "Best Practices for Reducing Bias in the Interview Process," *Current Urology Reports*, Vol. 23, No. 11 (2022), pp. 319–325.; Also see J. Levashina, C. Hartwell, F. Morgeson, and M. Campion, "The Structured Employment Interview: Narrative and Quantitative Review of the Research Literature," *Personnel Psychology*, Vol. 67, No. 1 (2014), pp. 241–293.

70. J. Levashina, C. Hartwell, F. Morgeson, and M. Campion, "The Structured Employment Interview: Narrative and Quantitative Review of the Research Literature," *Personnel Psychology* Vol. 67, No. 1 (2014), pp. 241–293.

71. "A Guide to Conducting Behavioral Interviews with Early Career Job Candidates," *SHRM*, 2016, https://www.shrm.org/LearningAndCareer/learning/Documents/Behavioral%20Interviewing%20Guide%20for%20Early%20Career%20Candidates.pdf.

72. Y. Kim and R. Ployhart, "The Strategic Value of Selection Practices: Antecedents and Consequences of Firm-Level Selection Practice Usage," *Academy of Management Journal*, Vol. 61, No. 1 (2018), pp. 46–66.

73. "Candidate FAQs," *National Testing Network*, https://nationaltestingnetwork.com/publicsafetyjobs/faqs.cfm. (accessed March 16, 2023).

74. "A Guide to Taking the Physical Abilities Test," *SoCalGas*, https://www.socalgas.com/1443740394085/PhysicalTestBattery.pdf (accessed March 16, 2023).

75. M. Mullenweb, "The CEO of Automattic on Holding 'Auditions' to Build a Strong Team," *Harvard Business Review*, April 2014, pp. 39–42.

76. M. Kleinmann and P. Ingold, "Toward a Better Understanding of Assessment Centers: A Conceptual Review," *Annual Review of Organizational Psychology and Organizational Behavior*, Vol. 6 (2019), pp. 349–372.

77. P. Sackett, O. Shewach, and H. Keiser, "Assessment Center versus Cognitive Ability Tests: Challenging the Conventional Wisdom on Criterion-Related Validity," *Journal of Applied Psychology*, 2017, pp. 1435–1447.

78. L. Watrin, L. Weihrauch, and O. Wilhelm, "The Criterion-Related Validity of Conscientiousness in Personnel Selection: A Meta-Analytic Reality Check," *International Journal of Selection and Assessment*, December 30, 2022; Also see M. Nordmo, H.O. Sørlie, O.C. Lang-Ree, and T.H. Fosse, "Decomposing the Effect of Hardiness in Military Leadership Selection and the Mediating Role of Self-Efficacy Beliefs", *Military Psychology*, Vol. 34, No. 6 (2022), pp. 697–705.

79. H. Claypool, "Job Hiring Increasingly Relies on Personality Tests, but That Can Bar People with Disabilities," *NBC News*, March 4, 2021, https://www.nbcnews.com/think/opinion/job-hiring-increasingly-relies-personality-tests-they-can-bar-people-ncna1259466.

80. "Types of Employment Tests," *Society for Industrial and Organizational Psychology*, http://www.siop.org/workplace/employment%20testing/testtypes.aspx (accessed March 21, 2018).

81. D.A. Cooper, J.E. Slaughter, and S.W. Gilliland, "Reducing Injuries, Malingering, and Workers' Compensation Costs by Implementing Overt Integrity Testing," *Journal of Business and Psychology*, Vol. 36 (2021), pp. 495–512.

82. S. Sajjadiani, A. Sojourner, J. Kammeyer-Mueller, and E. Mykerezi, "Using Machine Learning to Translate Applicant Work History into Predictors of Performance and Turnover," *Journal of Applied Psychology*, Vol. 104, No. 10 (2019), pp. 1207–1225.

83. "State Laws for Workplace Drug Testing," *NDS*, https://www.nationaldrugscreening.com/state-laws-for-workplace-drug-testing/ (accessed March 16, 2023).

84. E.G. Hammer and J. Kimbell, "Fair Chances for Work: Examining Hiring Practices for Background Checks and Disparate Impact," *The CASE Journal*, 19(2), 232–240.

85. "Employing Individuals with Criminal Records," *SHRM*, https://www.shrm.org/resourcesandtools/tools-and-samples/toolkits/pages/employing-individuals-with-criminal-records.aspx (accessed March 16, 2023); Also see D. Shoag and S. Veuger, "Ban-the-Box Measures Help High-Crime Neighborhoods," *The Journal of Law and Economics*, Vol. 64, No. 1 (2021), pp. 85–105.

86. Y. Lee, C. Berry, and E. Gonzalez-Mulé, "The Importance of Being Humble: A Meta-Analysis and Incremental Validity Analysis of the Relationship Between Honesty-Humility and Job Performance," *Journal of Applied Psychology*, Vol. 104, No. 12 (2019), pp. 1534–1546. Also see C. Van Iddekinge, H. Aguinis, J. Mackey, and P. DeOrtentiis, "A Meta-Analysis of the Interactive, Additive, and Relative Effects of Cognitive Ability and Motivation on Performance," *Journal of Management*, Vol. 44, No. 1 (2018), pp. 249–279.

87. Y. Lee, C. Berry, and E. Gonzalez-Mulé, "The Importance of Being Humble: A Meta-Analysis and Incremental Validity Analysis of the Relationship between Honesty-Humility and Job Performance," *Journal of Applied Psychology*, Vol. 104, No. 12 (2019), pp. 1534–1546. Also see C. Rockwood, "How Accurate Are Personality Assessments?" *SHRM*, November 21, 2019, https://www.shrm.org/hr-today/news/hr-magazine/winter2019/pages/how-accurate-are-personality-assessments.aspx.

88. "Pre-Offer Personality Testing in the Selection of California Peace Officers," *CA.gov*, https://post.ca.gov/Pre-Offer-Personality-Testing-in-the-Selection-of-California-Peace-Officers (accessed March 16, 2023); Also see "Pre-Offer Personality Testing in the Selection of Entry-Level California Peace Officers Resource Guide," *California Commission on Peace Officer Standards and Training—Resource Guide*, September 2015, https://post.ca.gov/Portals/0/Publications/Peace_Officer_Pre-Offer_Personality_Testing-Resource_Guide.pdf?ver=2019-07-12-131131-617.

89. L. Macabasco, "'They Become Dangerous Tools': The Dark Side of Personality Tests," *The Guardian*, March 4, 2021, https://www.theguardian.com/tv-and-radio/2021/mar/03/they-become-dangerous-tools-the-dark-side-of-personality-tests; Also see K. Rockwood, "Assessing Personalities," *SHRM*, February 29, 2020, https://www.shrm.org/hr-today/news/all-things-work/pages/personality-assessments.aspx; Also see R.P. Tett and D.V. Simonet, "Applicant Faking on Personality Tests: Good or Bad and Why Should We Care?" *Personnel Assessment and Decisions*, Vol. 7, No. 1 (2021), p. 2.

90. K. Parker and J. Horowitz, "Majority of Workers Who Quit a Job in 2021 Cite Low Pay, No Opportunities for Advancement, Feeling Disrespected," *Pew Research Center*, March 9, 2022, https://www.pewresearch.org/fact-tank/2022/03/09/majority-of-workers-who-quit-a-job-in-2021-cite-low-pay-no-opportunities-for-advancement-feeling-disrespected/#:~:text=Majorities%20of%20workers%20who%20quit,major%20reasons%20why%20they%20left.

91. S. Miller, "Employers Use Benefits and Perks to Counter Great Resignation," *SHRM*, November 29, 2021, https://www.shrm.org/resourcesandtools/hr-topics/benefits/pages/employers-use-benefits-and-perks-to-counter-great-resignation.aspx.

92. B. Martinson and J. De Leon, "Testing Horizontal and Vertical Alignment of HR Practices Designed to Achieve Strategic Organizational Goals," *Journal of Organizational Effectiveness*, Vol. 5, No. 2 (2018), pp. 158–181.

93. K. Baskin, "4 Things to Consider When Managing a Hybrid Workforce," *MIT Sloane School of Management*, February 9, 2022,

https://mitsloan.mit.edu/ideas-made-to-matter/4-things-to-consider-when-managing-a-hybrid-workforce.

94. P. Bergeron, "Fitting Hybrid Work Policy to Company Culture," *Society for Human Resource Management,* January 25, 2023, https://www.shrm.org/resourcesandtools/hr-topics/employee-relations/pages/fitting-hybrid-work-policy-to-company-culture.aspx.

95. "Employer Costs for Employee Compensation—September 2022," *Bureau of Labor Statistics,* December 15, 2022, https://www.bls.gov/news.release/pdf/ecec.pdf.

96. A. Kreacik, "Gen Z Is Bringing the Optimism on Gender Equity: Companies Need to Keep Up," *World Economic Forum,* March 14, 2023, https://www.weforum.org/agenda/2023/03/gen-z-workplace-equity/.

97. M. Freedman, "Understanding Generation Z in the Workplace," *Business News Daily,* February 21, 2023, https://www.businessnewsdaily.com/11296-what-gen-z-workers-want.html.

98. C. Berger, "For Gen Z, the 2-Year Plan Is the New 5-Year Plan in an Economy Where a Dream Job Doesn't Exist," *Fortune,* December 6, 2022, https://fortune.com/2022/12/06/gen-z-two-year-career-plan-dream-job/.

99. P. Wiseman et al., "Onboarding Salespeople: Socialization Approaches," *Journal of Marketing,* Vol. 86, No. 6 (2022), pp. 13–31.

100. J.G. Randall, R.R. Brooks, and M.J. Heck, "Formal and Informal Learning as Deterrents of Turnover Intentions: Evidence from Frontline Workers during a Crisis," *International Journal of Training and Development*, Vol. 26, No. 2 (2022), pp. 185–208.

101. D. Carhart, "People Are Quitting Jobs They Just Started: Here's What Managers Can Do," *Fast Company,* May 11, 2022, https://www.fastcompany.com/90750694/people-are-quitting-jobs-they-just-started-heres-what-managers-can-do.

102. R. Maurer, "New Employee Onboarding Guide," *SHRM,* https://www.shrm.org/resourcesandtools/hr-topics/talent-acquisition/pages/new-employee-onboarding-guide.aspx (accessed March 17, 2023).

103. K. Becker and A. Bish, "A Framework for Understanding the Role of Unlearning in Onboarding," *Human Resource Management Review* (2019), p. 100730.

104. K. Becker and A. Bish, "A Framework for Understanding the Role of Unlearning in Onboarding," *Human Resource Management Review,* Vol. 31, No. 1 (2021), p. 100730; Also see S. Sibisi and G. Kappers, "Onboarding Can Make or Break a New Hire's Experience," *Harvard Business Review Digital Articles,* 2022, pp. 1–7, (accessed March 17, 2023), <https://search.ebscohost.com/login.aspx?direct=true&AuthType=ip,sso&db=bth&AN=156333486&site=ehost-live&scope=site>.

105. S. Sibisi and G. Kappers, "Onboarding Can Make or Break a New Hire's Experience," *Harvard Business Review Digital Articles,* 2022, pp. 1–7, (accessed March 17, 2023), <https://search.ebscohost.com/login.aspx?direct=true&AuthType=ip,sso&db=bth&AN=156333486&site=ehost-live&scope=site>.

106. R. Maurer, "New Employee Onboarding Guide," *SHRM,* https://www.shrm.org/resourcesandtools/hr-topics/talent-acquisition/pages/new-employee-onboarding-guide.aspx (accessed March 17, 2023).

107. M. Driscoll and M.D. Watkins, "Onboarding a New Leader — Remotely," Harvard Business Review, May 18, 2020. https://hbr.org/2020/05/onboarding-a-new-leader-remotely.

108. R. Maurer, "The Brave New World of Onboarding," *SHRM,* August 20, 2022. https://www.shrm.org/topics-tools/news/all-things-work/brave-new-world-onboarding.

109. R. Carucci, "To Retain New Hires, Spend More Time Onboarding Them," *Harvard Business Review Digital Articles,* 2018, pp. 1–5.

110. S. Sibisi and G. Kappers, "Onboarding Can Make or Break a New Hire's Experience," *Harvard Business Review Digital Articles*, 2022, pp. 1–7.

111. "11 Examples of the Best Employee Onboarding Experiences out There," *Zavvy,* https://www.zavvy.io/blog/employee-onboarding-examples (accessed March 17, 2023).

112. K. Robertson, "How to Design Your Employee Onboarding Process (Step-by-Step)," *The Predictive Index,* July 16, 2019, https://www.predictiveindex.com/blog/design-employee-onboarding-process/.

113. S. Sibisi and G. Kappers, "Onboarding Can Make or Break a New Hire's Experience," *Harvard Business Review Digital Articles*, 2022, pp. 1–7.

114. "7 Examples of Killer Onboarding Programs We Can Learn From," *Employment Hero,* February 16, 2023, https://employmenthero.com/blog/killer-onboarding-programs/.

115. E. Andersen, "Learning to Learn," *Harvard Business Review*, 2019, pp. 14–18.

116. "Attract, Retain and Develop Talented People," *Carrefour,* 2022, https://www.carrefour.com/sites/default/files/2022-06/APznzaagEXVbOHaeqC_X2XFS9jtQCqQ_ViPkTnfgPNYxtxfsDa437Risv31JKaG-hVbDJOSOCIYAc1bTa1vhF8-w2o_MyP5OS72BkFmobLDSYih5aDTEvM2hMdtgCPKaMBdkrNx_payJyQdsABQJvGyI5JbgMjYIU7FE_Y4AKfli8qN2h_wCBq1Bg0Zqf55p_EAmmW11j0RkW63Ch0.pdf.

117. B. Wigert, "Quiet Firing: What It Is and How to Stop Doing It," *Gallup,* November 18, 2022, https://www.gallup.com/workplace/404996/quiet-firing-stop-doing.aspx.

118. F. Cespedes, "How to Conduct a Great Performance Review," *Harvard Business Review,* July 8, 2022.

119. D. Schleicher, H. Baumann, D. Sullivan, and J. Yim, "Evaluating the Effectiveness of Performance Management: A 30-Year Integrative Conceptual Review," *Journal of Applied Psychology*, Vol. 104, No. 7 (2019), p. 851.

120. Adapted from A.J. Kinicki, K.J.L. Jacobson, S.J. Peterson, and G.E. Prussia, "Development and Validation of the Performance Management Behavior Questionnaire," *Personnel Psychology,* Vol. 66 (2013), pp. 1–45.

121. "Regeneron Careers," *Regeneron,* https://careers.regeneron.com/life-at-regeneron (accessed March 19, 2023); Also see "100 Best Companies to Work For: Regeneron Pharmaceuticals," *Fortune*, https://fortune.com/company/regeneron-pharmaceuticals/best-companies/.

122. J. Courtney, "How Regeneron Built Their Performance Management System," *PerformYard,* February 22, 2021, https://blog.performyard.com/how-regeneron-built-their-performance-management-system.

123. P. Cappelli and A. Tavis, "HR Goes Agile," *Harvard Business Review*, Vol. 96, No. 2 (2018), pp. 46–52.

124. J. Courtney, "How Regeneron Built Their Performance Management System," *PerformYard,* February 22, 2021, https://blog.performyard.com/how-regeneron-built-their-performance-management-system.

125. "Foster a Culture of Integrity and Excellence," *Regeneron,* https://www.regeneron.com/responsibility/corporate-integrity (accessed April 27, 2020).

126. "Director Statistical Programming," *Regeneron Careers,* https://careers.regeneron.com/job/REGEA002619484BR5080/Director-Statistical-Programming (accessed April 26, 2020). Also see "Foster a Culture of Integrity and Excellence," *Regeneron,* https://www.regeneron.com/responsibility/corporate-integrity (accessed April 27, 2020); "2018 Responsibility Report, *Regeneron,* https://investor.regeneron.com/2018RR (accessed April 27, 2020).

127. D. Schleicher, H. Baumann, D. Sullivan, P. Levy, D. Hargrove, and B. Barros-Rivera, "Putting the System into Performance Management Systems: A Review and Agenda for Performance Management Research," *Journal of Management*, Vol. 44, No. 6 (2018), pp. 2209–2245.

128. D. Schleicher, H. Baumann, D. Sullivan, and J. Yim, "Evaluating the Effectiveness of Performance Management: A 30-Year Integrative Conceptual Review," *Journal of Applied Psychology*, Vol. 104, No. 7 (2019), pp. 851–887.

129. M. Brown, M. Kraimer, and V. Bratton, "Performance Appraisal Cynicism among Managers: A Job Demands Resources Perspective," *Journal of Business and Psychology*, 35, 2019, pp. 455–468.

130. E. Soltani and A. Wilkinson, "TQM and Performance Appraisal: Complementary or Incompatible?" *European Management Review,* Vol. 17, No. 1 (2018), pp. 57–82.

131. T. Agovino, "The Performance Review Problem," *HR Magazine,* March 15, 2023, https://www.shrm.org/hr-today/news/hr-magazine/spring-2023/pages/the-problem-with-performance-reviews.aspx.

132. M. Schaerer and R. Swaab, "Are You Sugarcoating Your Feedback without Realizing It?" *Harvard Business Review Digital Articles,* 2019, pp. 2–5.

133. L. Roepe, "6 Ways Managers Can Help Employees Achieve Their Performance Goals," *SHRM*, June 1, 2022, https://www.shrm.org/hr-today/news/hr-magazine/summer2022/pages/how-managers-can-help-employees-achieve-their-performance-goals.aspx. Also see K. Doheny, "Annual Performance Review Bows Out," *SHRM*, January 12, 2021, https://www.shrm.org/resourcesandtools/hr-topics/people-managers/pages/ditching-the-annual-performance-review-.aspx.

134. "Why Adobe Ditched Its Annual Performance Reviews," *Engagedly*, December 13, 2018, https://engagedly.com/adobe-annual-performance-reviews/.

135. B. Miller, "How We Inspire Great Performance at Adobe," *Adobe Blog*, May 9, 2022, https://blog.adobe.com/en/publish/2022/05/09/how-we-inspire-great-performance-at-adobe.

136. R. Carucci, "Giving Feedback to Someone Who Hasn't Had It in Years," *Harvard Business Review Digital Articles*, 2020, pp. 2–5.

137. L. Roepe, "6 Ways Managers Can Help Employees Achieve Their Performance Goals," *SHRM*, June 1, 2022, https://www.shrm.org/hr-today/news/hr-magazine/summer2022/pages/how-managers-can-help-employees-achieve-their-performance-goals.aspx.

138. H.K. Gardner and I. Matviak, "Performance Management Shouldn't Kill Collaboration," *Harvard Business Review*, Vol. 100, No. 5 (2022), pp. 118–127.

139. K.A. Indovina, A. Keniston, V. Manchala, and M. Burden, "Predictors of a Top-Box Patient Experience: A Retrospective Observational Study of HCAHPS Data at a Safety Net Institution," *Journal of Patient Experience*, Vol. 8 (2021), p. 23743735211034342.

140. B.J. Schneider, R. Ehsanian, D.J. Kennedy, A. Schmidt, L. Huynh, and D.P. Maher, "The Effect of Patient Satisfaction Scores on Physician Clinical Decision Making: A Possible Factor Driving Utilization of Opioid Prescriptions, Magnetic Resonance Imaging, and Interventional Spine Procedures," *Interventional Pain Medicine*, Vol. 1, No. 1 (2022), p. 100012.

141. "New Report Shows Benefit of Modernizing HCAHPS Patient Experience Survey," *American Hospital Association,* July 25, 2019, https://www.aha.org/press-releases/2019-07-25-new-report-shows-benefit-modernizing-hcahps-patient-experience-survey.

142. C. Rouvalis, "360-Degree Feedback Is Powerful Leadership Development Tool," *SHRM*, August 25, 2022, https://www.shrm.org/resourcesandtools/hr-topics/organizational-and-employee-development/pages/360-degreefeedback.aspx; Also see J. Zenger and J. Folkman, "What Makes a 360-Degree Review Successful?" *Harvard Business Review Digital Articles*, 2020, pp. 2–6.

143. C. Rouvalis, "360-Degree Feedback Is Powerful Leadership Development Tool," *SHRM*, August 25, 2022, https://www.shrm.org/resourcesandtools/hr-topics/organizational-and-employee-development/pages/360-degreefeedback.aspx.

144. J. Zenger and J. Folkman, "What Makes a 360-Degree Review Successful?" *Harvard Business Review Digital Articles*, 2020, pp. 2–6. ; Also see F. Shipper, R. Hoffman, and D. Rotondo, "Does the 360 Feedback Process Create Actionable Knowledge Equally across Cultures?" *Academy of Management Learning and Education,* Vol 6, No. 1 (March 2007), pp. 33–50.

145. J. Ghorpade, "Managing Five Paradoxes of 360-Degree Feedback," *Academy of Management Perspectives*, Vol. 14, No. 1 (2000), pp. 140–150.

146. A. Przystanski, "Performance Ranking Re-enters Legal Spotlight," *Namely*, February 10, 2016, https://hrnews.namely.com/hrnews/blog/2016/2/10/performance-ranking-re-enters-legal-spotlight.

147. C. Chambers and W. Baker, "Robust Systems of Cooperation in the Presence of Rankings: How Displaying Prosocial Contributions Can Offset the Disruptive Effects of Performance Rankings," *Organization Science*, Vol. 31, No. 2 (2020), pp. 287–307.; Also see G. Gupta, "Are You Still Using Force Rankings? Please Stop," *Forbes,* May 23, 2018, https://www.forbes.com/sites/johnkotter/2018/05/23/are-you-still-using-force-rankings-please-stop/#5b29e39334d2; Also see S. Thomason, A. Brownlee, A. Harris, and H. Rustogi, "Forced Distribution Systems and Attracting Top Talent," *International Journal of Productivity and Performance Management,* Vol. 67, No. 7 (2018), pp. 1171–1191; Also see H.K. Gardner and I. Matviak, "Performance Management Shouldn't Kill Collaboration," *Harvard Business Review*, Vol. 100, No. 5 (2022), pp. 118–127.

148. A. Hess, "Ranking Workers Can Hurt Morale and Productivity: Tech Companies Are Doing It Anyway," *Fast Company,* February 16, 2023, https://www.fastcompany.com/90850190/stack-ranking-workers-hurt-morale-productivity-tech-companies.

149. C. Colvin, "Why Some Employers Are Scrapping the Annual Review," *HR Dive,* December 14, 2021, https://www.hrdive.com/news/alternatives-to-performance-reviews/611485/.

150. L. Jampol, A. Rattan, and E. Wolf, "Women Get 'Nicer' Feedback—and It Holds Them Back," *Harvard Business Review*, January 25, 2023.

151. G. Leibowitz, "6 Ways Truly Effective Leaders Deliver Feedback," *Inc.*, February 13, 2018, https://www.inc.com/glenn-leibowitz/6-ways-truly-effective-leaders-deliver-feedback.html?cid=search. Also see P. Gasca, "Want to Deliver Effective Feedback? Try the 'You Suck Sandwich' Approach," *Inc.,* February 26, 2018, https://www.inc.com/peter-gasca/deliver-feedback-like-a-ninja-with-a-you-suck-sandwich.html?cid=search; J. Peterson, "Want to Be a Better Leader? Start by Giving Useful Feedback—Here's How," *Inc.*, January 12, 2018, https://www.inc.com/joel-peterson/3-ways-to-give-constructive-feedback-that-actually-works.html?cid=search; M. Schneider, "3 Steps to Give Tough but Effective Feedback to Your Employees," *Inc.,* September 27, 2017, https://www.inc.com/michael-schneider/3-steps-to-give-tough-but-effective-feedback-to-your-employees.html?cid=search.

152. S.-H. Jeong, H. Kim, and H. Kim, "Strategic Nepotism in Family Director Appointments: Evidence from Family Business Groups in South Korea," *Academy of Management Journal*, Vol. 65, No. 2 (2022), pp. 656–682.

153. Z. Zhu, X. Chen, Q. Wang, C. Jiao, and M. Yang, "Is Shooting for Fairness Always Beneficial? The Influence of Promotion Fairness on Employees' Cognitive and Emotional Reactions to Promotion Failure," *Human Resource Management*, Vol. 61, No. 6 (2022), pp. 643–661.

154. E. Pérez-Chiqués and E.V. Rubin, "Debasement of Merit: The Method and Experience of Political Discrimination by Public Employees in the Commonwealth of Puerto Rico," *Review of Public Personnel Administration*, Vol. 42, No. 4 (2022), pp. 669–685.

155. S. Joseph, "Passed over for a Promotion? Here's What to Do Next" *Forbes,* January 24, 2020, https://www.forbes.com/sites/shelcyvjoseph/2020/01/24/bypassed-for-a-promotion-heres-what-to-do-next/#3c8b437813df.

156. N. Vaduganathan, B. Zweig, C. McDonald, and L. Simon, "What Outperformers Do Differently to Tap Internal Talent," *MIT Sloan Management Review*, Vol. 64, No. 1 (2022), pp. 1–4.

157. N. Vaduganathan, B. Zweig, C. McDonald, and L. Simon, "What Outperformers Do Differently to Tap Internal Talent," *MIT Sloan Management Review*, Vol. 64, No. 1 (2022), pp. 1–4.

158. H.R. Costakis and J.S. Pickern, "Managing Human Capital through the Use of Performance Improvement Plans," *Journal of Applied Business & Economics*, Vol. 24, No. 6 (2022); Also see A. Smith, "PIPs: Write, Implement and Time Them Precisely," *Society for Human Resource Management,* February 17, 2023, https://www.shrm.org/resourcesandtools/legal-and-compliance/employment-law/pages/performance-improvement-plans-precise-implementation.aspx.

159. J. Marter, "Seven Ways to Deal with a Demotion at Work," *Psychology Today*, March 1, 2023, https://www.psychologytoday.com/us/blog/mental-wealth/202302/seven-ways-to-deal-with-a-demotion-at-work.

160. A. Smith, "Demotions Can Often Lead to Departures but Also to Fresh Starts," *SHRM,* August 22, 2018, https://www.shrm.org/resourcesandtools/legal-and-compliance/employment-law/pages/demotions-departures-fresh-starts.aspx.

161. S.J. Sucher and M. Morgan Westner, "What Companies Still Get Wrong about Layoffs," *Harvard Business Review Digital Articles*, 2022, pp. 1–12.

162. J. Karaian and L. Kelley, "Layoffs at Tech Giants Reverse Small Part of Pandemic Hiring Spree," *New York Times,* January 21, 2023, https://

www.proquest.com/newspapers/layoffs-at-tech-giants-reverse-small-part/docview/2767511078/se-2.

163. S. Shin, J. Lee, and P. Bansal, "From a Shareholder to Stakeholder Orientation: Evidence from the Analyses of CEO Dismissal in Large US Firms," *Strategic Management Journal*, Vol. 43, No. 7 (2022), pp. 1233–1257.

164. "Managing Difficult Employees and Disruptive Behaviors," *SHRM*, https://www.shrm.org/resourcesandtools/tools-and-samples/toolkits/pages/managingdifficultemployeesa.aspx (accessed March 20, 2023).

165. S. Sucher and M. Westner, "What Companies Still Get Wrong about Layoffs," *Harvard Business Review,* December 8, 2022, https://hbr.org/2022/12/what-companies-still-get-wrong-about-layoffs.

166. M. Frase-Blunt, "Making Exit Interviews Work," SHRM, August 1, 2004. https://www.shrm.org/topics-tools/news/hr-magazine/making-exit-interviews-work.

167. T. West, "The Lies We Tell at Work—And the Damage They Do; Lying at Our Jobs Feels So Harmless. Honestly, It Isn't," *Wall Street Journal (Online),* March 27, 2020, https://www.wsj.com/articles/the-lies-we-tell-at-workand-the-damage-they-do-11585319160.

168. L. Desjardins, "Congress Passes Law Banning Non-disclosure Agreements in Sexual Harassment Cases," *PBS,* November 23, 2022, https://www.pbs.org/newshour/show/congress-passes-law-banning-non-disclosure-agreements-in-sexual-harassment-cases#:~:text=Congress%20passes%20law%20banning%20non,sexual%20harassment%20cases%20%7C%20PBS%20NewsHour.

169. "Employment at Will," *SHRM,* https://www.shrm.org/resourcesandtools/tools-and-samples/hr-glossary/pages/employment-at-will.aspx (accessed March 20, 2023).

170. "Title VII of the Civil Rights Act of 1964," *U.S. Equal Employment Opportunity Commission*, https://www.eeoc.gov/statutes/title-vii-civil-rights-act-1964 (accessed April 5, 2020).

171. "Consolidated Minimum Wage Table," *U.S. Department of Labor,* January 1, 2023, https://www.dol.gov/agencies/whd/mw-consolidated; Also see "Minimum Wage," *U.S. Department of Labor,* https://www.dol.gov/general/topic/wages/minimumwage (accessed March 21, 2023); Also see K. Gibson, "After Inflation, Workers on Minimum Wage Haven't Made This Little since the 1950s," *CBS News,* July 18, 2022.

172. J. Bivens, "Inflation, Minimum Wages, and Profits," *Economic Policy Institute,* September 22, 2022, https://www.epi.org/blog/inflation-minimum-wages-and-profits-protecting-low-wage-workers-from-inflation-means-raising-the-minimum-wage/; Also see S. Higgins, "Inflation Numbers Show a Minimum Wage Hike Is Still A Bad Idea," *Competitive Enterprise Institute,* March 10, 2022, https://cei.org/blog/inflation-numbers-show-a-minimum-wage-hike-is-still-a-bad-idea/.

173. "FLSA Overtime Rule Resources," *SHRM,* https://advocacy.sba.gov/2023/09/12/dol-proposes-55k-overtime-rule-threshold/#:~:text=On%20August%2030%2C%202023%2C%20the,%2426.48%20per%20hour%2C%20respectively).

174. For more about legislation updating the Toxic Substances Control Act of 1976, see C. Davenport and E. Huetteman, "Deal Is Reached to Expand Rules on Toxic Chemicals," *The New York Times,* May 20, 2016, p. A3. Also see F. Krupp, "When Red and Blue in Congress Makes Green," *The Wall Street Journal,* June 10, 2016, p. A13.

175. "Affordable Care Act Tax Provisions for Employers," *Internal Revenue Service,* https://www.irs.gov/affordable-care-act/employers (accessed March 21, 2023).

176. A. Gunn and O. Dibinga, "Racial Equity in Health Series: Efforts to Expand Access to Healthcare in the United States," *U.S. Department of State*, FPC Briefing, April 8, 2022, https://www.state.gov/briefings-foreign-press-centers/efforts-to-expand-access-to-healthcare-in-the-united-states.

177. "What are disparate impact and disparate treatment?" *SHRM,* https://www.shrm.org/topics-tools/tools/hr-answers/disparate-impact-disparate-treatment#:~:text=Both%20disparate%20impact%20and%20disparate,sometimes%20used%20as%20an%20alternative.

178. A. Dalrymple, "Equal Pay in the United States," U.S. Department of Labor, https://www.dol.gov/sites/dolgov/files/WB/equalpay/WB_Brief_Equal_Pay_Salary_History_Bans_03072023.pdf.

179. "2021 EEOC Charges Show Decline in Most Categories," *Horton Management Law,* March 31, 2022, https://hortonpllc.com/2021-eeoc-charges-show-decline-in-most-categories/.

180. M. Gonzales, "Artificial Intelligence Takes Center Stage at EEOC," *Society for Human Resource Management,* January 18, 2023, https://www.shrm.org/resourcesandtools/hr-topics/behavioral-competencies/global-and-cultural-effectiveness/pages/artificial-intelligence-takes-center-stage-at-eeoc.aspx.

181. The Associated Press, "U.S. Warns of Discrimination in Using Artificial Intelligence to Screen Job Candidates," *NPR,* May 12, 2022, https://www.npr.org/2022/05/12/1098601458/artificial-intelligence-job-discrimination-disabilities.

182. "Affirmative Action Frequently Asked Questions," *U.S. Department of Labor,* https://www.dol.gov/agencies/ofccp/faqs/AAFAQs#Q4 (accessed March 21, 2023).

183. B. Sullivan, "How the Supreme Court Has Ruled in the Past about Affirmative Action," *NPR,* November 1, 2022, https://www.npr.org/2022/11/01/1132935433/supreme-court-affirmative-action-history-harvard-admissions-university-carolina.

184. S. Jaschik, "A Clear Divide for the Supreme Court," *Inside Higher Ed,* January 25, 2022, https://www.insidehighered.com/admissions/article/2022/01/25/universities-and-academics-offer-advice-supreme-court.

185. N. Totenberg, "Supreme Court Guts Affirmative Action, Effectively Ending Race-Conscious Admissions," NPR, June 29, 2023. https://www.npr.org/2023/06/29/1181138066/affirmative-action-supreme-court-decision.

186. S.L. Rawski, A.M. O'Leary-Kelly, and D. Breaux-Soignet, "It's All Fun and Games Until Someone Gets Hurt: An Interactional Framing Theory of Work Social Sexual Behavior," *Academy of Management Review*, Vol. 47, No. 4 (2022), pp. 617–636.

187. "Is an Employer Liable for Harassment by Coworkers?" *Kingsley & Kingsley Lawyers*, https://www.kingsleykingsley.com/employment-lawyer/sexual-harassment/employer-liable-harassment-coworkers#:~:text=Employer's%20Strict%20Liability&text=What%20this%20means%20that%20if,over%20whom%20it%20has%20control (accessed March 21, 2023).

188. "How Can I Prevent Harassment?" U.S. Equal Employment Opportunity Commission, https://www.eeoc.gov/employers/small-business/5-how-can-i-prevent-harassment.

189. L.N. Praslova, R. Carucci, and C. Stokes, "How Bullying Manifests at Work—and How to Stop It," *Harvard Business Review Digital Articles*, 2022, pp. 1–12.

190. L.N. Praslova, R. Carucci, and C. Stokes, "How Bullying Manifests at Work—and How to Stop It," *Harvard Business Review Digital Articles*, 2022, pp. 1–12.

191. T.Z. Buriro et al., "The Role of Perceived Organizational Support: Evidences from the Horizontal and Vertical Workplace Bullying," *Employee Responsibilities & Rights Journal*, Vol 34, No. 1 (2022), pp. 41–54.

192. T.Z. Buriro et al., "The Role of Perceived Organizational Support: Evidences from the Horizontal and Vertical Workplace Bullying," *Employee Responsibilities & Rights Journal*, Vol 34, No. 1 (2022), pp. 41–54.

193. S.R. Valentine, P.A. Meglich, and R.A. Giacalone, "Filling a Theoretical 'Black Box' between Workplace Bullying and Poor Attitudes: Psychological Contract Violation, Work Injustice, and Negative Environmental Contagion," *Employee Responsibilities & Rights Journal,* Vol. 35, No. 1 (2023), pp. 51–76; Also see M. Badenhorst and D. Botha"Workplace Bullying in a South African Higher Education Institution: Academic and Support Staff Experiences," *South African Journal of Human Resource Management,* Vol. 20 (2022), pp. 1–13; Also see Y.-C. Chen, H.-J. Tai, and H.-C. Chu, "Constructing Employee Assistance Program Measures against Workplace Bullying," *Employee Responsibilities & Rights Journal,* Vol. 34, No. 3 (2022), pp. 361–381. Also see T.Z. Buriro et al., "The Role of Perceived Organizational Support: Evidences from the Horizontal and Vertical Workplace Bullying." *Employee Responsibilities & Rights Journal,* Vol. 34, No. 1 (2022), pp. 41–54.

194. H. Benson, "Porters Found Road to Success Aboard Nation's 'Rolling Hotels,'" *San Francisco Chronicle,* February 11, 2009, pp. A1, A12.

195. J. McCarthy, "U.S. Approval of Labor Unions at Highest Point Since 1965," *Gallup,* August 30, 2022, https://news.gallup.com/poll/398303/approval-labor-unions-highest-point-1965.aspx.

196. "How Two-Tier Contracts Hurt Workers and Weaken Unions," *Teamsters for a Democratic Union,* February 18, 2023, https://www.tdu.org/how_two_tier_contracts_hurt_workers_and_weaken_unions#:~:text=Two%2Dtier%20contracts%20weaken%20the,it's%20really%20hard%20to%20reverse.

197. N. Dmitrovich, "Are Two Tiers a Bad Thing?" *Building Indiana,* April 19, 2022, https://buildingindiana.com/is-two-tier-compensation-a-bad-thing/.

198. Industry Week Staff, "Caterpillar Ratifies UAW Contract that Eliminates Two-Tier Wages, Prohibits Plant Closures," *Industry Week,* March 13, 2023, https://www.industryweek.com/talent/labor-employment-policy/article/21261869/caterpillar-ratifies-uaw-contract-that-eliminates-twotier-wages-prohibits-plant-closures; Also see B. Flowers, "Harley-Davidson and Union Employees Ratify Bargaining Agreement," *Reuters,* August 17, 2022, https://www.reuters.com/business/autos-transportation/harley-davidson-union-employees-ratify-bargaining-agreement-2022-08-17/; Also see D. Shepardson, "Boeing Defense Workers Ratify Revised Contract Offer," *Reuters,* August 3, 2022, https://www.reuters.com/business/aerospace-defense/boeing-defense-workers-ratify-revised-contract-offer-2022-08-03/.

199. J. Brown, "The US Labor Movement Notched Some Impressive Victories in 2022," *Jacobin,* December 22, 2022, https://jacobin.com/2022/12/2022-us-labor-movement-organizing-roundup-victories.

200. J. Silver-Greenberg and M. Corkery, "Bank Customers Likely to Regain Access to Courts," *The New York Times,* May 5, 2016, pp. A1, B3. Also see J. Silver-Greenberg and M. Corkery, "Start-Ups Turn to Arbitration in the Workplace," *The New York Times,* May 15, 2016, pp. News-1, News-4.

201. J. Silver-Greenberg and R. Gebeloff, "Arbitration Everywhere, Stacking Deck of Justice," *The New York Times,* November 1, 2015, pp. News-1, News-22, News-23. Also see J. Silver-Greenberg and M. Corkery, "A 'Privatization of the Justice System,'" *The New York Times,* November 2, 2015, pp. A1, B4, B5.

202. D. Gregorian, "Biden Signs Bill Ending Forced Arbitration in Sexual Misconduct Cases," *NBC News,* March 3, 2022, https://www.nbcnews.com/politics/white-house/biden-signs-bill-ending-ending-forced-arbitration-sexual-misconduct-ca-rcna18664.

203. E. Barends, D. Rousseau, E. Wietrak, and I. Cioca, *Performance Feedback: An Evidence Review: Scientific Summary.* London: Chartered Institute of Personnel and Development 2022).

204. A. Christensen, A. Kinicki, Z. Zhang, and F. Walumbwa, "Responses to Feedback: The Role of Acceptance, Affect, and Creative Behavior," *Journal of Leadership and Organizational Studies,* Vol. 25, No. 4 (2018), pp. 416–429.

205. D. Riegel, "How to Encourage Your Team to Give You Honest Feedback," *Harvard Business Review,* October 28, 2022.

206. C.C. Ferguson, "Patient Experience Surveys: Reflections on Rating a Sacred Trust," *BMJ Quality & Safety,* Vol. 28, No. 10 (2019), pp. 843–845.

207. S. Gupta, "Conversation Is More Than Nodding Your Head," *Chasing Life* (Podcast), *CNN,* June 14, 2022, https://www.cnn.com/audio/podcasts/chasing-life/episodes/090c60bd-290a-4896-8122-aeb300367f4f.

208. D. Riegel, "How to Encourage Your Team to Give You Honest Feedback," *Harvard Business Review,* October 28, 2022.

209. L. L. Holmer, "Understanding and Reducing the Impact of Defensiveness on Management Learning: Some Lessons from Neuroscience," *Journal of Management Education*, 38(5), October 2014, pp. 618–641.

210. S.J. Dodson and Y.T. Heng, "Self-Compassion in Organizations: A Review and Future Research Agenda," *Journal of Organizational Behavior*, Vol. 43, No. 2 (2022), pp. 168–196.

211. R.Y. Cai, A. Love, A. Robinson, and V. Gibbs, "The Inter-Relationship of Emotion Regulation, Self-Compassion, and Mental Health in Autistic Adults," *Autism in Adulthood,* Vol. 5, No. 3 (September 2023), pp. 335–342.

212. "4 Ways to Bounce Back after Negative Feedback," *The American Society of Administrative Professionals,* July 5, 2022, https://www.asaporg.com/4-ways-to-bounce-back-after-negative-feedback.

213. C.G. Coutifaris and A.M. Grant, "Taking Your Team behind the Curtain: The Effects of Leader Feedback-Sharing and Feedback-Seeking on Team Psychological Safety," *Organization Science*, Vol. 33, No. 4 (2022), pp. 1574–1598.

214. J. Luckoski, A. Thelen, D. Russell, B. George, and A. Krumm, "Feedback-Seeking Behavior and Practice Readiness for General Surgery," *Journal of Surgical Education*, Vol. 79, No. 2 (2022), pp. 295–301; Also see A. Christensen, A. Kinicki, Z. Zhang, and F. Walumbwa, "Responses to Feedback: The Role of Acceptance, Affect, and Creative Behavior," *Journal of Leadership and Organizational Studies,* Vol. 25, No. 4 (2018), pp. 416–429.

215. J. Kabat-Zinn, "Mindfulness-Based Interventions in Context: Past, Present, and Future," *Clinical Psychology: Science and Practice,* Summer 2003, p. 145.

216. M. Qasim, M. Irshad, M. Majeed, and S.T.H. Rizvi, "Examining Impact of Islamic Work Ethic on Task Performance: Mediating Effect of Psychological Capital and a Moderating Role of Ethical Leadership," *Journal of Business Ethics,* Vol. 180, No. 1 (2022), pp. 283–295.

CHAPTER 10

1. S. Harvey and J.W. Berry, "Toward a Meta-Theory of Creativity Forms: How Novelty and Usefulness Shape Creativity," *Academy of Management Review,* Vol. 48, No. 3 (July 2023), pp. 504–529.

2. N. Fedrizzi, "Am I Left or Right Brained?" *Smithsonian Science Education Center,* September 29, 2022, https://ssec.si.edu/stemvisions-blog/am-i-left-or-right-brained.

3. T. Donvito, "The Soft Skills That All Hiring Managers Are Looking For," *Reader's Digest,* January 13, 2023, https://www.rd.com/list/soft-skills/.

4. G. Levoy, "How to Avoid Adult-eration: The Value of Lifelong Learning," *Psychology Today,* July 1, 2022, https://www.psychologytoday.com/us/blog/passion/202207/how-avoid-adult-eration-the-value-lifelong-learning; Also see M. Anthony, "Creative Development in 3–5 Year Olds," *Scholastic,* https://www.scholastic.com/parents/family-life/creativity-and-critical-thinking/development-milestones/creative-development-3-5-year-olds.html (accessed April 4, 2023); Also see K. Good and A. Shaw, "Why Kids Are Afraid to Ask for Help," *Scientific American,* February 14, 2022, https://www.scientificamerican.com/article/why-kids-are-afraid-to-ask-for-help/.

5. C. Mornata and I. Cassar, "The Role of Insiders and Organizational Support in the Learning Process of Newcomers during Organizational Socialization," *Journal of Workplace Learning,* September–October, 2018, 30(7), pp. 562–575.

6. X. Chen and A.M. Padilla, "Emotions and Creativity as Predictors of Resilience among L3 Learners in the Chinese Educational Context," *Current Psychology,* Vol. 41 (2022), pp. 406–416.

7. Y.S. Chan, J.T. Jang, and C.S. Ho, "Effects of Physical Exercise on Children with Attention Deficit Hyperactivity Disorder," *Biomedical Journal,* Vol. 45, No. 2 (2022), pp. 265–270.

8. B. Robinson, "The Bitter Pill You Must Swallow If You Want Success," *Psychology Today,* June 10, 2019, https://www.psychologytoday.com/us/blog/the-right-mindset/201906/the-bitter-pill-you-must-swallow-if-you-want-success.

9. F. Gobet and G. Sala, "How Artificial Intelligence Can Help Us Understand Human Creativity," *Frontiers in Psychology,* Vol. 10 (2019), p. 1401.

10. S. Ellsworth, J. Sourges, M. Wahrendorff, and A. Egetenmeyer, "Turbocharging Industrial Speed to Market," *Accenture,* July 26, 2022, https://www.accenture.com/us-en/insights/industrial/accelerate-industrial-speed-to-market.

11. "LinkedIn CEO Ryan Roslansky: Skills, Not Degrees, Matter Most in Hiring: Even If You Don't Plan to Change Jobs, Your Job Is going to Change on You," *Harvard Business Review Digital Articles,* 2022, pp. 1–19.

12. K. Albrecht, "Eight Supertrends Shaping the Future of Business," *The Futurist,* September–October 2006, pp. 25–29. Also see J. C. Glenn, "Scanning the Global Situation and Prospects for the Future," *The Futurist,* January–February 2008, pp. 41–46; "The Future Issue," *Fortune,* January 13, 2014; "The Future of Everything," *The Wall Street Journal,* July 8, 2014, pp. R1–R24; "How to tackle challenge of workforce disruption, remote work," *Deloitte,* April 9, 2022, https://action.deloitte.com/insight/1745/how-to-tackle-challenge-of-workforce-disruption-remote-work.

13. P. Yakuel, "Why Personalized Marketing Is Key to Fostering Customer Loyalty in the New Age of Marketing," *Forbes,* December 16, 2022, https://www.forbes.com/sites/forbescommunicationscouncil/2022/12/16/why-personalized-marketing-is-key-to-fostering-customer-loyalty-in-the-new-age-of-marketing/?sh=1fd4a0a8a01e; Also see G. Esenduran, P. Letizia, and A. Ovchinnikov, "Why You Should Allow Returns on Customized Products," *Harvard Business Review Digital Articles,* 2022, pp. 1–7.

14. T. Levine, "What Does Today's Consumer Want? Personalized, Seamless, Omnichannel Experiences," *Forbes,* March 11, 2022, https://www.forbes.com/sites/forbesbusinesscouncil/2022/03/11/what-does-todays-consumer-want-personalized-seamless-omnichannel-experiences/?sh=158a891b1e1e.

15. G. Esenduran, P. Letizia, and A. Ovchinnikov, "Customization and Returns," *Management Science,* Vol. 68, No. 6 (2022), pp. 4517–4526.

16. "How Suitablee Became the World's Most Sophisticated Custom Suit Design Platform," *Men's Journal,* May 25, 2022, https://www.mensjournal.com/style/how-suitablee-became-the-worlds-most-sophisticated-custom-suit-design-platform; Also see G. Davis, "Custom Suit Brand Suitablee Combines the Art of Tailoring with AI," *Maxim,* March 5, 2023, https://www.maxim.com/partner/custom-suit-brand-suitablee-combines-the-art-of-tailoring-with-ai/; Also see Suitablee, https://suitablee.com/ (accessed April 12, 2023).

17. "Accenture Report Details How New Technologies Are Enabling Industrial Companies to Bring Products to Market Faster," *Business Wire,* September 8, 2022, https://www.businesswire.com/news/home/20220908005153/en/Accenture-Report-Details-How-New-Technologies-Are-Enabling-Industrial-Companies-to-Bring-Products-to-Market-Faster.

18. S. Ellsworth, J. Sourges, M. Wahrendorff, and A. Egetenmeyer, "Turbocharging Industrial Speed to Market," *Accenture,* July 26, 2022, https://www.accenture.com/us-en/insights/industrial/accelerate-industrial-speed-to-market.

19. J. Zinkula, "Electric Vehicles Accounted for 10% of Global Auto Sales Last Year—This Could Quadruple by 2030," *Business Insider,* January 16, 2023, https://www.businessinsider.com/electric-vehicles-accounted-global-auto-sales-could-quadruple-2030-report-2023-1; Also see "Electric Vehicles Are Forecast to Be Half of Global Car Sales by 2035," *Goldman Sachs,* February 10, 2023, https://www.goldmansachs.com/insights/pages/electric-vehicles-are-forecast-to-be-half-of-global-car-sales-by-2035.html#:~:text=EV%20sales%20will%20soar%20to,from%202%25%20during%20that%20span.

20. "Battery 2030: Resilient, Sustainable, and Circular," *McKinsey & Company,* January 16, 2023, https://www.mckinsey.com/industries/automotive-and-assembly/our-insights/battery-2030-resilient-sustainable-and-circular.

21. "ABB Unveils New Fast-Track Battery Manufacturing Methodology," *Assembly Magazine,* September 15, 2022, https://www.assemblymag.com/articles/97321-abb-unveils-new-fast-track-battery-manufacturing-methodology.

22. C. M. Christensen, *The Innovator's Dilemma: When New Technologies Cause Great Firms to Fail* (Boston: Harvard Business School Press, 1997). Also see J. Howe, "The Disruptor," *Wired,* March 2013, pp. 74–78; J. Lepore, "The Disruption Machine," *The New Yorker,* June 23, 2014, pp. 30–36.

23. T. Bureggemann, "Movie Theaters Endured Every Threat for over a Century, until Coronavirus Shut Them Down: A Timeline," *Indiewire,* March 18, 2020, https://www.indiewire.com/2020/03/coronavirus-american-movie-theaters-closed-1202217809/.

24. R. Rubin and B. Lang, "How 2020 Changed Hollywood, and the Movies, Forever," *Variety,* https://variety.com/2020/film/news/movie-theaters-hollywood-pandemic-2020-recap-1234874385/; Also see Staff, "When You Buy a Movie Ticket, Where Does That Money Go?" *The Week,* September 8, 2016, https://theweek.com/articles/647394/when-buy-movie-ticket-where-does-that-money.

25. E. Schwartzel, "'Trolls World Tour' Breaks Digital Records and Charts a New Path for Hollywood," *The Wall Street Journal,* April 28, 2020, https://www.wsj.com/articles/trolls-world-tour-breaks-digital-records-and-charts-a-new-path-for-hollywood-11588066202?mod=searchresults&page=1&pos=2.

26. "AMC Theatres Will No Longer Screen Universal Movies Due to 'Radical Change,'" *Blooloop,* April 29, 2020, https://blooloop.com/news/amc-theatres-universal-movies-trolls/.

27. M. Hughes, "Disney's Great Future Will Change the Movie Theater Industry Forever," *Forbes,* April 22, 2020, https://www.forbes.com/sites/markhughes/2020/04/22/disneys-great-future-will-change-the-movie-theater-industry-forever/#a2ebe0474737.

28. M. Bebernes, "Will Movie Theaters Survive the Pandemic?" *Yahoo News 360,* December 7, 2020, https://www.yahoo.com/entertainment/will-movie-theaters-survive-the-pandemic-192954518.html.

29. S. Whitten, "'We Do Crazy Stuff': How Cinemas Are Going beyond Studio Marketing to Lure Moviegoers Back," *CNBC,* May 1, 2022, https://www.cnbc.com/2022/05/01/how-cinemas-are-going-beyond-studio-marketing-to-lure-moviegoers-back.html; E. Blessing, "How Cinemark Is Approaching Dynamic Ticket Pricing," *The Hollywood Reporter,* March 8, 2022, https://www.hollywoodreporter.com/business/business-news/how-cinemark-is-approaching-dynamic-ticket-pricing-1235107334/.

30. N. Vega, "AMC and Zoom Want You to Take Your Next Work Meeting on the Big Screen," *CNBC,* November 10, 2022, https://www.cnbc.com/2022/11/10/amc-and-zoom-want-you-to-take-your-next-work-meeting-on-the-big-screen.html.

31. S. Whitten, "'We Do Crazy Stuff': How Cinemas Are Going beyond Studio Marketing to Lure Moviegoers Back," *CNBC,* May 1, 2022, https://www.cnbc.com/2022/05/01/how-cinemas-are-going-beyond-studio-marketing-to-lure-moviegoers-back.html.

32. N. Sheidlower, "Movie Theaters Get Creative with Food and Drink as They Struggle to Fill Seats," *CNBC,* February 8, 2023, https://www.cnbc.com/2023/02/08/movie-theaters-upscale-food-empty-seats.html.

33. R. Rubin, "'Top Gun: Maverick' Returns to Theaters for Limited Re-Release," *Variety,* November 29, 2022, https://variety.com/2022/film/box-office/top-gun-maverick-returns-theaters-1235444404/; D. Libby, "*Avatar: The Way of Water* Was a Massive Box Office Success, and James Cameron Got a Huge Payday Himself," *Cinema Blend,* February 14, 2023, https://www.cinemablend.com/movies/avatar-the-way-of-water-was-a-massive-box-office-success-and-james-cameron-got-a-huge-payday-himself#:~:text=Saying%20that%20Avatar%3A%20The%20Way,break%20the%20%242%20billion%20mark; I. Youngs, "Super Mario Movie's 'Sensational' Box Office Takings Defy Poor Reviews," *BBC,* April 11, 2023, https://www.bbc.com/news/entertainment-arts-65230431.

34. D. Sims, "Hollywood Cannot Survive without Movie Theaters," *The Atlantic,* January 19, 2023, https://www.theatlantic.com/culture/archive/2023/01/movie-theaters-streaming-film-industry-the-fabelmans/672766/.

35. T. Buckley and L. Shaw, "Apple to Spend $1 Billion a Year on Films to Break into Cinemas," *Bloomberg,* March 23, 2023, https://www.bloomberg.com/news/articles/2023-03-23/apple-to-splash-1-billion-a-year-on-films-to-break-into-cinemas#xj4y7vzkg; L. Shaw, "Amazon Plans to Invest $1 Billion a Year in Movies for Theaters," *Bloomberg,* November 23, 2022, https://www.bloomberg.com/news/articles/2022-11-23/amazon-plans-to-invest-1-billion-in-movies-for-theaters?leadSource=uverify%20wall.

36. F. Haron, "How Outsourcing Helps Tech Businesses Thrive in Times of Economic Uncertainty," *Forbes,* January 13, 2023, https://www.forbes.com/sites/forbestechcouncil/2023/01/13/how-outsourcing-

helps-tech-businesses-thrive-in-times-of-economic-uncertainty/?sh=301f95d02bd2.

37. L. Hoteit et al., "MENA Talent Map," *Boston Consulting Group,* February 15, 2023, https://www.bcg.com/publications/2023/future-of-outsourcing-mena-talent-map.

38. N. Rosen, "U.S. Engagement in Uruguay: The Tech Sector," *Center for Latin American & Latino Studies,* American University, https://www.american.edu/centers/latin-american-latino-studies/upload/uruguay-tech-sector_case-vignette.pdf.

39. "How Uruguay Established Itself as the Silicon Valley of South America," *Vesta Software Group,* https://www.vestasoftwaregroup.com/how-uruguay-established-itself-as-the-silicon-valley-of-south-america/ (accessed April 12, 2023).

40. T. Hansen, "The Future of Knowledge Work," *Intel Labs,* Tech. Rep., 2012.

41. "Gartner Forecasts 39% of Global Knowledge Workers Will Work Hybrid by the End of 2023," *Gartner,* March 1, 2023, https://www.gartner.com/en/newsroom/press-releases/2023-03-01-gartner-forecasts-39-percent-of-global-knowledge-workers-will-work-hybrid-by-the-end-of-2023.

42. W. Thomas, "Knowledge Workers in the Age of AI—Part 1," *Medium,* January 5, 2023, https://gumdropai.medium.com/knowledge-workers-in-the-age-of-ai-part-1-eb190cc46bfb.

43. "Cleary Announces $7.5m in Funding amid Strong Demand for Their Employee Experience Platform to Support Distributed Teams," *Cleary,* January 31, 2023, https://www.prnewswire.com/news-releases/cleary-announces-7-5m-in-funding-amid-strong-demand-for-their-employee-experience-platform-to-support-distributed-teams-301734120.html.

44. J. Dickie et al., "Can AI Really Help You Sell?" *Harvard Business Review,* Vol. 100, No. 6 (2022), pp. 120–129.

45. J. Nathan, "Four Ways Artificial Intelligence Can Benefit Robotic Surgery," *Forbes,* February 15, 2023, https://www.forbes.com/sites/forbestechcouncil/2023/02/15/four-ways-artificial-intelligence-can-benefit-robotic-surgery/; Also see "Robotic Surgery," *Mayo Clinic,* https://www.mayoclinic.org/tests-procedures/robotic-surgery/about/pac-20394974 (accessed April 16, 2023).

46. J. Constantz, "Why the Trend toward Remote Work Isn't Going to Fade in 2023," *Los Angeles Times,* December 23, 2022, https://www.latimes.com/business/story/2022-12-23/why-the-trend-toward-remote-work-isnt-going-to-fade-in-2023.

47. G. Iacurci, "Why Labor Economists Say the Remote Work 'Revolution' Is Here to Stay," *CNBC,* December 1, 2022, https://www.cnbc.com/2022/12/01/why-labor-economists-say-the-remote-work-revolution-is-here-to-stay.html.

48. S. Gupta, "How Companies Are Giving Workers the Hybrid Workplace They Want," *Fast Company,* April 27, 2023, https://www.fastcompany.com/90885802/companies-giving-workers-hybrid-workplace-mckinsey-state-organizations.

49. J. Constantz, "Why the Trend toward Remote Work Isn't Going to Fade in 2023," *Los Angeles Times,* December 23, 2022, https://www.latimes.com/business/story/2022-12-23/why-the-trend-toward-remote-work-isnt-going-to-fade-in-2023.

50. J. Constantz, "Why the Trend toward Remote Work Isn't Going to Fade in 2023," *Los Angeles Times,* December 23, 2022, https://www.latimes.com/business/story/2022-12-23/why-the-trend-toward-remote-work-isnt-going-to-fade-in-2023.

51. S. Gupta, "How Companies Are Giving Workers the Hybrid Workplace They Want," *Fast Company,* April 27, 2023, https://www.fastcompany.com/90885802/companies-giving-workers-hybrid-workplace-mckinsey-state-organizations.

52. H. Markell-Goldstein, "What We've Learned from Our First-Ever Life in Virtual First Survey," *Dropbox,* February 22, 2023, https://blog.dropbox.com/topics/company/what-weve-learned-from-our-firstever-life-in-virtual-first-survey.

53. G. Iacurci, "Why Labor Economists Say the Remote Work 'Revolution' Is Here to Stay," *CNBC,* December 1, 2022, https://www.cnbc.com/2022/12/01/why-labor-economists-say-the-remote-work-revolution-is-here-to-stay.html.

54. *Capitalizing on Complexity: Insights from the Global Chief Executive Officer Study,* International Business Machines, Somers, New York, 2010, www-01.ibm.com/common/ssi/cgi-bin/ssialias?htmlfid=GBE03301USEN&appname=wwwsearch. Also see *Leading through Connections: Insights from the IBM Global CEO Study,* International Business Machines, Somers, New York, 2012, www-935.ibm.com/services/us/en/c-suite/ceostudy2012; and *PwC's Annual Global CEO Survey,* PricewaterhouseCoopers, 2016, www.pwc.com/gx/en/ceo-agenda/ceosurvey/2016.html (all accessed June 17, 2016).

55. E. Garcia, "U.S. Solar Tax Credits Hike Factory Activity but Supply Lines Limit Growth," *Reuters,* November 10, 2022, https://www.reuters.com/business/energy/us-solar-tax-credits-hike-factory-activity-supply-lines-limit-growth-2022-11-10/; Also see D. DiGangi, "Solar Expected to See Demand Boom from Inflation Reduction Act in 2023 as Supply Chain Remains Uncertain," *Utility Dive,* January 19, 2023, https://www.utilitydive.com/news/solar-expected-to-see-demand-boom-from-inflation-reduction-act-in-2023-as-s/639784/.

56. P. Robertson, D. Roberts, and J. Porras, "Dynamics of Planned Organizational Change: Assessing Empirical Support for a Theoretical Model," *Academy of Management Journal,* Vol. 36, No. 3 (1993), pp. 619–634.

57. F. Taylor, "Is Microsoft Heading the Way of the Dinosaur?" *The Globe and Mail,* July 7, 2010, https://www.theglobeandmail.com/globe-investor/investment-ideas/is-microsoft-heading-the-way-of-the-dinosaur/article1390270/.

58. B. Tabrizi, "How Microsoft Became Innovative Again," *Harvard Business Review Digital Articles,* 2023, pp. 1–7.

59. D. Fadeyi and J. Horowitz, "Americans More Likely to Say It's a Bad Thing Than a Good Thing That More Young Adults Live with Their Parents," *Pew Research Center,* August 24, 2022, https://www.pewresearch.org/fact-tank/2022/08/24/americans-more-likely-to-say-its-a-bad-thing-than-a-good-thing-that-more-young-adults-live-with-their-parents/.

60. R. Burris, "Millennials Are Changing the Face of Adulthood," *Rocket Money,* November 24, 2022, https://www.rocketmoney.com/learn/personal-finance/millennials-are-changing-the-face-of-adulthood.

61. "Overcoming Social Isolation through Rendever's Purposeful VR Platform for Seniors," *Rendever,* https://www.rendever.com/ (accessed April 16, 2023).

62. M. Hickman, "AGING: OPPORTUNITIES IN THE SILVER TSUNAMI" *Urban-X,* https://urban-x.com/article/silver-tsunami/ (accessed April 16, 2023).

63. S. Scotti, "Supporting Older Adults with Approaches Spanning Multiple Policy Areas," *National Conference of State Legislatures,* January 18, 2023, https://www.ncsl.org/state-legislatures-news/details/supporting-older-adults-with-approaches-spanning-multiple-policy-areas.

64. T. Coop, "Don't Underestimate the Unexpected," *Medium,* February 3, 2023, https://medium.com/@strategicteams/dont-underestimate-the-unexpected-1ffb168814be.

65. S. Cain, "California Winemakers Are Using A.I. to Combat Climate Change Challenges," *Fortune,* August 23, 2022, https://fortune.com/2022/08/23/tech-forward-everyday-ai-california-winemakers/.

66. S. Thompson, "Autonomous Robots to Help Modernize Grape, Wine Industry," *Cornell,* November 16, 2022, https://news.cornell.edu/stories/2022/11/autonomous-robots-help-modernize-grape-wine-industry.

67. A. Moghe, "Artificial Intelligence Is Stepping into the Wine World," *Future Drinks Expo,* https://futuredrinksexpo.com/en/blog/insights-64/artificial-intelligence-is-stepping-into-the-wine-world-330.htm#:~:text=The%20AI%2Dbased%20recommendation%20platform,idea%20about%20their%20target%20clientele (accessed April 16, 2023).

68. I.M. García-Sánchez, C. Aibar-Guzmán, M. Núñez-Torrado, and B. Aibar-Guzmán, "Are Institutional Investors 'in Love' with the Sustainable Development Goals? Understanding the Idyll in the Case of Governments and Pension Funds," *Sustainable Development,* Vol. 30, No. 5 (2022), pp. 1099–1116.

69. "Find a B Corp," *B Corporation,* https://www.bcorporation.net/en-us/find-a-b-corp?refinement%5Bcountries%5D%5B0%5D=United%20States (accessed April 16, 2023).

70. "Our Story," *Follow This,* https://www.follow-this.org/our-story/ (accessed April 16, 2023).

71. M. McCormick and T. Wilson, "Activist Group Follow This Launches Climate Campaign against Big Oil," *Financial Times,* December 18, 2022, https://www.ft.com/content/c695432d-436a-4784-aa66-a06bfeec186d; Also see R. Bousso and S. Valle, "Investors Ramp Up Pressure on Big Oil Firms to Set 2030 Climate Targets," *Reuters,* December 18, 2022, https://www.reuters.com/business/sustainable-business/investors-ramp-up-pressure-big-oil-firms-set-2030-climate-targets-2022-12-19/.

72. M. Carnegie, "Gen Z: How Young People Are Changing Activism," *BBC,* August 8, 2022, https://www.bbc.com/worklife/article/20220803-gen-z-how-young-people-are-changing-activism.

73. C. Jin, "The Effects of Creating Shared Value (CSV) on the Consumer Self–Brand Connection: Perspective of Sustainable Development," *Corporate Social Responsibility and Environmental Management,* Vol. 25, No. 6 (2018), pp. 1246–1257.

74. "About Us," *To The Market,* https://tothemarket.com/pages/about-to-the-market (accessed April 16, 2023).

75. "2022 Impact Report," *To The Market,* https://www.flipsnack.com/B9BD9BFF8D6/to-the-market-impact-report-2022/full-view.html (accessed April 16, 2023).

76. "Overweight & Obesity Statistics," *National Institute of Diabetes and Digestive and Kidney Diseases,* https://www.niddk.nih.gov/health-information/health-statistics/overweight-obesity#:~:text=About%201%20in%206%20children,19%20(16.1%25)%20are%20overweight.&text=Almost%201%20in%205%20children,19%20(19.3%25)%20have%20obesity.&text=About%201%20in%2016%20children,6.1%25)%20have%20severe%20obesity (accessed April 16, 2023).

77. M. Krupnick, "'This Industry Will Stop at Nothing': Big Soda's Fight to Ban Taxes on Sugary Drinks," *The Guardian,* November 12, 2022, https://www.theguardian.com/environment/2022/nov/12/big-soda-industry-lobby-fight-ban-soda-taxes.

78. "Another Soda Tax Success Story: Sugary Beverage Consumption Drops in San Francisco," *Public Health Institute,* January 25, 2023, https://www.phi.org/press/another-soda-tax-success-story-sugary-beverage-consumption-drops-in-san-francisco/.

79. M. Catt, "U.S. Labor Strikes up 52% in 2022 as Worker Activism Rises," *Cornell Chronicle,* February 21, 2023, https://news.cornell.edu/stories/2023/02/us-labor-strikes-52-2022-worker-activism-rises.

80. S. Becker, "Labor Strikes Have Doubled in the Past Year. Is High Inflation Part of the Reason?" *Fast Company,* June 23, 2022, https://www.fastcompany.com/90763525/labor-strikes-have-doubled-in-the-last-year-is-high-inflation-part-of-the-reason.

81. A. Heath and M. Sato, "Hundreds of Employees Say No to Being Part of Elon Musk's 'Extremely Hardcore' Twitter," *The Verge,* November 17, 2022, https://www.theverge.com/2022/11/17/23465274/hundreds-of-twitter-employees-resign-from-elon-musk-hardcore-deadline.

82. This three-way typology of change was adapted from discussion in P.C. Nutt, "Tactics of Implementation," *Academy of Management Journal,* June 1986, pp. 230–261.

83. J. Valinsky, "Online Black Friday Sales Set a New Record," *CNN Business,* November 28, 2022, https://www.cnn.com/2022/11/28/business/black-friday-sales-numbers/index.html.

84. Radical organizational change is discussed by T.E. Vollmann, *The Transformational Imperative* (Boston: Harvard Business School Press, 1996).

85. A. Alexander, "Remote Work Challenges Company Culture," *SHRM,* March 7, 2022, https://www.shrm.org/hr-today/news/hr-magazine/spring2022/pages/remote-work-challenges-company-culture.aspx.

86. D. Waeger and K. Weber, "Institutional Complexity and Organizational Change: An Open Policy Perspective," *Academy of Management Review,* Vol. 44, No. 2 (2019), pp. 336–359.

87. K. Johnson, "Hospital Robots Are Helping Combat a Wave of Nurse Burnout," *Wired,* April 19, 2022, https://www.wired.com/story/moxi-hospital-robot-nurse-burnout-health-care/.

88. J. Constine, "Hospital Droid Diligent Robotics Raises $10M to Assist Nurses," *Tech Crunch,* March 20, 2020, https://techcrunch.com/2020/03/20/robot-nurse/.

89. M.A. Wolfson, S.I. Tannenbaum, J.E. Mathieu, and M.T. Maynard, "A Cross-Level Investigation of Informal Field-Based Learning and Performance Improvements," *Journal of Applied Psychology,* January 2018, pp. 14–36. Also see S. Hussain, S. Lei, T. Akram, M. Haider, S. Hussain, and M. Ali, "Kurt Lewin's Change Model: A Critical Review of the Role of Leadership and Employee Involvement in Organizational Change," *Journal of Innovation & Knowledge,* Vol. 3, No. 3 (2018), pp. 123–127.

90. J. Constine, "Hospital Droid Diligent Robotics Raises $10M to Assist Nurses," *Tech Crunch,* March 20, 2020, https://techcrunch.com/2020/03/20/robot-nurse/.

91. T. Lind, "Deaconess Rolls Out Nurse Robots amid Staff Shortages to Deliver Medications, Lab Work, Supplies," *The Spokesman-Review,* January 27, 2023, https://www.spokesman.com/stories/2023/jan/27/deaconess-rolls-out-nurse-robots-amid-staff-shorta/.

92. E. Winick, "Walmart's New Robots Are Loved by Staff—And Ignored by Customers," *Technology Review,* January 31, 2018, https://www.technologyreview.com/2018/01/31/145906/the-robots-patrolling-walmarts-aisles/.

93. T. Lind, "Deaconess Rolls Out Nurse Robots amid Staff Shortages to Deliver Medications, Lab Work, Supplies," *The Spokesman-Review,* January 27, 2023, https://www.spokesman.com/stories/2023/jan/27/deaconess-rolls-out-nurse-robots-amid-staff-shorta/.

94. E. Wee and M. Taylor, "Attention to Change: A Multilevel Theory on the Process of Emergent Continuous Organizational Change," *Journal of Applied Psychology,* Vol. 103, No. 1 (2018), pp. 1–13.

95. L.R. Hearld and J.A. Alexander, "Governance Processes and Change within Organizational Participants of Multi-Sectoral Community Health Care Alliances: The Mediating Role of Vision, Mission, Strategy Agreement, and Perceived Alliance Value," *American Journal of Community Psychology,* March 2014, pp. 185–197.

96. A.E. Rafferty, N.L. Jimmieson, and A.A. Armenakis, "Change Readiness: A Multilevel Review," *Journal of management,* 39(1), January 2013, pp. 110–135

97. "Rankings," *RepTrak,* https://www.reptrak.com/rankings/ (accessed April 14, 2023); Also see H. Bhasin, "Top 10 Toy Companies in the World in 2023," *Marketing,* Vol. 91 (February 8, 2023), https://www.marketing91.com/top-toy-companies-in-world/#:~:text=The%20Danish%20company%20The%20Lego,2022%20based%20on%20brand%20value.

98. P. Merrill, "Brick by Brick," *CEO Magazine,* June 14, 2022, https://digitalmag.theceomagazine.com/us/july-2022/innovate/lessons-from-lego/.

99. P. Merrill, "Brick by Brick," *CEO Magazine,* June 14, 2022, https://digitalmag.theceomagazine.com/us/july-2022/innovate/lessons-from-lego/.

100. J. Davis, "How Lego Clicked: The Super Brand That Reinvented Itself," *The Guardian,* June 4, 2017, https://www.theguardian.com/lifeandstyle/2017/jun/04/how-lego-clicked-the-super-brand-that-reinvented-itself.

101. J. Grieves, "Introduction: The Origins of Organizational Development," *Journal of Management Development,* Vol. 19, No. 5 (2000), pp. 345–447.

102. G.R. Bushe and S. Lewis, "Three Change Strategies in Organization Development: Data-Based, High Engagement and Generative," *Leadership & Organization Development Journal,* Vol. 44, No. 2 (April 2023), pp. 173–188.

103. "Executive and Professional Coaching," *University of Southern California,* https://employees.usc.edu/learn-grow/learning-and-professional-development/executive-and-professional-coaching/#wellness-resolution (accessed April 15, 2023).

104. M. Ballé, "Putting Customers First," *Lean Enterprise Institute,* December 8, 2022, https://www.lean.org/the-lean-post/articles/putting-customers-first/.

105. Y. Klok, D.P. Kroon, and S.N. Khapova, "The Role of Emotions during Mergers and Acquisitions: A Review of the Past and a Glimpse into the Future," *International Journal of Management Reviews,* 25(3), December 8, 2022, pp. 587–613.

106. P. Brennan and G. Dholakia, "M&A Activity Slumped in North America in 2022 after Record 2021," *S&P Global,* January 17, 2023, https://www.spglobal.com/marketintelligence/en/news-insights/latest-news-headlines/m-a-activity-slumped-in-north-america-in-2022-after-record-2021-73807615#:~:text=The%20total%20value%20of%20mergers,year%20over%20year%20to%2020%2C965.

107. Y. Klok, D.P. Kroon, and S.N. Khapova, "The Role of Emotions during Mergers and Acquisitions: A Review of the Past and a Glimpse into the Future," *International Journal of Management Reviews,* 25(3), December 8, 2022, pp. 587–613.

108. E. De Haan, D. Gray, and S. Bonneywell, "Executive Coaching Outcome Research in a Field Setting: A Near-Randomized Controlled Trial Study in a Global Healthcare Corporation," *Academy of Management Learning & Education*, Vol. 18, No. 4 (2019), pp. 581–605.

109. E. Gilbert, T. Foulk, and J. Bono, "Building Personal Resources through Interventions: An Integrative Review," *Journal of Organizational Behavior*, Vol. 39, No. 2 (2018), pp. 214–228.

110. "Change Management: The HR Strategic Imperative as a Business Partner," *Research Quarterly,* Fourth Quarter 2007, pp. 1–9. Also see D.A. Garvin, A.C. Edmondson, and F. Gino, "Is Yours a Learning Organization?" *Harvard Business Review,* March 2008, pp. 109–116.

111. D.M. Rousseau and S. ten Have, "Evidence-Based Change Management," *Organizational Dynamics*, Vol. 51, No. 3 (2022), p. 100899.

112. D.M. Rousseau and S. ten Have, "Evidence-Based Change Management," *Organizational Dynamics*, Vol. 51, No. 3 (2022), p. 100899.

113. S. Shrivastava, F. Pazzaglia, K. Sonpar, and D. McLoughlin, "Effective Communication during Organizational Change: A Cross-Cultural Perspective," *Cross Cultural & Strategic Management,* Vol. 29, No. 3 (July 2022), pp. 675–697; Also see E. Supriharyanti and B.M. Sukoco, "Organizational Change Capability: A Systematic Review and Future Research Directions," *Management Research Review*, Vol. 46, No. 1 (2023), pp. 46–81.

114. E. Newbery, "The Average American Spends This Much on Clothes Every Year," *The Motley Fool,* July 26, 2022, https://www.fool.com/the-ascent/personal-finance/articles/the-average-american-spends-this-much-on-clothes-every-year/; Also see "Fashion and Finance: The New Economic Realities of Luxury Consumers," *Vogue Business,* November 10, 2022, https://www.voguebusiness.com/consumers/fashion-and-finance-the-new-economic-realities-of-luxury-consumers-rakuten; Also see "Activewear Apparel Market Size to Grow by USD 157.1 billion," *PR Newswire,* March 30, 2022, https://www.prnewswire.com/news-releases/activewear-apparel-market-size-to-grow-by-usd-157-1-billion--technavio-301513001.html.

115. "What Is innovation?" *McKinsey & Company,* August 17, 2022, https://www.mckinsey.com/featured-insights/mckinsey-explainers/what-is-innovation.

116. A. Fisher, "America's Most Admired Companies," *Fortune,* March 17, 2008, p. 66.

117. "Dizolve Inside," *Dizolve,* https://dizolve.com/dizolve-inside#:~:text=Dizolve%20Group%20Corporation%20is%20the,the%20active%20composition%20delivery%20system (accessed April 16, 2023).

118. "Love This Sheet!" *Ecos,* https://www.ecos.com/lovethissheet/ (accessed April 16, 2023).

119. "Online Food Delivery Market Size, Share & Trends Analysis Report by Type (Platform to Consumer, Restaurant to Consumer), by Region (North America, Europe), and Segment Forecasts, 2023–2030," *Grand View Research,* https://www.grandviewresearch.com/industry-analysis/online-food-delivery-market-report#:~:text=Report%20Overview,10.3%25%20from%202023%20to%202030 (accessed April 16, 2023).

120. "The Food You Love, Sky Delivered in 5 Minutes," *Flytrex,* https://www.flytrex.com/ (accessed April 16, 2023).

121. J. Littman, "Flytrex Expands Delivery Radius to Service 100K Customers," *Restaurant Dive,* July 28, 2022, https://www.restaurantdive.com/news/flytrex-expands-drone-delivery-radius-to-service-100k-restaurant-and-retail-customers/628060/.

122. "J-Tip Needle-Free Injection for Virtually Pain Free Experiences," *J-Tip,* https://jtip.com/j-tip-landing-page/ (accessed April 16, 2023).

123. J. Shaver, "The State of Telehealth before and after the COVID-19 Pandemic," *Primary Care: Clinics in Office Practice*, Vol. 49, No. 4 (2022), pp. 517–530.

124. "Telehealth for Rural Areas," *Telehealth.HHS.gov,* https://telehealth.hhs.gov/providers/best-practice-guides/telehealth-for-rural-areas/getting-started#benefits-of-telehealth-in-rural-areas (accessed April 16, 2023).

125. S. D'Agostino, "GPT-4 Is Here. But Most Faculty Lack AI Policies," *Inside Higher Ed,* March 21, 2023, https://www.insidehighered.com/news/2023/03/22/gpt-4-here-most-faculty-lack-ai-policies.

126. G.P. Pisano, "You Need an Innovation Strategy," *Harvard Business Review,* June 2015, p. 46.

127. N. Anderson, K. Potocnik, and J. Zhou, "Innovation and Creativity in Organizations: A Stateof-the-Science Review, Prospective Commentary, and Guiding Framework," *Journal of Management*, 40(5), pp. 1297–1333.

128. S. Erzurumlu, "What Can the Innovator Learn from the Operations Manager? An Operations View of Innovation Strategy," *IEEE Engineering Management Review*, Vol. 46, No. 2 (2018), pp. 97–102.

129. "Innovation at Reckitt," *Reckitt,* https://www.reckitt.com/our-science/innovation/ (accessed April 16, 2023).

130. "Finish," *Reckitt,* https://www.reckitt.com/our-brands/hygiene/finish/ (accessed April 16, 2023).

131. Y. Dong, K. M. Bartol, Z-X Zhang, and C. Li, "Enhancing Employee Creativity via Individual Skill Development and Team Knowledge Sharing: Influences of Dual-Focused Transformational Leadership," *Journal of Organizational Behavior*, 38(3), 2017, pp. 439–458.

132. "Dr. Jin Huang Honored by CIO Views in '10 Most Innovative CEOs to Watch in 2023'," *PR Newswire,* March 9, 2023, https://www.prnewswire.com/news-releases/dr-jin-huang-honored-by-cio-views-in-10-most-innovative-ceos-to-watch-in-2023-301766411.html.

133. "Dr. Jin Huang: Transforming Lives through Enriched Education," *CIO Views,* https://cioviews.com/dr-jin-huang-transforming-lives-through-enriched-education/ (accessed April 16, 2023).

134. T. Joseph, "5 Biggest Innovation Barriers That Business Leaders Should Resolve in 2022," *Fingent,* July 1, 2022, https://www.fingent.com/blog/5-biggest-innovation-barriers-that-business-leaders-should-resolve-in-2022/.

135. K. AlKayid, K.M. Selem, A.E. Shehata, and C.C. Tan, "Leader Vision, Organizational Inertia and Service Hotel Employee Creativity: Role of Knowledge-Donating," *Current Psychology*, 2022, pp. 1–13.

136. B. Nottingham, "Inertia Is the Greatest Challenge to Innovation. Here's How to Counter It," *Fast Company,* November 3, 2022, https://www.fastcompany.com/90799603/inertia-is-the-greatest-challenge-to-innovation-heres-how-to-counter-it.

137. D. Sutardi, Y. Nuryanti, D.F.C. Kumoro, S. Mariyanah, and E. Agistiawati, "Innovative Work Behavior: A Strong Combination of Leadership, Learning, and Climate," *International Journal of Social and Management Studies*, Vol. 3, No. 1 (2022), pp. 290–301.

138. See M. Henderson, P. Abramson, M. Bangerter, M. Chen, I. D'Souza, J. Fulcher, V. Halupka, J. Hook, C. Horton, B. Macfarlan, and R. Mackay, "Educational Design and Productive Failure: The Need for a Culture of Creative Risk Taking," in *Handbook of Digital Higher Education* (Edward Elgar Publishing 2022), pp. 14–25; Also see S. Thomke, "Building a Culture of Experimentation," *Harvard Business Review*, Vol. 98, No. 2 (2020), pp. 40–48.

139. See "Flagship Pioneering Is an Experiment in Institutional Innovation," *Flagship Pioneering,* https://www.flagshippioneering.com/process (accessed April 16, 2023) ; Also see G. Pisano, "The Hard Truth about Innovative Cultures," *Harvard Business Review*, Vol. 97, No. 1 (2019), pp. 62–71.

140. "IDEO at a Glance," *IDEO,* https://www.ideo.com/about/ideo-at-a-glance (accessed April 16, 2023).

141. "An Overview of Our Best Design Thinking & Strategy Frameworks," *IDEO U,* https://www.ideou.com/blogs/inspiration/an-overview-of-our-best-design-thinking-strategy-frameworks (accessed April 16, 2023).

142. "Design Thinking Resources," *IDEO,* https://www.ideou.com/pages/design-thinking-resources (accessed April 16, 2023).

143. "An Overview of Our Best Design Thinking & Strategy Frameworks," *IDEO U,* https://www.ideou.com/blogs/inspiration/an-overview-of-our-best-design-thinking-strategy-frameworks (accessed April 16, 2023).

144. "Keysight Announces Winners of the 2022 Innovation Challenge," *Business Wire,* November 4, 2022, https://www.businesswire.com/news/home/20221104005366/en/Keysight-Announces-Winners-of-the-2022-Innovation-Challenge.

145. "The Future of Jobs Report 2020," *World Economic Forum,* October 2020, https://www3.weforum.org/docs/WEF_Future_of_Jobs_2020.pdf.

146. T. Wang and C. Zatzick, "Human Capital Acquisition and Organizational Innovation: A Temporal Perspective.," *Academy of Management Journal,* Vol. 62, No. 1 (2019), pp. 99–116. Also see X. Wang, Y. Fang, I. Qureshi, and O. Janssen, "Understanding Employee Innovative Behavior: Integrating the Social Network and Leader-Member Exchange Perspectives," *Journal of Organizational Behavior,* April 2015, pp. 403–420; F.C. Godart, W.W. Maddux, A.V. Shipilov, and A.D. Galinsky, "Fashion with a Foreign Flair: Professional Experiences Abroad Facilitate the Creative Innovations of Organizations," *Academy of Management Journal,* February 2015, pp. 195–220.

147. "The Future of Jobs Report 2020," *World Economic Forum,* October 2020, https://www3.weforum.org/docs/WEF_Future_of_Jobs_2020.pdf.

148. "Sparking Fresh Innovation," *Nestlé USA,* https://www.nestleusa.com/stories/sparking-fresh-innovation (accessed April 17, 2023).

149. S. Danley, "How Nestle New Business Ventures Sparks Fresh Innovation," *Food Business News,* October 24, 2022, https://www.foodbusinessnews.net/articles/22488-how-nestle-new-business-ventures-sparks-fresh-innovation.

150. "Innovation," *Nestlé USA,* https://www.nestleusa.com/innovation (accessed April 17, 2023).

151. R. Donnelly and E. Hughes, "The HR Ecosystem Framework: Examining Strategic HRM Tensions in Knowledge-Intensive Organizations with Boundary-Crossing Professionals," *Human Resource Management,* Vol. 62, No. 1 (2023), pp. 79–95.

152. G.M. Kankisingi and S. Dhliwayo, "Rewards and Innovation Performance in Manufacturing Small and Medium Enterprises (SMEs)," *Sustainability,* Vol. 14, No. 3 (2022), p. 1737.

153. G. Kane, D. Palmer, A. Phillips, D. Kiron, and N. Buckley, "Accelerating Digital Innovation Inside and Out," *Deloitte,* June 4, 2019, https://www2.deloitte.com/us/en/insights/focus/digital-maturity/digital-innovation-ecosystems-organizational-agility.html.

154. "Ep 2: Inside the Digital Transformation of CarMax with CITO Shamim Mohammad," *Enterprise Software Innovators,* February 1, 2022, https://www.enterprisesoftware.blog/episode/ep-2-inside-the-digital-transformation-of-carmax-with-shamim-mohammad.

155. S. Lake, "Investors Are Paying More Attention—and Money—to Upskilling," *Fortune Education,* June 8, 2022, https://fortune.com/education/articles/investors-are-paying-more-attention-and-money-to-upskilling/.

156. "Amazon Pledges to Upskill 100,000 U.S. Employees for In-Demand Jobs by 2025," *Amazon Press Center,* July 11, 2019, https://press.aboutamazon.com/news-releases/news-release-details/amazon-pledges-upskill-100000-us-employees-demand-jobs-2025; Also see S. Lake, "Investors Are Paying More Attention—and Money—to Upskilling," *Fortune Education,* June 8, 2022, https://fortune.com/education/articles/investors-are-paying-more-attention-and-money-to-upskilling/.

157. N. Sverdlik and S. Oreg, "Beyond the Individual-Level Conceptualization of Dispositional Resistance to Change: Multilevel Effects on the Response to Organizational Change," *Journal of Organizational Behavior,* 44(7), October 28, 2022, pp. 1066–1077.

158. N. Sverdlik and S. Oreg, "Beyond the Individual-Level Conceptualization of Dispositional Resistance to Change: Multilevel Effects on the Response to Organizational Change," *Journal of Organizational Behavior,* 44(7), October 28, 2022, pp. 1066–1077.

159. J. Vos and J. Rupert, "Change Agent's Contribution to Recipients' Resistance to Change: A Two-Sided Story," *European Management Journal,* Vol 36, No. 4 (2018), pp. 453–462.

160. B. Brandes and Y.-L. Lai, "Addressing Resistance to Change through a Micro Interpersonal Lens: An Investigation into the Coaching Process," *Journal of Organizational Change Management,* Vol. 35, No. 3 (May 2022), pp. 666–681.

161. A. Blaschka, "The 2 Seemingly Opposite Traits That Work Together to Drive Your Career," *Forbes,* April 9, 2022, https://www.forbes.com/sites/amyblaschka/2022/04/09/the-2-seemingly-opposite-traits-that-work-together-to-drive-your-career/?sh=7e8c01065951.

162. See S.B. Doeze Jager, M.P. Born, and H.T. van der Molen, "The Relationship between Organizational Trust, Resistance to Change and Adaptive and Proactive Employees' Agility in an Unplanned and Planned Change Context," *Applied Psychology,* Vol. 71, No. 2 (2022), pp. 436–460; Also see J. Vos and J. Rupert, "Change Agent's Contribution to Recipients' Resistance to Change: A Two-Sided Story," *European Management Journal,* Vol 36, No. 4 (2018), pp. 453–462.

163. J. Vos and J. Rupert, "Change Agent's Contribution to Recipients' Resistance to Change: A Two-Sided Story," *European Management Journal,* Vol 36, No. 4 (2018), pp. 453–462.

164. E. Andersen, "Change Is Hard. Here's How to Make It Less Painful," *Harvard Business Review Digital Articles,* 2022, pp. 1–8.

165. S.L. Reeves, T. Nguyen, A.A. Scholer, K. Fujita, and S.J. Spencer, "Examining Beliefs about the Benefits of Self-Affirmation for Mitigating Self-Threat," *Personality and Social Psychology Bulletin,* 2022, p. 01461672221120612.

166. A.J. Howell, "Self-Affirmation Theory and the Science of Well-Being," *Journal of Happiness Studies,* Vol. 18 (2017), pp. 293–311.

167. D.K. Sherman and G. L. Cohen, "The Psychology of Self-Defense: Self-Affirmation Theory," *Advances in Experimental Social Psychology,* 2006, pp. 183–242.

168. P. Soral, S.P. Pati, S.K. Singh, and F.L. Cooke, "Coping with Dirty Work: A Meta-Synthesis from a Resource Perspective," *Human Resource Management Review,* Vol. 32, No. 4 (2022), p. 100861.

169. C.R. Schneider and E.U. Weber, "Motivating Prosocial Behavior by Leveraging Positive Self-Regard through Values Affirmation," *Journal of Applied Social Psychology,* Vol. 52, No. 2 (2022), pp. 106–114.

170. P. Soral, S.P. Pati, S.K. Singh, and F.L. Cooke, "Coping with Dirty Work: A Meta-Synthesis from a Resource Perspective," *Human Resource Management Review,* Vol. 32, No. 4 (2022), p. 100861.

171. P. Onderko, "3 Tips to Open Your Heart, Mind and Life to Change," *Success,* August 6, 2015, https://www.success.com/article/3-tips-to-open-your-heart-mind-and-life-to-changeApply.

172. K.E. Wakelin, G. Perman, and L.M. Simonds, "Effectiveness of Self-Compassion-Related Interventions for Reducing Self-Criticism: A Systematic Review and Meta-Analysis," *Clinical Psychology & Psychotherapy,* Vol. 29, No. 1 (2022), pp. 1–25.

173. P. Onderko, "3 Tips to Open Your Heart, Mind and Life to Change," *Success,* August 6, 2015, https://www.success.com/article/3-tips-to-open-your-heart-mind-and-life-to-changeApply.

174. A. Abrams, "How to Cultivate More Self-Compassion," *Psychology Today,* March 3, 2017, https://www.psychologytoday.com/us/blog/nurturing-self-compassion/201703/how-cultivate-more-self-compassion.

175. K. Wong, "Why Self-Compassion Beats Self-Confidence," *The New York Times,* December 28, 2017, https://www.nytimes.com/2017/12/28/smarter-living/why-self-compassion-beats-self-confidence.html.

176. A. Abrams, "How to Cultivate More Self-Compassion," *Psychology Today,* March 3, 2017, https://www.psychologytoday.com/us/

blog/nurturing-self-compassion/201703/how-cultivate-more-self-compassion.

177. L. Eby, T. Allen, K. Conley, R. Williamson, T. Henderson, and V. Mancini, "Mindfulness-Based Training Interventions for Employees: A Qualitative Review of the Literature," *Human Resource Management Review*, Vol. 29, No. 2 (2019), pp. 156–178.

CHAPTER 11

1. D.M. Lewis, L. Al-Shawaf, A.Y. Semchenko, and K.C. Evans, "Error Management Theory and Biased First Impressions: How Do People Perceive Potential Mates under Conditions of Uncertainty?" *Evolution and Human Behavior*, Vol. 43, No. 2 (2022), pp. 87–96.
2. J. Kelly, "How To Make a Great First Impression in an Interview," *Forbes*, June 27, 2022, https://www.forbes.com/sites/jackkelly/2022/06/27/how-to-make-a-great-first-impression-in-an-interview/?sh=b043f39594bc.
3. M. Wroblewski, "The Importance of Making a Good First Impression in Business," *Houston Chronicle*, March 25, 2022, https://smallbusiness.chron.com/importance-making-good-first-impression-business-23065.html.
4. H. McGurgan, "How to Convince the Employer in a Job Interview," *Houston Chronicle*, September 2, 2022, https://work.chron.com/convince-employer-job-interview-17665.html.
5. M. Lyons, "Starting a New Job as a Mid-Career Professional," *Harvard Business Review Digital Articles*, 2022, pp. 1–5.
6. For a thorough discussion of personality psychology, see P.R. Sackett, F. Lievens, C.H. Van Iddekinge, and N.R. Kuncel, "Individual Differences and Their Measurement: A Review of 100 Years of Research," *Journal of Applied Psychology*, March 2017, pp. 254–273.
7. See L. Xu et al., "Leader Perfectionism—Friend or Foe of Employee Creativity? Locus of Control as a Key Contingency," *Academy of Management Journal*, Vol. 65, No. 6 (2022), pp. 2092–2117; Also see M. Mihalache and O.R. Mihalache, "How Workplace Support for the COVID-19 Pandemic and Personality Traits Affect Changes in Employees' Affective Commitment to the Organization and Job-Related Well-Being," *Human Resource Management*, Vol. 61, No. 3 (2022), pp. 295–314; Also see M. Pelster "Dark Triad Personality Traits and Selective Hedging," *Journal of Business Ethics*, Vol. 182, No. 1 (2023), pp. 261–286.
8. J.M. Digman, "Personality Structure: Emergence of the Five-Factor Model," *Annual Review of Psychology*, Vol. 41 (1990), pp. 417–440.
9. E. Goldberg, "The $2 Billion Question of Who You Are at Work," *The New York Times*, March 7, 2023.
10. A. Raval, "Psychological Tests Can Help Firms Hire Better—but Accuracy Is Not Guaranteed," *Financial Times*, April 23, 2023, https://www.ft.com/content/d8094b4e-5535-45a5-b3e2-5677637b6d28.
11. See B.S. Connelly et al. "A Multirater Perspective on Personality and Performance: An Empirical Examination of the Trait–Reputation–Identity Model," *Journal of Applied Psychology*, Vol. 107, No1 8 (2022), pp. 1352–1368; Also see F.Y. Wu et al. "Individual Differences at Play: An Investigation into Measuring Big Five Personality Facets with Game-Based Assessments," *International Journal of Selection & Assessment*, Vol. 30, No. 1 (2022), pp. 62–81.
12. See G. Coleman, A. Furnham, and L. Treglown, "Exploring the Dark Side of Conscientiousness: The Relationship between Conscientiousness and Its Potential Derailers: Perfectionism and Narcissism," *Current Psychology*, 42(31), 2022, pp. 27744–27757.
13. E. Kuijpers, J. Pickett, B. Wille, and J. Hofmans, "Do You Feel Better When You Behave More Extraverted Than You Are? The Relationship between Cumulative Counterdispositional Extraversion and Positive Feelings," *Personality and Social Psychology Bulletin*, Vol. 48, No. 4 (2022), pp. 606–623; B. Landis, J.M. Jachimowicz, D.J. Wang, and R.W. Krause, "Revisiting Extraversion and Leadership Emergence: A Social Network Churn Perspective," *Journal of Personality and Social Psychology*, Vol. 123, No. 4 (2022), p. 811; F. Chiesi, C. Tagliaferro, G. Marunic, and C. Lau, "Prioritize Positivity in Italians: A Validation and Measurement Invariance Study of an Italian Version of the Prioritizing Positivity Scale," *Current Psychology*, 2022, pp. 1–12; M.L. Huo and Z. Jiang, "Work–Life Conflict and Job Performance: The Mediating Role of Employee Wellbeing and the Moderating Role of Trait Extraversion," *Personality and Individual Differences*, Vol. 205 (2023), p. 112109; A. Wihler, G. Blickle, C. Ewen, H. Genau, S. Fritze, L. Völkl, R. Merkl, T. Missfeld, and M. Mützel, "An Integrative Approach to More Nuanced Estimates of Personality–Job–Performance Relations," *Applied Psychology*, Vol. 72, No. 2 (2023), pp. 588–624; J. Palomäki, M. Laakasuo, S. Castrén, J. Saastamoinen, T. Kainulainen, and N. Suhonen, "Online Betting Intensity Is Linked with Extraversion and Conscientiousness," *Journal of Personality*, Vol. 89, No. 5 (2021), pp. 1081–1094.

14. J.L. Pletzera, M. Bentvelzenb, J.K. Oostromc, R.E. de Vries, "A Meta-Analysis of the Relations between Personality and Workplace Deviance: Big Five versus HEXACO," *Journal of Vocational Behavior*, 2019, pp. 369–383.
15. L. Cassiday, "Lots of Companies Use Personality Tests for Hiring Decisions. Here's Why That Can Backfire," *Neuro Leadership*, April 27, 2023, https://neuroleadership.com/your-brain-at-work/personality-tests-for-hiring-decisions-can-backfire.
16. Y. Zhang, J. Sun, C. Lin, and H. Ren, "Linking Core Self-Evaluation to Creativity: The Roles of Knowledge Sharing and Work Meaningfulness," *Journal of Business and Psychology*, 2020, pp. 257–270. Also see T.A. Judge, H.M. Weiss, J.D. Kammeyer-Mueller, and C. L. Hulin, "Job Attitudes, Job Satisfaction, and Job Affect: A Century of Continuity and of Change," *Journal of Applied Psychology*, March 2017, pp. 356–374; Z. Wang, X. Bu, S. Cai, "Core Self-Evaluation, Individual Intellectual Capital and Employee Creativity," *Current Psychology*, 2018, https://doi.org/10.1007/s12144-018-0046-x; H. Ding and X. Lin, "Exploring the Relationship between Core Self-Evaluation and Strengths Use: The Perspective of Emotion," *Personality and Individual Differences*, 2020, https://doi.org/10.1016/j.paid.2019.109804; S. S. Kirmani, S. Attiq, H. Bakari, and M. Irfan, "Role of Core Self Evaluation and Acquired Motivations in Employee Task Performance," *Pakistan Journal of Psychological Research*, 2019; J. Ahn, S. Lee, and S. Yun, "Leaders' Core Self-Evaluation, Ethical Leadership, and Employees' Job Performance: The Moderating Role of Employees' Exchange Ideology," *Journal of Business Ethics*, 2018, pp. 457–470.
17. T.A. Judge, A. Earez, and J.A. Bono, "The Power of Being Positive: The Relation between Positive Self-Concept and Job Performance," *Journal of Human Performance*, June 1998, pp. 167–187.
18. D.J. Yoon et al. "Customer Courtesy and Service Performance: The Roles of Self-Efficacy and Social Context," *Journal of Organizational Behavior*, Vol. 43, No. 6 (2022), pp. 1015–1037; H. Bing, B. Sadjadi, M. Afzali, and J. Fathi, "Self-Efficacy and Emotion Regulation as Predictors of Teacher Burnout among English as a Foreign Language Teachers: A Structural Equation Modeling Approach," *Frontiers in Psychology*, Vol. 13 (2022); G. Affuso, A. Zannone, C. Esposito, M. Pannone, M.C. Miranda, G. De Angelis, S. Aquilar, M. Dragone, and D. Bacchini, "The Effects of Teacher Support, Parental Monitoring, Motivation and Self-Efficacy on Academic Performance over Time," *European Journal of Psychology of Education*, Vol. 38, No. 1 (2023), pp. 1–23; S. Machmud and S. Pasundan, "The Influence of Self-Efficacy on Satisfaction and Work-Related Performance," *International Journal of Management Science and Business Administration*, 2018, pp. 43–47; F. Cetin and D. Askun, "The Effect of Occupational Self-Efficacy on Work Performance through Intrinsic Work Motivation," *Management Research Review*, 2018, pp. 186–201.
19. W.S. Silver, T.R. Mitchell, and M.E. Gist, "Response to Successful and Unsuccessful Performance: The Moderating Effect of Self-Efficacy on the Relationship between Training and Newcomer Adjustment," *Journal of Applied Psychology*, April 1995, pp. 211–225.
20. J.V. Vancouver, K.M. More, and R.J. Yoder, "Self-Efficacy and Resource Allocation: Support for a Nonmonotonic, Discontinuous Model," *Journal of Applied Psychology*, January 2008, pp. 35–47.

21. V. Mattias, L. Bjørn, and R. Torleif, "Predictors of Return to Work 6 Months after the End of Treatment in Patients with Common Mental Disorders: A Cohort Study," *Journal of Occupational Rehabilitation,* December 2017, pp. 1–11. Also see Z. Millman, "Taking Control: Training in Verbal Self-Guidance to Enhance One's Performance," *Organizational Dynamics,* 2017, pp. 182–188; M.R. Chowdhury, "4 Ways To Improve and Increase Self-Efficacy," *Positive Psychology*, February 18, 2020, https://positivepsychology.com/3-ways-build-self-efficacy/.

22. M. Martinko and W.L. Gardner, "Learned Helplessness: An Alternative Explanation for Performance Deficits," *Academy of Management Review,* April 1982, pp. 195–204. Also see C.R. Campbell and M.J. Martinko, "An Integrative Attributional Perspective of Employment and Learned Helplessness: A Multimethod Field Study," *Journal of Management,* Vol. 2 (1998), pp. 173–200.

23. P. Filippello, C. Buzzai, S. Costa, S. Orecchio, and L. Sorrenti, "Teaching Style and Academic Achievement: The Mediating Role of Learned Helplessness and Mastery Orientation," *Psychology in the Schools*, 2019, https://doi.org/10.1002/pits.22315; C.H. Van Iddekinge and N.R. Kuncel, "Individual Differences and Their Measurement: A Review of 100 Years of Research," *Journal of Applied Psychology,* March 2017, pp. 254–273.

24. Y.Z. Yusuff, M. Mohamad, and N.Y. Ab Wahab, "The Influence of General Self-Efficacy on Women Entrepreneurs," *Academy of Entrepreneurship Journal*, 2019, DOI: 1528-2686-25-2-220. Also see R. Head, "Self-Efficacy and Sports Performance," *Sport Psychology Today*, October 8, 2019, http://www.sportpsychologytoday.com/youth-sports-psychology/self-efficacy-and-sports-performance/.

25. V. Gecas, "The Self-Concept," in R.H. Turner and J.F. Short Jr. (eds.), *Annual Review of Sociology*, Vol. 8 (Palo Alto, CA: Annual Reviews, 1982).

26. U. Orth and R.W. Robins, "Is High Self-Esteem Beneficial? Revisiting a Classic Question," *American Psychologist,* Vol. 77, No. 1 (2022), p. 5; W. Gao, Y. Luo, X. Cao, and X. Liu, "Gender Differences in the Relationship between Self-Esteem and Depression among College Students: A Cross-Lagged Study from China," *Journal of Research in Personality,* Vol. 97 (2022), p. 104202; C.E. Whelpley and M.A. McDaniel, "Self-Esteem and Counterproductive Work Behaviors: A Systematic Review," *Journal of Managerial Psychology,* 2016, pp. 850–863; K. Matzler, F.A. Bauer, and T.A. Mooradian, "Self-Esteem and Transformational Leadership," *Journal of Managerial Psychology,* 2015, pp. 815–831.

27. M. Rouault, G.J. Will, S.M. Fleming, and R.J. Dolan, "Low Self-Esteem and the Formation of Global Self-Performance Estimates in Emerging Adulthood, *Translational Psychiatry*," Vol. 12, No. 1 (2022), p. 272.

28. N. Niveau, B. New, and M. Beaudoin, "Self-Esteem Interventions in Adults—A Systematic Review and Meta-Analysis," *Journal of Research in Personality*, Vol. 94 (2021), p. 104131.

29. For an overall view of research on locus of control, see A. Hoffmann, D. Plotkina, P. Roger, and C. D'Hondt, "Superstitious Beliefs, Locus of Control, and Feeling at Risk in the Face of COVID-19," *Personality and Individual Differences*, Vol. 196 (2022), p. 111718.; Also see B.M. Galvin, A.E. Randel, B.J. Collins, and R.E. Johnson, "Changing the Focus of Locus (of Control): A Targeted Review of the Locus of Control Literature and Agenda for Future Research," *Journal of Organizational Behavior,* 2018, pp. 820–833. Also see M. Wilding, "Successful People Have a Strong 'Locus of Control.' Do You?" *Forbes*, March 2, 2020, https://www.forbes.com/sites/melodywilding/2020/03/02/successful-people-have-a-strong-locus-of-control-do-you/#5582d17d7af3.

30. Y.M. Kundi, S. Sardar, and K. Badar, "Linking Performance Pressure to Employee Work Engagement: The Moderating Role of Emotional Stability," *Personnel Review*, Vol. 51, No. 3 (2022), pp. 841–860.

31. J.D. Mayer, R.D. Roberts, and S.G. Barsade, "Human Abilities: Emotional Intelligence," *Annual Review of Psychology,* January 2008, http://papers.ssrn.com/sol3/papers.cfm?abstract_id=1082096 (accessed July 1, 2016).

32. S. Yu, G.J. Kilduff, and T. West, "Status Acuity: The Ability to Accurately Perceive Status Hierarchies Reduces Status Conflict and Benefits Group Performance," *Journal of Applied Psychology*, Vol. 108, No. 1 (2023), pp. 114–137.

33. A. Argianas, "Adopting Emotional Intelligence in the Workplace Is More Than a 'Nice to Have'," *Forbes,* May 4, 2022, https://www.forbes.com/sites/forbesbusinesscouncil/2022/05/04/adopting-emotional-intelligence-in-the-workplace-is-more-than-a-nice-to-have/?sh=6517bf995560.

34. Results are based on C. Miao, R.H. Humphrey, and S. Qian, "A Meta-Analysis of Emotional Intelligence and Work Attitudes," *Journal of Occupational and Organizational Psychology,* June 2017, pp. 177–202; C. Miao, R.H. Humphrey, and S. Qian, "Are the Emotionally Intelligent Good Citizens or Counterproductive? A Meta-Analysis of Emotional Intelligence and Its Relationships with Organizational Citizenship and Counterproductive Work Behavior," *Personality and Individual Differences,* October 2017, pp. 144–156. Also see A. Minbashian, N. Beckmann, and R.E. Wood, "Emotional Intelligence and Individual Differences in Affective Processes Underlying Task-Contingent Conscientiousness," *Journal of Organizational Behavior*, 2018, pp. 1182–1196; S.B. Dust, J.C. Rode, M.L. Arthaud-Day, S.S. Howes, A. Ramaswami, "Managing the Self-Esteem, Employment Gaps, and Employment Quality Process: The Role of Facilitation- and Understanding-Based Emotional Intelligence," *Journal of Organizational Behavior*, 2018, pp. 680–693.

35. D. Goleman, "What Makes a Leader," *Harvard Business Review,* November–December 1998, pp. 93–102.

36. J. DeSmet, "The Social and Emotional Skills New Leaders Need Most: Insights from Harvard Business Publishing," *Harvard Business Publishing*, March 3, 2023, https://www.harvardbusiness.org/the-social-and-emotional-skills-new-leaders-need-most-insights-from-harvard-business-publishing/.

37. A. Chapman, "Empathy, Trust, Diffusing Conflict and Handling Complaints," *Businessballs.com*, www.businessballs.com/empathy.htm (accessed July 19, 2016).

38. D. Limon and B. Plaster, "Can AI Teach Us How to Become More Emotionally Intelligent?" *Harvard Business Review Digital Articles*, 2022, pp. 1–7.

39. K. Aldrup, B. Carstensen, and U. Klusmann, "Is Empathy the Key to Effective Teaching? A Systematic Review of Its Association with Teacher-Student Interactions and Student Outcomes," *Educational Psychology Review*, Vol. 34, No. 3 (2022), pp. 1177–1216.

40. K. Aldrup, B. Carstensen, and U. Klusmann, "Is Empathy the Key to Effective Teaching? A Systematic Review of Its Association with Teacher-Student Interactions and Student Outcomes," *Educational Psychology Review,* Vol. 34, No. 3 (2022), pp. 1177–1216.

41. T. Oesch, "Developing Employee Empathy Using Virtual Reality," *Training Industry*, May 30, 2018, https://trainingindustry.com/articles/learning-technologies/developing-employee-empathy-using-virtual-reality/.

42. R. Carter, "Hilton Hotels and How VR Is Changing Hospitality," *XR Today,* May 20, 2022, https://www.xrtoday.com/virtual-reality/hilton-hotels-and-how-vr-is-changing-hospitality/.

43. "Building Empathy in Dementia Care with Virtual Reality Simulation," *Ohio State University Advanced Computing Center for the Arts and Design,* https://accad.osu.edu/research-gallery/building-empathy-dementia-care-virtual-reality-simulation (accessed May 8, 2023).

44. "The Random App of Kindness App," *Raki,* March 8, 2022, *Game,* https://www.rakigame.com/.

45. M. Rokeach, *Beliefs, Attitudes, and Values* (San Francisco: Jossey-Bass, 1968), p. 168.

46. A. Hlastec, D. Mumel, and L. Hauptman, "Is There a Relationship between Self-Enhancement, Conservation and Personal Tax Culture?" *Sustainability*, Vol. 15, No. 7 (2023), p. 5797.

47. H.N. Ismail, S. Karkoulian, and S.K. Kertechian, "Which Personal Values Matter Most? Job Performance and Job Satisfaction across Job Categories," *International Journal of Organizational Analysis*, 2019, pp. 109–124. Also see J. Weber, "Understanding the Millennials' Integrated Ethical Decision-Making Process: Assessing the Relationship between Personal Values and Cognitive Moral Reasoning," *Business and Society*, 2019, pp. 1671–1706.

48. M. Fishbein and I. Ajzen, *Belief, Attitude, Intention and Behavior: An Introduction to Theory and Research* (Reading, MA: Addison-Wesley Publishing, 1975), p. 6.

49. M. Reid and A. Wood, "An Investigation into Blood Donation Intentions among Non-Donors," *International Journal of Nonprofit and Voluntary Sector Marketing,* February 2008, pp. 31–43. Also see J. Ramsey, B.J. Punnett, and D. Greenidge, "A Social Psychological Account of Absenteeism in Barbados," *Human Resource Management Journal,* April 2008, pp. 97–117.

50. T.A. Judge, C.J. Thoresen, J.E. Bono, and G.K. Patton, "The Job Satisfaction–Job Performance Relationship: A Qualitative and Quantitative Review," *Psychological Bulletin,* May 2001, pp. 376–407.

51. R. Johnson, "A Change of Pace For Gen Z Employees Entering the Workforce," *Glassdoor,* August 16, 2022, https://www.glassdoor.com/research/gen-z-employees-entering-the-workforce/.

52. J. Fernandez, J. Lee, and K. Landis, "Helping Gen Z Employees Find Their Place at Work: Seven Strategies to Engage, Support, and Connect," *Harvard Business Review Digital Articles*, 2023, pp. 1–10.

53. J. Fernandez, J. Lee, and K. Landis, "Helping Gen Z Employees Find Their Place at Work," *Harvard Business Review,* January 18, 2023, https://hbr.org/2023/01/helping-gen-z-employees-find-their-place-at-work.

54. H.M. Woznyj et al., "Job Attitudes: A Meta-Analytic Review and an Agenda for Future Research," *Journal of Organizational Behavior,* Vol. 43, No. 5 (2022), pp. 946–964.

55. "Building Life Skills for Career Readiness and Workplace Success," *Committee for Children,* https://www.cfchildren.org/policy-collateral/one-pagers/building-life-skills-for-career-readiness-and-workplace-success/ (accessed May 5, 2023).

56. L. Festinger, *A Theory of Cognitive Dissonance* (Stanford, CA: Stanford University Press, 1957).

57. A.H. Tangari, J. Kees, J.C. Andrews, and S. Burton, "Can Corrective Ad Statements Based on *U.S. v. Philip Morris USA Inc.* Impact Consumer Beliefs about Smoking?" *Journal of Public Policy & Marketing.* Vol. 29, No. 2 (2010), pp. 153–169.

58. Adapted from R. Kreitner and A. Kinicki, *Organizational Behavior,* 10th ed. (New York: McGraw-Hill/Irwin, 2013), Figure 7-1, p. 181.

59. M. Anderson, "Most Americans Say Racial Bias Is a Problem in the Workplace. Can AI Help?" *Pew Research,* April 20, 2023, https://www.pewresearch.org/short-reads/2023/04/20/most-americans-say-racial-bias-is-a-problem-in-the-workplace-can-ai-help/; T. Brewer, "Gender Stereotypes Still Matter at Work but New Data Shows Progress," *Forbes,* October 10, 2022, https://www.forbes.com/sites/tracybrower/2022/10/10/gender-stereotypes-still-matter-at-work-but-new-data-shows-progress/?sh=58cd44c63f3c.

60. "Careers," *Aptive,* https://careers.goaptive.com/us/en/job/R101998/Pest-Control-Technician#:~:text=In%202021%2C%20Aptive%20was%20included,Magazine's%20Best%20Companies%20in%20America (accessed May 15, 2023); "Summer Sales Paid Internship," *Aptive,* https://elevate.iit.edu/jobs/aptive-environmental-corporate-summer-sales-paid-internship-2/ (accessed May 15, 2023); L. Martis, "10 Companies That Really Care about Their Older Workers," *Monster,* https://www.monster.com/career-advice/article/companies-friendly-toward-older-workers-1217 (accessed May 15, 2023).

61. "Explicit Bias," *Perception Institute*, https://perception.org/research/explicit-bias/ (accessed April 9, 2020).

62. P. Connor, M. Weeks, J. Glaser, S. Chen, and D. Keltner, "Intersectional Implicit Bias: Evidence for Asymmetrically Compounding Bias and the Predominance of Target Gender," *Journal of Personality and Social Psychology*, Vol. 124, No. 1 (2023), pp. 22–48.

63. A. Vaxquez, "How to Mitigate Your Unconscious Bias," *Gladstone,* August 2, 2022, https://gladstone.org/news/how-mitigate-your-unconscious-bias; K. Payne, L. Niemi, and J.M. Doris, "How to Think about 'Implicit Bias,'" *Scientific American*, March 27, 2018, https://www.scientificamerican.com/article/how-to-think-about-implicit-bias/.

64. P. Connor, M. Weeks, J. Glaser, S. Chen, and D. Keltner, "Intersectional Implicit Bias: Evidence for Asymmetrically Compounding Bias and the Predominance of Target Gender," *Journal of Personality and Social Psychology*, Vol. 124, No. 1 (2023), pp. 22–48.

65. J. Saunders and G. Midgette, "A Test for Implicit Bias in Discretionary Criminal Justice Decisions," *Law and Human Behavior*, Vol. 47, No. 1 (2023), p. 217; I. Krajbich, "Decomposing Implicit Bias," *Psychological Inquiry*, Vol. 33, No. 3 (2022), pp. 181–184.

66. G.B. Cunningham and H.R. Cunningham, "Bias among Managers: Its Prevalence across a Decade and Comparison across Occupations," *Frontiers in Psychology*, 2022, p. 7216.

67. "Racial and Ethnic Disparities in the Justice System," *National Conference of State Legislatures,* May, 2022, https://documents.ncsl.org/wwwncsl/Criminal-Justice/Racial-and-Ethnic-Disparities-in-the-Justice-System_v03.pdf.

68. K.D. Elsbach and I. Stigliani, "New Information Technology and Implicit Bias," *Academy of Management Perspective*, May 2019, pp. 185–206.

69. J. Pei, X. Yang, R. Zheng, and Z. Wang, "The Effects of Physical Discrimination on Income," in *5th International Conference on Humanities Education and Social Sciences* (ICHESS Atlantis Press 2022) pp. 56–62; H. Zacher and C. von Hippel, "Weight-Based Stereotype Threat in the Workplace: Consequences for Employees with Overweight or Obesity," *International Journal of Obesity*, Vol. 46, No. 4 (2022), pp. 767–773.

70. See example about traits in X. Fang, G.A. van Kleef, and D.A. Sauter, "Person Perception from Changing Emotional Expressions: Primacy, Recency, or Averaging Effect?" *Cognition and Emotion*, 2018, pp. 1597–1610. Also see S. Guéraud, E.K. Walsh, A.E. Cook, and E.J. O'Brien, "Validating Information during Reading: The Effect of Recency," *Journal of Research in Reading*, 2018, pp. S85–S101.

71. R. Pinsker and E. Taylor, "Leveling the Playing Field: How Assurance Mitigates the Negative Effect of Unfamiliarity among Nonprofessional Investors," in *Advances in Accounting Behavioral Research* (Emerald Publishing Limited 2023) pp. 79–101.

72. J. Denrell, C. Fang, and C. Liu, "In Search of Behavioral Opportunities from Misattributions of Luck," *Academy of Management Review*, October 2019, pp. 896–915.

73. S. Wen, "The Effect of Result Publicity on Self-Serving Attributional Bias—a Social Comparison Perspective," *Frontiers of Business Research in China*, 2018, https://doi.org/10.1186/s11782-018-0028-8.

74. K. Cherry, "How the Self-Serving Bias Protects Self-Esteem," *Verywellmind*, February 12, 2018, https://www.verywellmind.com/what-is-the-self-serving-bias-2795032.

75. J. Weaver, J.F. Moses, and M. Snyder, "Self-Fulfilling Prophecies in Ability Settings," *Journal of Social Psychology,* Vol. 156, no 2 (2016), pp. 179–189.

76. These recommendations were adapted from J. Keller, "Have Faith—in You," *Selling Power,* June 1996, pp. 84, 86. Also see R.W. Goddard, "The Pygmalion Effect," *Personnel Journal*, June 1985, p. 10; J.S. Livingston, "Pygmalion in Management," *Harvard Business Review,* January 2003, https://hbr.org/2003/01/pygmalion-in-management; R.E. Riggio, "Pygmalion Leadership: The Power of Positive Expectations," *Psychology Today,* April 18, 2009, https://www.psychologytoday.com/blog/cutting-edge-leadership/200904/pygmalion-leadership-the-power-positive-expectations; G. Swanson, "The Pygmalion Effect: How It Drives Employee Performance," *LinkedIn,* September 24, 2014, https://www.linkedin.com/pulse/20140924142003-9878138-the-pygmalion-effect-how-it-drives-employees-performance.

77. "About Erik," *Erik Weihenmayer*, https://erikweihenmayer.com/about-erik/ (accessed April 18, 2020).

78. N. Angley, "All of Us in a Way Are Climbing Blind," *CNN,* May 11, 2016, www.cnn.com/2016/05/11/health/turning-points-erik-weihenmayer/index.html.

79. *No Barriers,* https://www.nobarriersusa.org/?gclid=EAIaIQobChMIgvGIhNWU2gIVVpN-Ch2G2Q4vEAAYASAAEgLtMvD_BwE (accessed April 11, 2018).

80. J. Hoedel, "Erik Weihenmayer—Determination," *Character Development & Leadership,* https://characterandleadership.com/erik-weihenmayer-determination/ (accessed May 11, 2023).

81. J. Hoedel, "Erik Weihenmayer—Determination," *Character Development & Leadership,* https://characterandleadership.com/erik-weihenmayer-determination/ (accessed May 11, 2023).
82. *No Barriers,* https://www.nobarriersusa.org/?gclid=EAIaIQobChMIgvGlhNWU2gIVVpN-Ch2G2Q4vEAAYASAAEgLtMvD_BwE (accessed April 11, 2018).
83. M. Dabney, "At No Barriers Summit: Aira Is Showcased as the Novel Technology Service That Helps the Blind Become Even More 'Adventurous,'" *Medium,* July 6, 2016, https://medium.com/aira-io/at-no-barriers-summit-aira-is-showcased-as-the-novel-technology-service-that-helps-the-blind-become-5a98845242ce.
84. A. Hackett, "The Ends of the Earth," *Boston College,* January, 2022, https://www.bc.edu/bc-web/bcnews/campus-community/alumni/the-ends-of-the-earth-.html.
85. A. Hackett, "The Ends of the Earth," *Boston College,* January, 2022, https://www.bc.edu/bc-web/bcnews/campus-community/alumni/the-ends-of-the-earth-.html.
86. C. Marshall, "How the First Blind Man to Summit Mount Everest Changed My Perspective on Fear," *Huffington Post,* May 25, 2017, www.huffingtonpost.com/entry/how-the-first-blind-man-to-summit-mount-everest-changed_us_59161939e4b02d6199b2ef04.
87. E. Weihenmayer, interview with the American Foundation for the Blind, https://www.afb.org/node/11132?page=13 (accessed March 24, 2020).
88. R.M. Vogel, J.B. Rodell, and A. Agolli, "Daily Engagement and Productivity: The Importance of the Speed of Engagement," *Journal of Applied Psychology,* Vol. 107, No. 9 (2022), pp. 1579–1599.
89. M.A. Uddin, M. Mahmood, and L. Fan, "Why Individual Employee Engagement Matters for Team Performance?" *Team Performance Management: An International Journal,* March 2019, pp. 47–67. Also see B. Schneider, A.B. Yost, A. Kropp, C. Kind, and H. Lam, "Workforce Engagement: What It Is, What Drives It, and Why It Matters for Organizational Performance," *Journal of Organizational Behavior,* May 2018, pp. 462–480; "A.M. Saks, "Translating Employee Engagement Research into Practice," *Organizational Dynamics,* April–June 2017, pp. 76–86; J.P. Meyer, "Has Engagement Had Its Day: What's Next and Does It Matter," *Organizational Dynamics,* April–June 2017, pp. 87–95; R. Muller, E. Smith, and R. Lillah, "The Impact of Employee Engagement on Organisational Performance: A Balanced Scorecard Approach," *International Journal of Economics and Finance Studies,* 2018, pp. 22–38; A. Madden and C. Bailey, "Engagement: Where Has All the 'Power' Gone?" *Organizational Dynamics,* 2017, pp. 113–119; M.R. Antony, "Paradigm Shift in Employee Engagement—A Critical Analysis on the Drivers of Employee Engagement," *International Journal of Information, Business and Management,* 2018, pp. 32–46.
90. M. Hayes, F. Chumney, C. Wright, and M. Buckingham, "The Global Study of Engagement Technical Report," *ADP Research Institute,* 2019, https://www.adp.com/-/media/adp/resourcehub/pdf/adpri/adpri0102_2018_engagement_study_technical_report_release%20ready.ashx. Also see M. Perry, "Engagement around the World, Charted," *Harvard Business Review,* May 15, 2019, https://hbr.org/2019/05/engagement-around-the-world-charted.
91. J. Harter, "U.S. Employee Engagement Needs a Rebound in 2023," *Gallup,* January 25, 2023, https://www.gallup.com/workplace/468233/employee-engagement-needs-rebound-2023.aspx.
92. For a review, see: G. Boccoli, L. Gastaldi, and M. Corso, "The Evolution of Employee Engagement: Towards a Social and Contextual Construct for Balancing Individual Performance and Wellbeing Dynamically," *International Journal of Management Reviews,* Vol. 25, No. 1 (2023), pp. 75–98.
93. "Nordstrom, Inc." *Great Place to Work,* https://www.greatplacetowork.com/certified-company/1000395#:~:text=74%25%20of%20employees%20at%20Nordstrom,a%20typical%20U.S.%2Dbased%20company (accessed May 12, 2023).
94. "Code of Business Conduct and Ethics," *Nordstrom,* January, 2022, https://press.nordstrom.com/static-files/952f5e64-473c-47c2-a396-3ddb81b303db.
95. D. Fernandes, "15 Companies Taking Employee Engagement to the Next Level," *Nudge,* May 9, 2022, https://nudge.co/blog/brands-taking-the-employee-experience-to-the-next-level/.
96. G. Boccoli, L. Gastaldi, and M. Corso, "The Evolution of Employee Engagement: Towards a Social and Contextual Construct for Balancing Individual Performance and Wellbeing Dynamically," *International Journal of Management Reviews,* Vol. 25, No. 1 (2023), pp. 75–98.
97. J. Kelly, "If Your Work Lacks Purpose, Make It More Meaningful through Job Crafting," *Forbes,* April 6, 2019, https://www.forbes.com/sites/jackkelly/2019/08/06/if-your-work-lacks-purpose-make-it-more-meaningful-through-job-crafting/#4c1886336416.
98. For a review, see: G. Boccoli, L. Gastaldi, and M. Corso, "The Evolution of Employee Engagement: Towards a Social and Contextual Construct for Balancing Individual Performance and Wellbeing Dynamically," *International Journal of Management Reviews,* Vol. 25, No. 1 (2023), pp. 75–98.
99. A.M. Saks, "Caring Human Resources Management and Employee Engagement," *Human Resource Management Review,* Vol. 32, No. 3 (2022), p. 100835.
100. A. Chopra-McGowan, "Effective Employee Development Starts with Managers," *Harvard Business Review Digital Articles,* 2022, pp. 1–7.
101. "2022 Workplace Learning & Development Trends," *Society for Human Resource Management,* 2022, https://www.shrm.org/hr-today/trends-and-forecasting/research-and-surveys/Documents/2022%20Workplace%20Learning%20and%20Development%20Trends%20Report.pdf.
102. "We Hire Happy People," *1800-GOT-JUNK?,* https://jobs.1800gotjunk.com/us_en/its-all-about-people/starting-career-1-800-got-junk-franchise-journey-will-take-you-places (accessed May 9, 2023).
103. T.J. Wu, K.S. Yuan, D.C. Yen, and C.F. Yeh, "The Effects of JDC Model on Burnout and Work Engagement: A Multiple Interaction Analysis," *European Management Journal,* Vol. 43, No. 3 (2023), pp. 395–403.
104. K. Weise, "Doctors Fear Bringing Coronavirus Home: 'I Am Sort of a Pariah in My Family,'" *The New York Times,* March 17, 2020, https://www.nytimes.com/2020/03/16/us/coronavirus-doctors-nurses.html.
105. These five job dimensions are developed by researchers at Cornell University as part of the Job Descriptive Index. For a review of the development of the JDI, see P.C. Smith, L.M. Kendall, and C.L. Hulin, *The Measurement of Satisfaction in Work and Retirement* (Skokie, IL: Rand McNally, 1969).
106. K. Ng, E. Franken, D. Nguyen, and S. Teo, "Job Satisfaction and Public Service Motivation in Australian Nurses: The effects of Abusive Supervision and Workplace Bullying," *The International Journal of Human Resource Management,* 2022, pp. 1-30; K.N. Khan, A. Ali, A. Adnan, Z. Ibrahim, and A. Haider, "Impact of Job Involvement and Employee Engagement on Job Satisfaction under Empowering Leadership in Private Hospitals," *Journal of Management Info,* Vol. 9, No. 2 (2022), pp. 174–188; J. Wegge, K.H. Schmidt, C. Parkes, and R. Van Dick, "Taking a Sickie: Job Satisfaction and Job Involvement as Interactive Predictors of Absenteeism in a Public Organization," *Journal of Occupational and Organizational Psychology,* Vol. 80, No. 1 (2007), pp. 77–89; D.J. Prottas, "Perceived Behavioral Integrity: Relationships with Employee Attitudes, Well-Being, and Absenteeism," *Journal of Business Ethics,* Vol. 81 (2008), pp. 313–322.
107. J. Horowitz and K. Parker, "How Americans View Their Jobs," *Pew Research,* March 30, 2023, https://www.pewresearch.org/social-trends/2023/03/30/how-americans-view-their-jobs/.
108. T.A. Judge, C.J. Thoresen, J.E. Bono, and G.K. Patton, "The Job Satisfaction–Job Performance Relationship: A Qualitative and Quantitative Review," *Psychological Bulletin,* May 2001, pp. 376–407; R. Kreitner and A. Kinicki, *Organizational Behavior,* 10th ed. (New York: McGraw Hill/Irwin, 2013), pp. 168–170.
109. A. Katebi, M.H. HajiZadeh, A. Bordbar, and A.M. Salehi, "The Relationship between 'Job Satisfaction' and 'Job Performance': A Meta-Analysis," *Global Journal of Flexible Systems Management,* Vol. 23, No. 1 (2022), pp. 21–42; T.A. Judge, H.M. Weiss, J.D. Kammeyer-Mueller, and

C. L. Hulin, "Job Attitudes, Job Satisfaction, and Job Affect: A Century of Continuity and of Change," *Journal of Applied Psychology,* March 2017, pp. 356–374.

110. A. Shahjehan, B. Afsar, and S.I. Shah, "Is Organizational Commitment–Job Satisfaction Relationship Necessary for Organizational Commitment–Citizenship Behavior Relationships? A Meta-Analytical Necessary Condition Analysis," *Economic Research,* August 2019, pp. 2657–2679. Also see A. Berberoglu, "Impact of Organizational Climate on Organizational Commitment and Perceived Organizational Performance: Empirical Evidence from Public Hospitals," *BMC Health Services Research,* June 2018, https://doi.org/10.1186/s12913-018-3149-z; A.H. Kabins, X. Xu, M.E. Bergman, C.M. Berry, and V.L Wilson, "A Profile of Profiles: A Meta-Analysis of the Nomological Net of Commitment Profiles," *Journal of Applied Psychology,* June 2016, pp. 881–904.

111. W.M. To and G. Huang, "Effects of Equity, Perceived Organizational Support and Job Satisfaction on Organizational Commitment in Macao's Gaming Industry," *Management Decision,* Vol. 60, No. 9 (2022), pp. 2433–2454; For a further review of commitment research, see the entire May 2016 issue of *Journal of Organizational Behavior,* May 2016, pp. 489–632. Also see S. Belwalkar, V. Vohra, and A. Pandey, "The Relationship between Workplace Spirituality, Job Satisfaction and Organizational Citizenship Behaviors—An Empirical Study," *Social Responsibility Journal,* June 2018, pp. 410–430.

112. H.J. Anderson and M.C. Bolino, "Haunted by the Past: How Performing or Withholding Organizational Citizenship Behavior May Lead to Regret," *Journal of Organizational Behavior,* Vol. 44, No. 2 (2023), pp. 297–310.

113. A.C. Klotz, M.C. Bolino, H. Song, and J. Stornelli, "Examining the Nature, Causes, and Consequences of Profiles of Organizational Citizenship Behavior," *Journal of Organizational Behavior,* June 2018, pp. 629–647.

114. S. Belwalkar, V. Vohra, and A. Pandey, "The Relationship between Workplace Spirituality, Job Satisfaction and Organizational Citizenship Behaviors—an Empirical Study," *Social Responsibility Journal,* June 2018, pp. 410–430. Also see N.P. Podsakoff, S.W. Whiting, P.M. Podsakoff, and B.D. Blume, "Individual- and Organizational-Level Consequences of Organizational Citizenship Behaviors: A Meta-Analysis," *Journal of Applied Psychology,* January 2009, pp. 122–141; D.S. Whitman, D.L. Van Rooy, and C. Viswesvaran, "Satisfaction, Citizenship Behaviors, and Performance in Work Units: A Meta-Analysis of Collective Relations," *Personnel Psychology,* Spring 2010, pp. 41–81; A.C. Klotz, M.C. Bolino, H. Song, and J. Stornelli, "Examining the Nature, Causes, and Consequences of Profiles of Organizational Citizenship Behavior," *Journal of Organizational Behavior,* June 2018, pp. 629–647.

115. E. Netchaeva, R. Ilies, M. Magni, and J. Yao, "What We Are Pushed to Do versus What We Want to Do: Comparing the Unique Effects of Citizenship Pressure and Actual Citizenship Behavior on Fatigue and Family Behaviors," *Journal of Vocational Behavior,* 2023. p. 103845.

116. W. Zhang, S. Zheng, J. Luca Pletzer, D. Derks, K. Breevaart, and X. Zhang, "How to Cope with an Abusive Leader? Examinations of Subordinates' Affective Reactions, CWB-O and Turnover Intentions," *Journal of Leadership & Organizational Studies,* Vol. 29, No. 4 (2022), pp. 389–408.

117. E.L. Anderson, M. McGue, P.R. Sackett, and W.G. Iacono, "Familial Resemblance, Citizenship, and Counterproductive Work Behavior: A Combined Twin, Adoption, Parent–Offspring, and Spouse Approach," *Journal of Applied Psychology,* Vol. 107, No. 12 (2022), p. 2334; Also see P.E. Spector and S. Fox, "Theorizing about the Deviant Citizen: An Attributional Explanation of the Interplay of Organizational Citizenship and Counterproductive Work Behavior," *Human Resource Management Review,* June 2010, pp. 132–143; J. Wu and J.M. Lebreton, "Reconsidering the Dispositional Basis of Counterproductive Work Behavior: The Role of Aberrant Personality," *Personnel Psychology,* Vol. 64 (2011), pp. 593–626; L.L. Meier and P.E. Spector, "Reciprocal Effects of Work Stressors and Counterproductive Work Behavior: A Five-Wave Longitudinal Study," *Journal of Applied Psychology,* May 2013, pp. 529–539.

118. M. Lovett, *The Relationship between Experienced Workplace Incivility and Pre-Quitting Behaviors: A Model of Mediated Moderation* (Doctoral dissertation, Louisiana Tech University 2022).

119. N.C. Carpenter, B. Rangel, G. Jeon, and J. Cottrell, "Are Supervisors and Coworkers Likely to Witness Employee Counterproductive Work Behavior? An Investigation of Observability and Self-Observer Convergence," *Personnel Psychology,* Winter 2017, pp. 843–889.

120. J. Deng, X. Hao, and T. Yang, "The Increase of Counterproductive Work Behaviour from Organizational and Individual Level Due to Workplace Conflict: A Sequential Moderated Mediation Model," *International Journal of Conflict Management,* Vol. 34, No. 2 (2023), pp. 213–233.

121. J.J. Lavelle et al., "Multifoci Effects of Injustice on Counterproductive Work Behaviors and the Moderating Roles of Symbolization and Victim Sensitivity," *Journal of Organizational Behavior,* October 2018, pp. 1022–1039. Also see J.R. Detert, L.K. Treviño, E.R. Burris, and M. Andiappan, "Managerial Modes of Influence and Counterproductivity in Organizations: A Longitudinal Business-Unit-Level Investigation," *Journal of Applied Psychology,* July 2007, pp. 993–1005; Z.E. Zhou, E.M. Eatough, and D.R. Wald, "Feeling Insulted? Examining End-of-Work Anger as a Mediator in the Relationship between Daily Illegitimate Tasks and Next-Day CWB," *Journal of Organizational Behavior,* January 2018, pp. 911–921; J. Yang and D.C. Treadway, "A Social Influence Interpretation of Workplace Ostracism and Counterproductive Work Behavior," *Journal of Business Ethics,* April 2018, pp. 879–891.

122. I.M. Jawahar, B. Schreurs, "Supervisor Incivility and How It Affects Subordinates' Performance: A Matter of Trust," *Personnel Review,* April 2018, pp. 709–726.

123. X. Hu, M. Dong, Y. Li, and M. Wang, "The Cross-Level Influence of Authoritarian Leadership on Counterproductive Work Behavior: A Moderated Mediation Model," *Current Psychology,* 2022, pp. 1–14.

124. C. Porath, "How to Avoid Hiring a Toxic Employee," *Harvard Business Review,* February 3, 2016, https://hbr.org/2016/02/how-to-avoid-hiring-a-toxic-employee.

125. C. Porath, "How to Avoid Hiring a Toxic Employee," *Harvard Business Review,* February 3, 2016, https://hbr.org/2016/02/how-to-avoid-hiring-a-toxic-employee.

126. T. Foulk, quoted in R.E. Silverman, "Workplace Rudeness Is as Contagious as a Cold," *The Wall Street Journal,* August 12, 2015, p. B7. Also see T. Foulk, A. Woolum, and A. Erez, "Catching Rudeness Is Like Catching a Cold: The Contagion Effects of Low-Intensity Negative Behaviors," *Journal of Applied Psychology,* Vol. 101, No. 1 (2016), pp. 50–67.

127. L.S. Park and L.R. Martinez, "An 'I' for an 'I': A Systematic Review and Meta-Analysis of Instigated and Reciprocal Incivility," *Journal of Occupational Health Psychology,* Vol. 27, No. 1 (2022), p. 7.

128. C. Porath, "No Time to Be Nice," *The New York Times,* June 21, 2015, p. SR–1

129. G. Spreizer, quoted in B. Hyslop, "Bad Attitudes Can Sap Workers' Energy and Productivity," *Providence Journal,* July 4, 2015. Also see P. Korkki, "Thwarting the Jerk at Work," *The New York Times,* November 22, 2015, p. BU-4; C.L. Porath and A. Erez, "Does Rudeness Really Matter? The Effects of Rudeness on Task Performance and Helpfulness," *Academy of Management Journal,* Vol. 50, No. 5 (2007), pp. 1181–1197; A. Gerbasi, C.L. Porath, A. Parker, G. Spreitzer, and R. Cross, "Destructive De-energizing Relationships: How Thriving Buffers Their Effect on Performance," *Journal of Applied Psychology,* Vol. 100, No. 5 (2015), pp. 1423–1433; C.L. Porath, A. Gerbasi, and S.L. Schorch, "The Effects of Civility on Advice, Leadership, and Performance," *Journal of Applied Psychology,* Vol. 100, No. 5 (2015), pp. 1527–1541.

130. L.S. Park and L.R. Martinez, "An 'I' for an 'I': A Systematic Review and Meta-Analysis of Instigated and Reciprocal Incivility," *Journal of Occupational Health Psychology,* Vol. 27, No. 1 (2022), p. 7.

131. M. Feinberg, B.Q. Ford, and F.J. Flynn, "Rethinking Reappraisal: The Double-Edged Sword of Regulating Negative Emotions in the

132. L.S. Park and L.R. Martinez, "An 'I' for an 'I': A Systematic Review and Meta-Analysis of Instigated and Reciprocal Incivility," *Journal of Occupational Health Psychology*, Vol. 27, No. 1 (2022), p. 7.

133. M. Hershcovis, B. Ogunfowora, T. Reich, and A. Christie, "Targeted Workplace Incivility: The Roles of Belongingness, Embarrassment, and Power," *Journal of Organizational Behavior*, Vol. 38 (2017), pp. 1057–1075.

134. J. Mercer, "Google Searches for Excuses to Miss Work Are at a Five-Year High," *Frank Recruitment Group,* November 1, 2022, https://www.frankgroup.com/blog/google-searches-for-excuses-to-miss-work-are-at-a-five-year-high/.

135. M.C. Kocakulah, A.G. Kelley, K.M. Mitchell, and M.P. Ruggieri, "Absenteeism Problems and Costs: Causes, Effects, and Cures," *International Business & Economics Research Journal,* May/June 2016, pp. 81–88. Also see C.R.S. de Carvalho, M.A.R. Castro, L.P. da Silva, and L.O.P. de Carvalho, "The Relationship between Organizational Culture, Organizational Commitment and Job Satisfaction," *Revista Brasileira de Estrategia*, January 2018, pp. 201–215.

136. C.P. Maertz Jr, M.G. Keith, S. Raghuram, C.M. Porter, and G.L. Dalton, "Advancing Theory and Practice on Managing Dysfunctional Turnover: Developing an Improved Measure of Turnover Reasons," *Group & Organization Management*, Vol. 48, No. 5 (2022), 10596011211065880.

137. J. Stowers, "Employee Retention: What Does Your Turnover Rate Tell You?" *Business,* February 21, 2023, https://www.business.com/articles/employee-turnover-rate/.

138. C.P. Maertz Jr, M.G. Keith, S. Raghuram, C.M. Porter, and G.L. Dalton, "Advancing Theory and Practice on Managing Dysfunctional Turnover: Developing an Improved Measure of Turnover Reasons," *Group & Organization Management*, Vol. 48, No. 5 (2022), 10596011211065880.

139. K. Navarra, "The Real Costs of Recruitment," *SHRM,* April 11, 2022, https://www.shrm.org/resourcesandtools/hr-topics/talent-acquisition/pages/the-real-costs-of-recruitment.aspx.

140. C.P. Maertz Jr, M.G. Keith, S. Raghuram, C.M. Porter, and G.L. Dalton, "Advancing Theory and Practice on Managing Dysfunctional Turnover: Developing an Improved Measure of Turnover Reasons," *Group & Organization Management*, Vol. 48, No. 5 (2022), 10596011211065880; C.M. Porter, S.E. Woo, D.G. Allen, M.G. Keith, "How Do Instrumental and Expressive Network Positions Relate to Turnover? A Meta-Analytic Investigation," *Journal of Applied Psychology,* April 2019, pp. 511–536; C.M. Porter et al., "On-the-Job and Off-the-Job Embeddedness Differentially Influence Relationships between Informal Job Search and Turnover," *Journal of Applied Psychology*, May 2019, pp. 678–689.

141. R.S. Lazarus, *Psychological Stress and Coping Processes* (New York: McGraw-Hill, 1966); R.S. Schuler, "Definition and Conceptualization of Stress in Organizations," *Organizational Behavior and Human Performance,* April 1980, pp. 184–215.

142. "Work Related Stress on Employees Health," *EKU Online,* https://safetymanagement.eku.edu/resources/infographics/work-related-stress-on-employees-health/ (accessed March 31, 2020). Also see "Workplace Stress," *The American Institute of Stress*, https://www.stress.org/workplace-stress (accessed March 31, 2020).

143. H. Godman, "Top Ways to Reduce Daily Stress," *Harvard Health Publishing,* March 1, 2022, https://www.health.harvard.edu/staying-healthy/top-ways-to-reduce-daily-stress; Also see "Workplace Stress: A Silent Killer of Employee Health and Productivity," *Corporate Wellness Magazine,* https://www.corporatewellnessmagazine.com/article/workplace-stress-silent-killer-employee-health-productivity (accessed March 31, 2020). Also see E. Scott, "How to Deal With Stress-Related Insomnia," *Very Well Mind,* January 28, 2020, https://www.verywellmind.com/stress-related-insomnia-3144827.

144. "Workplace Stress," *The American Institute of Stress,* https://www.stress.org/workplace-stress (accessed May 12, 2023).

145. H. Cheng, Y. Fan, and H. Lau, "An Integrative Review on Job Burnout among Teachers in China: Implications for Human Resource Management," *The International Journal of Human Resource Management*, Vol. 34, No. 3 (2023), pp. 529–561.

146. W. Salama, A.H. Abdou, S.A.K. Mohamed, and H.S. Shehata, "Impact of Work Stress and Job Burnout on Turnover Intentions among Hotel Employees," *International Journal of Environmental Research and Public Health*, Vol. 19, No. 15 (2022), p. 9724.

147. K. du Bois, P. Sterkens, L. Lippens, S. Baert, and E. Derous, "Beyond the Hype: (How) Are Work Regimes Associated with Job Burnout?" *International Journal of Environmental Research and Public Health*, Vol. 20, No. 4 (2023), p. 3331.

148. H. Selye, *Stress without Distress* (New York: Lippincott, 1974), p. 27.

149. R. Koerber, M. Rouse, K. Stanyar, M. Pelletier, "Building Resilience in the Workforce," *Organizational Dynamics*, April 2018, pp. 124–134.

150. P.D. Bliese, J.R. Edwards, and S. Sonnentag, "Stress and Well-Being at Work: A Century of Empirical Trends Reflecting Theoretical and Societal Influences," *Journal of Applied Psychology,* March 2017, pp. 380–402.

151. C. Zhang, D.M. Mayer, and E. Hwang, "More Is Less: Learning but Not Relaxing Buffers Deviance under Job Stressors," *Journal of Applied Psychology*, February 2018, pp. 123–136; P.D. Bliese, J.R. Edwards, and S. Sonnentag, "Stress and Well-Being at Work: A Century of Empirical Trends Reflecting Theoretical and Societal Influences," *Journal of Applied Psychology,* March 2017, pp. 380–402.

152. T. He, Z. Wu, X. Zhang, H. Liu, Y. Wang, R. Jiang, C. Liu, K. Hashimoto, and C. Yang, "A Bibliometric Analysis of Research on the Role of BDNF in Depression and Treatment," *Biomolecules*, Vol. 12, No. 10 (2022), p. 1464.

153. M. Friedman and R.H. Rosenman, *Type A Behavior and Your Heart* (Greenwich, CT: Fawcett Publications, 1974), p. 84.

154. M.S. Taylor, E.A. Locke, C. Lee, and M.E. Gist, "Type A Behavior and Faculty Research Productivity: What Are the Mechanisms?" *Organizational Behavior and Human Performance,* December 1984, pp. 402–418; S.D. Bluen, J. Barling, and W. Burns, "Predicting Sales Performance, Job Satisfaction, and Depression by Using the Achievement Strivings and Impatience–Irritability Dimensions of Type A Behavior," *Journal of Applied Psychology,* April 1990, pp. 212–216.

155. S. Booth-Kewley and H.S. Friedman, "Psychological Predictors of Heart Disease: A Quantitative Review," *Psychological Bulletin,* May 1987, pp. 343–362; S.A. Lyness, "Predictors of Differences between Type A and B Individuals in Heart Rate and Blood Pressure Reactivity," *Psychological Bulletin,* September 1993, pp. 266–295; T.Q. Miller, T.W. Smith, C.W. Turner, M.L. Guijarro, and A.J. Hallet, "A Meta-Analytic Review of Research on Hostility and Physical Health," *Psychological Bulletin,* March 1996, pp. 322–348.

156. P. Watson, "Stress, PTSD, and COVID-19: The Utility of Disaster Mental Health Interventions during the COVID-19 Pandemic," *Current Treatment Options in Psychiatry*, Vol. 9, No. 1 (2022), pp. 14–40.

157. M. Richtel, "In Web World of 24/7 Stress, Writers Blog Till They Drop," *The New York Times,* April 6, 2008, news section, pp. 1, 23.

158. W.J. Hwang and E.H. Park, "Developing a Structural Equation Model from Grandey's Emotional Regulation Model to Measure Nurses' Emotional Labor, Job Satisfaction, and Job Performance," *Applied Nursing Research*, Vol 64 (2022), p. 151557.

159. "Stressful Jobs That Pay Badly," *CNN Money,* March 7, 2014, http://money.cnn.com/gallery/pf/jobs/2013/03/07/jobs-stress-pay (accessed July 19, 2016).

160. C. Hoare and C. Vandenberghe, "Are They Created Equal? A Relative Weights Analysis of the Contributions of Job Demands and Resources to Well-Being and Turnover Intention," *Psychological Reports*, 2022, p. 1.

161. K. Vangrieken, N. De Cuyper, and H. De Witte, "Karasek's Activation Hypothesis: A Longitudinal Test of Within-Person Relationships," *Journal of Organizational Behavior*, Vol. 44, No. 3 (2023), pp. 495–518.

162. E. Reid and L. Ramarajan, "Managing the High Intensity Workplace," *Harvard Business Review,* June 2016, pp. 85–90.

163. J.H. Wayne, M.M. Butts, W.J. Casper, and T.D. Allen, "In Search of Balance: A Conceptual and Empirical Integration of Multiple Meanings of Work-Family Balance," *Personnel Psychology,* Vol. 70, No. 1 (2017), pp. 167–210. Also see S.J. Wayne, G. Lemmon, J.M. Hoobler, G.W. Cheung, and M.S. Wilson, "The Ripple Effect: A Spillover Model of the Detrimental Impact of Work-Family Conflict on Job Success," *Journal of Organizational Behavior,* July 2017, pp. 876–894.

164. A. Moreira et al., "Conflict (Work-Family and Family-Work) and Task Performance: The Role of Well-Being in This Relationship," *Administrative Sciences (2076–3387),* Vol. 13, No. 4 (2023), p. 94.

165. A. Hirschi, K.M. Shockley, and H. Zacher, "Achieving Work-Family Balance: An Action Regulation Model," *Academy of Management Review,* January 2019, pp. 150–171. Also see A. Cazan, C. Truţă, M. Pavalache-Ilie, "The Work-Life Conflict and Satisfaction with Life: Correlates and the Mediating Role of the Work-Family Conflict," *Romanian Journal of Applied Psychology,* June 2019, pp. 3–10; R. Ilies, X-Y. Liu, Y. Liu, and X. Zheng, "Why Do Employees Have Better Family Lives When They Are Highly Engaged at Work?" *Journal of Applied Psychology,* June 2017, pp. 956–970; J.I. Menges, D.V. Tussing, A. Wihler, and A.M. Grant, "When Job Performance Is All Relative: How Family Motivation Energizes Effort and Compensates for Intrinsic Motivation," *Academy of Management Journal,* April 2017, pp. 695–719; J. Choi et al., "Antecedents and Consequences of Satisfaction with Work-Family Balance: A Moderating Role of Perceived Insider Status," *Journal of Organizational Behavior,* January 2018, pp. 1–11.

166. J. Alpert, "Yes, Secondhand Stress Is a Thing. Here's How to Protect Yourself—And Others," *Inc.,* March 31, 2017, https://www.inc.com/jonathan-alper/what-you-need-to-know-about-secondhand-stress.html.

167. J. Kim, "8 Traits of Toxic Leadership to Avoid," *Psychology Today,* July 6, 2016, https://www.psychologytoday.com/us/blog/culture-shrink/201607/8-traits-toxic-leadership-avoid.

168. G. Staglin, "Prioritizing Mental Health in a 'Remote First' Workplace," *Forbes,* May 31, 2022, https://www.forbes.com/sites/onemind/2022/05/31/prioritizing-mental-health-in-a-remote-first-workplace/?sh=7857a9102a51.

169. K. Bishop, "Is Remote Work Worse for WellBeing Than People Think?" *BBC,* June 17, 2022, https://www.bbc.com/worklife/article/20220616-is-remote-work-worse-for-wellbeing-than-people-think.

170. "The Invisible Strain of Screen Time: How It Impacts Remote Workers and Freelancer's Mental Health," *World Health.Net,* February 20, 2023, https://www.worldhealth.net/news/invisible-strain-screen-time-how-it-impacts-remote-workers-and-freelancers-mental-health/#:~:text=Research%20has%20shown%20that%20excessive,and%20other%20mental%20health%20issues.

171. E. Rohwer, J.C. Flöther, V. Harth, and S. Mache, "Overcoming the 'Dark Side' of Technology—A Scoping Review on Preventing and Coping with Work-Related Technostress," *International Journal of Environmental Research and Public Health,* Vol. 19, No. 6 (2022), p. 3625.

172. J. Kelly, "Belgium, Portugal and Other European Countries Prohibit Managers from Contacting Employees outside of Working Hours," *Forbes,* February 3, 2022, https://www.forbes.com/sites/jackkelly/2022/02/03/belgium-portugal-and-other-european-countries-are-ahead-of-the-us-prohibiting-managers-from-contacting-employees-outside-of-working-hours/?sh=565346b21d00.

173. S. Milligan, "Wellness Blows Up," *HRMagazine,* September 2017, pp. 61–67.

174. M. Yu, MJ. Wen, S.M. Smith, and P. Stokes, "Building-Up Resilience and Being Effective Leaders in the Workplace: A Systematic Review and Synthesis Model," *Leadership & Organization Development Journal,* Vol. 43, No. 7 (2022), pp. 1098–1117.

175. L. Parsons, "Building Resilience in the Workplace," *Human Resources Magazine,* Vol. 27, No. 1 (2022), pp. 34–37.

176. "#110: James Dyson," *Bloomberg Billionaires Index,* https://www.bloomberg.com/billionaires/profiles/james-dyson/#xj4y7vzkg (accessed May 13, 2023).

177. G. Tinline and C. Cooper, "Work-Related Stress: The Solution Is Management Not Mindfulness," *Organizational Dynamics,* Vol. 48, No. 3 (2019), pp. 93–97. Also see E. Dane, "Where Is My Mind? Theorizing Mind Wandering and Its Performance-Related Consequences in Organizations," *Academy of Management Review,* April 2018, pp. 179–197; K.M. Kiburz, T.D. Allen, and K.A. French, "Work-Family Conflict and Mindfulness: Investigating the effectiveness of a Brief Training Intervention," *Journal of Organizational Behavior,* September 2017, pp. 1016–1037; E. Bernstein, "A Daily Workout for the Brain," *The Wall Street Journal,* December 5, 2017, p. A13.

178. T. Parker-Pope, "How to Build Resilience in Midlife," *The New York Times,* July 25, 2017, https://www.nytimes.com/2017/07/25/well/mind/how-to-boost-resilience-in-midlife.html. Also see P.R. Pietromonaco and N.L. Collins, "Interpersonal Mechanisms Linking Close Relationships to Health," *American Psychologist,* September 2017, pp. 531–542; B. Litwiller, L.A. Snyder, W.D. Taylor, and L.M. Steele, "The Relationship between Sleep and Work: A Meta-Analysis," *Journal of Applied Psychology,* April 2017, pp. 682–699.

179. T. Long and F.L. Cooke, "Advancing the Field of Employee Assistance Programs Research and Practice: A Systematic Review of Quantitative Studies and Future Research Agenda," *Human Resource Management Review,* 2022, p.100941.

180. C. Stern, "A Slow-Motion Crisis: Gen Z's Battle against Depression, Addiction, Hopelessness," *The 74 Million,* September 7, 2022, https://www.the74million.org/article/a-slow-motion-crisis-gen-zs-battle-against-depression-addiction-hopelessness/.

181. C. Kabajwara, "Amidst the Chaos and Disruption Brought on by the COVID-19 Pandemic, the First Members of Generation Z Graduated from University," *PWC,* https://www.pwc.com/ug/en/press-room/how-prepared-are-employers-for-generation-z-.html#:~:text=According%20to%20recent%20studies%2C%20Gen,to%20about%2058%25%20by%202030 (accessed May 13, 2023).

182. M. Gill and T. Roulet, "Stressed at Work? Mentoring a Colleague Could Help," *Harvard Business Review,* March 1, 2019, https://hbr.org/2019/03/stressed-at-work-mentoring-a-colleague-could-help. Also see H. Aguinis, Y.H. Ji, and H. Joo, "Gender Productivity Gap among Star Performers in STEM and Other Scientific Fields," *Journal of Applied Psychology,* December 2018, pp. 1283–1306; "Mentors Help Reduce Stress, Burnout," *San Francisco Chronicle,* February 26, 2016, p. C2, reprinted from *Pittsburgh Post-Gazette.*

183. M.L. van Hooff and E.A. van Hooft, "Dealing with Daily Boredom at Work: Does Self-Control Explain Who Engages in Distractive Behaviour or Job Crafting as a Coping Mechanism?" *Work & Stress,* 2022, pp. 1–21.

184. C. Hogan, "Career Coaching Should Become a Standard Perk—Here's Why," *Worklife,* March 11, 2022, https://www.worklife.vc/blog/career-coaching.

185. "Be Your Authentic Self. Everyone Else Is Taken," *IBM Careers,* February 27, 2023, https://www.ibm.com/blogs/jobs/diversity-and-inclusion-at-ibm-be-your-authentic-self-everyone-else-is-taken/.

186. These questions were adapted from B. Tulgan, *Bridging the Soft Skills Gap* (Hoboken, NJ: John Wiley & Sons, 2015).

187. These steps were based on material in B. Tulgan, *Bridging the Soft Skills Gap* (Hoboken, NJ: John Wiley & Sons, 2015).

188. S. Algoe, (Apr 16, 2023). Why it's important to show gratitude at Work—and what's the best way to do it; research finds that even a simple thank-you can go a long way to making employees and colleagues feel valued and more collaborative. *Wall Street Journal (Online)* Retrieved from https://www.proquest.com/newspapers/why-important-show-gratitude-at-work-whats-best/docview/2801511050/se-2.

189. D. Meinert, "Are You an Emotional Genius?" *HRMagazine,* March 2018, pp. 17–19.

190. A. Gholamrezaei, I. Van Diest, Q. Aziz, A. Pauwels, J. Tack, J.W. Vlaeyen, and L. Van Oudenhove, "Effect of Slow, Deep Breathing on Visceral Pain Perception and Its Underlying Psychophysiological Mechanisms," *Neurogastroenterology & Motility,* Vol. 34, No. 4 (2022), p. e14242.

191. J. Shahbaz and J. Parker, "Workplace Mindfulness: An Integrative Review of Antecedents, Mediators, and Moderators," *Human Resource Management Review*, Vol. 32, No. 3 (2022), p. 100849.

192. C.S. Reina, M.J. Mills, and D.M. Sumpter, "A Mindful Relating Framework for Understanding the Trajectory of Work Relationships," *Personnel Psychology*, Vol. 42, No. 1 (2022).

CHAPTER 12

1. P.N.L. Shanmugam and R. Kayalvizhi, "Influence of Goal Orientation on Academic Self-Actualization of Prospective Teachers," *International Journal of Indian Psychology*, Vol. 11 (2023), https://doi.org/10.25215/1101.042.

2. "Motivation Statistics 2022: By the Numbers," *TeamStage*, https://teamstage.io/motivation-statistics/#:~:text=Companies%20with%20actively%20motivated%20employees (accessed March 2, 2023).

3. "How to Motivate Yourself: 10 Tips for Self Improvement," *Coursera*, February 21, 2023, https://www.coursera.org/articles/how-to-motivate-yourself.

4. "What Is Self-Motivation? Learn Efficient Self-Motivation Techniques," *Tony Robbins*, https://www.tonyrobbins.com/personal-growth/what-is-self-motivation (accessed March 2, 2023).

5. E. Kaplan, "How to Stay Insanely Self-Motivated, According to Science," *Medium.com*, September, 15, 2017, https://medium.com/the-mission/how-to-create-insane-change-in-your-life-according-to-science-bb3cddd1022.

6. R.A. Ravishankar and K. Alpaio, "5 Ways to Set More Achievable Goals," *Harvard Business Review*, August 30, 2022, https://hbr.org/2022/08/5-ways-to-set-more-achievable-goals.

7. A. Stahl, "This New Year's Set Goals, Not Resolutions," *Forbes*, December 9, 2021, https://www.forbes.com/sites/ashleystahl/2021/12/09/this-new-years-set-goals-not-resolutions/?sh=3d3f95c51ece. Also see S. Gardner, D. Albee, "Study Focuses on Strategies for Achieving Goals, Resolutions," *Press Releases*, February 1, 2015, p. 266, https://scholar.dominican.edu/news-releases/266.

8. W. Johnson, "Celebrate to Win," *Harvard Business Review*, January 26, 2022, https://hbr.org/2022/01/celebrate-to-win.

9. E. Segal, "The Most Effective Perks and Penalties to Get Workers to Return to Offices: New Surveys," *Forbes*, November 16, 2022, https://www.forbes.com/sites/edwardsegal/2022/11/16/the-most-effective-perks-and-penalties-to-get-workers-to-return-to-offices-new-surveys/?sh=1c7ce365324a. Also see M. Smith, "No. 1 Perk That Will Bring Workers back to Office: Microsoft Report," *CNBC*, September 30, 2022, https://www.cnbc.com/2022/09/30/no-1-perk-that-will-bring-workers-back-to-office-microsoft-report.html.

10. A. Hlehoski, R. Lane, and E. Haverstock, "Student Loan Debt Statistics: 2022," *NerdWallet*, January 31, 2023, https://www.nerdwallet.com/article/loans/student-loans/student-loan-debt#:~:text=Forty%2Dfive%20million%20Americans%20have. Also see D. Avery, "15 Companies That Help Employees Pay off Their Student Loans," *CNET*, September 22, 2022, https://www.cnet.com/personal-finance/15-companies-that-help-employees-with-student-loan-repayment-assistance/.

11. B. Luthi, "What Is Employer Student Loan Repayment?" *Bankrate*, October 28, 2022, https://www.bankrate.com/loans/student-loans/employer-student-loan-repayment/.

12. Adapted from definition in T.R. Mitchell, "Motivation: New Directions for Theory, Research, and Practice," *Academy of Management Review*, January 1982, p. 81.

13. R. Ryan and E. Deci, "Intrinsic and Extrinsic Motivations: Classic Definitions and New Directions," *Contemporary Educational Psychology*, January 2000, pp. 54–67.

14. C. Lin, H. Shipton, W. Teng, A. Kitt, H. Do, and C. Chadwick, "Sparking Creativity Using Extrinsic Rewards: A Self-Determination Theory Perspective," *Human Resource Management*, Vol. 61 (2022), pp. 723–735.

15. "100 Best Companies to Work For: American Express," *Fortune*, https://fortune.com/company/american-express/best-companies/ (accessed March 7, 2023). Also see "The 4 American Express Employee Benefits That Attract Top Talent," *PerkUp*, August 11, 2022, https://www.perkupapp.com/post/the-4-american-express-employee-benefits-that-attract-top-talent.

16. K. Murayama, "A Reward-Learning Framework of Knowledge Acquisition: An Integrated Account of Curiosity, Interest, and Intrinsic–Extrinsic Rewards," *Psychological Review*, Vol. 129 (2022), pp. 175–198.

17. R. Sheckler, "Disney Institute Cast Members Celebrate Education in Every Step of Storytelling at Work," *Disney Parks Blog*, January 26, 2023, https://disneyparks.disney.go.com/blog/2023/01/disney-institute-cast-members-celebrate-education-in-every-step-of-storytelling-at-work/.

18. S.L. Paredes, J.O. Salomón, and J.R. Camino, "Impact of Authentic Leadership on Work Engagement and Organizational Citizenship Behavior: The Meditating Role of Motivation for Work," *International Journal of Economics and Business Administration*, Vol. 9 (2021), pp. 3–31. Also see R. Kanfer, M. Frese, and R.E. Johnson, "Motivation Related to Work: A Century of Progress," *Journal of Applied Psychology*, Vol. 102 (2017), pp. 338–355.

19. A. Maslow, "A Theory of Human Motivation," *Psychological Review*, July 1943, pp. 370–396.

20. The Conference Board, "Survey: Professional Development Is Key to Retaining Talent, but People of Color Report Less Access," *PR Newswire*, July 5, 2022, https://www.prnewswire.com/news-releases/survey-professional-development-is-key-to-retaining-talent-but-people-of-color-report-less-access-301580611.html.

21. T. Bridgman, S. Cummings, and J. Ballard, "Who Built Maslow's Pyramid? A History of the Creation of Management Studies' Most Famous Symbol and Its Implications for Management Education," *Academy of Management Learning & Education*, Vol. 18, No. 1 (2019), pp. 81–98.

22. A. Janssen, "Work Culture: Engaged and Committed," *Auto Service World*, October 23, 2019, https://www.autoserviceworld.com/work-culture-engaged-and-committed/.

23. C. Connley, "Amazon, Facebook and 8 Other Companies That Have Committed to Raising Their Minimum Wage," *CNBC*, May 24, 2019, https://www.cnbc.com/2019/05/24/glassdoor-10-companies-that-have-committed-to-raising-minimum-wage.html.

24. M. Clendaniel, "The 10 Most Innovative Companies in Corporate Social Responsibility of 2022," *Fast Company*, March 8, 2022, https://www.fastcompany.com/90724377/most-innovative-companies-corporate-social-responsibility-2022.

25. D.C. McClelland, *Human Motivation* (Glenview, IL: Scott, Foresman, 1985).

26. J.A. de Andrade Baptista, A. Formigoni, S.A. da Silva, C.F. Stettiner, and R.A. Bueno de Novais, "Analysis of the Theory of Acquired Needs from McClelland as a Means of Work Satisfaction," *Timor Leste Journal of Business and Management*, Vol. 3 (2021), pp. 54–59.

27. A. Acquah, T.K. Nsiah, E.N.A. Antie, and B. Otoo, "Literature Review on Theories of Motivation," *EPRA International Journal of Economic and Business Review*, Vol. 9 (2021), pp. 25–29.

28. O-D.B. Abiola, O.M. David, N. Okutu, A.B. Hammed, and A.V. Ozioma, "McClelland Acquired Need and Skinner's Reinforcement Management Theories: Their Relevance in Today's Organization," *South Asian Research Journal of Business and Management*, Vol. 5 (2023), pp. 35–45.

29. R.M. Ryan and E.L. Deci, "Self-Determination Theory and the Facilitation of Intrinsic Motivation, Social Development, and Well-Being," *American Psychologist*, January 2000, pp. 68–78.

30. V. Good, D.E. Hughes, A.H. Kirca, and S. McGrath, "A Self-Determination Theory-Based Meta-Analysis on the Differential Effects of Intrinsic and Extrinsic Motivation on Salesperson Performance," *Journal of the Academy of Marketing Science*, Vol. 50 (2022), pp. 586–614. Also see E.L. Bradshaw, R. Ryan, J. Duineveld, S. Di Domenico, W.S. Ryan, and B.A. Steward, "We Know This Much Is (Meta-Analytically) True: A Meta-Review of Meta-Analytic Findings

Evaluating Self-Determination Theory," *PsyArXiv,* 2023, doi:10.31234/osf.io/gk5cy.

31. F. Martela and R.M. Ryan, "Clarifying Eudaimonia and Psychological Functioning to Complement Evaluative and Experiential Well-Being: Why Basic Psychological Needs Should Be Measured in National Accounts of Well-Being," *Perspectives on Psychological Science,* 2023, https://doi.org/10.1177/17456916221141099.

32. F. Martela A. Lehmus-Sun, P.D. Parker, A. Birgitta Pessi, and R.M. Ryan, "Needs and Well-Being across Europe: Basic Psychological Needs Are Closely Connected with Well-Being, Meaning, and Symptoms of Depression in 27 European Countries," *Social Psychological and Personality Science,* 2022, https://doi.org/10.1177/19485506221113678.

33. K.W. Rockmann and G.A. Ballinger, "Intrinsic Motivation and Organizational Identification among On-Demand Workers," *Journal of Applied Psychology,* September 2017, pp. 1305–1316.

34. M. Smith, "The 10 Best U.S. Companies for Career Growth, according to New Research," *CNBC,* July 17, 2022, https://www.cnbc.com/2022/07/17/the-10-best-us-companies-for-career-growth-according-to-new-research.html.

35. "Code of Business Conduct and Ethics," *Nordstrom,* https://press.nordstrom.com/static-files/952f5e64-473c-47c2-a396-3ddb81b303db#:~:text=Our%20number%20one%20goal%20is,companies%20we%20do%20business%20with (accessed March 13, 2023). Also see "Nordstrom," *Fortune,* https://fortune.com/company/nordstrom/worlds-most-admired-companies/ (accessed March 13, 2023).

36. "Frequently Asked Questions: What Is the Culture Like at In-N-Out Burger?" *In-N-Out Burger,* https://www.in-n-out.com/employment/corporate/faqs (accessed March 13, 2023). Also see M. Smith, "The 10 Best U.S. Places to Work in 2023, according to Glassdoor," *CNBC,* January 16, 2023, https://www.cnbc.com/2023/01/11/the-10-best-us-places-to-work-in-2023-according-to-glassdoor.html.

37. F. Herzberg, B. Mausner, and B.B. Snyderman, *The Motivation to Work* (New York: Wiley, 1959). Also see F. Herzberg, "One More Time: How Do You Motivate Employees?" *Harvard Business Review,* January–February 1968, pp. 53–62.

38. M.T. Prabhu, "Despite Raises, Turnover Remains High at Georgia Prisons, Juvenile Centers," *The Atlanta Journal-Constitution,* January 19, 2022, https://www.ajc.com/politics/despite-raises-turnover-remains-high-at-georgia-prisons-juvenile-centers/GQQFNTODNVBM7NW5F64YQ53HEQ/.

39. J. Peebles and D. Robbins, "Georgia Prison Employees Arrested for Drug Crimes, Battery, Sexual Assault of Inmates," *The Atlanta Journal-Constitution,* August 11, 2022, https://www.ajc.com/news/georgia-news/georgia-prison-employees-arrested-for-drug-crimes-battery-sexual-assault-of-inmates/C7K4ZWGOJVG35HMVZOECMDJ2UU/.

40. "David Weekley Homes: 2022 100 Best Companies," *Fortune,* https://fortune.com/company/david-weekley-homes/best-companies/ (accessed March 15, 2023).

41. A. Donaldson, "7 Benefits You Should Offer Your Employees in 2023," *Inc.,* January 13, 2023, https://www.inc.com/ali-donaldson/7-benefits-you-should-offer-your-employees-in-2023.html.

42. D. Miranda, "These Are the Best Employee Benefits in 2023," *Forbes,* February 6, 2023, https://www.forbes.com/advisor/business/best-employee-benefits/.

43. M. D'Sa-Wilson, "5 Companies with Exceptional Employee Development Programs," *Together,* April 29, 2022, https://www.togetherplatform.com/blog/best-training-and-development-programs.

44. J.S. Adams, "Toward an Understanding of Inequity," *Journal of Abnormal and Social Psychology,* November 1963, pp. 422–436; J.S. Adams, "Injustice in Social Exchange," in L. Berkowitz (ed.), *Advances in Experimental Social Psychology,* 2nd ed. (New York: Academic Press, 1965), pp. 267–300.

45. Perceptions of fairness are discussed by L.J. Barclay, M.R. Bashshur, and M. Fortin, "Motivated Cognition and Fairness: Insights, Integration, and Creating a Path Forward," *Journal of Applied Psychology,* June 2017, pp. 867–889.

46. J. Bivens and J. Kandra, "CEO Pay Has Skyrocketed 1,460% since 1978," *Economic Policy Institute,* October 4, 2022, https://www.epi.org/publication/ceo-pay-in-2021/#:~:text=CEO%20compensation%20growth%20in%202021&text=The%20granted%20measure%20of%20CEO.

47. D. Osiichuk, "The Driver of Workplace Alienation or the Cost of Effective Stewardship? The Consequences of Wage Gap for Corporate Performance," *Sustainability,* Vol. 14 (2022), p. 8006.

48. R. Cropanzano, D. Rupp, C. Mohler, and M. Schminke, "Three Roads to Organizational Justice," in G.R. Ferris (ed.), *Research in Personnel and Human Resources Management,* Vol. 20 (New York: JAI Press, 2001), pp. 269–329.

49. C. Roussillon Soyer, D.B. Balkin, and A. Fall, "Unpacking the Effect of Autonomous Motivation on Workplace Performance: Engagement and Distributive Justice Matter!" *European Management Review,* Vol. 19 (2022), pp. 138–153. Also see J.A. Colquitt, E.T. Hill, and D. De Cremer, "Forever Focused on Fairness: 75 Years of Organizational Justice in *Personnel Psychology*," *Personnel Psychology,* https://doi.org/10.1111/peps.12556.

50. J.A. Colquitt, E.T. Hill, and D. De Cremer, "Forever Focused on Fairness: 75 Years of Organizational Justice in *Personnel Psychology*," *Personnel Psychology,* https://doi.org/10.1111/peps.12556.

51. S. Qiu and L. Dooley, "How Servant Leadership Affects Organizational Citizenship Behavior: The Mediating Roles of Perceived Procedural Justice and Trust," *Leadership & Organization Development Journal,* Vol. 43 (2022), pp. 350–369. Also see J.A. Colquitt, B.A. Scott, J.B. Rodell, D.M. Long, C.P. Zapata, D.E. Conlon, and M.J. Wesson, "Justice at the Millennium, a Decade Later: A Meta-Analytic Test of Social Exchange and Affect-Based Perspectives," *Journal of Applied Psychology,* Vol. 98 (2013), pp. 199–236.

52. J.A. Colquitt, E.T. Hill, and D. De Cremer, "Forever Focused on Fairness: 75 Years of Organizational Justice in *Personnel Psychology*," *Personnel Psychology,* https://doi.org/10.1111/peps.12556.

53. M.S. Alqahtani, "The Impact of Interactional Justice on Employees' Job Performance and Assisting Behaviour," *Journal of Leadership, Accountability and Ethics,* Vol. 19 (2022), pp. 12–30.

54. M. Cohen, "A Vast Majority of Workers Aren't Happy with What They're Being Paid," *CNBC,* December 14, 2022, https://www.cnbc.com/2022/12/14/a-vast-majority-of-workers-arent-happy-with-what-theyre-being-paid.html#:~:text=The%20verdict%3A%20nearly%2070%25%20of.

55. "Nestle to Pay Ex Manager $2.2 Million over Bullying Case, Tages-Anzeiger Reports," *Reuters,* February 11, 2023, https://www.reuters.com/markets/europe/nestle-pay-ex-manager-22-mln-over-bullying-case-tages-anzeiger-2023-02-11/.

56. M. Mori, V. Cavaliere, S. Sassetti, and A. Caputo, "Employee Voice: A Knowledge Map to Provide Conceptual Clarity and Future Research Directions," *Journal of Management & Organization,* 2022, pp. 1–27.

57. E.W. Morrison, "Employee Voice and Silence: Taking Stock a Decade Later," *Annual Review of Organizational Psychology and Organizational Behavior,* Vol. 10 (2023), pp. 79–107.

58. C. Robinson, "Capitol Hill to Sports: This Executive Uses Active Listening to Enhance Leadership, Communication," *Forbes,* March 17, 2022, https://www.forbes.com/sites/cherylrobinson/2022/03/17/capitol-hill-to-sports-this-executive-uses-active-listening-to-enhance-leadership-communication/?sh=c073db9667c1.

59. "Grade Appeal Policy and Process," *ASU Mary Lou Fulton Teachers College,* https://education.asu.edu/sites/default/files/2022-11/Teachers_College_Grade_Appeal_Policy_and_Process_11-15-22.pdf (accessed March 16, 2023).

60. S. Lee, S. Hong, and B.G. Lee, "Is There a Right Way to Lay Off Employees in Times of Crisis?: The Role of Organizational Justice in the Case of Airbnb," *Sustainability,* Vol. 15 (2023), p. 4690, https://doi.org/10.3390/su15054690.

61. J. Green and Bloomberg, "American Express Joins the Pay Transparency Movement, Adding Salary Ranges to Its Job Listings Nationwide," *Fortune,* October 31, 2022, https://fortune.com/2022/10/31/american-express-pay-transparency-salary-ranges-job-listings/.

62. C.A. Hartnell, A. Christensen-Salem, F.O. Walumbwa, D.J. Stotler, F.F.T. Chiang, and T.A. Birtch, "Manufacturing Motivation in the Mundane: Servant Leadership's Influence on Employees' Intrinsic Motivation and Performance," *Journal of Business Ethics,* 2023, pp. 1–20, https://doi.org/10.1007/s10551-023-05330-2. Also see A. Li and R. Cropanzano, "Fairness at the Group Level: Justice Climate and Intraunit Justice Climate," *Journal of Management,* Vol. 35 (2009), pp. 564–599.

63. V.H. Vroom, *Work and Motivation* (New York: Wiley, 1964).

64. P. Prakash, "Jamie Dimon Is Going to Make a Lot Less Than He Did Last Year as He Joins Apple's Tim Cook as the Latest Big CEO to Lose out on a Bigger Payday," *Fortune,* January 20, 2023, https://fortune.com/2023/01/20/jamie-dimon-jpmorgan-compensation-special-award-tim-cook-apple-pay/.

65. S.M. Kalita, "What to Know When Five Generations Share an Office," *Time,* January 24, 2023, https://time.com/charter/6249581/what-to-know-when-five-generations-share-an-office/. Also see K. Mery, "How Different Generations Want to Be Recognized at Work," *Bamboo HR,* September 30, 2020, https://www.bamboohr.com/blog/how-different-generations-want-to-be-recognized#generation-z.

66. J.S. Eccles and A. Wigfield, "Expectancy-Value Theory to Situated Expectancy-Value Theory: Reflections on the Legacy of 40+ Years of Working Together," *Motivation Science,* Vol. 9, (2023), pp. 1–12.

67. H.T.W. Frankort and A. Avgoustaki, "Beyond Reward Expectancy: How Do Periodic Incentive Payments Influence the Temporal Dynamics of Performance?" *Journal of Management,* Vol. 48 (2022), pp. 2075–2107.

68. A.N. Li, E.N. Sherf, and S. Tangirala, "Team Adaptation to Discontinuous Task Change: Equity and Equality as Facilitators of Individual and Collective Task Capabilities Redevelopment," *Organization Science,* 2023, https://doi.org/10.1287/orsc.2022.1621.

69. E.A. Locke and G.P. Latham, "The Development of Goal Setting Theory: A Half Century Retrospective," *Motivation Science,* Vol. 5 (2019), pp. 93–105.

70. P.A. Heslin and U.-C. Klehe, "Goal Enablers: Evidence-Based Ways to Turn Your Goals into Reality," *Organizational Dynamics,* 2023, 100944, https://doi.org/10.1016/j.orgdyn.2022.100944.

71. S. Ahmadi, J.J.P. Jansen, and J.P. Eggers, "Using Stretch Goals for Idea Generation among Employees: One Size Does not Fit All!" *Organization Science,* Vol. 33 (2022), pp. 671–687.

72. F. Schneider, "The Stretch Goal Myth: When More Ambition Is Really Better," *Workpath,* February 22, 2023, https://www.workpath.com/en/magazine/the-stretch-goal-myth-when-more-ambition-is-really-better/.

73. I. Hamilton, "Meet the Coding Prodigy Who Has Prince Harry and Meghan Markle on Her Side in the Fight to Boost Women in Tech," *Business Insider,* October 4, 2018, https://www.businessinsider.com/anne-marie-imafidon-coding-prodigy-fighting-for-women-in-tech-2018-10.

74. "Dr. Anne-Marie Imafidon MBE," *Anne-Marie Imafidon,* https://aimafidon.com/ (accessed March 16, 2023).

75. "About Stemettes," *Stemettes,* https://stemettes.org/about-us/ (accessed March 16, 2023). See also Stemettes Annual Report 2021–2022.

76. J. Bush and M. Chui, "Forward Thinking on Democratizing Technology with Anne-Marie Imafidon," *McKinsey & Company,* May 4, 2022, https://www.mckinsey.com/featured-insights/diversity-and-inclusion/forward-thinking-on-democratizing-technology-with-anne-marie-imafidon.

77. I. Hamilton, "Meet the Coding Prodigy Who Has Prince Harry and Meghan Markle on Her Side in the Fight to Boost Women in Tech," *Business Insider,* October 4, 2018, https://www.businessinsider.com/anne-marie-imafidon-coding-prodigy-fighting-for-women-in-tech-2018-10.

78. C. Chen, Z. Zhang, and M. Jia, "Stretch Goals and Unethical Behavior: Role of Ambivalent Identification and Competitive Psychological Climate," *Management Decision,* Vol. 59 (2021), pp. 2005–2023.

79. C. Waters, "Here's What the Wells Fargo Cross-Selling Scandal Means for the Bank's Growth," *CNBC,* October 19, 2022, https://www.cnbc.com/2022/10/19/heres-what-the-wells-fargo-cross-selling-scandal-means-for-the-bank.html.

80. S. Ahmadi, J.J.P. Jansen, and J.P. Eggers, "Using Stretch Goals for Idea Generation among Employees: One Size Does not Fit All!" *Organization Science,* Vol. 33 (2022), pp. 671–687.

81. A. Adeel, D.M.H. Kee, A.S. Mubashir, S. Samad, and Y.Q. Daghriri, "Leaders' Ambition and Followers' Cheating Behavior: The Role of Performance Pressure and Leader Identification," *Frontiers in Psychology,* Vol. 14 (2023), 982328, doi:10.3389/fpsyg.2023.982328.

82. E.A. Locke and G.P. Latham, "The Development of Goal Setting Theory: A Half Century Retrospective," *Motivation Science,* Vol. 5 (2019), pp. 93–105. Also see E. Locke and G. Latham, "Building a Practically Useful Theory of Goal Setting and Task Motivation," *AmericanPsychologist,* September 2002, pp. 705–717.

83. "Mission & Goals," *FedEx,* https://investors.fedex.com/company-overview/mission-and-goals/default.aspx (accessed March 16, 2023).

84. E.A. Locke and G.P. Latham, "Building a Theory by Induction: The Example of Goal Setting Theory," *Organizational Psychology Review,* Vol. 10 (2020), pp. 223–239.

85. G. Latham, "Goal Setting: A Five-Step Approach to Behavior Change," in M.L. Di Domenico, S. Vangen, N. Winchester, D.K. Boojihawon, and J. Mordaunt (Eds.), *Organizational Collaboration* (New York, NY: Routledge, 2021), pp. 10–20.

86. "2022-2027 Strategic Intent," *Calvary Health Care,* https://www.calvarycare.org.au/about/strategy/ (accessed March 16, 2023).

87. J. Harter, "U.S. Employee Engagement Needs a Rebound in 2023," *Gallup,* January 25, 2023, https://www.gallup.com/workplace/468233/employee-engagement-needs-rebound-2023.aspx.

88. G.R. Oldham and Y. Fried, "Job Design Research and Theory: Past, Present and Future," *Organizational Behavior and Human Decision Processes,* Vol. 136 (2016), pp. 20–35.

89. D. Birnbaum and M. Somers, "Past as Prologue: Taylorism, the New Scientific Management and Managing Human Capital," *International Journal of Organizational Analysis,* 2022, https://doi.org/10.1108/IJOA-01-2022-3106.

90. C.L. Hulin and M.R. Blood, "Job Enlargement, Individual Differences, and Worker Responses," *Psychological Bulletin,* Vol. 69 (1968), pp. 41–55. Also see J.A. Carpini and S.K. Parker, "Job Enlargement," in *Encyclopedia of Human Resource Management* (Northampton, MA: Edward Elgar Publishing, 2023), pp. 218–219.

91. M.M. Siruri and S. Cheche, "Revisiting the Hackman and Oldham Job Characteristics Model and Herzberg's Two Factor Theory: Propositions on How to Make Job Enrichment Effective in Today's Organizations," *European Journal of Business and Management Research,* Vol. 6 (2021), pp. 162–167.

92. F. Herzberg, B. Mausner, and B.B. Snyderman, *The Motivation to Work* (New York: Wiley, 1959).

93. "CrowdStrike Promotes Michael Sentonas to President," *CrowdStrike,* February 8, 2023, https://www.crowdstrike.com/press-releases/crowdstrike-promotes-michael-sentonas-to-president/. Also see "Careers at CrowdStrike," *CrowdStrike,* https://www.crowdstrike.com/careers/ (accessed March 17, 2023).

94. J. Hackman and G. Oldham, *Work Redesign* (Reading, MA: Addison-Wesley, 1980).

95. B.A. Allan, C. Batz-Barbarich, H.M. Sterling, and L. Tay, "Outcomes of Meaningful Work: A Meta-Analysis," *Journal of Management Studies,* Vol. 56 (2019), pp. 500–528. Also see R. Kanfer, M. Frese, and R.E. Johnson, "Motivation Related to Work: A Century of Progress," *Journal of Applied Psychology,* Vol. 102 (2017), pp. 338–355.

96. K. Morgan, "The Search for 'Meaning' at Work," *BBC,* September 7, 2022, https://www.bbc.com/worklife/article/20220902-the-search-for-meaning-at-work.

97. S.K. Parker and G. Grote, "Automation, Algorithms, and Beyond: Why Work Design Matters More Than Ever in a Digital World," *Applied Psychology,* Vol. 71 (2022), pp. 1171–1204. Also see E.I. Lysova, B.A. Allan, B.J. Dik, R.D. Duffy, and M.F. Steger, "Fostering Meaningful Work in Organizations: A Multi-Level Review and Integration," *Journal of Vocational Behavior,* Vol. 110 (2019), pp. 374–389.

98. C. Serhan and H. Tsangari, "The Mediating Effects of Psychological States on the Relationship of Job Dimensions to Personal and Work Outcomes, for Fresh Graduates," *Journal of Management Development,* 2022, pp. 223–239.

99. "Corporate Overview" *USAA,* https://www.usaa.com/inet/wc/about_usaa_corporate_overview_main?akredirect=true (accessed March 18, 2023). Also see M. Mankins, E. Garton, and D. Schwartz, "3 Ways Companies Make Work Purposeful," *Harvard Business Review,* July 20, 2022, https://hbr.org/2022/07/3-ways-companies-make-work-purposeful.

100. A.M. Grant, "Does Intrinsic Motivation Fuel the Prosocial Fire? Motivational Synergy in Predicting Persistence, Performance, and Productivity," *Journal of Applied Psychology,* Vol. 93 (2008), pp. 48–58. Also see A.M. Grant, "Relational Job Design and the Motivation to Make a Prosocial Difference," *Academy of Management Review,* Vol. 32 (2007), pp. 393–417.

101. H. Liao, R. Su, T. Ptashnik, and J. Nielsen, "Feeling Good, Doing Good, and Getting Ahead: A Meta-Analytic Investigation of the Outcomes of Prosocial Motivation at Work," *Psychological Bulletin,* Vol. 148 (2022), pp. 158–198.

102. A.M. Grant and M.S. Shandell, "Social Motivation at Work: The Organizational Psychology of Effort for, against, and with Others," *Annual Review of Psychology,* Vol. 73 (2022), pp. 301–326.

103. A.M. Grant and M.S. Shandell, "Social Motivation at Work: The Organizational Psychology of Effort for, against, and with Others," *Annual Review of Psychology,* Vol. 73 (2022), pp. 301–326.

104. A.M. Grant and D.A. Hofmann, "Outsourcing Inspiration: The Performance Effects of Ideological Messages from Leaders and Beneficiaries," *Organizational Behavior and Human Decision Processes,* Vol. 116 (2011), pp. 173–187.

105. A.M. Grant, E.M. Campbell, G. Chen, K. Cottone, D. Lapedis, and K. Lee, "Impact and the Art of Motivation Maintenance: The Effects of Contact with Beneficiaries on Persistence Behavior," *Organizational Behavior and Human Decision Processes,* Vol. 103 (2007), pp. 53–67.

106. E. Thorndike, *Educational Psychology: The Psychology of Learning,* Vol. II (New York: Columbia University Teachers College, 1913). Also see B. Skinner, *Walden Two* (New York: Macmillan, 1948); B. Skinner, *Science and Human Behavior* (New York: Macmillan, 1953); D. Mozingo, "Contingencies of Reinforcement," in F. R. Volker (ed.), *Encyclopedia of Autism Spectrum Disorders* (New York: Appleton-Century-Crofts, 1969), p. 799.

107. E. Thorndike, *Educational Psychology: The Psychology of Learning,* Vol. II (New York: Columbia University Teachers College, 1913).

108. G. Freedman, D.N. Powell, B. Le, and K.D. Williams, "Emotional Experiences of Ghosting," The *Journal of Social Psychology,* 2022, pp. 1–20. Also see M. Locker, "Have You Been Ghosted? Relationship Experts Break down Why That Happens," *Health,* December 21, 2022, https://www.health.com/relationships/why-would-someone-ghost.

109. H. Martin, "Airlines Are Paying Fewer Fines. Are Regulators More Lenient or Are Airlines More Law Abiding?" *MSN,* January 13, 2020, https://www.msn.com/en-us/news/us/airlines-are-paying-fewer-fines-are-regulators-more-lenient-or-are-airlines-more-law-abiding/ar-BBYUyQ0.

110. "DOT Fines United Airlines for Violating Tarmac Delay Rule," *U.S. Department of Transportation,* September 24, 2021, https://www.transportation.gov/briefing-room/dot-fines-united-airlines-violating-tarmac-delay-rule.

111. A. Kinne, "What Are the Benefits of Employee Recognition?" *Workhuman,* December 23, 2022, https://www.workhuman.com/blog/benefits-of-employee-recognition/.

112. Y. Asulin, Y. Heller, and N. Munichor, "Comparing the Effects of Non-Monetary Incentives and Monetary Incentives on Prosocial Behavior," *SSRN,* 2023, http://dx.doi.org/10.2139/ssrn.4375009. Also see S. O'Flaherty, M.T. Sanders, and A. Whillans, "Research: A Little Recognition Can Provide a Big Morale Boost," *Harvard Business Review,* March 29, 2021, https://hbr.org/2021/03/research-a-little-recognition-can-provide-a-big-morale-boost.

113. T.A. Judge, R.F. Piccolo, N.P. Podsakoff, J.C. Shaw, and B.L. Rich, "The Relationship between Pay and Job Satisfaction: A Meta-Analysis of the Literature," *Journal of Vocational Behavior,* Vol. 77 (2010), pp. 157–167.

114. E. Barker, "To Keep Workers in Today's Economy, Flexibility Is More Important than Money," *Time,* April 24, 2022, https://time.com/6169927/marcus-buckingham-adp-love-work-book-interview/. Also see Entrepreneur Staff, "The Best Employees Want More Than Just Money. Here Are 6 Ways to Attract Them," *Entrepreneur,* November 27, 2022, https://www.entrepreneur.com/growth-strategies/the-best-employees-want-more-than-just-money-here-are-6/438820.

115. "Minimum Wage," *Worker.gov,* https://www.worker.gov/concerns/pay-minimum-wage/ (accessed March 20, 2023).

116. "Work Hard, Be Rewarded: Your Income Has No Ceiling," *Edward Jones,* http://careers.edwardjones.com/explore-opportunities/new-financial-advisors/compensation/compensation.html (accessed March 20, 2023).

117. B. Biron, "5 Jobs Offering Massive Signing Bonuses Right Now," *Business Insider,* August 12, 2022, https://www.businessinsider.com/jobs-offering-massive-signing-bonuses-to-combat-labor-crisis-2022-8#healthcare-3.

118. "Publix Super Markets," *Fortune,* https://fortune.com/company/publix-super-markets/ (accessed March 20, 2023). Also see J.B., "In the Words of Mr. George," *Publix Blog,* April 16, 2018, https://blog.publix.com/publix/in-the-words-of-mr-george/.

119. H. Bhasin, "Gains Sharing—Types, Advantages and Disadvantages," *Marketing91,* June 17, 2022, https://www.marketing91.com/gains-sharing/.

120. S. Ghamat, G.S. Zaric, and H. Pun, "Care-Coordination: Gain-Sharing Agreements in Bundled Payment Models," *Production and Operations Management,* Vol. 30 (2021), pp. 1457–1474.

121. T. Kim, "Tech Is Still Addicted to Stock Options. These 4 Companies Could Be Most at Risk," *Barron's,* March 5, 2023, https://www.barrons.com/articles/okta-confluence-snowflake-tech-stock-based-comp-33588231.

122. J. Csiszar, "The Cheesecake Factory and Other Major Companies That Offer Employee Stock Options," *GOBankingRates,* April 18, 2022, https://www.gobankingrates.com/investing/stocks/major-companies-that-offer-employee-stock-options/.

123. T. Kim, "Tech Is Still Addicted to Stock Options. These 4 Companies Could Be Most at Risk," *Barron's,* March 5, 2023, https://www.barrons.com/articles/okta-confluence-snowflake-tech-stock-based-comp-33588231. Also see R. Waters, "Reality Bites for the Stock-Based Pay Lottery," *Financial Times,* May 5, 2022, https://www.ft.com/content/0a45bf12-90f3-4473-8231-b91369226a67; P.R. La Monica, "Snowflake Shares More Than Double. It's the Biggest Software IPO Ever," *CNN,* September 17, 2020, https://www.cnn.com/2020/09/16/investing/snowflake-ipo/index.html.

124. "Knowledge-Based Pay—Definition and Meaning," *Market Business News,* https://marketbusinessnews.com/financial-glossary/knowledge-based-pay/ (accessed March 20, 2023).

125. "Executives Feel the Strain of Leading in the 'New Normal,'" *Future Forum,* https://futureforum.com/research/pulse-report-fall-2022-executives-feel-strain-leading-in-new-normal/ (accessed March 22, 2023).

126. D. Klinghoffer, "Hybrid Tanked Work-Life Balance. Here's How Microsoft Is Trying to Fix It," *Harvard Business Review,* December 8, 2021, https://hbr.org/2021/12/hybrid-tanked-work-life-balance-heres-how-microsoft-is-trying-to-fix-it.

127. Definition from I. Tatara, *Work-Life Benefits: Everything You Need to Know to Determine Your Work-Life Program* (Chicago, IL: CCH KnowledgePoint, 2002), p. 2.

128. K. Buchholz, "These Countries Have the Best Work-Life Balance," *World Economic Forum,* May 4, 2022, https://www.weforum.org/agenda/2022/05/the-countries-with-the-best-work-life-balance/.

129. M. Johnson-Jones, "The World's Most Flexible Companies to Work for in 2023," *the HR Director,* February 1, 2023, https://www

130. N.V. Shifrin and J.S. Michel, "Flexible Work Arrangements and Employee Health: A Meta-Analytic Review," *Work & Stress,* Vol. 36 (2022), pp. 60–85.

131. Glassdoor Team, "20 Companies Offering Unlimited PTO," *Glassdoor,* January 17, 2020, https://www.glassdoor.com/blog/cool-companies-offering-unlimited-vacation/.

132. L. Runkle and D. Miranda, "Unexpected Companies Offering Sabbaticals.," *The Penny Hoarder,* September 9, 2022, https://www.thepennyhoarder.com/make-money/career/companies-offering-sabbaticals/.

133. M.C. Perna, "Why Learning and Development Is Now a Competitive Differentiator," *Forbes,* April 12, 2022, https://www.forbes.com/sites/markcperna/2022/04/12/why-learning--development-is-now-a-competitive-differentiator-and-how-to-get-on-board/?sh=669bdeea30ff.

134. L. Freifeld, "2022 Training Industry Report," *Training Mag,* November 16, 2022. https://trainingmag.com/2022-training-industry-report/#:~:text=Average%20training%20expenditures%20for%20large.

135. M.E. Seligman, *Flourish* (New York: Free Press, 2011).

136. B.L. Fredrickson and M.F. Losada, "Positive Affect in the Complex Dynamics of Human Flourishing," *American Psychologist,* 2005, pp. 678–686.

137. M.F. Naim and A. Ozyilmaz, "Flourishing-at-Work and Turnover Intentions: Does Trust in Management Moderate the Relationship?" *Personnel Review,* 2022, https://doi.org/10.1108/PR-09-2020-0715. Also see W.D. Hunsaker and W. Ding, "Workplace Spirituality and Innovative Work Behavior: The Role of Employee Flourishing and Workplace Satisfaction," *Employee Relations,* 2022, pp. 1355–1371; S. Rothmann, K. Redelinghuys, and E. Botha, "Workplace Flourishing: Measurement, Antecedents and Outcomes," *SA Journal of Industrial Psychology,* Vol. 45 (2019), pp. 1–11.

138. "State of the Global Workplace Report," *Gallup,* https://www.gallup.com/workplace/349484/state-of-the-global-workplace.aspx#ite-393248 (accessed March 22, 2023).

139. A.B. Adler, P.D. Bliese, S.G. Barsade, and W.J. Sowden, "Hitting the Mark: The Influence of Emotional Culture on Resilient Performance," *Journal of Applied Psychology,* Vol. 107 (2022), pp. 319–327. Also see J.A.D. Datu, J.P.M. Valdez, D.M. McInerney, and R.F. Cayubit, "The Effects of Gratitude and Kindness on Life Satisfaction, Positive Emotions, Negative Emotions, and COVID-19 Anxiety: An Online Pilot Experimental Study," *Applied Psychology: Health and Well-Being,* Vol. 14 (2022), pp. 347–361.

140. K. Sun, "How to Create a Culture of Gratitude in the Workplace," *Charney & Associates,* https://nscharney.com/how-to-create-a-culture-of-gratitude-in-the-workplace/(accessed May 14, 2020).

141. P.M. Tang, R. Ilies, S.S.Y. Aw, K.J. Lin, R. Lee, and C. Trombini, "How and When Service Beneficiaries' Gratitude Enriches Employees' Daily Lives," *Journal of Applied Psychology,* Vol. 107 (2022), pp. 987–1008. Also see K.B. Sawyer, C.N. Thoroughgood, E.E. Stillwell, M.K. Duffy, K.L. Scott, and E.A. Adair, "Being Present and Thankful: A Multi-Study Investigation of Mindfulness, Fratitude, and Employee Helping Behavior," *Journal of Applied Psychology,* Vol. 107 (2022), pp. 240–262.

142. L.R. Locklear, S. Sheridan, and D.T. Kong, "Appreciating Social Science Research on Gratitude: An Integrative Review for Organizational Scholarship on Gratitude in the Workplace," *Journal of Organizational Behavior,* 2023, pp. 225–260.

143. "How to Express Gratitude," *Psych Central,* May 20, 2022, https://psychcentral.com/health/ways-to-express-gratitude.

144. J. Charles, "How I Used a Gratitude Intervention to Change Company Culture," *Ladders,* July 24, 2021, https://www.theladders.com/career-advice/how-i-used-a-gratitude-intervention-to-change-company-culture.

145. P.M. Tang, R. Ilies, S.S.Y. Aw, K.J. Lin, R. Lee, and C. Trombini, "How and When Service Beneficiaries' Gratitude Enriches Employees' Daily Lives," *Journal of Applied Psychology,* Vol. 107 (2022), pp. 987–1008. Also see W. Johnson and A. Humble, "Notes of Appreciation Can Boost Individual and Team Morale," *Harvard Business Review,* November 21, 2022. https://hbr.org/2022/11/notes-of-appreciation-can-boost-individual-and-team-morale.

146. L.C. Walsh, A. Regan, and S. Lyubomirsky, "The Role of Actors, Targets, and Witnesses: Examining Gratitude Exchanges in a Social Context," *The Journal of Positive Psychology,* Vol. 17 (2022), pp. 233–249.

147. L.R. Locklear, S. Sheridan, and D.T. Kong, "Appreciating Social Science Research on Gratitude: An Integrative Review for Organizational Scholarship on Gratitude in the Workplace," *Journal of Organizational Behavior,* 2023, pp. 225–260. Also see R. Fehr, A. Fulmer, E. Awtrey, and J.A. Miller, "The Grateful Workplace: A Multilevel Model of Gratitude in Organizations," *Academy of Management Review,* Vol. 42 (2017), pp. 361–381.

148. C. Castrillon, "How to Create a Culture of Gratitude at Work," *Forbes,* April 24, 2022, https://www.forbes.com/sites/carolinecastrillon/2022/04/24/how-to-create-a-culture-of-gratitude-at-work/?sh=2963bda73b1f.

149. Disney Ambassador Team, "Celebrating 100,000 Mobile Compliments for Disney Cast Members," *Disney Parks,* April 15, 2022, https://disneyparks.disney.go.com/blog/2022/04/celebrating-100000-mobile-compliments-for-disney-cast-members/#:~:text=Celebrating%20100%2C000%20Mobile%20Compliments%20for%20Disney%20Cast%20Members%20%7C%20Disney%20Parks%20Blog.

150. V. Gujral, R. Palter, A. Sanghvi, and A. Wolkomir, "In the Office of the Future, Magic Is in and the Cube Farm Is Out," *McKinsey,* April 27, 2021, https://www.mckinsey.com/industries/real-estate/our-insights/the-workplace-will-never-be-the-same-imperatives-for-real-estate-owners-and-operators.

151. P. Wahba, "Bosses Are Trying to Lure Workers Back to the Office with a Free, Coveted Perk: Quiet and Privacy," *Fortune,* February 17, 2023, https://fortune.com/2023/02/17/workers-return-office-design-quiet-amenities/.

152. J. Zenger and J. Folkman, "Quiet Quitting Is about Bad Bosses, Not Bad Employees," *Harvard Business Review,* August 31, 2022, https://hbr.org/2022/08/quiet-quitting-is-about-bad-bosses-not-bad-employees.

153. "Meaningful Work and Wealth," *U.S. Department of Health and Human Services,* https://health.gov/our-work/national-health-initiatives/equitable-long-term-recovery-and-resilience/framework/meaningful-work-and-wealth (accessed March 22, 2023).

154. "Most and Least Meaningful Jobs Full List," *PayScale,* https://www.payscale.com/data-packages/most-and-least-meaningful-jobs/full-list (accessed March 22, 2023).

155. V.E. Frankl, *Man's Search for Meaning* (New York: Pocket Books, 1959).

156. L. Garrad and T. Premuzic, "How to Make Work More Meaningful for Your Team," *Harvard Business Review,* August 9, 2017, https://hbr.org/2017/08/how-to-make-work-more-meaningful-for-your-team.

157. M.E. Seligman, *Flourish* (New York: Free Press, 2011).

158. "Mike Krzyzewski," *Duke University,* https://goduke.com/sports/mens-basketball/roster/coaches/mike-krzyzewski/4159 (accessed March 22, 2023). Also see P. Harlow, B. Church, and B. Morse, "Mike Krzyzewski: Legendary Duke Coach on the Secrets of His Success and Importance of His Family Name," *CNN,* March 15, 2023, https://www.cnn.com/2023/03/15/sport/mike-krzyzewski-duke-family-legacy-spt-intl/index.html.

159. S. Sorenson, "How Employees' Strengths Make Your Company Stronger," *Gallup,* https://www.gallup.com/workplace/231605/employees-strengths-company-stronger.aspx (accessed March 22, 2023). Also see K. Lundin, "Ten Ways Leaders Can Help Employees Find Meaning at Work," *Crowdspring,* May 6, 2022, https://www.crowdspring.com/blog/help-employees-cultivate-meaning-at-work/.

160. M.E. Seligman, *Flourish* (New York: Free Press, 2011).

161. M. Heron, "Bellhops CEO Gives New Employee Car after Walking 20 Miles to Work," *Local3News,* December 1, 2021, https://www.local3news.com/bellhops-ceo-gives-new-employee-car-after-walking-20-miles-to-work/article_f6561e68-65ab-5fa2-abed-dae5ff992bd6.html.

162. J. Porter, "How to Move from Self-Awareness to Self-Improvement," *Harvard Business Review*, November 2019, pp. 37–38.

163. "Productivity Stop Checking Off Easy To-Dos," *Harvard Business Review*, November–December 2017, p. 24.

164. E.B. Hemphill, "Uncomfortable (but Necessary) Conversations about Burnout," *Gallup*, December 6, 2022, https://www.gallup.com/workplace/406232/uncomfortable-necessary-conversations-burnout.aspx.

165. E. Saunders, "Working Parents, Give Yourself Permission to Recharge," *Harvard Business Review Digital Articles*, February 2020, pp. 1–5. Also see E. Cirino, "Recharge Your Personal Battery with These Activities," *Healthline*, October 26, 2018, https://www.healthline.com/health/how-to-recharge#overview.

CHAPTER 13

1. W. Elsey, "Conflict Management Tips: 4 Ways to Navigate Conflict at Work." Forbes, January 25, 2023, https://www.forbes.com/sites/forbesbusinessdevelopmentcouncil/2023/01/25/conflict-management-tips-4-ways-to-navigate-conflict-at-work/?sh=2d0b42dc6d3a. Also see P. Reynolds, "Preventing and Managing Team Conflict." Harvard DCE, October 31, 2022, https://professional.dce.harvard.edu/blog/preventing-and-managing-team-conflict/; T. West, "How to Deal with Office Jerks," *Wall Street Journal*, February 19, 2022, https://www.wsj.com/articles/how-to-deal-with-annoying-co-workers-11645222368.

2. M. Doblinger, "Individual competencies for self-managing team performance: A systematic literature review," *Small Group Research*, 53, 2022, pp. 128–180. Also see B. Salcinovic, M. Drew, P. Dijkstra, G. Waddington, and B. G. Serpell, "Factors influencing team performance: what can support teams in high-performance sport learn from other industries? A systematic scoping review," *Sports Medicine-Open*, 8, 2022, pp. 1–18, https://doi.org/10.1186/s40798-021-00406-7.

3. P.F. Drucker, "The Coming of the New Organization," *Harvard Business Review,* January–February 1988, pp. 45–53.

4. This definition is based in part on one found in D. Horton Smith, "A Parsimonious Definition of 'Group': Toward Conceptual Clarity and Scientific Utility," *Sociological Inquiry*, Spring 1967, pp. 141–167.

5. J.R. Katzenbach and D.K. Smith, "The Wisdom of Teams: Creating the High- Performance Organization," *Harvard Business Review*, March–April 1993, https://hbr.org/1993/03/the-discipline-of-teams-2.

6. J.R. Katzenbach and D.K. Smith, "The Wisdom of Teams: Creating the High- Performance Organization," *Harvard Business Review*, March–April 1993, https://hbr.org/1993/03/the-discipline-of-teams-2.

7. C. Towers-Clark, "Losing My Direction—Merging Formal and Informal Networks (Part 1—Formal Networks)," *Forbes*, October 31, 2022, https://www.forbes.com/sites/charlestowersclark/2022/10/31/losing-my-directionmerging-formal-and-informal-networks-part-1formal-networks/?sh=65ef4dfe2895. Also see C. Towers-Clark, "Losing My Direction—Merging Formal and Informal Networks (Part 2—Informal Networks)," *Forbes*, November 1, 2022, https://www.forbes.com/sites/charlestowersclark/2022/11/01/losing-my-directionmerging-formal-and-informal-networks-part-2informal-networks/?sh=5a91b5e878d6.

8. N. Catalino, N. Gardner, D. Goldstein, and J. Wong, "Effective Employee Resource Groups Are Key to Inclusion at Work. Here's How to Get Them Right," *McKinsey & Company*, December 7, 2022, https://www.mckinsey.com/capabilities/people-and-organizational-performance/our-insights/effective-employee-resource-groups-are-key-to-inclusion-at-work-heres-how-to-get-them-right. Also see S. Miller, "Employee Resource Groups Create a Sense of Belonging, Foster Engagement," *Society for Human Resource Management*, June 12, 2022, https://www.shrm.org/resourcesandtools/hr-topics/benefits/pages/employee-resource-groups-create-a-sense-of-belonging.aspx.

9. B.E. Ashforth and R.H. Humphrey, "Institutionalized Affect in Organizations: Not an Oxymoron," *Human Relations*, Vol. 75 (2022), pp. 1483–1517.

10. "2022 FIFA World Cup," *SKYMAGIC,* https://skymagic.show/project/2022-fifa-world-cup/ (accessed April 3, 2023). Also see "About SKYMAGIC," *SKYMAGIC,* https://skymagic.show/about/ (accessed April 3, 2023).

11. "Surgical Team," *Johns Hopkins Medicine,* https://www.hopkinsmedicine.org/health/treatment-tests-and-therapies/the-surgical-team (accessed April 3, 2023).

12. M.J. Vaulont, J.D. Nahrgang, M.M. Luciano, L. D'Innocenzo, and C.T. Lofgren, "The Room Where It Happens: The Impact of Core and Noncore Roles on Surgical Team Performance," *Journal of Applied Psychology,* Vol. 106 (2021), pp. 1767–1783.

13. F.T. Koe, "Instead of Putting People on Teams, Let Employees Form Their Own Teams. The Result May Surprise You," *Entrepreneur,* April 14, 2022, https://www.entrepreneur.com/leadership/instead-of-putting-people-on-teams-let-employees-form/423404.

14. M. Krzywdzinski and M. Greb, "Teamwork: From Self-Managed to Lean and Agile Teams," in *Shifting Categories of Work* (Routledge, 2022) pp. 73–86.

15. R.J. Ellis, "A Chronology of the Evolution of Self-Managed Teams: A Humanistic Organizational Structure," *Organization Development Journal,* Vol. 41 (2023), pp. 82–94. Also see N.C. Magpili and P. Pazos, "Self-Managing Team Performance: A Systematic Review of Multilevel Input Factors," *Small Group Research,* Vol. 49 (2018), pp. 3–33.

16. M. Doblinger, "Individual Competencies for Self-Managing Team Performance: A Systematic Literature Review," *Small Group Research,* Vol. 53 (2022), pp. 128–180.

17. "Remote Work Statistics: Shifting Norms and Expectations," *Flex Jobs,* February 13, 2020, https://www.flexjobs.com/blog/post/remote-work-statistics/.

18. "Is Remote Work Effective: We Finally Have the Data," *McKinsey,* June 23, 2022, https://www.mckinsey.com/industries/real-estate/our-insights/americans-are-embracing-flexible-work-and-they-want-more-of-it.

19. "Is Remote Work Effective: We Finally Have the Data," *McKinsey,* June 23, 2022, https://www.mckinsey.com/industries/real-estate/our-insights/americans-are-embracing-flexible-work-and-they-want-more-of-it.

20. "The Future of Work: A Trends Forecast for 2023," *International Workplace Group,* https://assets.iwgplc.com/image/upload/v1671807904/IWG/MediaCentre/IWG_White_Paper_Trends_Forecast_2023.pdf (accessed April 5, 2023).

21. M. Kilcullen, J. Feitosa, and E. Salas, "Insights from the Virtual Team Science: Rapid Deployment during COVID-19," *Human Factors,* Vol. 64 (2022), pp. 1429–1440.

22. K. Gilli, V. Veglio, M. Gunkel, and V. Taras, "In Search of the Holy Grail in Global Virtual Teams: The Mediating Role of Satisfaction on Performance Outcomes," *Journal of Business Research,* Vol. 146 (2022), pp. 325–337.

23. K. Gosnell, "Why Remote Work Is Good for Business," *Business.com,* June 29, 2022, https://www.business.com/articles/remote-work-good-for-business/.

24. "The State of Remote Work: 5 Trends to Know for 2023," *PR Newswire,* February 21, 2023, https://www.prnewswire.com/news-releases/the-state-of-remote-work-5-trends-to-know-for-2023-301751351.html.

25. "What Are the Challenges of Working in Virtual Teams?" *Experteer*, July 20, 2018, https://us.experteer.com/magazine/what-are-the-challenges-of-working-in-virtual-teams/. Also see "How-to Guide: How to Manage Team Time Zone Challenges," *1 Million for Work Flexibility*, https://www.workflexibility.org/how-to-manage-team-time-zone-challenges/ (accessed April 11, 2020).

26. J. Lauring, R. Drogendijk, and A. Kubovcikova, "The Role of Context in Overcoming Distance-Related Problems in Global Virtual Teams: An Organizational Discontinuity Theory Perspective," *The International Journal of Human Resource Management,* Vol. 33 (2022), pp. 4251–4283.

27. E.L. Keating, "Why Do Virtual Meetings Feel so Weird?" *American Scientist,* https://www.americanscientist.org/article/why-do-virtual-meetings-feel-so-weird (accessed April 5, 2023). See also A. Caputo, M. Kargina, and

M.M. Pellegrini, "Conflict in Virtual Teams: A Bibliometric Analysis, Systematic Review, and Research Agenda," *International Journal of Conflict Management,* Vol. 34 (2023), pp. 1–31; K. Swart, T. Bond-Barnard, and R. Chugh, "Challenges and Critical Success Factors of Digital Communication, Collaboration and Knowledge Sharing in Project Management Virtual Teams: A Review," *International Journal of Information Systems and Project Management,* Vol. 10 (2022), pp. 84–103.

28. I. Villamor, N.S. Hill, E.E. Kossek, and K.O. Foley, "Virtuality at Work: A Doubled-Edged Sword for Women's Career Equality?" *Academy of Management Annals,* Vol. 17 (2023), pp. 113–140.

29. "11 Effective Ways to Support Enhanced Virtual Communication," *Forbes,* October 20, 2021, https://www.forbes.com/sites/forbesbusinesscouncil/2021/10/20/11-effective-ways-to-support-enhanced-virtual-communication/?sh=4ed5f26e5e7b.

30. K. DePaul, "Is Remote Work Right for You?" *Harvard Business Review,* March 9, 2023, https://hbr.org/2023/03/is-remote-work-right-for-you.

31. "Virtual Team Building Activities: 43 BEST Ideas for Work in 2023," *Teambuilding.com,* November 30, 2022, https://teambuilding.com/blog/virtual-team-building-activities.

32. C. Breuer, J. Hüffmeier, F. Hibben, and G. Hertel, "Trust in Teams: A Taxonomy of Perceived Trustworthiness Factors and Risk-Taking Behaviors in Face-to-Face and Virtual Teams," *Human Relations,* Vol. 73 (2020), pp. 3–34.

33. M. Saratchandra and A. Shrestha, "The Role of Cloud Computing in Knowledge Management for Small and Medium Enterprises: A Systematic Literature Review," *Journal of Knowledge Management,* 2022, pp. 2668–2698. Also see F. Iddris, P.O. Mensah, R. Asiedu, and H.K. Mensah, "Student Innovation Capability in Virtual tTeam Projects: Lessons Learnt from COVID-19 Pandemic Dra," *International Journal of Innovation Science,* 2022, pp. 113–134.

34. "How to Work Remotely—and Enjoy It, Too," *Clevertech,* https://clevertech.biz/insights/discovering-remote-work (accessed April 5, 2023). Also see K. DePaul, "Is Remote Work Right for You?" *Harvard Business Review,* March 9, 2023, https://hbr.org/2023/03/is-remote-work-right-for-you.

35. "11 Effective Ways to Support Enhanced Virtual Communication," *Forbes,* October 20, 2021, https://www.forbes.com/sites/forbesbusinesscouncil/2021/10/20/11-effective-ways-to-support-enhanced-virtual-communication/?sh=4ed5f26e5e7b. Also see J.V. Dinh, D.L. Reyes, L. Kayga, C. Lindgren, J. Feitosa, and E. Salas, "Developing Team Trust: Leader Insights for Virtual Settings," *Organizational Dynamics,* Vol. 50 (2021), pp. 1–11.

36. S. Morrison-Smith and J. Ruiz, "Challenges and Barriers in Virtual Teams: A Lterature Review," *SN Applied Sciences,* Vol. 2 (2020), pp. 1–33.

37. D.P. Taylor, "Improve Face-To-Face Communication with These 5 Benefits," *The Motley Fool,* August 5, 2022, https://www.fool.com/the-ascent/small-business/video-conferencing/articles/face-to-face-communication/.

38. E. Goldberg, "Do We Know How Many People Are Working from Home?" *The New York Times,* April 2, 2023, https://www.nytimes.com/2023/03/30/business/economy/remote-work-measure-surveys.html#:~:text=Stanford.

39. C. Breuer, "Trust in Teams: A Taxonomy of Perceived Trustworthiness Factors and Risk-Taking Behaviors in Face-to-Face and Virtual Teams," *Human Relations*, Vol. 73 (2020), pp. 3–34. Also see K. Jaakson, A. Reino, and P. B. McClenaghan, "The Space between—Linking Trust with Individual and Team Performance in Virtual Teams," *Team Performance Management: An International Journal*, October 2018, pp. 30–46.

40. E.R. Crawford, "Team Processes," *Oxford Bibliographies,* July 29, 2020, https://www.oxfordbibliographies.com/display/document/obo-9780199846740/obo-9780199846740-0192.xml#:~:text=Team%20processes%20refer%20to%20the,or%20thoughts%20among%20team%20members.

41. B.W. Tuckman, "Developmental Sequence in Small Groups," *Psychological Bulletin,* June 1965, pp. 384–399; B.W. Tuckman and M.A.C. Jensen, "Stages of Small-Group Development Revisited," *Group & Organization Studies,* December 1977, pp. 419–427.

42. M. Kiweewa, D. Gilbride, M. Luke, and T. Clingerman, "Tracking Growth Factors in Experiential Training Groups through Tuckman's Conceptual Model," *The Journal for Specialists in Group Work*, July 2018, pp. 274–296.

43. E.J. Donald, and A. Carter, "Overview of Common Group Theories," *Group Development and Group Leadership in Student Affairs,* 2021, pp. 17–25. Also see D. Jones, "The Tuckman's Model Implementation, Effect, and Analysis & the New Development of Jones LSI Model on a Small Group," *Journal of Management,* Vol. 6 (2019), pp. 23–28.

44. J. Lim, "Navigating the Pathway to Leader Emergence in Self-Managed Work Groups over Time: Should I Self-Promote and Try to Emerge Initially as a Leader?" *Sex Roles,* April 2019, pp. 489–502.

45. M. Kankousky, "6 Ways to Help New Employees Mesh Well with Their Team," *Insperity,* https://www.insperity.com/blog/6-ways-help-new-employees-mesh-well-team/ (accessed April 5, 2023).

46. J. Stein, "Using the Stages of Team Development," *MIT,* https://hr.mit.edu/learning-topics/teams/articles/stages-development (accessed April 5, 2023).

47. J. Jyoti, "Fun at Workplace and Intention to Leave: Role of Work Engagement and Group Cohesion," *International Journal of Contemporary Hospitality Management,* Vol. 34 (2022), pp. 782–807.

48. J.M. Kiweewa, D. Gilbride, M. Luke, and T. Clingerman, "Tracking Growth Factors in Experiential Training Groups through Tuckman's Conceptual Model," *The Journal for Specialists in Group Work*, July 2018, pp. 274–296. Also see T. Hall, "Does Cohesion Positively Correlate to Performance in All Stages of a Group's Life Cycle," *Journal of Organizational Culture, Communications and Conflict,* January 2015, pp. 58–69.

49. U. Leicht-Deobald, C.F. Lam, H. Bruch, F. Kunze, and W. Wu, "Team Boundary Work and Team Workload Demands: Their Interactive Effect on Team Vigor and Team Effectiveness," *Human Resource Management,* Vol. 61 (2022), pp. 465–488. Also see M.S. Cole, H. Bruch, and B. Vogel, "Energy at Work: A Measurement Validation and Linkage to Unit Effectiveness," *Journal of Organizational Behavior,* May 2012, pp. 445–467.

50. C.J.G. Gersick, "Revolutionary Change Theories: A Multilevel Exploration of the Punctuated Equilibrium Paradigm," *Academy of Management Review,* Vol. 16 (1991), pp. 10–36.

51. J. Toonkel and S. Krouse, "Who Owns SpongeBob? AI Shakes Hollywood's Creative Foundation," *Wall Street Journal,* April 4, 2023, https://www.wsj.com/articles/ai-chatgpt-hollywood-intellectual-property-spongebob-81fd5d15.

52. B.L. Kirkman and A. Stoverink, *Unbreakable: Building and Leading Resilient Teams* (Stanford University Press, 2023). Also see A.N. Li and S. Tangirala, "How Employees' Voice Helps Teams Remain Resilient in the Face of Exogenous Change," *Journal of Applied Psychology,* Vol. 107 (2022), pp. 668–692; C.-Y. Chiu, P. Balkundi, B.P. Owens, and P.E. Tesluk, "Shaping Positive and Negative Ties to Improve Team Effectiveness: The Roles of Leader Humility and Team Helping Norms," *Human Relations,* Vol. 75 (2022), pp. 502–531; L.L. Martins and W. Sohn, "How Does Diversity Affect Team Cognitive Processes? Understanding the Cognitive Pathways Underlying the Diversity Dividend in Teams," *Academy of Management Annals,* Vol. 16 (2022), pp. 134–178.

53. Y. Yuan and D. Van Knippenberg, "Leader Network Centrality and Team Performance: Team Size as Moderator and Collaboration as Mediator," *Journal of Business and Psychology,* 2022, pp. 1–14.

54. "Realigning Incentives along the Value Chain to Reform Health Care," *Harvard Business Review*, May 2020.

55. A. Frederiksen, D.B.S. Hansen, and C.F. Manchester, "Does Group-Based Incentive Pay Lead to Higher Productivity? Evidence from a Complex and Interdependent Industrial Production Process," *IZA Institute of Labor Economics,* Discussion Paper No. 14986, 2022, Available at SSRN: https://ssrn.com/abstract=4114109 or http://dx.doi.org/10.2139/ssrn.4114109.

56. Y. Tian, H. Zhang, Y. Jiang, and Y. Yang, "Understanding Trust and Perceived Risk in Sharing Accommodation: An Extended Elaboration Likelihood Model and Moderated by Risk Attitude,"

57. K.T. Dirks and B. de Jong, "Trust within the Workplace: A Review of Two Waves of Research and a Glimpse of the Third," *Annual Review of Organizational Psychology and Organizational Behavior,* Vol. 9 (2022), pp. 247–276. Also see J. Feitosa, R. Grossman, W.S. Kramer, and E. Salas, "Measuring Team Trust: A Critical and Meta-Analytical Review," *Journal of Organizational Behavior,* Vol. 41 (2020), pp. 479–501; A.C. Costa, C.A. Fulmer, and N.R. Anderson, "Trust in Work Teams: An Integrative Review, Multilevel Model, and Future Directions," *Journal of Organizational Behavior,* Vol. 39 (2018), pp. 169–184; B.A. De Jong, K.T. Dirks, and N. Gillespie, "Trust and Team Performance: A Meta-Analysis of Main Effects, Moderators, and Covariates," *Journal of Applied Psychology,* Vol. 101 (2016), pp. 1134–1150.

58. W. Chen, J.-H. Zhang, and Y.-L. Zhang, "How Shared Leadership Affects Team Performance: Examining Sequential Mediation Model Using MASEM," *Journal of Managerial Psychology,* Vol. 37 (2022), pp. 669–682.

59. J. Thier, "Tim Cook Called Remote Work 'the Mother of All Experiments.' Now Apple Is Cracking down on Employees Who Don't Come in 3 Days a Week, Report Says," *Yahoo! Life,* March 24, 2023, https://www.yahoo.com/lifestyle/tim-cook-called-remote-mother-165415471.html.

60. F. Frei and A. Morriss, "Trust: The Foundation of Leadership," *Leader to Leader,* Vol. 99 (2021), pp. 20–25. Also see R. Carucci, "Build Your Reputation as a Trustworthy Leader," *Harvard Business Review,* June 11, 2021, https://hbr.org/2021/06/build-your-reputation-as-a-trustworthy-leader.

61. B. Salcinovic, M. Drew, P. Dijkstra, G. Waddington, and B.G. Serpell, "Factors Influencing Team Performance: What Can Support Teams in High-Performance Sport Learn from Other Industries? A Systematic Scoping Review," *Sports Medicine-Open,* Vol. 8 (2022), pp. 1–18, https://doi.org/10.1186/s40798-021-00406-7.

62. C. Gulledge, "Like a NASCAR Pit Crew, Here's How to Master Your Organizational Game Plan," *Forbes,* June 2, 2020, https://www.forbes.com/sites/forbescoachescouncil/2020/06/02/like-a-nascar-pit-crew-heres-how-to-master-your-organizational-game-plan/?sh=71b8d95955a7.

63. E. Bernstein, J. Bunch, N. Canner, and M. Lee, "Beyond the Holacracy Hype," *Harvard Business Review,* July–August 2016, p. 43.

64. S.H. Courtright, G.R. Thurgood, G.L. Stewart, and A.J. Pierotti, "Structural Interdependence in Teams: An Integrative Framework and Meta-Analysis," *Journal of Applied Psychology,* November 2015, pp. 1825–1846.

65. S.H. Courtright, G.R. Thurgood, G.L. Stewart, and A.J. Pierotti, "Structural Interdependence in Teams: An Integrative Framework and Meta-Analysis," *Journal of Applied Psychology,* November 2015, pp. 1825–1846.

66. I. Grabner, A. Klein, and G. Speckbacher, "Managing the Trade-Off between Autonomy and Task Interdependence in Creative Teams: The Role of Organizational-Level Cultural Control," *Accounting, Organizations and Society,* Vol. 101 (2022), 101347.

67. L.L. Martins and W. Sohn, "How Does Diversity Affect Team Cognitive Processes? Understanding the Cognitive Pathways Underlying the Diversity Dividend in Yeams," *Academy of Management Annals,* Vol. 16 (2022), pp. 134–178. Also see L. Patrício and M. Franco, "A Systematic Literature Review about Team Diversity and Team Performance: Future Lines of Investigation," *Administrative Sciences,* Vol. 12 (2022), p. 31.

68. J.G. Lu, R.I. Swaab, and A.D. Galinsky, "Global Leaders for Global Teams: Leaders with Multicultural Experiences Communicate and Lead More Effectively, Especially in Multinational Teams," *Organization Science,* Vol. 33 (2022), pp. 1554–1573.

69. H. Hajarolasvadi and V. Shahhosseini, "A System-Dynamic Model for Evaluating the Effect of Person–Team Fit on Project Performance," *Journal of Construction Engineering and Management,* Vol. 148 (2022), 04022126. Also see J. Billsberry, B.M. Hollyoak, and D.L. Talbot, "Insights into the Lived Experience of Misfits at Work: A Netnographic Study," *European Journal of Work and Organizational Psychology,* 2022, pp. 1–17; D. Memmert, H. Plessner, S. Hüttermann, G. Froese, C. Peterhänsel, and C. Unkelbach, "Collective Fit Increases Team Performances: Extending Regulatory Fit from Individuals to Dyadic Teams," *Journal of Applied Social Psychology,* Vol. 45 (2015), pp. 274–281.

70. K. Woo, "Why Cardinals' Paul Goldschmidt Is Valuing Leadership above All after MVP Season," *The Athletic,* February 21, 2023, https://theathletic.com/4232579/2023/02/21/cardinals-mlb-paul-goldschmidt-mvp/.

71. C. Bicchieri and A. Funcke, "Norm Change: Trendsetters and Social Structure," *Social Research,* April 2008, pp. 1–21.

72. D.C. Feldman, "The Development and Enforcement of Group Norms," *Academy of Management Review,* January 1984, pp. 47–53.

73. A. Schecter, A. Pilny, A. Leung, M.S. Poole, and N. Contractor, "Step by Step: Capturing the Dynamics of Work Team Process through Relational Event Sequences," *Journal of Organizational Behavior,* November 2018, pp. 1163–1181. Also see T. Friehe, "Predicting Norm Enforcement: The Individual and Joint Predictive Power of Economic Preferences, Personality, and Self-Control," *European Journal of Law and Economics,* February 2018, pp. 127–146.

74. D.C. Feldman, "The Development and Enforcement of Group Norms," *Academy of Management Review,* January 1984, pp. 47–53.

75. B. Laker, and V. Pereira, "4 Triggers Cause the Majority of Team Conflicts," *Harvard Business Review,* May 31, 2022, https://hbr.org/2022/05/conflict-is-not-always-bad-but-you-should-know-how-to-manage-it.

76. J.A. Wall Jr. and R. Robert Callister, "Conflict and Its Management," *Journal of Management,* Vol. 3 (1995), p. 517.

77. D. DeNatale, "Former MetroHealth CEO Akram Boutros Defied Board's Authority by Awarding Himself Bonus, Hospital Says in Court Filing," *WKYC,* January 31, 2023, https://www.wkyc.com/article/news/local/cleveland/former-metrohealth-ceo-akram-boutros-defied-board-authority-hospital-says-court-filing/95-5c429d77-6d0f-4487-8295-adda92a838f4.

78. D. Tjosvold, *Learning to Manage Conflict: Getting People to Work Together Productively* (New York: Lexington, 1993); D. Tjosvold and D. W. Johnson, *Productive Conflict Management Perspectives for Organizations* (New York: Irvington, 1983).

79. T. A. O'Neill, G.C. Hoffart, M.M.J.W. Mclarnon, H.J. Woodley, M. Eggermont, W. Rosehart, and R. Brennan, "Constructive Controversy and Reflexivity Training Promotes Effective Conflict Profiles and Team Functioning in Student Learning Teams," *Academy of Management Learning & Education,* June 2017, pp. 257–276.

80. M. Qi, S.J. Armstrong, Z. Yang, and X. Li, "Cognitive Diversity and Team Creativity: Effects of Demographic Faultlines, Subgroup Imbalance and Information Elaboration," *Journal of Business Research,* Vol. 139 (2022), pp. 819–830.

81. J. Dhar, S. Rafiq, and K. Gudziak, "Beyond 'Agree to Disagree': Why Leaders Need to Foster a Culture of Productive Disagreement and Debate," *BCG,* July 25, 2022, https://www.bcg.com/publications/2022/fostering-a-culture-of-productive-conflict. Also see "Pixar's Ed Catmull on Innovation (Part II): Why a 'Brain Trust' Is Key for Successful Team Collaboration," *Disney Institute,* September 10, 2019, https://www.disneyinstitute.com/blog/pixars-ed-catmull-on-innovation-part-ii-why-a-brain-trust-is-key-for-successful-team-collaboration/.

82. H. Wei, D. Shan, L. Wang, and S. Zhu, "Research on the Mechanism of Leader Aggressive Humor on Employee Silence: A Conditional Process Model," *Journal of Vocational Behavior,* Vol. 135 (2022), 103717. Also see K.L. Krueger, M.A. Diabes, and L.R. Weingart, "The Psychological Experience of Intragroup Conflict," *Research in Organizational Behavior,* Vol. 42 (2022), 100165.

83. B. Laker and V. Pereira, "4 Triggers Cause the Majority of Team Conflicts," *Harvard Business Review,* May 31, 2022, https://hbr.org/2022/05/conflict-is-not-always-bad-but-you-should-know-how-to-manage-it.

84. J. Yao, S. Lim, C.Y. Guo, A.Y. Ou, and J.W.X. Ng, "Experienced Incivility in the Workplace: A Meta-Analytical Review of Its Construct Validity and Nomological Network," *Journal of Applied Psychology,*

Vol. 107 (2022), pp. 193–120. Also see S. Han, C.M. Harold, I.-S. Oh, J.K. Kim, and A. Agolli, "A Meta-Analysis Integrating 20 Years of Workplace Incivility Research: Antecedents, Consequences, and Boundary Conditions," *Journal of Organizational Behavior,* Vol. 43 (2022), pp. 497–523.

85. A. Steingrad and T. Barrabi, "Disney Mired in Chaos as Bob Iger Takes Reins Back from 'Novice' CEO," *New York Post,* November 21, 2022, https://nypost.com/2022/11/21/disney-mired-in-chaos-as-bob-iger-takes-reins-back-from-novice-ceo/. Also see J. Flint, R. Whelan, E. Schwartzel, E. Glazer, and J. Toonkel, "Bob Iger vs. Bob Chapek: Inside the Disney Coup," *Wall Street Journal,* December 17, 2022, https://www.wsj.com/articles/bob-iger-bob-chapek-disney-coup-11671236928.

86. L. Battle and D.L. Diab, "Is Envy Always Bad? An Examination of Benign and Malicious Envy in the Workplace," *Psychological Reports,* 2022, 00332941221138476.

87. R. Yuniati and C. Sitinjak, "Upward Comparison at the Workplace: A Review," *East Asian Journal of Multidisciplinary Research,* Vol. 1 (2022), pp. 1377–1394.

88. D.V. Tussing, A. Wihler, T.V. Astandu, and J.I. Menges, "Should I Stay or Should I Go? The Role of Individual Strivings in Shaping the Relationship between Envy and Avoidance Behaviors at Work," *Journal of Organizational Behavior,* Vol. 43 (2022), pp. 567–583.

89. A. Wells, "Padres' Manny Machado Explains Contract Decision: 'Price of Eggs Is How Much?'" *Bleacher Report,* February 24, 2023, https://bleacherreport.com/articles/10066712-padres-manny-machado-explains-contract-decision-price-of-eggs-is-how-much#:~:text=Machado%20told%20reporters%20on%20Feb. Also see K. Acee, "Structure of Manny Machado's New Contract Leaves Padres Room to Add More Big Names," *San Diego Union-Tribune,* February 28, 2023, https://www.sandiegouniontribune.com/sports/padres/story/2023-02-28/padres-manny-machado-contract-shohei-ohtani-juan-soto-free-agents.

90. N.A. Den Nieuwenboer, J.J. Kish-Gephart, L.K. Treviño, A.C. Peng, and I. Reychav, "The Dark Side of Status at Work: Perceived Status Importance, Envy, and Interpersonal Deviance," *Business Ethics Quarterly,* 2022, pp. 1–35. Also see J.-Y. Mao, J. Quan, X. Liu, and X. Zheng, "Too Drained to Obey! A Daily Study on How Workplace Envy Fosters Employee Deviance and the Buffering Role of Ethical Leadership," *Applied Psychology,* Vol. 71 (2022), pp. 1304–1325.

91. A. Satariano, "Meta's Ad Practices Ruled Illegal under E.U. Law," *The New York Times,* January 4, 2023, https://www.nytimes.com/2023/01/04/technology/meta-facebook-eu-gdpr.html. Also see T. Collins, "EU Passes Historic Law to Hold Social Media Sites Accountable for Illegal Content," *USA Today,* April 22, 2022, https://www.usatoday.com/story/tech/2022/04/22/european-union-law-meta-facebook-google/7419892001/; M. Scott, "Why Facebook Is More Worried about Europe Than the U.S.," *Politico,* November 2, 2021, https://www.politico.com/news/agenda/2021/11/02/facebook-europe-privacy-content-laws-518514.

92. M. Moussa, T. Doumani, A. McMurray, N. Muenjohn, and L. Deng, "Performance Management Management across Cultures," in *Cross-Cultural Performance Management: Transcending Theory to a Practical Framework* (Cham: Springer International Publishing, 2022), pp. 1–21. Also see S. Kotiloglu, Y. Chen, and T. Lechler, "Organizational Responses to Performance Feedback: A Meta-Analytic Review," *Strategic Organization,* Vol. 19 (2021), pp. 285–311.

93. J.G. Lu, R.I. Swaab, and A.D. Galinsky, "Global Leaders for Global Teams: Leaders with Multicultural Experiences Communicate and Lead More Effectively, Especially in Multinational Teams," *Organization Science,* Vol. 33 (2022), pp. 1554–1573.

94. "Managing Workplace Conflict," *SHRM,* https://www.shrm.org/resourcesandtools/tools-and-samples/toolkits/pages/managingworkplaceconflict.aspx (accessed April 13, 2023).

95. S.G. Katzenstein, "The Debate on Structured Debate: Toward a Unified Theory," *Organizational Behavior and Human Decision Processes,* June 1996, pp. 316–332.

96. "Managing Workplace Conflict," *Society for Human Resource Management,* https://www.shrm.org/resourcesandtools/tools-and-samples/toolkits/pages/managingworkplaceconflict.aspx (accessed April 13, 2023). Also see W. Elsey, "Conflict Management Tips: 4 Ways to Navigate Conflict at Work," *Forbes,* January 25, 2023, https://www.forbes.com/sites/forbesbusinessdevelopmentcouncil/2023/01/25/conflict-management-tips-4-ways-to-navigate-conflict-at-work/?sh=4312a68f6d3a; B. Laker and V. Pereira, "4 Triggers Cause the Majority of Team Conflicts," *Harvard Business Review,* May 31, 2022, https://hbr.org/2022/05/conflict-is-not-always-bad-but-you-should-know-how-to-manage-it.

97. M.A. Rahim, "A Strategy for Managing Conflict in Complex Organizations," *Human Relations,* January 1985, p. 84. Also see M.A. Rahim and N.R. Magner, "Confirmatory Factor Analysis of the Styles of Handling Interpersonal Conflict: First-Order Factor Model and Its Invariance across Groups," *Journal of Applied Psychology,* February 1995, pp. 122–132.

98. S. Rispens, K.A. Jehn, and W. Steinel, "Conflict Management Style Asymmetry in Short-Term Project Groups," *Small Group Research,* Vol. 52 (2021), pp. 220–242.

99. S. Murphy, "10 Leadership Focus Areas That Build High Performing Teams," *Inc.*, January 15, 2018, https://www.inc.com/shawn-murphy/10-leadership-focus-areas-that-build-high-performing-teams.html. Also see M.K. Stewart, "How Can You Be a More Effective Team Member," *Meeteor,* August 11, 2016, http://blog.meeteor.com/blog/effective-team-member.

100. J. Haden, "Why the Best Teams—Why Your Team—Needs a Nikola Jokic," *Inc.,* May 1, 2023, https://www.inc.com/sarah-lynch/how-to-introduce-your-employees-to-artificial-intelligence.html.

101. D. Gervasi, G. Faldetta, M.M. Pellegrini, and J. Maley, "Reciprocity in Organizational Behavior Studies: A Systematic Literature Review of Contents, Types, and Directions," *European Management Journal,* Vol. 40 (2022), pp. 441–457.

102. H.C.Y. Ho, W.K. Hou, K.-T. Poon, A.N.M. Leung, and J.L.Y. Kwan, "Being Virtuous Together: A One-Year Prospective Study on Organizational Virtuousness, Well-Being, and Organizational Commitment," *Applied Research in Quality of Life,* Vol. 18 (2023), pp. 521–542. Also see N. Pillay, G. Park, Y.K. Kim, and S. Lee, "Thanks for Your Ideas: Gratitude and Team Creativity," *Organizational Behavior and Human Decision Processes*, January 2020, pp. 69–81; J. Peñalver, M. Salanova, I.M. Martínez, and W.B. Schaufeli, "Happy-Productive Groups: How Positive Affect Links to Performance through Social Resources," *The Journal of Positive Psychology*, Vol. 14 (2019), pp. 377–392.

103. M. Patrick, "Why Business Management Should Lead by Example," *Forbes,* January 9, 2023, https://www.forbes.com/sites/forbesbusinesscouncil/2023/01/09/why-business-management-should-lead-by-example/?sh=1264eda13175.

104. T.O. Philogène, "Why Creating a Culture of Collaboration Is Critical to Business Success in the Age of Remote Work and How to Achieve It," *Forbes,* February 28, 2022, https://www.forbes.com/sites/forbestechcouncil/2022/02/28/why-creating-a-culture-of-collaboration-is-critical-to-business-success-in-the-age-of-remote-work-and-how-to-achieve-it/?sh=618d73d452a7.

105. R. Abrahams and B. Groysberg, "How to Become a Better Listener," Harvard Business Review, December 21, 2021, https://hbr.org/2021/12/how-to-become-a-better-listener.

106. R. Carucci and L. Velasquez, "When Leaders Struggle with Collaboration," *Harvard Business Review,* December 2, 2022, https://hbr.org/2022/12/when-leaders-struggle-with-collaboration.

107. "Leader Chat: 60% of Work Teams Fail—Top 10 Reasons Why," *Vickihalsey.com,* Accessed April 16, 2023, http://www.vickihalsey.com/leader-chat/437-60-of-work-teams-fail%E2%80%94top-10-reasons-why.

108. P. Lencioni, The five dysfunctions of a team, John Wiley & Sons, 2002.

109. G. Tsipursky, "The Key to Success in Hybrid and Remote Work Is Trust," *Entrepreneur,* August 29, 2022, https://www.entrepreneur.com/leadership/the-key-to-success-in-hybrid-and-remote-work-is-trust/432686.

110. S. Madan, K. Nanakdewa, K. Savani, and H.R. Markus, "Research: What Makes Employees Feel Empowered to Speak Up?" *Harvard Business Review*, October 13, 2021, https://hbr.org/2021/10/research-what-makes-employees-feel-empowered-to-speak-up.

111. X. Zheng, X. Liu, H. Liao, X. Qin, and D. Ni, "How and when top manager authentic leadership influences team voice: A moderated mediation model," *Journal of Business Research*, 145, 2022, pp. 144–155.

112. "Council Post: 15 Ways Leaders Can Encourage Employees to Voice Their Concerns," *Forbes*, May 26, 2022, https://www.forbes.com/sites/forbescoachescouncil/2022/05/26/15-ways-leaders-can-encourage-employees-to-voice-their-concerns/?sh=63534f6e1af9.

113. K. Bain, T.A. Kreps, N.L. Meikle, and E.R. Tenney, 2021, "Research: Amplifying Your Colleagues' Voices Benefits Everyone," *Harvard Business Review*, June 17, 2021, https://hbr.org/2021/06/research-amplifying-your-colleagues-voices-benefits-everyone.

114. J. E. Mathieu and T. L. Rapp, "Laying the Foundation for Successful Team Performance Trajectories: The Roles of Team Charters and Performance Strategies," *Journal of Applied Psychology*, 2009, pp. 90–103, p. 92.

115. S. T. Bell, S. G. Brown, A. Colaneri, and N. Outland, "Team Composition and the ABCs of Teamwork," *American Psychologist*, May-June 2018, pp. 349–362. Also see S. H. Courtright, B. W. McCormick, S. Mistry, and J. Wang, "Quality Charters of Quality Members? A Control Theory Perspective on Team Charters and Team Performance," *Journal of Applied Psychology*, October 2017, pp. 1462–1470.

116. S. Shellenbarger, "The Invisible Walls at Work," *The Wall Street Journal*, November 29, 2017, p. A11.

117. D. Maloney, "The Ultimate Guide to Remote Working Team Collaboration," Slack, March 18, 2020, https://slack.com/intl/es-la/blog/collaboration/ultimate-guide-collaboration-in-the-workplace.

118. A. C. M. Abrantes, A.M. Passos, M. Pina e Cunha, and C.M. Santos. "Getting the knack for team-improvised adaptation: The role of reflexivity and team mental model similarity," *The Journal of Applied Behavioral Science*, 58, 2022, pp. 281–315.

119. P-M Leblanc, V. Rousseau, and J-F. Harvey, "Leader humility and team innovation: The role of team reflexivity and team proactive personality," Journal of Organizational Behavior, 43, 2022, pp. 1396–1409.

120. N.U.I. Hadi, and A. Chaudhary, "Impact of shared leadership on team performance through team reflexivity: examining the moderating role of task complexity," *Team Performance Management: An International Journal*, 27, 2021, pp. 391–405.

121. N. L. Keiser, and W. Arthur Jr, "A meta-analysis of the effectiveness of the after-action review (or debrief) and factors that influence its effectiveness," *Journal of Applied Psychology*, 106, 2021, pp. 1007–1032.

CHAPTER 14

1. "USMC Leadership Principles," Officer Candidate School, https://officercandidatesschool.com/2021/10/24/usmc-leadership-principles/ (accessed April 17, 2023).

2. K.L. Badura, E. Grijalva, B.M. Galvin, B.P. Owens, and D.L. Joseph, "Motivation to Lead: A Meta-Analysis and Distal-Proximal Model of Motivation and Leadership," *Journal of Applied Psychology*, Vol. 105 (2020), pp. 331–354.

3. H. Horner, "What Leadership Style Do You Major In?" *Harvard Business Review*, February 10, 2023, https://hbr.org/2023/02/what-leadership-style-do-you-major-in.

4. F. Brenton, "How to Commit to Lifelong Learning for Leadership Success," *Forbes*, December 9, 2022, https://www.forbes.com/sites/forbestechcouncil/2022/12/09/how-to-commit-to-lifelong-learning-for-leadership-success/?sh=46d934f175a7.

5. "99 Inspirational Leadership Quotes," *Indeed Career Guide*, February 20, 2023, https://www.indeed.com/career-advice/career-development/leadership-quotes.

6. B. Monnet, "3 Steps to Creating a Culture of Problem-Solvers," *Entrepreneur*, October 25, 2022, https://www.entrepreneur.com/leadership/3-steps-to-creating-a-culture-of-problem-solvers/436071.

7. A. Lewis, "Importance of Trust in Leadership," *Harvard Business Publishing*, October 26, 2022, https://www.harvardbusiness.org/good-leadership-it-all-starts-with-trust/.

8. C.S. Reina, G.E. Kreiner, A. Rheinhardt, and C.A. Mihelcic, "Your Presence Is Requested: Mindfulness Infusion in Workplace Interactions and Relationships," *Organization Science*, Vol. 34 (2023), pp. 722–753.

9. C.S. Reina, G.E. Kreiner, A. Rheinhardt, and C.A. Mihelcic, "Your Presence Is Requested: Mindfulness Infusion in Workplace Interactions and Relationships," *Organization Science*, Vol. 34 (2023), pp. 722–753.

10. P.G. Northouse, *Leadership: Theory and Practice,* 6th ed. (Thousand Oaks, CA: Sage, 2012), p. 3.

11. C.B. Jacobsen, L.B. Andersen, A. Bøllingtoft, and T.L.M Eriksen, "Can Leadership Training Improve Organizational Effectiveness? Evidence from a Randomized Field Experiment on Transformational and Transactional Leadership," *Public Administration Review*, Vol. 82 (2022), pp. 117–131. Also see S.J. Allen, D.M. Rosch, and R.E. Riggio, "Advancing Leadership Education and Development: Integrating Adult Learning Theory," *Journal of Management Education*, Vol. 46 (2022), pp. 252–283; A.B. Bakker, J. Hetland, O.K. Olsen, and R. Espevik, "Daily Transformational Leadership: A Source of Inspiration for Follower Performance?" *European Management Journal*, 2022, https://doi.org/10.1016/j.emj.2022.04.004.

12. S.N. Taylor, A.M. Passarelli, and E.B. Van Oosten, "Leadership Coach Effectiveness as Fostering Self-Determined, Sustained Change," *The Leadership Quarterly*, Vol. 30 (2019), 101313.

13. L. Zhou, "The Coaching Industry Market Size in 2023," *Luisa Zhou*, March 7, 2023, https://www.luisazhou.com/blog/coaching-industry-market-size/.

14. A. Christensen-Salem, A. Kinicki, J. Perrmann-Graham, and F.O. Walumbwa, "CEO Performance Management Behaviors' Influence on TMT Flourishing, Job Attitudes, and Firm Performance," *Human Relations*, 2022, 00187267221119767. Also see A.N. Kiss, A.F. Cortes, and P. Herrmann, "CEO Proactiveness, Innovation, and Firm Performance," *The Leadership Quarterly*, Vol. 33 (2022), 101545; R. Reyes, R.S. Vassolo, E.E. Kausel, D.P. Torres, and S. Zhang, "Does Overconfidence Pay Off When Things Go Well? CEO Overconfidence, Firm Performance, and the Business Cycle," *Strategic Organization*, Vol. 20 (2022), pp. 510–540.

15. Z. Lyubykh, D. Gulseren, N. Turner, J. Barling, and M. Seifert, "Shared Transformational Leadership and Safety Behaviours of Employees Leaders, and Teams: A Multilevel Investigation," *Journal of Occupational and Organizational Psychology*, Vol. 95 (2022), pp. 431–458.

16. J.R. Bailey, "The Best Managers Are Leaders—and Vice Versa," *Harvard Business Review*, September 22, 2022. https://hbr.org/2022/09/the-best-managers-are-leaders-and-vice-versa. Also see J. Kraaijenbrink, "There Is No Difference between Managers and Leaders," *Forbes*, April 7, 2022, https://www.forbes.com/sites/jeroenkraaijenbrink/2022/04/07/there-is-no-difference-between-managers-and-leaders/?sh=70d267186e73.

17. S. Volk, D.A. Waldman, and C.M. Barnes, "A Circadian Theory of Paradoxical Leadership," *Academy of Management Review*, Vol. 8, No. 4 (2023), https://doi.org/10.5465/amr.2020.0468. Also see M.J. Zhang, Y. Zhang, and K.S. Law, "Paradoxical Leadership and Innovation in Work Teams: The Multilevel Mediating Role of Ambidexterity and Leader Vision as a Boundary Condition," *Academy of Management Journal*, Vol. 65 (2022), pp. 1652–1679; C.L. Pearce, C.L. Wassenaar, Y. Berson, and R. Tuval-Mashiach, "Toward a Theory of Meta-Paradoxical Leadership," *Organizational Behavior and Human Decision Processes*, Vol. 155 (2019), pp. 31–41.

18. T.O. Peterson, D.D. Van Fleet, and C.M. Peterson, "What Members Need in Work Situations: Two Samples of Essential Managerial Leadership Behaviors," *Journal of Managerial Issues*, Vol. 34 (2022), pp. 100–124. Also see G. Yukl, "Managerial Leadership: A Review of

Theory and Research," *Journal of Management,* Vol. 15 (1989), pp. 251–289.

19. C.J. Torelli, L.M. Leslie, C. To, and S. Kim, "Power and Status across Cultures," *Current Opinion in Psychology,* Vol. 33 (2020), pp. 12–17.

20. M. Rickley, "A Systematic Review of Power in Global Leadership," *Advances in Global Leadership,* 2023, pp. 3–35. Also see M. Kovach, "Leader Influence: A Research Review of French & Raven's (1959) Power Dynamics," *The Journal of Values-Based Leadership,* Vol. 13 (2020), https://doi.org/10.22543/0733.132.1312.

21. "Supporting Freight Agents with Insane Awards," *Tallgrass Freight,* August 25, 2022, https://tallgrassfreight.com/supporting-freight-agents-with-insane-awards/.

22. M. Repko, "CVS Fires Several Employees and Executives after Internal Sexual Harassment Investigation," *CNBC,* March 11, 2022, https://www.cnbc.com/2022/03/11/cvs-ceo-karen-lynch-fires-executives-after-internal-sexual-harassment-probe.html.

23. B. Berkowitz, "If You Invested $5,000 in Berkshire Hathaway in 2000, This Is How Much You Would Have Today," *The Motley Fool,* October 10, 2022, https://www.fool.com/investing/2022/10/10/if-you-invested-5000-in-berkshire-hathaway-in-2000/#:~:text=Between%20 1965%20and%202021%2C%20Berkshire. Also see A. Otani, "Warren Buffett's Last Charity Lunch Auction Draws Record $19 Million Bid," *Wall Street Journal,* June 18, 2022, https://www.wsj.com/articles/warren-buffetts-last-charity-lunch-auction-draws-record-19-million-bid-11655554293.

24. "Top Instagram Influencers in United States in 2022," *Starngage,* https://starngage.com/app/global/influencer/ranking/united-states (accessed April 20, 2023). Also see V. Padia, "The 8 Biggest Business Ventures of Dwayne 'the Rock' Johnson," *The Richest,* December 19, 2022, https://www.therichest.com/rich-powerful/the-8-biggest-business-ventures-of-dwayne-the-rock-johnson/.

25. B. Raven, J. Schwarzwald, and M. Koslowsky, "Conceptualizing and Measuring a Power/Interaction Model of Interpersonal Influence," *Journal of Applied Social Psychology,* Vol. 28, No. 4 (1998), pp. 307–332.

26. N. Chhaya, "How to Figure out the Power Dynamics in a New Job," *Harvard Business Review,* August 29, 2022, https://hbr.org/2022/08/how-to-figure-out-the-power-dynamics-in-a-new-job.

27. E. Harrell, "Persuasion—And Resistance," *Harvard Business Review,* Vol. 97, No. 6 (2019), pp. 162–163.

28. K. Cullen, A. Gerbasi, and D. Chrobot-Mason, "Thriving in Central Network Positions: The Role of Political Skill," *Journal of Management,* Vol. 44, No. 2 (2018), pp. 682–706. Also see L. Maher, V. Gallagher, A. Rossi, G. Ferris, and P. Perrewé, "Political Skill and Will as Predictors of Impression Management Frequency and Style: A Three-Study Investigation," *Journal of Vocational Behavior,* Vol. 107 (2018), pp. 276–294; E. Lvina, G. Johns, and C. Vandenberghe. "Team Political Skill Composition as a Determinant of Team Cohesiveness and Performance," *Journal of Management,* Vol. 44, No. 3 (2018), pp. 1001–1028.

29. "The Digitization Imperative, Insurance, and Change with Bill Pieroni," *Planck,* https://planckdata.com/the-digitization-imperative-insurance-and-change-with-bill-pieroni/ (accessed April 21, 2023).

30. "Lisa Su Quotes," *BrainyQuote,* https://www.brainyquote.com/authors/lisa-su-quotes#:~:text=The%20world%20is%20starving%20 for (accessed April 21, 2023). Also see H. Khederian, "'The Biggest Risk Is Not Taking Any Risk': 3 Inspiring Quotes from AMD Boss Lisa Su on Business and Life," *Benzinga,* March 27, 2023, https://www.benzinga.com/news/23/03/31504904/the-biggest-risk-is-not-taking-any-risk-3-inspiring-quotes-from-amd-boss-lisa-su-on-business-and-lif.

31. A. Ignatius, "Former Best Buy CEO Hubert Joly: Empowering Workers to Create 'Magic,'" *Harvard Business Review,* December 2, 2021, https://hbr.org/2021/12/former-best-buy-ceo-hubert-joly-empowering-workers-to-create-magic.

32. "Notice of Exempt Solicitation," *US Securities and Exchange Commission,* https://www.sec.gov/Archives/edgar/data/12927/000121465920003218/p46203px14a6g.htm (accessed April 21, 2023). Also see "Boeing Co Profile," *OpenSecrets,* https://www.opensecrets.org/orgs/boeing-co/summary?id=d000000100 (accessed April 21, 2023).

33. C. Fairchild, "Are Your Friendships at Work Holding You Back?" *LinkedIn,* November 6, 2019, https://www.linkedin.com/pulse/your-friendships-work-holding-you-back-caroline-fairchild.

34. J. Constantz, "Work Shift: There's Another Reason Your Boss May Want You Back at the Office," *Bloomberg,* February 21, 2023, https://www.bloomberg.com/news/newsletters/2023-02-21/tax-breaks-threaten-work-from-home-as-ceo-s-get-return-to-office-incentives. Also see E. Segal, "How Employers Are Enticing Workers back to the Office," *Forbes,* April 22, 2022, https://www.forbes.com/sites/edwardsegal/2022/04/22/how-companies-are-getting-their-employees-to-return-to-the-workplace/?sh=4ba83f5b30b1.

35. "Frequently Asked Questions," *Graham Windham,* https://www.graham-windham.org/frequently-asked-questions/#:~:text=Graham%20 Windham%20was%20established%20in (accessed April 21, 2023).

36. C. Davenport, "E.P.A. Is Said to Propose Rules Meant to Drive up Electric Car Sales Tenfold," *The New York Times,* April 8, 2023, https://www.nytimes.com/2023/04/08/climate/biden-electric-cars-epa.html.

37. "What Is Legitimate Power? 5 Examples of Legitimate Power," *MasterClass,* June 17, 2022, https://www.masterclass.com/articles/legitimate-power#498LIRt3CKblDOS3ZzOo9h.

38. C.M. Falbe and G. Yukl, "Consequences for Managers of Using Single Influence Tactics and Combinations of Tactics," *Academy of Management Journal,* Vol. 35 (1992), pp. 638–652.

39. S. Lee, S. Han, M. Cheong, S.L. Kim, and S. Yun, "How Do I Get My Way? A Meta-Analytic Review of Research on Influence Tactics," *The Leadership Quarterly,* Vol. 28 (2017), pp. 210–228.

40. S. Lee, S. Han, M. Cheong, S.L. Kim, and S. Yun, "How Do I Get My Way? A Meta-Analytic Review of Research on Influence Tactics," *The Leadership Quarterly,* Vol. 28 (2017), pp. 210–228.

41. S. Lee, S. Han, M. Cheong, S.L. Kim, and S. Yun, "How Do I Get My Way? A Meta-Analytic Review of Research on Influence Tactics," *The Leadership Quarterly,* Vol. 28 (2017), pp. 210–228.

42. "Mary Barra," *GM,* https://www.gm.com/company/leadership.detail.html/Pages/bios/global/en/corporate-officers/Mary-Barra (accessed April 24, 2023).

43. R. M. Stogdill, *Handbook of Leadership* (New York: Free Press, 1974). Also see B.M. Bass and R. Bass, *The Bass Handbook of Leadership: Theory, Research, and Managerial Applications,* 4th ed. (New York: Free Press, 2008). An update on the role of intelligence can be found in M. Daly, M. Egan, and F. O'Reilly, "Childhood General Cognitive Ability Predicts Leadership Role Occupancy across Life: Evidence from 17,000 Cohort Study Participants," *The Leadership Quarterly,* 2015, pp. 323–341.

44. B.M. Bass and R. Bass, *The Bass Handbook of Leadership: Theory, Research, and Managerial Applications,* 4th ed. (New York: Free Press, 2008).

45. K.L. Badura, E. Grijalva, B.M. Galvin, B.P. Owens, and D.L. Joseph, "Motivation to Lead: A Meta-Analysis and Distal-Proximal Model of Motivation and Leadership," *Journal of Applied Psychology,* Vol. 105 (2020), pp. 331–354.

46. These results are based on A.B. Blake, V.H. Luu, O.V. Petrenko, W.L. Gardner, K.J.N. Moergen, and M.E. Ezerins, "Let's Agree about Nice Leaders: A Literature Review and Meta-Analysis of Agreeableness and Its Relationship with Leadership Outcomes," *The Leadership Quarterly,* 2022, 101593; Also see J.D. Mackey, B.P. Ellen III, C.P. McAllister, and K.C. Alexander, "The Dark Side of Leadership: A Systematic Literature Review and Meta-Analysis of Destructive Leadership Research," *Journal of Business Research,* Vol. 132 (2021), pp. 705–718; K.L. Badura, E. Grijalva, B.M. Galvin, B.P. Owens, and D.L. Joseph, "Motivation to Lead: A Meta-Analysis and Distal-Proximal Model of Motivation and Leadership," *Journal of Applied Psychology,* Vol. 105 (2020), pp. 331–354; A. König, L. Graf-Vlachy, J. Bundy, and L.M. Little, "A Blessing and a Curse: How CEOs' Trait Empathy Affects Their Management of Organizational Crises," *Academy of Management Review,* Vol. 45 (2020), pp. 130–153; J.M.

46. J.M. LeBreton, L.K. Shiverdecker, and E.M. Grimaldi, "The Dark Triad and Workplace Behavior," *Annual Review of Organizational Psychology and Organizational Behavior*, Vol. 5 (2018), pp. 387–414.

47. G. Hoang, T.T. Luu, T.T.T. Le, and A.K.T. Tran, "Dark Triad Traits Affecting Entrepreneurial Intentions: The Roles of Opportunity Recognition and Locus of Control," *Journal of Business Venturing Insights*, Vol. 17 (2022), e00310.

48. J.D. Mackey, B.P. Ellen III, C.P. McAllister, and K.C. Alexander, "The Dark Side of Leadership: A Systematic Literature Review and Meta-Analysis of Destructive Leadership Research," *Journal of Business Research*, Vol. 132 (2021), pp. 705–718.

49. B.M. Galvin, D.A. Waldman, and P. Balthazard, "Visionary Communication Qualities as Mediators of the Relationship Between Narcissism and Attributions of Leader Charisma," *Personnel Psychology*, Vol. 63 (2010), pp. 509–537. Also see J.M. LeBreton, L.K. Shiverdecker, and E.M. Grimaldi, "The Dark Triad and Workplace Behavior," *Annual Review of Organizational Psychology and Organizational Behavior*, Vol. 5 (2018), pp. 387–414.

50. M. Tiwari and R. Jha, "Narcissism, Toxic Work Culture and Abusive Supervision: A Double-Edged Sword Escalating Organizational Deviance," *International Journal of Organizational Analysis*, Vol. 30 (2022), pp. 99–114.

51. F.R. Fox, M.B. Smith, and B.D. Webster, "Take Your Ethics and Shove It! Narcissists' Angry Responses to Ethical Leadership," *Personality and Individual Differences*, Vol. 204 (2023), 112032.

52. A. Hammali and N. Nastiezaie, "The Effect of Machiavelli Leadership on Destructive Organizational Behaviors through Mediation Job Stress," *International Journal of Psychology and Educational Studies*, Vol. 9 (2022), pp. 272–282.

53. K. Landay, P. Harms, and M. Credé, "Shall We Serve the Dark Lords? A Meta-Analytic Review of Psychopathy and Leadership," *Journal of Applied Psychology*, Vol. 104, No. 1 (2019), p. 183.

54. S. McClean, S.H. Courtright, T.A. Smith, and J. Yim, "Stop Making Excuses for Toxic Bosses," *Harvard Business Review*, January 19, 2021, https://hbr.org/2021/01/stop-making-excuses-for-toxic-bosses. Also see C.A. O'Reilly, and J.A. Chatman, "Transformational Leader or Narcissist? How Grandiose Narcissists Can Create and Destroy Organizations and Institutions," *California Management Review*, Vol. 62 (2020), pp. 5–27.

55. S.-H. Jeong, S. Kang, and K. Byron, "Bottom-Up Effects of Female Executives: Firm Performance Effects through Middle and Lower Management," *Academy of Management Proceedings*, Vol. 2022, No. 1 (2022) p. 16981. Also see C.S. Halliday, S.C. Paustian-Underdahl, and S. Fainshmidt, "Women on Boards of Directors: A Meta-Analytic Examination of the Roles of Organizational Leadership and National Context for Gender Equality," *Journal of Business and Psychology*, Vol. 36 (2021), pp. 173–191; K. Dashper, "Mentoring for Gender Equality: Supporting Female Leaders in the Hospitality Industry," *International Journal of Hospitality Management*, Vol. 88 (2020), 102397.

56. L. Elting, "New Year, New Glass Heights: Women Now Comprise 10% of Top U.S. Corporation CEOs," *Forbes*, January 27, 2023, https://www.forbes.com/sites/lizelting/2023/01/27/new-year-new-glass-heights-for-the-first-time-in-history-over-10-of-fortune-500-ceos-are-women/?sh=15a4f878e77f.

57. "Maria Black," *ADP*, https://www.adp.com/about-adp/leadership/maria-black.aspx (accessed April 25, 2023). Also see "ADP President Maria Black to Succeed CEO Carlos Rodriguez, Effective January 1, 2023," *ADP*, October 26, 2022, https://investors.adp.com/press-releases/press-release-details/2022/ADP-President-Maria-Black-to-succeed-CEO-Carlos-Rodriguez-Effective-January-1-2023/default.aspx.

58. C.J. Eichenauer, A.M. Ryan, and J.M. Alanis, "Leadership during Crisis: An Examination of Supervisory Leadership Behavior and Gender during COVID-19," *Journal of Leadership & Organizational Studies*, Vol. 29 (2022), pp. 190–207. Also see G.J. Lemoine and T.C. Blum, "Servant Leadership, Leader Gender, and Team Gender Role: Testing a Female Advantage in a Cascading Model of Performance," *Personnel Psychology*, Vol. 74 (2021), pp. 3–28; K.L. Badura, E. Grijalva, D.A. Newman, T.T. Yan, and G. Jeon, "Gender and Leadership Emergence: A Meta-Analysis and Explanatory Model," *Personnel Psychology*, Vol. 71 (2018), pp. 335–367.

59. K.L. Badura, E. Grijalva, D.A. Newman, T.T. Yan, and G. Jeon, "Gender and Leadership Emergence: A Meta-Analysis and Explanatory Model," *Personnel Psychology*, Vol. 71 (2018), pp. 335–367.

60. K.L. Badura, B.M. Galvin, and M.Y. Lee, "Leadership Emergence: An Integrative Review," *Journal of Applied Psychology*, Vol. 107 (2022), pp. 2069–2100. Also see J.W. Cox, K. Madison, and N. Eva, "Revisiting Emergence in Emergent Leadership: An Integrative, Multi-Perspective Review," *The Leadership Quarterly*, Vol. 33 (2022), 101579.

61. E. Netchaeva, L.D. Sheppard, and T. Balushkina, "A Meta-Analytic Review of the Gender Difference in Leadership Aspirations," *Journal of Vocational Behavior*, Vol. 137 (2022), 103744.

62. N. Hsu, D.A. Newman, and K.L. Badura, "Emotional Intelligence and Transformational Leadership: Meta-Analysis and Explanatory Model of Female Leadership Advantage," *Journal of Intelligence*, Vol. 10 (2022), p. 104.

63. J.D. Mackey, R.E. Frieder, J.R. Brees, and M.J. Martinko, "Abusive Supervision: A Meta-Analysis and Empirical Review," *Journal of Management*, Vol. 43 (2017), pp. 1940–1965.

64. N. Hsu, K.L. Badura, D.A. Newman, and M.E.P. Speech, "'Gender,' 'Masculinity' and 'Femininity': A Meta-Analytic Review of Gender Differences in Agency and Communion," *Psychological Bulletin*, Vol. 147 (2021), pp. 987–1011. Also see K.L. Badura, E. Grijalva, D.A. Newman, T.T. Yan, and G. Jeon, "Gender and Leadership Emergence: A Meta-Analysis and Explanatory Model," *Personnel Psychology*, Vol. 71 (2018), pp. 335–367.

65. W. Shen and D.L. Joseph, "Gender and Leadership: A Criterion-Focused Review and Rsearch Agenda," *Human Resource Management Review*, Vol. 31 (2021), 100765.

66. T. Morgenroth, T.A. Kirby, M.K. Ryan, and A. Sudkämper, "The Who, When, and Why of the Glass Cliff Phenomenon: A Meta-Analysis of Appointments to Precarious Leadership Positions," *Psychological Bulletin*, Vol. 146 (2020), pp. 797–829.

67. S. Jeong and D. Harrison, "Glass Breaking, Strategy Making, and Value Creating: Meta-Analytic Outcomes of Women as CEOs and TMT Members," *Academy of Management Journal*, August 2017, pp. 1219–1252.

68. S. Creary, M-H. McDonnell, S. Ghai, and J. Scruggs, "When and Why Diversity Improves Your Board's Performance," *Harvard Business Review*, March 27, 2019, https://hbr.org/2019/03/when-and-why-diversity-improves-your-boards-performance.

69. A.H. Eagly, C. Nater, D.I. Miller, M. Kaufmann, and S. Sczesny, "Gender Stereotypes Have Changed: A Cross-Temporal Meta-Analysis of US Public Opinion Polls from 1946 to 2018," *American Psychologist*, Vol. 75 (2020), pp. 301–315.

70. C. Ammerman and B. Groysberg, "How to Close the Gender Gap," *Harvard Business Review*, May–June 2021, https://hbr.org/2021/05/how-to-close-the-gender-gap.

71. R. Hougaard, J. Carter, and M. Afton, "When Women Leaders Leave, the Losses Multiply," *Harvard Business Review*, March 8, 2022, https://hbr.org/2022/03/when-women-leaders-leave-the-losses-multiply.

72. P. Banerjee, "Shy, Intelligent Student with 'Big Handwriting': IIT Professors Remember Google CEO Sundar Pichai," *Hindustan Times*, August 26, 2018, https://www.hindustantimes.com/india-news/20-years-of-google-iit-kgp-remembers-sundar-the-student/story-m1A6akTDlLWQszk7uLBTIN.html.

73. J. Austin, "15 Company Culture Examples That Deserve Your Attention," *Atlassian*, April 3, 2020, https://www.atlassian.com/blog/leadership/15-company-culture-examples-that-deserve-your-attention. Also see P. Eggen, "Reflecting on the Zoom Investment: Getting It Right & Wrong," *LinkedIn*, April 26, 2019, https://www.linkedin.com/pulse/reflecting-zoom-investment-getting-right-wrong-patrick-eggen.

74. C. Bashar, "How the Art of Curiosity Transforms Leadership," *Forbes*, January 27, 2023, https://www.forbes.com/sites/forbesbusinessdevelopmentcouncil/2023/01/27/how-the-art-of-curiosity-transforms-leadership/?sh=5d2acaa94e98. Also see F.

Lievens, S.H. Harrison, P. Mussel, and J.A. Litman, "Killing the Cat? A Review of Curiosity at Work," *Academy of Management Annals,* Vol. 16 (2022), pp. 179–216.

75. J. Stillman, "15 Female CEOs Weighed in on the Most Important Personality Trait for Success. The 1 That Came up the Most: Curiosity," *Inc.,* March 12, 2020, https://www.inc.com/jessica-stillman/15-female-ceos-weighed-in-on-most-important-personality-trait-for-success-this-1-characteristic-came-up-most.html.

76. "Author Talks: IBM's Ginni Rometty on Leading with 'Good Power,'" *McKinsey,* March 10, 2023, https://www.mckinsey.com/featured-insights/mckinsey-on-books/author-talks-how-ibms-ginni-rometty-leads-with-good-power.

77. M. Curtin, "Billionaire CEO Sara Blakely Says These 7 Words Are the Best Career Advice She Ever Got," *Thrive Global,* April 26, 2018, https://thriveglobal.com/stories/billionaire-ceo-sara-blakely-says-these-7-words-are-the-best-career-advice-she-ever-got/.

78. A.B. Blake, V.H. Luu, O.V. Petrenko, W.L. Gardner, K.J.N. Moergen, and M.E. Ezerins, "Let's Agree about Nice Leaders: A Literature Review and Meta-Analysis of Agreeableness and Its Relationship with Leadership Outcomes," *The Leadership Quarterly,* 2022, 101593. Also see J.D. Mackey, B.P. Ellen III, C.P. McAllister, and K.C. Alexander, "The Dark Side of Leadership: A Systematic Literature Review and Meta-Analysis of Destructive Leadership Research," *Journal of Business Research,* Vol. 132 (2021), pp. 705–718.

79. "The 10 Characteristics of a Good Leader," *Center for Creative Leadership,* January 24, 2023, https://www.ccl.org/articles/leading-effectively-articles/characteristics-good-leader/#:~:text=A%20good%20leader%20should%20have.

80. C.A. O'Reilly III, J.A. Chatman, and B. Doerr, "When 'Me' Trumps 'We': Narcissistic Leaders and the Cultures They Create," *Academy of Management Discoveries,* Vol. 7 (2021), pp. 419–450.

81. P. Singh, "10 Companies That Use Psychometric Assessment," *CareerGuide,* February 20, 2023, https://www.careerguide.com/career/psychometric-test/companies-that-use-psychometric-tests.

82. "Screening by Means of Pre-Employment Testing," *Society for Human Resource Management,* https://www.shrm.org/resourcesandtools/tools-and-samples/toolkits/pages/screeningbymeansofpreemploymenttesting.aspx (accessed April 25, 2023).

83. C.W. Chang and H.C. Huang, "How Global Mindset Drives Innovation and Exporting Performance: The Roles of Relational and Bricolage Capabilities," *Journal of Business & Industrial Marketing,* 2022, pp. 2587–2602. Also see V. Ratanjee, "The Future of Leadership Development: A Global Mindset," *Gallup,* February 8, 2019, https://www.gallup.com/workplace/246551/future-leadership-development-global-mindset.aspx.

84. G. Yukl, R. Mahsud, G. Prussia, and S. Hassan, "Effectiveness of Broad and Specific Leadership Behaviors," *Personnel Review,* Vol. 48 (2019), pp. 774–783.

85. "Adidas—Adidas Results in 2022 Reflect Geopolitical, Macroeconomic, and Company-Specific Challenges," *Adidas-Group,* March 8, 2023, https://www.adidas-group.com/en/media/news-archive/press-releases/2023/adidas-results-in-2022-reflect-geopolitical-macroeconomic-and-company-specific-challenges/. Also see "Adidas Has Just Swiped Its New CEO from under the Nose of Its Local Rivals," *Fortune,* November 8, 2022, https://fortune.com/2022/11/08/adidas-swipes-new-ceo-bjorn-gulden-from-rivals-puma/.

86. Q. Zhou, J.-Y. Mao, S. Xiang, R. Huang, and B. Liu, "How Can Leaders Help? A Mediated Moderation Influence of Leader Consideration and Structure Initiation on Employee Learning from Work Failures," *Journal of Knowledge Management,* Vol. 27 (2023), pp. 566–583. Also see Z. Lyubykh, N. Turner, M.S. Hershcovis, and C. Deng, "A Meta-Analysis of Leadership and Workplace Safety: Examining Relative Importance, Contextual Contingencies, and Methodological Moderators," *Journal of Applied Psychology,* Vol. 107 (2022), pp. 2149–2175; D.S. Derue, J.D. Nahrgang, N. Wellman, and S.E. Humphrey, "Trait and Behavioral Theories of Leadership: An Integration and Meta-Analytic Test of Their Relative Validity," *Personnel Psychology,* Vol. 64 (2011), pp. 7–52.

87. R. Martin, O. Epitropaki, B. Erdogan, and G. Thomas, "Relationship Based Leadership: Current Trends and Future Prospects," *Journal of Occupational and Organizational Psychology,* Vol. 92 (2019), pp. 465–474.

88. A.N. Kluger and G. Itzchakov, "The Power of Listening at Work," *Annual Review of Organizational Psychology and Organizational Behavior,* Vol. 9 (2022), pp. 121–146.

89. P. Smirl, "'Leadership Gems' from TIAA CEO Thasunda Brown Duckett," *Wisconsin School of Business,* February 21, 2022, https://business.wisc.edu/news/leadership-gems-from-tiaa-ceo-thasunda-brown-duckett/.

90. Z. Lyubykh, N. Turner, M.S. Hershcovis, and C. Deng, "A Meta-Analysis of Leadership and Workplace Safety: Examining Relative Importance, Contextual Contingencies, and Methodological Moderators," *Journal of Applied Psychology,* Vol. 107 (2022), pp. 2149–2175. Also see D.S. Derue, J.D. Nahrgang, N. Wellman, and S.E. Humphrey, "Trait and Behavioral Theories of Leadership: An Integration and Meta-Analytic Test of Their Relative Validity," *Personnel Psychology,* Vol. 64 (2011), pp. 7–52.

91. C.A. Hartnell, A.J. Kinicki, L.S. Lambert, M. Fugate, and P.D. Corner, "Do Similarities or Differences between CEO Leadership and Organizational Culture Have a More Positive Effect on Firm Performance? A Test of Competing Predictions," *Journal of Applied Psychology,* Vol. 101 (2016), pp. 846–861.

92. F. Fiedler, "Assumed Similarity Measures as Predictors of Team Effectiveness," *Journal of Abnormal and Social Psychology,* Vol. 49 (1954), pp. 381–388. Also see F. Fiedler, *Leader Attitudes and Group Effectiveness* (Urbana, IL: University of Illinois Press, 1958); F. Fiedler, *A Theory of Leadership Effectiveness* (New York: McGraw-Hill, 1967).

93. B. Shala, A. Prebreza, and B. Ramosaj, "The Contingency Theory of Management as a Factor of Acknowledging the Leaders-Managers of Our Time Study Case: The Practice of the Contingency Theory in the Company Avrios," *Open Access Library Journal,* Vol. 8 (2021), pp. 1–20.

94. M.A. Omazić, D. Labaš, and P. Uroić, "Contingency Theory," in S.O. Idowu et al. (eds.), *Encyclopedia of Sustainable Management* (Springer Link, 2023), pp. 1–9.

95. "Fiedler's Contingency Theory: Why Leadership Isn't Uniform," *Asana,* October 7, 2022, https://asana.com/resources/fiedlers-contingency-theory.

96. M.V. Vugt, R. Hogan, and R. Kaiser, "Leadership, Followership, and Evolution," *American Psychologist,* April 2008, pp. 182–196.

97. O. Shenkar and S. Ellis, "The Rise and Fall of Structural Contingency Theory: A Theory's 'Autopsy'," *Journal of Management Studies,* 59, 2022, pp. 782–818.

98. R.J. House, "Path-Goal Theory of Leadership: Lessons, Legacy, and a Reformulated Theory," *The Leadership Quarterly,* Vol. 7 (1996), pp. 323–352.

99. R.P. Vecchio, J.E. Justin, and C.L. Pearce, "The Utility of Transactional and Transformational Leadership for Predicting Performance and Satisfaction within a Path-Goal Theory Framework," *Journal of Occupational and Organizational Psychology,* Vol. 81 (2008), pp. 71–82. Also see A. Khan, "Approaches in Leadership: Trait, Situational and Path-Goal Theory: A Critical Analysis," *Pakistan Business Review,* Vol. 14 (2013), pp. 830–842; C.A. Schriesheim and L.L. Neider, "Path-Goal Leadership Theory: The Long and Winding Road," *The Leadership Quarterly,* Vol. 7 (1996), pp. 317–321; P.M. Podsakoff, S.B. MacKenzie, M. Ahearne, and W.H. Bommer, "Searching for a Needle in a Haystack: Trying to Identify the Illusive Moderators of Leadership Behaviors," *Journal of Management,* 1995, pp. 422–470; J.C. Wofford and L.Z. Liska, "Path-Goal Theories of Leadership: A Meta-Analysis," *Journal of Management,* Vol. 19 (1993), pp. 857–876.

100. R.J. House, "Path-Goal Theory of Leadership: Lessons, Legacy, and a Reformulated Theory," *The Leadership Quarterly,* Vol. 7 (1996), pp. 323–352.

101. P. Goodman, "C.E.O.s Were Our Heroes, at Least according to Them," *New York Times,* January 13, 2022, https://www.nytimes.com/2022/01/13/business/davos-man-marc-benioff-book.html.

Also see P. Zaveri, "Tech Billionaire Marc Benioff Wants Every CEO to Take a 'No Layoff' Pledge as Part of an 8-Point Plan to Deal with Coronavirus," *Business Insider,* Accessed March 25, 2020, https://www.businessinsider.com/marc-benioff-no-layoffs-plan-coronavirus-2020-3.

102. D. Streitfeld, "Happiness or Success? Salesforce's Marc Benioff Doesn't Want to Choose," *New York Times,* February 13, 2023, https://www.nytimes.com/2023/02/13/technology/salesforce-marc-benioff-pressure.html. Also see T. Bove, "Salesforce Cuts 10% of Staff in Layoffs as Boss Admits He 'Hired Too Many People,'" *Fortune,* January 4, 2023, https://fortune.com/2023/01/04/salesforce-layoffs-10-percent-staff-office-space-marc-benioff/.

103. O. Uslu, "A General Overview of Leadership Theories from a Critical Perspective," *Marketing and Management of Innovations,* Vol. 1 (2019), pp. 161–172. Also see C.A. Schriesheim and L.L. Neider, "Path-Goal Leadership Theory: The Long and Winding Road," *The Leadership Quarterly,* Vol. 7 (1996), pp. 317–321.

104. G. Wang, I. Oh, S. Courtright, and A. Colbert, "Transformational Leadership and Performance Across Criteria and Levels: A Meta-Analytic Review of 25 Years of Research," *Group & Organization Management,* Vol. 36, No. 2 (2011), pp. 223–270.

105. M.J. Zhang, Y. Zhang, and K.S. Law, "Paradoxical Leadership and Innovation in Work Teams: The Multilevel Mediating Role of Ambidexterity and Leader Vision as a Boundary Condition," *Academy of Management Journal,* Vol. 65 (2022), pp. 1652–1679. Also see C.L. Pearce, C.L. Wassenaar, Y. Berson, and R. Tuval-Mashiach, "Toward a Theory of Meta-Paradoxical Leadership," *Organizational Behavior and Human Decision Processes,* Vol. 155 (2019), pp. 31–41.

106. C. Carvalho, F.K. Carvalho, and S. Carvalho, "Managerial Coaching: Where Are We Now and Where Should We Go in the Future?" *Development and Learning in Organizations: An International Journal,* Vol. 36 (2022), pp. 4–7. Also see L. Zheng, Y. Wang, Z. Guo, and Y. Zhu, "Effects of Managerial Coaching on Employees' Creative Performance: Cross-Level Moderating Role of a Climate for Innovation," *Leadership & Organization Development Journal,* Vol. 43 (2022), pp. 211–224.

107. C.A. Hartnell, A.J. Kinicki, L.S. Lambert, M. Fugate, and P.D. Corner, "Do similarities or differences between CEO leadership and organizational culture have a more positive effect on firm performance? A test of competing predictions," *Journal of Applied Psychology,* 101, 2016, pp. 846–861.

108. J. Jordan, M. Wade, and T. Yokoi, "Finding the Right Balance—and Flexibility—in Your Leadership Style," *Harvard Business Review,* January 11, 2022, https://hbr.org/2022/01/finding-the-right-balance-and-flexibility-in-your-leadership-style. Also see J. Zhuo, "As Your Team Gets Bigger, Your Leadership Style Has to Adapt," *Harvard Business Review,* March 13, 2019, https://hbr.org/2019/03/as-your-team-gets-bigger-your-leadership-style-has-to-adapt; The specific steps were developed by H.P. Sims Jr., S. Faraj, and S. Yun, "When Should a Leader Be Directive or Empowering? How to Develop Your Own Situational Theory of Leadership," *Business Horizons,* March–April 2009, pp. 149–158.

109. For a complete description of the full-range leadership theory, see B.J. Bass and B.J. Avolio, *Revised Manual for the Multi-Factor Leadership Questionnaire* (Palo Alto, CA: Mindgarden, 1997).

110. M. Abbas and R. Ali. "Transformational versus Transactional Leadership Styles and Project Success: A Meta-Analytic Review," *European Management Journal,* 2023, pp. 125–142. Also see T. Rockstuhl, D. Wu, J.H. Dulebohn, C. Liao, and J.E. Hoch, "Cultural Congruence or Compensation? A Meta-Analytic Test of Transformational and Transactional Leadership Effects across Cultures," *Journal of International Business Studies,* 2023, pp. 476–504.

111. A.J. Kaluza, D. Boer, C. Buengeler, and R. van Dick, "Leadership Behaviour and Leader Self-Reported Well-Being: A Review, Integration and Meta-Analytic Examination," *Work & Stress,* Vol. 34 (2020), pp. 34–56.

112. J.V. Pagaduan, "How Canva CEO Melanie Perkins Has Risen along with Tech Giants," *ITech Post,* January 12, 2023, https://www.itechpost.com/articles/116021/20230112/entertainmenttech-canva-ceo-melanie-perkins-rise-along-tech-giants.htm. Also see "It Took Melanie Perkins 100+ Rejections over 3 Yrs (& Some Faith!) to Give Life to Design Platform Canva," *The Economic Times,* July 13, 2022, https://economictimes.indiatimes.com/magazines/panache/it-took-melanie-perkins-100-rejections-over-3-yrs-some-faith-to-give-life-to-design-platform-canva/articleshow/92845505.cms?from=mdr; K. Caprino, "Canva Cofounder and CEO Melanie Perkins Leads Her Unicorn to New Heights," *Forbes,* April 5, 2019, https://www.forbes.com/sites/kathycaprino/2019/04/05/canva-cofounder-and-ceo-melanie-perkins-leads-her-unicorn-to-new-heights/?sh=37ff475f7547.

113. T. Rockstuhl, D. Wu, J.H. Dulebohn, C. Liao, and J.E. Hoch, "Cultural Congruence or Compensation? A Meta-Analytic Test of Transformational and Transactional Leadership Effects across Cultures," *Journal of International Business Studies,* 2023, pp. 476–504. Also see A. Lee, A. Legood, D. Hughes, A.W. Tian, A. Newman, and C. Knight, "Leadership, Creativity and Innovation: A Meta-Analytic Review," *European Journal of Work and Organizational Psychology,* Vol. 29 (2020), pp. 1–35; D. DeRue, J. Nahrgang, N. Wellman, and S. Humphrey, "Trait and Behavioral Theories of Leadership," *Personnel Psychology,* Vol. 64 (2011), pp. 7–52.

114. U.R. Dundum, K.B. Lowe, and B.J. Avolio, "A Meta-Analysis of Transformational and Transactional Leadership Correlates of Effectiveness and Satisfaction: An Update and Extension," in B.J. Avolio and F.J. Yammarino (eds.), *Transformational and Charismatic Leadership: The Road Ahead* (New York: JAI Press, 2002), p. 38.

115. N. Hasegawa, "A Quantitative Study of the Augmentation Hypothesis of Transformational-Transactional Leadership," *Journal of Management Science,* Vol. 12 (2023), pp. 31–35. Also see J.E. Hoch, W.H. Bommer, J.H. Dulebohn, and D. Wu, "Do Ethical, Authentic, and Servant Leadership Explain Variance above and beyond Transformational Leadership? A Meta-Analysis," *Journal of Management,* Vol. 44 (2018), pp. 501–529.

116. G. Paul, "What Companies Does Richard Branson Own?" *The Org,* February 15, 2023, https://theorg.com/iterate/what-companies-does-richard-branson-own. Also see J. Stillman, "The 2 Essential Ingredients for Radical Innovation, According to Richard Branson," *Inc.,* September 15, 2022, https://www.inc.com/jessica-stillman/richard-branson-google-x-audacity-humility.html; N. Juma, "26 Richard Branson Quotes on Leadership and Opportunity," *Everyday Power,* June 9, 2022, https://everydaypower.com/richard-branson-quotes/.

117. Supportive results can be found in N. Hsu, D.A. Newman, and K.L. Badura, "Emotional Intelligence and Transformational Leadership: Meta-Analysis and Explanatory Model of Female Leadership Advantage," *Journal of Intelligence,* Vol. 10 (2022), p. 104. Also see B. McCormick, R. Guay, A. Colbert, and G. Stewart, "Proactive Personality and Proactive Behaviour: Perspectives on Person–Situation Interactions," *Journal of Occupational and Organizational Psychology,* Vol. 92, No. 1 (2019), pp. 30–51; A. Deinert, A.C. Homan, D. Boer, S.C. Voelpel, and D. Gutermann, "Transformational Leadership Sub-dimensions and Their Link to Leaders' Personality and Performance," *The Leadership Quarterly,* Vol. 26 (2015), pp. 1095–1120; T. Judge and J. Bono, "Five-Factor Model of Personality and Transformational Leadership," *Journal of Applied Psychology,* October 2000, pp. 751–765.

118. C.A. Hartnell and F.O. Walumbwa, "Transformational Leadership and Organizational Culture," *The Handbook of Organizational Culture and Climate,* Vol. 2 (2011), pp. 225–248.

119. N. Hasegawa, "A Quantitative Study of the Augmentation Hypothesis of Transformational-Transactional Leadership," *Journal of Management Science,* Vol. 12 (2023), pp. 31–35. Also see G. Wang, I.-S. Oh, S.H. Courtright, and A.E. Colbert, "Transformational Leadership and Performance across Criteria and Levels: A Meta-Analytic Review of 25 Years of Research," *Group & Organization Management,* Vol. 36 (2011), pp. 223–270.

120. "The 50 Most Powerful Women," *Fortune,* https://fortune.com/ranking/most-powerful-women/ (accessed May 5, 2023).

121. "The Home Depot Leadership: Ann-Marie Campbell," *Home Depot,* https://corporate.homedepot.com/bio/ann-marie-campbell-executive-vice-president-us-stores-international-operations (accessed May 5, 2023).

122. "Ann-Marie Campbell," *Fortune,* https://fortune.com/ranking/most-powerful-women/2022/ann-marie-campbell/ (accessed May 5, 2023).
123. "Ann-Marie Campbell," *AACSB,* 2019, https://www.aacsb.edu/influential-leaders/honorees/2019/ann-marie-campbell.
124. E. Kinlin, "WE Interviews: Ann-Marie Campbell," *ECK Consulting,* https://www.kinlin.com/we-interviews-ann-marie-campbell/ (accessed May 5, 2023).
125. "Ann-Marie Campbell Nomination," *Leadership Character Awards,* April 2018, https://www.leadershipcharacterawards.org/wp-content/uploads/2018/04/Ann-Marie-Campbell-Nomination.pdf.
126. B. Woods, "What Home Depot's Billion-Dollar Pay Raise May Help Prove about Workers," *CNBC,* April 30, 2023, https://www.cnbc.com/2023/04/30/what-home-depots-billion-dollar-pay-raise-can-prove-about-workers.html.
127. "The Bold Leader," *Retail Today,* March 2020, https://magazine.retail-today.com/women_in_retail/the_home_depot.
128. V. Nguon, "Effect of Transformational Leadership on Job Satisfaction, Innovative Behavior, and Work Performance: A Conceptual Review," *International Journal of Business and Management,* Vol. 17 (2022), pp. 75–89.
129. J. Peng, M. Li, Z. Wang, and Y. Lin, "Transformational Leadership and Employees' Reactions to Organizational Change: Evidence from a Meta-Analysis," *The Journal of Applied Behavioral Science,* Vol. 57 (2021), pp. 369–397.
130. S. Ytterstad and J. Olaisen, "An Overview of Perspectives on Transformational Leadership," *Learning Transformational Leadership: A Pedagogical and Practical Perspective,* 2023, pp. 13–33.
131. D. Tokbaeva, "Charisma and Charismatic Leadership in Organizations," in *Research Handbook on the Sociology of Organizations* (Edward Elgar Publishing, 2022), pp. 311–328.
132. B. Nanus, *Visionary Leadership* (San Francisco: Jossey-Bass, 1992), p. 8.
133. M.S. Malone, "The Secret to Midcareer Success," *The Wall Street Journal,* February 12, 2018, p. A17.
134. P. Summitt, *Quotes from the Summit* (Premium Press America, 2019).
135. P. Summitt and S. Jenkins, *Reach for the Summit: The Definite Dozen System for Succeeding at Whatever You Do* (New York: Three Rivers Press, 1988).
136. M. Bonesteel, "Pat Summitt Remembered as 'a Hero and a Mentor,'" *Washington Post,* June 28, 2016, https://www.washingtonpost.com/news/early-lead/wp/2016/06/28/pat-summitt-remembered-as-a-hero-and-a-mentor/. Also see P. Summitt and S. Jenkins, *Reach for the Summit: The Definite Dozen System for Succeeding at Whatever You Do* (New York: Three Rivers Press, 1998).
137. J. Fournier, "Choosing Discipline," *Basketball Is Psychology,* August 19, 2019. https://www.basketballispsychology.com/post/choosing-discipline. Also see P. Summitt and S. Jenkins, *Reach for the Summit: The Definite Dozen System for Succeeding at Whatever You Do* (New York: Three Rivers Press, 1998).
138. M. Mach, A.I. Ferreira, and A.C.M. Abrantes, "Transformational Leadership and Team Performance in Sports Teams: A Conditional Indirect Model," *Applied Psychology,* Vol. 71 (2022), pp. 662–694. Also see A.B. Bakker, J. Hetland, O.K. Olsen, and R. Espevik, "Daily Transformational Leadership: A Source of Inspiration for Follower Performance?" *European Management Journal,* 2022, https://doi.org/10.1016/j.emj.2022.04.004; J.E. Hoch, W.H. Bommer, J.H. Dulebohn, and D. Wu, "Do Ethical, Authentic, and Servant Leadership Explain Variance above and beyond Transformational Leadership? A Meta-Analysis," *Journal of Management,* Vol. 44 (2018), pp. 501–529.
139. C. Cohrs, K.C. Bormann, M. Diebig, C. Millhoff, K. Pachocki, and J. Rowold, "Transformational Leadership and Communication: Evaluation of a Two-Day Leadership Development Program," *Leadership & Organization Development Journal,* Vol. 41 (2020), pp. 101–117.
140. S. E. Seibert, L. D. Sargent, M. L. Kraimer, and K. Kiazad, "Linking Developmental Experiences to Leader Effectiveness and Promotability: The Mediating Role of Leadership Self-Efficacy and Mentor Network," *Personnel Psychology,* April 2017, pp. 357–397. Also see D.V. Day and L. Dragoni, "Leadership Development: An Outcome-Oriented Review Based on Time and Levels of Analyses," *Annual Review of Organizational Psychology and Organizational Behavior,* Vol. 2 (2015), pp. 133–156.
141. R. Kark, B. Shamir, and G. Chen, "The Two Faces of Transformational Leadership: Empowerment and Dependency," *Journal of Applied Psychology,* Vol. 88 (2003), pp. 246–255.
142. Z. Yuan, U.Y. Sun, A.L. Effinger, and J. Zhang, "Being on the Same Page Matters: A Meta-Analytic Investigation of Leader–Member Exchange (LMX) Agreement," *Journal of Applied Psychology,* 2023, https://doi.org/10.1037/apl0001089. Also see E.Y. Liao and C. Hui, "A Resource-Based Perspective on Leader-Member Exchange: An Updated Meta-Analysis," *Asia Pacific Journal of Management,* Vol. 38 (2021), pp. 317–370; G. Graen and J. F. Cashman, "A Role-Making Model of Leadership in Formal Organizations: A Developmental Approach," in J.G. Hunt and L.L. Larson (eds.), *Leadership Frontiers* (Kent, OH: Kent State University Press, 1975), pp. 143–165; F. Dansereau Jr., G. Graen, and W.J. Haga, "A Vertical Dyad Linkage Approach to Leadership within Formal Organizations: A Longitudinal Investigation of the Role-Making Process," *Organizational Behavior and Human Performance,* February 1975, pp. 46–78.
143. M. Daneshvar, F.K. Jafari, and F. Saberi, "Systematic Review of the Impact of Leader-Member Exchange on Employee Voice: A Meta-Analysis Approach," *Journal of Sustainable Human Resource Management,* Vol. 4 (2022), pp. 197–219.
144. C. Buengeler, R.F. Piccolo, and L.R. Locklear, "LMX Differentiation and Group Outcomes: A Framework and Review Drawing on Group Diversity Insights," *Journal of Management,* Vol. 47 (2021), pp. 260–287.
145. H. Park, H. Park, and R.C. Liden, "Leader–Member Exchange Differentiation and Employee Performance: A Political Perspective," *Journal of Organizational Behavior,* Vol. 43 (2022), pp. 1121–1135.
146. W. Chang, A. Liu, X. Wang, and B. Yi, "Meta-Analysis of Outcomes of Leader–Member Exchange in Hospitality and Tourism: What Does the Past Say about the Future?" *International Journal of Contemporary Hospitality Management,* Vol. 32 (2020), pp. 2155–2173. Also see J.H. Dulebohn, W.H. Bommer, R.C. Liden, R.L. Brouer, and G.R. Ferris, "A Meta-Analysis of Antecedents and Consequences of Leader-Member Exchange: Integrating the Past with an Eye toward the Future," *Journal of Management,* Vol. 38 (2012), pp. 1715–1759.
147. H.R. Young, D.R. Glerum, D.L. Joseph, and M.A. McCord, "A Meta-Analysis of Transactional Leadership and Follower Performance: Double-Edged Effects of LMX and Empowerment," *Journal of Management,* Vol. 47 (2021), pp. 1255–1280. Also see R.K. Gottfredson and H. Aguinis, "Leadership Behaviors and Follower Performance: Deductive and Inductive Examination of Theoretical Rationales and Underlying Mechanisms," *Journal of Organizational Behavior,* May 2017, pp. 558–591.
148. "A Tactical Guide to Managing Up: 30 Tips from the Smartest People We Know," *First Round Review,* https://review.firstround.com/a-tactical-guide-to-managing-up-30-tips-from-the-smartest-people-we-know (accessed May 8, 2023).
149. A summary of servant leadership is provided by L. Spears, *Reflections on Leadership: How Robert K. Greenleaf's Theory of Servant-Leadership Influenced Today's Top Management Thinkers* (New York: Wiley, 1995).
150. "We're Here to Make Your Day," *Sodexo,* https://www.sodexo.com/en/about-us/our-purpose (accessed May 8, 2023). Also see B. Sampath, "'Making Others Successful'—an Important Leadership Trait," *Linkedin,* December 16, 2021, https://www.linkedin.com/pulse/making-others-successful-important-leadership-trait-bhavesh-sampath.
151. G.J. Lemoine, C.A. Hartnell., S. Hora, D. Watts, "Moral Minds: How and When Does Servant Leadership Influence Employees to Benefit Multiple Stakeholders?" *Personnel Psychology,* 2023, in press. Also see

A. Lee, J. Lyubovnikova, A.W. Tian, and C. Knight, "Servant Leadership: A Meta-Analytic Examination of Incremental Contribution, Moderation, and Mediation," *Journal of Occupational and Organizational Psychology,* Vol. 93 (2020), pp. 1–44; N. Eva, M. Robin, S. Sendjaya, D. van Dierendonck, and R. Liden, "Servant Leadership: A Systematic Review and Call for Future Research," *The Leadership Quarterly,* Vol. 30, No. 1 (2019), pp. 111–132.

152. M.J. Neubert, M. Sully de Luque, M.J. Quade, and E.M. Hunter, "Servant Leadership across the Globe: Assessing Universal and Culturally Contingent Relevance in Organizational Contexts," *Journal of World Business,* Vol. 57 (2022), 101268. Also see G.J. Lemoine, C.A. Hartnell, and H. Leroy, "Taking Stock of Moral Approaches to Leadership: An Integrative Review of Ethical, Authentic, and Servant Leadership," *Academy of Management Annals,* Vol. 13 (2019), pp. 148–187.

153. A.Y. Ou, A.S. Tsui, A.J. Kinicki, D.A. Waldman, Z. Xiao, and L.J. Song, "Humble Chief Executive Officers' Connections to Top Management Team Integration and Middle Managers' Responses," *Administrative Science Quarterly,* March 2014, pp. 34–72.

154. T.K. Kelemen, S.H. Matthews, M.J. Matthews, and S.E. Henry, "Humble Leadership: A Review and Synthesis of Leader Expressed Humility," *Journal of Organizational Behavior,* Vol. 44 (2023), pp. 202–224.

155. E.J. Krumrei-Mancuso and M.R. Begin, "Cultivating Intellectual Humility in Leaders: Potential Benefits, Risks, and Practical Tools," *American Journal of Health Promotion,* Vol. 36 (2022), pp. 1404–1411. Also see L. Wang, B. Owens, J. Li, and L. Shi, "Exploring the Affective Impact, Boundary Conditions, and Antecedents of Leader Humility," *Journal of Applied Psychology,* Vol. 103, No. 9 (2018), pp. 1019–1038.

156. G. Freeland, "Microsoft CEO Satya Nadella: Finding Success Out of the Spotlight," *Forbes,* March 18, 2019, https://www.forbes.com/sites/grantfreeland/2019/03/18/microsoft-ceo-satya-nadellas-success-secret/#27c736667efd.

157. D. Drake, "Career Insight: 5 Leadership Truths from Microsoft CEO Satya Nadella," *Wharton Global Youth Program,* May 27, 2022, https://globalyouth.wharton.upenn.edu/articles/career-insight/career-insight-5-leadership-truths-from-microsoft-ceo-satya-nadella/.

158. A. Papadopoulos, "The World's Most Influential CEOs and Business Executives of 2023," *CEOWORLD magazine,* March 17, 2023, https://ceoworld.biz/2023/03/17/the-worlds-most-influential-ceos-and-business-executives-of-2023/.

159. T.K. Kelemen, S.H. Matthews, M.J. Matthews, and S.E. Henry, "Humble Leadership: A Review and Synthesis of Leader Expressed Humility," *Journal of Organizational Behavior,* Vol. 44 (2023), pp. 202–224. Also see J.A. Chandler, N.E. Johnson, S.L. Jordan, and J.C. Short, "A Meta-Analysis of Humble Leadership: Reviewing Individual, Team, and Organizational Outcomes of Leader Humility," *The Leadership Quarterly,* 2022, 101660; based on results found in C. Chen, J. Feng, X. Liu, and J. Yao, "Leader Humility, Team Job Crafting and Team Creativity: The Moderating Role of Leader–Leader Exchange," *Human Resource Management Journal,* Vol. 31 (2021), pp. 326–340.

160. J. Stillman, "Humility Is an Undersung Leadership Skill. Adam Grant Says These 2 Interview Questions Screen for It," *Inc.,* September 13, 2021, https://www.inc.com/jessica-stillman/adam-grant-leadership-hiring-humility-job-interviews.html.

161. A. Beard, "To Get Ahead, You Need Both Ambition and Humility" *Harvard Business Review* January 11, 2022, https://hbr.org/podcast/2022/01/to-get-ahead-you-need-both-ambition-and-humility.

162. R. Cuenca, P.A. Tomei, and S.F. Mello, "How to Infuse an Organizational Culture with Humility: A Study of Humble Behaviors and Practices," *Global Business and Organizational Excellence,* Vol. 42 (2022), pp. 39–58.

163. "About," *Life Is Good,* https://www.lifeisgood.com/company/about.html (accessed May 8, 2023). Also see D. Ward, "Meet Bert Jacobs: Chief Executive Optimist," *Society for Human Resource Management,* August 27, 2021, https://www.shrm.org/hr-today/news/hr-magazine/fall2021/pages/meet-bert-jacobs-chief-executive-optimist.aspx.

164. D. Lancefield, "5 Strategies to Empower Employees to Make Decisions," *Harvard Business Review,* March 20, 2023, https://hbr.org/2023/03/5-strategies-to-empower-employees-to-make-decisions.

165. "Lauren Bush Lauren," *Feeding America,* https://www.feedingamerica.org/partners/entertainment-council/lauren-bush-lauren (accessed May 8, 2023).

166. L. Danziger, "FEED's Lauren Bush, on Giving Back and What She Eats in a Day," *The Beet,* November 12, 2021, https://thebeet.com/lauren-bush-and-feed-expand-from-bags-to-home-collection-to-feed-kids/.

167. L. Dunn, "Women in Business Q&A: Lauren Bush Lauren, Founder and CEO, FEED," *Huffington Post,* October 24, 2017, www.huffingtonpost.com/entry/women-in-business-qa-lauren-bush-lauren-founder_us_59ef70bee4b04809c0501185.

168. D. Lancefield, "5 Strategies to Empower Employees to Make Decisions," *Harvard Business Review,* March 20, 2023, https://hbr.org/2023/03/5-strategies-to-empower-employees-to-make-decisions.

169. A. Lee, S. Willis, and A.W. Tian, "Empowering Leadership: A Meta-Analytic Examination of Incremental Contribution, Mediation, and Moderation," *Journal of Organizational Behavior,* Vol. 39 (2018), pp. 306–325. Also see M. Cheong, F.J. Yammarino, S.D. Dionne, S.M. Spain, and C.-Y. Tsai, "A Review of the Effectiveness of Empowering Leadership," *The Leadership Quarterly,* Vol. 30 (2019), pp. 34–58; M. Kim and T.A. Beehr, "The Power of Empowering Leadership: Allowing and Encouraging Followers to Take Charge of Their Own Jobs," *The International Journal of Human Resource Management,* Vol. 32 (2021), pp. 1865–1898.

170. M.E. Brown, L.K. Treviño, and D.A. Harrison, "Ethical Leadership: A Social Learning Perspective for Construct Development and Testing," *Organizational Behavior and Human Decision Processes,* Vol. 97 (2005), pp. 117–134.

171. "The Biggest Business Scandals of 2020," *Fortune,* December 27, 2020, https://fortune.com/2020/12/27/biggest-business-scandals-of-2020-nikola-wirecard-luckin-coffee-twitter-security-hack-tesla-spx-mcdonalds-ceo-ppp-fraud-wells-fargo-ebay-carlos-ghosn/.

172. S. Berger, "Top Reason CEOs Were Ousted in 2018 Was Because of Scandal," *CNBC,* May 15, 2019, https://www.cnbc.com/2019/05/15/pwc-strategy-report-top-reason-ceos-were-ousted-in-2018-was-scandals.html.

173. "2023 Edelman Trust Barometer Reveals Business Is the Only Institution Viewed as Ethical and Competent; Emerges as Ethical Force for Good in a Polarized World," *PRN Newswire,* January 15, 2023, https://www.prnewswire.com/news-releases/2023-edelman-trust-barometer-reveals-business-is-the-only-institution-viewed-as-ethical-and-competent-emerges-as-ethical-force-for-good-in-a-polarized-world-301721906.html.

174. T. Ng and D. Feldman, "Ethical Leadership: Meta-Analytic Evidence of Criterion-Related and Incremental Validity," *Journal of Applied Psychology,* May 2015, pp. 948–965.

175. "Ethisphere Announces the 2023 World's Most Ethical Companies," *Business Wire,* March 13, 2023, https://www.businesswire.com/news/home/20230313005129/en/Ethisphere-Announces-the-2023-World%E2%80%99s-Most-Ethical-Companies.

176. As demonstrated in A. Legood, L. van der Werff, A. Lee, and D. Den Hartog, "A Meta-Analysis of the Role of Trust in the Leadership-Performance Relationship," European Journal of Work and Organizational Psychology, Vol. 30 (2021), pp. 1–22. Also see A.C. Peng and D. Kim, "A Meta-Analytic Test of the Differential Pathways Linking Ethical Leadership to Normative Conduct," *Journal of Organizational Behavior,* Vol. 41 (2020), pp. 348–368; M. Kuenzi, D. Mayer, and R. Greenbaum, "Creating an Ethical Organizational Environment: The Relationship between Ethical Leadership, Ethical Organizational Climate, and Unethical Behavior," *Personnel Psychology,* Vol. 73, No. 1 (2020), pp. 43–71; J.E. Hoch, W.H. Bommer, J.H. Dulebohn, and D. Wu, "Do Ethical, Authentic, and Servant Leadership Explain Variance above and beyond Transformational Leadership? A Meta-Analysis," *Journal of Management,* February 2018, pp. 501–529.

177. T. Matshoba-Ramuedzisi, D. De Jongh, and W. Fourie, "Followership: A Review of Current and Emerging Research," *Leadership & Organization Development Journal,* Vol. 43 (2022), pp. 653–668.

178. D. Pietraszewski, "The Evolution of Leadership: Leadership and Followership as a Solution to the Problem of Creating and Executing Successful Coordination and Cooperation Enterprises," *The Leadership Quarterly,* June 2019, p. 101299.

179. R.J. Plachy and T.L. Smunt, "Rethinking Managership, Leadership, Followership, and Partnership," *Business Horizons,* Vol. 65 (2022), pp. 401–411.

180. B.M. Bass and R. Bass, *The Bass Handbook of Leadership: Theory, Research, and Managerial Applications,* 4th ed. (New York: Free Press, 2008).

181. "What Is Followership? 14 Qualities of Good Followers," *Indeed,* March 10, 2023, https://www.indeed.com/career-advice/career-development/followership. Also see R. Farnell, "Toxic Followership and What Can Be Done," *Psychology Today,* June 21, 2021, https://www.psychologytoday.com/us/blog/leading-high-performing-team/202106/toxic-followership-and-what-can-be-done.

182. "What Is Followership? 14 Qualities of Good Followers," *Indeed,* March 10, 2023, https://www.indeed.com/career-advice/career-development/followership. Also see D. Brenner, "Don't Be Afraid to Be a Follower," *Forbes,* May 2, 2019, https://www.forbes.com/sites/forbescoachescouncil/2019/05/02/dont-be-afraid-to-follow/?sh=49f31fcf467b.

183. B. Tepper, "Consequences of Abusive Supervision," *Academy of Management Journal,* Vol. 43, No. 2 (2000), pp. 178–190.

184. A. Bhattacharjee and A. Sarkar, "Abusive Supervision: A Systematic Literature Review," *Management Review Quarterly,* 2022, pp. 1–34.

185. For a thorough review of the abusive supervision literature, see B. Tepper, L. Simon, and H. Park, "Abusive Supervision," *Annual Review of Organizational Psychology and Organizational Behavior,* Vol. 4 (2017), pp. 123–152. Also see J.D. Mackey, R.E. Frieder, J.R. Brees, and M.J. Martinko, "Abusive Supervision: A Meta-Analysis and Empirical Review," *Journal of Management,* Vol. 43 (2017), pp. 1940–1965; Y. Zhang, and T.C. Bednall, "Antecedents of Abusive Supervision: A Meta-Analytic Review," *Journal of Business Ethics,* Vol. 139 (2016), pp. 455–471.

186. W. Cao, P. Li, R.C. van der Wal, and T.W. Taris, "Leadership and Workplace Aggression: A Meta-Analysis," *Journal of Business Ethics,* 2022, pp. 1–21. Also see T. Fischer, A.W. Tian, A. Lee, and D.J. Hughes, "Abusive Supervision: A Systematic Review and Fundamental Rethink," *The Leadership Quarterly,* Vol. 32 (2021), 101540; J. Mackey, R. Frieder, J. Brees, and M. Martinko, "Abusive Supervision: A Meta-Analysis and Empirical Review," *Journal of Management,* Vol. 43 (2017), pp. 1940–1965.

187. "Workplace Violence," *OSHA,* https://www.osha.gov/workplace-violence (accessed May 8, 2023).

188. Y. Zhang, Y. Guo, M. Zhang, S. Xu, X. Liu, and A. Newman, "Antecedents and Outcomes of Authentic Leadership across Culture: A Meta-Analytic Review," *Asia Pacific Journal of Management,* Vol. 39 (2022), pp. 1399–1435.

189. M. Ong, S.J. Ashford, and U.K. Bindl, "The Power of Reflection for Would-Be Leaders: Investigating Individual Work Reflection and Its Impact on Leadership in Teams," *Journal of Organizational Behavior,* Vol. 44 (2023), pp. 19–41.

190. These questions were taken from B. Gardner, "Become a Better Leader with Disciplined Reflection," *Forbes,* December 28, 2015, https://www.forbes.com/sites/forbescoachescouncil/2015/12/28/become-a-better-leader-with-disciplined-reflection/#f60ae9f65c39.

191. J.R. Bailey and S. Rehman, "Don't Underestimate the Power of Self-Reflection," *Harvard Business Review,* March 4, 2022, https://hbr.org/2022/03/dont-underestimate-the-power-of-self-reflection.

192. H.M. Kraemer, "How Self-Reflection Can Make You a Better Leader," *Kellogg Insight,* December 2, 2016, https://insight.kellogg.northwestern.edu/article/how-self-reflection-can-make-you-a-better-leader.

193. A. Abell, "How to Break Free from the Imposter Syndrome Zone," *LinkedIn,* November 10, 2018, https://www.linkedin.com/pulse/how-break-free-from-imposter-syndrome-zone-alexander-abell.

194. M. Murphy, "The Dunning-Kruger Effect Shows Why Some People Think They're Great Even When Their Work Is Terrible," *LSA Psychology: University of Michigan,* January 26, 2017, https://lsa.umich.edu/psych/news-events/all-news/faculty-news/the-dunning-kruger-effect-shows-why-some-people-think-they-re-gr.html.

195. T. Herrera, "How to Spot and Overcome Your Hidden Weaknesses," *The New York Times,* April 23, 2018, https://www.nytimes.com/2018/04/23/smarter-living/how-to-spot-and-overcome-your-hidden-weaknesses.html.

CHAPTER 15

1. "Former Jamba Juice CEO James D. White: Empathy Is a Skill That Can Be Taught," *Harvard Business Review Digital Articles,* December 1, 2022, pp. 1–15.

2. C.S. Sunahara, D. Rosenfield, T. Alvi, Z. Wallmark, J. Lee, D. Fulford, and B.A. Tabak, "Revisiting the Association between Self-Reported Empathy and Behavioral Assessments of Social Cognition," *Journal of Experimental Psychology: General,* Vol. 151, No. 12 (2022), pp. 3304–3322.

3. J. Guttman, "How to Develop and Strengthen Your Empathy" *Psychology Today,* July 19, 2022, https://www.psychologytoday.com/us/blog/sustainable-life-satisfaction/202207/how-develop-and-strengthen-your-empathy.

4. A. König, J. Bundy, and L. M. Little, "A Blessing and a Curse: How CEOs' Trait Empathy Affects Their Management of Organizational Crises," *Academy of Management Review,* January 2020, pp. 130–153.

5. Z. Hu, Y. Wen, Y. Wang, Y. Lin, J. Shi, Z. Yu, Y. Lin, and Wang, "Effectiveness of Mindfulness-Based Interventions on Empathy: A Meta-Analysis," *Frontiers in Psychology,* Vol. 13 (2022).

6. J.A. Hall and R. Schwartz, "Empathy Present and Future," *The Journal of Social Psychology,* May 2019, pp. 225–243.

7. H. Gehlbach and N. Mu, "How We Understand Others: A Theory of How Social Perspective Taking Unfolds," *Review of General Psychology,* Vol. 27, No. 3 (2023), pp. 282–302.

8. P. Bregman, "Empathy Starts with Curiosity," *Harvard Business Review,* April 27, 2020, https://hbr.org/2020/04/empathy-starts-with-curiosity?ab=hero-subleft-1.

9. "Advance Your Career by Improving Communication Skills in the Workplace," *Entrepreneur,* September 16, 2022, https://www.entrepreneur.com/living/advance-your-career-by-improving-communication-skills-in/435491.

10. S. VanDerziel, "Future Forward: Key Issues and Recommendations for Success in 2022," *NACE,* February 1, 2022, https://www.naceweb.org/talent-acquisition/trends-and-predictions/future-forward-key-issues-and-recommendations-for-success-in-2022/.

11. J. Kotter, "Power, Dependence, and Effective Management," *Harvard Business Review,* Vol. 55 (1977), pp. 125–136.

12. These sources are discussed by A. Ahmed, "Noise in Business Communication," *bizfluent,* April 25, 2019, https://bizfluent.com/facts-6757500-noise-business-communication.html.

13. J. Thier, "Everyone Hates the Open Floor Office Plan, Meet Its Remote-Work-Friendly Replacement: 'Quiet Spaces'," *Fortune,* December 1, 2022, https://fortune.com/2022/12/01/quiet-spaces-replacing-open-office-floor-plans/.

14. T.S. Lau, "The Effect of Typewriting vs. Handwriting Lecture Notes on Learning: A Systematic Review and Meta-Analysis," (2022). *Electronic Theses and Dissertations,* 2022, paper 3982, https://doi.org/10.18297/etd/3982.

15. O. Drawhorn, "Community Expertise Improves Fish Advisory Signs," *Port Seattle,* May 3, 2022, https://www.portseattle.org/blog/community-expertise-improves-fish-advisory-signs.

16. M.P. Normand and H.E. Donohue, "Behavior Analytic Jargon Does Not Seem to Influence Treatment Acceptability Ratings," *Journal of Applied Behavior Analysis,* Vol. 55, No. 4 (2022), pp. 1294–1305.

17. T. Musbach, "The Most Annoying, Overused Words in the Workplace," *San Francisco Chronicle,* October 11, 2009, p. A1.

18. H. Nesher Shoshan and W. Wehrt, "Understanding 'Zoom fatigue': A Mixed-Method Approach," *Applied Psychology*, Vol. 71, No. 3 (2022), pp. 827–852.

19. R.L. Daft and R.H. Lengel, "Information Richness: A New Approach to Managerial Behavior and Organizational Design," in B.M. Staw and L.L. Cummings (eds.), *Research in Organizational Behavior* (Greenwich, CT: JAI Press, 1984), p. 196. Also see R.H. Lengel and R.L. Daft, "The Selection of Communication Media as an Executive Skill," *Academy of Management Executive*, August 1988, pp. 225–232.

20. S.-H. Chao, J. Jiang, C.-H. Hsu, Y.-T. Chiang, E. Ng, and W.-T. Fang, "Technology-Enhanced Learning for Graduate Students: Exploring the Correlation of Media Richness and Creativity of Computer-Mediated Communication and Face-to-Face Communication," *Applied Sciences*, Vol. 10 (2020), p. 1602, www.mdpi.com/journal/applsci. Also see F.-C. Tseng, T. Cheng, P.-L. Yu, T.-L. Huang, and C.-I. Teng, "Media Richness, Social Presence and Loyalty to Mobile Instant Messaging," *Industrial Management & Data Systems*, July 2019, pp. 1357–1373.

21. T. Neeley, "What Managers Need to Know about Social Tools," *Harvard Business Review*, November–December 2017, pp. 118–126. Also see T. Harbert, "Let's Chat," *HR Magazine*, November 2017, pp. 46–51.

22. S.M. Clor-Proell, K. Kadous, and C.A. Proell, "Do as I Say: A Look at the Supervisor Behaviors That Encourage Upward Communication on Audit Teams," *Accounting Horizons*, Vol. 37, No. 1 (2023), pp.15–24.

23. A. Bertello, P. De Bernardi, G. Santoro, and R. Quaglia, "Unveiling the Microfoundations of Multiplex Boundary Work for Collaborative Innovation," *Journal of Business Research*, Vol. 139 (2022), pp. 1424–1434.

24. "Future of Work Research," *Accenture*, November 29, 2022, https://www.accenture.com/us-en/insights/consulting/future-work?c=acn_glb_talentandorganimediarelations_12163686&n=mrl_0521.

25. A. Chaker, "Slack? Phone? Teams? Zoom? There Are Too Many Work Communications," *Wall Street Journal*, April 26, 2023, https://www.wsj.com/articles/so-many-ways-to-communicate-at-work-so-many-ways-to-misfire-ec7d9f07.

26. B. Lufkin, "Communicating Remotely Is Hard, with Far More Room for Ambiguity. That's Why Some Overthinkers Are Struggling," *BBC*, August 9, 2022, https://www.bbc.com/worklife/article/20220803-why-overthinkers-struggle-with-remote-work.

27. M. Rivera, "5 Remote Work Best Practices for 2023," *Motley Fool*, August 5, 2022, https://www.fool.com/the-ascent/small-business/video-conferencing/articles/remote-work-best-practices/.

28. Z. Wang, "How Wendy's Is Using the Metaverse to Win Gen Z Consumers," *Business Insider*, June 29, 2022, https://www.businessinsider.com/inside-wendys-metaverse-strategy-2022-6.

29. D. Chang, "Here Are the Most Popular Fast Food Brands in America," *Motley Fool*, October 8, 2022, https://www.fool.com/the-ascent/personal-finance/articles/here-are-the-most-popular-fast-food-brands-in-america/.

30. N. Duncan, "How Kristin Tormey Elevated Wendy's to Influencer Status," *QSR Magazine*, June 17, 2022, https://www.qsrmagazine.com/fast-food/how-kristin-tormey-elevated-wendys-influencer-status.

31. T. Sun, P. Schilpzand, and Y. Liu, "Workplace Gossip: An Integrative Review of Its Antecedents, Functions, and Consequences," *Journal of Organizational Behavior*, Vol. 44, No. 2 (2023), pp. 311–334.

32. K.L. Robinson and P.D. Thelen, 2018. What makes the grapevine so effective? An employee perspective on employee-organization communication and peer-to-peer communication. *Public Relations Journal*, 12(2), pp. 1–20. Vancouver.

33. These recommendations were based on "How to Stop Workplace Gossip," *Robert Half blog*, January 6, 2020, https://www.roberthalf.com/blog/management-tips/managing-the-rumor-mill-6-tips-on-dealing-with-office-gossip.

34. J. Humphrey "Why You Need to Master In-Person Conversations in Your Slack-Driven Office," *Fast Company*, July 1, 2016, http://www.fastcompany.com/3061470/how-to-be-a-success-at-everything/why-you-need-to-master-in-person-conversations-in-your-sla.

35. J. McKendrick, "Managing by Walking around—Digitally," *Forbes*, February 25, 2022, https://www.forbes.com/sites/joemckendrick/2022/02/25/managing-by-walking-around---digitally/?sh=425565fa2c2a.

36. K. Lobell, "How to Run Employee Town Hall Meetings Post-Pandemic," *Society for Human Resource Management*, August 8, 2022, https://www.shrm.org/resourcesandtools/hr-topics/employee-relations/pages/how-to-run-employee-town-hall-meetings-post-pandemic.aspx.

37. B. Laker, V. Pereira, A. Malik, and L. Soga, "Dear Manager, You're Holding Too Many Meetings," *Harvard Business Review*, March 9, 2022.

38. B. Laker, V. Pereira, A. Malik, and L. Soga, "Dear Manager, You're Holding Too Many Meetings," *Harvard Business Review*, March 9, 2022.

39. "What Is an Effective Meeting?" *McKinsey & Company*, May 8, 2023, https://www.mckinsey.com/featured-insights/mckinsey-explainers/what-is-an-effective-meeting.

40. These recommendations were largely based on D. Lancefield, "Stop Wasting People's Time with Meetings," *Harvard Business Review*, March 14, 2022, https://hbr.org/2022/03/stop-wasting-peoples-time-with-bad-meetings; Also see C. Castrillon, "How to Reduce Unnecessary Meetings at Work," *Forbes*, January 5, 2023, https://www.forbes.com/sites/carolinecastrillon/2023/01/05/how-to-reduce-unnecessary-meetings-at-work/?sh=399bdb794b20; Also see Abbajay, "9 Ways to Make Your Meetings Matter," *Forbes*, January 20, 2020, https://www.forbes.com/sites/maryabbajay/2020/01/20/9-ways-to-make-your-meetings-matter/#19a4a3203831. Also see S. Hyken, "Six Ways to Have Effective and Successful Meetings," *Forbes*, May 10, 2020, https://www.forbes.com/sites/shephyken/2020/05/10/six-ways-to-have-effective-and-successful-meetings/#1a50cd838b94.

41. N. Piñon, "No. 1 Lesson from 3 Years of No-Meeting Wednesdays, Says HR Expert: Meetings Aren't 'the Enemy'," *CNBC*, February 1, 2023, https://www.cnbc.com/2023/02/01/top-lesson-from-no-meeting-wednesdays-canva-hr-head-jennie-rogerson.html.

42. H. Field, "Survey: Here's How U.S. Workers Really Feel about Meetings," *Entrepreneur*, February 25, 2020, https://www.entrepreneur.com/article/346742.

43. E. Bernstein and B. Waber, "The Truth about Open Offices." *Harvard Business Review*, Vol. 97 (2019), pp. 82–91.

44. T. Mitchell, G.J. Lemoine, and D. Lee, "Inclined but Less Skilled? Disentangling Extraversion, Communication Skill, and Leadership Emergence," *Journal of Applied Psychology*, Vol. 107, No. 9 (2022), pp. 1524–1542.

45. S. Heathfield, "The Components of Communication in the Workplace," *The Balance Careers*, April 29, 2020, https://www.thebalancecareers.com/communication-in-the-workplace-1918089.

46. C. Yue, L. Men, and M Ferguson, "Bridging Transformational Leadership, Transparent Communication, and Employee Openness to Change: The Mediating Role of Trust," *Public Relations Review*, Vol. 45, No. 3 (2019). Also see H. Jiang and Y. Luo, "Crafting Employee Trust: From Authenticity, Transparency to Engagement," *Journal of Communication Management*, May 2018, pp. 138–160.

47. A. Lewis, "Good Leadership? It All Starts with Trust," *Harvard Business Publishing*, October 26, 2022, https://www.harvardbusiness.org/good-leadership-it-all-starts-with-trust/.

48. S. Camparo, P.Z. Maymin, C. Park, S. Yoon, C. Zhang, Y Lee, and E.J. Langer, "The Fatigue Illusion: The Physical Effects of Mindlessness," *Humanities and Social Sciences Communications*, Vol. 9, No. 1 (2022), pp. 1–16.

49. V. Greenwood, "Focus and the Organized Mind: A Cheat Sheet to Boost Productivity and Cope with Information Overload," *The Washington Center for Cognitive Therapy*, https://washingtoncenterforcognitivetherapy.com/focus-and-the-organized-mind/ (accessed May 14, 2023).

50. "Are There Benefits of Multitasking?" *USC*, https://appliedpsychologydegree.usc.edu/blog/benefits-of-multitasking/ (accessed May 14, 2023).

51. https://twitter.com/BernieSanders (accessed May 14, 2023).

52. D. Milmo and A. Packham, "'They're 25, They Don't Do Emails': Is Instant Chat Replacing the Inbox?" *The Guardian*, January 20, 2023, https://www.theguardian.com/technology/2023/jan/20/davos-elite-say-gen-z-workers-prefer-chat-to-email.

53. G. Ritzer, *Introduction to Sociology* (Thousand Oaks, CA: Sage Publications, 2013), p. 116.

54. Y. Cao, Y. Hou, Z. Dong, and L.J. Ji, "The Impact of Culture and Social Distance on Humor Appreciation, Sharing, and Production," *Social Psychological and Personality Science,* Vol. 14, No. 2 (2023), pp. 207–217.

55. I. West-Knights, "A Brit and Some Americans Have Words about a Facial-Expression Scandal That Blew Minds across the Atlantic," *Slate,* December 2, 2022, https://slate.com/human-interest/2022/12/frown-meaning-britain-america-scandal.html#:~:text=Imogen%20West%2DKnights%3A%20He%20had,is%20less%20good%20than%20good.

56. "'Dutch Working Environment Is Direct ... Elephants in the Room Are Introduced as Soon as They Appear'; Cork Woman at Home on the Continent Where She Has 'Become Who I'm Supposed to Be in my Working Life,'" *The Irish Times,* January 20, 2023.

57. "Strategies to Improve Intercultural Communication," *Notre Dame Online,* March 13, 2020, https://www.notredameonline.com/resources/intercultural-management/strategies-to-improve-intercultural-communication/.

58. Based on: P. Caligiuri and D. DeCaprio, "How to Prepare for a Cross-Cultural Interview," *HBR Ascend,* March 10, 2023, https://hbr.org/2023/03/how-to-prepare-for-a-cross-cultural-interview; "What Is Cultural Fluency? And Why Is It Important?" *NBC News,* October 15, 2019, https://www.nbcnews.com/better/lifestyle/what-cultural-fluency-why-it-important-ncna1061656. Also see "Strategies to Improve Intercultural Communication," *Notre Dame Online,* March 13, 2020, https://www.notredameonline.com/resources/intercultural-management/strategies-to-improve-intercultural-communication/; V. Gambhir, "Building Cultural Fluency," *LinkedIn,* May 13, 2019, https://www.linkedin.com/pulse/building-cultural-fluency-vivek-gambhir.

59. P. Caligiuri and D. DeCaprio, "How to Prepare for a Cross-Cultural Interview," *HBR Ascend,* March 10, 2023, https://hbr.org/2023/03/how-to-prepare-for-a-cross-cultural-interview.

60. H. Bedir and A. Daskan, "The Significance of Body Language in Foreign Language Learning and Teaching," *International Journal of Social Sciences & Educational Studies*, Vol. 10, No. 1 (2023), p. 111.

61. S. Anders, "What Are You Really Saying? The Importance of Nonverbal Clues," *American Association for Physician Leadership*, December 5, 2018, https://www.physicianleaders.org/news/what-are-you-really-saying-importance-nonverbal-clues.

62. S. Helou, E. El Helou, N. Evans, T. Shigematsu, J. El Helou, M. Kaneko, and K. Kiyono, "Physician Eye Contact in Telemedicine Video Consultations: A Cross-Cultural Experiment," *International Journal of Medical Informatics*, Vol 165 (2022), p. 104825.

63. "Understanding Cross-Cultural Differences in Engagement," *Wake Forest University,* July 31, 2022, https://prod.wp.cdn.aws.wfu.edu/sites/445/2022/07/Understanding-Cross-Cultural-Differences-in-Engagement.mri-AH.pdf.

64. J. Steinhoff, "The Science behind a Smile," *Wisconsin Alumni Association,* May 28, 2022, https://onwisconsin.uwalumni.com/the-science-behind-a-smile/.

65. "Russia Training Their People to Smile for World Cup", *OHO Feed*, June 21, 2018, https://www.ohofeed.com/russia-training-people-smile-fifa-world-cup/.

66. "15 Common Body Language Mistakes to Avoid When Talking to VIPs," *Forbes,* August 1, 2022, https://www.forbes.com/sites/forbesbusinesscouncil/2022/08/01/15-common-body-language-mistakes-to-avoid-when-talking-to-vips/?sh=41025e4f5d28.

67. Based on "Why You Shouldn't Hug Your Colleagues," *BBC,* October 16, 2018, https://www.bbc.com/news/business-45680670. Also see K. Vasel, "To Hug or Not to Hug: A 5-Step Guide to Embracing at Work," *CNN,* July 12, 2019, https://www.cnn.com/2019/07/12/success/hugging-at-work/index.html.

68. C.M. Portengen, A.L. van Baar, and J.J. Endendijk, 2023. A Neurocognitive Approach to Studying Processes Underlying Parents' Gender Socialization. *Frontiers in Psychology*, 13, p. 1054886.

69. "Social Media Users by Country 2023," *World Population Review*, https://worldpopulationreview.com/country-rankings/social-media-users-by-country; "Social Media Advertising Segment Projected to Surpass the $300 Billion Dollar Mark by 2024," *PR Newswire,* March 10, 2023, https://www.prnewswire.com/news-releases/social-media-advertising-segment-projected-to-surpass-the-300-billion-dollar-mark-by-2024-301768534.html; "Smartly.io Survey: 82% of Gen Z Consumers Use Social Media to Find New Brands," *Business Wire*, June 30, 2022, https://www.businesswire.com/news/home/20220630005082/en/Smartly.io-Survey-82-of-Gen-Z-Consumers-Use-Social-Media-to-Find-New-Brands.

70. F. Colcol, "Six Ways to Use Social Media to Strengthen Your Business's Brand," *Forbes,* March 17, 2023, https://www.forbes.com/sites/theyec/2023/03/17/six-ways-to-use-social-media-to-strengthen-your-businesss-brand/?sh=6a5842ff57e8/.

71. "Natgeo," *Instagram,* https://www.instagram.com/natgeo/?hl=en (accessed May 15, 2023); K. Amaria, "National Geographic Hit 100 Million Instagram Followers. To Celebrate, It Wants Your Images for Free," *Vox,* February 20, 2019.

72. C. Johnson, "Best Brands on Social Media: 10 Inspiring Examples to Follow," Nextiva, October 25, 2023. https://www.nextiva.com/blog/best-brands-on-social-media.html.

73. "Our Focus," *National Geographic,* https://www.nationalgeographic.org/society/our-focus/#:~:text=Spark%20curiosity%2C%20empower%20exploration%2C%20inspire%20change&text=We%20are%20a%20global%20non,the%20wonder%20of%20our%20world (accessed May 15, 2023).

74. E. Barry, "These Are the Countries Where Twitter, Facebook and TikTok Are Banned," *Time,* January 18, 2022, https://time.com/6139988/countries-where-twitter-facebook-tiktok-banned/.

75. "Find Top Talent through Social Media Recruiting," *Monster,* January 29, 2022, https://hiring.monster.com/resources/recruiting-strategies/screening-candidates/recruiting-using-social-media/.

76. A. Barinka, "Meta's Instagram Users Reach 2 Billion, Closing in on Facebook," *Bloomberg,* October 26, 2022, https://www.bloomberg.com/news/articles/2022-10-26/meta-s-instagram-users-reach-2-billion-closing-in-on-facebook#xj4y7vzkg; "About LinkedIn," *LinkedIn,* https://about.linkedin.com/#:~:text=930%20million%20members%20in%20more,member%20of%20the%20global%20workforce (accessed May 15, 2023).

77. D. Cotriss, "Keep It Clean: Social Media Screenings Gain in Popularity," *Business News Daily,* May 11, 2023, https://www.businessnewsdaily.com/2377-social-media-hiring.html.

78. "How to Use Social Media for Applicant Screening," *Society for Human Resource Management,* https://www.shrm.org/resourcesandtools/tools-and-samples/how-to-guides/pages/howtousesocialmediaforapplicantscreening.aspx (accessed May 15, 2023).

79. J. Semetaite, "The Pitfalls of Pre-Employment Social Media Screening," *Toggl,* April 17, 2023, https://toggl.com/blog/social-media-screening.

80. "How to Use Social Media for Applicant Screening," *Society for Human Resource Management,* https://www.shrm.org/resourcesandtools/tools-and-samples/how-to-guides/pages/howtousesocialmediaforapplicantscreening.aspx (accessed May 15, 2023).

81. H. Xu, Y. Wu, and J. Hamari, "What Determines the Successfulness of a Crowdsourcing Campaign: A Study on the Relationships between Indicators of Trustworthiness, Popularity, and Success," *Journal of Business Research*, Vol. 139 (2022), pp. 484–495.

82. "51 Product Ideas Qualify for the Second 2022 LEGO Ideas Review," *LEGO Ideas,* September 5, 2022, https://ideas.lego.com/blogs/a4ae09b6-0d4c-4307-9da8-3ee9f3d368d6/post/8ddbf903-64e7-4821-9cac-3eee6030fe63; "New Challenge—100 Years of Fairytales!" *LEGO Ideas,* May 1, 2023, https://ideas.lego.com/blogs/a4ae09b6-0d4c-4307-9da8-3ee9f3d368d6/post/ff80199d-d31c-4d89-9a05-2bb87a3f8f6d.

83. K.B. Wilson, V. Bhakoo, and D. Samson, "Crowdsourcing: A Contemporary Form of Project Management with Linkages to Open Innovation and Novel Operations," *International Journal of Operations & Production Management*, Vol. 38, No. 6 (2018), pp. 1467–1494.

84. N.V.Q. Truong, L.C. Dinh, S. Stein, L. Tran-Thanh, and N.R. Jennings, "Efficient and Adaptive Incentive Selection for Crowdsourcing Contests," *Applied Intelligence,* 2022, pp. 1–31; "How Do You Engage and Reward Your Crowd and Open Source Contributors?" *LinkedIn,* April 27, 2023, https://www.linkedin.com/advice/0/how-do-you-engage-reward-your-crowd-open-source.

85. M. Allen, "Five Ways to Increase Brand Recognition," *Forbes,* July 21, 2022, https://www.forbes.com/sites/forbesbusinesscouncil/2022/07/21/five-ways-to-increase-brand-recognition/?sh=5c95ee2051bc.

86. K. Reddy, K. Sravanth, and N. Sundaram, "The Role of Social Media Communication in Small Business Organisations," *Test Engineering and Management,* July 2022, https://www.researchgate.net/publication/361989810_The_Role_of_Social_Media_Communication_in_Small_Business_Organisations.

87. A. Poulis, I. Rizomyliotis, and K. Konstantoulaki, "Do Firms Still Need to Be Social? Firm Generated Content in Social Media," *Information Technology & People*, April 2019, pp. 387–404. Also see Y. Bilgin, "The Effect of Social Media Marketing Activities on Brand Awareness, Brand Image and Brand Loyalty," *Business & Management Studies: An International Journal*, April 2018, pp. 128–148; Y. Liu and R.A. Lopez, "The Impact of Social Media Conversations on Consumer Brand Choices," *Marketing Letters*, August 2014, pp. 1–13; A. Dwivedi, L.W. Johnson, D.C. Wilkie, and L. De Araujo-Gil, "Consumer Emotional Brand Attachment with Social Media Brands and Social Media Brand Equity," *European Journal of Marketing*, June 2019, pp. 1176–1204.

88. R. Guesalaga, "The Use of Social Media in Sales: Individual and Organizational Antecedents, and the Role of Customer Engagement in Social Media," *Industrial Marketing Management*, April 2016, pp. 71–79. Also see L. Collier, "Should You Let Your Employees Shop Online at Work?" *Office-Depot Solutions Center,* October 26, 2015, http://solutions.officedepot.com/leadership/article/should-you-let-your-employees-shop-online-at-work.

89. A.C.C. Tiong, "Corporate Reputation: Building and Maintaining," *Journal of Digital Marketing and Communication*, Vol. 2, No. 1 (2022), pp. 25–29.

90. A. Petrilli, "Five Tips for Repairing Your Brand Reputation (and Reaching More Customers on the Web)," *Forbes,* August 16, 2022, https://www.forbes.com/sites/forbesbusinesscouncil/2022/08/16/five-tips-for-repairing-your-brand-reputation-and-reaching-more-customers-on-the-web/?sh=478395556eb3.

91. A. Lake, "Burger King's 7 Most Controversial Ads of All Time," *Eat This, Not That!,* April 3, 2022, https://www.eatthis.com/news-burger-king-controversial-ads/.

92. "What Are the Pros and Cons of Using Social Media in the Workplace? What Should We Include in a Policy?" *Society for Human Resource Management,* https://www.shrm.org/ResourcesAndTools/tools-and-samples/hr-qa/Pages/socialnetworkingsitespolicy.aspx (accessed May 15, 2022).

93. K. Kuligowski, "Small Business Guide to Hiring a Social Media Manager," *Business,* February 21, 2023, https://www.business.com/articles/hiring-social-media-manager/.

94. Microsoft Create Team, "How to Avoid—or Apologize for—Social Media Disasters," *Microsoft,* March 23, 2023, https://create.microsoft.com/en-us/learn/articles/how-to-avoid-apologize-social-media-disasters.

95. A. Lake, "Burger King's 7 Most Controversial Ads of All Time," *Eat This, Not That!,* April 3, 2022, https://www.eatthis.com/news-burger-king-controversial-ads/.

96. B. Cherry, "The Dos and Don'ts of Responding to Negative Social Media Comments," *BlueLeadz*, December 31, 2018, https://www.bluleadz.com/blog/the-dos-and-donts-of-responding-to-negative-social-media-comments.

97. C.A. Henle, "Shifting the Literature from Who and When to Why: Identifying Cyberloafing Motives," *Applied Psychology*, April 2, 2023.

98. A. Reizer, B.L. Galperin, M. Chavan, A. Behl, and V. Pereira, "Examining the Relationship between Fear of COVID-19, Intolerance for Uncertainty, and Cyberloafing: A Mediational Model," *Journal of Business Research,* Vol. 145 (2022), pp. 660–670; C. Kolmar, "30 Surprising Social Media at Work Statistics [2023]: What Every Manager Should Know," *Zippia,* February 2, 2023, https://www.zippia.com/advice/social-media-at-work-statistics/#:~:text=The%.

99. C. Goerner, "Practical Advice on Work and Careers from Dr. Carolyn Goerner," *Practical Paradigms*, April 24, 2019, https://www.practicalparadigms.com/blog-content/2019/4/22/stop-the-cyberloafing.

100. I.A. Smith and A. Griffiths, "Microaggressions, Everyday Discrimination, Workplace Incivilities, and Other Subtle Slights at Work: A Meta-Synthesis," *Human Resource Development Review*, Vol 21, No. 3 (2022), pp. 275–299.

101. L.C. Chi, T.C. Tang, and E. Tang, "The Phubbing Phenomenon: A Cross-Sectional Study on the Relationships among Social Media Addiction, Fear of Missing Out, Personality Traits, and Phubbing Behavior," *Current Psychology*, Vol. 41, No. 2 (2022), pp. 1112–1123.

102. R. Newsom and A. Rehman, "Sleep and Social Media," *Sleep Foundation,* December 15, 2022, https://www.sleepfoundation.org/how-sleep-works/sleep-and-social-media.

103. P. Seciu, "Hackers Use ChatGPT to Spread Malware on Facebook, Instagram and WhatsApp," *Forbes,* May 3, 2023, https://www.forbes.com/sites/petersuciu/2023/05/03/hackers-use-chatgpt-to-spread-malware-on-facebook-instagram-and-whatsapp/?sh=7bbcbadb7e61.

104. J. Koziol and C. Bottorff, "Passwords and People: Your Secret Weapons against Cybercriminals," *Forbes,* August 8, 2022, https://www.forbes.com/advisor/business/passwords-and-people-against-cybercriminals/.

105. E. Charlton, "Gen Z Might Think They're Cyber Secure—but Baby Boomers Have Better Passwords," *World Economic Forum,* May 11, 2023, https://www.weforum.org/agenda/2023/05/cybersecurity-passwords-boomers-genz/.

106. Derived from B.K. Williams and S.C. Sawyer, *Using Information Technology: A Practical Introduction*, 11th ed. (New York: McGraw Hill Education, 2015), pp. 94, 100, 101, 357, 478.

107. "What Is Encryption & How Does It Work?" *Medium*, November 27, 2017, https://medium.com/searchencrypt/what-is-encryption-how-does-it-work-e8f20e340537.

108. I. Rijnetu, "The Most Popular Free Encryption Software Tools to Protect Your Data," *Heimdal Security*, April 15, 2019, https://heimdalsecurity.com/blog/free-encryption-software-tools/.

109. H. Reissman, "Americans Don't Understand What Companies Can Do with Their Personal Data—and That's a Problem," *University of Pennsylvania,* February 7, 2023, https://www.asc.upenn.edu/news-events/news/americans-dont-understand-what-companies-can-do-their-personal-data-and-thats-problem.

110. S. Hargadon, "Nothing Is Private," *Northwestern University,* April 18, 2023, https://magazine.northwestern.edu/features/nothing-is-private-protection-personal-information-privacy-matthew-kugler-lara-liss-caitin-fennessy/.

111. Z. Corbyn, "'Bossware Is Coming for Almost Every Worker': The Software You Might Not Realize Is Watching You," *The Guardian,* April 27, 2022, https://www.theguardian.com/technology/2022/apr/27/remote-work-software-home-surveillance-computer-monitoring-pandemic.

112. H. Tan, "96% of Remote Companies Say They're Using Some Kind of Software to Monitor Employees Who Work from Home, Survey Finds," *Business Insider,* March 30, 2023, https://www.businessinsider.com/majority-remote-hybrid-work-companies-wfh-monitor-employees-rto-2023-3.

113. S. Hargadon, "Nothing Is Private," *Northwestern University,* April 18, 2023, https://magazine.northwestern.edu/features/nothing-is-private-protection-personal-information-privacy-matthew-kugler-lara-liss-caitin-fennessy/.

114. J. Valverde-Berrocoso, A. González-Fernández, and J. Acevedo-Borrega, "Disinformation and Multiliteracy: A Systematic Review of the Literature," *Comunicar*, Vol. 30, No. 70 (2022), pp. 97–110.

115. C. Melchior and M. Oliveira, "Health-Related Fake News on Social Media Platforms: A Systematic Literature Review," *New Media & Society*, Vol. 24, No. 6 (2022), pp. 1500–1522.

116. A. Knuutila, L. Neudert, and P. Howard, "Who Is Afraid of Fake News? Modeling Risk Perceptions of Misinformation in 142 Countries," *Harvard Kennedy School,* April 12, 2022, https://misinforeview.hks.harvard.edu/article/who-is-afraid-of-fake-news-modeling-risk-perceptions-of-misinformation-in-142-countries/.

117. P. Madrid, "USC Study Reveals the Key Reason Why Fake News Spreads on Social Media," *USC News,* January 17, 2023, https://news.usc.edu/204782/usc-study-reveals-the-key-reason-why-fake-news-spreads-on-social-media/.

118. "'Fake News,' Lies and Propaganda: How to Sort Fact from Fiction," *University of Michigan Library,* August 4, 2022, https://guides.lib.umich.edu/c.php?g=637508&p=4462444.

119. D. Ruby, "69+ Fake News Statistics Revealed for 2023 (Updated)," *Demand Sage,* April 17, 2023, https://www.demandsage.com/fake-news-statistics/.

120. D. Georgiev, "18 Eye-Opening Fake News Statistics for 2023," *Tech Jury,* April 19, 2023, https://techjury.net/blog/fake-news-statistics/#gref.

121. "The Data Will Save Us: An Interview with CSSLab Director Duncan Watts," *CSS Lab,* April 18, 2022, https://css.seas.upenn.edu/the-data-will-save-us-an-interview-with-csslab-director-duncan-watts/.

122. J. Murray, "Stop Believing Every Statistic You Hear," *The Michigan Daily,* March 22, 2023, https://www.michigandaily.com/opinion/stop-believing-every-statistics-you-hear/.

123. "Misinformation and Disinformation: Thinking Critically about Information Sources," *CUNY Library,* January 23, 2023, https://library.csi.cuny.edu/c.php?g=619342&p=4376665.

124. R. Zhou, Z. Luo, S. Zhong, X. Zhang, and Y. Liu, "The Impact of Social Media on Employee Mental Health and Behavior Based on the Context of Intelligence-Driven Digital Data," *International Journal of Environmental Research and Public Health*, Vol. 19, No. 24 (2022), p. 16965.

125. E. Gonzalez, "How to Write the Ultimate Social Media Policy," *Motley Fool,* August 5, 2022, https://www.fool.com/the-ascent/small-business/human-resources/articles/social-media-policy/.

126. M. Porter and N. Nohria, "How CEOs Manage Time," *Harvard Business Review*, Vol. 96, No. 4 (July 2018), pp. 42–51. Also see P. Pehar, "Five Communication Barriers in Business and How to Fix Them," *Forbes,* April 5, 2022, https://www.forbes.com/sites/forbescommunicationscouncil/2022/04/05/five-communication-barriers-in-business-and-how-to-fix-them/?sh=105d784f780f.

127. M. Collins, "Recruiters and Students Have Differing Perceptions of New Grad Proficiency in Competencies," *NACE,* October 24, 2022, https://www.naceweb.org/career-readiness/competencies/recruiters-and-students-have-differing-perceptions-of-new-grad-proficiency-in-competencies/.

128. R. Bailey and E. Bailey, "Effective Communication with Participants in Court Hearings: Using Polyvagal Theory in the Courtroom," *Juvenile and Family Court Journal*, Vol. 73, No. 1 (2022), pp. 57–66.

129. D. Booher, "5 Defensive Habits That Cut off Communication and Creativity," *Forbes,* August 15, 2022, https://www.forbes.com/sites/womensmedia/2022/08/15/5-defensive-habits-that-cut-off-communication-and-creativity/?sh=6205e47255e3.

130. K. Aldrup, B. Carstensen, and U. Klusmann, "Is Empathy the Key to Effective Teaching? A Systematic Review of Its Association with Teacher-Student Interactions and Student Outcomes," *Educational Psychology Review*, Vol. 34, No. 3 (2022), pp. 1177–1216.

131. J. Alexander and C. Andersson, "Fællesskab and Belonging," *Berkeley Othering & Belonging Institute,* February 15, 2022, https://belonging.berkeley.edu/democracy-belonging-forum/papers/faellesskab#:~:text=From%20the%20age%20of%206,and%20social%20skills%20it%20teaches.

132. These definitions were taken from "Nice Guys Finish First," *Mindful*, October 2017, p. 32.

133. Thomas Jefferson University, "Medical Students Become Less Empathic Toward Patients throughout Medical School," *Medical Express,* February 5, 2020, https://medicalxpress.com/news/2020-02-medical-students-empathic-patients-school.html.

134. C. O'Connell, J. McCauley, and L. Herbert, "Improvisation-Based Workshop to Build Empathy in Mentor-Mentee Relationships and Support Academic Equity," *Journal of Student Affairs Research and Practice*, Vol. 59, No. 1 (2022), pp. 87–100.

135. Young Entrepreneur Council, "Speak Like a Leader: 7 Effective Communication Skills," *Inc.*, December 18, 2018, https://www.inc.com/young-entrepreneur-council/7-communication-secrets-of-great-leaders.html.

136. R.D. Minehart, B.B. Symon, and L.K. Rock, "What's Your Listening Style?" *Harvard Business Review Digital Articles*, 2022, pp. 1–8.

137. S. Illing, "Are You a Good Listener? The Answer May Surprise You," *Vox,* April 24, 2023, https://www.vox.com/the-gray-area/23692685/how-to-listen-gray-area-kate-murphy-good-listener.

138. J. Agbanyim, "3 Ways to Communicate Better Amid Uncertainty," *Psychology Today,* March 26, 2023, https://www.psychologytoday.com/intl/blog/humanizing-the-world-of-work/202303/3-ways-to-communicate-better-amid-uncertainty.

139. M. Hagerty, "5 Things to Know about the Lost Art of Listening," *Houston Public Media,* February 26, 2020, https://www.houstonpublicmedia.org/articles/shows/houston-matters/2020/02/26/361969/listening-a-skill-that-takes-effort-and-practice/.

140. C. Headlee, "10 Ways to Have a Better Conversation," *TED,* https://www.ted.com/talks/celeste_headlee_10_ways_to_have_a_better_conversation?language=en (accessed May 15, 2023).

141. J. Kavanaugh, "'Pro Listener' and NPR Guest Faith Salie Coming to Annual Meeting," *MMA,* September 16, 2019, https://www.mma.org/pro-listener-and-npr-guest-faith-salie-coming-to-annual-meeting/.

142. Based on advice in J. Kerr, "How to Talk to People, According to Terry Gross," *The New York Times*, November 17, 2018, https://www.nytimes.com.

143. Based on C. Headlee, "10 Ways to Have a Better Conversation," *TED,* https://www.ted.com/talks/celeste_headlee_10_ways_to_have_a_better_conversation?language=en (accessed May 28, 2020). Also see K. Murphy, "Talk Less. Listen More. Here's How," *The New York Times*, January 9, 2020, https://www.nytimes.com.

144. C. Headlee, "10 Ways to Have a Better Conversation," *TED,* https://www.ted.com/talks/celeste_headlee_10_ways_to_have_a_better_conversation?language=en (accessed May 15, 2023). Also see M. Hagerty, "5 Things to Know about the Lost Art of Listening," *Houston Public Media,* February 26, 2020, https://www.houstonpublicmedia.org/articles/shows/houston-matters/2020/02/26/361969/listening-a-skill-that-takes-effort-and-practice/.

145. J. Stich, M. Tarafdar, and C. Cooper, "Electronic Communication in the Workplace: Boon or Bane?" *Journal of Organizational Effectiveness: People and Performance*, March 2018, pp. 98–106.

146. C. Gallo, "Public Speaking Is No Longer a 'Soft Skill.' It's Your Key to Success in Any Field," *Inc.*, January 4, 2019, https://www.inc.com/carmine-gallo/public-speaking-is-no-longer-a-soft-skill-its-your-key-to-success-in-any-field.html.

147. "The Chapman Survey of American Fears, Wave 8: The Complete List of Fears, 2022," *Chapman University*, 2022, https://www.chapman.edu/wilkinson/_files/fear-8-alphabetical-list_-22.pdf.

148. "TED Talks: The Official TED Guide to Public Speaking," *TED,* https://www.ted.com/read/ted-talks-the-official-ted-guide-to-public-speaking (accessed May 15, 2023).

149. G. Genard, "How to Open a Presentation: Tell 'Em What You're Going to Say," *Genard Method,* November 22, 2015, http://www.genardmethod.com/blog/bid/192061/How-to-Open-a-Presentation-Tell-Em-What-You-re-Going-to-Say.

150. "5 Elements of Public Speaking," *UNC Greensboro,* https://speakingcenter.uncg.edu/resources/5-elements-of-public-speaking/ (accessed May 15, 2023).

151. J. Moglia, "Why Storytelling Is a Leader's Most Powerful Defense against the Great Resignation," *Forbes,* February 22, 2022, https://

www.forbes.com/sites/joemoglia/2022/02/22/why-storytelling-is-a-leaders-most-powerful-defense-against-the-great-resignation/?sh=4963eed16650.

152. "TED Talk Takeaways: 8 Ways to Hook Your Audience," July 30, 2014, https://blog.slideshare.net/2014/07/30/set-your-hook-to-capture-your-audience.

153. "Networking Basics," *UNC Chapel Hill,* https://careers.unc.edu/students/step-4-self-marketing-professional-branding/networking-and-social-media/networking-basics/ (accessed May 15, 2023).

154. "Virtual Networking: Why Networks Matter for MBA Graduates," *Washington State University,* February 24, 2022, https://onlinemba.wsu.edu/mba/careers/why-mba-networking-matters/; R. Lotfi, "8 Tips to Help College Students Start Networking," *CNBC,* August 23, 2022, https://www.cnbc.com/2022/08/23/8-tips-to-help-college-students-start-networking.html.

155. D. Burkus, "Networking for Actual Human Beings," *The Wall Street Journal,* April 21–22, 2018, p. C3.

156. A. Tracy, "The Importance of Networking," *University of Illinois,* February 22, 2022, https://blogs.illinois.edu/view/8605/805793343.

157. "Network Marketing: How a Positive Attitude Determines Your Success," *Teamzy,* December 30, 2019, https://teamzy.com/network-marketing-how-a-positive-attitude-determines-your-success.

158. M. Moore, "4 Tips to Get Your Career Unstuck through Networking," *Forbes,* April 11, 2023, https://www.forbes.com/sites/forbescoachescouncil/2023/04/11/4-tips-to-get-your-career-unstuck-through-networking/?sh=21e20e0c40eb.

159. K. Klyver and P. Arenius, "Networking, Social Skills and Launching a New Business: A 3-Year Study of Nascent Entrepreneurs," *Entrepreneurship Theory and Practice,* Vol. 46, No. 5 (2022), pp. 1256–1283; Z. Ahmad, S.H. Soroya, and K. Mahmood, "Bridging Social Capital through the Use of Social Networking Sites: A Systematic Literature Review," *Journal of Human Behavior in the Social Environment,* 33(4), pp. 473–489, 2022.

160. Indeed Editorial Team, "47 Great Questions to Ask at a Networking Event," *Indeed,* February 3, 2023, https://www.indeed.com/career-advice/interviewing/questions-to-ask-at-a-networking-event.

CHAPTER 16

1. S. Rodríguez, R. González-Suárez, T. Vieites, I. Piñeiro, and F.M. Díaz-Freire, "Self-Regulation and Students Well-Being: A Systematic Review 2010–2020," *Sustainability,* Vol. 14 (2022), p. 2346. Also see M. Inzlicht, K.M. Werner, J.L. Briskin, and B.W. Roberts, "Integrating Models of Self-Regulation," *Annual Review of Psychology,* Vol. 72 (2021), pp. 319–345.

2. S.R. Covey, *The 7 Habits of Highly Effective People* (Simon & Schuster, 2020).

3. S.R. Covey, *The 7 Habits of Highly Effective People* (Simon & Schuster, 2020).

4. H. Liao, R. Su, T. Ptashnik, and J. Nielsen, "Feeling Good, Doing Good, and Getting Ahead: A Meta-Analytic Investigation of the Outcomes of Prosocial Motivation at Work," *Psychological Bulletin,* Vol. 148 (2022), pp. 158–198. Also see F. Righetti, J.K. Sakaluk, R. Faure, and E.A. Impett, "The Link between Sacrifice and Relational and Personal Well-Being: A Meta-Analysis," *Psychological Bulletin,* Vol. 146 (2020), pp. 900–921.

5. S.R. Covey, *The 7 Habits of Highly Effective People* (Simon & Schuster, 2020).

6. E-L. Elsey, "Coaching Tools 101: The Urgent Important Matrix—What Is It and How to Use It!" *The Coaching Tools Company,* September 22, 2022, https://www.thecoachingtoolscompany.com/coaching-tools-101-what-is-the-urgent-important-matrix/.

7. A. Boyes, "How to Focus on What's Important, Not Just What's Urgent," *Harvard Business Review,* July 3, 2018, https://hbr.org/2018/07/how-to-focus-on-whats-important-not-just-whats-urgent.

8. S.R. Covey, *The 7 Habits of Highly Effective People* (Simon & Schuster, 2020).

9. "What Is a Win Win Situation?" *Program on Negotiation at Harvard Law School,* https://www.pon.harvard.edu/tag/a-win-win-situation/ (accessed May 16, 2023).

10. E. Laurence, "10 Easy Self-Care Ideas That Can Help Boost Your Health," *Forbes,* January 26, 2023, https://www.forbes.com/health/mind/self-care-ideas/. Also see A.F. Westring, "There's No 'Right' Way to Do Self-Care," *Harvard Business Review,* April 20, 2021, https://hbr.org/2021/04/theres-no-right-way-to-do-self-care.

11. J. Cox, "Layoffs Are up Nearly Fivefold so Far This Year with Tech Companies Leading the Way," *CNBC,* April 6, 2023, https://www.cnbc.com/2023/04/06/layoffs-are-up-nearly-fivefold-so-far-this-year-with-tech-companies-leading-the-way.html.

12. L. Gupta, "Disney's Revenue Breakdown Worldwide (2016–2022)," *Business Quant,* https://businessquant.com/disney-revenue-breakdown-worldwide#:~:text=The%20company (accessed May 15, 2023).

13. "Revenue of the Walt Disney Company Worldwide in 2nd Quarter 2022 and 2nd Quarter 2023, by Segment," *Statista,* https://www.statista.com/statistics/1028537/quarterly-revenue-walt-disney-company-by-segment/ (accessed May 15, 2023). Also see B. Reed, "Disney Cuts Thousands of Jobs in Second Wave of Layoffs," *The Guardian,* April 24, 2023, https://www.theguardian.com/film/2023/apr/24/disney-latest-job-layoffs; A. Levy, "Here's Exactly When Disney+ Plans to Become Profitable," *The Motley Fool,* November 17, 2022, https://www.fool.com/investing/2022/11/17/heres-exactly-when-disney-plans-to-become-profitab/.

14. "Peloton Interactive Inc (PTON)," *Google Finance,* https://www.google.com/finance/quote/PTON:NASDAQ?sa=X&ved=2ahUKEwj3uZXeiPj-AhUXkGoFHUgoDU0Q3ecFegQIKhAf&window=5Y (accessed May 15, 2023). Also see S. Berkman, "Peloton Bike Recall: What Owners Need to Know," *New York Times,* May 11, 2023, https://www.nytimes.com/wirecutter/blog/peloton-bike-recall-may-2023/.

15. S. Van Kuiken, "Tech Trends Reshaping the Future of IT and Business," *McKinsey Digital,* October 21, 2022, https://www.mckinsey.com/capabilities/mckinsey-digital/our-insights/tech-at-the-edge-trends-reshaping-the-future-of-it-and-business.

16. X. Sobrepere i Profitós, T. Keil, and P. Kuusela, "The Two Blades of the Scissors: Performance Feedback and Intrinsic Attributes in Organizational Risk Taking," *Administrative Science Quarterly,* Vol. 67 (2022), pp. 1012–1048.

17. C. Wang, H. Jiao, and J. Song, "Wear Glasses for Supervisors to Discover the Beauty of Subordinates: Supervisor Developmental Feedback and Organizational Ambidexterity," *Journal of Business Research,* Vol. 158 (2023), 113650. Also see A. Christensen, A. Kinicki, Z. Zhang, and F. Walumbwa, "Responses to Feedback: The Role of Acceptance, Affect, and Creative Behavior," *Journal of Leadership and Organizational Studies,* February 2018, pp. 416–429.

18. "Welcome to the New Era of Microsoft Teams," *Microsoft 365 Blog,* March 27, 2023, https://www.microsoft.com/en-us/microsoft-365/blog/2023/03/27/welcome-to-the-new-era-of-microsoft-teams/.

19. S. Su, K. Baird, and A. Tung, "Controls and Performance: Assessing the Mediating Role of Creativity and Collegiality," *Journal of Management Control,* 2022, pp. 1–34.

20. "A Guide to Organisational Performance Measures (with Types)," *Indeed,* October 16, 2022, https://in.indeed.com/career-advice/career-development/organizational-performance-measures.

21. "List of Objective and Subjective Data/Data Sources..." *Department of Commerce,* https://www.commerce.gov/sites/default/files/2018-12/caps-1-report-d2-data-sources.pdf (accessed May 16, 2023). Also see R. Izquierdo, "5 Best Employee Performance Metrics to Track in 2022," *The Motley Fool,* August 5, 2022, https://www.fool.com/the-ascent/small-business/human-resources/articles/performance-metrics/.

22. B. Nordmeyer, "The Importance of Variation in Manufacturing," *Small Business Chronicle,* https://smallbusiness.chron.com/importance-variation-manufacturing-36996.html (accessed May 16, 2023).

23. "Celebrating the 5th Anniversary of Atlanta's Mercedes-Benz Stadium," *HOK,* August 26, 2022, https://www.hok.com/news/2022-08/

celebrating-the-5th-anniversary-of-atlantas-mercedes-benz-stadium/. Also see N.M. Post, "The Agonies of Building Atlanta's Mercedes-Benz Stadium," *ENR,* July 26, 2017, https://www.enr.com/articles/42419-the-agonies-of-building-atlantas-mercedes-benz-stadium.

24. "What Are Control Charts?" *National Institute of Standards and Technology,* https://www.itl.nist.gov/div898/handbook/pmc/section3/pmc31.htm (accessed May 16, 2023). Also see "Control Chart," *American Society for Quality,* https://asq.org/quality-resources/control-chart (accessed May 16, 2023).

25. "Control Chart," *American Society for Quality,* https://asq.org/quality-resources/control-chart (accessed May 16, 2023).

26. L. Kudrna, P. Bird, K. Hemming, L. Quinn, K. Schmidtke, and R. Lilford, "Retrospective Evaluation of an Intervention Based on Training Sessions to Increase the Use of Control Charts in Hospitals," *BMJ Quality & Safety,* Vol. 32 (2023), pp. 100–108. Also see A.G. Abdulaziz, C.S. Ribas, and G.S. Weheba, "Application of Group Control Charts for Multiple Parts Manufacturing," *Journal of Management and Engineering Integration,* Vol. 12 (2019), pp. 41–48.

27. "Southwest Airlines Customer Service Plan-English Version," *Southwest Airlines,* August 30, 2022, https://www.southwest.com/assets/pdfs/corporate-commitments/customer-service-plan.pdf?clk=7396032.

28. M. Fairlie, "Best GPS Fleet Management Services of 2023," *Business.com,* May 1, 2023, https://www.business.com/categories/best-gps-fleet-tracking-services/#Force-by-Mojio.

29. R.S. Kaplan and D.P. Norton, "The Balanced Scorecard—Measures That Drive Performance," *Harvard Business Review,* January–February 1992, pp. 71–79.

30. C. Mio, A. Costantini, and S. Panfilo, "Performance Measurement Tools for Sustainable Business: A Systematic Literature Review on the Sustainability Balanced Scorecard Use," *Corporate Social Responsibility and Environmental Management,* Vol. 29 (2022), pp. 367–384. Also see R.E. Freeman, S.D. Dmytriyev, and R.A. Phillips, "Stakeholder Theory and the Resource-Based View of the Firm," *Journal of Management Studies,* Vol. 58 (2021), pp. 1441–1470.

31. R.S. Kaplan and D.P. Norton, "The Balanced Scorecard—Measures That Drive Performance," *Harvard Business Review,* January–February 1992, pp. 71–79.

32. F. Amer, S. Hammoud, H. Khatatbeh, S. Lohner, I. Boncz, and D. Endrei, "The Deployment of Balanced Scorecard in Health Care Organizations: Is It Beneficial? A Systematic Review," *BMC Health Services Research,* Vol. 22 (2022), pp. 1–14.

33. A. Tawse and P. Tabesh, "Thirty Years with the Balanced Scorecard: What We Have Learned," *Business Horizons,* Vol. 66 (2023), pp. 123–132. Also see F. Amer, S. Hammoud, H. Khatatbeh, S. Lohner, I. Boncz, and D. Endrei, "The Deployment of Balanced Scorecard in Health Care Organizations: Is It Beneficial? A Systematic Review," *BMC Health Services Research,* Vol. 22 (2022), pp. 1–14.

34. J. Clement, "Electronic Arts (EA) Net Revenue 2016–2022, By Composition," *Statista,* May 30, 2022, https://www.statista.com/statistics/269698/revenue-of-electronic-arts-by-composition/.

35. A. Hartmans, "Macy's Is Closing Another Batch of Stores in 2023—Here's the Full List," *Business Insider,* January 5, 2023, https://www.businessinsider.com/macys-store-closings-2023-full-list-2023-1.

36. S. Freakley and L. Donahue, "Setting Your Annual Budget amid Economic Uncertainty," *Harvard Business Review,* September 1, 2022, https://hbr.org/2022/09/setting-your-annual-budget-amid-economic-uncertainty. Also see C. Cote, "Why Is Budgeting Important in Business? 5 Reasons," *Harvard Business School Online,* July 6, 2022, https://online.hbs.edu/blog/post/importance-of-budgeting-in-business.

37. J.P. DeMuro, "Best Budgeting Software of 2023," *Tech Radar Pro,* April 17, 2023, https://www.techradar.com/best/best-budgeting-software.

38. S. Freakley and L. Donahue, "Setting Your Annual Budget amid Economic Uncertainty," *Harvard Business Review,* September 1, 2022, https://hbr.org/2022/09/setting-your-annual-budget-amid-economic-uncertainty.

39. N. Zhexembayeva, "3 Ways to Bring Flexibility to Budgeting," *Harvard Business Review,* September 28, 2022, https://hbr.org/2022/09/3-ways-to-bring-flexibility-to-budgeting.

40. A. Naim, "Role of Accounting and Finance in Performance Appraisal," *American Journal of Sociology, Economics and Tourism,* Vol. 1 (2022), pp. 1–17. Also see M.A. Rashid, A. Al-Mamun, H. Roudaki, and Q.R. Yasser, "An Overview of Corporate Fraud and Its Prevention Approach," *Australasian Accounting Business & Finance Journal,* Vol. 16 (2022), pp. 101–118.

41. S. Valle, "Exxon Smashes Western Oil Majors' Profits with $56 Billion in 2022," *Reuters,* January 31, 2023, https://www.reuters.com/business/energy/exxon-smashes-western-oil-majors-earnings-record-with-59-billion-profit-2023-01-31/.

42. "How the 3 Financial Statements Are Linked," *Corporate Finance Institute,* April 18, 2023, https://corporatefinanceinstitute.com/resources/accounting/3-financial-statements-linked/.

43. E. Yoon and C. Lochhead, "5 Ways to Stimulate Cash Flow in a Downturn," *Harvard Business Review,* April 8, 2020, https://hbr.org/2020/04/5-ways-to-stimulate-cash-flow-in-a-downturn.

44. A.R. Sorkin, R. Mattu, B. Warner, S. Kessler, M.J. de la Merced, L. Hirsch, and E. Livni, "Why Bed Bath & beyond Is Weighing Bankruptcy," *The New York Times,* January 6, 2023, https://www.nytimes.com/2023/01/06/business/dealbook/bed-bath-beyond-bankruptcy.html. Also see G. Fonrouge, "Bed Bath & beyond Files for Bankruptcy Protection after Failed Turnaround Efforts," *CNBC,* April 23, 2023, https://www.cnbc.com/2023/04/23/bed-bath-beyond-files-for-bankruptcy-protection.html.

45. "Financial Ratios," Inc., https://www.inc.com/encyclopedia/financial-ratios.html (accessed May 3, 2023).

46. S. Kumar, "Customer Retention versus Customer Acquisition," *Forbes,* Accessed December 12, 2022, https://www.forbes.com/sites/forbesbusinesscouncil/2022/12/12/customer-retention-versus-customer-acquisition/?sh=7ed3fe741c7d.

47. G.T.M. Hult and F. Morgeson, "10 Ways to Boost Customer Satisfaction," *Harvard Business Review,* January 12, 2023, https://hbr.org/2023/01/10-ways-to-boost-customer-satisfaction.

48. J. Aten, "LEGO Customers Lose Millions of Pieces a Year. The Company's 4-Word Response Is the Best I've Ever Seen," *Inc,* November 7, 2021, https://www.inc.com/jason-aten/lego-customers-lose-millions-of-pieces-a-year-companys-4-word-response-is-best-ive-ever-seen.html.

49. "Converting Disconnects into Loyalty Opportunities: PwC Customer Loyalty Executive Survey 2023," *PwC,* https://www.pwc.com/us/en/services/consulting/business-transformation/library/building-customer-loyalty-guide.html (accessed May 17, 2023).

50. G.T.M. Hult and F. Morgeson, "10 Ways to Boost Customer Satisfaction," *Harvard Business Review,* January 12, 2023, https://hbr.org/2023/01/10-ways-to-boost-customer-satisfaction. Also see J. Michelli, "Being the Ritz Carlton of Your Industry: How to Deliver Delight," *Linkedin,* July 26, 2022, https://www.linkedin.com/pulse/being-ritz-carlton-your-industry-how-deliver-delight-michelli-ph-d-; T. Matthews-El and C. Bottorff, "14 Customer Retention Strategies That Work in 2022," *Forbes Advisor,* August 22, 2022, https://www.forbes.com/advisor/business/customer-retention-strategies/.

51. S. Hyken, "58% of Customers Will Pay More for Better Customer Service," *Forbes,* April 24, 2022, https://www.forbes.com/sites/shephyken/2022/04/24/fifty-eight-percent-of-customers-will-pay-more-for-better-customer-service/?sh=75ee881413f1.

52. "Converting Disconnects into Loyalty Opportunities: PwC Customer Loyalty Executive Survey 2023," *PwC,* https://www.pwc.com/us/en/services/consulting/business-transformation/library/building-customer-loyalty-guide.html (accessed May 17, 2023).

53. C. Mio, A. Costantini, and S. Panfilo, "Performance Measurement Tools for Sustainable Business: A Systematic Literature Review on the Sustainability Balanced Scorecard Use," *Corporate Social Responsibility and Environmental Management,* Vol. 29 (2022), pp. 367–384.

54. "About Us," *J.D. Power,* https://www.jdpower.com/business/about-us (accessed May 17, 2023).

55. A. Hayes, "Best Practices: Definition in Business, How to Develop, Examples," *Investopedia,* December 26, 2022, https://www.investopedia.com/terms/b/best_practices.asp.

56. M. Angell, "Adam Grant to Entrepreneurs: It's Time to Rethink 'Best Practices,'" *Inc.,* July 28, 2022, https://www.inc.com/melissa-angell/adam-grant-american-express-best-practice.html.

57. B. Schafer, "Amazon's CEO Says 2023 Will Be a Year of Efficiency. Does That Make the Stock a Buy?" *The Motley Fool,* April 21, 2023, https://www.fool.com/investing/2023/04/21/amazons-ceo-says-2023-will-be-a-year-of-efficiency/.

58. D. Shvartsman, "Apple Inc.: Our Modern-Day Symbol of Knowledge, Power, and Wealth," *Investing.com,* May 7, 2023, https://www.investing.com/academy/statistics/apple-facts/.

59. F. Richter, "How Happy and Loyal Are U.S. Smartphone Users?" *Statista,* June 28, 2022, https://www.statista.com/chart/27694/satisfaction-and-brand-loyalty-among-us-smartphone-users/.

60. J. Antony, V. Swarnakar, E. Cudney, and M. Pepper, "A Meta-Analytic Investigation of Lean Practices and Their Impact on Organisational Performance," *Total Quality Management & Business Excellence,* Vol. 33 (2022), pp. 1799–1825. Also see E.C. Ong and C.L. Tan, "Soft TQM, Agility, and Knowledge Management Deliver Organizational Performance: A Study of Malaysian Manufacturing Organizations in the Electrical and Electronics Sector," *Global Business and Organizational Excellence,* Vol. 41 (2022), pp. 28–47.

61. T. Fatima and S. Elbanna, "Corporate Social Responsibility (CSR) Implementation: A Review and a Research Agenda towards an Integrative Framework," *Journal of Business Ethics,* Vol. 183 (2023), pp. 105–121.

62. "Phoenix Sintered Metals, LLC, Recognized for Excellent Safety Practices," *Occupational Safety and Health Administration,* https://www.osha.gov/successstories/psmllc (accessed May 17, 2023).

63. J.G. Meijerink, S.E. Beijer, and A.C. Bos-Nehles, "A Meta-Analysis of Mediating Mechanisms between Employee Reports of Human Resource Management and Employee Performance: Different Pathways for Descriptive and Evaluative Reports?" *The International Journal of Human Resource Management,* Vol. 32 (2021), pp. 394–442. Also see J.K. Harter, F.L. Schmidt, S. Agrawal, S.K. Plowman, and A.T. Blue, "Increased Business Value for Positive Job Attitudes during Economic Recessions: A Meta-Analysis and SEM Analysis," *Human Performance,* Vol. 33 (2020), pp. 307–330.

64. E.E.T. Bolt, J. Winterton, and K. Cafferkey, "A Century of Labour Turnover Research: A Systematic Literature Review," *International Journal of Management Reviews,* Vol. 24 (2022), pp. 555–576. Also see J. Park and H.K. Min, "Turnover Intention in the Hospitality Industry: A Meta-Analysis," *International Journal of Hospitality Management,* Vol. 90 (2020), p. 102599.

65. C.P. Maertz Jr, M.G. Keith, S. Raghuram, C.M. Porter, and G.L. Dalton, "Advancing Theory and Practice on Managing Dysfunctional Turnover: Developing an Improved Measure of Turnover Reasons," *Group & Organization Management,* Vol. 48, No. 5 (2022), pp. 1387–1429, https://doi.org/10.1177/10596011211065880.

66. P.W. Hom, T.W. Lee, J.D. Shaw, and J.P. Hausknecht, "One Hundred Years of Employee Turnover Theory and Research," *Journal of Applied Psychology,* March 2017, pp. 530–545.

67. "Exit Interview: How to Conduct Exit Interviews," *MasterClass,* November 3, 2022, https://www.masterclass.com/articles/exit-interview.

68. J. Hall, "Why Businesses Should Invest in Employee Learning Opportunities," *Forbes,* February 26, 2023, https://www.forbes.com/sites/johnhall/2023/02/26/why-businesses-should-invest-in-employee-learning-opportunities/?sh=1c0078d61548.

69. "CarMax," *Fortune,* https://fortune.com/company/carmax/best-companies/ (accessed May 17, 2023). Also see "There's a Lot to Love about CarMax," *CarMax,* https://www.carmax.com/about-carmax (accessed May 17, 2023).

70. Sample strategy maps for different industries can be found in T. Jackson, "A Complete Strategy Map Template (Including Examples)," *ClearPoint Strategy,* April 28, 2023, https://www.clearpointstrategy.com/blog/complete-strategy-map-template-examples.

71. I. Adeinat, "Mediating Effects between Perspectives in Strategy Maps," *Administrative Sciences,* February 2019, https://doi.org/10.3390/admsci9010014. Also see R. Armstrong, "Revisiting Strategy Mapping for Performance Management: A Realist Synthesis," *International Journal of Productivity and Performance Management,* April 2019, pp. 721–752.

72. An example of creating scorecards for projects is illustrated in M. Scheiblich, M. Maftei, V. Just, and M. Studeny, "Developing a Project Scorecard to Measure the Performance of Project Management in Relation to EFQM Excellence Model," *Total Quality Management,* November 2017, pp. 966–980.

73. "Converting Disconnects into Loyalty Opportunities: PwC Customer Loyalty Executive Survey 2023," *PwC,* https://www.pwc.com/us/en/services/consulting/business-transformation/library/building-customer-loyalty-guide.html (accessed May 17, 2023).

74. W.E. Deming, *Out of the Crisis* (Cambridge, MA: MIT Press, 1986), p. 5.

75. R.N. Lussier, *Management: Concepts, Applications, Skill Development* (Cincinnati, OH: South-Western College Publishing, 1997), p. 260.

76. A. Goodwin, "Genesis, Hyundai Dominate J.D. Power 2022 Tech Experience Study," *CNET,* August 25, 2022, https://www.cnet.com/roadshow/news/jd-power-2022-tech-experience-study-genesis-hyundai-kia/.

77. A. Honeyman, "How Did Hyundai Do It with Genesis?—Quality, the Only Game in Town," *Torque News,* June 28, 2017, https://www.torquenews.com/3793/hyundai-genesis-quality-game-town.

78. "Our Core Values" *Hyundai USA,* https://www.hyundaiusa.com/us/en/careers/core-values (accessed May 18, 2023).

79. "Awards and Accolades," *Genesis,* https://www.genesis.com/us/en/awards.html (accessed May 18, 2023).

80. J. Garcia-Bernal and M. Ramirez-Aleson, "Why and How TQM Leads to Performance Improvements," *Quality Management Journal,* November 2017, pp. 23–37.

81. A. Ganz, "How Kia Went from Worst to First in Reliability," *Capital One Auto Navigator,* March 25, 2022, https://www.capitalone.com/cars/learn/finding-the-right-car/how-kia-went-from-worst-to-first-in-reliability/1383.

82. I.W. Rusdiana and D. Soediantono, "Kaizen and Implementation Suggestion in the Defense Industry: A Literature Review," *Journal of Industrial Engineering & Management Research,* Vol. 3 (2022), pp. 35–52.

83. "What Kind of Training Do Publix Employees Receive?" *JobzMall,* https://www.jobzmall.com/publix-super-markets-1/faqs/what-kind-of-training-do-publix-employees-receive (accessed May 18, 2023). Also see A.L. "Job Spotlight: Education and Training Development," *The Publix Checkout,* August 5, 2019, https://blog.publix.com/publix/publix-job-spotlight-education-and-training-development/.

84. "Research: 80% of Customers Said They Have Switched Brands because of Poor Customer Experience, and Poor Customer Service Experiences Drove the Most People to Switch," *Qualtrics,* December 15, 2021, https://www.qualtrics.com/blog/qualtrics-servicenow-customer-service-research/.

85. N. Meyersohn, "Wait, Trader Joe Was a Real Guy?" *CNN,* May 7, 2022, https://www.cnn.com/2022/05/07/business/trader-joes-history-joe-coulombe/index.html.

86. R. Redman "Customer Satisfaction Stays Strong at Grocery Stores," *Winsight Grocery Business,* February 24, 2023, https://www.winsightgrocerybusiness.com/retailers/customer-satisfaction-stays-strong-grocery-stores.

87. K. Wood, "11 'Secret' Trader Joe's Tips Straight from Store Employees," *Tinybeans,* April 6, 2023, https://tinybeans.com/trader-joes-secrets-from-an-employee/.

88. K. Wood, "11 'Secret' Trader Joe's Tips Straight from Store Employees," *Tinybeans,* April 6, 2023, https://tinybeans.com/trader-joes-secrets-from-an-employee/.

89. B. Morgan, "The Five Lessons from Trader Joe's Unbeatable Customer Experience," *Forbes,* October 24, 2019, https://www.forbes.com/sites/blakemorgan/2019/10/24/the-5-lessons-from-trader-joes-unbeatable-customer-experience/?sh=54c50bca4776.

90. M.-J. Gambal, A. Asatiani, and J. Kotlarsky, "Strategic Innovation through Outsourcing—A Theoretical Review," *The Journal of Strategic Information Systems,* Vol. 31 (2022), 101718. Also see J. Mageto, "Current and Future Trends of Information Technology and Sustainability in Logistics Outsourcing," *Sustainability,* Vol. 14 (2022), p. 7641.

91. E. Boskamp, "40+ Vital Outsourcing Statistics [2023]: How Many Jobs Lost to Outsourcing?" *ZIPPIA,* February 15, 2023, https://www.zippia.com/advice/outsourcing-statistics/.

92. L. Gualtieri, I. Palomba, F.A. Merati, E. Rauch, and R. Vidoni, "Design of Human-Centered Collaborative Assembly Workstations for the Improvement of Operators' Physical Ergonomics and Production Efficiency: A Case Study," *Sustainability,* Vol. 12 (2020), 3606. Also see J.V. Kovach and D. Ingle, "Using Lean Six Sigma to Reduce Patient Cycle Time in a Nonprofit Community Clinic," *Quality Management in Healthcare,* Vol. 28 (2019), pp. 169–175.

93. M. Heric and P. Doddapaneni, "Intelligent Automation: Getting More Bang from the Bots," *CFO,* May 7, 2020, https://www.cfo.com/applications/2020/05/intelligent-automation-getting-more-bang-from-the-bots/.

94. M. Sagnak and Y. Kazancoglu, "Fuzzy Analytic Hierarchy Process Integrated Statistical Process Control: An Application of Demerit Chart at Furniture Manufacturing Company," *Journal of Multi-Criteria Decision Analysis*, May 2020, pp. 96–103.

95. J. Arthur, "Statistical Process Control for Health Care," *Quality Digest,* https://www.qualitydigest.com/june08/articles/03_article.shtml (accessed May 18, 2023).

96. "Why Is It Called 'Six Sigma'?" *Six Sigma Daily,* January 4, 2022, https://www.sixsigmadaily.com/why-is-it-called-six-sigma/.

97. R. Yanamandra and H.M. Alzoubi, "Empirical Investigation of Mediating Role of Six Sigma Approach in Rationalizing the COQ in Service Organizations," *Operations and Supply Chain Management: An International Journal,* Vol. 15 (2022), pp. 122–135. Also see H.M. Alzoubi, M. In'airat, and G. Ahmed, "Investigating the Impact of Total Quality Management Practices and Six Sigma Processes to Enhance the Quality and Reduce the Cost of Quality: The Case of Dubai," *International Journal of Business Excellence,* Vol. 27 (2022), pp. 94–109.

98. J. Antony, O. McDermott, D. Powell, and M. Sony, "The Evolution and Future of Lean Six Sigma 4.0," *The TQM Journal,* Vol. 35 (2023), pp. 1030–1047.

99. "Lean Six Sigma Solves a Commercial Bank's Growth Problem," *Bain & Company,* https://www.bain.com/client-results/lean-six-sigma-solves-a-commercial-banks-growth-problem/ (accessed May 18, 2023). Also see "Benefits of Six Sigma in Finance & Accounting," *Purdue University,* June 25, 2021, https://www.purdue.edu/leansixsigmaonline/blog/benefits-of-six-sigma-in-finance-accounting/.

100. J. Antony, O. McDermott, D. Powell, and M. Sony, "The Evolution and Future of Lean Six Sigma 4.0," *The TQM Journal,* Vol. 35 (2023), pp. 1030–1047. Also see S. Tissir, A. Cherrafi, A. Chiarini, S. Elfezazi, and S. Bag, "Lean Six Sigma and Industry 4.0 Combination: Scoping Review and Perspectives," *Total Quality Management & Business Excellence,* Vol. 34 (2023), pp. 261–290.

101. S.N. Rinalducci, "9 Smart Manufacturing Examples of Industry 4.0," *Sustainability Success,* March, 28, 2023, https://sustainability-success.com/smart-manufacturing-examples-of-industry-4-0/. Also see D. Lawson, "How Advanced Industry 4.0 Solutions Are Proliferating Smart Factories," *Forbes,* April 20, 2023, https://www.forbes.com/sites/forbestechcouncil/2023/04/20/how-advanced-industry-40-solutions-are-proliferating-smart-factories/?sh=1a609d787b4b.

102. "Digital Transformation: Leading by Example," *Siemens,* https://www.siemens.com/global/en/company/stories/industry/electronics-digitalenterprise-futuretechnologies.html (accessed May 18, 2023). Also see D. Greenfield, "How Siemens' Amberg Factory Uses Red Hat OpenShift," *Automation World,* December 9, 2022, https://www.automationworld.com/analytics/article/22591938/how-siemens-amberg-factory-uses-red-hat-openshift.

103. "What Is the ISO 9000 Series of Standards," *ASQ,* https://asq.org/quality-resources/iso-9000 (accessed May 18, 2023).

104. B. Kumar, "What's the Differences between ISO 9000 & ISO 9001?" *Quora,* May 25, 2015, https://www.quora.com/What%E2%80%99s-the-difference-between-ISO-9000-9001.

105. "Members," *ISO,* https://www.iso.org/members.html (accessed May 18, 2023).

106. "What Is ISO 14001:2015—Environmental Management Systems?" *ASQ,* https://asq.org/quality-resources/iso-14001 (accessed May 18, 2023).

107. J. Antony, V. Swarnakar, E. Cudney, and M. Pepper, "A Meta-Analytic Investigation of Lean Practices and Their Impact on Organisational Performance," *Total Quality Management & Business Excellence,* Vol. 33 (2022), pp. 1799–1825; E.C. Ong and C.L. Tan, "Soft TQM, Agility, and Knowledge Management Deliver Organizational Performance: A Study of Malaysian Manufacturing Organizations in the Electrical and Electronics Sector," *Global Business and Organizational Excellence,* Vol. 41 (2022), pp. 28–47.

108. L.L. Bernardino, F. Teixeira, A.R. de Jesus, A. Barbosa, M. Lordelo, and H.A. Lepikson, "After 20 Years, What Has Remained of TQM?" *International Journal of Productivity and Performance,* March 2016, pp. 378–400. Also see R. Merriman, "A Review of Current Implementations of Statistical Process Control in Large Organizations," *Journal of Management and Engineering Integration*, January 2018, pp. 46–54.

109. N. Mittal, I. Saif, and B. Ammanath, "State of AI in the Enterprise 2022," 5th edition, *Deloitte,* https://www2.deloitte.com/us/en/pages/consulting/articles/state-of-ai-2022.html (accessed May 19, 2023).

110. A. Rao and B. Greenstein, "PwC 2022 AI Business Survey," *PwC,* https://www.pwc.com/us/en/tech-effect/ai-analytics/ai-business-survey.html (accessed May 19, 2023).

111. A. Rao, "PwC's Global Artificial Intelligence Study: Sizing the Prize," *PwC,* https://www.pwc.com/gx/en/issues/data-and-analytics/publications/artificial-intelligence-study.html#:~:text=AI%20could%20contribute%20up%20to (accessed May 19, 2023).

112. I. Anwar, "Five Reasons AI Makes Sense for the Rail Industry," *LinkedIn,* March 7, 2023, https://www.linkedin.com/pulse/five-reasons-ai-makes-sense-rail-industry-imran-anwar. Also see B. Mario, V. Mezhuyev, and M. Tschandl, "Predictive Maintenance for Railway Domain: A Systematic Literature Review," *IEEE Engineering Management Review*, 2023, pp. 1–18.

113. "System Uses AI and Industrial IoT to Usher in New Era of Predictive Maintenance in Rail," *Cordis Europa,* https://cordis.europa.eu/article/id/418452-system-uses-ai-and-industrial-iot-to-usher-in-new-era-of-predictive-maintenance-in-rail (accessed May 19, 2023).

114. "LNER Leads the Way in Railway Innovation and Investment," *LNER,* July 19, 2021, https://www.lner.co.uk/news/lner-leads-the-way-in-railway-innovation-and-investment/.

115. J. McKendrick, "Artificial Intelligence: Not a Panacea for Supply Chain Issues, but Extremely Helpful," *Forbes,* July 14, 2022, https://www.forbes.com/sites/joemckendrick/2022/07/14/artificial-intelligence-not-a-panacea-for-supply-chain-issues-but-extremely-helpful/?sh=7fe37965821f.

116. "Lower Last Mile Costs by Optimizing the Entire Supply Chain," *Lineage Logistics,* April 24, 2023, https://lineagelogistics.com/news-stories/lower-last-mile-costs-optimizing-entire-supply-chain. Also see "Automation Is Using Software to Transform the Cold Chain," *Lineage Logistics,* March 24, 2022, https://www.lineagelogistics.com/news-stories/automation-using-software-transform-cold-chain.

117. C. Berger, "Bosses Giving up the Return-to-Office Fight Have Found Another Way to Win: Tracking Their Remote Workers' Every Move," *Fortune,* August 18, 2022, https://fortune.com/2022/08/18/bosses-monitoring-remote-workers-digital-productivity/. Also see B. Lufkin, "The Companies Doubling down on Remote Work," *BBC,* July 24, 2022, https://www.bbc.com/worklife/article/20220722-the-companies-doubling-down-on-remote-work.

118. M. Freedman, "The Laws and Ethics of Workplace Privacy and Employee Monitoring," *Business News Daily,* March 29, 2023, https://www.businessnewsdaily.com/6685-employee-monitoring-privacy.html.

119. "ELD—Electronic Logging Devices," *United States Department of Transportation,* https://eld.fmcsa.dot.gov/ (accessed May 19, 2023).

120. J. Kantor, A. Sundaram, A. Aufrichtig, and R. Taylor, "The Rise of the Worker Productivity Score," *The New York Times,* August 15, 2022, https://www.nytimes.com/interactive/2022/08/14/business/worker-productivity-tracking.html?te=1&nl=the-morning&emc=edit_nn_20220815.

121. G.C. Tong, "Employee Surveillance Is on the Rise—and That Could Backfire on Employers," *CNBC,* April 26, 2023, https://www.cnbc.com/2023/04/24/employee-surveillance-is-on-the-rise-that-could-backfire-on-employers.html. Also see "ExpressVPN Survey Shows Widespread Surveillance on Remote Workers," *ExpressVPN,* May 20, 2021, https://www.expressvpn.com/blog/expressvpn-survey-surveillance-on-the-remote-workforce/.

122. M. Freedman, "The Laws and Ethics of Workplace Privacy and Employee Monitoring," *Business News Daily,* March 29, 2023, https://www.businessnewsdaily.com/6685-employee-monitoring-privacy.html.

123. "Survey: Remote Workers Are Working 1/3 of the Time," *ExpressVPN,* March 20, 2023, https://www.expressvpn.com/blog/how-much-do-remote-workers-work/.

124. D.M. Ravid, J.C. White, D.L. Tomczak, A.F. Miles, and T.S. Behrend, "A Meta-Analysis of the Effects of Electronic Performance Monitoring on Work Outcomes," *Personnel Psychology,* Vol. 76 (2023), pp. 5–40.

125. R.N. Murty and S. Karanth, "Monitoring Individual Employees Isn't the Way to Boost Productivity," *Harvard Business Review,* October 27, 2022, https://hbr.org/2022/10/monitoring-individual-employees-isnt-the-way-to-boost-productivity.

126. C.E. Thiel, J. Bonner, J.T. Bush, D.T. Welsh, and N. Garud, "Stripped of Agency: The Paradoxical Effect of Employee Monitoring on Deviance," Journal of Management, Vol. 49 (2023), pp. 709–740. Also see J. Kantor, A. Sundaram, A. Aufrichtig, and R. Taylor, "The Rise of the Worker Productivity Score," *The New York Times,* August 15, 2022, https://www.nytimes.com/interactive/2022/08/14/business/worker-productivity-tracking.html?te=1&nl=the-morning&emc=edit_nn_20220815; R.N. Murty and S. Karanth, "Monitoring Individual Employees Isn't the Way to Boost Productivity," *Harvard Business Review,* October 27, 2022, https://hbr.org/2022/10/monitoring-individual-employees-isnt-the-way-to-boost-productivity; T. Kalischko and R. Riedl, "Electronic Performance Monitoring in the Digital Workplace: Conceptualization, Review of Effects and Moderators, and Future Research Opportunities," *Frontiers in Psychology,* Vol. 12 (2021), 633031.

127. R.N. Murty and S. Karanth, "Monitoring Individual Employees Isn't the Way to Boost Productivity," *Harvard Business Review,* October 27, 2022, https://hbr.org/2022/10/monitoring-individual-employees-isnt-the-way-to-boost-productivity. Also see T. Kalischko and R. Riedl, "Electronic Performance Monitoring in the Digital Workplace: Conceptualization, Review of Effects and Moderators, and Future Research Opportunities," *Frontiers in Psychology,* Vol. 12 (2021), 633031.

128. P. Neale, "Career Management: For You and Your Leadership," *Forbes,* August 13, 2021, https://www.forbes.com/sites/forbescoachescouncil/2021/08/13/career-management-for-you-and-your-leadership/?sh=351ebffa43f3.

129. C. Duhigg, *The Power of Habit: Why We Do What We Do in Life and Business* (Random House, 2012).

130. A.B. Bakker, K. Breevaart, Y.S. Scharp, and J.D. de Vries, "Daily Self-Leadership and Playful Work Design: Proactive Approaches of Work in Times of Crisis," *The Journal of Applied Behavioral Science,* Vol. 59 (2023), pp. 314–336; K. Knotts, J.D. Houghton, C.L. Pearce, H. Chen, G.L. Stewart, and C.C. Manz, "Leading from the Inside Out: A Meta-Analysis of How, When, and Why Self-Leadership Affects Individual Outcomes," *European Journal of Work and Organizational Psychology,* Vol. 31 (2022), pp. 273–291.

131. L. Llovio, "2023 Top Entrepreneur: Brad Oleshansky, Founder, CEO and Developer of the Motor Enclave in Tampa," *Business Observer,* May 4, 2023, https://www.businessobserverfl.com/news/2023/may/04/2023-top-entrepreneur-brad-oleshansky-founder-ceo-and-developer-of-the-motor-enclave-in-tampa/.

132. B. Scott, "Diane Von Furstenberg on Self-Discovery, Acceptance, and the American Dream," *Inc.,* http://www.inc.com/bartie-scott/diane-von-furstenberg-and-seth-meyers- on-becoming-the-woman-you-want-to-be.html (accessed July 2016).

133. D.G. Riegel, "How to Encourage Your Team to Give You Honest Feedback," *Harvard Business Review,* October 28, 2022, https://hbr.org/2022/10/how-to-encourage-your-team-to-give-you-honest-feedback.

134. D. Kragt, "How Busy People Can Develop Leadership Skills," *Harvard Business Review,* December 7, 2022, https://hbr.org/2022/12/how-busy-people-can-develop-leadership-skills.

135. V. Lipman, "The Hardest Thing for New Managers," *Forbes,* http://www.forbes.com/sites/victorlipman/2016/06/01/the-hardest-thing-for-new-managers/#2d3a7bca218f (accessed July 2016).

136. C. Simpson, "Adaptability: The Secret Sauce of Leadership," *Forbes,* March 13, 2023, https://www.forbes.com/sites/forbesbooksauthors/2023/03/13/adaptability-the-secret-sauce-of-leadership/?sh=7dbaacec42da.

137. "Stop Taking Yourself so Seriously: 10 Quotes about Happiness, Laughter and Letting Go," *SUCCESS,* February 4, 2023, https://www.success.com/stop-taking-yourself-so-seriously-10-quotes-about-happiness-laughter-and-letting-go/.

138. D. Overbye, "Stephen Hawking Dies at 76; His Mind Roamed the Cosmos," *The New York Times,* March 14, 2018, https://www.nytimes.com/2018/03/14/obituaries/stephen-hawking-dead.html.

139. M.P. Seligman, *Flourish* (New York: Free Press, 2011).

Note: Page numbers in *italics* represent figures, tables, and illustrations.

Abbott, Bill, 224
Acosta, David, *514*
Adams, J. Stacey, 434
Aguinis, Herman, 39, 41
Ahmadi, K., *132*
Ain, Aron, 312
Akinci, C., *378*
Alamba, Sunday, *23*
Alexander, Dorothy, *606*
Allenden, Ian, *374*
Almeida, José, *273*
Ammanath, B., *241, 244*
Amodeo, David, 605
Anandan, Rajesh, DEI-10
Andersen, Erika, 379
Arnau, Xavier, *253*
Arnof-Fenn, Paige, 150
Aron, Adam, 352
Aufrichtig, A., *613*
Avolio, Bruce, 520

Bagley, E., *228*, 228
Ballmer, Steve, 174
Bankman-Fried, Sam, 179
Barra, Mary, 4, *4,* 14, 16, *16,* 17, 25, 508, *509*
Barth, P., *231*
Bass, Bernard, 520
Bean, R., *231*
Beckham, Robin, *172*
Bedford, Keith, *593*
Behrend, T.S., *613*
Belichick, Bill, DEI-14
Bell, C. H., Jr., *367*
Benioff, Marc, *518,* 519
Bennett, Karen, 327
Berra, Yogi, 179
Bezos, Jeffrey, 4-5, 209, 225
Bhagra, Ashita, *30*
Biden, Joe, 343
Bilous, Jon, *159*
Black, Maria, 510
Blakely, Sara, 512
Blanchard, Ken, 491, 492
Bloom, Nicholas, 354
Blount, S., *149*
Bohnet, Iris, DEI-24
Bohr, Niels, 350
Bonner, J.M., *613*
Bonno, K.D., *481*
Borges, R., *378*
Bossidy, Larry, 154, 190-191, 193
Bottorff, C., *206*
Boutros, Akram, Dr., 483
Bozeman, J., *73*
Branson, Richard, 224-225, 521
Bregman, Peter, 61
Breslin, D., *378*
Brin, Sergey, 200, 283
Brofsky, Keith, *494*
Brown, Dave L., *485*
Brown, Jenny, 342
Bruneau, Megan, 382
Bruxelle, Marc, *179*
Brynjolfsson, Erik, 242
Buac, K.M., *378*
Buakaew, Neramit, *278*
Buchanan, Ryan, DEI-26
Buck, Michele, 4
Buckingham, M., *403*
Buffett, Warren, 81, 505, *505*

Bukovski, Max, *555*
Burnett, Jennifer, 427
Burrow, Joe, 31
Burrows, Charlotte, 336
Bush, J.T., *613*

Cameron, K. S., *272*
Camp, Garret, 209
Campbell, Ann-Marie, 522
Campion, M.A., *512*
Cantarero, K., *132*
Carnegie, Andrew, 81
Carroll, Archie B., 79, *79*
Carr, Walter, 459
Carter, Christine, Dr., 381
Cash, Mel, 375
Catmull, Ed, 484
Catz, Safra, 4
Chambers, Kevin, 75
Charan, Ram, 154, 190-191, 193
Cheboi, Nelly, 270, 271
Cheong, M., *507*
Chilazi, Siri, DEI-24
Chirot, Daniel, 41
Choi, D., *275*
Choi, Y., *149*
Christensen, Clayton M., 39, 41, 151, 351
Christie, Agatha, 349
Chugh, Dolly, DEI-27, DEI-28
Chumney, F., *403*
Churchill, Robert, *285*
Clouse, Mark, 12
Cochrane, John, 257
Collins, Jim, 54
Collison, John, 206
Collison, Patrick, 206
Comer, Debra, 61
Cook, Rebecca, *16*
Cook, Tim, 11
Corcoran, Barbara, *200*
Cosier, R.A., *256, 257*
Covey, Stephen, 579
Cronin, Matthew, 39, 41
Csikszentmihalyi, Mihaly, 18
Cuban, Mark, *200*
Cummings, T. G., *367*

Daft, Richard, 543
D'Amelio, A., *378*
Dansereau, Fred, 525
Darlington, Molly, *611*
Davenport, T.H., *231*
Davidson, Kate, 29
Davis, Karen Niovitch, 269
Davis, Robert, 98
Dawkins, Ceejay, 169
DeAngelo, Joseph, 21
De Burca, Sean, *494*
Deci, Edward, 426, 429, 433
de Geus, Arie, 321
Degraff, J., *272*
Del Greco, Kimberly, 238
Deming, W. Edwards, 324, 601, *602,* 613
Denison, Mungo, 470
Devgan, Anirudh, 269
Diesel, Vin, 147
Dimon, Jamie, 440
Dixon, Monica, 437
Dorsey, Jack, 200
Dowling, B., *319*
Doyle, Alison, *30*
Doyle, Arthur Conan, 349
Drobot, Dean, *369*

Drucker, Peter, 9-10, 40-41, 118, 150, 156, 192, 468
DuBois, Cathy, Dr., 101
Duckett, Thasunda Brown, 4, 514, *514*
Duhigg, Charles, 617
Dumaguing, L.I., *378*
Dunning, David, Dr., 535
Dutton, Jane, DEI-24
Dyson, James, 413

Easterbrook, Stephen, 226
Einstein, Albert, 225
Ekman, Paul, 567
Emmert, Mark, DEI-18
Emmons, Robert, 457
Epstein, Jeffrey, 71
Eyal, N., *613*

Falbe, C.M., *507*
Farley, Jim, 281
Fayol, Henri, 44, 51
Feldman, Daniel, 271
Fiedler, F. E., *517,* 518
Flores, Brian, DEI-14
Fogg, B. J., Dr., 34
Foley, John, 50
Folkman, Zenger, 458
Follett, Mary Parker, 45, 46
Fong, Serena, DEI-5
Ford, J.D., *378*
Ford, L.W., *378*
Foulk, Trevor, 406
Frackowiak, T., *132*
Frankel, Matt, 239
Frankl, Viktor, 458
Frazier, David R., *95*
Frazier, Kenneth, 98
Freeman, Louis, *266*
Freight, Tallgrass, 504
French, W. L., *367*
Friedman, Milton, 62, 80, 90
Fry, W., *DEI-6*
Fults, Christopher, 424
Fuqua, D. R., *363*
Fürstenberg, Diane von, 81

Gallo, Carmine, 570
Gandhi, V., *319*
Gantt, Henry L., 624
Gardenswartz, Lee, *64*
Gardiner, Judith, 554
Garud, N., *613*
Gates, Bill, 238-239
Gavin, M., *503*
Gennette, Jeff, 588
Gentile, Mary, 77
Gentry, W.A., *512*
Gibb, J.R., *566*
Gilbert, Cecilia, DEI-11
Gilbreth, Frank, 43, 44
Gilbreth, Lillian, 43, 44
Ginzburg, Jean, 567
Gladwell, Malcolm, 263
Goldberg, Nick, 548
Goldschmidt, Paul, 480
Goldstein, D., *319*
Goleman, Daniel, 392
Goodrich, B.F., 368
Gore, W.L., 370
Goswami, R., *73*
Graen, George, 525
Grant, Adam, 447, 594

Name Index IND1

NAME INDEX

Gray, A.M., 501
Greenleaf, Robert, 527
Greenwood, Vincent, 553
Greiner, Lori, 200
Grinvalds, Kaspars, *589*
Gulden, Bjørn, 514
Gutierrez, Felipe, 249

Haas, M., *319*
Hackman, Richard J., *445*, 445
Hagen, Torstein, 187
Hall, Edward T., 127
Hamel, Gary, 147
Han, S., *507*
Hanks, Tom, 147
Harris, Helen, DEI-11
Hartnell, Chad A., *275, 446, 480*, 619
Hasan, Md Morshadul, *231*
Hawking, Stephen, 242, 619
Hawkins, B.W., *DEI-4*
Hayes, M., *403*
Headlee, Celeste, 344, 568
Heathfield, Susan, 552
Heaphy, Emily, DEI-24
Hennessy, John, 523
Herjavec, Robert, *200*
Hershcovis, M.S., *73*
Herzberg, Frederick, 426, 431, 432, 433, 444
Hilpert, P., *132*
Hinch, A.J., 23–24
Hindriks, Karoli, 109
Hirsch, A., *564*
Hobfoll, S.E., *409*
Hofstede, Geert, 128
Hojat, Mohammadreza, Dr., 567
House, Robert J., 128, *517*
Huang, Jin, Dr., *373*
Hubbard, Elbert, 619
Hubbart, J.A., *378*
Hughes, Harold, 277, *277*
Humpton, Barbara, 62
Hunsberger, Ariel, 497
Huse, E. G, *367*
Hutchins, Kathy, *200*
Hyatt, Amber, 320

Iger, Bob, 485, 581
Ignatius, Adi, 539
Imafidon, Anne-Marie, Dr., 441, 442, *442*
Ingram, P., *149*

Jackson, Brian A., *422*
Jacobsen, Eric, 152
Jacobson, K.J.L., *323*
Jaiswal, S., *503*
Jassy, Andy, 595
Javaid, Usman, 100
Jenkins, George, 453
Jensen, Anne Flemmert, Dr., 365
Jensen, Todd, *73*
Jobs, Steve, 199, 201
Johnson, Dwayne, 251, 505
Johnson, Whitney, 421
Johnson, William, 267
Jokic, Nikola, 491
Jones, Edward, 453

Kalanick, Travis, 209
Kalinichenko, Alexey, 206
Kalischko, T., *613*

Kantor, J., *613*
Kanter, Rosabeth Moss, 111
Kaplan, Robert S., 588, *589*, 599
Karam, E. P., *275*
Karasek, R.A., Jr., *409*
Karayaneva, Natalia, DEI-3
Karuza, J., *DEI-6*
Katz, Robert, 16
Katzenbach, Jon R., 468
Kell, G., *73*
Kelley, David, 374
Kennedy, John F., 121, 459
Kennedy, Kathleen, 11
Kennell, Krista, 505
Khokthong, Nopparat, *173*
Kidman, Nicole, 352
Kim, S.L., *507*
King, B., *517*
King, Mark, 160
Kinicki, Angelo J., 126, 151, *265, 275, 306,* 323, *363, 475,* 534, 542, *579,* 600, 602, 619, DEI-22
Kirch, Alexander, 587
Knotts, Perry, *584*
Knudstorp, Jørgen Vig, 365
Kohlberg, Lawrence, 76
Koo, Chung Mong, 604
Kopp, Rochelle, 128
Kotter, J.P., *503*
Kramer, Mark, Dr., 90, 96
Krause, Aaron, 211
Kreitner, R., *363, 475*
Kruger, Justin, Dr., 535
Krzyzewski, Mike, 459
Kumar Sharma, Dinesh, *30*
Kurpius, D. J., *363*

Laguarta, Ramon, 530
Lang, Gordon S., *101*
Lapidez, W.D., *378*
Lass, Imke, *402*
Latham, Gary P., *156, 157,* 441
Lauder, Estée, 226, 280
Lauren, Lauren Bush, 529, *529*
Lauren, Ralph, 226
Laurian, Lucie, 100
Lazarus, R.S., *409*
Lee, S., *507*
Leinwand, P., *149*
Lencioni, Patrick, 493
Lengel, Robert, 543
Lennihan, Mark, *4*
Leventhal, G., *DEI-6*
Levine, Zach, 239
Lewin, Kurt, 361, DEI-13
Lewis, Nea, DEI-16
Liao, H., *447*
Linwei, Lou, 112
Locke, A. Edwin, *156,* 441
Lofgren, Jenn, 219
Lombardi, Vince, 491
Lucas, Wonya, 224
Luhnow, Jeff, 23–24
Lund, Jacob, *390*
Lütke-Daldrup, Monika, 593
Lynch, Karen, 504
Lynch, S., *378*
Lyubykh, Z., *73*

MacDonald, C.J., 206
Machado, Manny, 485–486
Machiavelli, Niccolò, 509
Macpherson, A., *378*

Macron, Emmanuel, 133
Main, K., *206*
Maitlis, S., *378*
Malik, Z., *81*
Manfred, Robert, 24
Marklin, Luke, 459
Martel, Éric, 182
Maslow, Abraham, 46, 426, 427, 428
Mason, Jeanne, 273
Matthews, Gail, Dr., 421
Mauboussin, M.J., *503*
Mayo, Elton, 45, 46
Mazliah, Mandy, 169
McCarrick, Chris, 190
McCartney, S., *181*
McChrystal, Stanley, 5
McClelland, David, 426, 428
McCormack, Eamonn, *529*
McGrath, R.G., *503*
McGregor, Douglas, 46, 47
McIlhenny, Edmund, 182
McLean, M., *202*
McLuhan, Marshall, 111
Meadows, Dennis, 55
Meadows, Donella, 55
Melamed, Yulia, 555
Messi, Lionel, 491
Metayer, Sylvia, 527
Meyers, Aaron, 219
Michel, Aaron, 31
Mikells, Kathryn, 590
Mikulka, G., *DEI-6*
Miles, A.F., *613*
Mintzberg, Henry, 13–15, 36
Mitchell, Kimberly P., *509*
Mittal, N., *241, 244*
Mohammad, Shamim, 376
Montgomery, Scott, 41, 81
Morgeson, F.P., *512*
Morris, Jane Mosbacher, 358
Morris, M., *DEI-4*
Mors, M., *378*
Motarjemi, Yasmine, 437
Muhammad, R. S., *265, 306*
Mumford, T.V., *512*
Murray, Ken, *31*
Musk, Elon, 146, 223, 242, 544

Nadella, Satya, *10,* 158, 174–175, 265, 355, 528, *528*
Nadler, D. A., *363*
Nahm, Sarah, 270
Nanus, Burt, *149,* 523
Nassetta, Christopher, 64
Neff, Kristen, 381
Nguyen, T., *DEI-4*
Nielsen, J., *447*
Nohria, Nitin, 13–14
Noonan, Eóin, *521*
Norton, David P., 588, *589,* 599
Nyholm, Kasper, 567

Ochoa, L., *73*
Oláh, Judit, *231*
Oldham, Greg R., *445,* 445
O'Leary, Kevin, *200*
Oleshansky, Brad, 618
Osborn, A. F., 254
Osterwalder, Alexander, 210
Ostroff, C., *265, 306*
Otero, L.M., *266*
Ottley, Sonja Gittens, DEI-21
Ou, A. Y., *275*

NAME INDEX

Packer, B., *319*
Page, Larry, 200, 283
Palamarchuk, Sergiy, *179*
Pangilinan, C.A., *378*
Pardee, B., *202*
Parisi-Carew, Eunice, Dr., 492
Park, M., *319*
Patel, N., *613*
Peek, S., *149*
Pelen, François, 213
Pelosi, Nancy, *103*
Peredo, A.M., *202*
Perkins, Melanie, 521, *521*
Perry, Mike, 224
Peters, Tom, 40
Peterson, S.J., 323
Pfeffer, Jeffrey, 49, 54
Pichai, Sundar, 15, 512
Pilarski, Jan, 208
Plato, 255
Pollak, Julia, 354
Popov, Andrey, *240, 245, 411*
Popp, József, *231*
Porath, Christine, 406
Porter, Michael, 13-14, 55, 90, 185
Pouts, Patrice, 213
Powell, Colin, 501
Price, H., *319*
Prince, Sedona, DEI-18
Prussia, G.E., 323
Ptashnik, T., *447*

Quain, S., *149*
Quinn, R. E., *272*
Quintas, C.A., *378*

Radin, Lev, *518*
Rahim, M.A., *489*
Ravid, D.M., *613*
Raynor, Michael, 39, 41
Redzepi, René, 269
Reid, Grant, 372
Reif, L. Rafael, 71
Reilly, Ed, 14
Reyes, M.E., *378*
Richmond, Kristin, 105, *105*
Riedl, R., *613*
Riegel, Deborah Grayson, 618
Rinn, Thomas, 351
Ripley, Amanda, 569
Robbie, Margot, 147
Rodriguez, Carlos, 510
Roekdeethaweesab, Prachaya, *182*
Rogerson, Jennie, 549
Romero, Anthony, 12
Rometty, Ginni, 306, 357, 512
Roslansky, Ryan, 350
Rowling, J.K., 200
Ryan, Richard, 426, 429, 433

Saif, I., *241, 244*
Samuelson, Paul, 80
Sandberg, Sheryl, 65
Santos, George, 313
Sargut, G., *503*
Sato, Koji, 179
Schaninger, Bill, 271
Schein, Edgar, 285
Schnitzer, Raphael, 213

Schubert, Aba, DEI-7
Schwab, Charles, 180
Schwab, Klaus, 236
Schwartz, Barry, 7
Schwenk, R.C., *256, 257*
Scott, MacKenzie, 81
Seagal, Steven, 534
Segre, Alex, *45*
Seijts, G., *157*
Sekerka, Leslie, 61
Seligman, Martin, 456
Selye, Hans, 409
Senge, Peter, 53
Shah, Dharmesh, 278
Shan, J.V., *73*
Shaw, George Bernard, 401, 553
Shell, Jeff, 352
Shepherd, L., *319*
Sheeran, Ed, 67
Shewhart, Walter, 601
Shoats, P., *481*
Siegel, J., *DEI-4*
Sigalos, M., *73*
Simon, Herbert, 223
Simpson, Cicely, 619
Skinner, B. F., 448
Slocum, J., *157*
Smith, Adam, 220
Smith, Douglas K., 468
Smith, E., *202*
Smith, James, 339
Snyder, Kieran, DEI-18
Soeripto, Janti, 12
Soignet, Denise Breaux, 554, 568, 619, DEI-22, DEI-23
Sorokowska, A., *132*
Sorokowski, P., *132*
Soros, Lucy, 227
Spaulding, Charles Clinton, 44, 51
Spinoy, Bernadette, 283
Spreitzer, Gretchen, 406
Springmann, Marco, 6
Squeiri, Stephen, 438
Steib, Mike, 497
Stogdill, Ralph, 509
Stoller, Jonathan, 100
Stone, Biz, 198
Stone, Sharon, 534
Streufert, S., *517*
Stupple, Laura, 224
Su, R., *447*
Suleman, Fatima, *30*
Sullivan, Justin, *10*
Summerville, K.M., *512*
Summitt, Pat, *523*, 524
Sundaram, A., *613*
Sutton, Robert, 49
Sweet, Julie, 314
Swift, Taylor, 67
Sy, W.P., *378*
Syse, Henrik, 82
Syvak, Pavlo, *532*

Taylor, Frederick W., 43, *43*, 51, 601
Taylor, R., *613*
Tengberg, Carl, 249
Tepper, B.J., *73*
Terrazas, Aaron, 354
Thakor, A. V., *272*
Thiel, C.E., *613*

Thomas, Ed, 311
Thomas, K.W., *489*
Thomaz, Andrea, 361
Thorndike, Edward L., 448
Thunberg, Greta, 68
Tidmarsh, Chris, 208
Tinyakov, Sergey, 527
Tobey, Kirsten, 105, *105*
Tomczak, D.L., *613*
Tomé, Carol, 267
Tonidandel, S., *512*
Tormey, Kristin, 547
Torres, Gabriel, 100
Totty, M., *73*
Toyoda, Akio, 179
Trivedi, S., *613*
Truex Jr., Martin, *479*
Tulgan, Bruce, 138
Tuleja, Elizabeth, Dr., 554
Turner, N., *73*
Tushman, M. L., *363*
Tweney, D., *231*

Ubaldo, J.S., *378*
Unahalekhaka, Aukrit, 100

Vaara, E., *378*
van Baal, Mark, 357
Vardell, E., *DEI-4*
Verret, Grady, 568
Vilimek, Adam, *208*
Villeneuve, Daniel, *571*
Vopson, Melvin, 233

Walsh, Bryan, 242
Walsh, Patrick Parker, 75
Webb, Michael, 243
Weber, Max, 44
Wegman, Colleen, 40, 273
Weihenmayer, Erik, 402
Weiss, Emily, 12
Weitzman-Garcia, Michelle, 324
Welch, Jack, 185, 188, 305
Welch, Suzy, 263
Welsh, D.T., *613*
White, J.C., *613*
Whittle, A., *378*
Widyawati, Nicke, 12
Wilson, Rob, *210*
Winfrey, Oprah, 200
Witte, Martin, *237*
Wojcicki, Susan, DEI-27
Wong, Debby, *523*
Wong, T., *73*
Wright, C., *403*
Wright, Frank Lloyd, 6
Wright, Matthew Micah, 367

Yakowicz, Will, *70*
Youn, J.Y., *507*
Young, S.F., *512*
Yuan, Eric, 512
Yukl, G., *507*
Yun, S., *507*

Zinkevych, Dmytro, *407*
Zuckerberg, Mark, 65, 147, 479

Name Index   IND3

ORGANIZATION INDEX

Note: Page numbers in *italics* represent figures, tables, and illustrations.

ABB Ltd., 351
Abbott, 422
Accenture, 25, 305, 314, 350, 351
Acer, 187
ACORD, *506*
Acura, 119
Adelphia, 75, 417
Adidas, 514, 608
Adobe, 12, 69, 325, 458, 612
ADP Research Institute, 403
Aetna, 417
Airbus, 307, *373*, 612
Airbus, stretch goals and, 441
Air France-KLM, 155
Alameda Research, *73*
Alaska Airlines, *181*
Aldi, 115, 187
Allbirds, 67, 357
Allegiant Airlines, *181*
Allied Signal, 154, 190
Allstate, 12
Alphabet, 114, 331, 523
Amazon, 5, 25, 47, 52, 147, 173, 174, 184, 211, 234, 239, 240, *240*, 331, 352, 473, 595, 606, 608, DEI-15
 acquisition of Whole Foods by, 185
 brand recognition, 169
 competition for, 66
 corporate-level strategy of, 171
 decision making at, 225
 high-quality products, 54
 history of, 4, 209
 as multinational corporation, 114
 overseas operations, 117
 ranking for employment attractiveness, 27
 reliance on Taylor's scientific management principles, 43
 streaming wars, 186, *186*
 web services, 175
Ambow Education, 372-373
AMC, 352
American Airlines, *181*, 368
American Civil Liberties Union (ACLU), 12
American Express, 305, 424, 438
American Federation of Teachers, 67, 340
American Institute of Architects, 6
American Management Association, 14
AmerisourceBergen, 114
Anheuser-Busch, 115
Apple Inc., 17, 25, 184, 185, 239, *240*, 352, 370, 374, 473, 612
 big businesses, 98
 brand recognition, 169
 high-quality products, 595
 history of, 199, 291
 innovation by, 147
 leadership of, 11
 low labor costs, 117
 as multinational corporation, 114
 ranking for employment attractiveness, 27
 response to customer complaints, 209
 stock options in, 454
 streaming wars, 186
 stretch goals and, 441
 supply chain, 116
Aramis Group, 366-367

Arizona State University, 19, 616
Armis, *373*
Articulate, 227
Association to Advance Collegiate Schools of Business (AACSB), 100-101
AT&T, 111, 458, 527
Audi, 66

Bain Capital Double Impact, *202*
Bain & Company, 180
Bandwagon, 277, *277*
Bank of America, *202*, 608, DEI-15
Barrio Brewing Company, 65
Baruch College, 313
Baseload Capital, 119
Baxter International, 273
Bed Beth & Beyond, 592
Bellhops, 459
Bell Telephone Labs, 601
Ben & Jerry's, 428
Berkshire Hathaway, 505
 as multinational corporation, 114
Best Buy, *506*
B.F. Goodrich, 368
Bic, 187
Bloomberg, DEI-20
Bloomingdale, 358
BMW, 23, 66
Boeing, 295, 342, *506*
Bombardier, 182
Bombas, 357
Boring Company, 223
Bosch, 608
Boston Consulting Group (BCG), 181, 182, 430
Boston University, 17
BP, 357
Burberry, 55
Burger King, 119, 560
buy buy BABY, 170
ByteDance, 205

Cadence, 269
California Rail Authority, 250
Calm, 417
Calvary Health Care, 443
Campbell Soup Company, 12, 95, *95*
Canva, 521, *521*, 549
Capital One Financial, 305, 608
CareerBuilder, 311
CarMax, 376, 597
Caterpillar Inc., 118, 342, 608
CBS, 186
Chapman University, 570
Charles Schwab, 180
Cheesecake Factory, 454
Chevron, 118, 119, 357
Chick-fil-A, 209-210
China Investment Corporation (CIC), 117
China National Petroleum, 114
China State Construction Engineering, 114
Cinemark, 352
Cisco, 93, 305, *506*, 612, DEI-15, DEI-20
Citigroup, 313, 513
Citrix, 494
Claremont Graduate University, 18
Clearasil, 372
CNN, 112, 226, 271

Coca-Cola Company, 25, 45, *112*, 117, *151*, 234
 brand recognition, 169
 mission, vision and values, 150-151
 strategies of, 153
CollegeGrad.com, 54
Columbia University
 Columbia College at New York, 100
Confédération générale du travail (CGT), 133
Container Store, 456
Core Hydration, 184
Costco, 117
Cotopaxi, *202*
Cox, 186
Crowdstrike, 445
CVS Health, *74*, 114, 504

DataRobot, 226
David Weekley Homes, 305, 432
Dell, DEI-111
Deloitte, 52, 118, 169, 240, 325, 513, 610, 612
Delta Airlines, 180, *181*
Diligent Robotics, 361-362
Dior, 55
Discovery, 186
Disruption Advisors, 421
Dizolve Group Corporation, 370
Dollar Tree, 187
Dominican University, 421
DoorDash, 65
Dropbox, 65, 354, 412, 472
Duke University, 459, 618
Dunkin', 171
Duolingo, 131
DuPont, 118, 119, 609

Economic Policy Institute, 122
Edelman, 530
Edward Jones, 453
Electronic Arts (EA), 588
Enron, 75, 82
Enterprise Rent-A-Car, 54
Equal Employment Opportunity Commission (EEOC), 336
Equinix, 554
Ernst & Young, 77
Estée Lauder, 226, 280
ExpressVPN, 612
ExxonMobil, 76, 78, 114, 134, 292, 357-358, 590
EZRA, 548

Facebook, 52, 67, 90, 147, 233, 248, 486, 557, *557*, 558, 562
 board of directors at, 65
 media richness of, 544
Fakespot, 234
Federal Aviation Agency (FAA), 68
Federal Bureau of Investigation (FBI), 238
Federal Reserve, 69
Federal Trade Commission, 234
Fédération Internationale de Football Association (FIFA), 555
FedEx, 25, 443, 454
FEED, 529, *529*
Fidelity Investments, 330
Finless Foods, 5
FleetUp, 586

IND4 Organization Index

Flex Ltd. (Flex), 93
Flytrex, 370
Ford Motor Co., 66, 281, 459, 513
   matrix structure of, 293
Forrester Research, 20
FromSoftware, *373*
Frontier Airlines, *181*
FTX, *73*, 226
Fusion Technologies, 596
Future Meat Technologies, 5, 6

Gallup, 72, 192, 323, 354, 395, 403, 443, 456, 459, 461
Gartner, 19, 353
General Electric (GE), 185, 188, 305, 325, 368
   forced ranking, 328
General Mills, 417
General Motors (GM), *4*, 14, *16*, 18, 44, 49, 508, *509*
   big businesses, 98
   decentralized authority and, 289
   leadership of, 4, 10, 16–17
   stockholders of, 65
Georgia Department of Corrections, 431
Glassdoor, 57, 230, 354, 431
   recruitment on, 311
Global Entrepreneurship Monitor, 202, 207
Glossier, 12
GoFundMe, 215
Goldman Sachs, 117, 313, 318, 440, 612
   ranking for employment attractiveness, 27
Google, 3, 15, 52, 71, 131, 172, *172*, 173, 184, 200, 233, 239, *240*, 283, 321, 322, 359, 407, 472, 512, 562, 582
   brand recognition, 169
   failed product of, 51
   functional management at, 12
   informational roles at, 17
   inspirational motivation, 523
   ranking for employment attractiveness, 27
   stretch goals and, 441
Grammarly, 205
Great Lakes Brewing Company, 160
Green Bridge Growers, 208
GroupMe, 546
Gusto, *268*

Hallmark, 223, 224
Hammer and Nails, 219
Harbor Freight, 187
Harley-Davidson, 289, 342
Harpo Productions, 200
Harvard Business School, 90, 111, 251, 351
Harvard University, 17, 55, 151, 336–337
HBO, 186, *186*
Hershey, 4
Hertz, 119
Hewlett-Packard (HP), 291, 513
Hilton Hotels, 65, 119, 305, 393
H&M, 295
HOKA, 182, *373*
Holdfast Collective, *373*
Home Depot, 211, 267, 522
   cost-leadership strategy of, 187
Honda Motor Company, 119, 171
Honeywell International, Inc., 154, 190, 368
HSBC Financial, 330
Hubspot, 239, 278, 279
Hulu, streaming wars, 186, *186*

HumanGood, 257
Hyatt, 320
Hydrema, 478
Hyundai Motor Co., 604

IBM, 25, 28, 231, 306, 353, *512*
   big businesses, 98
   career planning at, 414
   employee benefits at, 227
   leadership of, 357
IDEO, 254, 374
IKEA, 240, 359, 428
   cost-leadership strategy of, 187
Indeed, 8, 14, 16, 41, 45, 74, 78, 80, 127, 132, 145, 205, 222, 247, 293, 305, 351, 353, 390, 442, 483, 522, 558, 570
   recruitment on, 311
Infosys, 115
In-N-Out Burger, 431
Instacart, 205
Instagram, 35, 52, 169, 248, 505, 557, *557*
Intel, 353, 607, 608
Internal Revenue Service (IRS), 212
International Institute for Management Development (IMD), 110
International Monetary Fund (IMF), 120–121, *122*
International Organization for Standardization (ISO), 609
International Red Cross, 114
Intuit, 454
ITT, 368

JAB Holdings, 184
Japan Intercultural Consulting, 128
J.D. Power, 594, 605
Jefferson Medical College, 567
JetBlue, 180
JetBlue Airlines, *181*
Jobbatical, 109
Johnson & Johnson, 115
J.P. Morgan Chase & Co., 440, 513, 612
   psychometric testing by, 513
   ranking for employment attractiveness, 27

Kawasaki, 295
Ken Blanchard Companies, 492
Kent State University College of Business, 101
Kentucky Fried Chicken, 119
Keurig Dr Pepper, 184, 226, *600*
Kia Motors, 66, 66, 604, 605, *605*
Kickstarter, 68, 559
Kroger, 47, 55, 189, 190, *190*, 191, 211
Kronos, 312

Land O'Lakes, 428
LEGO, 365, 559, *559*, 593, *593*
Lemonade, *202*
Levi Strauss & Co., 145
Lexus, 187
LG, 118, 119
Lighthouse Family Retreat, *202*
Lineage Logistics, 611
LinkedIn, 30, 52, 53, 57, 169, 350, 434, 456, *557*
   media richness of, 544
   recruitment on, 558
Little League, 67
LiveNation, 66
LJS Content, 224

London North Eastern Railway, 611
Louis Vuitton, 55
Lucasfilm, 11
Lucid Motors, 178
Lucid Software, 457
Luckin Coffee, 530
Lululemon, 152

Maastricht University, the Netherlands, 5
Macy's, 588
Marriott International, 115, 119, *119*
Mars UK, 372, 455
Massachusetts Institute of Technology (MIT), 53, 71, 100
Mastercard, 55, 55
Mattel, 147
Mavens & Moguls, 150
McDonald's, 45, *45*, 71, 114, 119, 177, 180, 209, 210, 226, 274, 289, 370, 373, *373*, 607, 611
McIlhenny Company, 182
McKesson, 114
McKinsey & Company, *81*, 180, 220, 234, 242, 271, 354, 373, 458, 468, 471, 611
Meijer, 211
Memrise, 131
Mercedes-Benz, 270, 584, *584*
Merck & Co., 98
Meta, 65, 147, 331, 471, 479, 486
MetroHealth, 483
Microsoft, *10*, 53, *53*, 71, 115, 152, *157*, 158, *172–173*, 172–175, 184, 238, 239, 242, 265, 296, 331, 353, 355, *373*, 422, 454, 471, *528*, *528*, 553, *562*, 582, *589*, 607, 608, 622, 623
   brand recognition, 169
Morgan Stanley, 440
Mosa Meat, 5
Mosbacher Morris, 358
Moscow Metro, 555
Mothers Against Drunk Driving, 68
Motorola, 607, 608

Namely, 456
NASA, 459
National Association of Colleges and Employers (NACE), 540
National Basketball Association (NBA), 48
National Center for Charitable Statistics (NCCS), 12
National Education Association, 67
National Labor Relations Board (NLRB), 340
National Organization for Women, 68
National Rifle Association, 68
Nationwide, 412
NBC, 186
Nestlé, 115, *351*, 375, 437, 546
Netflix, 88, 145, 184, 186, *186*, 230, 270, 456, 462
   ranking for employment attractiveness, 27
Networking Academy, 93
Neuralink, 223
Neutrogena, 170
Newspaper Guild, 67
New York Metropolitan Transportation Authority, 282
New York Stock Exchange, 65
Nike, 125, 270
   ranking for employment attractiveness, 27
Nio, 178

Noma, 73
Nordstrom, 403, 404, 430, *430*, 482
North Carolina Mutual Life Insurance Company, 44
Norton, 588, 599
Novartis, 49, 92
NOX US LLC, *73*
Nubank, *373*
NVIDIA, 305, 422

Occupational Safety and Health Administration (OSHA), *73*, 78, 532, 595
OECD, 125
Ohio State University, 393
On, *373*
Oneota Community Food Cooperative, *202*
OpenAI, *373*
Operator Collective, *506*
Oracle, 4, 184, 505

Paramount, 352
Patagonia, 357, 456
PathSource, 31
PayPal, 65
PayScale, 458
PCMag.com, 234
Peloton, 50, 581, *581*
People for the Ethical Treatment of Animals, 68
Peppers Pizzeria, 568
PepsiCo, 170, 530
Pertamina, 12
Pew Research Center, 405
Pfizer, 213
Phoenix Sintered Metals, 595, *595*
Pinterest, *557*
Pixar Animation Studios, 484
Planet Fitness, 209
PricewaterhouseCoopers (PwC), 102, 226, 229, 422, 530, 594, 610, 611
Procter & Gamble (P&G), 266, 309, 368, 513
  psychometric testing by, 513
Prolific, 455
Prudential, 368
Publix, 453, 605
Purina, 456

Ralph Lauren, 226
Ramp, *373*
Reckitt Benckiser (RB), 372
Recreational Equipment, Inc. (REI), 56
Red Box, 187
Red Bull Media House, 147
Red Cross, 12
Reddit, *557*
Regal, 352
Regeneron, 324
REI, 56
Reliance Jio, 90-91
Renown Regional Medical Center, 226
ReviewMeta, 234
Revolution Foods, 104, 105, *105*
Ricult, 100
Ritz-Carlton, 54, 187, 593, *593*, 594
Rivian, 178
Roblox, *373*
Rockefeller Foundation, 19
Rocket Companies, 305, 308
Rothco, 67
Russian Railways, 555

Salesforce, 26, 239, 296, 305, 350, 454, 473, *518*, 519
Salvation Army, 12
Samsung Electronics, 114
Saudi Aramco, 114
Save the Children, 12
Seagate, 230, 330
Securities and Exchange Commission (SEC), 75, 76, 78, 226
Service Employees International Union, 67, 340
7-Eleven, 119, 209
Shell, 114, 357
Shell Energy, 180
Shopify, 213, 412, 549
Siemens, 62, 608, *609*
Sinopec Group, 114
SKYMAGIC, *470*
Slack, 296, 412, 416, 472, 497, 546, 548, 549, 553
Snapchat, 557, *557*
Snowflake, 454
Society for Human Resource Management (SHRM), 135, 407, 558
Society of Industrial Engineers, 44
Sodexo, 527
SolarCity, 223
Sony, 171
Southern California Gas Company (SoCalGas), 315
Southwest Airlines, *181*, 265, 266, *266*, 586
SpaceX, 205, 223
Spectrum, 186
Spirit Airlines, *181*
Spotify, 184, 270, 612
  ranking for employment attractiveness, 27
Stanford University, 12, 523
Starbucks, 39, 61, 71, 147, 185, 473
State Grid, 114
Stemettes, 442, *442*
Stitch Fix, 370
St. Jude Children's Research Hospital, 26
Stripe Inc., 213
StubHub, 66
Summit Public Affairs, 619
SuperMeat, 5
Sweetgreen, 428
SweetRush, 393
Swissair, 252
Synchrony Financial, 325

Tabasco, 182, *182*
Taiwan Semiconductor Manufacturing Company, 112
Tallgrass Freight Company, 504
Target, 47, 66, 211, 358, DEI-23
  competition for, 66
Teamsters Union, 67, 340
TechLit Africa, 270
Teflon, 118
TELUS International, 455
Tesla, 44, 178, 223, 242, *370*, 608, 612
  ranking for employment attractiveness, 27
Texas Instruments, 368
Theranos, 530
3M, 608
  stretch goals and, 441
TIAA, 4, 514, *514*
Ticketmaster, 66, 67

Tiffany & Co., *373*
TikTok, 52, 71, 147, 205, 553, 557, *557*, 563
Timex, 187
Toyota Motor, 114, 115, 178, 179, *179*, 479
Trader Joe's, 605, 606, *606*
Trenitalia, 611
Trifigura Group, 114
Tumblr, *557*
20th Century Studios, 352
Twitch, 557, *557*
Twitter, 52, 57, 146, 169, 198, 200, 223, 248, 359, 519, 553, 557, *557*, 563
  media richness of, 544
Tyco, 75, 82
Tyson Foods, 274, 611, DEI-24

Uber, 209, 454
UC Berkeley, 105
UKG, 312
Uncommon Goods, 357
Unilever, 115, 126, 235
United Airlines, *181*
United Auto Workers, 67, 340
UnitedHealth Group, 47, 114, 282
United Nations (UN), 24, 25, 80, 88-89, 96, *97*, 98, 103, *124*, 134, 281
United Way, 67
Universal Studios, 352
University of Arkansas, DEI-24
University of California, 12
University of Georgia, 79
University of Guelph, Canada, *101*
University of Illinois Leadership Center, 573
University of Iowa, 100
University of Michigan, 17
  Marsal Family School of Education, 100
University of Oxford, 6
University of Pennsylvania, 342
University of Rochester, 429
University of Southern California (USC), 366
University of Tennessee, 523, *523*
Uno, 147
UPS, 47
Upside Foods, 5
UPS Store, 209
U.S. Air and Space Forces, 311, *478*
U.S. Army, 10, 255
U. S. Automobile Association (USAA), 447
U.S. Bureau of Labor Statistics, 144, 342
U.S. Congress, 332, 355
U.S. Department of Corrections, 431
U.S. Department of Health and Human Services, 158
U.S. Department of Justice, 75
U.S. Department of Labor (DOL), 76, 307, 334
U.S. Department of Transportation (DOT), 450
U.S. Marine Corps, 308-309, 501
U.S. Office of Disease Prevention and Health Promotion, 458
U.S. Small Business Administration, 198, 206
U.S. State Department, 135
U.S. Treasury, 590

Vanguard Group, 170
Verizon, 279
Viking Cruises, 187
Virgin Group, 163, 224–225, 521
Virgin Media O$_2$, 455
Volkswagen, 23, *73*, 178, 530
    as multinational corporation, 114

Walker & Dunlop, 154
Walmart, 66, 114, 211, 235, 289, 360, 611
    big businesses, 98
    cost-leadership strategy of, 187
    as multinational corporation, 187
    stockholders of, 65
Walt Disney Company, 55, 72, 119, 145, 184, *424*, 424, 458, 473, 484, 485, 581, *581*
    Disney+, 581
    Disney Institute, 424
    ranking for employment attractiveness, 27
    streaming wars, 186, *186*
Warby Parker, 67, 187, *187*

Warner Bros., 352
WarnerMedia, 186
Warner Music, 67
Waymo, *370*
Weber, 44, 45
WebEx, 471–472
WebFX, 241
Webtoon, *373*
Wegmans Food Markets, 40, 273, 305
Wells Fargo, 442, 530
Wendy's, 547
Western Electric, 46
Westinghouse Canada, 368
WhatsApp, 233
Whole Foods, 54, 56, 171, 185
W. L. Gore & Associates, 370
Woolite, 372
Workers United, *373*
World Bank, 120–121, *122*
WorldCom, 75, 82
World Economic Forum (WEF), 19, 375
World Health Organization (WHO), 114

World Trade Organization (WTO), 68, 120–121, *122*

X, formerly known as Twitter, *557*
Xfinity, 186
Xiaopeng Motors, 178

YouTube, 169, 184, 186, 187, 233, 248, 311, *557*, DEI-27

Zappos, 282
Zendesk, 55
Zenger Folkman, 458
Zest AI, 241
Zillow, 12
Zipline, 99
ZipRecruiter, 17, 354
Zola, 224
Zoom, 263, 270, 296, 303, 352, 387, 456, 471, 472, *512*, 541, 543, 546, 548, 551, 582

Note: Page numbers in *italics* represent figures, tables, and illustrations and numbers in **bold** represent glossary terms

Ability tests, 315

Absenteeism, 407

Abusive supervision *Occurs when supervisors repeatedly display verbal and nonverbal hostility toward their subordinates,* **73**, 532

Accountability *Describes expectation that managers must report and justify work results to the managers above them,* **287**

Achievement, need for, 428, 429

Acquired needs theory *Theory that states that there are three needs—achievement, affiliation, and power—that are the major motives determining people's behavior in the workplace,* 428, **428**-429

Acquisitions and mergers, 367

Action plans *Course of action needed to achieve a stated goal,* **154**, 443

Active listening *The process of actively decoding and interpreting verbal messages,* 492, **567**-568

ADA. *See* Americans with Disabilities Act

Adaptive change *Reintroduction of a familiar practice,* **360**

ADEA. *See* Age Discrimination in Employment Act

Adhocracy culture *Type of organizational culture that has an external focus and values flexibility,* 272, **273**, 275

Adjourning *One of five stages of forming a team; the stage in which members of an organization prepare for disbandment,* **477**

Administrative management *Management concerned with managing the total organization,* 42, **44**-45

Adverse impact *Effect an organization has when it uses an employment practice or procedure that results in unfavorable outcomes to a protected class (such as Hispanics) over another group of people (such as non-Hispanic whites),* **335**

Affective component of an attitude *The feelings or emotions one has about a situation,* **396**

Affiliation needs, 428, 429

Affirmative action *The focus on achieving equality of opportunity,* **336**-337

Affordable Care Act (2010), 333, 335

Age Discrimination in Employment Act (ADEA) (1967), *333*

Agency shop, 341

Agreeableness, 388

AI. *See* Artificial intelligence

After action review *A review of recent decisions in order to identify possible future improvements,* **255**

Project teams, 470-471

Promotions, 281, 329-330

Ally *Is a member of a majority group who champions DE&I by publicly and proactively calling attention to DE&I issues and working to drive improvements to an organization's systems,* **DEI-26**-DEI-27

Ambiguity
role, 411
tolerance for, 204, 244, *244*

Analyze (biometric AI), 237-238

Analytical decision-making style, 245

Anchoring and adjustment bias *The tendency to make decisions based on an initial figure,* **248**-249

Angel investors *Wealthy individuals or retired executives who invest in small firms,* **215**

Antecedents of communication, 566, *566*

Anticipatory socialization phase, organizational socialization, 271

APEC. *See* Asia-Pacific Economic Cooperation

Arbitration *The process in which a neutral third party, an arbitrator, listens to both parties in a dispute and makes a decision that the parties have agreed will be binding on them,* **343**

Artificial intelligence (AI) *A set of technologies that develop humanlike capabilities such as gathering and interpreting information, generating responses, and learning from decisions to attain specific objectives,* **21**, 231, 610-611
benefits, 240-241, *241*
as decision-making resource, 236-243
drawbacks, 241-243
and human replacement, 242-243
implementation, 241
and productivity, 610-611
and supply chain management, 611
types of, 236-240
weaponizing, 242

ASEAN. *See* Association of Southeast Asian Nations

Assertiveness, 129, *130*

Assessment center *Company department where management candidates participate in activities for a few days while being assessed by evaluators,* **316**

Association to Advance Collegiate Schools of Business (AACSB), 100, *101*

Attainable goals, 156

Attentional issues, 552-553

Attire, 109, 351

Attitudes *Learned predisposition toward a given object,* **31**, 308, **395**
behavior and, 397
career readiness and, 414-416
collision between reality and, 396-397
components of, 396
work-related, 402-407

Fundamental attribution error *The tendency to assume that others' negative outcomes are attributable to their person factors rather than to factors in their environment,* **DEI-14**-DEI-15

Authenticity, 479

Authority *The right to perform or command; also, the rights inherent in a managerial position to make decisions, give orders, and utilize resources,* **287**-288, 504
centralized, 289
decentralized, 289

Authorization cards, 340

Automate (robotic AI), 236-237, *237*

Automated experience, 224

Autonomous devices *Collect data from situations to make calculations, define probabilities, and make reason-based decisions according to programmed goals,* **236**

Autonomy, 287, 430, 446, 529

Availability bias *The use of information readily available from memory to make judgments,* **247**

Avoiding conflict, 488-489

Background checks, 303, 316

Background information, 313-314

Balanced scorecard *Gives top managers a fast but comprehensive view of the organization via four indicators: (1) financial measures, (2) customer outcomes, (3) internal business processes, and (4) the organization's innovation and learning activities,* **588**, *589*
customer perspective, 592-594
financial perspective, 588-592
innovation, 596-599
internal business perspective, 594-595

Balance sheet *A summary of an organization's overall financial worth—assets and liabilities—at a specific point in time,* **590**

Bank loans, 214

Bargaining unit, 340

BARS. *See* Behaviorally anchored rating scale

Base pay *Consists of the basic wage or salary paid employees in exchange for doing their jobs,* **318**

Basic assumptions, 269-270

BCG matrix *A management strategy by which companies evaluate their strategic business units on the basis of (1) their business growth rates and (2) their share of the market,* **182**-184, *183*

Behavior *Actions and judgments,* 308, **397**
effect of attitudes and values on, 397
individual attitudes and, 395-397
perception and, 397-402
personality and, 388-394
stress and, 408-414
values and, 395, 397
workplace, 405-407
work-related attitudes and, 402-407

Behavioral appraisals, 326

IND8 Glossary/Subject Index

Behavioral component of an attitude
Also known as intentional component, this refers to how one intends or expects to behave toward a situation, **396**

Behavioral decision-making style, 246

Behavioral-description interview
Type of structured interview in which the interviewer explores what applicants have done in the past, **315**

Behavioral leadership approaches
Attempts to determine the key behaviors displayed by effective leaders, **513**-515
  task-oriented, 514
  task-oriented behavior, 612
  relationship-orineted behavior, 613

Behavioral science approach Relies on scientific research for developing theories about human behavior that can be used to provide practical tools for managers, **47**

Behavioral viewpoint Emphasizes the importance of understanding human behavior and of motivating employees toward achievement, **45**-47

Behaviorally anchored rating scale (BARS) Employee gradations in performance rated according to scales of specific behaviors, **326**

Behavioral objectives, *157*

Behavior modification, 449
  to motivate employees, 450-451
  types of, 449-451, *449*

Belongingness, DEI-7, DEI-21-DEI-22

Benchmarking A process by which a company compares its performance with that of high-performing organizations, **180**-181, *181*, 594

Benefits Additional nonmonetary forms of compensation, **319**, *333*

Best practices A set of guidelines, ethics or ideas that have been shown to produce optimal results, **594**

Bias
  anchoring and adjustment, 248-249
  availability, 247
  categorical thinking, 250
  confirmation, 248
  decision making, 247-250
  in decision making, 218
  escalation of commitment, 250
  explicit, 399
  framing, 249-250
  fundamental attribution, 401
  hindsight, 249
  implicit, 399-400
  judicial, 399
  overconfidence, 249
  representativeness, 247-248
  self-serving, 401
  sunk-cost, 248

Big data An extremely large quantity of data that is too large for a typical computer to handle and requires you to adopt new technologies and statistical approaches to process it, **20**, 21, 230, **232**-236, *235*
  HR analysts, 234-235
  up and down hierarchy, 235-236

value, 234
variety, 233
velocity, 233
veracity, 233-234
volume, 233

Big Five personality dimensions
They are (1) extroversion, (2) agreeableness, (3) conscientiousness, (4) emotional stability, and (5) openness to experience, **388**-389

Board of directors Group of people elected to oversee the firm's activities and ensure that management acts in the shareholders' best interests, 63, **65**

Body language, 387, 539, 555

Bonuses Cash awards given to employees who achieve specific performance objectives, 281, **453**

Boomerangs Former employees who return to the organization, **312**

Boundaryless organization A fluid, highly adaptive organization whose members, linked by information technology, come together to collaborate on common tasks; the collaborators may include competitors, suppliers, and customers, **294**-296, *295*

Bounded rationality One type of nonrational decision making; the ability of decision makers to be rational is limited by numerous constraints, **223**

Brainstorming Technique used to help groups generate multiple ideas and alternatives for solving problems; individuals in a group meet and review a problem to be solved, then silently generate ideas, which are collected and later analyzed, **254**-255, *255*

Brand recognition, 169, 559-560

Brazil, emerging economy of, 125-126

Break-even analysis, 625, *625*
  benefits of, 626
  limitations of, 626

Bribes, 134

BRICS countries, 125-126

Broader stakeholders, 358

Budgets A formal financial projection, **589**-590

Buffers Administrative changes that managers can make to reduce the stressors that lead to employee burnout, **413**

Bullying Repeated mistreatment of one or more persons by one or more perpetrators. It's abusive, physical, psychological, verbal, or nonverbal behavior that is threatening, humiliating, or intimidating, **338**-339

Bureaucracy, 44-45

Burnout State of emotional, mental, and even physical exhaustion, **408**

Business, core processes of, 191

Business ethics, 226-227

Business-level strategy Focuses on individual business units or product/service lines, *171*, **171**

Business plan A document that outlines a proposed firm's goals, the strategy for achieving them, and the standards for measuring success, **145**, 210-212

Business schools, role in creating shared value, 100-101

Business skills, *512*

Buyers, bargaining power of, 186

Buzzwords, 543

CAFTA-DR. *See* Central America Free Trade Agreement

Canada
  individualism in, 128
  in NAFTA, 122

Career counselling, 414

Career readiness Represents the extent to which an individual possess the knowledge, skills, and attributes desired by employers, **27**
  competencies needed for, 29, *29*-30
  critical thinking/problem solving and, 258
  cross-cultural awareness and, 109, 137
  development of, 32-33
  emotional regulation and, 416
  interventions, 368
  levels of, 27, *27*
  management of, 33-35, 55-57
  management of, 379-382
  model of, *28*, *28*-32, *56*
  networking skills and, 572-574
  openness to change and, 379-382
  personal adaptability and, 136
  positive approach and, 414-416
  process for developing, 33-34
  professionalism and work ethic in, 83
  receiving feedback, 343-345
  self-awareness and, 136, 534-535
  strategic thinking and, 193-194
  task-based/functional knowledge and, 194
  understanding business and personal adaptability, *296*, 296-298
  understanding the business and, 194

Cascading goals Objectives are structured in a unified hierarchy, becoming more specific at lower levels of the organization, **159**

Cash cows, 184

Categorical thinking bias Tendency of decision makers to classify people or information based on observed or inferred characteristics, **250**

Causal attribution The activity of inferring causes for observed behavior, **400**-401

C corporations, 213

Cell phones, 553

Centralized authority Organizational structure in which important decisions are made by upper managers—power is concentrated at the top, **289**

Change. *See* Organizational change

Change agent A person inside or outside the organization who can be a catalyst in helping deal with old problems in new ways, **366**, 377-378

Change and acquisition phase, organizational socialization, 271

Changing stage of organizational change, 361–362

Charisma *Form of interpersonal attraction that inspires acceptance and support,* **523**

Charismatic leadership *Once assumed to be an individual inspirational and motivational characteristic of particular leaders, now considered part of transformational leadership,* **523**

Cheating, 24

China
   collectivism in, 128
   emerging economy of, 125
   foreign investments by, 117
   import quotas by, 121
   labor costs in, 117
   lower labor costs in, 117
   middle class growth in, 117
   tariff dispute with, 120
   zero-COVID policy, 113

Civil Rights Act (1991), *333*

Civil Rights Act, Title VII (1964), *333*

Clan culture *Type of organizational culture that has an internal focus and values flexibility rather than stability and control, 272,* **273,** *276*

Classical viewpoint *Emphasized finding ways to manage work more efficiently, assumed that people are rational. It had two branches–scientific and administrative,* **42–45**

Clawbacks *Rescinding the tax breaks when firms don't deliver promised jobs,* **67**

Climate *Is defined as the set of perceptions that employees share, based on their interrelated experiences, regarding the organization's procedures and policies,* **DEI-8**

Climate change *Refers to major changes in temperature, precipitation, wind patterns, and similar matters occurring over several decades,* **80**

Closed shop, 340

Closed system *A system that has little interaction with its environment,* **50**

Cloud computing *The storing of software and data on gigantic collections of computers located away from a company's principal site,* **20**

Clusters *Geographic concentrations of interrelated entities such as competitors, suppliers, universities, and other organizations that result in benefits for the firm in the local operating environment,* **93**

Coaching, 280

Coalition tactics, *507*

COBRA. *See* Consolidated Omnibus Budget Reconciliation Act

Code of ethics *A formal, written set of ethical standards that guide an organization's actions,* **77–78**

Coercive power *One of five sources of a leader's power that results from the authority to punish,* **504–505**

Cognitive abilities, *512*

Cognitive component of an attitude *The beliefs and knowledge one has about a situation,* **396**

Cognitive dissonance *Psychological discomfort a person experiences between his or her cognitive attitude and incomparable behavior,* **396–397,** 434

Cognitive empathy, 567

COLA. *See* Cost-of-living adjustment clause

Collaboration *Act of sharing information and coordinating efforts to achieve a collective outcome,* **478,** 484, 487–488, 491

Collective bargaining *Negotiations between management and employees regarding disputes over compensation, benefits, working conditions, and job security,* **334**

Collaborative computing *Using state-of-the-art computer software and hardware, to help people work better together,* **22**

Collectivism, 128, 129, *129*

Common purpose *A goal that unifies employees or members and gives everyone an understanding of the organization's reason for being,* **286**

Commonweal organization, 12–13

Communication barriers
   cross-cultural barriers, 553–554
   gender differences as, 556
   nonverbal, 555–556
   overview, 550–551
   personal, 551–553
   physical, 551

Communication *The transfer of information and understanding from one person to another,* **540**
   barriers to (*see* Communication barriers)
   cross-cultural, 553–554
   cultural differences in, 131
   empathy, 539
   face-to-face, 544, 548–549
   formal channels of, 545–547
   gender differences in, 556
   improving effectiveness of, 565–572
   informal channels of, 547–579
   medium for, 543–544, *544*
   nonverbal, 539, 555–556
   oral/written, 488
   process, 540–543, *541*
   social media and (*see* Social media)

Communities, as stakeholders, 67

Compassionate empathy, 567

Compensation *Payment comprising three parts: wages or salaries, incentives, and benefits,* **317,** 334
   issues related to, 342

Competence needs, 429

Competing values framework (CVF), 272–274, *272*

Competition
   conflict and, 487
   globalization and, 110–111
   international, 110
   organizational change and, 351

Competitive advantage *The ability of an organization to produce goods or services more effectively than competitors do, thereby outperforming them,* **18–20**
   cultural differences and, 131
   strategic management and, 147
   sustainable, 175

Competitors *People or organizations that compete for customers or resources,* **66**
   rivalry among, 186

Complexity theory *The study of how order and pattern arise from very complicated, apparently chaotic systems,* **60**

Compromising, conflict and, 489

Conceptual decision-making style, 245

Conceptual skills *Skills that consist of the ability to think analytically, to visualize an organization as a whole and understand how the parts work together,* **16–17,** *512*

Concurrent control *Entails collecting performance information in real time,* **586–587**

Confirmation bias *Biased way of thinking in which people seek information to support their point of view and discount data that do not support it,* **248**

Conflict *Process in which one party perceives that its interests are being opposed or negatively affected by another party,* **483**
   constructive, 487
   cross-cultural, 486
   dysfunctional, 483
   envy-based, 485–486
   functional, 484
   handling, 487–488, *489*
   intergroup, 486
   nature of, 483–484
   performance and, 484, *485*
   personality, 485
   programmed, 487
   resistance to change and, 379
   role, 411
   team conflict, 467

Conscientiousness, 388

Consensus *General agreement; group solidarity,* **254**

Consideration *A leadership behavior that is concerned with group members' needs and desires and that is directed at creating mutual respect or trust,* **514**
   individualized, 524

Consolidated Omnibus Budget Reconciliation Act (COBRA) (1985), *333*

Consultation, *506*

Consumer price index (CPI), 342

Contemporary control issues
   artificial intelligence, 610–611
   employee tracking and monitoring, 612–614

Contemporary perspective *In contrast, ..., these approaches focus on the leader-member exchange (LMX) model of leadership (624) and servant leadership (626),* **525–533**
   leader-member exchange model of leadership, 525–526

Content perspectives *Also known as need-based perspectives; theories that emphasize the needs that motivate people,* **426**
  Deci and Ryan's self-determination theory, 429–431
  Herzberg's two-factor theory, 431–433, *432*
  Maslow's hierarchy of needs, 46, 426–428, *427*
  McClelland's acquired needs theory, *428*, 428–429

Context *The situational or environmental characteristics that influence our behavior,* **137**–138

Contingency factors, 446

Contingency leadership model *A model that determines if a leader's style is (1) task-oriented or (2) relationship-oriented and if that style is effective for the situation at hand,* **515**–517, *517*

Contingency plans *Responses to possible future events that could threaten a company's operations,* **154**–155

Contingency viewpoint *The belief that a manager's approach should vary according to-that is, be contingent on-the individual and the environmental situation,* 51–52

Continuous improvement *Ongoing, small, incremental improvements in all parts of an organization,* **604**–605

Continuous self-improvement model, *616*, 616–618

Contract negotiation, 340

Control charts *A visual statistical tool used for quality-control purposes,* **584**–586, *585*

Control/control systems. *See also* Total quality management (TQM)
  balanced scorecard and, 588, *589*
  contemporary issues, 610–614
  need for, 580–582
  productivity and, 581
  strategy map and, 599–600, *600*
  types of, 586–587

Controlling *Monitoring performance, comparing it with goals, and taking corrective action as needed,* **9**, 580, *580*

Control process steps *The four steps in the process of controlling: (1) establish standards; (2) measure performance; (3) compare performance to standards; and (4) take corrective action, if necessary,* **582**–586, *583*

Control standard *The first step in the control process; the performance standard (or just standard) is the desired performance level for a given goal,* **583**

Coordinated effort *The coordination of individual efforts into a group or organization-wide effort,* **286**

Core competencies *Competencies that are vital across jobs, occupations, and industries,* **28**

Core self-evaluation (CSE) *Represents a broad personality trait comprising four positive individual traits: (1) self-efficacy,* (2) self-esteem, (3) locus of control, and (4) emotional stability, **389**–392

Core values statement, 56–57

Coronavirus (COVID-19) pandemic. *See* COVID-19 pandemic

Corporate culture *Set of shared taken for granted implicit assumptions that group holds and that determines how it perceives, thinks about, and reacts to its various environments,* 56–57, **265**, *265*. *See also* Organizational culture

Corporate governance *The system of governing a company so that the interests of corporate owners and other stakeholders are protected,* **82**–83
  and ethics, 82
  and social responsibility, 82–83

Corporate-level strategy *Focuses on the organization as a whole,* **171**, *171*

Corporate reputation, 560

Corporate social responsibility (CSR) *The notion that corporations are expected to go above and beyond following the law and making a profit, to take actions that will benefit the interests of society as well as of the organization,* **78**
  climate change and, 80
  creating shared value *vs.*, 95
  philanthropy and, 81
  pyramid of, 79, *79*
  traditional, 90
  viewpoints on, 80

Corporation *An entity that is separate from its owners, meaning it has its own legal rights, independent of its owners—it can sue, be sued, own and sell property, and sell the rights of ownership in the form of stocks,* **213**

Corruption, 134

Cost-focus strategy *One of Porter's four competitive strategies; keeping the costs, and hence prices, of a product or service below those of competitors and to target a narrow market,* **187**

Cost-leadership strategy *One of Porter's four competitive strategies; keeping the costs, and hence prices, of a product or service below those of competitors and to target a wide market,* **187**

Cost-of-living adjustment (COLA) clause *Clause in a union contract that ties future wage increases to increases in the cost of living,* **342**

Counterproductive work behavior (CWB) *Type of behavior that harms employees and the organization as a whole,* **406**

Counterthrusters, 364

Countertrading *Bartering goods for goods,* **118**

Courage *Taking intentional action in a worthy cause and enduring in this act despite the risk of serious personal consequences,* **61**

COVID-19 pandemic, 69
  China's governmental policies, 113
  downward communication during, 545
  lockdowns, 48
  need for control during, 580–582
  negative impacts of, 103
  scenario analysis, 180

Creating shared value (CSV) *Implementing policies and operating practices that enhance the competitiveness of a company while simultaneously advancing the economic and social conditions in the communities in which it operates,* **90**–91
  challenges for, 102–104
  corporate social responsibility *vs.*, 95
  model of, 91–95, *92*
  progress for, 102–104
  recommendations for transitioning, 104–105
  role of businesses in, 98–99
  role of business schools in, 100–101
  roles of stakeholders in, 96–101

Creativity *Process of generating novel ideas,* 204, **349**

Credibility, 552
  as entrepreneur trait, 99

Crime, white-collar, 75–77

Criminal background checks, 316

Crises, responses to organizational, 280

Critical thinking, 162, 258

Cross-cultural awareness *The ability to operate in different cultural settings,* 109, **126**, 136–138

Cross-cultural communication barriers, 553–554

Cross-cultural conflict, 486

Cross-functional teams *A team that is staffed with specialists pursuing a common objective,* 294, **470**

Crowdfunding *Raising money for a project or venture by obtaining many small amounts of money from many people ("the crowd"),* **68**, 559

Crowd investing *Allows a group of people—the crowd—to invest in an entrepreneur or business online,* **215**

Crowdsourcing *The practice of obtaining needed services, ideas, or content by soliciting contributions from a large group of people and especially from the online community, such as Facebook and Twitter users,* **375**, 559

CSR. *See* Corporate social responsibility

CSR contracting *Linking executive compensation to CSR criteria such as environment and social performance,* **82**, 83

Cultural differences. *See also* Diversity
  communication and, 131
  competitive advantage and, 131
  dimensions of, 128–130, *129–130*
  GLOBE project and, 128–130, *129–130*
  interpersonal space and, 131–132, *132*
  language and, 131
  law and political stability and, 133–134
  national culture and, 127
  overview of, 126
  religion and, 133, *134*
  stereotypes and, 398–399
  time orientation and, 132–133
  tipping customs and, 127

Culture Code, 278

Culture *The shared set of beliefs, values, knowledge, and patterns of behavior common to a group of people,* **127.** *See also* Organizational culture
    adhocracy, 273
    business travel and, 109
    clan, *272*, 273
    hierarchy, *272*, 274
    high-context, 127
    importance of, 274–276, *275*
    of innovation, 373
    low-context, 127
    market, *272*, 273–274
    safety, 283–284
    tipping, 127
    transmission of, 270–272

Curiosity, genuine sense of 554, 569

Current assets, 590

Current reality assessment *Assessment to look at where the organization stands and see what is working and what could be different so as to maximize efficiency and effectiveness in achieving the organization's mission,* **173**

Customer divisions *Divisional structures in which activities are grouped around common customers or clients,* **292**, *292*

Customer retention *Refers to the actions companies take to reduce customer defections,* **593–594**

Customer satisfaction *Measure of how products or services provided by a firm meet customer expectations,* **593**

Customers *Those who pay to use an organization's goods or services,* **66**
    foreign, 114
    organizational change and, 357
    performance appraisals by, 327
    social responsibility effect on, *81*
    as stakeholders, 66

CVF. *See* Competing values framework

CWB. *See* Counterproductive work behaviors

Cyberloafing *Using the Internet at work for personal use,* **560–561**

Data analysis, 237–238

Data analytics *Process of examining data sets in order to draw conclusions about the information they contain,* **232**

Databases *Computerized collections of interrelated files,* **20**

Decentralized authority *Organizational structure in which important decisions are made by middle-level and supervisory-level managers—power is delegated throughout the organization,* **289**

Decision *A choice made from among available alternatives,* **220**

Decision-making styles *Styles that reflect the combination of how an individual perceives and responds to information,* **243**
    tolerance for ambiguity, 244, *244*
    types of, *244*, 244–246
    value orientation, 244, *244*

Decision making *The process of identifying and choosing alternative courses of action,* **220**
    bias in, 219, 247–250
    decentralization of, 582
    ethical, 225–228, *228*, 243
    evidence-based, 229–232
    group (*see* Group decision making)
    implicit bias and, 399
    methodology, 259
    rational model, 220–222
    strategies for, 219

Decision trees *Graph of decisions and their possible consequences, used to create a plan to reach a goal,* **227–228**, *228*

Decisional roles *Managers use information to make decisions to solve problems or take advantage of opportunities. The four decision-making roles are entrepreneur, disturbance handler, resource allocator, and negotiator,* **15**, *15*

Decoding barrier, *550*

Decoding *Interpreting and trying to make sense of a message,* **540–541**

Defensive communication *Form of communication that is either aggressive, attacking, angry, passive, or withdrawing,* **566**, *566*

Defensiveness *Occurs when people perceive they are being attacked or threatened,* **345**

Defensive strategy *Also called retrenchment strategy, one of three grand strategies, this strategy involves reduction in the organization's efforts,* **182**, *183*

DE&I *An acronym that stands for diversity, equity, and inclusion,* **DEI-3**

DE&I Management *The process of identifying, acquiring, developing, deploying, and integrating diverse perspectives throughout an organization,* **DEI-3**
    accept feedback, DEI-27
    career readiness, DEI-25, DEI-25–DEI-28
    challenges of, DEI-12–DEI-20
    diversity, DEI-3–DEI-4, *DEI-4*
    equity, DEI-5–DEI-6
    evolution of, DEI-9–DEI-12
    inclusion, DEI-6–DEI-8
    intersectionality, DEI-5
    managerial practices, DEI-21–DEI-22
    organizational practices, DEI-22–DEI-24
    pay gaps, DEI-23

Delegation *The process of assigning managerial authority and responsibility to managers and employees lower in the hierarchy,* **288**

Deming management *Ideas proposed by W. Edwards Deming for making organizations more responsive, more democratic, and less wasteful,* **601–602**

Demographic forces *Influences on an organization arising from changes in the characteristics of a population, such as age gender, or ethnic origin,* **70**, 356–357, *356*

Demotions, 331

Descriptive analytics *identifies trends and relationships within big data,* **230–231**

Devil's advocacy *Role-playing criticism to test whether a proposal is workable,* 255, **256**, **487**

Diagnosis *Analyzing the underlying causes,* **221**, 367, 368

Dialectic method *Role-playing two sides of a proposal to test whether it is workable,* 255, **256**, **487**

Differential rate system, 43

Differentiation strategy *One of Porter's four competitive strategies; offering products or services that are of unique and superior value compared with those of competitors but to target a wide market,* **187**

Digital communication. *See* Social media

Direct-to-consumer genetics testing, 21

Directive decision-making style, 244–245

Discrimination. *See* Workplace discrimination

Discovery of new products/services, 91

Disinformation *Information that is false and deliberately misleading,* **563**

Dismissals, 331–332

Disparate treatment *Results when employees from protected groups (such as disabled individuals) are intentionally treated differently,* **336**

Disruptive innovation, 351

Distress, 381

Distributive justice *Reflects the perceived fairness of how resources and rewards are distributed or allocated,* **436**

Distributors *People or organizations that help another organization sell its goods and services to customers,* **66–67**

Diversification *Strategy by which a company operates several businesses in order to spread the risk,* **184**

Diversity *Refers to the presence of differences among a group of people,* **DEI-3–DEI-4**. *See also* Cultural differences
    managing for, 22
    stereotypes and, 398–399

Divisional structure *The third type of organizational structure, whereby people with diverse occupational specialties are put together in formal groups according to products and/or services, customers and/or clients, or geographic regions,* **292**, *292*

Division of labor *Also known as work specialization; arrangement of having discrete parts of a task done by different people. The work is divided into particular tasks assigned to particular workers,* **286**

Dominating, conflict and, 489

Downsizings, 331

Downward communication *Communication that flows from a higher level to a lower level,* **545**

Dress code, 303

Drones, *242*, 290, *357*, 470

Drug and alcohol tests, 316

Dunning-Kruger effect *A cognitive bias whereby people who are incompetent at something are unable to recognize their own incompetence. And not only do they fail to recognize their incompetence, they're also likely to feel confident that they actually are competent,* 534-**535**

Dynamic inputs, 94-95

Dysfunctional conflict *Conflict that hinders the organization's performance or threatens its interests,* **483**

Dysfunctional turnover, 596

EAPs. *See* Employee assistance programs

E-business *Using the Internet to facilitate every aspect of running a business,* **20**

E-commerce *Electronic commerce—the buying and selling of goods or services over computer networks,* **20, 111**

Economic community. *See* Trading bloc

Economic forces *General economic conditions and trends—unemployment, inflation, interest rates, economic growth—that may affect an organization's performance,* **69**

Economy, global, 111-112

EEOC. *See* Equal Employment Opportunity Commission

Effectiveness *To achieve results, to make the right decisions, and to successfully carry them out so that they achieve the organization's goals,* **5-6**

Efficiency *To use resources—people, money raw materials, and the like—wisely and cost effectively,* **5**, 20, 595
  big data and, 235
  effectiveness *vs.*, 5-6

Effort-to-performance expectancy, 439

Egypt's Suez Canal blockage, 113

Electronic brainstorming *Technique in which members of a group come together over a computer network to generate ideas and alternatives,* **254-255**

Embargoes *A complete ban on the import or export of certain products,* **121**

Emotional empathy, 567

Emotional intelligence *Ability to monitor your and others' feelings and to use this information to guide your thinking and actions,* 392, **392**-393, 488

Emotional regulation, 416

Emotional stability *Is the extent to which people feel secure and unworried and how likely they are to experience negative emotions under pressure,* 388, **392**

Empathy *Represents the ability to recognize and understand another person's feelings and thoughts,* 393-394, 479, 539, **567**

Employee assistance programs (EAPs) *Host of programs aimed at helping employees to cope with stress, burnout, substance abuse, health-related problems, family and marital issues, and any general problems that negatively influence job performance,* **413**

Employee-centered leader behaviors *Emphasize relationships with subordinates and attention to their individual needs,* **514**

Employee engagement *A mental state in which a person performing a work activity is fully immersed in the activity, feeling full of energy and enthusiasm for the work,* 403, **403**-404

Employee referrals *Tap into existing employees' social networks to fill open positions with outside applicants,* **311**-312

Employee Retirement Income Security Act (ERISA) (1974), *333*

Employees. *See also* Human resource management (HRM)
  as owners, 65
  as stakeholders, 64, *64*
  foreign, 115
  perceptions, 437
  profiles, 310
  promotion of, 329-330
  resistance to change in, *377*, 377-379
  social media policy for, 560
  social responsibility effect on, *81*
  voice of, 437

Employee socialization, 320

Employee tracking and monitoring
  advantages of, 613
  disadvantages of, 613
  overview, 612

Employment at will *Governing principle of employment in the great majority of states, that anyone can be dismissed at any time for any reason at all-or for no reason,* **332**

Employment interviews, 56-57, 258, 303, 314-315

Employment landscape, 354

Employment tests *Standardized devices organizations use to measure specific skills, abilities, traits, and other tendencies,* **315**-317

Empowering leadership *A form of leadership that represents the extent to which a leader creates perceptions of psychological empowerment in others,* **529**-530

Empowerment
  leadership and, 529-530
  worker, 46

Enacted values *Values and norms actually exhibited in the organization,* **269**

Encoding barrier, 550

Encoding *Translating a message into understandable symbols or language,* **540**

Encounter phase, organizational socialization, 271

Entrepreneurship *The pursuit of opportunity beyond resources controlled,* **200**-203
  global importance of, 205-207
  innovation and, 206
  self-employment *vs.*, 201
  social, 201-203
  standard of living and, 207

Entrepreneurial confidence *An individual's generalized sense of self-assurance and control over outcomes,* **205**

Entrepreneurial mindset *Reflects an individual's adaptive ability to continuously gather information and make decisions in a complex, uncertain, and dynamic environment,* **204**

Entrepreneurial orientation *An individual's tendency to engage in innovative, risk-taking, and proactive behaviors,* **204**

Entrepreneurial self-efficacy, 205

Entrepreneurs *Someone who identifies a business opportunity and takes the risk of creating or running an independent business to exploit the business opportunity,* **200**
  characteristics of, 203-205, *203*
  role in creating shared value, 99

Environmental factors *External forces and elements that contribute to people's outcomes,* **DEI-13**

Envy-based conflicts, 485-486

Epiphany, 224

Equal employment opportunity, 335

Equal Employment Opportunity Commission (EEOC) *U.S. panel whose job it is to enforce anti-discrimination and other employment related laws,* **335**

Equal Pay Act (1963), *333*

Equity *Exists when employees perceive that they receive fair and unbiased treatment with respect to their opportunities, resources, and outcomes in organizations,* **DEI-5**-DEI-6

Equity theory *In the area of employee motivation, the focus on how employees perceive how fairly they think they are being treated compared with others,* **434**-438, *435*

ERISA. *See* Employee Retirement Income Security Act

Escalation of commitment bias *When decision makers increase their commitment to a project despite negative information about it,* **250**

Espoused values *Explicitly stated values and norms preferred by an organization,* **269**

Esteem needs, 426, *427*

Ethical behavior *Behavior that is accepted as "right" as opposed to "wrong" according to those standards,* **72**, 78

Ethical climate *A term that refers to employees' perceptions about the extent to which work environments support ethical behavior,* **77**

Ethical dilemma *A situation in which you have to decide whether to pursue a course of action that may benefit you or your organization but that may harm one or more stakeholders in your environment,* 72-75, *73*

Ethical leadership *A form of leadership that focuses on being a moral role model and encouraging others to do the right thing,* **530**

Ethical/legal issues
   approaches to, 74-75
   in human resource management, 332-339
   for managers, 23-24
   white-collar crime and, 75-77

Ethics *The standards of right and wrong that influence behavior. It is behavior that is accepted as "right" as opposed to "wrong" according to prevailing standards,* **72**, **79**
   in business, 225-227
   codes of, 77-78
   in consumer behavior, 84-85
   corporate governance and, 82
   in decision making, 225-228, *228*, 243
   leadership and, 524
   methods to promote, 77-78
   moral development and, 76-77
   overview of, 72
   social responsibilities and, 78-82
   standards, managing for, 23-24
   strategies for being more ethical, 84
   values and, 72

Ethics officers *Individuals trained in matters of ethics in the workplace, particularly about resolving ethical dilemmas,* **227**

Ethnocentric managers *Managers who believe that their native country, culture, language, and behavior are superior to all others,* **115**

European Union (EU) *Union of 27 trading partners in Europe,* **123**
   imports by, 110

Evaluation
   of organizational development, *367*
   in rational model of decision making, 222

Evidence-based decision making *The process of gathering and analyzing high-quality data to develop and implement a plan of action,* **229**-232

Evidence-based management *Translation of principles based on best evidence into organizational practice, bringing rationality to the decision-making process,* **49**-50, 229-232, *230*

Exchange, *507*

Exchange rates *The rate at which the currency of one area or country can be exchanged for the currency of another's,* **124**, *124-125*

Execution: The Discipline of Getting Things Done (Bossidy and Charan), 190

Execution *Using questioning, analysis, and follow-through in order to mesh strategy with reality, align people with goals, and achieve the results promised,* **190**
   roadblocks, 192

Exit interview *A formal conversation between a manager and a departing employee to find out why he or she is leaving and to learn about potential problems in the organization,* **332**

Expatriate selection, 135

Expatriates *People living or working in a foreign country,* **135**

Expectancy *The belief that a particular level of effort will lead to a particular level of performance,* **439**

Expectancy theory *Based on notion that motivation is a two staged sequence of expectations–moving from effort to performance and then from performance to outcomes,* **439**-441, *439*

Expertise, 224, 505

Expert power *One of five sources of a leader's power, resulting from specialized information or expertise,* **505**

Explicit bias *Refers to the attitudes or beliefs that affect our understanding, actions, and decisions in a conscious manner,* **399**

Exporting *Producing goods domestically and selling them outside the country,* **118**, *118*

Expropriation *A government's seizure of a domestic or foreign company's assets,* **134**

External communication *Communication between people inside and outside an organization,* **547**

External fit, strategic HRM, 305

External locus of control, 391

External stakeholders *People or groups in the organization's external environment that are affected by it,* **63**, *64*
   in general environment, 68-71
   in task environment, 66-68

External recruiting *Attracting job applicants from outside the organization,* **311**

Extinction *The weakening of behavior by ignoring it or making sure it is not reinforced,* **450**

Extrinsic rewards *The payoff, such as money, that a person receives from others for performing a particular task,* **424**

Extroversion, 388, 389

Eye contact, 555

Face-to-face communication, 544, 548-549

Face-to-face interactions, 69, 473

Facial expressions, 555

Facial recognition system, 238

Failure and mistakes, 378

Fair Labor Standards Act *Legislation passed in 1938 that established minimum living standards for workers engaged in interstate commerce, including provision of a federal minimum wage,* **334**

Fair Minimum Wage Act (2007), *333*

Fairness, 74-75, 329-330

Family and Medical Leave Act (1963), *333*

Family demands, 412

Feedback *The receiver expresses their reaction to the sender's message,* **541**-542
   barrier, 550
   in communication process, 540, 542
   control function of, 582
   in goal-setting theory, 443
   job design and, 446
   organizational change and, 364
   in organizational development, 368
   and performance appraisals, 324, 325
   performance goals for, 479
   receiving, 343-345
   on teams, 479

Feedback control *Collecting performance information after a task or project is done,* **587**

Feedforward control *Focuses on preventing future problems,* **586**

Femininity *vs.* masculinity, 128

Financial background checks, 316

Financial capital, access to, 117

Financial institutions, as stakeholders, 67-68

Financial perspective
   budget, 589-590
   financial statements, 590-592

Financial ratios *Indicators determined from a company's financial information and used for comparison purposes,* **592**, *592*

Financial statements *Summary of some aspect of an organization's financial status,* **590**-592, *591*

Financing activities, *591*

Firings, 331-332

First impressions, 263, 387

First-line managers *One of four managerial levels; they make short-term operating decisions, directing the daily tasks of non-managerial personnel,* **11**

Fit, 170, 297

Fixed assets, 590

Fixed budgets *Allocation of resources on the basis of a single estimate of costs,* **590**

Flat organization *Organizational structure with few or no levels of middle management between top managers and those reporting to them,* **286**

Flexible budget, 590

Flourishing *Represents the extent to which our lives contain PERMA resulting in "goodness . . . growth, and resilience,* **456**

Flowchart, 622
   benefits of, 622
   for improving a company's advertising, 623
   limitations of, 622-623

Focused-differentiation strategy *One of Porter's four competitive strategies; offering products or services that are of unique and superior value compared to those of competitors and to target a narrow market,* **187**-188

Followers, 531

FOMO *Fear of missing out or of being out of touch with something happening in your social network,* **561**, 574

For-profit organizations, 12

Forced ranking performance review systems *Performance review systems whereby all employees within a business unit are ranked against one another, and grades are distributed along some sort of bell curve, like students being graded in a college course,* **328**

Force-field analysis *A technique to determine which forces could facilitate a proposed change and which forces could act against it,* **364**

Forcing, conflict and, 489

Forecast *A vision or projection of the future,* **179**-180

Foreign Corrupt Practices Act (1978) *Act that makes it illegal for employees of U.S. companies to make "questionable" or "dubious" contributions to political decision makers in foreign nations,* **134**

Formal communication channels *Communications that follow the chain of command and are recognized as official,* **545**-547

Formal group *A group assigned by organizations or its managers to accomplish specific goals,* **469**

Formal statements, 278-279

Forming *The first of the five stages of forming a team, in which people get oriented and get acquainted,* **475**

Fortune 500, 4, 90, 145, 328, 388, 510

Fortune 1000, 471

Fortune (magazine), 4, 26, 40, 64, 91, 99, 270, 273, 305, 308, 312

Four management functions *The management process that "gets things done": planning, organizing, leading, and controlling,* **8**

Framing bias *The tendency of decision makers to be influenced by the way a situation or problem is presented to them,* **119**, **249**-250

Franchising *A form of licensing in which a company allows a foreign company to pay it a fee and a share of the profit in return for using the first company's brand name and a package of materials and services,* **119**, 209-210

Free trade *The movement of goods and services among nations without political or economic obstruction,* **120**

Fringe benefits. *See* Benefits

Full-range leadership *Approach that suggests that leadership behavior varies along a full range of leadership styles, from take-no-responsibility (laissez-faire) "leadership" at one extreme through transactional leadership, to transformational leadership at the other extreme,* **520**-525

Functional conflict *Conflict that benefits the main purposes of the organization and serves its interests,* **484**

Functional knowledge, 162

Functional-level strategy *Plan of action by each functional area of the organization to support higher level strategies,* **171**, **171**-172

Functional manager *Manager who is responsible for just one organizational activity,* **12**

Functional strategy, 189

Functional structure *The second type of organizational structure, whereby people with similar occupational specialties are put together in formal groups,* **291**, *291*

Functional turnover, 596

Fundamental attribution bias *Tendency whereby people attribute another person's behavior to his or her personal characteristics rather than to situational factors,* **401**, **DEI-14**

Future orientation, 129, *130*

Gainsharing *The distribution of savings or "gains" to groups of employees who reduce costs and increase measurable productivity,* **453**

Gantt chart, 624
　benefits of, 624
　for designing a website, *624*
　limitations of, 624

Gender identity *Refers to a person's internal sense of being male, female, a combination of both, or neither,* **DEI-11**

Gender, traits and, 509-512

Gender differences, as communication barrier, 556

Gender egalitarianism, 129, *129*

General and Industrial Management (Fayol), 44

General environment *Also called macroenvironment; in contrast to the task environment, it includes six forces: economic, technological, sociocultural, demographic, political-legal, and international,* **63**, 68-71

General manager *Manager who is responsible for several organizational activities,* **12**

Generalized self-efficacy *Represents the belief in one's general ability to perform across different situations,* **389**-390

Generational differences, communication and, 553

Genuine sense of curiosity, 539, 554, 569

Gen Y. *See* Millennials

Gen Z, 53, 63, 100, 319, 358, 395, 414

Geocentric managers *Managers who accept that there are differences and similarities between home and foreign personnel and practices and that they should use whatever techniques are most effective,* **116**

Geographic divisions *Divisional structures in which activities are grouped around defined regional locations,* **292**, *292*

Gestures, 555

Gig economy, 607

Givebacks *Negotiation tactic in which the union agrees to give up previous wage or benefit gains in return for something else,* **342**

Giving Voice to Values (GVV), 77

Global economy *The increasing tendency of the economies of the world to interact with one another as one market instead of many national markets,* **111**-112

Globalization *The trend of the world economy toward becoming a more interdependent system,* **111**
　competition and, 110
　cultural awareness and, 109, 126, 136-138
　managing for, 22-23
　and supply chain vulnerabilities, 113

Global management
　attitudes and, 115-116
　benefits of learning about, 114-115
　BRICS countries, 125-126, *125*
　cross-cultural awareness and, 109
　cultural differences and, 126-134
　electronic commerce, 111
　exchange rates and, 124-125, *125*
　expansion methods and, 116-119, *117*
　expatriates and, 135
　global competition, 111-112
　global economy, 111-112
　international markets, growing, 116-119
　most favored nation trading status and, 124
　organizations promoting trade and, 121-122
　trade issues and, 120-126
　trading blocs and, 122-124, *122*
　travel issues and, 109

Global mindset *Your belief in your ability to influence dissimilar others in a global context,* **513**

Global outsourcing *Also called offshoring; use of suppliers outside the United States to provide labor, goods, or services,* 117-**118**

Global village *The "shrinking" of time and space as air travel and the electronic media have made it easier for the people around the globe to communicate with one another,* **111**

Global warming *One aspect of climate change, refers to the rise in global average temperature near the Earth's surface, caused mostly by increasing concentrations in the atmosphere of greenhouse gases, such as carbon emissions from fossil fuels,* **80**

GLOBE project *A massive and ongoing cross-cultural investigation of nine cultural dimensions involved in leadership and organizational processes,* **127**-130

Goal displacement *The primary goal is subsumed to a secondary goal,* **252**

Goals *Also known as objective; a specific commitment to achieve a measurable result within a stated period of time,* **154**, 443
　of business, 62-63
　cascading, 159
　long-term, 154, 460

Glossary/Subject Index　IND15

setting, 441–443, 579
setting, for career, 143
short-term, 154, 460–461
SMART, 155–156

Goal-setting theory *Employee-motivation approach that employees can be motivated by goals that are specific and challenging but achievable,* **441**–443

Government regulators *Regulatory agencies that establish ground rules under which organizations may operate,* **68**

Grand strategies, 181–185

Grapevine *The unofficial communication system of the informal organization,* **547**

Great Recession (2007–2009), 68

Greenfield venture *A foreign subsidiary that the owning organization has built from scratch,* **119**

Grievance *Complaint by an employee that management has violated the terms of the labor-management agreement,* **342**–343

Group cohesiveness *A "we feeling" that binds group members together,* **476**

Group decision making, 250–251. *See also* Decision making
advantages, 251
characteristics of, 253
disadvantages, 251–252
participation in, 254

Groups *Two or more freely interacting individuals who share collective norms, share collective goals, and have a common identity,* **468**. *See also* Teams
demands of, 412
formal *vs.* informal, 469
managing conflict in, 483–489
stages of development for, 474–477, *475*
teams *vs.*, 468

Groupthink *A cohesive group's blind unwillingness to consider alternatives. This occurs when group members strive for agreement among themselves for the sake of unanimity and avoid accurately assessing the decision situation,* **251**, 252, *252*, 487
symptoms of, 252

Growth strategy *One of three grand strategies, this strategy involves expansion—as in sales revenues, market share, number of employees, or number of customers or (for nonprofits) clients served,* **182**, *183*

Halo effect *We form an impression of an individual based on a single trait,* **400**

Happiness, managing for, 25–26

Hawthorne effect *Employees work harder if they receive added attention, if they think managers care about their welfare and if supervisors pay special attention to them,* **46**

Hawthorne studies, 46

Health Insurance Portability and Accountability Act (HIPAA) (1996), *333*

Hero *A person whose accomplishments embody the values of the organization,* **270**–271

Heuristics *Strategies that simplify the process of making decisions,* **247**

Hierarchy culture *Type of organizational culture that has an internal focus and values stability and control over flexibility,* **274**–275, 328

Hierarchy of authority *Also known as chain of command; a control mechanism for making sure the right people do the right things at the right time,* **286**

Hierarchy of needs theory *Psychological structure proposed by Maslow whereby people are motivated by five levels of needs: (1) physiological, (2) safety, (3) love, (4) esteem, and (5) self-actualization,* **426**–427
background of, 46
explanation of, 426–428, *427*

High-context culture *Culture in which people rely heavily on situational cues for meaning when communicating with others,* **127**

High-control situation, 516–*517*

High-performance work practices (HPWPs) *Improve an organization's ability to effectively attract, select, hire, develop and retain high-performing personnel,* **54**, 275

High-performance work system (HPWS) *Approach to strategic HRM deploys bundles of internally consistent HR practices in order to improve employee ability, motivation, and opportunities across the entire organization,* **309**

Hindsight bias *The tendency of people to view events as being more predictable than they really are,* **249**

HIPAA. *See* Health Insurance Portability & Accountability Act

Hiring decisions, social media and, 303, 558

Hofstede model of four cultural dimensions *Identifies four dimensions along which national cultures can be placed: (1) individualism/collectivism, (2) power distance, (3) uncertainty avoidance, and (4) masculinity/femininity,* **128**

Holistic hunch, 224

Holistic wellness program *Program that focuses on self-responsibility, nutritional awareness, relaxation techniques, physical fitness, and environmental awareness,* **414**

Hollow structure *Often called network structure, structure in which the organization has a central core of key functions and outsources other functions to vendors who can do them cheaper or faster,* **295**, *295*

Horizontal communication *Communication that flows within and between work units; its main purpose is coordination,* **546**

Horizontal design *Arrangement in which teams or workgroups, either temporary or permanent, are used to improve collaboration and work on shared tasks by breaking down internal boundaries,* **294**, *294*

Horizontal loading, 444–445

Horizontal specialization, 289–290

Horn-and-halo effect, 400

Hostile environment, 337

HR practices
performance evaluations, DEI-18–DEI-19
recruiting, DEI-16
selection, DEI-16–DEI-17
training, DEI-17–DEI-18

HubSpot, 239

Horizontal structure *Also called a team-based design, teams or workgroups, either temporary or permanent, are used to improve collaboration and work on shared tasks by breaking down internal boundaries,* **294**

Hubris *Extreme and inflated sense of pride, certainty, and confidence,* **223**–224

Human capital *Economic or productive potential of employee knowledge, experience, and actions,* **307**, 375

Humane orientation, 129–*130*

Human replacement, artificial intelligence and, 242–243

Human relations movement *The movement that proposed that better human relations could increase worker productivity,* **46**–47

Human resource management (HRM) *The activities managers perform to plan for, attract, develop, and retain a workforce,* **304**–305
demotions, 330–331
dismissals, 331–332
employee selection and, 312–317
innovation and, 375
labor-management issues, 339–343, *340*, *341*
legal requirements, 332–339
performance management and, 323–328
promotions, 329–330
recruitment and, 309–312
strategic (*see* Strategic human resource management)
transfer, 330

Human resource practices *Consist of all of the activities an organization uses to manage its human capital, including staffing, appraising, training and development, and compensation,* **266**, 304–305
leading for alignment among organizational culture/organizational structure and, 267
strategy implementation and, *265*, 266, 265–267

Human skills *Skills that consist of the ability to work well in cooperation with other people to get things done,* **17**

Humility, 527–530

Hygiene factors *Factors associated with job dissatisfaction—such as salary, working conditions, interpersonal relationships, and company policy—all of which affect the job context or environment in which people work,* **431**–432, *432*

Identity *It represents your own description of who you are,* **DEI-4**

Identity theft *A violation of privacy in which thieves hijack your name and identity and use your good credit rating to get cash or buy things,* 118, **561**-563

Imitability (in VRIO framework), 178, *178*

Immigration Reform & Control Act (1986), *333*

Implementation
artificial intelligence, 241
in rational model of decision making, 221-222

Implicit bias *Is the attitudes or beliefs that affect our understanding, actions, and decisions in an unconscious manner,* **399**-400

Importing *Buying goods outside the country and reselling them domestically,* **118**

Import quotas *A trade barrier in the form of a limit on the numbers of a product that can be imported,* 117, **121**

Improvement innovations, 370-371

Improvement orientation, 604-605

Incentives, 318-319

Inclusion *Represents the extent to which employees feel heard, valued, involved, and respected,* **DEI-6**-DEI-8
decision making, DEI-8
hallmarks of, DEI-7-DEI-8

Inclusion climate *Represents employees' shared beliefs about the degree to which they feel valued, welcomed, accepted, and important in the organization,* **DEI-8**

Inclusive language, DEI-2, *DEI-2*

Income statement *Summary of an organization's financial results—revenues and expenses—over a specified period of time,* **590**-591, *591*

Incremental budgeting *Allocating increased or decreased funds to a department by using the last budget period as a reference point; only incremental changes in the budget request are reviewed,* **589**

India
emerging economy of, 125
lower labor costs in, 117
offshoring to, 118

Individual approach *One of four approaches to solving ethical dilemmas; ethical behavior is guided by what will result in the individual's best long-term interests, which ultimately are in everyone's self-interest,* **74**

Individualism, 128

Industry 4.0 *A management perspective that uses digital transformation technologies (cloud computing, artificial intelligence [AI], robotics, and the Internet of Things [IoT]) to develop agile and adaptable processes that meet diverse customers' unique needs,* **608**

Industrial engineering, 43-44

Inertia *The tendency for firms to resist change in favor of their current modes of operation,* **99**

Influence tactics *Are conscious efforts to affect and change behaviors in others,* **506**-508, *506*-*507*

Informal communication channels *Communication that develops outside the formal structure and does not follow the chain of command,* **547**-549

Informal group *A group formed by people whose overriding purpose is getting together for friendship or a common interest,* **469**

Informal influence, 469, *469*

Informal nominations, 310

Informational power *Power deriving from one's access to information,* **505**

Informational roles *Managers as monitors, disseminators, and spokespersons,* **15**, *15*

Information oversimplification, 544

Information processing, 552

Information technology application skills *The extent to which you can effectively use information technology and learn new applications on an ongoing basis,* **20**

Ingratiation, *506*, 508

In-group collectivism, 129, *130*

In-group exchange, 526

Initiating-structure leadership *A leadership behavior that organizes and defines—that is, "initiates the structure for"—what employees should be doing to maximize output,* **514**

Innovation *Introduction of something new or better, as in goods or services,* **19**. *See also* Organizational change
balanced scorecard and, 596-599
control function of, 582
crowdsourcing and, 559
disruptive, 351
employee attitudes, 596
employee turnover, 596
entrepreneurship and, 206
focus of, 370-371
human capital and, 375
organizational culture, 597-599
process, 370
product, 370, *370*, 371
resource capabilities, 597
resources and, 375-376
structure and processes for, 373-375
type of, 370, *370*

Innovation strategy *Grows market share or profits by improving existing products and services or introducing new ones,* **182**, **372**

Innovation system *A set of mutually reinforcing structures, processes, and practices that drive an organization's choices around innovation and its ability to innovate successfully,* **371**-376, *372*

Innovative change *The introduction of a practice that is new to the organization,* **360**

The Innovator's Dilemma (Christensen), 351

In-person meetings, 548

Inputs, 362-363

In Search of Excellence (Peters), 40

Insider trading *The illegal trading of a company's stock by people using confidential company information,* **75**

Inspirational appeals, *506*

Instability, international, 133

Institutional collectivism, 129, *129*

Instrumentality *The expectation that successful performance of the task will lead to the outcome desired,* **439**-440

Integrating, conflict and, 489

Integrity tests, 316

Intelligence, emotional, *392*, **392**-393

Interactional justice *Relates to how organizational representatives treat employees in the process of implementing procedures and making decisions,* **436**

Intercultural communication apprehension *Represents the anxiety, stress, and general avoidance we experience when we are confronted with the possibility of spending time with someone we perceive as different,* **DEI-13**

Interest rates, 69

Intergroup conflicts, 486

Internal business perspective, 594-595
efficiency, 595
productivity, 594-595

Internal fit, strategic HRM, 306

Internal job postings, 310

Internal locus of control, 205, 391

Internal recruiting *Hiring from the inside, or making people already employed by the organization aware of job openings,* **310**-311

Internal Revenue Service (IRS), 78

Internal stakeholders *Employees, owners, and the board of directors, if any,* **63**-65, *64*

International forces *Changes in the economic, political, legal, and technological global system that may affect an organization,* **71**

International management. *See* Global management

Interpersonal roles *Of the three types of managerial roles, the roles in which managers interact with people inside and outside their work units. The three interpersonal roles include figurehead, leader, and liaison activities,* **14**, *15*

Interpersonal skills, 512

Interpersonal space, 131-132, *132*

Intersectionality *The way various dimensions of individual identity overlap to create unique experiences not attributable to individual dimensions,* **DEI-5**

Intervention *Interference in an attempt to correct a problem,* **368**

Interviews
employment, 259, 303, 314-315
exit, 332

Intrapreneurs *Someone who works inside an existing organization who sees an opportunity for a product or service and mobilizes the organization's resources to try to realize it,* **201**

Intrinsic rewards *The satisfaction, such as a feeling of accomplishment, a person receives from performing a task,* **424**

Intuition *Making a choice without the use of conscious thought or logical inference,* **224**-225

Investment activities, *591*

IoT. *See* Internet of Things

ISO 9000 series *Quality-control procedures companies must install—from purchasing to manufacturing to inventory to shipping—that can be audited by independent quality-control experts, or "registrars,"* **609**

ISO 14000 series *Set of quality-control procedure that extends the concept of the ISO 9000 series, identifying standards for environmental performance,* **609**

Jargon *Terminology specific to a particular profession or group,* **542**

Job characteristics model *The job design model that consists of five core job characteristics that affect three critical psychological states of an employee that in turn affect work outcomes—the employee's motivation, performance, and satisfaction, 445,* **445**-448

Job design *The division of an organization's work among its employees and the application of motivational theories to jobs to increase satisfaction and performance,* **444**
    fitting jobs to people, 444-445
    fitting people to jobs, 444
    job characteristics model, *445,* 445-448

Job enlargement *Increasing the number of tasks in a job to increase variety and motivation,* **444**

Job enrichment *Building into a job such motivating factors as responsibility, achievement, recognition, stimulating work, and advancement,* **444**-445

Job performance. *See* Performance

Job postings
    internal, 310
    online, 311

Job satisfaction *The extent to which one feels positive or negative about various aspects of one's work,* **405**

Job security, 378

Jointly set objectives, 157-158

Joint venture *Also known as a strategic alliance; a U.S firm may form a joint venture with a foreign company to share the risks and rewards of starting a new enterprise together in a foreign country,* **119**

Judgements, avoid to make, 569

Judicial bias, *399, 399*

Justice approach *One of four approaches to solving ethical dilemmas; ethical behavior is guided by respect for impartial standards of fairness and equity,* **74**-75

Justice climate *Relates to the shared sense of fairness felt by the entire workgroup,* **438**

Justice theory, 434, 436-438

Kaizen *A Japanese philosophy of small continuous improvement that seeks to involve everyone at every level of the organization in the process of identifying opportunities and implementing and testing solutions,* **605**

Kindness, 462

Knowledge
    competitive advantage as, 353-354
    in career readiness, 29
    learning organizations and, 52-54
    task-based/functional, 162

Knowledge management *Implementation of systems and practices to increase the sharing of knowledge and information throughout an organization,* **22**

KSAs *(essential knowledge, skills, and abilities),* 10

Labor abuses, 134

Labor costs, multinationals and, 117

Labor-management issues
    arbitration and, 343
    compensation and, 342
    contract negotiation, 340, *340*
    grievance procedures, 342-343
    mediation and, 343
    union formation and, 340
    union security and workplace types, 340-341

Labor unions *Organizations of employees formed to protect and advance their members' interests by bargaining with management over job-related issues,* **339**
    formation of, 340
    as stakeholders, 67

Language differences, 131, 553

Law of effect *Behavior with favorable consequences tends to be repeated, while behavior with unfavorable consequences tends to disappear,* **448**

Layoffs, 331

Leader–member exchange (LMX) model of leadership *Model of leadership that emphasizes that leaders have different sorts of relationships with different subordinates,* **525**-526

Leader-member relations, 516, *517*

Leadership coaching *The process of enhancing the skills and abilities that a leader needs in order to help the organization achieve its goals,* **502**

Leadership *The ability to influence employees to voluntarily pursue organizational goals,* **502**
    alignment, DEI-15
    behavioral approaches, 513-515
    characteristics of, 502

    and commitment, 372-373
    contemporary perspectives, 525-533
    empowering, 529-530
    ethical, 530
    followers and, 531
    full-range model of, 520-525
    humility and, 527-528
    influence and, 506-508, *506-507*
    leader-member exchange, 525-526
    management *vs.,* 502-503, *503*
    power sources for, 504-505
    relationship-oriented, 514
    representation, DEI-15
    servant, 527
    situational approaches to, 515-517
    skills needed for, 512, *512*
    strategies for competency development, 501
    and superior performance, 522
    trait approaches to, 508-513
    transactional, 521
    transformational, 520-525

Leading *Motivating, directing, and otherwise influencing people to work hard to achieve the organization's goals,* **9**, 388, 580

Lean medium, 544

Lean Six Sigma *Quality-control approach that focuses on problem solving and performance improvement—speed with excellence—of a well-defined project,* **608**

Lean Six Sigma 4.0 *A new approach that combines the quality control and efficiency of Lean Six Sigma with the technological connectivity of Industry 4.0 (a reference to the fourth industrial revolution),* **608**-609

Learned helplessness *The debilitating lack of faith in your ability to control your environment,* **390**

Learning, 456

Learning and development (L&D)
    example, 322
    goal of, 321-322
    process of, 321-322, *322*

Learning objectives, *157*

Learning organization *An organization that actively creates, acquires, and transfers knowledge within itself and is able to modify its behavior to reflect new knowledge,* 52-54, *53, 53*

Legal defensibility *The extent to which the selection device measures job-related criteria in a way that is free from bias,* **313**

Legal issues. *See* Ethical/legal issues

Legends, 279-280

Legitimate power *One of five sources of a leader's power that results from formal positions with the organization,* **504**

Legitimating tactics, *507*

Lewin's change model, *361,* 361-362

Liabilities, 590

Licensing *Company X allows a foreign company to pay it a fee to make or distribute X's product or service,* **118**-119

Limited liability company (LLC) *A hybrid structure that combines elements of sole proprietor, partnership, and corporation,* **213**

Listening skills, 492, 539, 567–569

LLC. *See* Limited liability company

LMX model. *See* Leader-member exchange model of leadership

Local communities, as stakeholders, 67

Locus of control *Measure of how much people believe they control their fate through their own efforts,* 205, **391**

Logic, 479

Long-term goals *Tend to span one to five years and focus on achieving the strategies identified in a company's strategic plan,* **154**, 460

Love needs, 426, *427*

Low-context culture *Culture in which shared meanings are primarily derived from written and spoken words,* **127**

Low-control situation, 516, *517*

Lying, 314

Machiavellianism *A cynical view of human nature and condoning opportunistic and unethical ways of manipulating people, putting results over principles,* **509**

Machine learning *The process by which computers use algorithms and statistical models to detect patterns in data without being explicitly programmed,* **231**

Macroenvironment *In contrast to the task environment, it includes six forces: economic, technological, sociocultural, demographic, political-legal, and international,* **63**, 68–71

Maintenance role *Relationship-related role consisting of behavior that fosters constructive relationships among team members,* *481*, **481**

Management by exception *Control principle that states that managers should be informed of a situation only if data show a significant deviation from standards,* **586**

Management by objectives (MBO) *Four-step process in which (1) managers and employees jointly set objectives for the employee, (2) managers develop action plans, (3) managers and employees periodically review the employee's performance, and (4) the manager makes a performance appraisal and rewards the employee according to results,* **156**–158
  types of objectives in, *157*

Management, leadership *vs.*, 502, *503*

Managerial leadership *Involves both influencing followers to internalize and commit to a set of shared goals, and facilitating the group and individual work that is needed to accomplish those goals,* **503**–504

Managerial practices
  belongingness, DEI-21–DEI-22
  value uniqueness, DEI-22

Management theory, 39
  administrative management, 42, 44–45
  behavioral science approach, 47
  behavioral viewpoint, 45–47
  classical viewpoint, 42–45
  contingency viewpoint, 51–52
  human relations movement, 46–47
  learning organizations, 52–54, *53*
  operations management, 48–49
  quantitative viewpoints, 48–49
  reasons to study, 41
  scientific management, 43–44
  systems viewpoints, 49–51
  viewpoints om, 41, *42*

Management *The pursuit of organizational goals efficiently and effectively by integrating the work of people through planning, organizing, leading, and controlling the organization's resources,* 4, **5**
  areas of, 9–10, *10*, 11–12
  levels of, 9–11, *10*
  modern, creation of, 40–41
  organization types and, 12–13
  process of, 8, *8*
  rewards of practicing, 7–8
  rewards of studying, 7
  skills, 3
  viewpoints, progression of, 41, *42*

Managers
  and control of organizational effectiveness, 587–600
  challenges facing, 18–26
  communication channels and, 545–549
  ethical responsibilities, 71–78
  expatriate, 135
  international, 115
  international, 115–116
  leaders *vs.*, 502–503, *503*
  multiplier effect, 6
  organizational change and behavior of, 358–359
  rewards for, 7–8
  roles of, 13–15, *15*
  skill requirements for, 16–18
  social responsibilities, 78–82
  stress created by, 412
  thoughtfulness of, 458
  traits in, 18

Man's Search for Meaning (Frankl), 458–459

Maquiladoras *Foreign-owned manufacturing plants allowed to operate in Mexico with special privileges in return for employing Mexican citizens,* **117**

Market culture *Type of organizational culture that has a strong external focus and values stability and control,* **273**–274, 275

Markets, access to new markets, 117

Masculinity *vs.* femininity, 128

Matrix structure *Fourth type of organizational structure, which combines functional and divisional chains of command in a grid so that there are two command structures vertical and horizontal,* **293**, 294

MBO. *See* Management by objectives

Meaningfulness *Is characterized by a sense of being part of something you believe is bigger than yourself,* **25**, **459**

Means-end chain *A hierarchy of goals; in the chain of management (operational, tactical, strategic), the accomplishment of low-level goals are the means leading to the accomplishment of high-level goals or ends,* **25–26**, **154**

Measurable and controllable activities, 282

Measurable goals, 156

Media richness *Indication of how well a particular medium conveys information and promotes learning,* **543**–544

Mediation *The process in which a neutral third party, a mediator, listens to both sides in a dispute, makes suggestions, and encourages them to agree on a solution,* **343**

Medium *The pathway by which a message travels,* **541**

Meetings, 548–549

Men. *See* Gender

Mentor *An experienced person who provided guidance to someone new in the work world,* **8**

Mergers and acquisitions (M&A), 367

Message, 541, *541*

#MeToo movement, 332

Mexico
  collectivism in, 128
  imports from, 118
  in NAFTA, 122
  maquiladoras in, 117
  masculinity in, 139

Microaggressions *Acts of unconscious bias; include a number of seemingly tiny but repeated actions, like interrupting others, mispronouncing or mistaking someone's name, and avoiding eye contact,* **561**

Middle managers *One of four managerial levels; they implement the policies and plans of the top managers above them and supervise and coordinate the activities of the first-line managers below them,* **11**

Millennials, 53

Mindfulness 345, 417, 501, 539, 569, 574

Mindlessness *A state of reduced attention expressed in behavior that is rigid, or thoughtless,* **552**–553

Minority dissent *Dissent that occurs when a minority in a group publicly opposes the beliefs, attitudes, ideas, procedures, or policies assumed by the majority of the group,* **253**

Misinformation *Information that is false but not created with the intention of causing harm,* **563**

Mission *An organization's purpose or reason for being,* **150**
  strategic management and, 148–150

Mission statements *Statement that expresses the purpose of the organization,* 56, *148*, *149*, 149, **150**
  example of, 150

Mistakes and failure, *378*

Modular structure *Seventh type of organizational structure, in which a firm assembles product chunks, or modules, provided by outside contractors*, **295**

Monochronic time *The standard kind of time orientation in U.S. business; a preference for doing one thing at a time*, **132**-133

Moral development, ethics and, 76-77

Moral-rights approach *One of four approaches to solving ethical dilemmas; ethical behavior is guided by respect for the fundamental rights of human beings*, **74**

Most favored nation *This trading status describes a condition in which a country grants other countries favorable trading treatment such as the reduction of import duties*, **124**

Motion studies, 43

Motivating *factors* *Factors associated with job satisfaction—such as achievement, recognition, responsibility, and advancement—all of which affect the job content or the rewards of work performance*, **124, 432**

Motivating potential score (MPS), 447

Motivation *Psychological processes that arouse and direct goal-directed behavior*, **423**-425, *423*
   to become manager, 26
   compensation and rewards as, 424, 451-459
   content perspectives on, 426-433
   importance of, 425
   inspirational, 523
   intrinsic, 429
   job design perspectives on, 443-448
   for job performance, 423-426
   management by objectives and, 157-159
   managing for, 421
   model of, 423, *423*
   nonmonetary methods for, 454-459
   perspectives on, 425-426
   process perspectives on, 434-443
   reinforcement perspectives on, 448-451, 449
   on teams, 480

Multinational corporations *A business firm with operations in several countries*, **114**
   expansion and, 116-119, *118*

Multinational organization *A nonprofit organization with operations in several countries*, **114**

Multiplier effect, 6

Muslims, *133*

Mutual-benefit organizations, 13

Myths, 279

NAFTA. *See* North American Free Trade Agreement

Narcissism *A self-centered perspective, feelings of superiority, and a drive for personal power and glory*, **509**

Narrow recruiting efforts, DEI-16

Narrow span of control, 287

National Labor Relations Board (NLRB) *Legislated in 1935, U.S. commission that enforces procedures whereby employees may vote to have a union and for collective bargaining*, **334**, 340

Natural capital *The value of natural resources, such as topsoil, air, water, and genetic diversity, which humans depend on*, **80**

Needs *Physiological or psychological deficiencies that arouse behavior*, **426**

Negative reinforcement *Process of strengthening a behavior by withdrawing something negative*, **450**

Negotiated labor-management contract, 340

Networking, 163, 169, 263, 572-574

Neurodiversity *The idea that there are differences in the way people learn, think, and interact*, **DEI-10**-DEI-11

New-direction innovations, 371

Niche products, 350-351

NLRB, National Labor Relations Board

Noise *Any disturbance that interferes with the transmission of a message*, **541**, 542-543
   as communication barrier, 551
   physical, 542
   physiological, 543
   psychological, 542
   semantic, 542

Nondefensive communication *Communication that is assertive, direct, and powerful*, **566**, *566*

Nondisparagement agreement *Is a contract between two parties that prohibits one party from criticizing the other; it is often used in severance agreements to prohibit former employees from criticizing their former employers*, **332**

Nonmanagerial employees *Those who either work alone on tasks or with others on a variety of teams*, **11**

Nonprofit organizations, 12-13, 114

Nonrational models of decision making *Models of decision-making style that explain how managers make decisions; they assume that decision making is nearly always uncertain and risky, making it difficult for managers to make optimum*, **223**-225

Nonverbal communication *Messages in a form other than the written or the spoken word*, **539**, *555*-556

Norming *One of five stages of forming a team; stage three, in which conflicts are resolved, lose relationships develop, and unity and harmony emerge*, **476**

Norm of reciprocity *A powerful social norm by which we feel obligated to return favors or assistance after people have provided favors or assistance to us*, **491**

Norms *General guidelines or rules of behavior that most group or team members follow*, **482**

North American Free Trade Agreement (NAFTA) *A trading bloc consisting of the United States, Canada, and Mexico*, **122**-123

Nurture diverse relationships, DEI-26

OB. *See* Organizational behavior

Objective *Also known as goal; a specific commitment to achieve a measurable result within a stated period of time*, **154**
   types of, *157*

Objective appraisals *Also called results appraisals; performance evaluations that are based on facts and that are often numerical*, **325**-326

Obliging, conflict and, 489

Observable artifacts, 268, 268-269

Occupational Safety and Health Act (OSHA) (1970), 78, *333*, 335

OD. *See* Organizational development

Offshoring *Also called global outsourcing; use of suppliers outside the United States to provide labor, goods, or services*, **118**

Onboarding *Programs that help employees to integrate and transition to new jobs by making them familiar with corporate policies, procedures, culture, and politics by clarifying work-role expectations and responsibilities*, **320**
   best practices, 320-321
   outcomes of, 320, 320-321

Online collaboration, 471

Online job postings, 311

On-the-job activities, 32

Open-ended questions, 568

Open mind, 163-164

Open-mind, 492

Openness to change, *30*, 243, 257, 344

Openness to experience, 488

Open shop, 341

Open system *System that continually interacts with its environment*, **50**

Operant conditioning, 448

Operating activities, 592

Operating plan *Typically designed for a 1-year period, this plan defines how a manager will conduct his or her business based on the action plan; the operating plan identifies clear targets such as revenues, cash flow, and market share*, **154**

Operations management *A branch of quantitative management; focuses on managing the production and delivery of an organization's products or services more effectively*, **48**-49

Organizational change, 21-22

Operational goals *Goals that are set by and for first-line managers and are concerned with short-term matters associated with realizing tactical goals*, **154**

Operational planning *Determining how to accomplish specific tasks with available resources within the next 1-week to 1-year period; done by first-line managers,* 148, **152**

Opportunities *Situations that present possibilities for exceeding existing goals,* **221**
   controls to detect, 581

Oral/written communication, 488

Organization (in VRIO framework), 177-178

Organization *A group of people who work together to achieve some specific purpose. A system of consciously coordinated activities of two or more people,* 5, **285**
   boundaryless, 294-296, *295*
   demands, 412
   experience from, 33
   features of, 285-290, *285*
   flat, 286
   learning, 52-54, *53*
   multinational, 114
   process of, 435-436, *436*
   promotion of ethics within, 77-78
   responsibilities of, 78-82
   types of, 12-13

Organizational behavior (OB) *Behavior that is dedicated to better understanding and managing people at work,* **394**

Organizational change. *See also* Innovation
   adapting to, 581
   conflict and, 487
   external forces of, 356-358, *356*
   forms of, 359-360
   internal forces of, *356*, 358-359
   Lewin's change model, *361*, 361-362
   mechanisms to drive, 283
   nature of, 350-359
   proactive, 355, 376
   process of, 278-284
   reactive, 376
   resistance to change in, 377-379
   systems approach to, 362-365
   target elements of, 364
   technology and, *356*, 357
   as threat, 360, 376-379

Organizational chart *Box-and-lines illustration of the formal relationships of positions of authority and the organization's official positions or work specializations,* **289**-290

Organizational citizenship behaviors (OCBs) *Employee behaviors that are not directly part of employees' job descriptions—that exceed their work-role requirements—such as constructive statements about the department,* **405**-406

Organizational commitment *Behavior that reflects the extent to which an employee identifies with an organization and is committed to its goals,* **405**

Organizational culture *The set of shared, taken-for-granted implicit assumptions that a group holds and that determines how it perceives, thinks about, and reacts to its various environments,* **265**, *265*, 597
   role in DE&I
   change in, 278-284, 487
   fitting into, 263

   importance of, 215, 274-276, *275*
   leading for alignment among organizational structure/ HR practices and, 267
   learning prior to job interview, 56-57
   levels of, 268-270, *268*
   P-O fit, 276
   strategy implementation and, 264-265, *265*
   transmission of, 269-272
   types of, 272-274, *272*

Organizational design *Creating the optimal structures of accountability and responsibility that an organization uses to execute its strategies,* **290**
   boundaryless, 294-296, *295*
   horizontal, 294, *294*
   traditional, 291-293, *291-293*

Organizational development (OD) *Set of techniques for implementing planned change to make people and organizations more effective,* **366**
   applications of, 366-367
   effectiveness of, 368-369

Organizational goals and criteria, 281, DEI-20

Organizational opportunities *Environmental factors that the organization may exploit for competitive advantage,* **177**

Organizational practices
   business strategy, DEI-23
   data tracking, DEI-24
   meaningful conversations, DEI-23-DEI-24

Organizational socialization *The process by which people learn the values, norms, and required behaviors that permit them to participate as members of an organization,* **271**-272

Organizational strengths *The skills and capabilities that give the organization special competencies and competitive advantages in executing strategies in pursuit of its mission,* **177**

Organizational structure *A formal system of task and reporting relationships that coordinates and motivates an organization's members so that they can work together to achieve the organization's goals,* **265**-266, 282
   hollow, 294-295, *295*
   horizontal, 294, *294*
   for innovation, 373-374
   leading for alignment among organizational culture/ HR practices and, 267
   modular, 295
   strategy implementation and, 265, 266
   traditional, 291-293, *291-293*
   types of, 290-296
   virtual, 295-296

Organizational systems and procedures, 282

Organizational threats *Environmental factors that hinder an organization's achieving a competitive advantage,* **177**

Organizational weaknesses *The drawbacks that hinder an organization in executing strategies in pursuit of its mission,* **177**

Organization chart *Box-and-lines illustration of the formal relationships of positions of authority and the organization's official positions or work specializations,* **289**-290, *290*

Organizing *Arranging tasks, people, and other resources to accomplish the work,* **9**, **580**, *580*

OSHA. *See* Occupational Safety and Health Act

Out-group exchange, 526

Outputs, 364

Outsourcing *Using suppliers outside the company to provide goods and services,* **117**, **607**
   quality improvement and, 607

Overconfidence bias *Bias in which people's subjective confidence in their decision making is greater than their objective accuracy,* **249**

Overdelivering, 263

Overloading, 544

Oversimplification, information, 544

Owners *All those who can claim the organization as their legal property,* **65**

Paraphrasing *Form of communication that occurs when people restate in their words the crux of what they heard or read,* **542**, 552

Parochialism *A narrow view in which people see things solely through their own perspective,* **115**

Partnership *A relationship between two or more persons who join to carry on a trade or business,* 65, **212**-213

Patents *Licenses with which the government authorizes a person or company to exclude others from making using or selling an invention for a time,* **206**

Path–goal leadership model *Approach that holds that the effective leader makes available to followers desirable rewards in the workplace and increases their motivation by clarifying the paths, or behavior, that will help them achieve those goals and providing them with support,* **517**-519, *518*

Patient Protection and Affordable Care Act (2010), *333*, 335

Pay for knowledge *Situation in which employees' pay is tied to the number of job-relevant skills they have or academic degrees they earn,* **454**

Pay for performance *Situation in which an employee's pay is based on the results he or she achieves,* **453**

Pay gaps, DEI-23

PDCA cycle *A Plan-Do-Check-Act cycle using observed data for continuous improvement of operations,* **602**, *602*

Peer pressure, 378

People orientation, 604

Perception *Awareness; interpreting and understanding one's environment*, **398**
and behavior, 397–402
casual attribution and, 400–401
distortions in, 398–401
halo effect and, 400
recency effect and, 400
self-fulfilling prophecy and, 401–402
steps in process of, 398, *398*

Performance
controls to monitor, 580–582
effect of conflict on, 484, *485*
evaluation of, 158, 407
standards of, 584–586
stress and, 408, *410*

Performance appraisal *A management process that consists of (1) assessing an employee's performance and (2) providing him or her with feedback; also called a performance review*, **324**–325

Performance improvement plans (PIPs) *Formal policies of progressive discipline that outline employee performance problems, routes to and timelines for improvement, and consequences for not meeting plan objectives*, **331**

Performance management *A set of processes and managerial behaviors that involve defining, monitoring, measuring, evaluating, and providing consequences for performance expectations*, **192, 323**
example of, 324
procedural steps, 323, *323*

Performance measures, 583–584

Performance objectives, *157*

Performance orientation, 129, 130

Performance tests, 316

Performance-to-reward expectancy, 439

Performing *The fourth of five stages of forming a team, in which members concentrate on solving problems and completing the assigned task*, **476**, 477

Personal adaptability, 136, 297–298

Personal appeals, 506

Personal brand, 169

Personal communication barriers, 551–553

Personality *The stable psychological traits and behavioral attributes that give a person his or her identity*, **388**
core self-evaluations, 389–392
dimensions, 388–389
emotional intelligence, 392–394
tests, 388

Personality conflict *Interpersonal opposition based on personal dislike, disagreement, or differing styles*, **485**

Personality tests, 316, 388

Personalized power *Power directed at helping oneself*, **504**

Personal power, 509

Person factors *The various individual differences that make individuals the unique people they are*, **DEI-13**–DEI-15

expectations and attributions, DEI-14–DEI-15
fear, DEI-13
misperceptions, DEI-13–DEI-14

Person–job (P–J) fit *The extent to which a worker's competencies and needs match with a specific job*, **312**

Person–organization (PO) fit *The extent to which your personality and values match the climate and culture of an organization*, **276, 312**, 284

Perspective taking *Viewing the world from another person's perspective*, **DEI-26**

Philanthropy *Making charitable donations to benefit humankind*, **81**

Phubbing, 561, 574

Physical communication barriers, 551, *551*

Physical design, 280–281

Physical distance, as communication barrier, 551

Physical noise, 542

Physiological needs, 426, *427*

Physiological noise, 543

Piece rate *Pay based on how much output an employee produces*, **453**

Plan *A document that outlines how goals are going to be met*, **145**

Planning *Setting goals and deciding how to achieve them; also, coping with uncertainty by formulating future courses of action to achieve specified results*, 9, **144**–146. *See also* Decision making; Strategic management; Strategic planning
for career, 143
control and, 580, *580*
fundamentals of, 148–153
importance of, 146–147

Planning/control cycle *A continuous process managers use to evaluate the progress in achieving strategic goals and to make modifications as needed*, *161*, **160**–161

PO fit. *See* Person-organization fit

Political stability, 133–134

Political–legal forces *Changes in the way politics shape laws and laws shape the opportunities for and threats to an organization*, **70**

Politics, 358

Polycentric managers *Managers who take the view that native managers in the foreign offices best understand native personnel and practices, and so the home office should leave them alone*, **116**

Polychronic time *The standard kind of time orientation in Mediterranean, Latin American, and Arab cultures; a preference for doing more than one thing at a time*, **133**

Porter's four competitive strategies *Also called four generic strategies; (1) cost leadership, (2) differentiation, (3) cost-focus, and (4) focused-differentiation. The first two strategies focus on wide markets, the last two on narrow markets*, **186**–188

Porter's model for industry analysis *Model proposes that business-level strategies originate in five primary competitive forces in the firm's environment: (1) threats of new entrants, (2) bargaining power of suppliers, (3) bargaining power of buyers, (4) threats of substitute products or services, and (5) rivalry among competitors*, **185**–186

Position power, 516, 517

Positiveness, 349, 414–415, 573

Positive reinforcement *The use of positive consequences to strengthen a particular behavior*, **449**–451

Power distance, 128, *129*

Power *The ability to marshal human, informational, and other resources to get something done*, **504**
need for, 427–428, 429
position, 516, *517*
sources of, 504–505

Pressure, *507*

The Practice of Management (Drucker), 40

Predictive analytics *Combines historical data with statistical models and machine learning to specify the likelihood of future outcomes*, **231**

Private investors, 65

Privacy Act (1974), *333*

Privacy *The right of people not to reveal information about themselves*, **561**–563

Proactive change *Planned change; making carefully thought-out changes in anticipation of possible or expected problems or opportunities; opposite of reactive change*, **355**

Proactive learning orientation *The desire to learn and improve your knowledge, soft skills, and other characteristics in pursuit of personal development*, **32**, 163, 501

Proactivity, 204

Problems *Difficulties that inhibit the achievement of goals*, **221**
causes of occurrence, 39
defined, 39

Problem solving, 39, 162, 258, 349

Procedural justice *The perceived fairness of the process and procedures used to make allocation decisions*, **436**

Process *A series of actions or steps followed to bring about a desired result*, **33**, 34

Process innovation *A change in the way a product or service is conceived, manufactured, or disseminated*, **370**

Process perspectives *Theories of employee motivation concerned with the thought processes by which people decide how to act*, **434**
equity/justice theory, 433–434, *435*
expectancy theory, 439–440, *439*
goal-setting theory, 441–443

Product divisions *Divisional structures in which activities are grouped around similar products or services,* **292**

Product innovation *A change in the appearance or the performance of a product or a service or the creation of a new one,* **370–371,** *370*

Production-centered leader behaviors *Emphasize the technical or task-related aspects of employees' roles,* **514**

Productivity, **407,** **594**
benchmarking and, 594
best practices and, 594–595
control systems and, 581

Professionalism, 83

Profit sharing *The distribution to employees of a percentage of the company's profits,* **453**

Profit, social responsibility and, *81*

Programmed conflict *Conflict designed to elicit different opinions without inciting people's personal feelings,* **487**

Project management software *Programs for planning and scheduling the people, costs, and resources to complete a project on time,* **22**

Prosocial behavior (PSB) *Voluntary behavior intended to benefit another, such as helping, donating, sharing, and comforting,* **447,** 480, 481

Prosocial motivation (PSM) *The desire to promote the well-being of others,* **447–448**

Protected class *Refers to a group of people protected from employment discrimination based on a specific characteristic or identity they share,* **DEI-9,** **DEI-9–DEI-10**

Protective tariffs, 120

Psychological capital *Positive state of psychological development that is characterized by high levels of hope, resiliency, optimism, and self-efficacy,* **345**

Psychological contract *Represents your perception of the terms that govern your exchange relationship with another party,* **18–19**

Psychological empowerment *Employees' belief that they have control over their work,* **529–530**

Psychological noise, 542

Psychopathy *A lack of concern for others, impulsive behavior, and a dearth of remorse when the psychopath's actions harm others,* **510**

Punctuated equilibrium *Establishes periods of stable functioning until an event causes a dramatic change in norms, roles, and/or objectives resulting in the establishment and maintenance of new norms of functioning, returning to equilibrium,* **477,** 477

Punishment *The process of weakening behavior by presenting something negative or withdrawing something positive,* **450**

Pygmalion effect, 401–402

Quality *The total ability of a product or service to meet customer needs,* 595, **20,** **601**

Deming management and, 601–602

Quality assurance *A means of ensuring quality that focuses on the performance of workers, urging employees to strive for "zero defects,"* **601**

Quality control *A means of ensuring quality whereby errors are minimized by managing each stage of production,* **601**

Quantitative management *The application to management of quantitative techniques, such as statistics and computer simulations. Two branches of quantitative management are management science and operations management,* **48**

Quantitative viewpoint, 48–49

Questions
curious, 569
judgmental, 569
noncurious, 569
nonjudgmental, 569
open-ended, 568

Quid pro quo harassment, 337

Quotas
avoidance of, 117
import, 120

Radically innovative change *Introduces a practice that is new to the industry,* **360**

Rarity (in VRIO framework), 177–178, *178*

Rational model of decision making *Also called the classical model; the style of decision making that explains how managers should make decisions; it assumes that managers will make logical decisions that are the optimal means of furthering the organization's best interests,* **220**
problems related to, 222, *222*
stages in, *220,* 221–222

Rational persuasion, 603

Reactive change *Change made in response to problems or opportunities as they arise; compare proactive change,* **355**

Readiness for change *The beliefs, attitudes, and intentions of the organization's staff regarding the extent of the changes needed and how willing and able they are to implement them,* **362–363**

Receiver barrier, 550

Receiver *The person for whom the message is intended,* **540,** *541*

Recency effect *The tendency of people to remember recent information better than earlier information,* **400**

Recharging, self-motivation strategy, 461

Recruiting *The process of locating and attracting qualified applicants for jobs open in the organization,* **307–312**

Reduced cycle time *The reduction of steps in the work process,* **607**

Referent power *One of five sources of a leader's power deriving from personal attraction,* **505**

Reflection, 258

Refreezing stage of organizational change, 361, 362

Reinforcement *Anything that causes a given behavior to be repeated or inhibited; the four types are positive, negative, extinction, and punishment,* **449**

Reinforcement theory *The belief that behavior reinforced by positive consequences tends to be repeated, whereas behavior reinforced by negative consequences tends not to be repeated,* **448–**449

Related diversification *When a company purchases a new business that is related to the company's existing business portfolio,* **184**

Relatedness needs, 429–430

Relationship management, *392*

Relationship-oriented leadership *Form of leadership that is primarily concerned with the leader's interactions with their people,* **514**

Relationship-oriented role, 481

Reliability *Degree to which a test measures the same thing consistently, so that an individual's score remains about the same over time, assuming the characteristics being measured also remain the same,* **313**

Religious practices, during COVID-19, 355

Religious values, 133

Repatriation, 135

Representative bias *The tendency to generalize from a small sample or a single event,* 247–**248**

Reputation, corporate, 560

Resentments, 330

Reshoring, 118

Resilience *Generally defined as the ability to recover from setbacks, adapt well to change, and keep going in the face of adversity,* **31–32,** 413–414

Resistance to change *An emotional/behavioral response to real or imagined threats to an established work routine,* **377,** 377–379

Responsibility *The obligation one has to perform the assigned tasks,* **288**

Results-oriented goals, 156

Résumés, 313–314

Retrenchment strategy. *See* Defensive strategy

Revenue, social responsibility and, *81*

Revenue tariffs, 120

Revised path–goal theory, 517–518, *518*

Reward power *One of five sources of a leader's power that results from the authority to reward subordinates,* **504**

Rewards, 281, DEI–20
extrinsic, 424

intrinsic, 424
for managers, 7–8
as motivation, 424
nonreinforcing, 378

Rich medium, 544

Right-to-work laws *Statutes that prohibit employees from being required to join a union as a condition of employment,* **341**, *341*

Risk propensity, 204
as entrepreneur trait, 99

Rites and rituals *The activities and ceremonies, planned and unplanned, that celebrate important occasions and accomplishments in an organization's life,* **271**, 279, DEI-20

Robots, 243

Role ambiguity, 411–412

Role conflict, 411

Role modeling, 280

Role overload, 411

Roles *Socially determined expectations of how individuals should behave in a specific position,* **411**–412, **480**–481, *481*

Russia, emerging economy of, 125, 130

Russia–Ukraine War, 113

Sabbaticals, 456

Safety, 595

Safety culture, 283

Safety needs, 426, *427*

Salaries, 318

Sales, social media and, 559–560

Sales commission *The percentage of a company's earnings as the result of a salesperson's sales that is paid to that salesperson,* **453**

Sanction *The trade prohibition on certain types of products, services, or technology to another country for a specific reason,* **121**

Sarbanes-Oxley Act of 2002 *Often shortened to SarbOx or SOX, established requirements for proper financial record keeping for public companies and penalties for noncompliance,* **75**–76, *333*

Satisficing model *One type of nonrational decision-making model; managers seek alternatives until they find one that is satisfactory, not optimal,* **223**

Sayings, 279

Scenario analysis *The creation of alternative hypothetical but equally likely future conditions,* **180**

Scientific management *Management approach that emphasizes the scientific study of work methods to improve the productivity of individual workers,* **43**–44, *444*

S corporations, 213

Securities and Exchange Commission (SEC), 75, 78, 226

Security *A system of safeguards for protecting information technology against disasters, system failures, and unauthorized access that result in damage or loss,* **561**, 562

Selection process *The screening of job applicants to hire the best candidate,* **313**
background information for, 313–314
interviews for, 314–315

Self-actualization needs, 426, *427*

Self-affirmations *Positive statements that impact your subconscious mind by drawing attention to your values and positive attributes and away from negative self-perceptions,* 61, **379**–381

Self-appraisals, 326

Self-assessments
acquired needs, 429
adaptability, 377
assessing groupthink, 253
attitudes toward unions, 343
balanced scorecard, 597
Big Five dimensions of personality, 389
climate, 567
communication competence, 565
conflict-management style, 489
consumer ethnocentrism, 115
corporate responsibility attitudes, 82
decision-making style, 246
emotional intelligence level, 394
employment in learning organizations, 54
engagement in studies, 404
entrepreneurial spirit, 205
experience, 606
extrinsic or intrinsic rewards, 425
generalized self-efficacy, 390
global manager potential, 136
influence tactics, 507
innovation in organizational climate, 373
interpersonal conflict tendencies, 484
intuition level, 225
job satisfaction, 405
leader-member exchange, 526
leadership role, 503
listening style, 570
measuring perceived fair interpersonal treatment, 437
motivation to lead, 26
needs for self-determination, 431
obstacles to strategic execution, 192
openness to change at work, 355
organizational culture, 274
organizational culture, preferred type of, 284
participation in group decision making, 254
person-job fit, 312
positive approach at work, 396
power, preference of, 506
proactive learning orientation, 158
problem-solving potential, 222
productive energy of team, 477
quality of HR practices, 305
readiness for change, 363
resistance to change, 379
responsibility for actions, 31
social media readiness, 565
social networking, 558
standing on GLOBE dimensions, 130
strategic planning, 188

strategic thinking, 175
task-and relationship-oriented leader behavior, 515
team effectiveness, 482
teamwork, attitudes toward, 469
total quality management, 610
transformational leadership, 524
Theory X *vs.* Theory Y orientation, 47

Self-awareness, 32, 136, 534–535

Self-compassion *Tendency to be understanding, kind, and warm toward yourself in the process of pain or failure, instead of being self-critical or over-identifying with negative emotions,* 61, **345**, 381–382

Self-determination theory *Theory that assumes that people are driven to try to grow and attain fulfillment, with their behavior and well-being influenced by three universal needs: competence, autonomy, and relatedness,* **429**–431

Self-efficacy *Belief in one's personal ability to do a task,* 316, **389**–390, 528

Self-employment *A way of working for yourself as a freelancer or the owner of a business rather than for an employer,* **201**

Self-esteem *Self-respect; the extent to which people like or dislike themselves,* **391**

Self-fulfilling prophecy *Also known as the Pygmalion effect; the phenomenon in which people's expectations of themselves or others leads them to behave in ways that make those expectations come true,* **401**

Self-managed teams *Groups of workers who are given administrative oversight for their task domains,* **471**

Self-management, 392, 416–417

Self-motivation, 421

Self-regulation *The process of managing your attitudes, emotions, and motivation as you achieve your goals,* **579**

Self-serving bias *The attributional tendency to take more personal responsibility for success than for failure,* **401**

Semantic noise, 542–543

Sender barrier, *550*

Sender *The person wanting to share information,* **540**, *541*

Servant leadership *A model of leadership that focuses on benefiting multiple stakeholders,* **527**

Services companies, 605–606

Sexual harassment *Unwanted sexual attention that creates an adverse work environment,* **337**–338
actions to prevent, 337–338
types of, 337

Sham participation *Occurs when powerless, but useful individuals are selected by leaders to rubber stamp decisions and work hard to implement them,* **251**

Shared values, 55

Shareholders, 588–592

Short-term goals *Tend to span 12 month and are connected to strategic goals in a hierarchy known as a means-end chain,* **154, 251,** 460-461

Simple structure *The first type of organizational structure, whereby an organization has authority centralized in a single person, as well as a flat hierarchy, few rules, and low work specialization,* **291**

Situational approaches *An approach to leadership where it is believed that effective leadership behavior depends on the situation at hand,* 515-520

Situational interview *A structured interview in which the interviewer focuses on hypothetical situations,* **314**

Six Sigma *A rigorous statistical analysis process that reduces defects in manufacturing and service-related industries,* **608**

Skills. *See also* Soft skills
 and communication, 552
 business, *512*
 conceptual, 16-17
 conceptual, 512
 human, 17
 interpersonal, 512
 listening, 491-492, 539, 568-569
 management, 3
 soft, 17
 speaking, 570-572, *572*
 technical, 16
 writing, 570

Skill variety, 445

Slogans, 279

Small businesses, 198, 206

SMART goals *A goal that is Specific, Measurable, Attainable, Results oriented, and has Target dates,* **155**-156

Smart manufacturing, 608

Social awareness, 392

Social capital *Economic or productive potential of strong, trusting, and cooperative relationships,* **307**

Social entrepreneurship *Identifies and pursues business opportunities to change society for the better,* **201**-203, *202*

Social intelligence, 488

Social loafing *A phenomenon in which a team member puts forth less effort in the team than they would if they were working alone,* **494**

Socialized power *Power directed at helping others,* **504**

Social media *Internet-based and mobile technologies used to generate interactive dialogue with members of a network,* 169, **556-565**
 age distribution of usage, 557, *557*
 brand recognition and, 559-560
 crowdsourcing and, 559
 downsides of, 560-564
 as external recruitment source, 311
 hiring decisions and, 303, 558
 impact of, 556-557
 innovation in, 559

 networks, 558
 policy creation for, 564-565, *564*
 sales and, 559-560

Social media policy *Describes the who, how, when, and for what purposes of social media use, and the consequences for non-compliance,* **564-565,** *564*

Social responsibility
 climate change and, 80
 corporate, 79-80
 philanthropy and, 81
 viewpoints on, 80

Social Security Act of 1935 *Established the U.S. retirement system,* **334**

Social support, 61

Society for Human Resource Management (SHRM), 407, DEI-24

Sociocultural forces *Influences and trends originating in a country's, a society's, or a culture's human relationships and values that may affect an organization,* **69**-70, *70*

Soft skills *The interpersonal "people" skills needed for success at all levels,* **17,** 30-31

Sole proprietor *Someone who completely owns an unincorporated business,* 65, **212**

South Africa, emerging economy of, 125, *125*

Span of control *The number of people reporting directly to a given manager,* **287,** 287

Speaking skills, 571-572, *571*

Special-interest groups *Groups whose members try to influence specific issues,* **68**

Specificity of goals, 156, 443

Stability strategy *One of three grand strategies, this strategy involves little or no significant change,* **182**

Stakeholders *People whose interests are affected by an organization's activities,* **63,** 357-358
 external, 63, *64*, 65-71
 internal, 63-65, *64*
 roles in creating shared value, 96-101

Standard of living *Is the level of necessaries, comforts and luxuries that a person is accustomed to enjoy,* **207**

Start-up *Newly created company designed to grow fast,* **205**
 considerations for, 198-199
 culture and design for, 215
 failure, causes for, 216
 financing for, 213-215
 ideas for, 208-209
 legal structure for, 212-213
 plans for, 210-212
 trends for, 198, *198*

Statement of cash flows *Reports the cash generated and used over a specific period of time,* **590-592**

Static budget, 589

Statistical process control *A statistical technique that uses periodic random samples from production runs to see if quality is being maintained within a standard range of acceptability,* **607**

Stereotypes *Are generalizations that we make about groups of people,* **DEI-13**

Stereotyping *The tendency to attribute to an individual the characteristics one believes are typical of the group to which that individual belongs,* **398**-399

Stockholders, 65

Stock options *The right to buy a company's stock at a future date for a discounted price,* **453-454**

Storming *The second of five stages of forming a team in which individual personalities, roles, and conflicts within the group emerge,* **475-476**

Story *A narrative based on true events, which is repeated—and sometimes embellished upon—to emphasize a particular value,* **270,** 279

Strategic allies *The relationship of two organizations who join forces to achieve advantages neither can perform as well alone,* **67,** 119

Strategic control *Monitoring performance to ensure that strategic plans are being implemented and taking corrective action as needed,* **174,** 192-193

Strategic goals *Goals that are set by and for top management and focus on objectives for the organization as a whole,* **154**

Strategic human resource management *The process of designing and implementing systems of policies and practices that align an organization's human capital with its strategic objectives,* **305**
 approach to, 307-309
 external fit, 307
 human capital, 307
 internal fit, 306

Strategic implementation, 189-193, 231

Strategic management *A process that involves managers from all parts of the organization in the formulation and the implementation of strategies and strategic goals,* **145,** *146*, 146-147
 BCG matrix and, 182-184, *183*
 forecasting and, 179-180
 importance of, 146-147
 levels of, 171-172
 mission statement and, 148-150, *149*
 process of, *173*, 173-175
 strategic positioning, 170
 SWOT analysis and, **175**-177, *176*
 VRIO analysis and, 177-179, *178*

Strategic planning *Determines what the organization's long-term goals should be for the next one to five years with the resources they expect to have available,* *146*, 146-148, **152**

Strategic positioning *Strategy that attempts to achieve sustainable competitive advantage by preserving what is distinctive about a company,* **170**

Strategic thinking, 194-195

Strategy *A large-scale action plan that sets the direction for an organization,* **145**

Strategy formulation *The process of choosing among different strategies and altering them to best fit the organization's needs,* **174**

Strategy implementation *The implementation of strategic plans,* **174**

Strategy map *A visual representation of the four perspectives of the balanced scorecard that enables managers to communicate their goals so that everyone in the company can understand how their jobs are linked to the overall objectives of the organization,* **599**–**600**

Stress *The tension people feel when they are facing or enduring extraordinary demands, constraints, or opportunities and are uncertain about their ability to handle them effectively,* **408**
   components of, 409–410
   effects of, 408–410
   methods to reduce, 413–414
   sources of, 410–413

Stressors *Environmental characteristics that cause stress,* **404**, 409–410
   methods to reduce, 413–414

Stretch goals *Goals beyond what someone actually expects to achieve,* **441**

Structured interviews *Interviews in which the interviewer asks each applicant the same questions and then compares the responses to a standardized set of answers,* **314**

Student loans, 422

Styles, communication, 554

Subjective appraisals *Performance evaluations based on a manager's perceptions of an employee's traits or behaviors,* **326**

Substitute products/services, 186

Subsystems *The collection of parts making up the whole system,* **50**

Sunk-cost bias *Way of thinking in which managers add up all the money already spent on a project and conclude it is too costly to simply abandon it; also called the sunk-cost fallacy,* **248**
   bargaining power of, 186

Suppliers *People or organizations that provide supplies—that is, raw materials, services, equipment, labor, or energy—to other organizations,* **66**

Supplies, availability of, 116

Supply chain *The sequence of suppliers that contribute to creating and delivering a product, from raw materials to production to final buyers,* 48, **611**

Suspending judgment, 163–164

Sustainable competitive advantage *Exists when other companies cannot duplicate the value delivered to customers,* **175**

Sustainable development *Focuses on meeting present needs while simultaneously ensuring that future generations will be able to meet their needs,* 24–**25**
   shared value and, 55

Sustainable Development Goals (SDGs), 24–25, 102–103
   for creating shared value, 96–98, *97*

SWOT analysis *Also known as a situational analysis, the search for the Strengths, Weaknesses, Opportunities, and Threats affecting the organization,* **175**–177, *176*

Symbol *An object, act, quality, or event that conveys meaning to others,* **270**

Synergy *Situation in which the economic value of separate, related businesses under one ownership and management is greater together than the businesses are worth separately,* **50**

System *A set of interrelated parts that operate together to achieve a common purpose,* **50**

Systems approach to organizational change, 362–365, *363*

Systems viewpoint *Perspective that regards the organization as a system of interrelated parts,* 49–51, **50**

Tactical goals *Goals that are set by and for middle managers and focus on the actions needed to achieve strategic goals,* **154**

Tactical planning *Determining what contributions departments or similar work units can make with their given resources during the next 6 months to 2 years; done by middle management,* 148, **152**, *153*

Tactics, influence, **506**–508

Taft-Hartley Act (1947), 334

Talent management *Approach to strategic HRM that matches high-potential employees with an organization's most strategically valuable positions,* **308**–309

Talent marketplaces *Digital platforms that use AI to match existing employees with job openings, training opportunities, and mentoring relationships,* **311**

Target dates, for goals, 156

Tariffs *A trade barrier in the form of a customs duty, or tax, levied mainly on imports,* 117, **120**

Task-based knowledge, 162

Task environment *Eleven groups that present you with daily tasks to handle: customers, competitors, suppliers, distributors, strategic allies, employee organizations, local communities, financial institutions, government regulators, special-interest groups, and mass media,* **63**, 66–68

Task identity, 446

Task-oriented leadership behaviors *Ensure that human, physical, and other resources are deployed efficiently and effectively to accomplish the group's or organization's goals,* **514**–515

Task role *Behavior that concentrates on getting the team's task done,* **480**–481, *481*

Task significance, 446

Task structure, 516, *517*

Team *A small group of people working together with a common purpose, performance goals, and mutual accountability,* **468**. *See also* Groups
   accountability of, 479–480
   building, 478–482
   composition of, 480
   effect of controls on, 582
   groups *vs.*, 468
   high-performance, 482
   managing conflict in, 483–489
   member, 490–491
   motivation of, 479–480
   norms for, 482
   project, 470
   roles of individuals on, **480**–481, *481*
   self-managed, 471
   stages of development for, 474–477, *475*
   trust on, 479
   types of, 469–474
   virtual, *471*, 471–474
   work, 469–470

Team-based design. *See* Horizontal design

Team charter *Outlines how a team will manage teamwork activities,* **496**, 497

Team composition *Reflects the collection of jobs, personalities, values, knowledge, experience, and skills of team members,* **480**

Team conflict, 467

Team design *Involves choosing the best type of team to accomplish a goal,* **473**

Team development *The process of assembling individuals in a team, getting acquainted with each other, and working together to achieve a common goal,* **473**

Team leaders *Facilitate team members' activities to help teams achieve their goals,* **11**

Team management processes *The actions, feelings, and thoughts that influence team members interactions and the team's effectiveness,* **473**

Team member interdependence *The extent to which team members rely on common task-related team inputs, such as resources, information, goals, and rewards, and the amount of interpersonal interactions needed to complete the work,* **480**

Team processes *Team members' interdependent acts that transform inputs to outcomes through activities directed toward organizing taskwork to achieve collective goals,* **496**–497

Team reflexivity *A collective process by which members reflect on the team's objectives, strategies, methods, and processes and adapt accordingly,* **497**

Team viability *Team members' satisfaction with and desire to remain a member in the team,* **473**–474

Team voice *The extent to which team members feel free to express opinions, concerns, proposals, or thoughts about work-related issues,* **496**

Teamwork, 487–488

Technical skills *Skills that consist of the job-specific knowledge needed to perform well in a specialized field,* **16**

Technological forces *New developments in methods for transforming resources into goods or services,* **69**

Technology *Not just computer technology; refers to any machine or process that enables an organization to gain a competitive advantage in changing materials used to produce a finished product,* **357**
    communication and, 556–565
    empathy and, 393–394
    implicit bias and, 399–400
    managing for, 20–22
    organizational change and, 356, 356–358

TED talks, 571

Telecommute *To work from home or remote locations using a variety of information technologies,* **21**

Telecommuting, 455

Tensions, DEI-11–DEI-12

Tests. *See* Employment tests

Theories, 39

Theory X, 47

Theory Y, 47

Thoughtfulness, 458

360-degree assessment/feedback appraisal *A performance appraisal in which employees are appraised not only by their managerial superiors but also by peers, subordinates, and sometimes clients,* **327–328**

Thrusters, 364

Time orientation, 132

Time schedule, 461

Tipping culture, *127*

Titles, 281

Tolerance for ambiguity, 244, *244*

Top managers *Managers who determine what the organization's long-term goals should be for the next 1–5 years with the resources they expect to have available,* **10–11**

Total quality management (TQM) *A comprehensive approach—led by top management and supported throughout the organization—dedicated to continuous quality improvement, training, and customer satisfaction,* **604**
    applied to services, 605–606
    core principles of, 604–605
    Deming management, 601–602
    overview, 601
    quality assurance, 601
    quality control, 601
    research takeaways, 609–610
    tools and techniques, 556–557

Touch, 555–556

Toxic Substances Control Act (1976), 335

TPP. *See* Trans-Pacific Partnership

TQM. *See* Total quality management

Trade, 120–121, *122*

Trade balance *Difference between a country's imports' and exports' monetary value,* **69**

Trade deficit, 69

Trade protectionism *The use of government regulations to limit the import of goods and services,* **120**

Trade surplus, 69

Trading bloc *Also known as an economic community, it is a group of nations within a geographical region that have agreed to remove trade barriers with one another,* 122–124, *123*

Training, in organizational values, 280

Trait appraisals, 326

Trait approaches to leadership *Attempts to identify distinctive characteristics that account for the effectiveness of leaders,* 509–513

Traits
    dark triad, 513
    of entrepreneurs, 99
    gender and, 510–512
    in managers, 18
    positive, 509–510, *509*

Transactional leadership *Leadership style that focuses on clarifying employees' roles and task requirements and providing rewards and punishments contingent on performance,* 520–**521**

Transfer *Movement of an employee to a different job with similar responsibility,* **330**

Transformational leadership *Leadership style that transforms employees to pursue organizational goals over self-interests,* **521**–524

Travel, international, 109, 194

Trend analysis *A hypothetical extension of a past series of events into the future,* **179**–180

Triple bottom line (TBL) *Representing people, planet, and profit (the 3 Ps)-measures an organization's social, environmental, and financial performance,* **62**

Trust *Reciprocal faith in others' intentions and behaviors,* **479**
    of teams, 479

Trustworthiness, 552

Tuition reimbursement, 456

Turnover, 407

Two core principles of TQM (1) *People orientation—everyone involved with the organization should focus on delivering value to customers—and (2) improvement orientation—everyone should work on continuously improving the work processes,* **604**–605

Two-factor theory *Theory that proposes that work satisfaction and dissatisfaction arise from two different work factors—work satisfaction from so-called motivating factors and work dissatisfaction from so-called hygiene factors,* **431**–433

Two-tier wage contracts *Contracts in which new employees are paid less or receive lesser benefits than veteran employees have,* **342**

Type A behavior pattern *Behavior describing people involved in a chronic, determined struggle to accomplish more in less time,* **411**

Uncertainty, adapting to, 581

Uncertainty avoidance, 129, *129*

Unfreezing stage of organizational change, 361–362

Ukraine, Russian invasion of, 113

Unemployment, 69

Unions. *See* Labor unions

Union security clause *Part of a labor-management agreement that states that employees who receive union benefits must join the union, or at least pay dues to it,* **340**

Union shop, 341

Uniqueness, DEI-7

United Nations (UN), 24–25
    Sustainable Development Goals, 24–25, 96–98, *97*, 102–103

United States–Mexico–Canada Agreement (USMCA) *The United States, Mexico, and Canada renegotiated NAFTA in November 2018, drafting a new policy known as the United States-Mexico-Canada Agreement (USMCA)* **122–123**

Unity of command *Principle that stresses an employee should report to no more than one manager in order to avoid conflicting priorities and demands,* **286**

Unrelated diversification *Occurs when a company acquires another company in a completely unrelated businesses,* **185**

Unstructured interviews *Interviews in which the interviewer asks probing questions to find out what the applicant is like,* **314**–315

Upward communication *Communication that flows from lower levels to higher levels,* 545–546, *545*

Utilitarian approach *One of four approaches to solving ethical dilemmas; ethical behavior is guided by what will result in the greatest good for the greatest number of people,* **74**

Vacations, 456

Valence *The value or the importance a worker assigns to a possible outcome or reward,* **440**

Validity *Extent to which a test measures what it purports to measure and extent to which it is free of bias,* **313**

Value *The extent to which analyzing data produces insights that contribute to an organization's effectiveness,* **134, 234**

Value (in VRIO framework), 177

Value orientation, 244

Value chain *Consists of all of the processes a company uses to add value to its products or services,* 92-93, 94

Values *Abstract ideals that guide one's thinking and behavior across all situations; the relatively permanent and deeply held underlying beliefs and attitudes that help determine a person's behavior,* 72, **234**, **395**
  behavior and, 394-395, 397
  enacted values, 269
  espoused, 269
  example of, 151

Value system *The pattern of values within an organization,* **72**

Values statement *Expresses what the company stands for, its core priorities, the values its employees embody, and what its products contribute to the world,* 148, **151**, 173, 269

Variable budgets *Allowing the allocation of resources to vary in proportion with various levels of activity,* **590**

Variety *Different sources of data generated by humans or machines,* **283**

Velocity *The speed at which data accumulates,* **233**

Venezuela, expropriations in, 134

Venture capital *Is money provided by investors to start-up firms and small businesses with high risk but perceived long-term growth potential, in return for an ownership stake,* **68**

Venture capitalists (VCs) *Those who exchange funds for an ownership share in the company,* **214**

Veracity *The degree to which data is of high quality and comes from a trustworthy source,* **233**-234

Vertical communication, 545-546

Vertical hierarchy of authority, 289

Vertical integration *Diversification strategy where a firm expands into businesses that provide the supplies it needs to make its products or that distribute and sells its products,* **185**

Vertical loading, 444-445

Videoconferencing *Using video and audio links along with computers to let people in different locations see, hear, and talk with one another,* **22**

Virtual structure *An organization whose members are geographically apart, usually working with e-mail, collaborative computing, and other computer connections,* **295**-296

Virtual teams *A team composed of members in different geographic locations who use technology to work together and achieve common goals,* **471**-473

Vision *A long-term goal describing "what" an organization wants to become; it casts a clear and motivational picture of the ultimate goal the organization wants to pursue,* 149, **150**-154

Vision statements *Statement that expresses what the organization should become and where it wants to go strategically,* 56, *149*, **150**-152, 173, 362
  example of, 150-151

Voice *Employees' expression of work-related concerns, ideas, and/or constructive suggestions to managers,* **437**

Volume *Refers to the quantity of data and the storage capacity required to house it,* **233**

VRIO *Is a framework for analyzing a resource of capability to determine its competitive strategic potential by answering four questions about its Value, Rarity, Imitability, and Organization,* **177**-179

Wage reopener clause, 342

Wages, 317, 342

Well-being *The combined impact of five elements—positive emotions, engagement, relationships, meaning, and achievement (PERMA),* **456**

Whistleblower *An employee who reports organizational misconduct to the public,* **78**

White-collar crime, 75-77

Wholly owned subsidiary *A foreign subsidiary, or subordinate section of an organization, that is totally owned and controlled by an organization,* **119**

Wide span of control, 287

Women. *See* Gender

Work ethics, 83

Work–family conflict *Occurs when the demands or pressures from work and family domains are mutually incompatible,* **412**

Work–life benefits *Consist of initiatives and programs that employers implement in an effort to help employees balance the often competing needs of their work and home lives,* **455**

Workplace
  behaviors in, 405-408
  bullying, 338-339, *338*
  courageous at, 61
  design, 294-296
  flexible, 455
  hostile environment, 337
  incivility, 485
  labor agreements, 340
  positive environment, 456-458
  sexual harassment at, 337, *337*
  stress in, 408-414

Workplace cheating *Unethical behaviors that result in employees receiving benefits or advantages to which they are otherwise not entitled,* **76**-77

Workplace discrimination *Type of discrimination that occurs when people are hired or promoted—or denied hiring or promotion—for reasons not relevant to the job,* **335**
  stereotyping, 398-399

Work specialization, 286

Work teams, 469 *See also* Team

Writing skills, 401